www.wileyplus.com

ALL THE HELP, RESOURCES, AND PERSONAL SUPPORT YOU AND YOUR STUDENTS NEED!

www.wileyplus.com/resources

2-Minute Tutorials and all of the resources you & your students need to get started.

Student support from an experienced student user.

Collaborate with your colleagues, find a mentor, attend virtual and live events, and view resources.
www.WhereFacultyConnect.com

Pre-loaded, ready-to-use assignments and presentations. Created by subject matter experts.

Technical Support 24/7 FAQs, online chat, and phone support.
www.wileyplus.com/support

Your *WileyPLUS* Account Manager. Personal training and implementation support.

MANAGEMENT

SECOND CANADIAN EDITION

John R. Schermerhorn, Jr.

Barry Wright

John Wiley & Sons Canada, Ltd.

Library and Archives Canada Cataloguing in Publication

Schermerhorn, John R.
    Management / John R. Schermerhorn Jr., Barry Wright. — 2nd Canadian ed.

ISBN 978-0-470-67886-2 (bound).—ISBN 978-0-470-67973-9 (looseleaf)

    1. Management—Textbooks.   I. Wright, Barry, 1954– II. Title.
HD31.S33 2011   658   C2010-905810-0

Images are from iStockphoto unless otherwise noted.

Production Credits

Acquisitions Editor: Darren Lalonde
Vice President & Publisher: Veronica Visentin
Vice President, Publishing Services: Karen Bryan
Creative Director, Publishing Services: Ian Koo
Senior Marketing Manager: Aida Krneta
Editorial Manager: Karen Staudinger
Developmental Editor: Daleara Jamasji Hirjikaka
Media Editor: Channade Fenandoe
Editorial Assistant: Laura Hwee
Interior Design: Joanna Vieira
Cover Design: Interrobang Graphic Design, Inc.
Typesetting: Thomson Digital
Cover Photo: David Trood/Stone+/Getty Images
Printing & Binding: Quad/Graphics

Printed and bound in the United States of America
1 2 3 4 5 QG 15 14 13 12 11

John Wiley and Sons Canada Ltd.
6045 Freemont Blvd.
Mississauga, Ontario L5R 4J3
WILEY Visit our website at www.wiley.ca

About the Authors

Barry Wright is Associate Dean of the Faculty of Business at Brock University in St. Catharines, Ontario. Dr. Wright has over 20 years of experience in the classroom. Prior to joining the faculty at Brock, he worked as a professor at St. Francis Xavier University, and taught at the International Study Centre in Herstmonceux, United Kingdom, and at Queen's University in Kingston, Ontario. He has also worked as an administrator with the City of Red Deer, Alberta. During his career as an educator, Barry has received several excellence in teaching awards at both the undergraduate and graduate student levels.

At home in the classroom, Barry is also comfortable in the boardroom. He has provided a variety of training and research consultations to a number of Canadian private and public organizations. These services have included the development and implementation of programs in leadership, employee motivation, strategic planning, diversity management, stress management, and managing organizational change. Barry also provides one-on-one "coaching" sessions for senior executives who have expressed a desire for outside counsel.

He received his MA (Sport Psychology) and Ph.D. (Management) degrees from Queen's University. His academic research focuses on understanding and solving leadership challenges, change and its influence on organizational members, and creating effective work environments.

Barry enjoys being married and being a father, coaching sports, a trip to the art gallery, travelling, and a good laugh.

John R. Schermerhorn, Jr. is the Charles G. O'Bleness Professor of Management Emeritus in the College of Business at Ohio University, where he teaches graduate and undergraduate courses in management. Dr. Schermerhorn earned a Ph.D. in Organizational Behavior from Northwestern University, an MBA (with distinction) in Management and International Business from New York University, and a BS in Business Administration from the State University of New York at Buffalo. He has taught at Tulane University, the University of Vermont, and Southern Illinois University at Carbondale, where he also served as Head of the Department of Management and Associate Dean of the College of Business Administration.

At Ohio University, Dr. Schermerhorn has been named a University Professor, the university's highest campus-wide honour for excellence in undergraduate teaching. International experience also adds a unique global dimension to Dr. Schermerhorn's teaching and textbooks. Currently he is adjunct professor at the National University of Ireland at Galway, a member of the graduate faculty at Bangkok University in Thailand, and advisor to the Lao-American College in Vientiane, Laos.

He serves as a guest speaker at colleges and universities, lecturing on developments in higher education for business and management, as well as on instructional approaches and innovations. Dr. Schermerhorn has also published numerous articles in academic journals. He is co-author of *Organizational Behaviour* (Wiley, 2005).

Preface

Countless elements are vying for the attention of today's managers and students. Not only must they master skills and knowledge in their fields, but they must handle pressure to keep up with technology, beat the competition, excel as individuals, and be the first and the fastest in a world of constant change. But as shown on the cover of this book, the best results are achieved not only through teamwork, but by focusing on one goal at a time, sometimes taking just tiny steps.

Not everyone will climb a mountain, but everyone can learn about the roles they will play in an organization to meet daily goals, achieve long-term success, and inspire others to reach for the top as well. To succeed, managers and their co-workers must challenge themselves to operate outside their familiar boundaries and contribute to the organization—and society—as a whole.

Just as there are many routes to reaching the summit, there are many paths to success in today's global workplace. Some will be quicker than others, but they will all be challenging and will require taking risks. Whether someone begins on the management path from the start of their career or specializes in a profession and becomes a valued team member because of their expertise, the tools to succeed are presented from a Canadian perspective in *Management 2e*.

MANAGEMENT 2E PHILOSOPHY

Today's students are tomorrow's leaders and managers. They are our hope for the future. And just as the Canadian workplace is rapidly changing, so too must our teaching and learning environments change from the comforts and successes of days gone by. Management educators must confidently move students forward on paths that, although at times uncertain and even troublesome, will be full of promise and great opportunities. New values and management approaches are appearing; the nature of work and organizations is changing; the age of information is a major force in our lives; and the intricacies of globalization are not only proving complex, they are presenting major organizational and economic challenges.

Our students, well prepared, can be leaders and major players in organizations during this time of continuing social transformation. *Management 2e* was written to help centre students' attention on the usefulness of what they are reading and to find significance in the study of management. The focus is on helping them to understand their personal responsibilities for developing management skills and competencies and then using them for positive social impact. The goal is to enhance our students' career readiness, help make them attractive as intern and job candidates, and inspire them toward lifelong learning of essential career and life skills.

MANAGEMENT 2E PEDAGOGY

The pedagogical foundations of *Management 2e* are based on four constructive balances. We believe each remains essential to the agenda of higher education for business and management.

- **The balance of research insights with formative education.** As educators, we must be willing to make choices when bringing the theories and concepts of our discipline to the attention of the introductory student. We cannot do everything in one course. The goal should be to make good content choices and to set the best possible foundations for lifelong learning.

- **The balance of management theory with management practice.** As educators, we must understand the compelling needs of students to learn and appreciate the applications of the material they are reading and thinking about. We must continually bring to their attention good, interesting, and recognizable examples.

- The balance of present understandings with future possibilities. As educators, we must continually search for the directions in which the real world of management is heading. We must select and present materials that can both point students in the right directions and help them develop the confidence and self-respect needed to best pursue them.

- The balance of what "can" be done with what is, purely and simply, the "right" thing to do. As educators, we are role models; we set the examples. We must be willing to take stands on issues such as managerial ethics and corporate social responsibility. We must be careful not to let the concept of "contingency" betray the need for positive "action" and "accountability" in managerial practice.

Today, more than ever before, students have pressing needs for direction as well as suggestion. They have needs for application as well as information. They have needs for integration as well as presentation. Instructional approaches and materials must deliver on all of these dimensions and more. Our goal is to put into your hands and into those of your students a learning resource that can help meet these needs. *Management 2e* and its supporting on-line resources are our contributions to the future careers of your students and ours.

MANAGEMENT 2E HIGHLIGHTS

Management 2e introduces the essentials of management as they apply within the contemporary work environment. The subject matter is carefully chosen to meet AACSB accreditation guidelines, while still allowing extensive flexibility to fit various course designs and class sizes. There are many new things to look for in this edition. Along with updates of core material, *Management 2e* offers a number of changes in organization, content, and design that respond to current themes and developments in management theory and practice.

Chapter Organization

Management 2e is now divided into six parts. Within each part you will notice some chapter realignment that is designed to make the new edition as useful and flexible as possible in meeting your course objectives. All chapters have also been updated and enriched with new materials and examples from the latest current events.

- *Part 1: Management*—Shortened to include two chapters that introduce management in terms of both present-day dynamics and historical foundations—Introducing Management, and Management Learning Past to Present.

- *Part 2: Environment*—Retains three chapters that set the environmental context—Global Dimensions of Management; Ethics, Social Responsibility, and Sustainability; and Entrepreneurship and Small Business Management.

- *Part 3: Planning*—Now includes two chapters—Planning Processes and Techniques, and Strategy and Strategic Management.

- *Part 4: Organizing*—Includes three chapters for an improved flow—Organization Structure and Design, Innovation and Organizational Change, and Human Resource Management.

- *Part 5: Leading*—Contains five chapters rearranged into a building block sequence—Leading and Leadership Development; Individual Behaviour; Information and Decision-Making; Motivation Theory and Practice; and Teams, Teamwork, and Collaboration.

- *Part 6: Controlling*—Includes two chapters—Control Processes and Systems, and Operations and Services Management.

Integrated Learning Model

An important foundation of *Management 2e* is the use of an integrated learning model. From the chapter opener, through chapter content, to end-of-chapter support, this integrated learning model (a) helps guide students as they read and study for exams, (b) encourages students to engage in self-reflection about personal development of management skills and competencies, (c) challenges students to engage in critical thinking and active learning, and (d) informs students of how management issues and themes apply both in our careers and in current events that affect everyday living. Look for the following chapter features that bring the learning model alive.

Reading and Studying

Each chapter has *Study Questions* that are linked to the major headings in the chapter. These headings and their major contents are highlighted in a *Visual Chapter Overview* that precedes the text discussion. Well-designed *Figures* provide backup to solidify student comprehension as concepts, theories, and terms are introduced. Where appropriate, *Small Boxed Figures and Summaries* are embedded with the discussion to help summarize and clarify major points. A *Learning Check* follows each major section as a point of self-assessment prior to continuing with the reading. A *Study Questions Summary* and a chapter *Self-Test* tie things together at the end of the chapter.

Critical Thinking and Active Learning

Within the chapter are special features that not only introduce students to examples, current events, and applications of chapter material, but also engage them in critical thinking and active learning opportunities. *Real Ethics* challenges students to respond to an ethics problem or dilemma. *Issues and Situations* raises questions about personal behaviour in common organizational situations. *Research Brief* both summarizes recent research on a chapter topic and suggests how the students might pursue further research of their own. *Going Global* highlights management trends and practices around the world, while *Canadian Company in the News* and *Canadian Managers* provide examples close to home.

At the end of the chapter, a *Case* asks students to answer questions relating the case study to chapter content. It also proposes *Further Research* to follow up on the case, find current information, track the latest developments, and refine understanding of the case and chapter content in a dynamic context. The cases are useful for in-class discussions, and their Further Research questions offer additional opportunities for both individual and team writing and presentation assignments.

Practical Applications

Learning from Others opens each chapter with an example that places chapter content in the context of real people and organizations. The examples are chosen to both capture student interest in the chapter and remind them that many insights into chapter topics and themes can be found in everyday experiences. Included in the opening is an embedded *Benchmark* that summarizes a management lesson or question based on the example used.

Within a chapter, *Management Smarts* offers a bullet list summary of applications for a chapter concept or theory to support the focus on practical applications. And at the end of the chapter, the *Team Exercise* and *Case* have been carefully chosen to further extend the students' understanding and abilities in applying chapter content to real situations.

Self-Reflection

Each chapter also opens with *Learning About Yourself*, a feature that focuses on a critical personal skill or characteristic relevant to chapter content, such as "self-awareness" in Chapter 1. Students are provided with information and insight on the topic, but are also asked to engage in a process of self-reflection. An integrated *Get to Know Yourself Better* box sets forth a further personal development challenge and directs students toward self-assessment instruments at the end of the chapter and in the on-line resources.

Each chapter ends with a *Self-Assessment* section with three components to further help consolidate the self-reflection process. *Back to Yourself* reminds students about how chapter discussion relates back to the chapter-opening Learning About Yourself segment. *Further Reflection* provides a self-assessment instrument, along with scoring and interpretation, for additional personal insights relevant to the chapter.

MANAGEMENT 2E TEACHING AND LEARNING RESOURCES

Instructor's Resource Manual

Updated by Richard Michalski, the Instructor's Resource Manual offers helpful teaching ideas; advice on course development; sample assignments; and chapter-by-chapter text highlights, learning objectives, lecture outlines, class exercises, lecture notes, answers to end-of-chapter material, and tips on using cases.

Test Bank

Revised by Ryaan Sudally, this comprehensive Test Bank (available on the instructor portion of the website) will consist of more than 200 questions per chapter. Each chapter will have true/false, multiple-choice, and short-answer questions. The questions are designed to vary in degree of difficulty to challenge your *Management 2e* students. The Computerized Test Bank, for use on a PC running Windows, is from a test-generating program that allows instructors to modify and add questions to the Test Bank, and to customize their exams.

Web Quizzes

On-line quizzes of varying levels of difficulty are designed to help your students evaluate their individual progress through a chapter. They are available on the student portion of the Schermerhorn *Management 2e* website.

Pre- and Post-Lecture Quizzes

Adapted by Richard Michalski and included in WileyPLUS, the Pre- and Post-Lecture Quizzes consist of questions varying in level of detail and difficulty. They focus on the key terms and concepts within each chapter, so that professors can evaluate their students' progress from before the lecture to after it.

Personal Response System

The Personal Response System questions (PRS, or "Clickers") for each chapter of the *Management 2e* textbook are designed to spark discussion and debate in the classroom. For more information on PRS, please contact your local Wiley sales representative.

PowerPoint Presentation Slides

Revised by Shavin Malhotra of Ryerson University, this robust set of slides for each chapter will enhance your students' overall experience in the management classroom.

Videos

Six video cases accompany selected chapters of the text. In addition, Lecture Launcher short video clips that are tied to the major topics and developed from CBS and CBC are available on-line. They provide an excellent starting point for lectures or for general class discussion. Teaching notes for using the video clips are available on the instructor's portion of the website.

MP3 Downloads

A complete playlist of MP3 downloads is available for all text chapters. The MP3 downloads provide easy-to-access and ever-ready audio files that provide an overview of key chapter topics, terms, and potential test materials.

Student Portfolio Builder

This special guide to building a student portfolio is complete with professional resumé and competency documentations. It can be found on the student companion website.

Companion Website

The text's website at www.wiley.com/canada/management contains myriad tools and links to aid both teaching and learning, including resources described above.

Business Extra Select On-Line Courseware System

Wiley has launched a program that provides instructors with content resources from an extensive database of cases, journals, periodicals, newspapers, and supplemental readings. This courseware system integrates real-world content that helps instructors to convey the relevance of the course content to their students. It is available at www.wiley.com/college/bxs.

WileyPLUS

WileyPLUS is an innovative, research-based on-line environment for effective teaching and learning.

WileyPLUS builds students' confidence because it takes the guesswork out of studying by providing students with a clear road map: what to do, how to do it, whether they did it right. This interactive approach focuses on:

DESIGN: Research-based design is based on proven instructional methods. Content is organized into small, more accessible amounts of information, helping students build better time management skills.

ENGAGEMENT: Students can visually track their progress as they move through the material at a pace that is right for them. Engaging in individualized self-quizzes followed by immediate feedback helps to sustain their motivation to learn.

OUTCOMES: Self-assessment lets students know the exact outcome of their effort at any time. Advanced reporting allows instructors to easily spot trends in the usage and performance data of their class in order to make more informed decisions.

With *WileyPLUS*, students take more initiative so you'll have a greater impact on their achievement in the classroom and beyond.

What do students receive with *WileyPLUS?*

- Confidence-boosting feedback and proof of progress, 24/7
- Context-sensitive feedback as they work on problems that are linked to relevant sections in the on-line digital textbook
- An easy-to-navigate framework, calendars, visual progress tracking, and self-evaluation tools that help students study more effectively

What do instructors receive with *WileyPLUS?*

- Reliable resources that reinforce course goals inside and outside of the classroom
- Media-rich course materials and assessment content—Instructor's Manual, Test Bank, PowerPoint® Slides, Learning Objectives, Computerized Test Bank, Pre- and Post- Lecture Quizzes, and much more

Acknowledgements

Writing a book is always a big task and there are many people who have contributed greatly to this project. Special thanks go to Darren Lalonde, Acquisitions Editor, for his support and vision for the project and for his friendship. My thanks go to Daleara (Dela) Hirjikaka, Developmental Editor, for her gentle yet strong, steady, and unwearied guidance on the day-to-day aspects of the project. Dela truly epitomizes the "family" characteristic that distinguishes Wiley culture. I am blessed to be able to work with her. I would like to thank Aida Krneta, Marketing Manager, for her very helpful counsel on making the book student-friendly. I would also like to thank Alison Arnot, Laurel Hyatt (a truly gifted writer), and Zofia Laubitz for their editorial contributions. And I would like to thank Deanna Durnford for coordinating the supplements for the text. I would like to offer my particular thanks to Melissa Linseman, who was an exceptional research assistant, and finally to Michelle Leece, who was both innovative and instrumental in creating several of the cases, including the integrative case on Rogers Communications. To all, my heartfelt thanks.

I am grateful to the following colleagues who offered their insightful and very useful comments at different stages of this book's development.

Colin Boyd	University of Saskatchewan
Lewie Callahan	University of Lethbridge
Tyler Chamberlin	University of Ottawa
Choon Hian Chan	Kwantlen University College
Kay Devine	Athabasca University
Victoria Digby	Fanshawe College
Richard Field	University of Alberta
Douglas Fletcher	Kwantlen University College
Paul Gallina	Bishop's University
Jane Haddad	Seneca College
Don Haidey	Mount Royal University
Don Hill	Kwantlen University College
Cyndi Hornby	Fanshawe College
Michael Khan	University of Toronto
Barbara Lipton	Seneca College
Ed Leach	Dalhousie University
Brad Long	St. Francis Xavier University
Sean MacDonald	University of Manitoba
Shavin Malhotra	Ryerson University
Trecia McLennon	Ryerson University
Bonnie Milne	British Columbia Institute of Technology
Kerry Rempel	Okanagan College
Ron Shay	Kwantlen University College
Patricia Stoll	Seneca College
Susan Thompson	Trent University
Joe Trubic	Ryerson University
Debra Warren	Centennial College
Bruce Weir	Kwantlen University College
Wallace John Whistance-Smith	Ryerson University
Don Valeri	Douglas College
Heather White	Georgian College
David Wright	Kwantlen University College
Allen Zhu	Capilano University

I would especially like to thank my family—my lovely wife Mary, darling daughters Monica and Kit, and happy son John Emmett—who all offered hugs and help along the way.

To my mother and father, for all your guidance, strength, and love, I dedicate this book.

Barry Wright
St. Catharines, Ontario
November 2010

How to Use This Book

LEARNING FROM OTHERS

We can make the world a better place

A couple of guys did, and they made ice cream to boot. You know the ice cream for sure—you may have tasted a Ben & Jerry's Cherry Garcia® cone or enjoyed a scoop of Chunky Monkey® banana. But do you really know the company? Ben & Jerry's earned its reputation not just from great ice cream, but also from the concept of "linked prosperity"—sharing prosperity with its employees and the communities in which it operates.

It was 1977 when friends Ben Cohen and Jerry Greenfield moved from Long Island, New York, to Burlington, Vermont. Needing a source of income, they took a university correspondence course on ice cream making. A year later, Ben & Jerry's Homemade, created on a $12,000 investment, sold its first ice cream cones from a converted gas station. It was a "different" ice cream store right from the start, and on the firm's first anniversary, the first annual Free Cone Day—free ice cream all day—was held to celebrate.

LEARNING ABOUT YOURSELF

Individual Character

There is no doubt that individual character is a foundation for all that we do. It establishes our integrity and provides an ethical anchor for how we behave at work and in life overall. Persons of high character can always be confident in the self-respect it provides, even in the most difficult of situations. Those who lack it are destined to perpetual insecurity, acting inconsistently, and suffering not only in self-esteem but also in the esteem of others.

How strong is your individual character? How well do your values prepare you to deal with the inevitable ethical dilemmas and challenges that pop up at school, in work, and in life?

STUDY QUESTIONS

- What is ethical behaviour?

- How do ethical dilemmas complicate the workplace?

- How can high ethical standards be maintained?

- What are social responsibility, governance, and sustainability?

VISUAL CHAPTER OVERVIEW

ETHICS, SOCIAL RESPONSIBILITY, AND SUSTAINABILITY

Study Question 1	Study Question 2	Study Question 3	Study Question 4
What Is Ethical Behaviour?	**Ethics in the Workplace**	**Maintaining High Ethical Standards**	**Social Responsibility, Governance, and Sustainability**
■ Laws, values, and ethical behaviour	■ Ethical dilemmas	■ Whistleblower protection	■ Stakeholder issues and analysis
■ Alternative views of ethics	■ Ethical decision-making	■ Ethics training	■ Perspectives on corporate social responsibility
■ Cultural issues in ethical behaviour	■ Rationalizations for unethical behaviour	■ Codes of ethical conduct	■ Evaluating corporate social performance
		■ Ethical role models	■ Directions in corporate governance
		■ Moral management	
		■ Social entrepreneurship	
✓ Learning Check 1	✓ Learning Check 2	✓ Learning Check 3	✓ Learning Check 4

Learning from Others opens each chapter with an example that places chapter content in the context of real people and organizations.

Each chapter also opens with **Learning About Yourself**, a feature that focuses on a critical personal skill or characteristic.

Each chapter opens with a set of **Study Questions** that provide learning objectives for the chapter and a framework for the end-of-chapter review.

The **Visual Chapter Overview** includes a graphic outline of major topics.

☘ Canadian Company in the News

FREE THE CHILDREN

Since its founding in 1995, Free The Children has built more than 650 schools in developing countries, improved over 1 million people's access to clean water, and helped start 30,000 microbusinesses. Pretty good results, but what is truly amazing is that this non-profit company was started by, at the time, 12-year-old Craig Kielburger. After reading a story in the newspaper—"Battled Child Labour, Boy 12 Murdered"—he gathered together a group of school friends to fight against child labour. Today, Free The Children is the world's largest network of children helping other children. A motivated 12-year-old, Craig has developed into a self-confident, passionate, and energetic adult who still has the leadership drive to change the world.

Courtesy Free The Children

CANADIAN MANAGERS
Bonnie Brooks and The Bay ☘

Mario Beauregard/CPI
The Canadian Press

In 2009, Bonnie Brooks took over Canada's largest and oldest merchandise retailer as president and CEO of the Hudson's Bay Company. Her task: to revitalize and differentiate The Bay's brand. Some would say this would be a daunting task during good economic times, but it would be overwhelming with Canada in the midst of a recession. But Brooks, who came with over two decades of leadership experience, including as the president of the Lane Crawford Group in Hong Kong, editor-in-chief of *Flare* magazine, and executive vice-president for Holt Renfrew, has taken a strategic approach to meeting this challenge. Her priority has been to recognize customer needs by dropping brands, adding lines, and slowly making over The Bay. Brooks understands that pleasing customers is central to improving The Bay's bottom line. It is a challenging task, but she's getting the job done.

The **Canadian Company in the News** and **Canadian Managers** features bring real-life examples of management skills and innovation into the classroom

GOING GLOBAL

A Better World Courtesy of Cirque du Soleil

This Quebec company, which began in 1984 as a group of 20 street performers, is world-famous for its artistic circus show. Cirque du Soleil's mission is to "invoke the imagination, provoke the senses and evoke the emotions of people around the world" and it has brought delight to over 90 million spectators worldwide. However, it sees its role as more than just entertaining the world. In expressing its terminal values, the company says, "Cirque du Soleil's citizenship principles are founded on the conviction that the arts, business and social initiatives can, together, contribute to making a better world." How does it do this? Cirque du Soleil tracks its environmental performance and has implemented water, waste, and power initiatives in its Montreal headquarters and on the road; it has launched a $100-million project entitled ONE DROP to provide the world's poorest with access to drinking water; and it gives an amount equivalent to 1 percent of Cirque du Soleil's earnings to cultural and social action programs each year. As founder Guy Laliberté shares, "life pays you back what you have given to it." It is safe to say he has earned a wonderful payback!

The **Going Global** feature introduces students to global management trends and practices.

REAL ETHICS

Resumé Lies

From *The Wall Street Journal*—Employers are looking for resumé lies; senders beware! Don't assume that, because so many resumés are in the stack for a position, the employer won't bother to check details. They do. The Society for Human Resource Management surveyed 2,500 members, and 96 percent said that they checked up on references and/or stated credentials. When ResumeDoctor.com checked resumés submitted for its review by job hunters, 42.7 percent had at least one inaccuracy and 12.6 percent had more.

research analyst, but they're really an associate." At her firm, that's cause for automatic rejection.

YOU DECIDE

Although it may be tempting to "beef up" one's resumé, it's the wrong thing to

Real Ethics challenges students to respond to an ethics problem or dilemma.

RESEARCH BRIEF

Issues management pacesetters influence pharmaceutical industry's response to AIDS in Africa

Writing in *Business & Society*, Cedric E. Dawkins describes an "issues management pacesetter" as a company in an industry that addresses an external issue in a unique and different way. His article first develops a pacesetters model and then applies it to case studies of responses by global pharmaceutical firms to the AIDS crisis in Africa over a three-year period. In his words, the article analyzes "the confrontation between the mainline pharmaceutical industry and AIDS activists and stakeholders over access to AIDS medications in Africa."

Dawkins views organizational decision-making as a process of negotiation between external normative and competitive pressures. Issues pacesetters are firms that change in response to pressures from external stakeholders and then stimulate further changes by other industry

that were consolidating around a new set of expectations. He concludes that the pacesetters model is accurate in explaining the industry events, and that the perceptions of organizational decision-makers of stakeholder interests and demands are a critical factor in the process. He also suggests that stakeholder groups that understand how firms make decisions will be able to gain more influence over firm behaviour.

In a postscript to the article, Dawkins also notes increased cooperation among countries in the fight against AIDS. But he also points out that, in Africa and elsewhere, more still needs to be done to "widen access to HIV medicines and technologies."

You be the researcher

Can you come up with other examples or cases where the issues pacesetters model helps explain how organizations deal with stakeholder issues and concerns? Iden-

Research Brief both summarizes recent research on a chapter topic and suggests how the students might pursue further research of their own.

ISSUES AND SITUATIONS
Ethics Training

Lots of organizations provide some form of ethics training for employees. At Lockheed Martin, employees watch DVD scenes involving ethically suspect actions. In one scene, a manager gives a bad assignment to a direct report who had earlier criticized her behaviour in a staff meeting. The scenes are discussed for their ethical implications.

The assumption in ethics training is that such exercises will raise ethical awareness and confidence, creating a more ethical workplace. But does ethics training really work? The Ethics Resource Center finds that no more than 55 percent of persons who observe unethical acts actually report them.

CRITICAL RESPONSE

Put yourself in the shoes of someone observing questionable practices at work. How would you respond? Now, put your own shoes back on. Suppose you learn of someone who bullied another student into allowing him to "read over" her

have had ethics training at work and, if so, what it covered and what it meant in terms of personal impact.

Report from the Ethics Resource Center

- 3,015 U.S. workers surveyed
- 69 percent work for employers providing ethics training
- About 50 percent observed unethical behaviour in the past 12 months at work
- The most observed unethical actions are:

Issues and Situations raises questions about personal behaviour in common organizational situations.

Procedural justice is concerned that policies and rules are fairly applied.

Distributive justice is concerned that people are treated the same regardless of personal characteristics.

Interactional justice is the degree to which others are treated with dignity and respect.

Key terms are called out and defined in the margins, forming a **Margin Running Glossary**.

4.1 MANAGEMENT SMARTS
Checklist for dealing with ethical dilemmas

Step 1. Recognize the ethical dilemma.

Step 2. Get the facts.

Step 3. Identify your options.

Step 4. Test each option: Is it legal? Is it right? Is it beneficial?

Step 5. Decide which option to follow.

Step 6. Double-check with the *spotlight questions:*
"How will I feel if my family finds out about my decision?"
*"How will I feel about this if my decision is reported in the local newspaper
or posted on the Internet?"*

Step 7. Take action.

Management Smarts
in each chapter offers
lists of helpful "do's" and
"don'ts" of managerial
behaviour.

 Learning Check **1**   **BE SURE YOU CAN**

• define *ethics* • list and explain four views of ethical behaviour • give examples showing violation of procedural, distributive, and interactional justice • differentiate between cultural relativism and universalism in international business ethics

At the end of each section, **Learning Checks** prompt you to stop and review the key points you have just studied. If you cannot answer these questions, you should go back and read the section again.

MANAGEMENT LEARNING REVIEW

STUDY QUESTIONS SUMMARY

1. What is ethical behaviour?

• Ethical behaviour is that which is accepted as "good" or "right" as opposed to "bad" or "wrong."

• Because an action is not illegal does not necessarily make it ethical in a given situation.

• Because values vary, the question "What is ethical behaviour?" may be answered differently by different people.

• The utilitarian, individualism, moral rights, and justice views offer alternative ways of thinking about ethical behaviour.

• Cultural relativism argues that no culture is ethically superior to any other; universalism argues that certain ethical standards apply everywhere.

FOR DISCUSSION Is there ever a justification for cultural relativism in international business ethics?

2. How do ethical dilemmas complicate the workplace?

The **Study Questions Summary** is a bullet list summary of key points for each chapter-opening Study Question.

SELF-TEST

Multiple-Choice Questions

1. Values are personal beliefs that help determine whether a behaviour will be considered ethical or unethical. An example of a terminal value is _____.

   (a) ambition (b) self-respect (c) courage (d) imagination

2. Under the _____ view of ethical behaviour, a business owner would be considered ethical if she reduced a plant's workforce by 10 percent in order to cut costs to keep the business from failing and thus save jobs for the other 90 percent.

   (a) utilitarian (b) individualism (c) justice (d) moral rights

3. A manager's failure to enforce a late-to-work policy the same way for all employees is an ethical violation of _____ justice.

   (a) ethical (b) moral (c) distributive (d) procedural

4. The Sarbanes-Oxley Act of 2002 makes it easier for corporate executives to _____.

   (a) protect themselves from shareholder lawsuits (b) sue employees who commit illegal acts (c) be tried and sentenced to jail for financial misconduct (d) shift blame for wrongdoing to boards of directors

An end-of-chapter **Self-Test** helps assess your understanding of key chapter topics, including multiple-choice, short response, and application (essay) questions.

SELF-ASSESSMENT

Back to Yourself: Individual Character

Individual character is something that people tend to think a lot about during parliamentary election periods. But, as suggested in the chapter opener, character and its underlying foundation of personal integrity isn't something that should only be an occasional concern; it deserves more than passing and even reluctant attention. The ethics and social responsibility issues facing organizations today put individual character to the test. Ethical dilemmas can arise on any given day. To deal with them, we have to know ourselves well enough to make principled decisions, ones that we can be proud of and that others will respect. After all, it's the character of people making key decisions that determines whether our organizations act in socially responsible or irresponsible ways. And an understanding of personal values is very helpful as we try to stay on course with individual character.

Further Reflection: Terminal Values

Instructions

Rate each of the following values in terms of its importance to you. Think about each value in terms of its importance as a guiding principle in your life. Consider each value in relation to all the other values listed in the survey.

Terminal Values

1. A comfortable life	Of lesser importance	1 2 3 4 5 6 7	Of greater importance
2. An exciting life	Of lesser importance	1 2 3 4 5 6 7	Of greater importance
3. A sense of accomplishment	Of lesser importance	1 2 3 4 5 6 7	Of greater importance
4. A world at peace	Of lesser importance	1 2 3 4 5 6 7	Of greater importance
5. A world of beauty	Of lesser importance	1 2 3 4 5 6 7	Of greater importance
6. Equality	Of lesser importance	1 2 3 4 5 6 7	Of greater importance
7. Family security	Of lesser importance	1 2 3 4 5 6 7	Of greater importance
8. Freedom	Of lesser importance	1 2 3 4 5 6 7	Of greater importance

Each chapter ends with a **Self-Assessment** section with three components to further help consolidate the self-reflection process.

CASE 4

Tom's of Maine: "Doing Business" Means "Doing Good"

Tom's of Maine was one of the first natural health care companies to distribute outside normal channels. The company holds fast to the values that got owners Tom and Kate Chappell started more than three decades ago, providing insight into how a small firm can grow while staying true to its founding principles in the midst of competition. Now that Tom's has been sold to Colgate, one wonders if those principles can be sustained in a large corporate environment.

Courtesy Tom's of Maine, Inc

against "business as usual" made the company wait seven years longer and spend about 10 times the usual sum to get the American Dental Association's seal of approval for its fluoride toothpastes. And mistakes were made. At a time when deodorant made up 25 percent of the business, Chappell reformulated the product for ecological reasons. Later, he realized that the new formulation "magnified the human bacteria that cause odor" in half its users. After much agonizing, Chappell took the product from his shelves at a cost of $400,000, 30 percent of the firm's projected profits for the year. Dissatisfied consumers were sent refunds and a letter of apology.

A **Case** for critical thinking for each chapter applies the case to the material being discussed.

Integrated Case

Rogers Communications Inc. – The Next Generation of Communications

The **Integrated Case** is a multi-faceted cross-functional case that allows you to apply an extensive amount of course material.

that there was a real person behind it. As founder and major shareholder, Ted Rogers had always had the final say in what happened.[7]

Mohamed also knew that, while he would be responsible for leading RCI into the future, the Rogers children, Edward III and Melinda, had inherited their father's 91 percent of RCI's class A voting shares, effectively ensuring continued control of the company to the Rogers family.[8] He wondered what problems, if any, would arise if his vision for RCI was not the same as the family's. As Mohamed prepared for his first day of work, the question was where to start and what to do first to ensure that Ted Rogers' legacy continued.

How Do You Learn Best?

This questionnaire aims to find out something about your preferences for the way you work with information. You will have a preferred learning style. One part of that learning style is your preference for the intake and the output of ideas and information.

Circle the letter of the answer that best explains your preference. Circle more than one if a single answer does not match your perception. Leave blank any question that does not apply.

1. You are helping someone who wants to go to your airport, town centre, or railway station. You would:
   V) draw, or give her a map.
   A) tell her the directions.
   R) write down the directions.
   K) go with her.

2. You are not sure whether a word should be spelled "dependent" or "dependant." You would:
   V) see the words in your mind and choose by the way they look.
   A) think about how each word sounds and choose one.
   R) find it in a dictionary.
   K) write both words on paper and choose one.

3. You are planning a holiday for a group. You want some feedback from them about the plan. You would:
   V) use a map or website to show them the places.
   A) phone, text, or e-mail them.
   R) give them a copy of the printed itinerary.
   K) describe some of the highlights.

4. You are going to cook something as a special treat for your family. You would:
   V) look through the cookbook for ideas from the pictures.
   A) ask friends for suggestions.
   R) use a cookbook where you know there is a good recipe.
   K) cook something you know without the need for instructions.

5. A group of tourists wants to learn about the parks and wildlife reserves in your area. You would:
   V) show them Internet pictures, photographs, or picture books.
   A) talk about or arrange a talk for them to learn about parks or wildlife reserves.
   R) give them a book or pamphlets about the parks or wildlife reserves.
   K) take them to a park or wildlife reserve and walk with them.

6. You are about to purchase a digital camera or mobile phone. Other than price, what would most influence your decision?
   V) It is a modern design and looks good.
   A) The salesperson telling me about its features.
   R) Reading the details about its features.
   K) Trying or testing it.

7. Remember a time when you learned how to do something new. Try to avoid choosing a physical skill, such as riding a bike. You learned best by:
   V) diagrams and charts—visual clues.
   A) listening to somebody explaining it and asking questions.
   R) written instructions—e.g., a manual or textbook.
   K) watching a demonstration.

8. You have a problem with your knee. You would prefer that the doctor:
   V) showed you a diagram of what was wrong.
   A) described what was wrong.
   R) gave you a web address or something to read about it.
   K) used a plastic model of a knee to show what was wrong.

9. You want to learn a new program, skill, or game on a computer. You would:
   V) follow the diagrams in the book that came with it.
   A) talk with people who know about the program.
   R) read the written instructions that came with the program.
   K) use the controls or keyboard.

10. You like websites that have:
    V) interesting design and visual features.
    A) audio channels where you can hear music, radio programs, or interviews.
    R) interesting written descriptions, lists, and explanations.
    K) things you can click on, shift, or try.

11. Other than price, what would most influence your decision to buy a new, non-fiction book?
    V) The way it looks is appealing.
    A) A friend talks about it and recommends it.
    R) Quickly reading parts of it.
    K) It has real-life stories, experiences, and examples.

12. You are using a book, CD, or website to learn how to take photos with your new digital camera. You would like to have:
    V) diagrams showing the camera and what each part does.
    A) a chance to ask questions and talk about the camera and its features.
    R) clear written instructions with lists and bullet points about what to do.
    K) many examples of good and poor photos and how to improve them.

13. Do you prefer an instructor who likes to use
    V) diagrams, charts, or graphs?
    A) question and answer, talk, group discussions, or guest speakers?
    R) handouts, books, or readings?
    K) demonstrations, models, or practical sessions?

14. You have finished a competition or test and would like some feedback. You would like to have feedback:
    V) using graphs showing you what you had achieved.
    A) from somebody who talks it through with you.
    R) using a written description of your results.
    K) using examples from what you have done.

15. You are going to choose food at a restaurant or café. You would:
    V) look at what others are eating or look at pictures of each dish.
    A) listen to the waiter or ask friends to recommend choices.
    R) choose from descriptions on the menu.
    K) choose something that you have had there before.

16. You have to make an important speech at a conference or special occasion. You would:
    V) make diagrams or get graphs to help explain things.
    A) write a few key words and practise saying your speech over and over.
    R) write your speech and learn from reading it over several times.
    K) gather many examples and stories to make the talk real and practical.

Count your choices: ☐ ☐ ☐ ☐
                            V   A   R   K

Determine whether your learning style is primarily visual (V), aural (A), reading/writing (R), or kinesthetic (K). You may have more than one learning style preference—many people do. This is known as a multimodal (MM) style. Look at the learning styles chart below and on the next page to determine what will help you learn the best.

LEARNING STYLES CHART

 Visual

WHAT TO DO IN CLASS	WHAT TO DO WHEN STUDYING	TEXT FEATURES THAT MAY HELP YOU	WHAT TO DO PRIOR TO EXAMS
• Pay close attention to charts, drawings, and handouts your instructor uses. • Underline and highlight. • Use different colours. • Use symbols, flow charts, graphs, different arrangements on the page, white space.	Convert your lecture notes into "page pictures." To do this: • Reconstruct images in different ways. • Redraw pages from memory. • Replace words with symbols and initials. • Look at your pages.	• Chapter opener vignettes • Visual chapter overview • Photos • Figures • Key Terms in brown • Words in italics • Learning Checks • Self-Tests • Video news clips (available in your instructor's Video Package)	• Recall your "page pictures." • Draw diagrams where appropriate. • Practise turning your visuals back into words.

Aural

WHAT TO DO IN CLASS	WHAT TO DO WHEN STUDYING	TEXT FEATURES THAT MAY HELP YOU	WHAT TO DO PRIOR TO EXAMS
• Attend lectures and tutorials. • Discuss topics with students and instructors. • Explain new ideas to other people. • Use a tape recorder. • Leave spaces in your lecture notes for later recall. • Describe overheads, pictures, and visuals to somebody who was not in class.	You may take poor notes because you prefer to listen. Therefore: • Expand your notes by talking with others and with information from your textbook. • Listen to the pre-recorded chapter summaries (available on the companion website). • Read summarized notes out loud. • Explain your notes to another "aural" person.	• Chapter study questions • Visual chapter overview • Photos/Figures • Study Questions Summary • Self-Tests • Cases • Team exercises • Self-Assessments • Glossary	• Talk with the instructor. • Spend time in quiet places recalling the ideas. • Practise writing answers to old exam questions. • Say your answers out loud.

Reading/Writing

WHAT TO DO IN CLASS	WHAT TO DO WHEN STUDYING	TEXT FEATURES THAT MAY HELP YOU	WHAT TO DO PRIOR TO EXAMS
• Use lists and headings. • Use dictionaries, glossaries, and definitions. • Read handouts, textbooks, and supplemental library readings. • Use lecture notes.	• Write out words again and again. • Reread notes silently. • Rewrite ideas and principles into other words. • Turn charts, diagrams, and other illustrations into statements.	• Chapter opener vignettes • Chapter study questions • Visual chapter overview • Learning Checks • Key term definitions in margins • Study Questions Summary • Self-Tests, especially the Short-Response Questions and the Application Questions • Cases • Glossary	• Write exam answers. • Practise with multiple-choice questions. • Write paragraphs, beginnings and endings. • Write your lists in outline form. • Arrange your words into hierarchies and points.

Kinesthetic

WHAT TO DO IN CLASS	WHAT TO DO WHEN STUDYING	TEXT FEATURES THAT MAY HELP YOU	WHAT TO DO PRIOR TO EXAMS
• Use all your senses. • Go to labs, take field trips. • Listen to real-life examples. • Pay attention to applications. • Use hands-on approaches. • Use trial-and-error methods.	You may take poor notes because topics do not seem concrete or relevant. Therefore: • Put examples in your summaries. • Use case studies and applications to help with principles and abstract concepts. • Talk about your notes with another "kinesthetic" person. • Use pictures and photographs that illustrate an idea.	• Chapter opener vignettes • Visual chapter overview • Canadian Company in the News boxes • Canadian Managers boxes • Going Global boxes • Study Questions Summary • Self-Tests • Integrated Case • Cases, especially the questions on Further Research • Team exercises • Self-Assessments	• Write practice answers. • Role-play the exam situation.

For all learning styles: Be sure to use the learning aids on the companion website to enhance your understanding of the concepts and procedures of the text.

Brief Contents

Contents

PART 5: LEADING

CHAPTER 11

LEADING AND LEADERSHIP DEVELOPMENT 314

THE NATURE OF LEADERSHIP 317

LEADERSHIP TRAITS AND BEHAVIOURS 320

CONTINGENCY APPROACHES TO LEADERSHIP 323

ISSUES IN LEADERSHIP DEVELOPMENT 329

THE COMMUNICATION PROCESS 334

IMPROVING COMMUNICATION 339

CHAPTER 12

INDIVIDUAL BEHAVIOUR 354

PERCEPTION 357

PERSONALITY 361

ATTITUDES 365

EMOTIONS, MOODS, AND STRESS 369

Introducing Management

Smart people create their own futures

Akin to many great business deals, the concept for Workopolis was sketched out on a napkin over lunch. Two competitors, the head of the *Toronto Star's* electronic division and the head of *The Globe and Mail's* electronic division, looked at the evolving on-line job market in the United States and determined that if newspapers were to survive in the employment category they needed to embrace new technologies and become partners, not competitors. Workopolis.com was launched in 2000 with 15,000 job listings and was almost immediately a phenomenal success, becoming Canada's leading provider of Internet recruitment and job search solutions.

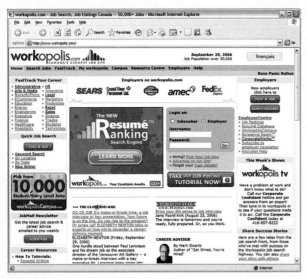

Courtesy Workopolis.com

Workopolis is still a top destination for job seekers and job providers. The site represents itself as a network that serves everyone from recent college and university graduates all the way up to seasoned executives. But in the new age of multimedia resumés and high-tech employment searches, networking and career sites such as Monster, CareerBuilder, LinkedIn, and ZoomInfo offer additional alternatives.

To respond, Workopolis has learned to keep adapting and updating. It has done such things as adding the "Learn More" feature that allows job seekers to see what it would be like to work for a particular employer, launching a smarter job search engine, simplifying site navigation, and making search tools easier to use. Like the rest of us, Workopolis needs to keep changing with the times.

The same challenge holds true of you—you need to keep changing to stay ahead of the times. This book and your management course offer many ways to explore career skills and capabilities and to identify and develop new ones. Take good advantage of the opportunity and always remember: What happens is up to you! There is no better time than the present to commit to learning and personal growth.

> **BENCHMARK** You don't need to create your own company like Workopolis did to achieve career success. What you must do, however, is to commit to academic success and career development. Remember—smart people create their own futures!

Self-Awareness

When it comes to doing well as a student and in a career, a lot rests on how well you know yourself and what you do with this knowledge. Self-awareness is an important career skill, but it is also one of those concepts that is easy to talk about and hard to master.

What do you really know about yourself? How often do you take a critical look at your attitudes, behaviours, skills, personal characteristics, and accomplishments? Do you ever realistically assess your strengths and weaknesses from a career perspective—both as you see them and as others do?

A high degree of self-awareness is essential for personal adaptability, to be able to learn, grow, and develop in changing times. It sets a strong foundation for stepping forward and making adjustments so that we can always move confidently toward the future. But true self-awareness means not just knowing your idealized self, the person you want or hope to be. It also means getting to know how you are perceived through the eyes of others.[1]

	Unknown to you	Known to you
Known to others	Blind Spot	Open Area
Unknown to others	The Unknown	Hidden Self

This figure, called the *Johari Window*, offers a way of comparing what we know about ourselves with what others know about us.[2] Our "open" areas known to ourselves and others are often small. The "blind spot," "the unknown," and the "hidden" areas can be quite large; they challenge our willingness and capacities for self-discovery.

Think about the personal implications of the Johari Window. Are you willing to probe the unknown, uncover your blind spots, and discover talents and weaknesses that may be hidden? As your self-awareness expands, you will find many insights for personal growth and development.

❖ Get to Know Yourself Better

Put the Johari Window to work. Think about your career skills and personal characteristics. Jot down aspects of your "Open Area" and "Hidden Self." Confront "The Unknown" by speculating on what might be listed there. Ask friends, family members, and co-workers to comment on your "Blind Spot." Analyze the results in a short self-reflection paper. End it with a set of goals for your continued personal and professional development.

CHAPTER 1 STUDY QUESTIONS

- What are the challenges of working in the new economy?

- What are organizations like in the new workplace?

- What is the makeup of the external environment of organizations and how is an organization linked to its environment?

- Who are managers and what do they do?

- What is the management process and how do you learn managerial skills and competencies?

VISUAL CHAPTER OVERVIEW

CHAPTER 1 INTRODUCING MANAGEMENT

Study Question 1	Study Question 2	Study Question 3	Study Question 4	Study Question 5
Working Today	**Organizations in the New Workplace**	**Organizational Environment**	**Managers in the New Workplace**	**The Management Process**
■ Talent ■ Diversity ■ Globalization ■ Technology ■ Ethics ■ Careers	■ What is an organization? ■ Organizations as systems ■ Organizational performance ■ Changing nature of organizations	■ Dynamic forces and the general environment ■ Stakeholders and the specific environment ■ Competitive advantage ■ Environmental uncertainty ■ Organizational effectiveness	■ What is a manager? ■ Levels of managers ■ Types of managers ■ Managerial performance ■ Changing nature of managerial work	■ Functions of management ■ Managerial roles and activities ■ Managerial agendas and networks ■ Essential managerial skills ■ Developing managerial competencies ■ *Management* learning model
✓ Learning Check 1	✓ Learning Check 2	✓ Learning Check 3	✓ Learning Check 4	✓ Learning Check 5

Welcome to *Management* and its career development theme—"Get to know yourself better." We live and work in very complex times. Financial turmoil, great resource and environmental challenges, uncertain international relations, the economics of globalization, and complexities of balancing work and personal lives are just some of the forces and trends that are having an undeniable impact on our society. The dynamics of ever-present change extend into the workplace and raise for all of us a host of new career challenges. There is no better time than now to commit your energies and intellect to continuous learning and personal development. Indeed, your future depends on it.

We are dealing with a new workplace, one in which everyone must adapt to a rapidly changing society with constantly shifting demands and opportunities. Learning and speed are in; habit and complacency are out. Organizations are fast changing, as is the nature of work itself. The economy is global, driven by innovation and technology. Even the concept of success, personal and organizational, is evolving as careers are transformed. Can there be any doubt that this is a time when smart people and smart organizations create their own futures?[3]

In the quest for the future, the best employers share an important commitment—they value people! They are extremely good at attracting and retaining talented employees, and they excel at creating high-performance settings in which talented people achieve great results—individually and collectively. In their book *Everything I Needed to Know About Business . . . I Learned from a Canadian*, Leonard Brody and David Raffa credit leading beyond managing to create challenging and enriched jobs for employees as "Leaders inspire, motivate, and influence an organization, coaxing the best performance from their staff, often by personal example."[4]

What often sets great organizations apart today is that they offer creative and inspiring leadership and supportive work environments that reward and respect people, allowing their talents to be fully utilized.[5] The themes of the day are "respect," "participation," "empowerment," "involvement," "teamwork," and "self-management." All of this, and more, is what *Management* and your management course are about. They are designed to introduce you to the concepts, themes, and directions that are consistent with career success and organizational leadership in the high-performance settings of today's new workplace.

WORKING TODAY

Expectations for organizations and their members are very high. Organizations are expected to continuously excel on performance criteria that include concerns for ethics and social responsibilities, innovativeness, and employee development, as well as more traditional measures of profitability and investment value. When they fail, customers, investors, and employees are quick to let them know. For individuals, there are no guarantees of long-term employment. Jobs are increasingly earned and re-earned every day through one's performance accomplishments. Careers are being redefined in terms of "flexibility," "free agency," "skill portfolios," and "entrepreneurship." Career success takes lots of initiative and discipline, as well as continuous learning.

TALENT

If you follow the news, you'll find many examples of great organizations, and there should be many right in your local community. One that often makes the management news is Herman Miller, an innovative manufacturer of designer furniture. Respect for employees is a rule of thumb at the firm, whose core values include this statement: "Our greatest assets as a corporation are the gifts, talents and abilities of our employee-owners . . . . When we as a corporation invest in developing people, we are investing in our future." Former CEO Max DePree says, "We talk about the difference between being successful and being exceptional. Being successful is meeting goals in a good way—being exceptional is reaching your potential."[6]

Herman Miller seems to fit the notion of a high-involvement organization. It also seems consistent with results from a study of high-performing companies by management scholars Charles

O'Reilly and Jeffrey Pfeffer. They concluded that high performers achieve success because they are better than their competitors at getting extraordinary results from the people working for them. "These companies have won the war for talent," they say, "not just by being great places to work—although they are that—but by figuring out how to get the best out of all of their people, every day."[7]

The point of these examples is that people and their talents—what they know, what they learn, and what they do with it—are the ultimate foundations of organizational performance. They represent what managers call **intellectual capital**, the collective brainpower or shared knowledge of a workforce that can be used to create value.[8] Indeed, the ultimate challenge of

Intellectual capital is the collective brainpower or shared knowledge of a workforce.

$$\text{Intellectual Capital} = \text{Competency} \times \text{Commitment}$$

any organization is to combine the talents of many people, sometimes thousands of them, to achieve unique and significant results.

Consider this intellectual capital equation as a way of personalizing this discussion. If you want a successful career, you must be a source of intellectual capital for employers. You must be someone willing to reach for the heights of personal competency and accomplishment. This means being a self-starter willing to continuously learn from experience. And it means becoming a valued **knowledge worker**—someone whose mind is a critical asset to employers and adds to the intellectual capital of the organization. The late management guru Peter Drucker once said: "Knowledge workers have many options and should be treated as volunteers. They're interested in personal achievement and personal responsibility. They expect continuous learning and training. They will respect and want authority. Give it to them."[9]

A **knowledge worker** is someone whose mind is a critical asset to employers.

DIVERSITY

Workforce diversity describes differences among workers in gender, race, age, ethnicity, religion, sexual orientation, and able-bodiedness.

The term **workforce diversity** describes the composition of a workforce in terms of differences among people according to gender, age, race, ethnicity, religion, sexual orientation, and able-bodiedness.[10] The diversity trends of changing demographics are well recognized: more seniors, women, members of visible minorities, and immigrants are in the workforce. Statistics Canada predicts that by 2031 three in 10 Canadians (between 29 and 32 percent) will be members of visible minority groups. South Asians and Chinese compose the largest portion of the visible minority, while Arabs and West Asians are predicted to be the fastest-growing minority groups in Canada between 2006 and 2031. And while aging baby boomers are a growing proportion of the population, more of them are postponing retirement.[11]

Even though our society is diverse, diversity issues in employment are not always handled very well. How, for example, can we explain research in which resumés with white-sounding first names, such as Brett, received 50 percent more responses from potential employers than those with black-sounding first names, such as Kareem?[12] The fact that these resumés were created with equal credentials suggests diversity bias, whether unconscious or deliberate.

Prejudice is the display of negative, irrational attitudes toward members of diverse populations.

Prejudice, or the holding of negative, irrational opinions and attitudes regarding members of diverse populations, sets the stage for diversity bias. It becomes active **discrimination** when visible minority members are unfairly treated and denied the full benefits of organizational membership. A subtle form of discrimination is called the **glass ceiling effect**, an invisible barrier or "ceiling" that prevents women and members of visible minorities from rising above a certain level of organizational responsibility. Scholar Judith Rosener warns that the loss caused by any form of discriminatory practice is "undervalued and underutilized human capital."[13]

Discrimination actively denies minority members the full benefits of organizational membership.

The **glass ceiling effect** is an invisible barrier limiting career advancement of women and minorities.

Many voices call diversity a "business imperative," meaning that today's increasingly diverse and multicultural workforce should be an asset that, if tapped, creates opportunities for performance gains. A female vice president at Avon once posed the diversity challenge this way: "Consciously creating an environment where everyone has an equal shot at contributing, participating, and most of all advancing."[14] But even when such awareness exists, consultant R. Roosevelt Thomas says that too many employers still address diversity with the goal of "making their numbers," rather than truly valuing and managing diversity.[15]

GOING GLOBAL

DIVERSITY FACTS

- While women in the United States make up 47 percent of the workforce and hold 50.3 percent of managerial jobs, in Canada women also account for 47 percent of the workforce but hold only 36 percent of managerial roles.

- People of Chinese descent make up 3.6 percent of Canada's workforce; those of South Asian background make up 3.8 percent.

- For each $1 earned by men, Canadian women earn $0.705.

GLOBALIZATION

Japanese management consultant Kenichi Ohmae suggests that the national boundaries of world business have largely disappeared.[16] What is the likelihood that you will someday work domestically for a foreign employer? When you call a customer service help line, do you know which country the service agent is speaking from? Can you state with confidence where a pair of your favourite athletic shoes or the parts for your personal computer were manufactured? More and more products are designed in one country, whereas their components are sourced, and final assembly is contracted in others, and all are for sale in still others. We have reached the point where top managers at Starbucks, IBM, Sony, Toyota, and other global corporations have little need for the word "overseas" in everyday business vocabulary. They operate as global businesses that are equidistant from customers and suppliers, wherever in the world they may be located.

These are all part of the forces of **globalization**, the worldwide interdependence of resource flows, product markets, and business competition that characterizes our new economy.[17] It is described as a process in which "improvements in technology (especially in communications and transportation) combine with the deregulation of markets and open borders to bring about vastly expanded flows of people, money, goods, services, and information."[18]

Globalization is the worldwide interdependence of resource flows, product markets, and business competition.

Globalization isn't an abstract concept. It is increasingly a part of the fabric of our everyday lives, and with particular consequences for work and careers. In our global world, countries and peoples are increasingly interconnected through the news, in travel and lifestyles, in labour markets and employment patterns, and in financial and business dealings. Government leaders now worry about the competitiveness of nations, just as corporate leaders worry about business competitiveness.[19] Employees in a growing number of occupations must worry about being replaced by workers in other countries who are willing and able to perform their jobs through outsourcing and at lower cost to employers. Even new graduates must worry about lower-priced competition for the same jobs from graduates in other parts of the world.

Thomas Friedman, author of *The World Is Flat*, summarizes the challenge of globalization through comments made to him by one of India's business entrepreneurs: "Any activity where we can digitize and decompose the value chain, and move the work around, will get moved around."[20] At a time when more Canadians find that their customer service call is answered in India, their company's website is designed in Malaysia, and their tax return is prepared by an accountant in the Philippines, the fact that globalization offers both opportunities and challenges is quite clear indeed.

TECHNOLOGY

In many ways, the forces of globalization ride on the foundations of the Internet and a continuing explosion in communication technologies. For better or worse, we live and work in a

(AP Photo)

technology-driven world increasingly dominated by bar codes, automatic tellers, e-mail, instant messaging, text messaging, web blogs, on-line media, electronic commerce, social networks, and more. And for a glimpse at what the future might hold, consider how many major firms are now participating in the virtual world of Second Life. If you log in and roam as an avatar, you can visit such major corporations as Toyota, IBM, and Sony to sample and learn about new products and services.

From Second Life to real life, from the small retail store to the large multinational firm, technology is an indispensable part of everyday business—whether one is checking inventory, making a sales transaction, ordering supplies, or analyzing customer preferences. Physical distance hardly matters anymore; in "virtual space," people hold meetings, access common databases, share information and files, make plans, and solve problems together—all without ever meeting face to face. The new technologies have also added great flexibility to work arrangements, allowing people to telecommute, work from home, and maintain mobile offices while working in non-traditional ways and free from the constraints of the normal 9-to-5 schedules.

As all this transpires, everyone has to rush to stay informed and build what we might call their "Tech IQ." For example, job searches now increasingly involve multimedia resumés, and electronic portfolios that display skills and job qualifications. More than 31 percent of employers responding to one survey report using social networking sites in recruitment efforts.[21] Some 44 percent or more of employers say they are now checking the on-line profiles of their job applicants.[22] And, although an electronic persona is fun, it pays to remember that the "brand" one conveys on-line can spill over to affect one's reputation as a job candidate.

ETHICS

When former CEO Jeffrey Skilling was sentenced to 24-plus years in jail for crimes committed during the sensational collapse of Enron Corporation, the message was crystal clear. There is no excuse for senior executives in any organization to act illegally and to tolerate management systems that enrich the few while damaging the many. The harm done at Enron affected company employees who lost retirement savings and shareholders who lost investment values, as well as customers and society at large who paid the price as the firm's business performance deteriorated.[23]

Ethics set moral standards of what is "good" and "right" in one's behaviour.

The issue raised here is **ethics**—a code of moral principles that sets standards of what is "good" and "right" as opposed to "bad" and "wrong" in the conduct of a person or group.[24] And even though ethical failures like those at Enron are well publicized and should be studied, there are a plethora of positive cases and ethical role models to be studied as well.

The former CEO of Dial Corporation, Herb Baum, is one of the positive ethics examples. In his book *The Transparent Leader*, Baum argues that integrity is a key to leadership success and that the responsibility to set the ethical tone of an organization begins at the top. Believing that most CEOs are overpaid, he once gave his annual bonus to the firm's lowest-paid workers. Baum also tells the story of an ethical role model—a rival CEO, Reuben Mark, of Colgate Palmolive. Mark called him one day to say that a newly hired executive had brought with him to Colgate a disk containing Dial's new marketing campaign. Rather than read it, he returned the disk to Baum—an act Baum called "the clearest case of leading with honor and transparency I've witnessed in my career."[25]

You will find in this book many people and organizations that are exemplars of ethical behaviour and whose integrity is unquestioned. They meet the standards of a new ethical reawakening and expectations for ethical leadership at all levels in an organization. They also show respect for such things as sustainable development and protection of the natural environment, protection of consumers through product safety and fair practices, and protection of human rights in all aspects of society, including employment.

CAREERS

Globalization, emerging technologies, and the demand for talent make very personal the importance of initiative and self-renewal when it comes to careers. For most recent graduates, an immediate challenge is getting the first full-time job. And when the economy is down and employment markets are tight, the task of finding a career entry point can be daunting. It always pays to remember the importance of on-line resumés and job searches, and the power of social networking with established professionals. It's also helpful to pursue internships as pathways to first job placements.[26]

Today's career challenge isn't just finding your first job; it's also about successful career planning. British scholar Charles Handy[27] uses the analogy of the Irish shamrock to discuss career patterns characteristic of the new economy. In one leaf of Handy's shamrock are the core workers. These full-time employees pursue traditional career paths. With success and the maintenance of critical skills, they can advance within the organization and may remain employed for a long time. In the second leaf are contract workers. They perform specific tasks as needed by the organization and are compensated on a fee-for-services basis rather than by a continuing wage or salary. They sell a skill or service and contract with many different employers over time. In the third leaf are part-time workers hired only as needed and for as long as needed. Employers expand and reduce their part-time staffs as business needs rise and fall.

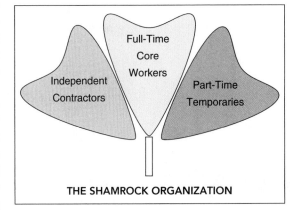

THE SHAMROCK ORGANIZATION

You should be prepared to prosper in any of the shamrock's three leaves. It's likely that you will be changing jobs and employers over time, so your skills must be portable and always of value. These skills aren't gained once and then forgotten; they must be carefully maintained and upgraded all the time. For Handy, this means being a **portfolio worker**, someone who always has the skills needed to readily shift jobs and even careers.[28] Another career consultant describes this career challenge with the analogy of a surfer: "You're always moving. You can expect to fall into the water any number of times, and you have to get back up to catch the next wave." Later in this chapter, we'll be talking more about important career skills and competencies, and how the learning opportunities in *Management* and your course can help strengthen your personal portfolio of capabilities.

A **portfolio worker** has up-to-date skills that allow for job and career mobility.

REAL ETHICS

$100 Laptops

"When you have both Intel and Microsoft on your case, you know you're doing something right," says Nicholas Negroponte. He's a professor at MIT and head of One Laptop Per Child, a non-profit association. Negroponte's goal was to build and distribute laptops for $100 (U.S.) to the world's children. When the first ones were produced in China, the cost came to $188; the "X02" version is shooting for $75. Negroponte is convinced that this is a way to vastly improve the quality of children's educations and life opportunities. Once a child is given a laptop, Negroponte says, "The speed with which this child will acquire the knowledge to use the device is so astonishing, you risk thinking it is genetic."

The One Laptop Per Child project has been backed by Google, chip maker AMD, and Linux software distributor Red Hat. Intel joined and then, after choosing to build its own version, dropped out. A spokesperson says that its alternative, a PC it calls the

"classmate," is a further help in supplying computing power to third-world children.

Negroponte still hopes that soon "every child on the planet will be connected." Meanwhile, he is searching for a CEO to help move his non-profit forward. Says Negroponte: "Management and administration details are my weakness; I'm much better at the vision, big-picture side of the house."

YOU DECIDE

As you think about the goal—making computers available to the world's poor children—tackle this question: Is cooperation or competition the best way to rally the world's non-profits and greatest businesses around positive social change and development in the world's poorest nations?

✓ Learning Check ❶

BE SURE YOU CAN

• describe how intellectual capital, ethics, diversity, globalization, technology, and the changing nature of careers influence working in the new economy • define *intellectual capital, workforce diversity*, and *globalization* • explain how prejudice, discrimination, and the glass ceiling effect can hurt people at work

---

ORGANIZATIONS IN THE NEW WORKPLACE

In his article "The Company of the Future," Robert Reich says: "Everybody works for somebody or something—be it a board of directors, a pension fund, a venture capitalist, or a traditional boss. Sooner or later you're going to have to decide who you want to work for."[29] In order to make good employment choices and perform well in a career, you need a fundamental understanding of the nature of organizations. Management Smarts 1.1 provides a first look at some of the critical survival skills that you should acquire to work well in the organizations of today and tomorrow.[30]

1.1 MANAGEMENT SMARTS
Early career survival skills

- *Mastery:* You need to be good at something; you need to be able to contribute something of value to your employer.

- *Networking:* You need to know people; links with peers and others within and outside the organization are essential to get things done.

- *Entrepreneurship:* You must act as if you are running your own business, spotting ideas and opportunities and stepping out to embrace them.

- *Love of technology:* You have to embrace technology; you don't have to be a technician, but you must be willing and able to fully utilize information technology.

- *Marketing:* You need to be able to communicate your successes and progress, both yours personally and those of your work group.

- *Passion for renewal:* You need to be continuously learning and changing, always updating yourself to best meet future demands.

CANADIAN MANAGERS
Do What You Love!

Courtesy Jacquelyn Cyr

Jacquelyn Cyr, CEO and partner of Toronto-based marketing agency Espresso, has some wise words for business students. Cyr, recognized as a top performer by *Women's Post*, has guided the agency through a major relaunch including rebranding the company. Cyr recommends:

Do what you love. There isn't a possible way to get downtrodden and bored with what you're doing if you're crazy and joyfully obsessed with your work. Of course, doing what you love alone clearly isn't enough—as such, I am a firm believer in being completely imbalanced in order to ensure ongoing motivation. I have no guilt about the imbalance that comprises my life—to me, balance is stagnation, because you're not unleashing the parts of you that are fiery and excited and compelled to do something you used to think wasn't possible. To me, that's the whole reason to work—the whole reason to be!

WHAT IS AN ORGANIZATION?

An **organization** is a collection of people working together to achieve a common purpose. It is a unique social phenomenon that enables its members to perform tasks far beyond the reach of individual accomplishment. This description applies to organizations of all sizes and types, from large corporations to the small businesses that make up the life of any community, to non-profit organizations such as schools, government agencies, and hospitals.

An **organization** is a collection of people working together to achieve a common purpose.

All organizations share a broad purpose—providing goods or services of value to customers and clients. A clear sense of purpose tied to "quality products and services" and "customer satisfaction" is an important source of organizational strength and performance advantage. At Skype (now owned by eBay), founders Niklas Zennstrom and Janus Friis began with a straightforward sense of purpose: they wanted the whole world to be able to talk by telephone for free. When you open Skype on your computer and notice that there are millions of users making calls, you'll see the appeal of what Zennstrom and Friis set out to accomplish.

ORGANIZATIONS AS SYSTEMS

An **open system** transforms resource inputs from the environment into product outputs.

Organizations are **open systems** that interact with their environments in the continual process of obtaining resource inputs and then transforming them into outputs in the form of finished goods and services for their customers.[31] As shown in Figure 1.1, the external environment is both the supplier of resources and the source of customers. Feedback from the environment indicates how well an organization is doing. When customers stop buying a firm's products, it will be hard to stay in business for long unless something soon changes for the better. Any time you hear or read about bankruptcies, for example, remember that they are often stark testimonies to this fact of the marketplace: without loyal customers, a business can't survive.

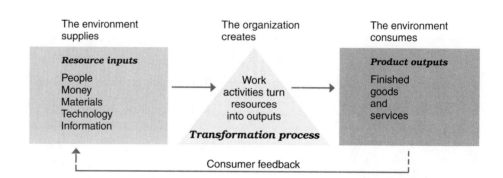

Figure 1.1 Organizations as open systems.

ORGANIZATIONAL PERFORMANCE

If an organization is to perform well, its resources must be well utilized and its customers must be well served. This is a process of value creation through organizational performance. If operations add value to the original cost of resource inputs, then (1) a business organization can earn a profit—that is, sell a product for more than the cost of making it—or (2) a non-profit organization can add wealth to society—that is, provide a public service that is worth more than its cost (e.g., fire protection in a community).

Productivity is the quantity and quality of work performance, with resource utilization considered.

A common way to describe how well an organization is performing overall is **productivity**. It measures the quantity and quality of outputs relative to the cost of inputs. Productivity can be measured at the individual and group as well as organizational levels. And as Figure 1.2 shows, productivity involves two common performance measures: effectiveness and efficiency.

Performance effectiveness is an output measure of task or goal accomplishment.

Performance effectiveness is an output measure of task or goal accomplishment. If you are working as a software engineer for a computer game developer, performance effectiveness may mean that you meet a daily production target in terms of the quantity and quality of lines of code written. This adds to productivity, helping the company as a whole maintain its production schedule and meet customer demands for timely delivery and high-quality gaming products.

Performance efficiency is an input measure of the resource costs associated with goal accomplishment. Returning to the gaming example, the most efficient software production is accomplished at a minimum cost in materials and labour. If you are producing fewer lines of code in a day than you are capable of, this amounts to inefficiency; if you make a lot of mistakes that require extensive rewrites, this is also inefficient work. Such inefficiencies reduce productivity.

Performance efficiency is an input measure of resource cost associated with goal accomplishment.

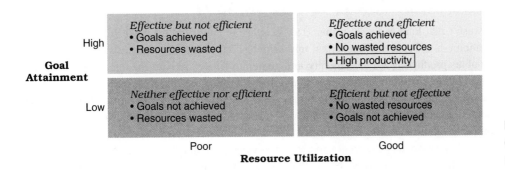

Figure 1.2 Productivity and the dimensions of organizational performance.

CHANGING NATURE OF ORGANIZATIONS

Change is a continuing theme in society, and organizations are certainly undergoing dramatic changes today. Although not exhaustive, the following list of organizational trends and transitions is relevant to your study of management.[32]

- *Renewed belief in human capital:* Demands of the new economy place premiums on high-involvement and participatory work settings that rally the knowledge, experience, and commitment of all members.

- *Demise of "command-and-control":* Traditional hierarchical structures with "do as I say" bosses are proving too slow, conservative, and costly to do well in today's competitive environments.

- *Emphasis on teamwork:* Today's organizations are less vertical and more horizontal in focus; they are increasingly driven by teamwork that pools talents for creative problem solving.

- *Pre-eminence of technology:* New opportunities appear with each development in computer and information technology; they continually change the way organizations operate and how people work.

- *Embrace of networking:* Organizations are networked for intense, real-time communication and coordination, internally among parts and externally with partners, contractors, suppliers, and customers.

- *New workforce expectations:* A new generation of workers brings to the workplace less tolerance for hierarchy, more informality, and more attention to performance merit than to status and seniority.

- *Concern for work-life balance:* As society increases in complexity, workers are forcing organizations to pay more attention to balance in the often-conflicting demands of work and personal affairs.

- *Focus on speed:* Everything moves fast today; in business, those who get products to market first have an advantage, and in any organization, work is expected to be done both well and in a timely manner.

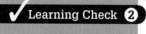 **Learning Check 2** **BE SURE YOU CAN**

• describe how organizations operate as open systems • explain productivity as a measure of organizational performance • distinguish between performance effectiveness and performance efficiency • list several ways in which organizations are changing today

ORGANIZATIONAL ENVIRONMENT

It wasn't that long ago that former U.S. Secretary of Labor Robert Reich said: "The emerging economy is offering unprecedented opportunities, an ever-expanding choice of terrific deals, fabulous products, good investments, and great jobs for people with the right talents and skills. Never before in human history have so many had access to so much so easily."[33] In these terms, things couldn't have been better for organizations and career seekers. But times have changed quite dramatically. We've been dealing with a severe financial crisis, mortgage foreclosures and property value meltdowns in the United States, stimulus packages that have increased long-term debt, global monetary challenges, major energy woes, job cutbacks in many employment sectors, and more. What is now very clear is that the environment in which we live and work includes substantial threats as well as great opportunities. What will the future bring?

We begin this section by reviewing the external environments of organizations and continue by discussing the relationship between the organization and the external environment and how to make good decisions in response to the opportunities and threats posed by the external environment. In this regard, managers continually wrestle with the notion of competitive advantage, the challenges of environmental uncertainty, and the quest for organizational effectiveness.

DYNAMIC FORCES AND THE GENERAL ENVIRONMENT

The **general environment** is composed of economic, legal-political, technological, socio-cultural, and natural environment conditions.

The **general environment** of organizations consists of all external conditions that set the context for managerial decision-making. You might think of it as a broad envelope of dynamic forces within which the organization exists and important decisions must be made. We classify these forces as economic, legal-political, technological, socio-cultural, and natural environment conditions. And as suggested by the Starbucks example in Figure 1.3, it can be quite challenging to understand and deal with the full complexity of an organization's external environment.

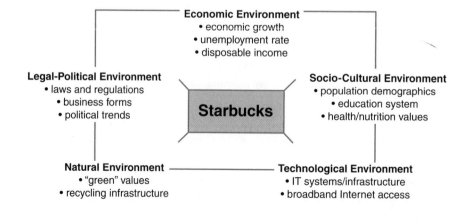

Figure 1.3 Sample general environment conditions faced by firms like Starbucks.

Economic Conditions

Managers must be concerned about *economic conditions* in the general environment, particularly those that influence customer spending, resource supplies, and investment capital. Things like the overall health of the economy in terms of financial markets, inflation, income levels, gross domestic product, unemployment, and job outlook are always important. They affect the amount of wealth available to consumers, and that affects product markets and spending patterns.

Changing economic conditions were major concerns for retail executives at the Bay, Canadian Tire, Walmart, and other stores as they faced the challenges of recessionary forces. When Canadians were hit with losses in investment and retirement accounts and negative economic forecasts, they cut back on consumer spending. Among the retailers, discounters benefited, or at least held their own, while the premium sellers suffered.

CANADIAN MANAGER

Courtesy Ann Kaplan

Publically funded health care is under attack in Canada. With an aging population and shrinking health care budgets, Ann Kaplan, the president and CEO of Medicard Finance Inc., is keeping an eye on government policy around elective medical procedures. Ann launched her company in 1996 as an innovative way for Canadians to pay for elective surgery; it is now the largest medical procedure finance company in Canada. Her business model relies on finding the medical procedures that provincial governments are unable or unwilling to pay for and offering patients ways to assist them to pay for them themselves.

Legal-Political Conditions

Managers must also stay abreast of developments in *legal-political conditions* as represented by existing and proposed laws and regulations, government policies, and the philosophy and objectives of political parties. The last Canadian federal elections were full of debates on issues such as health care, sales taxes, environmental waste, and Canadian troop involvement in Afghanistan. Corporate executives follow such debates and developments closely to monitor trends that can affect the regulation and oversight of their businesses.

The global business environment presents many challenges in respect to legal-political conditions. In 2008, the European Union fined Microsoft $1.35 billion (U.S.) for antitrust violations. The EU ruling targeted Microsoft's practice of bundling media and Windows software, and making the source code for compatibility with other systems unavailable to competitors.[34] Google also faced problems during China's crackdown in Tibet when unrest broke out prior to the Beijing Olympics. After video images from Tibet were posted on Google's YouTube site, the Chinese government cut off access to it and Google acquiesced. The action received lots of criticism, especially given the firm's avowed commitment to information freedom.[35] A company spokesperson said: "We have a delicate balancing act between being a platform for free expression and also obeying local laws around the world."[36]

Reporters Without Borders Top 13 Internet Enemies	
Belarus	Saudi Arabia
China	Syria
Cuba	Tunisia
Egypt	Turkmenistan
Iran	Uzbekistan
Myanmar	Vietnam
North Korea	

Internet censorship is the deliberate blockage and denial of public access to information posted on the Internet.

The Google case raises the issue of **Internet censorship**, the deliberate blockage and denial of public access to information posted on the Internet. National policies on Internet censorship vary around the world, and, as highlighted in the box, organizations like Reporters Without Borders offer periodic reports on censorship policies and press freedom in various countries.[37] With encouragement from the Canadian government and U.S. Senate, Yahoo, Microsoft, Google, and other global companies are supposed to have reached agreement on an Internet Freedom Code of Conduct. This code would voluntarily govern firm behaviour in environments like China where Internet access is restricted by the government.[38]

Technological Conditions

Speaking of the Internet, perhaps nothing gets as much attention these days as developments in the *technological conditions* of the general environment. And if we think changes to date have been something, what about the future? Steve Ballmer, Microsoft's CEO, believes we're just on the edge of yet another technology revolution, one involving personal empowerment and social interaction. He says that, by 2015, among other things, "We will each have a single digital identity; software will learn our habits; and personal information will be instantly and ubiquitously accessible."[39]

Not only must managers stay abreast of the latest technologies for their work applications, they must also be aware of their work implications. You are familiar with YouTube, Facebook, Google Maps, and other Internet resources, but are you aware that one of the growing concerns of employers is just how much time their "tech-savvy" employees spend browsing the Web and engaging in such diversionary pastimes? After finding out that 70 percent of workers spent over an hour a day watching Web-based videos, one employer said: "I almost fell out of my chair when I saw how many people were doing it."[40] And on the employee side of the equation, how often do you hear people talking about how they're "never free from the job" because their work follows them home, on vacation, and just about everywhere in the form of the ubiquitous notebook computer and BlackBerry device?

Socio-Cultural Conditions

The *socio-cultural* conditions of a society or region take meaning as norms, customs, and social values on such matters as ethics, human rights, gender roles, and lifestyles. They also include environmental trends in education and related social institutions, as well as demographic patterns. All such changes have consequences for how organizations are managed. There was a time, for example, when the pay of Canadian CEOs wouldn't have been the subject of much public attention. No more. With a depressed economy and wide gaps between the average worker's pay ($42,305) and the average CEO's ($7.3 million), complaints are flying.[41] Public values are shifting toward intolerance of perceived pay inequities. We have reached the point where in the United States, Congressional discussions have been held on executive pay, and many firms are facing shareholder resolutions asking for more input on executive compensation.

Business executives go to great lengths to track demographic and social trends, and anticipate shifting values that will affect customer tastes and preferences. Not long ago, for example, research was reporting that only about 10 percent of consumers would "go out of their way to purchase environmentally sound products."[42] But dramatic shifts in energy prices and increased attention on global warming seem to be quickly increasing consumer preferences for "green" products—everything from automobiles to energy to building materials to the food we eat. Research also shows that many consumers are now willing to pay more for ethical products (e.g., fair trade coffee) and to punish sellers of products that are unethically made (e.g., rugs made with child labour).[43]

Natural Environment Conditions

When it comes to *natural environment* conditions, "green" is certainly an issue in our communities. Just look at the variety of initiatives likely to be in place on your campus to reduce paper usage, recycle, buy local produce, and adopt energy-saving practices. It's also increasingly evident in job markets, where growth in industries like renewable power is creating new opportunities for "green-collar" employment.[44]

As public concerns for global warming, carbon emissions, and protection of the natural environment grow in strength, their impact on government and business grows as well. We increasingly expect businesses to supply us with environmentally friendly products and to operate in ways that preserve and respect the environment. If you buy Timberland shoes, you'll soon find them labelled with a carbon rating to show how much greenhouse gas was released during the production.[45] This is but one of any number of initiatives you can find in respect to **sustainable business**, where firms operate in ways that both meet the needs of customers and protect or advance the well-being of our natural environment. Business is "sustainable" in the sense that it minimizes our impact on the environment and helps preserve it for the benefit of future generations.[46] The hallmarks of sustainable business practices include less waste, less toxic materials, resource efficiency, energy efficiency, and renewable energy.[47] They represent a transition away from traditional practices that took an exploitative approach to nature and toward ones that demonstrate a desire to live in harmony with nature.[48]

Sustainable business both meets the needs of customers and protects the well-being of our natural environment.

More and more today, you will also hear and read about **sustainable innovation** as businesses strive to create new products and production methods that have lower environmental impacts than the available alternatives. Sustainable innovations are found in areas like energy use, water use, packaging, waste management, and transportation practices, as well as in product development. At Procter & Gamble, for example, researchers identified that the major energy consumption by customers of its laundry products occurred as they used warm or hot water for washing.[49] The firm created Tide Cold Water laundry detergents to eliminate the need for its customers to do this. P&G's goal is to have $20 billion (U.S.) in sustainable innovation products on the market by 2012.

Sustainable innovation creates new products and production methods that have reduced environmental impact.

STAKEHOLDERS AND THE SPECIFIC ENVIRONMENT

The **specific environment**, also called the *task environment*, consists of the actual organizations, groups, and persons with whom an organization interacts and conducts business. Members of the specific environment are often described as **stakeholders**, the persons, groups, and institutions affected in one way or another by the organization's performance.[50] Stakeholders are key constituencies that have a stake in the organization's performance; they are influenced by how it operates, and can influence it in return. Figure 1.4 shows that the important stakeholders for most organizations include customers, suppliers, competitors, regulators, and investors/owners as well as employees. Note also that "society at large" and "future generations" are part of the stakeholder map.

The **specific environment**, or task environment, includes the people and groups with whom an organization interacts.

Stakeholders are the persons, groups, and institutions directly affected by an organization.

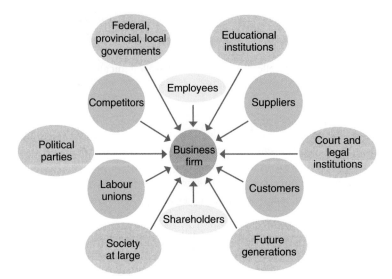

Figure 1.4 Multiple shareholders in the specific or task environment of a typical business firm.

Value creation is the creation of value for and satisfying needs of stakeholders.

For each stakeholder or task environment element, there are many possible interests and considerations for managers. Top-level decisions are often made with the assistance of stakeholder analysis focusing on **value creation**. This is an analysis of the extent to which the organization is creating value for and satisfying the needs of its multiple stakeholders. For example, businesses create value for customers through product pricing and quality; for owners, the value is represented in realized profits and losses. Businesses can create stakeholder value for suppliers through the benefits of long-term business relationships; for local communities, this value can be found in such areas as the citizenship businesses display in using and contributing to public services. Value creation for employees takes such forms as wages earned and job satisfaction. And businesses can even create value for competitors. An example is Starbucks, where coffee industry experts claim that having a Starbucks open in a neighbourhood stimulates the growth of small independent coffee shops. Why? The answer is that Starbucks creates "a clientele for coffee that wouldn't otherwise exist."[51]

Of course, the interests of multiple stakeholders sometimes conflict, and management decisions have to address different priorities and trade-offs among them. In a study conducted a few years ago, for example, MBA students were asked a question regarding what a business's top priorities should be. Some 75 percent answered "maximizing shareholder value," and 71 percent answered "satisfying customers." Only 25 percent included "creating value for communities," and only 5 percent noted "concern for environmentalism."[52] It would be interesting to repeat the survey today, at a time when the stakeholder concerns of society at large and future generations are driving more emphasis on sustainable business practices.

COMPETITIVE ADVANTAGE

Competitive advantage allows an organization to deal with market and environmental forces better than its competitors.

Competitors are a key element in any analysis of the specific or task environment of the organization. The term **competitive advantage** refers to something that an organization does extremely well, a core competency that clearly sets it apart from competitors and gives it an advantage over them in the marketplace.[53] Competitive advantage is an ability to do things better than one's competitors. When these are things others cannot quickly copy or easily learn to do, the competitive advantage becomes more sustainable over time.

The notion of competitive advantage may be best summed up as an answer to this question: "What does my organization do best?" Legendary investor Warren Buffet is often quoted as saying "sustainable competitive advantage" is what he first looks for in a potential investment. Examples of what might attract Buffet as an investor and that represent the essence of competitive advantage include Walmart's inventory management technology, which enables a low cost structure, and Coca-Cola's brand management, which helps maintain a loyal customer base.

When strategic management is examined in Chapter 7, competitive advantage is linked with what Harvard scholar Michael Porter calls **strategic positioning**—helping one's firm or organization do different things or the same things in different ways from one's major competitors.[54] For Porter and others, this quest for competitive advantage can be pursued in a variety of ways, most of which fall into one or more of the following categories.

Strategic positioning occurs when an organization does different things or the same things in different ways from its major competitors.

- *Competitive advantage can be achieved through costs*—finding ways to operate with lower costs than one's competitors and thus earn profits with prices that competitors have difficulty matching.

- *Competitive advantage can be achieved through quality*—finding ways to create products and services than are of demonstrably and consistently higher quality for customers than what is offered by one's competitors.

- *Competitive advantage can be achieved through delivery*—finding ways to outperform competitors by delivering products and services to customers faster and consistently on time, and to continue to develop timely new products.

- *Competitive advantage can be achieved through flexibility*—finding ways to adjust and tailor products and services to fit customer needs in ways that are difficult for one's competitors to match.

 Canadian Company in the News

RIM NOW PLAYING CATCH-UP

Waterloo, Ontario–based Research In Motion (RIM) carved a front-runner place in the smart phone market because it recognized consumer desires to keep connected. With its handheld BlackBerry and the technology that goes with it, RIM cornered the market in the way business communicates in the new economy. Other companies took note and then took aim at RIM by releasing their own smart phones.

The Canadian Press Images/Stephen C. Host

Reacting to competition, RIM introduced a new BlackBerry called the Torch and with it a new operating system. Some worry that it looks all too familiar with its thumb-friendly keyboard and staid business design. Will consumers ignore it in favour of the iPhone or latest Android handset? Will times be less rosy for RIM? In the fiercely competitive world of smart phones, standing still is not an option.

ENVIRONMENTAL UNCERTAINTY

Environmental uncertainty is a lack of complete information about the environment.

As managers pursue competitive advantage in dealing with opportunities and threats in the external environment, decision-making is often complicated by uncertainty. **Environmental uncertainty** means that there is a lack of complete information regarding what exists and what developments may occur. This makes it difficult to analyze general environment conditions and deal more specifically with stakeholders' needs. With greater uncertainty, it becomes harder to predict future states of affairs and understand their potential implications for the organization.

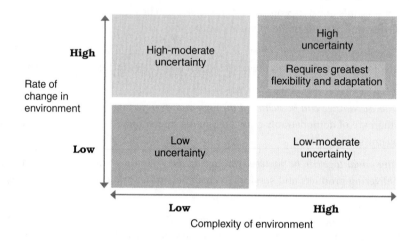

Figure 1.5 Dimensions of uncertainty in the external environments of organizations.

Researchers describe the two dimensions of environmental uncertainty shown in Figure 1.5.[55] The first is the *degree of complexity*, or the number of different factors in the environment. An environment is typically classified as relatively simple or complex. The second is the *rate of change* in and among these factors. An environment is typically classified as stable or dynamic. The most challenging of the four possible combinations is the environment that is complex and dynamic, perhaps well represented by what faces automobile industry executives today. Such high-uncertainty environments require flexibility and adaptability in organizational designs and work practices. Because of uncertainty, organizations must be able to respond quickly as new circumstances arise and new information becomes available.

ORGANIZATIONAL EFFECTIVENESS

Organizational effectiveness is sustainable high performance in using resources to accomplish a mission.

A basic indicator of management success in dealing with complex and changing environments is **organizational effectiveness**—sustainable high performance in using resources to accomplish mission and objectives. Theorists view and analyze organizational effectiveness from different vantage points.[56]

- The *systems resource approach* looks at the input side and defines organizational effectiveness in terms of success in acquiring needed resources from the organization's environment.

- The *internal process approach* looks at the transformation process and defines organizational effectiveness in terms of how efficiently resources are utilized to produce goods and services.

- The *goal approach* looks at the output side and defines organizational effectiveness in terms of how to measure achievement of key operating objectives.

- The *strategic constituencies approach* looks at the external environment and defines organizational effectiveness in terms of the organization's impact on key stakeholders and their interests.

Organizational effectiveness can also be evaluated on a time line.[57] In the short run, the criteria focus on performance effectiveness in goal accomplishment and performance efficiency in resource utilization, as well as stakeholder satisfaction—including customers, employees, owners, and society at large. In the medium term, two more criteria become important: adaptability in the face of changing environments, and development of people and systems to meet new challenges. And in the long run, the criterion is prosperity under conditions of uncertainty.

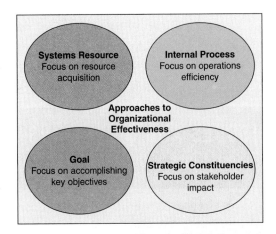

Systems Resource
Focus on resource acquisition

Internal Process
Focus on operations efficiency

Approaches to Organizational Effectiveness

Goal
Focus on accomplishing key objectives

Strategic Constituencies
Focus on stakeholder impact

BE SURE YOU CAN

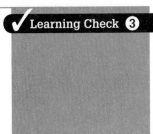 Learning Check ❸

- list key elements in the general and specific environments of organizations • define *sustainable business* and *sustainable innovation* • describe how a business can create value for four key stakeholders • define *competitive advantage* and give examples of how a business might achieve it • analyze the uncertainty of an organization's external environment • describe the systems resource, internal process, goal, and strategic constituencies approaches to organizational effectiveness

MANAGERS IN THE NEW WORKPLACE

This chapter opened with an emphasis on people, along with their talents and intellectual capital, as key foundations of organizational success. In an article entitled "Putting People First for Organizational Success," Jeffrey Pfeffer and John F. Veiga argue forcefully that organizations perform better when they treat their members better.[58] They note that "managers" in high-performing organizations act in ways that truly value people. They don't treat people as costs to be controlled; they treat them as valuable strategic assets to be carefully nurtured and developed. So, who are these "managers" and just what do they do?

WHAT IS A MANAGER?

You find them in all organizations. They work with a wide variety of job titles—team leader, department head, supervisor, project manager, dean, president, administrator, and more. They always work directly with other persons who rely on them for critical support and assistance in their own jobs. Peter Drucker described their job as "to make work productive and workers effective."[59] We call them **managers**, people in organizations who directly support, supervise, and help activate the work efforts and performance accomplishments of others.

For those serving as managers, the job is challenging and substantial. Any manager is responsible not just for her or his own work but for the overall performance accomplishments of a team, work group, department, or even organization as a whole. Whether they are called direct reports, team members, work associates, or subordinates, these "other people" are the essential human resources whose contributions represent the real work of the organization. And as pointed out by Canadian management theorist Henry Mintzberg, being a manager remains an important and socially responsible job:[60]

A **manager** is a person who supports, activates, and is responsible for the work of others.

No job is more vital to our society than that of the manager. It is the manager who determines whether our social institutions serve us well or whether they squander our talents and resources. It is time to strip away the folklore about managerial work, and time to study it realistically so that we can begin the difficult task of making significant improvement in its performance.

ISSUES AND SITUATIONS
Talent Wars

Scene: Executive conference room at a large corporation.
Action: The vice president for human resource development is convening a staff meeting.

"Welcome all. The purpose of today's meeting is to get everyone's attention focused on a fundamental issue, one that may well determine the future of our company. I'm speaking about TALENT, the lifeblood of any organization. And I'm concerned about the implications of this PowerPoint slide— 'Conversation Starters.'

"Now, here's the task. Each year we hire many newcomers into the firm; we also make a fair number of offers that are rejected. Think about our university recruiting and the management of newcomers. Think of everything that you believe we can and should be doing in order to attract, hold, nurture, and develop the most talented workforce possible.

"Tell me what you think we need to do in order to win what some people are starting to call the 'war for talent.' Jot down your ideas as two lists: List A for best practices in university recruiting, and List B for best practices in managing newcomers."

CRITICAL RESPONSE

Project yourself into the conference room. Respond to the VP's charge by preparing A and B lists based on your needs,

aspirations, and experiences. Include insights gained from your friends and acquaintances, and the conversations you share with them.

Conversation Starters

- We face major hiring needs now and for several years as our aging "baby boomers" phase into retirement.
- "Gen Ys" graduating from post-secondary education have strong skills; they also have unique career needs and aspirations.
- Our management ranks are increasingly diverse, but most top managers are older white males.
- Recruiting and training budgets are shrinking as the firm deals with a sagging economy.

LEVELS OF MANAGERS

Top managers guide the performance of the organization as a whole or of one of its major parts.

At the highest levels of organizations, as shown in Figure 1.6, common job titles are chief executive officer (CEO), president, and vice president. These **top managers** are responsible for the performance of an organization as a whole or for one of its larger parts. They are supposed to pay special attention to the external environment, be alert to potential long-run problems and opportunities, and develop appropriate ways of dealing with them. Top managers also create and communicate long-term vision, and ensure that strategies and objectives are consistent with the organization's purpose and mission.

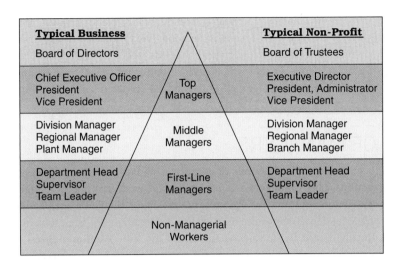

Figure 1.6 Management levels in typical business and non-profit organizations.

Top managers should be future-oriented, strategic thinkers capable of making decisions under competitive and uncertain conditions. Newly repurchased Canadian chocolatier Laura Secord will emulate strategic planning as executives with parent company Nutriart begin to rebuild and reposition the brand to appeal to younger demographics in addition to their existing clientele. With the brand's current strategic positioning between premium brands such as Godiva chocolates and convenience brands such as Cadbury, the president of Laura Secord, Jean Leclerc, highlights: "It's always a challenge to follow new trends and keep customers coming . . . There is a lot of work to do on the brand, but we're not going to apologize for being nearly 100 years old."[61]

Reporting to top managers are **middle managers** who are in charge of relatively large departments or divisions consisting of several smaller work units. Examples are clinic directors in hospitals; deans in universities; and division managers, plant managers, and regional sales managers in businesses. Middle managers work with top managers and coordinate with peers to develop and implement action plans to accomplish organizational objectives.

Middle managers oversee the work of large departments or divisions.

Team leaders report to middle managers and supervise non-managerial workers.

Even though most people enter the workforce as technical specialists such as auditor, market researcher, or systems analyst, sooner or later they advance to positions of initial managerial responsibility. A first job in management typically involves serving as a **team leader** or supervisor—someone in charge of a small work group composed of nonmanagerial workers. Job titles for these first-line managers include such designations as department head, group leader, and unit manager. For example, the leader of an auditing team is considered a first-line manager, as is the head of an academic department in a university.

People serving in team leader positions create the building blocks for organizational performance.[62] Jean Leclerc's goals for Laura Secord could be met only with the contributions of people like his brother Jacques Leclerc, head of the research and

1.2 MANAGEMENT SMARTS
Advice for front-line managers

1. Plan meetings and work schedules.

2. Clarify goals and tasks, and gather ideas for improvement.

3. Appraise performance and counsel team members.

4. Recommend pay increases and new assignments.

5. Recruit, train, and develop team members.

6. Encourage high performance and teamwork.

7. Inform team members about organizational goals.

8. Inform higher levels of team needs and accomplishments.

9. Coordinate activities with other teams.

development division, who has been leading the team responsible for ensuring that the traditional taste of Laura Secord chocolates remains the same. "We have state of the art machinery and we have been doing tests for more than six months," attests Jacques Leclerc, who is committed to maintaining Canadian suppliers while bringing select production to in-house facilities at parent company Nutriart.[63] Management Smarts 1.2 offers advice for team leaders and other first-line managers.

TYPES OF MANAGERS

Line managers directly contribute to producing the organization's goods or services.

Staff managers use special technical expertise to advise and support line workers.

Functional managers are responsible for one area such as finance, marketing, production, personnel, accounting, or sales.

General managers are responsible for complex, multifunctional units.

An **administrator** is a manager in a public or non-profit organization.

In addition to serving at different levels of authority, managers work in different capacities within organizations. **Line managers** are responsible for work that makes a direct contribution to the organization's outputs. For example, the president, retail manager, and department supervisors of a local department store all have line responsibilities. Their jobs in one way or another are directly related to the sales operations of the store. **Staff managers**, by contrast, use special technical expertise to advise and support the efforts of line workers. In a department store, again, the director of human resources and chief financial officer would have staff responsibilities.

In business, **functional managers** have responsibility for a single area of activity such as finance, marketing, production, human resources, accounting, or sales. **General managers** are responsible for activities covering many functional areas. An example is a plant manager who oversees purchasing, manufacturing, warehousing, sales, personnel, and accounting functions. In public or non-profit organizations, it is common for managers to be called **administrators**. Examples include hospital administrators, public administrators, and city administrators.

MANAGERIAL PERFORMANCE

Accountability is the requirement to show performance results to a supervisor.

An **effective manager** helps others achieve high performance and satisfaction at work.

Quality of work life is the overall quality of human experiences in the workplace.

All managers help people, working individually and in groups, to perform. They do this while being held personally "accountable" for results achieved. **Accountability** is the requirement of one person to answer to a higher authority for performance results in his or her area of work responsibility. The team leader is accountable to a middle manager, the middle manager is accountable to a top manager, and even the top manager is accountable to a board of directors or board of trustees.

But what actually constitutes managerial performance? When is a manager "effective"? A good answer is that **effective managers** successfully help others achieve both high performance and satisfaction in their work. This dual concern for performance and satisfaction introduces the concept of **quality of work life** (QWL). It is an indicator of the overall quality of human experiences in the workplace. A "high-QWL" workplace offers such things as fair pay, safe working conditions, opportunities to learn and use new skills, room to grow and progress in a career, protection of individual rights, and pride in the work itself and in the organization. Would you agree that both performance and satisfaction are important management goals, and that productivity and quality of work life can and should go hand in hand?

CHANGING NATURE OF MANAGERIAL WORK

Mark Jones, President and CEO of pharmaceutical company AstraZeneca Canada, can attest to the importance of engaging employees in opportunity development in the modern workplace. In the development of Frontline Health, AstraZeneca's program to support health care providers that helps Canadians with limited or no access to health services, Jones has heavily involved employees in the development process right from the beginning. As he offers: "Building employee consensus and involvement may be more complex and time-consuming than an executive decision, but it is ultimately a much stronger foundation on which to build one's program."[64] As Jones's comments highlight, we are in a time when the best managers are known more for "helping" and "supporting" than for "directing" and "order giving." The words "coordinator," "coach," and "team leader" are heard as often as "supervisor" or "boss." The best managers are well informed regarding the needs of those reporting to or dependent on them. They can often be found providing advice and developing the support needed for others to perform to the best of their abilities.

The concept of the **upside-down pyramid** fits well with Mark Jones's description of his job as a manager and in general reflects the changing nature of managerial work today. Shown in Figure 1.7, the pyramid offers an alternative and suggestive way of viewing organizations and the role played by managers within them. Notice that the operating workers are at the top of the upside-down pyramid, just below the customers and clients they serve. They are supported in their work efforts by managers below them. These managers clearly aren't just order-givers; they are there to mobilize and deliver the support others need to do their jobs best and serve customer needs. The upside-down pyramid view leaves no doubt that the whole organization is devoted to serving the customer, and that the job of managers is to support the workers.

In the **upside-down pyramid**, operating workers are at the top, serving customers, while managers are at the bottom supporting them.

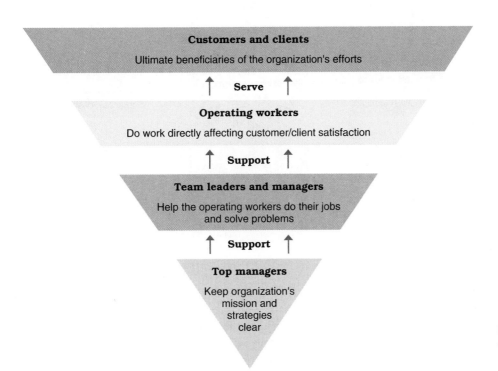

Figure 1.7 The organization viewed as an upside-down pyramid.

BE SURE YOU CAN

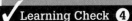 Learning Check ❹

• describe the various types and levels of managers • define *accountability* and *quality of work life*, and explain their importance to managerial performance • discuss how managerial work is changing today • explain the role of managers in the upside-down pyramid view of organizations

THE MANAGEMENT PROCESS

If productivity in the form of high levels of performance effectiveness and efficiency is a measure of organizational success, managers are largely responsible for its achievement. The ultimate "bottom line" in every manager's job is to help an organization achieve high performance by best utilizing its human and material resources.

FUNCTIONS OF MANAGEMENT

Management is the process of planning, organizing, leading, and controlling the use of resources to accomplish performance goals.

The process of **management** involves planning, organizing, leading, and controlling the use of resources to accomplish performance goals. These four management functions and their interrelationships are shown in Figure 1.8. All managers, regardless of title, level, type, and organizational setting, are responsible for the four functions. However, they are not accomplished in a linear, step-by-step fashion. The reality is that these functions are continually engaged as a manager moves from task to task and opportunity to opportunity in his or her work.

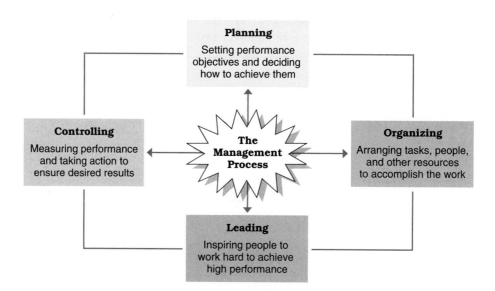

Figure 1.8 Four functions of management.

Planning

Planning is the process of setting objectives and determining what should be done to accomplish them.

In management, **planning** is the process of setting performance objectives and determining what actions should be taken to accomplish them. Through planning, a manager identifies desired results and ways to achieve them.

Take, for example, an Ernst & Young initiative that was developed to better meet the needs of the firm's female professionals. This initiative grew out of top management's concern about the firm's retention rates for women.[65] The firm's chairman at the time, Philip A. Laskawy, launched a Diversity Task Force with the planning objective to reduce turnover rates for women. When the task force began its work, this turnover was running some 22 percent per year, and it cost the firm about 150 percent of a departing employee's annual salary to hire and train each replacement.

Organizing

Organizing is the process of assigning tasks, allocating resources, and coordinating work activities.

Even the best plans will fail without strong implementation. This begins with **organizing**: the process of assigning tasks, allocating resources, and coordinating the activities of individuals and groups to implement plans. Through organizing, managers turn plans into actions by defining jobs, assigning personnel, and supporting them with technology and other resources.

At Ernst & Young, Laskawy organized to meet the planning objective by first creating a new Office of Retention and then hiring Deborah K. Holmes to head it. As retention problems were identified in various parts of the firm, Holmes also took initiative. She convened special task forces to tackle problems and recommend location-specific solutions. For example, a Woman's Access Program was started to give women access to senior executives for mentoring and career development.

Leading

In management, **leading** is the process of arousing people's enthusiasm to work hard and inspiring their efforts to fulfill plans and accomplish objectives. By leading, managers build commitments to a common vision, encourage activities that support goals, and influence others to do their best work on the organization's behalf.

Leading is the process of arousing enthusiasm and inspiring efforts to achieve goals.

At Ernst & Young, Deborah Holmes identified a core problem: work at the firm was extremely intense, and women were often stressed because their spouses also worked. She became a champion for improved work-life balance and pursued it relentlessly. Although admitting that "there's no silver bullet" in the form of a universal solution, her office supported and encouraged better balance in a variety of ways. She started "call-free holidays," when professionals did not check voice mail or e-mail on weekends and holidays. She also started a "travel sanity" program that limited staffers' travel to four days a week so that they could get home for weekends.

Controlling

The management function of **controlling** is the process of measuring work performance, comparing results with objectives, and taking corrective action as needed. Through controlling, managers maintain active contact with people in the course of their work, gather and interpret reports on performance, and use this information to make constructive changes. In today's dynamic times, such control and adjustment are indispensable. Things don't always go as anticipated, and plans must be modified and redefined for future success.

Controlling is the process of measuring performance and taking action to ensure desired results.

At Ernst & Young, Laskawy and Holmes had documented what the firm's retention rates for women were when they started the new program. With this baseline, they were subsequently able to track progress to verify real improvements. Through measurement, they were able to compare actual results with planning objectives, and identify changes in work-life balance and retention rates over time. As they reviewed the results, they continually adjusted their plans and activities to improve future performance.

MANAGERIAL ROLES AND ACTIVITIES

Although the management process as just described may seem straightforward, planning, organizing, leading, and controlling are more complicated than they appear at first glance. In his classic book *The Nature of Managerial Work*, for example, Henry Mintzberg describes the daily work of corporate chief executives as follows: "There was no break in the pace of activity during office hours. The mail . . . telephone calls . . . and meetings . . . accounted for almost every minute from the moment these executives entered their offices in the morning until they departed in the evenings."[66] Today we would complicate things even further by adding everpresent e-mail, instant messages, text messages, and voice mail to Mintzberg's list of executive preoccupations.

RESEARCH BRIEF

Worldwide study identifies success factors in global leadership

Robert J. House and colleagues developed a network of 170 researchers to study leadership around the world. Over a 10-year period, they investigated cultural frameworks, cultural differences, and their leadership implications as part of Project GLOBE. The results are summarized in the book *Culture, Leadership, and Organizations: The GLOBE Study of 62 Societies* (Sage, 2004).

Data from over 17,000 managers working in 62 national cultures were collected and analyzed. In respect to leadership effectiveness, the researchers found that the world's cultures share certain universal facilitators and impediments to leadership success, while also having some unique cultural contingencies. In terms of leadership development, the GLOBE researchers concluded that global mindsets, tolerance for ambiguity, cultural adaptability, and flexibility are essential as leaders seek to influence persons whose cultural backgrounds are different from their own. Personal aspects that seemed most culturally sensitive in terms of leadership effectiveness were being individualist, being status conscious, and being open to risk.

Universal facilitators of leadership effectiveness

- *Trustworthy, honest, just*
- *Foresight, ability to plan ahead*
- *Positive, dynamic, encouraging, motivating*
- *Communicative, informed, integrating*

Universal impediments to leadership effectiveness

- *Loner, asocial, self-protective*
- *Non-cooperative, irritable*
- *Dictatorial and autocratic*

You be the researcher

Take a survey of workers at your university, place of employment, or a local organization. Ask them to describe their best and worst leaders. Use the results to answer the question: How closely do local views of leadership match with findings of the GLOBE study?

As informative as the GLOBE project is, don't you agree that we still have a lot more to learn about how leadership success is viewed in the many cultures of the world? The links between culture and leadership seem particularly important, not only in a business context, but also as governments try to work together both bilaterally and multilaterally in forums such as the United Nations.

Managerial Roles

In trying to better understand and describe the nature of managerial work, Mintzberg also identified a set of 10 roles that managers fulfill.[67] The roles fall into three categories: informational, interpersonal, and decisional roles.

A manager's informational roles involve the giving, receiving, and analyzing of information. A manager fulfilling these roles will be a *monitor*, scanning for information; a *disseminator*, sharing information; and a *spokesperson*, acting as official communicator. The interpersonal roles involve interactions with people inside and outside the work unit. A manager fulfilling these roles will be a *figurehead*, modelling and setting forth key principles and policies; a *leader*, providing direction and instilling enthusiasm; and a *liaison*, coordinating with others. The decisional roles involve using information to make decisions to solve problems or address opportunities. A manager fulfilling these roles will be a *disturbance handler*, dealing with problems and conflicts; a *resource allocator*, handling budgets and distributing resources; a *negotiator*, making deals and forging agreements; and an *entrepreneur*, developing new initiatives. Figure 1.9 further describes all 10 roles.

Interpersonal roles	Informational roles	Decisional roles
How a manager interacts with other people	How a manager exchanges and processes information	How a manager uses information in decision-making
• Figurehead • Leader • Liaison	• Monitor • Disseminator • Spokesperson	• Entrepreneur • Disturbance handler • Resource allocator • Negotiator

Figure 1.9 Mintzberg's 10 managerial roles.

Managerial Activities

Managers must not only understand and master their roles, they must also have the ability to implement them in an intense and complex work setting. The managers Mintzberg observed had little free time to themselves; unexpected problems and continuing requests for meetings consumed almost all the time that became available. Their workdays were hectic, and the pressure for continuously improving performance was all-encompassing. Mintzberg summarized his observations this way: "The manager can never be free to forget the job, and never has the pleasure of knowing, even temporarily, that there is nothing else to do . . . . Managers always carry the nagging suspicion that they might be able to contribute just a little bit more. Hence they assume an unrelenting pace in their work."[68]

Without any doubt, managerial work is busy, demanding, and stressful for all levels of responsibility in any work setting. However, it is worth noting that managerial work is also intellectually challenging and personally and financially rewarding. A summary of continuing research on the nature of managerial work offers this important reminder:[69]

- Managers work long hours.

- Managers work at an intense pace.

- Managers work at fragmented and varied tasks.

- Managers work with many communication media.

- Managers accomplish their work largely through interpersonal relationships.

MANAGERIAL AGENDAS AND NETWORKS

On his way to a meeting, a GM bumped into a staff member who did not report to him. Using this opportunity, in a two-minute conversation, he (a) asked two questions and received the information he needed; (b) reinforced their good relationship by sincerely complimenting the staff member on something he had recently done; and (c) got the staff member to agree to do something that the GM needed done.

This brief incident provides a glimpse of an effective general manager (GM) in action.[70] It portrays two activities that management consultant and scholar John Kotter considers critical to a manager's success: agenda setting and networking. Through **agenda setting**, good managers develop action priorities that include goals and plans spanning long and short time frames. These agendas are usually incomplete and loosely connected in the beginning, but they become more

Agenda setting develops action priorities for accomplishing goals and plans.

specific as the manager utilizes information continually gleaned from many different sources. The agendas are always kept in mind and are "played out" whenever an opportunity arises, as in the preceding example.

Good managers implement their agendas by working with many people inside and outside the organization. This is made possible by **networking**, the process of building and maintaining positive relationships with people whose help may be needed to implement one's agendas. Such networking creates **social capital**—a capacity to attract support and help from others in order to get things done. In Kotter's example, the GM received help from a staff member who did not report directly to him. His networks and social capital would also include relationships with peers, a boss, higher-level executives, subordinates, and members of their work teams, as well as with external customers, suppliers, and community representatives.

Networking is the process of creating positive relationships with people who can help advance agendas.

Social capital is a capacity to get things done with support and help of others.

ESSENTIAL MANAGERIAL SKILLS

Today's turbulent times present an ever-shifting array of problems, opportunities, and performance expectations for organizations, their managers, and their members. All of this, of course, means that your career success depends on a real commitment to **learning**—changing behaviour through experience. In management, the learning focus is on developing skills and competencies to deal with the complexities of human behaviour and problem solving in organizations. When you think about this goal, don't forget that it's not just formal learning in the classroom that counts. Indeed the long-term difference in career success may well rest with **lifelong learning**—the process of continuous learning from all of our daily experiences and opportunities.

A **skill** is the ability to translate knowledge into action that results in desired performance. Harvard scholar Robert L. Katz has classified the essential, or baseline, skills of managers into three useful categories: technical, human, and conceptual.[71] He suggests that their relative importance tends to vary by level of managerial responsibility, as shown in Figure 1.10.

Learning is a change in behaviour that results from experience.

Lifelong learning is continuous learning from daily experiences.

A **skill** is the ability to translate knowledge into action that results in desired performance.

Lower-level managers	Middle-level managers	Top-level managers
Conceptual skills—The ability to think analytically and achieve integrative problem solving		
Human skills—The ability to work well in cooperation with other persons; emotional intelligence		
Technical skills—The ability to apply expertise and perform a special task with proficiency		

Figure 1.10 Katz's essential managerial skills.

Technical Skills

A **technical skill** is the ability to use a special proficiency or expertise to perform particular tasks. Accountants, engineers, market researchers, financial planners, and systems analysts, for example, possess technical skills. These skills are initially acquired through formal education and are further developed by training and job experience. Figure 1.10 shows that technical skills are very important at career entry levels. The critical question for you in preparation for any job interview comes down to this simple test: "What can I really do right from the start that offers value for an employer?"

A **technical skill** is the ability to use expertise to perform a task with proficiency.

Human and Interpersonal Skills

The ability to work well in cooperation with other persons is a **human skill** or an interpersonal skill. Given the highly interpersonal nature of managerial work, human skills are consistently important across all the managerial levels. They emerge in the workplace as the capacity to collaborate and network with others, to engage others with a spirit of trust, enthusiasm, and positive engagement. The next time you sign on to Facebook or Bebo or LinkedIn, for example, think about how these social networking experiences can translate into workplace networking skills.

> A **human skill** or interpersonal skill is the ability to work well in cooperation with other people.

A manager with good human skills will have a high degree of self-awareness and a capacity to understand or empathize with the feelings of others. This relates to **emotional intelligence**. Discussed also in later chapters for its leadership implications, "EI" is defined by scholar and consultant Daniel Goleman as the "ability to manage ourselves and our relationships effectively."[72] Emotional intelligence is reflected in how well or poorly you recognize, understand, and manage feelings while interacting and dealing with others. Someone high in emotional intelligence will know when her or his emotions are about to become disruptive, and act to control them. This same person will sense when another person's emotions are negatively influencing a relationship, and make attempts to understand and better deal with them.[73] If you are willing to ask, a straightforward question can put your interpersonal skills and emotional intelligence to the test: "Just how well do I relate with and work with others?"

> **Emotional intelligence** is the ability to manage ourselves and our relationships effectively.

Conceptual and Analytical Skills

The ability to think critically and analytically is a **conceptual skill**. It involves the capacity to break problems into smaller parts, to see the relations between the parts, and to recognize the implications of any one problem for others.

> A **conceptual skill** is the ability to think analytically to diagnose and solve complex problems.

In the classroom, we often call this "critical thinking." It is a diagnostic skill that facilitates effective decision-making and problem solving. As people assume ever-higher responsibilities in organizations, they are called upon to deal with more ambiguous problems that have many complications and longer-term consequences. This is why Figure 1.10 shows that conceptual skills gain in relative importance for top managers. In respect to long-term career readiness, the question to ask is: "Am I developing the critical-thinking and problem-solving capabilities I will need for long-term career success?"

DEVELOPING MANAGERIAL COMPETENCIES

Katz's notion of essential managerial skills is taken further in ideas expressed by futurist Daniel Pink. In his book *A Whole New Mind,* Pink points out that our societal transition from information age into a new conceptual age is demanding a combination of conceptual and human skills that makes us good at both creating and empathizing.[74] This "right brain" skills package is both *high concept*—the ability to see the big picture, identify patterns, and combine ideas—and *high touch*— the ability to empathize and enjoy others in the pursuit of a purpose.

Management educators are devoted to helping students and practising managers acquire and continually develop the skills needed for managerial success. To personalize the challenge, you might think of a **managerial competency** as a skill-based capability that contributes to high performance in a management job.[75] A number of high-concept and high-touch competencies are listed here as a baseline checklist for you to consider.

> A **managerial competency** is a skill-based capability for high performance in a management job.

- *Communication*—Ability to share ideas and findings clearly in written and oral expression— includes writing, oral presentation, giving/receiving feedback, technology utilization.

- *Teamwork*—Ability to work effectively as a team member and team leader—includes team contribution, team leadership, conflict management, negotiation, consensus building.

- *Self-management*—Ability to evaluate oneself, modify behaviour, and meet performance obligations—includes ethical reasoning and behaviour, personal flexibility, tolerance for ambiguity, performance responsibility.

- *Leadership*—Ability to influence and support others to perform complex and ambiguous tasks—includes diversity awareness, global understanding, project management, strategic action.

- *Critical thinking*—Ability to gather and analyze information for creative problem solving—includes problem solving, judgement and decision-making, information gathering and interpretation, creativity/innovation.

- *Professionalism*—Ability to sustain a positive impression, instill confidence, and maintain career advancement—includes personal presence, personal initiative, career management.

MANAGEMENT LEARNING MODEL

Management is written and organized to help you learn managerial skills and competencies while deepening your understanding of the knowledge base to which they are linked. The emphasis is on both studying key management concepts, theories, and research, and understanding their implications for improved management practice and performance.

You have already experienced the learning model of *Management* by reading this first chapter. The model initiates learning with the all-important commitment to *experience and self-assessment*—engaging experience and coming to terms with where you presently stand in respect to skills, personal characteristics, and understandings. Each chapter opens with a "Learning from Others" example to demonstrate how we can learn about management from experience and by following the news and current events on people and organizations. Each chapter also opens with a "Learning about Yourself" section that highlights an essential management skill or competency for personal inquiry. It ties in with an end-of-chapter "Self-Assessment" section that includes both "Back to Yourself"—a reflection on how the focus of the chapter opener fits with chapter content—and "Further Reflection"—a self-assessment instrument that can be taken to gain added personal insights.

Next in the learning model is *inquiry and reflection*—the process of discovering, thinking about, and understanding the knowledge base of management. The chapter content is written and organized to clearly present core theories and concepts. Many examples are interspersed to help show the relevance of the theories and concepts to real-world settings. Also, a "Research Brief" illustrates the types of questions researchers are trying to answer in their scientific inquiries into matters relevant to chapter content. "Learning Checks" at the end of each major heading are chances to pause and check understanding before reading further. The end-of-chapter "Self-Test" includes multiple-choice, short answer, and essay questions to further check comprehension and exam readiness.

The process of *analysis and application* completes the learning model. It is facilitated by chapter features such as "Real Ethics" and "Issues and Situations." They present incidents that pose common management challenges and dilemmas, and then ask you to engage in critical thinking about how best to deal with them. "Going Global" boxes illustrate how globalization is affecting management trends, and how managers around the world carry out their work. "Canadian Companies in the News" and "Canadian Managers" spotlight management issues close to home. "Management Smarts" summaries in each chapter also provide bullet list pointers on how to put the theories and concepts into practice. The end-of-chapter "Class Exercise" and "Case Study" offer further opportunities to wrestle with theory-into-practice applications relevant to chapter content, and to test your problem-solving capabilities in management.

BE SURE YOU CAN

• define and give examples of each of the management functions—*planning, organizing, leading,* and *controlling* • explain Mintzberg's view of what managers do, including the 10 key managerial roles • explain Kotter's points on how managers use agendas and networks to fulfill their work responsibilities • define three essential managerial skills—*technical, human,* and *conceptual skills* • explain Katz's view of how these skills vary in importance across management levels • define *emotional intelligence* as an important human skill • list and give examples of personal competencies important for managerial success

MANAGEMENT LEARNING REVIEW

STUDY QUESTIONS SUMMARY

1. What are the challenges of working in the new economy?

• Work in the new economy is increasingly knowledge based, and people, with their capacity to bring valuable intellectual capital to the workplace, are the ultimate foundation of organizational performance.

• Organizations must value the talents and capabilities of a workforce whose members are increasingly diverse with respect to gender, age, race and ethnicity, able-bodiedness, and lifestyles.

• The forces of globalization are bringing increased interdependencies among nations and economies, as customer markets and resource flows create intense business competition.

• Ever-present developments in information technology are reshaping organizations, changing the nature of work, and increasing the value of knowledge workers.

• Society has high expectations for organizations and their members to perform with commitment to high ethical standards and in socially responsible ways.

• Careers in the new economy require great personal initiative to build and maintain skill "portfolios" that are always up to date and valuable to employers challenged by the intense competition and the information age.

FOR DISCUSSION How is globalization creating career challenges for today's university and college graduates?

2. What are organizations like in the new workplace?

• Organizations are collections of people working together to achieve a common purpose.

• As open systems, organizations interact with their environments in the process of transforming resource inputs into product and service outputs.

• Productivity is a measure of the quantity and quality of work performance, with resource costs taken into account.

• High-performing organizations are both effective, in terms of goal accomplishment, and efficient, in terms of resource utilization.

FOR DISCUSSION Is it ever acceptable to sacrifice performance efficiency for performance effectiveness?

KEY TERMS

administrators, 24
accountability, 24
agenda setting, 29
competitive advantage, 18
conceptual skill, 31
controlling, 27
discrimination, 6
effective managers, 24
emotional intelligence, 31
environmental
    uncertainty, 20
ethics, 8
functional managers, 24
general environment, 14
general managers, 24
glass ceiling effect, 6
globalization, 7
human skill, 31
intellectual capital, 6
Internet censorship, 16
knowledge worker, 6
leading, 27
learning, 30
lifelong learning, 30
line managers, 24
management, 26
manager, 21
managerial competency, 31
middle managers, 23
networking, 30
open systems, 12
organization, 11

3. What is the makeup of the external environment of organizations and how is an organization linked to its environment?

- The general environment includes background economic, socio-cultural, legal-political, technological, and natural environment conditions.

- The specific environment or task environment consists of suppliers, customers, competitors, regulators, and other groups with which an organization interacts.

- Stakeholders are people and constituents affected by an organization's performance and for whom it creates value.

- Stakeholder analysis focuses on the extent to which an organization is creating value for each of its many stakeholders.

FOR DISCUSSION If interests of a firm's owners/investors conflict with those of the community, which stakeholder gets preference?

4. Who are managers and what do they do?

- Managers directly support and facilitate the work efforts of other people in organizations.

- Top managers scan the environment, create vision, and emphasize long-term performance goals; middle managers coordinate activities in large departments of divisions; team leaders and supervisors support performance at the team or work-unit level.

- Functional managers work in specific areas such as finance or marketing; general managers are responsible for larger multifunctional units; administrators are managers in public or non-profit organizations.

- Managers are held accountable for performance results that the manager depends on other persons to accomplish.

- The upside-down pyramid view of organizations shows operating workers at the top serving customer needs while being supported from below by various levels of management.

- The changing nature of managerial work emphasizes being good at "coaching" and "supporting" others, rather than simply "directing" and "order-giving."

FOR DISCUSSION In what ways could we expect the work of a top manager to differ from that of a team leader?

5. What is the management process and how do you learn managerial skills and competencies?

- The management process consists of the four functions of planning, organizing, leading, and controlling.

- Planning sets the direction; organizing assembles the human and material resources; leading provides the enthusiasm and direction; controlling ensures results.

- Managers implement the four functions in daily work that is intense and stressful, involving long hours and continuous performance pressures.

- Managerial success in this demanding context requires the ability to perform well in interpersonal, informational, and decision-making roles.

- Managerial success also requires the ability to use interpersonal networks to accomplish well-selected task agendas.

- Careers in the new economy demand continual attention to lifelong learning from all aspects of daily experience and job opportunities.

- Skills considered essential for managers are broadly described as technical—ability to use expertise; human—ability to work well with other people; and conceptual—ability to analyze and solve complex problems.

- Competencies considered as foundations for managerial success include communication, teamwork, self-management, leadership, critical thinking, and professionalism.

FOR DISCUSSION Among the various skills and competencies for managerial success, which do you consider the most difficult to develop, and why?

SELF-TEST

Multiple-Choice Questions

1. The process of management involves the functions of planning, _____, leading, and controlling.

    (a) accounting   (b) creating   (c) innovating   (d) organizing

2. An effective manager achieves both high-performance results and high levels of _____ among people doing the required work.

    (a) turnover   (b) effectiveness   (c) satisfaction   (d) stress

3. Performance efficiency is a measure of the _____ associated with task accomplishment.

    (a) resource costs   (b) goal specificity   (c) product quality   (d) product quantity

4. Two dimensions that determine the level of environmental uncertainty are the number of factors in the external environment and the _____ of these factors.

    (a) location   (b) rate of change   (c) importance   (d) interdependence

5. Productivity is a measure of the quantity and _____ of work produced, with resource utilization taken into account.

    (a) quality   (b) cost   (c) timeliness   (d) value

6. _____ managers pay special attention to the external environment, looking for problems and opportunities and finding ways to deal with them.

    (a) Top   (b) Middle   (c) Lower   (d) First-line

7. The accounting manager for a local newspaper would be considered a _____ manager, whereas the plant manager in a manufacturing firm would be considered a _____ manager.

    (a) general, functional   (b) middle, top   (c) staff, line   (d) senior, junior

8. When a team leader clarifies desired work targets and deadlines for a work team, he or she is fulfilling the management function of _____.

    (a) planning   (b) delegating   (c) controlling   (d) supervising

9. The process of building and maintaining good working relationships with others who may help implement a manager's work agendas is called _____.

   (a) governance   (b) networking   (c) authority   (d) entrepreneurship

10. In Katz's framework, top managers tend to rely more on their _____ skills than do first-line managers.

    (a) human   (b) conceptual   (c) decision-making   (d) technical

11. The research of Mintzberg and others concludes that managers _____.

    (a) work at a leisurely pace   (b) have blocks of private time for planning   (c) always live with the pressures of performance responsibility   (d) have the advantages of short workweeks

12. When someone with a negative attitude toward members of visible minorities makes a decision to deny advancement opportunities to an Indo-Canadian worker, this is an example of _____.

    (a) discrimination   (b) emotional intelligence   (c) control   (d) prejudice

13. Among the trends in the new workplace, one can expect to find _____.

    (a) more order-giving   (b) more valuing people as human assets   (c) less teamwork   (d) reduced concern for work-life balance

14. The manager's role in the "upside-down pyramid" view of organizations is best described as providing _____ so that operating workers can directly serve _____.

    (a) direction, top management   (b) leadership, organizational goals   (c) support, customers   (d) agendas, networking

15. The management function of _____ is being performed when a retail manager measures daily sales in the women's apparel department and compares them with daily sales targets.

    (a) planning   (b) agenda setting   (c) controlling   (d) delegating

Short-Response

16. Discuss the importance of managerial ethics in the workplace.

17. Explain how "accountability" operates in the relationship between (a) a manager and her subordinates, and (b) the same manager and her boss.

18. Explain how the "glass ceiling effect" may disadvantage newly hired African-Canadian graduates in a large corporation.

19. What is "globalization" and what are its implications for working in the new economy?

Application Question

20. You have just been hired as the new supervisor of an audit team for a national accounting firm. With four years of experience, you feel technically well prepared for the assignment. However, this is your first formal appointment as a "manager." Things are complicated at the moment. The team has 12 members with diverse demographic and cultural backgrounds, as well as work experience. There is an intense workload and lots of performance pressure. How will this situation challenge you to develop and use essential managerial skills and related competencies to successfully manage the team to high levels of auditing performance?

MANAGEMENT SKILLS AND COMPETENCIES

SELF-ASSESSMENT

Back to Yourself: Self-Awareness

The chapter opener used the Johari Window to introduce you to possible "blind spots" and other facets of your self-awareness. Now that you have had the chance to think about current trends in the workplace, how organizations are changing today, and the nature of managerial work, the importance of self-awareness to your career should be very evident. The following chapters will be introducing other key skills and personal characteristics that should also be placed high on your list of professional development goals. With effort on your part, this book and your management course can become fine resources to help you start turning self-awareness, which is a key component of emotional intelligence, into a source of career advantage.

Further Reflection: Emotional Intelligence

Instructions

Rate yourself on how well you are able to display the abilities for each item listed below. As you score each item, try to think of actual situations in which you have been called upon to use the ability. Use the following scale.

1	2	3	4	5	6	7

Low   Neutral   High
Ability   Ability

1 2 3 4 5 6 7   **1.** Identify changes in physiological arousal.

1 2 3 4 5 6 7   **2.** Relax when under pressure in situations.

1 2 3 4 5 6 7   **3.** Act productively when angry.

1 2 3 4 5 6 7   **4.** Act productively in situations that arouse anxiety.

1 2 3 4 5 6 7   **5.** Calm yourself quickly when angry.

1 2 3 4 5 6 7   **6.** Associate different physical cues with different emotions.

1 2 3 4 5 6 7   **7.** Use internal "talk" to affect your emotional states.

1 2 3 4 5 6 7   **8.** Communicate your feelings effectively.

1 2 3 4 5 6 7   **9.** Reflect on negative feelings without being distressed.

1 2 3 4 5 6 7   **10.** Stay calm when you are the target of anger from others.

1 2 3 4 5 6 7   **11.** Know when you are thinking negatively.

1 2 3 4 5 6 7   **12.** Know when your "self-talk" is instructional.

1 2 3 4 5 6 7   **13.** Know when you are becoming angry.

1 2 3 4 5 6 7   **14.** Know how you interpret events you encounter.

1 2 3 4 5 6 7   **15.** Know what senses you are currently using.

1 2 3 4 5 6 7   **16.** Accurately communicate what you experience.

1 2 3 4 5 6 7   **17.** Identify what information influences your interpretations.

1 2 3 4 5 6 7   **18.** Identify when you experience mood shifts.

1 2 3 4 5 6 7   **19.** Know when you become defensive.

1 2 3 4 5 6 7   **20.** Know the impact your behaviour has on others.

1 2 3 4 5 6 7   **21.** Know when you communicate incongruently.

1 2 3 4 5 6 7   **22.** "Gear up" at will.

1 2 3 4 5 6 7   **23.** Regroup quickly after a setback.

1 2 3 4 5 6 7   **24.** Complete long-term tasks in designated time frames.

1 2 3 4 5 6 7   **25.** Produce high energy when doing uninteresting work.

1 2 3 4 5 6 7   **26.** Stop or change ineffective habits.

1 2 3 4 5 6 7   **27.** Develop new and more productive patterns of behaviour.

1 2 3 4 5 6 7   **28.** Follow words with actions.

1 2 3 4 5 6 7   **29.** Work out conflicts.

1 2 3 4 5 6 7   **30.** Develop consensus with others.

1 2 3 4 5 6 7   **31.** Mediate conflict between others.

1 2 3 4 5 6 7   **32.** Exhibit effective interpersonal communication skills.

1 2 3 4 5 6 7   **33.** Articulate the thoughts of a group.

1 2 3 4 5 6 7   **34.** Influence others, directly or indirectly.

1 2 3 4 5 6 7   **35.** Build trust with others.

1 2 3 4 5 6 7   **36.** Build support teams.

1 2 3 4 5 6 7   **37.** Make others feel good.

1 2 3 4 5 6 7   **38.** Provide advice and support to others, as needed.

1 2 3 4 5 6 7   **39.** Accurately reflect people's feelings back to them.

1 2 3 4 5 6 7   **40.** Recognize when others are distressed.

1 2 3 4 5 6 7   **41.** Help others manage their emotions.

1 2 3 4 5 6 7   **42.** Show empathy to others.
1 2 3 4 5 6 7   **43.** Engage in intimate conversations with others.
1 2 3 4 5 6 7   **44.** Help a group to manage emotions.
1 2 3 4 5 6 7   **45.** Detect incongruence between others' emotions or feelings and their behaviours.

Scoring

This instrument measures dimensions of your emotional intelligence. Find your scores as follows.

Self-awareness—Add scores for items 1, 6, 11, 12, 13, 14, 15, 16, 17, 18, 19, 20, 21

Managing emotions—Add scores for items 1, 2, 3, 4, 5, 7, 9, 10, 13, 27

Self-motivation—Add scores for items 7, 22, 23, 25, 26, 27, 28

Relating well—Add scores for items 8, 10, 16, 19, 20, 29, 30, 31, 32, 33, 34, 35, 36, 37, 38, 39, 42, 43, 44, 45

Emotional mentoring—Add scores for items 8, 10, 16, 18, 34, 35, 37, 38, 39, 40, 41, 44, 45

Interpretation

The prior scoring indicates your self-perceived abilities in these dimensions of emotional intelligence. To further examine your tendencies, go back for each dimension and sum the number of responses you had that were 4 and lower (suggesting lower ability), and sum the number of responses you had that were 5 or better (suggesting higher ability). This gives you an indication by dimension of where you may have room to grow and develop your emotional intelligence abilities.

Source: Scale from Hendrie Weisinger, *Emotional Intelligence at Work* (San Francisco: Jossey-Bass, 1998), pp. 214–15. Used by permission.

TEAM EXERCISE

My Best Manager

Preparation

Working alone, make a list of the *behavioural attributes* that describe the "best" manager you have ever had. This could be someone you worked for in a full-time or part-time job, summer job, volunteer job, student organization, or elsewhere. If you have trouble identifying an actual manager, make a list of behavioural attributes of the manager you would most like to work for in your next job.

Instructions

Form into groups as assigned by your instructor, or work with a nearby classmate. Share your list of attributes and listen to the lists of others. Be sure to ask questions and make comments on items of special interest. Work together to create a master list that combines the unique attributes of the "best" managers experienced by members of your group. Have a spokesperson share that list with the rest of the class for further discussion.

Source: Adapted from John R. Schermerhorn, Jr., James G. Hunt, and Richard N. Osborn, *Managing Organizational Behavior*, 3rd ed. (New York: Wiley, 1988), pp. 32–33. Used by permission.

CASE 1

Vancity: On Top of Its Game

What makes a great organization? Well, if winning multiple national and international awards is a positive signal, Vancity Credit Union is definitely on the right path! Vancity was on Mediacorp Canada Inc.'s list of Canada's top 100 employers for 2011, it was recognized as one of the Globe *and Mail's* Top 50 Employers for Young People, *and it was one of Canada's Top 30 Greenest Employers. In 2010, Vancity was also one of the Corporate Knights Best 50 Corporate Citizens in Canada as well as being on* Fast Company's *Most Innovative Companies, Finance Section, where it was listed as the eighth most innovative financial company in the world. What does Vancity do right to deserve all this external recognition?*

Keeping Employees Happy and Healthy

This Vancouver-based co-operative was founded in 1946; it began with only $22 in total assets, aiming to lend money to those the banks ignored. Today, it is Canada's largest credit union, with over 2,400 employees and more than $14.5 billion in assets. As a member-owned credit union, it provides a complete range of financial services to its 400,000 members. Vancity continues to be committed to its original purpose and values: working with people and communities to help them thrive and prosper, all the while operating with integrity, innovation, and responsibility.[1]

Courtesy Vancity

Vancity acknowledges that a healthy and committed workforce is the reason it is able to sustain productivity and financial success within a competitive industry. Vancity provides its employees with the opportunity to help set corporate policies and procedures that impact both their work and home life. At work, employees enjoy business casual dress, listening to music while they work, participating on Vancity sports teams, and attending a host of social events. Vancity has other family-friendly programs as well. For example, the co-operative understands that if an employee has a young child, it may be necessary to build a workday that allows for flexibility. This positive approach recognizes the challenges of balancing work and life commitments and empowers employees to create the right environment to thrive at both.

The organization offers several alternative work options, including telecommuting, flexible hours, shortened work weeks (fewer hours with less pay), and compressed work weeks. Employees are given full pay for working 35 hours a week.[2]

Over the years and primarily driven by the employees' desire for personal development, Vancity has initiated a number of programs to help employees adopt a plan for a healthier life. Programs have included opportunities to work with Employee Assistance Providers (EAP) for developing personal plans for health and wellness.

Vancity offers a competitive pay and benefits program that includes dental and life insurance, three to six weeks of annual vacation, maternity and paternity leave top-ups, and care days that can be used for personal and family illness or injury. Other rewards include profit-sharing, tuition reimbursement, retirement planning, and reduced rates on personal financial services such as mortgages and loans. Employees also have a chance to attend Vancity's co-operative studies program in Italy, where co-ops are well-established.

Vancity has a young corporate culture—the average age of its employees is 39 and 94 percent of its new recruits are under 40. Even its CEO, Tamara Vrooman, was only 39 when she took the helm. The co-operative once threw a party for 2,200 employees and guests, and hip-hop dancers and a slam poet entertained the crowd until 3 a.m. Young employees organized the event for their peers. "We're interested in creating energy, we're interested in having people connect," Vrooman says. "And young people tell us that's an important part of the entire employee experience that they come to Vancity to enjoy."[3]

There are some challenges in human resources, too. Every year, the co-operative surveys employees, and it did not meet its targets for employee engagement for three years in a row, which it blamed partly on workforce and budgetary reductions. The employee engagement target is set at 75 percent but in those years it did not reach beyond 64 percent. "The Executive Leadership Team's compensation is tied to achieving this significant stretch target, reflecting how important it is we improve employee engagement and their pivotal role and responsibility in making this happen," Vancity said in its annual accountability report to members.[4]

In response to the first disappointing employee survey, the co-operative held focus groups with 120 employees, who said they were concerned, among other things, that individual goals were not aligned with those of the organization; that work processes, tools, and resources were not streamlined to improve efficiency; and that managers lacked support to manage performance effectively.[5] To reengage employees, Vrooman said Vancity would increase investment in training and development, renewing the organization's IT infrastructure and providing employees with growth opportunity by focusing on new areas.[6] Among other things, the organization examined its process for conducting employee performance reviews; as a result, it clarified the process, told managers to focus on ongoing employee coaching, and provided employees with on-line training and support materials to help them improve in areas identified during their performance reviews. It then planned on examining its monetary and non-monetary compensation strategies.[7]

Keeping the Organization Healthy

Vancity uses a triple bottom line business model; it is driven to achieve financial success but also focuses on environmental and social sustainability. Vancity is in a healthy financial position, with rising membership, because it takes an innovative approach in serving the financial needs of its members. It was the first Canadian financial institution to offer mortgages to women, first to use traditional media to market directly to the gay and lesbian community, the first North American credit union to receive an R1 rating from the Dominion Bond Rating Service, and the first financial institution to offer its own socially responsible mutual fund.

Vancity's vision to achieve positive social change has succeeded through a number of programs, such as one called Shared Success. Through this program, Vancity gives back each year a significant portion of net profits (generally 30 percent) to members and to communities. Since the program was introduced, a total of $130 million has been redistributed as community grants and other funding initiatives. Among the grant recipients was Just Beginnings Flowers, a non-profit florist that provides jobs to people with barriers to employment, which was selected to provide victory ceremony bouquets for the 2010 winter Olympics in Vancouver.[8] Other successful Vancity programs include its Pigeon Park Savings program, which provides banking services to the poor,[9] and, Each One, Teach One, which trains selected employees to teach basic financial literacy skills to newcomers to Canada.[10]

A focus on giving back to the community makes decision-making in a credit union more challenging, since maximizing shareholder profit is not the only goal. An employee survey found that 81 percent of workers agreed that the co-operative considers long-term social and environmental concerns when it makes decisions. Vancity managers take leadership training in values-based decision-making.[11]

"What makes a credit union is that we are community-based," Vrooman says. "We make decisions locally, we get to know our members, we live and work where they live and work, and when you start to expand beyond that we need to make sure that we keep the key thing that differentiates us from a large bank, which is the local decision-making. That's the biggest challenge: how to keep the credit union niche while you grow."[12]

Starting in 1995, before doing so was popular, Vancity focused on its own environmental performance. Vancity achieved its target of being the first carbon neutral North American-based financial institution. Through its climate change strategy, Vancity has supported innovative partnerships involving public transportation and green building projects. It also invests in organizations doing climate change work.

The organization is also a strong supporter of women. For example, among its recent board of directors, all but two of nine directors, including the chair, were women.[13]

Banking on the unbankable is one of the cornerstones of the Vancity story and today this financial institution continues to look for ways to improve. Vrooman, who was given an accolade herself by being named by the *Vancouver Sun* as one of British Columbia's most influential women in business,[14] says, "We're owned by our members, who have a say in the way our organization is run and a vested interest in how we do things, and we're accountable to them to deliver positive financial, social and environmental returns."[15] And deliver they do—that and win awards!

Discussion Questions

1. What is Vancity's competitive advantage over other types of financial institutions?

2. What does Vancity do to keep its stakeholders happy?

3. Which of the four functions of management does Vancity appear to be doing quite well? Draw from the case to support your answer.

4. FURTHER RESEARCH—What new initiatives is Vancity Credit Union undertaking right now for both employees and members?

Management Learning Past to Present

With the right foundations, practice makes perfect

"Googol" is a mathematical term standing for the number 1 followed by 100 zeros. That's a really big number. It's also symbolic of the reach and impact achieved by Google, a firm that is so successful its name has become a common verb. The firm's origins trace to the day when Larry Page and Sergey Brin met as students at Stanford University in California. Their conversations led to collaboration on a search engine they called BackRub. It became so popular on campus that they kept refining and expanding the service as they worked in Larry's dormitory room.

Courtesy Google Inc.

Google Inc. began with a goal of bringing order and transparency to the information available on the Internet. Even though it hasn't stopped running, or growing, since, the goal endures. The firm's mission is: "To organize the world's information and make it universally accessible and useful." And if you want to talk about success, take a look at Google's corporate information and follow its new initiatives in the news.

What is the Google difference? How did it gain such runaway popularity? The answers start with a commitment to performance excellence based on solid foundations of speed, accuracy, and ease of use. These have been the guiding performance criteria from the beginning, the basis for generating user appeal and competitive advantage for Google's products in the marketplace.

Google's belief in people also sets it apart. Recently ranked #1 on *Fortune* magazine's list of best workplaces, the firm gets over 2,000 job applications per day. It runs with an informal culture and small-company feel, reminiscent of a college campus. *BusinessWeek* says that CEO Eric Schmidt and founders Brin and Page have built "a unique, just-do-it culture." The firm's website declares: "we do everything we can to make sure our employees not only have great jobs, but great lives," and that its approach to staffing is "aggressively non-discriminatory, and favors ability over experience."[1]

> **BENCHMARK** Just as a Google search churns billions of websites, Google's founders and staffers learn from experience and strive to continuously improve. Google today is built upon foundations set yesterday and guided by aspirations for a greater tomorrow. Every day is a test, but this firm's story shows how practice makes perfect.

Learning Style

Speaking about foundations for performance success, what about you? Now is a very good time for you to examine your learning style. Some people learn by watching; they observe others and model what they see. Others learn by doing; they act and experiment, learning as they go. Some people are feelers for whom emotions and values count a lot; others are thinkers who emphasize reason and analysis.[2]

These preferences come together in the learning styles shown here. Look at the figure and then "shade" in each circle to show the degree to which you believe that description applies to you.

After you have turned the figure into your personal learning style profile, ask: "What are the implications of my learning style for how I perform academically, and how well I perform at work?" Ask also: "How does my learning style influence how I relate to others in my study groups and work teams, including those with different styles?"

Every person a manager deals with is unique, most problem situations are complex, and things are always changing. Success only comes to managers who thrive on learning. It's a personal challenge to

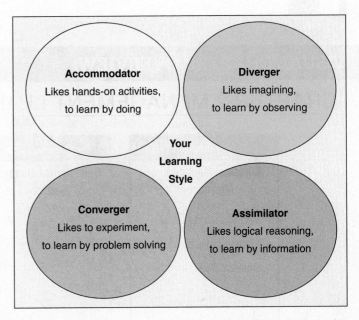

learn something new every day, and it's a big managerial challenge to help others learn things as well. A senior PepsiCo executive says: "I believe strongly in the notion that enhancing managers' knowledge of their strengths and particularly their weaknesses is integral to ensuring long-term sustainable performance improvement and executive success."[3]

❖ **Get to Know Yourself Better**

Why not take the executive's words to heart and start building a *personal learning scorecard*?

Make lists of your learning strengths and your learning weaknesses. Write a set of goals to take full advantage of the learning available from this book, your management course, and your academic program of studies.

CHAPTER 2 STUDY QUESTIONS

- What can be learned from classical management thinking?

- What are the insights of the behavioural management approaches?

- What are the foundations of modern management thinking?

VISUAL CHAPTER OVERVIEW

CHAPTER 2 MANAGEMENT LEARNING PAST TO PRESENT

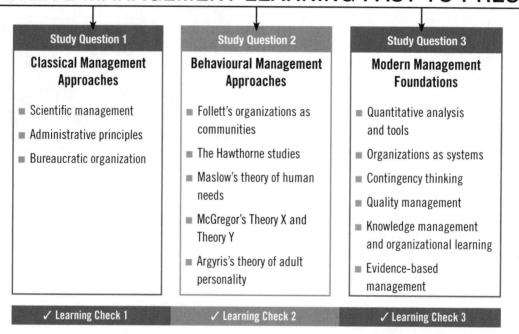

Study Question 1	Study Question 2	Study Question 3
Classical Management Approaches	**Behavioural Management Approaches**	**Modern Management Foundations**
■ Scientific management	■ Follett's organizations as communities	■ Quantitative analysis and tools
■ Administrative principles	■ The Hawthorne studies	■ Organizations as systems
■ Bureaucratic organization	■ Maslow's theory of human needs	■ Contingency thinking
	■ McGregor's Theory X and Theory Y	■ Quality management
	■ Argyris's theory of adult personality	■ Knowledge management and organizational learning
		■ Evidence-based management
✓ Learning Check 1	✓ Learning Check 2	✓ Learning Check 3

In *The Evolution of Management Thought*, Daniel Wren traces management as far back as 5000 B.C.E., when ancient Sumerians used written records to assist in governmental and business activities.[4] Management was important to the construction of the Egyptian pyramids, the rise of the Roman Empire, and the commercial success of fourteenth-century Venice. By the time of the Industrial Revolution in the 1700s, great social changes had helped prompt a major leap forward in the manufacturing of basic staples and consumer goods. Industrial development was accelerated by Adam Smith's ideas of efficient production through specialized tasks and the division of labour. At the turn of the twentieth century, Henry Ford and others were making mass production a mainstay of the emerging economy. Since then, the science and practices of management have been on a rapid and continuing path of development.

One pathway in management is summarized in *Mary Parker Follett—Prophet of Management: A Celebration of Writings from the 1920s*. The book is a reminder of the wisdom of history.[5]

Although Follett wrote in a different day and age, her ideas are rich with foresight. She advocated cooperation and better horizontal relationships in organizations, taught respect for the experience and knowledge of workers, warned against the dangers of too much hierarchy, and called for visionary leadership. Today we pursue similar themes while using terms like "empowerment," "involvement," "flexibility," and "self-management."

There are many useful lessons in the history of management thought. Rather than naively believing that we are always reinventing management practice today, it is wise to remember the historical roots of many modern ideas and admit that we are still trying to perfect them.

CLASSICAL MANAGEMENT APPROACHES

Our study of management begins with the classical approaches: (1) scientific management, (2) administrative principles, and (3) bureaucratic organization.[6] Figure 2.1 associates each with a prominent person in the history of management thought, and their names are still widely used in management conversations today. The figure also shows that the classical approaches share a common assumption: people at work act in a rational manner that is primarily driven by economic concerns. Workers are expected to rationally consider opportunities made available to them and to do whatever is necessary to achieve the greatest personal and monetary gain.[7]

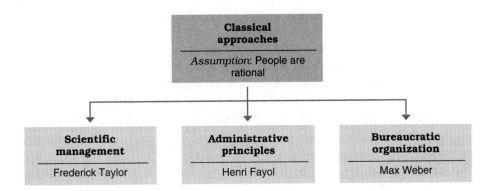

Figure 2.1 Major branches in the classical approach to management.

SCIENTIFIC MANAGEMENT

In 1911, Frederick W. Taylor published *The Principles of Scientific Management*, in which he made the following statement: "The principal object of management should be to secure maximum prosperity for the employer, coupled with the maximum prosperity for the employee."[8] Taylor, often called the "father of scientific management," noticed that many workers did their jobs in their own ways and without clear and uniform specifications. He believed this caused them to lose efficiency and underperform. He also believed that this problem could be corrected if workers were taught and then helped by supervisors to always do their jobs in the right ways.

Taylor's goal was to improve the productivity of people at work. He used the concept of "time study" to analyze the motions and tasks required in any job and to develop the most efficient ways to perform them.[9] He then linked these job requirements to both training for the worker and support from supervisors in the form of proper direction, work assistance, and monetary incentives. Taylor's approach is known as **scientific management** and includes four guiding action principles.

Scientific management emphasizes careful selection and training of workers and supervisory support.

1. Develop for every job a "science" that includes rules of motion, standardized work implements, and proper working conditions.

2. Carefully select workers with the right abilities for the job.

3. Carefully train workers to do the job and give them the proper incentives to cooperate with the job "science."

4. Support workers by carefully planning their work and by smoothing the way as they go about their jobs.

GOING GLOBAL

ONE-BEST-WAY APPROACH

When Mercedes-Benz started manufacturing in North America, the best of its German management practices came, too. Apparently subscribing to the scientific management approach, the German automaker expects and teaches its North American workers to follow precise standard methods and procedures (SMPs), which specify everything right down to the way a lug nut should be tightened. Mercedes believes this is the key to maintaining high-quality and high-performance standards, no matter where in the world its automobiles are manufactured. In 2010, Mercedes-Benz was ranked third in overall quality (behind Porsche and Acura) by J. D. Power and Associates; it looks like Mercedes-Benz's "one-best-way approach" is working.

Motion study is the science of reducing a task to its basic physical motions.

Mentioned in Taylor's first principle, **motion study** is the science of reducing a job or task to its basic physical motions. Two of Taylor's contemporaries, Frank and Lillian Gilbreth, pioneered the use of motion studies as a management tool.[10] In one famous case, they reduced the number of motions used by bricklayers and tripled their productivity. The Gilbreths' work led to later advances in the areas of job simplification, work standards, and incentive wage plans—all techniques still used in the modern workplace. For example, speed was the focus in a recent study of workers editing computer documents and copying data among spreadsheets. It was found that persons using 24-inch monitors did tasks 52 percent faster than those using 18-inch monitors. Researchers estimated that use of the larger monitors could save up to 2.5 labour hours per day.[11]

Some lessons from scientific management are shown in Management Smarts 2.1. An example of its present-day influence can be seen at United Parcel Service (UPS), where many workers are guided by carefully calibrated productivity standards. Sorters at regional centres are timed according to strict task requirements and are expected to load vans at a set number of packages per hour. Global positioning technology plots the shortest routes; delivery stops are studied and carefully timed; supervisors generally know within a few minutes how long a driver's pickups and deliveries will take. Industrial engineers also devise precise routines for drivers, who are trained to knock on customers' doors rather than spend even a few seconds looking for the doorbell. At UPS, and in classic scientific management fashion, the point is that savings of seconds on individual stops add up to significant increases in productivity.[12]

2.1 MANAGEMENT SMARTS
Practical lessons from scientific management

- Make results-based compensation a performance incentive.
- Carefully design jobs with efficient work methods.
- Carefully select workers with the abilities to do these jobs.
- Train workers to perform jobs to the best of their abilities.

ADMINISTRATIVE PRINCIPLES

In 1916, after a career in French industry, Henri Fayol published *Administration Industrielle et Générale.*[13] The book outlines his views on the proper management of organizations and of the people within them. Henri Fayol identified 14 principles of management that he felt should be taught to all aspiring managers like yourselves. Fayol derived these principles from his own experiences as an engineer leading large-scale enterprises of thousands of employees. His 14 principles are as follows:

1. Division of Labour—Specialization of work will result in continuous improvements in skills and methods.

2. Authority—Managers and workers need to understand that managers have the right to give orders.

3. Discipline—Behaviour needs to be grounded in obedience and derived from respect. There will be no slacking or bending of rules.

4. Unity of Command—Each employee should have one, and only one, manager.

5. Unity of Direction—The leader generates a single plan, and all play their part in executing that plan.

6. Subordination of Individual Interests—While at work, only work issues should be undertaken or considered.

7. Remuneration—All should receive fair payment for their work; employees are valuable and not simply an expense.

8. Centralization—While recognizing the difficulties in large organizations, decisions are primarily made from the top.

9. Scalar Chain (line of authority)—Organizations must have clear, formal chains of command running from the top to the bottom of the organization.

10. Order—There is a place for everything, and all things should be in their place.

11. Equity—Managers should be kind and fair.

12. Personnel Tenure—Unnecessary turnover is to be avoided, and there should be lifetime employment for good workers.

13. Initiative—Undertake work with zeal and energy.

14. Esprit de corps—Work to build harmony and cohesion among personnel.

Fayol identified the following five "rules" or "duties" of management, which closely resemble the four functions of management—planning, organizing, leading, and controlling—that we talk about today:

1. *Foresight*—to complete a plan of action for the future.

2. *Organization*—to provide and mobilize resources to implement the plan.

3. *Command*—to lead, select, and evaluate workers to get the best work toward the plan.

4. *Coordination*—to fit diverse efforts together and to ensure information is shared and problems solved.

5. *Control*—to make sure things happen according to plan and to take necessary corrective action.

Importantly, Fayol believed that management could be taught. He was very concerned about improving the quality of management and set forth a number of "principles" to guide managerial action. A number of them are still part of the management vocabulary. They include Fayol's *scalar chain principle*—there should be a clear and unbroken line of communication from the top to the bottom in the organization; *the unity of command principle*—each person should receive orders from only one boss; and the *unity of direction principle*—one person should be in charge of all activities that have the same performance objective.

BUREAUCRATIC ORGANIZATION

Max Weber was a late–nineteenth-century German intellectual whose insights have had a major impact on the field of management and the sociology of organizations. His ideas developed in reaction to his belief that the organizations of his day often failed to reach their performance potential. Among other things, Weber was concerned that people were in positions of authority not because of their job-related capabilities, but because of their social standing or "privileged" status in German society.

At the heart of Weber's thinking was a specific form of organization he believed could correct the problems just described—a **bureaucracy**.[14] For him it was an ideal, intentionally rational, and very efficient form of organization founded on principles of logic, order, and legitimate authority. The defining characteristics of Weber's bureaucratic organization are as follows:

A **bureaucracy** is a rational and efficient form of organization founded on logic, order, and legitimate authority.

- *Clear division of labour:* Jobs are well defined, and workers become highly skilled at performing them.

- *Clear hierarchy of authority:* Authority and responsibility are well defined for each position, and each position reports to a higher-level one.

- *Formal rules and procedures:* Written guidelines direct behaviour and decisions in jobs, and written files are kept for historical record.

- *Impersonality:* Rules and procedures are impartially and uniformly applied, with no one receiving preferential treatment.

- *Careers based on merit:* Workers are selected and promoted on ability, competency, and performance, and managers are career employees of the organization.

The Classic Bureaucracy

Impersonal
Career managers
Clear division of labour
Promotion based on merit
Formal hierarchy of authority
Written rules and standard procedures

Weber believed that bureaucracies would have the advantages of efficiency in utilizing resources, and of fairness or equity in the treatment of employees and clients. In his words:[15]

The purely bureaucratic type of administrative organization . . . is, from a purely technical point of view, capable of attaining the highest degree of efficiency . . . It is superior to any other form in precision, in stability, in the stringency of its discipline, and in its reliability. It thus makes possible a particularly high degree of calculability of results for the heads of the organization and for those acting in relation to it.

This is the ideal side of bureaucracy. However, the terms "bureaucracy" and "bureaucrat" are now often used with negative connotations. The possible disadvantages of bureaucracy include excessive paperwork or "red tape," slowness in handling problems, rigidity in the face of shifting customer or client needs, resistance to change, and employee apathy.[16] These disadvantages are most likely to cause problems for organizations that must be flexible and quick in adapting to changing circumstances—a common situation today. Current trends in management include many innovations that seek the same goals as Weber but use different approaches to how organizations can be structured.

✓ Learning Check ❶

BE SURE YOU CAN
• state the underlying assumption of the classical management approaches • list the principles of Taylor's scientific management • list three of Fayol's "principles" for guiding managerial action • list the key characteristics of bureaucracy and explain why Weber considered it an ideal form of organization • identify possible disadvantages of bureaucracy in today's environment

---

Behavioural Management Approaches

During the 1920s, an emphasis on the human side of the workplace began to influence management thinking. Major branches in the behavioural or human resource approaches to management are shown in Figure 2.2. They include Follett's notion of organizations as communities, the famous Hawthorne studies, and Maslow's theory of human needs, as well as theories generated from these foundations by Douglas McGregor, Chris Argyris, and others. The behavioural approaches maintain that people are social and self-actualizing. People at work are assumed to seek satisfying social relationships, respond to group pressures, and search for personal fulfillment.

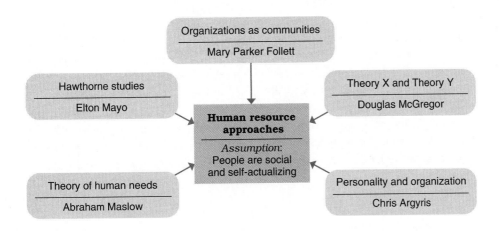

Figure 2.2 Foundations in the behavioural or human resource approaches to management.

FOLLETT'S ORGANIZATIONS AS COMMUNITIES

The work of Mary Parker Follett, briefly mentioned earlier, was part of an important transition from classical thinking into behavioural management. She was eulogized upon her death in 1933 as "one of the most important women America has yet produced in the fields of civics and sociology."[17]

In her writings, Follett views organizations as "communities" in which managers and workers should labour in harmony without one party dominating the other, and with the freedom to talk over and truly reconcile conflicts and differences. For her, groups were mechanisms through which diverse individuals could combine their talents for a greater good. And she believed it was the manager's job to help people in organizations cooperate with one another and achieve an integration of interests.

Follett's emphasis on groups and her commitment to human cooperation are still highly relevant themes today.[18] Follett believed that making every employee an owner in a business would create feelings of collective responsibility. Today, we address the same issues under such labels as "employee ownership," "profit sharing," and "gain sharing plans." Follett believed that business problems involve a wide variety of factors that must be considered in relationship to one another. Today, we talk about "systems" and "contingency thinking." Follett also believed that businesses were service organizations and that private profits should always be considered vis-à-vis the public good. Today, we pursue the same issues under the labels "managerial ethics" and "corporate social responsibility."

REAL ETHICS

Employment Agreements

Nelsonville, Ohio—Rocky Brands chief executive Mike Brooks filed a suit in Athens County Common Pleas Court against Joe P. Marciante, former regional vice president for sales. Marciante had resigned from Rocky, and Brooks believed he was going to work for a competitor. The suit claimed Marciante violated a "no-compete" agreement he had signed, which stipulated he would not go to work for a competitor for one year after leaving Rocky Brands. The court was asked to enforce the one-year waiting period and require that Marciante return all materials in his possession that provided inside information on Rocky Brands. Marciante's attorney said: "Right now, we're involved in a concerted effort to settle."

YOU DECIDE

No-compete clauses and nondisclosure agreements are increasingly common in employment contracts. Chances are that you will be asked to sign one someday. Is it ethical for a firm to ask a new hire to sign such an agreement? Is it ethical for someone leaving a firm to try to break such an agreement?

Ask your friends, co-workers, and family for their views and even their personal experiences. What advice about employment agreements is available from the professionals, and perhaps from your university or campus placement services?

THE HAWTHORNE STUDIES

In 1924 the Western Electric Company commissioned a research program to study individual productivity at the Hawthorne Works of the firm's Chicago plant.[19] The initial "Hawthorne studies" had a scientific management perspective and sought to determine how economic incentives and physical conditions of the workplace affected the output of workers. An initial focus was on the level of illumination in the manufacturing facilities; it seemed reasonable to expect that better lighting would improve performance. After failing to find this relationship, however, the researchers concluded that unforeseen "psychological factors" somehow interfered with their illumination experiments. This finding and later Hawthorne studies directed research attention toward better understanding human interactions in the workplace.

Relay Assembly Test-Room Studies

A team led by Harvard's Elton Mayo set out to examine the effect of worker fatigue on output. Care was taken to design a scientific test that would be free of the psychological effects thought to have confounded the earlier illumination studies. Six workers who assembled relays were isolated for intensive study in a special test room. They were given various rest pauses, as well as workdays and workweeks of various lengths, and production was regularly measured. Once again, researchers failed to find any direct relationship between changes in physical working conditions and output. Productivity increased regardless of the changes made.

Mayo and his colleagues concluded that the new "social setting" created for workers in the test room accounted for the increased productivity. Two factors were singled out as having special importance. One was the group atmosphere. The workers shared pleasant social relations with one another and wanted to do a good job. The other was more participative supervision. Test-room workers were made to feel important, were given a lot of information, and were frequently asked for their opinions. This was not the case in their regular jobs back in the plant.

Employee Attitudes, Interpersonal Relations, and Group Processes

Mayo's research continued until the worsening economic conditions of the Depression forced the studies' termination in 1932. By then, interest in the human factor had broadened to include employee attitudes, interpersonal relations, and group dynamics. In one study, over 21,000 employees were interviewed to learn what they liked and disliked about their work environment. "Complex" and "baffling" results led the researchers to conclude that the same things (e.g., work conditions or wages) could be sources of satisfaction for some workers and of dissatisfaction for others.

The final Hawthorne study was conducted in the bank wiring room and centred on the role of the work group. A finding here was that people would restrict their output in order to avoid the displeasure of the group, even if it meant sacrificing pay that could otherwise be earned by increasing output. The researchers concluded that groups can have strong negative, as well as positive, influences on individual productivity.

Lessons of the Hawthorne Studies

As scholars now look back, the Hawthorne studies are criticized for poor research design, weak empirical support for the conclusions drawn, and the tendency of researchers to overgeneralize their findings.[20] Yet their significance as turning points in the evolution of management thought remains intact. The studies helped shift the attention of managers and researchers away from the technical and structural concerns of the classical approach and toward social and human concerns as keys to productivity. They brought visibility to the notions that people's feelings, attitudes, and relationships with co-workers affected their work, and that groups were important influences on individuals. They also identified the **Hawthorne effect**—the tendency of people who are singled out for special attention to perform as anticipated because of expectations created by the situation.

The Hawthorne studies contributed to the emergence of the **human relations movement**, which influenced management thinking during the 1950s and 1960s. This movement was largely based on the viewpoint that managers who used good human relations in the workplace would achieve productivity. Importantly, this movement set the stage for what evolved into the field of **organizational behaviour**, the study of individuals and groups in organizations.

The **Hawthorne effect** is the tendency of persons singled out for special attention to perform as expected.

The **human relations movement** suggested that managers using good human relations will achieve productivity.

Organizational behaviour is the study of individuals and groups in organizations.

ISSUES AND SITUATIONS
Management Candour

To: Sales Team List
From: Heather
Subject: Management Training Workshop

Dear Team Members:

We have scheduled a management development workshop for Thursday of next week. It will be a half-day session (1–4:30 P.M.) in the 4th-floor seminar room for our entire sales management team.

I apologize for the short notice, but it is the only day this month that we can get Prof. Lenie Holbrook from Western University to be with us. His reputation is really great, and I hope that the workshop will stimulate us to work together and improve our managerial performance.

Prof. Holbrook wants everyone, including me, as national sales manager, to do the pre-workshop homework attached to this e-mail. I know you can identify with this. Be sure to bring your responses to his questions on Thursday. I am looking forward to the workshop and hope you are too.

Thanks,

/electronically signed Heather/

CRITICAL RESPONSE

Answer the pre-workshop activity questions based on your own personal experiences, and about managers for whom you have actually worked. First consider the differences between the two lists (of best and worst managers). How well do your lists fit what might be predicted by management theories?

Second, assume you are a member of Heather's sales management team, and your lists will be shared at the workshop. It's decision time.

- Would you have any reservations about sharing your lists in open discussion with Heather and other members of the sales team?
- Put yourself in Heather's shoes. As Heather, how would you react to items on team members' "worst" manager lists? Would you take them as personal criticisms?
- Be the professor and consultant. How can you conduct this management workshop to make sure that it is positive and developmental for everyone?

Pre-Workshop Activity: "My Best Manager"

Think back to all the managers you have worked for in your career. Make a list of behaviours and characteristics that answer the following questions:

1. *How would you describe your "best" manager?*
2. *How would you describe your "worst" manager?*

MASLOW'S THEORY OF HUMAN NEEDS

A **need** is a physiological or psychological deficiency that a person wants to satisfy.

The work of psychologist Abraham Maslow in the area of human "needs" has had a major impact on management.[21] He described a **need** as a physiological or psychological deficiency a person feels the compulsion to satisfy, suggesting that needs create tensions that can influence a person's work attitudes and behaviours. He also placed needs in the five levels shown in Figure 2.3. From lowest to highest in order, they are physiological, safety, social, esteem, and self-actualization needs.

Maslow's theory is based on two underlying principles. The first is the *deficit principle*—a satisfied need is not a motivator of behaviour. People act to satisfy "deprived" needs, those for which a satisfaction "deficit" exists. The second is the *progression principle*—the five needs exist in a hierarchy of "prepotency." A need at any level is activated only when the next-lower-level need is satisfied.

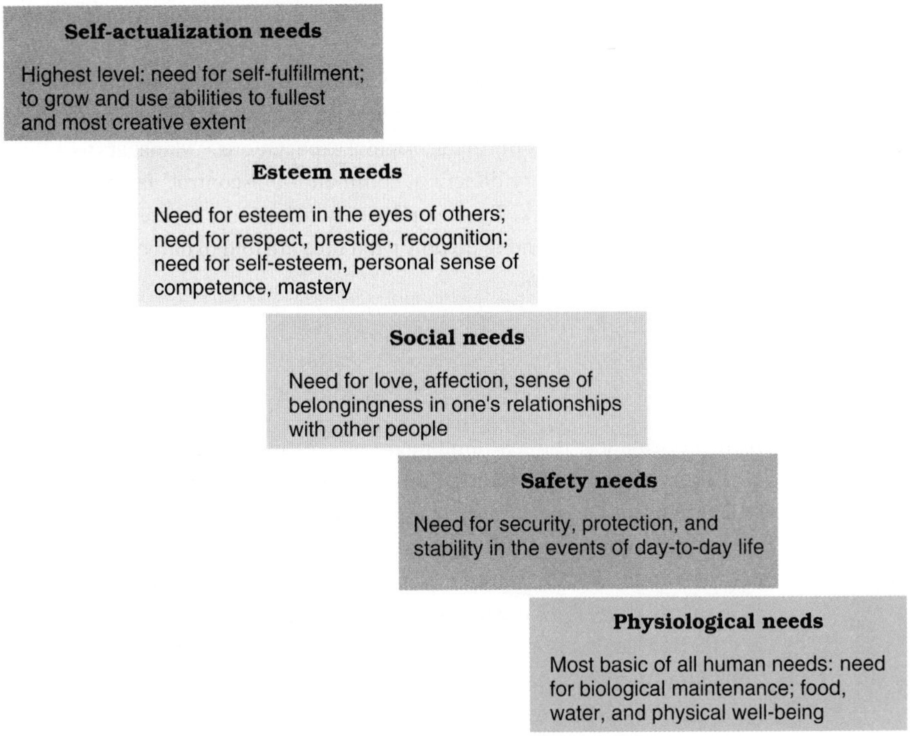

Self-actualization needs

Highest level: need for self-fulfillment; to grow and use abilities to fullest and most creative extent

Esteem needs

Need for esteem in the eyes of others; need for respect, prestige, recognition; need for self-esteem, personal sense of competence, mastery

Social needs

Need for love, affection, sense of belongingness in one's relationships with other people

Safety needs

Need for security, protection, and stability in the events of day-to-day life

Physiological needs

Most basic of all human needs: need for biological maintenance; food, water, and physical well-being

Figure 2.3 Maslow's hierarchy of human needs.

According to Maslow, people try to satisfy the five needs in sequence. They progress step by step from the lowest level in the hierarchy up to the highest. Along the way, a deprived need dominates individual attention and determines behaviour until it is satisfied. Then, the next-higher-level need is activated. At the level of self-actualization, the deficit and progression principles cease to operate. The more this need is satisfied, the stronger it grows.

Consistent with human relations thinking, Maslow's theory implies that managers who understand and help people satisfy their important needs at work will achieve productivity. Although scholars now recognize that things are more complicated than this, Maslow's ideas are still relevant. Consider, for example, the case of volunteer workers who do not receive any monetary compensation. Managers in non-profit organizations have to create jobs and work environments that satisfy the many different needs of volunteers. If their work isn't fulfilling, the volunteers will lose interest and probably redirect their efforts elsewhere.

McGREGOR'S THEORY X AND THEORY Y

Douglas McGregor was heavily influenced by both the Hawthorne studies and Maslow. His classic book, *The Human Side of Enterprise*, advances the thesis that managers should give more attention to the social and self-actualizing needs of people at work.[22] McGregor called upon managers to shift their view of human nature away from a set of assumptions he called "Theory X" and toward ones he called "Theory Y." You can check your managerial assumptions by completing the self-assessment at the end of the chapter.

According to McGregor, managers holding **Theory X** assumptions approach their jobs believing that those who work for them generally dislike work, lack ambition, are irresponsible, are resistant to change, and prefer to be led rather than to lead. McGregor considers such thinking inappropriate. He argues instead for **Theory Y** assumptions in which the manager believes people

Theory X assumes people dislike work, lack ambition, act irresponsibly, and prefer to be led.

Theory Y assumes people are willing to work, like responsibility, and are self-directed and creative.

are willing to work, capable of self-control, willing to accept responsibility, imaginative and creative, and capable of self-direction.

An important aspect of McGregor's ideas is his belief that managers who hold either set of assumptions can create **self-fulfilling prophecies**—that is, through their behaviour they create situations where others act in ways that confirm the original expectations.[23] Managers with Theory X assumptions, for example, act in a very directive "command-and-control" fashion that gives people little personal say over their work. These supervisory behaviours create passive, dependent, and reluctant subordinates, who tend to do only what they are told to or required to do. This reinforces the original Theory X viewpoint.

A **self-fulfilling prophecy** occurs when a person acts in ways that confirm another's expectations.

In contrast to Theory X, managers with Theory Y assumptions tend to behave in "participative" ways that allow subordinates more job involvement, freedom, and responsibility. This creates opportunities to satisfy esteem and self-actualization needs; workers tend to behave as expected with initiative and high performance. The self-fulfilling prophecy thus becomes a positive one.

Theory Y thinking is consistent with developments in the new workplace and its emphasis on employee participation, involvement, empowerment, and self-management.[24] When Betsy Holden became the president and CEO of Kraft Foods, Inc., for example, she had risen from division brand manager to CEO in just 16 years. She also showed a lot of Theory Y in her approach to leadership. Holden was praised for a "positive, upbeat, enthusiastic, collaborative, and team-oriented" management style, one that seems evident in the accompanying photo. She emphasized career development and focused on helping others with questions like these: "What skills do you need? What experiences do you need? What development do you need? How do we help you make that happen?"[25]

ARGYRIS'S THEORY OF ADULT PERSONALITY

Ideas set forth by the well-regarded scholar and consultant Chris Argyris also reflect the belief in human nature advanced by Maslow and McGregor. In his book *Personality and Organization*, Argyris contrasts the management practices found in traditional and hierarchical organizations with the needs and capabilities of mature adults.[26] He concludes that some practices, especially those influenced by the classical management approaches, are inconsistent with the mature adult personality.

Consider these examples. In scientific management, the principle of specialization assumes that people will work more efficiently as tasks become better defined. Argyris believes that this limits opportunities for self-actualization. In Weber's bureaucracy, people work in a clear hierarchy of authority, with higher levels directing and controlling lower levels. Argyris worries that this creates dependent, passive workers who feel they have little control over their work environments. In Fayol's administrative principles, the concept of unity of direction assumes that efficiency will increase when a person's work is planned and directed by a supervisor. Argyris suggests that this may create conditions for psychological failure; conversely, psychological success occurs when people define their own goals.

Like McGregor, Argyris believes that managers who treat people positively and as responsible adults will achieve the highest productivity. His advice is to expand job responsibilities, allow more task variety, and adjust supervisory styles to allow more participation and promote better human relations. He believes that the common problems of employee absenteeism, turnover, apathy, alienation, and low morale may be signs of a mismatch between management practices and mature adult personalities.

Canadian Company in the News

PEOPLE HOLD THE KEYS TO LONG-TERM PERFORMANCE SUCCESS

Toronto-based Four Seasons Hotels and Resorts seeks employees who are friendly, committed to teamwork, and, of course, highly talented. The firm declares that quality of service is "so critically important to our guests, and the degree to which we can provide and evolve it, worldwide, is also the degree to which we can differentiate ourselves and stay ahead of the rest." Four Seasons is a leader in the luxury segment of the hospitality industry. Its strengths and reputation are cultivated with leadership commitment to a fundamental principle: The key to sustained performance success is people. Among the guiding values of the firm is: "we believe that each of us needs a sense of dignity, pride, and satisfaction in what we do." It is obvious that Chris Argyris would be happy with the Four Seasons approach!

✔ Learning Check ❷

BE SURE YOU CAN
- explain Follett's concept of organizations as communities • define the *Hawthorne effect*
- explain how the Hawthorne findings influenced the development of management thought
- explain how Maslow's hierarchy of needs operates in the workplace • distinguish between Theory X and Theory Y assumptions, and explain why McGregor favoured Theory Y • explain Argyris's criticism that traditional organizational practices are inconsistent with mature adult personalities

MODERN MANAGEMENT FOUNDATIONS

The concepts, models, and ideas discussed so far helped set the stage for continuing developments in management thought. The many themes reflected throughout this book build from them as well as from modern management foundations that include the use of quantitative analysis and tools, a systems view of organizations, contingency thinking, commitment to quality, the role of knowledge management, learning organizations, and the importance of evidence-based management.

QUANTITATIVE ANALYSIS AND TOOLS

About the same time that some scholars were developing human resource approaches to management, others were investigating how quantitative analysis could improve managerial decision-making. The foundation of these approaches is the notion that mathematical tools can be used for better problem solving. Today such applications in analytical decision sciences, often described by the terms **management science** and **operations research**, are increasingly supported by computer technology and software programs.

A typical quantitative approach to managerial problem solving proceeds as follows. A problem is encountered, it is systematically analyzed, appropriate mathematical models and calculations

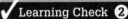

Management science and **operations research** use quantitative analysis and applied mathematics to solve problems.

are applied, and an optimum solution is identified. Consider these examples of real problems and how they can be addressed by using quantitative tools.

Problem: An oil exploration company is worried about future petroleum reserves in various parts of the world. Quantitative approach—*Mathematical forecasting* helps make future projections for reserve sizes and depletion rates that are useful in the planning process.

Problem: A real estate developer wants to control costs and finish building a new apartment complex on time. Quantitative approach—*Network models*, such as the Gantt chart pictured here

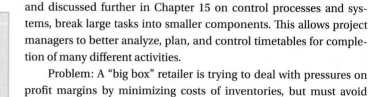

SIMPLIFIED GANTT CHART FOR APARTMENT COMPLEX

and discussed further in Chapter 15 on control processes and systems, break large tasks into smaller components. This allows project managers to better analyze, plan, and control timetables for completion of many different activities.

Problem: A "big box" retailer is trying to deal with pressures on profit margins by minimizing costs of inventories, but must avoid being "out of stock" for customers. Quantitative approach—*Inventory analysis*, discussed in Chapter 16 on operations and services management, helps control inventories by mathematically determining how much to automatically order and when.

Problem: A grocery store is getting complaints from customers that waiting times for checkouts are too long during certain times of the day. Quantitative approach—*Queuing theory* helps allocate service personnel and workstations based on alternative workload demands and in a way that minimizes both customer waiting times and costs of service workers.

Problem: A manufacturer wants to maximize profits for producing three different products on three different machines, each of which can be used for different periods of time and run at different costs. Quantitative approach—*Linear programming* is used to calculate how best to allocate production among different machines.

> **Operations management** is the study of how organizations produce goods and services.

The field of **operations management** uses such quantitative approaches and applied mathematics to systematically examine how organizations can produce goods and services most efficiently and effectively. Chapter 16 reviews operations management in manufacturing and service settings. Topics include value chain analysis, supply chain management, inventory management, and quality control, as well as business process analysis.

ORGANIZATIONS AS SYSTEMS

> A **system** is a collection of interrelated parts working together for a purpose.

Operations management tries to understand an organization as a **system** of interrelated parts that function together to achieve a common purpose. This includes the roles of **subsystems**, or smaller components of a larger system.[27]

> A **subsystem** is a smaller component of a larger system.

An early management writer who used a systems perspective was Chester Barnard. His 1938 groundbreaking book, *Functions of the Executive*, was based on years of experience as a telephone company executive.[28] Like Mary Parker Follett, Barnard described organizations as cooperative systems that achieve great things by integrating the contributions of many individuals to achieve a common purpose. He considered cooperation a "conscious, deliberate, and purposeful" feature of organizations. He also believed an executive's primary responsibility was to use communication to create cooperation.

> An **open system** interacts with its environment and transforms resource inputs into outputs.

In Chapter 1, organizations were described as **open systems** that interact with their environments in the continual process of transforming inputs from suppliers into outputs for customers. Figure 2.4 also shows that within the total system of the organization a number of critical subsystems make things happen. In the figure, the operations and service management subsystems centre the transformation process while integrating with other subsystems such as purchasing, accounting, sales, and information. High performance by the organization occurs only when each subsystem both performs its tasks well and works well in cooperation with others.

Figure 2.4 Organizations as complex networks of interacting subsystems.

CONTINGENCY THINKING

Modern management is situational in orientation; that is, it attempts to identify practices that are best fits with the demands of unique situations. This requires **contingency thinking** that tries to match managerial responses with the problems and opportunities specific to different settings, particularly those posed by individual and environmental differences. There is no expectation that one can or should find the "one best way" to manage in all circumstances. Rather, the contingency perspective tries to help managers understand situational differences and respond to them in ways appropriate to their unique characteristics.[29]

Contingency thinking tries to match management practices with situational demands.

Contingency thinking is an important theme in this book, and its implications extend to all of the management functions—from planning and controlling for diverse environmental conditions, to organizing for different strategies, to leading in different performance situations. Consider the concept of bureaucracy. Weber offered it as an ideal form of organization. But from a contingency perspective, the bureaucratic form is only one possible way of organizing things. What turns out to be the "best" structure in any given situation will depend on many factors, including environmental uncertainty, an organization's primary technology, and the strategy being pursued. As the figure suggests, a tight bureaucracy works best when the environment is relatively stable and operations are predictable and uncomplicated. In complex and changing situations, more flexible structures are needed.[30]

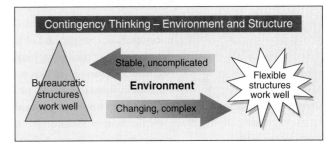

QUALITY MANAGEMENT

The work of W. Edwards Deming is a cornerstone of the quality movement in management.[31] His story begins in 1951 when he was invited to Japan to explain quality control techniques that had been developed in the United States. The result was a lifelong relationship epitomized in the Deming Application Prize, which is still awarded annually in Japan for companies achieving extraordinary excellence in quality.

"When Deming spoke," we might say, "the Japanese listened." The principles he taught the Japanese were straightforward and they worked: tally defects, analyze and trace them to the source, make corrections, and keep a record of what happens afterward. Deming's approach to quality emphasizes constant innovation, use of statistical methods, and commitment to training in the fundamentals of quality assurance.[32]

Total quality management is managing with an organization-wide commitment to continuous improvement, product quality, and customer needs.

One outgrowth of Deming's work was the emergence of **total quality management**, or TQM. This is a process that makes quality principles part of the organization's strategic objectives, applying them to all aspects of operations and striving to meet customers' needs by doing things right the first time. Most TQM approaches begin with an insistence that the total quality commitment applies to everyone and everything in an organization—from resource acquisition and supply chain management, through production and into the distribution of finished goods and services, and ultimately to customer relationship management.

Joseph Juran was one of Deming's contemporaries in the quality movement and his long career also included consultations at major companies around the world.[33] Juran is known for the slogan "There is always a better way" and for his three guiding principles—"plan, control, improve."[34] This search for and commitment to quality is now tied to the emphasis modern management gives to **continuous improvement**—always looking for new ways to improve on current performance.[35] The notion is that one can never be satisfied; something always can and should be improved upon.

Continuous improvement involves always searching for new ways to improve work quality and performance.

ISO certification indicates conformity with a rigorous set of international quality standards.

An indicator of just how important quality objectives have become is the value given to **ISO certification** by the International Organization for Standardization in Geneva, Switzerland. It has been adopted by many countries of the world as a quality benchmark. Businesses that want to compete as "world-class companies" are increasingly expected to have ISO certification at various levels. To do so, they must refine and upgrade quality in all operations, and then undergo a rigorous assessment by outside auditors to determine whether they meet ISO requirements.

KNOWLEDGE MANAGEMENT AND ORGANIZATIONAL LEARNING

Our technology-driven world is both rich with information and demanding in the pace and uncertainty of change. And although this is a setting rich in possibilities, Peter Drucker warned that "knowledge constantly makes itself obsolete."[36] His message suggests that neither people nor organizations can afford to rest on their laurels; future success will be earned only by those who continually build and use knowledge to the fullest extent possible.

Knowledge management is the process of using intellectual capital for competitive advantage.

The term **knowledge management** describes the processes through which organizations use information technology to develop, organize, and share knowledge to achieve performance success.[37] You can spot the significance of knowledge management with the presence of an executive job title—chief knowledge officer. The "CKO" is responsible for energizing learning processes and making sure that an organization's portfolio of intellectual assets is well managed and continually enhanced. These assets include such things as patents, intellectual property rights, trade secrets, and special processes and methods, as well as the accumulated knowledge and understanding of the entire workforce.

Google, featured in the chapter opener, can be considered a knowledge management company. It not only runs a business model based on information searches, it operates with an information-rich culture driven by creativity and knowledge. Google morphs and grows and excels, in part, because it continually taps the ever-expanding knowledge of its members. Its information technologies and management philosophies help and encourage employees located around the world to share information and collaborate. The net result is a firm that, so far at least, keeps competitors guessing what its next steps might be.

Courtesy Google Inc.

An emphasis on knowledge management is characteristic of what consultant Peter Senge calls a **learning organization**, popularized in his book *The Fifth Discipline*.[38] A learning organization, he says, is one that "by virtue of people, values, and systems is able to continuously change and improve its performance based upon the lessons of experience."[39] He describes learning organizations as encouraging and helping all members to learn continuously, while emphasizing information sharing, teamwork, empowerment, and participation.

> A **learning organization** continuously changes and improves, using the lessons of experience.

Organizations can learn from many sources. They can learn from their own experience. They can learn from the experiences of their contractors, suppliers, partners, and customers. And they can learn from firms in unrelated businesses. All of this, of course, depends on creating an organizational culture in which people are enthusiastic about learning opportunities and in which information sharing is an expected and valued work behaviour. Senge believes that those meeting his criteria for learning organizations tend to display the following characteristics:

1. Mental models—everyone sets aside old ways of thinking.

2. Personal mastery—everyone becomes self-aware and open to others.

3. Systems thinking—everyone learns how the whole organization works.

4. Shared vision—everyone understands and agrees to a plan of action.

5. Team learning—everyone works together to accomplish the plan.

When Google's CEO Eric Schmidt and his colleague Hal Varian describe their guiding management principles, they very much seem to fit the learning organization prototype.[40] The Google principles of managing for knowledge development and organizational learning are:

- *Hire by committee*—let great people hire other great people.

- *Cater to every need*—make sure nothing gets in anyone's way.

- *Make coordination easy*—put people in close proximity to one another, physically and electronically.

- *Encourage creativity*—let people spend some time on projects they choose.

- *Seek consensus*—get inputs before decisions are made.

- *Use data*—make informed decisions based on solid quantitative analysis.

- *Don't be evil*—create a climate of respect, tolerance, and ethical behaviour.

RESEARCH BRIEF

Great companies make the leap from doing good to doing great, while the others do not.

That's one of the messages in Jim Collins's best-selling book *Good to Great*. He opens the book with this sentence: "Good is the enemy of great." He goes on to describe an extensive study that compares companies that had moved to and then sustained "great" performance in cumulative stock returns over a 15-year period with those that hadn't. The study started by examining the records of 1,435 companies; only 11 made the final cut, joining the good-to-great set. The basic question addressed by Collins and his team of 21 researchers was "What did the good-to-great companies share in common that distinguishes them from the comparison companies?"

One of the major findings was that great companies demonstrate a unique form of leadership that Collins calls "Level 5." He says it is not leadership by celebrity, or leadership driven by compensation, or leadership based on a perfect strategy. Rather, Level 5 leadership is focused on people—getting the right people in, getting the wrong

ones out; ambitious—wanting the best for the company and for the long term; resolute—showing a determination to succeed in creating a great firm; and modest—not taking personal credit but recognizing the contributions of others.

Collins summarizes it as a combination of personal will and humility, stating that Level 5 leaders want to build "something larger and more lasting than themselves." While the comparison leaders were seeking fame, fortune, and power, the great company leaders were trying to create and contribute.

You be the researcher

Would these findings on Level 5 leadership in business hold true in government or in non-profit organizations? Can Level 5 leadership alone create long-term organizational greatness? Identify organizations in your community that have reputations for great performance. Conduct your own study: interview the leaders and other workers. How well do the findings fit Collins's model?

EVIDENCE-BASED MANAGEMENT

A book published by Tom Peters and Robert Waterman in 1982, *In Search of Excellence: Lessons from America's Best-Run Companies*, helped kindle interest in the attributes of organizations that achieve performance excellence.[41] Peters and Waterman highlighted things like "closeness to customers," "bias toward action," "simple form and lean staff," and "productivity through people," all of which seemed to make good sense. Later findings, however, showed that many of the companies deemed to be "excellent" at the time encountered future problems.[42]

A **high-performance organization** consistently achieves excellence while creating a high-quality work environment.

Today's management scholars are trying to move beyond generalized impressions of excellence to understand more empirically the characteristics of **high-performance organizations**. You can think of these as ones that consistently achieve high-performance results while also creating high-quality-of-work-life environments for their employees. A brief summary, for example, suggests that many high-performance organizations are:[43]

- *People-oriented*—they value people as human assets, respect diversity, empower members to fully use their talents, and are high in employee involvement.

- *Team-oriented*—they achieve synergy through teamwork, emphasize collaboration and group decisions, and allow teams to be self-directing.

- *Information-oriented*—they mobilize the latest information technologies to link people and information for creative problem solving.

- *Achievement-oriented*—they are focused on the needs of customers and stakeholders, and are committed to quality operations and continuous improvement.

- *Learning-oriented*—they operate with an internal culture that respects and facilitates learning, innovation, and constructive change.

Even with the above broad points available, managers and management scholars are always searching for scientific answers to even more precise questions like these: What is the best way to do performance appraisals? How do you select members for high-performance teams? How should a merit pay system be designed and implemented? How directive should a leader be? How do you structure organizations for innovation?

When such questions are posed, furthermore, the goal is to answer them with empirically sound and scientifically supported findings.[44] A book by Jeffrey Pfeffer and Robert Sutton makes the case for **evidence-based management**, or EBM, defined as the process of making management decisions on "hard facts"—that is, about what really works—rather than on "dangerous half-truths"—things that sound good but lack empirical substantiation.[45]

Evidence-based management involves making decisions based on hard facts about what really works.

In pursuing his own research in this area, Pfeffer, for example, has studied the ways in which organizations achieve competitive advantage through human resource management practices.[46] Using data from a sample of some 1,000 firms, a colleague and he found that firms using a mix of selected practices had more sales per employee and higher profits per employee than those that didn't. The positive human resource management practices included employment security, selective hiring, self-managed teams, high wages based on performance merit, training and skill development, minimal status differences, and shared information. Examples of other principles of EBM include: challenging goals accepted by an employee are likely to result in high performance and unstructured employment interviews are unlikely to result in the best person being hired to fill a vacant position.[47]

As scholars use scientific methods to advance knowledge in management, some carve out new and innovative territories while others build upon and extend knowledge that has come down through the history of management thought. The *Research Brief* feature, found earlier and in each chapter, introduces the types of studies that are being done and the types of evidence that are being accumulated. By staying abreast of

Basic Scientific Methods

- A research question or problem is identified.

- One or more hypotheses, or possible explanations, are stated.

- A research design is created to systematically test the hypotheses.

- Data gathered through the research are analyzed and interpreted.

- The hypotheses are accepted or rejected based upon the evidence.

such developments and findings, managers can have more confidence that they are approaching decisions from a solid foundation of evidence rather than on mere speculation or hearsay.

TWENTY-FIRST-CENTURY LEADERSHIP

There is no doubt that today's social, political, and economic forces make it necessary for people and organizations to continually adapt to new situations if they are to survive and prosper over the long run. Learning, learning, and more learning is the new reality of work in the twenty-first century. This fact carries with it distinctive personal development and leadership challenges. And when it comes to leadership, history once again sets the stage for the future. In his book *No Easy Victories,* John Gardner speaks of leadership as a special responsibility, and his words are well worth considering today:

> *Leaders have a significant role in creating the state of mind that is the society. They can serve as symbols of the moral unity of the society. They can express the values that hold the society together. Most important, they can conceive and articulate goals that lift people out of their petty preoccupations, carry them above the conflicts that tear a society apart, and unite them in the pursuit of objectives worthy of their best efforts.*[48]

Leadership and the new directions of learning organizations are singled out again and again in *Management* as important keys to personal and organizational performance.

Managers of the twenty-first century will have to excel as never before to meet the expectations held of them and of the organizations they lead. Importantly, we must all recognize that new managerial outlooks and new managerial competencies appropriate to the new times are requirements for future leadership success. At the very least, the twenty-first-century manager must display these attributes:

- *Global strategist*—understanding the interconnections among nations, cultures, and economies; planning and acting with due consideration of these interconnections.

- *Master of technology*—comfortable with information technology, understanding technological trends and their implications, able to use technology to best advantage.

- *Inspiring leader*—attracting highly motivated workers and inspiring them with a high-performance culture where individuals and teams can do their best work.

- *Model of ethical behaviour*—acting ethically in all ways, setting high ethical standards for others to follow, building a work culture that values ethics and social responsibility.

Management scholar and consultant Peter Drucker called this the age of information and considered knowledge the principal resource of a competitive society. Drucker also cautioned that knowledge constantly makes itself obsolete.[49] In a society where knowledge workers are increasingly important, this means that new managers must be well educated . . . and they must continue that education throughout their careers. Success in turbulent times comes only through learning and continuous improvement.

The new economy requires everyone—you included—to be unrelenting in efforts to develop, refine, and maintain job-relevant skills and competencies. It requires leaders with strong people skills, ones attuned to the nature of an information/service society, ones who understand the international dimensions, and ones who establish commitments to work-life balance. And the new economy places a premium on high-performance leadership. Consider, for example, this comment by former corporate CEO and college president Ralph Sorenson: "It is the ability to make things happen that most distinguishes the successful manager from the mediocre or unsuccessful one. . . . The most cherished manager is the one who says 'I can do it,' and then does."[50]

"Do it," advises Sorenson. "Of course," you may quickly answer. But don't forget that the twenty-first-century manager must also do the "right" things—the things that really count, the things that add value to the organization's goods and/or services, the things that make a real difference in performance results and competitive advantage, and the ethical things. Those are challenging directions for leadership and career success in the new economy.

BE SURE YOU CAN ....

• define *system, subsystem,* and *open system* • apply these concepts to describe the operations of an organization in your community • define *contingency thinking, knowledge management,* and *learning organization* • list characteristics of learning organizations • describe evidence-based management and its link with scientific methods • understand trends in twenty-first-century leadership

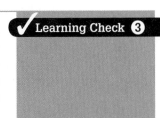
✓ Learning Check ❸

MANAGEMENT LEARNING REVIEW

STUDY QUESTIONS SUMMARY

1. What can be learned from classical management thinking?

• Frederick Taylor's four principles of scientific management focused on the need to carefully select, train, and support workers for individual task performance.

• Henri Fayol suggested that managers should learn what are now known as the management functions of planning, organizing, leading, and controlling.

• Max Weber described bureaucracy with its clear hierarchy, formal rules, and well-defined jobs as an ideal form of organization.

FOR DISCUSSION Should Weber's notion of the ideal bureaucracy be scrapped, or is it still relevant today?

2. What are the insights of the behavioural management approaches?

• The behavioural approaches shifted management attention toward the human factor as a key element in organizational performance.

• Mary Parker Follett described organizations as communities within which people combine talents to work for a greater good.

• The Hawthorne studies suggested that work behaviour is influenced by social and psychological forces and that work performance may be improved by better "human relations."

• Abraham Maslow's hierarchy of human needs introduced the concept of self-actualization and the potential for people to experience self-fulfillment in their work.

• Douglas McGregor urged managers to shift away from Theory X and toward Theory Y thinking, which views people as independent, responsible, and capable of self-direction in their work.

• Chris Argyris pointed out that people in the workplace are adults and may react negatively when constrained by strict management practices and rigid organizational structures.

FOR DISCUSSION How can a manager, even today, benefit by insights from Maslow's hierarchy of needs theory?

3. What are the foundations of modern management thinking?

• Advanced quantitative techniques in decision sciences and operations management can help managers solve complex problems.

KEY TERMS

bureaucracy, 48
contingency thinking, 57
continuous improvement, 58
evidence-based
    management, 61
Hawthorne effect, 51
high-performance
    organization, 60
human relations movement, 51
ISO certification, 58
knowledge management, 58
learning organization, 59
management science, 55
motion study, 46
need, 52
open systems, 56
operations management, 56
operations research, 55
organizational behaviour, 51
scientific management, 45
self-fulfilling prophecy, 54
subsystems, 56
system, 56
Theory X, 53
Theory Y, 53
total quality management 58

- Organizations are open systems that interact with their external environments, while consisting of many internal subsystems that must work together in a coordinated way to support the organization's overall success.

- Contingency thinking avoids "one-best-way" arguments, instead recognizing the need to understand situational differences and respond appropriately to them.

- Quality management focuses on making a total commitment to product and service quality throughout an organization, maintaining continuous improvement, and meeting worldwide quality standards such as ISO certification.

- Knowledge management is a process for developing, organizing, sharing, and using knowledge to facilitate organizational performance and create an environment for ongoing learning.

- Evidence-based management uses findings from rigorous scientific research to identify management practices for high performance.

FOR DISCUSSION Can system and subsystem dynamics describe performance problems for an organization in your community?

SELF-TEST

Multiple-Choice Questions

1. The assumption that people are complex with widely varying needs is most associated with the _____ management approaches.

    (a) classical   (b) neoclassical   (c) behavioural   (d) modern

2. The father of scientific management is _____.

    (a) Weber   (b) Taylor   (c) Mintzberg   (d) Katz

3. When the registrar of a university deals with students by an identification number rather than a name, which characteristic of bureaucracy is being displayed and what is its intended benefit?

    (a) division of labour; competency   (b) merit-based careers; productivity   (c) rules and procedures; efficiency   (d) impersonality; fairness

4. If an organization was performing poorly and Henri Fayol were called in as a consultant, what would he most likely suggest to improve things?

    (a) teach managers to better plan and control   (b) teach workers more efficient job methods   (c) promote to management only the most competent workers   (d) find ways to increase corporate social responsibility

5. One example of how scientific management principles are applied in organizations today would be:

    (a) a results-based compensation system.   (b) a bureaucratic structure.   (c) training in how to better understand worker attitudes.   (d) focus on groups and teamwork rather than individual tasks.

6. The Hawthorne studies are important because they raised awareness of the important influences of _____ on productivity.

    (a) structures   (b) human factors   (c) physical work conditions   (d) pay and rewards

7. Advice to study a job, carefully train workers to do that job, and link financial incentives to job performance would most likely come from:

    (a) scientific management.   (b) contingency management.   (c) Henri Fayol.   (d) Abraham Maslow.

8. The highest level in Maslow's hierarchy is the level of _____ needs.

    (a) safety   (b) esteem   (c) self-actualization   (d) physiological

9. Conflict between the mature adult personality and a rigid organization was a major concern of:

    (a) Argyris.   (b) Follett.   (c) Gantt.   (d) Fuller.

10. When people perform in a situation as they are expected to, this is sometimes called the _____ effect.

    (a) Hawthorne   (b) systems   (c) contingency   (d) open-systems

11. Resource acquisition and customer satisfaction are important when an organization is viewed as a(n):

    (a) bureaucracy.   (b) closed system.   (c) open system.   (d) pyramid.

12. When your local bank or credit union is viewed as an open system, the loan-processing department would be considered a:

    (a) subsystem.   (b) closed system.   (c) resource input.   (d) value centre.

13. When a manager notices that Sheryl has strong social needs and assigns her a job in customer relations, while also being sure to give Kwabena lots of praise because of his strong ego needs, the manager is displaying:

    (a) systems thinking.   (b) Theory X.   (c) motion study.   (d) contingency thinking.

14. In a learning organization, as described by Peter Senge, one would expect to find:

    (a) priority placed on following rules and procedures.   (b) promotions based on seniority.   (c) employees who are willing to set aside old thinking and embrace new ways.   (d) a strict hierarchy of authority.

15. The key outcomes of high-performance organizations are both consistent high performance and:

    (a) high public support   (b) high-quality work life environments.   (c) effective cost controls.   (d) high turnover

Short-Response Questions

16. Explain how McGregor's Theory Y assumptions can create self-fulfilling prophecies consistent with the current emphasis on participation and involvement in the workplace.

17. How do the deficit and progression principles operate in Maslow's hierarchy of needs theory?

18. Define contingency thinking and give an example of how it might apply to management.

19. Explain why the external environment is so important in the open-system view of organizations.

Application Question

20. Enrique Temoltzin has just been appointed the new manager of your local university bookstore. Enrique would like to make sure the store operates according to Weber's bureaucracy. Describe the characteristics of bureaucracy and answer this question: is bureaucracy a good management approach for Enrique to follow? Discuss the possible limitations of bureaucracy and the implications for managing people as key assets of the store.

MANAGEMENT SKILLS AND COMPETENCIES

Back to Yourself: Learning Style

People tend to learn in different ways, and the chapter opener was a chance for you to think about your learning style. Given that learning is any change of behaviour that results from experience, one of our most significant challenges is to always embrace experience and try our best to learn from it. A good way of mastering this challenge is to understand your learning style so that it works best for you in all types of experiences, whether in school, at work, or in everyday living. And when it comes to experience as a foundation for learning, let's always remember the wisdom of the past. This chapter has been a reminder about the importance of management history and how the achievements of the past can still provide insights that can help us deal with the present.

Further Reflection: Managerial Assumptions

Instructions

Read the following statements. Use the space in the margins to write "Yes" if you agree with the statement, or "No" if you disagree with it. Force yourself to take a Yes or No position.

1. Is good pay and a secure job enough to satisfy most workers?

2. Should a manager help and coach subordinates in their work?

3. Do most people like real responsibility in their jobs?

4. Are most people afraid to learn new things in their jobs?

5. Should managers let subordinates control the quality of their work?

6. Do most people dislike work?

7. Are most people creative?

8. Should a manager closely supervise and direct the work of subordinates?

9. Do most people tend to resist change?

10. Do most people work only as hard as they have to?

11. Should workers be allowed to set their own job goals?

12. Are most people happiest off the job?

13. Do most workers really care about the organization they work for?

14. Should a manager help subordinates advance and grow in their jobs?

Scoring

Count the number of yes responses to items 1, 4, 6, 8, 9, 10, 12; write that number here as [X = ___]. Count the number of yes responses to items 2, 3, 5, 7, 11, 13, 14; write that score here [Y = ___].

Interpretation

This assessment provides insight into your orientation toward Douglas McGregor's Theory X (your "X" score) and Theory Y (your "Y" score) assumptions. You should review the discussion of McGregor's thinking in this chapter and consider further the ways in which you are likely to behave toward other people at work. Think, in particular, about the types of "self-fulfilling prophecies" you are likely to create.

TEAM EXERCISE

Evidence-Based Management Quiz

Instructions

1. For each of the following questions, answer "T" (true) if you believe the statement is backed by solid research evidence, or "F" (false) if you do not believe it is an evidence-based statement.

    T F 1. Intelligence is a better predictor of job performance than having a conscientious personality.

    T F 2. Screening job candidates for values results in higher job performance than screening for intelligence.

    T F 3. A highly intelligent person will have a hard time performing well in a low-skill job.

    T F 4. "Integrity tests" are good predictors of whether employees will steal, be absent, or take advantage of their employers in other ways.

    T F 5. Goal setting is more likely to result in improved performance than is participation in decision-making.

    T F 6. Errors in performance appraisals can be reduced through proper training.

    T F 7. People behave in ways that show pay is more important to them than what they indicate on surveys.

2. Share your answers with others in your assigned group. Discuss the reasons why members chose the answers they did; arrive at a final answer to each question for the group as a whole.

3. Compare your results with these answers "from the evidence" — 1. T, 2. F, 3. F, 4. T, 5. F, 6. T, 7. T

4. Engage in a class discussion of how "common sense" answers can sometimes differ from answers provided by "evidence." Ask: What are the implications of this discussion for management practice?

Source: Developed from Sara L. Rynes, Tamara L. Giluk, and Kenneth G. Brown, "The Very Separate Worlds of Academic and Practitioner Periodicals in Human Resource Management: Implications for Evidence-Based Management," *Academy of Management Journal*, Vol. 50 (October, 2008), p. 986.

CASE 2

Zara International: Fashion at the Speed of Light

At the announcement of her engagement to Spain's Crown Prince Felipe, Letizia Ortiz Rocasolano wore a chic white trouser suit; within a few weeks, hundreds of European women sported the same look. Welcome to fast fashion, an emerging force that sees clothing retailers frequently purchasing small quantities of merchandise to stay on top of emerging trends. In this world of "hot today, gauche tomorrow," no company does fast fashion better than Zara International. Shoppers in 70 countries have taken to Zara's knack for bringing the latest styles from sketchbook to clothing rack in record time.

In Fast Fashion, Moments Matter

Because style-savvy customers expect shorter and shorter delays from runway to store, Zara International employs a stable of more than 200 designers to help it keep up with the latest fashions.[1] In two weeks, the company updates existing garments and has them in stores; new pieces hit the market in five. By year's end, Zara will have introduced about 11,000 new items, casting a long shadow over the 2,000 to 4,000 pieces that Gap or Swedish competitor H&M would expect to launch.[2]

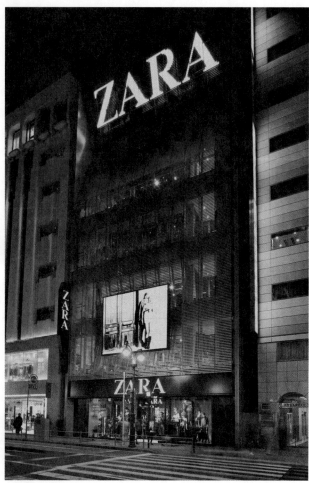

Courtesy ZARA

Parent company Inditex Group shortens the time from order to arrival by a complex system of just-in-time production and inventory reporting that keeps Zara ahead. Zara distribution centres can have items in European stores within 24 hours of receiving an order, and in American and Asian stores in under 48 hours.[3] "They're a fantastic case study in terms of how they manage to get product to their stores so quick," said Stacey Cartwright, CFO of Burberry Group PLC. "We are mindful of their techniques."[4]

Inditex's history in fabrics manufacturing made it good business sense to vertically integrate as many points in the supply chain as possible. Inditex controls design, production, distribution, and retail sales so as to optimize the flow of goods without having to share profits with wholesalers or intermediary partners. Customers win by having access to new fashions while they're still fresh off the runway. During a Madonna concert tour in Spain, Zara's quick turnaround let young fans at the last show wear Madonna's outfit from the first one.[5]

Inditex subcontracts much of its garment production to specialist companies, located on the Iberian peninsula, that it often supplies with its own fabrics. Although some pieces and fabrics are purchased in Asia—many undyed or only partly finished—the company manufactures about half its clothing in its hometown of La Coruña, Spain.[6]

Zara's finished garments are shipped to logistical centres that all simultaneously distribute product twice weekly to stores worldwide—small production batches avoid the risk of oversupply. Because batches always contain new products, Zara's stores perpetually energize their inventories.[7]

Inditex considers the interior and exterior design of retail outlets (which are specially dressed to amplify the brand) to be of the utmost importance—for outlets are where shoppers ultimately decide which fashions make the cut. In a faux shopping street in the basement of the company's headquarters, stylists craft and photograph eye-catching layouts that are e-mailed every two weeks to store managers for replication.[8] Most clothing lines are not replenished, but are replaced with new designs to create scarcity value—shoppers cannot be sure that designs in stores one day will be available the next.

Store managers track sales data with handheld computers, reordering hot items in less than an hour. This lets Zara know what's hot and what's not; when a look doesn't pan out, designers promptly put together new products. According to Dilip Patel, U.K. commercial director for Inditex, new arrivals are rushed to store sales floors still on the black plastic hangers used in shipping. Shoppers who are in the know recognize these designs as the newest of the new; soon after, any items left over are rotated to Zara's standard wood hangers.[9]

Catfights on the Catwalk

Zara is not the only player in fast fashion. Competition is fierce, but Zara's overwhelming success (recent sales were almost US$10 billion) has the competition scrambling to keep up. Esprit, for example, cut clothing prices by up to 25 percent for the first time in 19 years to cope with diminishing sales and decreased consumer purchasing power. According to Mathew Kichodhan, chief operating officer of Minor Corporation PLC, the importer and distributor of Esprit in Thailand, "Some global brands, in particular the newcomers Zara and MNG, have driven market change and impacted our business."[10] New Look, a British clothing retailer, is embarking on an Inditex-inspired international expansion to fend off competition from Inditex brands such as Zara and Massimo Dutti.[11]

Some fashion analysts are referring to this as the democratization of fashion: bringing high(er) fashion to low(er)-income shoppers. According to James Hurley, a senior research analyst with New York–based Telsey Advisory Group LLC, big box discount stores such as Target and Walmart are emulating Zara's ability to study emerging fashions and knock out look-alikes in a matter of weeks. "In general," Hurley said, "the fashion cycle is becoming sharper and more immediately accessible."[12]

A Single Fashion Culture

With a network of over 1,400 stores around the world, Zara International is Inditex's largest and most profitable brand, bringing home 72 percent of international sales and nearly 67 percent of revenues.[13] The first Zara outlet opened shop in 1975 in La Coruña.[14] It remained solely a Spanish chain until opening a store in Oporto, Portugal, in 1988. The brand reached the United States and France in 1989 and 1990 with outlets in New York and Paris, respectively.[15]

Inditex's 100-plus textile design, manufacturing, and distribution companies employ more than 80,000 workers who are integral to Zara's growth and success.[16] The Inditex group began in 1963 when Amancio Ortega Gaona, chairman and founder of Inditex, got his start in textile manufacturing.[17] After a period of growth, he assimilated Zara into a new holding company, Industria de Diseño Textil.[18] Inditex has a tried-and-true strategy for entering new markets: start with a handful of stores and gain a critical mass of customers. Generally, Zara is the first Inditex chain to break ground in new countries, paving the way for the group's other brands, including Pull and Bear, Massimo Dutti, and Bershka.[19]

Inditex CEO Pablo Isla believes in cutting expenses wherever and whenever possible. Zara spends just 0.3 percent of sales on ads, making the 3 to 4 percent typically spent by rivals seem excessive in comparison. Isla disdains markdowns and sales, as well.[20]

Few can criticize the results of Isla's frugality. Inditex recently opened 439 stores in a single year and was simultaneously named Retailer of the Year during the World Retailer Congress meeting, after raking in net profits of almost US$2 billion.[21,22] Perhaps most important in an industry predicated on image, Inditex secured bragging rights as Europe's largest fashion retailer by overtaking H&M.[23] According to José Castellano, the group plans to double in size in the coming years while making sales of more than US$15 billion with most of this growth taking place in Europe—especially in trend-savvy Italy.[24]

Fashion of the Moment

Although Inditex's dominance of fast fashion seems virtually complete, it isn't without its challenges. For instance, keeping production so close to home becomes difficult when an increasing number of Zara stores are far-flung across the globe. "The efficiency of the supply chain is coming under more pressure the farther abroad they go," notes Nirmalya Kumar, a professor at London Business School.[25] When Inditex overlooked a series of key fashion trends a few years ago, analysts at investment bank CSFB blamed the misses on factors of complexity and control, raising concern for a company with such aggressive growth goals.

Despite this, José Luis Nueno of IESE, a business school in Barcelona, says that Zara is here to stay. Consumers have become more demanding and more arbitrary, he says—and fast fashion is better suited to these changes.[26] But does Zara International have what it takes to succeed in the hypercompetitive world of fast fashion? Or is the company trying to expand too quickly?

Discussion Questions

1. In what ways are elements of the classical management approaches evident at Zara International?

2. What elements of the behavioural management approaches are being used by Zara's management team?

3. How can systems concepts and contingency thinking explain some of the distinctive practices underlying Zara's success?

4. FURTHER RESEARCH—Gather the latest information on competitive trends in the apparel industry, and the latest actions and innovations of Zara. Is the firm continuing to do well? Is it adapting in ways needed to stay abreast of both its major competition and the pressures of a changing global economy?

Whose Life Is It Anyway?

Video Summary and Discussion

The Scotts Miracle-Gro Company, a leader in lawn and garden products, offers a benefits package with a heavy emphasis on wellness and prevention. The company boasts an on-site fitness and medical facility complete with a gym (at no cost to those who exercise more than twice a week), free visits to an on-site doctor, a clinic, and a drive-through pharmacy. The company also offers healthy fare at its cafeteria.

In October 2006, Scotts started requiring its employees to be tobacco-free, even on their own time, or they would lose their jobs. The company gave employees a year to quit smoking, and provided free counselling, classes, and nicotine patches.

The reason for the wellness programs, including the nicotine ban, argues Scotts CEO Jim Hagedorn, is not only the company's bottom line, but also the desire to help employees achieve a healthy work–life balance. Estimates are that for each smoker employee, a company loses about $4,000 in productivity and health care costs. (In Canada, smoking can cost an employer over $3,000 per smoker each year in health care costs, absenteeism, and productivity losses, according to a 2006 report by the Conference Board of Canada.)

Running an effective wellness program, argues Hagedorn, will keep costs from rising well beyond the rate of inflation.

The question is whether the smoking ban goes too far. As of January 2009, most American states had laws making it illegal for companies to impose such bans on smokers when not at work. Ohio, home base for Scotts, is not one such state. Lawyer Marvin Gittler argues in the video that it's not a company's business what employees do on their own time, and moreover, that it sets a dangerous precedent. Viewers are left to decide for themselves.

In Canada, employers are taking a more voluntary approach to wellness issues, setting up initiatives such as smoking cessation programs that encourage employees to adopt a healthier lifestyle. To help abate continually rising group health care plan costs, Canadian employers are implementing wellness programs and prescription drug cost-containment strategies, according to a new survey conducted by the International Foundation of Employee Benefit Plans.

Group Health Care Cost Control in Canada 2010 includes responses from 665 Canadian individuals representing a cross-section of employee benefit sectors: corporations, multi-employer benefit plans, public/governmental plans, and professional service firms serving the employee benefits industry.

According to the survey, the proportion of employers offering wellness initiatives rose from 61 percent of employers in 2009 to 78 percent in 2010. In addition, nearly 1 in 5 organizations currently not offering wellness initiatives anticipated doing so in the future.

The most prevalent wellness initiatives in Canada included flu shot programs (71 percent), complementary and alternative medicine (52 percent), and smoking cessation programs (48 percent). Other common initiatives were wellness competitions (37 percent), off-site fitness program subsidies (31 percent), and healthy food choices in cafeterias or vending machines (26 percent). Nearly 1 in 10 plan sponsors offering wellness initiatives reported that they measured the return on investment of their programs, and a clear majority (88 percent) found the results are positive.

Looking to the future, a large majority (83 percent) of Canadian employers cited building a culture of health (encouraging employees to be healthy, to minimize risk factors, and to choose appropriate health services) as part of their strategy to improve health care quality and contain costs in the next two years.

Questions for Students

1. How can employers like Scotts Miracle-Gro justify the expense of providing employees with free access to doctors, a pharmacy, gyms, and personal trainers?

2. What lifestyle changes might employers encourage in the future to increase performance efficiency and performance effectiveness?

3. Should employers regulate your behaviour after work hours? Why or why not?

4. As stated in Chapter 1, there is more emphasis on respecting people as valuable strategic assets to be nurtured and developed, not as costs to be controlled. Do you believe the programs and policies at Scotts nurture and develop employees or treat them as costs to be controlled?

Global Dimensions of Management

LEARNING FROM OTHERS

With globalized businesses, there is much to watch, much to do!

A Montreal-based clothing company deciding to take on the global manufacturing giants. Seems foolish, right? That's exactly what Gildan Activewear is doing—and doing well. Starting in 1999, the company undertook a global survey of clothing prices. "The first thing we did from Day 1 was to make sure that we benchmarked ourselves against the global market," says Glenn Chamandy, the CEO of Gildan. To maintain its competitive advantage and remain a global player, Gildan recognized that it also had to establish operations offshore, first in Honduras, then later expanding to Mexico, Nicaragua, the Dominican Republic, and Bangladesh. For Gildan, there was a steep learning curve around locating offshore. Initially, the company was accused of poor working conditions and infringements on workers' rights, which may have negatively impacted its share price at the time. However, Gildan joined the Fair Labor Association and worked hard to develop solid labour relationships and a positive reputation for corporate social responsibility. The upside was that the strategic placement of these facilities allowed Gildan to benefit from bilateral and multilateral trade agreements, permitting the company to ship duty-free anywhere in North America, the European Union, and Australia.

(CP PHOTO/Ryan Remiorz)

Gildan has other things to watch out for as well. When you are dealing globally, currency fluctuations can have a large impact. So far the company has not been hurt by changing Canadian-U.S. exchange rates; however, the euro's decline in 2010 prompted the company to adjust its strategy. Gildan had to raise its prices in Europe to counter the effect of the falling euro. Gildan also keeps a close eye on cotton prices and energy costs across all of its manufacturing centres to adjust its product mix to ensure positive financial performance. All of this plus developing advanced technology has kept Gildan in the game. It isn't easy going global![1]

BENCHMARK There is more to Gildan Activewear than its T-shirts. Standing behind the garments is an operation that depends on vast worldwide networks of suppliers and subcontractors. But as with other international firms, Gildan's global reach must be well managed, and its ethical standards must be maintained. Any misstep will quickly be met by bad press, public and shareholder criticism, damaged reputation, and customer defections.

Cultural Awareness

The complications and dramas of global events are ever-present reminders that cultural awareness is one of the great challenges of our century. Consultant Richard Lewis warns of "cultural spectacles" that limit our vision, causing us to see and interpret things with the biases of our own culture.[2] Each of us has a responsibility to take off the blinders that limit our vision to the culture that we were raised in. We need to broaden our cultural horizons to embrace the full diversity of the world's peoples.

Many say this will be the "Asian" century. We're dealing with rising economic and geopolitical powers in China and India; it's hard to pass a day without bumping into one of these forces in the garments we wear and the customer services we seek.

Yet, it's a fact that even the most active global businesses don't always pass the cultural awareness test. In China, Nike featured NBA star LeBron James in a TV ad where he played the role of kung-fu master and battled dragons and Chinese symbols. The ad had to be pulled when Chinese critics claimed it wounded the "national dignity." Also in China, McDonald's aired an ad that showed a Chinese man asking for a discount. It was pulled after locals considered the ad "humiliating."[3]

Confucian Values in Asian Cultures

- *Harmony*—works well in a group, doesn't disrupt group order, puts group before self-interests

- *Hierarchy*—accepts authority and hierarchical nature of society, doesn't challenge superiors

- *Benevolence*—acts kindly and understandingly toward others; paternalistic, willing to teach and help subordinates

- *Loyalty*—loyal to organization and supervisor, dedicated to job, grateful for job and supportive of superior

- *Learning*—eager for new knowledge, works hard to learn new job skills, strives for high performance

---

How informed are you regarding Asian cultures and how they might differ from both yours and those in other parts of the world? Do you know, for example, that in Japan, China, and Korea, Confucian values such as those shown in the box are very influential?[4] When our business and government leaders venture into Asia, they must be informed about such cultural dynamics and their implications for international business and politics. And as to the rest of us, can we afford not to understand how these values match up with our own?

❖ Get to Know Yourself Better

The university and college campus is a great place to start building competencies in cultural awareness. Make a commitment tomorrow to carefully monitor yourself as you meet, interact with, and otherwise come into contact with persons from other cultures. Jot notes on what you perceive as cultural differences. Note also your "first tendencies" in reacting to these differences, and ponder their implications for your managerial skills and competencies.

CHAPTER 3 STUDY QUESTIONS

- What are the management challenges of globalization?

- What are global businesses, and what do they do?

- What is culture, and how does it impact global management?

- How can we benefit from global management learning?

VISUAL CHAPTER OVERVIEW

CHAPTER 3 GLOBAL DIMENSIONS OF MANAGEMENT

Study Question 1	Study Question 2	Study Question 3	Study Question 4
Management and Globalization	**Global Businesses**	**Culture and Global Diversity**	**Global Management Learning**
■ Global management ■ Why companies go global ■ How companies go global ■ Global business environments	■ Types of global businesses ■ Pros and cons of global corporations ■ Ethics challenges for global managers	■ Cultural intelligence ■ Silent languages of culture ■ Values and national cultures	■ Are management theories universal? ■ Cultural insights from Project GLOBE ■ Global management attitudes and learning
✓ Learning Check 1	✓ Learning Check 2	✓ Learning Check 3	✓ Learning Check 4

Our global community is rich with information, opportunities, controversies, and complications. The Internet and television bring on-the-spot news from around the world into our homes; most of the world's newspapers can be read on-line. It is possible to board a plane in Toronto and fly nonstop to Beijing, China, or Karachi, Pakistan, or Dubai in the United Arab Emirates. Colleges and universities offer a growing variety of study-abroad programs. And in the business world, an international MBA is an increasingly desirable credential.

Speaking of businesses travelling the globe, IBM employs more than 40,000 software developers in India. Labatt is now owned by the Belgian firm InBev. The Volkswagen Jetta is built in Mexico, Mercedes builds M-class vehicles in Alabama, while India's Tata Group owns Jaguar and Land Rover. The front fuselage of Boeing's new 787 Dreamliner is made by a Japanese company, with 60 percent of the plane's components made by foreign firms. Nike earns the vast majority of its sales outside of the United States, with its complex worldwide web of contractors including more than 120 factories in China alone.[5]

Similar trends and patterns are evident in other industries, and the growing power of global businesses affects all of us in our roles as citizens, consumers, and career-seekers. If at all in doubt, take a look at what you are wearing. You might be surprised how hard it is to find a garment or a shoe that is "Made in Canada."

MANAGEMENT AND GLOBALIZATION

This is the age of the **global economy**, in which resource supplies, product markets, and business competition are worldwide, rather than local or national in scope.[6] It is also a time heavily influenced by the forces of **globalization**, defined in previous chapters as the process of growing interdependence among the components in the global economy.[7] Harvard scholar and consultant Rosabeth Moss Kanter describes globalization as "one of the most powerful and pervasive influences on nations, businesses, workplaces, communities, and lives."[8] America Online's cofounder Stephen M. Case once described the scene this way: "I sometimes feel like I'm behind the wheel of a race car. One of the biggest challenges is there are no road signs to help navigate. And in fact . . . no one has yet determined which side of the road we're supposed to be on."[9]

> In the **global economy**, resources, markets, and competition are worldwide in scope.
>
> **Globalization** is the process of growing interdependence among elements of the global economy.

GLOBAL MANAGEMENT

The term used to describe management in businesses and organizations with interests in more than one country is **global management**, and there is no denying its importance. Procter & Gamble, for example, pursues a global strategy with a presence in more than 70 countries. The majority of McDonald's sales are now coming from outside of North America, with the "Golden Arches" prominent on city streets from Moscow to Tokyo to Budapest to Rio de Janeiro. Ben & Jerry's Homemade is owned by the Dutch multinational Unilever, and when IBM exited the personal computer business, its former Chinese supplier Lenovo took over and is now a global brand.

> **Global management** involves managing operations in more than one country.

As the leaders of these and other companies press forward with global initiatives, the management challenges and opportunities of working across national and cultural borders must be mastered. Consider two short cases—one rather a success story, and the other still a "work in progress."

Honda—Honda Canada opened its first Ontario plant in 1986 and was producing nearly 400,000 vehicles before the car market softened. Overall, the company has invested more than $2.6 billion in its plants in Alliston, Ont. "All around the world we build our products close to our customers," explains Manabu Nishimae, President and CEO of Honda Canada. "This allows us to become part of their community and helps us anticipate and meet their needs."[10]

(AP Photo/Tom Strattman)

Haier—You may know the brand as a popular name in dorm-room refrigerators; there's hardly a consumer in China who doesn't know it—the Haier Group is one of the country's best-known appliance makers. With the goal of becoming a major player in the North American market, Zhang Ruimin, Haier's CEO, built a factory in South Carolina. The idea was to manufacture in North America and take a larger share of the refrigerator market. But the plant was expensive by Chinese standards and it started production just at the time when the North American economy was slowing down. Furthermore, Haier's organizational culture, with a top-down management style and required work hats that showed different ranks and seniority, didn't fit well with American workers. But Zhang is committed to global expansion for his firm. "First the hard, then smooth," he says. "That's the way to win."[11]

What about you? Is it possible that you will work at home some day for a foreign employer? Are you interested in an assignment abroad as an "expatriate" employee of your domestic employer? Are you informed about the world and what is taking place amid the forces of globalization? A new breed of manager, the **global manager**, is increasingly sought after. This is someone informed about international developments, transnational in outlook, competent in working with people from different cultures, and always aware of regional developments in a changing world.

> A **global manager** is culturally aware and informed on international affairs.

WHY COMPANIES GO GLOBAL

John Chambers, chairman of Cisco Systems Inc., has said: "I will put my jobs anywhere in the world where the right infrastructure is, with the right educated workforce, with the right supportive government."[12] Cisco and other firms like it are global businesses that conduct for-profit transactions of goods and services across national boundaries. Global businesses are the foundations of world trade, helping to move raw materials, finished products, and specialized services from one country to another in the global economy.

Courtesy Nike

Nike is one of those brands that may come to mind as an exemplar of international businesses; its swoosh is one of the world's most globally recognized logos. But did you know that Nike does no domestic manufacturing? All of its products come from sources abroad. The story of its competitor New Balance is a bit different. This Boston firm has been in business for more than 100 years, and it too sells in some 120 countries. But New Balance still produces at factories in the United States, even though it also manufactures in China and elsewhere.[13]

While competing in the same industry, Nike and New Balance are pursuing somewhat different strategies as they deal with the opportunities and threats of a global economy. Both stories are good examples of how businesses naturally grow and go international for reasons such as these:

- *Profits*—Global operations offer greater profit potential.
- *Customers*—Global operations offer new markets to sell products.
- *Suppliers*—Global operations offer access to needed products and services.
- *Capital*—Global operations offer access to financial resources.
- *Labour*—Global operations offer access to lower labour costs.

HOW COMPANIES GO GLOBAL

A **global business** conducts commercial transactions across national boundaries.

The common forms of **global business** are shown in Figure 3.1. When a business is just getting started internationally, global sourcing, exporting/importing, and licensing and franchising are the usual ways to begin. These are *market-entry strategies* that involve the sale of goods or services to foreign markets without expensive investments. Strategic alliances, joint ventures, and wholly owned subsidiaries are *direct investment strategies*. They require major capital commitments, but they also create rights of ownership and control over operations in the foreign country.

Figure 3.1 Common forms of international business—from market entry to direct investment strategies.

Market entry strategies			Direct investment strategies	
Global sourcing	Exporting and importing	Licensing and franchising	Joint ventures	Foreign subsidiaries

Increasing involvement in ownership and control of foreign operations →

Global Sourcing

In **global sourcing**, materials or services are purchased around the world for local use.

A common first step into international business is **global sourcing**—the process of purchasing materials, manufacturing components, or business services from around the world. It is an international division of labour in which activities are performed in countries where they can be done well at the lowest cost. In auto manufacturing, global sourcing may mean local assembly but using, for example, windshields and instrument panels from Mexico and electrical components from Vietnam. In the service sector, it may mean setting up toll-free customer support call centres in the Philippines, or contracting for research and development by computer software engineers in Russia.

Firms selling toys, shoes, electronics, furniture, and clothing are among those that make extensive use of global sourcing. The goal is to take advantage of the international wage gaps by sourcing products in countries that can produce them at the lowest costs.[14] China, as suggested by the box, is a major outsourcing destination and in many areas of manufacturing has become the factory for the world.[15]

> *China Manufactures for the World*
> - 70 percent of the world's umbrellas
> - 60 percent of the world's buttons
> - 72 percent of U.S. shoes
> - 50 percent of U.S. appliances
> - 80 percent of U.S. toys

Exporting and Importing

A second form of international business involves **exporting**—selling locally made products in foreign markets. The flip side of exporting is **importing**—buying foreign-made products and selling them in domestic markets. Exporting is a significant pathway to business growth for both individual firms and economies. For businesses, the goal of exporting is to find new customers and expanded markets by selling one's products and services in other countries. For governments concerned about economic growth, expanding exports helps keep local businesses strong at a time when the potential is high for job loss to lower-wage countries.

In **exporting**, local products are sold abroad to foreign customers.

Importing involves the selling in domestic markets of products acquired abroad.

Because the growth of export industries creates local jobs, governments often offer special advice and assistance to businesses that are trying to develop or expand their export markets. One case in point is Richards Industries. After visiting a trade fair in China, the president of Richards Industries, Bruce Boxerman, decided to take advantage of the growing market for precision valves. In 10 years, he doubled export sales, and with more expansion in the China and India markets soon, he expects them to account for one-half the firm's revenues. One of his employees says: "It wasn't long ago that guys looked at globalization like it is going to cause all of us to lose our jobs. Now it's probably going to save our jobs."[16]

Licensing and Franchising

Another form of international business is the **licensing agreement**, where foreign firms pay a fee for rights to make or sell another company's products in a specified region. The licence typically grants access to a unique manufacturing technology, special patent, or trademark. In effect, the foreign firm provides the local firm with the technology and knowledge to offer its products or services for local sales. Such licensing involves some potential risk.[17] New Balance, for example, licensed a Chinese supplier to produce one of its brands. Even after New Balance revoked the licence, the supplier continued to produce and distribute the shoes around Asia. New Balance ended up facing costly and complex litigation in China's courts.[18]

In a **licensing agreement**, a local firm pays a fee to a foreign firm for rights to make or sell its products.

Franchising is a form of licensing in which the foreign firm buys the rights to use another's name and operating methods in its home country. The international version operates similarly to domestic franchising agreements. Firms such as McDonald's, Wendy's, Subway, and others sell facility designs, equipment, product ingredients and recipes, and management systems to foreign investors, while retaining certain product and operating controls.

In **franchising**, a fee is paid to a foreign business for rights to locally operate using its name, branding, and methods.

Joint Ventures and Strategic Alliances

Sooner or later, some firms decide to make substantial investments in operations in foreign countries. Such **foreign direct investment**, or FDI, involves setting up, buying all, or buying part of a business in another country. For many countries, the ability to attract foreign business investors has been a key to succeeding in the global economy. The term **insourcing** is often used to

Foreign direct investment is building, buying all, or buying part ownership of a business in another country.

Insourcing is job creation through foreign direct investment.

describe job creation that results from foreign direct investment. Its effects can be very positive for the local economy; for example, statistics show that $45.4 billion in investments flowed into Canada in 2008,[19] with insourced plants being more productive, more innovative, and more technology-intensive, and paying higher wages and using more skilled workers than domestic-controlled plants.[20]

A **joint venture** operates in a foreign country through co-ownership by foreign and local partners.

When foreign firms do invest in a new country, a common way to start is with a **joint venture**. This is a co-ownership arrangement in which the foreign and local partners agree to pool resources, share risks, and jointly operate the new business. Sometimes the joint venture is formed when a foreign partner buys part ownership in an existing local firm. In other cases, it is formed as an entirely new operation that the foreign and local partners jointly invest in and start up together.

A **global strategic alliance** is a partnership in which foreign and domestic firms share resources and knowledge for mutual gains.

International joint ventures are types of **global strategic alliances** in which foreign and domestic firms act as partners by sharing resources and knowledge for mutual benefit. Each partner hopes to gain through cooperation things they couldn't do or would have a hard time doing alone. For the local partner, an alliance may bring access to technology and opportunities to learn new skills. For the outside partner, an alliance may bring access to new markets and the expert assistance of locals that understand them.[21]

Joint ventures and strategic alliances were the business forms of choice for most of the world's large automakers when they decided to pursue major operations in China. Recognizing the local complexities, they decided it was better to cooperate with local partners than try to enter the Chinese markets on their own. Of course, any such business deals pose potential risks. Not long ago, GM executives noticed that a new car from a fast-growing local competitor, partially owned by GM's Chinese joint venture partner, looked very similar to one of its models. GM claims its design was copied. The competitor denied it, and even pursued plans to export the cars, called "Cherys," for sale in North America.[22]

Criteria for Choosing a Joint Venture Partner

- Is familiar with your firm's major business

- Employs a strong local workforce

- Values its customers

- Has potential for future expansion

- Has strong local market for its own products

- Has good profit potential

- Has sound financial standing

GOING GLOBAL

IS CANADA OPEN FOR BUSINESS?

Wind Mobile entered the Canadian wireless market in December 2009 but it took a lot of determination, deal making, and political intervention to do so. When Industry Canada auctioned broadband spectrum in 2008, University of Toronto grad Tony Lacavera set out to find investors to start a wireless business. He found no investors in Canada and, while he saw interest abroad, once international investors learned of the labyrinth known as Canada's telecommunications regulatory environment, only one remained. Egypt's Orascom Telecom provided financing to purchase licences to enter the Canadian wireless market. Yet, after Globalive purchased the spectrum for $442 million, the Canadian Radio-television and Telecommunications Commission (CRTC) ruled that it was an illegally constituted company. "You can imagine the chaos when I had to say to my foreign investor, I do not know how to fix this," Lacavera said. Only after a rare political intervention made by Industry Minister Tony Clement and the federal cabinet was Globalive's Wind service able to launch. Lacavera warned that the situation could repeat itself and keep needed international investment at bay. The world wants to know: is Canada open for business?

Foreign Subsidiaries

One way around some of the risks and problems associated with strategic alliances and joint ventures is full ownership of the foreign operation. A **foreign subsidiary** is a local operation completely owned and controlled by a foreign firm. These subsidiaries may be set up by **greenfield investments**, in which the foreign operation is built entirely new. They can also be established by acquisition, in which the outside firm purchases a local operation in its entirety. Although a foreign subsidiary represents the highest level of involvement in international operations, it can make very good business sense.

A **foreign subsidiary** is a local operation completely owned by a foreign firm.

A **greenfield investment** builds an entirely new operation in a foreign country.

GLOBAL BUSINESS ENVIRONMENTS

A lot of what takes place in foreign business environments is very different from what is common at home. Not only must global managers master the demands of operating with worldwide suppliers, distributors, customers, and competitors, they must deal successfully with a variety of forces in the general environment that can pose unique challenges. Among those forces are differences in legal and political systems, complexities in trade agreements and barriers, and the roles of regional economic alliances.

Legal and Political Systems

When it comes to risk in international business, some of the biggest complications come from differences in legal and political systems. A major planning concern in global management, for example, involves **political risk**—the potential loss in value of an investment in or managerial control over a foreign asset because of instability and political changes in the host country. The major threats of political risk today come from terrorism, civil wars, armed conflicts and military disruptions, shifting government systems through elections or forced takeovers, and new laws and economic policies. Although such things can't be prevented, they can be anticipated. Most global firms use a planning technique called **political-risk analysis** to forecast the probability of disruptive events that can threaten the security of a foreign investment.

Political risk is the potential loss in value of a foreign investment due to instability and political changes in the host country.

Political-risk analysis tries to forecast political disruptions that can threaten the value of a foreign investment.

Global managers must also be prepared to deal with differences between home-country and host-country laws and politics. And the greater the differences, the more difficult and complex it is for international businesses to operate successfully in the local context. Global firms are expected to abide by local laws, some of which may be unfamiliar. In the United States and Canada, for example, executives of foreign-owned companies must comply with antitrust laws that prevent competitors from regularly talking to one another, something that they may not be used to at home. They also must deal with a variety of special laws regarding occupational health and safety, employment equity, sexual harassment, and other matters, all of which, again, may be different from the legal environments they are used to at home.

Common legal problems faced by international businesses involve incorporation practices and business ownership; negotiating and implementing contracts with foreign parties; handling foreign exchange; and intellectual property rights—patents, trademarks, and copyrights. You might know the intellectual property issue best in terms of concerns about movie and music downloads, photocopying of books and journals, and sale of fake designer fashions. Laws on intellectual property protection are quite strict in Canada, but can be lax in other countries. Companies like Microsoft, Sony, and Louis Vuitton are among those that often lose profits when their products or designs are copied and sold as imitations abroad.

Trade Agreements and Trade Barriers

When international businesses believe they are being mistreated in foreign countries, or when local companies believe foreign competitors are disadvantaging them, their respective governments

REAL ETHICS

Bolivia's Nationalization of the Oil and Gas Industry

Although executives from the world's oil industry couldn't say that it wasn't anticipated as a possibility, it still must have been a shock when Bolivia's government announced that it was taking control of the country's oil and gas fields. The announcement said: "We are beginning by nationalizing oil and gas; tomorrow we will add mining, forestry, and all natural resources, what our ancestors fought for."

As soon as the announcement was made, Bolivia's armed forces secured all oil and gas fields in the country. The country's newly elected president, Evo Morales, set forth new terms that gave a state-owned firm 82 percent of all revenues, leaving 18 percent for the foreign firms. He said: "Only those firms that respect these new terms will be allowed to operate in the country." The implicit threat was that any firms not willing to sign new contracts would be sent home.

While foreign governments described this nationalization as an "unfriendly move," Morales considered it patriotic. His position was that any existing contracts with the state were in violation of the constitution, and that Bolivia's natural resources belonged to its people.

YOU DECIDE

Exxon-Mobil and BP were among the firms affected by Bolivia's new law. If you were the CEO of one of these firms, how would you react to this nationalization? Do you raise the ethics of honouring your "old" contracts with the Bolivian government? Do you resist, or do you comply with the new terms being offered?

Now, be what you are—an everyday citizen of the world. Consider Morales's argument that Bolivia's natural resources are a national treasure belonging to the people. Do you agree or disagree that a country has a right to protect its natural resources from exploitation by foreigners? Just what are the ethics of Morales's decision to nationalize the oil and gas industry?

World Trade Organization member nations agree to negotiate and resolve disputes about tariffs and trade restrictions.

might take the cases to the **World Trade Organization**. The "WTO" is a global organization whose member nations, currently 153 of them, agree to negotiate and resolve disputes about tariffs and trade restrictions.

The WTO was established to promote free trade and open markets around the world. Its website declares that: "Liberal trade policies—which allow the unrestricted flow of goods and services—sharpen competition, motivate innovation, and breed success. They multiply the rewards that result from producing the best products, with the best design, at the best price."[23]

Although members agree to work together within the WTO framework to resolve international business problems, controversies still develop. In one claim filed with the WTO, for example, the United States complained that China's "legal structure for protecting and enforcing copyright and trademark protections" was "deficient" and not in compliance with WTO rules.

China's official response was that the suit was out of line with WTO rules and that "we strongly oppose the U.S. attempt to impose on developing members through this case."[24]

WTO members are supposed to give one another **most favoured nation status**—the most favourable treatment for imports and exports. Yet trade barriers that limit freedom of trade are still common. They include **tariffs**, which are basically taxes that governments impose on imports, and other forms of **protectionism** that give favourable treatment to domestic businesses.

The goal of most tariffs and protectionism is to protect local firms from foreign competition and save jobs for local workers. You will see such issues reflected in political campaigns and debates. And the issues aren't easy. Government leaders face the often-conflicting goals of seeking freer international trade while still protecting domestic industries. Such political dilemmas sometimes make it difficult to reach international agreements on trade matters, and they create controversies for the WTO in its role as a global arbiter of trade issues.

Most favoured nation status gives a trading partner most favourable treatment for imports and exports.

Tariffs are taxes governments levy on imports from abroad.

Protectionism is a call for tariffs and favourable treatments to protect domestic firms from foreign competition.

Regional Economic Alliances

In 1994, Canada, the United States, and Mexico joined in the North American Free Trade Agreement, or **NAFTA**. This alliance creates a trade zone with minimal barriers, which frees the flow of goods and services, workers, and investments among the three countries. One of the global businesses that embraced NAFTA is GE, and the firm has moved many jobs and production activities to Mexico. Between its own facilities and joint ventures, GE employs some 30,000 Mexicans at lower wages than those earned by American workers. Mexican engineers, for example, earn one-third the pay of their counterparts in the United States.[25] Cases like this have stimulated many debates about NAFTA's pros and cons.

NAFTA is the North American Free Trade Agreement linking Canada, the United States, and Mexico in an economic alliance.

Arguments on the positive side of NAFTA include greater cross-border trade, benefits to farm exports, greater productivity of manufacturers, and reform of the Mexican business environment. The head of GE's Mexican operations, Rafael Diaz-Granados, says: "NAFTA has been an unparalleled success; it helped turn GE from a very America-centered company into a much more global one." By contrast, the United Auto Workers union blames NAFTA and low Mexican wages for the loss of 200,000 auto-related jobs. Other arguments on the negative side of NAFTA include job losses to Mexico, lower wages for Canadian and American workers wanting to keep their jobs, and the lack of protection of Canadian fresh water and natural resources.[26]

Another well-known regional alliance is the **European Union** or EU. It now links 27 countries that agree to support mutual economic growth by removing barriers that previously limited cross-border trade and business development. A common currency, the **euro**, has grown to the point where it is a major alternative—indeed, competitor—to the U.S. dollar. And, when one looks toward Asia, the Asia Pacific Economic Cooperation, APEC, was established to promote free trade and investment in the Pacific region. It has 21 members, including Canada, the United States, and Australia. The 10 nations of Southeast Asia also belong to the Association of Southeast Asian Nations (ASEAN) with a stated goal of promoting economic growth and progress.

The **European Union** is a political and economic alliance of European countries.

The **euro** is the common European currency.

Africa is also making headlines in the business news.[27] The United Nations reports that 34 African countries rank in the bottom 40 of the world's nations on health, education, and economic progress.[28] Yet the region's economies are growing, and there is a promising rise in

entrepreneurship. Says Coby Asmah, who runs a successful design and printing business in Ghana: "It's a young economy, and anyone who looks into that will see . . . returns on investment here are 20 percent higher than anywhere else."[29] The Southern Africa Development Community, SADC, links 14 countries of southern Africa in trade and economic development efforts. Its objectives include harmonizing and rationalizing strategies for sustainable development among member countries. The SADC website posts this vision: ". . . a future in a regional community that will ensure economic well-being, improvement of the standards of living and quality of life, freedom and social justice, and peace and security for the peoples of Southern Africa."[30]

✔ **Learning Check 1**

BE SURE YOU CAN

• define *globalization* and discuss its implications for international management • list five reasons why companies pursue international business opportunities • describe and give examples of global sourcing, exporting/importing, franchising/licensing, joint ventures, and foreign subsidiaries • discuss how differences in legal environments can affect businesses operating internationally • explain the goals of the WTO • discuss the significance of regional economic alliances such as NAFTA, the EU, and SADC

GLOBAL BUSINESSES

Big Mac Index (2010 Data)	
United States	$3.73
Canada	$4.00
Australia	$3.84
Brazil	$4.91
China	$1.95
Euro area	$4.33
Russia	$2.33
Norway	$7.20
Turkey	$3.89

A **global corporation**, or MNC, is a multinational business with extensive operations in more than one foreign country.

If you travel abroad these days, many of your favourite brands and products will travel with you. You can have a McDonald's sandwich in 119 countries, follow it with a Haagen-Dazs ice cream in some 50 countries, and then brush up with Procter & Gamble's Crest toothpaste in 80 countries. Economists even use the "Big Mac" index to track purchasing power parity among the world's currencies. The index compares the price in a currency like the U.S. dollar of the McDonald's sandwich around the world.[31]

Global corporations, also called multinational corporations or "MNCs," are business firms with extensive international operations in many foreign countries. The largest MNCs are identified in annual listings such as *Fortune* magazine's Global 500 and the *Financial Times* FT Global 500. They include familiar names such as Walmart, Toyota, Nestlé, BMW, Hitachi, Caterpillar, Sony, and Samsung, as well as others you might not recognize such as big oil and gas producers like PetroChina (China), Gazprom (Russia), and Total (France). Indeed, in the last 10 years, the geographical distribution of the world's largest and most powerful companies has shifted, with North America and Japan showing declines while countries like China, Russia, India, South Korea, and Mexico show substantial gains.[32]

Also important on the world scene are multinational organizations with non-profit missions. Examples include the International Federation of Red Cross and Red Crescent Societies, the United Nations, and the World Bank.

TYPES OF GLOBAL BUSINESSES

Although any global corporation, or MNC, operates in many countries, its founding history and corporate headquarters give it a strong national identification. Is there any doubt in your mind that Hewlett-Packard and Dell are American firms, Sony and Honda are Japanese, and BMW and Daimler are German? Most likely not; yet that may not be how their executives want the firms to be viewed. Each of these and many other global firms are acting more like **transnational corporations**. That is, they try to operate as "borderless firms" with worldwide presences, and without being identified with one national home.[33]

A **transnational corporation** is an MNC that operates worldwide on a borderless basis.

Executives of transnationals view the entire world as their domain for acquiring resources, locating production facilities, marketing goods and services, and communicating brand image. They seek total integration of global operations, try to operate across borders without home-based prejudices, make major decisions from a global perspective, distribute work among world-wide points of excellence, and employ senior executives from many different countries. Aldi is an example in groceries, Nestlé is a good example in foods, and Asea Brown Boveri (ABB) is another in diversified conglomerates. When buying a Hugo Boss item, would you know it's a German company? When buying a Nestlé product or learning that a new neighbour works for ABB in Toronto, would you know that both are registered Swiss companies? And finally consider this: Which company is really more North American—the Indian giant Tata, which gets 51.4 percent of its revenues from North America, or IBM, which earns 65 percent of its revenues outside of the United States?[34]

PROS AND CONS OF GLOBAL CORPORATIONS

The recent global economic downturn raised important questions that relate, in part at least, to the growth of the "transnational" concept of global business. For example, does a company's nationality matter to the domestic economy? Does it matter to a Canadian whether local jobs come from a domestic giant like Tim Hortons or a foreign one like Toyota?[35] And what about what some call the "globalization gap"? Is it wrong for large multinationals to gain disproportionately from the forces of globalization, while many smaller firms and many countries do not?[36]

Did you know, for example, that global firms hold one-third of the world's productive assets and control 70 percent of world trade? Or that more than 50 of the largest 100 economies in the world are multinational corporations? Or that more than 90 percent of MNCs are based in the Northern Hemisphere?[37] Although such facts may bring a sense of both accomplishment and future opportunity to global business leaders, they can also be very threatening to small and less-developed countries, and to their domestic industries.

Host-Country Issues

Global corporations and the countries that "host" their foreign operations should ideally both benefit. But, as shown in Figure 3.2, things can go both right and wrong in MNC relationships with their host countries.

The potential host-country benefits of MNCs include larger tax bases, increased employment opportunities, technology transfers, introduction of new industries, and development of local resources. The potential host-country costs include complaints that MNCs extract excessive profits, dominate the local economy, interfere with the local government, do not respect local customs and laws, fail to help domestic firms develop, hire the most talented of local personnel, and fail to transfer their most advanced technologies.[38]

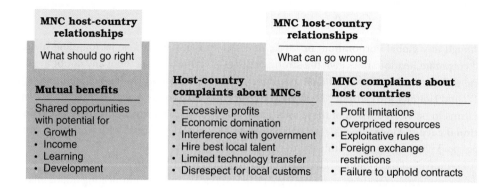

Figure 3.2 What should go right and what can go wrong in MNC host-country relationships.

Home-Country Issues

An MNC may also encounter difficulties in its home country, the one where it was founded and where its headquarters is located. Even as many global firms try to operate as transnationals, home-country governments and citizens still tend to identify them with local and national interests. They also expect the MNCs to act as good domestic citizens. That's one of the arguments against NAFTA. Many Americans resent the fact that firms such as GE employ so many people in their Mexican operations.[39]

Whenever a domestic employer outsources jobs, or cuts back or closes a domestic operation in order to shift work to lower-cost international destinations, the loss of local jobs is controversial. Corporate decision-makers are likely to be engaged by government and community leaders in critical debates about a firm's domestic social responsibilities. Other home-country criticisms of MNCs include complaints about sending capital investments abroad and engaging in corrupt practices in foreign settings.

ETHICS CHALLENGES FOR GLOBAL MANAGERS

The ethical aspects of international business are often in the news. In just one day—March 24, 2008, for example—the *Wall Street Journal* contained articles reporting on Brazil—where Alcoa is spending over $35 million on health services, a water system, and technical training for local residents in the area of a mine it wants to expand; Indonesia—where locals suffer shortages of coal, natural gas, and palm oil at the same time that exports of the same commodities are increasing to China, India, and Japan; and China—where the government's harsh treatment of Tibetan unrest dampened prospects for foreign direct investments in the region.[40] Take a moment to about think where you stand on the underlying issues in these examples, and think also about other areas of ethical challenge that face global corporations.

Corruption

Corruption involves illegal practices to further one's business interests.

Corruption—engaging in illegal practices to further one's business interests—is a source of continuing controversy in any setting, international or domestic.[41] As the accompanying table suggests, bribery and other forms of corruption can pose significant challenges as global managers travel the world. Whereas Transparency International scores Somalia, Iraq, Myanmar, and Haiti among the worst countries in respect to corruption, the best are Denmark, New Zealand, Sweden, and Singapore.[42]

Canada and the United States have similar anti-bribery laws making it illegal for domestic firms and their managers to engage in corrupt practices with foreign officials. While Canada's Corruption of Foreign Public Officials Act requires that the illegal activity took place in Canada or had a "real and substantial" impact on Canada, the U.S. Foreign Corrupt Practices Act also applies to the activities of American firms overseas, banning payoffs to foreign officials to obtain or keep businesses.

Some critics believe the Foreign Corrupt Practices Act fails to recognize the "reality" of business as practised in many foreign nations. They complain that American companies are at a competitive disadvantage because they can't offer the same "deals" as competitors from other nations—deals that locals may regard as standard business practices. However, many nations are starting to pass similar laws. And the U.S. Department of Justice has also stepped up the heat. In one year alone, the caseload under the act doubled to 150 possible violations.[43]

Child Labour and Sweatshops

One of the issues in the cultural relativism–ethical absolutism debate (which will be discussed more in the next chapter) is **child labour**, the full-time employment of children for work otherwise done by adults. It remains one of the major ethics issues and challenges in international business. A frequent target of activist groups, for example, is the use of child labour to manufacture handmade carpets in countries such as India and Pakistan. Initiatives to eliminate child labour include an effort by the Rugmark Foundation to discourage purchases of carpets that do not carry its label. The Rugmark label is earned by a certification process to guarantee that a carpet manufacturer does not use illegal child labour.[44]

As timely and appropriate as concerns about child labour are, this isn't the only labour issue facing global managers. **Sweatshops**, business operations that employ workers at low wages for long hours and in poor working conditions, are another concern. Networks of outsourcing contracts are now common as manufacturers follow the world's low-cost labour supplies—countries such as the Philippines, Sri Lanka, and Vietnam are popular destinations. And the many players in these supply chains are often difficult to identify, let alone control. Nike Inc., for example, revised its global labour practices after a review by the consulting firm Goodworks International. Nike now hosts a special website with reports and audit results on more than 750 manufacturing sites and contractors in some 50 countries.[45]

> **Transparency International— Countries Most Affected by Corruption**
>
> - Somalia
> - Myanmar
> - Iraq
> - Haiti
> - Afghanistan
> - Sudan
> - Chad
> - Guinea

Child labour is the full-time employment of children for work otherwise done by adults.

Sweatshops employ workers at very low wages for long hours and in poor working conditions.

ISSUES AND SITUATIONS
Sweatshop Hunter

Help Wanted: Sweatshop Hunter—One of the world's premier fashion merchandisers seeks an experienced executive to head staff in charge of monitoring international suppliers for ethics and social responsibility practices. The successful candidate will have a strong commitment to ethics and social responsibility in business, strong communication skills and cultural intelligence, confidence in handling conflict situations, and the capacity to work well in relationships spanning from shop-floor workers to chief executives.

This ad is fabricated; the job it features is real. At Hewlett-Packard, it's filled by Bonnie Nixon-Gardiner. She has a middle-management appointment, overseeing the work of some 70 auditors and with major responsibilities for keeping track of more than 200 supplier factories. Nixon-Gardiner and her staff travel the world inspecting HP suppliers, with the

(continued on next page)

ISSUES AND SITUATIONS (*continued*)

Traveling with a Sweatshop Hunter

Bonnie Nixon-Gardiner arrives at Foxconn Electronics in Long Hua, China. Her hosts try to move her into a conference room, but she declines and opts to walk about the factory with its multiple buildings and 200,000 employees. "Look," she tells her hosts when they balk, "this isn't going to work unless you're totally transparent with me."

When she found that the noise was too loud for the workers on some machines, the firm agreed to purchase ear protectors. On a later visit, she called for and got more changes: special enclosures for the machines and purchase of the best ear protection devices available. Her no-nonsense but polite approach has been described by a colleague as "like being kissed and slapped at the same time."

goal of making sure that working conditions are up to HP's standards. She describes her goal this way: "My 10-year vision is for [consumers to know that] when you touch a technology product, you are guaranteed it was made in a socially and environmentally responsible way."

CRITICAL RESPONSE

Would you like a job like this? Should all international businesses have a similar position? What special skills and capabilities does Nixon-Gardiner need to succeed in this job? Were you surprised that she is described as a "middle manager"? With these responsibilities, should she be on the top management team?

Sustainable Development

Global warming, industrial pollution, hazardous waste disposal, depletion of natural resources, and related concerns are now worldwide issues. Yet we also want the products and economic development that come from using environmental resources—everything from timber, to iron ore and minerals, to oil and water. How do we satisfy the needs of the present without sacrificing the welfare of future generations? What are the implications of the growing resource needs in rapidly growing economies such as India and China? In a book entitled *Collapse*, scholar Jared Diamond argues that "resource exhaustion" is linked with "social catastrophe," and that both are of increasing likelihood on the world stage. He suggests that, if China's 1.3 billion people were to reach the prosperity of Americans, the worldwide demand for resources would double and require "another earth" to provide them.[46]

Sustainable development meets the needs of the present without hurting future generations.

Concerns for our natural environment and its resources are embodied in the notion of **sustainable development**, a popular guideline advanced by activist groups and one increasingly accepted as a social responsibility goal by global corporations. The term describes "development that meets the needs of the present without compromising the ability of future generations to meet their own needs."[47] For a firm to fulfill a commitment to sustainable development, its executives must lead in ways that demonstrate stewardship in protecting the natural environment and preserving its resources for the future.

Davos Awards: Most Sustainable Global Corporations in Information Technology

- SAP AG—Germany

- Indra Sistemas SA—Spain

- Advanced Micro Devices—USA

- Google Inc.—USA

- Hewlett-Packard—USA

- Intel Inc.—USA

As a step in this direction of sustainability, several of the world's largest mining firms—including DeBeers, Rio Tinto, Newmont, and Anglo-American—have proposed that the United Nations develop a "budget of excellence" establishing environmental and safety standards in the mining industry.[48] The Davos World Economic Forum publishes an annual list of the Global 100 Most Sustainable Corporations in the World.[49] And sustainable development is a top priority for the International Organization for Standardization, whose "ISO" designations for world-class quality were first introduced in Chapter 2. Organizations meeting the ISO 14000 standards are certified to have management systems that identify and control the environmental impacts of their activities, systematically develop environmental targets and objectives, and continuously improve environmental performance.[50] Another forthcoming standard, ISO 26000, will set further guidelines for social responsibility practices.[51]

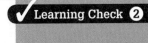

BE SURE YOU CAN

• differentiate a multinational corporation from a transnational corporation • list at least three host-country complaints and three home-country complaints about MNC operations • give examples of corruption, sweatshops, and child labour in international businesses • define *sustainable development* and explain what international businesses might do to make it a priority

CULTURE AND GLOBAL DIVERSITY

Here's the situation. An American businessperson goes to meet a Saudi Arabian official. He sits in the office with crossed legs and the sole of his shoe exposed, an unintentional sign of disrespect in the local culture. He passes documents to the host using his left hand, which Muslims consider unclean. He declines when coffee is offered, suggesting criticism of the Saudi's hospitality. What is the price for these cultural miscues? A $10-million contract is lost to a Korean executive better versed in Arab ways.[52]

"Culture" matters, as we often say, and here are its basic terms and considerations. **Culture** is the shared set of beliefs, values, and patterns of behaviour common to a group of people.[53] **Culture shock** is the confusion and discomfort a person experiences when in an unfamiliar culture; Management Smarts 3.1 is a reminder that these feelings must be mastered in order to travel comfortably and do business around the world. **Ethnocentrism** is the tendency to view one's culture as superior to others.

Culture is a shared set of beliefs, values, and patterns of behaviour common to a group of people.

Culture shock is the confusion and discomfort a person experiences when in an unfamiliar culture.

Ethnocentrism is the tendency to consider one's culture superior to others.

CULTURAL INTELLIGENCE

The American's behaviour in Saudi Arabia was ethnocentric, so self-centred that he ignored and showed no concern for the culture of his Arab host. Some might excuse him as suffering from culture shock. Maybe he was so uncomfortable upon arrival in Saudi Arabia that all he could think about was offering his contract and leaving as quickly as possible. Still others might give him the benefit of the doubt. It could have been that he was well intentioned but didn't have time to learn about Saudi culture before making the trip. But regardless of the possible reasons for the cultural miscues, they still worked to his disadvantage. There is little doubt that he lacked **cultural intelligence**— the ability to adapt and adjust to new cultures.[54]

Cultural intelligence is the ability to accept and adapt to new cultures.

3.1 MANAGEMENT SMARTS
Culture shock: Stages in adjusting to a new culture

• *Confusion*: First contacts with the new culture leave you anxious, uncomfortable, and in need of information and advice.

• *Small victories*: Continued interactions bring some "successes," and your confidence grows in handling daily affairs.

• *The honeymoon*: A time of wonderment, cultural immersion, and even infatuation, with local ways viewed positively.

• *Irritation and anger*: A time when the "negatives" overwhelm the "positives," and the new culture becomes a target of your criticism.

• *Reality*: A time of rebalancing; you are able to enjoy the new culture while accommodating its less desirable elements.

People with cultural intelligence have high cultural self-awareness and are flexible in dealing with cultural differences. In cross-cultural situations, they are willing to learn from what is unfamiliar; they modify their behaviours to act with sensitivity to another culture's ways. In other words, someone high in cultural intelligence views cultural differences not as threats, but as learning opportunities. This personal quality is a good indicator of someone's capacity for success in international assignments and in relationships with persons of different cultures.[55]

Executives at China's Haier Group showed cultural intelligence in the way they responded to problems at the firm's new factory in South Carolina.[56] As part of Haier's commitment to quality, workers who make mistakes in its Chinese factories are made to stand on special footprints and publicly criticize themselves. They are expected to point out what they did wrong and what lessons they have learned. When this practice was implemented at the U.S. factory, American workers protested—they thought it was humiliating. In response, Haier executives didn't force the practice; they changed their approach. The footprints and quality commitment still exist, but American workers stand in the footprints as a form of public recognition when they do exceptional work. It seems that the Chinese managers listened and learned from the initial bad experience, ending up with a local practice that fits both corporate values and the local culture.

SILENT LANGUAGES OF CULTURE

The capacities to listen, observe, and learn are building blocks of cultural intelligence. These skills and competencies can be developed by better understanding what anthropologist Edward T. Hall calls the "silent" languages of culture.[57] He believes that these silent languages are found in a culture's approach to context, time, and space.

Context

Low-context cultures emphasize communication via spoken or written words.

High-context cultures rely on nonverbal and situational cues as well as on spoken or written words in communication.

If we look and listen carefully, Hall believes we should recognize that cultures differ in how their members use language in communication.[58] In **low-context cultures**, most communication takes place via the written or spoken word. This is common in the United States, Canada, and Germany, for example. As the saying goes, we say or write what we mean, and we mean what we say.

In **high-context cultures**, things are different. What is actually said or written may convey only part, and sometimes a very small part, of the real message. The rest must be interpreted from nonverbal signals and the situation as a whole, including body language, the physical setting, and even past relationships among the people involved. Dinner parties and social gatherings in high-context cultures like Thailand and Malaysia, for example, are ways for potential business partners to get to know one another. Only after the relationships are established and a context for communication exists is it possible to make business deals.

Time

The way people approach and deal with time varies across cultures. You might think of this in terms of punctuality and sticking to schedules. Hall takes this a step further and describes differences between "monochronic" and "polychronic" cultures.

A **monochronic culture** is one in which people tend to do one thing at a time. This is typical of the United States, where most business people schedule a meeting for one person or group to focus on one issue for an allotted time.[59] And if someone is late for one of those meetings or brings an uninvited guest, Americans tend not to like it. Members of a **polychronic culture** are more flexible toward time and who uses it. They often try to work on many different things at once, perhaps not in any particular order. A Canadian visitor (from a monochronic culture) to an Egyptian client (in a polychronic culture) may be frustrated, for example, by continued interruptions as the client greets and deals with people flowing in and out of his office.

> In **monochronic cultures**, people tend to do one thing at a time.

> In **polychronic cultures**, time is used to accomplish many different things at once.

Space

Hall also considers the use of space part of the silent language of culture. He points out that most North Americans like and value their own space, perhaps as much space as they can get. We like big offices, big homes, and big yards. We get uncomfortable in tight spaces and when others stand too close to us in lines. When someone "talks right in our face," we don't like it; the behaviour may even be interpreted as an expression of anger. Members of other cultures may view such things as quite normal.

Hall describes these cultural tendencies in terms of **proxemics**, or how people use interpersonal space to communicate.[60] If you visit Japan, you would notice the difference in proxemics very quickly. Space is precious in Japan; its use is carefully planned and it is respected. Small, tidy homes, offices, and shops are the norm; gardens are tiny, but immaculate; public spaces are carefully organized for most efficient use.

> **Proxemics** is how people use space to communicate.

VALUES AND NATIONAL CULTURES

The work of Geert Hofstede is often considered a benchmark for how cultural differences can influence management and organizational practices. After studying employees of a global corporation operating in 40 countries, Hofstede identified four cultural dimensions: power distance, uncertainty avoidance, individualism–collectivism, and masculinity–femininity.[61] Later studies added a fifth: time orientation.[62] Figure 3.3 shows how national cultures can vary on these dimensions.

Imagine what the cultural differences shown in Figure 3.3 might mean when international business executives try to make deals around the world, or when representatives of national governments try to work out problems. But remember, Hofstede's dimensions offer only a ballpark look; his model is best considered a starting point for developing cross-cultural awareness. In fact, Hofstede warns about the **ecological fallacy** that occurs when someone acts with the mistaken assumption that a generalized cultural value, such as individualism in American culture or masculinity in Japanese culture, applies equally to all members of the culture.[63]

> The **ecological fallacy** assumes that a generalized cultural value applies equally well to all members of the culture.

Power Distance

Power distance is the degree to which a society accepts or rejects the unequal distribution of power among people in organizations and the institutions of society. In high-power-distance cultures, such as Japan, we expect to find great respect for age, status, and titles. People in these cultures tend to be tolerant of power; they are prone to follow orders and accept differences in rank. Picture a Canadian businessperson visiting her firm's joint-venture partner in high-power-distance Malaysia. Could her tendencies toward informality—using first names to

> **Power distance** is the degree to which a society accepts unequal distribution of power.

address superiors and dressing casually in the office—create discomfort for local executives less accustomed to such practices?

Individualism–Collectivism

Individualism–collectivism is the degree to which a society emphasizes individuals and their self-interests.

Individualism–collectivism is the degree to which a society emphasizes individual accomplishments and self-interests versus collective accomplishments and the interests of groups.[64] In Hofstede's data, the United States had the highest individualism score of any country, with Canada not too far behind. Think about it; have you found that "I" and "me" words are used a lot in our conversations and meetings, or even when students are making team presentations in class? Such expressions reflect a cultural tendency toward individualism. Contrast this with the importance placed on group harmony in the Confucian cultures of Asia. What are the implications when those of us from more individualistic settings try to work with colleagues from more collectivist national cultures? How, for example, are individualistic Canadians perceived on work teams that include members from Japan or Thailand?

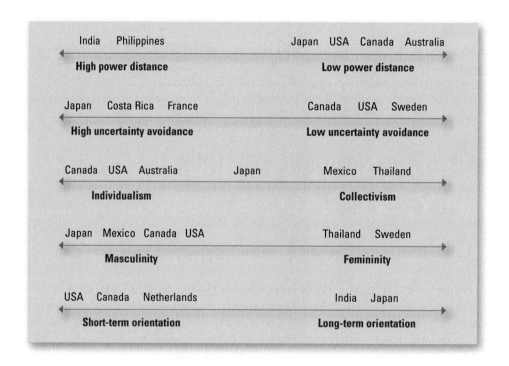

Figure 3.3 How countries compare on Hofstede's dimensions of national culture.

Uncertainty Avoidance

Uncertainty avoidance is the degree to which a society tolerates risk and uncertainty.

Uncertainty avoidance is the degree to which a society is uncomfortable with risk, change, and situational uncertainty, versus having tolerance for them. Low-uncertainty-avoidance cultures display openness to change and innovation. In high-uncertainty-avoidance cultures, by contrast, one would expect to find a preference for structure, order, and predictability. Persons in these cultures may have difficulties dealing with ambiguity, tend to follow rules, and prefer structure in their lives. Could high uncertainty avoidance be one of the reasons why some Europeans, perhaps the French, seem to favour employment practices that provide job security? Could the entrepreneurial tendencies toward business risks that are characteristic of Hong Kong Chinese reflect a low-uncertainty-avoidance culture?

RESEARCH BRIEF

Stable personality traits and behavioural competencies linked with expatriate effectiveness

A research collaboration brought together teams of scholars from Hong Kong and the United States to investigate the effectiveness of *expatriate workers*. The results of three empirical studies reported in the *Journal of Applied Psychology* by Margaret Shaffer and her colleagues show that individual differences have an impact on expatriate effectiveness.

When organizations send employees to work as expatriates in foreign countries, the assignments can be challenging, and the expatriate's performance can turn out lower than anticipated. Nevertheless, many employers fail to make fully informed decisions on expatriate assignments.

Expatriate Effectiveness Model

Individual Differences
• Stable dispositions
• Dynamic competencies

Expatriate Effectiveness
• Adjustment
• Withdrawal cognitions
• Performance

The researchers propose a model in which expatriate effectiveness is a function of *individual differences* in personalities and competencies. Specifically, they address *stable dispositions* in terms of the *"Big Five" personality traits:* conscientiousness, emotional stability,

agreeableness, intellectance (openness to new experiences), and extroversion; and the *dynamic competencies* of cultural flexibility, task orientation, people orientation, and ethnocentrism.

The research model was tested in samples of expatriates working in Hong Kong and Korean expatriates working in other nations. Results show that each of the Big Five traits, except conscientiousness, predicts some aspect of expatriate effectiveness. Emotional stability was the strongest predictor of withdrawal cognitions, while intellectance was the only predictor of task and contextual performance. Results were less uniform with respect to the link between dynamic competencies and performance, and the researchers believe that study design and/or the presence of unmeasured moderator variables might account for the mixed findings. One of their suggestions is that future research look at the entire model in the context of one well-designed study.

You be the researcher

Chances are that there are international students in your class or on campus who have worked with or as expatriates. You may also have family and friends with expatriate experience. Why not interview them to gather their views about how expatriates adapt and perform in foreign cultures? Compare the results of your investigation with the model and findings of this research study.

Masculinity–Femininity

Masculinity–femininity is the degree to which a society values assertiveness and materialism, versus feelings, relationships, and quality of life.[65] You might think of it as a tendency for members of a culture to show stereotypical masculine or feminine traits and reflect different attitudes toward gender roles. Visitors to Japan, which has the highest masculinity score in Hofstede's research, may be surprised at how restricted career opportunities can be for women.[66] The *Wall Street Journal* comments: "In Japan, professional women face a set

Masculinity–femininity is the degree to which a society values assertiveness and materialism.

of socially complex issues—from overt sexism to deep-seated attitudes about the division of labor." One female Japanese manager says: "Men tend to have very fixed ideas about what women are like."[67]

Time Orientation

Time orientation is the degree to which a society emphasizes short-term or long-term goals.

Time orientation is the degree to which a society emphasizes short-term or long-term goals and gratifications.[68] North American tendencies toward impatience and desire for quick, even instantaneous, gratifications, show short-term thinking. Even our companies are expected to achieve short-term results; those failing to meet quarterly financial targets often suffer immediate stock price declines. Many Asian cultures are quite the opposite, displaying more Confucian values of persistence, thrift, patience, and willingness to work for long-term success. This might help explain why Japan's auto executives were willing to invest in hybrid engine technologies and stick with them, even though market demand was very low at first and any return on the investments would be long-term at best.

✔ **Learning Check ③**   **BE SURE YOU CAN**

• define *culture* • explain how ethnocentrism can create difficulties for people working across cultures • differentiate between low-context and high-context cultures, and monochronic and polychronic cultures • list and illustrate Hofstede's five dimensions of value differences among national cultures

GLOBAL MANAGEMENT LEARNING

Comparative management studies how management practices differ among countries and cultures.

The management process—planning, organizing, leading, and controlling—is as relevant to international operations as to domestic ones. Yet, as the preceding discussions of global business environments and cultures should suggest, just how these functions are applied may vary somewhat from one country and culture to the next. Scholars in the area of **comparative management** study how management perspectives and practices differ systematically among countries and cultures.[69]

ARE MANAGEMENT THEORIES UNIVERSAL?

An important question in global management is: "Are management theories universal?" Geert Hofstede, whose framework for understanding national cultures was just discussed, believes the answer is clearly "no." He worries that many theories are ethnocentric and fail to take into account cultural differences.[70] Hofstede argues, for example, that Canadian and American emphasis on participation in leadership reflects the culture's moderate stance on power distance. National cultures with lower scores, such as Sweden and Israel, are characterized by even more "democratic" leadership initiatives. By contrast, the cultures of France and some Asian countries with higher power-distance scores are comfortable with hierarchy and less concerned with participative leadership.

Hofstede also points out that the motivation theories of western scholars tend to value individual performance. This is consistent with the high individualism found in Anglo-American countries such as the United States, Canada, and the United Kingdom. In other countries, where values are more collectivist, the theories may be less applicable. Until recently, practices in the United States largely emphasized redesigning jobs for individuals. Elsewhere in the world, such as in Sweden, the emphasis has been on redesigning jobs for groups of workers.

Consider as well some of the Japanese management practices that have attracted great interest over the years.[71] Lifetime employment, gradual career advancement, and collective decision-making have all been associated in one way or another with past successes in Japanese industry.[72] But as interesting as the practices may be, attempts to transfer them elsewhere should take into account the distinctive Japanese cultural traditions within which they emerged—long-term orientation, collectivism, and high power distance.[73]

CULTURE INSIGHTS FROM PROJECT GLOBE

In an effort to integrate and extend insights on cultural influences on management, a team of international researchers led by Robert House convened to study leadership, organizational practices, and diversity among world cultures.[74] They called the effort Project GLOBE, short for Global Leadership and Organizational Behavior Effectiveness. In studying data from 170,000 managers in 62 countries, the GLOBE researchers discovered that these countries fall into 10 culture clusters.[75] They report that societal culture practices tend to be more similar among countries within a cluster than across them. As shown in Figure 3.4, the researchers use nine dimensions to explore and describe cultural differences among the country clusters.

Two of the GLOBE dimensions are direct fits with Hofstede's framework. They are *power distance*, which is higher in Confucian Asia and lower in Nordic Europe, and *uncertainty avoidance*, which is high in Germanic Europe and low in the Middle East.

	Low-score clusters	Mid-score clusters	High-score clusters
Power distance	Nordic Europe	Sub-Saharan Africa	—
Uncertainty avoidance	Latin America	Southern Asia	Germanic Europe
Gender egalitarianism	Middle East	Anglo	Eastern Europe
Future orientation	Eastern Europe	Latin Europe	Nordic Europe
Institutional collectivism	Latin America	Anglo	Confucian Asia
In-group collectivism	Anglo	Latin Europe	Middle East
Assertiveness	Nordic Europe	Confucian Asia	Germanic Europe
Performance orientation	Eastern Europe	Southern Asia	Confucian Asia
Humane orientation	Germanic Europe	Middle East	Sub-Saharan Africa

Figure 3.4 Sample scores on nine cultural dimensions used by Project GLOBE.

Four GLOBE dimensions are similar to Hofstede's. *Gender egalitarianism* is the degree to which a culture minimizes gender inequalities. Similar to Hofstede's masculinity–femininity, it is high in the cultures of Eastern and Nordic Europe and low in those of the Middle East. *Future orientation* is the degree to which members of a culture are willing to look ahead, delay gratifications, and make investments in the expectation of longer-term payoffs. It is similar to Hofstede's time orientation. Germanic and Nordic Europe are high on future orientation; Latin America and the Middle East are low. *Institutional collectivism* is the extent to which a society emphasizes and rewards group action and accomplishments versus individual ones. It is similar to Hofstede's individualism–collectivism. Confucian Asia and Nordic Europe score high in institutional collectivism, whereas Germanic and Latin Europe score low. *In-group collectivism* is the extent to which people take pride in their families, small groups, and organizational memberships, acting loyally and cohesively regarding them. This form of collectivism runs high in Latin America and the Middle East, but tends to be low in Anglo and Germanic European cultures.

The remaining three GLOBE dimensions offer additional cultural insights. *Assertiveness* is the extent to which a culture emphasizes competition and assertiveness in social relationships, valuing behaviour that is tough and confrontational as opposed to modest and tender. Cultures in Eastern and Germanic Europe score high in assertiveness; those in Nordic Europe and Latin America score low. *Performance orientation* is the degree of emphasis on performance excellence and improvements. Anglo and Confucian Asian cultures tend to be high in performance orientation. Countries in these clusters can be expected to reward performance accomplishments and invest in training to encourage future performance gains. *Humane orientation* reflects tendencies toward fairness, altruism, generosity, and caring as people deal with one another. It tends to be high in Southern Asia and Sub-Saharan Africa, and to be low in Latin and Germanic Europe.

The GLOBE research offers a timely, systematic, and empirical look at culture and management across a large sample of countries. And, as the table shows, it is shedding new light on the debate over universality of management theories and practices. GLOBE researchers, for example, are starting to draw evidence-based conclusions about universal facilitators and inhibitors of leadership success.[76] Yet, as with other cross-cultural research, the GLOBE project is insightful but not definitive. It should be used along with the insights of Hall, Hofstede, and others to help us better understand the diversity of global cultures.[77]

> ### *Universal Facilitators of Leadership Success*
>
> - Acting trustworthy, just, honest
> - Showing foresight, planning
> - Being positive, dynamic, motivating
> - Inspiring confidence
> - Being informed and communicative
> - Being a coordinator and team builder
>
> ### *Universal Inhibitors of Leadership Success*
>
> - Being a loner
> - Acting uncooperative
> - Being irritable
> - Acting autocratic

GLOBAL MANAGEMENT ATTITUDES AND LEARNING

We live at a fortunate time when researchers and managers around the world are realizing they have much to share with and learn from one another. But when it comes to global management attitudes and learning, we have to be realistic: not everyone and not every organization is ready to embrace cultural diversity.

Global Management Attitudes

Managers with **ethnocentric attitudes** believe the best approaches are found at home and tightly control foreign operations.

For some managers and in some global businesses, **ethnocentric attitudes** still predominate.[78] Ethnocentric managers tend to believe that the best approaches are always found at home. They often fail to respect other practices and people. They are likely to keep tight control over foreign operations and find little to learn from their international counterparts.

Managers with **polycentric attitudes** respect local knowledge and allow foreign operations to run with substantial freedom.

For other managers and in other businesses, more **polycentric attitudes** predominate. Polycentric managers tend to respect the knowledge and practices of locals and allow them greater freedom to run business operations in their countries. Yet they often fail to encourage transfers of knowledge and experience between local operations and the parent company, and from one foreign location to the next.

Truly global managers and transnational corporations display **geocentric attitudes** that create global learning environments. Geocentric managers place a high value on cultural intelligence. They tend toward collaborative management approaches that link colleagues around the world in vast learning networks rich in ideas, information sharing, and performance opportunities. Their management style is to find, respect, and support the best practices and the best people, wherever in the world they may be located. McDonald's, for example, seems to be moving in a geocentric direction as it operates globally. If you stop in at a recently remodelled restaurant, see if you can spot the influence of *feng shui,* 風水— a Chinese practice of arranging spaces and choosing locations to maximize harmony and balance. Look for colour tones, seating arrangements, plants, and even water. The belief is that work and living spaces based on feng shui designs will bring positive energy and balance to a location. McDonald's of course hopes that this will also mean more satisfied and loyal customers.[79]

Managers with **geocentric attitudes** are high in cultural intelligence and take a collaborative approach to global management practices.

CANADIAN MANAGERS
From Global Manager to CEO

(AP Photo/Laurent Cipriani, file)

Christopher A. Viehbacher, a graduate of Queen's University and a certified public accountant, was recently named CEO of French drug maker Sanofi-Aventis. His path to success included being a global manager. After beginning his career at PricewaterhouseCoopers, Viehbacher spent the major part of his professional life in pharmaceuticals with Glaxo Wellcome and then GlaxoSmithKline. He acquired broad international experience in different positions across Europe, in the United States, and in Canada. Apparently demonstrating a geocentric attitude, Viehbacher is fluent in French, English, and German, and while living in France he was made a knight of the French Legion of Honour in 2003 for service to business and health.

Global Management Learning

We have a lot to learn about management and organizational practices from one country and culture to the next. When casting the global learning net, however, it is important to both identify the potential merits of management practices in other countries and understand how cultural differences can affect their success when applied elsewhere.[80] Consider the earlier example of "quality footprints" at Haier's Chinese and South Carolina factories. Instead of just taking a "best practice" from China and forcing it into the U.S. operation, Haier's managers recognized cultural differences and modified the practice to find a good fit with the American workers.[81]

Without any doubt, we should always be looking everywhere for new management ideas. But we should hesitate to accept any practice, no matter how well it appears to work somewhere else, as a universal prescription to action. The goal of comparative management studies is not to find universal principles. It is to engage in critical thinking about the way managers around the world do things and about whether they can and should be doing them better. As Hofstede states: "Disregard of other cultures is a luxury only the strong can afford . . . increase in cultural awareness represents an intellectual and spiritual gain."[82]

 **Learning Check ④** **BE SURE YOU CAN**
- answer this question: "Do management theories apply universally around the world?"
- identify the major components in Project GLOBE's model of cultural differences • list and explain three global management attitudes • describe the concept of global organizational learning

MANAGEMENT LEARNING REVIEW

STUDY QUESTIONS SUMMARY

1. What are the management challenges of globalization?

- Global managers are informed about international developments and are competent in working with people from different cultures.

- The forces of globalization create international business opportunities to pursue profits, customers, capital, and low-cost suppliers and labour in different countries.

- Market entry strategies for international business include global sourcing, exporting and importing, and licensing and franchising.

- Direct investment strategies of international business establish joint ventures or wholly owned subsidiaries in foreign countries.

- General environment differences, including legal and political systems, often complicate international business activities.

- Regional economic alliances such as NAFTA, the EU, APEC, and SADC link nations of the world with the goal of promoting economic development.

- The World Trade Organization (WTO) is a global institution that promotes free trade and open markets around the world.

FOR DISCUSSION What aspects of the Canadian legal-political environment could prove difficult for a Chinese firm operating a factory in Canada?

2. What are global businesses, and what do they do?

- A global corporation, or MNC, is a business with extensive operations in multiple foreign countries.

- A transnational corporation tries to operate globally without a strong national identity and with a worldwide mission and strategies.

- MNCs can benefit host countries by offering broader tax bases, new technologies, and employment opportunities.

- MNCs can cause problems for host countries if they interfere in local government, extract excessive profits, and dominate the local economy.

- Ethics challenges facing MNCs include corruption, child labour and sweatshops, and sustainable development.

FOR DISCUSSION Is the U.S. Foreign Corrupt Practices Act unfair to American firms trying to compete for business around the world?

3. **What is culture, and how does it impact global management?**
- Culture is a shared set of beliefs, values, and behaviour patterns common to a group of people.
- Culture shock is the discomfort people sometimes experience when interacting with persons from cultures different from their own.
- Cultural intelligence is an individual capacity to understand, respect, and adapt to cultural differences.
- Hall's "silent" languages of culture include the use of context, time, and interpersonal space.
- Hofstede's five dimensions of value differences in national cultures are power distance, uncertainty avoidance, individualism–collectivism, masculinity–femininity, and time orientation.

FOR DISCUSSION Should religion be included on Hall's list of the silent languages of culture?

4. **How can we benefit from global management learning?**
- The field of comparative management studies how management is practised around the world and how management ideas are transferred from one country or culture to the next.
- Project GLOBE is an extensive worldwide study of management and leadership that identified country clusters that varied on nine cultural dimensions.
- Attitudes toward global management and global learning vary from ethnocentric (home is best) to polycentric (respect others but keep home paramount) to geocentric (respect, value, and learn from others).
- Because management practices are influenced by cultural values, global management learning must recognize that successful practices in one culture may work less well in others.

FOR DISCUSSION Even though cultural differences are readily apparent, is the tendency today for the world's cultures to converge and become more alike?

SELF-TEST

Multiple-Choice Questions

1. The reasons why businesses go international include gaining new markets and the search for _____.

   (a) political risk   (b) protectionism   (c) lower labour costs   (d) most favoured nation status

2. When Rocky Brands decided to buy full ownership of a manufacturing company in the Dominican Republic, Rocky was engaging in which form of international business?

   (a) import/export   (b) licensing   (c) foreign subsidiary   (d) joint venture

3. A form of international business that falls into the category of a direct investment strategy is _____.

   (a) exporting   (b) joint venture   (c) licensing   (d) global sourcing

4. The World Trade Organization, or WTO, would most likely become involved in disputes between countries over _____.

   (a) exchange rates   (b) ethnocentrism   (c) nationalization   (d) tariffs

5. Business complaints about copyright protection and intellectual property rights in some countries illustrate how differences in _____ can impact international operations.

    (a) legal environments   (b) political stability   (c) sustainable development   (d) economic systems

6. In _____ cultures, members tend to do one thing at a time; in _____ cultures, members tend to do many things at once.

    (a) monochronic, polychronic   (b) polycentric, geocentric   (c) collectivist, individualist   (d) neutral, affective

7. A culture that places great value on meaning expressed in the written or spoken word would be described as _____ by Hall.

    (a) monochronic   (b) proxemic   (c) collectivist   (d) low-context

8. It is common in Malaysian culture for people to value teamwork and to display great respect for authority. Hofstede would describe this culture as high in both _____.

    (a) uncertainty avoidance and feminism   (b) universalism and particularism   (c) collectivism and power distance (d) long-term orientation and masculinity

9. In Hofstede's study of national cultures, America was found to be the most _____ compared with other countries in his sample.

    (a) individualistic   (b) collectivist   (c) feminine   (d) long-term oriented

10. It is _____ when a foreign visitor takes offence at a local custom such as dining with one's fingers, considering it inferior to the practices of his or her own culture.

    (a) universalist   (b) prescriptive   (c) monochronic   (d) enthnocentric

11. When a clothing manufacturer buys cotton in Egypt, has tops sewn from it in Sri Lanka according to designs made in Italy, and then offers them for sale in Canada, this form of international business is known as _____.

    (a) licensing   (b) importing   (c) joint venturing   (d) global sourcing

12. The difference between an international business and a transnational corporation is that the transnational _____.

    (a) tries to operate without a strong national identity   (b) does business in only one or two foreign countries   (c) is led by managers with ethnocentric attitudes   (d) is ISO 14000–certified

13. The Corruption of Foreign Public Officials Act makes it illegal for _____.

    (a) Canadians to engage in joint ventures abroad   (b) Canadian businesses to pay bribes to foreign government officials (c) Canadian businesses to make "payoffs" abroad to gain international business contracts   (d) foreign businesses to steal intellectual property from Canadian firms operating in their countries

14. In a culture described by Project GLOBE as high in _____, one would expect to find men and women treated equally in terms of job and career opportunities.

    (a) humane orientation   (b) institutional collectivism   (c) gender egalitarianism   (d) performance orientation

15. Hofstede would describe a culture whose members respect age and authority and whose workers defer to the preferences of their supervisors as _____.

    (a) low masculinity   (b) high particularism   (c) high power distance   (d) monochronic

Short-Response Questions

16. Why do host countries sometimes complain about how MNCs operate within their borders?

17. Why is the "power-distance" dimension of national culture important in management?

18. What is the difference between institutional collectivism and in-group collectivism as described by Project GLOBE?

19. How do regional economic alliances impact the global economy?

Application Question

20. Monique has just returned from her first business trip to Japan. While there, she was impressed with the intense use of work teams. Now back in Manitoba, she would like to totally reorganize the workflows and processes of her canoe manufacturing company and its 75 employees around teams. There has been very little emphasis on teamwork, and she now believes this is "the way to go." Based on the discussion of culture and management in this chapter, what advice would you offer Monique?

MANAGEMENT SKILLS AND COMPETENCIES

SELF-ASSESSMENT

Back to Yourself: Cultural Awareness

The forces of globalization are often discussed in respect to job migration, outsourcing, currency fluctuations, and the fortunes of global corporations. But it's important to remember, as was pointed out in the chapter, that these and other aspects of globalization are best understood and dealt with in a context of cultural awareness. It's only natural that we become comfortable with and used to the ways of our culture; it's natural too for cultural differences to be frustrating and even threatening when we come face to face with them. The models discussed in this chapter are a good basis for cultural understanding. National economies are now global, business is now global, and our personal thinking must be global as well.

Further Reflection: Global Intelligence

Instructions

Rate yourself on each of the following items: 1 = Very Poor   2 = Poor   3 = Acceptable   4 = Good   5 = Very Good

1. I understand my own culture in terms of its expectations, values, and influence on communication and relationships.

2. When someone presents me with a different point of view, I try to understand it rather than attack it.

3. I am comfortable dealing with situations where the available information is incomplete and the outcomes unpredictable.

4. I am open to new situations and am always looking for new information and learning opportunities.

5. I have a good understanding of the attitudes and perceptions toward my culture as they are held by people from other cultures.

6. I am always gathering information about other countries and cultures and trying to learn from them.

7. I am well informed regarding the major differences in the government, political, and economic systems around the world.

8. I work hard to increase my understanding of people from other cultures.

9. I am able to adjust my communication style to work effectively with people from different cultures.

10. I can recognize when cultural differences are influencing working relationships, and I adjust my attitudes and behaviour accordingly.

Interpretation

To be successful in the global economy, you must be comfortable with the cultural diversity that it holds. This requires a global mindset that is receptive to and respectful of cultural differences, global knowledge that includes the continuing quest to know and learn more about other nations and cultures, and global work skills that allow you to work effectively across cultures.

Scoring

The goal is to score as close to a perfect "5" as possible on each of the three dimensions of global intelligence. Develop your scores as follows:

- Items $(1 + 2 + 3 + 4)/4 = $ _____ Global Mindset Score
- Items $(5 + 6 + 7)/3 = $ _____ Global Knowledge Score
- Items $(8 + 9 + 10)/3 = $ _____ Global Work Skills Score

Source: Developed from "Is Your Company Really Global?" *BusinessWeek* (December 1, 1997).

TEAM EXERCISE

Hockey

Instructions

Form into groups as assigned by the instructor. In the group, do the following:

1. Discuss hockey—the rules, the way the game is played, the way players and coaches behave, and the roles of owners and fans.

2. Use hockey as a metaphor to explain the way Canadian corporations run and how they tend to behave in terms of strategies and goals.

3. Prepare a class presentation for a group of visiting Japanese business executives. In this presentation, use the metaphor of hockey to (1) explain Canadian business strategies and practices to the Japanese, and (2) critique the potential strengths and weaknesses of the Canadian business approach in terms of success in the global marketplace.

CASE 3

McCain Foods Limited: Global Fries—Good in Any Language!

What do you get when you mix the lowly potato with a passion for growth? The answer is as close as your freezer! McCain Foods Limited, maker of frozen fries, pizzas, appetizers, and entrees, is one of Canada's most famous world brands.[1] The maker of Canada's favourite french fries started in 1957 in Florenceville, New Brunswick, with brothers Wallace and Harrison McCain, with one plant, 30 employees, and sales of just over $157,000. Over 50 years later, McCain employs over 20,000 people at 53 facilities worldwide generating over $6 billion in sales.[2] Currently producing nearly one-third of the world's french fries for fast food giants McDonald's and KFC,[3] McCain also supplies frozen products for restaurants and grocery stores in over 166 countries.[4]

How did a homegrown Canadian company become an international success story? Co-owner Harrison McCain had always been interested in emerging markets as a way to grow and expand the business.[5] McCain embraces multicultural experiences and traditions, which translate into new ways of thinking and doing business. Based on this principle, McCain pursued global expansion with passion; he focused on entering new markets through a variety of strategies including direct selling, joint ventures, acquisitions of existing local businesses, and greenfield developments by building new production facilities.[6] Currently, McCain has 53 manufacturing facilities on six continents today, 41 of which are outside Canada.[7]

One major advantage McCain had was the success of its largest client, McDonald's. Harvard's James L. Watson, author of *Golden Arches East: McDonald's in East Asia*, offers that the secret to McDonald's global popularity has almost certainly been its french fries, which he writes are "consumed with great gusto by Muslims, Jews, Christians, Buddhists, Hindus, vegetarians, communists, Tories, marathoners, and armchair athletes." McDonald's fries made from McCain products have resonated with local tastes across the globe.

Globalization: Successes and Challenges

Like many in the North American food industry, McCain has struggled over the past few years with a slowed U.S. economy, high Canadian dollar, increased cost of fuel, and low-priced competition from Europe.[8] While most of the company's revenue is generated in the United States, Canada, the United Kingdom, and Australia, emerging countries such as China and India are becoming increasingly important to McCain's future profitability.[9] To compensate for decreasing demand in North America, where fast-food suppliers are increasingly under scrutiny for rising obesity rates,[10] McCain is focusing on strengthening its share in foreign markets, especially Asia.[11]

With a population of over 1.3 billion people, China is an attractive market but success will not be easy for McCain. China, the world's largest potato producer, often uses potatoes in traditional dishes but the average annual per capita consumption of fries is less than 100 grams. Compare that with the 13 kilograms that the average Canadian consumes per year and McCain has one tough market to crack. Back in 1988, McCain was hesitant to get into China; the Chinese market, while exciting, wasn't strong enough to warrant setting up operations. McCain's clients, KFC and McDonald's, were just breaking into China but neither was doing well enough to warrant McCain's investment in on-the-ground operations.[12]

Yet by 1995, McCain became interested again as China's economy started to emerge. Practising a "beachhead" strategy, McCain began in 1997 by developing a sales force in Shanghai to start building relationships with fast-food chains such as McDonald's and KFC, as well as hotel chains and grocery stores, to further expand its sales base and introduce a range of products to Chinese consumers.[13] By 2005, McCain had built its own processing plant surrounded by land on which Chinese farmers had been growing potatoes for centuries.[14] McCain employs mostly local workers at its processing plant in Harbin. Facility managers and line workers are largely hired from

Courtesy McCain Foods

within the local community and are sent abroad to be educated in the McCain culture. Joining other production facilities on six continents, McCain's investment in China responded to rising demand from its restaurant and retail markets and helped solidify the company's position as a major supplier to the Chinese market.[15]

Despite years of experience with setting up global operations, McCain's entrance into China will be far from easy, as the company feels the french fry market still needs to mature. With McCain's biggest fast-food clients forecast to grow by 20 percent annually, the potential for development is there, but the company predicts that it will still take a few generations for the Chinese to accept western food.[16] Will the change be too slow for McCain to justify its investment in China?

Discussion Questions

1. If you were in charge of the Asian operations for McCain, how would you recommend the company overcome the challenges in the Chinese market?

2. Drawing from Hofstede and Trompenaar's work on global diversity and cultures, what challenges might Canadian managers at McCain face when interacting with their Chinese business colleagues?

3. Much of McCain's global success seems to be closely tied to the success and efforts of its clients, McDonald's and KFC. Describe how successful you think McCain would have been if it had gone into China with just its own brand name.

4. FURTHER RESEARCH—Are the fast-food industry and, in turn, McCain's sales growing in China?

04 Ethics, Social Responsibility, and Sustainability

LEARNING FROM OTHERS

We can make the world a better place

A couple of guys did, and they made ice cream to boot. You know the ice cream for sure—you may have tasted a Ben & Jerry's Cherry Garcia® cone or enjoyed a scoop of Chunky Monkey® banana. But do you really know the company? Ben & Jerry's earned its reputation not just from great ice cream, but also from the concept of "linked prosperity"—sharing prosperity with its employees and the communities in which it operates.

ANP ADE JOHNSON

It was 1977 when friends Ben Cohen and Jerry Greenfield moved from Long Island, New York, to Burlington, Vermont. Needing a source of income, they took a university correspondence course on ice cream making. A year later, Ben & Jerry's Homemade, created on a $12,000 investment, sold its first ice cream cones from a converted gas station. It was a "different" ice cream store right from the start, and on the firm's first anniversary, the first annual Free Cone Day—free ice cream all day—was held to celebrate.

When the Ben & Jerry's Foundation was established in 1985 as a way of funding community-oriented projects, the company pledged 7.5 percent of the annual pretax profits to support the foundation. In 1988, when sales were $47 million, Ben & Jerry's received the Corporate Giving Award from the Council on Economic Priorities for its foundation's philanthropy. And then in 1989, when sales were $59 million, the company introduced Rainforest Crunch® ice cream, with sales helping to support rainforest preservation efforts.

By the time the firm's 30th birthday was celebrated in 2008, with the introduction of Cake Batter ice cream, Ben & Jerry's had become a global operation owned by the multinational giant Unilever. But with its own board of directors and mission statement, and guided by core values of the founders, Ben & Jerry's remains devoted to linked prosperity and the three P's of people, profits, and planet. The test will be how well this all holds up inside Unilever's global business portfolio.[1]

BENCHMARK You have to appreciate what Ben Cohen and Jerry Greenfield accomplished at Ben & Jerry's. But what's the lesson? It isn't just that they were able to grow a well-regarded global company from a small start-up. It's the nature of the company they developed—one with a commitment to ethical behaviour, social responsibility, and sustainability—that is the true hallmark. The lesson is profits with principles. In how many other ways can business performance, ethical behaviour, social responsibility, and sustainability go hand in hand?

Individual Character

There is no doubt that individual character is a foundation for all that we do. It establishes our integrity and provides an ethical anchor for how we behave at work and in life overall. Persons of high character can always be confident in the self-respect it provides, even in the most difficult of situations. Those who lack it are destined to perpetual insecurity, acting inconsistently, and suffering not only in self-esteem but also in the esteem of others.

How strong is your individual character? How well do your values prepare you to deal with the inevitable ethical dilemmas and challenges that pop up at school, in work, and in life?

How does your behaviour as a student stack up on ethics issues? Do you engage in plagiarism, copy homework, purchase term papers, or cheat on exams? Do you tolerate others who do these things? What does this say about your integrity and how you're likely to behave at work—handling expense accounts, using company cars and cell phones, calling in sick, tolerating anti-social behaviour, or reporting work performance?

Take this opportunity to do some self-assessment on issues of individual character. A good starting point is found in the *Six Pillars of Character* identified by the Josephson Institute of Ethics and shown in the box.[2] Why not take a moment to go through the principles and see if you can give specific examples showing how your behaviour lives up to them?

SIX PILLARS OF CHARACTER

- **Trustworthiness**—Honesty, integrity, reliability in keeping promises, loyalty
- **Respect**—Civility, courtesy and decency, dignity, tolerance, and acceptance
- **Responsibility**—Sense of accountability, pursuit of excellence, self-restraint
- **Fairness**—Commitment to process, impartiality, equity
- **Caring**—Concern for others, benevolence, altruism
- **Citizenship**—Knowing the law, being informed, volunteering

❖ Get to Know Yourself Better

Make a list of at least three incidents that you have been involved in and that posed ethical dilemmas. Put yourself in the position of being your parent, a loved one, or a good friend. Using their vantage points, write a letter to yourself that critiques your handling of each incident and summarizes the implications in terms of your individual character.

CHAPTER 4 STUDY QUESTIONS

- What is ethical behaviour?
- How do ethical dilemmas complicate the workplace?
- How can high ethical standards be maintained?
- What are social responsibility, governance, and sustainability?

VISUAL CHAPTER OVERVIEW

CHAPTER 4 ETHICS, SOCIAL RESPONSIBILITY, AND SUSTAINABILITY

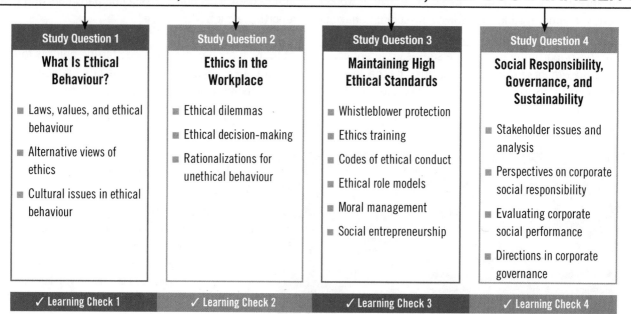

Study Question 1	Study Question 2	Study Question 3	Study Question 4
What Is Ethical Behaviour?	**Ethics in the Workplace**	**Maintaining High Ethical Standards**	**Social Responsibility, Governance, and Sustainability**
■ Laws, values, and ethical behaviour	■ Ethical dilemmas	■ Whistleblower protection	■ Stakeholder issues and analysis
■ Alternative views of ethics	■ Ethical decision-making	■ Ethics training	■ Perspectives on corporate social responsibility
■ Cultural issues in ethical behaviour	■ Rationalizations for unethical behaviour	■ Codes of ethical conduct	■ Evaluating corporate social performance
		■ Ethical role models	■ Directions in corporate governance
		■ Moral management	
		■ Social entrepreneurship	
✓ Learning Check 1	✓ Learning Check 2	✓ Learning Check 3	✓ Learning Check 4

The opening example of how Ben Cohen and Jerry Greenfield started a successful company with a commitment to "profits with principles" should get you thinking. Look around; there are many cases of people and organizations operating in socially responsible ways out there. Some are quite well known—The Body Shop, Stantec Inc., and Loblaws, for example. Surely there are others right in your local community. But as you think of the organizations, don't forget that the underlying foundations rest with people, individuals like you and me. This is where individual character comes into play; it largely determines the ethics of our decisions and actions.

As we move into the issues of management ethics and social responsibility in this chapter, the following reminder from Desmond Tutu, Archbishop of Capetown, South Africa, and winner of the Nobel Peace Prize, is well worth consideration.[3]

> *You are powerful people. You can make this world a better place where business decisions and methods take account of right and wrong as well as profitability . . . . You must*

take a stand on important issues: the environment and ecology, affirmative action, sexual harassment, racism and sexism, the arms race, poverty, the obligations of the affluent West to its less-well-off sisters and brothers elsewhere.

WHAT IS ETHICAL BEHAVIOUR?

For our purposes, **ethics** is defined as the code of moral principles that sets standards of good or bad, or right or wrong, in one's conduct.[4] Ethics provides principles to guide behaviour and help people make moral choices among alternative courses of action. In practice, **ethical behaviour** is that which is accepted as "good" and "right" as opposed to "bad" or "wrong" in the context of the governing moral code.

Ethics sets standards of good or bad, or right or wrong, in one's conduct.

Ethical behaviour is "right" or "good" in the context of a governing moral code.

LAWS, VALUES, AND ETHICAL BEHAVIOUR

It makes sense that anything legal should be considered ethical. Yet slavery was once legal in the United States, and laws once permitted only men to vote.[5] That doesn't mean the practices were ethical. Just because an action is not strictly illegal doesn't make it ethical.[6] Living up to the "letter of the law" is not sufficient to guarantee that one's actions will or should be considered ethical. Is it truly ethical, for example, for an employee to take longer than necessary to do a job? To make personal telephone calls on company time? To call in sick to gain a day off for leisure? To fail to report rule violations by a co-worker? Although none of these acts are strictly illegal, many would consider them unethical.

Most ethical problems in the workplace arise when people are asked to do, or find they are about to do, something that violates their personal beliefs. For some, if the act is legal, they proceed with confidence. For others, the ethical test goes beyond the legality of the act alone. The ethical question extends to personal **values**—the underlying beliefs and attitudes that help determine individual behaviour. The value pattern for any one person is very enduring, but values vary from one person to the next. And to the extent that they do, we can expect different interpretations of what behaviour is ethical or unethical in a given situation.

Values are broad beliefs about what is appropriate behaviour.

The psychologist Milton Rokeach makes a distinction between "terminal" and "instrumental" values.[7] **Terminal values** are preferences about desired ends, such as the goals one strives to achieve in life. Examples of terminal values considered important by managers include self-respect, family security, freedom, inner harmony, and happiness. **Instrumental values** are preferences regarding the means for accomplishing these ends. Among the instrumental values held important by managers are honesty, ambition, courage, imagination, and self-discipline.

Terminal values are preferences about desired end states.

Instrumental values are preferences regarding the means to desired ends.

Variation in terminal and instrumental values is a reason why people respond quite differently to situations and their ethical challenges. When commenting on cheating tendencies among business school students, for example, an ethics professor at INSEAD in France says, "The academic values of integrity and honesty in your work can seem to be less relevant than the instrumental goal of getting a good job."[8] In a study published in the *Canadian Journal of Higher Education*, authors Julia Christensen and Donald McCabe note that of 14,913 undergraduate students surveyed across five provinces, 18 percent admit to engaging in one or more instances of serious test cheating behaviour, while an overwhelming 53 percent report one or more instances of engaging in serious written work cheating behaviour.[9] These students are part and parcel of the Internet age—big on music downloads, file sharing, open source software, text messaging, and electronic collaboration. Some say that cheating is a good example of "postmodern learning"—we should expect such behaviour from students who are taught to collaborate and work in teams and use the latest communication technologies. For others, there is no doubt that the instrumental values driving such behaviour are unacceptable—if it was an individual exam and the students cheated, they should be penalized.

GOING GLOBAL

A BETTER WORLD COURTESY OF CIRQUE DU SOLEIL

This Quebec company, which began in 1984 as a group of 20 street performers, is world-famous for its artistic circus show. Cirque du Soleil's mission is to "invoke the imagination, provoke the senses and evoke the emotions of people around the world" and it has brought delight to over 90 million spectators worldwide. However, it sees its role as more than just entertaining the world. In expressing its terminal values, the company says, "Cirque du Soleil's citizenship principles are founded on the conviction that the arts, business and social initiatives can, together, contribute to making a better world." How does it do this? Cirque du Soleil tracks its environmental performance and has implemented water, waste, and power initiatives in its Montreal headquarters and on the road; it has launched a $100-million project entitled ONE DROP to provide the world's poorest with access to drinking water; and it gives an amount equivalent to 1 percent of Cirque du Soleil's earnings to cultural and social action programs each year. As founder Guy Laliberté shares, "life pays you back what you have given to it." It is safe to say he has earned a wonderful payback!

ALTERNATIVE VIEWS OF ETHICS

Figure 4.1 shows four views of ethical behaviour that philosophers have discussed over the years—the utilitarian, individualism, moral rights, and justice views.[10] Depending on which perspective one adopts in a given situation, the resulting behaviours may be considered ethical or unethical.

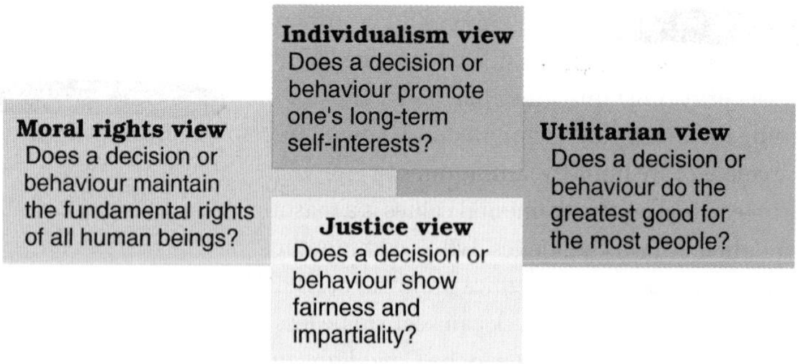

Individualism view
Does a decision or behaviour promote one's long-term self-interests?

Moral rights view
Does a decision or behaviour maintain the fundamental rights of all human beings?

Utilitarian view
Does a decision or behaviour do the greatest good for the most people?

Justice view
Does a decision or behaviour show fairness and impartiality?

Figure 4.1 Four views of ethical behaviour.

In the **utilitarian view**, ethical behaviour delivers the greatest good to the most people.

Behaviour that would be considered ethical from the **utilitarian view** delivers the greatest good to the greatest number of people. Based on the work of nineteenth-century philosopher John Stuart Mill, this results-oriented point of view assesses the moral implications of actions in terms of their consequences. Business decision-makers, for example, are inclined to use profits, efficiency, and other performance criteria to judge what is best for the most people. In a recession or when a firm is suffering hard times, an executive may make a decision to cut 30 percent of a plant's workforce in order to keep the plant profitable and save the remaining jobs. She could justify this decision based upon a utilitarian sense of business ethics.

The **individualism view** of ethical behaviour is based on the belief that one's primary commitment is long-term advancement of self-interests. People supposedly become self-regulating as they pursue long-term individual advantage. For example, lying and cheating for short-term gain should not be tolerated. If one person does it, everyone will do it, and no one's long-term interests will be served. The individualism view is supposed to promote honesty and integrity. But in business practice it may result in greed, a pecuniary ethic described by one executive as the tendency to "push the law to its outer limits" and "run roughshod over other individuals to achieve one's objectives."[11]

In the **individualism view**, ethical behaviour advances long-term self-interests.

Ethical behaviour under a **moral rights view** is that which respects and protects the fundamental rights of people. Then–Prime Minister Pierre Trudeau heavily influenced the recognition of such rights for all Canadian citizens through the enactment of the Canadian Charter of Rights and Freedoms under the Constitution Act in 1982. In organizations, the moral rights concept extends to ensuring that employees are always protected in rights to privacy, due process, free speech, free consent, health and safety, and freedom of conscience. The issue of human rights, a major ethical concern in the international business environment, is central to this perspective. The United Nations, as indicated in the accompanying box, stands by the Universal Declaration of Human Rights passed by the General Assembly in 1948.[12]

In the **moral rights view**, ethical behaviour respects and protects fundamental rights.

The **justice view** of moral behaviour is based on the belief that ethical decisions treat people impartially and fairly, according to legal rules and standards. This approach evaluates the ethical aspects of any decision on the basis of whether it is "equitable" for everyone affected.[13] Justice issues in organizations are typically addressed on three dimensions—procedural, distributive, and interactional.[14]

Procedural justice involves the degree to which policies and rules are fairly administered. For example, does a sexual harassment charge levied against a senior executive receive the same full hearing as one made against a first-level supervisor? **Distributive justice** involves the degree to which outcomes are allocated fairly among people and without respect to individual characteristics based on ethnicity, race, gender, age, or other particular criteria. For example, does a woman with the same qualifications and experience as a man receive the same consideration for hiring or promotion? **Interactional justice** involves the degree to which people treat one another with dignity and respect. For example, does a bank loan officer take the time to fully explain to an applicant why he or she was turned down for a loan?[15]

> **Selections from Universal Declaration of Human Rights**
>
> - All human beings are born free and equal in dignity and rights.
>
> - Everyone has the right to life, liberty and security of person.
>
> - No one shall be held in slavery or servitude . . . .
>
> - No one shall be subjected to torture or to cruel, inhuman or degrading treatment or punishment.
>
> - All are equal before the law and are entitled without any discrimination to equal protection of the law.

In the **justice view**, ethical behaviour treats people impartially and fairly.

Procedural justice is concerned that policies and rules are fairly applied.

Distributive justice is concerned that people are treated the same regardless of personal characteristics.

Interactional justice is the degree to which others are treated with dignity and respect.

CULTURAL ISSUES IN ETHICAL BEHAVIOUR

Picture the situation: a 12-year-old boy working in a garment factory in Bangladesh. He is the sole income earner for his family. He often works 12-hour days and was once burned quite badly by a hot iron. One day he is fired. His employer had been given an ultimatum by a major American customer: "no child workers if you want to keep our contracts." The boy says: "I don't understand. I could do my job very well. I need the money."

Should this boy be allowed to work? This difficult and perplexing question is one example of the many ethics challenges faced in international business. Former Levi CEO Robert Haas once said that an ethical problem "becomes even more difficult when you overlay the complexities of different cultures and values systems that exist throughout the world."[16]

Those who believe that behaviour in foreign settings should be guided by the classic rule of "when in Rome, do as the Romans do" reflect an ethical position of **cultural relativism**.[17] This is the belief that there is no one right way to behave, and that ethical behaviour is always determined by its cultural context. An American international business executive guided by rules of cultural relativism, for example, would argue that the use of child labour is OK in another country as long as it is consistent with local laws and customs.

Figure 4.2 contrasts cultural relativism with the alternative of **universalism**. This is an absolutist ethical position suggesting that, if a behaviour or practice is not OK in one's home environment, it is not acceptable practice anywhere else. In other words, ethical standards are universal and should apply absolutely across cultures and national boundaries. In the former example, the American executive would not do business in a setting where child labour was used, since it is unacceptable at home. Critics of such a universal approach claim that it is a form of **ethical imperialism**, an attempt to externally impose one's ethical standards on others.

> **Cultural relativism** suggests there is no one right way to behave; ethical behaviour is determined by its cultural context.
>
> **Universalism** suggests ethical standards apply absolutely across all cultures.
>
> **Ethical imperialism** is an attempt to impose one's ethical standards on other cultures.

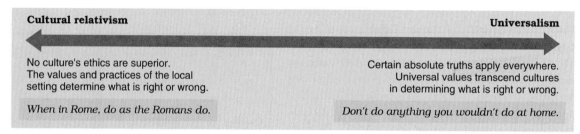

Figure 4.2 Cultural relativism and universalism in international business ethics.

Source: Developed from Thomas Donaldson, "Values in Tension: Ethics Away from Home," *Harvard Business Review*, vol. 74 (September–October 1996), pp. 48–62.

Business ethicist Thomas Donaldson has discussed the debate between cultural relativism and ethical imperialism. Although there is no simple answer, he finds fault with both extremes. He argues instead that certain fundamental rights and ethical standards can be preserved at the same time that values and traditions of a given culture are respected.[18] The core values or "hyper-norms" that should transcend cultural boundaries focus on human dignity, basic rights, and good citizenship. Donaldson believes international business behaviours can be tailored to local and regional cultural contexts while still upholding these core values. In the case of child labour, again, the American executive might ensure that any children working in a factory under contract to his or her business would be provided with daily scheduled schooling as well as employment.[19]

✓ **Learning Check 1**

BE SURE YOU CAN
• define *ethics* • list and explain four views of ethical behaviour • give examples showing violation of procedural, distributive, and interactional justice • differentiate between cultural relativism and universalism in international business ethics

ETHICS IN THE WORKPLACE

The real test of ethics occurs when you or anyone encounters a situation that challenges personal values and standards. Often ambiguous and unexpected, these ethical challenges are inevitable, and everyone has to be prepared to deal with them, even students.

A university student may get a job offer and accept it, only to get a better offer two weeks later. Is it right for her to renege on the first job to accept the second? A student knows that in a certain course his roommate submitted a term paper purchased on the Internet. Is it right for him not to tell the instructor? One student tells another that a faculty member promised her a high final grade in return for sexual favours. Is it right for him not to vigorously encourage her to inform the instructor's department head?

ETHICAL DILEMMAS

An **ethical dilemma** is a situation that requires a choice regarding a possible course of action that, although offering the potential for personal or organizational benefit, or both, may be considered unethical. It is often a situation in which action must be taken but for which there is no clear consensus on what is "right" and "wrong."

An **ethical dilemma** is a situation that offers potential benefit or gain and is also unethical.

The burden in confronting ethical dilemmas is on the individual to make good choices. An engineering manager speaking from experience sums it up this way: "I define an unethical situation as one in which I have to do something I don't feel good about."[20] Some common ethical dilemmas that entrap managers include the following:[21]

- *Discrimination*—denying promotion or appointment to a job candidate because of the candidate's race, religion, gender, age, or other non-job-relevant criterion.

- *Sexual harassment*—making a co-worker uncomfortable because of inappropriate comments or actions regarding sexuality; requesting sexual favours in return for favourable job treatment.

- *Conflicts of interest*—taking a bribe or kickback or extraordinary gift in return for making a decision favourable to the gift giver.

- *Customer confidence*—giving to another party privileged information regarding the activities of a customer.

- *Organizational resources*—using official stationery or a company e-mail account to communicate personal opinions or make requests from community organizations.

A survey of *Harvard Business Review* subscribers showed an interesting pattern in the ethical dilemmas reported by managers. Many of the dilemmas involved conflicts with superiors, customers, and subordinates.[22] The most frequent issues involved dishonesty in advertising and communications with top management, clients, and government agencies. Problems in dealing with special gifts, entertainment, and kickbacks were also reported. Significantly, the managers' bosses sometimes pressured them to engage in such unethical activities as supporting incorrect viewpoints, signing false documents, overlooking the boss's wrongdoings, and doing business with the boss's friends.

ETHICAL DECISION-MAKING

Management Smarts 4.1 presents a seven-step checklist for dealing with an ethical dilemma. It is a way to double-check the ethics of decisions before taking action. The key issue in the checklist may well be Step 6: the risk of public disclosure. Asking and answering the *spotlight questions* is a powerful way to test whether a decision is consistent with your personal ethical standards. They're worth repeating: "How will I feel about this if my family finds out, or if it's reported in the local newspaper or posted on the Internet?"

4.1 MANAGEMENT SMARTS
Checklist for dealing with ethical dilemmas

Step 1. Recognize the ethical dilemma.

Step 2. Get the facts.

Step 3. Identify your options.

Step 4. Test each option: Is it legal? Is it right? Is it beneficial?

Step 5. Decide which option to follow.

Step 6. Double-check with the *spotlight questions:*
> *"How will I feel if my family finds out about my decision?"*
> *"How will I feel about this if my decision is reported in the local newspaper or posted on the Internet?"*

Step 7. Take action.

Even with this checklist for ethical decision-making, it is almost too easy to confront ethical dilemmas from the safety of a textbook or a classroom discussion. In real life, it's often a lot harder to consistently choose ethical courses of action. We end up facing ethical dilemmas at unexpected and inconvenient times, the events and facts can be ambiguous, and other performance pressures can be unforgiving and intense. Is it any surprise, therefore, that 56 percent of U.S. workers in one survey reported feeling pressured to act unethically in their jobs? Or that 48 percent said they had committed questionable acts within the past year?[23]

Increased awareness of the typical influences on ethical decision-making can help you better deal with future ethical pressures and dilemmas. A basic model for understanding these influences, as shown here, includes the situational context, personal factors, organizational culture, and the external environment.

Situational Context and Ethics Intensity

Ethics intensity or issue intensity indicates the degree to which an issue or situation is recognized to pose important ethical challenges.

Ethical dilemmas often appear unexpectedly or in ambiguous conditions; we're caught off guard and struggle to respond. Other times, we might even fail to see that an issue or situation has an ethics component. This may happen, for example, when students find cheating so commonplace on campus that it becomes an accepted standard of behaviour. Scholars use the concept of **ethics intensity** or issue intensity to describe the extent to which a situation is perceived to pose important ethics challenges.[24]

The conditions that raise the ethics intensity of a situation include the magnitude, probability, and immediacy of any potential harm; the proximity and concentration of the effects; and social consensus. A decision situation will elicit greater ethical attention when the potential harm is perceived as great, likely, and imminent; the potential victims are visible and close by; and there is more social agreement on what is good or bad about what is taking place. Take, for example, the issue of pirated music downloads. Run it through each of these ethics intensity factors. Can we say that low ethics intensity contributes to the likelihood of music pirating? In general, the greater the ethical intensity of the situation, the more aware the decision-maker is about ethics issues and the more likely that his or her behaviour will be ethical.

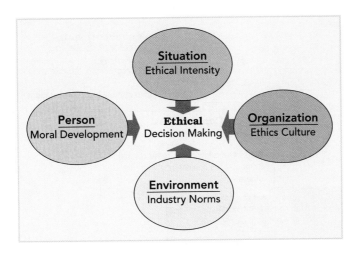

Personal Factors and Moral Development

It isn't always easy to stand up for what you believe in as a person, especially in a social context full of contradictory or just plain bad advice. Consider these words from a commencement address delivered some years ago at a well-known school of business administration. "Greed is all right," the speaker said. "Greed is healthy. You can be greedy and still feel good about yourself." The students, it is reported, greeted these remarks with laughter and applause. The speaker was Ivan Boesky, once considered the "king of the arbitragers."[25] It wasn't long after his commencement speech, however, that Boesky was arrested, tried, convicted, and sentenced to prison for trading on inside information.

Values, family, religion, and personal needs, financial and otherwise, all help determine a person's ethics. Managers who lack a strong and clear set of personal ethics will find that their decisions vary from situation to situation. Those with solid **ethical frameworks**, ones that provide personal rules or strategies for ethical decision-making, will act more consistently and confidently. The foundations for strong ethical frameworks are personal values that give priority to such virtues as honesty, fairness, integrity, and self-respect. These anchors can help us make ethical decisions even when circumstances are ambiguous and situational pressures are difficult.

An **ethical framework** is a personal rule or strategy for making ethical decisions.

The many personal influences on ethical decision-making come together in the three levels of moral development described by Lawrence Kohlberg and shown in Figure 4.3: preconventional, conventional, and postconventional.[26] There are two stages in each level and Kohlberg believes that we move step by step through them as we grow in maturity and education. Not everyone—perhaps only a few of us—reaches the postconventional level.

In Kohlberg's *preconventional level* of moral development, the individual is self-centred. Moral thinking is largely limited to issues of punishment, obedience, and personal interest. Decisions made in the preconventional stages of moral development are likely to be directed toward personal gain and based on obedience to rules.

In the *conventional level* of moral development, the individual is more social-centred. Decisions made in these stages are likely to be based on following social norms, meeting the expectations of others, and living up to agreed-upon obligations.

At the *postconventional level* of moral development, the individual is strongly principle-centred. This is where a strong ethics framework is evident and the individual is willing to break with norms and conventions, even laws, to make decisions consistent with personal principles. Kohlberg believes that only a small percentage of people progress to the postconventional

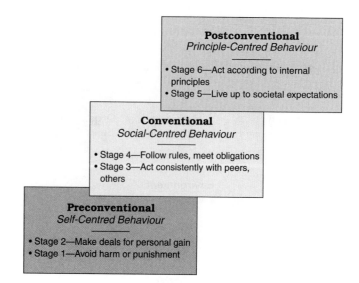

Figure 4.3 Kohlberg's levels of individual moral development.

stages. An example might be the student who passes on an opportunity to cheat on a take-home examination because he or she believes it is just wrong, even though the consequence will be a lower grade on the test. Another might be someone who refuses to use pirated computer software easily available through the Internet and social networks, preferring to purchase it and respect others' intellectual property rights.

Internal Environment and Ethics Culture

The ways and culture of an organization are important influences on ethics in the workplace. Bosses, in particular, can have a major impact on their subordinates' behaviours. How a supervisor behaves, what he or she requests, and which actions are rewarded or punished can certainly affect the ethics of an individual's decisions and actions. The expectations and reinforcement provided by peers and group norms are likely to have a similar impact. Formal policy statements and written rules are also influential.

Consider the story behind The Body Shop, quite well known for its entrepreneurial beginnings and worldwide growth. Right from her first store in Brighton, England, the late founder Dame Anita Roddick built an organizational culture around "profits with principles" values. She created an 11-point charter to guide the company's employees. It included this statement: "Honesty, integrity and caring form the foundations of the company and should flow through everything we do—we will demonstrate our care for the world in which we live by respecting fellow human beings, by not harming animals, by preserving our forests." Now owned by L'Oreal, The Body Shop grew rapidly, and Roddick's firm struggled at times with ethical criticisms.[27] The case demonstrates both the importance and the difficulties of maintaining an ethics-driven organizational culture when operations are scattered around the world—now among more than 2,500 shops in 60 countries.[28]

External Environment and Industry Norms

Wherever they operate, domestically or internationally, organizations are influenced by government laws and regulations as well as social norms and expectations. Laws interpret social values to define appropriate behaviours for organizations and their members; regulations help governments monitor these behaviours and keep them within acceptable standards. For example, the Enron and Arthur Andersen scandals led to U.S. federal legislation that attempts to substitute external controls for any lack of ethical leadership at the firm and industry levels in business. The Sarbanes-Oxley Act of 2002 makes it easier for corporate executives to be tried and sentenced to jail for financial misconduct. It also created the Public Company Accounting Oversight Board and set a new standard for auditors to verify reporting processes in the companies they audit.

The climate of competition in an industry also sets a standard of behaviour for those who hope to prosper within it. Sometimes the pressures of competition contribute to the ethical dilemmas of managers. When WestJet Airlines was caught spying on its fellow Canadian competitor Air Canada in 2005, Air Canada sued the low-cost airline for $220 million. Eventually a settlement was reached wherein WestJet paid Air Canada $5.5 million in legal fees and donated $10 million to Canadian charities in the name of both corporations. WestJet also issued a press release apology to Air Canada, stating that the unethical misconduct was "undertaken with the knowledge and direction of the highest management levels."[29] Montreal-born lawyer Richard Sanders notes in the article "Corporate Espionage: A By-Product of Today's Global Economy", "Corporate espionage is nothing new. Then, as now, what makes corporate espionage so hard to police is that it can pay so well."[30]

RATIONALIZATIONS FOR UNETHICAL BEHAVIOUR

Consider the possibility of being asked to place a bid for a business contract using insider information, paying bribes to obtain foreign business, or falsifying expense account bills. "How," you should be asking, "do people explain doing things like this?" In fact, there are at least four common rationalizations that may be used to justify misconduct in these situations and others that pose ethical dilemmas.[31]

- Convincing yourself that a behaviour is not really illegal.
- Convincing yourself that a behaviour is in everyone's best interests.
- Convincing yourself that nobody will ever find out what you've done.
- Convincing yourself that the organization will "protect" you.

After doing something that might be considered unethical, a rationalizer says: "*It's not really illegal.*" This expresses a mistaken belief that one's behaviour is acceptable, especially in ambiguous situations. When dealing with shady or borderline situations in which you are having a hard time precisely determining right from wrong, the advice is quite simple: when in doubt about a decision to be made or an action to be taken, don't do it.

Another common statement by a rationalizer is: "*It's in everyone's best interests.*" This response involves the mistaken belief that, because someone can be found to benefit from the behaviour, the behaviour is also in the individual's or the organization's best interests. Overcoming this rationalization depends in part on the ability to look beyond short-run results to address longer-term implications, and to look beyond results in general to the ways in which they are obtained. In response to the question "How far can I push matters to obtain this performance goal?", the best answer may be "Don't try to find out."

Sometimes rationalizers tell themselves that "*no one will ever know about it.*" They mistakenly believe that a questionable behaviour is really "safe" and will never be found out or made public. Unless it is

Inappropriate Rationalizations for Unethical Behaviour
"It isn't really illegal."
"It's in everybody's best interests."
"No one will ever find out."
"The organization will protect me."

discovered, the argument implies, no crime was really committed. Lack of accountability, unrealistic pressures to perform, and a boss who prefers "not to know" can all reinforce such thinking. In this case, the best deterrent is to make sure that everyone knows that wrongdoing will be punished whenever it is discovered.

Finally, rationalizers may proceed with a questionable action because of a mistaken belief that *"the organization will stand behind me."* This is misperceived loyalty. The individual believes that the organization's best interests stand above all others. In return, the individual believes that top managers will condone the behaviour and protect the individual from harm. But loyalty to the organization is not an acceptable excuse for misconduct; it should not stand above the law and social morality.

REAL ETHICS

Resumé Lies

From *The Wall Street Journal*—Employers are looking for resumé lies; senders beware! Don't assume that, because so many resumés are in the stack for a position, the employer won't bother to check details. They do. The Society for Human Resource Management surveyed 2,500 members, and 96 percent said that they checked up on references and/or stated credentials. When ResumeDoctor.com checked resumés submitted for its review by job hunters, 42.7 percent had at least one inaccuracy and 12.6 percent had more.

One of the most common resumé lies is the out-of-work cover-up: people try to hide periods of unemployment. Michael Worthington of ResumeDoctor.com says that "people are lying when they don't have to. Companies understand that being out of work can be the norm." Another lie is the inflated credential—job title or education. Elaine Hahn of Hahn Capital Management says that "someone says they're a senior research analyst, but they're really an associate." At her firm, that's cause for automatic rejection.

YOU DECIDE

Although it may be tempting to "beef up" one's resumé, it's the wrong thing to do—unethical and potentially hazardous to a career. Go through your resumé and get it up to date for a serious internship or new job search. Then check it thoroughly for "resumé lies" or anything that may be viewed by a potential employer as of questionable accuracy. Don't rationalize: remember there is only one ethics standard in resumé writing—100 percent truthfulness.

✔ **Learning Check ❷** | **BE SURE YOU CAN**

• define *ethical dilemma* and give workplace examples • explain how ethics intensity influences ethical decision-making • identify Kohlberg's stages of moral development • explain how ethics decisions are influenced by the organization's culture and external environment • list four common rationalizations for unethical behaviour

Maintaining High Ethical Standards

We all know that news from the corporate world is not always positive when it comes to ethics. Here are some reports that quickly come to mind. Item: Firm admits lowering phone contract bid after receiving confidential information from an insider that an initial bid "was not good enough to win." Item: Company admits overcharging consumers and insurers more than $13 million for repairs to damaged rental cars. Item: In June 2008, three former executives of Toronto-based Nortel Networks Corp. were charged with fraud after financial audits uncovered grossly misleading financial reports. Item: Ontario Auditor General Jim McCarter unearthed eHealth Ontario's waste of over $1 billion in taxpayer money through misuse of electronic medical information tracking programs. Item: Alcoa is charged with paying illegal "kickbacks" to an official in Bahrain.[32]

Yes, ethics problems are out there. But as quick as we are to recognize the bad news about ethical behaviour in organizations, we shouldn't forget that there is a lot of good news, too. There are many organizations, like Ben & Jerry's, whose leaders and members set high ethics standards for themselves and others. Tom's of Maine, the end of chapter case, is another good example. You'll find that organizations like these engage in a variety of methods to encourage consistent ethical behaviours by everyone they employ.

WHISTLEBLOWER PROTECTION

- Agnes Connolly pressed her employer to report two toxic chemical accidents.

- Dave Jones reported that his company was using unqualified suppliers in the construction of a nuclear power plant.

- Margaret Newsham revealed that her firm was allowing workers to do personal business while on government contracts.

- Herman Cohen charged that a humane society was mistreating animals.

- Barry Adams complained that his hospital followed unsafe practices.[33]

These persons in different work settings and linked to various issues share two important things in common. First, each was a **whistleblower**. They exposed the misdeeds of others in their organizations in order to preserve ethical standards and protect against further wasteful, harmful, or illegal acts.[34] Second, each was fired from their job.

A **whistleblower** exposes the misdeeds of others in organizations.

At the same time that we can admire whistleblowers for their intent and ethical stances, there is no doubt that they face risks in taking such actions. Research by the Ethics Resource Center has found that some 44 percent of workers in the United States fail to report the wrongdoings they observe at work. The top reasons for not reporting are "(1) the belief that no corrective action would be taken and (2) the fear that reports would not be kept confidential."[35]

Whistleblowers are known to suffer impaired career progress and other forms of organizational retaliation, up to and including termination. Although laws in the United States such as the Whistleblower Protection Act of 1989 offer whistleblowers some defence against "retaliatory discharge," legal protections are continually being tested in court, and many consider them inadequate at best.[36] American laws vary from state to state, and federal laws mainly protect government workers. In Canada, specific whistleblower protection is only found in New Brunswick and Saskatchewan. Otherwise, Canadians may have vague coverage under the Public Servants Disclosure Act of Bill C-11.[37] Within an organization, furthermore, typical barriers to whistleblowing include a strict chain of command that makes it hard to bypass the boss; strong work group identities that encourage loyalty and self-censorship; and ambiguous priorities that make it hard to distinguish right from wrong.[38]

ETHICS TRAINING

Ethics training seeks to help people understand the ethical aspects of decision-making and to incorporate high ethical standards into their daily behaviour.

Ethics training takes the form of structured programs to help participants understand the ethical aspects of decision-making. It is designed to help people incorporate high ethical standards into their daily behaviours. The CEO of Weaver Investment Companies, M. Lee McAllister, uses ethics training to help build and support an ethical organizational culture. He says, "We're basically setting the bar; we're setting the standard. We're putting ethical behaviour at a level where we think it ought to be."[39] He also describes how his firm provides its employees with "wallet cards" that are printed with the firm's code of conduct. Whenever an employee encounters another engaging in a questionable practice, he or she pulls the card out and hands it to the other party. McAllister even admits to having had this happen to him: "I was actually carded for gossip one time," he says.

There are lots of options in ethics training. Canadian university and college curricula include course work on ethics, and seminars on the topic are popular in the corporate world. But regardless of where or how the ethics training is conducted, it is important to keep things in perspective. Training is an ethics development aid; it isn't a guarantee of ethical behaviour. A banking executive once summed things up this way: "We aren't teaching people right from wrong—we assume they know that. We aren't giving people moral courage to do what is right—they should be able to do that anyhow. We focus on dilemmas."[40]

CODES OF ETHICAL CONDUCT

A **code of ethics** is a formal statement of values and ethical standards.

Ethics training often includes the communication of a **code of ethics**, a formal statement of an organization's values and ethical principles. Such codes are important anchor points in professions such as engineering, medicine, law, and public accounting. In organizations, they identify expected behaviours in such areas as general citizenship, the avoidance of illegal or improper acts in one's work, and good relationships with customers. Specific guidelines are often set for bribes and kickbacks, political contributions, honesty of books or records, customer–supplier relationships, co-worker relationships, and confidentiality of corporate information.

Ethics codes are also common in the complicated world of international business. For example, global manufacturing at Gap Inc. is governed by a Code of Vendor Conduct.[41] The document addresses discrimination— "Factories shall employ workers on the basis of their ability to do the job, not on the basis of their personal characteristics or beliefs"; forced labour—"Factories shall not use any prison, indentured or forced labor"; working conditions—"Factories must treat all workers with respect and dignity and provide them with a safe and healthy environment"; and freedom of association—"Factories must not interfere with workers who wish to lawfully and peacefully associate, organize or bargain collectively."

But even though they have ethics codes in place, global companies, including The Gap, sometimes find they are contracted with suppliers using unacceptable practices. It is hard for even the most ethically committed firms to police practices when they have many, even hundreds, of suppliers from different parts of the world. You might remember the recall of some 25 million toys, the large majority of which were made in China. Toy sellers like Walmart have ethics codes and the Canadian government has toy safety regulations. Yet, the tainted toys got through to customers. Walmart responded to the crisis by tightening its code and requiring suppliers to meet safety standards that are even higher than Canadian government requirements.[42]

Although codes of ethical conduct are helpful, they cannot guarantee ethical behaviour either by members of an organization or by outsiders that the organization does business with. Ultimately, the value of any ethics code still rests on the human resource foundations of the organization. There is no replacement for effective management practices that staff organizations with honest people. And there is no replacement for having ethical leaders that set positive examples and always act as ethical role models.

ISSUES AND SITUATIONS
Ethics Training

Lots of organizations provide some form of ethics training for employees. At Lockheed Martin, employees watch DVD scenes involving ethically suspect actions. In one scene, a manager gives a bad assignment to a direct report who had earlier criticized her behaviour in a staff meeting. The scenes are discussed for their ethical implications.

The assumption in ethics training is that such exercises will raise ethical awareness and confidence, creating a more ethical workplace. But does ethics training really work? The Ethics Resource Center finds that no more than 55 percent of persons who observe unethical acts actually report them.

CRITICAL RESPONSE

Put yourself in the shoes of someone observing questionable practices at work. How would you respond? Now, put your own shoes back on. Suppose you learn of someone who bullied another student into allowing him to "read over" her answers to a take-home exam. Or suppose you spot someone during an exam using a cell phone to take photos of test questions and send those photos to someone who is text messaging back answers. What do you do?

Conduct a brief survey of friends and acquaintances. Ask them about unethical practices in their work settings, and about what they and others do about them. Ask whether they have had ethics training at work and, if so, what it covered and what it meant in terms of personal impact.

Report from the Ethics Resource Center

- 3,015 U.S. workers surveyed
- 69 percent work for employers providing ethics training
- About 50 percent observed unethical behaviour in the past 12 months at work
- The most observed unethical actions are:
  - 21 percent: abusive or intimidating behaviour toward employees
  - 19 percent: lying to employees, customers, vendors, public
  - 16 percent: misreporting actual time worked
  - 12 percent: race, sex, or other discrimination
  - 11 percent: theft
  - 9 percent: sexual harassment

ETHICAL ROLE MODELS

Gabrielle Melchionda was a young entrepreneur in Portland, Maine, when she started Mad Gab's Inc. She was a college student and Mad Gab's was an all-natural skin care business—another "profits with principles" business example. After sales reached over $300,000, an exporter offered Gabrielle a deal to sell $2 million of her products abroad. She turned it down. Why? She learned that the exporter also sold weapons, and that was against her values. Gabrielle's principles trumped the allure of profits, an indicator that she was comfortably operating at Kohlberg's postconventional level of moral development.[43] Her values are reflected in other business decisions at Mad Gab's—from setting up an employee profit-sharing plan, to hiring disabled adults, to using only packaging designs that minimize waste. Mad Gab's mission statement declares that it aims "to participate in revolutionizing capitalism with honesty, integrity and sound business practices."[44]

Top managers, in large and small enterprises, have the power to shape an organization's policies and set its moral tone by serving as ethical role models. The day-to-day behaviour of

those at the top should be the epitome of high ethical conduct; their words and actions should be consistent in communicating ethics expectations throughout the organization. But even though top managers bear a special responsibility for setting the ethical tone of an organization, all managers should act as ethics role models and both expect and support ethical behaviour by others. The important supervisory act of setting goals and communicating performance expectations is a good case in point. A surprising 64 percent of 238 executives in one study, for example, reported feeling stressed to compromise personal standards to achieve company goals. A *Fortune* survey also reported that 34 percent of its respondents felt a company president can create an ethical climate by setting reasonable goals "so that subordinates are not pressured into unethical actions."[45]

MORAL MANAGEMENT

An **immoral manager** chooses to behave unethically.

An **amoral manager** fails to consider the ethics of her or his behaviour.

A **moral manager** makes ethical behaviour a personal goal.

Management scholar Archie Carroll makes a distinction between immoral, amoral, and moral managers.[46] The **immoral manager** chooses to behave unethically. He or she does something purely for personal gain and intentionally disregards the ethics of the action or situation. The **amoral manager** also disregards the ethics of an act or decision, but does so unintentionally. This manager simply fails to consider the ethical consequences of his or her actions. The **moral manager** considers ethical behaviour as a personal goal. He or she makes decisions and acts always in full consideration of ethical issues. In Kohlberg's terms, this manager is operating at the postconventional or principled level of moral development.[47]

Think about these three types of managers and how common they might be in the real world of work. Although it may seem surprising, Carroll suggests that most of us act amorally. Although well intentioned, we remain mostly uninformed or undisciplined in considering the ethical aspects of our behaviour.

Ethics mindfulness is enriched awareness that leads to consistent ethical behaviour.

Think also about how management morality can influence organizations. Figure 4.4 shows how it can affect the "ethics centre of gravity" for the organization as a whole. The key is **ethics mindfulness**—a state of enriched awareness that causes a person to behave ethically from one situation to the next.[48] Moral managers are leaders with ethics mindfulness. By communicating ethical values and serving as ethics role models, they help move the ethics centre of gravity of the whole organization in a positive direction, contributing to a virtuous shift. Of course, amoral and immoral leaders can be just as influential, but their impact on the ethics centre of gravity is largely negative rather than positive.

Figure 4.4 Moral management and the ethics centre of gravity in an organization.

Source: Developed from Terry Thomas, John R. Schermerhorn Jr., and John W. Dienhart, "Strategic Leadership of Ethical Behavior in Business," *Academy of Management Executive*, vol. 18 (May 2004), pp. 56–66.

SOCIAL ENTREPRENEURSHIP

Speaking of moral management and ethics role models, consider the following social issues: housing and job training for the homeless, bringing technology to poor families, improving literacy among disadvantaged youth, making small loans to start multicultural-owned businesses. What do these examples and others like them have in common? They are all targets for **social entrepreneurship**, a unique form of ethical entrepreneurship that seeks novel ways to solve pressing social problems. Social entrepreneurs are different from other entrepreneurs in that they are driven by a social mission. They pursue innovations that help solve social problems, or at least help make lives better for people who are disadvantaged.[49]

Social entrepreneurship has a mission to solve pressing social problems.

John Wood is a social entrepreneur.[50] Once comfortably immersed in his career as a Microsoft executive, his life changed on a vacation to the Himalayas of Nepal. Wood was shocked at the lack of schools. He discovered a passion that determines what he calls the "second chapter" in his life: to provide the lifelong benefits of education to poor children. He quit his Microsoft job and started a non-profit organization called Room to Read. So far, the organization has built over 400 schools and 5,000 libraries in Cambodia, India, Nepal, Vietnam, and Laos. Noting that one-seventh of the global population can't read or write, Wood says: "I don't see how we are going to solve the world's problems without literacy." The Room to Read model is so efficient that it can build schools for as little as $6,000. *Time* magazine has honoured Wood and his team as "Asian Heroes," and *Fast Company* magazine tapped his organization for a Social Capitalist Award.

BE SURE YOU CAN

✔ **Learning Check ③**

• define *whistleblower* • list three organizational barriers to whistleblowing • compare and contrast ethics training, codes of ethical conduct, and ethical role models as methods for encouraging ethical behaviour in organizations • differentiate between amoral, immoral, and moral management • describe ethics mindfulness and how moral management can shift an organization's ethics centre of gravity • explain and give an example of social entrepreneurship

---

SOCIAL RESPONSIBILITY, GOVERNANCE, AND SUSTAINABILITY

The social entrepreneurship of John Wood sets a high ethics standard. But he's not alone. Here are a few Canadians among the many examples you can find of people who have made the commitment to create and work for organizations that follow ethical and socially responsible practices.[51]

• David Suzuki's commitment to educating and promoting environmental sustainability led him to start the Davis Suzuki Foundation in 1990. Today, the foundation focuses on "working with government, business and individuals to conserve our environment by providing science-based

© E1 Films Canada/courtesy Everett Collection

education, advocacy and policy work, and acting as a catalyst for the social change that today's situation demands."

- Rick Hanson began the Rick Hanson Foundation 25 years ago in his quest to make the world accessible to those with disabilities. Since its inception, the foundation has raised over $200 million for spinal cord injury research and quality of life programs.

- Craig Kielburger was 12 when he read a newspaper article about a boy killed in South Asia for speaking out against child labour. With a group of his classmates, Craig formed Free the Children, an organization focused on advocating children's rights to free them from poverty and exploitation. Free the Children is now active in over 45 countries as Craig continues to support his quest for children helping children.

- Nina Gupta recognized an opportunity to contribute positively to the environmental sustainability movement through providing energy-efficient light sources. Her organization, Greenlite Lighting Corporation, now operates internationally while raising awareness for reducing greenhouse gas emissions both on an individual and corporate level.

The importance of such examples hits close to home as university and college students search for internships and new jobs. Members of the millennial generation, in particular, seem to be casting a cautious eye on potential employers. "These students grew up amidst the corporate scandals," says an observer. "Students nowadays want to work for companies that help enhance the quality of life in their surrounding community."[52] In one survey, 70 percent of students report that "a company's reputation and ethics" is "very important" when deciding whether or not to accept a job offer; in another survey, 79 percent of 13- to 25-year-olds say they "want to work for a company that cares about how it affects or contributes to society."[53]

Corporate social responsibility is the obligation of an organization to serve its own interests and those of society.

In management, we use the term **corporate social responsibility** or "CSR" to describe an organization's obligation to act in ways that serve both its own interests and the interests of society at large. Some discuss this commitment to social responsibility in respect to a *double bottom line*—financial performance and social impact. Others go even further in referring to the *triple bottom line*—economic, social, and environmental performance.[54]

STAKEHOLDER ISSUES AND ANALYSIS

Organizational **stakeholders** are directly affected by the behaviour of the organization and hold a stake in its performance.

Any discussion of social responsibility needs to recognize a point from the last chapter—organizations exist in a network of **stakeholders**. These are the persons, groups, and other organizations that are directly affected by the behaviour of the organization and hold a stake in its performance.[55] From the perspective of a stakeholder model, any organization has a social responsibility to serve the interests of its many stakeholders. Consider again the prior example of Walmart's response to toy safety problems. Where would the firm be without the loyalty of its customers? When toy safety was at issue, Walmart hardly had any choice. In order to protect its reputation with customers and other stakeholders, it had to respond vigorously by raising standards and tightening controls on foreign suppliers.

Respect for stakeholders has been a guiding principle at Tom's of Maine, as discussed in the end of chapter case. Founders Tom and Kate Chappell clearly state: "When we founded the company, it was our goal to make a different kind of business, one where people, the environment, and animals are seen as inherently worthy and deserving of respect. We remain committed to this mission, now more than ever." One of Tom's initiatives has been to offset 100 percent of its factory electricity usage with wind energy.[56]

Stakeholder respect is also present in Hot Fudge, a venture capital fund started by Ben Cohen, of Ben & Jerry's fame.[57] The fund supports small business development in depressed communities. And stakeholder respect is found at Timberland Company, where each full-time employee gets 40 hours of paid time per year for community volunteer work. Timberland's motto is "when you come to work in the morning, don't leave your values at the door."[58]

The importance of understanding stakeholder issues cannot be overstated. Consumers, activist groups, non-profit organizations, employees, and governments are often vocal and influential in pushing organizations toward socially responsible practices. Also, in today's information age, business activities are increasingly transparent. Irresponsible practices are difficult to hide for long, wherever in the world they take place. Not only do news organizations find and disseminate information on bad practices, activist organizations do the same. They also lobby, campaign, and actively pressure organizations to respect and protect everything from human rights to the natural environment. Furthermore, some investment funds only own shares in businesses that they evaluate as performing in socially responsible ways.[59]

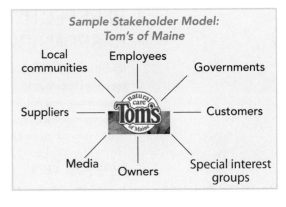

Sample Stakeholder Model: Tom's of Maine

RESEARCH BRIEF

Issues management pacesetters influence pharmaceutical industry's response to AIDS in Africa

Writing in *Business & Society*, Cedric E. Dawkins describes an "issues management pacesetter" as a company in an industry that addresses an external issue in a unique and different way. His article first develops a pacesetters model and then applies it to case studies of responses by global pharmaceutical firms to the AIDS crisis in Africa over a three-year period. In his words, the article analyzes "the confrontation between the mainline pharmaceutical industry and AIDS activists and stakeholders over access to AIDS medications in Africa."

Dawkins views organizational decision-making as a process of negotiation between external normative and competitive pressures. Issues pacesetters are firms that change in response to pressures from external stakeholders and then stimulate further changes by other industry firms.

In the article, Dawkins examines two pacesetting pharmaceuticals that initiated pressures for change in Africa—one by substantially lowering prices of AIDS drugs, and the other by freeing patents on these drugs. Both pacesetters were responding to stakeholder views that were consolidating around a new set of expectations. He concludes that the pacesetters model is accurate in explaining the industry events, and that the perceptions of organizational decision-makers of stakeholder interests and demands are a critical factor in the process. He also suggests that stakeholder groups that understand how firms make decisions will be able to gain more influence over firm behaviour.

In a postscript to the article, Dawkins also notes increased cooperation among countries in the fight against AIDS. But he also points out that, in Africa and elsewhere, more still needs to be done to "widen access to HIV medicines and technologies."

You be the researcher

Can you come up with other examples or cases where the issues pacesetters model helps explain how organizations deal with stakeholder issues and concerns? Identify a social issue that is being voiced in your community. Study the issue, the stakeholders, and the businesses or other organizations whose products or services are in question. Test how well the issues pacesetters model helps to explain events to date and predict what might happen in the future.

PERSPECTIVES ON CORPORATE SOCIAL RESPONSIBILITY

It may seem that corporate social responsibility, or CSR, is one of those concepts and goals that most everyone would agree upon. However, there are two contrasting views that stimulate debate in academic and public-policy circles.[60] On one side the classical view takes a stand against making corporate social responsibility a top business priority, while on the other side the socio-economic view advocates for it.

Classical View

The **classical view of CSR** is that business should focus on profits.

The **classical view of CSR** holds that management's only responsibility in running a business is to maximize profits. In other words, "the business of business is business," and the principal obligation of management should always be to owners and shareholders. This classical view takes a very narrow stakeholder perspective and puts the focus on the single bottom line of financial performance. It is supported by Milton Friedman, a respected economist and Nobel Laureate. He says: "Few trends could so thoroughly undermine the very foundations of our free society as the acceptance by corporate officials of social responsibility other than to make as much money for their stockholders as possible."[61]

The arguments against corporate social responsibility include fears that its pursuit will reduce business profits, raise business costs, dilute business purpose, give business too much social power, and do so without business accountability to the public. Although not against corporate social responsibility in its own right, Friedman and other proponents of the classical view believe that society's best interests are always served in the long run by executives who focus on profit maximization by their businesses.

Socio-Economic View

The **socio-economic view of CSR** is that business should focus on broader social welfare as well as profits.

The **socio-economic view of CSR** holds that management of any organization must be concerned with the broader social welfare and not just with corporate profits. This view takes a broad stakeholder perspective and puts the focus on an expanded bottom line that includes not just financial performance but also social and environmental performance. It is supported by Paul Samuelson, another distinguished economist and Nobel Laureate. He states: "A large corporation these days not only may engage in social responsibility, it had damn well better try to do so."[62]

Among the arguments in favour of corporate social responsibility are that it will add long-run profits for businesses, improve the public image of businesses, and help them avoid government regulation. Furthermore, businesses often have vast resources with the potential to have enormous social impact. Thus, business executives have ethical obligations to ensure that their firms act responsibly in the interests of society at large.

The **virtuous circle** occurs when CSR improves financial performance, which leads to more CSR.

There is little doubt today that the public at large wants businesses and other organizations to act with genuine social responsibility. Stakeholder expectations are increasingly well voiced and include demands that organizations integrate social responsibility into their core values and daily activities. Also, a growing body of research links social responsibility and financial performance. One report showed that, among Standard & Poor's 500 firms, those with strong commitments to corporate philanthropy outperformed in respect to operating earnings.[63] More generally, research indicates that social responsibility can be associated with strong financial performance; at worst, it has no adverse financial impact.[64] The argument that acting with a commitment to social responsibility will negatively affect the "bottom line" is hard to defend. Indeed, evidence points toward a **virtuous circle** in which corporate social responsibility leads to improved financial performance for the firm, and this in turn leads to more socially responsible actions in the future.[65]

EVALUATING CORPORATE SOCIAL PERFORMANCE

If we are to get serious about social responsibility, we need to get rigorous about measuring corporate social performance and holding business leaders accountable for the results. A **social responsibility audit** can be used at regular intervals to report on and systematically assess an organization's performance in various areas of corporate social responsibility.

A **social responsibility audit** assesses an organization's accomplishments in areas of social responsibility.

Criteria for Evaluating Social Performance

The social performance of business firms varies along a continuum that ranges from *compliance*—acting to avoid adverse consequences, to *conviction*—acting to create positive impact.[66] As shown in Figure 4.5, the continuum also varies in commitments to four criteria for evaluating social responsibility practices: economic, legal, ethical, and discretionary.[67] Thus, an audit of corporate social performance might cover these four questions:

1. Is the organization's economic responsibility met—is it profitable?

2. Is the organization's legal responsibility met—does it obey the law?

3. Is the organization's ethical responsibility met—is it doing the "right" things?

4. Is the organization's discretionary responsibility met—does it contribute to the broader community?

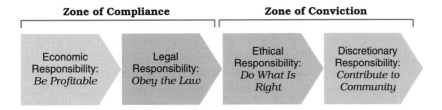

Figure 4.5 Criteria for evaluating corporate social performance.

An organization is meeting its *economic responsibility* when it earns a profit through the provision of goods and services desired by customers. *Legal responsibility* is fulfilled when an organization operates within the law and according to the requirements of various external regulations. An organization meets its *ethical responsibility* when its actions voluntarily conform not only to legal expectations but also to the broader values and moral expectations of society. The highest level of social performance comes through the satisfaction of *discretionary responsibility*. At this level, the organization moves beyond basic economic, legal, and ethical expectations to provide leadership in advancing the well-being of individuals, communities, and society as a whole.

Social Responsibility Strategies

The decisions of people working at all levels in organizations ultimately determine whether or not practices are socially responsible. At the executive level, these decisions can be viewed as "strategic"—ones designed to move the organization forward in its environment according to a long-term plan. And, of course, those plans can vary greatly depending on the executives' viewpoints, organizational histories, and other factors.[68]

Figure 4.6 describes four corporate social responsibility strategies, with the commitment to social performance increasing as the strategy shifts from "obstructionist" at the lowest end to "proactive" at the highest.[69] The **obstructionist strategy** ("Fight social demands") focuses mainly on economic priorities in respect to social responsibility. Social demands lying outside the organization's perceived self-interests are resisted. If the organization is criticized for wrongdoing, it can be expected to deny the claims.

An **obstructionist strategy** avoids social responsibility and reflects mainly economic priorities.

Canadian Company in the News

CANADIAN STORE IS NUMBER ONE AT DOING GOOD

Vancouver-based Mountain Equipment Co-op (MEC) was recently named by the Conference Board of Canada as the best in Canada for governance because of its environmentally sustainable approach to business. But actions speak louder than awards. MEC joined One Percent for the Planet, which encourages businesses to donate 1 percent of sales to environmental groups. To date, MEC has donated over $17 million to support conservation efforts. The co-op also strives for environmentally friendly products; it chooses organic cotton, recycled polyester, and PVC-free fabrics. Products that meet MEC's stringent sustainable products criteria proudly display the sustainability symbol. The company cites open communications as a key success contributor. MEC produces an annual accountability report posted to its website so everyone can see how it is doing in terms of achieving its sustainability goals.

Courtesy MEC

A **defensive strategy** seeks protection by doing the minimum legally required.

A **defensive strategy** ("Do the minimum legally required") seeks to protect the organization by doing the minimum legally necessary to satisfy expectations. Corporate behaviour at this level conforms only to legal requirements, competitive market pressure, and perhaps activist voices. If criticized, wrongdoing on social responsibility matters is likely to be denied.

An **accommodative strategy** accepts social responsibility and tries to satisfy economic, legal, and ethical criteria.

Organizations pursuing an **accommodative strategy** ("Do the minimum ethically required") accept their social responsibilities. They try to satisfy economic, legal, and ethical criteria. Corporate behaviour at this level is consistent with society's prevailing norms, values, and expectations, often reflecting the demands of outside pressures. An oil company, for example, may be willing to "accommodate" with appropriate cleanup activities when a spill occurs, yet it may remain quite slow in taking actions to prevent spills in the first place.

A **proactive strategy** meets all the criteria of social responsibility, including discretionary performance.

The **proactive strategy** ("Take leadership in social initiatives") is designed to meet all prior criteria of social performance plus engage in discretionary performance. Corporate behaviour at this level takes preventive action to avoid adverse social impacts from company activities, and it takes the lead in identifying and responding to emerging social issues.

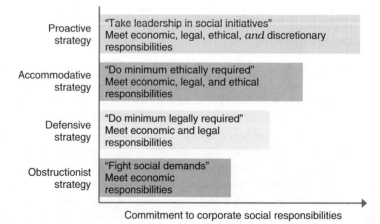

Figure 4.6 Four strategies of corporate social responsibility—from obstructionist to proactive behaviour.

DIRECTIONS IN CORPORATE GOVERNANCE

When you read and hear about business ethics failures, issues relating to **corporate governance** are often raised. The term refers to the active oversight of management decisions and company actions by boards of directors.[70] Businesses by law must have boards of directors that are elected by shareholders to represent their interests. The governance exercised by these boards most typically involves hiring, firing, and compensating the CEO; assessing strategy; and verifying financial records. The expectation is that board members will hold management accountable for ethical and socially responsible leadership.[71]

Corporate governance is the oversight of top management by a board of directors.

It is tempting to think that corporate governance is a clear-cut way to ensure that organizations behave with social responsibility and that their members always act ethically. But the recent financial crisis and related banking scandals show once again that corporate governance can be inadequate and in some cases ineffectual. Consider controversies with CEO pay and the roles of corporate boards in setting such pay. CEOs of major financial firms made millions while their companies—and shareholders—lost billions. During the first stages of the U.S. mortgage crisis, Angelo Mozilo made $120 million at Countrywide Financial, Stanley O'Neal retired with a $161-million package from Merrill Lynch, and Citigroup CEO Charles Prince made $39.5 million.[72]

The examples just cited were from United States Congressional hearings on what was called the "lavish pay" of corporate CEOs.[73] Where, you might ask, were the boards and corporate governance in such situations? When corporate failures and controversies occur, weak governance often gets blamed. And when it does, you will sometimes see government stepping in to try to correct things for the future. In addition to holding hearings, as in the case of CEO pay or "bailout" loans to U.S. and Canadian automakers, governments also pass laws and establish regulating agencies in attempts to better control and direct business behaviour. For example, the Sarbanes-Oxley Act, mentioned earlier, was passed by the U.S. Congress in response to public outcries over major ethics and business scandals. Its goal is to ensure that top managers properly oversee and are held accountable for the financial conduct of their organizations. All Canadian publicly traded firms that do business in the United States must adhere to this act as well.

But even as one talks about corporate governance reform and the accountability of top management, it is important to remember that all managers must accept personal responsibility for doing the "right" things.[74] Figure 4.7 highlights what might be called the need for ethics self-governance in day-to-day work behaviour. It is not enough to fulfill one's performance accountabilities; they must be fulfilled in an ethical and socially responsible manner. The full weight of this responsibility holds in every organizational setting, from small to large and from private to non-profit, and at every managerial level from top to bottom. There is no escaping the ultimate reality—being a manager at any level is a very socially responsible job!

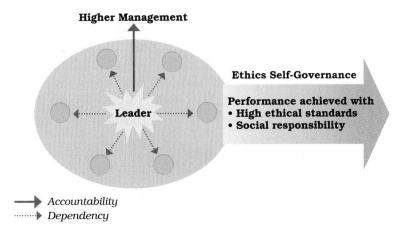

Figure 4.7 Ethics self-governance in leadership and the managerial role.

DIRECTIONS IN SUSTAINABILITY

As a socially responsible manager, take a look at a developing problem. Water is central to life. Yet it is becoming an increasingly scarce resource for most of the planet. While water appears to be abundant on earth, only 3 percent of water is fresh water and, of that, only 5 percent is readily available for human use. Right now, 20 percent of the world's population lacks access to safe drinking water and within 15 years that number is predicted to grow to about 40 percent of the world's population.[75] We are becoming a thirsty planet.

This might be difficult to appreciate in Canada as most of us have ready access to seemingly unlimited amounts of freshwater. And we take full advantage of this; Canadians are the second highest per capita users of fresh water in the world, behind only the United States. It is not seen as a problem for us. Many organizations have also been slow to pick up on this developing challenge, but are now coming face to face with the problem. We turn to the companies involved in the "cola wars" as an example.

Both Coca-Cola and Pepsi have been singled out as large users of water. For example, Coca-Cola sells 1.5 billion beverages each day in over 200 countries, and it takes about 2.5 litres of water to produce just one litre of its products at Coke's bottling plants.[76] Facing difficult questions in water-scarce India and China around the company's use of water, Coke knows the risks well. In 2002, villagers in India accused the company's nearby bottling plant of first depleting and then polluting their groundwater. This resulted in the forced shutdown of the plant. In 2006, when a New Delhi research group purportedly found high levels of pesticides in Coca-Cola and PepsiCo's locally produced soft drinks, a charge Coke denies, several Indian states banned their sale.[77] In response, Coke has spent $10 million to establish the Coca-Cola India Foundation to install rainwater harvesting structures across India to provide clean drinking water to 1,000 schools.[78]

The company is likewise trying to avoid incurring public wrath in water-thirsty China. "We recognize the need to be more vigilant in how we manage our water," says C. B. Chiu, vice president and technical director of Coca-Cola China. "If we don't contribute to the community, the community will see us as outsiders."[79]

It is clear that businesses must do their part to solve this and other sustainability challenges. Sustainability can be defined as "development that meets the needs of the present without compromising the ability of future generations to meet their own needs."[80] Central to sustainability is finding a balance between present and future needs, focusing on social rights, environmental protection, and economic development.

There is a strong business case why businesses should focus on sustainability. Reasons include:

1. Cost reduction: sustainability provides a mechanism to reduce costs by focusing attention on efficiency. This might be achieved by reducing waste produced, increasing recycling, or a host of other strategies. For example, Procter Gamble's "waste-out" program saved the company over $500 million and eliminated 2 million tonnes of waste.[81]

2. Resource preservation: It is recognized that the raw materials we are all dependent upon are being used up quicker than they can be replenished. We only need to look to the Grand Banks off Newfoundland to recognize the problems of overfishing and the impact this has had. However, other materials are not replenishable and when they are used they are gone from the planet for good.

3. Legislative compliance: Governments around the world are putting in place more regulations and standards that speak to sustainability needs. Organizations must work closely with regulators to ensure compliance and to build commitment to ensure all are following the rules.

4. Reputation: Being seen as a promoter of environmental and social performance is now essential for organizations to maintain a positive reputation among stakeholders. Failing to do so may come at a high price to the organization and to the senior management team; we only need to look to BP and its recent oil spill in the Gulf of Mexico to appreciate this truth. A solid reputation allows organizations to attract and retain quality employees, to differentiate itself from competitors in the marketplace, and to attract "socially responsible" capital investors and consumers. It makes sense strategically to focus on sustainability.

5. Right initiative: There is a clear business case why organizations should embrace sustainability but another reason is that it is the right thing to do. Sustainability is likely already happening in most organizations. Whether management- or employee-driven, it is taking hold. Is the organization willing to be a leader or a laggard when it comes to sustainability?

What does a sustainable company look like? While there is no firm answer as to how to determine if an organization embraces sustainability, there are things to look for when determining how important sustainability is to the company.

1. Who is leading the initiative? If the CEO is leading the charge, there is a strong sense that the company is making a serious commitment.

2. Who understands the initiative? If the board of directors and the employees know the details of the sustainability strategy, it is likely that the cause is widely embraced.

3. What resources are allocated to sustainability? Organizations and people vote with their wallets. How many people are assigned to this project and what resources they have to tackle the challenge all send signals as to the importance of the program.

4. Is it holistic? Is the company being proactive or reactive? Is it talking sustainability with all of its business partners? Is it working with industry peers? Is it involved with sustainability networks or coalitions? Has it publicly stated measurable short-, medium-, and long-range goals on sustainability initiatives and does it regularly report whether it is achieving these goals?

5. Is it recognized as a sustainability leader? While awards are only one measure, they can signal that peer groups or interest groups recognize that an organization is on the right track. Some signals include inclusion on lists such as the Global 100 list of the most sustainable large corporations in the world, The Sustainability Yearbook, and *Business Ethics* magazine's 100 best corporate citizens. These are all positive indicators that a firm is pursuing the right sustainability initiatives.

What Can You Do Now?

The path to sustainable prosperity will be a long one, yet each journey begins with a first step. Likely you have already been walking this journey for some time or maybe this is the moment when you embrace sustainability in a serious way. The key thing is to take on a leadership role. Lead first by example; whether it is through reducing waste or water use, turning off lights, purchasing from sustainable companies, or living a life with as small an environmental "footprint" as possible, the first task is to walk the sustainability path. Then, look for or create a green job, in fields such as green credit trading, community banking, social marketing, sustainability investment, eco-efficiency operational models, and eco-packaging. To build a sustainable future requires us to take action now. The best tree planted was one planted 50 years ago; the second best tree planted is the one planted today.

✓ **Learning Check ❹** **BE SURE YOU CAN**

• define *corporate social responsibility* • summarize arguments for and against corporate social responsibility • identify four criteria for measuring corporate social performance • explain four possible social responsibility strategies • define *corporate governance* and discuss its importance in organization–society relationships • define *sustainability* and highlight five reasons why it is an effective strategy for businesses to follow

MANAGEMENT LEARNING REVIEW

STUDY QUESTIONS SUMMARY

KEY TERMS

1. What is ethical behaviour?

• Ethical behaviour is that which is accepted as "good" or "right" as opposed to "bad" or "wrong."

• Because an action is not illegal does not necessarily make it ethical in a given situation.

• Because values vary, the question "What is ethical behaviour?" may be answered differently by different people.

• The utilitarian, individualism, moral rights, and justice views offer alternative ways of thinking about ethical behaviour.

• Cultural relativism argues that no culture is ethically superior to any other; universalism argues that certain ethical standards apply everywhere.

FOR DISCUSSION Is there ever a justification for cultural relativism in international business ethics?

2. How do ethical dilemmas complicate the workplace?

• An ethical dilemma occurs when someone must decide whether to pursue a course of action that, although offering the potential for personal or organizational benefit or both, may be unethical.

• Managers report that their ethical dilemmas often involve conflicts with superiors, customers, and subordinates over such matters as dishonesty in advertising and communications, as well as pressure from bosses to do unethical things.

• Common rationalizations for unethical behaviour include believing the behaviour is not illegal, is in everyone's best interests, will never be noticed, or will be supported by the organization.

FOR DISCUSSION Are ethical dilemmas always problems, or can they also be opportunities?

3. How can high ethical standards be maintained?

• Ethics training can help people better deal with ethical dilemmas in the workplace.

• Whistleblowers expose the unethical acts of others in organizations, even while facing career risks for doing so.

• Top management sets an ethical tone for the organization as a whole, while all managers are responsible for acting as positive models of ethical behaviour.

• Written codes of ethical conduct formally state what an organization expects of its employees regarding ethical behaviour at work.

- Immoral managers intentionally choose to behave unethically; amoral managers disregard the ethics of their actions or decisions; moral managers consider ethical behaviour a personal goal.

- Moral managers can shift the ethics centre of gravity in organizations in a positive direction and strengthen ethics mindfulness by others.

- Social entrepreneurs pursue ethics goals in seeking novel ways to help solve social problems.

FOR DISCUSSION Is it right for organizations to require employees to sign codes of conduct and undergo ethics training?

4. What are social responsibility, governance, and sustainability?

- Social responsibility is an obligation of the organization to act in ways that serve both its own interests and the interests of its many stakeholders.

- An organization's social performance can be evaluated on how well it meets economic, legal, ethical, and discretionary responsibilities.

- Corporate strategies in response to demands for socially responsible behaviour include obstruction, defence, accommodation, and proaction.

- Corporate governance is the responsibility of a board of directors to oversee the performance by top management of a firm.

- Managers should exercise ethical self-governance by making sure that performance is achieved with commitments to high ethical standards and by socially responsible means.

- There are many reasons why an organization's sustainability focus makes business sense, including cost reduction, preserving resources, legislative compliance, reputation, and being the right thing to do.

FOR DISCUSSION What questions would you include on a sustainability audit for an organization in your community?

SELF-TEST

Multiple-Choice Questions

1. Values are personal beliefs that help determine whether a behaviour will be considered ethical or unethical. An example of a terminal value is _____.

    (a) ambition (b) self-respect (c) courage (d) imagination

2. Under the _____ view of ethical behaviour, a business owner would be considered ethical if she reduced a plant's workforce by 10 percent in order to cut costs to keep the business from failing and thus save jobs for the other 90 percent.

    (a) utilitarian (b) individualism (c) justice (d) moral rights

3. A manager's failure to enforce a late-to-work policy the same way for all employees is an ethical violation of _____ justice.

    (a) ethical (b) moral (c) distributive (d) procedural

4. The Sarbanes-Oxley Act of 2002 makes it easier for corporate executives to _____.

    (a) protect themselves from shareholder lawsuits (b) sue employees who commit illegal acts (c) be tried and sentenced to jail for financial misconduct (d) shift blame for wrongdoing to boards of directors

5. Two "spotlight" questions for conducting the ethics double-check of a decision are (a) "How would I feel if my family found out about this?" and (b) "How would I feel if _____?"

    (a) my boss found out about this (b) my subordinates found out about this (c) this was printed in the local newspaper or appeared on the Internet (d) this went into my personnel file

6. Research on ethical dilemmas indicates that _____ is/are often the cause of unethical behaviour by people at work.

    (a) declining morals in society (b) lack of religious beliefs (c) the absence of whistleblowers (d) pressures from bosses and superiors

7. Customers, investors, employees, and regulators are examples of _____ that are important in the analysis of corporate social responsibility.

    (a) special interest groups (b) stakeholders (c) ethics advocates (d) whistleblowers

8. Two employees are talking about their employers. Sayed says that ethics training and codes of ethical conduct are worthless; Maura says these are the best ways to ensure ethical behaviour in the organization. Who is right and why?

    (a) Sayed—no one cares. (b) Maura—only the organization can influence ethical behaviour. (c) Neither Sayed nor Maura—training and codes can aid but never guarantee ethical behaviour. (d) Neither Sayed nor Maura—only the threat of legal punishment will make people act ethically.

9. A proponent of the classical view of corporate social responsibility would most likely agree with which of these statements?

    (a) Social responsibility improves the public image of business. (b) The primary responsibility of business is to maximize business profits. (c) By acting responsibly, businesses avoid government regulation. (d) Businesses can and should do "good" while doing business.

10. An amoral manager _____.

    (a) always acts in consideration of ethical issues (b) chooses to behave unethically (c) makes ethics a personal goal (d) acts unethically but not intentionally

11. An organization that takes the lead in addressing emerging social issues is being _____, showing the most progressive corporate social responsibility strategy.

    (a) accommodative (b) defensive (c) proactive (d) obstructionist

12. The criterion of _____ responsibility identifies the highest level of conviction by an organization to operate in a responsible manner.

    (a) economic (b) legal (c) ethical (d) discretionary

13. Which ethical position has been criticized as a source of "ethical imperialism"?

    (a) individualism (b) absolutism (c) utilitarianism (d) relativism

14. A manager supports an organization's attempts at self-governance when he or she always tries to achieve performance objectives in ways that are _____.

    (a) performance effective (b) cost efficient (c) quality oriented (d) ethical and socially responsible

15. Which of the following is NOT a reason why a company should focus on sustainability?

    (a) legislative compliance (b) cultural relativism (c) cost reduction (d) reputation

Short-Response Questions

16. Explain the difference between the individualism and justice views of ethical behaviour.

17. List four common rationalizations for unethical managerial behaviour.

18. What are the major arguments in the socio-economic view of corporate social responsibility?

19. What decisions should a board of directors oversee in order to fulfill its governance responsibilities?

Application Question

20. A small outdoor clothing company has just received an attractive offer from a business in Bangladesh to manufacture its work gloves. The offer would allow for substantial cost savings over the current supplier. The company manager, however, has read reports that some Bangladeshi businesses break their own laws and operate with child labour. How would differences in the following corporate responsibility strategies affect the manager's decision regarding whether to accept the offer: obstruction, defence, accommodation, and proaction?

MANAGEMENT SKILLS AND COMPETENCIES

SELF-ASSESSMENT

Back to Yourself: Individual Character

Individual character is something that people tend to think a lot about during parliamentary election periods. But, as suggested in the chapter opener, character and its underlying foundation of personal integrity isn't something that should only be an occasional concern; it deserves more than passing and even reluctant attention. The ethics and social responsibility issues facing organizations today put individual character to the test. Ethical dilemmas can arise on any given day. To deal with them, we have to know ourselves well enough to make principled decisions, ones that we can be proud of and that others will respect. After all, it's the character of people making key decisions that determines whether our organizations act in socially responsible or irresponsible ways. And an understanding of personal values is very helpful as we try to stay on course with individual character.

Further Reflection: Terminal Values

Instructions

Rate each of the following values in terms of its importance to you. Think about each value in terms of its importance as a guiding principle in your life. Consider each value in relation to all the other values listed in the survey.

Terminal Values

1. A comfortable life	Of lesser importance	1 2 3 4 5 6 7	Of greater importance
2. An exciting life	Of lesser importance	1 2 3 4 5 6 7	Of greater importance
3. A sense of accomplishment	Of lesser importance	1 2 3 4 5 6 7	Of greater importance
4. A world at peace	Of lesser importance	1 2 3 4 5 6 7	Of greater importance
5. A world of beauty	Of lesser importance	1 2 3 4 5 6 7	Of greater importance
6. Equality	Of lesser importance	1 2 3 4 5 6 7	Of greater importance
7. Family security	Of lesser importance	1 2 3 4 5 6 7	Of greater importance
8. Freedom	Of lesser importance	1 2 3 4 5 6 7	Of greater importance

9. Happiness	Of lesser importance	1 2 3 4 5 6 7	Of greater importance
10. Inner harmony	Of lesser importance	1 2 3 4 5 6 7	Of greater importance
11. Mature love	Of lesser importance	1 2 3 4 5 6 7	Of greater importance
12. National security	Of lesser importance	1 2 3 4 5 6 7	Of greater importance
13. Pleasure	Of lesser importance	1 2 3 4 5 6 7	Of greater importance
14. Salvation	Of lesser importance	1 2 3 4 5 6 7	Of greater importance
15. Self-respect	Of lesser importance	1 2 3 4 5 6 7	Of greater importance
16. Social recognition	Of lesser importance	1 2 3 4 5 6 7	Of greater importance
17. True friendship	Of lesser importance	1 2 3 4 5 6 7	Of greater importance
18. Wisdom	Of lesser importance	1 2 3 4 5 6 7	Of greater importance

Interpretation

Terminal values reflect a person's preferences concerning the "ends" to be achieved. They are the goals individuals would like to achieve in their lifetimes. Different value items receive different weights in this scale. (Example: "A comfortable life" might receive a weight of "5" while "Freedom" receives a weight of "1.") Subtract your Social Values score from your Personal Values score to determine your Terminal Values score.

Scoring

To score this instrument, multiply your score for each item times a "weight"—e.g., (#3 $\times$ 5) = your new question 3 score.

1. Calculate your Personal Values score as:
    (#1 $\times$ 5) + (#2 $\times$ 4) + (#3 $\times$ 4) + (#7) + (#8) + (#9 $\times$ 4) + (#10 $\times$ 5) + (#11 $\times$ 4) + (#13 $\times$ 5) + (#14 $\times$ 3) + (#15 $\times$ 5) + (#16 $\times$ 3) + (#17 $\times$ 4) + (#18 $\times$ 5)

2. Calculate your Social Values score as (#4 $\times$ 5) + (#5 $\times$ 3) + (#6 $\times$ 5) + (#12 $\times$ 5)

3. Calculate your Terminal Values score as Personal Values – Social Values

Source: Adapted from James Weber, "Management Value Orientations: A Typology and Assessment," *International Journal of Value Based Management*, vol. 3, no. 2 (1990), pp. 37–54.

TEAM EXERCISE

Confronting Ethical Dilemmas

Preparation

Read and indicate your response to each of the situations below.

a. Ron Christopoulos, vice president of a large construction firm, receives in the mail a large envelope marked "personal." It contains a competitor's cost data for a project that both firms will be bidding on shortly. The data are accompanied by a note from one of Ron's subordinates saying: "This is the real thing!" Ron knows that the data could be a major advantage to his firm in preparing a bid that can win the contract. What should he do?

b. Arya Ibrahim is one of your top-performing subordinates. She has shared with you her desire to apply for promotion to a new position just announced in a different division of the company. This will be tough on you since recent budget cuts mean you will be unable to replace anyone who leaves, at least for quite some time. Arya knows this and, in all fairness, has asked your permission before she submits an application. It is rumoured that the son of a good friend of your boss is going to apply for the job. Although his credentials are less impressive than Arya's, the likelihood is that he will get the job if she doesn't apply. What will you do?

c. Marty Jose got caught in a bind. She was pleased to represent her firm as head of the local community development committee. In fact, her supervisor's boss once held this position and told her in a hallway conversation, "Do your best and give them every support possible." Going along with this, Marty agreed to pick up the bill (several hundred dollars) for a dinner meeting with local civic and business leaders. Shortly thereafter, her supervisor informed everyone that the entertainment budget was being eliminated in a cost-saving effort. Marty, not wanting to renege on supporting the community development committee, was able to charge the dinner bill to an advertising budget. Eventually, an internal auditor discovered the mistake and reported it to you, the personnel director. Marty is scheduled to meet with you in a few minutes. What will you do?

Instructions

Working alone, make the requested decisions in each of these incidents. Think carefully about your justification for the decision. Meet in a group assigned by your instructor. Share your decisions and justifications in each case with other group members. Listen to theirs. Try to reach a group consensus on what to do in each situation and why. Be prepared to share the group decisions, and any dissenting views, in general class discussion.

CASE 4

Tom's of Maine: "Doing Business" Means "Doing Good"

Tom's of Maine was one of the first natural health care companies to distribute outside normal channels. The company holds fast to the values that got owners Tom and Kate Chappell started more than three decades ago, providing insight into how a small firm can grow while staying true to its founding principles in the midst of competition. Now that Tom's has been sold to Colgate, one wonders if those principles can be sustained in a large corporate environment.

Courtesy Tom's of Maine, Inc

Getting Tom's of Maine Going

Tom and Kate Chappell, dreaming of a line of all-natural, environmentally friendly household products, started Tom's of Maine in 1970. The company's first product, a phosphate-free detergent, was environmentally friendly, Tom Chappell says, but "it didn't clean so well."[1] But consumers were interested in environmentally friendly products—and the toothpaste and soap that followed were more successful.

All of Tom's products were made with all-natural ingredients and packaged in recycled materials whenever possible. New personal care products, including shampoo and deodorant, were developed without animal testing.[2] But the road to success wasn't always direct or fast. Tom's stand

against "business as usual" made the company wait seven years longer and spend about 10 times the usual sum to get the American Dental Association's seal of approval for its fluoride toothpastes. And mistakes were made. At a time when deodorant made up 25 percent of the business, Chappell reformulated the product for ecological reasons. Later, he realized that the new formulation "magnified the human bacteria that cause odor" in half its users. After much agonizing, Chappell took the product from his shelves at a cost of $400,000, 30 percent of the firm's projected profits for the year. Dissatisfied consumers were sent refunds and a letter of apology.

One pivotal event was the introduction of baking soda toothpaste. The gritty product had none of the sweetness of commercial toothpastes, and the marketing manager told Chappell, "In all candor, I don't know how we're going to sell it."[3] Tom insisted that the product be test-marketed. It became a best-seller and was quickly copied by Arm and Hammer and Procter & Gamble.[4]

As the company moved from experience to experience, it gained strength and customers, but Tom was still unhappy, saying he was tired of simply "creating new brands and making money." He felt that something was missing.[5] It seemed to him that sales potential was becoming more important than product quality. "We were working for the numbers, and we got the numbers. But I was confused by success, unhappy with success," said Chappell.[6] He later wrote, "I had made a real go of something I'd started. What more could I do in life except make more money? Where was the purpose and direction for the rest of my life?"[7] Following this line of thinking, Tom Chappell entered Harvard Divinity School.[8]

Sharpening the Company's Focus

The years that Chappell spent as a part-time divinity student gave him a new understanding of his role. "For the first time in my career, I had the language I needed to debate my bean-counters."[9] He realized that his company was his ministry: "I'm here to succeed . . . according to my principles."[10]

Tom's new mission statement reflected both business aspiration and social responsibility, spelling out guiding values for the company that included natural ingredients and high quality. It talked of respecting employees by providing meaningful work, as well as fair pay. Concern for the community and the world required that Tom's of Maine "be a profitable and successful company, while acting in a socially responsible manner."[11] The company began donating 10 percent of pretax profits to charities—from arts organizations and environmental groups to curbside recycling programs—and supported the Rainforest Alliance.

Tom's also urged its employees to work with charitable causes and allowed them to donate 5 percent of their work time to volunteer activities. Employees enthusiastically took advantage of the opportunity—when one employee began teaching art classes for emotionally disturbed children, nearly all the employees got involved.[12] Others worked in soup kitchens and homeless shelters.

The volunteer program required other employees to cover for absent volunteers for an equivalent of 20 days each month, but Colleen Myers, vice president of community life, called volunteer activities valuable to the company as well as the community. "After spending a few hours at a soup kitchen or a shelter, you're happy to have a job. It's a morale booster, and better morale translates pretty directly into better productivity."[13] Sometimes the company benefited even more directly: "The woman who headed up those art classes—she discovered she's a heck of a project manager. We found that out, too."[14]

Not all employee benefits were strictly psychological. The company offered flexible four-day scheduling and subsidized day care, designing even coffee breaks with employee preference in mind. Individual employees were helped to earn high school equivalency diplomas and to develop skills required for new positions.[15]

Even as product distribution expanded across the United States, Tom's marketing efforts remained low-key, according to Katie Shisler, vice president of marketing. "We just tell them our story," she said. "We tell them why we have such a loyal base of consumers who vote with their dollars every day. A number of trade accounts appreciate our social responsibility."[16] Tom Chappell agreed: "We're selling a lot more than toothpaste; we're selling a point of view—that nature is worth protecting."[17] He stuck by those notions even in the face of increased competition. Tom's prices were similar to those of national competitors for baking soda toothpaste, but 20 to 40 percent higher for deodorant and mouthwash. But Tom, unworried, believed that "[t]hat's not the way you're going to get market share—you're going to get it by being who you are."[18] He explained his philosophy: "If we try to act like commodities, act like a toothpaste, we give up our souls. Instead, we have to be peculiarly authentic in everything we do.[19] When you start doing that, customers are very aware of your difference," says Tom. "And they like the difference."[20]

Selling the Company

In 2006, Tom's of Maine entered into what Tom and Kate called a "partnership" with a global conglomerate, the Colgate-Palmolive Company. For approximately $100 million—or 84 percent of outstanding shares—they sold the company and retained a minority interest, with Tom staying on as CEO of Tom's of Maine as a free-standing division of Colgate.[21] The Chappells stated in a letter to employees and stakeholders that "after much soul-searching, and many conversations with our children and trusted advisors, we realized that we cannot meet this growing demand alone. We decided to seek a partner to help us. It's been a quest that we entered with trepidation and excitement because we wanted to find a company that would honor our values, and we were unwavering in our commitment to stay intact in Maine as Tom's of Maine."[22] Afterward, Chappell compared Colgate to a big Tom's of Maine: "I find that we have more in common than we have differences. They have an organization run by human beings, and they're very capable, savvy, and caring human beings."[23]

Tom's Future: A Different Kind of Company?

Tom's of Maine stresses the "common good" in everything and is passionately concerned about corporate, customer, product, community, environmental, and employee wellness. The firm uses the services of a wellness advisory council, provides wellness education, and practises stewardship by using natural, sustainable, and responsible ingredients, products, and packaging. In "doing well by doing good," Tom's has also been recognized as an exemplar for "common good" capitalism.[24]

In order to pass his knowledge on to others, Tom Chappell has authored two books—*The Soul of a Business: Managing for Profit and the Common Good* and *Managing Upside Down: Seven Intentions for Values-Centered Leadership*. He also created the Saltwater Institute, a non-profit organization providing training in the Seven Intentions:[25]

1. *Connect with goodness.* Non-work discussions with an upbeat spin usually draw people to common ground, away from hierarchical titles.

2. *Know thyself, be thyself.* Discovering and tapping people's passions, gifts, and strengths generates creative energy.

3. *Envision your destiny.* The company is better served if its efforts are steered by strengths, instead of following market whims.

4. *Seek counsel.* The journey is long, and assistance from others is absolutely necessary.

5. *Venture out.* The success of any business hinges on pushing value-enhanced products into the market.

6. *Assess.* Any idea must be regularly reviewed, and refined if necessary.

7. *Pass it on.* Since developing and incorporating values is a trial-and-error process, sharing ideas and soliciting feedback allows for future growth.[26]

Tom's of Maine achieved financial success while following its principles. But will the acquisition by a large, profit-seeking corporation make it hard to hold fast to those principles in the future? Will Tom's reputation for commitment to the environment and ethical behaviour be threatened in the large corporate environment, or can a little company from Maine teach a cosmetics giant a thing or two about corporate responsibility?

Discussion Questions

1. Does the Tom's of Maine experience prove that one can "do business with principles," or are there business realities that make it hard for others to copy this principled management model?

2. What examples and incidents from this brief history of Tom's of Maine illustrate how the personal ethics and values of founders can positively influence a firm and its culture as it deals with the challenges of start-up and growth?

3. What are the biggest threats that Tom's faces in its new life within Colgate's global corporate structure, and especially with respect to maintaining what Tom and Kate call "the character, spirit, and values of our company"?

4. FURTHER RESEARCH—Find news items reporting on what has happened at Tom's of Maine since being purchased by Colgate. Has the firm been able to operate with the ethics and independence that Tom and Kate had hoped for? Is the company starting to lose its way now that it's part of a global corporate giant?

VIDEO CASE 2

Workplace Misconduct Rising

Video Summary and Discussion

It is probably not that easy to take an accurate measure of the impacts of absenteeism and pilferage on corporate health against the background of the economic downturn. But CCH Inc., which conducts annual surveys in the field, says it remains a paramount concern. The latest survey put the absenteeism rate in the United States at an all-time high, and also found the number of offences, from resumé fraud to stealing office supplies, to be uncomfortably high. CCH called it "a troubling indication of a breakdown in workplace ethics—which costs companies money and reduces productivity."

It may sound or look harmless, and you could call it "office misconduct" if you must. But when CBS News correspondent Susan McGinnis researched this topic, it was dubbed "a disturbing trend to many experts and to the economy at large."

Needless to say, employees who engaged in illegitimate absenteeism appeared on the program in silhouette. Silhouette A could then talk freely about "an elderly parent being an excellent excuse." A fall down the stairs, he notes, is "two days off work—mandatory." Adds Silhouette B: "kidney stones—totally fail-safe. No one wants to know; no one needs to know. They hear 'kidney stones' and they start shifting workloads and sending out the get-well-soon cards."

Outfits like Phenix Investigations, the Ethics Resource Center, and the Society for Human Resource Management are making careers out of studying the problem.

The causes can stem from both sides, says Susan Meisinger of the Society for Human Resource Management. She pins employee misbehaviour on the reputations earned by corporate leaders of scandal-ridden companies such as Enron, Tyco, and their likes.

In Canada, employment candidates continue to lie about their pasts in an effort to secure their next job. Nearly a third of all job candidates in our unsteady economy continue to present falsehoods on their resumés. Employers unacquainted with these trends are in danger of making poor hiring decisions. And poor hiring decisions often contribute to employee turnover, which can be very costly to an organization.

According to a 2008 survey by CareerBuilder.ca, office misconduct is alive and well in Canada. Examples of such misconduct that Canadian workers have admitted to committing include: stealing from the office (28 percent), spreading a rumour about a co-worker (26 percent), snooping after hours (22 percent), lying about an academic background (9 percent), and taking credit for someone else's work (4 percent). The survey strongly suggests that a higher percentage of younger age groups commit such acts.

Workplace absenteeism also continues to rise in Canada according a recent Conference Board of Canada survey. The absenteeism rate has been increasing steadily in the first decade of the new century, rising to 6.6 days per full-time employee in 2008–09 from 5.7 days in 2000–01. The 6.6 figure represents the highest point since the Board began surveying employee absences 20 years ago.

The implications of absenteeism for organizations are significant in terms both of lost wages and productivity. The cost of absenteeism—defined as time off from work that is avoidable, habitual, and unscheduled—is estimated at 2.6 percent of payroll.

The more troubling issue, the Conference Board says, is that currently fewer than half of the 255 mid- to large-size organizations surveyed for its study even track absenteeism rates, and only 15 percent know the direct costs of absenteeism to their organizations.

Questions for Students

1. List categories of unethical workplace conduct and rate them in terms of seriousness.

2. What employee actions might be considered legal but not ethical?

3. Why do you think the workers in the video did not feel much or any guilt about their unethical actions? Try to reference the concept of ethics intensity in your answer.

4. How might you avoid getting trapped in unethical behaviour or ethical dilemmas like the ones posed in the video? You can use Management Smarts 4.1 to help with your answer.

Entrepreneurship and Small Business Management

LEARNING FROM OTHERS

The ACEs are flying high

Do you see yourself as a Bill Gates, a Heather Reisman, a Richard Branson, or a Frank Stronach? If you do, your local ACE team (Advancing Canadian Entrepreneurs) may be for you. Founded in 1987, this national not-for-profit organization challenges university and college students to "address economic, social and environmental

issues in their own entrepreneurial ventures and in their communities." Located at 50 campuses across Canada, there are over 60,000 individuals impacted by ACE projects, with more than 1,600 student leaders donating in excess of 260,000 volunteer hours.

In 2000, ACE developed a strategic alliance with Students in Free Enterprise (SIFE), an international non-profit group that works with student teams on campuses in over 40 countries. Through the alliance, ACE operates SIFE programs in which student teams led by faculty advisors are challenged to develop community outreach projects.

Courtesy ACE

There are many entrepreneurial success stories. For example, the 2010 SIFE Canada National Championship team from Ryerson University, a group of 120 students, dedicated thousands of volunteer hours in their local community and operated 47 community outreach projects that positively affected 4,500 people. The SIFE team from Niagara College, who were the Entrepreneurial National Champions, worked with over 300 international entrepreneurs from countries such as South Africa, Peru, and Brazil, developing their own entrepreneurial skills as they went overseas to work one-on-one with these businesses.

ACE also develops individual entrepreneurs. For Vincent Cheung, a winner of ACE's Student Entrepreneur of the Year Award, it has opened many doors. While a full-time student at the University of Toronto, Vincent owned and operated Shape Collage Inc., a digital media software company with an automatic photo collage-making software program. On winning the award, he said, "With the competitions finally done, the real work begins, and I hope that I can live up to the title." This award, sponsored by CIBC, supports budding entrepreneurs with $10,000. Are you an entrepreneur looking for opportunity?[1]

BENCHMARK Even if you don't go into business for yourself, having entrepreneurial skills will stand you in good stead in your career. More employers are expecting their managers to think like entrepreneurs and take calculated risks to result in good returns on investment. Surveying competitors, pouncing on unfilled niches in the market, and presenting a solid business case for new ventures will add value to your organization—and yourself.

Entrepreneurial Mindset

In the new economy, managers using conventional approaches are losing out to risk-taking entrepreneurs who move on innovative ideas others failed to see and who assertively act while others wait. We don't need to tell you that personal and organizational success will depend upon your adopting such an *entrepreneurial mindset*. Essentially, developing an entrepreneurial mindset is about learning to succeed in an unpredictable, dynamic world.

To help keep things in perspective, let's debunk some common myths about entrepreneurship.[2]

- *Entrepreneurs are born, not made.* Not true! Talent gained and enhanced by experience is a foundation for entrepreneurial success.

- *Entrepreneurs are gamblers.* Not true! Entrepreneurs are risk takers, but the risks are informed and calculated.

- *Money is the key to entrepreneurial success.* Not true! Money is no guarantee of success. There's a lot more to it than that; many entrepreneurs start with very little.

- *You have to be young to be an entrepreneur.* Not true! Age is no barrier to entrepreneurship; with age often come experience, contacts, and other useful resources.

- *You have to have a degree in business to be an entrepreneur.* Not true! You may not need a degree at all. Although a business degree is not necessary, it helps to study and understand business fundamentals.

Important for you to recognize as you develop an entrepreneur's mindset is that you will need to become a free thinker (along your journey, some might actually call you a dreamer). You must also learn to seek out difficult challenges and see them not as problems but as opportunities. You must learn to dedicate yourself to things of interest, and embark on quests of insight trying to find better, distinctive, or more efficient ways to do things. And, you must learn to be a troubleshooter, problem solver, and one who is willing to fail a few times before eventually winning.

Are you willing to join the ranks of the entrepreneurs? The tools and knowledge are available to anyone who wants to learn; Chapter 5 is ready for you. Remember, the secret is being willing to dream and willing to act. Are you willing?

❖ Get to Know Yourself Better

A question you might be asking yourself is, "Do I currently have the same orientation as an entrepreneur?" Not to worry: if you don't, there is time to change!

CHAPTER 5 STUDY QUESTIONS

- What is entrepreneurship?

- What is special about small businesses?

- How does one start a new venture?

VISUAL CHAPTER OVERVIEW

CHAPTER 5 ENTREPRENEURSHIP AND SMALL BUSINESS MANAGEMENT

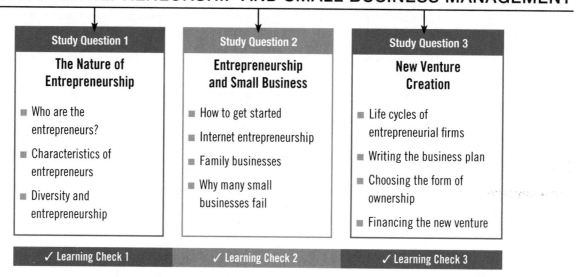

Study Question 1

The Nature of Entrepreneurship

- Who are the entrepreneurs?
- Characteristics of entrepreneurs
- Diversity and entrepreneurship

✓ Learning Check 1

Study Question 2

Entrepreneurship and Small Business

- How to get started
- Internet entrepreneurship
- Family businesses
- Why many small businesses fail

✓ Learning Check 2

Study Question 3

New Venture Creation

- Life cycles of entrepreneurial firms
- Writing the business plan
- Choosing the form of ownership
- Financing the new venture

✓ Learning Check 3

People with innovative ideas for new businesses don't always get the chance to turn them into reality. And a good percentage of them are women. Count Me In for Women's Economic Independence is trying to turn the tables and give female entrepreneurs a chance to get started. Co-founded by Nell Merlino (who also created Take Our Daughters to Work Day) and Iris Burnett, Count Me In provides "microcredit" loans in amounts from US$500 to US$10,000 to help women start and expand small businesses. Women qualify for the loans by a unique credit scoring system that doesn't hold against them things such as a divorce, time off to raise a family, or age—all things that might discourage conventional lenders. Merlino says: "Women own 38 percent of all businesses in this country, but still have far less access to capital than men because of today's process." Count Me In is out to change all that, and has many success stories to show.[3]

- Geneva Francais received a $1,500 loan from Count Me In to build storage shelves for her special cooking sauce "Geneva's Splash," brewed and bottled in her kitchen. Francais is a

65-year-old widow. She says: "A bank would not loan a woman money when she is 65 years old. It's as simple as that."

- Heather McCartney is married to a high school principal in New York. She received a US$5,000 loan to expand "Ethnic Edibles," her line of cookies and cookie cutters designed according to traditional African motifs. The money will be used for packaging and marketing.

Think about it. There is so much one can do with creativity and initiative. In fact, this is a chapter of examples. The goal is not only to inform but to better familiarize you with the nature of entrepreneurship, small business, and new venture creation. The objective is also to stimulate you to consider starting your own business, become your own boss, and make your own special contribution to society. What about it? Can we interest you in the world of entrepreneurship and small business?

THE NATURE OF ENTREPRENEURSHIP

Success in a highly competitive business environment depends on **entrepreneurship**. This term is used to describe strategic thinking and risk-taking behaviour that result in the creation of new opportunities. H. Wayne Huizenga, who started Waste Management with just $5,000 and who once owned Blockbuster Video and the Miami Dolphins NFL team, describes it this way: "An important part of being an entrepreneur is a gut instinct that allows you to believe in your heart that something will work even though everyone else says it will not. You say, 'I am going to make sure it works. I am going to go out there and make it happen.'"[4]

> **Entrepreneurship** is risk-taking behaviour that results in new opportunities.

> An **entrepreneur** is willing to pursue opportunities in situations others view as problems or threats.

WHO ARE THE ENTREPRENEURS?

An **entrepreneur** is a risk-taking individual who takes action to pursue opportunities others fail to recognize, or may even view as problems or threats. Business entrepreneurs start new ventures that bring to life new products or service ideas. Their stories are rich with ideas for all of us to consider. Although the people in the following examples are different, they share something in common. Each built a successful long-term business from good ideas and hard work.[5]

Want to start an airline? Richard Branson decided he would and called it Virgin Atlantic. His career began in his native England with a student literary magazine and small mail-order record business. Since then he's built "Virgin" into one of the world's most recognized brand names. Virgin Group is a business conglomerate employing some 25,000 people around the globe. It holds over 200 companies, including Virgin Mobile, Virgin Records, and even a space venture—Virgin Galactic. It's all very creative and ambitious—but that's Sir Richard. "I love to learn things I know little about," he says.

When Frank Stronach was 22, he left his native Austria to come to Montreal. With just a few hundred dollars, a suitcase, and an entrepreneurial willingness to work hard, he drew from his toolmaking know-how to build what is one of the world's largest automotive parts manufacturing companies. He did all of this by holding true to his vision of building a culture known as Fair Enterprise, which ensures the rights of employees, management, and investors to share in the profits they all help produce. Stronach wanted to give every employee a share of the company's profits, in a way making each of them a part-owner of the business with a stake in the company's success. It helped propel Magna to the world stage and enshrine Stronach as one of Canada's premier entrepreneurs.[6]

(AP Photo/Susan Montoya Bryan)

Courtesy Frank Stronach

Heather Reisman was born in Montreal and received her university education at McGill University. Early in her career, she co-founded Paradigm Consulting, a strategy and change-management firm. Paradigm was the world's first strategic change consultancy and helped develop many organizational change strategies still in use today. She left Paradigm to take on the challenge of being president of Cott Corporation. During her time at the helm, Cott grew from a Canadian-based regional bottler to become the world's largest retailer-branded beverage supplier. In 1996, Reisman returned to her entrepreneurial roots and launched Indigo Books & Music Inc. Using a strong growth and change strategy, Indigo is now the largest book retailer in Canada, operating bookstores all across the country.[7]

Tim Horton opened his first doughnut and coffee store in 1964 in Hamilton, Ontario. Ron Joyce, a former police constable, saw through a newspaper advertisement that the NHL hockey player was looking for help in running his store. The two teamed up and Joyce proceeded to take out a $10,000 loan from the credit union to invest in the store. In 1965, Joyce took over the original Tim Hortons store with aspirations of expanding it to include 10 outlets. He acquired the whole operation in 1976 and, drawing on unique products such as Timbits, creative marketing strategies like "Roll up the Rim," and a partnership with Dave Thomas of Wendy's, Joyce grew the company into Canada's largest national chain of coffee and doughnut shops.[8]

In 1973, Anita Roddick was a 33-year-old housewife looking for a way to support herself and her two children. She spotted an opportunity for natural-based skin and health care products, and started mixing and selling them from a small shop in Brighton, England. The Body Shop has grown to some 2,500 outlets in 61 countries, selling a product every half-second to one of its 86 million customers. Known for her commitment to human rights, the environment, and economic development, Dame Anita once said: "If you think you're too small to have an impact, try going to bed with a mosquito." Following her death in 2007, then British Prime Minister Gordon Brown paid tribute to Dame Anita, calling her "one of the country's true pioneers." He said: "She campaigned for green issues for many years before it became fashionable to do so and inspired millions to the cause by bringing sustainable products to a mass market."[9]

CHARACTERISTICS OF ENTREPRENEURS

A common image of an entrepreneur is as the founder of a new business enterprise that achieves large-scale success, like the ones just mentioned. But entrepreneurs also operate on a smaller and less public scale. Those who take the risk of buying a local McDonald's or Harvey's hamburger franchise, opening a small retail shop, or going into a self-employed service business are also entrepreneurs. Similarly, anyone who assumes responsibility for introducing a new product or change in operations within an organization is also demonstrating the qualities of entrepreneurship.

Research suggests that entrepreneurs tend to share certain *attitudes and personal characteristics*. The general profile is of an individual who is very self-confident, determined, resilient, adaptable, and driven by excellence.[10] You should be able to identify these attributes in the prior examples. As shown in Figure 5.1, typical personality traits and characteristics of entrepreneurs include the following.[11]

- *Internal locus of control:* Entrepreneurs believe that they are in control of their own destiny; they are self-directing and like autonomy.

- *High energy level:* Entrepreneurs are persistent, hard working, and willing to exert extraordinary efforts to succeed.

- *High need for achievement:* Entrepreneurs are motivated to accomplish challenging goals; they thrive on performance feedback.

- *Tolerance for ambiguity:* Entrepreneurs are risk takers; they tolerate situations with high degrees of uncertainty.

- *Self-confidence:* Entrepreneurs feel competent, believe in themselves, and are willing to make decisions.

- *Passion and action orientation:* Entrepreneurs try to act ahead of problems; they want to get things done and not waste valuable time.

- *Self-reliance and desire for independence:* Entrepreneurs want independence; they are self-reliant; they want to be their own bosses, not work for others.

- *Flexibility:* Entrepreneurs are willing to admit problems and errors, and are willing to change a course of action when plans aren't working.

Entrepreneurs also tend to have unique backgrounds and personal experiences.[12] *Childhood experiences and family environment* seem to make a difference. Evidence links entrepreneurs with parents who were entrepreneurial and self-employed. And entrepreneurs are often raised in families that encourage responsibility, initiative, and independence. Another issue is *career or work history*. Entrepreneurs who try one venture often go on to others. Prior work experience in the business area or industry is helpful.

Entrepreneurs also tend to emerge during certain *windows of career opportunity*. Most start their businesses between the ages of 22 and 45, an age spread that seems to allow for risk taking. However, age shouldn't be viewed as a barrier. When Tony DeSio was 50, he founded the Mail Boxes Etc. chain. He sold it for US$300 million when he was 67. Within a year he launched PixArts, another franchise chain based on photography and art.[13]

Figure 5.1 Personality traits and characteristics of entrepreneurs.

Finally, a report in the *Harvard Business Review* suggests that entrepreneurs may have unique and *deeply embedded life interests*. The article describes entrepreneurs as having strong interests in creative production: enjoying project initiation, working with the unknown, and finding unconventional solutions. They also have strong interests in enterprise control: finding enjoyment from running things. The combination of creative production and enterprise control is characteristic of people who want to start things and move things toward a goal.[14]

Undoubtedly, entrepreneurs seek independence and the sense of mastery that comes with success. That seems to keep driving Tony DeSio from the earlier example. When asked by a reporter what he liked most about entrepreneurship, he replied: "Being able to make decisions without having to go through layers of corporate hierarchy—just being a master of your own destiny."

DIVERSITY AND ENTREPRENEURSHIP

When economists speak about entrepreneurs, they differentiate between those who are driven by the quest for new opportunities and those who are driven by absolute need.[15] Those in the latter group pursue **necessity-based entrepreneurship**; they start new ventures because they have few or no other employment and career options. Sometimes these are women and members of visible minorities who have suffered the "glass ceiling" effect and have found career doors closed.

Necessity-based entrepreneurship takes place because other employment options don't exist.

Entrepreneurship offers women and members of visible minorities opportunities to strike out on their own and gain economic independence, providing a pathway for career success that may be blocked otherwise.[16] According to Statistics Canada, there are more than 821,000 women entrepreneurs in Canada and growing; the number of women who are self-employed rose at a rate of over 8 percent annually. Women entrepreneurs are increasing in numbers everywhere: they make up 38 percent of the self-employed Aboriginal population, 45 percent of ownership of Canadian small and medium enterprises (SMEs), and 31-percent ownership of both knowledge-based industry firms and manufacturing firms.[17]

CANADIAN MANAGERS
Dreaming Big Dreams

Courtesy Thomas Benjoe

The dream of one day operating your own business is enticing for many Aboriginal youths, but becoming your own boss has its challenges. For most, a lack of business training is a large obstacle in the way of developing good ideas. With the support of the Aboriginal Youth Entrepreneurship Camp run by First Nations University of Canada, students gain necessary business skills and help to turn their dreams into reality. Aboriginal students in Grades 11 and 12 attend a six-day camp where they learn about marketing, advertising, preparing cash flow projections, and creating a new business plan. "It gives students a better heads up into what has become the fastest growing market out there for First Nations people," said Thomas Benjoe, coordinator with the Entrepreneurship Camp. "We have businesses opening up everywhere. It is growing at a pretty good rate for Saskatchewan, so we want to make sure our First Nations people are getting those skills they need in order to be successful."

A 2005 report by Industry Canada shows that entrepreneurship is opening business doors for visible minorities in Canada.[18] In that year, SMEs owned by visible minorities employed more than 500,000 people and generated revenues of more than $48.5 billion, an important contribution to Canada's economy. About 7 percent of Canada's 1.5 million SMEs were owned by visible minorities, and the percentage is growing, as this group is now entering the SME marketplace at more than one and a half times the rate per year of other entrepreneurs. While most heavily concentrated in the service-based industries, the minority-owned SMEs are also twice as likely to be in a knowledge-based industry and are more likely to invest in research and development than are other SMEs.

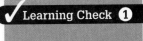

BE SURE YOU CAN

• define *entrepreneurship* • list key personal characteristics of entrepreneurs • explain the influence of background and experience on entrepreneurs • define necessity-based entrepreneurship • discuss motivations for entrepreneurship by women and minorities

Entrepreneurship and Small Business

Industry Canada defines a **small business** as one with 100 or fewer employees, and almost 98 percent of Canadian businesses fall into this category. The small business sector is very important in most nations because small businesses offer major economic advantages. In Canada, for example, they employ 5 million workers or 48 percent of the workforce. Small businesses in Canada spent close to $4 billion on research and development (R&D), spending a larger percentage of their revenue on R&D than larger firms.[19] Smaller businesses are prevalent in the service and retailing sectors of the economy. Higher costs of entry make them less common in other industries, such as manufacturing and transportation.

A **small business** has fewer than 100 employees, is independently owned and operated, and does not dominate its industry.

HOW TO GET STARTED

There are many reasons why entrepreneurs launch their own small businesses. One study reports the following motivations: #1 wanting to be your own boss and control your future; #2 going to work for a family-owned business; and #3 seeking to fulfill a dream.[20] Once a decision is made to go the small business route, the most common ways to get involved are start one, buy an existing one, or buy and run a **franchise**—where a business owner sells to another the right to operate the same business in another location. A franchise, such as Subway, Tim Hortons, or Pizza Pizza, runs under the original owner's business name and guidance. In return, the franchise parent receives a share of income or a flat fee from the franchisee.

A **franchise** is a form of business where one business owner sells to another the right to operate the same business in another location.

INTERNET ENTREPRENEURSHIP

Have you started a "dot-com" today? The Internet creates an array of entrepreneurial possibilities. Just take a look at the action on eBay and imagine how many people are now running small trading businesses from their homes.

The Small Business Administration (SBA) says that some 85 percent of small firms are already conducting business over the Internet.[21] Many of these firms are existing firms that modified traditional ways to pursue new Internet-driven opportunities. For others, the old ways of operating from a bricks-and-mortar retail establishment have given way to entirely on-line business activities. That's what happened to Rod Spencer and his S&S Sportscards store in Worthington, Ohio. He closed his store, not because business was bad; it was really good. But the nature of the business was shifting into cyberspace. When sales over the Internet became much greater than in-store sales, Spencer decided to follow the world of e-commerce. He now works from his own home with a computer and high-speed Internet connection. This saves the cost of renting retail space and hiring store employees. "I can do less business overall," he says, "to make a higher profit."[22]

FAMILY BUSINESSES

A **family business** is owned and controlled by members of a family.

Family businesses, ones owned and financially controlled by family members, represent the largest percentage of businesses operating worldwide. The Family Firm Institute reports that family businesses account for 78 percent of new jobs created in the United States and provide 60 percent of that nation's employment.[23]

REAL ETHICS

Social Entrepreneurship in Action

Social entrepreneurs identify and solve social problems on a local and large scale. They act as social change agents for societies by seizing opportunity to create a better world.

Andrew Mawson made such a mark with his social entrepreneurship that he was made a Lord by the former British Prime Minister, Tony Blair. Mawson came to understand what it takes to make a community work: how a merchant relates to the school teacher and the hospital relies on the business environment. He was the change agent who set up the Bromley by Bow Centre that now runs a large number of community projects ranging from creating jobs, to helping raise individual hope, to supporting people as they transform their lives. By creating an enterprising community, Mawson has helped build dreams.

Mary Gordon is recognized internationally as an educator, child advocate and social entrepreneur. Gordon has created groundbreaking programs teaching children how to relate to others. Her organization, Roots of Empathy, designs classroom empathy curricula with the goal being to develop more respectful and caring relationships while also reducing bullying and aggression. Gordon was the first female Canadian Ashoka Fellow, which identifies her as a select member of an international circle of social entrepreneurs.

Muhammad Yunus, a Bangladeshi economist and Nobel Peace Prize laureate has harnessed the power of free markets to help eradicate poverty. After visiting a rural village on a university trip in the 1980s, he and his students thought about what they might do to help poor people's existence. One of his ideas has had a great impact. Yunus developed the concept of microcredit, an innovative banking program that provides poor people—primarily women—with small loans to start businesses. In 1983, he formed Grameen Bank or "Village" Bank and started giving out small loans; this economic revolution, which has now gone worldwide, has helped lift millions of families out of poverty.

YOU DECIDE

According to Ashoka International, a group designed to create global change-makers, "Social entrepreneurs often seem to be possessed by their ideas, committing their lives to changing the direction of their field. They are both visionaries and ultimate realists, concerned with the practical implementation of their vision above all else." Might this be a career for you?

Family businesses must solve the same problems as other small or large businesses—meeting the challenges of strategy, competitive advantage, and operational excellence. When everything goes right, the family firm is almost an ideal situation—everyone working together, sharing values and a common goal, and knowing that what they do benefits the family. But it doesn't always work out this way—or stay this way, as a business changes hands over successive generations. Indeed, family businesses often face quite unique problems.

"Okay, Dad, so he's your brother. But does that mean we have to put up with inferior work and an erratic schedule that we would never tolerate from anyone else in the business?"[24] This complaint introduces a problem that can all too often set the stage for failure in a family business: the **family business feud**. Simply put, members of the controlling family get into disagreements about work responsibilities, business strategy, operating approaches, finances, or other matters. The example is indicative of an intergenerational problem, but the feud can be between spouses, among siblings, or between parents and children. It really doesn't matter. Unless family disagreements are resolved to the benefit of the business itself, the firm will have difficulty surviving in a highly competitive environment.

> A **family business feud** occurs when family members have major disagreements over how the business should be run.

Another common problem faced by family businesses is the **succession problem**—transferring leadership from one generation to the next. A survey of small and mid-sized family businesses indicated that 66 percent planned on keeping the business within the family. But the management question is: how will the assets be distributed and who will run the business when the current head leaves? Although this problem is not specific to the small firm, it is especially significant in the family business context. A family business that has been in operation for some time is often a source of both business momentum and financial wealth. Ideally, both are maintained in the succession process. But data on succession are eye-opening. About 30 percent of family firms survive to the second generation; only 12 percent survive to the third; and only 3 percent are expected to survive beyond that.[25]

> The **succession problem** is the issue of who will run the business when the current head leaves.

Business advisors recommend a **succession plan**—a formal statement that describes how the leadership transition and related financial matters will be handled when the time for changeover arrives. A succession plan should include at least procedures for choosing or designating the firm's new leadership, legal aspects of any ownership transfer, and financial and estate plans relating to the transfer. The foundations for effective implementation of a succession plan are set up well ahead of the need to use it. The plan should be shared and understood by all affected by it. The chosen successor should be prepared, through experience and training, to perform the new role when needed.

> A **succession plan** describes how the leadership transition and related financial matters will be handled.

WHY MANY SMALL BUSINESSES FAIL

Small businesses have a high failure rate—one high enough to be intimidating. The SBA reports that as many as 60 to 80 percent of new businesses fail in their first five years of operation.[26] Part of this is a "counting" issue—the SBA counts as a "failure" any business that closes, whether it is because of the death or retirement of an owner, sale to someone else, or the inability to earn a profit.[27] Nevertheless, the fact remains: a lot of small business start-ups don't make it. And as shown in Figure 5.2, most of the failures are the result of bad judgement and management mistakes of several types.[28]

- *Lack of experience*—not having sufficient know-how to run a business in the chosen market or area.

- *Lack of expertise*—not having expertise in the essentials of business operations, including finance, purchasing, selling, and production.

- *Lack of strategy and strategic leadership*—not taking the time to craft a vision and mission, nor to formulate and properly implement a strategy.

- *Poor financial control*—not keeping track of the numbers, and failure to control business finances.

- *Growing too fast*—not taking the time to consolidate a position, fine-tune the organization, and systematically meet the challenges of growth.

- *Insufficient commitment*—not devoting enough time to the requirements of running a competitive business.

- *Ethical failure*—falling prey to the temptations of fraud, deception, and embezzlement.

Figure 5.2 Eight reasons why many small businesses fail.

✔ Learning Check ❷ **BE SURE YOU CAN**

- give the Industry Canada definition of small business • illustrate opportunities for entrepreneurship on the Internet • discuss the succession problem in family-owned businesses and possible ways to deal with it • list several reasons why many small businesses fail

NEW VENTURE CREATION

Whether your interest is low-tech or high-tech, on-line or off-line, opportunities for new ventures are always there for the true entrepreneur. To pursue entrepreneurship and start a new business, you need good ideas and the courage to give them a chance. But you must also be prepared to meet and master the test of strategy and competitive advantage. Can you identify a market niche that is being missed by other established firms? Can you identify a new market that has not yet been discovered by existing firms? Can you generate **first-mover advantage** by exploiting a niche or entering a market before competitors? These are among the questions that entrepreneurs must ask and answer in the process of beginning a new venture.

A **first-mover advantage** comes from being first to exploit a niche or enter a market.

LIFE CYCLES OF ENTREPRENEURIAL FIRMS

Figure 5.3 describes the stages common to the life cycles of entrepreneurial companies. It shows the relatively predictable progression of the small business. The firm begins with the *birth stage—* where the entrepreneur struggles to get the new venture established and survive long enough to test the viability of the underlying business model in the marketplace. The firm then passes into the *breakthrough stage—*where the business model begins to work well, growth is experienced, and the complexity of managing the business operation expands significantly. Next comes the *maturity stage—*where the entrepreneur experiences the advantages of market success and financial stability, while also facing the continuing management challenge of remaining competitive in a changing environment.

Entrepreneurs must often deal with substantial control and management dilemmas when their firms experience growth, including possible diversification or global expansion. They encounter a variation of the succession problem described earlier for family businesses. This time, the problem is transition from entrepreneurial leadership to professional strategic leadership. The former brings the venture into being and sees it through the early stages of life; the latter manages and leads the venture into maturity as an ever-evolving and perhaps still-growing corporate enterprise. If the entrepreneur is incapable of meeting or unwilling to meet the firm's strategic leadership needs in later life-cycle stages, continued business survival and success may well depend on the business being sold, or management control being passed to professionals.

Figure 5.3 Stages in the life cycle of an entrepreneurial firm.

WRITING THE BUSINESS PLAN

When people start new businesses or even start new units within existing ones, they can benefit from a good **business plan**. This plan describes the details needed to obtain start-up financing and operate a new business.[29] Banks and other financiers want to see a business plan before they loan money or invest in a new venture; senior managers want to see a business plan before they allocate scarce organizational resources to support a new entrepreneurial project. There's good reason for this. The detailed thinking required to prepare a business plan can contribute to the success of the new initiative. It forces the entrepreneur to think through important issues and challenges before starting out. Importantly, the detailed thinking required to prepare a business plan can contribute to the success of the new initiative. As an old adage states, "If you fail to plan, you plan to fail."

A **business plan** describes the direction for a new business and the financing needed to operate it.

Or, in the case of Rootcellar Village Green Grocer, plan well and then plan again! Launched in February 2008 in Victoria, B.C., Rootcellar had a strong business plan that pointed them in the right direction. Within the first year, their 450-square-metre (5,000-square-foot) store won them a number of awards including the Business Development Bank of Canada's 2009 Young Entrepreneurs of the Year Award. After Rootcellar exceeded projected sales in its first year by 430 percent, owner Daisy Orser said, "our business plan was tossed three months in. At this point, we expected to have 15 employees." The second year saw sales triple again and they now have 57 people working for them![30]

Although there is no single template for a successful business plan, there is general agreement on the framework presented in Management Smarts 5.1. Every business plan should have an executive summary, cover certain business fundamentals, be well organized with headings and easy to read, and run no more than about 20 pages in length. In addition to advice you find in books and magazines, there are many on-line resources available to assist in the development of a business plan.[31]

5.1 MANAGEMENT SMARTS
What to include in a business plan

- *Executive summary*—overview of the business purpose and highlight of key elements of the plan.

- *Industry analysis*—nature of the industry, including economic trends, important legal or regulatory issues, and potential risks.

- *Company description*—mission, owners, and legal form.

- *Products and services description*—major goods or services, with competitive uniqueness.

- *Market description*—size of market, competitor strengths and weaknesses, five-year sales goals.

- *Marketing strategy*—product characteristics, distribution, promotion, pricing, and market research.

- *Operations description*—manufacturing or service methods, supplies and suppliers, and control procedures.

- *Staffing description*—management and staffing skills needed and available, compensation, and human resource systems.

- *Financial projection*—cash flow projections for one to five years, break-even points, and phased investment capital.

- *Capital needs*—amount of funds needed to run the business, amount available and amount requested from new sources.

- *Milestones*—a timetable of dates showing when key stages of the new venture will be completed.

CHOOSING THE FORM OF OWNERSHIP

One of the important planning choices that must be made in starting a new venture is the legal form of ownership. There are a number of alternatives, and the choice among them requires careful consideration of their respective advantages and disadvantages. Briefly, the ownership forms include the following:

A **sole proprietorship** is simply an individual or a married couple pursuing business for a profit. This does not involve incorporation. One does business, for example, under a personal name, such as "Aalya Bardai Designs." A sole proprietorship is simple to start, run, and terminate, and it is the most common form of small business ownership in Canada. However, the business owner is personally liable for business debts and claims.

A **partnership** is formed when two or more people agree to contribute resources to start and operate a business together. It is usually backed by a legal and written partnership agreement. Business partners agree on the contribution of resources and skills to the new venture, and on the sharing of profits and losses. In a *general partnership*, the simplest and most common form, they also share management responsibilities. A *limited partnership* consists of a general partner and one or more "limited" partners who do not participate in day-to-day business management. They share in the profits, but their losses are limited to the amount of their investment. A *limited liability partnership*, common among professionals such as accountants and lawyers, limits the liability of one partner for the negligence of another.

A **corporation**, commonly identified by the "Inc." designation in a name, is a legal entity that is chartered by the government and exists separately from its owners. The corporation can be for-profit, such as Microsoft Inc., or non-profit, such as Count Me In. The corporate form offers two major advantages: (1) it grants the organization certain legal rights (e.g., to engage in contracts), and (2) the corporation becomes responsible for its own liabilities. This separates the owners from personal liability and gives the firm a life of its own that can extend beyond that of its owners. The disadvantage of incorporation rests largely with the cost of incorporating and the complexity of the documentation required to operate an incorporated business.

Recently, the **limited liability corporation**, or LLC, has gained popularity. A limited liability corporation combines the advantages of the other forms—sole proprietorship, partnership, and corporation. For liability purposes, it functions like a corporation, protecting the assets of owners against claims made against the company. For tax purposes, it functions as a partnership in the case of multiple owners, and as a sole proprietorship in the case of a single owner.

A **sole proprietorship** is a form of business where an individual pursues a profit.

A **partnership** is a form of business where two or more people agree to contribute resources to start and operate a business together.

A **corporation** is a legal entity that exists separately from its owners.

A **limited liability corporation** is a hybrid business form combining advantages of the sole proprietorship, partnership, and corporation.

FINANCING THE NEW VENTURE

Starting a new venture takes money, and that money often must be raised. Realistically speaking, the cost of a new business start-up can easily exceed the amount a would-be entrepreneur has available from personal sources.

There are two major ways an entrepreneur can obtain outside financing for a new venture. **Debt financing** involves going into debt by borrowing money from another person, bank, or financial institution. This loan must be paid back over time, with interest. It also requires collateral that pledges business assets or personal assets, such as a home, to secure the loan in case of default. **Equity financing** involves giving ownership shares in the business to outsiders in return for their cash investments. This money does not need to be paid back. It is an investment, and the investor assumes the risk for potential gains and losses. In return for taking that risk, the equity investor gains some proportionate ownership control.

Debt financing involves borrowing money that must be repaid over time, with interest.

Equity financing involves exchanging ownership shares for outside investment monies.

GOING GLOBAL

FOSTERING ENTREPRENEURSHIP IN ISRAEL

With the highest number of start-ups per capita, Israel is one of the world's leading entrepreneurship centres. It is recognized as a country that focuses heavily on R&D (Israel has the highest percentage of GDP that goes to R&D), and the world's top technology companies regularly shop for ideas and for companies to buy there. What makes Israel so innovative and entrepreneurial? The book *Start-Up Nation* lists the close proximity of creative businesses, universities, and start-up firms, as well as a strong supplier support system, skilled workers, and venture capital (per capita more than 2.5 times that of the United States and 30 times that of Europe). It is also due to Israel's culture being "built on a rich stew of aggressiveness and team orientation, on isolation and connectedness, and on being small and aiming big." Can Canada develop this kind of entrepreneurial spirit and know-how?

Venture capitalists make large investments in new ventures in return for an equity stake in the business.

An initial public offering, or IPO, is an initial selling of shares of stock to the public at large.

Equity financing is usually obtained from **venture capitalists**, companies and individuals that make investments in new ventures in return for an equity stake in the business. Most venture capitalists tend to focus on relatively large investments of $1 million or more, and they usually take a management role, such as a board of directors' seat, in order to oversee business growth. The hope is that a fast-growing firm will gain a solid market base and either be sold at a profit to another firm or become a candidate for an **initial public offering**. This "IPO" is when shares of stock in the business are first sold to the public and then begin trading on a major stock exchange. When an IPO is successful and the share prices are bid up by the market, the original investments of the venture capitalist and entrepreneur rise in value. The anticipation of such return on investment is a large part of the venture capitalist's motivation; indeed, it is the business model of the venture capitalist.

An angel investor is a wealthy individual willing to invest in a new venture in return for equity in a new venture.

When large amounts of venture capital aren't available to the entrepreneur, another important financing option is the **angel investor**. This is a wealthy individual who is willing to make an investment in return for equity in a new venture. Angel investors are especially common and helpful in the very early start-up stage. Their presence can raise investor confidence and help attract additional venture funding that would otherwise not be available. For example, when Liz Cobb wanted to start her sales compensation firm, Incentive Systems, she contacted 15 to 20 venture capital firms. She was interviewed by 10 and turned down by all of them. After she located US$250,000 from two angel investors, the venture capital firms got interested again. She was able to obtain her first US$2 million in financing and has since built the firm into a 70-plus employee business.[32]

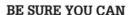 **Learning Check 3**

BE SURE YOU CAN

• explain the concept of first-mover advantage • illustrate the life cycle of an entrepreneurial firm • identify the major elements in a business plan • differentiate sole proprietorship, partnership, and corporation • differentiate debt financing and equity financing • explain the roles of venture capitalists and angel investors in new venture financing

MANAGEMENT LEARNING REVIEW

STUDY QUESTIONS SUMMARY

1. What is entrepreneurship?

- Entrepreneurship is risk-taking behaviour that results in the creation of new opportunities.

- An entrepreneur takes risks to pursue opportunities in situations that others may view as threats.

- Entrepreneurs tend to be creative people who are self-confident, determined, resilient, adaptable, and driven to excel; they like to be masters of their own destinies.

- Women and members of visible minorities are well represented among entrepreneurs, with some being driven by necessity or the lack of alternative career options.

FOR DISCUSSION: Do successful local entrepreneurs in your region fit the personality profile discussed in this chapter?

2. What is special about small businesses?

- Entrepreneurship results in the founding of many small businesses that offer job creation and other benefits to economies.

- The Internet has opened a whole new array of entrepreneurial possibilities for small businesses.

- Family businesses, ones owned and financially controlled by family members, represent the largest percentage of businesses operating worldwide; they sometimes have succession problems.

- Small businesses have a high failure rate, with as many as 60 to 80 percent failing within five years; many failures are the result of poor management.

FOR DISCUSSION: What is the business failure rate in your area? Whom would you have to contact to answer this question?

3. How does one start a new venture?

- Entrepreneurial firms tend to follow the life-cycle stages of birth, breakthrough, and maturity, with each stage offering different management challenges.

- A new start-up should be guided by a good business plan that describes the intended nature of the business, how it will operate, and how financing will be obtained.

- An important choice is the form of business ownership, with the proprietorship, corporate, and limited liability forms offering different advantages and disadvantages.

- Two basic ways of financing a new venture are through debt financing—by taking loans—and equity financing—exchanging ownership shares in return for outside investment.

- Venture capitalists pool capital and invest in new ventures in return for equity in the business; an angel investor is a wealthy individual who invests money in return for equity in a new venture.

FOR DISCUSSION: What venture capital groups or angel networks operate in your region?

KEY TERMS

angel investor, 152
business plan, 149
corporation, 151
debt financing, 151
entrepreneur, 141
entrepreneurship, 141
equity financing, 151
family business, 146
family business feud, 147
first-mover advantage, 148
franchise, 145
initial public offering, 152
limited liability corporation, 151
necessity-based
     entrepreneurship, 144
partnership, 151
small business, 145
sole proprietorship, 151
succession plan, 147
succession problem, 147
venture capitalists, 152

SELF-TEST

Multiple-Choice Questions

1. _____ is one of the personality characteristics commonly found among entrepreneurs.

     (a) External locus of control   (b) Inflexibility   (c) Self-confidence   (d) Low self-reliance

2. When an entrepreneur is comfortable with uncertainty and willing to take risks, these are indicators of someone with a(n) _____.

    (a) high tolerance for ambiguity   (b) internal locus of control   (c) need for achievement   (d) action orientation

3. Almost _____ percent of Canadian businesses meet the definition of "small business" used by the Industry Canada.

    (a) 48   (b) 98   (c) 78   (d) 85

4. When a business owner sells to another person the right to operate that business in another location, this is a _____.

    (a) conglomerate   (b) franchise   (c) joint venture   (d) limited partnership

5. A small business owner who is concerned about passing the business on to heirs after retirement or death should prepare a formal _____ plan.

    (a) retirement   (b) succession   (c) franchising   (d) liquidation

6. Among the most common reasons that new small business start-ups fail is_____.

    (a) lack of business expertise   (b) strict financial controls   (c) slow growth   (d) high ethical standards

7. When a new business is quick to capture a market niche before competitors, this is called _____.

    (a) intrapreneurship   (b) an initial public offering   (c) succession planning   (d) first-mover advantage

8. When a small business is just starting, the business owner is typically struggling to _____.

    (a) gain acceptance in the marketplace   (b) find partners for expansion   (c) prepare an initial public offering   (d) bring professional skills into the management team

9. A venture capitalist who receives an ownership share in return for investing in a new business is providing _____ financing.

    (a) debt   (b) equity   (c) corporate   (d) partnership

10. In _____ financing, the business owner borrows money as a loan that must eventually be repaid, along with agreed-upon interest to the lender.

    (a) debt   (b) equity   (c) partnership   (d) limited

11. _____ take ownership shares in a new venture in return for providing the entrepreneur with critical start-up funds.

    (a) Business incubators   (b) Angel investors   (c) Franchisees   (d) Intrapreneurs

12. Among the forms of small business ownership, a _____ protects the owners from any personal liabilities for business losses.

    (a) sole proprietorship   (b) franchise   (c) limited partnership   (d) corporation

13. The first component of a good business plan is usually _____.

    (a) an industry analysis   (b) a marketing strategy   (c) an executive summary   (d) a set of milestones

14. Current trends in small business ownership in Canada would most likely show that _____.

    (a) the numbers of women- and minority-owned businesses are declining   (b) the majority of small businesses conduct some business by Internet   (c) large businesses create more jobs than small businesses   (d) very few small businesses engage in international import/export activities

15. If a new venture has reached the point where it is pursuing an IPO, the firm is most likely _____.

    (a) going into bankruptcy   (b) trying to find an angel investor   (c) filing legal documents to become an LLC   (d) successful enough that the public at large will buy its shares

Short-Response Questions

16. What is the relationship between diversity and entrepreneurship?

17. What are the major stages in the life cycle of an entrepreneurial firm, and what are the management challenges at each stage?

18. What are the advantages of the limited partnership form of small business ownership?

19. What is the difference, if any, between a venture capitalist and an angel investor?

Application Question

20. Assume for the moment that you have a great idea for a potential Internet-based start-up business. When you discuss the idea with a friend, she advises you to be very careful to tie your business idea to potential customers and then describe it well in a business plan. "After all," she says, "you won't succeed without customers, and you'll never get a chance to succeed if you can't attract financial backers through a good business plan." With these words to the wise, you proceed. What questions will you ask and answer to ensure that you are customer-focused in this business? What are the major areas that you would address in writing your initial business plan?

MANAGEMENT SKILLS AND COMPETENCIES

SELF-ASSESSMENT

Back to Yourself: Entrepreneurial Mindset

If you are wondering whether you have an entrepreneurial spirit inside of you waiting to break out, take the time to do this self-assessment. This assessment compares your characteristics to those of typical entrepreneurs. Find out if you have an Anita Roddick, Steve Jobs, Heather Reisman or Mark Zuckerberg hidden within!

Further Relection: Entrepreneurship Orientation

Instructions:

Answer the following questions.

1. What portion of your university expenses did you earn (or are you earning)?
    (a) 50% or more
    (b) less than 50%
    (c) none

2. In university, your academic performance was/is
    (a) above average.
    (b) average.
    (c) below average.

3. What is your basic reason for considering opening a business?
    (a) I want to make money.
    (b) I want to control my own destiny.
    (c) I hate the frustration of working for someone else.

4. Which phrase best describes your attitude toward work?
    (a) I can keep going as long as I need to; I don't mind working for something I want.
    (b) I can work hard for a while, but when I've had enough, I quit.
    (c) Hard work really doesn't get you anywhere.

5. How would you rate your organizing skills?
    (a) super-organized
    (b) above average
    (c) average
    (d) I do well if I can find half the things I look for.

6. You are primarily a(n)
    (a) optimist.
    (b) pessimist.
    (c) neither.

7. You are faced with a challenging problem. As you work, you realize you are stuck. You will most likely
    (a) give up.
    (b) ask for help.
    (c) keep plugging; you'll figure it out.

8. You are playing a game with a group of friends. You are most interested in
    (a) winning.
    (b) playing well.
    (c) making sure that everyone has a good time.
    (d) cheating as much as possible.

9. How would you describe your feelings toward failure?
    (a) Fear of failure paralyzes me.
    (b) Failure can be a good learning experience.
    (c) Knowing that I might fail motivates me to work even harder.
    (d) "Damn the torpedoes! Full speed ahead."

10. Which phrase best describes you?
    (a) I need constant encouragement to get anything done.
    (b) If someone gets me started, I can keep going.
    (c) I am energetic and hard-working—a self-starter.

11. Which bet would you most likely accept?
    (a) a wager on a dog race
    (b) a wager on a racquetball game in which you play an opponent
    (c) Neither. I never make wagers.

12. At the Kentucky Derby, you would bet on
   (a) the 100-to-1 long shot.
   (b) the odds-on favourite.
   (c) the 3-to-1 shot.
   (d) none of the above.

Scoring

Give yourself 10 points for each of the following answers: 1a, 2a, 3c, 4a, 5a, 6a, 7c, 8a, 9c, 10c, 11b, 12c; total the scores and enter the results here [I = ___]. Give yourself 8 points for each of the following answers: 3b, 8b, 9b; total the scores and enter the results here [II = ___]. Give yourself 6 points for each of the following answers; 2b, 5b; total the scores and enter the results here [III = ___]. Give yourself 5 points for this answer: 1b; enter the result here [IV = ___]. Give yourself 4 points for this answer: 5c; enter the result here [V = ___]. Give yourself 2 points for each of the following answers: 2c, 3a, 4b, 6c, 9d, 10b, 11a, 12b; total the scores and enter the results here [VI = ___]. Any other scores are worth 0 points. Total your summary scores for I + II + III + IV + V + VI and enter the result here [EP = ___].

Interpretation

This assessment offers an impression of your *entrepreneurial profile,* or EP. It compares your characteristics with those of typical entrepreneurs. Your instructor can provide further information on each question as well as some additional insights into the backgrounds of entrepreneurs. You may locate your EP score on the following grid.

100 + = Entrepreneur extraordinaire
80–99 = Entrepreneur
60–79 = Potential entrepreneur
0–59 = Entrepreneur in the rough

Source: Instrument adapted from Norman M. Scarborough and Thomas W. Zimmerer, *Effective Small Business Management,* 3rd ed. (Columbus: Merrill, 1991), pp. 26–27.

TEAM EXERCISE

Community Entrepreneurs

Michael Gerber, author and entrepreneur, says: "The entrepreneur in us sees opportunities everywhere we look, but many people see only problems everywhere they look." The entrepreneurs he describes are everywhere; some might live next door and one might be you; many own and operate the small businesses of your community.

Question: Who are the entrepreneurs in your community and what are they accomplishing?

Research Directions:

Read the local news, talk to your friends and locals, consider where you shop. Make a list of the businesses and other organizations that have an entrepreneurial character. Be as complete as possible—look at both businesses and non-profits.

For each of the organizations, do further research to identify the entrepreneurs responsible for them.

Contact as many of the entrepreneurs as possible and interview them. Try to learn how they got started, why, what they encountered as obstacles or problems, what they learned about entrepreneurship that could be passed along to others. Add to these questions a list of your own: what do you want to know about entrepreneurship?

Analyze your results for class presentation and discussion. Look for patterns and differences in terms of entrepreneurs as persons, the entrepreneurial experience, and potential insights into business versus social entrepreneurship.

Consider writing short cases that summarize the "founding stories" of the entrepreneurs you find especially interesting.

The Simply Sweet Taste of Success

Along a strip of Vancouver's West Broadway, where fresh fruit and vegetable stands spill out on the sidewalk beside trendy coffee shops and Greek restaurants, you'll find the bubblegum-pink canopy of Cupcakes by Heather and Lori. Inside is a bakery decorated in the basic candy colours of chocolate brown, soft vanilla, and sweet pink, and offering one simple treat—cupcakes—the brainchild of two best friends. How did two entrepreneurs go from leaving their corporate jobs to peddling products with names like Sweet 16, Caramella, and Mochamotion?[1]

Where Ideas Come From

Best friends since their high school days in Victoria, B.C., Heather White and Lori Joyce had always wanted to go into business together but thought it would probably be in fashion or other areas in which they had sales experience. Then, one afternoon in 2001 while both were working in New York City, Joyce took White for a treat at the popular Magnolia Bakery. White looked around at the long line-ups and was convinced that this was what they should do.

"I really liked the company that I was working for at the time, but within a couple months, I was really hitting the ceiling there," Joyce explains. "I realized that ultimately I wouldn't be satisfied unless I had my own company."

Flash forward a few months: the young women were both back in Canada and working in Vancouver. While out for a jog, they passed a "For lease" sign on Denman Street in the city's downtown. On February 13, 2002, the friends incorporated their company and signed a lease with little more than their idea for a cupcakes-only bakery. "We decided to make some cupcakes for our boyfriends. They were horrible because we don't bake," Joyce laughs. "But the cupcakes looked great. We had this cute little box we had made up . . . It was clear where our talent was, and it wasn't in the baking. That taught us not to be the bakers, but to hire bakers."

The women knew their skills weren't in the actual making of the product, but in developing and marketing the business. They got to work researching the bakery business, establishing contracts with suppliers, and hiring the help they needed, while also developing their concept and brand. "We didn't have the skills, so we didn't have the ego," Joyce says. "We were really open to advice." The women sought and accepted the help of family and friends wherever possible.

Two months later, in April 2002, their first location on Denman Street opened. "We were actually the first cupcakes-branded concept in all of North America," says Joyce. It seems they tapped into a burgeoning trend, now seen in the popularity of Sprinkles Cupcakes, which originated in Beverly Hills and is a favourite stop for many celebrities, and in features on cupcakes in magazines like *Gourmet*.

Courtesy Cupcakes by Heather and Lori

"Stick to What You're Good At"

White and Joyce, in their late 20s at the time, did all this without a formal business plan. They simply started with a basic food product—a cupcake—and took advice and flavour ideas from customers. "We stood in front of the customer and asked for feedback, and we just evolved the recipes constantly," Joyce says, adding that many of the flavour names, like Cosmopolitan and Obsession, actually came from the names of the paint samples they were looking at when choosing colours for the store.

"Our vision was to have the bakery look like you're standing inside a cupcake. It was very whimsical, it was very fantasy, it was very childhood-like, it was very unlike anything you'd seen before," Joyce says. "After September 11th, there was a real big movement toward comfort food," she continues. "It was all about family values and bringing it back to simplicity and that's how our brand tied in." Low-carb diets had been popular at that time, but their bakery offered a change, a treat, a mini-escape in the form of a single-size cake.

White's focus was on developing the product. She spent her time in the store and connecting with the customers and the bakers, while Joyce focused on public relations, getting the cupcakes known by handing out samples at every opportunity. "You should really stick to what you're good at," she says. "If you can eventually do what you're good at and delegate or employ out the rest of the jobs, that will help you make your business successful."

Joyce admits the first year was very hard and there were times when she and White considered calling it quits. They each invested $40,000 into the business and neither got paid that first year. "We both learned the hard way," she admits. "But we both loved the brand. . . . we were really lucky with the timing."

The idea caught on—first with the urban trendsetters who came in for cupcakes because it was cool, then with parents bringing their kids in for a nostalgic taste of their own childhoods, and then with the kids dragging their grandparents in for a treat. And, Joyce says, there is little difference in numbers between men and women. "The most rugged dirty construction worker would come in and have no problem asking for a Diva cupcake [chocolate cake frosted with pink]."

Evolving the Business

Cupcakes by Heather and Lori now also offers wedding cakes, though this was not part of the original plan. Like much of their business, the wedding cake side grew out of a customer request. One of their urban trendsetter customers came in and asked if they could provide cupcakes on tiers for her wedding, Joyce explains. "That was before the Martha Stewart issue [featuring a tiered stand of cupcakes] . . . When that came out, everyone thought it was us. Then every bride in town wanted that, and we were the only ones doing it." And that evolved into offering cakes, for weddings or other occasions, as well. In keeping with the retro feel of the bakery, the cake names, like Annette, Veronica, Dean, and Ricky, have the nostalgic echo of simpler times.

Still, about 80 percent of the business is from the retail sale of cupcakes. The most basic flavours—the Diva and the Sweet 16—are by far the most popular, Joyce says. And this reflects the approach of the company as a whole: "keep it simple."

But life for enterprising young women is never simple. After an appearance on the Women's Network show *The Shopping Bag Girls* in 2005, White and Joyce were approached by the same production company a couple of years later with the idea for their own reality television show. Now the lives of *The Cupcakes Girls*—both their business dealings and personal challenges—are documented and broadcast weekly across Canada. "Because we were at the beginning of expansion, I took this opportunity as a great commercial essentially," says Joyce, whose efforts to start a family while also running the business have been a regular feature on the show.

Plans are to continue to expand—both their families (soon after Joyce gave birth to her son, White became pregnant as well) and the business. By 2010, Cupcakes by Heather and Lori had six locations in the Greater Vancouver Area (including the one on West Broadway): four franchises and two corporate-owned. Another location in Victoria was coming soon, and plans were in the works for expansion in Toronto. Their long-term plans included international franchise development outside of North America.

Any future expansion will be through franchising, Joyce confirms. "We found that, once we opened up three corporate stores, there was only Heather and I, so there was always a store that was left out," she explains. She feels that if you expand too much corporately, you lose touch with the customer. "As we were expanding, we weren't working *in* the business anymore; we were working *on* the business. What's really important at the end of the day is not only the product that you're selling, but also the service that you're providing with the product. And that was missing. With franchising, I want to get the right person in place and have them recreate the whole Denman experience we had in the beginning."

And she and White are confident their business will continue to evolve to satisfy the needs of their customers. After all, as Joyce says, "the customer determines your success."

Discussion Questions

1. What entrepreneurial traits and personal characteristics do Heather White and Lori Joyce display in the case?

2. If White and Joyce wished to expand their operation by opening new stores, what ownership approach would you recommend they use?

3. What would you include in a business plan for a new venture on your campus called "Sweet Bites," a new cupcake-only eatery?

4. FURTHER RESEARCH—How can a cupcake-only business grow? Gather current information on Cupcakes by Heather and Lori and do a "venture capitalists" analysis. What makes the firm attractive to an investor and what are its downsides? Is Cupcakes a good fit for the future?

Planning Processes and Techniques

Think now and embrace the future

The aim of Cognos, a software company owned by IBM and located in Ottawa, is to help businesses "crunch the numbers" in order to yield better organizational planning and control. And businesses like what they do; more than 23,000 organizations worldwide have elected to adopt Cognos performance management solutions.

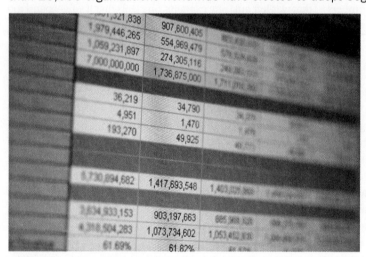

Courtesy Cognos

With businesses facing an ever-changing marketplace, Cognos has set out to help companies gain a flexible approach to their strategic plans by providing software to analyze business data. A world leader in business intelligence and performance planning software, the company provides businesses with a competitive advantage by integrating key areas of budgeting, performance, and sales so companies can analyze the numbers to monitor and change strategic direction. This ensures resources are directed toward areas that are financially and commercially viable.

What is Cognos's own plan? It continues to research and develop new software. With products like Cognos 8 Business Intelligence, Cognos TM1, Cognos Express and Cognos Now!, the company has a full line of enterprise planning software for budgeting, forecasting and analysis. As IT consultant Philip Howard notes, "What Cognos has recognized is that planning is more than just a financial activity—that it is something that needs to spread across the enterprise and be coordinated across multiple departments. However, appreciating that fact and supporting it in principle in the planning software is one thing; supporting it in practice is another. This is where the Cognos blueprints come in, enabling users to adopt these practices relatively easily." It sounds as if Cognos has a plan.[1]

BENCHMARK "The best plans often go wrong." "The problem is with the details." We often hear these expressions. But Cognos shows that you can make great things happen with good insight and the right plans. Even when things don't go as intended, plans and their implementation can often be adjusted to achieve important goals.

Time Management

Time is one of our most precious resources, and time management is an essential skill in today's high-pressure, fast-paced world of work. Some 77 percent of managers in one survey said the new digital age has increased the number of decisions they have to make; 43 percent complained there was less time available to make them. *BusinessWeek* reports that interruptions steal 28 percent of the average worker's day and that the lost productivity costs the U.S. economy $650 billion per year.[2]

Don't you wonder about the time you waste dealing with e-mail, instant messages, voice and text messages, drop-in visits from co-workers and friends, waiting on the phone for customer service, and more?

Of course, you have to be careful in defining "waste." It isn't a waste of time to occasionally relax, take a breather from work, and find humour and pleasure in social interactions. Such breaks help us gather and replenish energies to do well in our work. But it is a waste to let friends dominate your time so that you don't work on a term paper until it is too late to write a really good one, or delay a decision to apply for an internship until the deadline is passed.

Perhaps you are one of those who plan to do so many things in a day that you never get to the most important ones. Perhaps you hardly plan, letting events take you where they may. And perhaps on many days you end up not accomplishing much at all.

> **Time Management Planner**
>
> List 1 – What I have to do tomorrow
>   (A) Most important, top priority
>   (B) Important, not top priority
>   (C) Least important, low priority
>
> List 2 – Time wasters
>   (A) Things I can control
>   (B) Things I can't control

Learning to better manage your time can serve you very well in the future, both at work and in your personal life. Take a step forward in time management. Complete the lists requested in the boxed time management planner. Double-check all the List 1 "B" activities. Reclassify any that are really "A's" or "C's." Look at your "A's" and reclassify any that are really "B's" or "C's." Also check your time wasters. Make a commitment to take charge of the controllables, and see if you really could do something about items marked "uncontrollable."

❖ Get to Know Yourself Better

One of the best ways to improve time management is to keep a daily time log for a day or two—listing what you do and how long it takes. Make such a log, and then analyze it to determine where you seem to be wasting time and where you are using it well. Use the Time Management Profile at the end of the chapter to help you think further about your time management skills.

CHAPTER 6 STUDY QUESTIONS

- Why and how do managers plan?

- What types of plans do managers use?

- What are the useful planning tools and techniques?

- How can plans be well implemented?

VISUAL CHAPTER OVERVIEW

CHAPTER 6 PLANNING PROCESSES AND TECHNIQUES

Study Question 1	Study Question 2	Study Question 3	Study Question 4
Why and How Managers Plan	**Types of Plans Used by Managers**	**Planning Tools and Techniques**	**Implementing Plans to Achieve Results**
■ Importance of planning ■ The planning process ■ Benefits of planning ■ Planning and time management	■ Long-range and short-range plans ■ Strategic and tactical plans ■ Operational plans	■ Forecasting ■ Contingency planning ■ Scenario planning ■ Benchmarking ■ Use of staff planners	■ Goal setting and goal alignment ■ Management by objectives ■ Participation and involvement
✓ Learning Check 1	✓ Learning Check 2	✓ Learning Check 3	✓ Learning Check 4

To survive and succeed, IBM's Cognos knows it has to plan for the future by constantly reinventing itself and its products. In Chapter 6, you will learn how managers use planning to help turn insight and opportunity into real performance accomplishments. Managers need the ability to look ahead, make good plans, and help themselves and others meet the challenges of the future. However, the future is full of uncertainty; the likelihood is that even the best of plans will have to be adjusted and changed at some point. Thus, managers need the insight and courage to be flexible in response to new circumstances. They also need the discipline to stay focused on goals even as complications and problems arise.

WHY AND HOW MANAGERS PLAN

Planning is the process of setting objectives and determining how to accomplish them.

In Chapter 1, the management process was described as planning, organizing, leading, and controlling the use of resources to achieve performance objectives. The first of these functions, **planning**, sets the stage for the others by providing a sense of direction. It is a process of setting objectives and determining how best to accomplish them. Said a bit differently, planning involves deciding exactly what you want to accomplish and how best to go about it.

IMPORTANCE OF PLANNING

When planning is done well, it creates a solid platform for the other management functions: organizing—allocating and arranging resources to accomplish tasks; leading—guiding the efforts of human resources to ensure high levels of task accomplishment; and controlling—monitoring task accomplishments and taking necessary corrective action. This centrality of planning in management is shown in Figure 6.1. In today's demanding organizational and career environments, it is essential to stay one step ahead of the competition. This involves always striving to become better at what you are doing and to be action-oriented. An annual report for power management company Eaton Corporation, for example, once stated: "Planning at Eaton means making the hard decisions before events force them upon you, and anticipating the future needs of the market before the demand asserts itself."[3]

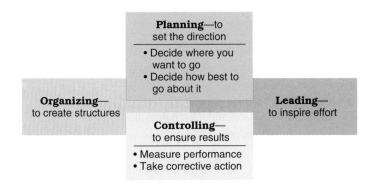

Figure 6.1 The roles of planning and controlling in the management process.

THE PLANNING PROCESS

Planning should focus attention on **objectives** that identify the specific results or desired outcomes that one intends to achieve. Planning should also create a real **plan**, a statement of action steps to be taken in order to accomplish the objectives. Furthermore, planning should result in plans being well implemented so that objectives are accomplished. Planning in this sense is an application of the decision-making process that will be more fully discussed in Chapter 12, and involves five steps.

Objectives are specific results that one wishes to achieve.

A **plan** is a statement of intended means for accomplishing objectives.

1. *Define your objectives*—Identify desired outcomes or results in very specific ways. Know where you want to go; be specific enough that you will know you have arrived when you get there, or know how far off the mark you are at various points along the way.

2. *Determine where you stand vis-à-vis objectives*—Evaluate current accomplishments relative to the desired results. Know where you stand in reaching the objectives; know what strengths work in your favour and what weaknesses may hold you back.

3. *Develop premises regarding future conditions*—Anticipate future events. Generate alternative "scenarios" for what may happen; identify for each scenario things that may help or hinder progress toward your objectives.

4. *Analyze alternatives and make a plan*—List and evaluate possible actions. Choose the alternative most likely to accomplish your objectives; describe what must be done to follow the best course of action.

5. *Implement the plan and evaluate results*—Take action and carefully measure your progress toward objectives. Follow through by doing what the plan requires; evaluate results, take corrective action, and revise plans as needed.

Good Planning Helps Make Us

- *Priority-oriented*—making sure the most important things get first attention

- *Action-oriented*—keeping a results-driven sense of direction

- *Advantage-oriented*—ensuring that all resources are used to best advantage

- *Change-oriented*—anticipating problems and opportunities so they can be best dealt with

The planning process as just described all seems simple and straightforward enough. But remember, planning is not something managers do while working alone in quiet rooms, free from distractions, and at scheduled times. It is an ongoing process, often continuously being done even while dealing with an otherwise busy and demanding work setting.[4] And like other decision-making in organizations, the best planning is done with the active participation of those people whose work efforts will eventually determine whether or not the plans are well implemented.

BENEFITS OF PLANNING

The pressures organizations face come from many sources. Externally, these include ethical expectations, government regulations, uncertainties of a global economy, changing technologies, and the sheer cost of investments in labour, capital, and other supporting resources. Internally, they include the quest for operating efficiencies, new structures and technologies, alternative work arrangements, greater diversity in the workplace, and related managerial challenges. As you would expect, planning in such conditions has a number of benefits for both organizations and individuals.

REAL ETHICS

Fighting Poverty

Facts: Developing countries send $100+ billion (U.S.) in aid to poor countries; private foundations and charities spend $70+ billion (U.S.) more fighting poverty and its effects around the world.

Question: Are these monies being well spent? Answer: Not all of them, that's for sure. And that's a problem being tackled by the Poverty Action Lab at the Massachusetts Institute of Technology. The director, Abhijit Banerjee, a development economist, says: "We aren't really interested in the more-aid-less-aid debate. We're interested in seeing what works and what doesn't."

Ruth Levine, director of programs for the Center for Global Development, says: "You don't see many reports of projects that fail. But it's very hard to learn what works if you are only exposed to a nonrandom subset of things that work." The Poverty Action Lab

pans "feel-good" evaluations and pushes for rigorous evaluations of poverty-fighting programs using scientific methods. Here's an example.

The Indian anti-poverty group Sevi Mandir was concerned about teacher absenteeism and low performance by rural schoolchildren. Its original plan was to pay extra tutors to assist teachers in 120 rural schools. The Poverty Lab Plan suggested paying extra tutors in 60 schools, making no changes in the other 60, and then comparing outcomes to see if the plan worked. An evaluation of results showed no difference in children's performance, even with the higher costs of extra tutors.

A new plan was made to buy cameras for 60 teachers, have them take time-and-date-stamped photos with children at the start and end of each school day, and have the photos analyzed each month. Teachers would receive bonuses or fines based on their absenteeism and student performance. Again, no changes were made in the other 60 schools. Evaluation revealed that teacher absenteeism was 20 percent lower and student performance was significantly higher in the camera schools. With the Poverty Lab's help, Sevi Mandir concluded that investing in closely monitored pay incentives could improve teacher attendance in rural schools.

YOU DECIDE

Look around organizations you know and at cases reported in the news. How often do we draw conclusions that "plans are working" based on feel-good evaluations rather than solid scientific evaluations? What are the consequences in our personal lives, at work, and in society at large when plans are implemented at great cost, but without defensible systems of evaluation?

Planning Improves Focus and Flexibility

Good planning improves focus and flexibility, both of which are important for performance success. An organization with focus knows what it does best, knows the needs of its customers, and knows how to serve them well. An individual with focus knows where he or she wants to go in a career or situation, and in life overall. An organization with flexibility is willing and able to change and adapt to shifting circumstances, and operates with an orientation toward the future rather than the past. An individual with flexibility adjusts career plans to fit new and developing opportunities.

Planning Improves Action Orientation

Planning is a way for people and organizations to stay ahead of the competition and become better at what they are doing. It keeps the future visible as a performance target and reminds us that the best decisions are often those made before events force problems upon us. It helps avoid the **complacency trap**—simply being carried along by the flow of events.

The **complacency trap** is being carried along by the flow of events.

Management consultant Stephen R. Covey talks about the importance of priorities. He points out that the most successful executives "zero in on what they do that 'adds value' to an organization."[5] Instead of working on too many things, they work on the things that really count. Covey says that good planning makes us more (1) results-oriented—creating a performance-oriented sense of direction; (2) priority-oriented—making sure the most important things get first attention; (3) advantage-oriented—ensuring that all resources are used to best advantage; and (4) change-oriented—anticipating problems and opportunities so they can be best dealt with.

Planning Improves Coordination and Control

Planning improves coordination.[6] The different individuals, groups, and subsystems in organizations are each doing many different things at the same time. But their efforts must add up to meaningful contributions to the organization as a whole. When plans are coordinated among people and subsystems, there is greater likelihood that their combined accomplishments will advance performance for the organization.

When planning is done well, it also facilitates control. The first step in the planning process is to set objectives and standards, and this is a prerequisite to effective control. The objectives set by good planning make it easier to measure results and take action to improve things as necessary. If results are less than expected, either the objectives or the actions being taken, or both, can be evaluated and adjusted. In this way, planning and controlling work closely together in the management process. Without planning, control lacks objectives and standards for measuring how well things are going and what could be done to make them go better. Without control, planning lacks the follow-through needed to ensure that things work out as planned.

PLANNING AND TIME MANAGEMENT

Daniel Vasella is CEO of Novartis AG and its 98,000 employees spread across 140 countries. He's also calendar-bound. He says: "I'm locked in by meetings, travel and other constraints . . . I have to put down in priority things I like to do." Kathleen Murphy is CEO of ING US Wealth Management. She's also calendar-bound, with conferences and travel booked a year ahead. She schedules meetings at half-hour intervals, works 12-hour days, and spends 60 percent of her time travelling. She also makes good use of her time on planes. "No one can reach me by phone and I can get reading and thinking done."[7]

These are common executive stories—tight schedules, little time alone, lots of meetings and phone calls, and not much room for spontaneity. The keys to success in such classic management scenarios rest, in part at least, with another benefit of good planning—time management. Management Smarts 6.1 offers some good tips on developing this important management skill and competency. And a lot of time management comes down to discipline and priorities. Lewis Platt, former chairman of Hewlett-Packard, once said: "Basically, the whole day is a series of choices."[8] These choices have to be made in ways that allocate your time to the most important priorities. Platt said that he was "ruthless about priorities" and that you "have to continually work to optimize your time."

Most of us have experienced the difficulties of balancing available time with our many commitments and opportunities. It is easy to lose track of time and fall prey to what consultants identify as "time wasters." Too many of us allow our time to be dominated by other people or to be misspent on non-essential activities.[9] "To do" lists can help, but they have to contain the right things. In daily living and in management, it is important to distinguish between things that you must do (top priority), should do (high priority), would be nice to do (low priority), and really don't need to do (no priority).

6.1 MANAGEMENT SMARTS
Personal time management tips

1. *Do* say "No" to requests that divert you from what you really should be doing.

2. *Don't* get bogged down in details that you can address later or leave for others.

3. *Do* have a system for screening telephone calls, e-mails, and requests for meetings.

4. *Don't* let drop-in visitors or instant messages use too much of your time.

5. *Do* prioritize what you will work on in terms of importance and urgency.

6. *Don't* become calendar-bound by letting others control your schedule.

7. *Do* follow priorities; work on the most important and urgent tasks first.

✔ **Learning Check** ❶   **BE SURE YOU CAN**

• explain the importance of planning as the first of four management functions • list the steps in the formal planning process • illustrate the benefits of planning for an organization familiar to you • illustrate the benefits of planning for your personal career development • list at least three things you can do now to improve your time management

Types of Plans Used by Managers

I am the master of my fate: I am the captain of my soul. How often have you heard this phrase? The lines are from *Invictus*, written by British poet William Earnest Henley in 1875. He was sending a message, one of confidence and control, as he moved forward into the future. That notion, however, worries a planning scholar by the name of Richard Levin. His response to Henley is: *Not without a plan you're not.*[10]

Managers use a variety of plans as they face different challenges in the flow and pace of activities in organizations. In some cases, the planning environment is stable and quite predictable; in others, it is more dynamic and uncertain. Different needs call for different types of plans.

LONG-RANGE AND SHORT-RANGE PLANS

Generally, long-range plans look three or more years into the future, intermediate-range plans cover one to two years, and short-range plans cover one year or less. Top management is most likely to be involved in setting long-range plans and directions for the organization as a whole, whereas lower management levels focus more on short-run plans that help achieve long-term objectives.

Unless everyone understands an organization's long-term plans, there is always a risk that the pressures of daily events will divert attention from important tasks. In other words, without a sense of long-term direction, people can end up working hard and still not achieve significant results. Auto industry executives know this only too well. Their firms are operating today in what used to be the far-off "future," and they have arrived here only to be in lots of trouble. Was it the inability to think long term that got them here, or was it an inability to anticipate, recognize, and adjust to changing events that led to their downfalls?

Canadian-born management researcher Elliott Jaques suggested that people vary in their capability to think with different time horizons.[11] In fact, he believed that most people work comfortably with only 3-month time spans; a smaller group works well with a 1-year span; and only the very rare person can handle a 20-year time frame. These are provocative ideas, and personally challenging ones. Although a team leader's planning may fall mainly in the weekly or monthly range, a chief executive is expected to have a vision extending several years into the future. Career progress to higher management levels requires the conceptual skills to work well with longer-range time frames.

Jaques's Findings on Planning Horizons

Most of us — 3-month time frame

A few of us — 1-year time frame

Very few of us ↓ — 20-year time frame

CANADIAN MANAGERS
When a Plan Wows!

Courtesy Steam Whistle Brewing

Cameron Heaps, 36, is co-founder of Steam Whistle Brewing Company based in Toronto. For Heaps, Steam Whistle's start-up was a "thrill of a lifetime" that allowed him and business partners to combine their experience in the beer industry into a successful business. But they didn't get where they are without a plan. Heaps offered: "If you believe strongly enough in what you are doing, you never stop to see the risks. That being said, the best way to reduce the potential of entering a risky endeavour is with a business plan that you circulate to many people for feedback. When you get to the point where 7 out of 10 people go 'wow' then you're probably on to something. One of the great things about a business plan is you don't need to quit your job to write it. You can wait until you know you have something worth pursuing."

Would you agree that the complexities and uncertainties of today's environments challenge how we go about planning and how far ahead we can really plan? In an increasingly global economy, planning opportunities and challenges are often worldwide in scope, not just local. And of course, the information age is also ever-present in its planning implications. We now talk about planning in Internet time, where businesses are continually changing and updating plans. Even top managers now face the reality that Internet time keeps making the "long" range of planning shorter and shorter.

STRATEGIC AND TACTICAL PLANS

Plans also differ in scope and purpose served. At the top of the traditional organizational pyramid, senior executives deal mainly with strategic plans; in the middle, managers deal with tactical plans; at lower levels, managers focus on operating plans.

Strategic Plans

A **strategic plan** identifies long-term directions for the organization.

A **vision** clarifies the purpose of the organization and expresses what it hopes to be in the future.

When planning for the organization as a whole or a major component, the focus is on **strategic plans**. These are longer-term plans that set broad directions for an organization and create a framework for allocating resources for maximum long-term performance impact. Strategic planning is part of the strategic management process discussed in the next chapter. It begins with a **vision** that clarifies the purpose of the organization and expresses what it hopes to be in the future, and it involves determining the goals and objectives that will be pursued in order to accomplish that vision.

Even though strategic plans are long term, they are also dynamic. Consider the example of Skype, the Internet telephone service now owned by eBay. Skype began with the genius of its founders, Niklas Zennstrom and Janus Friis, and morphed into a company that quickly outgrew its original goals.[12] The firm was just three years old when it was bought by eBay for US$ 2.6 billion. That was quite a payoff for investors and the firm's founders. But it wasn't their plan to just start the company, move it fast, and sell quickly to the highest bidder. Says Zennstrom: "Our objective was to build the business." Once started, however, Skype quickly gained 54 million users and became an acquisition target. The deal was sealed after Zennstrom and Friis had a breakthrough meeting with eBay's CEO, Meg Whitman. According to Zennstrom, it was an *Aha!* experience: "We went crazy on the whiteboard, mapping out ideas." The rest is business history—a strategic plan that worked so well it moved faster than Skype's founders ever anticipated.

Tactical Plans

A **tactical plan** helps to implement all or parts of a strategic plan.

Functional plans indicate how different operations within the organization will help advance the overall strategy.

When a sports team enters a game or contest, it typically does so with a "strategy" in hand. Most often, this strategy is set by the head coach in conjunction with assistants. The goal is clear and long term: win the game or contest. As the game unfolds, a variety of situations arise that require immediate adjustments to solve problems or exploit opportunities. They call for "tactics" that deal with a current situation in ways that advance the overall strategy for winning.

The same logic holds true for organizations. **Tactical plans** are developed and used to implement strategic plans. They tend to be intermediate-term plans that specify how the organization's resources can be used to put strategies into action. In the sports context, you might think of tactical plans as involving "special teams," or as "special plays," designed to meet a particular threat or opportunity. In business, tactical plans often take the form of **functional plans** that indicate how different components of the enterprise will contribute to the overall strategy. Such functional plans might include:

- *Production plans*—dealing with work methods and technologies
- *Financial plans*—dealing with money and capital investments

- *Facilities plans*—dealing with facilities and work layouts
- *Logistics plans*—dealing with suppliers and acquiring resource inputs
- *Marketing plans*—dealing with selling and distributing goods or services
- *Human resource plans*—dealing with building a talented workforce

OPERATIONAL PLANS

Operational plans describe what needs to be done in the short term and in response to different situations. They include both standing plans such as policies and procedures that are used over and over again, and single-use plans such as budgets that apply to one specific task or time period.

An **operational plan** identifies short-term activities to implement strategic plans.

Policies and Procedures

A **policy** communicates broad guidelines for making decisions and taking action in specific circumstances. Organizations operate with lots of policies, and they set expectations for many aspects of employee behaviour. Typical human resource policies, for example, cover employee hiring, termination, performance appraisals, pay increases, promotions, and discipline. Another important policy area is sexual harassment, and it's one that Judith Nitsch made a top priority when starting her engineering consulting business.[13] Nitsch defined a sexual harassment policy, took a hard line on its enforcement, and appointed both a male and a female employee for others to talk with about sexual harassment concerns.

A **policy** is a standing plan that communicates broad guidelines for decisions and action.

Procedures or **rules** describe exactly what actions are to be taken in specific situations. They are stated in employee handbooks and often called "SOPs"—standard operating procedures. Whereas a policy sets a broad guideline, procedures define precise actions to be taken. In the prior example, Judith Nitsch was right to establish a sexual harassment policy for her firm. But she should also put into place procedures that ensure everyone receives fair, equal, and non-discriminatory treatment under the policy. Everyone in her firm should know how to file a sexual harassment complaint and how that complaint will be handled.

A **procedure** or **rule** precisely describes actions that are to be taken in specific situations.

Budgets

Budgets are single-use plans that commit resources for specific time periods to activities, projects, or programs. Managers typically spend a fair amount of time bargaining with higher levels to get adequate budgets to support the needs of their work units or teams. They are also expected to achieve work objectives while keeping within the allocated budget. To be "over budget" is generally bad; to come in "under budget" is generally good.

A **budget** is a plan that commits resources to projects or activities.

Managers deal with and use a variety of budgets. *Financial budgets* project cash flows and expenditures; *operating budgets* plot anticipated sales or revenues against expenses; *non-monetary budgets* allocate resources like labour, equipment, and space. A *fixed budget* allocates a stated amount of resources for a specific purpose, such as $50,000 for equipment purchases in a given year. A *flexible budget* allows resources to vary in proportion with various levels of activity, such as having extra money available to hire temporary workers when workloads exceed certain levels.

All budgets link planned activities with the resources needed to accomplish them. And because they are clear in identifying financial or other resource constraints, budgets are useful for tracking and controlling performance. But budgets can get out of control, creeping higher and higher without getting sufficient critical attention.

One of the most common budgeting problems is that resource allocations get "rolled over" from one time period to the next without a rigorous performance review; the new budget is simply

A zero-based budget allocates resources as if each budget were brand new.

an incremental adjustment to the previous one. In a major division of Campbell Soups, for example, managers once discovered that 10 percent of the marketing budget was going to sales promotions no longer relevant to current product lines. A **zero-based budget** deals with this problem by approaching each new budget period as it if were brand new. In zero-based budgeting, there is no guarantee that any past funding will be renewed; all proposals must compete anew for available funds at the start of each new budget cycle.

RESEARCH BRIEF

You've got to move beyond planning by the calendar

Organizations today need executives who can make faster and better decisions, and that means strategic planning must be done continuously. Michael C. Mankins and Richard Steele, writing in the *Harvard Business Review*, express their concerns that planning is too often viewed as an annual activity focused more on documenting plans for the record than on action. Little wonder, they suggest, that only 11 percent of executives in a survey of 156 firms with sales of US$ 1+ billion were highly satisfied that strategic planning is worthwhile.

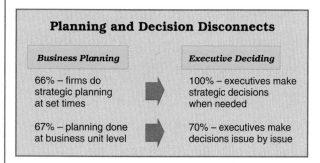

Planning and Decision Disconnects

Business Planning	Executive Deciding
66% – firms do strategic planning at set times	100% – executives make strategic decisions when needed
67% – planning done at business unit level	70% – executives make decisions issue by issue

The research, conducted in collaboration with Marakon Associates and the Economist Intelligence Unit, inquired as to how long-range strategic planning was conducted and how effective these planning activities were. Results showed that executives perceived a substantial disconnect between the way many firms approached strategic planning and the way they approached strategic decisions. Some 66

percent of the time, executives said that strategic planning at their firms was conducted only at set times, and very often was accomplished by a formal and structured process. Survey respondents also indicated that planning was often considered as only a "periodic event" and not something to be engaged in continuously. Mankins and Steele call such planning "calendar driven," and they question its effectiveness.

In calendar-driven planning, the researchers found that firms averaged only 2.5 major strategic decisions per year, with "major" meaning a decision that could move profits by more than 10 percent. They also point out that when planning is disconnected from the calendar, companies make higher-quality and more strategic decisions. The researchers call this alternative planning approach "continuous review" and argue it is more consistent with the way executives actually make decisions and with business realities.

You be the researcher

Why is it that tying the planning process to certain calendar dates may be dysfunctional for a business? On the other hand, how can we plan almost continuously? Choose two or three organizations in your community for some field research. Arrange interviews with a senior executive at each. Find out if they plan on a set schedule and if so, what that schedule might be. Probe further to find out how effective they consider planning in their organization to be.

BE SURE YOU CAN

• differentiate between short-range and long-range plans • differentiate between strategic and operational plans and explain their relationships to one another • define *policy* and *procedure* and give an example of each in the university setting • explain how a zero-based budget works

Planning Tools and Techniques

The benefits of planning are best realized when the foundations are strong. Among the useful tools and techniques of managerial planning are forecasting, contingency planning, scenarios, benchmarking, and the use of staff planners.

FORECASTING

Who would have predicted even a few years ago that China would now be the second-largest car market in the world? Would you believe that by 2025 China will have more cars on the roads than the United States has now?[14] Planning in business and our personal lives often involves **forecasting**, the process of predicting what will happen in the future.[15] Periodicals such as *Canadian Business*, *Maclean's*, and the *Financial Post* regularly report forecasts of economic conditions, interest rates, unemployment, and trade deficits, among other issues. Some are based on qualitative forecasting, which uses expert opinions to predict the future. Others involve quantitative forecasting, which uses mathematical models and statistical analyses of historical data and surveys to predict future events.

> **Forecasting** attempts to predict the future.

Although useful, all forecasts should be treated cautiously. They are planning aids, not substitutes. It is said that a music agent once told Elvis Presley: "You ought to go back to driving a truck, because you ain't going nowhere." He was obviously mistaken, and that's the problem with forecasts. They rely on human judgement—and they can be wrong.

CONTINGENCY PLANNING

Picture the scene. It is shortly before the Vancouver Olympic Winter Games are to begin and there is little snow on Cypress Mountain, home to freestyle skiing, snowboard half-pipe, and snowboard cross events. Fortunately, the Vancouver Olympic Committee (VANOC) had a backup plan. The warm weather forced VANOC to turn to its contingency plan, which included using straw and wood to build the courses with real and artificial snow. A few short days later, on Cypress Mountain, Alexandre Bilodeau, a 22-year-old from Rosemère, Que., became the first Canadian to win an Olympic gold medal at home.[16] Planning is often like that. By definition, it involves thinking ahead. But the more uncertain the planning environment, the more likely that one's original forecasts and intentions may prove inadequate or wrong. **Contingency planning** identifies alternative courses of action that can be implemented if circumstances change.

> **Contingency planning** identifies alternative courses of action to take when things go wrong.

Coke and Pepsi spend hundreds of millions of dollars on advertising as they engage one another in the ongoing "Cola Wars." It may seem that they have nothing to worry about except each other and a few discounters. But more than 50 percent of their revenues comes internationally and it's a pretty safe bet that they have contingency plans in place to deal with any variety of global events, everything from currency fluctuations to social trends to changing politics. One thing they've had to deal with was anti-American backlash from the Iraq war, including the emergence of new competitors Mecca Cola and Qibla Cola. These colas entered European markets riding a wave of resentment of U.S. brands and multinationals. The founder of Qibla says: "By choosing to boycott major

© VANOC/COVAN

brands, consumers are sending an important signal—that the exploitation of Muslims cannot continue unchecked."[17]

SCENARIO PLANNING

Scenario planning identifies alternative future scenarios and makes plans to deal with each.

A long-term version of contingency planning, called **scenario planning**, involves identifying several alternative future scenarios or states of affairs that may occur. Plans are then made to deal with each should it actually happen.[18] At Royal Dutch/Shell, scenario planning began years ago when top managers asked themselves: "What will Shell do after its oil supplies run out?" Although scenario planning can never be inclusive of all future possibilities, a Shell executive once said that it helps "condition the organization to think" and better prepare for "future shocks."

Shell's recent planning includes a "worst-case" scenario—global conflict occurring as nations jockey with one another to secure supplies of oil and other resources; the effects are devastating for the natural environment. It also includes an alternative "best-case" scenario—governments work together to find mutual pathways that take care of resource needs while supporting the sustainability of global resources. It's anyone's guess which scenario will materialize, or if something else altogether will happen. In any event, Shell CEO Jeroen van der Veer says: "This will require hard work and time is short."[19]

BENCHMARKING

Benchmarking uses external and internal comparisons to plan for future improvements.

Planners sometimes become too comfortable with the ways things are going and overconfident that the past is a good indicator of the future. It is often better to keep challenging the status quo and not simply accept things as they are. One way to do this is through **benchmarking**, the use of external and internal comparisons to better evaluate one's current performance and identify possible ways to improve for the future.[20]

Best practices are things people and organizations do that lead to superior performance.

The purpose of benchmarking is to find out what other people and organizations are doing very well, and then plan how to incorporate these ideas into one's own operations. One benchmarking technique is to search for **best practices**—things people and organizations do that help them achieve superior performance. Well-run organizations emphasize internal benchmarking that encourages all members and work units to learn and improve by sharing one another's best practices. They also use external benchmarking to learn from competitors and non-competitors alike.

GOING GLOBAL

ENGINEERING SOLUTIONS THAT PLAN FIRST AND THEN PERFORM

With head offices located in Kitchener, Ontario, Brock Solutions has completed over 4,000 automation projects worldwide. Brock Solutions helps Fortune 500 corporations reduce operating costs within their manufacturing and processing facilities by providing real-time automation systems for manufacturing, transportation, and logistics. One of Brock's best practices is that it plans well and thus minimizes risk through using structured processes such as functional testing before installing systems on site. And the company is good at it; Brock was honoured by the Ontario government for outstanding export growth and job creation and has been selected as one of the 50 Best Privately Managed Companies for fourteen years in a row!

In the fast-moving apparel industry, the Spanish retailer Zara has exploded on the world scene and become a benchmark for both worried competitors and others outside the industry.[21] Zara is praised for excellence in "fast fashion." The firm's design and manufacturing systems allow it to get new fashions from design to stores in two weeks; competitors may take months. Zara produces only in small batches that sell out and create impressions of scarcity. Shoppers at Zara know they have to buy now because an item will not be replaced. At its competitors, shoppers can often wait for sales and inventory clearance bargains. And if something doesn't sell at Zara, it's not a big problem since there wasn't a large stock of the item to begin with.

(Photo by Gong Wenbao/ ChinaFotoPress)

USE OF STAFF PLANNERS

As organizations grow, so do the planning challenges. Cisco Systems, for example, is already planning that a lot of its growth is going to come from investments overseas. And, it wasn't too long ago that China was the big target in Asia. It still is a big one, but "big" got smaller when Cisco's planners analyzed their planning premises and projected future scenarios for both India and China. It turns out that they found a lot to like about India: excellence in software design, need for Cisco's products, and weak local competition. They also found some major things to worry about in China: centrally planned economy, government favouring local companies, and poor intellectual property protection.[22] In another example of a planning challenge, Toronto-based CCL Industries is already planning that a lot of its growth is going to come from following overseas customers. Operating as a labelling and packaging supplier within the consumer packaged goods industry, CCL recognizes that hosting locations throughout the world to ease workflow processes for their customers is integral to its international success. Therefore, planning has become an integral component of CCL's business model as it continually learns about and adjusts to new global markets.[23]

In many organizations, as with Cisco and CCL, staff planners are employed to help coordinate and energize planning. These specialists are skilled in all steps of the planning process, as well as in the use of planning tools and techniques. They can help bring focus and expertise to accomplish important, often strategic, planning tasks. But one risk is a tendency for a communication gap to develop between staff planners and line managers. Unless everyone works closely together, the resulting plans may be inadequate, and people may lack commitment to implement the plans, no matter how good they are.

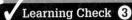

Learning Check 3

BE SURE YOU CAN
• define *forecasting, contingency planning, scenario planning*, and *benchmarking* • explain the values of contingency planning and scenario planning • describe pros and cons of using staff planners

IMPLEMENTING PLANS TO ACHIEVE RESULTS

In a book entitled *Doing What Matters*, Jim Kilts, the former CEO of Gillette, quotes an old management adage: "In business, words are words, promises are promises, but only performance is reality."[24] The same applies to plans—plans, we might say, are words with promises attached. These promises are only fulfilled when plans are implemented so that their purposes are achieved. The implementation of plans is largely driven by the solid management practices discussed throughout the rest of this book. Among the foundation issues, however, are goal setting and alignment, management by objectives, and participation.

GOAL SETTING AND GOAL ALIGNMENT

In the dynamic and highly competitive technology industry, CEO T. J. Rodgers of Cypress Semiconductor Corp. values both performance goals and accountability. He supports a planning system where employees work with clear and quantified work goals that they help set. He believes the system helps people find problems before they can interfere with performance. Says Rodgers: "Managers monitor the goals, look for problems, and expect people who fall behind to ask for help before they lose control of or damage a major project."[25]

Goal Setting

Rodgers' commitment to goals isn't unique among successful managers. In fact, it's standard practice. Here's another example. When Jim Kilts took over as CEO of Gillette, he realized that the firm needed work.[26] In analyzing the situation, however, he was very disciplined in setting planning goals or objectives. He identified core problems that were highly consequential and tagged them with measurable targets for improvement. In respect to *sales*, the company's big brands were losing sales to competitors. Kilts made plans to *increase market shares* for these brands. In respect to *earnings*, the company had missed its estimates for 15 quarters in a row. Kilts made plans to *meet earnings estimates* and raise the company's share price.

Although both Rodgers and Kilts make us aware of the importance of goal setting in management, they may make it look a bit too easy. The way goals are set can make a big difference in how well they do in pointing people in the right directions and inspiring them to work hard. The following guidelines are starting points in moving from "no goals" or even just run-of-the-mill "average goals" to having really "great goals"—ones that result in plans being successfully implemented. Great goals are SMART:

1. *Specific*—clearly target key results and outcomes to be accomplished

2. *Measurable*—described so results can be measured without ambiguity

3. *Attainable*—challenging, including a stretch factor that moves toward real gains, yet is realistic and possible to achieve

4. *Referred to*—goals need to be referred to regularly to keep people focused on the task at hand

5. *Timely*—linked to specific timetables and "due dates"

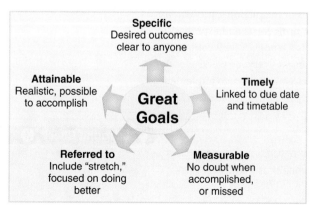

ISSUES AND SITUATIONS
Camp Samsung

Call it planning with a difference. Better yet, call it market-driven planning. And even better, call it creativity-based planning for high-value product innovations. That's what Camp Samsung is all about. Samsung Electronics Corp. is one of South Korea's giant multinational corporations. Its CEO, Yun Jong Yong, wants to double its present sales to US$ 170 billion by 2010. To meet this ambitious goal, however, Yong admits that the firm has a long way to go. It's "a good company," he says, while adding that "we still have a lot of things to do before we're a great company."

As an example, he points out that the firm brought out an MP3 player two years ahead of Apple, but that Apple's iPod took the market by storm. His plan for the future includes making Samsung a hotbed of market-driven product innovations; Camp Samsung is one of its launching pads.

Camp Samsung is really the Value Innovation Program (VIP) Center. It's a place where teams come together to work on new product ideas. For example, product planners, designers, programmers, and engineers working on a new flat-screen TV do so with the guidance of a "value innovation specialist." Driven by a tight timetable, separated from other work pressures and responsibilities, kept together until the project is completed, guided and supported by all sorts of technical and team-oriented staff members, and nurtured by communal leisure activities, the innovation teams do it.

In one year alone, Samsung sent 2,000 employees through the VIP Center, and they created 90 new products. Look for a Samsung notebook computer that doubles as a mobile TV, or a colour laser printer selling at the same price as "old" black-and-whites. With CEO Yong focusing on stretch goals and supporting them with investments like Camp Samsung, where else might this company go in the future?

CRITICAL RESPONSE

In your personal and work experiences, can you spot examples of goals that aren't well supported by plans, and of plans that aren't well implemented? What makes the difference between planning with success and just planning? Is this one of the key differentiators between the great managers and the also-rans?

Goal Alignment

It is one thing to set good goals and make them part of a plan. It is quite another to make sure that goals and plans are well integrated across the many people, work units, and levels of an organization as a whole. Goals set anywhere in the organization should ideally help advance its overall mission or purpose. Yet, we sometimes work very hard to accomplish things that simply don't make much of a difference in organizational performance. This is why goal alignment is an important part of managerial planning.

Figure 6.2 shows how a **hierarchy of goals** or **hierarchy of objectives** helps with goal alignment. When a hierarchy of objectives is well defined, the accomplishment of lower-level objectives is the means to the accomplishment of higher-level ones. The example in the figure is built around quality goals in a manufacturing setting. Strategic goals set by top management cascade down the organization step by step to become quality management objectives for lower levels. Ideally, everything works together in a consistent "means-end" fashion so that the organization becomes "the number one supplier of recyclable food containers."

In a **hierarchy of goals** or **objectives**, lower-level objectives are means to accomplishing higher-level ones.

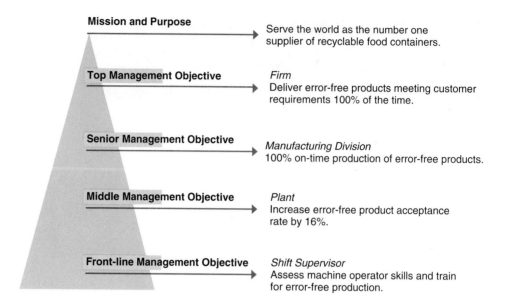

Figure 6.2 A sample hierarchy of objectives for quality management in a manufacturing firm.

MANAGEMENT BY OBJECTIVES

Management by objectives or **MBO** is a process of joint objective-setting between a superior and subordinate.

A useful planning technique that builds on the notions of goal setting and goal alignment, and that also helps integrate planning and controlling, is **management by objectives** or just **MBO**. This is a structured process of regular communication in which a supervisor or team leader works with subordinates or team members to jointly set performance objectives and review results accomplished.[27]

As shown in Figure 6.3, MBO creates an agreement between the two parties regarding (1) performance objectives for a given time period, (2) plans through which they will be accomplished, (3) standards for measuring whether they have been accomplished, and (4) procedures for reviewing performance results. Of course, both parties in any MBO agreement are supposed to work closely together to fulfill the terms of the agreement.

Performance Objectives in MBO

Improvement objectives describe intentions for specific performance improvements.

Personal development objectives describe intentions for personal growth through knowledge and skills development.

Three types of objectives may be specified in an MBO contract. **Improvement objectives** document intentions for improving performance in a specific way. An example is "to reduce quality rejects by 10 percent." **Personal development objectives** pertain to personal growth activities, often those resulting in expanded job knowledge or skills. An example is "to learn the latest version of a computer spreadsheet package." Some MBO contracts also include *maintenance objectives* that formally express intentions to maintain performance at an existing level.

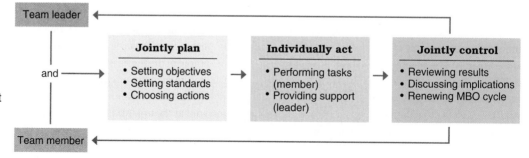

Figure 6.3 Management by objectives as an integrated planning and control framework.

One of the more difficult aspects of MBO is the need to make performance objectives as measurable as possible. Ideally, there is agreement on a *measurable end product*; for example, "to reduce travel expenses by 5 percent by the end of the fiscal year." But performance in some jobs, particularly managerial ones, is hard to quantify. Rather than abandon MBO in such cases, it is often possible to agree on performance objectives that are stated as *verifiable work activities*. The accomplishment of the activities serves as an indicator of performance progress. An example is "to improve communications with my team in the next three months by holding weekly team meetings." Whereas it can be difficult to measure "improved communications," it is easy to document whether the weekly team meetings have been held.

MBO Pros and Cons

MBO is one of the most talked-about and debated management concepts.[28] As a result, good advice is available. Things to avoid include tying MBO to pay, focusing too much attention on easy objectives, requiring excessive paperwork, and having supervisors simply tell subordinates their objectives. The advantages are also clear. MBO focuses workers on the most important tasks and objectives; and it focuses supervisors on areas of support that can truly help subordinates meet the agreed-upon objectives. Because of the direct face-to-face communication, MBO also contributes to relationship building. By giving people the opportunity to participate in decisions that affect their work, MBO encourages self-management.[29]

PARTICIPATION AND INVOLVEMENT

Planning is a process, not an event, and "participation" is one of its keywords. The best planning in organizations probably begins at the top of the organization or work unit, and then proceeds in a participatory fashion to actively involve others from lower levels. **Participatory planning** includes in all planning steps the people who will be affected by the plans and asked to help implement them.

Participatory planning includes the persons who will be affected by plans and/or those who will implement them.

One of the things that research is most clear about is that, when people participate in setting goals, they gain motivation to work hard to accomplish them.[30] Whether the focus is on planning for a team, a large division, or the entire organization, involving more people creates benefits. It goes a long way toward gaining their commitment to work hard and support the implementation of plans.

This role of participation and involvement in the planning process is shown in Figure 6.4, and there are many benefits when and if it can be followed in practice. Participation can increase the creativity and information available for planning. It can also increase the understanding and acceptance of plans, as well as commitment to their success. And even though participatory planning takes more time, it can improve results by improving implementation.

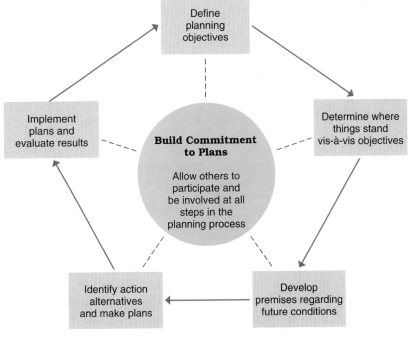

Figure 6.4 How participation and involvement help build commitment to plans.

An example of the benefits of a participatory approach to planning is found at Boeing. Former CEO Alan Mulally faced indecision in the firm's management ranks after the attacks on September 11, 2001, left the airline industry in turmoil and new plane orders plummeted. To regain momentum, he instituted a new planning approach that started with strategy sessions on Thursdays with 30 top executives. His message was to look ahead to the time when the "slump" in airplane orders would be over and plan now for a new generation of planes. Every other Thursday, he added 60 new lower-level managers to the process. He credits this approach with bringing to market the 787 "Dreamliner," the fastest-selling plane in the firm's history. About the benefits of engaging so many managers in the planning process, he says: "They gave us a wider perspective and could tell us if what we were planning actually worked and made sense."[31]

✔ **Learning Check ④**   **BE SURE YOU CAN**

• list the criteria of great goals • describe the value of a hierarchy of objectives • give examples of improvement and personal development objectives in MBO • explain how MBO can operate between a team leader and team members

---

MANAGEMENT LEARNING REVIEW

STUDY QUESTIONS SUMMARY

KEY TERMS

benchmarking, 172
best practices, 172
budget, 169
complacency trap, 165
contingency planning, 171
forecasting, 171
functional plans, 168
hierarchy of goals, 175
hierarchy of objectives, 175
improvement objectives, 176
management by objectives
    (MBO), 176
objectives, 163
operational plans, 169
participatory planning, 177
personal development
    objectives, 176
plan, 163
planning, 162
policy, 169
procedures, 169
rules, 169
scenario planning, 172
strategic plans, 168
tactical plans, 168
vision, 168
zero-based budget, 170

1. Why and how do managers plan?

• Planning is the process of setting performance objectives and determining what should be done to accomplish them.

• A plan is a set of intended actions for accomplishing important objectives.

• Five steps in the planning process are: (1) define your objectives, (2) determine where you stand vis-à-vis your objectives, (3) develop your premises regarding future conditions, (4) identify and choose among alternative ways of accomplishing objectives, and (5) implement action plans and evaluate results.

• The benefits of planning include better focus and flexibility, action orientation, coordination, control, and time management.

FOR DISCUSSION Which step in the planning process is likely to cause the most difficulties for managers?

2. What types of plans do managers use?

• Short-range plans tend to cover a year or less; long-range plans extend up to three years or more.

• Strategic plans set critical long-range directions; operational plans are designed to implement strategic plans.

• Policies, such as a sexual harassment policy, are plans that set guidelines for the behaviour of organizational members.

• Procedures and rules are plans that describe actions to be taken in specific situations, such as the steps to be taken when persons believe they have been subjected to sexual harassment.

• Budgets are plans that allocate resources to activities or projects.

FOR DISCUSSION Is there any real value to long-term planning in today's rapidly changing environment?

3. What are the useful planning tools and techniques?

- Forecasting, which attempts to predict what might happen in the future, is a planning aid but not a planning substitute.

- Contingency planning identifies alternative courses of action that can be implemented if and when circumstances change.

- Scenario planning analyzes the implications of alternative versions of the future.

- Planning through benchmarking uses external and internal comparisons to identify best practices for possible adoption.

- Staff planners with special expertise are often used to assist in the planning process, but the risk is a lack of involvement by managers and others essential to plan implementation.

FOR DISCUSSION Shouldn't all plans really be contingency plans?

4. How can plans be well implemented?

- Great goals are specific, timely, measurable, referred to, and attainable.

- A hierarchy of objectives helps to align goals from top to bottom in organizations.

- MBO is a participative process for clarifying performance objectives for an individual and identifying helpful support that can be provided by the manager.

- Participation and involvement open the planning process to valuable inputs from people whose efforts are essential to the effective implementation of plans.

FOR DISCUSSION Given its potential advantages, why isn't MBO standard practice in all organizations?

SELF-TEST

Multiple-Choice Questions

1. Planning is the process of _____ and _____.

    (a) developing premises about the future, evaluating them   (b) measuring results, taking corrective action   (c) measuring past performance, targeting future performance   (d) setting objectives, deciding how to accomplish them

2. The benefits of planning include _____.

    (a) improved focus   (b) lower labour costs   (c) more accurate forecasts   (d) guaranteed profits

3. In order to implement its strategy, a business firm would likely develop a (an) _____ plan for the marketing function.

    (a) benchmarking IT   (b) operational   (c) productivity   (d) zero-based

4. _____ planning identifies alternative courses of action that can be taken if and when certain situations arise.

    (a) Zero-based   (b) Participative   (c) Strategic   (d) Contingency

5. The first step in the control process is to _____.

    (a) measure actual performance   (b) establish objectives and standards   (c) compare results with objectives   (d) take corrective action

6. A sexual harassment policy is an example of _____ plans used by organizations.

    (a) long-range   (b) single-use   (c) standing-use   (d) operational

7. When a manager is asked to justify a new budget proposal on the basis of projected activities rather than past practices, this is an example of _____ budgeting.

    (a) zero-based   (b) variable   (c) fixed   (d) contingency

8. One of the benefits of participatory planning is _____.

    (a) reduced time for planning   (b) less need for forecasting   (c) greater attention to contingencies   (d) more commitment to implementation

9. In a hierarchy of objectives, the ideal situation is that plans set at lower levels become the _____ for accomplishing higher-level plans.

    (a) means   (b) ends   (c) scenarios   (d) benchmarks

10. When managers use the benchmarking approach to planning, they _____.

    (a) use flexible budgets   (b) identify best practices used by others   (c) are seeking the most accurate forecasts that are available   (d) focus more on the short term than the long term

11. One of the problems in relying too much on staff planners is _____.

    (a) a communication gap between planners and implementers   (b) lack of expertise in the planning process   (c) short-term rather than long-term focus   (d) neglect of budgets as links between resources and activities

12. The planning process isn't complete until _____.

    (a) future conditions have been identified   (b) stretch goals have been set   (c) plans are implemented and results evaluated   (d) budgets commit resources to plans

13. Review of an individual's performance accomplishments in an MBO system is done by _____.

    (a) the person   (b) the person's supervisor   (c) the person and the supervisor   (d) the person, the supervisor, and a lawyer

14. A good performance objective is written in such a way that it _____.

    (a) has no precise timetable   (b) is general and not too specific   (c) is almost impossible to accomplish   (d) can be easily measured

15. A manager is failing to live up to the concept of MBO when he or she _____.

    (a) sets performance objectives for subordinates   (b) actively supports subordinates in their work   (c) jointly reviews performance results with subordinates   (d) keeps a written record of subordinates' performance objectives

Short-Response Questions

16. List five steps in the planning process and give examples of each.

17. How might planning through benchmarking be used by the owner of a local bookstore?

18. How does planning help to improve focus?

19. Why does participatory planning facilitate implementation?

Application Question

20. Put yourself in the position of a management trainer. You have been asked to make a short presentation to the local Small Business Enterprise Association at its biweekly luncheon. The topic you are to speak on is "How Each of You Can Use Management by Objectives for Better Planning and Control." What will you tell them and why?

MANAGEMENT SKILLS AND COMPETENCIES

SELF-ASSESSMENT

Back to Yourself: Time Management

Time management is consistently rated one of the top "must have" skills for new graduates entering fast-paced and complicated careers in business and management. Many, perhaps most, of us keep To Do lists. But it's the rare person who is consistently successful in living up to one. Time management is a form of planning, and planning can easily suffer the same fate as the To Do lists—put together with the best of intentions, but with little or nothing to show for it in terms of results at the end of the day. There were a lot of good ideas in this chapter on how to plan, both in management and in our personal lives. Now is a good time to get in touch with your time management skills, and to start improving your capabilities to excel with planning as a basic management function.

Further Reflection: Time Management Profile

Instructions

Complete the following questionnaire by indicating "Y" (yes) or "N" (no) for each item. Be frank and allow your responses to create an accurate picture of how you tend to respond to these kinds of situations.

1. When confronted with several items of urgency and importance, I tend to do the easiest first.

2. I do the most important things during that part of the day when I know I perform best.

3. Most of the time, I don't do things someone else can do; I delegate this type of work to others.

4. Even though meetings without a clear and useful purpose upset me, I put up with them.

5. I skim documents before reading and don't finish any that offer little value for my time.

6. I don't worry much if I don't accomplish at least one significant task each day.

7. I save the most trivial tasks for that time of day when my creative energy is lowest.

8. My workspace is neat and organized.

9. My office door is always "open"; I never work in complete privacy.

10. I schedule my time completely from start to finish every workday.

11. I don't like "to do" lists, preferring to respond to daily events as they occur.

12. I "block" a certain amount of time each day or week that is dedicated to high-priority activities.

Scoring

Count the number of "Y" responses to items 2, 3, 5, 7, 8, 12. Enter that score here [___.] Count the number of "N" responses to items 1, 4, 6, 9, 10, 11. Enter that score here [___.] Add the two scores together here [___.]

Interpretation

The higher the total score, the closer your behaviour matches recommended time management guidelines. Reread those items where your response did not match the desired one. Why don't they match? Do you have reasons why your behaviour in this instance should be different from the recommended time management guideline? Think about what you can do to adjust your behaviour to be more consistent with these guidelines.

Source: Suggested by a discussion in Robert E. Quinn, Sue R. Faerman, Michael P. Thompson, and Michael R. McGrath, *Becoming a Master Manager: A Contemporary Framework* (New York: Wiley, 1990), pp. 75–76.

TEAM EXERCISE

Personal Career Planning

Preparation

Complete the following activities and bring the results to class. Your work should be in a written form suitable for grading.

Activity 1   Strengths and Weaknesses Inventory Different occupations require special talents, abilities, and skills. Each of us, you included, has a repertoire of existing strengths and weaknesses that are the "raw materials" we presently offer a potential employer. Actions can (and should!) be taken over time to further develop current strengths and to turn weaknesses into strengths. Make a list identifying your most important strengths and weaknesses in relation to the career direction you are likely to pursue upon graduation. Place a * next to each item you consider most important to focus on for continued personal development.
Activity 2   Five-Year Career Objectives Make a list of three career objectives that you hope to accomplish within five years of graduation. Be sure they are appropriate given your list of personal strengths and weaknesses.
Activity 3   Five-Year Career Action Plans Write a specific action plan for accomplishing each of the five objectives. State exactly what you will do, and by when, in order to meet each objective. If you will need special support or assistance, identify it and state how you will obtain it. An outside observer should be able to read your action plan for each objective and end up feeling confident that he or she knows exactly what you are going to do and why.

Instructions

Form into groups as assigned by the instructor. Share your career-planning analysis with the group and listen to those of others. Participate in a discussion that examines any common patterns and major differences among group members. Take advantage of any opportunities to gather feedback and advice from others. Have one group member be prepared to summarize the group discussion for the class as a whole.

Source: Developed in part from Roy J. Lewicki, Donald D. Bowen, Douglas T. Hall, and Francine S. Hall, *Experiences in Management and Organizational Behavior*, 3rd ed. (New York: Wiley, 1988), pp. 261–267. Used by permission.

CASE 6

Lands' End: Living the Golden Rule

What's so interesting about a company that just wants to be nice? Longevity and year-after-year success, for starters. From a no-questions-asked return policy to patient, limitless customer support, Lands' End has developed a solid business model around treating customers the way they'd like to be treated. See how this former retailer of sailing products turned good manners into healthy profits.

Customers Come First

Lands' End, a clothing retailer out of Dodgeville, Wisconsin, is known for its generous return policy. But no customer request tested this more than that of a car collector who asked to return a taxicab his wife had purchased for him more than 20 years before. In a novel departure from its normal trade, Lands' End had featured the vintage taxi on the cover of its 1984 holiday catalogue and sold it to the woman for $19,000. In 2005, the man contacted Lands' End and inquired about a full refund on the car. Cheerfully, Lands' End obliged and returned the woman's full purchase price.

This sort of humble business practice seems unusually generous in today's hypercompetitive retail market. But Lands' End has built a cult following—and consistently strong profits—on the basis of kindness and durable, high-quality clothes. When on-line retail sales top US$ 131 billion, companies need any edge they can get.[1] Lands' End gets its edge simply by living in accordance with the Golden Rule. All business practices—customer service, phone support, return procedures, employee treatment, and even relationships with suppliers—flow from the company's principled ideals. Lands' End refers to this philosophy in one simple notion: "What is best for our customer is best for all of us."[2]

John Gress/Reuters/Landov

Lands' End's customer-first policies are necessary to distinguish the company from such catalogue-based competitors as L. L. Bean, a company that has been around more than 50 years longer and has deeper brand equity. And, the firm's inimitable customer experience has long been a shopper's favourite, especially during the holiday season. Though more and more customers order via the company's website, many still prefer to work with the well-trained phone staff, who receive 70 to 80 hours of product, customer service, and computer training when hired. They also respond to e-mails with a personal response, in most cases within three hours.[3]

Jeanne Bliss, author of *Chief Customer Officer* and a 25-year customer service veteran, started her career at Lands' End. She noted, "You've got to do reliability first: 24-hour delivery and answering the phone on the second ring 99.9 percent of the time. Then you've earned the right to do more." If you're Lands' End, "doing more" means adding fun touches, such as

including holiday poems or instructions for turning shipping cartons into barnyard animals.[4]

Born from Boating

Lands' End began in 1963 when founder Gary Comer established the company to sell racing sailboat equipment, along with a handful of sweaters and raincoats. Comer, a 10-year copywriting veteran at the Chicago office of Young & Rubicam, sought a change of pace after leaving the ad industry and struck up a partnership with like-minded sailing enthusiasts.[5] For several years, the company focused on sailing-related products until it became clear that what had been its peripheral merchandise—clothing, canvas luggage, and shoes—was in fact its most profitable.[6]

As the company's focus shifted to the casual, durable clothing it is known for today, its size and its profits continued to grow. By the spring of 1977, the company discontinued carrying sailing equipment altogether. One year later, Comer moved operations from Chicago to Dodgeville, Wisconsin. "I fell in love with the gently rolling hills and woods and cornfields, and being able to see the changing seasons," Comer said. He also likely fell in love with the substantially lower cost of operations.[7]

Lands' End continued to grow and diversify its clothing line for the next 20 years, culminating in a sale to Sears in 2002 for US$ 1.9 billion. Sears planned to expand on the relatively small number of Lands' End stores (only 12 outlet stores existed at the time) by creating a store-within-a-store concept. Some analysts considered this a brilliant move, especially because Lands' End was the top specialty catalogue and top specialty on-line retailer at the time. But the execution floundered when Sears failed to promote the integration. And when faithful Lands' End customers did come to Sears, they found the stock scattered throughout the store.[8]

Lands' End shops are now demarcated from Sears by navy blue signs and columns and occupy an average of 900 square metres (10,000 square feet) per store. According to Sears spokesman Christian Brathwaite, "The idea is to enhance the customer experience and make it easy for customers to shop for Lands' End apparel, coupled with the Lands' End service model. We've seen a very positive customer response."[9]

It's a solid bet for Sears, according to Christopher T. Shannon, managing director at the investment bank Berkery, Noyes & Co., who perceived that the store-within-a-store model was gaining steam. He noted a "rise in demand from the public for more specialty retailers. I believe the goal is to have more of a one-on-one relationship with the end-buyer and offer as many different ways to make a purchase as possible."[10]

Standing Out from the Crowd

To maintain a competitive presence in the crowded retail clothing market, Lands' End employs a number of creative strategies to stay at the forefront of customers' minds and wallets. Its website was the first to offer a feature called "My Virtual Model," a tool that uses customer-supplied measurements to generate a 3-D likeness that can be used to "try on" merchandise. To answer customers' questions as they occur, while maintaining a seamless web shopping experience, Lands' End installed a chat module called "Lands' End Live."

Banking on the durability and conservative styling of its clothes, Lands' End branched out of the traditional retail model to market directly to businesses, institutions, and schools. LEBO—the company's business outfitting division—strives to free organizations from the monotony of stuffy, starched uniforms. To attract attention to this program, LEBO provided a free apparel makeover to three companies, partnering to develop new looks that were eventually highlighted in the LEBO catalog.[11]

When the annual holiday shopping season approaches, Lands' End kicks its customer-retention efforts into high gear. In a recent holiday season, one customer service representative from each of the company's three call centres was chosen to serve as Elf of the Day from November 28 to December 18 and given the discretion to offer randomly selected customers complementary upgrades, such as free gift boxing or monogramming. "It's a way to spread a little extra surprise and happiness to customers," said Lands' End spokesperson Amanda Broderick.[12]

But as other clothing retailers follow suit and improve their customer service skills, Lands' End may begin to find itself with stiff competition and pinched profit margins. Do you think the company has what it takes to distinguish itself in the crowded apparel marketplace?

Discussion Questions

1. How could the planning process be followed to create a plan for continuous improvements in Lands' End's online customer service?

2. If you were hired by Lands' End to help benchmark its customer service performance, which three companies would you choose and why?

3. How could MBO at Lands' End build a clear hierarchy of objectives, improve goal alignment, and help with implementing plans within the customer services area?

4. FURTHER RESEARCH—Browse the Lands' End website and check the business news for updates to learn as much as you can about the company. Do the same for L.L. Bean. Does one firm or the other have any special advantage in respect to planning for future success? Why or why not?

Strategy and Strategic Management

Get ahead and stay ahead with strategy

Coffee just might be the most popular drink in the world. And the well-known Starbucks may hold claim to the most valuable brand name in the industry. But how long can Starbucks keep brewing a better cup of coffee?[1]

"Forever," might answer Howard Schultz, founding chairman and chief global strategist of the company. When he joined Starbucks in 1982 as director of retail operations, the firm was a small coffee retailer in Seattle. But Schultz

(AP Photo/Kin Cheung, file)

had the idea to build a coffee bar culture with Starbucks at its centre. The rest is history. The Seattle-based firm grew to cover over 12,000 locations worldwide—its goal is 40,000.

Schultz's vision was to build Starbucks into an international chain offering the finest coffee drinks and "educating consumers everywhere about fine coffee." He backed the vision with core values that set standards and expectations for everyone. "Provide a great work environment and treat each other with respect and dignity" was one core value; "embrace diversity as an essential component in the way we do things" was another. And the firm prospered.

But with a changing environment, Starbucks faces many hurdles; past successes are not future guarantees. McDonald's, of all chains, has made a major challenge with its new and cheaper upgraded coffee line—including premium roast and even cappuccinos. Tim Hortons is challenging as well with its national and United States expansion plans. While these firms have been on the upswing, Starbucks is struggling with some major problems.[2]

Shortly after Starbucks' board brought Schultz back from retirement to run day-to-day affairs, the firm announced hundreds of store closings and job cutbacks. Most analysts expect that future growth will depend on strategic changes as well as modifications to the product mix.[3] As for Schultz, he says: "Moving forward, we will continue to pursue opportunities that increase long-term value for our shareholders and our partners, provide unique experiences for our customers, and bring us ever closer to our goal of becoming the most recognized and respected brand of coffee in the world."[4] We wonder what Tim Hortons has up its sleeve to respond to Starbucks' strategic goal.

BENCHMARK Most likely, you're not very far away from a cup of Starbucks coffee. The smells of those fresh brews are reminders of how Schultz got his firm out ahead of the pack with his strategy. But to stay ahead, Starbucks' recent experience shows that strategies also need to be continuously tuned to changing times and supported by great implementation.

Critical Thinking

There shouldn't be any disagreement that crafting great strategies requires critical thinking. It is an analytical skill that involves the ability to gather and interpret information for decision-making in a problem context. How good are you at making critical connections in unusual situations? Take a stab at the two puzzles. Get help from a friend if you have trouble finding the solutions.[5]

A good way to develop critical thinking skills is through case studies and problem-solving projects in your courses. But beware—one of the risks of our information-rich environment is over-reliance on what we hear or read, especially when it comes from the Web. A lot of what circulates is anecdotal, superficial, irrelevant, and even just plain inaccurate. You must be disciplined, cautious, and discerning in interpreting the credibility and usefulness of information.

Whether you are searching the Web, talking with others, listening to presentations, or browsing reports and other information sources, critical thinking demands more than the ability to read and hear. Accessing information is one thing; sorting through it to identify what is solid and what is weak or pure nonsense is another. Determining what information is useful in a specific problem context is one thing; analyzing and integrating that information to make it useful for solid problem solving is yet another. Once you understand this and are willing to invest the time for critical thinking, the returns can be great.

Puzzle 1
Divide this shape into four shapes that are exactly the same size as one another.

Puzzle 2
Draw no more than four lines that cross all nine dots; don't lift your pencil while drawing.

❖ Get to Know Yourself Better

Sometimes our careers can be a lot like puzzles; everything looks pretty easy until you get down to the task. Is your personal career strategy well attuned to the future job market, not just the present one? Are you showing strong critical thinking skills as you make academic choices and prepare for your career? Make a list of information you need to best make solid career choices. Identify where you can obtain this information and how credible the sources might be. Write a short plan that uses this information and commits you to activities in this academic year that can improve your career readiness.

CHAPTER 7 STUDY QUESTIONS

- What is strategic management?
- What are the essentials of strategic analysis?
- What are corporate strategies and how are they formulated?
- What are business strategies and how are they formulated?
- What are some current issues in strategy implementation?

VISUAL CHAPTER OVERVIEW

CHAPTER 7 STRATEGY AND STRATEGIC MANAGEMENT

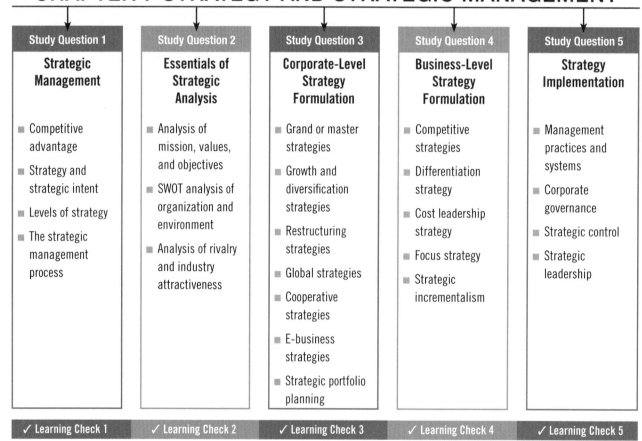

Study Question 1	Study Question 2	Study Question 3	Study Question 4	Study Question 5
Strategic Management	**Essentials of Strategic Analysis**	**Corporate-Level Strategy Formulation**	**Business-Level Strategy Formulation**	**Strategy Implementation**
■ Competitive advantage ■ Strategy and strategic intent ■ Levels of strategy ■ The strategic management process	■ Analysis of mission, values, and objectives ■ SWOT analysis of organization and environment ■ Analysis of rivalry and industry attractiveness	■ Grand or master strategies ■ Growth and diversification strategies ■ Restructuring strategies ■ Global strategies ■ Cooperative strategies ■ E-business strategies ■ Strategic portfolio planning	■ Competitive strategies ■ Differentiation strategy ■ Cost leadership strategy ■ Focus strategy ■ Strategic incrementalism	■ Management practices and systems ■ Corporate governance ■ Strategic control ■ Strategic leadership
✓ Learning Check 1	✓ Learning Check 2	✓ Learning Check 3	✓ Learning Check 4	✓ Learning Check 5

Set the opening Starbucks story aside for a moment and switch to another global name—Walmart Canada. Its master plan is elegant in its simplicity: to deliver consistently low prices and high-quality customer service.[6] The plan is pursued with the latest technology and sophisticated logistics. Inventories are monitored around the clock, and a world-class distribution system ensures that stores are rarely out of the items customers are seeking.

All systems and people are rallied to deliver on the objectives—low prices and quality service. At least, that's the plan.

As with Starbucks, times have changed; even Walmart can't rest on its laurels. It's been challenged on everything from its wage levels, to employee benefits, to its impact on competition in local communities, to the sustainability of its low-price business model.[7] Not too long ago, Walmart's competitors were consistently asking: "How can we keep up?" Now Canadian retailers such as Canadian Tire, Giant Tiger, and Zellers have become not just competitors, but a nemesis. In conversations in Walmart's Canadian headquarters in Mississauga, Ontario, you're likely to hear the strategists asking: "Are we still ahead, and if so, how can we stay ahead?"

Strategic Management

The forces and challenges evident in the opening examples confront managers in all organizations and industries. The result is that today's management environment places a great premium on "competitive advantage" and how it is achieved, or not, through "strategy" and "strategic management."

COMPETITIVE ADVANTAGE

One of Walmart's major strengths is its ability to cut costs, or "drive them out of the system," as its CEO says. To do this, the retailer makes aggressive use of the latest computer technologies to gain efficiencies in its supply chains, track sales, and quickly adjust orders and inventories to match buying trends. This is all part of Walmart's quest for **competitive advantage**, operating with a combination of attributes that allow it to outperform rivals. You should remember this term from earlier chapters. It is an ability to use resources so well that the organization performs better than the competition. Typical sources of competitive advantage include:[8]

> **Competitive advantage** is the ability to do something so well that one outperforms competitors.

- *Cost and quality*—where strategy drives an emphasis on operating efficiency and product or service quality.

- *Knowledge and speed*—where strategy drives an emphasis on innovation and speed of delivery to market for new ideas.

- *Barriers to entry*—where strategy drives an emphasis on creating a market stronghold that is protected from entry by others.

- *Financial resources*—where strategy drives an emphasis on investments or loss absorption that competitors can't match.

As just suggested, organizations pursue competitive advantage in different ways. Dell Computer eliminates wholesale supplier markups by marketing directly to consumers; Toyota's manufacturing systems reduce cycle times and allow it to carry a smaller work-in-process inventory; Mozilla's open-source networks allow for continual improvements to its Firefox web browser. But even as these organizations do such things very well, rivals try to duplicate the success stories. Thus, the goal becomes creating **sustainable competitive advantage**, one that is difficult or costly for others to copy or imitate.

> **Sustainable competitive advantage** is the ability to outperform rivals in ways that are difficult or costly to imitate.

STRATEGY AND STRATEGIC INTENT

If sustainable competitive advantage is the goal, "strategy" is the means to its achievement.[9] A **strategy** is a comprehensive action plan that identifies the long-term direction for an organization and guides resource utilization to achieve sustainable competitive advantage. It is a "best

> A **strategy** is a comprehensive plan guiding resource allocation to achieve long-term organization goals.

guess" about what must be done for future success in the face of rivalry and changing conditions. As BC Business Online notes: "Despite today's emphasis on strategic planning, few businesses actually think very long-term. Bigger market-listed businesses focus on the quarter to keep their stock up; small businesses are notorious for believing long-term means anything beyond next month."[10]

The "long-term" aspect of strategy is becoming ever shorter in a world of globalization and changing technologies. As it does, the challenges to the strategist become even greater. It used to be that companies could count on traditional "build-and-sell" business models that largely put them in control of their markets and made strategies long-lasting. In the early days of the automobile industry, Henry Ford once said: "The customer can have any color he wants as long as it's black." His firm, quite literally, was in the driver's seat. Today's auto executives have learned that they must come up with strategies that are driven by customers and economic realities. Stephen Haeckel, director of strategic studies at IBM's Advanced Business Institute, describes the shift in strategic thinking this way: "It's a difference between a bus, which follows a set route, and a taxi, which goes where customers tell it to go."[11]

Strategic intent focuses and applies organizational energies on a unifying and compelling goal.

All of this increases the importance of strategy as a plan that helps allocate resources among alternative uses. Just as with our personal resources, organizational resources like time, money, and people can sometimes get wasted on things that don't really add up to much value. A strategy helps ensure that resources are used with consistent **strategic intent**, that is, with all energies directed toward accomplishing a long-term target or goal.[12] At Coca-Cola, for example, strategic intent has been described as "to put a Coke within 'arm's reach' of every consumer in the world." Given this, we would not expect to find Coca-Cola investing in snack and convenience foods, as does its archrival PepsiCo. Yet such investments are consistent with Pepsi's strategic intent of being "the world's premier consumer products company focused on convenient food and beverages."[13]

GOING GLOBAL

LEHMAN BROTHERS—STRATEGY GONE WRONG

On September 15, 2008, Lehman Brothers, a global financial services firm with headquarters in New York City, London, and Tokyo and offices around the world, filed for bankruptcy protection. This was the largest bankruptcy filing in U.S. history. What went wrong? Lehman's losses were partially due to its strategy of holding on to large positions in subprime mortgages during the financial crisis, although allegations of short-selling and poor leadership are also cited. Richard S. "Dick" Fuld, Jr., who was the CEO in 2008, is widely held responsible for this strategic disaster. Interestingly, in 2006 Fuld was named #1 CEO by *Institutional Investor* magazine and in 2007 he received a $22-million bonus for his efforts. After the collapse and when it was clear how adrift Lehman Brothers had been, CNBC named Fuld the "Worst American CEO of All Time."

LEVELS OF STRATEGY

Three levels of strategy guide the activities of most enterprises. Shown in Figure 7.1, they are corporate strategy, business strategy, and functional strategy.

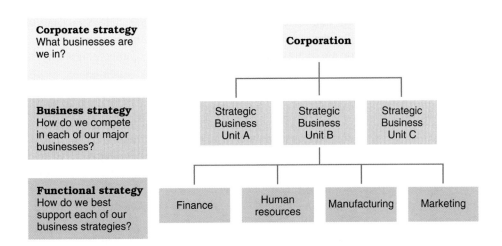

Figure 7.1 Three levels of strategy in organizations—corporate, business, and functional strategies.

Corporate-Level Strategy

The level of **corporate strategy** directs the organization as a whole toward sustainable competitive advantage. It describes the scope of operations by answering the following strategic question: "In what industries and markets should we compete?" The purpose of corporate strategy is to set direction and guide resource allocations for the entire enterprise.

In large, complex organizations, corporate strategy identifies how the company intends to compete across multiple industries and markets. General Electric, for example, owns over 100 businesses in a wide variety of areas, including aircraft engines, appliances, capital services, medical systems, broadcasting, and power systems. Typical strategic decisions for GE at the corporate level relate to things like acquisitions, expansions, and cutbacks across this complex portfolio.

A **corporate strategy** sets long-term direction for the total enterprise.

Business-Level Strategy

Business strategy is the strategy for a single business unit or product line. The selection of strategy at the business level involves answering this question: "How are we going to compete for customers in this industry and market?" Typical business strategy decisions include choices about product and service mix, facilities locations, new technologies, and the like.

In single-product enterprises, business strategy is the corporate strategy. But in large conglomerates like General Electric, a variety of business strategies will be followed. The term *strategic business unit* (SBU) is often used to describe a single business firm within a larger enterprise. Whereas the enterprise as a whole will have a corporate strategy, each SBU will have its own business strategy.

A **business strategy** identifies how a division or strategic business unit will compete in its product or service domain.

Functional Strategy

Functional strategy guides the use of organizational resources to implement business strategy. This level of strategy focuses on activities within a specific functional area such as marketing, manufacturing, finance, or human resources. The strategic question to be answered in selecting functional strategies is: "How can we best utilize resources within a function to implement our business strategy?" Answers to this question typically involve the choice of management practices within each function that improve operating efficiency, product or service quality, customer service, or innovativeness.

A **functional strategy** guides activities within one specific area of operations.

THE STRATEGIC MANAGEMENT PROCESS

Developing strategy for a business may seem a deceptively simple task: find out what customers want, provide it for them at the best prices and service, and make sure competitors can't

Strategic management is the process of formulating and implementing strategies.

Strategic analysis is the process of analyzing the organization, the environment, and the organization's competitive position and current strategies.

Strategy formulation is the process of crafting strategies to guide the allocation of resources.

Strategy implementation is the process of putting strategies into action.

copy what you are doing well. In practice, things can get very complicated.[14] Strategies don't just happen; they must be developed and then well implemented. And at the same time that managers in one organization are trying to craft a great strategy, their competitors are trying to do the same.

Strategic management is the process of formulating and implementing strategies to accomplish long-term goals and sustain competitive advantage. You can think of it as making decisions that allocate an organization's resources so as to consistently outperform rivals. As shown in Figure 7.2, the process begins with **strategic analysis** to assess the organization, its environment, its competitive positioning, and its current strategies. Next is **strategy formulation**, developing a new or revised strategy with the goal of sustainable competitive advantage. The final phase in the process is **strategy implementation**, using resources to put strategies into action, and then evaluating results. As the late management consultant and guru Peter Drucker once said: "The future will not just happen if one wishes hard enough. It requires decision—now. It imposes risk—now. It requires action—now. It demands allocation of resources, and above all, of human resources—now. It requires work—now."[15]

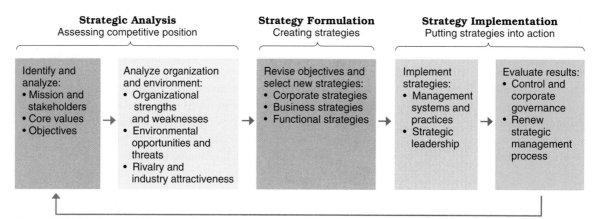

Figure 7.2 Major elements in the strategic management process.

✔ **Learning Check 1**

BE SURE YOU CAN

• define *competitive advantage*, *strategy*, and *strategic intent* • explain the concept of sustainable competitive advantage • differentiate corporate, business, and functional strategies • differentiate strategy formulation from strategy implementation • list the major components in the strategic management process

ESSENTIALS OF STRATEGIC ANALYSIS

Can you name this firm? Its headquarters is in Toronto, Ontario. It sells outdoor clothing and gear, and its products are top-quality and high-priced. It is known for a commitment to sustainability and respect for the natural environment. Its larger competitors include Northface and Columbia Sportsgear. Its earnings are consistently above the industry average. Its workforce is loyal and inspired, and you are as likely to find its CEO Dani Reiss protecting polar bears in the Arctic as working in the office. It is also a strategic success story.[16]

The firm is Canada Goose Inc. Keep it in mind as we now consider the foundation issues in strategic analysis. Think too about this set of questions that Peter Drucker often asked of his clients when consulting with them about strategic management: (1) What is your business mission? (2) Who are your customers? (3) What do your customers value? (4) What have been your results? (5) What is your plan?[17]

ANALYSIS OF MISSION, VALUES, AND OBJECTIVES

The strategic management process begins with a review and clarification of **mission**, values, and objectives. This sets the stage for assessing the organization's resources and capabilities, as well as competitive opportunities and threats in its external environment.

A **mission** statement expresses the organization's reason for existence in society.

Mission and Stakeholders

As first discussed in Chapter 1, the mission or purpose of an organization may be described as its reason for existence in society.[18] Strategy consultant Michael Hammer believes that a mission should represent what the strategy or underlying business model is trying to accomplish. To clarify mission, he suggests asking: "What are we moving to?" "What is our dream?" "What kind of a difference do we want to make in the world?" "What do we want to be known for?"[19]

The mission of outdoor clothing maker Patagonia is straightforward: "Build the best product, cause no unnecessary harm, use business to inspire and implement solutions to the environmental crisis."[20] In this mission, one finds not only a business direction but also a distinctive value commitment, one that gives Patagonia a unique identity as it competes with much larger rivals in its industry.

A clear sense of mission helps managers keep organizations on track and use resources with strategic intent. Starbucks' mission is to be "the premier purveyor of the finest coffee in the world, while maintaining our uncompromising principles as we grow." Over at Canadian coffee giant Tim Hortons, you will find its mission is "to deliver superior quality products and services for our customers and communities through leadership, innovation and partnerships. Our vision is to be the quality leader in everything we do."[21] It might be seen as a fine line—finest versus superior quality—but one does notice a difference in the price charged for the finest quality compared with a superior quality coffee, although in this case, quality is truly judged by the holder of the cup!

Stakeholders are individuals and groups directly affected by the organization and its strategic accomplishments.

A clear sense of mission also helps managers inspire the support and respect of an organization's **stakeholders**. You should recall that these are individuals and groups—including customers, shareholders, suppliers, creditors, community groups, and others—who are directly affected by the organization and its accomplishments. A **strategic constituencies analysis** is a useful tool in the strategic management process. It assesses the specific interests of each stakeholder, along with the organization's record in responding to them. Figure 7.3 gives an example of how stakeholder interests can be linked with the mission of a business firm.

A **strategic constituencies analysis** assesses interests of stakeholders and how well the organization is responding to them.

Employees
We respect the individuality of each employee . . . creativity and productivity are encouraged, valued, and rewarded.

Communities
We are committed to being caring and supportive corporate citizens within the worldwide communities in which we operate.

Mission

Shareholders
We are dedicated to . . . performing in a manner that will enhance returns on investments.

Customers
We are committed to providing superior value in our products and services.

Suppliers
We think of our suppliers as partners who share our goal of . . . highest quality.

Figure 7.3 External stakeholders as strategic constituencies in an organization's mission statement.

Core Values

Behaviour in and by organizations will always be affected in part by **core values**, which are broad beliefs about what is or is not appropriate behaviour. Canada Goose CEO Dani Reiss says: "It's about

Core values are broad beliefs about what is or is not appropriate behaviour.

authenticity, and how we believe in being real. So much stuff is made offshore, but part of corporate responsibility is about making sure everyone has a good place to work that adds to the quality of their life. That's very much part of our core values." Reiss leads Canada Goose with a personal commitment to sustainability, particularly within the Canadian economy. He expects the firm to live up to his values and fulfill its responsibilities as a steward of the natural environment. In his words: "That's because sustainability means more than watching your carbon output; by keeping positions in Canada, the company helps to build vibrant communities through good-paying jobs."[22]

Organizational culture is the predominant value system for the organization as a whole.

The Canada Goose example shows how the personal values of a founder and leader can become part of the **organizational culture**, more fully discussed in Chapter 10 as the predominant value system of the organization as a whole.[23] In the strategic management process, core values and the organizational culture should be assessed to determine how well they align with and support the organization's mission.[24] The presence of strong core values helps build organizational identity, giving a sense of character to the organization in the eyes of its employees and external stakeholders. Core values also back up the mission by helping guide the behaviour of organization members in meaningful and consistent ways. When browsing Canada Goose's website, for example, the message about the corporate values is consistent: "Canada Goose is deeply committed to the preservation of our global environment and the humane treatment of animals."[25]

REAL ETHICS

Customers Hurt by Skybus Failure

High fuel prices, a bad economy, and perhaps a flawed business model led to the folding of Skybus Airlines at midnight one Friday in 2008. The closure of the discount carrier cost 450 employees their jobs, and it hit many passengers where it hurts most—stranded with no flight home and facing costly alternative transportation choices.

Scene: Passengers were waiting to board their Skybus flight in Columbus, Ohio. Rumours moved through the line that the company was going "belly up." Sure enough, when they boarded the plane, the pilot had an announcement: There would be no return flight. He also said he would hold the plane for 20 minutes while they each decided what to do; his conscience wouldn't allow him to do otherwise, he said.

Scene: Same airport, same airline, same day, but another flight. This time, passengers boarded their plane and flew off without knowing it was a one-way trip. The pilots and crew said nothing. When the plane landed, they heard the standard message: "Thanks again for flying Skybus; don't forget to check our website for great deals."

One passenger, Tech Sergeant Gary Patterson, had flown into Columbus from his Air Force base to visit his girlfriend. After learning that Skybus had folded and he had no flight back, Patterson said "common courtesy" should have allowed passengers at least a week's notice to make other arrangements.

YOU DECIDE

Is it acceptable for a company to simply fold like this without any warning to employees and customers? How could this situation have been handled better by Skybus? And why can a pilot do the "right" thing by customers while executives seem unable to act? Is it because the pilot is close to the customers, and the executives too far removed? What does this say about the airline's core values?

Objectives

Whereas a mission statement sets forth an organization's purpose, and core values establish standards for accomplishing it, **operating objectives** direct activities toward key performance areas. They turn a broad sense of mission into specific performance targets. Although organizations pursue a wide variety of operating objectives, those typical of a business often include the following.[26]

Operating objectives are specific results that organizations try to accomplish.

- *Profitability*—operating with a net profit.
- *Financial health*—acquiring capital; earning positive returns.
- *Cost efficiency*—using resources well to operate at low cost.
- *Customer service*—meeting customer needs and maintaining loyalty.
- *Product quality*—producing high-quality goods or services.
- *Market share*—gaining a specific share of possible customers.
- *Human talent*—recruiting and maintaining a high-quality workforce.
- *Innovation*—developing new products and processes.
- *Social responsibility*—making a positive contribution to society.

The strategic management process should make sure that operating objectives align with and drive the organization toward its mission. In the case of Canada Goose, the mission, values, and operating objectives seem to fit well together as a coherent whole. CEO Reiss shares that: "The key for us is to stay authentic. It is important to stay true to who we are. The goal," he says, "is to stay relevant without going down-market." Although one of the firm's objectives is growth, for Reiss it isn't just any growth or growth at any cost; the objective lies in limiting supply to maintain exclusivity using controlled growth.[27]

SWOT ANALYSIS OF ORGANIZATION AND ENVIRONMENT

After the assessment of mission, values, and objectives, the next step in the strategic management process is to analyze the organization and its environment using a technique known as **SWOT analysis**. As shown in Figure 7.4, this is an internal analysis of *organizational strengths and weaknesses* as well as the external analysis of *environmental opportunities and threats*.

A **SWOT analysis** examines organizational strengths and weaknesses and environmental opportunities and threats.

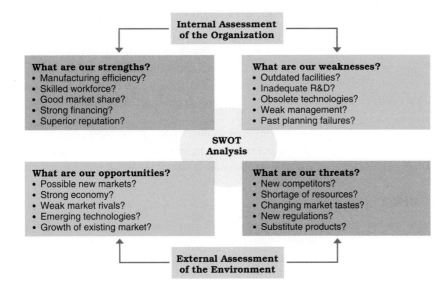

Figure 7.4 SWOT analysis of strengths, weaknesses, opportunities, and threats.

Organizational Strengths and Weaknesses

A SWOT analysis begins with a systematic evaluation of the organization's resources and capabilities—its basic strengths and weaknesses. You can think of this as an analysis of organizational capacity for action, or capacity to achieve its objectives. A major goal in assessing strengths is to identify **core competencies**—things that the organization has or does exceptionally well in comparison with competitors. They are capabilities that, because they are rare, costly to imitate, and cannot be substituted, become potential sources of competitive advantage.[28] Core competencies may be found in special knowledge or expertise, superior technologies, or unique distribution systems, among many other possibilities.

Organizational weaknesses are the other side of the picture. The goal in assessing weaknesses is to identify things that inhibit performance and hold the organization back from fully accomplishing its objectives. Examples might be outdated products, lack of capital, shortage of talented workers, or poor technology. When weaknesses are identified, plans can be set to eliminate or reduce them, or to possibly turn them into strengths. Even if some weaknesses cannot be corrected, they need to be understood. Strategies should ideally build upon organizational strengths and minimize the negative impact of weaknesses.

Environmental Opportunities and Threats

No SWOT analysis is complete until opportunities and threats in the external environment are also analyzed. As shown in Figure 7.4, opportunities may exist as possible new markets, a strong economy, weaknesses in competitors, and emerging technologies. Environmental threats may be such things as the emergence of new competitors, resource scarcities, changing customer tastes, new government regulations, and a weak economy. Imagine, for example, the threats faced by airline executives when the world economy headed toward recession and oil prices vacillated. These forces upset existing strategies and caused major rethinking about what to do next. Some airlines adjusted tactically through reduced flight schedules, fleet cutbacks, and employee layoffs. Others made substantial strategy shifts; Air Canada and WestJet adapted while the low-fare start-up Zoom Airlines went out of business.

ANALYSIS OF RIVALRY AND INDUSTRY ATTRACTIVENESS

When it comes to strategic analysis, Harvard scholar and consultant Michael Porter further points our attention toward what he calls the nature of rivalry and competition within the industry. The ideal condition for a firm is to operate in *monopoly* conditions as the only player in an industry; that is, to have no rivals to compete with for resources or customers. Although the firm's strategy is largely unchallenged due to its monopoly status, this ideal is rare except in highly regulated settings. The reality for most businesses is rivalry and competition that unfolds either under conditions of *oligopoly*—facing just a few competitors, such as in a consolidated airline industry; or *hyper-competition*—facing several direct competitors, such as in the fast-food industry.[29] Both oligopoly and hyper-competition are strategically challenging, and the latter is especially so because any competitive advantage tends to be short-lived.

Porter's Five Forces Model

Porter offers the five forces model shown in Figure 7.5 as a framework for competitive industry analysis. An understanding of these five forces can help managers make strategic choices that best position a firm within its industry.[30]

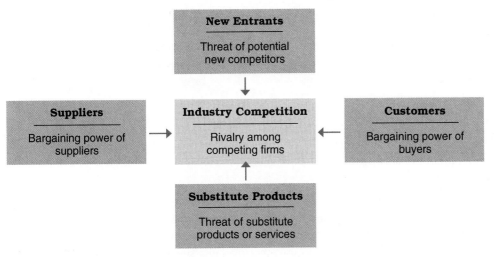

Figure 7.5 Porter's model of five strategic forces affecting industry competition.

Source: Adapted with permission of The Free Press, a Division of Simon & Schuster, Inc., from *Competitive Strategy* by Michael E. Porter. Copyright 1980, 1988 by The Free Press.

1. *Industry competition*—the intensity of rivalry among firms in the industry and the ways they behave competitively toward one another.

2. *New entrants*—the threat of new competitors entering the market, based on the presence or absence of barriers to entry.

3. *Substitute products or services*—the threat of substitute products or services, based on the ability of consumers to find what they want from other sellers.

4. *Bargaining power of suppliers*—the ability of resource suppliers to influence the price that one has to pay for their products or services.

5. *Bargaining power of customers*—the ability of customers to influence the price that they will pay for the firm's products or services.

Industry Attractiveness

The five competitive forces constitute what Porter calls the "industry structure," and it establishes the industry's attractiveness or potential to generate long-term returns. The less attractive the industry structure, the harder it will be to make good strategic choices and realize a sustained competitive advantage relative to rivals. According to a five forces analysis, an *unattractive industry* is one in which rivalry among competitors is intense, substantial threats exist in the form of possible new entrants and substitute products, and suppliers and buyers are very powerful in bargaining over such things as prices and quality. An *attractive industry*, by contrast, has less existing competition, few threats from new entrants or substitutes, and low bargaining power among suppliers and buyers.

BE SURE YOU CAN

 **Learning Check ❷**

• explain what a mission statement is and illustrate how a good mission statement helps organizations • list several operating objectives of organizations • define *core competency* • explain SWOT analysis • explain how Porter's five forces model can be used to assess the attractiveness of an industry

CORPORATE-LEVEL STRATEGY FORMULATION

The CEO and the senior management team in a business focus on corporate-level strategy formulation. The goal at this level of strategic analysis is to plot the overall direction of the organization in the competitive setting of its industry.

GRAND OR MASTER STRATEGIES

The choice of corporate-level strategies generally begins with what are called "grand" or "master" strategies. These are the growth, stability, renewal, and combination strategies.[31]

Growth Strategy

A growth strategy involves expansion of the organization's current operations.

Growth strategies seek to expand the size and scope of operations in respect to such things as total sales, market shares, and operating locations. When you hear terms like "acquisition," "merger," and "global expansion," for example, the underlying master strategy is one of growth. Although there is a tendency to equate growth with effectiveness, that is not necessarily the case. It is possible to get caught in an "expansion trap" where growth outruns an organization's capacity to run effectively.

Mark Zuckerberg, founder and chief executive at Facebook, knows the challenges of a growth strategy pretty well. Zuckerberg started Facebook as a college student. When it was opened to the public in 2006, it quickly generated over 14 million site visits; by 2008, monthly visitors topped 100 million. But spending was still outrunning revenues, and the *Wall Street Journal* claimed the firm had "growing pains." Zuckerberg asked: "Is being a CEO always this hard?" His response was to hire an experienced Google vice president, Sheryl Sandberg, as Chief Operating Officer to lead Facebook's continued expansion.[32]

Stability Strategy

A stability strategy maintains current operations without substantial changes.

Stability strategies try to maintain an existing course of action without major changes. At a retail firm, for example, stability may mean working with current customers in the same markets and in mostly the same ways as in the past, while avoiding any major investments in new initiatives. Stability is sometimes pursued when an organization is performing well, already operating at capacity, or when the environment appears stable or exceptionally risky. In the latter case, strategic managers may make the decision to "wait," rather than "leap," until current conditions change for the better.

Renewal Strategy

A renewal strategy tries to solve problems and overcome weaknesses that are hurting performance.

Renewal strategies, also called *retrenchment strategies* or *defensive strategies*, try to solve problems and overcome weaknesses. They often cut size and rearrange operations to improve performance. When *Globe and Mail* chief executive and publisher Phillip Crawley faced problems with dropping customer demand in a recessionary economy, for example, he announced a voluntary severance plan for some 80 workers, or 10 percent of its Canadian staff.[33]

In **liquidation**, business operations cease and assets are sold to pay creditors.

A decision to retrench, like Crawley's, can be difficult to make; it seems to be an admission of failure. But retrenchment is a viable strategic option under appropriate circumstances. When you hear terms like "restructuring," "divestiture," and "bankruptcy," the underlying master strategy is renewal and retrenchment. In fact, U.S. law allows firms to file for bankruptcy protection while they regroup and make changes to restore profitability. In Canada, bankruptcy is set out by a federal law called the *Bankruptcy and Insolvency Act* and is applicable to both businesses and individuals. The most extreme form of retrenchment is **liquidation**, where business ceases and assets are sold to pay creditors.

Combination Strategy

Combination strategies pursue one or more of the other strategies at the same time. This is common in complex and diversified firms, which may be retrenching in one major business line while seeking growth in another, and operating with stability in still another. In the case of *The Globe and Mail* again, at the same time that the newspaper was announcing plans to reduce domestic capacity by 10 percent, it was also announcing plans to introduce new printing technology to modernize and improve the quality of colour advertisements.[34]

A **combination strategy** pursues growth, stability, and/or retrenchment in some combination.

GROWTH AND DIVERSIFICATION STRATEGIES

Growth is one of the most common and popular of the grand strategies. It is popular in part because growth is viewed as necessary for long-run survival in some industries, and also because organizations have a variety of strategic options in how to pursue growth.

One approach to growth is through **concentration**, where expansion is within the same business area. Tim Hortons, Canadian Tire, Roots, and others pursue growth strategies while still concentrating on their primary business areas. Because of limits to growth in domestic markets, some Canadian firms are aggressively expanding into markets south of the border and around the world.

Growth through **concentration** is growth within the same business area.

Growth can also be pursued through **diversification**, where expansion takes place in new and different business areas. A strategy of *related diversification* pursues growth by acquiring new businesses or entering business areas that are related to what one already does. An example is the acquisition of Tropicana by PepsiCo. Although Tropicana specializes in fruit juices, the business is related to PepsiCo's expertise in the beverages industry. A strategy of *unrelated diversification* pursues growth by acquiring businesses or entering business areas that are different from what one already does. Tata Group, for example, is a $30-billion (U.S.) Indian conglomerate and FT Global 500 company. It started as a textile firm, but now owns 98 companies in diverse industries such as steel, chemicals, telecommunications, communications and outsourcing, hotels, mining, and automobiles—with brands including Jaguar and Land Rover. As Tata continues to grow and diversify, Chairman Ratan N. Tata says: "We have been thinking bigger . . . we have been bolder . . . we have been more aggressive in the marketplace."[35]

Growth through **diversification** is growth by acquisition of or investment in new and different business areas.

Diversification can also take the form of **vertical integration**, where a business acquires suppliers (backward vertical integration) or distributors (forward vertical integration). Backward vertical integration was once common in the automobile industry, as firms purchased suppliers to ensure quality and control over the availability of key parts. In beverages, both Coca-Cola and PepsiCo have pursued forward vertical integration by purchasing some of their major bottlers.

Growth through **vertical integration** is growth by acquiring suppliers or distributors.

RESTRUCTURING STRATEGIES

When organizations are in trouble, perhaps experiencing problems brought about by a bad economy or too much growth and diversification, the goal shifts toward renewal.[36] A **restructuring** strategy tries to correct weaknesses by changing the mix or reducing the scale of operations. The idea is to reverse or change an approach that isn't working, and reorganize to compete better in the future.

Restructuring changes the mix or reduces the scale of operations.

Restructuring by **turnaround** focuses on fixing specific performance problems. When McDonald's executives realized they were largely missing the boom in coffee sales led by Starbucks and Tim Hortons in Canada, they crafted a turnaround strategy called Plan to Win. It included adding wireless Internet to restaurants and changing internal décor and seating to encourage more of a "coffee house" atmosphere. The coffee blend was changed and specialty coffees added to menus. Plan to Win delivered as hoped, with McDonald's experiencing rising coffee sales.[37]

A **turnaround** strategy tries to fix specific performance problems.

A **downsizing** strategy decreases the size of operations.

Restructuring by **downsizing** decreases the size of operations, often by reducing the workforce.[38] A dramatic example was the release of tens of thousands of auto workers in Canada and across the globe. Such cutbacks are most successful when done in targeted ways that advance specific performance objectives, rather than being simple "across the board cuts."[39] The term *rightsizing* is used to describe downsizing with a clear strategic focus.

Divestiture sells off parts of the organization to refocus attention on core business areas.

Restructuring by **divestiture** also reduces size, this time by selling off parts of the organization to refocus on core competencies, cut costs, and improve operating efficiency. This strategy is followed when organizations become over-diversified and have problems managing so much complexity. It is also a strategy followed by organizations that want to profit from the value of internal assets by selling them off as independent businesses.

GLOBAL STRATEGIES

Very few businesses operate today without some exposure to and direct involvement in international operations. A key aspect of corporate strategy, therefore, is how the firm approaches the global economy and its mix of business risks and opportunities. Very often, a grand or master strategy of growth is pursued with the support of an accompanying global strategy.[40]

A **globalization strategy** adopts standardized products and advertising for use worldwide.

An easy way to spot differences in global strategies is to notice how products are developed and advertised around the world. A firm pursuing a **globalization strategy** tends to view the world as one large market, making most decisions from the corporate home base and trying as much as possible to standardize products and their advertising for use everywhere. The latest Gillette razors, for example, are typically sold and advertised similarly around the world. This reflects a somewhat ethnocentric view, assuming that everyone everywhere wants the same thing.

A **multi-domestic strategy** customizes products and advertising to best fit local needs.

Firms using a **multi-domestic strategy** try to customize products and their advertising as much as possible to fit the local needs of different countries or regions. Local and regional managers are given authority to provide this differentiation. Many consumer goods companies, such as Bristol Myers, Procter & Gamble, and Unilever, take this polycentric view and vary their products to fit consumer preferences in different countries and cultures. McDonald's is another example. Although you can get your standard fries and Big Mac in most locations, you can have a McVeggie in India, a McArabia Kofta in Saudi Arabia, a Croque McDo in France, and poutine in Canada.[41]

A **transnational strategy** seeks efficiencies of global operations with attention to local markets.

A third approach is the **transnational strategy** that tries to balance efficiencies in global operations and responsiveness to local markets. The transnational firm, first described in Chapter 3, tries to operate without a strong national identity and blend seamlessly with the global economy to fully tap its business potential. Resources are acquired worldwide; manufacturing and other business functions are performed wherever in the world they can be done best at lowest cost. Ford, for example, draws upon design, manufacturing, and distribution expertise all over the world to build car "platforms" that can then be efficiently modified to meet regional tastes. This geocentric view respects diversity and values talents around the world. Transnational firms like Ford are highly networked, with information and learning continually flowing between headquarters and subsidiaries, and among the subsidiaries themselves.

COOPERATIVE STRATEGIES

In a **strategic alliance**, organizations join together in partnership to pursue an area of mutual interest.

One of the trends today is toward more cooperation among organizations, such as the joint ventures that are common in international business. They are a form of **strategic alliance** in which two or more organizations join together in partnership to pursue an area of mutual interest. One way to cooperate strategically is through *outsourcing alliances*—contracting to purchase important services from another organization. Many organizations, for example, are outsourcing their IT function to firms such as EDS, Infosys, and IBM, in the belief that these services are better provided by a firm with specialized expertise. Cooperation in the supply chain takes the form of *supplier alliances,* in which preferred supplier relationships guarantee a smooth and timely flow of quality supplies among alliance partners. Another common approach today is cooperation in *distribution alliances,* in which firms join together to accomplish sales and distribution of products or services.

A term used to describe cooperation strategies that involve strategic alliances among competitors is **co-opetition**. It applies to situations in which competitors work cooperatively on projects that can benefit all parties. Airlines like United and Lufthansa are major international competitors, but they cooperate in the "Star Alliance," which provides their customers with code-sharing on flights and shared frequent flyer programs. Likewise, luxury car competitors Daimler and BMW are cooperating to co-develop new motors and components for hybrid cars. Such examples of co-opetition reflect what scholars Adam M. Brandenburger and Barry J. Nalebuff call a "revolution mindset," in which strategists recognize that business can be conducted on a playing field of both competitors and cooperating partners.[42]

Co-opetition is the strategy of working with rivals on projects of mutual benefit.

ISSUES AND SITUATIONS
Video Game Contrarian

You may be seeing less sex and gore in video games these days. The industry is broadening markets and responding to criticisms of its traditional product lines. It's moving from the violence of "Mortal Kombat" and sexual situations embedded in "Grand Theft Auto's" secret room into a new world of gaming options. And standing in the middle of the new direction is video game contrarian Will Wright. He was the originator of "Sim City," which earned US$ 320 million for its publisher, and co-created "The Sims," which was also a best seller. His latest is "Spore," in which players create their own whimsical creatures and a full universe emerges from one single-celled organism. To fully explore the possibilities of "Spore," Wright says it would take "79 years if you never slept."

When Wright was a kid, his mother said he used to love to take things apart to see how they worked, including her sewing machine. As a game creator, however, he hasn't always had an easy time. After years of successes with follow-ups to "Sim City," he wanted to work on a new version based on people. An analyst said that executives of Electronic Arts, which by then owned Wright's original firm, "had a hard time communicating with Will." But Wright persevered, even against internal opposition from the sales and marketing departments. At one point, they forecast that "The Sims" would sell 400,000 units

lifetime. Were they ever wrong—2 million shipped within two months of its publication.

CRITICAL RESPONSE

Don't you wonder why Will Wright met such resistance to his idea for "The Sims"? The facts are undeniable: younger people are shifting away from TV time to gaming time, more women are becoming regular gamers, and the average age of gamers is now up to 33. In an environment like this, no wonder the executives are shifting their strategies. But do we pay CEOs to be "followers," reaping the benefits of existing markets? Or do we pay them to be "strategic leaders" who move businesses toward new and profitable markets of the future?

E-BUSINESS STRATEGIES

One of the most frequently asked questions these days for the business executive is "What is your **e-business strategy**?" This refers to strategic use of the Internet to gain competitive advantage—see

An **e-business strategy** strategically uses the Internet to gain competitive advantage.

Management Smarts 7.1.[43] Popular e-business strategies involve B2B (business-to-business) and B2C (business-to-consumer) applications.

A B2B business strategy
uses IT and web portals to link organizations vertically in supply chains.

B2B business strategies use IT and web portals to vertically link organizations with members of their supply chains. When Dell Computer sets up special website services that allow its major corporate customers to manage their accounts on-line, when Walmart suppliers are linked to the firm's information systems and manage inventories for their own products electronically, and even when a business uses an on-line auction site to bid for supplies at the cheapest prices, they are using B2B in various forms.

A B2C business strategy
uses IT and web portals to link businesses with customers.

Most of us probably are more aware of **B2C business strategies** that use IT and web portals to link organizations with their customers. But there is more to success with B2C than simply advertising and selling on-line. The B2C strategy must be fully integrated with supporting functional strategies and operations. Among the e-tailers, for example, Dell has set a benchmarking standard. Its easy-to-use website allows customization of an individual's computer order, in effect offering a design-your-own-product capability. Then a highly efficient and streamlined manufacturing and distribution system takes over to build and quickly ship the computer.

7.1 MANAGEMENT SMARTS
Web-based business models

- *Brokerage model*—bringing buyers and sellers together to make transactions (e.g., CarsDirect.com).

- *Advertising model*—providing information or services while generating revenue from advertising (e.g., Yahoo!).

- *Merchant model*—selling products wholesale and retail through the Web—e-tailing (e.g., chapters.indigo.ca).

- *Subscription model*—selling access to a website through subscription (e.g., *Wall Street Journal* Interactive).

- *Infomediary model*—collecting information on users and selling it to other businesses (e.g., ePinions.com).

- *Community model*—supporting sites by donations from a community of users (e.g., Wikipedia.org).

STRATEGIC PORTFOLIO PLANNING

A portfolio planning approach seeks the best mix of investments among alternative business opportunities.

When firms are highly diversified, like General Electric and the Tata Group, they operate in multiple industries and deal with many products and services. They are also internally complex and often very large in size. This makes resource allocation a challenging strategic management task. The problem is similar to that faced by an individual with limited money who must allocate it among stocks, bonds, and real estate in a personal investment portfolio. In multi-business situations, corporate-level strategy formulation can make use of **portfolio planning** to help allocate scarce resources among competing uses.[44]

The **BCG matrix** analyzes business opportunities according to market growth rate and market share.

Figure 7.6 summarizes an approach to business portfolio planning developed by the Boston Consulting Group and known as the **BCG matrix**. This framework analyzes business

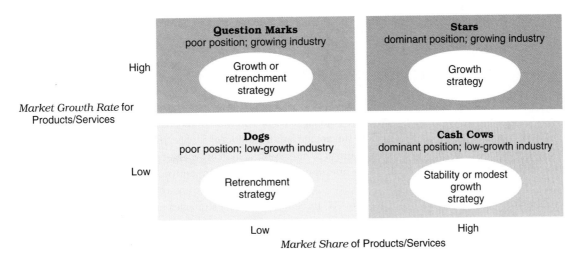

Figure 7.6 The BCG matrix approach for portfolio planning in corporate-level strategy formulation.

opportunities according to industry or market growth rate and market share.[45] As shown in the figure, this comparison results in four possible business conditions, each associated with a strategic implication.

- *Stars*—are high-market-share businesses in high-growth markets. They produce large profits through substantial penetration of expanding markets. The preferred strategy for stars is growth, and further resource investments in them are recommended.

- *Question marks*—are low-market-share businesses in high-growth markets. They do not produce much profit, but they compete in rapidly growing markets. The preferred strategy is growth, but the risk exists that further investments will not result in improved market share. Only the most promising question marks should be targeted for growth; others are candidates for retrenchment by restructuring or divestiture.

- *Cash cows*—are high-market-share businesses in low-growth markets. They produce large profits and a strong cash flow. Because the markets offer little growth opportunity, the preferred strategy is stability or modest growth. "Cows" should be "milked" to generate cash that can be used to support investments in stars and question marks.

- *Dogs*—are low-market-share businesses in low-growth markets. They do not produce much profit, and they show little potential for future improvement. The preferred strategy for dogs is retrenchment by divestiture.

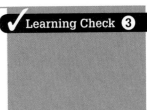

✓ Learning Check ❸

BE SURE YOU CAN
- differentiate the three levels of strategy—corporate, business, and functional • list and explain the major types of growth and diversification strategies and restructuring and divestiture strategies • list and give examples of global strategies • define *strategic alliance* • explain cooperation as a business strategy • explain B2B and B2C as e-business strategies • describe the BCG matrix as a way of strategic portfolio planning

BUSINESS-LEVEL STRATEGY FORMULATION

Michael Porter says that "the company without a strategy is willing to try anything."[46] With a good strategy in place, by contrast, he believes a business can achieve superior profitability or above-average returns within its industry. The key question in business-level strategy formulation is: "How can we best compete for customers in our market and with our products or services?"

COMPETITIVE STRATEGIES

Figure 7.7 shows the model Porter proposes for making choices among possible competitive strategies. He bases business-level strategic decisions on two main considerations: (1) market scope, and (2) source of competitive advantage for the product or service. In respect to *market scope,* the strategic planner asks: "How broad or narrow is the market or target market?" In respect to *source of competitive advantage,* the question is: "Do we seek competitive advantage primarily through low price or product uniqueness?" When these questions are answered and the results analyzed in the matrix shown in Figure 7.7, three business-level strategies are possible: cost leadership, differentiation, and focus. The focus strategy exists in two combinations: focused cost leadership and focused differentiation.

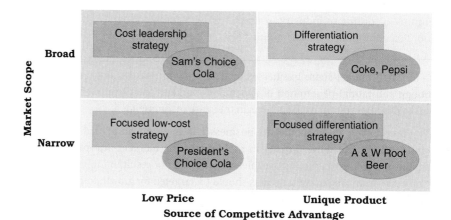

Figure 7.7 Porter's competitive strategies framework: soft drink industry examples.

DIFFERENTIATION STRATEGY

A **differentiation strategy** offers products that are different from the competition.

Organizations pursuing a **differentiation strategy** seek competitive advantage through uniqueness. They try to develop goods and services that are clearly different from the competition or that, through successful advertising, are perceived as clearly different. The objective is to build a strong base of customers that are loyal to the organization's products and lose interest in those of competitors.

To succeed with a differentiation strategy, an organization must have strengths in research and development, marketing, and advertising. An example in the apparel industry is Polo Ralph Lauren, retailer of upscale classic fashions and accessories. In Ralph Lauren's words, "Polo redefined how American style and quality is perceived. Polo has always been about selling quality products by creating worlds and inviting our customers to be part of our dream."[47] Another example of differentiation can be seen in Walmart's recent foray into the Canadian banking industry. In establishing the Walmart Bank Canada, chief executive Trudy Fahie notes, "Walmart will always look to save customers more so they can live better."[48]

In soft drinks, as shown in Figure 7.7, the differentiation examples are Coke and Pepsi. The two are always battling for customer attention and loyalty. Although part of their product differentiation may be in actual taste, another very important part is pure perception. And that is driven by advertising. Coke and Pepsi spend enormous amounts on advertising to create and maintain perceptions that their products are somehow unique.

CANADIAN MANAGERS
Bonnie Brooks and The Bay

In 2008, Bonnie Brooks took over Canada's largest and oldest merchandise retailer as President and CEO of The Bay. Her task: to revitalize and differentiate The Bay's brand. Some would say this would be a daunting task during good economic times, but it would be overwhelming with Canada in the midst of a recession. But Brooks, who came with over two decades of leadership experience,

Mario Beauregard/CPI/ The Canadian Press

including as the president of the Lane Crawford Group in Hong Kong, editor-in-chief of *Flare* magazine, and executive vice-president for Holt Renfrew, has taken a strategic approach to meeting this challenge. Her priority has been to recognize customer needs by dropping brands, adding lines, and slowly making over The Bay. Brooks understands that pleasing customers is central to improving The Bay's bottom line. It is a challenging task, but she's getting the job done.

COST LEADERSHIP STRATEGY

Organizations pursuing a **cost leadership strategy** try to have low costs so that they can sell products and services at low prices. While the low prices drive sales, the low cost structure allows them to still make profits even when selling at low prices that competitors can't match. Success with the cost leadership at low prices strategy requires a continuing search for innovations that increase operating efficiencies throughout purchasing, production, distribution, and other organizational systems.

The classic benchmark for cost leadership in discount retailing is Walmart. The firm is a master at using technology, mass purchasing, and retail savvy to keep its costs so low that it can offer customers the lowest prices and still make a reasonable profit. Whereas most discounters operate with 18-to 20-percent gross margins, Walmart can accept less and still make good returns. Walmart's cost leadership strategy in soft drinks is represented in Figure 7.7 by Sam's Choice Colas. In the financial services industry, President's Choice Financial is a benchmark for cost leadership. By providing limited service yet offering customers lower banking fees and low-cost borrowing, the company is able to attract customers to its cost-saving banking alternatives.

> A **cost leadership strategy** seeks to operate with low costs so that products can be sold at low prices.

FOCUS STRATEGY

Organizations pursuing **focus strategies** concentrate on a special market segment—niche customer group, geographical region, or product or service line. The objective is to serve the needs of the segment better than anyone else. Competitive advantage is achieved by combining focus with either differentiation or cost leadership. In airlines, for example, NetJets focuses on private, secure, and luxury air services for those who can pay a high fee, such as wealthy media stars and executives. This is **focused differentiation**; the firm sells a unique product to a special niche market. Also in airlines, you find carriers like Ryanair and easyJet in Europe offering heavily discounted fares and "no frills" flying. They focus on budget travellers and make profits through lowering costs by flying to regional airports and cutting out free services such as bag checks and in-flight snacks. This is **focused cost leadership**.

> A **focus strategy** concentrates on serving a unique market segment better than anyone else.

> A **focused differentiation** strategy offers a unique product to a special market segment.

> A **focused cost leadership** strategy seeks the lowest costs of operations within a special market segment.

Figure 7.7 shows how both types of focus strategies play out in the soft drink industry. Specialty drinks like A&W Root Beer, Dr. Pepper, and Mountain Dew represent the focused differentiation strategy. Each focuses on a special market segment and tries to compete on the basis of product uniqueness. Other drinks like Equality Cola, Compliments Black Cherry Cola, and Life Brand Lemon Lime Cola represent the focused cost leadership strategy. They also focus on special market segments, but try to compete on low prices made possible by low costs.

You might be wondering at this point about another possible combination—cost leadership and differentiation. In fact, Porter does discuss this, but isn't enthusiastic. He believes that it is hard for a firm to stick with cost leadership when also pursuing differentiation, because differentiation most often drives up costs. "You can compete on price or you can compete on product, but you can't compete on both," the marketers tend to say. And Porter generally agrees. He refers to this strategy combination as *stuck in the middle* and believes it is rarely successful. An example to ponder in the airline industry is Southwest's decision to add premium prices for "business class" and preferred seating. This moves Southwest away from its traditional strength in cost leadership; time will tell if its attempt to combine cost leadership and differentiation will be successful.

STRATEGIC INCREMENTALISM

Strategic incrementalism makes modest changes in strategy as experience builds over time.

Not all strategies are created in systematic and deliberate fashion and then implemented step by step. Instead, strategies often take shape, change, and develop over time as modest adjustments to past patterns. James Brian Quinn calls this a process of **strategic incrementalism**, whereby modest and incremental changes in strategy occur as managers learn from experience and make adjustments.[49]

This approach has much in common with Henry Mintzberg's and John Kotter's descriptions of managerial behaviour, as described in Chapter 1.[50] They view managers as planning and acting in complex interpersonal networks and in hectic, fast-paced work settings. Given these challenges, effective managers must have the capacity to stay focused on long-term objectives while still remaining flexible enough to master short-run problems and opportunities as they occur.

An **emergent strategy** unfolds over time as managers learn from and respond to experience.

Such reasoning has led Mintzberg to identify what he calls **emergent strategies**.[51] These are strategies that develop progressively over time as managers make "streams" of decisions while they learn from and respond to experience. There is an important element of "craftsmanship" here, something that Mintzberg worries may be overlooked by managers who choose and discard strategies in rapid succession while using the formal planning models. He also believes that incremental or emergent strategic planning allows managers and organizations to become really good at implementing strategies, not just formulating them.

✓ Learning Check ④   **BE SURE YOU CAN**

• list and explain the four competitive strategies in Porter's model • illustrate how these strategies apply to products in a market familiar to you • explain the concepts of strategic incrementalism and emergent strategy

STRATEGY IMPLEMENTATION

A discussion of the corporate history on Patagonia Inc.'s website includes this statement: "During the past thirty years, we've made many mistakes but we've never lost our way for very long."[52] Not only is the firm being honest in its public information, it is also communicating an important point about strategic management—mistakes will be made. Sometimes those mistakes will be in poor strategy selection, other times they will be implementation failures. Among the current issues in strategy implementation are needs for excellence in all management systems and practices, the responsibilities of corporate governance, and the importance of strategic control and leadership.

RESEARCH BRIEF

Female directors on corporate boards linked with positive management practices

A growing body of research links the composition of boards of directors with both the financial performance of the firms and their social responsibility behaviours. Building on prior studies, Richard Vernardi, Susan Bosco, and Katie Vassill examined the gender diversity of board membership as an indicator of corporate social responsibility.

The research question guiding their article in *Business and Society* was: "Do firms listed in *Fortune*'s '100 Best Companies to Work For' have a higher percentage of female directors than do *Fortune* 500 companies?" The researchers chose the "100 Best" listing because it includes firms whose employees consider them to have positive organizational cultures and supportive work practices. The evaluations were measured on a 225-item Great Place to Work Trust Index, sent to a random sample of employees in each company. Documentation of female board representatives was obtained by examining company annual reports.

Results confirmed expectations: the percentage of female directors was higher for firms on the "100 Best" list than for those in the *Fortune* 500 overall. In discussing the finding, the researchers suggest that gender diversity on boards of directors may bring about positive organizational changes that make firms better places to work. They also cite the growing presence of women on corporate boards as evidence that firms are changing board memberships to be "more representative of its employee and customer pools."

You be the researcher

Why would the presence of more female directors on a board cause better corporate social performance? Does board diversity, including members of visible minorities and women, lead to different agendas, deliberations, concerns, and strategies? Does it lead to better strategy implementation through greater employee involvement and loyalty? Look at organizations with which you are familiar. Can you see where greater membership diversity in general, not just at the top, makes a difference in the way an organization performs?

MANAGEMENT PRACTICES AND SYSTEMS

The rest of *Management* is really all about strategy implementation. In order to successfully put strategies into action, the entire organization and all of its resources must be mobilized in support of them. This, in effect, involves the complete management process—from planning and controlling through organizing and leading.

No matter how well or elegantly selected, a strategy requires supporting structures, a good allocation of tasks and workflow designs, and the right people to staff all aspects of operations. The strategy needs to be enthusiastically supported by leaders who are capable of motivating everyone, building individual performance commitments, and utilizing teams and teamwork to their best advantage. And the strategy needs to be well and continually communicated to all relevant parties.

Poor management practices hinder strategy implementation in a number of ways. Among them are *failures of substance*. They reflect inadequate attention to the major strategic planning elements, resulting in poor strategic analysis and bad strategy formulation. Other strategic errors are *failures of process*. They reflect poor handling of the ways in which strategic management is accomplished. A common process failure is the **lack of participation error**, discussed in the last chapter as failure to include key persons in the planning process.[53] As a result, they lack commitment to

Lack of participation error is a failure to include key persons in strategic planning.

all-important action and follow-through. Process failure also occurs with too much centralization of planning in top management, or too much delegation to staff planners or separate planning departments. Another process failure is *goal displacement*. This is the tendency to get so bogged down in details that the planning process becomes an end in itself, instead of a means to an end.

CORPORATE GOVERNANCE

Corporate governance is the system of control and performance monitoring of top management.

As was pointed out in Chapter 4 on ethics and social responsibility, organizations today are experiencing lots of pressures at the level of **corporate governance**. This is the system of control and monitoring of top management performance that is exercised by boards of directors and other major stakeholder representatives.

In businesses, members of a board of directors are expected to make sure that an organization operates in the best interests of its owners and that the strategic management of the enterprise is successful.[54] But boards are sometimes too compliant in endorsing or confirming the strategic initiatives of top management. This is one of the concerns raised in the collapse of the U.S. automakers during the economic crisis. People asked: "Did the boards of these firms allow top management to pursue flawed strategies? And if so, how and why did this happen?"

When corporate governance is weak and top management isn't subjected to rigorous oversight and accountability, blame may be placed on the individual board members or on the composition of the board overall. Controversies can arise over the role of inside directors, who are chosen from the senior management of the organization, and outside directors, who are chosen from other organizations and positions external to the organization. In some cases, insiders may have too much control; in others, the outsiders may be selected because they are friends of top management or at least sympathetic to them.

You should recall from Chapter 4 on ethics and social responsibility that corporate boards are under pressure to exercise stronger governance over CEO pay. When, for example, the CEO of Merrill Lynch received total direct compensation of US$ 78.5 million in a year when shareholder return was −41 percent, shareholders and the public at large were vocal in expressing their concerns.[55] The *Wall Street Journal* reports that the chair of one board's compensation committee said: "We understand it is an obligation we have to our shareholders." Of course, the same article notes that many boards are facing shareholder resolutions calling for major revisions in CEO pay policies.[56] "If you won't do it," they seem to be saying to the boards, "we will."

STRATEGIC CONTROL

For sure, the current trend is toward greater emphasis on the responsibilities of corporate governance. Top managers probably feel more performance accountability today than ever before to boards of directors and other stakeholder interest groups. But just as a board of directors is expected to exercise its governance, the top leadership of a firm or organization is expected to

Strategic control makes sure strategies are well implemented and that poor strategies are scrapped or modified.

exercise **strategic control** of the enterprise. That is, they are supposed to make sure strategies are well implemented and that poor strategies are scrapped or modified to quickly meet the performance demands of changing conditions.

And just where, you might ask, was strategic control at Chrysler, Ford, and General Motors over the past years? Was top management in control of these firms in the run-up to the economic crisis and collapse of their markets, or was a lack of control in part to blame for their inability to achieve and maintain competitive advantage versus foreign rivals? Basic management practice would have CEOs and other senior executives always "in control" in the sense of measuring results, evaluating the success of existing strategies, and taking action to improve things in the future. Yet many critics believe strategic control was inadequate at the automakers; top management was simply "going along for the ride"—content to find excuses, rather than solutions, for poor results.

Perhaps the best evidence for strategic control problems at these firms emerged in Congressional hearings where the three CEOs—Robert Nardelli of Chrysler, Alan Mulally of Ford, and Richard Wagoner of GM—asked the (U.S.) government for a US$ 25-billion bailout loan to save them from bankruptcy. One analyst was harshly critical, saying that the firms were "already bankrupt." The message was that their troubles were caused by decision-making failures and the CEOs should be held accountable to the point of two, Wagoner and Nardelli, being removed from their jobs and replaced by newcomers with "fresh ideas to fix things." The review of Ford's Mulally was more forgiving, stating that: "He seems to be making the right moves—cutting costs, eliminating the dividend early on, revamping product plans, mortgaging assets to raise money to fund the turnaround, etc."[57]

The low point in the hearing came when Congressional Representative Brad Sherman asked if any of the CEOs had flown into Washington by commercial airline. "Let the record show," he said, "that no hands went up." The estimated cost of the private jet travel was $20,000 per CEO; a standard economy fare round-trip ticket from Detroit to Washington would have been about $500. This left a negative impression of the CEOs' abilities to exercise strategic control and reinforced concerns about their decision-making abilities. It didn't make sense to most at the hearing for the CEOs to spend that kind of money and then beg for a huge bailout from the government.[58]

STRATEGIC LEADERSHIP

In our dynamic and often uncertain environment, the premium in strategy implementation is on **strategic leadership**—the capability to inspire people to successfully engage in a process of continuous change, performance enhancement, and implementation of organizational strategies.[59] In this respect and as just pointed out, one of the big lessons learned in studying how business firms fared in the economic crisis is: *A strategic leader has to maintain strategic control.* This means that the CEO and other top managers should always be in touch with the strategy, how well it is being implemented, whether the strategy is generating performance success or failure, and the need for the strategy to be tweaked or changed.

Strategic leadership inspires people to continuously change, refine, and improve strategies and their implementation.

Michael Porter, whose five forces and competitive strategy models for strategic management were discussed earlier, places a great emphasis on the role of the CEO as chief strategist. He describes additional aspects of the strategic leadership task in the following ways.[60]

- *A strategic leader has to be the guardian of trade-offs.* It is the leader's job to make sure that the organization's resources are allocated in ways consistent with the strategy. This requires the discipline to sort through many competing ideas and alternatives, stay on course, and not get sidetracked.

- *A strategic leader needs to create a sense of urgency,* not allowing the organization and its members to grow slow and complacent. Even when doing well, the leader keeps the focus on getting better and being alert to conditions that require adjustments to the strategy.

- *A strategic leader needs to make sure that everyone understands the strategy.* Unless strategies are understood, the daily tasks and contributions of people lose context and purpose. Everyone might work very hard, but without alignment to strategy the impact is dispersed and fails to advance common goals.

- *A strategic leader needs to be a teacher.* It is the leader's job to teach the strategy and make it a "cause," says Porter. In order for strategy to work it must become an ever-present commitment throughout the organization. This means that a strategic leader must be a great communicator. Everyone must understand the strategy and how it makes their organization different from others.

To the items on Porter's list, Michael Dell, founder and chairman of Dell Computer, might add a final point: *A strategic leader must be a team player*. He began the firm in 1984 with US$ 1,000, selling computers out of his dormitory room in college. Dell was the youngest CEO to lead a *Fortune 500* company and is also on record as an advocate of top management teams. "We bounce ideas off one another," he says, "and at the end of the day if we say 'who did this?' the only right answer is that we all did. Three heads are better than one."[61]

✓ **Learning Check ⑤**

BE SURE YOU CAN

• explain how the management process supports strategy implementation • define *corporate governance* • explain why boards of directors sometimes fail in their governance responsibilities • define *strategic control* and *strategic leadership* • list the responsibilities of a strategic leader in today's organizations

MANAGEMENT LEARNING REVIEW

STUDY QUESTIONS SUMMARY

KEY TERMS

B2B business strategies, 202
B2C business strategies, 202
BCG matrix, 202
business strategy, 191
combination strategies, 199
competitive advantage, 189
concentration, 199
co-opetition, 201
core competency, 196
core values, 193
corporate governance, 208
corporate strategy, 191
cost leadership strategy, 205
differentiation strategy, 204
diversification, 199
divestiture, 200
downsizing, 200
e-business strategy, 201
emergent strategies, 206
focus strategies, 205
focused costs leadership, 205
focused differentiation, 205
functional strategy, 191
globalization strategy, 200
growth strategy, 198
lack of participation error, 207
liquidation, 198
mission, 193
multi-domestic strategy, 200

1. What is strategic management?

• Competitive advantage is achieved by operating in ways that allow an organization to outperform its rivals; a competitive advantage is sustainable when it is difficult for competitors to imitate.

• A strategy is a comprehensive plan that sets long-term direction and guides resource allocation for sustainable competitive advantage.

• Corporate strategy sets direction for an entire organization; business strategy sets direction for a business division or product/service line; functional strategy sets direction for the operational support of business and corporate strategies.

• Strategic management is the process of formulating and implementing strategies that achieve goals in a competitive environment.

FOR DISCUSSION Can an organization have a good strategy and still fail to achieve competitive advantage?

2. What are the essentials of strategic analysis?

• The strategic management process begins with analysis of mission, clarification of core values, and identification of objectives.

• A SWOT analysis systematically assesses organizational strengths and weaknesses, and environmental opportunities and threats.

• Porter's five forces model analyzes industry attractiveness in terms of competitive rivalry, new entrants, substitute products, and the bargaining powers of suppliers and buyers.

FOR DISCUSSION Would a monopoly get a perfect score for industry attractiveness in Porter's five forces model?

3. What are corporate strategies and how are they formulated?

• The grand or master strategies used by organizations include growth—pursuing expansion through concentration and diversification; stability—maintaining existing operations; and renewal—pursuing ways to correct performance problems.

- Global strategies take advantage of international business opportunities; cooperative strategies use strategic alliances and co-opetition as pathways to performance gains.

- E-business strategies use information technology and the Internet to pursue competitive advantage in business-to-business and business-to-consumer transactions.

- The BCG matrix is a portfolio planning approach that classifies businesses or product lines as "stars," "cash cows," "question marks," or "dogs" for purposes of strategy formulation.

FOR DISCUSSION Is it good news or bad news for investors when a firm announces that it is restructuring?

4. What are business strategies and how are they formulated?

- Potential sources of competitive advantage in business-level strategy formulation include lower costs, better quality, more knowledge, greater speed, and strong financial resources.

- Porter's model of competitive strategy includes: differentiation—distinguishing one's products from the competition; cost leadership—minimizing costs relative to the competition; and focus—concentrating on a special market segment.

- The incremental or emergent model recognizes that many strategies are formulated and implemented incrementally over time.

FOR DISCUSSION Can a business ever be successful with a combined cost leadership and differentiation strategy?

5. What are some current issues in strategy implementation?

- Management practices and systems—including the functions of planning, organizing, leading, and controlling—must be mobilized to support strategy implementation.

- Pitfalls that inhibit strategy implementation include failures of substance—such as poor analysis of the environment; and failures of process—such as lack of participation in the planning process.

- Boards of directors play important roles in corporate governance, including monitoring how well top management fulfills strategic management responsibilities.

- Strategic leadership inspires the process of continuous evaluation and improvement of strategies and their implementation.

FOR DISCUSSION Is strategic leadership capable of making up for poor corporate governance?

SELF-TEST

Multiple-Choice Questions

1. The most appropriate first question to ask in strategic planning is _____.

   (a) "Where do we want to be in the future?"   (b) "How well are we currently doing?"   (c) "How can we get where we want to be?"   (d) "Why aren't we doing better?"

2. The ability of a firm to consistently outperform its rivals is called _____.

   (a) vertical integration   (b) competitive advantage   (c) incrementalism   (d) strategic intent

3. In a complex conglomerate business such as General Electric, a(n) _____-level strategy sets strategic direction for a strategic business unit.

   (a) institutional   (b) corporate   (c) business   (d) functional

4. An organization that is downsizing to reduce costs is implementing a grand strategy of _____.

    (a) growth   (b) cost differentiation   (c) renewal   (d) stability

5. The _____ is a predominant value system for an organization as a whole.

    (a) strategy   (b) core competency   (c) mission   (d) corporate culture

6. A _____ in the BCG matrix would have a high market share in a low-growth market.

    (a) dog   (b) cash cow   (c) question mark   (d) star

7. In Porter's five forces framework, having _____ increases industry attractiveness.

    (a) many rivals   (b) many substitute products   (c) low bargaining power of suppliers   (d) few barriers to entry

8. When PepsiCo acquired Tropicana, a maker of orange juice, the firm's strategy was growth by _____.

    (a) related diversification   (b) concentration   (c) vertical integration   (d) cooperation

9. Cost efficiency and product quality are two examples of _____ objectives of organizations.

    (a) official   (b) operating   (c) informal   (d) institutional

10. Restructuring by reducing staff and scale of operations is a form of _____ strategy.

    (a) turnaround   (b) growth   (c) concentration   (d) incremental

11. Among the global strategies that might be pursued by international businesses, the _____ strategy is the most targeted on local needs, local management, and local products.

    (a) ethnocentric   (b) transnational   (c) geocentric   (d) multi-domestic

12. According to Porter's model of competitive strategies, a firm that wants to compete with its rivals in a broad market by selling a very low-priced product would need to successfully implement a _____ strategy.

    (a) retrenchment   (b) differentiation   (c) cost leadership   (d) diversification

13. When Coke and Pepsi spend millions on ads trying to convince customers that their products are unique, they are pursuing a _____ strategy.

    (a) transnational   (b) concentration   (c) diversification   (d) differentiation

14. The role of the board of directors as an oversight body that holds top executives accountable for the success of business strategies is called _____.

    (a) strategic leadership   (b) corporate governance   (c) logical incrementalism   (d) strategic opportunism

15. An example of a process failure in strategic planning is _____.

    (a) lack of participation   (b) poorly worded mission   (c) incorrect core values   (d) insufficient financial resources

Short-Response Questions

16. What is the difference between corporate strategy and functional strategy?

17. What would a manager look at in a SWOT analysis?

18. Explain the differences between B2B and B2C as e-business strategies.

19. What is strategic leadership?

Application Question

20. Tashlin Masrani owns and operates a small retail store selling the outdoor clothing of a Canadian manufacturer to a predominantly university-student market. Lately, a large department store outside of town has started selling similar but lower-priced clothing manufactured in China, Thailand, and Bangladesh. Tashlin believes she is starting to lose business to this store. Assume you are part of a student team assigned to do a management class project for Tashlin. Her question for the team is: "How can I best deal with my strategic management challenges in this situation?" How will you reply?

MANAGEMENT SKILLS AND COMPETENCIES

SELF-ASSESSMENT

Back to Yourself: Critical Thinking

Strategic management is one of the most significant planning challenges faced by managers. It requires managers to deal with a complex array of forces and uncertainties, all of which must be consolidated and integrated to craft a strategy that moves an organization forward with success. Critical thinking, introduced in the opener, is an essential foundation for all aspects of strategic management discussed in this chapter. The same critical thinking that is part of a case study in your course is what helps strategic leaders create strategies that result in competitive advantage. But with all the uncertainties that exist today, managers rarely have the luxury of full information that is boxed up for analysis in a nice neat case format. Rather, critical thinking in the real world must be multi-dimensional, embracing both the systematic and intuitive aspects of decision-making.

Further Reflection: Intuitive Ability

Instructions

Complete this survey as quickly as you can. Be honest with yourself. For each question, select the response that most appeals to you.

1. When working on a project, do you prefer to
   (a) be told what the problem is but be left free to decide how to solve it?
   (b) get very clear instructions for how to go about solving the problem before you start?

2. When working on a project, do you prefer to work with colleagues who are
   (a) realistic?
   (b) imaginative?

3. Do you most admire people who are
   (a) creative?
   (b) careful?

4. Do the friends you choose tend to be
   (a) serious and hard-working?
   (b) exciting and often emotional?

5. When you ask a colleague for advice on a problem you have, do you
   (a) seldom or never get upset if he or she questions your basic assumptions?
   (b) often get upset if he or she questions your basic assumptions?

6. When you start your day, do you
    (a) seldom make or follow a specific plan?
    (b) usually first make a plan to follow?

7. When working with numbers, do you find that you
    (a) seldom or never make factual errors?
    (b) often make factual errors?

8. Do you find that you
    (a) seldom daydream during the day and really don't enjoy doing so when you do it?
    (b) frequently daydream during the day and enjoy doing so?

9. When working on a problem, do you
    (a) prefer to follow the instructions or rules that are given to you?
    (b) often enjoy circumventing the instructions or rules that are given to you?

10. When you are trying to put something together, do you prefer to have
    (a) step-by-step written instructions on how to assemble the item?
    (b) a picture of how the item is supposed to look once assembled?

11. Do you find that the person who irritates you *the most* is the one who appears to be
    (a) disorganized?
    (b) organized?

12. When an unexpected crisis comes up that you have to deal with, do you
    (a) feel anxious about the situation?
    (b) feel excited by the challenge of the situation?

Scoring

Total the number of "a" responses selected for questions 1, 3, 5, 6, 11; enter the score here [a = ___]. Total the number of "b" responses for questions 2, 4, 7, 8, 9, 10, 12; enter the score here [b = ___]. Add your "a" and "b" scores and enter the sum here [a + b = ___]. This is your intuitive score. The highest possible intuitive score is 12; the lowest is 0.

Interpretation

In his book *Intuition in Organizations* (Newbury Park, CA: Sage, 1989), pp. 10–11, Weston H. Agor states, "Traditional analytical techniques . . . are not as useful as they once were for guiding major decisions . . . . If you hope to be better prepared for tomorrow, then it only seems logical to pay some attention to the use and development of intuitive skills for decision making." Agor developed the preceding survey to help people assess their tendencies to use intuition in decision-making. Your score offers a general impression of your strength in this area. It may also suggest a need to further develop your skill and comfort with more intuitive decision-making approaches.

Source: AIM Survey (El Paso, TX: ENFP Enterprises, 1989). Copyright ©1989 by Weston H. Agor.

TEAM EXERCISE

Strategic Scenarios

Preparation

In today's turbulent economies, it is no longer safe to assume that an organization that was highly successful yesterday will continue to be so tomorrow—or that it will even be in existence. Changing times exact the best from strategic planners. Think about the situations currently facing the following well-known organizations. Think, too, about the futures they may face.

McDonald's	Ford	Sony
Apple Computer	Yahoo.ca	The Bay
Electronic Arts	Bell Canada	RW & Co.
Federal Express	Air Canada	Nortel

Instructions

Form into groups as assigned by your instructor. Choose one or more organizations from the prior list (or as assigned) and answer the following questions for each one:

1. What in the future might seriously threaten the success, perhaps the very existence, of this organization? As a group, develop at least three such *future scenarios*.

2. Estimate the probability (0 to 100 percent) of each future scenario occurring.

3. Develop a strategy for each scenario that will enable the organization to successfully deal with it.

Thoroughly discuss these questions within the group and arrive at your best possible consensus answers. Be prepared to share and defend your answers in general class discussion.

Source: Suggested by an exercise in John F. Veiga and John N. Yanouzas, *The Dynamics of Organization Theory: Gaining a Macro Perspective* (St. Paul, MN: West, 1979), pp. 69–71.

CASE 7

HBC: From Fur to Fendi

After 300 years, Canada's oldest retailer knows a thing or two about change. Older than the country it serves, Hudson's Bay Company (HBC) has remained a landmark institution in Canada, navigating its way from rural outposts to over 600 locations and nearly 60,000 associates located in every province in Canada. Known best for its flagship department store The Bay, HBC currently operates three additional retailers: Zellers, Home Outfitters, and Fields.

Despite its long and glorious past, all is not well at Canada's historic company. Leadership changes, increased competition, a fragmenting retail market, and plummeting sales have plagued HBC well into the new millennium. Will HBC be able to successfully weather the seas of change or will it sink into history?

History

Two centuries before confederation, a pair of European explorers discovered a wealth of fur in the interior of Canada accessible by an inland sea, Hudson's Bay. In 1670, with permission from the King of England, trading began and the first century found HBC trading goods and furs in a few forts and posts around the James and Hudson Bays. Later, competition forced HBC to expand into Canada's interior and a string of outposts grew up along river networks that would eventually become the modern cities of Winnipeg, Calgary, and Edmonton.

By the end of the nineteenth century, changing tastes caused the fur trade to lose importance, while western settlements and the gold rush quickly introduced new clientele to HBC—ones who paid in cash, not fur. Trading posts began to give way to sales shops with a greater selection of goods, transforming HBC into a modern retail organization. During this

The Canadian Press Images/Francis Vachon

time, HBC also started selling homesteads to newly arrived settlers, eventually diversifying into a full-scale commercial property holding and development organization. Shipping and natural resources, particularly oil and gas, were important sidelines.

Challenges

Flash forward to the 1980s. The pace of HBC's retail acquisition and the economic downturn left The Bay with major debt and caused HBC to rethink its priorities. Like many other firms at the time, HBC decided to return to its core business. Non-strategic assets were sold, as were the company's last natural resource holdings. Strategic expansion followed to strengthen its share of the market with the acquisition of other retailers, such as K-Mart Canada.

Since the 1980s, the company has continued to navigate its way through the wake of a weakened economy, changing consumer tastes, and intense competition. The popularity of big-box stores, such as Old Navy, Future Shop, and Walmart, have changed consumer behaviour away from department store shopping, forcing retailers like The Bay and Zellers to compete on selection of merchandise and price.

With its reputation for unfocused collections of merchandise, shabby stores, and unhelpful sales staff, HBC tried a number of strategies to entice customers back to its stores. Some strategies, such as the HBC Rewards program and on-line shopping, have been successful; however, other strategies haven't fared as well. Early in 2001, it tried to reinvent itself with a more fashionable image for The Bay and it reduced the focus on steep discounts. The economy, and frustrated customers, forced it to abandon the move and return to its value-based focus. To try to remain competitive with other low-cost retailers, HBC diversified, although unsuccessfully, through Designer Depot/Style Depot, which operated from 2004 to 2008.

After remaining a Canadian company for over 330 years, HBC was bought in 2006 by U.S. financier Jerry Zucker, who sought to revive the firm by focusing on improving operations and customer satisfaction. In 2008, after Zucker's death, HBC was bought by U.S. private equity firm NRDC Equity Partners. NRDC's strategy was once again to revitalize HBC with better brands and better service.

Under NRDC's leadership, The Bay quickly focused on reattracting customers by dropping over 60 percent of its former brands and relaunching the "Room," a plush VIP suite at one of its Toronto locations, with high-end designers such as Armani, Ungaro, and Chanel. Despite the economic downturn in 2008 and the resulting layoffs, The Bay was in the black.

Another coup for HBC was becoming an official sponsor for the 2010 Olympics in Vancouver. Now that it was official outfitter of the Canadian Olympics team and exclusive supplier of Olympic-branded merchandise, new customers and those who hadn't shopped at The Bay or Zellers in years flocked back to HBC to snap up hoodies, coats, hats, and the iconic red mittens as fast as they could put the merchandise on the shelves.

HBC will try to repeat its current successes by introducing new products, redesigning stores, and launching the "Room" in other major cities. In particular, it hopes to bring customers back by capitalizing on its Canadian history by redesigning its Signature Line, adding a modern twist to HBC classics such as its striped "point" blankets, sweaters, coats, canoes, trapper hats, and maple syrup, reminiscent of its early trading days.

Based on its recent successes, HBC seems to be on the right track, but will it be enough to make it once again a premier Canadian shopping destination or is it too late to revive the historic department store?

Discussion Questions

1. What does an analysis using Porter's five forces model reveal about the industry that HBC competes within and what are its strategic implications for HBC?

2. Describe the competitive strategy used by HBC prior to its sale to Zucker and NRDC. What strategy has HBC adopted since the sale?

3. As a strategic consultant hired by HBC, discuss what strategies and implementation processes you would recommend for capitalizing on its Olympic success.

4. FURTHER RESEARCH—Are there other successful chains in the world that HBC could learn from by examining their strategic path? If so, which ones, and why?

Starbucks' New Everyday Brew

Video Summary and Discussion

When news broke that Starbucks was losing customers in Seattle, Washington, its birthplace, and further news surfaced of shrinking profits, store closings, and layoffs, CBS News decided to investigate.

The consensus among coffee customers in Seattle was that something was wrong with Starbucks: perhaps too many shops, coffee that was good but indistinguishable, and maybe even an overabundance of expensive, exotic beverages.

The video then shows Starbucks CEO and Chairman Howard Schultz being interviewed by Harry Smith. Schultz used the occasion to launch a new coffee line for Starbucks, representing a change in strategy designed to reinvigorate the company's business.

While acknowledging the emergence of significant competition, he stated that competition is not the motivation for launching its new product line. More of a factor is the overall worsening economy, where a luxury item such as Starbucks' $4 cup of latte and exotic brews may no longer suit the tenor of the times. Schultz wanted to get back to basics and give customers a high-quality cup of basic coffee (not espresso-based like most of its offerings) at under $2 a cup.

The new brew, named Pike Place Roast after the Seattle site where Starbucks began, was carefully selected from some 30 beans and 30 blends. In keeping with Starbucks' core values and stated mission, it is produced in a manner that is environmentally friendly, with no pesticides, and from suppliers that meet high workplace and environmental standards.

Furthermore, the new brew is roasted in the shop and brewed every 30 minutes, a departure from the current method where the brew is brought into the shop prepackaged. As one orders a cup of coffee, it is assembled but not brewed, lacking the aroma of freshly brewing coffee that permeated the earlier shops.

Schultz talks about his company's new "everyday" brew, which he hopes will revive slumping sales in a crucial U.S. market. This strategy marks a "back to basics" approach, which is meant to propel Starbucks past key American competitors like McDonald's and Dunkin' Donuts.

Schultz appears optimistic in the video that Starbucks can reclaim its position as the premier coffee seller and win back a loyal, passionate clientele. But we now know that the introduction of the new blend has been controversial. While it has succeeded in improving Starbucks' lagging sales in North America, it has alienated some of its long-time customers. Such customers have complained that the company is "selling out" by introducing a tamer brew for the masses. They contend that it has compromised itself by straying away from its approach of providing bold coffee for coffee connoisseurs.

More recently, amid the controversy, Starbucks in Canada has been using the Pike Place Roast blend for promotional purposes, whereby customers who do something "green" for their community are given a coupon entitling them to a free cup of it. Starbucks Canada asked Canadians to join them in doing so as part of the company's support for the stewardship and restoration program of Evergreen, a non-profit group that aims to protect and revitalize public urban green spaces across Canada.

Consumers who made a formal pledge on Facebook to devote time to greening their local community and inspire others to do the same received a free tall cup of Pike Place Roast at participating Starbucks locations across Canada.

Questions for Students

1. Is growth a necessary progression for a company or can it do well in the niche it has created? You can use Starbucks as an example if desired.

2. Is Starbucks' dependence on essentially one product a source of great vulnerability? If not, is that because coffee is omnipresent in daily life? If coffee is omnipresent, did Starbucks help make it so? What are other weaknesses in the Starbucks brand?

3. Compare Starbucks' strategy over the past five years to that of Tim Hortons and McDonald's. How are they similar and how are they different?

4. Using only the information in the video, prepare a SWOT analysis for Starbucks. Note: this would be a good activity for a small group.

5. How would you classify Starbucks in the BCG Matrix? Why?

08 Organization Structures and Design

Structure supporting strategy

Edward Jones is an investment firm that does not operate like other investment firms. Rather than develop large offices with many employees, Edward Jones has opened up many smaller offices, each staffed with one invest-

Courtesy Edward Jones

ment representative, a licensed broker, and one branch office administrator. Edward Jones's core strategic belief is that face-to-face interaction with clients is the best way to build their business; something best done at small, highly personal, focused centres. While some branches may have additional brokers and office staff, depending on the level of business, Edward Jones believes that the one-broker-per-office model allows clients the opportunity to choose their broker and then to deal only with that broker.

With a strong core surrounded by largely independent satellite units, the Edward Jones structure is unique. Noted organizational theorist Peter Drucker described this company as "a confederation of highly autonomous entrepreneurial units bound together by a highly centralized core of values and services." And the approach is working. In the 1980s, it was a small regional firm only in the United States. Today, Edward Jones has over 10,000 offices in the United States, Canada, and the United Kingdom.

Edward Jones's way of organizing also seems to be working for its clients. Edward Jones was ranked "Highest in Investor Satisfaction with Full Service Brokerage Firms" by J.D. Power and Associates. It is easy to see that Edward Jones has found both an inventive and a successful way to organize.[1]

| **BENCHMARK** | The success of Edward Jones is classic management—tackling opportunities and handling growth without compromising principles. It isn't easy to stay on course while expanding into new territories. But with the right organizational structure, firms such as Edward Jones can only get better as they get bigger. |

Empowerment

It takes a lot of trust to be comfortable with empowerment—letting others make decisions and exercise discretion in their work. But if you aren't willing and able to empower others, you may try to do too much on your own and end up accomplishing too little.

How often are you stressed out by group projects at school, feeling like you're doing all the work? Do you seem to be always rushing while your peers have time for coffee and chats? If so, perhaps you have a problem "letting go," or being willing to let others do their share of the work.

If the above description fits you, your assumptions probably align with those in the upper left box in the Empowerment Quick Test. Alternatively, you could be in the lower right box and perhaps find that you work smarter and better while making others happier, too.

The beauty of organizations is synergy—bringing together the contributions of many people to achieve something that is much greater than what any individual can accomplish alone. Empowerment gives synergy a chance. It means joining with others to get things done; allowing and helping them to do even things that you might be very good at doing yourself.

Many of us suffer from control anxiety. We don't empower others because we fear losing control. Being "unwilling to let go," we try to do too much and end up running the risk of missed deadlines and even poor performance. This behaviour denies others opportunities to contribute. We end up losing the benefits of their talents and often alienating them in the process.

EMPOWERMENT QUICK TEST

In a team situation, which square best describes your beliefs and behaviours?

- It's faster to do things myself than explain how to do them to others
- Some things are just too important not to do yourself

?

- People make mistakes, but they also learn from them
- Many people are ready to take on more work, but are too shy to volunteer

❖ Get to Know Yourself Better

Are you someone who easily and comfortably empowers others? Or do you suffer from control anxiety and lack the willingness to delegate? The next time you are in a study or work group, be a self-observer. Write a short narrative that would accurately describe your behaviour to someone who wasn't present. Compare that narrative with where you stand on the Empowerment Quick Test.

CHAPTER 8 STUDY QUESTIONS

- What is organizing as a management function?
- What are the traditional organization structures?
- What are the newer types of organization structures?
- How are organizational designs changing the workplace?

VISUAL CHAPTER OVERVIEW

CHAPTER 8 ORGANIZATION STRUCTURES AND DESIGN

Study Question 1	Study Question 2	Study Question 3	Study Question 4
Organizing as a Management Function	**Traditional Organization Structures**	**Horizontal Organization Structures**	**Organizational Designs**
■ What is organization structure? ■ Formal structures ■ Informal structures	■ Functional structures ■ Divisional structures ■ Matrix structures	■ Team structures ■ Network structures ■ Boundaryless structures	■ Mechanistic and organic designs ■ Subsystems design and integration ■ Trends in organizational design

✓ Learning Check 1	✓ Learning Check 2	✓ Learning Check 3	✓ Learning Check 4

Management scholar and consultant Henry Mintzberg points out that, as organizations change rapidly in today's world, people within them are struggling to find their places.[2] One of his points is that people need to understand how their organizations work if they are to work well within them. Mintzberg notes some common questions: "What parts connect to one another?" "How should processes and people come together?" "Whose ideas have to flow where?" These and related questions raise critical issues about organization structures and how well they meet an organization's performance needs.

ORGANIZING AS A MANAGEMENT FUNCTION

Organizing arranges people and resources to work toward a goal.

Organizing is the process of arranging people and other resources to work together to accomplish a goal. As one of the basic functions of management, it involves creating a division of labour and then coordinating results to achieve a common purpose.

Figure 8.1 shows the central role that organizing plays in the management process. Once plans are created, the manager's task is to see to it that they are carried out. Given a clear mission, core values, objectives, and strategy, organizing begins the process of implementation by clarifying jobs and working relationships. It identifies who is to do what, who is in charge of whom, and how different people and parts of the organization relate to and work with one another. All of this, of course, can be done in different ways. The strategic leadership challenge is to choose the best organizational form to fit the strategy and other situational demands.

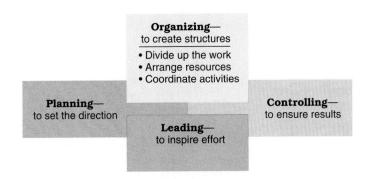

Figure 8.1 Organizing viewed in relationship with the other management functions.

WHAT IS ORGANIZATION STRUCTURE?

The way in which the various parts of an organization are formally arranged is usually referred to as the **organization structure**. It is the system of tasks, workflows, reporting relationships, and communication channels that link together the work of diverse individuals and groups. Any structure should both allocate tasks through a division of labour and provide for the coordination of performance results. A structure that does both of these things well is an important asset, helping to implement an organization's strategy.[3] Unfortunately, it is easier to talk about good structures than it is to actually create them. This is why you often read and hear about organizations changing their structures in an attempt to improve performance.

Organization structure is a system of tasks, reporting relationships, and communication linkages.

FORMAL STRUCTURES

You may know the concept of structure best in the form of an **organization chart**. This is a diagram that shows reporting relationships and the formal arrangement of work positions within an organization.[4] A typical organization chart identifies various positions and job titles, as well as the lines of authority and communication between them. It shows the **formal structure**, or the structure of the organization in its official state. This is how the organization is intended to function. By reading an organization chart, you can learn the basics of an organization's formal structure, including:

- *Division of work:* Positions and titles show work responsibilities.

- *Supervisory relationships:* Lines show who reports to whom.

- *Communication channels:* Lines show formal communication flows.

- *Major subunits:* Positions reporting to a common manager are shown.

- *Levels of management:* Vertical layers of management are shown.

An **organization chart** describes the arrangement of work positions within an organization.

Formal structure is the official structure of the organization.

ISSUES AND SITUATIONS
Nokia Reorganizes

The cell phone industry is one of the most competitive in the world and the Finnish firm Nokia is one of the major brand leaders. When the firm announced that it was reorganizing its cell phone unit, it drew lots of attention from investors and analysts. Nokia switched from a structure based on customer or market segment divisions (consumer phones, smart phones, and business phones) to one based on product divisions (phones and software and services development). The goal of the change is to "unlock" the software and services businesses from their existing attachment to phones, giving them more operating freedom since these markets were starting to take on lives of their own.

Nokia's new formal structure is part of CEO Olli-Pekka Kallasvuo's agenda to make the firm capable of reinventing itself to meet changing market conditions. One of his strategists says that the new structure is "unstable by design" and that the two new units will be expected to collaborate while still challenging one another. As for CEO Kallasvuo, he's a fan of creative tension. The *Wall Street Journal* reports that he didn't inform other top executives about what roles they would have in the new structure until just before it was officially announced.

The last time Nokia went through a major reorganization, four top executives left the firm, and analysts were critical that the aftermath contributed to the firm's missing some major

market trends and falling behind competitors. The question now is whether or not the new structure will result in sufficient cooperation between the two divisions, or if they will end up competing with each other to the point that Nokia loses competitive ground.

CRITICAL RESPONSE

Does this change of structure make sense to you? What is the likelihood that the new software and services division will start to flourish with its new-found freedom and forget that it is supposed to be a good partner to the cell phone division? Is there anything that CEO Kallasvuo could do structurally or managerially to make sure that there is enough "cooperation" between the two divisions and still take full advantage of creative tension within the firm?

INFORMAL STRUCTURES

Informal structure is the set of unofficial relationships among an organization's members.

Behind every formal structure typically lies an **informal structure**. This is a "shadow" organization made up of the unofficial, but often critical, working relationships between organizational members. If the informal structure could be drawn, it would show who talks to and interacts regularly with whom, regardless of their formal titles and relationships. The lines of the informal structure would cut across levels and move from side to side. They would show people meeting for coffee, in exercise groups, and in friendship cliques. No organization can be fully understood without gaining insight into the informal structure as well as the formal one.[5]

Social network analysis identifies the informal structures and their embedded social relationships that are active in an organization.

A tool known as **social network analysis** is one way of identifying informal structures and their embedded social relationships. Such an analysis typically asks people to identify others whom they turn to for help most often, and with whom they communicate regularly, and who energize and de-energize them.[6] Social networks are then drawn with lines running from person to person according to the frequency and type of relationship maintained. The result is an organizational map that shows how a lot of work really gets done in organizations, in contrast to the formal arrangements depicted on organization charts. This information is useful for redesigning the formal structure for better performance, and it also legitimizes the informal networks people use in their daily work.

Informal structures and social networks are in many ways essential to organizational success. This is especially true during times of change, when out-of-date formal structures may fail to provide the support people need to deal with new or unusual situations. Because it takes time to change or modify formal structures, the informal structure helps fill the void. The emergent and spontaneous relationships of informal structures allow people to make contacts with others who can help them get things done. Informal learning also takes place as people work and interact together throughout the workday. And informal structures are sources of emotional support and friendship that satisfy important social needs.

Of course, informal structures have potential disadvantages. Because they exist outside the formal authority system, informal structures can be susceptible to rumour, carry inaccurate information, breed resistance to change, and even divert work efforts from important objectives. Also, "outsiders"—people who are left out of informal groupings—may feel less a part of daily activities and become dissatisfied. Some American managers of Japanese firms, for example, have complained about being excluded from what they call the "shadow cabinet"—an informal group of Japanese executives who hold the real power to get things done and sometimes act to the exclusion of others.[7]

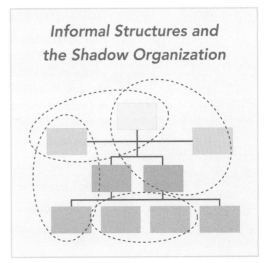

Informal Structures and the Shadow Organization

BE SURE YOU CAN

• define *organizing as a management function* • explain the difference between formal and informal structures • discuss the potential advantages and disadvantages of informal structures in organizations

✓ Learning Check ❶

TRADITIONAL ORGANIZATION STRUCTURES

A basic principle of organizing is that performance should improve when people are allowed to specialize and become experts in specific jobs or tasks. Given this division of labour, however, decisions must be made regarding **departmentalization**—how to group work positions into formal teams or departments that are linked together in a coordinated way. These decisions have traditionally resulted in three major types of organizational structures: functional, divisional, and matrix structures.[8]

Departmentalization is the process of grouping people and jobs into work units.

FUNCTIONAL STRUCTURES

In **functional structures**, people with similar skills and performing similar tasks are grouped together into formal work units. Members of functional departments share technical expertise, interests, and responsibilities. The first example in Figure 8.2 shows a functional structure common in business firms, with top management arranged by the functions of marketing, finance, production, and human resources. In this functional structure, manufacturing problems are the responsibility of the production vice president, marketing problems are the responsibility of the marketing vice president, and so on. The key point is that members of a function work within their areas of expertise. If each function does its work properly, the expectation is that the business as a whole will operate successfully.

A **functional structure** groups together people with similar skills who perform similar tasks.

Advantages of Functional Structures

Functional structures are not limited to businesses. Figure 8.2 also shows how they are used in other types of organizations, such as banks and hospitals. Most typically, functional structures work well for smaller organizations dealing with only one or a few products or services. They also tend to work best in relatively stable environments where problems are predictable and the demands for change and innovation are limited. The major advantages of functional structures include the following:

- Economies of scale with efficient use of resources.
- Task assignments consistent with expertise and training.
- High-quality technical problem solving.
- In-depth training and skill development within functions.
- Clear career paths within functions.

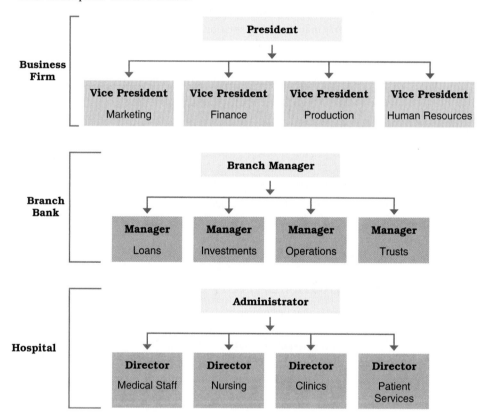

Figure 8.2 Functional structures in a business, branch bank, and hospital.

Disadvantages of Functional Structures

There are also potential disadvantages of functional structures. Common problems include difficulties in pinpointing responsibilities for things like cost containment, product or service quality, and innovation. A significant concern is with the **functional chimneys problem**—a lack of communication, coordination, and problem solving across functions. Because the functions become formalized not only on the organization chart but also in mindsets, people's cooperation can break down as everyone goes about the daily work. The sense of common purpose gets lost to self-centred and narrow viewpoints. When problems occur between functions, they are too often referred up to higher levels for resolution, rather than being addressed by people at the same level. This slows decision-making and can harm organizational performance.

The **functional chimneys problem** is a lack of communication and coordination across functions.

DIVISIONAL STRUCTURES

A second organizational alternative is the **divisional structure**. As illustrated in Figure 8.3, it groups together people who work on the same product or process, serve similar customers, or are located in the same area or geographical region. Divisional structures are common in complex organizations with diverse operations that extend across many products, territories, customers, and work processes.[9]

> A **divisional structure** groups together people working on the same product, in the same area, with similar customers, or on the same processes.

Product Structures

Product structures group together jobs and activities focused on a single product or service. They clearly identify costs, profits, problems, and successes in a market area with a central point of accountability. This prompts managers to be responsive to changing market demands and customer tastes. Common in large organizations, product structures may even extend into global operations. When taking over as H. J. Heinz's CEO, William R. Johnson decided that a change in the company's international structure could help improve performance. The existing structure that emphasized countries and regions was changed to global product divisions. The choice was based on Johnson's belief that a product structure would bring the best brand management to all countries and increase cooperation within product lines around the world.

> A **product structure** groups together people and jobs focused on a single product or service.

Geographical Structures

Geographical structures, sometimes called area structures, group together jobs and activities being performed in the same location. They are typically used when there is a need to differentiate products or services in various locations, such as in different parts of a country. They are also quite common in international operations, where they help to focus attention on the unique cultures and requirements of particular regions. As United Parcel Service's operations expanded worldwide, for example, the company announced a change from a product structure to a geographical structure. Two geographical divisions were created—the Americas and Europe/Asia. Each area was given responsibility for its own logistics, sales, and other business functions.

> A **geographical structure** groups together people and jobs performed in the same location.

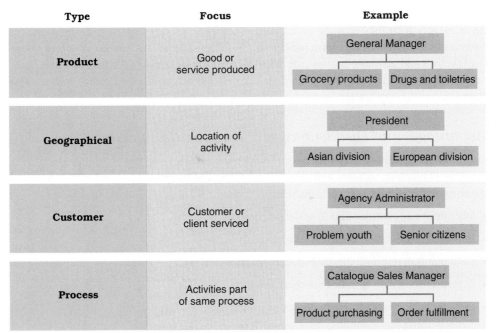

Figure 8.3 Divisional structures based on product, geography, customer, and process.

Customer Structures

A **customer structure** groups together people and jobs that serve the same customers or clients.

Customer structures group together jobs and activities that are serving the same customers or clients. The goal is to best serve the special needs of the different customer groups. This is a common structure in the consumer products industry. 3M Corporation structures itself to focus attention on such diverse markets as consumer and office, specialty materials, industrial, health care, electronics and communications, transportation, graphics, and safety. Customer structures are also useful in services. Banks, for example, use them to give separate attention to consumer and commercial customers for loans. Figure 8.3 also shows a government agency serving different client populations.

GOING GLOBAL

P&G GIVES BEAUTY DIVISION A MAKEOVER

Procter & Gamble division chief Ed Shirley recognized that, with the consumer products giant's current organizational structure, employees "experienced frustration with the complexity and slow pace of working across our business matrix." During boom times, the company bet that its beauty products line would return higher profit margins than its other lines. However, with the recent economic woes, P&G's beauty division's sales sagged. The company plans to reorient its beauty business by gender, to better serve "Him and Her," rather than organize around product categories. "We have announced organizational changes designed to support our plans for growth," a P&G spokeswoman said. "We're beginning to communicate to employees how we will bring the business vision to life through our organizational design."

Process Structures

A **work process** is a group of related tasks that collectively creates a valuable work product.

A **process structure** groups jobs and activities that are part of the same processes.

A **work process** is a group of related tasks that collectively creates something of value to a customer.[10] An example is order fulfillment by a catalogue retailer, a process that takes an order from point of initiation by the customer to point of fulfillment by a delivered product. A **process structure** groups together jobs and activities that are part of the same processes. Figure 8.3 shows how this might take the form of product-purchasing teams and order-fulfillment teams for a mail-order catalogue business.

Advantages and Disadvantages of Divisional Structures

Organizations use divisional structures for a variety of reasons, including the desire to avoid the functional chimneys problem and other disadvantages of functional structures. The potential advantages of divisional structures include:

- More flexibility in responding to environmental changes.
- Improved coordination across functional departments.
- Clear points of responsibility for product or service delivery.
- Expertise focused on specific customers, products, and regions.
- Greater ease in changing size by adding or closing down divisions.

As with other structural alternatives, there are also potential disadvantages to divisional structures. They can reduce economies of scale and increase costs through the duplication of resources and efforts across divisions. They can also create unhealthy rivalries as divisions compete for resources and top management attention, and emphasize division needs to the detriment of the goals of the organization as a whole.

MATRIX STRUCTURES

The **matrix structure**, often called the *matrix organization*, combines the functional and divisional structures. In effect, it is an attempt to gain the advantages and minimize the disadvantages of each. This is accomplished in the matrix by using permanent teams that cut across functions to support specific products, projects, or programs.[11] As shown in Figure 8.4, workers in a matrix structure belong to at least two formal groups at the same time—a functional group and a product, program, or project team. They also report to two bosses—one within the function and the other within the team.

A **matrix structure** combines functional and divisional approaches to emphasize project or program teams.

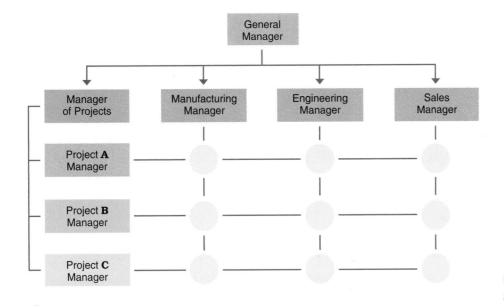

Persons assigned to both projects and functional departments

Figure 8.4 Matrix structure in a small, multi-project business firm.

The matrix organization has gained a strong foothold in the workplace, with applications in such diverse settings as manufacturing (e.g., aerospace, electronics, pharmaceuticals), service industries (e.g., banking, brokerage, retailing), professional fields (e.g., accounting, advertising, law), and the non-profit sector (e.g., municipal, provincial, and federal agencies, hospitals, universities). Matrix structures are also found in multinational corporations, where they offer the flexibility to deal with regional differences as well as multiple product, program, or project needs.

Advantages of Matrix Structures

The main benefits of matrix structures rest with the teams whose members work closely together to share expertise and information in a timely manner to solve problems. The potential advantages of matrix structures include:

- Better cooperation across functions.

- Improved decision-making; problem solving takes place at the team level where the best information is available.

- Increased flexibility in adding, removing, or changing operations to meet changing demands.

- Better customer service; there is always a program, product, or project manager informed and available to answer questions.

- Better performance accountability through the program, product, or project managers.

- Improved strategic management; top managers are freed from lower-level problem solving to focus more time on strategic issues.

Disadvantages of Matrix Structures

Predictably, there are potential disadvantages of matrix structures. The two-boss system is susceptible to power struggles, as functional supervisors and team leaders vie with one another to exercise authority. The two-boss system can also be frustrating if it creates task confusion and conflicting work priorities. Team meetings in the matrix can take lots of time, and the teams may develop "groupitis"—strong team loyalties that cause a loss of focus on larger organizational goals. The requirement of adding the team leaders to a matrix structure can also result in higher costs.

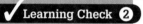
Learning Check 2

BE SURE YOU CAN
- explain the differences between functional, divisional, and matrix structures • list advantages and disadvantages of a functional structure, divisional structure, and matrix structure • draw charts to show how each type of structure is used in organizations familiar to you

Horizontal Organization Structures

The matrix structure is a step toward better cross-functional integration in an organization. But it is just one part of a broader movement toward more horizontal structures that try to improve communication and flexibility by decreasing hierarchy, increasing empowerment, and better mobilizing human talents.[12]

TEAM STRUCTURES

A **team structure** uses permanent and temporary cross-functional teams to improve lateral relations.

A **cross-functional team** brings together members from different functional departments.

Project teams are convened for a particular task or project and disband once it is completed.

As traditional vertical structures give way to more horizontal ones, teams serve as the basic building blocks.[13] Organizations with **team structures** extensively use both permanent and temporary teams to solve problems, complete special projects, and accomplish day-to-day tasks.[14] As illustrated in Figure 8.5, these are often **cross-functional teams** composed of members from different areas of work responsibility.[15] As with the matrix structure, the intention is to break down functional chimneys and create more effective lateral relations. There are also many **project teams** that are convened for a particular task or "project" and that disband once it is completed. The intention here is to quickly convene people with the needed talents and focus their efforts intensely to solve a problem or take advantage of a special opportunity.

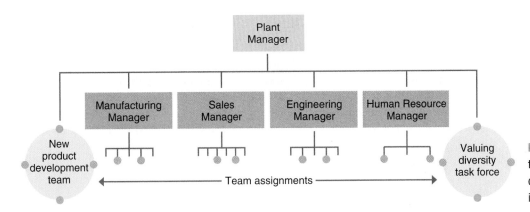

Figure 8.5 How a team structure uses cross-functional teams for improved lateral relations.

Advantages of Team Structures

Team structures help eliminate difficulties with communication and decision-making that result from the functional chimneys problem. Team assignments break down barriers between departments as people from different parts of an organization get to know one another. This can also boost morale; people working in teams often experience a greater sense of involvement and identification, increasing their enthusiasm for the job. Because teams focus shared knowledge and expertise on specific problems, they can also improve the speed and quality of decisions in many situations. Teamwork has proven to be a key component to success in the animation industry, as Toronto-based Soho VFX has learned. "In the visual effects sector, timing and teamwork are critical, since multiple studios work on movie projects at any one time. That means no one can afford to drop the ball on any part of a project," Soho President Allan Magled says. "A lot of this work is relationship dependent so you have to be able to deliver."[16]

CANADIAN MANAGERS
Don Carmody, Executive Producer

THE CANADIAN PRESS/Chris Young

Don Carmody has been in the film industry for more than 45 years. Immigrating to Canada with his parents as a young boy, Carmody got interested in films and graduated from film school in Montreal. He started in the movie industry first as a cast driver on Robert Altman's *McCabe and Mrs. Miller* before climbing up the ladder working as a gofer, production assistant, location manager, and eventually vice-president of production for Cinepix (now Lions Gate Films). After starting his own production company in 1980, Carmody produced comedy smash hits such as *Porky's, Porky's II, Weekend at Bernie's,* and a host of other top films. He was co-producer of the hit musical *Chicago* starring Renée Zellweger, Catherine Zeta-Jones, and Richard Gere, which won seven Academy Awards in 2002. When talking about how teams are put together to make a film, Carmody likens it to throwing a party: you invite people you have enjoyed working with previously with a few new people added in as well. The crew works together for a few months to shoot the film and then everyone says goodbye. It is apparent that producing films depends upon one's network of relationships; having strong ties with many talented people is essential.

Disadvantages of Team Structures

The complexities of teams and teamwork contribute to the potential disadvantages of team structures. These include conflicting loyalties for persons with both team and functional assignments. They also include issues of time management and group process. By their very nature, teams spend a lot of time in meetings. Not all of this time is productive. How well team members spend their time together often depends on the quality of interpersonal relations, group dynamics, and team management. But, as described in Chapter 15 on teams and teamwork, all of these concerns are manageable.

NETWORK STRUCTURES

A **network structure** uses information technologies to link with networks of outside suppliers and service contractors.

Organizations using a **network structure** operate with a central core that is linked through "networks" of relationships with outside contractors and suppliers of essential services.[17] The old model was for organizations to own everything. The new model is to own only the most essential, or "core," components of the business, and then use strategic alliances and outsourcing to provide the rest.

Figure 8.6 shows how a network structure might work for a mail-order company selling lawn and deck furniture through a catalogue and website. The firm itself is very small, consisting of relatively few full-time core employees. Beyond that, it is structured as a network of outsourcing and partner relationships that are maintained by the latest in information technology.

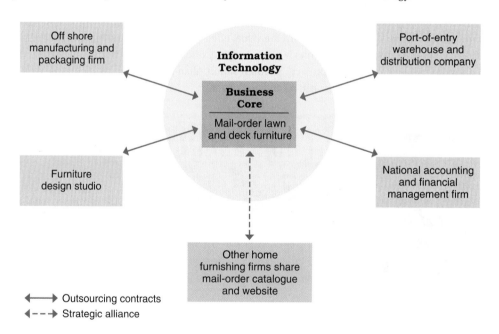

Figure 8.6 A network structure for a web-based retail business.

⟷ Outsourcing contracts
◀– – ▶ Strategic alliance

Merchandise in this networked firm is designed on contract with a furniture designer—which responds quickly as designs are shared and customized via computer networking. The furniture is manufactured and packaged by subcontractors located around the world—wherever materials are found at the lowest cost and best quality. Stock is maintained and shipped from a contract warehouse—ensuring quality storage and on-time expert shipping. All of the accounting and financial details are managed on contract with an outside firm—providing better technical expertise than the merchandiser could afford to employ on a full-time basis. The quarterly catalogue is designed, printed, and mailed cooperatively as a strategic alliance with two other firms that sell different home furnishings with a related price appeal. All of this is supported by a company website and information system maintained by an outside contractor.

Advantages of Network Structures

With the right use of technology, the mail-order company in this example can operate with fewer full-time employees and less complex internal systems. Network structures are lean and stream-lined, helping organizations stay cost-competitive through reduced overhead and increased operating efficiency. Network concepts allow organizations to employ outsourcing strategies and contract out specialized business functions. Information technology makes it easy to manage these contracts and business alliances, even across great distances. Within the operating core of a network structure, furthermore, interesting jobs are created for those who coordinate the entire system of relationships.

Disadvantages of Network Structures

The potential disadvantages of network structures largely lie with the demands of new management responsibilities. The more complex the business or mission of the organization, the more complicated it is to control and coordinate the network of contracts and alliances. If one part of the network breaks down or fails to deliver, the entire system suffers. Also, there is the potential to lose control over activities contracted out, and to experience a lack of loyalty among contractors who are used infrequently rather than on a long-term basis. Some worry that outsourcing can become so aggressive as to be dangerous to the firm, especially when critical activities such as finance, logistics, and human resources management are outsourced.[18]

BOUNDARYLESS STRUCTURES

It is popular today to speak about creating a **boundaryless organization** that eliminates many of the internal boundaries among subsystems and external boundaries with the external environment.[19] The boundaryless structure can be viewed as a combination of the team and network structures just described, with the addition of "temporariness."

> A **boundaryless organization** eliminates internal boundaries among subsystems and external boundaries with the external environment.

Internal to the boundaryless organization, teamwork and communication—either spontaneous, as needed, or intense—replace formal lines of authority. Meetings and spontaneous sharing are happening continuously. Perhaps thousands of people work together in hundreds of teams that form and disband as needed. There is an absence of boundaries that separate organizational members from one another. At consulting giant PricewaterhouseCoopers, for example, knowledge sharing brings together 160,000 partners spread across 150 countries in a vast virtual-learning and problem-solving network. Partners collaborate electronically through on-line databases, where information is stored, problems posted, and questions asked and answered in real time by those with experience and knowledge relevant to the problem at hand. Technology makes collaboration instantaneous and always possible, breaking down boundaries that might otherwise slow or impede the firm's performance. At Toronto-based marketing firm Eloqua, knowledge sharing brings together hundreds of people stationed across the world in a vast, virtually accessible problem-solving network. Eloqua uses its own marketed software services to host operations entirely through virtual networks, enabling employees to access databases on-line and communicate in real time to complete client projects. Breaking down technology barriers has enabled Eloqua to increase revenues by 747 percent over five years.[20]

In the external context, organizational needs are met by a shifting mix of outsourcing contracts and operating alliances that form and disband with changing circumstances. A "photograph" that documents an organization's configuration of external relationships today will look different from one taken tomorrow, as the form naturally adjusts to new pressures and circumstances. Figure 8.7 shows how the absence of internal and external barriers helps people work in ways that bring speed and flexibility to the boundaryless firm.

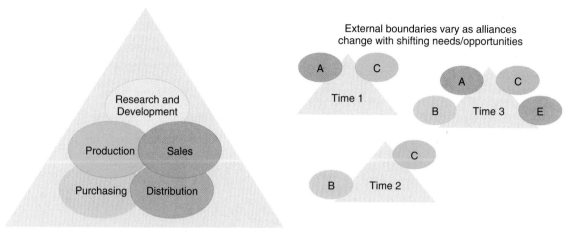

Figure 8.7 The boundaryless organization eliminates internal and external barriers.

Key requirements of boundaryless structures are the absence of hierarchy, empowerment of team members, technology utilization, and acceptance of impermanence. Knowledge sharing is both a goal and an essential component. One way to think of this is in the context of a very small organization, perhaps a start-up. In the small firm, everyone pitches in to help out as needed and when appropriate to get things done. There are no formal assignments, and there are no job titles or job descriptions standing in the way. People with talent work together as needed to get the job done. The boundaryless organization, in its pure form, is like this.

A **virtual organization** uses IT and the Internet to engage a shifting network of strategic alliances.

The **virtual organization** takes the boundaryless concept to the extreme.[21] It operates as a shifting network of alliances that are engaged as needed, using IT and the Internet. The boundaries that traditionally separate a firm from its suppliers, customers, and even competitors are largely eliminated. The virtual organization calls an alliance into action to meet specific operating needs and objectives; when the work is complete, the alliance rests until next called into action. The mix of mobilized alliances is continuously shifting, and an expansive pool of potential alliances is always ready to be called upon.

✓ **Learning Check ③**

BE SURE YOU CAN

• describe how organizations can use cross-functional teams and project teams in their structures • define *network structure* • illustrate how a new venture, such as a web-based retailer, might use a network structure to organize its various operations • discuss the potential advantages and disadvantages of a network structure • explain the concept of the boundaryless organization

---

ORGANIZATIONAL DESIGNS

Organizational design is the process of creating structures that accomplish mission and objectives.

Organizational design is the process of choosing and implementing structures to accomplish the organization's mission and objectives.[22] Because every organization faces its own set of unique problems and opportunities, the best design at any moment is the one that achieves a good match between structure and situational contingencies—including task, technology, environment, and people.[23] The process of organizational design is thus a problem-solving activity; no one design applies in all circumstances. The goal is to achieve a best fit among structures and the unique situation faced by each organization. The choices among design alternatives are broadly framed in the distinction between mechanistic or bureaucratic designs at one extreme, and organic or adaptive designs at the other.

MECHANISTIC AND ORGANIC DESIGNS

As first introduced in the discussion of management history in Chapter 2, a **bureaucracy** is a form of organization based on logic, order, and the legitimate use of formal authority.[24] It is a classic vertical structure, and its distinguishing features include a clear-cut division of labour, strict hierarchy of authority, formal rules and procedures, and promotion based on competency.

A **bureaucracy** emphasizes formal authority, order, fairness, and efficiency.

According to sociologist Max Weber, bureaucracies were supposed to be orderly, fair, and highly efficient. In short, they were a model form of organization.[25] Yet, the bureaucracies that we know are often associated with "red tape." And instead of being orderly and fair, they are often seen as cumbersome and impersonal to customer or client needs.[26] But rather than view all bureaucratic structures as inevitably flawed, management theory asks the contingency questions: When is a bureaucratic form a good choice for an organization? What alternatives exist when it is not a good choice?

Pioneering research conducted in England during the early 1960s by Tom Burns and George Stalker helps answer these questions.[27] After investigating 20 manufacturing firms, they concluded that two quite different organizational forms could be successful, depending on the nature of a firm's external environment. A more bureaucratic form, which Burns and Stalker called "mechanistic," thrived when the environment was stable. But it experienced difficulty when the environment was rapidly changing and uncertain. In these dynamic situations, a much less bureaucratic form, called "organic," performed best. Figure 8.8 portrays these two approaches as opposite extremes on a continuum of organizational design alternatives.

Mechanistic Designs

Organizations with more **mechanistic designs** are highly bureaucratic. As shown in the figure, they are vertical structures that typically operate with centralized authority, many rules and procedures,

A **mechanistic design** is centralized, with many rules and procedures, a clear-cut division of labour, narrow spans of control, and formal coordination.

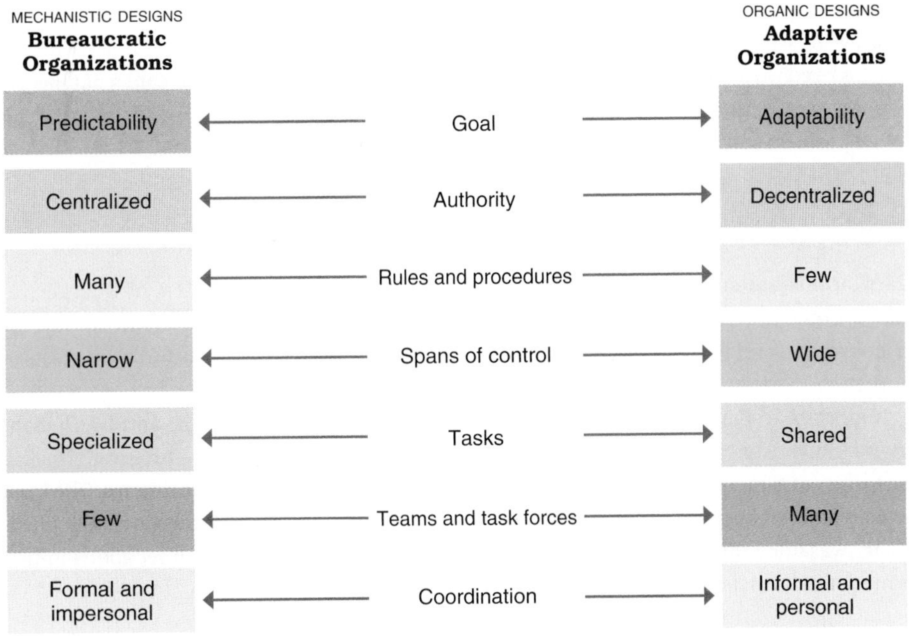

MECHANISTIC DESIGNS **Bureaucratic Organizations**		ORGANIC DESIGNS **Adaptive Organizations**
Predictability	← Goal →	Adaptability
Centralized	← Authority →	Decentralized
Many	← Rules and procedures →	Few
Narrow	← Spans of control →	Wide
Specialized	← Tasks →	Shared
Few	← Teams and task forces →	Many
Formal and impersonal	← Coordination →	Informal and personal

Figure 8.8 Organizational design alternatives: from bureaucratic to adaptive organizations.

a precise division of labour, narrow spans of control, and formal means of coordination. They can be described as "tight" structures of the traditional pyramid form.[28]

Mechanistic designs work best for organizations doing routine tasks in stable environments. For a good example, visit your local fast-food restaurant. As a relatively small operation, each store operates quite like others in the franchise chain and according to rules established by the corporate management. Service personnel work in orderly and disciplined ways, guided by training, rules and procedures, and close supervision of crew leaders who work alongside them. Even their appearance is carefully regulated, with everyone wearing a standardized uniform. These restaurants perform well as they repetitively deliver items that are part of their standard menus. You quickly encounter the limits, however, if you try to order something not on the menu. The chains also encounter difficulty when consumer tastes change or take on regional preferences that are different from what the corporate menu provides. Making adjustments to these mechanistic systems takes a long time.

Organic Designs

The limits of mechanistic designs are especially apparent in organizations that operate in dynamic, often uncertain, environments. It is hard, for example, to find a technology company, consumer products firm, or dot-com retailer that isn't making continual adjustments in operations and organizational design. Their effectiveness depends on being able to change with the times.

The ability to respond quickly to shifting environmental challenges is characteristic of organizations with more **organic designs**.[29] As portrayed in Figure 8.8, they use horizontal structures with decentralized authority, fewer rules and procedures, less precise division of labour, wider spans of control, and more personal means of coordination. These features create **adaptive organizations** with horizontal structures and cultures that encourage worker empowerment and teamwork. Within these relatively "loose" systems, a lot of work gets done through informal structures and networking.[30]

Organic designs work well for organizations facing dynamic environments that demand flexibility in dealing with changing conditions. They are built upon a foundation of trust that people will do the right things on their own initiative. This means letting workers take over production scheduling and problem solving; it means letting workers set up their own control systems; it means letting workers use their ideas to improve customer service; and it means that workers are given the freedom to do what they can do best—get the job done. This helps create what has been described in earlier chapters as a learning organization, one designed for continuous adaptation through problem solving, innovation, and learning.[31]

An **organic design** is decentralized, with fewer rules and procedures, open divisions of labour, wide spans of control, and more personal coordination.

An **adaptive organization** operates with a minimum of bureaucratic features and encourages worker empowerment and teamwork.

SUBSYSTEMS DESIGN AND INTEGRATION

A **subsystem** is a work unit or smaller component within a larger organization.

Organizations are composed of **subsystems** that operate as smaller parts of a larger total organizational system. A major challenge of organizational design is to create subsystems and coordinate relationships among them so that the entire organization's interests are best met.

Important research in this area was initiated in 1967 by Paul Lawrence and Jay Lorsch of Harvard University.[32] They studied 10 firms in three different industries—plastics, consumer goods, and containers. The firms were chosen because they differed in performance. The industries were chosen because they faced different levels of environmental uncertainty. The plastics industry was uncertain; the containers industry was more certain; the consumer goods industry was moderately uncertain.

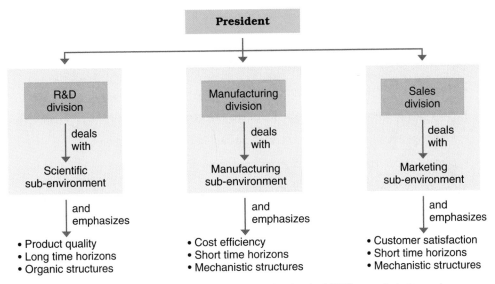

Figure 8.9 Subsystems differentiation among research and development (R&D), manufacturing, and sales divisions.

The results of the Lawrence and Lorsch study can be summarized as follows. First, successful plastics firms in uncertain environments had more organic designs; successful container firms in certain environments had more mechanistic designs. This result was consistent with the research by Burns and Stalker discussed earlier.[33] Second, subsystems in the successful firms used different structures to accommodate the special problems and opportunities of their sub-environments. Third, subsystems in the successful firms worked well with one another, even though they were also very different from one another.

Figure 8.9 shows how research and development, manufacturing, and sales subsystems operate in response to unique needs. This illustrates **differentiation**—the degree of difference that exists between the internal components of the organization. It also suggests the need for **integration**—the level of coordination achieved among an organization's internal components. The creation of both differentiated subsystems and appropriate integrating mechanisms is a particularly challenging managerial task. Increased differentiation creates the need for greater integration, but integration becomes harder to achieve as differentiation increases.

Management Smarts 8.1 identifies several mechanisms for achieving subsystem integration.[34] When differentiation is low, the integrating mechanisms that rely on vertical coordination and the use of authority relationships work best. They include use of rules and procedures, hierarchical referral, and planning. When differentiation is high, the integrating mechanisms that emphasize horizontal coordination and improved lateral relations work better.[35] They include the use of direct contact between managers, liaison roles, task forces, teams, and matrix structures.

Differentiation is the degree of difference between subsystems in an organization.

Integration is the level of coordination achieved between subsystems in an organization.

TRENDS IN ORGANIZATIONAL DESIGN

The complexity, uncertainty, and change characteristic of today's environment have prompted more and more organizations to shift toward horizontal structures and organic designs. As they do so, a number of trends in organizational design are evident.

8.1 MANAGEMENT SMARTS
How to improve subsystem integration

- *Rules and procedures:* Clearly specify required activities.

- *Hierarchical referral:* Refer problems upward to a common superior.

- *Planning:* Set targets that keep everyone headed in the same direction.

- *Direct contact:* Have subunit managers coordinate directly.

- *Liaison roles:* Assign formal coordinators to link subunits together.

- *Task forces:* Form temporary task forces to coordinate activities and solve problems on a timetable.

- *Teams:* Form permanent teams with the authority to coordinate and solve problems over time.

- *Matrix organizations:* Create a matrix structure to improve coordination on specific programs.

Fewer Levels of Management

The **chain of command** links all persons with successively higher levels of authority.

Span of control is the number of subordinates directly reporting to a manager.

A typical organization chart shows the **chain of command**, or the line of authority that vertically links each position with successively higher levels of management. When organizations grow in size, they tend to get "taller" as more and more levels of management are added to the chain of command. Yet, high-performing firms like the Jim Pattison Group, a Vancouver-based company with a wide range of product and service offerings throughout multiple industries—from car dealerships to radio stations—show preferences for fewer management levels. The Jim Pattison Group's management hierarchy is defined by its "separate operating divisions and a simple organizational structure." This structure is used to encourage an entrepreneurial spirit within the company while maintaining efficient business practices.[36]

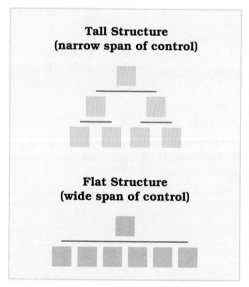

Tall Structure (narrow span of control)

Flat Structure (wide span of control)

One of the influences on management levels is **span of control**—the number of persons directly reporting to a manager. Tall structures have narrow spans of control and many levels of management. Because tall organizations have more managers, they are more costly than flatter ones. They also tend to be less efficient, less flexible, and less customer-sensitive. Flat structures have wider spans of control and fewer levels of management, and this reduces overhead costs. The wider spans of control also allow workers more empowerment and independence.[37]

Researchers now suggest that the use of new information technologies makes it possible to manage with wider spans of control. At Gemesa, one of PepsiCo's Mexico operations, some managers have as many as 56 direct reports; a few years ago, it was rare to see more than 12. The firm believes that the new flat structure focuses managers more on training, coaching, and motivating.[38] In another case, Cindy Zollinger supervises some 24 workers at a litigation consulting firm. She says: "They largely run themselves. I help them in dealing with obstacles they face, or in making the most of opportunities they find."[39]

Trend: Organizations are cutting unnecessary levels of management and shifting to wider spans of control. Managers are taking responsibility for larger numbers of subordinates who operate with less direct supervision.

More Delegation and Empowerment

> **Delegation** is the process of distributing and entrusting work to other persons.

All managers must decide what work they should do themselves and what should be left for others. At issue here is **delegation**—the process of entrusting work to others by giving them the right to make decisions and take action.

Delegation can be described as a set of three action steps. In *step 1*, the manager assigns responsibility by carefully explaining the work or duties someone else is expected to do. This responsibility is an expectation that the other person will perform assigned tasks. In *step 2*, the manager grants authority to act. Along with the assigned task, the right to take necessary actions (for example, to spend money, direct the work of others, or use resources) is given to the other person. In *step 3*, the manager creates accountability. By accepting an assignment, the person takes on a direct obligation to the manager to complete the job as agreed.

> **Three Steps in Delegation**
>
> 1. *Assign responsibility*—explain task and expectations
>
> 2. *Grant authority*—allow others to make decisions and act
>
> 3. *Create accountability*—require others to report back on results

REAL ETHICS

Flattened into Exhaustion

Dear Stress Doctor:

My boss has come up with this great idea of laying off some supervisors, assigning more workers to those of us who remain, and calling us "coaches" instead of supervisors. She says this is all part of a new management approach to operate with a flatter structure and more empowerment.

For me, this means a lot more work coordinating the activities of 17 operators instead of the six that I previously supervised. I can't get everything cleaned up on my desk most days, and I end up taking a lot of paperwork home.

As my organization "restructures" and cuts back staff, it puts a greater burden on those of us that remain. We get exhausted, and our families get shortchanged and even angry. I even feel guilty now taking time to watch my daughter play soccer on Saturday mornings. Sure, there's some decent pay involved, but that doesn't make up for the heavy price I'm paying in terms of lost family time.

But you know what? My boss doesn't get it. I never hear her ask: "Henry, are you working too much? Don't you think it's time to get back on a reasonable schedule?" No! What I often hear instead is "Look at Andy; he handles our new management model really well, and he's a real go-getter. I don't think he's been out of here one night this week before 8 p.m."

What am I to do, just keep it up until everything falls apart one day? Is a flatter structure with fewer managers always best? Am I missing something in regard to this "new management"?

Sincerely,
Overworked in Regina

YOU DECIDE

Is it ethical to restructure, cut management levels, and expect the remaining managers to do more work? Or is it simply the case that managers used to the "old" ways of doing things need extra training and care while learning "new" management approaches? And what about this person's boss—is she on track with her management skills? Aren't managers supposed to help people understand their jobs, set priorities, and fulfill them, while still maintaining a reasonable work–life balance?

A classic principle of organization warns managers not to delegate without giving the other person sufficient authority to perform. Without authority, it is very hard for someone to live up to another's performance expectations. The *authority-and-responsibility principle* states that authority should equal responsibility when work is delegated from a supervisor to a subordinate.

Unwillingness to delegate is a common management failure. Whether this comes from a lack of trust in others or from a manager's personal inflexibility, it can still be damaging. Too little delegation overloads the manager with work that could be done by others; it also denies others many opportunities to fully utilize their talents on the job.

Empowerment allows others to make decisions and exercise discretion in their work.

When well done, delegation leads to **empowerment**, defined as letting others make decisions and exercise discretion in their work. Empowerment results when delegation moves decisions to people who are most capable of doing the work. It builds performance potential by allowing people freedom to use their talents, contribute ideas, and do their jobs in the best possible ways. And because empowerment creates a sense of ownership, it also increases commitment to decisions and work goals.

Trend: Managers are delegating more. They are finding ways to empower people at all levels to make more decisions that affect themselves and their work.

Decentralization with Centralization

"Should most decisions be made at the top levels of an organization, or should they be dispersed by extensive delegation throughout all levels of management?" The former approach is referred to as **centralization**; the latter is called **decentralization**. But the management issue here doesn't have to be framed as an either/or choice. Today's organizations use information technology to operate with greater decentralization without giving up centralized control.[40]

Centralization is the concentration of authority for most decisions at the top level of an organization.

Decentralization is the dispersion of authority to make decisions throughout all organization levels.

With computer networks and advanced information systems, managers at higher levels can more easily stay informed about a wide range of day-to-day performance matters. Because they have information on results readily available, they can allow more decentralization in decision-making. If something goes wrong, presumably the information systems will sound an alarm and allow corrective action to be taken quickly.

Trend: Delegation, empowerment, and horizontal structures are contributing to more decentralization in organizations; at the same time, advances in information technology are allowing for adequate centralized control.

RESEARCH BRIEF

Making schools work better

Scholar and consultant William Ouchi believes that our public schools can be improved through organizational design. In his book *Making Schools Work: A Revolutionary Plan to Get Your Children the Education They Need*, Ouchi points out that as organizations grow in size, they tend to "bulk up" with staff personnel and higher-level managers who are distant from customers and operating workers. He finds many less-successful schools following this pattern.

Ouchi's study of 223 school districts suggests that adding administrative weight and cost at the top does little to improve organizational performance, and can actually harm it. Even though most school districts are highly centralized, he finds that decentralization is a characteristic of the more successful ones. The better districts in his study had fewer central office staff personnel per student and allowed maximum autonomy to school principals. Ouchi advocates redesigning schools so that decision-making is more decentralized. He believes in allowing principals more autonomy to control school budgets and work with their staffs, and in allowing teachers more freedom to solve their own problems.

You be the researcher

Does Ouchi offer us a general organizational design principle—systems perform best with streamlined

designs and greater decentralization? Or can you come up with examples of organizations that perform well with large staffs and lots of centralization? What follow-up research questions do you think Ouchi and others should consider pursuing in the future?

Don't you wonder how School District B justifies the size of its administrative staff and a centralized approach when School District A, with a far different configuration, has a reputation for success? What is the ratio of administrative to instructional staff at your college or university? Is it possible that "performance" could be improved along the lines suggested by Ouchi?

Reduced Use of Staff

When it comes to coordination and control in organizations, the issue of line–staff relationships is important. Chapter 1 described staff roles as providing expert advice and guidance to line personnel. Persons appointed in **staff positions** perform a technical service or provide special problem-solving expertise for other parts of the organization. This could be a single person, such as a corporate safety director, or a complete unit, such as a corporate safety department.

Staff positions provide technical expertise for other parts of the organization.

Many organizations rely on staff specialists to maintain coordination and control over a variety of matters. In a large retail chain, line managers in each store typically make daily operating decisions regarding direct sales of merchandise. But staff specialists at the corporate or regional levels often provide direction and support so that all the stores operate with the same credit, purchasing, employment, and advertising procedures.

Problems in line–staff distinctions can and do arise, and organizations sometimes find that staff size grows to the point where it costs more than it is worth. This is why staff cutbacks are common in downsizing and other turnaround efforts. There is no one best solution to the problem of how to divide work between line and staff responsibilities. What is best for any organization will be a cost-effective staff component that satisfies, but doesn't overreact to, needs for specialized technical assistance to line operations.

Trend: Organizations are reducing the size of staff. They are lowering costs and increasing efficiency by employing fewer staff personnel and using smaller staff units.

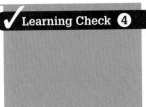
✓ **Learning Check ④**

BE SURE YOU CAN
....
• define *organizational design* • describe the characteristics of mechanistic and organic designs • explain when the mechanistic design and the organic design work best • define *differentiation* and *integration* • list ways to improve subsystem integration in organizations • describe trends in levels of management, delegation and empowerment, decentralization and centralization, and use of staff

MANAGEMENT LEARNING REVIEW

STUDY QUESTIONS SUMMARY

KEY TERMS

adaptive organization, 234
boundaryless organization, 231
bureaucracy, 233
centralization, 238
chain of command, 236
cross-functional team, 228
customer structure, 226
decentralization, 238
delegation, 237
departmentalization, 223
differentiation, 235
divisional structure, 225
empowerment, 238
formal structure, 221
functional chimneys
    problem, 224
functional structure, 223
geographical structure, 225
informal structure, 222
integration, 235
matrix structure, 227
mechanistic design, 233
network structure, 230
organic design, 234
organization chart, 221
organization structure, 221
organizational design, 232
organizing, 220
process structure, 226
product structure, 225
project teams, 228
social network analysis, 222
span of control, 236
staff positions, 239
subsystem, 234
team structure, 228
virtual organization, 232
work process, 226

1. What is organizing as a management function?

- Organizing is the process of arranging people and resources to work toward a common goal.

- Organizing decisions divide up the work that needs to be done, allocate people and resources to do it, and coordinate results to achieve productivity.

- Structure is the system of tasks, reporting relationships, and communication that links people and positions within an organization.

- The formal structure, such as shown on an organization chart, describes how an organization is supposed to work.

- The informal structure of an organization consists of the unofficial relationships that develop among members.

FOR DISCUSSION If organization charts are imperfect, why bother with them?

2. What are the traditional organization structures?

- In functional structures, people with similar skills who perform similar activities are grouped together under a common manager.

- In divisional structures, people who work on a similar product, work in the same geographical region, serve the same customers, or participate in the same work process are grouped together under common managers.

- A matrix structure combines the functional and divisional approaches to create permanent cross-functional project teams.

FOR DISCUSSION Why use functional structures if they are prone to functional chimneys problems?

3. What are the newer types of organization structures?

- Team structures use cross-functional teams and task forces to improve lateral relations and problem solving at all levels.

- Network structures use contracted services and strategic alliances to support a core business or organizational centre.

- Boundaryless structures or boundaryless organizations combine team and network structures with the advantages of technology to accomplish tasks and projects.

- Virtual organizations use information technology to mobilize a shifting mix of strategic alliances to accomplish tasks and projects.

FOR DISCUSSION How can problems with group decision-making hurt team structures?

4. How are organizational designs changing the workplace?

- Mechanistic designs are bureaucratic and vertical, performing best for routine and predictable tasks; organic designs are adaptive and horizontal, performing best in conditions requiring change and flexibility.

- Differentiation is the degree of difference that exists between various subsystems; integration is the level of coordination achieved among them.

- Organizations with little internal differentiation can be integrated vertically through authority relationships; greater differentiation requires more intense horizontal integration, emphasizing cross-functional teams and lateral relations.

- Key organizing trends include fewer levels of management, more delegation and empowerment, decentralization with centralization, and fewer staff positions.

FOR DISCUSSION Which of the organizing trends is most subject to change under current conditions?

SELF-TEST

Multiple-Choice Questions

1. The main purpose of organizing as a management function is to _____.

    (a) make sure that results match plans   (b) arrange people and resources to accomplish work   (c) create enthusiasm for the work to be done   (d) match strategies with operational plans

2. _____ is the system of tasks, reporting relationships, and communication that links together the various parts of an organization.

    (a) Structure   (b) Staff   (c) Decentralization   (d) Differentiation

3. Transmission of rumours and resistance to change are potential disadvantages often associated with _____.

    (a) virtual organizations   (b) informal structures   (c) delegation   (d) specialized staff

4. An organization chart showing vice presidents of marketing, finance, manufacturing, and purchasing all reporting to the president is depicting a _____ structure.

    (a) functional   (b) matrix   (c) network   (d) product

5. The "two-boss" system of reporting relationships is found in the _____ structure.

    (a) functional   (b) matrix   (c) network   (d) product

6. A manufacturing business with a functional structure has recently developed two new product lines. The president of the company might consider shifting to a(n) _____ structure to gain a stronger focus on each product.

    (a) virtual   (b) informal   (c) divisional   (d) network

7. Better lower-level teamwork and more top-level strategic management are among the expected advantages of a _____ structure.

    (a) divisional   (b) matrix   (c) geographical   (d) product

8. "Tall" organizations tend to have long chains of command and _____ spans of control.

    (a) wide   (b) narrow   (c) informal   (d) centralized

9. The functional chimneys problem occurs when people in different functions _____.

    (a) fail to communicate with one another   (b) try to help each other work with customers   (c) spend too much time coordinating decisions   (d) focus on products rather than functions

10. A _____ structure tries to combine the best elements of the functional and divisional forms.

    (a) virtual   (b) boundaryless   (c) team   (d) matrix

11. A student volunteers to gather information on a company for a group case analysis project. The other members of the group agree, and tell her to go ahead and choose the information sources. In terms of delegation, this group is giving the student _____ to fulfill the agreed-upon task.

    (a) responsibility   (b) accountability   (c) authority   (d) decentralization

12. The current trend in the use of staff in organizations is to _____.

    (a) give staff personnel more authority over operations   (b) reduce the number of staff personnel   (c) remove all staff from the organization   (d) combine all staff functions in one department

13. The bureaucratic organization described by Max Weber is similar to the _____ organization described by Burns and Stalker.

    (a) adaptive   (b) mechanistic   (c) organic   (d) adhocracy

14. A basic paradox in subsystem design is that as differentiation increases, the need for _____ also increases—but becomes harder to accomplish.

    (a) cost efficiency   (b) innovation   (c) integration   (d) transformation

15. When the members of a marketing department pursue sales volume objectives, and those in manufacturing pursue cost efficiency objectives, this is an example of _____.

    (a) simultaneous systems   (b) subsystems differentiation   (c) long-linked technology   (d) small-batch production

Short-Response Questions

16. What symptoms might indicate that a functional structure is causing problems for the organization?

17. Explain by example the concept of a network organization structure.

18. Explain the practical significance of this statement: "Organizational design should always be addressed in contingency fashion."

19. Describe differentiation and integration as issues in subsystem design.

Application Question

20. Faisal Sham supervises a group of seven project engineers. His unit is experiencing a heavy workload, as the demand for different versions of one of his firm's computer components is growing. Faisal finds that he doesn't have time to follow up on all design details for each version. Up until now, he has tried to do this all by himself. Two of the engineers have shown an interest in helping him coordinate work on the various designs. As a consultant, how would you advise Faisal in terms of delegating work to them?

MANAGEMENT SKILLS AND COMPETENCIES

SELF-ASSESSMENT

Back to Yourself: Empowerment

Structures help bring order to organizational complexity; they put people together in ways that, on paper at least, make good sense in terms of getting tasks accomplished. But although there are many structural alternatives, as described in this chapter, they all struggle for success at times. Things can change so fast that you might think of today's structures as solutions to yesterday's problems. This puts a great burden on people to fill in the gaps and deal spontaneously with things that structures don't or can't cover at any point in time. Empowerment is a way of unlocking talent and motivation so that people can act in ways that make a performance difference; it gives them freedom to make decisions about how they work. As discussed in the chapter, many managers fail when it comes to empowerment. And when they do, their organizations often under-perform.

Further Reflection: Empowering Others

Instructions

Think of times when you have been in charge of a group—this could be a full-time or part-time work situation, a student work group, a volunteer initiative, or whatever. Complete the following questionnaire by recording how you feel about each statement according to this scale:

1 = Strongly disagree   2 = Disagree   3 = Neutral   4 = Agree   5 = Strongly agree

When in charge of a team, I find that

1. Most of the time, other people are too inexperienced to do things, so I prefer to do them myself.

2. It often takes more time to explain things to others than to just do them myself.

3. Mistakes made by others are costly, so I don't assign much work to them.

4. Some things simply should not be delegated to others.

5. I often get quicker action by doing a job myself.

6. Many people are good only at very specific tasks, so they can't be assigned additional responsibilities.

7. Many people are too busy to take on additional work.

8. Most people just aren't ready to handle additional responsibilities.

9. In my position, I should be entitled to make my own decisions.

Scoring

Total your responses and enter the score here _____.

Interpretation

This instrument gives an impression of your willingness to delegate. Possible scores range from 9 to 45. The lower your score, the more willing you appear to be to delegate to others. Willingness to delegate is an important managerial characteristic: it is how you—as a manager—can "empower" others and give them opportunities to assume responsibility and exercise self-control in their work. With the growing importance of horizontal organizations and empowerment in the new workplace, your willingness to delegate is worth thinking about seriously.

Source: Questionnaire adapted from L. Steinmetz and R. Todd, *First Line Management, 4th ed.* (Homewood, IL: BPI/Irwin, 1986), pp. 64–67. Used by permission.

The Future Workplace

Instructions

Form groups as assigned by the instructor. Brainstorm to develop a master list of the major workplace characteristics you expect to find in the year 2020. Use this list as background for completing the following tasks:

1. Write a one-paragraph description of what the typical "Workplace 2020" manager's workday will be like.

2. Draw a "picture" representing what the Workplace 2020 organization will look like.

3. State why your Workplace 2020 organization does or does not conform with the organizational design trends discussed in this chapter.

4. Write a "short story" (10 sentences maximum) that portrays a manager in trouble in your Workplace 2020 because of a failure to empower others.

Choose a spokesperson to share your results with the class as a whole and explain their implications for the class members.

Nike: Spreading Out to Stay Together

Nike is indisputably a giant in the athletics industry. But the Oregon company has grown large precisely because it knows how to stay small. By focusing on its core competencies—and outsourcing all others—Nike has managed to become a sharply focused industry leader. But can it stay in front?

Courtesy Nike

What Do You Call a Company of Thinkers?

It's not a joke or a Buddhist koan. Rather, it's a conundrum about one of the most successful companies in the United States—

a company known worldwide for its products, none of which it actually makes. This raises two questions: If you don't make anything, what do you actually do? If you outsource everything, what's left?

A whole lot of brand recognition, for starters. Nike, famous for its trademark Swoosh™, is still among the most recognized brands in the world and is an industry leader in the US$ 79-billion sports footwear and apparel market.[1] And its 33-percent market share is the largest in the global athletic shoe market.[2]

Since captivating the shoe-buying public in the early 1980s with indomitable spokesperson Michael Jordan, Nike continues to outpace the athletic shoe competition while spreading its brand through an ever-widening universe of sports equipment, apparel, and paraphernalia. The omnipresent Swoosh graces everything from bumper stickers to sunglasses to high school sports uniforms.

Not long after Nike's introduction of Air Jordans, the first strains of the "Just Do It" ad campaign sealed the company's reputation as a megabrand. When Nike made the strategic image shift from simply selling products to embodying a love of sport, discipline, ambition, practice, and all the other desirable traits of athleticism, it became among the first in a long line of brands to represent itself as aiding customers in their self-expression as part of its marketing strategy.

Advertising has played a large part in Nike's continued success. In the United States alone, Nike recently spent US$ 1.7 billion annually on advertising,[3] with a recent combined total of US$ 220 million in measured media.[4] Portland ad agency Wieden & Kennedy has been instrumental in creating and perpetuating Nike's image—so much so that the agency has a large division in-house at Nike headquarters. This intimate relationship between the two companies allows the agency's creative designers to focus solely on Nike work and gives them unparalleled access to executives, researchers, and anyone else who might provide advertisers with their next inspiration for marketing greatness.

What's Left, Then?

Although Nike has cleverly kept its ad agency nestled close to home, it has relied on outsourcing many non-executive responsibilities in order to reduce overhead. It can be argued that Nike, recognizing that its core competency lies in the design—not the manufacturing—of shoes, was wise to transfer production overseas.

But Nike has taken outsourcing to a new level, barely producing any of its products in its own factories. All its shoes, for instance, are made by subcontractors. Although this allocation of production hasn't hurt the quality of the shoes at all, it has challenged Nike's reputation among fair-trade critics.

After initial allegations of sweatshop labour surfaced at Nike-sponsored factories, the company tried to reach out and reason with its more moderate critics. But this approach failed, and Nike found itself in the unenviable position of trying to defend its outsourcing practices while withholding the locations of its favoured production shops from the competition.

Boldly, in a move designed to turn critics into converts, Nike posted information on its website detailing every one of the approximately 700 factories it uses to make shoes, apparel, and other sporting goods.[5] It released the data in conjunction with a comprehensive new corporate responsibility report summarizing the environmental and labour situations of its contract factories.[6]

"This is a significant step that will blow away the myth that companies can't release their factory names because it's proprietary information," said Charles Kernaghan, executive director of the National Labor Committee, a New York–based anti-sweatshop group that has been no friend to Nike over the years. "If Nike can do it, so can Wal-Mart and all the rest."[7]

Jordan Isn't Forever

Knowing that shoe sales alone wouldn't be enough to sustain continued growth, Nike decided, in a lateral move, to learn more about its customers' involvement in sports, identifying what needs it might be able to fill. Banking on the star power of its Swoosh, Nike has successfully branded apparel, sporting goods, sunglasses, and even an MP3 player made by Philips. Like many large companies who have found themselves at odds with the possible limitations of their brands, Nike realized that it would have to master the one-two punch: identifying new needs and supplying creative and desirable products to fill those needs.

In keeping with the times, Nike's head designer, John R. Hoke III, is encouraging his designers to develop environmentally sustainable designs. This may come as a surprise to anyone who has ever thought about how much foam and plastic goes into the average Nike sneaker, but a corporate-wide mission called "Considered" has designers rethinking the materials used to put the spring in millions of steps. The company even launched a line of environmentally sustainable products under the same name, all of them built under the principle established in the Considered program. "I'm very passionate about this idea," Hoke said. "We are going to challenge ourselves to think a little bit differently about the way we create products."[8]

Nipping at Nike's Heels

Despite Nike's success and retention of its market share, things haven't been a bed of roses in the past few years. When CEO Phil Knight decided to step down, he handed the reins to Bill Perez, former CEO of S. C. Johnson and Sons, who became the first outsider recruited for the executive tier since Nike's founding in 1968. But after barely a year with Perez on the job, Knight, who remained in the inner circle in his position as chairman of the board, decided Perez couldn't "get his arms around the company." Knight accepted Perez's resignation and promoted Mark Parker, a 27-year veteran who was then co-president of the Nike brand, as a replacement.[9]

And pressures are mounting from outside its Beaverton, Oregon, headquarters. German rival Adidas drew a few strides closer to Nike when it purchased Reebok for approximately US$ 3.8 billion.[10] Joining forces will help the brands collectively negotiate shelf space and other sales issues in American stores and will aid the Adidas group in its price discussions with Asian manufacturers. With recent combined global sales of US$ 15 billion,[11] the new supergroup of shoes isn't far off from Nike's US$ 16 billion.[12]

According to Jon Hickey, senior vice president of sports and entertainment marketing for the ad agency Mullen, with the combination of Adidas and Reebok, Nike has its "first real, legitimate threat since the '80s. There's no way either one would even approach Nike, much less overtake them, on their own." But now, adds Hickey, "Nike has to respond. This new, combined entity has a chance to make a run. Now, it's game on."[13] But when faced with a challenge, Nike simply knocks its bat against its cleats and steps up to the plate. "Our focus is on growing our own business," said Nike spokesman Alan Marks. "Of course we're in a competitive business, but we win by staying focused on our strategies and our consumers. And from that perspective nothing has changed."[14] One new place the shoe wars were fought was at the 2010 World Cup. A Nielsen study released before the soccer extravaganza began showed that Nike had double the buzz levels of the official sponsor, Adidas. Alas for Nike, this changed once the games began as Adidas overtook Nike as the top brand, climbing to 25 percent of all buzz among brands monitored.[15]

Putting It All Together

Nike has balanced its immense size and tremendous pressures to remain successful by leveraging a decentralized corporate structure. Individual business centres—such as research, production, and marketing—are free to focus on their core competencies without worrying about the effects of corporate bloat. Similarly, Nike has found continued marketplace success by positioning itself not simply as a sneaker company but as a brand that fulfills the evolving needs of today's athletes and does so in a sustainable and, now, in an ethical way. Will Nike continue to profit from its increasingly decentralized business model, or will it spread itself so thin that its competition will overtake it?

Discussion Questions

1. When Nike CEO Phil Knight stepped down and handed his job to Bill Perez, he stayed on as chairman of the board. In what ways could Knight's continued presence on the board have created an informal structure that prevented Perez from achieving full and complete leadership of Nike?

2. How can Nike utilize both traditional and newer organization structures to support the firm's heavy strategic commitment to outsourcing?

3. Given the problems that Nike had with sweatshop labour being used by some of its foreign contractors, are there subsystems of the firm that need to be run with a mechanistic rather than organic design? Give examples to support your answer.

4. FURTHER RESEARCH—Gather information on Nike's recent moves and accomplishments, and those of its rival Adidas. Are both firms following the same strategies and using the same structures to support them? Or is one doing something quite different from the other? Based on what you learn, what do you predict for the future? Will Nike stay on top, or is Adidas the next industry leader?

VIDEO CASE 4

The First Western CEO of Sony

Video Summary and Discussion

What do Queen Elizabeth II, David Letterman, and Sony have in common? The answer is Howard Stringer. Knighted by the queen and responsible for bringing David Letterman to CBS, Stringer has the challenge of being the first "Western" (non-Japanese) chairman and CEO of Sony. This CBS news interview by Lesley Stahl shows the balance Stringer has had to maintain running a company whose language he does not speak and whose culture, corporate or otherwise, he does not share.

Sony hired Stringer to turn the company around after a run of product disappointments and missed market opportunities. It hoped the British-born, American-made knight, already known as the "affable axe-wielder," could restructure, cutting factories and thousands of jobs in the process—something Japanese executives wouldn't want to do. In Japan, jobs are held for life and loyalty runs both ways. But cut he did: 9,000 jobs and 11 factories, with nary a bad reputation.

Indeed, while president of CBS News in the late 1980s, when the network needed to cut costs, Stringer personally delivered the bad news to all 200 employees slated for layoffs. "I didn't send a memo to somebody and say 'your job is over.' It was emotionally very draining. And it affected me," he said.

In his restructuring of Sony, Stringer has had to meld the old with the new, the Western and Eastern business models. "This is a company with great traditions . . . that's why this company was successful in the first place. And I'm not sure that leaping on board an American business model of ruthlessness and viciousness and counter-attacks all the time is a good thing necessarily for somebody else. And, so, taking care of somebody else's culture is part of the joy and opportunity of this job. I have things to learn from the Japanese. And not just the other way around."

Canadian managers would also benefit greatly from familiarizing themselves with the organizational cultures of foreign countries such as Japan to function effectively in them. For example, if a Canadian manager had assumed the role of Howard Stringer, he or she would benefit from knowing the following additional aspects of Japanese organizational culture:

1. Japanese organizational culture emphasizes lifetime employment and would only lay off employees as a last resort.

2. The career paths of typical employees in Japanese organizations span several business functions.

3. In Japanese firms, decisions are typically made in groups by consensus, and such decisions are based on principles.

4. In Japanese firms, the cultural value that dominates is a holistic concern for workers and managers. Holistic concern extends beyond concern for a person simply as a worker or a manager to concern about that person's home life, hobbies, personal beliefs, hopes, fears, and aspirations.

It should be clear that these aspects of Japanese organizational culture are not generally shared by Canadian companies.

For example, Canadian organizational culture tends not to emphasize lifetime employment, and layoffs are not uncommon. It tends to emphasize specialized career paths as opposed to those spanning several business functions. Canadian organizational culture emphasizes individual as opposed to group decision-making. Canadian employers' concern for workers tends to be confined primarily to their work life.

It is evident, therefore, that knowledge of Japanese organizational culture would be essential for a Canadian manager if he or she were to be able to operate effectively within that culture, given the stark differences between the two organizational cultures.

Questions for Students

1. Based on the video, explain why you believe Sony has a mechanistic or organic design.

2. Your textbook explains that successful organizations tend to have strong and positive cultures. How would you explain the core culture or core values of Sony?

3. If you were Howard Stringer, how would an understanding of the organizational culture help you in leading the company?

09 Innovation and Organizational Change

New thinking deserves to be pampered

Millions of babies owe thanks to Victor Mills. Concerned in the 1950s that his grandchildren should have a better experience with their diapers, he invented the disposable diaper. It was commercialized by Procter & Gamble as Pampers. Fortunately for babies and their parents, Mills worked for a company that valued creativity and innovation. It still does, although the road has sometimes been a rocky one.

The company's former CEO A. G. Lafley took the reins when P&G was a bit in the doldrums, stuck in a culture *BusinessWeek* described as "stodgy" and "insular." But as Lafley's leadership took hold, innovation again became a way of life and a competitive advantage for the global firm—138,000 employees and operations in 80 countries. Looking back, Lafley says: "We were trying to do too much, too fast, and nothing was being done well." He set out to change things.

To boost innovation, Lafley reinvigorated research and development. He broke barriers within the firm; his message was that there was nothing wrong with introducing products that were "not invented here." He pushed employees to scour the environment; he asked them to find and bring into the firm great ideas and technologies from the outside.

Lafley also expanded the push for innovation beyond new products and into a quest for new processes, improved operations, and better ways of working. "To succeed," he says, "companies need to see innovation not as something special that only special people can do, but as something that can become routine and methodological, taking advantage of the capabilities of ordinary people." He backed that notion with a commitment to fuelling innovation with an understanding of customer wants and needs. Rather than pushing products on customers, he believes the firm needs to provide products for customers.

This means keeping customers "at the center of all our decisions," he says. With Lafley at the helm, you'll find that P&G ranked high on *Fortune* magazine's listing of the world's most admired companies.[1]

BENCHMARK Procter & Gamble is a huge global firm, and it's easy to see how size alone might drain creativity and innovation. But with Lafley's focus on the employees and customers, innovation seemed back on track. The story should make you think about what it takes for any organization to embrace new ideas, stimulate creativity, and make positive changes.

Tolerance for Ambiguity

Even through creativity and innovation can be exciting, change and uncertainty also evoke anxiety. Change breaks us from past habits and conditions; uncertainty moves many things out of our direct control. Depending on your tolerance for ambiguity, you may be comfortable or uncomfortable dealing with these realities.

Consider the boxed questions. Which best describes how you respond to different courses and instructors? What are the insights concerning your tolerance for ambiguity?

It takes personal flexibility and lots of confidence to cope well with unpredictability, whether in a university course or a work situation. Some, probably many, people are uneasy when dealing with the unfamiliar. They prefer to work with directions that provide clear decision-making rules and minimize ambiguity. They like the structure of mechanistic organizations with bureaucratic features. They tend to get comfortable with fixed patterns in life and can be afraid of anything "new."

> **In a typical course, do you prefer . . .**
>
> 1. An instructor who gives precise assignments and accepts no deviations, or one who gives open-ended assignments and lets students suggest alternatives?
>
> 2. An instructor who gives out a general syllabus and then modifies it over time based on student feedback, or one who gives out a detailed syllabus and sticks to it?

Does the latter description apply to you? Or are you among those who are willing, able, and happy to work in less structured settings—ones that allow lots of flexibility in responding to changing situations? Such people like the freedom and spontaneity allowed in organic organizations that are designed for innovation and adaptation. They are excited by the prospects of change and new opportunities.

Many, perhaps even most, management challenges today fall into the change category, and many personal challenges do so as well. In this regard, it's important to find a good fit between your personal preferences and the pace and nature of change in the organizations in which you choose to work. To achieve this fit, you have to understand your tolerance for ambiguity and how you react in change situations.

❖ Get to Know Yourself Better

Write a short narrative describing your "ideal" employer in terms of structure, culture, management styles, and frequency of major changes. Add a comment that explains how this ideal organization fits your personality, including insights from self-assessments such as those recommended here. What does this say about your capability to be a change leader?

CHAPTER 9 STUDY QUESTIONS

- How do organizations accomplish innovation?

- What is the nature of organizational change?

- How can planned organizational change be managed?

- What is organization development?

VISUAL CHAPTER OVERVIEW

CHAPTER 9 INNOVATION AND ORGANIZATIONAL CHANGE

Study Question 1	Study Question 2	Study Question 3	Study Question 4
Innovation in Organizations	**Organizational Change**	**Managing Planned Change**	**Organization Development**
■ Creativity and innovation	■ Change leaders	■ Phases of planned change	■ Organization development goals
■ Types of innovations	■ Models of change leadership	■ Change strategies	■ How organization development works
■ The innovation process	■ Incremental and transformational change	■ Resistance to change	■ Organization development interventions
■ Characteristics of innovative organizations	■ Forces and targets for change	■ Challenges of technological change	
✓ Learning Check 1	✓ Learning Check 2	✓ Learning Check 3	✓ Learning Check 4

Harvard scholars Michael Beer and Nitin Nohria point out that "The new economy has ushered in great business opportunities and great turmoil. Not since the Industrial Revolution have the stakes of dealing with change been so high. Most traditional organizations have accepted, in theory at least, that they must either change or die."[2] John Chambers, CEO of Cisco Systems, says "Companies that are successful will have cultures that thrive on change, even though change makes most people uncomfortable," and Gabrielle Chevalier, CEO of Mississauga-based Solutions to Go Inc., agrees: "Our organization is a high-performance culture that recognizes continuous change in the marketplace and in our customers' needs."[3]

It's accurate to say that the watchwords of today continue to be change, change, and change. But it's also true that many organizations and leaders are slow or unsuccessful in dealing with it. Creating positive change in organizations is not easy. Change threatens those with low tolerance for ambiguity, as discussed in the chapter opener; it involves risk, complexity, anxiety, and stress. For all of these reasons and more, it takes special understanding to manage people and organizations in ways that fully unlock their potential for creativity and innovation.

INNOVATION IN ORGANIZATIONS

In his book *The Circle of Innovation*, consultant Tom Peters urges managers to refocus away from past accomplishments and toward the role of innovation as the primary source of competitive advantage.[4] His message is that individuals and organizations alike must change and adapt and innovate as the environment changes around them. For organizations, this places primacy on **strategic leadership**, defined in Chapter 7 as the "ability to anticipate, envision, maintain flexibility, think strategically, and work with others to initiate changes that will create a viable future for the organization."[5] Strategic leaders are change leaders who build organizations that, by constantly renewing themselves, are able to thrive even in the most difficult and uncertain times.

Strategic leadership creates the capacity for ongoing strategic change.

CREATIVITY AND INNOVATION

Creativity is the generation of a novel idea or unique approach to solving problems or crafting opportunities.[6] And it is one of the great assets of human capital. People have ideas in organizations, people possess ingenuity, and people drive innovation. Managers who understand this are able to work with people in ways that allow their creativity to prosper. Among the forces known to foster creative work environments are challenging work, freedom to exercise talent and initiative, encouragement by peers and supervisors, supportive organizational cultures, and a lack of performance obstacles.[7]

Creativity exerts its influence in organizations through **innovation**, the process of coming up with new ideas and putting them into practice.[8] When the environment is right and creativity thrives, people are able to turn technologies and other resources into innovations that, in turn, can make the accomplishments of an organization truly distinctive.

Creativity is the generation of a new idea or unique approach that solves a problem or crafts an opportunity.

Innovation is the process of taking a new idea and putting it into practice.

Creative Work Environments				
Challenging work	Freedom to apply talents	Encouraging peers, bosses	Supportive culture	Lack of obstacles

TYPES OF INNOVATIONS

When you think innovation, products like the iPod, Post-It Notes, and even a Super-Soaker water gun might come to mind. Or you might think about self-scanning checkouts at the grocery store, or on-line check-in for air travel. All are part and parcel of a whole host of business innovations available today. But don't forget that innovations can also take positive steps toward social responsibility. Some seek sustainability in relationship with our natural environment; some tackle social problems like poverty and disease.

Business Innovations

Innovation in and by organizations has traditionally been addressed in three broad forms: (1) **product innovations**, which result in the creation of new or improved goods and services;

Product innovations result in new or improved goods or services.

Process innovations result in better ways of doing things.

Business model innovations result in ways for firms to make money.

Canadian Press/AP Photo/Rafiq Maqbool

(2) **process innovations**, which result in better ways of doing things; and (3) **business model innovations**, which result in new ways of making money for the firm.[9] Consider these examples from *BusinessWeek's* listing of "The World's Most Innovative Companies."[10]

- *Product Innovation*—Apple introduced us to the "iPod world"; Toyota has been the market mover in new hybrid vehicles; the BlackBerry from Research In Motion ushered in a new era of handheld mobile devices; Pure Digital technologies came out with the low-cost Flip Video camcorder selling at about $120; Tata Group of India has introduced a $2,500 car, the Nano, for low-income earners.

- *Process Innovation*—WestJet continues to improve operations supporting its low-cost business strategy; IKEA transformed retail shopping for furniture and household items; Amazon.com keeps improving the online shopping experience; Procter & Gamble reorganized to bring design executives into the top management circle; Facebook opened its software platform to third-party developers, with Yahoo! and Google soon following.

- *Business Model Innovation*—Virgin Group Ltd. uses "hip lifestyle" branding to infuse its traditional industries and is ready to launch a new era of space travel; Starbucks continues to turn coffee selling into a global branding business; eBay created the world's largest on-line marketplace; Google thrives on advertising revenues driven by web technology; Amazon.com sells its proprietary web services to other firms.

Sustainable Innovations

Sustainable innovation creates new products and processes that have lower environmental impact.

In Chapter 4 on ethics and social responsibility we discussed **sustainable innovation** as the creation of new products and processes that have lower environmental impacts than the available alternatives. The goal is to find ways to do business while having minimal impact on the natural environment or, even better, to improve it. Sustainable innovations are found in areas like energy use, water use, packaging, waste management, and transportation practices, as well as in product development. At the United Nations–sponsored Global Forum for Business as an Agent of World Benefit, attendees pointed out directions for sustainable innovation when they described the ideal world of 2020 with characteristics such as these: "bright-green restorative economy that purifies the air that we breathe . . . has eliminated the waste and toxic byproducts . . . powered through renewable energy."[11]

Green innovation is the process of turning ideas into innovations that reduce the carbon footprint of an organization or its products.

What some call **green innovations** fits this notion of sustainability. They reduce the carbon footprint of an organization or its products, sometimes in quite simple ways. Replacement of air travel with new videoconferencing technologies is one example. Vodafone estimates that in one year it eliminated 13,500 flights employees would otherwise have taken to attend meetings; carbon emissions were lowered by some 4,500 tonnes. At Sierra Nevada Brewing Company, green innovation involved blending purchased natural gas with biogas from its water treatment plant to fuel generators for heat. When solar power is added to the mix, the firm generates 80 percent of its own power and also reduces air pollution. Quebec's Cascades, a paper products manufacturer, works to reduce its use of water and currently consumes six times less water than the industry average. Toronto chef Mark McEwan, who heads upscale restaurants including North 44 and Bymark, is reducing the carbon footprint and promoting local sustainability by selling only domestically produced water in reusable glass bottles. Bayer Canada has adopted a green innovation program called "Operation Zero Waste" to divert 80 percent of its waste from landfills through aggressive recycling efforts. And at Walmart, CEO Lee Scott's green innovation goal is ultimately expansive; he wants Walmart to totally eliminate waste.[12]

REAL ETHICS

Corporate Greens and Global Warming

Get ready—you'll be reading and hearing a lot more about "corporate greens." No, we're not talking about a new political party; we're talking about a growing message from the business community that it really does care about global warming and is going to do its share to respond to the threats. There's emerging consensus not only that global warming is harming our planet even faster than expected, but that business innovation is needed to deal with it.

HSBC was the first large bank to declare that it was going "carbon neutral," committing to cut its carbon output as much as possible and then offsetting the remainder by paying to reduce emissions elsewhere. As concerns about global warming build, so, too, do pressures for change in traditional business methods. More business leaders seem to be taking the challenge seriously.

Ryan Wright is manager in charge of utility and sustainability at the Bellisio Foods plant in Jackson, Ohio. You may not think there's a lot that can be done to "green up" a manufacturing facility, but he's found the way. A large treatment plant digests food waste, using bio-organisms to create the methane that becomes fuel to run the factories' boilers. Wright believes the process cuts carbon dioxide output by 43,000 tons per year by saving on natural gas and transporting waste to a landfill. Although the price of the system was more than $4.6 million, he says: "It's a great project; we're proud of it: it's the right thing to do."

YOU DECIDE

Is it ethical for a business to pursue anything but "carbon neutrality" in today's world? What differentiates executives who resist from those willing to innovate and make changes in response to global warming challenges? And, while you are thinking about the issues, is it ethical to claim social responsibility for pursuing environmentally friendly practices only to avoid government regulation or adverse publicity? In other words, does it make a difference if a firm does "good things" for selfish reasons?

Social Business Innovations

Management consultant Peter Drucker called innovation "an effort to create purposeful, focused change in an enterprise's economic or social potential."[13] Said a bit differently, it is the act of converting new ideas into usable applications with positive economic or social value. And although the tendency is to view innovation in an economic context, it's important to remember that it applies equally well when we talk about the world's social problems: poverty, famine, illiteracy, disease, and the general conditions for economic and social development.

A good example is Mohammad Yunus, the Bangladeshi economist who developed the Grameen Bank to lend small amounts of money to entrepreneurs in developing countries. On one level, it is a business model innovation—micro-credit lending. But at another level, it is a **social business innovation**—using micro-credit lending to help create small enterprises and fight poverty. In this case, the underlying business model directly addresses a social problem. And it's

Social business innovation finds ways to use business models to address important social problems.

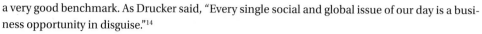

a very good benchmark. As Drucker said, "Every single social and global issue of our day is a business opportunity in disguise."[14]

Social entrepreneurship
pursues innovative ways to create change that benefits society.

Social business innovation stems from creativity that also manifests itself as **social entrepreneurship**. This term was first used in Chapter 4 in a discussion of ethics and social responsibility. It is a unique form of entrepreneurship that finds novel ways to create changes that solve pressing social problems. You can think of it as entrepreneurship and innovation for social good.[15] Rather than financial gain, the goal is social change; for example, change toward what the U.N. Global Forum for Business as an Agent of World Benefit described as a world that has "eradicated poverty and preventable disease" and "made empowered prosperity accessible to everyone."[16]

What can be done, for example, about chronic hunger—the leading cause of death among African children? Sympathy wasn't enough for Andrew Youn. He's a social entrepreneur whose creativity has made a world of difference for many African families. After returning from a Northwestern University internship in South Africa, Youn attacked the problem of chronic child hunger with an innovative program: the One Acre Fund. It provides small loans to Kenya's poor families, enabling them to work their land with high-quality seed, fertilizer, equipment, and training. The goal is to help farmers "grow their way out of poverty" by finding ways to increase crop yields and avoid the devastating effects of Kenya's three-month "hunger season."[17]

THE INNOVATION PROCESS

The innovation process begins with *invention*—the act of discovery—and ends with *application*—the act of use. One way to describe it is in the five steps consultant Gary Hamel calls the wheel of innovation.[18]

1. *Imagining*—thinking about new possibilities; making discoveries by ingenuity or communicating with others; extending existing ways

2. *Designing*—testing ideas in concept; discussing them with peers, customers, clients, or technical experts; building initial models, prototypes, or samples

3. *Experimenting*—examining practicality and financial value through experiments and feasibility studies

4. *Assessing*—identifying strengths and weaknesses, potential costs and benefits, and potential markets or applications, and making constructive changes

5. *Scaling*—gearing up and implementing new processes; putting to work what has been learned; commercializing new products or services

The ultimate test of successful innovation is whether the entire process meets the real needs of the organization and its marketplace. In talking about Procter & Gamble's approach to innovation, former CEO A. G. Lafley says: "We have figured out how to keep the consumer at the center of all our decisions, so as a result, we don't go wrong."[19] Canadian National Railway's approach to innovation focuses on the marketplace. According to CN CEO Claude Mangeau, innovations are "driven by normal commercial incentives in a market place where there is substantial and effective competition. The deregulation of the rail industry has been a true success in Canada. It helped to revive the industry, improve service, generate competitive rates for customers, and encouraged railways to step up investment in their networks."[20]

Commercializing Innovation

In business, the process of **commercializing innovation** turns new ideas into actual products, services, or processes that can increase profits through greater sales or reduced costs. For example, 3M Corporation generates as much as one-third or more of its revenues from products that didn't exist four years ago. The firm, where product innovation is a way of life, owes its success to the imagination of employees like Art Fry. He's the person whose creativity turned an adhesive that "wasn't sticky enough" into the blockbuster product known worldwide today as Post-It Notes.

Commercializing innovation turns ideas into economic value added.

Figure 9.1 shows the typical steps in commercializing innovation. It's tempting to think that the process for a product like the Post-It Note is easy, straightforward, even a "no brainer." But it isn't necessarily so. Fry and his colleagues had to actively "sell" the Post-It idea to 3M's marketing group and then to senior management before getting substantial support for its development as a saleable product. And at Patagonia, its Common Threads innovation—collecting old garments and breaking them down to create reusable fibres—was almost four years in the making.[21]

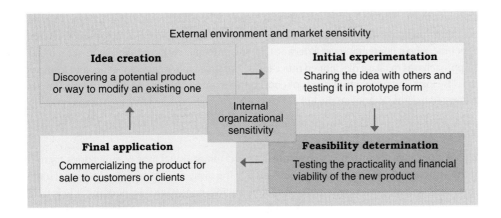

Figure 9.1 The process of commercializing innovation: an example of new product development.

CHARACTERISTICS OF INNOVATIVE ORGANIZATIONS

Innovative organizations such as Google, RIM, eBay, and Apple Computer have the capacity to move fast with innovations and this helps deliver competitive advantage. But how do you view Microsoft? Do you see a firm whose strategy and culture drive an innovation powerhouse? Or do you see what *PC World* describes as "a stodgy old corporation churning out boring software"? Craig Mundie, Microsoft's chief research and strategy officer, claims the criticisms are more perception than fact, and that his firm hasn't lost its innovative edge. He pledges to do a better job "communicating about the tremendous things this company does."[22] But claiming innovation and demonstrating innovation are two different things; the proof for Mundie will be in what Microsoft delivers in the future and how its products are received in the marketplace.

Even though 72 percent of executives in one survey considered innovation a top priority at their firms, about one-third said they were not happy with how fast companies innovate.[23] Such data raise an important question: what does it take to create a highly innovative organization? The answers boil down most often to strategy, culture, structure, top management, and staffing.

Strategy and Culture

Insights from the literature tell us that in highly innovative organizations, the corporate strategy and culture support innovation. The strategies of the organization, the visions and values of senior management, and the framework of policies and expectations all emphasize an entrepreneurial spirit. The culture is driven by values that let everyone know that innovation is expected, failure is accepted, and the organization is willing to take risks.

Such priorities are evident in these examples. Johnson & Johnson's former CEO James Burke once said: "I try to give people the feeling that it's okay to fail, that it's important to fail." His point is that managers should eliminate risk-averse climates and replace them with organizational cultures in which innovation is the norm. Vancouver's 1-800-GOT-JUNK Founder and CEO Brian Scudamore agrees to a certain extent: "Taking risks is good, but sticking to smart risks is even better." His point is that risk-averse climates should not be avoided, but a meticulous appraisal should be done prior to embracing risk.[24] Jack Welch, former CEO of GE, says that innovation occurs when "the whole organization buys into a mindset that innovation is so deeply ingrained in everyone's job that employees arrive each day thinking, 'Is there a better way to do everything we do around here?'"[25] When he took over as CEO at Sony, Howard Stringer was concerned that the firm was not as innovative as it could be. He placed a large part of the blame on a cumbersome corporate culture and told the executives "I'm asking you to get mad," and pointedly said he wanted their businesses run in more "energetic," "bold," and "imaginative" ways.[26] When Irene Lewis, President and CEO of Calgary-based SAIT Polytechnic, began her tenure over a decade ago, she immediately introduced large-scale changes. Her approach was to take a disciplined move toward strategic thinking, innovation, and implementation. "By inspiring people to the acts of courage necessary to believe and live the plan, we have transformed the little 'school on the hill' into a globally-recognized polytechnic," Lewis says.[27]

Structures

In highly innovative organizations, structures support innovation. Large organizations try to capture the structural flexibility of smaller ones by moving away from hierarchical and mechanistic designs and operating with more horizontal and organic ones. One way of doing this is to form special creative units (stars in the boxed diagram) that are set free from the normal structure. Sometimes called "skunkworks," these units are often given separate locations, special resources, and their own managers.

Yahoo!, often viewed as less innovative than Google, for example, has created a skunkworks known as the "Brickhouse." It's basically an idea incubator set up in a separate facility where Yahoo! staffers, some in beanbag chairs and others playing with Nerf balls, work on ideas submitted from all over the company. "The goal," says Salim Ismail, who heads Brickhouse, "is to take the idea, develop it, and make sure it's seen by senior management quickly."[28] In other words, Brickhouse exists so that good ideas don't get lost in Yahoo's bureaucracy.

An **ambidextrous organization** uses integrated creative teams to simultaneously be good at both producing and creating.

Scholars Charles O'Reilly and Michael Tushman describe an **ambidextrous organization** that is simultaneously good at both producing and creating.[29] Rather than assigning innovation to a separate creative unit such as a skunkworks, this approach scatters creative project teams throughout an organization. The teams operate with unique and creative work environments, but are managed as part of an integrated and team-driven horizontal structure. O'Reilly and Tushman's research suggests that, by integrating the creative units, as opposed to separating them, ambidextrous organizations are often more successful than skunkworks in coming up with breakthrough innovations.

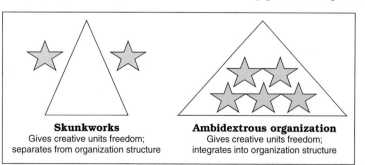

Skunkworks
Gives creative units freedom;
separates from organization structure

Ambidextrous organization
Gives creative units freedom;
integrates into organization structure

Systems

Highly innovative organizations use special information and knowledge management systems to support innovation. Internally, the basic notion is to break traditional barriers of structures, time, and physical distance, and use the latest technologies to help employees collaborate by becoming known to one another, posting and sharing information, and staying abreast of each other's expertise and latest thinking. IBM, for example, uses an internal version of Facebook known as BeeHive. Employees post profiles on BeeHive and engage in networking through the site. It also has a program called SmallBlue that searches internal blogs, e-mail, instant messages, and files to maintain an up-to-date database of experts who can be contacted by other employees.[30]

Externally, the systems focus in innovative organizations is often on setting up mechanisms for customers to provide ideas, and then getting these ideas considered for possible innovations. At Starbucks, for example, CEO Howard Schultz created the MyStarbucksIdea.com website for customers to provide suggestions on how the company could improve. Based on "Ideas" software from Salesforce.com, the site is monitored by 48 "idea partners" who facilitate the discussion and then act as idea champions within the firm. Among the early ideas for innovations were ice cubes made of coffee so that iced coffees aren't diluted as added ice melts; shelves in bathroom cubicles to hold drink cups; and hole plugs in coffee lids to prevent splashing.[31]

ISSUES AND SITUATIONS
Innovators-in-Chief

IBM's CEO, Samuel J. Palmisano, says: "The way you will thrive in this environment is by innovating—innovating in technologies, innovating in strategies, innovating in business models." His words speak volumes. Innovation is a top theme in most executive suites, and the CEO is increasingly expected to be the "innovator-in-chief."

But top CEOs know that innovation doesn't come easily. It has to be nurtured constantly, and the innovation "killers" have to be dealt with: lengthy development times, poor coordination, risk-averse cultures, little customer insight, and more. Lots needs to be done to keep the innovation pipeline flowing. BMW relocates engineers and designers to a central location for face-to-face product development; GE measures and tracks innovation records; 3M expects its "old-timers" to pass along stories and values associated with the firm's long-standing commitment to innovation; Research In Motion CEO Mike Lazaridis holds weekly "vision sessions" to get everyone excited; and Procter & Gamble created a new vice-president position for innovation and knowledge.

Innovator-in-chief CEOs seem to recognize that you can't innovate if key players aren't talking to and working closely with one another. You can't innovate consistently if the "we believe in innovation" message isn't consistently delivered from the top. At IBM, Palmisano pushes internal collaboration among employees across some 173 countries, and he pushes external collaboration with other firms, governments, and educational institutions. His message seems to be: You can't always innovate alone. Whether you are an individual or a multinational corporation, good partners can often help greatly.

CRITICAL RESPONSE

It doesn't seem hard to agree that innovation needs to be spearheaded and championed by top management. But shouldn't every manager view himself or herself as "innovator-in-chief"? Shouldn't "demonstrated excellence in fostering innovation" be a part of any manager's individual performance scorecard?

Top Management

In highly innovative organizations, top management supports innovation. In the case of 3M, many top managers have been the innovators and product champions in the company's past. They understand the innovation process, are tolerant of criticisms and differences of opinion, and take all possible steps to keep innovation goals clear and prominent. The key in top management support for innovation is to lead in ways that encourage and allow people's creative potential to operate fully. Quoting Jack Welch again: "often innovation doesn't arrive like a thunderbolt. It emerges incrementally, in bits and chugs, forged by a mixed bag of coworkers from up, down, and across an organization."[32] Top management might also create innovation. Consider the test created by the CEO of Ontario's Goldcorp Inc. when Rob McEwen rocked the mining industry by launching the Internet-based Goldcorp Challenge. In an industry defined by secretive practices, McEwen sought outside submissions by releasing proprietary exploration data on-line for "contest" purposes, asking the public where they should search for gold. It proved to be an abundantly successful initiative, allowing the firm to find a large gold deposit at one of its mines in Canada.[33]

Highly Innovative Organizations

Strategy includes innovation	Culture values innovation	Responsive structures and systems	Top management support	Staffing for creativity and innovation

Staffing

In highly innovative organizations, staffing supports innovation. Step one is to make creativity an important criterion when hiring and moving people into positions of responsibility. Step two is allowing their creative talents to fully operate by following through on the practices just discussed: strategy, culture, structure, and leadership. Google engineers, for example, are allowed to spend 20 percent of their time on projects of their own choosing. And the firm's CEO, Eric Schmidt, is considered a master at fuelling innovation. He says: "The story of innovation has not changed. It has been a small team of people who have a new idea, typically not understood by people around them and their executives. This is a systematic way of making sure that a middle manager does not eliminate that innovation."[34] Step three in staffing for innovation is putting people in key roles that are focused on meeting the needs of the innovation process itself. These critical innovation roles include:

- *Idea generators*—create new insights from internal discovery or external awareness or both

- *Information gatekeepers*—link between people and groups within the organization and with external sources

- *Product champions*—advocate and push for change and innovation, and for the adoption of specific product or process ideas

- *Project managers*—perform technical functions needed to keep an innovative project on track with necessary resource support

- *Innovation leaders*—encourage, sponsor, and coach others to keep the innovation values, goals, and energies in place

✓ **Learning Check ❶**

BE SURE YOU CAN

• define *creativity* and *innovation* • discuss differences between process, product, business model, and sustainable and social innovations • list the five steps in Hamel's wheel of innovation • explain how innovations get commercialized • list and explain the characteristics of innovative organizations • identify the critical innovation roles in organizations

ORGANIZATIONAL CHANGE

With innovation in our society so positively valued, the tendency may be to make change sound almost a matter of routine, something readily accepted by everyone involved. But the realities of trying to change organizations and the behaviours of people within them can be quite different.[35] When Angel Martinez became CEO of Rockport Company, for example, he sought to move the firm from traditional ways that were not aligned with future competition. Rather than embrace the changes he sponsored, employees resisted. Martinez said they "gave lip service to my ideas and hoped I'd go away."[36] And after Bank of America announced a large quarterly operating loss, the new CEO at the time, Samuel Armacost, complained about the lack of "agents of change" among his top managers. Claiming that managers seemed more interested in taking orders than initiating change, he said: "I came away quite distressed from my first couple of management meetings. Not only couldn't I get conflict, I couldn't even get comment. They were all waiting to see which way the wind blew."[37]

CHANGE LEADERS

A **change leader**, or **change agent**, is someone who takes leadership responsibility for changing the existing pattern of behaviour of another person or social system. Change leaders make things happen. They are alert to situations or people needing change, open to good ideas and opportunities, and ready and able to support the implementation of new ideas in actual practice.

> A **change leader**, or **change agent**, tries to change the behaviour of another person or social system.

MODELS OF CHANGE LEADERSHIP

Figure 9.2 contrasts a true "change leader" with a "status quo manager." The former is forward-looking, proactive, and supportive of new ideas; the latter is backward-looking, reactive, and comfortable with habit. Obviously, the new workplace demands change leadership at all levels of management.

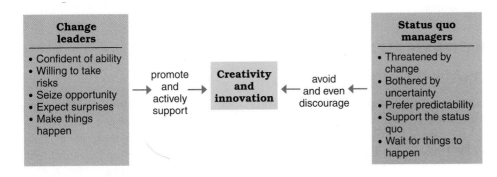

Figure 9.2 Change leaders versus status quo managers.

Top-Down Change

In **top-down change**, senior managers initiate changes with the goal of improving organizational performance. This is the domain of strategic leadership, as discussed earlier in the chapter. Importantly, however, research indicates that some 70 percent or more of large-scale change efforts in North American firms actually fail; only 20 percent of European firms report "substantial success" with large-scale change, while 63 percent report "occasional" success. The most common reason for the lack of change success is poor implementation.[38]

> In **top-down change**, the change initiatives come from senior management.

Change programs have little chance of success without the support of those who must implement them. Any change that is driven from the top and perceived as insensitive to the needs of lower-level personnel can easily fail. Successful top-down change is led in ways that earn the support of others throughout the organization.

Bottom-Up Change

In **bottom-up change**, change initiatives come from all levels in the organization.

In **bottom-up change**, the initiatives for change come from any and all parts of the organization, not just from top management. Such change is made possible by management commitments to empowerment, involvement, and participation.

Bottom-up change is essential to organizational innovation and very useful in adapting operations and technologies to the changing requirements of work. For example, at Canadian legal firm Stikeman Elliot LLP, a young lawyer named Valérie Mac-Seing was labelled the "green terrorist" when she began a green movement by removing all of her firm's plastic cutlery and paper cups. Despite the initial backlash the lawyer received from co-workers in her efforts to fuel eco-friendly initiatives in her company, Stikeman now boasts of its sustainability initiatives and its carbon neutral position.[39]

Integrated Change Leadership

The most successful and enduring change leadership harnesses the advantages of both top-down and bottom-up change. Top-down initiatives may be needed to break habits and traditional patterns, or make difficult economic adjustments; bottom-up initiatives help build institutional capability for sustainable change and organizational learning.

When first taking over as CEO of General Electric, Jack Welch took the integrated approach to change leadership. He began with an aggressive top-down restructuring that led to major workforce cuts and a trimmer organization structure. Next, he started bottom-up change, using a widely benchmarked program called Work-Out to gain employee involvement in a process of continuous reassessment and planned change. In Work-Out sessions, employees confront their managers in a town meeting format, with the manager in front listening to suggestions. The managers are expected to respond immediately and support positive change initiatives raised during the session. Welch says that approaches like this facilitate change because they "bring an innovation debate to the people closest to the products, services, and processes."[40]

Reactive change responds to events as or after they occur.

A **performance gap** is a discrepancy between a desired and an actual state of affairs.

Planned change aligns the organization with anticipated future challenges.

INCREMENTAL AND TRANSFORMATIONAL CHANGE

Some changes occur spontaneously in organizations, largely in response to unanticipated events. Managers deal with them by **reactive change**, hopefully doing a good job of responding to events as or after they occur. But the really great managers are not satisfied with being reactive. They are forward-thinking and always on the lookout for **performance gaps**, or discrepancies between desired and actual states of affairs that indicate potential problems to be resolved or opportunities to be explored. They pursue **planned change**—taking steps to best align the organization with future challenges.[41]

One way to consider planned change is in respect to what might be called an *organizational change pyramid*.[42] In this view, planned changes at top levels are likely to be large-scale and strategic repositioning changes focused on big issues that affect the organization as a whole. Middle-level changes often deal with major adjustments in structures, systems, technologies, products, and people to support strategic positioning. At the lower levels, frequent and smaller-scale changes seek continuous improvements in performance.

Organizational Change Pyramid

Few strategic, large-scale changes to reposition organization

Major changes to improve performance through new structures, systems, technologies, products, and people

Frequent smaller-scale changes to fine-tune performance, enable short-term gains and provide continuous improvements in operations

Incremental Change

Incremental change is a modest, frame-bending version of planned organizational change. It bends and nudges existing systems and practices to better align them with emerging problems and opportunities. The intent isn't to break and remake the system but to move it forward through continuous improvements. Common incremental changes in organizations involve evolutions in products, processes, technologies, and work systems.

Incremental change bends and adjusts existing ways to improve performance.

Transformational Change

Transformational change is radical or frame-breaking planned change that results in a major and comprehensive redirection of the organization.[43] It creates fundamental shifts in strategies, culture, structures, and even the underlying sense of purpose or mission. Transformational change is led from the top and designed to change the basic character of the organization. For example, it was only a short time ago that General Motors announced that nearly 6,000 of the remaining 10,000 positions in Canada would be gone by 2014, and that hundreds of GM's Canadian auto dealers would also close. It looked like the end of an era.[44]

Transformational change results in a major and comprehensive redirection of the organization.

As you might expect, such change is intense, highly stressful, and very complex to achieve. Management Smarts 9.1 offers several lessons learned from studies of large-scale transformational change in business.[45]

Both incremental change and transformational change are important in the organizational change pyramid just described. Incremental changes keep things tuned up (like the engine on a car) in between transformations (as when the old car is replaced with a new one).

9.1 MANAGEMENT SMARTS
How to lead transformational change

- Establish a sense of urgency for change.

- Form a powerful coalition to lead the change.

- Create and communicate a change vision.

- Empower others to move change forward.

- Celebrate short-term "wins" and recognize those who help.

- Build on success; align people and systems with the new ways.

- Stay with it; keep the message consistent; champion the vision.

FORCES AND TARGETS FOR CHANGE

The impetus for organizational change can arise from a variety of external forces.[46] These include globalization, market competition, local economic conditions, government laws and regulations, technological developments, market trends, and social forces and values, among others. As an organization's general and specific environments develop and change over time, the organization has to adapt or suffer the consequences.

Internal forces for change are important too. Indeed, any change in one part of an organization can often create the need for change in another part of the system. The common internal organizational targets for change—tasks, people, culture, technology, and structure—are highly interrelated.[47]

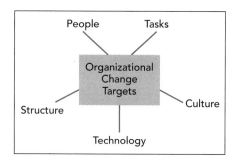

- *Tasks*—nature of work as represented by mission, objectives, strategy, and the job designs for individuals and groups.

- *People*—attitudes and competencies of employees and the human resource systems that support them.

- *Culture*—value system for the organization as a whole, and norms guiding individual and group behaviour.

- *Technology*—operations and information technology used to support job designs, arrange workflows, and integrate people and machines in systems.

- *Structure*—configuration of the organization, including its design features and lines of authority and communication.

GOING GLOBAL

BIG COMPANIES CHANGE TOO

Japan's Mitsubishi Corporation (MC) has for years been seen as a leading global company and is Japan's largest general trading company. Located in over 80 countries worldwide, MC is a conglomerate made up of over 500 companies with a multinational workforce of more than 54,000. Mitsubishi is confronting change not only in the global economy but in broader society. The company is driving into new territories by investing in new areas including the Business Service Group and the Global Environment Business Development Group. Commenting on present economic events, President and CEO Ken Kobayashi says: "While the world economy appears to be gradually recovering, growth in developed countries remains stagnant. The presence of China and other emerging countries as leaders of global growth is increasing, and 'boom-and-bust' economic cycles are no longer attracting attention. In this new era of structural change and uncertainty, MC must be prepared to compete further in global markets." It is interesting to note that even large companies are adapting to keep up with the changing times.

✔ Learning Check ②   **BE SURE YOU CAN**
- define *change agent* • discuss pros and cons of top-down change and bottom-up change
- differentiate planned and unplanned change • differentiate transformational and incremental change • list common organizational targets for change

MANAGING PLANNED CHANGE

The many complications of managing planned change begin with human nature. People tend to act habitually and in stable ways over time. They may not want to change even when circumstances require it. Any manager needs to recognize, understand, and deal with such tendencies in order to successfully lead planned change.

PHASES OF PLANNED CHANGE

The noted psychologist Kurt Lewin recommends that any planned change be viewed as a process with the three phases shown in Figure 9.3: (1) *unfreezing*—preparing a system for change;

(2) *changing*—making actual changes in the system; and (3) *refreezing*—stabilizing the system after change.[48]

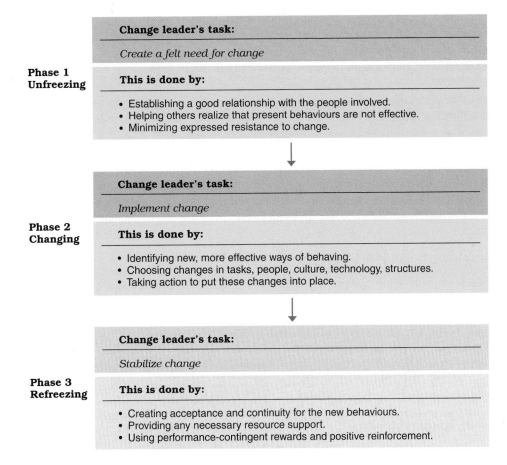

**Phase 1
Unfreezing**

Change leader's task:

Create a felt need for change

This is done by:

- Establishing a good relationship with the people involved.
- Helping others realize that present behaviours are not effective.
- Minimizing expressed resistance to change.

**Phase 2
Changing**

Change leader's task:

Implement change

This is done by:

- Identifying new, more effective ways of behaving.
- Choosing changes in tasks, people, culture, technology, structures.
- Taking action to put these changes into place.

**Phase 3
Refreezing**

Change leader's task:

Stabilize change

This is done by:

- Creating acceptance and continuity for the new behaviours.
- Providing any necessary resource support.
- Using performance-contingent rewards and positive reinforcement.

Figure 9.3 Lewin's three phases of planned organizational change.

Unfreezing

Change has a better chance for success when people are ready for it and open to doing things differently. **Unfreezing** is the phase in which a situation is prepared for change and felt needs for change are developed. It can be facilitated in several ways: through environmental pressures for change, declining performance, recognition of problems or opportunities, observation of behavioural models or benchmarks, or the presence of conflict that helps people break old habits and recognize alternative ways of thinking about or doing things. Common errors at the unfreezing stage include not creating a sense of urgency for change and neglecting to build a coalition of influential persons who support it.

Unfreezing is the phase during which a situation is prepared for change.

Changing

In the **changing** phase, something new takes place in a system and change is actually implemented. This is the point where changes are made in such organizational targets as tasks, people, culture, technology, and structure. The changing phase is ideally reached after unfreezing, and after a good diagnosis of a problem and a careful examination of alternatives. However, Lewin believes that many change agents commit the error of entering the changing phase prematurely. They are too quick to change things and end up creating harmful resistance. The lesson is that, if you implement change before people feel a need for it, there is an increased likelihood of failure.

Changing is the phase where a planned change actually takes place.

Refreezing

Refreezing is the phase at which change is stabilized.

The final phase in the planned change process is **refreezing**. Here, the manager is concerned about stabilizing the change and creating the conditions for its long-term continuity. Refreezing is accomplished by linking change with appropriate rewards, positive reinforcement, and resource support. It is also important in this phase to evaluate results carefully, provide feedback to the people involved, and make any required modifications in the original change. When refreezing is done well, change should last longer because people have incorporated it into their normal routines. When it is done poorly, changes are too easily forgotten or abandoned with the passage of time. The most common error at the refreezing stage is declaring victory too soon and withdrawing support before the change is really fixed in normal routines.

Of course, there may not always be a lot of time for refreezing before things are ready to change again. In other words, we are often preparing for more changes even while trying to take full advantage of the present one. Although Lewin's model depicts change as a linear, step-by-step process, the reality is that change is dynamic and complex. Managers must not only understand all phases of planned change, they must be prepared to deal with them simultaneously.

CHANGE STRATEGIES

The act of actually changing or moving people to do things differently, the middle phase of Lewin's change model, can be pursued in different ways. Figure 9.4 summarizes three common change strategies known as force-coercion, rational persuasion, and shared power.[49] Managers, as change agents and leaders, should understand each strategy and its likely results.

Change Strategy	Power Bases	Managerial Behaviour	Likely Results
Force-Coercion Using formal authority to create change by decree and position power	Legitimacy Rewards Punishments	*Direct forcing* and unilateral action *Political manoeuvring* and indirect action	Faster, but low commitment and only temporary compliance
Rational Persuasion Creating change through rational persuasion and empirical argument	Expertise	*Informational efforts* using credible knowledge, demonstrated facts, and logical argument	
Shared Power Developing support for change through personal values and commitments	Reference	*Participative efforts* to share power and involve others in planning and implementing change	Slower, but high commitment and longer-term internalization

Figure 9.4 Alternative change strategies and their leadership implications.

Force-Coercion Strategies

A **force-coercion strategy** pursues change through formal authority and/or the use of rewards or punishments.

A **force-coercion strategy** uses formal authority as well as rewards and punishments as the primary inducements to change. A change agent that seeks to create change through force-coercion believes that people are motivated by self-interest and by what the situation offers in terms of potential personal gains or losses.[50] This change agent tries to find out where vested interests lie, and then puts the pressure on. Once a weakness is found, it is exploited.

In a *direct forcing* strategy, the change agent takes direct and unilateral action to "command" that change take place. In *political manoeuvring*, the change agent works indirectly to gain special advantage over other persons and thereby make them change. This involves bargaining, obtaining control of important resources, forming alliances, or granting small favours.

Force-coercion usually produces limited results. Although it can be quickly tried, most people respond to this strategy out of fear of punishment or hope for a reward. The likely result is temporary compliance with the change agent's desires; that is, the new behaviour continues only so long as the rewards and punishments are present. For this reason, force-coercion may be most useful as an unfreezing strategy that helps people break old patterns and gain impetus to try new ones.

The earlier example of General Electric's Work-Out program applies here.[51] Jack Welch started Work-Out to create a forum for active employee empowerment for continuous change. But he didn't make the program optional; participation in Work-Out was mandatory. Part of Welch's commitment to change leadership was a willingness to use authority to unfreeze situations and get new things started. Once the program was under way, he was confident it would survive and prosper on its own—and it did.

Rational Persuasion Strategies

Change agents using a **rational persuasion strategy** attempt to bring about change through persuasion backed by special knowledge, empirical data, and rational argument. A change agent following this strategy believes that people are inherently rational and guided by reason. Once a specific course of action is demonstrated by information and facts, the change agent assumes that reason and rationality will cause the person to adopt it.

A **rational persuasion strategy** pursues change through empirical data and rational argument.

The likely outcome of rational persuasion is compliance with reasonable commitment. When successful, a rational persuasion strategy helps both unfreeze and refreeze a change situation. Although slower than force-coercion, it can result in longer-lasting and more internalized change.

To succeed at rational persuasion, a manager must convince others that a change will leave them better off than before. This persuasive power can come directly from the change agent if she or he has personal credibility as an "expert." It can also be borrowed in the form of consultants and other outside experts, or gained from credible demonstration projects and identified benchmarks. Many firms, for example, use Disney as a benchmark to demonstrate to their own employees how changes in customer orientation can improve operations. A Ford vice president says: "Disney's track record is one of the best in the country as far as dealing with customers."[52] In this sense, the power of rational persuasion is straightforward: if it works for Disney, why can't it work for us?

Courtesy Julie Jeffries

Shared Power Strategies

A **shared power strategy** uses collaboration to identify values, assumptions, and goals from which support for change will naturally emerge. The process is slow, but it is likely to yield high commitment. Sometimes called a *normative-re-educative strategy*, this approach is empowerment-based and highly participative. It involves others in examining personal needs and values, group norms, and operating goals as they relate to the issues at hand. Power is shared as the change agent and others work together to develop a new consensus to support needed change. Because it entails a high level of involvement, this strategy is often quite time-consuming. But power sharing is likely to result in longer-lasting, internalized change.

A **shared power strategy** pursues change by participation in assessing change needs, values, and goals.

A change agent who shares power begins by recognizing that people have varied needs and complex motivations. Changes in organizations are understood to involve changes in attitudes, values, skills, and significant relationships, not just changes in knowledge, information, or practices. Thus, this change agent is sensitive to the way group pressures can support or inhibit change. In working with people, every attempt is made to gather their opinions, identify their feelings and expectations, and incorporate them fully into the change process.

The great "power" of sharing power in the change process lies with unlocking the creativity and experience of people within the system. Some managers hesitate to engage this strategy for fear of losing control or of having to compromise on important organizational goals. However, Harvard scholar Teresa M. Amabile points out that they should have the confidence to share power regarding means and processes, if not overall goals. "People will be more creative," she says, "if you give them freedom to decide how to climb particular mountains. You needn't let them choose which mountains to climb."[53]

RESISTANCE TO CHANGE

We all know that change very often brings resistance with it.[54] When people resist change, furthermore, they are most often defending something important that appears threatened. A change of work schedules for workers in ON Semiconductor's Rhode Island plant, for example, may not have seemed like much of an issue to top management. But to the workers it was significant enough to bring about an organizing attempt by the Teamsters union. When management delved into the issues, they found that employees viewed changes in weekend work schedules as threatening to their personal lives. The problem was resolved when the new schedule was developed with input from the workers.[55]

Why People Resist Change

There are a number of reasons why people in organizations may resist planned change. Change is often viewed as a threat to something of value, as a source of uncertainty, or as something that is high in cost or limited in benefits. These and other common sources of resistance are shown in Management Smarts 9.2.

Change agents and managers can view resistance as something that must be "overcome" in order for change to be successful. But resistance is better viewed as feedback. The presence of resistance usually means that something can be done to achieve a better "fit" among the planned change, the situation, and the people involved.

9.2 MANAGEMENT SMARTS
Why people may resist change

- *Fear of the unknown*—not understanding what is happening or what comes next

- *Disrupted habits*—feeling upset to see the end of the old ways of doing things

- *Loss of confidence*—feeling incapable of performing well under the new ways of doing things

- *Loss of control*—feeling that things are being done "to" you rather than "by" or "with" you

- *Poor timing*—feeling overwhelmed by the situation, or that things are moving too fast

- *Work overload*—not having the physical or emotional energy to commit to the change

- *Loss of face*—feeling inadequate or humiliated because the "old" ways weren't "good" ways

- *Lack of purpose*—not seeing a reason for the change and/or not understanding its benefits

Dealing with Resistance to Change

Four basic checkpoints can help greatly in dealing with resistance and in leading successful organizational changes.[56]

1. *Check the benefits*—make sure the people involved see a clear advantage in making the change; people should know "what is in it for me" or "what is in it for our group or the organization as a whole."

2. *Check the compatibility*—keep the change as close as possible to the existing values and ways of doing things; minimizing the scope of change helps keep it more acceptable and less threatening.

3. *Check the simplicity*—make the change as easy as possible to understand and use; people should have access to training and assistance to make the transition to new ways as easy as possible.

4. *Check the "tryability"*—allow people to try the change little by little, making adjustments as they go; don't rush the change, but adjust the timing to best fit work schedules and cycles of high/low workloads.

In addition to following these checkpoints for dealing with resistance to change, other techniques can also be used.[57] *Education and communication* uses discussions, presentations, and demonstrations to educate people beforehand about a change. *Participation and involvement* allows others to contribute ideas and help design and implement the change. *Facilitation and support* provides encouragement and training, actively listening to problems and complaints, and helping to overcome performance pressures. *Negotiation and agreement* provides incentives that appeal to those who are actively resisting or ready to resist.

Two other approaches to resistance are risky in terms of potentially negative side effects. *Manipulation and co-optation* tries to covertly influence others by selectively providing information and structuring events in favour of the desired change. *Explicit and implicit coercion* forces people to accept change by threatening resistors with undesirable consequences if they do not do what is being asked.

CANADIAN MANAGERS

Don Tapscott: The Net Generation Changing the World

(Globe and Mail-Tibor Kolley)

Don Tapscott is a Toronto-born entrepreneur who understands the strategic value of information technology. He is a visionary who also writes very successful books, his latest being *Growing Up Digital: How the Next Generation Will Change the World*. Looking into the future, Tapscott sees a period of extreme upheaval for companies as they must keep up with fast-paced technological change but must also recruit and retain a young workforce. Creating organizations that appeal to the "Net" generation will require a tremendous amount of change in order to be successful. Tapscott's point is that organizations and managers need to embrace change or be left in the dust!

CHALLENGES OF TECHNOLOGICAL CHANGE

Ongoing technological change is a way of life in today's organizations, but it also raises special challenges for change leaders. For the full advantages of new technologies to be realized, a good fit must be achieved with work needs, practices, and people. This task has been described using the analogy of navigators from the Micronesian island of Truk and their European counterparts.[58]

The European navigator works from a plan, relates all moves during a voyage to the plan, and tries to always stay "on course." When something unexpected happens, the plan is revised systematically, and the new plan is followed until the navigator again finds the ship to be off course. The Trukese navigator, in contrast, starts with an objective and moves off in its general direction. Always alert to information from waves, clouds, winds, etc., the navigator senses subtle changes in conditions and steers and alters the ship's course continually to reach the ultimate objective.

Like Trukese navigation, technological change may best be approached as an ongoing process. This involves **improvisational change**, where adjustments are continually made as things are being implemented. Because new technologies are often designed out-side the organization in which they are to be used, the implications for local applications may be hard to anticipate. A technology that is attractive in concept may appear complicated to the new users; the full extent of its benefits or inadequacies may not become known until it is tried. Thus, the change leader should be alert to resistance, continually gather and process information relating to the change, and be willing to customize the new technology to best meet local needs.

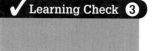

Improvisational change makes continual adjustments as changes are implemented.

✓ **Learning Check ❸**

BE SURE YOU CAN

• describe Lewin's three phases of planned change • explain the force-coercion, rational persuasion, and shared power change strategies • discuss pros and cons of each change strategy • list several reasons why people resist change • identify strategies for dealing with resistance to change • discuss the challenges of leading technological change

---

Organization Development

There will always be times when the members of organizations should sit together and systematically reflect on strengths and weaknesses, performance accomplishments and failures, and the future. One way to ensure that this happens in a participative and action-oriented environment is through **organization development**. This is a shared power approach to planned organizational change that involves the application of behavioural science in a systematic and long-range effort to improve organizational effectiveness.[59] Although "OD" often involves the assistance of a consultant with special training, all managers can and should use it in their change leadership agendas.

Organization development is a shared power effort to improve an organization's ability to solve problems and improve performance.

ORGANIZATION DEVELOPMENT GOALS

Two goals are pursued simultaneously in organization development. The *outcome goals* of OD focus on task accomplishments, while the *process goals* of OD focus on the ways people work together. The process goals are what strongly differentiate OD from more general attempts at planned change in organizations. In this sense, you may think of OD as a form of "planned change plus." The "plus" means that change is accomplished in a collaborative way so that organization members develop a capacity for continued self-renewal. That is, OD tries to achieve change in ways that help organization members become more active and self-reliant in their ability to continue changing in the future.

What also makes OD unique is its commitment to strong humanistic values and established principles of behavioural science. The processes of OD try to improve organizations through freedom of choice, shared power, and self-reliance, and by taking the best advantage of what we know about human behaviour in organizations.

HOW ORGANIZATION DEVELOPMENT WORKS

The first step in the OD process is for the consultant or facilitator to *establish a working relationship* with members of the client system. The next step is *diagnosis*—gathering and analyzing data to assess the situation and set appropriate change objectives. This helps with unfreezing and also clarifies possible action directions. Diagnosis leads to *active intervention*, where change objectives are pursued at the individual, group, and organization levels. The next step is *evaluation* to determine whether things are proceeding as desired and whether further action is needed. Finally, the OD consultant or facilitator should *achieve a terminal relationship* that leaves the client able to function on its own. These steps are shown in Figure 9.5, which presents a general model of OD and shows its relationship to Lewin's three phases of planned change.

The success or failure of any OD program lies in part in the strength of its diagnosis. And this is based on the methodological foundations of **action research**. This is a process of systematically collecting data on an organization, feeding the information back to the members for action planning, and evaluating results by collecting more data and repeating the process as necessary. The data gathering can be done in several ways. Interviews are a common means, and formal surveys of employee attitudes and needs are also popular. Many such "climate," "attitude," or "morale" questionnaires have been tested for reliability and validity. Some have norms that allow one organization to compare its results with those from a broad sample of counterparts.

Action research is a collaborative process of collecting data, using it for action planning, and evaluating the results.

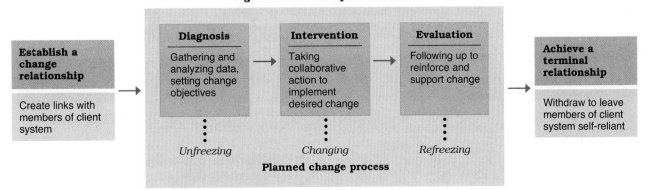

Figure 9.5 Organization development and the planned change process.

ORGANIZATION DEVELOPMENT INTERVENTIONS

In many ways, organization development is employee involvement in action. The process uses a variety of **OD interventions** to activate participation in collaborative and self-directed change efforts.[60]

An **OD intervention** is a structured activity that helps create change for organization development.

Individual Interventions

Organization development practitioners accept the premise that most people are capable of assuming responsibility for their own actions and of making positive contributions to organizational performance. Based on these principles, some of the more popular OD interventions to help improve individual effectiveness include:

- *Sensitivity training*—unstructured sessions where participants learn interpersonal skills and increased sensitivity to other people.

- *Management training*—structured educational opportunities for developing important managerial skills and competencies.

- *Role negotiation*—structured interactions to clarify and negotiate role expectations among people who work together.

- *Job redesign*—realigning task components to better fit the needs and capabilities of individuals.

- *Career planning*—structured advice and discussion sessions to help individuals plan career paths and personal development programs.

Team Interventions

The team plays a very important role in organization development. OD practitioners view teams as important vehicles for helping people satisfy important needs, and they believe that improved collaboration within and among teams can improve organizational performance. Selected OD interventions designed to improve team effectiveness include:

- *Team building*—structured experiences to help team members set goals, improve interpersonal relations, and become a better-functioning team.

- *Process consultation*—third-party observation and advice on critical team processes, such as communication, conflict, and decision-making.

- *Intergroup team building*—structured experiences to help two or more teams set shared goals, reduce conflict, improve intergroup relations, and become better coordinated.

RESEARCH BRIEF

Top management must get—and stay—committed in order for organization development to work in tandem with top-down change

Harry Sminia and Antonie van Nistelrooij's case study of a public-sector organization in the Netherlands sheds light on what happens when top-down change and organization development are used simultaneously.

Writing in the *Journal of Change Management*, they describe how top management initiated a strategic change involving organization design, procedures, work standards, and systems. Called the "project strand," this change was well structured with deadlines and a management hierarchy. Simultaneously, a "change strand" was initiated with organization development interventions to develop information and create foundations helpful to the success of the project strand. The change strand involved conferences, workshops, and meetings. The goal was for both strands to operate in parallel and eventually converge in joint implementation.

RESEARCH BRIEF (*continued*)

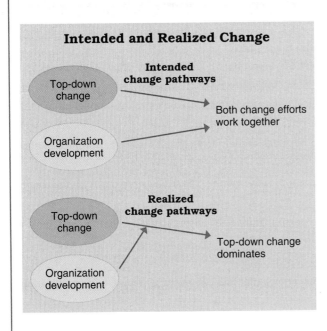

Intended and Realized Change

Intended change pathways

Top-down change
Organization development
→ Both change efforts work together

Realized change pathways

Top-down change
Organization development
→ Top-down change dominates

What the researchers found was that top management favoured the project strand and resisted challenges to its decision-making prerogatives that came from the change strand. Eventually, the OD aspects of the change initiative pretty much disappeared, and activities centred around completing the project changes as scheduled. Although the workforce "embraced" the OD methods, Sminia and van Nistelrooij conclude that their success was hampered by "management refusal to share power with the employees."

You be the researcher

Is it realistic to expect that top-down and bottom-up changes can operate simultaneously? Can any organization's development activity be successful without continuing support and legitimacy from top management? How would you design research projects to test these questions?

Organization-Wide Interventions

At the level of the total organization, OD practitioners operate on the premise that any change in one part of the system will also affect other parts. The organization's culture is considered to have an important impact on member attitudes and morale. The belief is also that structures and jobs can be designed to bring together people, technology, and systems in highly productive and satisfying working combinations. OD interventions with an emphasis on overall organizational effectiveness include:

- *Survey feedback*—comprehensive and systematic data collection to identify attitudes and needs, analyze results, and plan for constructive action

- *Confrontation meeting*—one-day intensive, structured meetings to gather data on workplace problems and plan for constructive actions

- *Structural redesign*—realigning the organization structure to meet the needs of environmental and contextual forces

- *Management by objectives*—Formalizing MBO throughout the organization to link individual, group, and organizational objectives

✔ Learning Check ❹

BE SURE YOU CAN
- define *organization development* • differentiate outcome and process goals of OD • explain the steps in the OD process • explain the role of action research in OD • list OD interventions focusing on individuals, teams, and the organization as a whole

MANAGEMENT LEARNING REVIEW

STUDY QUESTIONS SUMMARY

KEY TERMS

1. How do organizations accomplish innovation?

- Organizations need strategic leaders who initiate and successfully implement changes that help them perform well in changing environments.

- Organizations pursue process innovations, product innovations, business model innovations, and sustainable or green innovations.

- Social business innovations use business models to help address social problems; social entrepreneurship seeks social change rather than financial gains.

- Highly innovative organizations have supportive cultures, strategies, structures, systems, staffing, and management.

FOR DISCUSSION Can a creative person prosper in an organization that doesn't have an innovation-driven culture?

2. What is the nature of organizational change?

- Change leaders are change agents who change the behaviour of people and organizational systems.

- Organizational change can proceed with a top-down emphasis, with a bottom-up emphasis, or a combination of both.

- Incremental change makes continuing adjustments to existing ways and practices; transformational change makes radical changes in organizational directions.

- The many possible targets for change include organizational tasks, people, cultures, technologies, and structures.

FOR DISCUSSION Is it better for a new leader in an organization to focus first on transformational or incremental change?

3. How can planned organizational change be managed?

- Lewin's three phases of planned change are unfreezing—preparing a system for change; changing—making a change; and refreezing—stabilizing the system.

- Change agents should understand the force-coercion, rational persuasion, and shared power change strategies.

- People resist change for a variety of reasons, including fear of the unknown and force of habit.

- Good change agents deal with resistance positively and in a variety of ways, including education, participation, support, and facilitation.

- Success with technological change requires being alert to resistance and willingness to improvise as implementation proceeds.

FOR DISCUSSION Can the refreezing stage of planned change ever be satisfied in today's dynamic environments?

4. What is organization development?

- Organization development, OD, is a shared power approach to planned organization change that uses principles of behavioural science to improve long-term organizational effectiveness.

- Outcome goals of OD focus on improved task accomplishment; process goals of OD focus on improvements in the way people work together.
- The OD process involves action research, where people work together to collect and analyze data on system performance and decide what actions to take to improve things.
- OD interventions are structured activities at the individual, group, and organizational levels that help people work together to accomplish change.

FOR DISCUSSION Does the leader lose control of the change process in organization development?

SELF-TEST

Multiple-Choice Questions

1. Product innovation creates new goods or services and _____ innovation creates new ways of doing things.

   (a) content   (b) process   (c) quality   (d) task

2. The first step in Hamel's wheel of innovation is _____.

   (a) imagining   (b) assessing   (c) experimenting   (d) scaling

3. An executive pursuing transformational change would give highest priority to which one of these change targets?

   (a) An out-of-date policy   (b) The organizational culture   (c) A new management information system   (d) Job designs in a customer service department

4. A manager using a force-coercion strategy will rely on _____ to bring about change.

   (a) expertise   (b) benchmarking   (c) formal authority   (d) information

5. The most participative of the planned change strategies is _____.

   (a) force-coercion   (b) rational persuasion   (c) shared power   (d) command and control

6. Trying to covertly influence others, offering only selective information, and structuring events in favour of the desired change is a way of dealing with resistance by _____.

   (a) participation   (b) manipulation and co-optation   (c) force-coercion   (d) facilitation

7. In organization development, both _____ and _____ goals are important.

   (a) task, maintenance   (b) management, labour   (c) outcome, process   (d) profit, market share

8. Sensitivity training and role negotiation are examples of organization development interventions targeted at the _____ level.

   (a) individual   (b) group   (c) system-wide   (d) organization

9. The concept of empowerment is most often associated with the _____ strategy of planned change.

   (a) market-driven   (b) rational persuasion   (c) direct forcing   (d) normative-re-educative

10. Unfreezing occurs during the _____ step of organizational development.

    (a) diagnosis   (b) intervention   (c) evaluation   (d) termination

11. The quality concept of continuous improvement is most consistent with the notion of _____.

    (a) incremental change   (b) transformational change   (c) radical change   (d) reactive change

12. True internalization and commitment to a planned change is most likely to occur when a manager uses a(n) _____ change strategy.

    (a) education and communication   (b) rational persuasion   (c) manipulation and co-optation   (d) shared power

13. When a manager listens to users, makes adaptations, and continuously tweaks and changes a new management information system as it is being implemented, the approach to technological change can be described as _____.

    (a) top-down   (b) improvisational   (c) organization development   (d) frame-breaking

14. In change management, the recommendation is to view resistance to change as _____.

    (a) feedback of potential value   (b) an indicator of political manoeuvring   (c) a sign that change is moving too slowly   (d) a warning that force-coercion may be needed

15. When an organization development consultant uses process consultation as an intervention, the target is change at the _____ level of analysis.

    (a) individual   (b) group   (c) organization   (d) organization-environment

Short-Response Questions

16. How do product, process, and business model innovations differ from one another?

17. What are the three phases of change described by Lewin, and what are their implications for change leadership?

18. What are the major differences in potential outcomes of the force-coercion, rational persuasion, and shared power strategies of planned change?

19. What does the statement "OD equals planned change plus" mean?

Application Question

20. As a newly appointed manager in any work setting, you are likely to spot many things that could be done better and to have many new ideas that you would like to implement. Based on the ideas presented in this chapter, how should you go about effecting successful planned change in such situations?

MANAGEMENT SKILLS AND COMPETENCIES

SELF-ASSESSMENT

Back to Yourself: Tolerance for Ambiguity

The next time you are driving somewhere and following a familiar route only to find a "detour" sign ahead, test your tolerance for ambiguity. Is the detour no big deal and you go forward without any further thought? Or is it a bit of a deal, perhaps causing anxiety and anger? The chapter opener links tolerance for ambiguity with the processes of innovation and organizational change discussed in this chapter. People are being asked today to be ever more creative and innovative in their work; organizations are too. Managers are expected to support change initiatives launched from the top; they are also expected to be change leaders in their own teams and work units. This is a good time to check your readiness to meet the challenges of innovation and change in organizations.

Further Reflection: Change Leadership IQ

Instructions

Indicate whether each of the following statements is true (T) or false (F).

T F   1. People invariably resist change.

T F   2. One of the most important responsibilities of any change effort is that the leader clearly describes the expected future state.

T F   3. Communicating what will remain the same after change is as important as communicating what will be different.

T F   4. Planning for change should be done by a small, knowledgeable group, and then that group should communicate its plan to others.

T F   5. Managing resistance to change is more difficult than managing apathy about change.

T F   6. Complaints about a change effort are often a sign of change progress.

T F   7. Leaders find it more difficult to change organizational goals than to change the ways of reaching those goals.

T F   8. Successful change efforts typically involve changing reward systems to support change.

T F   9. Involving more members of an organization in planning a change increases commitment to making the change successful.

T F 10. Successful organizational change requires certain significant and dramatic steps or "leaps," rather than moderate or "incremental" ones.

Scoring

Questions 2, 3, 6, 8, 9, 10 are true; the rest are false. Tally the number of correct items to indicate the extent to which your change management assumptions are consistent with findings from the discipline.

Source: Based on an instrument developed by W. Warner Burke. Used by permission.

TEAM EXERCISE

Force-Field Analysis

Instructions

1. Form into your class discussion groups and review this model of force-field analysis—the consideration of forces driving support of a planned change and forces resisting the change.

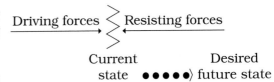

2. Use force-field analysis and make lists of driving and resisting forces for one of the following situations:

(a) Because of rapid advances in web-based computer technologies, the possibility exists that the course you are currently taking could be, in part, offered on-line. This would mean a reduction in the number of required class sessions but an increase in students' responsibility for completing learning activities and assignments through computer mediation. The dean wants all faculty to put at least part of their courses on-line.

(b) A new owner has just taken over a small by-the-slice pizza shop in a university town. There are eight employees, three of whom are full-time and five of whom are part-time. The shop is open seven days a week from 10:30 a.m. to midnight. The new owner believes there is a market niche available for late-night pizza and would like to stay open each night until 4 a.m. She wants to make the change as soon as possible.

(c) A situation assigned by the instructor.

3. Choose the three driving forces that are most significant for the proposed change. For each force, develop ideas on how it could be further increased or mobilized in support of the change.

4. Choose the three resisting forces that are most significant for the proposed change. For each force, develop ideas on how it could be reduced or turned into a driving force.

5. Be prepared to participate in a class discussion led by your instructor.

CASE 9

Apple, Inc.: People and Design Create the Future

Over a span of more than 30 years, Apple Computer paradoxically existed both as one of America's greatest business successes and as one of the greatest failures of a company to realize its potential. Apple, Inc. ignited the personal computer industry in the 1970s,[1] bringing such behemoths as IBM and Digital Equipment almost to their knees; stagnated when a series of CEOs lost opportunities; and rebounded tremendously since the return of its co-founder and former CEO, Steve Jobs. The firm represents a fascinating microcosm of American business as it continues to leverage its strengths while reinventing itself.

Corporate History

The history of Apple, Inc. is a history of passion, whether on the part of its founders, its employees, or its loyal users.[2] It was begun by a pair of Stevens who, from an early age, had an interest in electronics. Steven Wozniak and Steven Jobs initially put their skills to work at Hewlett-Packard and Atari, respectively. But then Wozniak constructed his first personal computer—the Apple I—and, along with Jobs, created Apple Computer on April 1, 1976. Right from the start, Apple exhibited an extreme emphasis on new and innovative styling in its computer offerings. Jobs took a personal interest in the development of new products, including the Lisa and the first, now legendary, Macintosh, or "Mac."

The passion that Apple is so famous for was clearly evident in the design of the Mac. Project teams worked around the clock to develop the machine and its operating system, Mac OS. The use of graphical icons to create simplified user commands was an immensely popular alternative to the command-line structure of DOS found on IBM's first PCs.

When Apple and IBM began to clash head-on in the personal computer market, Jobs recognized the threat and realized that it was time for Apple to "grow up" and be run in a more businesslike fashion. In early 1983, he persuaded John Sculley, at that time president of Pepsi-Cola, to join Apple as president. The two men clashed almost from the start, with Sculley eventually ousting Jobs from the company.

The launch of the Mac reinvigorated Apple's sales. However, by the 1990s, IBM PCs and clones were saturating the personal computer market. Furthermore, Microsoft launched Windows 3.0, a greatly improved version of the Wintel operating system, for use on IBM PCs and clones. Although in 1991 Apple had contemplated licensing its Mac

Courtesy Apple Computer, Inc.

operating system to other computer manufacturers, making it run on Intel-based machines, the idea was nixed by then chief operating officer Michael Spindler in a move that would ultimately give Windows the nod to dominate the market.

Innovative Design to the Rescue

Apple continued to rely on innovative design to remain competitive in the 1990s. It introduced the very popular Power-Book notebook computer line, as well as the unsuccessful Newton personal digital assistant. Sculley was forced out and replaced by Michael Spindler. He oversaw a number of innovations, including the PowerMac family—the first Macs based on the PowerPC chip, an extremely fast processor co-developed with IBM and Motorola. In addition, Apple finally licensed its operating system to a number of Mac cloners, although never in significant numbers.

After a difficult time in the mid-1990s, Spindler was replaced with Gil Amelio, the former president of National Semiconductor. This set the stage for one of the most famous returns in corporate history.

Jobs's Return

After leaving Apple, Steven Jobs started NeXT Computer, which produced an advanced personal computer with a sleek, innovative design. However, the computer, which entered the market late in the game and required proprietary software, never gained a large following. Jobs then co-founded the Pixar computer-animation studio, which co-produced a number of movies with Walt Disney Studios, including the popular *Toy Story*.[3]

In late 1996, Apple purchased NeXT, and Jobs returned to Apple in an unofficial capacity as advisor to the president. When Amelio resigned, Jobs accepted the role of "interim CEO" of Apple Computer and wasted no time in making his return felt. He announced an alliance with Apple's former rival, Microsoft. In exchange for $150 million in Apple stock, Microsoft and Apple would share a five-year patent cross-licence for their graphical interface operating systems. He revoked licences allowing the production of Mac clones and started offering Macs over the Web through the Apple Store.

Beginning with the iMac and the iBook, its laptop cousin, Jobs has continually introduced a series of increasingly popular products that have captured the buying public's imagination. Upon their release, the iPod, MacBook, Apple TV, and iPhone instantly spawned imitators that mimicked the look of these products, but they couldn't duplicate Apple's acute ability to integrate design with usability. Once again, Apple became an industry innovator by introducing certifiably attractive—and powerful—consumer electronics products such as the iPad. Its recent successes have included growing to command approximately 21 percent of the total computer market[4] and 66 percent of the market share for computers priced over $1,000.[5] It also tends to earn more revenue per computer sold than its value-priced competitors.

What Does the Future Hold?

Whenever critics argued that Apple should reinvent itself again, it did just that—and then some. Now it is setting standards with new corporate strategy, taking advantage of the explosion of personal electronic devices. In its first week, iTunes sold 1.5 million songs and captured 80 percent of the market share of legal music downloads. And now we're into the new generation of successful iPhones and iPods, which leaves us wondering what Jobs will come up with next.

It is Jobs's hope that making its products the hub of a "digital lifestyle" will cement Apple's sales and guarantee the company's long-term security. But can the Cupertino, California, company maintain its lead? Although Apple's designs are widely lauded by both critics and customers, will it ever earn a majority share of the personal computer market? Does it really need to? When Jobs was running Pixar and it was struggling, his co-founder Alny Ray Smith says: "We should have failed, but Steve just wouldn't let it go."[6] If Steve Jobs is the key to Apple's success, what would the firm do without him?

Discussion Questions

1. Apple sells stylish and functional computers as well as a variety of electronic devices, and it operates retail stores. Which type of organization structure would best help Apple keep its creative edge, and why?

2. Should Apple's board of directors be expecting the CEO to push transformational change or incremental change, or both, at this point in time? Why?

3. How could organization development be used to help the teams involved with iPhone development make sure that they are always working together in the best ways as they pursue the next generations of iPhones and innovative product extensions?

4. FURTHER RESEARCH—Review what the analysts are saying about Apple. Make a list of all the praises and criticisms, organize them by themes, and then put them in the priority order you would tackle if taking over from Steve Jobs as Apple's new CEO. In what ways can the praises and criticisms be used to create a leadership agenda for positive change?

LEARNING FROM OTHERS

Great companies attract and value great people

Research In Motion (RIM), based in Waterloo, Ont., is the creator, manufacturer, and marketer of the acclaimed Black-Berry line of wireless products, selected by presidents, princes, and professionals. Founded in 1984, the company celebrates over 32 million worldwide subscribers (and growing). RIM has been named as one of the top 10 places to work in Canada. What makes this company extraordinary? How does it attract, develop, and keep a quality workforce?

It starts with space: RIM's work atmosphere is exceptional. The head office includes a comfy employee lounge, religious observance room, on-site cafeteria (with subsidized meals and free coffee and tea), free parking for your car and secure parking for your bike, shower facilities, self-serve kitchen areas, an outdoor eating area, and a walking trail.

Courtesy The Canadian Press Images/Stephen C. Host

Compensation is competitive; RIM participates in outside salary surveys every 12 months and individual salaries are reviewed annually. RIM also provides signing bonuses for some employees, year-end bonuses for all employees, and a profit-sharing plan too. And RIM knows how to celebrate significant milestones and holidays. Employees are treated to "RIM Rocks" concerts featuring Canadian artists such as the Tragically Hip and the Barenaked Ladies and international groups like Van Halen, Aerosmith, and U2. To borrow from the Hip: RIM employees have music @ work!

The company makes people feel valued. New employees feel appreciated right away as they receive an excellent benefit package, start off with three weeks of vacation and, as important, a free BlackBerry on their first day.

What are the measures that show that RIM is successful? One way it keeps on top of what is happening in employee ranks is by hiring outside consultants to conduct confidential employee satisfaction and engagement surveys with its 12,000 employees. Another way is looking at voluntary turnover, recently at a very low 7 percent. And there is no shortage of people who want to work with RIM. Nearly 375,000 applications were sent its way, with 2,746 lucky enough to join this very successful firm. Co-CEOs Mike Lazaridis and Jim Balsillie have designed both an ingenious smartphone and a high-performance corporate culture.[1]

BENCHMARK Check out how other top Canadian employers are doing by reviewing the Canadian Top 100 website at canadastop100.com. Do your homework—what quality company deserves to get you?

Professionalism

It isn't just a word—it's a commitment. Speak the word aloud: professionalism. Ask: what does it really mean? And, more importantly, ask: what does being "professional" mean to me?

Medicine, law, and accounting are examples of occupations governed by professional codes. We take some comfort in knowing that those who practise in these fields are held accountable by peers for meeting professional standards. Professionalism is also part of business and management careers, and we are most often expected to be and act just as professionally in a management job as a lawyer is in hers.

Take a moment and picture yourself in your ideal job. Then check off the items in the box that best describe you and how you expect to work in that job. While doing so, think about how a real professional would act in that job.

The code of ethics of the Canadian Council of Human Resources Associations offers a framework for professionalism that is worth considering, especially in the context of this chapter. CCHRA, as the council is often called, identifies and describes the commitment expected within the Certified Human Resources Professional (CHRP) designation through knowledge of core competencies and understanding legal requirements while maintaining the standards of behaviour relating to fairness, justice, truthfulness, and social responsibility.[2]

How I Work
• Like to read journal articles in my field of work
• Like to make own decisions
• Believe in my competence
• Want to help society through my work
• Feel responsible for good work
• Rate job significance above pay received
• Enjoy learning and training
• Willing to be judged by peers
• Willing to judge my peers
• Accept external standards of excellence

Not every manager meets the standards for professionalism just described. But might we say they that they should? From a personal perspective, isn't professionalism the way each of us should always approach our future jobs and career?

❖ Get to Know Yourself Better

If you checked off each of the items in the short "How I Work" exercise, you're on the right pathway. Based on a scale developed for the health professions, the items are indicators of professionalism.[3] Put yourself in the employer's seat. Think again about your ideal job, then write a list of questions that you, as the employer, would ask of a candidate for this job and that would help you get a sense of his or her professionalism. Be prepared to share your questions with the class.

CHAPTER 10 STUDY QUESTIONS

- What is human resource management?
- How do organizations attract a quality workforce?
- How do organizations develop a quality workforce?
- How do organizations maintain a quality workforce?
- What are the links between organizational culture and diversity?

VISUAL CHAPTER OVERVIEW

CHAPTER 10 HUMAN RESOURCE MANAGEMENT

Study Question 1	Study Question 2	Study Question 3	Study Question 4	Study Question 5
Human Resource Management	**Attracting a Quality Workforce**	**Developing a Quality Workforce**	**Maintaining a Quality Workforce**	**Organizational Culture and Diversity**
■ Human resource management process ■ Strategic human resource management ■ Global human resource management ■ Legal environment of human resource management	■ Human resource planning ■ Recruiting techniques ■ Selection techniques	■ Orientation and socialization ■ Training and development ■ Performance management	■ Flexibility and work–life balance ■ Compensation and benefits ■ Retention and turnover ■ Labour–management relations	■ What is organizational culture? ■ Levels of organizational culture ■ Values and organizational culture ■ Multicultural organizations ■ Diversity and organizational subcultures ■ Managing diversity
✓ Learning Check 1	✓ Learning Check 2	✓ Learning Check 3	✓ Learning Check 4	✓ Learning Check 5

The key to managing people in ways that lead to profit, productivity, innovation, and real organizational learning ultimately lies in how you think about your organization and its people. When you look at your people, do you see costs to be reduced? Or, when you look at your people do you see intelligent, motivated, trustworthy individuals—the most critical and valuable strategic assets your organization can have?

With these words from his book *The Human Equation: Building Profits by Putting People First*, scholar Jeffrey Pfeffer challenges managers to invest in people and their talents. He believes, and has research evidence, that organizations that do invest in people outperform the ones that don't.[4] High-performing organizations thrive on strong foundations of **human capital**, first defined in Chapter 1 as the economic value of people with job-relevant abilities, knowledge, experience, ideas, energies, and commitments. This chapter explores how organizations build human capital by managing their essential human resources in ways that unleash and respect talents and value diversity.

Human capital is the economic value of people with job-relevant abilities, knowledge, ideas, energies, and commitments.

Human Resource Management

Author and consultant Lawrence Otis Graham suggests a simple test that tells a lot about someone's approach to managing human resources.[5] Question 1 is: "Which of the following qualities would you look for in anyone who works for you—work ethic, ambition and energy, knowledge, creativity, motivation, sincerity, outlook, collegiality and collaboration, curiosity, judgment and maturity, and integrity?" In answering, you most likely selected all of these qualities, or at least you should have, according to Graham. Question 2 is: "Where can you find people with these workplace qualities?" The correct answer is "everywhere."

HUMAN RESOURCE MANAGEMENT PROCESS

A marketing manager at Ideo, a California-based industrial design firm, once said: "If you hire the right people, if you've got the right fit, then everything will take care of itself."[6] This is what **human resource management**, or HRM, is all about: attracting, developing, and maintaining a talented and energetic workforce. If an organization can't do this right and doesn't have the right people available to do the required work, it has very little chance of long-term success.

Human resource management is the process of attracting, developing, and maintaining a high-quality workforce.

The goal of human resource management is to build organizational performance capacity through people; to ensure that highly capable and enthusiastic people are always in the right positions and working with the support they need to be successful. The three major responsibilities of human resource management are typically described as:

1. *Attracting a quality workforce*—human resource planning, employee recruitment, and employee selection.

2. *Developing a quality workforce*—employee orientation, training and development, and performance management.

3. *Maintaining a quality workforce*—career development, work–life balance, compensation and benefits, retention and turnover, and labour–management relations.

STRATEGIC HUMAN RESOURCE MANAGEMENT

As VP of Human Resources for the Yellow Pages Group, Josée Dubuc was tasked with a key role in redefining the organization when it became independent in 2002. To identify the culture, values, and behaviour the company wanted to foster, Dubuc went back to the basics to develop key objectives to establish a foundation to drive performance. Management internally marketed six values or "ground rules" for its employees: customer focus, compete to win, teamwork, passion, respect, and open communication.[7] These initiatives are consistent with the concept of **strategic human resource management**—mobilizing human capital through the HRM process to best implement organizational strategies.[8]

Strategic human resource management mobilizes human capital to implement organizational strategies.

One indicator that HRM is truly strategic to an organization is when it is headed by a senior executive reporting directly to the chief executive officer. When Denis Donovan became the Home Depot's first executive vice president for human resources, he said: "CEOs and boards of directors are learning that human resources can be one of your biggest game-changers in terms of competitive advantage."[9] The strategic importance of HRM has been further accentuated by the spate of corporate ethics scandals. Journalist John Hobel offers that, "For HR professionals with mandates to create productive workplaces, the negative impact on morale caused by leaders taking greed and corruption to new heights undermines the very goal of improving worker productivity."[10]

There are many career opportunities in the human resource management profession. HR specialists within organizations and HR consulting or outsourcing firms deal with hiring, compensation and benefits, training, employee relations, and more. Their expertise is highly important in an environment complicated by legal issues, labour shortages, economic turmoil, new corporate strategies, and changing social values. Scholar and consultant Edward E. Lawler III argues that the HR staff should be the "expert resource on the state of an organization's work force and its ability to perform."[11] He describes the ideal as a human resources department, supported by HR outsourcing, led by a senior executive, and staffed by professionals devoted to human capital development.[12]

GLOBAL HUMAN RESOURCE MANAGEMENT

Huge size and a global workforce put lots of demands on human resource management practices. At IBM, the goal is "global integration," locating jobs wherever in the world they can be done best. In a three-year period, this translated into hiring 90,000 new workers in Brazil, China, and India, alone. Company-wide, IBM employs 375,000+ workers in six continents. William J. Amelio, CEO of PC maker Lenovo, uses the term "world sourcing" to describe his firm's global workforce strategy. With major offices in five countries, he says, "you operate as if there's just one time zone, and you're always on."[13] Originating in Montreal, the multinational engineering and construction firm SNC-Lavalin shares on its company website: "The world is our worksite. Make it yours." With major offices in over 35 countries, SNC-Lavalin works hard at being an international employer of choice.[14]

One of the challenges in managing a global workforce is keeping track of expertise. IBM, for example, uses a global database called Marketplace to track employee skills. When new project teams are being formed, Marketplace helps match IBMers worldwide with possible jobs. And like other global firms, IBM also faces hiring challenges. It is always competing to hire the best workers all over the world and to retain them in face of different local environmental and cultural conditions. In India, for example, job hopping is common and a new generation of workers is described as "in a hurry," wanting "immediate rewards," and yet still "traditional" in many cultural ways. A sought-after perk among India's young professionals, for example, is support to help pay for the care of aging parents.[15]

Another challenge in global hiring is legal; the availability of visas for foreign workers. It's something, in fact, that took Microsoft Chairman Bill Gates to Washington, D.C., to testify before

---

Global Workforce Perks

China—perk: payments to employee housing fund; days off: 23.

India—perk: pay for care of aging parents; days off: 31.

Japan—perk: *kazoku teiate*, or family allowances, on top of pay; days off: 35.

Hong Kong—perk: health benefits cover traditional Chinese medicines; days off: 26.

Russia—perk: company-sponsored mortgages; days off: 39.

a special Senate committee. He pleaded for changes to limitations on the number of visas that can be issued to import skilled workers into the United States from other countries.[16] According to Gates, "It makes no sense to tell well-trained, highly skilled individuals—many of whom are educated at our top universities—that the U.S. does not welcome or value them." Senators disagreed. Gates responded by expanding operations in Canada, where the visa restrictions don't apply. Microsoft opened a satellite facility in Richmond, British Columbia, only 200 km from its headquarters in Redmond, Washington. The Canada office already employs more than 125 engineers from 26 countries.

LEGAL ENVIRONMENT OF HUMAN RESOURCE MANAGEMENT

Microsoft's problems with skilled worker visas point to the importance of valuing human capital in all of its diversity and in a fully inclusive manner. Job-relevant talent is not restricted because of anyone's national origin, race, gender, religion, marital or parental status, sexual orientation, ethnicity, or other diversity characteristics. And any time these characteristics interfere with finding, hiring, and using the best employees, one organization's loss in human capital can be another's gain.[17]

Laws against Employment Discrimination

Discrimination in employment occurs when someone is denied a job or a job assignment for reasons that are not job-relevant. Canada has established extensive laws to offer protection from various forms of discrimination. One such act is the Canadian Human Rights Act, which applies to federal government departments and agencies and to private-sector employers that are governed by federal legislation, such as banks, broadcasters, and transportation companies, as well as Aboriginal band councils. Established in 1977, this act covers various forms of employee discrimination, including race, colour, national or ethnic origin, religion, age, sexual orientation, pregnancy, marital status, family status, physical or mental disability, and pardoned criminal conviction. Another federal law is the Employment Equity Act, whose aim is to "achieve equality in the workplace so that no person shall be denied employment opportunities or benefits for reasons unrelated to ability and, in the fulfillment of that goal, to correct the conditions of disadvantage in employment experienced by women, aboriginal peoples, persons with disabilities, and members of visible minorities by giving effect to the principle that employment equity means more than treating persons in the same way but also requires special measures and the accommodation of differences."[18] Criticisms of **employment equity** tend to focus on the use of group membership (e.g., female or minority status) as a criterion in employment decisions.[19] The issues raised include claims of reverse discrimination by members of majority populations. White males, for example, may claim that preferential treatment given to members of visible minorities in a particular situation interferes with their individual rights.

This federal legislation often provides the framework for provinces and municipalities when drafting their own legislation, which may vary slightly from province to province. The intent is to ensure all citizens the right to gain and keep employment based only on their ability to do the job and their performance once on the job. Each provincial human rights commission has the power to impose remedies on organizations that do not provide a timely resolution to any discrimination charges brought against them. For example, the British Columbia Human Rights Tribunal has the power to order an organization to cease the discriminatory behaviour; make available the right, opportunity, or privilege that was denied; compensate for any wages lost or any expenses incurred; and provide damages for injury to feelings and self-respect.[20] Samples of major grounds on which discrimination is prohibited are provided in Figure 10.1.

Discrimination occurs when someone is denied a job or job assignment for reasons not job-relevant.

Employment equity is the right to employment and advancement without regard to race, sex, religion, colour, or national origin.

Prohibited Grounds for Discrimination	Provinces and Territories
Race or colour	All
Religion	All
Physical or mental disability	All
Age if 18–64/65	All except Ont., Que., and Man.
Sex (includes pregnancy and childbirth)	All
Marital status	All
Dependence on drugs/alcohol	All except Y.T. and N.W.T.
Family status	All except N.B. and N.L.
Sexual orientation	All except N.W.T.
National or ethnic origin	All except B.C. and Alta.
Ancestry or place of origin	Y.T., B.C., Alta., Man., Sask., N.W.T., Ont., N.B.
Language	Y.T., Ont., Que.
Social condition or origin	Que., N.L.
Source of income	Alta., Sask., Man., Que., P. E. I., N.S.
Political belief	Y.T., B.C., Man., Que., N.S., P.E.I., N.L.
Criminal conviction	Y.T., B.C., Que., P.E.I.
Pardoned conviction	B.C., N.W.T., Ont.

Source: <www.chrc-ccdp.ca>

Figure 10.1 A sample of prohibited grounds of employment discrimination in Canadian provinces and territories.

Current Legal Issues in Human Resource Management

Because the legal environment is dynamic, managers and human resource professionals have to stay informed about new laws and changes to existing ones. Failure to follow the laws is not only unjustified in civil society, it can also be an expensive mistake that results in fines and penalties. But things aren't always clear-cut and managers must be prepared to deal with a wide variety of employment issues of potential legal consequence. A brief sampler of current issues follows.

Sexual harassment is behaviour of a sexual nature that affects a person's employment situation.

Sexual harassment occurs when people experience conduct or language of a sexual nature that affects their employment situation. Sexual harassment can be defined as behaviour that creates a hostile work environment, interferes with a person's ability to do a job, or interferes with their promotion potential. Organizations should have clear sexual harassment policies in place along with fair and equitable procedures for implementing them. Both the Canadian Human Rights Act and the Canada Labour Code protect federally regulated employees from sexual harassment in the workplace.[21] Organizations should have clear sexual harassment policies in place, along with fair and equitable procedures for implementing them.

Comparable worth holds that persons performing jobs of similar importance should be paid at comparable levels.

Men and women in the same organization should be paid equally for doing equal work in terms of skills, responsibilities, and working conditions. But a lingering issue with gender disparities in pay involves **comparable worth**, the notion that persons performing jobs of similar importance should be paid at comparable levels. Why should a long-distance truck driver, for example, be paid more than an elementary teacher in a public school? Does it make any difference that the former is a traditionally male occupation and the latter a traditionally female occupation? Advocates of comparable worth argue that such historical disparities result from gender bias. They would like to have the issue legally resolved.

Pregnancy discrimination penalizes a woman in a job or as a job applicant for being pregnant.

Pregnancy discrimination is against the law, but pregnancy bias complaints are still commonly filed by provincial human rights commissions, increasingly so in wake of the recent economic downturn in 2009. A staff lawyer for the Ontario Human Rights Legal Support Centre reaffirms that "Pregnant women have a role to play in the workplace and efforts to exclude them will not be tolerated and will attract liability."[22] Recent research paints a bleak picture. In one study, actors played roles of visibly pregnant and non-pregnant applicants for jobs as corporate lawyers and university professors. Results showed that interviewers were more negative toward the "pregnant" females, making comments such as "she'll try to get out of doing work" and "she would be too moody."[23]

ISSUES AND SITUATIONS
Sexual Harassment Laws Are Strict

"If I had known you were getting married, I wouldn't have bothered you."

That statement, allegedly made by the former CEO of Toyota's North American operations, Hideaki Otaka, was part of a US$190-million lawsuit filed by his former personal assistant, Sayaka Kobayashi. She claimed that Otaka sexually harassed her with unwelcome romantic overtures, physical contact, and personal gifts. When she reported the problem to one of the firm's human resource executives, she was advised to meet one on one with Otaka to discuss the matter. Within a month, the firm's general counsel suggested she might want to consider leaving the firm.

Kobayashi believes that Otaka's behaviours reflected patterns of "sexual discrimination" in Japanese culture. But whether culturally linked or not, sexual harassment laws are strict in the United States, and employers are expected to protect workers from "hostile work environments." Toyota responded to the lawsuit by placing Otaka on leave (he later stepped down), and reiterated corporate policy: "zero tolerance toward sexual harassment or discrimination of any kind."

Legal experts say that any sexual harassment charge needs to be fully and fairly investigated, even when the accused is the chief executive. Because this might place a human resources director in a difficult position, the recommendation is that such complaints be reviewed by neutral outside experts or taken directly to the board of directors. In respect to the suggestion that Kobayashi meet alone with Otaka to discuss her claims, a legal expert says: "Having those two individuals meet alone is probably the worst way to bring about a resolution."

CRITICAL RESPONSE

Should foreign employers in North America be forgiven, or at least face relaxed penalties, when they run afoul of Canadian, American, or Mexican employment laws that are very different from those of their home countries? Does this example prompt you to think about personal situations or cases where sexual harassment is an issue? Suppose you learn from another student or co-worker that she or he is the target of romantic overtures from an instructor or boss. What do you do, if anything?

The legal status and employee entitlements of part-time workers and **independent contractors** are also being debated. In today's era of downsizing and outsourcing, more persons are hired as temporary workers who do not become part of an organization's permanent workforce. But even though they work only "as needed," many are engaged regularly by the same organization and become what some call "permatemps." Because they most often work without benefits such as health insurance and pensions, legal cases are now before the courts seeking to make independent contractors eligible for benefits.

Workplace privacy is the right of individuals to privacy on the job.[24] It is acceptable for employers to monitor the work performance and behaviour of their employees. But employer practices can become invasive and cross legal and ethical lines, especially with the capabilities of information technology. Computers can easily monitor e-mails and Internet searches to track personal and unauthorized usage, they can identify who is called by telephone and how long conversations

Independent contractors are hired as needed and are not part of the organization's permanent workforce.

Workplace privacy is the right to privacy while at work.

last, they can document work performance moment to moment, and they can easily do more. All of this information, furthermore, can be stored in vast databases that make it available to others, even without the individual's permission. Until the legal status of electronic surveillance is cleared up, one consultant says the best approach is to "assume you have no privacy at work."[25]

✓ **Learning Check** ❶

BE SURE YOU CAN

• explain the human resource management process • define *discrimination* and *employment equity* • identify major laws that protect against discrimination in employment • discuss legal issues of sexual harassment, comparable worth, pregnancy discrimination, independent contractors, and workplace privacy

ATTRACTING A QUALITY WORKFORCE

The first responsibility of human resource management is to attract to the organization a high-quality workforce whose talents match well with the jobs to be done. Edmonton-based Stantec Consulting clearly identifies its "people strategy" hiring goal on its corporate website: "The key to our success is our people. People, passion, and progress have made our Company what it is today, and create the foundation for what it will be tomorrow." To attract the right people, an organization must first know exactly what it is looking for; it must have a clear understanding of the jobs to be done and the talents required to do them well. Then it must have the systems in place to excel at employee recruitment and selection.

HUMAN RESOURCE PLANNING

Human resource planning
analyzes staffing needs and
identifies actions to fill those
needs.

Human resource planning is the process of analyzing an organization's staffing needs and determining how to best fill them. As shown in Figure 10.2, human resource planning identifies staffing needs, assesses the existing workforce, and determines what additions or replacements are required for the future. The process becomes strategic when this is all done in specific reference to organizational mission, objectives, and strategies.

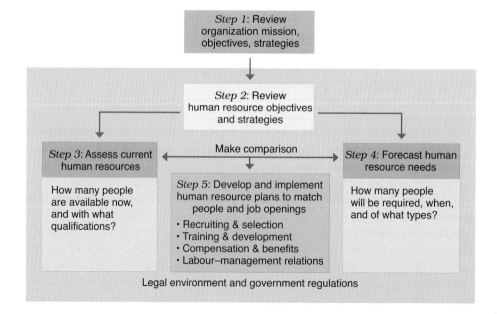

Step 1: Review organization mission, objectives, strategies

Step 2: Review human resource objectives and strategies

Step 3: Assess current human resources

How many people are available now, and with what qualifications?

Make comparison

Step 4: Forecast human resource needs

How many people will be required, when, and of what types?

Step 5: Develop and implement human resource plans to match people and job openings
• Recruiting & selection
• Training & development
• Compensation & benefits
• Labour–management relations

Legal environment and government regulations

Figure 10.2 Steps in strategic human resource planning.

The foundations for human resource planning include **job analysis**—the orderly study of job facts to determine what is done when, where, how, why, and by whom.[26] The job analysis provides information that can then be used to write or update **job descriptions**. These are written statements of job duties and responsibilities. The information in a job analysis can also be used to create **job specifications**. These are lists of the qualifications—such as education, prior experience, and skill requirements—needed by someone hired for a given job.

RECRUITING TECHNIQUES

Recruitment is a set of activities designed to attract a qualified pool of job applicants to an organization. The word "qualified" is important; recruiting should bring employment opportunities to the attention of people whose abilities and skills meet job specifications. Three steps in a typical recruitment process are (1) advertisement of a job vacancy, (2) preliminary contact with potential job candidates, and (3) initial screening to create a pool of qualified applicants.

External and Internal Recruitment

The recruiting that takes place on university and college campuses is one example of **external recruitment**, in which job candidates are sought from outside the hiring organization. Websites such as Eluta.ca and Workopolis.com, newspapers, employment agencies, universities and colleges, technical training centres, personal contacts, walk-ins, employee referrals, and even persons in competing organizations are all sources of external recruits. **Internal recruitment** seeks applicants from inside the organization. Most organizations have a procedure for announcing vacancies through newsletters, electronic postings, and the like. They also rely on managers to recommend candidates for advancement.

Both recruitment methods have potential advantages and disadvantages. External recruitment brings in outsiders with fresh perspectives, expertise, and work experience. Internal recruitment is usually less expensive, and it deals with persons whose performance records are well known. A history of serious internal recruitment also builds employee loyalty and motivation, showing that one can advance by working hard and doing well when given responsibility.

Realistic Job Previews

In what may be called **traditional recruitment**, the emphasis is on selling the job and organization to applicants. The focus is on communicating the most positive features, perhaps to the point where negatives are concealed. This may create unrealistic expectations that cause costly turnover when new hires become disillusioned and quit. The individual suffers a career disruption; the employer suffers lost productivity and the added costs of having to recruit again.

The alternative is to provide **realistic job previews** that give the candidate all pertinent information about the job and organization without distortion, and before the job is accepted.[27] Instead of "selling" only positive features, realistic recruitment tries to be open and balanced in describing the job and organization. Both favourable and unfavourable aspects are covered. The interviewer in a realistic job preview might use phrases such as "Of course, there are some downsides." "Things don't always go the way we hope." "Something that you will want to be prepared for is. . . ." "We have found that some new hires have difficulty with . . . ." Such conversations help candidates establish realistic expectations and better prepare for the inevitable "ups and downs" of a new job. Higher levels of early job satisfaction and less inclination to quit prematurely are among the expected benefits of realistic recruiting practices.

A **job analysis** studies exactly what is done in a job, and why.

A **job description** details the duties and responsibilities of a job holder.

Job specifications list the qualifications required of a job holder.

Recruitment is a set of activities designed to attract a qualified pool of job applicants.

External recruitment seeks job applicants from outside the organization.

Internal recruitment seeks job applicants from inside the organization.

Traditional recruitment focuses on selling the job and organization to applicants.

Realistic job previews provide job candidates with all pertinent information about a job and organization.

REAL ETHICS

Help Wanted: Saleswoman

Are you successful working in sales at mall fashion clothing and retail shops? If so, a new and higher-paying option may be right for you. A local car dealership selling luxury vehicles wants outgoing, helpful women for client sales positions. Applicants should be honest and money-motivated, with high initiative and excellent communication skills. Pay based on wages, commissions, and bonuses can reach $80,000 per year. Watch for our recruiters at your mall this weekend.

This ad isn't real; you're unlikely to see anything like it in your local paper. But it is reflective of a trend in automobile sales—trying to hire more women and trying to recruit them in non-traditional settings.

Marketing surveys show that women influence some 80 percent of car purchases, and that many men prefer dealing with a female salesperson. At a St. Louis dealership, the female owner claims that women are better organized and better at building a client base than are men; she wants to hire more.

One New York dealer wants to move his sales force from 11 to 50 percent female. A law professor at Washington University in St. Louis says that it's okay to try to hire more women if the dealers aren't getting enough applicants.

YOU DECIDE

Suppose you're a qualified man, working in sales at a mall fashion store; you're honest, self-starting, a good communicator, motivated by money, and in love with cars. Where does this ad leave you? Is it ethical for the car dealer to interview only women for this position?

SELECTION TECHNIQUES

Selection is choosing individuals to hire from a pool of qualified job applicants.

The process of **selection** involves choosing from a pool of applicants the person or persons who offer the greatest performance potential. Steps in a typical selection process are shown in Figure 10.3. They are (1) completion of a formal application, (2) interviewing, (3) testing, (4) reference checks,

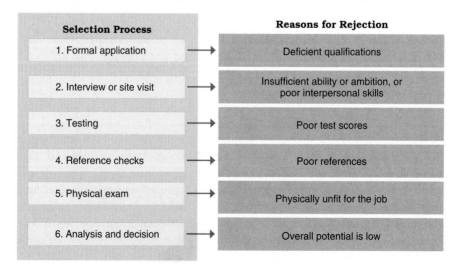

Figure 10.3 Steps in the selection process: the case of a rejected job applicant.

(5) physical examination, and (6) final analysis and decision to hire or reject. The goal in selection decisions is to get the best fit between the new hire and the organization.

Applications and Interviews

The application declares the individual as a job candidate and documents his or her background and qualifications. The personal resumé is often included with the job application. This important document should accurately summarize a person's special qualifications and accomplishments. A job applicant should exercise great care in preparing the resumé for job searches; a recruiter should know how to screen resumés to make good selection decisions.

Interviews are times in the selection process when both the job applicant and the potential employer can learn a lot about one another. However, they can be difficult experiences for both parties. Sometimes interviewers ask the wrong things, sometimes they talk too much, and sometimes their personal biases prevent an applicant's capabilities from being fully considered. Interviewees can fail, too. They may be unprepared, they may be poor communicators, and they may lack interpersonal skills. An increasingly common and challenging interview setting for job applicants—the telephone interview—is highlighted in Management Smarts 10.1.

10.1 MANAGEMENT SMARTS
How to succeed in a telephone interview

- *Prepare ahead of time*—study the organization; carefully list your strengths and capabilities.

- *Take the call in private*—make sure you are in a quiet room, with privacy and without the possibility of interruptions.

- *Dress as a professional*—don't be casual; dressing right increases confidence and sets a tone for your side of the conversation.

- *Practise your interview "voice"*—your impression will be made quickly; how you sound counts; it even helps to stand up while you talk.

- *Have reference materials handy*—your resumé and other supporting documents should be within easy reach.

- *Have a list of questions ready*—don't be caught hesitating; intersperse your best questions during the interview.

- *Ask what happens next*—find out how to follow up by telephone or e-mail; ask what other information you can provide.

Employment Tests

Common employment tests are designed to identify intelligence, aptitudes, personality, interests, and even ethics. But whenever tests are used, they should meet the criteria of reliability and validity. **Reliability** means that the test is consistent in measurement; it returns the same results time after time. **Validity** means that there is a demonstrable relationship between a person's test score and eventual job performance; that is, a good test score really does predict good performance.

Reliability means that a selection device gives consistent results over repeated measures.

Validity means that scores on a selection device have demonstrated links with future job performance.

An assessment centre examines how job candidates handle simulated work situations.

New developments in employment testing extend into actual demonstrations of job-relevant skills and personal characteristics. An **assessment centre** evaluates a person's potential by observing his or her performance in experiential activities designed to simulate daily work. A related approach is **work sampling**, which asks applicants to do actual job tasks while being graded by observers on their performance.

Reference and Background Checks

In **work sampling**, applicants are evaluated while performing actual work tasks.

Reference checks are inquiries to previous employers, academic advisors, co-workers, or acquaintances regarding the qualifications, experience, and past work records of a job applicant. Although they may be biased if friends are prearranged "to say the right things if called," reference checks are important. An American organization, the Society for Human Resources Management, has estimated that 25 percent of job applications and resumés contain errors.[28] Reference checks can verify resumé material and better inform the potential employer. They can also add credibility to the candidate if they back up what is said on a resumé and in an application.

Physical Examinations

Many organizations ask job applicants to take a physical examination. This health check helps ensure that the person is physically capable of fulfilling job requirements. It may also be used as a basis for enrolling the applicant in health-related fringe benefits such as life, health, and disability insurance programs. A controversial development is drug testing, used for pre-employment health screening and even as a basis for continued employment in some organizations. In Canada, both physical examinations and drug testing have been scrutinized and limited by human rights cases.

Final Decisions to Hire or Reject

The best selection decisions are most likely to be those involving extensive consultation among an applicant, the future manager or team leader, and new co-workers, as well as the human resource staff. Importantly, the emphasis in selection should focus on the person's capacity to perform well. Just as a "good fit" can produce long-term advantage, a "bad fit" can be the source of many long-term problems.

 **Learning Check 2**

BE SURE YOU CAN
- explain the difference between internal recruitment and external recruitment • discuss the value of realistic job previews to employers and job candidates • differentiate reliability and validity as two criteria of selection devices • illustrate the operation of an assessment centre • discuss the importance of conducting background and reference checks

DEVELOPING A QUALITY WORKFORCE

When people join an organization, they must "learn the ropes" and become familiar with "the way things are done." It is important to help newcomers learn the organizational culture and fit into the work environment in a way that furthers their development and performance potential.

ORIENTATION AND SOCIALIZATION

Orientation familiarizes new employees with jobs, co-workers, and organizational policies and services.

The first formal experience of workplace newcomers often begins with some form of **orientation**— a set of activities designed to familiarize new employees with their jobs, co-workers, and key aspects of the organization as a whole. A good orientation program clarifies mission and goals, explains the culture, and communicates key policies and procedures. With the tagline "Try Different Things. Build New Skills. Gain Experience," Canadian grocery parent company Loblaw takes orientation to a new level by offering a new graduate orientation program that includes 18 months of paid rotational training. During this time, corporate hires work directly on store floors to develop a thorough insight into the company and its foundation.[29]

Orientation is a form of **socialization**, a process that helps new members learn and adapt to the ways of the organization.[30] The socialization that occurs during the first six months or so of employment often determines how well someone is going to fit in and perform. When orientation is weak or neglected, socialization largely takes place informally as newcomers learn about the organization and their jobs through casual interactions with co-workers.[31] It is easy in such situations for even well-intentioned and capable people to learn the wrong things and pick up bad attitudes. By contrast, a good orientation like that offered to new employees at the Walt Disney World resort in Florida, where they learn that everyone is a "cast member" whose role is to help guests have fun, helps ensure that socialization sets the right foundations for high performance, job satisfaction, and work enthusiasm.

Courtesy Julie Jeffries

Socialization is a process of learning and adapting to the organizational culture.

Training provides learning opportunities to acquire and improve job-related skills.

In **job rotation**, people switch tasks to learn multiple jobs.

Coaching occurs as an experienced person offers performance advice to a less-experienced person.

TRAINING AND DEVELOPMENT

Training is a set of activities that helps people acquire and improve job-related skills. This applies both to initial training of an employee and to upgrading or improving skills to meet changing job requirements. Organizations committed to their employees invest in extensive training and development programs to ensure that everyone always has the capabilities needed to perform well.[32]

On-the-Job Training

On-the-job training takes place in the work setting while someone is doing a job. A common approach is **job rotation**, which allows people to spend time working in different jobs and thus expands the range of their job capabilities. Another is **coaching**, in which an experienced person provides performance advice to someone else. **Mentoring** is a form of coaching in which early-career employees are formally assigned as proteges to senior persons. The mentoring relationship gives them regular access to advice on developing skills and getting better informed about the organization. **Modelling** is another type of coaching in which someone demonstrates through their behaviour that which is expected of others. A good example is how the behaviours of senior managers help set the ethical culture and standards for other employees.

> **Sample Training Goals and Options**
>
> - *Acquire information*—videos, lectures, readings, interactive software
>
> - *Improve analytical skills*—cases, coaching, mentoring, interactive software
>
> - *Learn job behaviours*—on-the-job training, simulations, apprenticeships, interactive software

Mentoring assigns early-career employees as proteges to more senior ones.

Modelling uses personal behaviour to demonstrate the performance expected of others.

Off-the-Job Training

Off-the-job training is accomplished outside the work setting. An example is **management development**—training designed to improve a person's knowledge and skill in the fundamentals of management. Beginning managers often benefit from training that emphasizes team leadership and communication. Middle managers may benefit from training to better understand

Management development is training to improve knowledge and skills in the management process.

multifunctional viewpoints. Top managers may benefit from advanced management training to sharpen their decision-making and negotiating skills, and to expand their awareness of corporate strategy and direction.

PERFORMANCE MANAGEMENT

A **performance management system** sets standards, assesses results, and plans for performance improvements.

An important part of human resource management is the design and implementation of a successful **performance management system**. This system ensures that performance standards and objectives are set, that performance is regularly assessed, and that actions are taken to improve future performance.

RESEARCH BRIEF

Racial bias may exist in supervisor ratings of workers

That is a conclusion of a research study by Joseph M. Stauffer and M. Ronald Buckley reported in the *Journal of Applied Psychology*. The authors point out that it is important to have performance criteria and supervisory ratings that are free of bias. They cite a meta-analysis by Kraiger and Ford (1985) that showed raters who are Caucasian tending to rate white employees more favourably than black employees, whereas black raters rated

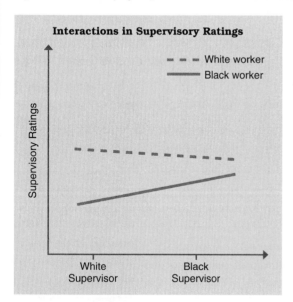

Interactions in Supervisory Ratings

- - - White worker
—— Black worker

Supervisory Ratings

White Supervisor   Black Supervisor

blacks more favourably than did whites. They also cite a later study by Dackett and DuBois (1991) that disputed the finding that raters tended to favour members of their own racial groups.

In their study, Stauffer and Buckley reanalyzed the Dackett and DuBois data for possible interactions between rater and ratee. The data included samples of military and civilian workers, each of whom was rated by black and white supervisors. In both samples, white supervisors gave significantly higher ratings to white workers than they did to black workers; black supervisors also tended to favour white workers in their ratings.

Stauffer and Buckley advise caution in concluding that the rating differences are the result of racial prejudice, saying the data aren't sufficient to address this issue. They call for future studies to examine both the existence of bias in supervisory ratings and the causes of such bias. In terms of present implications, however, the authors say: "If you are a White ratee, then it doesn't matter if your supervisor is Black or White. If you are a Black ratee, then it is important whether your supervisor is Black or White."

You be the researcher

Why would white supervisors rate black workers lower than white workers in this study if the rating weren't based on racial prejudice? Why would black supervisors consistently favour white workers over black workers in their ratings? As you ponder this study, what research questions come to mind that you would like to see definitively answered through rigorous scientific studies in the future? Is it possible that such findings could be replicated with respect to teacher ratings of student performance in our primary and secondary schools, as well as in university? Suggest a study design that would examine this possibility.

Performance Appraisal Purposes

The process of formally assessing someone's work accomplishments and providing feedback is **performance appraisal**, and it serves both evaluation and development purposes.[33] The *evaluation purpose* of performance appraisal focuses on past performance and measures results against standards. Performance is documented for the record and for allocating rewards. The manager acts in a judgemental role, giving a direct evaluation of the other person's accomplishments. The *development purpose* focuses on future performance. Performance goals and obstacles are identified, along with possible training and supervisory support. The manager acts in a counselling role and gives attention to the other person's developmental needs.

Performance appraisal is the process of formally evaluating performance and providing feedback to a job holder.

Performance Appraisal Methods

Organizations use a variety of performance appraisal methods and, just as with employment tests, they should be as reliable and valid as possible.[34] To be reliable, the method should consistently yield the same result over time or for different raters. To be valid, it should be unbiased and measure only factors directly relevant to job performance. At a minimum, written documentation of rigorous performance appraisals and a record of consistent past actions will be required to back up any contested evaluations.

One of the simplest performance appraisal methods is a **graphic rating scale**. It is basically a checklist for rating an individual on traits or performance characteristics such as quality of work, job attitude, and punctuality. Although this approach is quick and easy, it has poor reliability and validity.

A **graphic rating scale** uses a checklist of traits or characteristics to evaluate performance.

The **behaviourally anchored rating scale**, or BARS, is a more advanced approach. It describes actual behaviours for various levels of performance achievement in a job, such as the case of a customer service representative illustrated in Figure 10.4. "Extremely poor" performance is clearly defined as rude or disrespectful treatment of a customer. Because performance assessments are anchored to specific descriptions of work behaviour, the BARS is more reliable and valid than the graphic rating scale.

A **behaviourally anchored rating scale** uses specific descriptions of actual behaviours to rate various levels of performance.

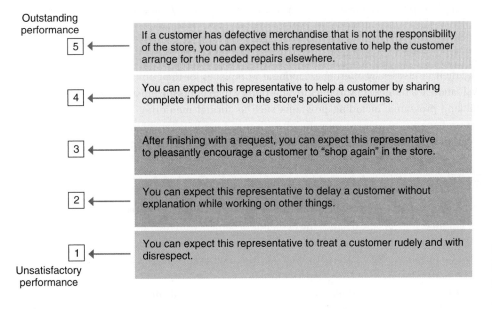

Outstanding performance

5 — If a customer has defective merchandise that is not the responsibility of the store, you can expect this representative to help the customer arrange for the needed repairs elsewhere.

4 — You can expect this representative to help a customer by sharing complete information on the store's policies on returns.

3 — After finishing with a request, you can expect this representative to pleasantly encourage a customer to "shop again" in the store.

2 — You can expect this representative to delay a customer without explanation while working on other things.

1 — You can expect this representative to treat a customer rudely and with disrespect.

Unsatisfactory performance

Figure 10.4 Sample of a behaviourally anchored rating scale for performance appraisal.

The **critical-incident technique** keeps a running log or inventory of effective and ineffective job behaviours. This written record of success and failure patterns can be specifically discussed with the individual. Using the case of the customer service representative again, a critical-incidents log

The **critical-incident technique** keeps a log of someone's effective and ineffective job behaviours.

might contain the following entries: Positive example—"Took extraordinary care of a customer who had purchased a defective item from a company store in another city"; negative example—"Acted rudely in dismissing the complaint of a customer who felt that a sale item was erroneously advertised."

A multi-person comparison compares one person's performance with that of others.

Some performance appraisals use **multi-person comparisons** that formally compare one person's performance with that of one or more others. Comparisons can be done in different ways. In *rank ordering*, all persons being rated are arranged in order of performance achievement. The best performer goes at the top of the list, the worst performer at the bottom; no ties are allowed. In *paired comparisons*, each person is formally compared with every other person and rated as either the superior or the weaker member of the pair. Each person then receives a summary ranking based on the number of superior scores achieved. In *forced distribution*, each person is placed into a frequency distribution, which requires that a certain percentage fall into specific performance classifications, such as top 10 percent, next 40 percent, next 40 percent, and bottom 10 percent.

360° feedback includes superiors, subordinates, peers, and even customers in the appraisal process.

It is increasingly popular to include more than the immediate boss in the appraisals process. *Peer appraisals* include in the process others who work regularly and directly with a job holder; *upward appraisals* include subordinates reporting to the job holder. An even broader approach is **360° feedback**, where superiors, subordinates, peers, and even internal and external customers are involved in the appraisal of a job holder's performance.[35]

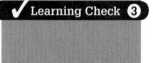

✓ Learning Check **3**   **BE SURE YOU CAN**

• define *socialization* and describe its importance to organizations • explain coaching, mentoring, and modelling as on-the-job training approaches • discuss strengths and weaknesses of performance appraisal methods: graphic rating scales, behaviourally anchored rating scales, critical-incident technique, and multi-person comparisons • explain 360° feedback

Maintaining a Quality Workforce

"Hiring good people is tough," states an article in the *Harvard Business Review*. The sentence finishes with "keeping them can be even tougher."[36] The point is that it isn't enough to hire and train workers to meet an organization's immediate needs; they must also be successfully nurtured, supported, and retained. Canada's Top 100 Employers competition recognizes employers that lead their industries by offering exceptional workplaces for their employees. Organizations are evaluated on a number of variables to determine which offers the most progressive and forward-thinking programs, including programs such as formal mentoring programs, parental leave top-up benefits, retirement preparation with matching RSP contributions, employee wellness program with free memberships, and share purchase plan open to all employees.[37]

FLEXIBILITY AND WORK–LIFE BALANCE

Work–life balance involves balancing career demands with personal and family needs.

Today's fast-paced and complicated lifestyles have contributed to increased concerns for **work–life balance**: how people balance the demands of careers with their personal and family needs.[38] Not surprisingly, the "family-friendliness" of an employer is now frequently used as a screening criterion by job candidates. It is also used in "best employer" rankings by publications like Eluta.ca, *Canadian Business,* and *Working Mother*.

Work–life balance is enhanced when workers have flexibility in scheduling work hours, work locations, and even such things as vacations and personal time off. Flexibility allows people to more easily balance personal affairs and work responsibilities, and it has been shown that workers who have flexibility, at least with start and stop times, are less likely to leave their jobs.[39] Job designs that include flexible work hours and other alternative work schedules are increasingly popular, and they are examined in Chapter 14 on motivation theory and practice. Two quick examples are the Information Services Corporation of Saskatchewan, a Crown corporation, where all employees are allowed flexible work hours and telecommuting options, and *The Halifax Herald,* a regional Nova Scotia newspaper company that offers employees shortened workweeks and earned days off alternatives in addition to flexible hours.[40]

In some industries and labour markets, flexibility programs are becoming essential for employers to attract and retain the talented workers they need. Some employers create flexibility by helping workers handle family matters through such things as on-site daycare and elder care, and concierge services for miscellaneous needs such as dry cleaning and gift purchasing. Others have moved into innovative programs such as work sabbaticals. A study of 164 Canadian companies by Hewitt Associates, a global human resources company, revealed that 36 percent offer sabbatical leave; other organizations such as OMNI Health Care Limited offer employees top-up payment to 75 percent of their salary for 17 weeks for compassionate leave to care for a loved one.[41]

Stockbyte/Alamy

COMPENSATION AND BENEFITS

Pay! It may be that no other work issue receives as much attention. **Base compensation** in the form of a market-competitive salary or hourly wage helps in hiring the right people. The way pay increases are subsequently handled can have a big impact on their job attitudes, motivation, and performance, and also influence their tendencies to "look around" for better jobs elsewhere.

Base compensation is a salary or hourly wage paid to an individual.

Benefits! They rank right up there in importance with pay as a way of helping to attract and retain workers. How many times does a graduating university or college student hear "be sure to get a job with benefits!"?[42]

Merit Pay Systems

The trend in compensation today is largely toward "pay-for-performance."[43] If you are part of a **merit pay** system, your pay increases will be based on some assessment of how well you perform. The notion is that a good merit raise is a positive signal to high performers and a negative signal to low performers, thus encouraging both to work hard in the future. Although this logic makes sense, merit systems are not problem-free. A survey reported by the *Wall Street Journal* found that only 23 percent of employees believed they understood their companies' reward systems.[44] Typical questions are: Who assesses performance? Suppose the employee doesn't agree with the assessment? Is the system fair and equitable to everyone involved? Is there enough money available to make the merit increases meaningful?

Merit pay awards pay increases in proportion to performance contributions.

A good merit pay system that is based on a solid foundation of agreed-upon and well-defined performance measures can handle these questions and more. At the restaurant chain Applebee's International, Inc., managers know that part of their merit pay will be determined by what percentage of their best workers are retained. In an industry known for high turnover, Applebee's makes retention a high-priority goal for managers, and makes their pay increases contingent on how well they do.[45] But this system can still break down if Applebee's managers don't perceive that it is administered in a fair, consistent, and credible fashion.

Bonuses and Profit-Sharing Plans

There's a bit more to the Applebee's story. If you are one of the employees whom managers want to retain, you might be on the receiving end of "Applebucks"—small cash bonuses that are given to reward performance and raise loyalty to the firm.[46] This is a modest example of a pay bonus, but there are larger possibilities as well. How would you like to someday receive a letter like this one, once sent to two top executives by Amazon.com's chairman Jeff Bezos? "In recognition and appreciation of your contributions," his letter read, "Amazon.com will pay you a special bonus in the amount of $1,000,000."[47]

Bonus pay plans provide one-time or lump-sum payments to employees who meet specific performance targets or make some other extraordinary contribution, such as an idea for a work improvement. Bonuses have been most common at the executive level, but many companies now use them more extensively across levels.[48] Whereas some bonus systems award bonuses to individuals—such as the Applebee's and Amazon examples—others award them to everyone in the group or division responsible for high performance. Home Depot, for example, once paid out US$90 million in cash bonuses in one year to employees in stores that met special financial goals.[49]

In contrast to straight bonuses, **profit-sharing** plans distribute to employees a proportion of net profits earned by the organization in a performance period. **Gain-sharing** plans extend the profit-sharing concept by allowing groups of employees to share in any savings or "gains" realized when their efforts result in measurable cost reductions or productivity increases.

Stock Ownership and Stock Options

Some employers provide employees with ways to accumulate stock in their companies and thus develop a sense of ownership. The idea is that stock ownership will motivate employees to work hard so that the company stays successful. In an **employee stock ownership plan**, employees purchase stock directly through their employing companies and sometimes at special discounted rates. West-Jet takes great pride in its employee stock ownership program, recently launching a commercial campaign promoting the slogan "Why do WestJetters care so much? Because we're also WestJet owners." Building stock ownership into their corporate culture has enabled WestJet employees to relentlessly pursue the corporate vision through unified goals and values. The Executive Vice-President of People and Culture at WestJet, Ferio Pugliese, notes: "Our culture drives a superior guest experience that is brought to our guests consistently every day. That's because we have the right people on our team. That's what makes me a proud WestJetter."[50] Of course, recent economic events show the risks of such ownership. When a company's market value falls, so too does the value of any employee-owned stock.

Another approach is to grant employees **stock options** linked to their performance or as part of their hiring packages.[51] Stock options give the owner the right to buy shares of stock at a future date at a fixed price. Employees gain financially as the stock price rises above the option price; they lose if the stock price ends up lower. Some companies "restrict" stock options so that they come due only after designated periods of employment. This practice is meant to tie high performers to the employer and is often called the "golden handcuff." The Hay Group reports that the most admired North American companies are also ones that offer stock options to a greater proportion of their workforces.[52]

Fringe Benefits

Fringe benefits packages include non-monetary forms of compensation such as health insurance and retirement plans. They can add as much as 30 percent or more to a typical worker's earnings. The ever-rising costs of benefits, especially medical insurance and pensions, are a major worry for employers. Many are attempting to gain control over health care expenses by shifting more of the insurance costs to the employees and by restricting options in choosing health care benefits. Some are also encouraging healthy lifestyles as a way of decreasing health insurance claims.

Flexible benefits programs are increasingly common. They let the employee choose a set of benefits within a certain dollar amount. The trend is also toward more **family-friendly benefits** that help employees to better balance work and non-work responsibilities. These include child care, elder care, flexible schedules, parental leave, and part-time employment options, among others. Increasingly common as well are **employee assistance programs** that help employees

---

Bonus pay plans provide one-time payments based on performance accomplishments.

Profit sharing distributes to employees a proportion of net profits earned by the organization.

Gain-sharing plans allow employees to share in cost savings or productivity gains realized by their efforts.

Employee stock ownership plans help employees purchase stock in their employing companies.

Stock options give the right to purchase shares at a fixed price in the future.

Fringe benefits are non-monetary forms of compensation such as health insurance and retirement plans.

Flexible benefits programs allow employees to choose from a range of benefit options.

Family-friendly benefits help employees achieve better work–life balance.

Employee assistance programs help employees cope with personal stresses and problems.

deal with troublesome personal problems. Such programs may offer assistance in dealing with stress, counselling on alcohol and substance abuse problems, referrals for domestic violence and sexual abuse, and sources for family and marital counselling.

RETENTION AND TURNOVER

The several steps in the human resource management process both conclude and recycle with replacement. Some replacement decisions transfer and promote people among positions; others involve terminations, layoffs, and retirements. Any replacement situation is an opportunity to review human resource plans, update job analyses, rewrite job descriptions and job specifications, renew hiring, and ensure that retention and turnover are well managed.

Retirement is one of those things that can often raise fears and apprehensions when it is close at hand. Many organizations offer special counselling and other forms of support for retiring employees, including advice on company benefits, money management, estate planning, and use of leisure time. Increasingly you will hear about **early retirement incentive programs**. These are programs that give workers financial incentives to retire early. For the employers, the potential benefits are opportunities to lower payroll costs by replacing higher-wage workers with less expensive newer hires, assist with staff reductions during downsizing, or create openings that can be used to hire workers with different skills and talents.

Early retirement incentive programs offer workers financial incentives to retire early.

The most extreme replacement decisions involve **termination**, or the involuntary and permanent dismissal of an employee. In some cases, the termination is based on performance problems or violation of organizational policy. In other cases, the persons involved may be performing well, but they are being terminated as part of a workforce reduction. In any and all cases, terminations should be handled fairly according to organizational policies and in full legal compliance. Under the principle of **wrongful dismissal**, workers have legal protections against discriminatory firings; employers must have bona fide job-related reasons for any termination decisions. In situations where workers belong to unions, terminations also become subject to labour contract rules and regulations.

Termination is the involuntary dismissal of an employee.

Wrongful dismissal is a doctrine giving workers legal protections against discriminatory firings.

 Canadian Company in the News

ONTARIO POWER GENERATION: ONE OF CANADA'S TOP 100 EMPLOYERS

With its head office in Toronto and offices across Ontario, Ontario Power Generation (OPG) has approximately 12,000 full-time employees. The company has some impressive HRM numbers: voluntary employee turnover in a recent year was 3.3 percent; the percentage of employees who are women was 22 percent, and the percent of managers who are women was 17 percent. Some 12 percent of employees and 16 percent of managers are members of visible minorities. OPG also provides a quality working environment that includes an on-site fitness facility, employee lounge, and religious observance room. OPG hosts employee social events, solicits outside salary surveys every 12 months, and provides a competitive health plan, including dental, orthodontics, eye care, and massage therapy. OPG also has formal mentoring programs, management training programs, and specialized sustainable development training for supervisors.

The Canadian Press Images/ Stephen C. Host

LABOUR–MANAGEMENT RELATIONS

A **labour union** is an organization that deals with employers on the workers' collective behalf.

Labour unions are organizations to which workers belong that deal with employers on the workers' behalf.[53] Unions are found in many industrial and business occupations, as well as among public-sector employees like teachers, professors, police officers, and government workers. The Trade Unions Act of 1985 protects employees by recognizing their right to join unions and engage in union activities.[54] The Canada Labour Code consolidates the various statutes relating to labour practices in Canada. It aims to protect both employees and employers that are both unionized and non-unionized. The Canada Industrial Relations Board is responsible for interpreting and administering the various elements of the Canada Labour Code.[55]

Although union membership has been waxing and waning, unions remain important forces in the workplace. As a comparison, unions in the United States cover approximately 12 percent of workers, while unions in Canada encompass over 29 percent of workers.[56] Canada's largest union, the Canadian Union of Public Employees (CUPE), boasts a membership of over 600,000 workers nationwide. CUPE represents workers in health care, education, municipalities, libraries, universities, social services, public utilities, transportation, emergency services, and airlines. Its stated goal is to achieve fair wages, negotiate working conditions, and speak out on behalf of employee labour disputes.[57] In just one example of CUPE's activism in the Canadian workplace, the union recently negotiated a collective agreement for Sodexo Canada employees at Acadia University allowing for vacation time increases and standardized wage increase structures.[58]

Collective bargaining is the process of negotiating, administering, and interpreting a labour contract.

Collective bargaining is the process through which labour and management representatives negotiate, administer, and interpret **labour contracts**. It typically occurs in face-to-face meetings between labour and management representatives. During this time, a variety of demands, proposals, and counterproposals are exchanged. Several rounds of bargaining may be required before a contract is reached or a dispute over a contract issue is resolved. And, as you might expect, the process can lead to problems. When telecommunications company Verizon and its unions were recently negotiating a new contract, disagreements and the possibility of a strike arose over issues of employee and retiree health care, job security, and outsourcing.

A **labour contract** is a formal agreement between a union and employer about the terms of work for union members.

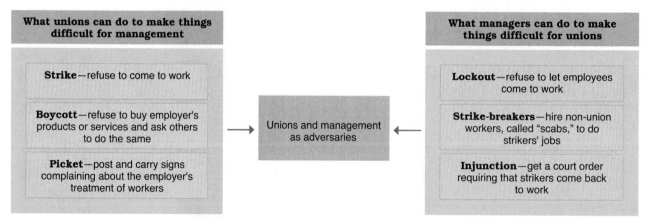

Figure 10.5 Traditional adversarial view of labour–management relations.

Two-tier wage systems pay new hires less than workers already doing the same jobs with more seniority.

In Figure 10.5, labour and management are viewed as "win-lose" adversaries destined to be in opposition and possessed of certain weapons with which to fight one another. This adversarial approach is, to some extent, giving way to a more collaborative one. The emergence of so-called **two-tier wage systems** offers a case in point of an issue that could go either way. These are controversial systems that pay new hires less than workers already doing the same jobs with more seniority. Some of the main concerns about two-tier wage systems are that they promote "ageism" and inhibit the skill development of young, inexperienced, and/or low-income earners in the workforce. The Canadian Auto Workers Union recently declined Air Canada's proposal for two-tier wage systems among customer service and sales agents.[59] However, proponents of this wage system argue that two-tier systems enable companies to keep jobs in Canada that would otherwise be lost due to foreign outsourcing.

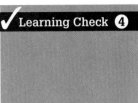

BE SURE YOU CAN

• define *work–life balance* • explain why compensation and benefits are important elements in human resource management • explain potential problems of merit pay plans • differentiate bonuses, profit sharing, and stock options • define *labour union, labour contract*, and *collective bargaining* • contrast the adversarial and cooperative approaches to labour–management relations

ORGANIZATIONAL CULTURE AND DIVERSITY

A key factor in human resource management is developing a performance culture where everyone feels "a part of" the company rather than "apart from" the organization. In his book *Beyond Race and Gender*, consultant R. Roosevelt Thomas Jr. makes the link between organizational culture and diversity.[60] He believes that the way people are treated at work—with respect and inclusion, or with disrespect and exclusion—is a direct reflection of the organization's culture. For sure, we would expect to find respect for diversity central to organizational cultures that are value-based and high on workplace spirituality. And if an organization's culture fails to respect the diversity of its membership, what would that be saying to us as customers or as actual or potential members?

Thomas pushes the discussion even further by arguing that organizational cultures that respect diversity are potential sources of competitive advantage. He believes such cultures offer organizations the wherewithal to mobilize a mixture of talents and perspectives to deal best with the complexities and uncertainty of the ever-changing environment. Research reported in the *Gallup Management Journal*, for example, shows that establishing a racially and ethnically inclusive workplace is good for morale. In a study of 2,014 North American workers, those who felt included were more likely to stay with their employers and recommend them to others. Survey questions asked such things as "Do you always trust your company to be fair to all employees?" "At work, are all employees always treated with respect?" "Does your supervisor always make the best use of employees' skills?"[61]

WHAT IS ORGANIZATIONAL CULTURE?

The organizational culture is what one sees and hears when walking around an organization as a visitor, a customer, or an employee. Look carefully, check the atmosphere, and listen to the conversations. Whenever someone, for example, speaks of "the way we do things here," that person is shedding insight into the organization's culture. Just as nations, ethnic groups, and families have cultures, organizations also have cultures that help to distinguish them from one another and bind members together with some sense of collective identity.

The best organizations are likely to have cultures that are customer-driven and performance-oriented.[62] Have you visited Disneyland or Disney World? If so, you've experienced first-hand an organization with a "strong" organizational culture. Think about how the employees acted, how the park ran, and how consistently and positively all visitors were treated. Strong organizational cultures like Disney's are clear, well defined, and widely shared among members. They encourage positive work behaviours and discourage dysfunctional ones. They also commit members to doing things for and with one another that are in the best interests of the organization.

One of the ways organizations build strong cultures is through socialization. As mentioned in the section on Developing a Quality Workforce, this is the process of helping new members learn the culture and values of the organization, as well as the behaviours and attitudes that are shared among its members.[63] Such socialization often begins in an anticipatory sense with one's education, such as the importance of professional appearance and interpersonal skills for business students. It then continues with an employer's orientation and training programs, which, when well done, can be strongly influential on the new member.

Disney is one of those employers that invest heavily in socialization and training of their members. Founder Walt Disney is quoted as saying: "You can dream, create, design and build the most wonderful place in the world, but it requires people to make the dream a reality."[64] Each new Disney employee attends a program called "traditions." It informs them on the company history, its language and lore, and its founding story. The goal is to help ensure that people do, indeed, help make the Disney dream a reality. And it works; Walt Disney's legacy has even endured to the point where the Disney Institute offers similar training for other employers.

LEVELS OF ORGANIZATIONAL CULTURE

Organizational culture is usually described from the perspective of the two levels shown in Figure 10.6. The outer level is the "observable" culture and the inner level is the "core" culture.[65] As suggested by the figure, you might think of this in terms of an iceberg. What lies below the surface and is harder to see is the core culture. That which stands out above the surface and is more visible to the discerning eye is the observable culture. Managers need to understand both.

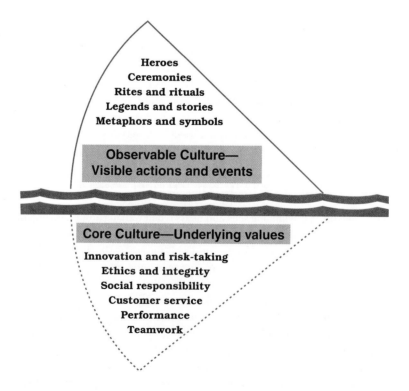

Figure 10.6 Levels of organizational culture—observable culture and core culture in the organizational "iceberg."

Heroes
Ceremonies
Rites and rituals
Legends and stories
Metaphors and symbols

Observable Culture—Visible actions and events

Core Culture—Underlying values

Innovation and risk-taking
Ethics and integrity
Social responsibility
Customer service
Performance
Teamwork

Observable Culture

The first and most visible part of the organizational culture, the observable culture, is readily apparent. As suggested in the opening discussion on RIM, this is what one sees and hears when walking around an organization as a visitor, a customer, or an employee. It is expressed in the way people dress at work, how they arrange their offices, how they speak to and behave toward one another, the nature of their conversations, and how they talk about and treat their customers.

Most discussions of organizational culture identify the following elements of daily organizational life. Each is an essential aspect of the observable culture.[66]

- *Heroes*—the people singled out for special attention and whose accomplishments are recognized with praise and admiration; they include founders and role models.

- *Ceremonies, rites, and rituals*—the ceremonies and meetings, planned and spontaneous, that celebrate important occasions and performance accomplishments.

- *Legends and stories*—oral histories and tales, told and retold among members, about dramatic sagas and incidents in the life of the organization.

- *Metaphors and symbols*—the special use of language and other non-verbal expressions that communicate important themes and values of the organization.

Core Culture

The second and deeper level of organizational culture is the core culture. As also shown in the iceberg model, it consists of the **core values**, or underlying assumptions and beliefs that shape and guide people's behaviours.

Strong-culture organizations typically operate with a small but enduring set of core values that are widely shared among members. At highly successful companies, these core values often emphasize customer service, performance excellence, innovation, social responsibility, integrity, worker involvement, and teamwork.[67] Examples of values statements at strong-culture firms include "service above all else" at Nordstrom; "science-based innovation" at Merck; "encouraging individual initiative and creativity" at Sony; and an aspiration "to be Canada's most trusted company" at Canadian Tire. Another example of a strong core culture is found at Herman Miller, the innovative and award-winning manufacturer of designer furniture. The firm calls itself "a high-performance, values-driven community of people tied together by a common purpose."[68]

> **Core values** are beliefs and values shared by organization members.

VALUES AND ORGANIZATIONAL CULTURE

Although it is clear that culture is not the sole determinant of what happens in organizations, it is an important influence on what they accomplish and how. A widely discussed study of successful businesses, for example, concluded that organizational culture has the potential to shape attitudes, reinforce beliefs, direct behaviour, and establish performance expectations and the motivation to fulfill them.[69] Importantly, the cultures in high-performing firms provided clear values and a vision of what each organization was attempting to accomplish, allowing individuals to rally around the vision and work hard to support and accomplish it.

Reading Values and Organizational Cultures

When IBM's research director, John E. Kelly III, says, "If we don't fail a third of the time, we're not stretching enough," he's not just making a point; he's describing part of IBM's values and corporate culture.[70] From his comments, you should be picturing an organization that encourages risk-taking while seeking extraordinarily high performance.

Management Smarts 10.2 offers ideas for reading the dimensions of organizational cultures. Consider the possible ways organizations like IBM and its competitors can vary on things like innovation and risk-taking, team emphasis, people orientation, emphasis on outcomes, and more.

10.2 MANAGEMENT SMARTS
Questions for reading an organization's culture

- How tight or loose is the *structure*?

- Do most decisions reflect *change* or the status quo?

- What *outcomes* or results are most highly valued?

- What is the climate for *risk-taking* and *innovation*?

- How widespread are *empowerment* and *worker involvement*?

- What is the *competitive style*, internal and external?

- What value is placed on *people*, as customers and employees?

- Is *teamwork* a way of life in this organization?

Reading values and organizational cultures is a useful skill to cultivate and, if you master it, you might make better job choices. We should all aspire to a good fit between ourselves and the culture of our employing organization. Indeed, it was a lack of such fit that was offered as an explanation for a talent drain in Hyundai's American operations. One former sales executive observes: "It's a very feudal approach to management, there's a king, he rules, and everyone curries his favor. It's very militaristic."[71]

Value-Based Management

Organizations often publicize core values in corporate mission statements and on their websites. But mere testimonies to values are not enough to create a strong organizational culture and derive its benefits. The values must be practised. They must be real, they must be shared, and they must be modelled and reinforced by managers from top to bottom. This is where good management comes into play.

Value-based management
actively develops,
communicates, and enacts
shared values.

The term **value-based management** describes managers who actively help develop, communicate, and enact shared values within an organization. Although you might tend to associate this with top management, the responsibility for value-based management extends to all managers and team leaders. Like the organization as a whole, any work team or group will have a culture. How well this culture operates to support the group and its performance objectives will depend in part on the strength of the core values and the team leader's role as a values champion. A good test of the value-based management of any organization or team includes criteria such as these.[72]

- *Relevance*—Core values support key performance objectives.

- *Integrity*—Core values provide clear, consistent ethical anchors.

- *Pervasiveness*—Core values are understood by all members.

- *Strength*—Core values are accepted by all members.

Workplace Spirituality

It is becoming popular to discuss **workplace spirituality** along with value-based management. Although the first tendency might be to associate "spirituality" with religion, the term is used more broadly in management to describe an organizational culture in which people are able to experience meaning in their work and a sense of shared community through their role in the organization. The foundations for workplace spirituality are set in management practices that respect and nurture the full value of human beings. The guiding principle is that people are inwardly enriched when they find real value in their work and are able to share that value through a sense of personal connection with others inside and outside of the organization.[73]

The core values in a culture of workplace spirituality will have strong ethics foundations, recognize human dignity, respect diversity, and focus on creating jobs that contribute in meaningful ways to an organization that offers identifiable value to society. When someone works in a culture of workplace spirituality, in other words, the person should derive pleasure from knowing that what is being accomplished is personally meaningful, created through community, and valued by others.

Meeting the standards for workplace spirituality isn't easy, and not all organizational cultures will hold up to the test. As a starting point, you might consider an organization's ethics and social responsibility practices. At Tom's of Maine, for example, CEO Tom Chappell didn't hesitate to recall a new all-natural deodorant when customers were dissatisfied. It cost the company some US$400,000, but Chappell confidently did the "right" thing. His company is founded on values that include fairness and honesty, and he lived up to them, setting a positive example for others to follow.[74]

Workplace spirituality creates meaning and shared community among organizational members.

Symbolic Leadership

A **symbolic leader** is someone who uses symbols well to communicate values and maintain a desired organizational culture. Symbolic managers and leaders both act and talk the "language" of the organization. They are always careful to behave in ways that live up to the core values; they are ever-present role models for others to emulate and follow.

Symbolic leaders use spoken and written words to describe people, events, and even the competition in ways that reinforce and communicate core values. Language metaphors—the use of positive examples from another context—are very powerful in this regard. For example, newly hired workers at Disney World and Disneyland are counselled to always think of themselves as more than employees; they are key "members of the cast," and they work "on stage." After all, they are told, Disney isn't just any business; it is an "entertainment" business.

Good symbolic leaders highlight and even dramatize core values and the observable culture. They tell key stories over and over again, and they encourage others to tell them. They may refer to the "founding story" about the entrepreneur whose personal values set a key tone for the enterprise. They remind everyone about organizational heroes, past and present, whose performances exemplify core values. They often use rites and rituals to glorify the performance of the organization and its members. At Mary Kay Cosmetics, gala events at which top sales performers share their tales of success are legendary. So, too, are the lavish incentive awards presented at these ceremonies, especially the pink luxury cars given to the most successful salespeople.[75]

A **symbolic leader** uses symbols to establish and maintain a desired organizational culture.

MULTICULTURAL ORGANIZATIONS

In studying the business case for diversity, Thomas Kochan and his colleagues at MIT found that the presence of diversity alone does not guarantee a positive performance impact. Only when diversity is leveraged through training and supportive human resource practices are the advantages gained. In other words, only when respect for diversity is embedded in the organizational culture can we expect such positive performance results. Kochan et al. summarize their findings with this guidance on diversity and organizational culture:[76]

> *To be successful in working with and gaining value from diversity requires a sustained, systemic approach and long-term commitment. Success is facilitated by a perspective that considers diversity to be an opportunity for everyone in an organization to learn from each other how better to accomplish their work and an occasion that requires a supportive and cooperative organizational culture as well as group leadership and process skills that can facilitate effective group functioning.*

The best organizational cultures, as described by Thomas Kochan et al., are inclusive in that they value the talents, ideas, and creative potential of *all* members. In management, the term **multiculturalism** refers to inclusivity, pluralism, and respect for diversity in the workplace. A truly **multicultural organization** is one where the organizational culture communicates and supports core values that respect and empower the full diversity of its members. Such a multicultural organization has these characteristics:[77]

Multiculturalism involves pluralism and respect for diversity.

A **multicultural organization** is based on pluralism and operates with inclusivity and respect for diversity.

- *Pluralism*—Members of both minority cultures and majority cultures are influential in setting key values and policies.

- *Structural integration*—Minority-culture members are well represented in jobs at all levels and in all functional responsibilities.

- *Informal network integration*—Various forms of mentoring and support groups assist in the career development of minority-culture members.

- *Absence of prejudice and discrimination*—A variety of training and task-force activities address the need to eliminate culture-group biases.

- *Minimum intergroup conflict*—Diversity does not lead to destructive conflicts between members of majority and minority cultures.

GOING GLOBAL

SCOTIABANK: INTERNATIONAL TIES ADD TO MULTICULTURALISM

The Bank of Nova Scotia, more commonly known as Scotiabank, was founded in Halifax in 1832. Now headquartered in Toronto, it is Canada's third-largest bank, with nearly 69,000 employees worldwide. It expanded earlier than most Canadian banks into the United States, setting up a branch in Minneapolis in 1885. Due to its original focus on transatlantic trade, it has always enjoyed a strong merchant and investment banking arm. Of the "big five" Canadian banks, it is the most international, with over 2,500 branches in 50 countries, and is the largest Canadian bank in China. During the financial crisis, it was identified as one of the 10 most stable banks in the world. Scotiabank is seen as an employer of choice: recent surveys of staff yielded a satisfaction score of over 85 percent. Strong international connections, strong financial footing, and strong HR performance as well!

Organizational subcultures exist among people with similar values and beliefs based on shared work responsibilities and personal characteristics.

Ethnocentrism is the belief that one's membership group or subculture is superior to all others.

DIVERSITY AND ORGANIZATIONAL SUBCULTURES

Like society as a whole, organizations contain a mixture of **subcultures**. These are cultures common to groups of people with similar values and beliefs based on shared work responsibilities and personal characteristics. And just as with life in general, **ethnocentrism**—the belief that one's membership group or subculture is superior to all others—can creep into the workplace and adversely affect the way people relate to one another.

Occupations and Functions

The many possible subcultures in organizations include *occupational subcultures*.[78] Salaried professionals such as lawyers, scientists, engineers, and accountants have been described as having special needs for work autonomy and empowerment that may conflict with traditional management methods of top-down direction and control. Unless these needs are recognized and properly dealt with, salaried professionals may prove difficult to integrate into the culture of the larger organization.

There are also *functional subcultures* in organizations, and people from different functions often have difficulty understanding and working well with one another. For example, employees of a business may consider themselves "systems people" or "marketing people" or "manufacturing people" or "finance people." When such identities are overemphasized, members of the functional groups may spend most of their time with each other, develop a "jargon" or technical language that is shared among them, and view their role in the organization as more important than the contributions of the other functions.

Ethnicity and National Cultures

Differences in *ethnic or national cultures* exist as people from various countries and regions of the world meet and work together in the global economy. And as we all know, it can sometimes be hard to work well with persons whose home cultures are different from our own. The best international understanding is most likely gained through direct contact and from being open-minded. The same advice holds true with respect to ethnic and racial subcultures. Although one may speak in everyday conversations about "francophone" or "Aboriginal" or "anglophone" cultures, current events demonstrate how difficult it can be for members of cultural communities to understand one another. If improved cross-cultural understanding can help people work better across national boundaries, how can we create the same understanding to help people from different racial subcultures work better together?

Gender and Generations

Relationship issues and discrimination based on *gender subcultures* also continue to complicate the workplace. Some research shows, that when men work together, a group culture forms around a competitive atmosphere. Sports metaphors are common, and games and stories often deal with winning and losing.[79] When women work together, a rather different culture may form, with more emphasis on personal relationships and collaboration.[80]

We live at a time when the influence of *generational subcultures* is often a topic for workplace conversations. Think about how age might affect a person's work attitudes and preferences. A survey by Leadership IQ, a training firm, found differences in the job satisfactions of younger and older workers.[81] Younger workers express desires for greater performance recognition, while older workers downplay praise and want more clarity regarding what their bosses expect from them. It probably isn't possible to use a "one size fits all" approach to manage a workforce with generational diversity.[82]

Issues of generational subcultures are often expressed in labels such as "baby boomer" and "Millennial." And indeed, generational gaps exist among baby boomers, now in their fifties and early sixties; Generation Xers, now in their thirties and early forties; Millennials or Gen Ys, now in their twenties; and the new Internet generation, moving through their teenage years. Members of these generations grew up in quite different worlds and were influenced by different values and opportunities. Someone who is 60 years old today, a common age for senior managers, was a teenager in the 1960s. Such a person may have difficulty understanding, working with, and leading younger managers who were teens during the 1970s, 1980s, and especially the 1990s. And if you belong to one of the latter generations—perhaps a Millennial—you'll need to ponder how well you will do in the future when working with still younger colleagues.

MANAGING DIVERSITY

The very term "diversity" basically means the presence of differences. But what happens when those differences are distributed unequally among organizational subcultures and in the governing power structures? What happens when one subculture is in "majority" status while others become "minorities"? Even though organizations are changing today, there is likely to be more workforce diversity at the lower and middle levels of most organizations than at the top. Most senior executives in large organizations are still older, white, and male; only 11 CEOs of Fortune Global 500 companies in 2009 were women.[83]

Glass Ceilings

The **glass ceiling** is a hidden barrier to the advancement of women and members of visible minorities.

Take a look at Figure 10.7. It depicts the **glass ceiling**, defined in Chapter 1 as an invisible barrier that limits the advancement of women and members of visible minorities in some organizations. What are the implications for minority members, such as women or persons of colour, seeking to advance and prosper in an organization dominated by a majority culture of white males? Consider the situation faced by Jesse Spaulding when he was a regional manager for a restaurant chain owned by Shoney's. He says that the firm used to operate on the "buddy system," which "left people of colour by the wayside" when it came to promotions. Things changed when new leadership rewarded Spaulding with new opportunities and Shoney's gained a ranking among *Fortune* magazine's list of America's 50 Best Companies for Minorities.[84]

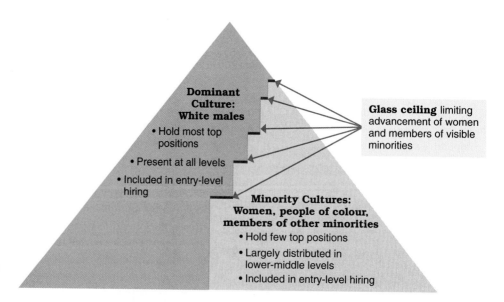

Figure 10.7 Glass ceilings as barriers to women and members of minority cultures in traditional organizations.

Harassment and Discrimination

The daily work challenges faced by members of visible minorities and women can range from misunderstandings and lack of sensitivity on the one hand, to glass ceiling limitations, to even outright harassment and discrimination. Data from the U.S. Equal Employment Opportunity Commission, for example, report a growing number of bias suits filed by workers, with sex discrimination being a factor in some 30 percent of them.[85] The commission also reports an increase in pregnancy discrimination complaints.[86] Pay discrimination is another issue. A senior executive in the computer industry reported her surprise at finding out that the top performer in her work group, an African-American male, was paid 25 percent less than anyone else. This wasn't because his pay had been cut to that level, she said. It was because his pay increases had always trailed those given to his white co-workers. The differences added up significantly over time, but no one noticed or stepped forward to make the appropriate adjustment.[87]

Sexual harassment in the form of unwanted sexual advances, requests for sexual favours, and sexually laced comments is a problem female employees in particular may face. It's not uncommon for minority workers to be targets of cultural jokes; one survey reports some 45 percent of respondents had encountered such abuse. Sometimes members of minority cultures try to adapt through tendencies toward **biculturalism**. This is the display of majority culture characteristics that seem necessary to succeed in the work environment. For example, one might find gays and lesbians hiding their sexual orientation from co-workers out of fear of prejudice or discrimination. Similarly, one might find an Aboriginal employee carefully training herself to not use certain words or phrases at work that might be considered as subculture colloquial speech by white co-workers.

Biculturalism occurs when minority members adopt characteristics of majority cultures in order to succeed.

Diversity Leadership

There should be no doubt today that minority workers want the same things everyone wants. They want respect for their talents and a work setting that allows them to achieve their full potential. It takes the best in diversity leadership at all levels of organizational management to meet these expectations.

R. Roosevelt Thomas describes the continuum of leadership approaches to diversity shown in Figure 10.8.[88] The first is *affirmative action*, in which leadership commits the organization to hiring and advancing members of certain groups. In Canada, this concept is behind the Employment Equity Act, which legislates employers in any federally regulated industry to ensure a proportionate representation in their workforces of four selected groups: women, people with disabilities, Aboriginal people, and members of visible minorities. The second is *valuing diversity*, in which leadership commits the organization to education and training programs designed to help people better understand and respect individual differences. The third and most comprehensive is **managing diversity**, in which leadership builds an organizational culture that allows all employees to reach their full potential.

Thomas believes that leaders committed to managing diversity create the most value in respect to competitive advantage.[89] They build organizations that are what Thomas calls "diversity mature." In these organizations, there is a diversity mission as well as an organizational mission. Diversity is viewed as a strategic imperative; the members understand diversity concepts and are themselves diversity-mature. Such an organization, as Thomas might say, is truly multicultural.

Managing diversity is building an inclusive work environment that allows everyone to reach their full potential.

Figure 10.8 Leadership approaches to diversity—from employment equity to managing diversity.

Source: Adapted by permission of the publisher, from *Beyond Race and Gender* by R. Roosevelt Thomas © 1991 R. Roosevelt Thomas, Jr., AMACOM Books, division of American Management Association, New York, New York. All rights reserved. www. amacombooks.org.

Affirmative Action
Create upward mobility for members of visible minorities and women

Valuing Differences
Build quality relationships with respect for diversity

Managing Diversity
Achieve full utilization of diverse human resources

✓ **Learning Check ⑤**

BE SURE YOU CAN

• define *organizational culture* and explain the importance of strong cultures to organizations
• distinguish between the observable and core cultures • explain how value-based management helps build strong culture organizations • describe how workplace spirituality and symbolic leadership relate to organizational culture • explain multiculturalism and the concept of a multi-cultural organization • identify common organizational subcultures • discuss glass ceilings and employment problems faced by members of visible minorities and women • explain Thomas's concept of managing diversity

MANAGEMENT LEARNING REVIEW

STUDY QUESTIONS SUMMARY

1. What is human resource management?

• The human resource management process involves attracting, developing, and maintaining a quality workforce.

• Human resource management becomes strategic when it is integrated into the organization's top management structure.

• Employees have legal protections against employment discrimination; human rights laws guarantee people the right to employment and advancement without discrimination.

• Current legal issues in human resource management include sexual harassment, comparable worth, rights of independent contractors, and employee privacy.

FOR DISCUSSION What gaps in legal protection against employment discrimination still exist?

2. How do organizations attract a quality workforce?

• Human resource planning analyzes staffing needs and identifies ways to fill these needs over time.

• Recruitment is the process of attracting qualified job candidates to fill positions.

• Realistic job previews offer candidates accurate information on the job and the organization.

• Interviews, employment tests, and reference checks help managers make selection decisions.

• The use of assessment centres and work sampling is becoming widespread in the selection process.

FOR DISCUSSION Can you expect a potential employer to give you a "realistic" job preview?

3. How do organizations develop a quality workforce?

• Orientation is the process of formally introducing new employees to their jobs, performance expectations, and the organization.

• On-the-job training includes coaching, modelling, and mentoring; off-the-job training includes formal job training and management development programs.

• Performance management systems establish work standards and the means for assessing performance results.

- Common performance appraisal methods are graphic rating scales, behaviourally anchored rating scales, and multi-person comparisons.

FOR DISCUSSION What are the potential downsides of being on the receiving end of 360° feedback?

4. How do organizations maintain a quality workforce?

- Complex demands of job and family responsibilities have made work–life balance programs increasingly important in human resource management.

- Compensation and benefits packages must be attractive so that an organization stays competitive in labour markets.

- Merit pay plans link compensation and performance; examples include bonuses, profit sharing, and stock options.

- Replacement decisions in human resource management involve promotions, transfers, retirements, and/or terminations.

- The collective bargaining process and labour–management relations are governed by law.

FOR DISCUSSION Given current trends in globalization, will labour unions gain in popularity?

5. What are the links between organizational culture and diversity?

- In organizations with strong cultures, members behave with shared understandings and act with commitment to core values.

- Multicultural organizations operate with internal cultures that value pluralism, respect diversity, and build strength from an environment of inclusion.

- Organizations have many subcultures, including those based on occupational, functional, ethnic, racial, age, and gender differences.

- Challenges faced by members of minority subcultures in organizations include sexual harassment, pay discrimination, job discrimination, and the glass ceiling effect.

- Managing diversity is the process of developing an inclusive work environment that allows everyone to reach their full potential.

FOR DISCUSSION What can a manager do, at the work team level, to reduce diversity bias in the workplace?

SELF-TEST

Multiple-Choice Questions

1. Human resource management is the process of _____, developing, and maintaining a high-quality workforce.

    (a) attracting (b) compensating (c) appraising (d) selecting

2. Which is not a major responsibility of human resource management?

    (a) attracting a quality workforce (b) developing a quality workforce (c) maintaining ISO 14001 (d) performance management

3. _____ regulations are designed to ensure equal employment opportunities for persons historically underrepresented in the workforce.

    (a) Realistic recruiting (b) External recruiting (c) Employment equity (d) Employee assistance

4. If an employment test yields different results over time when taken by the same person, it lacks _____.

    (a) validity   (b) specificity   (c) realism   (d) reliability

5. The assessment centre approach to employee selection relies heavily on _____.

    (a) pencil-and-paper tests   (b) simulations and experiential exercises   (c) 360° feedback   (d) formal one-on-one interviews

6. _____ is a form of on-the-job training wherein an individual learns by observing others who demonstrate desirable job behaviours.

    (a) Case study   (b) Work sampling   (c) Modelling   (d) Simulation

7. The first step in strategic human resource planning is to _____.

    (a) forecast human resource needs   (b) forecast labour supplies   (c) assess the existing workforce   (d) review organizational mission, objectives, and strategies

8. In Canada, the _____ protects employees' right to join unions and engage in union activities.

    (a) Canadian Human Rights Act   (b) Trade Unions Act of 1985   (c) Canada Labour Code   (d) Employment Equity Act

9. Socialization of newcomers occurs during the _____ step of the staffing process.

    (a) recruiting   (b) orientation   (c) selecting   (d) training

10. In human resource planning, a(n) _____ is used to determine exactly what is done in an existing job.

    (a) critical-incident technique   (b) assessment centre   (c) job analysis   (d) multi-person comparison

11. Which of the following is not an on-the-job training program?

    (a) gain sharing   (b) job rotation   (c) coaching   (d) modelling

12. The _____ purpose of performance appraisal is being addressed when a manager describes training options that might help an employee improve future performance.

    (a) development   (b) evaluation   (c) judgemental   (d) legal

13. Whether a structure is tight or loose and whether decisions are change-oriented or driven by the status quo are indicators of an organization's _____.

    (a) inclusivity   (b) culture   (c) competitive advantage   (d) multiculturalism

14. Pluralism and the absence of discrimination and prejudice in policies and practices are two important hallmarks of _____.

    (a) the glass ceiling effect   (b) a multicultural organization   (c) quality circles   (d) employment equity

15. A manager who _____ is displaying a commitment to valuing human capital.

    (a) believes payroll costs should be reduced wherever possible   (b) is always looking for new ways to replace people with machines   (c) protects workers from stress by withholding information from them about the organization's performance   (d) views people as assets to be nurtured and developed over time

Short-Response Questions

16. How do internal recruitment and external recruitment compare in terms of advantages and disadvantages for the employer?

17. Why is orientation an important part of the human resource management process?

18. What is the difference between the graphic rating scale and the BARS as performance appraisal methods?

19. Why is it important for managers to understand subcultures in organizations?

Application Question

20. Sy Dabrowski is not doing well in his job. The problems began to appear shortly after Sy's job was changed from a manual to a computer-based operation. He has tried hard but is just not doing well in learning to use the computer, and as a result he is having difficulty meeting performance expectations. As a 55-year-old employee with over 30 years with the company, Sy is both popular and influential among his work peers. Along with his performance problems, you have also noticed the appearance of some negative attitudes, including a tendency for Sy to sometimes "badmouth" the firm. As Sy's manager, what options would you consider in terms of dealing with the issue of his retention in the job and in the company? What would you do, and why?

MANAGEMENT SKILLS AND COMPETENCIES

SELF-ASSESSMENT

Back to Yourself: Professionalism

All managers should show professionalism in their own areas of expertise and work responsibility by behaving with internalized commitments to external standards. And, of course, they should be thoroughly professional in all aspects of human resource management discussed in this chapter—from recruiting and selecting new hires, to training and developing them, to appraising performance, to handling issues like compensation and work–life balance.

Further Reflection: Performance Appraisal Assumptions

Instructions

In each of the following pairs, check the statement that best reflects your assumptions about performance evaluation.

Performance evaluation is

1. (a) a formal process that is done annually.
   (b) an informal process done continuously.

2. (a) a process that is planned for subordinates.
   (b) a process that is planned with subordinates.

3. (a) a required organizational procedure.
   (b) a process done regardless of requirements.

4. (a) a time to evaluate subordinates' performance.
   (b) a time for subordinates to evaluate their manager.

5. (a) a time to clarify standards.
   (b) a time to clarify the subordinate's career needs.

6. (a) a time to confront poor performance.
   (b) a time to express appreciation.

7. (a) an opportunity to clarify issues and provide direction and control.
   (b) an opportunity to increase enthusiasm and commitment.

8. (a) only as good as the organization's forms.
   (b) only as good as the manager's coaching skills.

Scoring

There is no formal scoring for this assessment, but there may be a pattern to your responses.

Interpretation

In general, the "a" responses represent a more traditional approach to performance appraisal that emphasizes its evaluation function. This approach largely puts the supervisor in the role of documenting a subordinate's performance for control and administrative purposes. The "b" responses represent more emphasis on the counselling or development role. Here, the supervisor is concerned with helping the subordinate do better and with learning from the subordinate what he or she needs to be able to do better. This role is consistent with new directions and values emerging in today's organizations.

Source: Developed in part from Robert E. Quinn, Sue R. Faerman, Michael P. Thompson, and Michael R. McGrath, *Becoming a Master Manager: A Contemporary Framework* (New York: Wiley, 1990), p. 187. Used by permission.

Which Organizational Culture Fits You?

Instructions

Indicate which one of the following organizational cultures you feel most comfortable working in.

1. A culture that values talent, entrepreneurial activity, and performance over commitment; one that offers large financial rewards and individual recognition.

2. A culture that stresses loyalty, working for the good of the group, and getting to know the right people; one that believes in "generalists" and step-by-step career progress.

3. A culture that offers little job security; one that operates with a survival mentality, stresses that every individual can make a difference, and focuses attention on "turn-around" opportunities.

4. A culture that values long-term relationships; one that emphasizes systematic career development, regular training, and advancement based on gaining functional expertise.

Interpretation

These labels identify the four different cultures: 1 = "the baseball team," 2 = "the club," 3 = "the fortress," and 4 = "the academy."

Discuss your preferences in groups assigned by the instructor. Your future career success may depend on working for an organization in which there is a good fit between you and the prevailing corporate culture. This exercise can help you learn how to recognize various cultures, evaluate how well they can serve your needs, and realize how they may change with time. A risk-taker, for example, may be out of place in a "club" but fit right in with a "baseball team." Someone who wants to seek opportunities wherever they may occur may be out of place in an "academy" but fit right in with a "fortress."

Source: Developed from Carol Hymowitz, "Which Corporate Culture Fits You?" *Wall Street Journal* (July 17, 1989), p. B1.

Royal Bank of Canada: Progressive HR Makes Good Business Sense

Started in 1864 as a small group of enterprising Halifax merchants, Royal Bank of Canada (RBC) has grown to be Canada's largest bank, specializing in personal and business banking, full-service brokerage services, insurance, and corporate and investment banking.[1] RBC has a strong commitment to its approximately 80,000 employees worldwide through progressive human resources strategies, policies, and practices.[2] However, it's the company's total commitment to diversity and inclusion and a strong culture of employee engagement that provide the foundation for its employees and, in turn, RBC to succeed.[3]

Human Resource Practices

Committed to remaining an employer of choice, RBC goes beyond traditional HR programs to offer competitive compensation, flexible benefits, and training and career development opportunities that make RBC a great place to work.[4]

In addition to providing signing and referral bonuses, a share-purchase plan for all employees, defined benefit and defined contribution pension plans, and retirement planning assistance, RBC participates in annual outside salary surveys to make sure its compensation remains competitive.[5]

THE CANADIAN PRESS/Nathan Denette

RBC offers a flexible health plan covering both part-time and full-time employees with adjustable premiums and coverage levels. RBC also offers family-friendly benefits such as maternity top-up payments, pre-arranged emergency short-term daycare, and assistance finding family care services, such as daycare and elder care. Its "Living Well" intranet site encourages employees to remain healthy through an on-line resource guide with information on topics such as nutrition, physical exercise, and mental well-being.

Employees at RBC receive tuition subsidies for courses whether or not they are related to their current position. In addition to full tuition subsidies, the bank supports employees' career development with subsidies for professional accreditations, in-house apprenticeship and skilled trades internships, in-house and on-line training programs, a formal mentoring program, career planning services, and financial bonuses for the completion of certain professional accreditations.[6]

Diversity

For RBC, diversity in its workforce is one of its greatest competitive advantages for developing intellectual capital and ensuring continued growth, not only within Canada but around the world. With Canada becoming more ethnically diverse and the company itself expanding globally, RBC has committed to embedding diversity objectives into its recruiting, hiring, and promotion practices.[7] Having a workforce that fully reflects its clients and the communities in which it does business serves as a basic premise of diversity at RBC.[8]

RBC's focus on diversity dates back to the early 1970s when it developed an internal task force on the status of women, followed by a focus on employment equity groups in the 1980s and comprehensive work–life initiatives in the 1990s.[9] The Advisory Task Force on the Status of Women in Royal Bank of Canada in 1977 examined the bank's systems and practices toward women, the first of its kind for a Canadian bank.[10] Today, RBC continues to strive to build and sustain an inclusive work environment in many ways. For example, it was a founding sponsor of Career Bridge, which provides a four-month Canadian internship to foreign-trained professionals to help them integrate into the Canadian workforce.[11]

An important measure of RBC's success is the composition of its workforce. Of the more than 21,000 people RBC has hired since 2006, 52 percent have been women and 26 percent have been members of visible minorities. RBC actively recruits immigrants and has some 2,600 interpreters on call to help translate 180 different languages, including indigenous Canadian languages like Cree and Inuktitut.

Women now hold 40 percent of the executive positions at RBC, up from 35 percent in 2005, and members of visible minorities hold 14 percent, up from 5 percent. Perhaps most notably, three of the nine top executive jobs are held by women and two of them, chief financial officer Janice Fukukusa and human resources chief Zabeen Hirji, are members of visible minorities.[12]

RBC's commitment to diversity has won the company acclaim. In 2009 and 2010 alone, RBC was recognized twice as one of Canada's Top 100 Employers, received a Catalyst Award for Diversity, and was recognized for a second year running as one of Canada's Best Diversity Employers[13] for developing exemplary diversity initiatives in five employee groups: women; members of visible minorities; persons with disabilities; Aboriginal peoples; and lesbian, gay, bisexual, and transgendered/transsexual (LGBT) people.[14] It has also been named a "best place to work" for gays and lesbians and working mothers[15] and was inducted into the Canada's 10 Most Admired Corporate Cultures Hall of Fame by Waterstone Human Capital Ltd. for its strong organizational culture and commitment to "doing the right thing for the organization."[16]

Does diversity work at RBC? Based on its recent accolades, the answer is yes!

Discussion Questions

1. Using the three major responsibilities of human resources management, describe how RBC can be considered an employer of choice.

2. Assume you are hired as a consultant to create a plan to improve the development of RBC's workforce. What recommendations would you make for RBC to further develop its workforce? Explain your reasoning.

3. How does RBC work to maintain its workforce? Do you think the strategy is effective? Why or why not?

4. FURTHER RESEARCH—Compare RBC with Bank of Montreal (BMO), a competitor in the banking industry, in terms of approaches to attracting, developing, and maintaining a diverse workforce.

11 Leading and Leadership Development

Developing leaders: A firm's most important job

On July 1, A. G. Lafley woke up at his usual time of 6 a.m., worked out, showered, and headed to his office in downtown Cincinnati. What was different was that after 10 years he was no longer the chief executive of Procter & Gamble (P&G), having turned the company around, as described in the opener to Chapter 9. Instead, the new boss starting that day would be Bob McDonald. Later, at the weekly meeting of executives, Lafley chose a chair far from the one he'd regularly sat in. Everyone turned to McDonald as soon as he sat down. "It felt exactly like it was intended to" Lafley said later. "The king is dead. Long live the king!"

P&G's new CEO, Bob McDonald, has had a global career. For example, in 1989, McDonald was asked to go to Canada to turn around the struggling laundry products division. He accepted the promotion, he moved his family here, he joined the P&G hockey team, and he read every Canadian book he could find. Most importantly, he learned that you never say, "Here's how we do it in the United States." He aced the assignment—his superiors and staff recognized attention to detail and his love of mentoring.

At P&G, a successful leadership transition is not surprising. Why? Because P&G recognizes the importance of developing excellent leaders.

AP Photo/Al Behrman

One way P&G develops leadership is captured in a blue binder called the Talent Portfolio; it contains the names of P&G's up-and-coming leaders. There are sections that show who has consistently outperformed others, who is considered "at risk," who is ready to be promoted next, and who will need more time. There are at least three possible candidates for each major job. This kind of bench strength is something all companies wish they had.

The blue binder has been helping P&G for decades. All executives who become general managers are evaluated every six months, focusing on relevant financial measures and, equally important, assessing leadership and team-building abilities. All managers are evaluated by their bosses, by lateral managers who have worked with them, and by their own direct reports.

P&G knows how to grow leaders, who in turn know how to grow the business![1]

BENCHMARK Leadership development at P&G is supported right from the top. Executives are expected to be willing to develop leadership skills in themselves and in others. Shouldn't this be the task of all leaders? P&G executives do it so well, the company was recently selected as one of the World's Best Companies for Leaders by *Fortune* magazine. Check out what other organizations make developing leaders a priority by viewing *Fortune*'s list of top companies for leaders.

Integrity

Whether you call it ethical leadership or moral leadership, the personal implications are the same: respect flows toward leaders who behave with *integrity*. You should understand that integrity is defined as being honest, credible, and consistent in all that we do. On the flip side, here are some of the things that cause people to say someone lacks integrity.

- Giving special treatment to favoured people

- Willing to lie

- Blaming others for personal mistakes

- Letting others take blame for personal mistakes

- Wanting others to fail

- Falsifying reports and records

- Instigating conflict and disharmony

- Taking credit for others' ideas

- Stealing

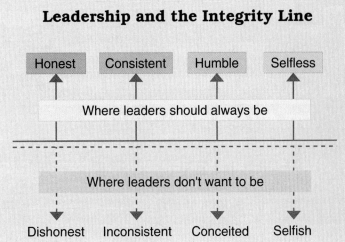

Leadership and the Integrity Line

What are the elements of leadership integrity? According to the late management guru Peter Drucker, the notion of "service" is central. He says leaders with integrity "are servants of the organization—whether elected or appointed, whether the organization is a government, a government agency, a business, a hospital, a diocese. It's their duty to subordinate their likes, wishes, preferences to the welfare of the institution." Drucker went on to say that to be such a leader you must have "the ability to see the world as it is, not as you want it to be."[2]

❖ Get to Know Yourself Better

How often have you worked for someone who behaved below the "integrity line" depicted in the figure above? How did you feel about it, and what did you do? Write a set of notes on your behaviour in situations—work, study groups, sports, shopping, friendship gatherings, or whatever—in which your leadership integrity could be questioned. What are the lessons for the future?

CHAPTER 11 STUDY QUESTIONS

- What is the nature of leadership?

- What are the important leadership traits and behaviours?

- What are the contingency theories of leadership?

- What are current issues in leadership development?

- What is the communication process?

- How can communication be improved?

VISUAL CHAPTER OVERVIEW

CHAPTER 11 LEADING AND LEADERSHIP DEVELOPMENT

Study Question 1	Study Question 2	Study Question 3	Study Question 4	Study Question 5	Study Question 6
The Nature of Leadership	**Leadership Traits and Behaviours**	**Contingency Approaches to Leadership**	**Issues in Leadership Development**	**The Communication Process**	**Improving Communication**
■ Leadership and power	■ Leadership traits	■ Fiedler's contingency model	■ Transformational leadership	■ Effective communication	■ Active listening
■ Leadership and vision	■ Leadership behaviours	■ Hersey–Blanchard situational leadership model	■ Emotional intelligence and leadership	■ Persuasion and credibility in communication	■ Constructive feedback
■ Leadership as service	■ Classic leadership styles	■ Path–goal leadership theory	■ Gender and leadership	■ Communication barriers	■ Space design
		■ Leader–member exchange theory	■ Moral leadership		■ Channel selection
		■ Leader–participation model	■ Drucker's "old-fashioned" leadership		■ Electronic communication
					■ Interactive management
					■ Cross-cultural communication

✓ Learning Check 1   ✓ Learning Check 2   ✓ Learning Check 3   ✓ Learning Check 4   ✓ Learning Check 5   ✓ Learning Check 6

The late Grace Hopper, management expert and the first female admiral in the U.S. Navy, once said: "You manage things; you lead people."[3] Leadership scholar and consultant Barry Posner believes that managers need to spend less time dealing with the status quo and focus more on "figuring out what needs to be changed." He says: "The present moment is the domain of managers. The future is the domain of leaders."[4] Consultant and author Tom Peters points out that the leader is "rarely—possibly never?—the best performer."[5] His point is that leaders thrive through and by the successes of others.

These are all good points and they are among many leadership insights that will be discussed in this chapter. If we go right to the heart of the matter, however, the consensus is that leaders become great by bringing out the best in people. This is part of Procter & Gamble's success story and it's a lesson well worth remembering.

But we also have to be realistic when studying leadership and working on personal leadership development. Managers today face often daunting responsibilities. The time frames for getting things accomplished are becoming shorter. Leaders are expected to get things right the first time, with second chances often few and far between. The problems to be resolved are complex, ambiguous, and multidimensional. Leaders are expected to stay focused on long-term goals even while dealing with problems and pressures in the short term.[6] It takes hard work to be a great leader; there are lots of challenges to be mastered. All the skills and competencies discussed in *Management* must be acquired and used to their full advantage.

THE NATURE OF LEADERSHIP

A glance at the shelves in your local bookstore will quickly confirm that **leadership**—the process of inspiring others to work hard to accomplish important tasks—is one of the most popular management topics.[7] As shown in Figure 11.1, it is also one of the four functions that constitute the management process. Planning sets the direction and objectives; organizing brings together resources to turn plans into action; leading builds the commitments and enthusiasm for people to apply their talents to help accomplish plans; controlling makes sure things turn out right.

Leadership is the process of inspiring others to work hard to accomplish important tasks.

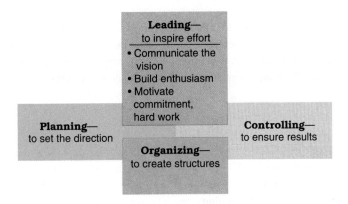

Figure 11.1 Leading viewed in relationship to the other management functions.

LEADERSHIP AND POWER

The foundation for leadership success rests with an ability to make things happen in ways that serve the goals of the team or organization. This is an issue of "power," and leadership essentially begins with the ways a manager uses power to influence the behaviour of other people. **Power** in this sense is the ability to get someone else to do something you want done, or to make things happen the way you want.[8] Although a need for power is essential to executive success, it is not a desire to control for the sake of personal satisfaction. It is a desire to influence and control others

Power is the ability to get someone else to do something you want done or to make things happen the way you want.

for the good of the group or organization as a whole.[9] This "positive" face of power is the foundation of effective leadership.

Figure 11.2 shows that leaders gain power both from the positions they hold and from their personal qualities.[10] Anyone holding a managerial position theoretically has power, but how well it is used will vary from one person to the next. The three bases of position power are reward power, coercive power, and legitimate power. The two bases of personal power are expertise and reference.

Sources of power...

Power of the POSITION: *Based on things managers can offer to others.*	**Power of the PERSON:** *Based on how managers are viewed by others.*
Rewards: "If you do what I ask, I'll give you a reward."	**Expertise**—"You should do what I want because of my special expertise or information."
Coercion: "If you don't do what I ask, I'll punish you."	**Referent**—You should do what I want in order to maintain a positive, self-defined relationship with me."
Legitimacy: "Because I am the boss, you *must* do as I ask."	

Figure 11.2 Sources of position power and personal power used by leaders.

Position Power

Reward power is the capacity to offer something of value as a means of influencing other people.

Reward power is the ability to influence through rewards. It is the capacity to offer something of value—a positive outcome—as a means of influencing another person's behaviour. This involves use of incentives such as pay raises, bonuses, promotions, special assignments, and verbal or written compliments. To mobilize reward power, a manager says, in effect: "If you do what I ask, I'll give you a reward."

Coercive power is the capacity to punish or withhold positive outcomes as a means of influencing other people.

Coercive power is the ability to influence through punishment. It is the capacity to punish or withhold positive outcomes as a way to influence the behaviour of other people. A manager may attempt to coerce someone by threatening him or her with verbal reprimands, pay penalties, and even termination. To mobilize coercive power, a manager says, in effect: "If you don't do what I want, I'll punish you."

Legitimate power is the capacity to influence other people by virtue of formal authority, or the rights of office.

Legitimate power is the ability to influence through authority—the right by virtue of one's organizational position or status to exercise control over persons in subordinate positions. It is the capacity to influence the behaviour of other people by virtue of the rights of office. To mobilize legitimate power, a manager says, in effect: "I am the boss; therefore, you are supposed to do as I ask."

Personal Power

Expert power is the capacity to influence other people because of specialized knowledge.

Expert power is the ability to influence through special expertise. It is the capacity to influence the behaviour of other people because of one's knowledge and skills. Expertise derives from the possession of technical understanding or special information. It is developed by acquiring relevant skills or competencies and by gaining a central position in relevant information networks. It is maintained by protecting one's credibility and not overstepping the boundaries of true expertise. When a manager uses expert power, the implied message is: "You should do what I want because of my special expertise or information."

Referent power is the capacity to influence other people because of their desire to identify personally with you.

Referent power is the ability to influence through identification. It is the capacity to influence the behaviour of other people because they admire you and want to identify positively with you. Reference is a power derived from charisma or interpersonal attractiveness. It is developed and maintained through good interpersonal relations that encourage the admiration and respect of others. When a manager uses referent power, the implied message is: "You should do what I want in order to maintain a positive, self-defined relationship with me."

LEADERSHIP AND VISION

"Great leaders," it is said, "get extraordinary things done in organizations by inspiring and motivating others toward a common purpose."[11] In other words, they use their power exceptionally well. And frequently, successful leadership is associated with **vision**—a future that one hopes to create or achieve in order to improve upon the present state of affairs. But simply having the vision of a desirable future is not enough. Truly great leaders are really good at turning their visions into accomplishments.

The term **visionary leadership** describes a leader who brings to the situation a clear and compelling sense of the future, as well as an understanding of the actions needed to get there successfully.[12] This means having a clear vision, communicating the vision, and getting people motivated and inspired to pursue the vision in their daily work. Think of it this way. Visionary leadership brings meaning to people's work; it makes what they do seem worthy and valuable.

At the Lorraine Monroe Leadership Institute, founder Lorraine Monroe brings visionary leadership to life. The institute's mission statement reads with a sense of inspiration: "to develop and support public school leaders who view solid education as a necessity for transforming children's lives and who are committed to leading consistently high achieving schools where all students, beginning with kindergarten, are prepared to enter and graduate from college." The mission is backed with values and principles described in the Monroe Doctrine: "We can reform society only if every place we live—every school, workplace, church, and family—becomes a site of reform." Monroe's personal leadership emphasizes what she calls the "heart of the matter." "Leadership is about making a vision happen," she says: "The job of a good leader is to articulate a vision that others are inspired to follow. That leader makes everybody in an organization understand how to make the vision active."[13]

Vision is a clear sense of the future.

Visionary leadership brings to the situation a clear sense of the future and an understanding of how to get there.

CANADIAN MANAGERS

Colleen Johnston: Having a Vision Helps You See Clearly

Courtesy TD Bank Financial Group

Colleen Johnston is the CFO of the TD Bank Financial Group. A chartered accountant and a graduate from York University, Johnston feels the key to building a business (or a bank) is to have a great team and to make developing people a priority. Having a vision is also important. She recalls that earlier in her career, when morale was low in her work group, she worked to develop and then share a vision. "It involved excellence in everything we did, partnership, teamwork and establishing the highest level of employee satisfaction," Johnston says. And it worked. Within a few years, they were known as one of the most service-oriented groups within the bank. She continues to seek out visions and wins. For example, she led a sustainability initiative by implementing an on-line expense reporting system, which eliminated the printing of an estimated 1.8 million pages.

LEADERSHIP AS SERVICE

Servant leadership is follower-centred and committed to helping others in their work.

When thinking about leadership, power, and vision, it is important to revisit the issue of integrity, as mentioned in the chapter opener. In the words of Peter Drucker again, the concept of "service" is central to integrity and leaders who have integrity act as "servants of the organization."[14] **Servant leadership** is leadership based on a commitment to serving others—to helping people use their talents to full potential while working together for organizations that benefit society.[15] You might think of servant leadership with this question in mind: who is most important in leadership, the leader or the followers? For those who believe in servant leadership, there is no doubt about the correct answer: the followers. Servant leadership is "other-centred," and not "self-centred."

Empowerment enables others to gain and use decision-making power.

If one shifts the focus away from the self and toward others, what does that generate in terms of leadership directions and opportunities? The answer is **empowerment**. This is the process through which managers enable and help others gain power and achieve influence within the organization. Servant leaders empower others by providing them with the information, responsibility, authority, and trust to make decisions and act independently. They expect that, when people feel empowered to act, they will follow through with commitment and high-quality work. Realizing that power in organizations is not a "zero-sum" quantity, they reject the idea that in order for one person to gain power, someone else needs to give it up.[16] In this way, servant leadership becomes empowering for everyone, making the whole organization more powerful in serving its cause or mission.

Consider how servant leadership is described by those who excel at it. Robert Greenleaf, who is actually credited with coining the term, says: "Institutions function better when the idea, the dream, is to the fore, and the person, the leader, is seen as servant to the dream."[17] Max DePree of Herman Miller praises leaders who "permit others to share ownership of problems—to take possession of the situation."[18] Lorraine Monroe, as discussed earlier, says: "The real leader is a servant of the people she leads. A really great boss is not afraid to hire smart people. You want people who are smart about things you are not smart about."[19]

✓ **Learning Check ❶**   **BE SURE YOU CAN**
- define *power* • illustrate three types of position power and discuss how managers use each
- illustrate two types of personal power and discuss how managers use each • define *vision*
- explain the concept of visionary leadership • define *empowerment* • explain the notion and benefits of servant leadership

---

LEADERSHIP TRAITS AND BEHAVIOURS

For centuries, people have recognized that some persons perform very well as leaders, whereas others do not. The question still debated is why. Historically, the issue of leadership success has been studied from the perspective of the trait, behavioural, and contingency approaches. Each offers a slightly different explanation of leadership effectiveness and the pathways to leadership development.

LEADERSHIP TRAITS

An early direction in leadership research involved the search for universal traits or distinguishing personal characteristics that would separate effective from ineffective leaders.[20] Sometimes called the "great person theory," the results of many years of research in this direction can be summarized as follows.

Physical characteristics such as a person's height, weight, and physique make no difference in determining leadership success. On the other hand, certain personal traits do seem common among the best leaders. A study of more than 3,400 managers, for example, found that followers rather consistently admired leaders who were honest, competent, forward-looking, inspiring, and credible.[21] A comprehensive review by Shelley Kirkpatrick and Edwin Locke identifies these personal traits of many successful leaders:[22]

- *Drive:* Successful leaders have high energy, display initiative, and are tenacious.

- *Self-confidence:* Successful leaders trust themselves and have confidence in their abilities.

- *Creativity:* Successful leaders are creative and original in their thinking.

- *Cognitive ability:* Successful leaders have the intelligence to integrate and interpret information.

- *Job-relevant knowledge:* Successful leaders know their industry and its technical foundations.

- *Motivation:* Successful leaders enjoy influencing others to achieve shared goals.

- *Flexibility:* Successful leaders adapt to fit the needs of followers and the demands of situations.

- *Honesty and integrity:* Successful leaders are trustworthy; they are honest, predictable, and dependable.

 ## Canadian Company in the News

FREE THE CHILDREN

Since its founding in 1995, Free The Children has built more than 650 schools in developing countries, improved over 1 million people's access to clean water, and helped start 30,000 microbusinesses. Pretty good results, but what is truly amazing is that this non-profit company was started by, at the time, 12-year-old Craig Kielburger. After reading a story in the newspaper—"Battled Child Labour, Boy 12 Murdered"—he gathered together a group of school friends to fight against child labour. Today, Free The Children is the world's largest network of children helping other children. A motivated

Courtesy Free The Children

12-year-old, Craig has developed into a self-confident, passionate, and energetic adult who still has the leadership drive to change the world.

LEADERSHIP BEHAVIOURS

Moving on from the early trait studies, researchers next turned their attention toward how leaders behave when dealing with followers. Work in this tradition investigated **leadership styles**—the recurring patterns of behaviours exhibited by leaders.[23] If the best style could be identified, the implications were straightforward and practical: train leaders to become skilled at using it.

A stream of research that began in the 1940s, spearheaded by studies at Ohio State University and the University of Michigan, focused attention on two dimensions of leadership style: (1) concern for the task to be accomplished, and (2) concern for the people doing the work.

Leadership style is the recurring pattern of behaviours exhibited by a leader.

The Ohio State studies used the terms *initiating structure* and *consideration* for the respective dimensions; the University of Michigan studies called them *production-centered* and *employee-centered*.[24] But regardless of the terminology used, the behaviours characteristic of each leadership dimension were quite clear.

- *A leader high in concern for the task* plans and defines the work to be done, assigns task responsibilities, sets clear work standards, urges task completion, and monitors performance results.

- *A leader high in concern for people* acts warm and supportive toward followers, maintains good social relations with them, respects their feelings, is sensitive to their needs, and shows trust in them.

The results of leader behaviour research at first suggested that followers of people-oriented leaders would be the most productive and satisfied.[25] However, researchers eventually moved toward the position that truly effective leaders were high in both concerns for people and concerns for task. Figure 11.3 shows one of the popular versions of this conclusion—the Leadership Grid™ of Robert Blake and Jane Mouton.[26] It describes how leaders vary in tendencies toward people and production concerns. The preferred combination of "high-high" leadership is called the *team manager*. This leader shares decisions with team members, empowers them, encourages participation, and supports teamwork.

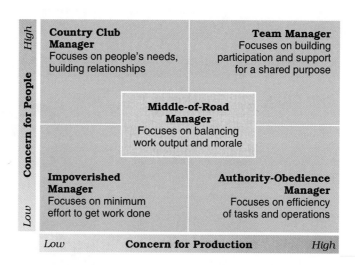

Figure 11.3 Managerial styles in Blake and Mouton's Leadership Grid.

A leader with an **autocratic style** acts in a unilateral, command-and-control fashion.

A leader with a **human relations style** emphasizes people over tasks.

A leader with a **laissez-faire style** displays a "do the best you can and don't bother me" attitude.

A leader with a **democratic style** emphasizes both tasks and people.

CLASSIC LEADERSHIP STYLES

Even today, when people talk about the leaders with whom they work, their vocabulary often describes classic styles of leadership relating back to the behavioural leadership theories.[27] A leader identified with an **autocratic style**, Blake and Mouton's authority-obedience manager, emphasizes task over people, retains authority and information, and acts in a unilateral, command-and-control fashion. A leader with a **human relations style**, the country club manager in the grid, does just the opposite, emphasizing people over tasks. A leader with a **laissez-faire style**, the impoverished manager, shows little concern for the task, letting the group make decisions and acting with a "do the best you can and don't bother me" attitude. A leader with a **democratic style**, Blake and Mouton's "high-high" team manager, is committed to both task and people, trying to get things done while sharing information, encouraging participation in decision-making, and otherwise helping others develop their skills and capabilities.

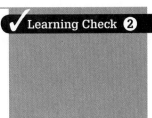

BE SURE YOU CAN ....

• contrast the trait and leader behaviour approaches to leadership research • identify five personal traits of successful leaders • illustrate leader behaviours consistent with a high concern for task • illustrate leader behaviours consistent with a high concern for people • explain the leadership development implications of Blake and Mouton's Leadership Grid • describe four classic leadership styles

CONTINGENCY APPROACHES TO LEADERSHIP

As leadership research continued, scholars became increasingly uncomfortable with the notion that a "high-high" leader was always best. They recognized the need to examine yet another question: when and under what circumstances is any one leadership style preferable to others? They developed the following contingency approaches with the goal of understanding the conditions for leadership success in different situations.

FIEDLER'S CONTINGENCY MODEL

An early contingency leadership model was developed by Fred Fiedler. He proposed that good leadership depends on a match between leadership style and situational demands.[28]

Understanding Leadership Style

Leadership style in Fiedler's model is measured on the *least-preferred co-worker scale*, known as the LPC scale and found as the end-of-chapter self-assessment. It describes tendencies to behave either as a task-motivated leader (low LPC score) or as a relationship-motivated leader (high LPC score). This "either/or" concept is important. Fiedler believes that leadership style is part of one's personality; therefore, it is relatively enduring and difficult to change. He doesn't place much hope on trying to train a task-motivated leader to behave in a relationship-motivated manner, or vice versa. Rather, Fiedler believes that the key to leadership success is putting our existing styles to work in situations for which they are the best "fit." We might think of it as avoiding the "square peg in a round hole" problem.

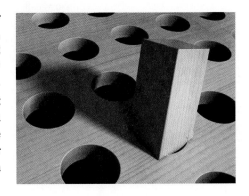

Understanding Leadership Situations

In Fiedler's model, the amount of control a situation allows the leader is a critical issue in determining the correct style–situation fit. Three contingency variables are used to diagnose situational control. The *quality of leader–member relations* (good or poor) measures the degree to which the group supports the leader. The degree of *task structure* (high or low) measures the extent to which task goals, procedures, and guidelines are clearly spelled out. The amount of *position power* (strong or weak) measures the degree to which the position gives the leader power to reward and punish subordinates.

Figure 11.4 shows eight leadership situations that result from different combinations of these contingency variables. They range from the most favourable situation of high control (good leader–member relations, high task structure, strong position power) to the least favourable situation of low control (poor leader–member relations, low task structure, weak position power).

Matching Leadership Style and Situation

In Fiedler's research, neither the task-oriented nor the relationship-oriented leadership style proved effective all the time. Instead, each style seemed to work best when used in the right situation. His findings are summarized in Figure 11.4 and can be stated as two propositions.

Proposition 1—a task-oriented leader will be most successful in either very favourable (high-control) or very unfavourable (low-control) situations.
Proposition 2—a relationship-oriented leader will be most successful in situations of moderate control.

Assume, for example, that you are the leader of a team of bank tellers. The tellers seem highly supportive of you, and their job is clearly defined regarding what needs to be done. You have the authority to evaluate their performance and to make pay and promotion recommendations. This is a high-control situation consisting of good leader–member relations, high task structure, and high position power. Figure 11.4 shows that a task-motivated leader would be most effective in this situation.

Now, suppose that you are chairperson of a committee asked to improve student–faculty relations in a university. Although the goal is clear, no one can say for sure how to accomplish it. Task structure is low, and because committee members are free to quit any time they want, the chairperson has little position power. Because not all members believe the committee is necessary, poor leader–member relations are apparent. According to the figure, this low-control situation also calls for a task-motivated leader.

Finally, assume that you are the new head of a fashion section in a large department store. Because you were selected over a popular sales clerk you now supervise, leader–member relations are poor. Task structure is high, because the clerk's job is well defined. Your position power is low, because the clerks work under a seniority system and fixed wage schedule. Figure 11.4 shows that a relationship-motivated leader is the best fit for this moderate-control situation.

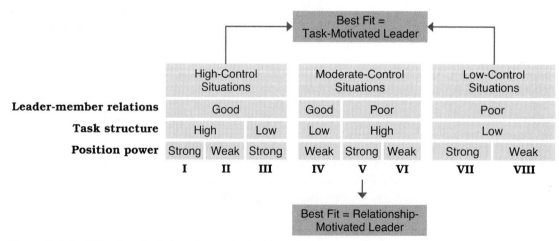

Figure 11.4 Predictions from Fiedler's contingency leadership model.

ISSUES AND SITUATIONS
Managing the Boss

To: Megan Leung

From: Glenn Pool

Subject: Performance Review

Hi Megan:

My To-Do List indicates that it's time for us to meet and discuss your six-month performance. I know we haven't spoken for quite a while, but we need to get this scheduled. Just access my on-line calendar and choose at least a one-hour block of time during the third week of the month when I am free. We'll meet in my office. Bring a list of your major accomplishments and also be prepared to discuss any problems that you have been having. We should also set some concrete goals for your next performance period, so be thinking of those as well.

See you in a couple of weeks.

Glenn

CRITICAL RESPONSE

Focus on Glenn: How is he doing as a manager? How should he deal with Megan?

■ Point out the troublesome aspects of his memo to Megan.

■ Recommend a set of goals for Glenn to accomplish in this meeting.

■ Prepare an agenda and script to help Glenn when he speaks with Megan.

Focus on Megan: Does she have a "managing the boss" problem? How should she handle this e-mail?

■ Recommend a set of goals for Megan to accomplish in the meeting with Glenn.

■ Prepare an agenda and script that she can use to achieve her goals in the meeting.

■ Advise Megan on how to get Glenn to understand her side of the employee–boss relationship.

HERSEY–BLANCHARD SITUATIONAL LEADERSHIP MODEL

In contrast to Fiedler's notion that leadership style is hard to change, the Hersey–Blanchard situational leadership model suggests that successful leaders do adjust their styles. They do so contingently and based on the maturity of followers, as indicated by their readiness to perform in a given situation.[29] "Readiness," in this sense, is based on how able and willing or confident followers are to perform required tasks. As shown in Figure 11.5, the possible combinations of task-oriented and relationship-oriented behaviours result in four leadership styles.

- *Delegating*—allowing the group to take responsibility for task decisions; a low-task, low-relationship style.

- *Participating*—emphasizing shared ideas and participative decisions on task directions; a low-task, high-relationship style.

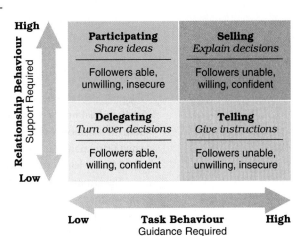

Figure 11.5 Leadership implications of the Hersey–Blanchard situational leadership model.

- *Selling*—explaining task directions in a supportive and persuasive way; a high-task, high-relationship style.

- *Telling*—giving specific task directions and closely supervising work; a high-task, low-relationship style.

The delegating style works best in high-readiness situations with able and willing, or confident followers. The telling style works best at the other extreme of low readiness, where followers are unable and unwilling, or insecure. The participating style is recommended for low-to-moderate-readiness followers—able but unwilling, or insecure; the selling style is for moderate-to-high-readiness followers—unable, but willing or confident.

Hersey and Blanchard also believe that leadership styles should be adjusted as followers change over time. The model implies that, if the correct styles are used in lower-readiness situations, followers will "mature" and grow in ability, willingness, and confidence. This allows the leader to become less directive as followers mature. Although the Hersey–Blanchard model is intuitively appealing, limited research has been accomplished on it to date.[30]

PATH–GOAL LEADERSHIP THEORY

A third contingency leadership approach is the path–goal theory advanced by Robert House.[31] This theory suggests that an effective leader is one who clarifies paths by which followers can achieve both task-related and personal goals. The best leaders help followers move along these paths by clarifying goals, removing barriers, and providing valued rewards for goal accomplishment. Path–goal theorists believe leaders should shift back and forth among these four leadership styles to create positive path–goal linkages.

- *Directive leadership*—letting subordinates know what is expected; giving directions on what to do and how; scheduling work to be done; maintaining definite standards of performance; clarifying the leader's role in the group.

- *Supportive leadership*—doing things to make work more pleasant; treating group members as equals; being friendly and approachable; showing concern for the well-being of subordinates.

- *Achievement-oriented leadership*—setting challenging goals; expecting the highest levels of performance; emphasizing continuous improvement in performance; displaying confidence in meeting high standards.

- *Participative leadership*—involving subordinates in decision-making; consulting with subordinates; asking for suggestions from subordinates; using these suggestions when making a decision.

Path–Goal Contingencies

The path–goal theory, summarized in Figure 11.6, advises managers to use leadership styles that fit situational needs. This allows the leader to add value by contributing things that are missing from the situation or that need strengthening, and by avoiding redundant behaviours. For example, when team members are expert and competent at their tasks, it is unnecessary and even dysfunctional for the leader to tell them how to do things.

The important contingencies for making good path–goal leadership choices include follower characteristics—ability, experience, and locus of control—and work environment characteristics—task structure, authority system, and work group. For example, when job assignments are unclear, directive leadership is appropriate to clarify task objectives and expected rewards. When worker self-confidence is low, supportive leadership is appropriate to increase confidence by emphasizing individual abilities and offering needed assistance. When performance incentives are poor, participative leadership is appropriate to clarify individual needs and identify appropriate

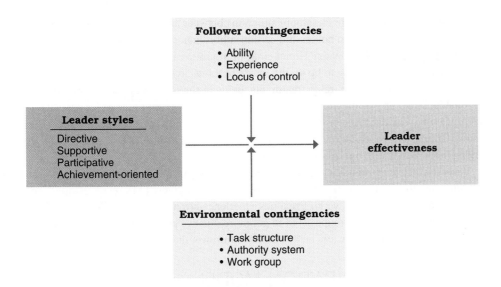

Figure 11.6 Contingency relationships in House's path–goal leadership theory.

rewards. When task challenge is insufficient in a job, achievement-oriented leadership is appropriate to set goals and raise performance aspirations.[32]

Substitutes for Leadership

Path–goal theory has contributed to the recognition of what are called **substitutes for leadership**.[33] These are aspects of the work setting and the people involved that can reduce the need for a leader's personal involvement. In effect, they make leadership from the "outside" unnecessary because leadership is already provided from within the situation.

Possible substitutes for leadership include subordinate characteristics such as ability, experience, and independence; task characteristics such as routineness and the availability of feedback; and organizational characteristics such as clarity of plans and formalization of rules and procedures. When these substitutes for leadership are present, managers are advised to avoid duplicating them. Instead, they should concentrate on making other and more important leadership contributions.

Substitutes for leadership are factors in the work setting that direct work efforts without the involvement of a leader.

LEADER–MEMBER EXCHANGE THEORY

One of the things you may have noticed in your work and study groups is the tendency of leaders to develop "special" relationships with some team members. This notion is central to leader–member exchange theory, or LMX theory, as it is often called.[34] The theory, described in Figure 11.7, recognizes that in most, or at least many, leadership situations, not everyone is treated the same by the leader. People fall into "in-groups" and "out-groups," and the group you are in can have quite a significant influence on your experience with the leader. Those in the "in-group" are often considered the best performers. They enjoy special and trusted high-exchange relationships with the leaders that can translate into special assignments, privileges, and access to information. Those in the "out-group" are often excluded from these attributions and benefits; they have a low-exchange relationship with the leader.

The premise underlying leader–member exchange theory is that, as a leader and follower interact over time, their exchanges end up defining the follower's role.[35] Look around, and you're

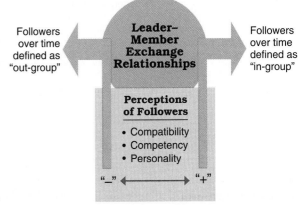

Figure 11.7 Elements of leader–member exchange (LMX) theory.

likely to see examples of this in classroom situations between instructors and certain students, and in work situations between bosses and certain subordinates. For the follower in a high-LMX relationship, being part of the leader's inner circle or in-group can have positive implications. It's often motivating and satisfying to be on the inside of things in terms of getting rewards, access to information, and other favourable treatments. Being in the out-group because of a low-LMX relationship, however, can mean fewer rewards, less information, and little or no special attention. And as to the leader, it is nice to be able to call on and depend upon the loyal support of those in the in-group. But the leader may also be missing out on opportunities that would come from working more closely with out-group members.

Research on leader–member exchange theory places most value on its usefulness in describing leader–member relationships. The notions of high-LMX and low-LMX relationships seem to make sense and correspond to working realities experienced by many people. Also, research finds that members of leaders' in-groups seem to get more positive performance evaluations, report higher levels of job satisfaction, and be less prone to turnover than are members of out-groups.[36]

LEADER–PARTICIPATION MODEL

The Vroom–Jago leader–participation model indicates that leadership success results when the decision-making method used by a leader best fits the problem being faced.[37] As shown in Figure 11.8, the leader's choices for making decisions fall into three categories: authority, consultative, or group decisions.[38] An **authority decision** is made by the leader and then communicated to the group. A **consultative decision** is made by the leader after gathering information and advice from others. A **group decision** is made by the group with the leader's support as a contributing member.

The Vroom–Jago model specifies that the leader's choice among the decision-making methods is governed by three rules: (1) *decision quality*—based on who has the information needed for problem solving; (2) *decision acceptance*—based on the importance of follower acceptance of the decision for its eventual implementation; and (3) *decision time*—based on the time available to make and implement the decision.

Authority decisions work best when leaders personally have the expertise needed to solve the problem; they are confident and capable of acting alone; others are likely to accept and implement the decision they make; and little or no time is available for discussion. By contrast, consultative and group decisions work best when:

- The leader lacks sufficient expertise and information to solve the problem alone.
- The problem is unclear and help is needed to clarify the situation.
- Acceptance of the decision and commitment by others are necessary for implementation.
- Adequate time is available to allow for true participation.

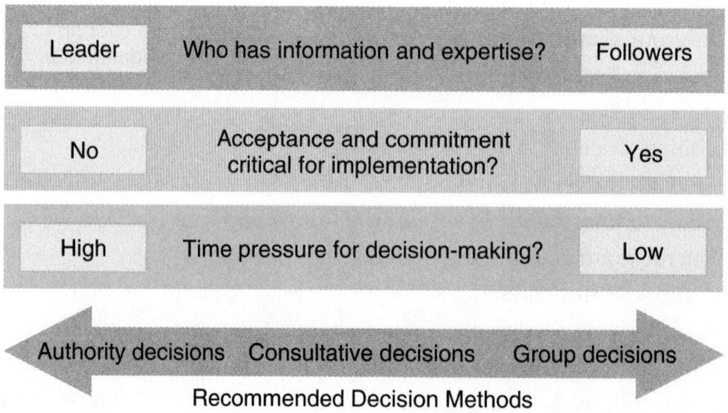

An **authority decision** is made by the leader and then communicated to the group.

A **consultative decision** is made by a leader after receiving information, advice, or opinions from group members.

A **group decision** is made by group members themselves.

Figure 11.8 Leadership implications of Vroom–Jago leader–participation model.

Consultative and group decisions offer important leadership benefits.[39] Participation helps improve decision quality by bringing more information to bear on the problem. It helps improve decision acceptance as participants gain understanding and become committed to the process. It also contributes to leadership development by allowing others to gain experience in the problem-solving process. However, a potential cost of participation is lost efficiency. Participation adds to the time required for decision-making, and leaders don't always have extra time available. When problems must be resolved immediately, the authority decision may be the only option.[40]

In its current version, the Vroom–Jago model views a manager as using the five options shown in Management Smarts 11.1. And in true contingency fashion, no one option is universally superior. Each of the decision methods is appropriate in certain situations, and each has advantages and disadvantages, as just discussed.[41] We should expect to find effective leaders continually shifting among individual, consultative, and group decisions as they deal with the problems and opportunities of daily events.

11.1 MANAGEMENT SMARTS
Five ways for leaders to make decisions

1. *Decide alone*—This is an authority decision; the manager decides how to solve the problem and communicates the decision to the group.

2. *Consult individually*—The manager makes the decision after sharing the problem and consulting individually with group members to get their suggestions.

3. *Consult with group*—The manager makes the decision after convening the group, sharing the problem, and consulting with everyone to get their suggestions.

4. *Facilitate group*—The manager convenes the group, shares the problem, and facilitates discussion to make a decision.

5. *Delegate to group*—The manager convenes the group and delegates authority to define the problem and make a decision.

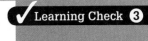
✓ Learning Check ❸

BE SURE YOU CAN
• contrast the leader behaviour and contingency approaches to leadership research • explain Fiedler's contingency model • identify the four leadership styles in the Hersey–Blanchard situational model • explain House's path–goal theory • define *substitutes for leadership* • explain LMX leadership theory • contrast the authority, consultative, and group decisions in the Vroom–Jago model

Issues in Leadership Development

There is a great deal of interest today in "superleaders," persons whose visions and strong personalities have an extraordinary impact on others. They are often called **charismatic leaders** because of their special powers to inspire others in exceptional ways. Although charisma was traditionally thought of as being limited to a few lucky persons who were born with it, it is now considered part of a broader set of personal leadership qualities that can be developed with foresight and practice.[42]

A **charismatic leader** develops special leader–follower relationships and inspires followers in extraordinary ways.

TRANSFORMATIONAL LEADERSHIP

Transactional leadership uses tasks, rewards, and structures to influence and direct the efforts of others.

Leadership scholars James MacGregor Burns and Bernard Bass suggest that the research and models we have discussed so far tend toward **transactional leadership**.[43] The impression is that, if you learn the frameworks, you can apply them systematically to keep others moving forward to achieve performance goals. Burns sees this as a very analytical approach in which transactional leaders change styles, adjust tasks, and allocate rewards to achieve positive influence.

Transformational leadership is inspirational and arouses extraordinary effort and performance.

Notably absent from this description of transactional leadership is any evidence of "enthusiasm" and "emotion," which are inspirational qualities more characteristic of superleaders with charismatic appeal. Importantly, these are the very qualities that Burns and Bass associate with **transformational leadership**. This describes someone who is truly inspiring as a leader, who is personally excited about what she or he is doing, and who arouses others to seek extraordinary performance accomplishments. A transformational leader raises aspirations and shifts people and organizational systems into new, high-performance patterns. The presence of transformational leadership is reflected in followers who are enthusiastic about the leader and his or her ideas, who work very hard to support them, who remain loyal and devoted, and who strive for superior performance accomplishments.

The goal of achieving excellence in transformational leadership is a stiff personal development challenge. It is not enough to possess leadership traits, know the leadership behaviours, and understand leadership contingencies. One must also be prepared to lead in an inspirational way and with a compelling personality, something shown by Martin Luther King and well evident in his famous "I have a dream" speech. Transformational leaders like King bring a strong sense of vision and a contagious enthusiasm to a situation. They substantially raise the confidence, aspirations, and performance commitments of followers through special qualities like the following.[44]

- *Vision*—having ideas and a clear sense of direction; communicating these to others; developing excitement about accomplishing shared "dreams."

- *Charisma*—using the power of personal reference and emotion to arouse others' enthusiasm, faith, loyalty, pride, and trust in themselves.

- *Symbolism*—identifying "heroes" and holding spontaneous and planned ceremonies to celebrate excellence and high achievement.

- *Empowerment*—helping others develop by removing performance obstacles, sharing responsibilities, and delegating truly challenging work.

- *Intellectual stimulation*—gaining the involvement of others by creating awareness of problems and stirring their imaginations.

- *Integrity*—being honest and credible, acting consistently out of personal conviction, and following through on commitments.

EMOTIONAL INTELLIGENCE AND LEADERSHIP

Emotional intelligence is the ability to manage our emotions in social relationships.

A popular issue in leadership development is **emotional intelligence**. It was first introduced in Chapter 1 as part of the essential human skills of managers, and will be examined again in Chapter 12 in a discussion of emotions and moods. You should recall that "EI" is defined by Daniel Goleman as "the ability to manage ourselves and our relationships effectively."[45] His research links emotional intelligence with leadership effectiveness, especially in more senior management positions. In Goleman's words: "the higher the rank of the person considered to be a star performer, the more emotional intelligence capabilities showed up as the reason for his or her effectiveness."[46] This is a strong endorsement for considering whether or not EI is one of your leadership assets.

Goleman believes that emotional intelligence skills can be learned. And for purposes of leadership development, he focuses on a core set of EI competencies.[47] A leader strong in emotional intelligence possesses *self-awareness*. This is the ability to understand our own moods and emotions, and to understand their impact on our work and on others. The emotionally intelligent leader is good at *self-management,* or self-regulation. This is the ability to think before we act and to control otherwise disruptive impulses. Emotional intelligence in leadership involves *motivation* in being able to work hard with persistence and for reasons other than money and status. Leaders with emotional intelligence display *social awareness,* or empathy. They have the ability to understand the emotions

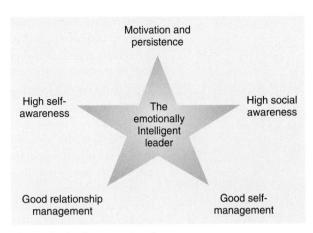

of others and to use this understanding to better relate to them. And a leader high in emotional intelligence has social awareness that makes her or him good at *relationship management*. This is the ability to establish rapport with others and to build good relationships and networks.

GENDER AND LEADERSHIP

Sara Levinson, former President of NFL Properties Inc. of New York and current director of Macy's, once asked the all-male members of her NFL management team this question: "Is my leadership style different from a man's?" "Yes," they replied, suggesting that the very fact that she was asking the question was evidence of the difference. They also indicated that her leadership style emphasized communication, as well as gathering ideas and opinions from others. When Levinson probed further by asking, "Is this a distinctly 'female' trait?" they said that they thought it was.[48]

This example poses an interesting question: are there gender differences in leadership? As we ponder the question, two background points deserve highlighting. First, social science research largely supports the **gender similarities hypothesis**; that is, males and females are very similar to one another in terms of psychological properties.[49] Second, research leaves no doubt that both women and men can be equally effective as leaders.[50]

The **gender similarities hypothesis** holds that males and females have similar psychological properties.

Having acknowledged these points, however, Sara Levinson's experience isn't an anomaly. It's real; such things happen. Perceptions of gender differences in leadership do exist. Research shows that men and women are sometimes perceived differently as leaders, and that these perceptions fit traditional stereotypes. That is, women may be expected to act as "take care" leaders who behave in supportive and nurturing ways; men may be expected to act as "take charge" leaders who are task-oriented and directive, getting things done in traditional command-and-control ways.[51]

When researchers push beyond the use of gender stereotypes, however, the most confident conclusion is that women and men may achieve leadership success from slightly different angles.[52] The most significant difference seems to rest with the use of participation. For example, Victor Vroom and his colleagues have investigated gender differences in respect to the leader-participation model discussed earlier.[53] They find women managers to be more participative in decision-making than men. They are also strong on motivating others, fostering communication, listening, mentoring, and supporting high-quality work.[54] This participative pattern of behaviours has been called an **interactive leadership** style.[55]

Leaders with an interactive style are good communicators and typically act in a democratic and participative manner—showing respect for others, caring for others, and sharing power and information with others. These leaders focus on using communication and involvement to build consensus and good interpersonal relations. And they display many qualities in common with transformational leadership.[56] An interactive leader tends to use personal power, and gains influence over others through support and good interpersonal

Interactive leadership leaders are strong communicators and act in a democratic and participative manner with followers.

relationships. This contrasts with transactional approaches that rely more on directive and assertive behaviours, and on using position power in traditional command-and-control ways. If interactive leadership is something women tend to excel at, these comments by Rosabeth Moss Kanter are worth thinking about: "Women get high ratings on exactly those skills required to succeed in the global information age, where teamwork and partnering are so important."[57]

But one of the risks in any discussion of gender and leadership is falling prey to stereotypes that place men and women into leadership boxes in which they don't necessarily belong.[58] Perhaps we should set gender issues aside for the moment, accept the gender similarities hypothesis, and focus instead on the notion of interactive leadership. The likelihood is that an interactive leadership style is a very good fit with the needs of today's organizations and workers. Furthermore, there is no reason why men and women can't do it equally well. All indications are that future leadership success for anyone will require the capacity to lead through openness, positive relationships, support, and empowerment.[59]

RESEARCH BRIEF

Charismatic leaders display positive emotions that followers find contagious

When leaders show positive emotions, the effect on followers is positive, creating positive moods and also creating tendencies toward positive leader ratings and feelings of attraction to the leader. These are the major conclusions from four research studies conducted by Joyce E. Bono and Remus Ilies, and reported in *Leadership Quarterly*.

Noting the growing interest in the role of emotions in leadership and recognizing the emotional aspects of transformational leadership, Bono and Ilies set out to examine how

Leader Charisma and Emotional Contagion

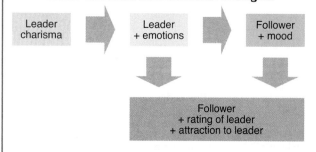

charismatic leaders "use emotion to influence followers." They advanced hypotheses as indicated in the figure, expecting to find that charismatic leaders display positive emotions, that positive leader emotions create positive follower moods, and that positive follower moods generate both positive

ratings of the leader and attraction toward the leader. These hypotheses were examined in a series of four empirical studies.

The researchers concluded that positive emotions are an important aspect of charismatic leadership. They found that leaders rated high in charisma choose words with more positive emotional content for vision statements and speeches. They also found that the positive emotions of leaders were transferred into positive moods among followers; that is, the positive leader moods were contagious. They also found that followers with positive moods had more positive perceptions of leader effectiveness.

One of the limitations of these studies, as pointed out by Bono and Ilies, is that they only focused on positive leader emotions. This leaves open the questions of how leaders use negative emotions and how these emotions affect followers. Also, the researchers suggest the need to examine the impact of leader moods on follower performance and creativity.

You be the researcher

While perhaps agreeing with the logic of emotional contagion, should we conclude that a leader can never have a "bad" day and can never communicate, verbally or nonverbally, anything other than positive emotional messages? Is it realistic for managers to live up to these expectations to always be positive?

MORAL LEADERSHIP

As discussed many times in this book, society expects organizations to be run with **moral leadership**. This is leadership by ethical standards that clearly meet the test of being "good" and "correct."[60] The expectation is that anyone in a leadership position will practise high ethical standards of behaviour, help to build and maintain an ethical organizational culture, and both help and require others to behave ethically in their work.

Moral leadership begins with personal integrity, a concept fundamental to the notion of transformational leadership. As noted in the chapter opener, a leader with **integrity** is honest, credible, and consistent in putting values into action. When a leader has integrity, he or she earns the trust of followers. And when followers believe leaders are trustworthy, they try to behave in ways that live up to the leader's expectations. For managers in our high-pressure and competitive work environments, nothing can substitute for leadership strongly anchored in personal integrity. When viewed through the lens of what is truly the right thing to do, even the most difficult decisions become easier.

In his book *Transforming Leadership: A New Pursuit of Happiness*, James MacGregor Burns explains that transformational leadership creates significant, even revolutionary, change in social systems, while still based on integrity. Notably, he eliminates certain historical figures from this definition: Napoleon is out—too much order-and-obey in his style; Hitler is out—no moral foundations; Mao is out, too—no true empowerment of followers. Among Burns's positive role models from history are Gandhi, George Washington, and Eleanor Roosevelt. Burns firmly believes that such great leaders follow agendas true to the wishes of their followers. He quotes Franklin Delano Roosevelt: "If we do not have the courage to lead the American people where they want to go, someone else will." Burns also says that wherever in the world great leadership is found, it will always have a moral anchor point.[61]

The concept of servant leadership is consistent with this thinking. So, too, is the notion of **authentic leadership** advanced by Fred Luthans and Bruce Avolio.[62] An authentic leader has a high level of self-awareness and clearly understands his or her personal values. This leader also acts consistently with those values, being honest and avoiding self-deception. Because of this, the authentic leader is perceived as genuine, gaining the respect of followers and developing a capacity to positively influence their behaviours. Luthans and his colleagues believe that authentic leadership is activated by the positive psychological states of confidence, hope, optimism, and resilience. The result is positive self-regulation that helps authentic leaders clearly frame moral dilemmas, transparently respond to them, and consistently serve as ethical role models.[63]

Moral leadership is always "good" and "right" by ethical standards.

Integrity in leadership is honesty, credibility, and consistency in putting values into action.

Bettmann/© Corbis

Authentic leadership activates positive psychological states to achieve self-awareness and positive self-regulation.

DRUCKER'S "OLD-FASHIONED" LEADERSHIP

The late management consultant Peter Drucker took a time-tested and very pragmatic view of leadership. It is based on what he refers to as a "good old-fashioned" look at the plain hard work it takes to be a successful leader. Consider, for example, his description of a telephone conversation with a potential consulting client: "We'd want you to run a seminar for us on how one acquires charisma," she said. Drucker's response was not what she expected. He advised her that there was more to leadership than the popular emphasis on personal "dash" or charisma. In fact, he said that "leadership is work."[64]

Drucker's many books and articles remind us that leadership effectiveness must have strong foundations. He believed that the basic building block of effective leadership is defining and establishing a sense of mission. A good leader sets the goals, priorities, and standards. A good

Drucker's Leadership Wisdom

- Define and communicate a clear vision.

- Accept leadership as a responsibility, not a rank.

- Surround yourself with talented people.

- Don't blame others when things go wrong.

- Keep your integrity; earn the trust of others.

- Don't be clever, be consistent.

leader keeps them all clear and visible, and maintains them. In Drucker's words: "The leader's first task is to be the trumpet that sounds a clear sound."

Drucker also believes in accepting leadership as a responsibility rather than a rank. Good leaders surround themselves with talented people. They are not afraid to develop strong and capable subordinates, and they do not blame others when things go wrong. The adage "The buck stops here" is still good to remember.

Finally, Drucker stresses the importance of earning and keeping the trust of others. The key here is the leader's personal integrity, the point on which the chapter began. The followers of good leaders trust them. They believe the leader means what he or she says, and that his or her actions will be consistent with what is said. In Drucker's words again: "effective leadership is not based on being clever; it is based primarily on being consistent."[65]

✔ **Learning Check ❹**

BE SURE YOU CAN

• differentiate transformational leadership and transactional leadership • explain how emotional intelligence contributes to leadership success • discuss research insights on the relationship between gender and leadership • define *interactive leadership* • discuss integrity as a foundation for moral leadership • list Drucker's essentials of good old-fashioned leadership

THE COMMUNICATION PROCESS

Communication is the process of sending and receiving symbols with meanings attached.

As Peter Drucker highlighted, leaders need to be that trumpet that sounds a clear sound. Key then to being an effective leader is to be an effective communicator. **Communication** is an interpersonal process of sending and receiving symbols with messages attached to them. One way to view the communication process is as a series of questions. "Who?" (sender) "says what?" (message) "in what way?" (channel) "to whom?" (receiver) "with what result?" (interpreted meaning).

The key elements in the communication process are shown in Figure 11.9. They include a sender who is responsible for encoding an intended message into meaningful symbols, both verbal and nonverbal. The message is sent through a communication channel to a receiver, who then decodes or interprets its meaning. This interpretation may or may not match the sender's original intentions. Feedback, when present, reverses the process and conveys the receiver's response back to the sender.

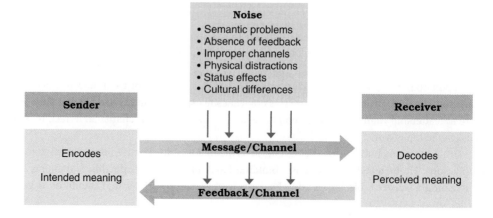

Figure 11.9 The interactive two-way process of interpersonal communication.

EFFECTIVE COMMUNICATION

The ability to communicate well both orally and in writing is a critical managerial skill and the foundation of effective leadership. Through communication, people exchange and share information with one another, and influence one another's attitudes, behaviours, and understandings. Communication allows managers to establish and maintain interpersonal relationships, listen to others, deal with conflicts, negotiate, and otherwise gain the information needed to create a high-performance workplace.

Effective communication occurs when the sender's message is fully understood by the receiver. **Efficient communication** occurs at minimum cost in terms of resources expended. It's nice to be effective and efficient. But, as we all know, this is not always achieved. Poor skills can limit communication effectiveness, and efficiency is sometimes traded for effectiveness.

> In **effective communication** the intended meaning is fully understood by the receiver.
>
> **Efficient communication** occurs at minimum cost.

Picture your instructor taking the time to communicate individually with each student about this chapter. It would be virtually impossible. Even if it were possible, it would be costly. This is why managers often leave voice-mail messages and interact by e-mail, rather than visit people personally. These alternatives are more efficient than one-on-one and face-to-face communications, but they may not always be effective. A low-cost approach such as an e-mail note to a distribution list may save time, but it may not result in everyone getting the same meaning from the message. Without opportunities to ask questions and clarify the message, erroneous interpretations are possible.

By the same token, an effective communication may not always be efficient. If a team leader visits each team member individually to explain a new change in procedures, this may guarantee that everyone truly understands the change. But it may also take a lot of the leader's time. A team meeting would be more efficient. In these and other ways, potential trade-offs between effectiveness and efficiency must be recognized in communication.

GOING GLOBAL

EFFECTIVE COMMUNICATION CREATES A COMMUNITY FIRST; A BUSINESS SECOND

A Fortune 500 company, DaVita, Inc., delivers dialysis services and education to patients with chronic kidney failure. It has also been recognized as a democratic workplace. "It is an honor to be named to the WorldBlu List of Most Democratic Workplaces for the third consecutive year," said Kent Thiry, Chairman and Chief Executive Officer of DaVita. "We consider DaVita a community first and a company second. This recognition reflects the two-way dialogue we strive to have with our 34,000 teammates around the country." As an example of how the company works, when looking to rename the firm, Thiry invited over 600 mid-managers to come up with the name. "DaVita" is Italian for "giving life."

PERSUASION AND CREDIBILITY IN COMMUNICATION

Communication is not only about sharing information or being "heard"; it often includes the intent of one party to influence or motivate the other in a desired way. **Persuasive communication** results in a recipient agreeing with or supporting the message being presented.[66] Managers get things done by working with and persuading others who are their peers, teammates, and co-workers. They often get things done more by convincing than by giving orders. Furthermore, they must be able to persuade others over and over again; once is not enough.

> **Persuasive communication** presents a message in a manner that causes the other person to support it.

Scholar and consultant Jay Conger says that many managers "confuse persuasion with taking bold stands and aggressive arguing."[67] He points out that this often leads to "counter-persuasion" responses and may even raise questions regarding the managers' credibility. **Credible communication** earns trust, respect, and integrity in the eyes of others. And without credibility, Conger sees little chance that persuasion can be successful. Conger's advice is to build credibility for persuasive communication through expertise and relationships.

Credible communication earns trust, respect, and integrity in the eyes of others.

To build credibility through expertise, you must be knowledgeable about the issue in question or have a successful track record in dealing with similar issues in the past. In a hiring situation where you are trying to persuade team members to select candidate A rather than B, for example, you must be able to defend your reasons. And it will always be better if your past recommendations turned out to be good ones. To build credibility through relationships, you must have a good working relationship with the person to be persuaded. And it is always easier to get someone to do what you want if that person likes you. In the prior example, where you want to persuade your boss to provide a special bonus package to attract top job candidates, having a good relationship with your boss can add credibility to your request.

COMMUNICATION BARRIERS

When Yoshihiro Wada was president of Mazda Corporation, he once met with representatives of the firm's American joint venture partner, Ford. But he had to use an interpreter. He estimated that 20 percent of his intended meaning was lost in the exchange between himself and the interpreter; another 20 percent was lost between the interpreter and the Americans.[68]

> **Millennial text to baby boomer**
>
> Omg sorry abt mtg nbd 4 now b rdy nxt time g2g ttl
>
> **Baby boomer text to millennial**
>
> Missed you at meeting. It was important. Don't forget next one. Stop by office.

Noise, as previously shown in Figure 11.9, is anything that interferes with the effectiveness of the communication process. The potential for noise is quite evident in foreign language situations like Wada's. But do you recognize it in everyday text messaging, such as the boxed exchange between a high-tech millennial and a low-tech baby boomer manager? Common sources of noise that often create communication barriers include poor choice of channels, poor written or oral expression, failures to recognize nonverbal signals, physical distractions, and status effects.

Poor Choice of Channels

A **communication channel** is the pathway through which a message moves from sender to receiver.

A **communication channel** is the pathway or medium through which a message is conveyed from sender to receiver. Good managers choose the right communication channel, or combination of channels, to accomplish their intended purpose.[69] In general, written channels—paper or electronic—are acceptable for simple messages that are easy to convey and for those that require extensive dissemination quickly. They are also important as documentation when formal policies or directives are being conveyed. Spoken channels work best for messages that are complex and difficult to convey, and where immediate feedback to the sender is valuable. They are also more personal and can create a supportive, even inspirational, climate.

Poor Written or Oral Expression

Communication will be effective only to the extent that the sender expresses a message in a way that can be clearly understood by the receiver. This means that words must be well chosen and properly used to express the sender's intentions. Consider the following "bafflegab" found in some executive communications.

A business report said: "Consumer elements are continuing to stress the fundamental necessity of a stabilization of the price structure at a lower level than exists at the present time." (Translation: consumers keep saying that prices must go down and stay down.)

A manager said: "Substantial economies were affected in this division by increasing the time interval between distributions of data-eliciting forms to business entities." (Translation: the division saved money by sending out fewer questionnaires.)

A survey of 120 companies by the National Commission on Writing found that over one-third of their employees were considered deficient in writing skills, and that employers were spending over US$3 billion each year on remedial training.[70] Such training typically covers both written and oral communication. It isn't easy, for example, to write a concise, clear, and understandable e-mail. Like any written message, the e-mail can easily be misunderstood. It takes practice and hard work to express one's intentions well in the space of an e-mail message.

The same holds true for oral communication that takes place in telephone calls, face-to-face meetings, formal briefings, video conferences, and the like. See Management Smarts 11.2 for guidelines on an important communication situation: the executive briefing or formal presentation.[71]

11.2 MANAGEMENT SMARTS
How to make a successful presentation

- *Be prepared:* know what you want to say; know how you want to say it; rehearse saying it.
- *Set the right tone:* act audience-centred; make eye contact; be pleasant and confident.
- *Sequence points:* state your purpose; make important points; follow with details; then summarize.
- *Support your points:* give specific reasons for your points; state them in understandable terms.
- *Accent the presentation:* use good visual aids; provide supporting handouts when possible.
- *Add the right amount of polish:* attend to details; have room, materials, and arrangements ready to go.
- *Check your technology:* test out everything ahead of time; make sure it works and know how to use it.
- *Don't bet on the Internet:* beware of real-time Internet visits; save sites on a disk and use a browser to open the file.
- *Be professional:* be on time; wear appropriate attire; act organized, confident, and enthusiastic.

Failure to Recognize Nonverbal Signals

Nonverbal communication takes place through such things as hand movements, facial expressions, body posture, eye contact, and the use of interpersonal space. It can be a powerful means of transmitting messages, with research showing that up to 55 percent of a message's impact may come through nonverbal communication.[72] In fact, a potential problem in the growing use of voice mail, text messaging, computer networking, and other electronic communications is

Nonverbal communication takes place through gestures and body language.

that gestures and other nonverbal signals are lost. Their absence may lower communication effectiveness.

Think of how nonverbal signals play out in your own communications. The astute observer notes the "body language" expressed by other persons; gestures, for example, can make a difference in whether someone's speech is positive or negative, excited or bored, or even engaged with or disengaged from you.[73] And we can't forget that sometimes our body may be "talking" for us, even as we otherwise maintain silence. When we do speak, our body may sometimes "say" different things than our words convey.

A **mixed message** occurs when a person's words communicate one message while his or her actions, body language, appearance, or use of interpersonal space communicate something else. Watch how people behave in a meeting. A person who feels under attack may move back in a chair or lean away from the presumed antagonist, even while expressing verbal agreement. All of this is done quite unconsciously, but it sends a message that will be picked up by those who are on the alert.

> A **mixed message** results when words communicate one message while actions, body language, or appearance communicate something else.

Physical Distractions

Any number of physical distractions can interfere with communication effectiveness. Some of these distractions, such as telephone interruptions, drop-in visitors, and lack of privacy, are evident in the following conversation between an employee, George, and his manager.[74]

> *Okay, George, let's hear your problem [phone rings, boss picks it up, promises to deliver a report "just as soon as I can get it done"]. Uh, now, where were we? Oh, you're having a problem with your technician. She's . . . [manager's assistant brings in some papers that need his immediate signature; assistant leaves] you say she's overstressed lately, wants to leave. I tell you what, George, why don't you [phone rings again, lunch partner drops by] uh, take a stab at handling it yourself? I've got to go now.*

Besides what may have been poor intentions in the first place, the manager in this example did not do a good job of communicating with George. This problem could easily be corrected; many communication distractions can be avoided or at least minimized through proper planning. If George has something important to say, the manager should set aside adequate time for the meeting. Additional interruptions such as telephone calls and drop-in visitors could easily be eliminated by good planning.

Status Effects

"Criticize my boss? I don't have the right to." "I'd get fired." "It's her company, not mine." As these comments suggest, the hierarchy of authority in organizations creates another potential barrier to effective communications. Consider the "corporate cover-up" once discovered at an electronics company. Product shipments were being predated and papers falsified as salespersons struggled to meet unrealistic sales targets set by the president. At least 20 persons in the organization cooperated in the deception and it was months before the president found out. What happened in this case was **filtering**—the intentional distortion of information to make it appear favourable to the recipient.

> **Filtering** is the intentional distortion of information to make it appear most favourable to the recipient.

Information filtering is often found in communications between lower and higher levels in organizations. Tom Peters, management author and consultant, has called information distortion "Management Enemy Number 1."[75] It most often involves someone "telling the boss what he or she wants to hear." Whether the reason behind this is a fear of retribution for bringing bad news, an unwillingness to identify personal mistakes, or just a general desire to please, the end result is the same. The higher-level person receiving filtered communications from below can end up making poor decisions because of a biased and inaccurate information base.

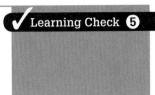

✓ Learning Check ⑤

BE SURE YOU CAN
• describe the communication process and identify its key components • differentiate between effective and efficient communication • explain the role of credibility in persuasive communication • list the common sources of noise that inhibit effective communication • explain how mixed messages and filtering interfere with communication

IMPROVING COMMUNICATION

A number of things can be done to reduce noise, overcome barriers, and improve the process of communication. They include active listening, constructive feedback, use of space, choosing channels, understanding electronic communication, interactive management, and cross-cultural sensitivity.

ACTIVE LISTENING

Managers must be very good at listening. When people "talk," they are trying to communicate something. That "something" may or may not be what they are saying. **Active listening** is the process of taking action to help someone say exactly what he or she really means.[76] It involves being sincere and trying to find out the full meaning of what is being said. It also involves being disciplined in controlling emotions and withholding premature evaluations or interpretations.

Different responses to the following two questions contrast how a "passive" listener and an "active" listener might act in real workplace conversations. Question 1: "Don't you think employees should be promoted on the basis of seniority?" Passive listener's response: "No, I don't!" Active listener's response: "It seems to you that they should, I take it?" Question 2: "What does the supervisor expect us to do about these out-of-date computers?" Passive listener's response: "Do the best you can, I guess." Active listener's response: "You're pretty frustrated with those machines, aren't you?"

These examples help show how active listening can facilitate rather than discourage communication in difficult circumstances. As you think further about active listening, keep these rules in mind.[77]

1. *Listen for message content:* Try to hear exactly what content is being conveyed in the message.

2. *Listen for feelings:* Try to identify how the source feels about the content in the message.

3. *Respond to feelings:* Let the source know that her or his feelings are being recognized.

4. *Note all cues:* Be sensitive to nonverbal and verbal messages; be alert for mixed messages.

5. *Paraphrase and restate:* State back to the source what you think you are hearing.

CONSTRUCTIVE FEEDBACK

The process of telling other people how you feel about something they did or said, or about the situation in general, is called **feedback**. Consider these examples of the types of feedback we might receive and deliver in our interactions with others.[78] *Evaluative feedback:* "You are unreliable and always late for everything." *Interpretive feedback:* "You're coming late to meetings; you might be spreading yourself too thin and have trouble meeting your obligations." *Descriptive feedback:* "You were 30 minutes late for today's meeting and missed a lot of the context for our discussion."

> **Active listening** helps the source of a message say what he or she really means.

> **Feedback** is the process of telling someone else how you feel about something that person did or said.

The art of giving feedback is an indispensable skill, particularly for managers, who must regularly give feedback to other people. This often takes the form of performance feedback given as evaluations and appraisals. When poorly done, feedback can be threatening to the recipient and cause resentment. When properly done, feedback—even performance criticism—can be listened to, accepted, and used to good advantage by the receiver.[79] When Lydia Whitfield, a marketing vice president at Avaya, asked one of her managers for feedback, she was surprised. He said: "You're angry a lot." Whitfield learned from the experience, saying: "What he and other employees saw as my anger, I saw as my passion."[80]

There are ways to help ensure that feedback is useful and constructive, rather than harmful. To begin, one must learn to recognize when the feedback will really benefit the receiver, and when it will mainly satisfy some personal need of the sender. A supervisor who berates a computer programmer for errors, for example, may actually be angry about personally failing to give clear instructions in the first place. A manager should also make sure that feedback is always understandable, acceptable, and plausible. Some guidelines for giving "constructive" feedback are:[81]

- Give feedback directly and with real feeling, based on trust between you and the receiver.

- Make sure that feedback is specific rather than general; use good, clear, and preferably recent examples to make your points.

- Give feedback at a time when the receiver seems most willing or able to accept it.

- Make sure the feedback is valid; limit it to things the receiver can be expected to do something about.

- Give feedback in small doses; never give more than the receiver can handle at any particular time.

REAL ETHICS

Difficult Employees

Conversation starts:

"We just got a new transfer into our office. Whew, he's a handful! Some days he comes in happy and pleasant; most days he's a real bear. Technically, his work is fine, but his behaviour is getting very disruptive. The others are starting to complain that his 'bad days' are becoming 'bad days' for everyone. And I'm starting to notice that on his bad days, the whole team's performance drops."

Points to ponder:

- Sometimes managers transfer their "problem workers" to other departments. Although this isn't fair to the receiving unit, it is an easy, although self-centred, solution for the sending unit.

- Different management styles apply best in different situations. This is point-of-contingency leadership thinking. "Calm and supportive" may fit one employee type or situation; "directive and firm" might be better for others.

- People's work and non-work lives don't always fall into neat and separate compartments. Things that happen at home can spill over to affect work behaviour, and vice versa.

- Managers are supposed to engage in "performance management" discussions with their direct reports. This is easy when things are all positive, but it's a lot harder to hold the conversation with an employee who has a performance problem.

Conversation continues:

"I've tried to be supportive and understanding with the guy, but I'm starting to lose patience. I've got to do something or the situation will get out of hand. As a manager, am I supposed to be a 'boss' or a 'therapist'? Or should I be both?"

YOU DECIDE

What are the best ways to deal with a disruptive employee like this? Is it time for constructive feedback or active listening, or are things past the point where those techniques would be useful? And let's not forget the other members of the team. How can they be best dealt with, or even brought into the "solution"?

SPACE DESIGN

An important but sometimes neglected part of communication involves **proxemics**, or the use of space.[82] The distance between people conveys varying intentions in terms of intimacy, openness, and status in interpersonal communications. And the physical layout of an office or room is a form of nonverbal communication. Check it out. Offices with chairs available for side-by-side seating convey different messages than those where the manager's chair sits behind the desk and those for visitors sit facing it in front.

Architects and consultants specializing in organizational ecology are helping executives build offices conducive to the intense communication needed in today's more horizontal organizational designs. When Sun Microsystems built its San Jose, California, facility, public spaces were designed to encourage communication among persons from different departments. Many meeting areas had no walls, and most walls were glass. As manager of planning and research, Ann Bamesberger, said: "We were creating a way to get these people to communicate with each other more."[83] At the Google headquarters, or "googleplex," telecommuters work in specially designed office "tents." These are made of acrylics to allow both the sense of private, personal space and transparency.[84] And at b&a advertising in Dublin, Ohio, "open space" supports the small ad agency's emphasis on creativity; after all, its web address is www.babrain.com. There are no offices or cubicles, and all office equipment is portable. Desks have wheels so that informal meetings can happen by people repositioning themselves for spontaneous collaboration. Even the formal meetings are held "standing up" in the company kitchen. Face-to-face communication is the rule at b&a to the point where internal e-mail among employees is banned.[85]

Proxemics involves the use of space in communication.

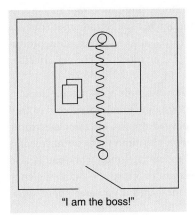

"I am the boss!"

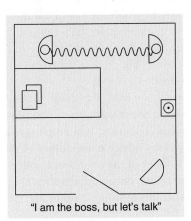

"I am the boss, but let's talk"

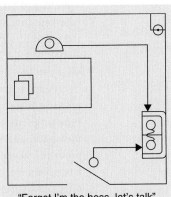

"Forget I'm the boss, let's talk"

CHANNEL SELECTION

Channel richness is the capacity of a communication channel to effectively carry information.

People communicate with one another using a variety of channels that vary in **channel richness**—the capacity to carry information in an effective manner.[86] Figure 11.10 shows that face-to-face communication is very high in richness, enabling two-way interaction and real-time feedback. Communications such as written reports, memos, and text messages are very low in richness because of impersonal, one-way interaction with limited opportunity for feedback. Managers need to understand the limits of the possible channels and choose wisely when using them for communication.

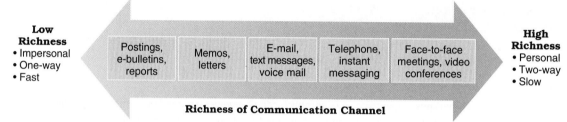

Low Richness
- Impersonal
- One-way
- Fast

| Postings, e-bulletins, reports | Memos, letters | E-mail, text messages, voice mail | Telephone, instant messaging | Face-to-face meetings, video conferences |

Richness of Communication Channel

High Richness
- Personal
- Two-way
- Slow

Figure 11.10 Channel richness and the use of communication media.

ELECTRONIC COMMUNICATION

When IBM surveyed employees to find out how they learned what was going on at the company, executives were not surprised that co-workers were perceived as credible and useful sources. But they were surprised that the firm's intranet ranked equally high. IBM's internal websites were ranked higher than news briefs, company memos, and information from managers.[87] The new age of communication is heavily electronic—one of e-mail, voice mail, text messages, instant messaging, teleconferencing, on-line discussions, video conferencing, virtual or computer-mediated meetings, intranets, and web portals. But the many implications for technology utilization must be understood.

Knowing how and when to use e-mail and text messaging is a growing communication concern. "Thnx for the IView! I Wud Luv to Work 4 U!! ;)" may be quite understandable "text-speak," but it isn't the follow-up message that most employers like to receive from job candidates.[88] When Tory Johnson, president of Women for Hire Inc., received a thank-you note by e-mail from an intern candidate, it included "hiya," "thanx," three exclamation points, and two emoticons. She says: "That e-mail just ruined it for me." The risk of everyday shorthand in e-mails and texting is that we become too casual in its use, forgetting that how a message is received is in large part determined by the receiver. Even though textspeak and emoticons are the norm in social networks, they may not fit the work culture. For example, staffing professionals at KPMG, which hires hundreds of new university grads and interns each year, consider their use "not professional."

Purpose and privacy are also important issues in the electronic workplace. Employers are concerned that too much work time gets spent handling personal e-mail and in web browsing; employees are concerned that employers are eavesdropping on their electronic messages. The best privacy advice comes down to this—don't assume that you have computer privacy at work; find out the employer's policy and follow it. E-mail workload is also a concern. Intel, for example, once initiated a training program to improve e-mail efficiency after discovering that employees faced up to 300 e-mail messages a day and spent some

2.5 hours per day dealing with them.[89] Tips on managing your e-mail are presented in Management Smarts 11.3.[90]

11.3 MANAGEMENT SMARTS
Tips on managing your e-mail

- Read items only once.

- Take action immediately to answer, move to folders, or delete.

- Purge folders regularly of useless messages.

- Send group mail and use "reply to all" only when really necessary.

- Get off distribution lists that are without value to your work.

- Send short messages in the subject line, avoiding a full-text message.

- Put large files on websites instead of sending them as attachments.

- Use instant messaging as an e-mail alternative.

- Don't forget the basic rule of e-mail privacy: there isn't any.

Another thing to remember is that technology offers the power of the **electronic grapevine**, speeding messages and information from person to person. The members of a Grade 6 class in Taylorsville, North Carolina (population 1,566), once sent out the e-mail message: "Hi! We are curious to see where in the world our e-mail will travel." They were surprised. More than a half-million replies flooded in, overwhelming not only the students but the school's computer system as well.[91] Electronic messages fly with equal speed and intensity around organizations. The results can be both functional—when the information is accurate and useful; and dysfunctional—when the information is false, distorted, or simply based on rumour. Managers need to be quick to correct misimpressions and inaccuracies; they should also be alert to using electronic grapevines to quickly move factual and relevant information to organizational members.

Electronic grapevines use electronic media to pass messages and information among members of social networks.

INTERACTIVE MANAGEMENT

Interactive management approaches use a variety of means to keep communication channels open between organizational levels. A popular choice is **management by wandering around** (MBWA)—dealing directly with subordinates or team members by regularly spending time walking around and talking with them. It is basically communicating face to face to find out what is going on. Patricia Gallup, CEO of PC Connection, made MBWA part of her style by spending as much time as possible out of her office and interacting with others.[92] Another practice designed to open channels and improve upward communications involves open office hours, whereby busy senior executives like Gallup set aside time in their calendars to welcome walk-in visits during certain hours. A rotating schedule of "shirtsleeve" meetings can also bring top managers into face-to-face contact with mixed employee groups throughout an organization. And, some organizations form groups such as elected employee advisory councils whose members meet with management on a regular schedule to share information and discuss issues.

In **management by wandering around (MBWA)**, managers spend time outside their offices to meet and talk with workers at all levels.

Interactive management also takes many electronic forms—including on-line discussion forums, chat rooms, electronic office hours, executive blogs, and video conferences. These options help managers overcome time and distance limitations that might otherwise make communication more difficult and less regular. At Royal Mail Group in the United Kingdom, for example, Chairman Allan Leighton's MBWA approach includes many personal visits to the more than 1,600 offices. But he also has an "Ask Allan" e-mail account to which everyone has access. He gets as many as 200 messages a day, each of which gets an immediate acknowledgement and is fully answered within seven days.[93]

When executives suspect that they are having communication problems, communication consultants can be hired to conduct interviews and surveys of employees on their behalf. Marc Brownstein, president of a public relations and advertising firm, for example, was surprised when managers complained in an anonymous survey that he was a poor listener who gave them insufficient feedback. They also felt inadequately informed about the firm's financial health. In other words, poor communication was hurting staff morale. With help from consultants, Brownstein started to hold more meetings, and he worked to share information and communicate regularly with the firm's employees.[94]

CROSS-CULTURAL COMMUNICATION

Communicating when the sender and receiver are from different cultures is a significant challenge, one that is well recognized by international travellers and executives. It's hard to communicate when you don't speak each other's languages. And messages even get lost in translation, as classic advertising miscues such as these demonstrate: A Pepsi ad in Taiwan intended to say "The Pepsi Generation" came out as "Pepsi will bring your ancestors back from the dead;" a KFC ad in China intended to convey "finger lickin' good" came out as "eat your fingers off."[95] Cultural differences are also common in nonverbal communication, everything from the use of gestures to interpersonal space. As illustrated in the box, the interpretation of nonverbal aspects of communication can be subtle and complicated.[96]

One of the enemies of effective cross-cultural communication is **ethnocentrism**, the tendency to consider one's culture superior to any and all others. It can hurt communication in at least three major ways. First, it may cause someone to not listen well to what others have to say. Second, it may cause someone to address or speak with others in ways that alienate them. And third, it may lead to the use of inappropriate stereotypes when dealing with persons from other cultures.[97]

Sample Cultural Variations in Nonverbal Communications

- *Eye movements (oculesics)*—Chinese and Japanese may only show anger in their eyes, a point often missed by westerners.

- *Touching (haptics)*—Asian cultures typically dislike touching behaviours; Latin cultures tend to use them in communicating.

- *Body motions (kinesics)*—gestures, shrugs, and blushes can mean different things; "thumbs up" means "A-OK" in North America, but is vulgar in the Middle East.

Ethnocentrism is the tendency to consider one's culture superior to any and all others.

✔ **Learning Check 6**

BE SURE YOU CAN
- define *active listening* and list active listening rules • illustrate the guidelines for constructive feedback • explain how and why space design influences communication • discuss the influence of technology utilization on communication • explain how MBWA can improve upward communication • explain the impact of ethnocentrism on cross-cultural communication

MANAGEMENT LEARNING REVIEW

STUDY QUESTIONS SUMMARY

1. What is the nature of leadership?

- Leadership is the process of inspiring others to work hard to accomplish important tasks.

- The ability to communicate a vision—a clear sense of the future—is essential for effective leadership.

- Power is the ability to get others to do what you want them to do through leadership.

- Sources of position power include rewards, coercion, and legitimacy or formal authority; sources of personal power include expertise and reference.

- Effective leaders empower others, allowing them to make job-related decisions on their own.

- Servant leadership is follower-centred, focusing on helping others fully utilize their talents.

FOR DISCUSSION When is a leader justified in using coercive power?

2. What are the important leadership traits and behaviours?

- Traits that seem to have a positive impact on leadership include drive, integrity, and self-confidence.

- Research on leader behaviours has focused on alternative leadership styles based on concerns for the task and concerns for people.

- One suggestion of leader behaviour researchers is that effective leaders are team-based and participative, showing both high task and people concerns.

FOR DISCUSSION Are any personal traits indispensable "must haves" for success in leadership?

3. What are the contingency theories of leadership?

- Contingency leadership approaches point out that no one leadership style always works best; the best style is one that properly matches the demands of each unique situation.

- Fiedler's contingency model matches leadership styles with situational differences in task structure, position power, and leader–member relations.

- The Hersey–Blanchard situational model recommends using task-oriented and people-oriented behaviours, depending on the "maturity" levels of followers.

- House's path–goal theory points out that leaders add value to situations by using supportive, directive, achievement-oriented, or participative styles.

- The Vroom–Jago leader-participation theory advises leaders to choose decision-making methods—individual, consultative, group—that best fit the problems to be solved.

FOR DISCUSSION What are the career development implications of Fiedler's contingency model of leadership?

4. What are current issues in leadership development?

- Transformational leaders use charisma and emotion to inspire others toward extraordinary efforts and performance excellence.

- Emotional intelligence—the ability to manage our relationships and ourselves effectively—is an important leadership capability.

KEY TERMS

active listening, 339
authentic leadership, 333
authority decision, 328
autocratic style, 322
channel richness, 342
charismatic leader, 329
coercive power, 318
communication, 334
communication
    channel, 336
consultative decision, 328
credible communication, 336
democratic style, 322
effective communication, 335
efficient communication, 335
electronic grapevine, 343
emotional intelligence, 330
empowerment, 320
ethnocentrism, 344
expert power, 318
feedback, 339
filtering, 338
gender similarities
    hypothesis, 331
group decision, 328
human relations style, 322
integrity, 333
interactive leadership, 331
laissez-faire style, 322
leadership, 317
leadership style, 321
legitimate power, 318
management by wandering
    around (MBWA), 343
mixed message, 338
moral leadership, 333
nonverbal communication, 337
persuasive communication, 335
power, 317
proxemics, 341
referent power, 318
reward power, 318
servant leadership, 320

- The interactive leadership style emphasizes communication, involvement, and interpersonal respect.
- Managers are expected to be moral leaders who communicate high ethical standards and show personal integrity in all dealings with other people.

FOR DISCUSSION Is transformational leadership always moral leadership?

5. What is the communication process?

- Communication is the interpersonal process of sending and receiving symbols with messages attached to them.
- Effective communication occurs when the sender and the receiver of a message both interpret it in the same way.
- Efficient communication occurs when the message is sent at low cost for the sender.
- Persuasive communication results in the recipient acting as intended by the sender; credibility earned by expertise and good relationships is essential to persuasive communication.
- Noise is anything that interferes with the effectiveness of communication; common examples are poor utilization of channels, poor written or oral expression, physical distractions, and status effects.

FOR DISCUSSION When is it okay to accept less effectiveness to gain efficiency in communication?

6. How can communication be improved?

- Active listening, through reflecting back and paraphrasing, can help overcome barriers and improve communication.
- Constructive feedback is specific, direct, well timed, and limited to things the receiver can change.
- Office architecture and space designs can be used to improve communication in organizations.
- Proper choice of channels and use of information technology can improve communication in organizations.
- Interactive management through MBWA, structured meetings, suggestion systems, and advisory councils can improve upward communication.
- The negative influences of ethnocentrism on communication can be offset by greater cross-cultural awareness and sensitivity.

FOR DISCUSSION What rules of active listening do most people break?

SELF-TEST

Multiple-Choice Questions

1. Someone with a clear sense of the future and the actions needed to get there is considered a _____ leader.

    (a) task-oriented   (b) people-oriented   (c) transactional   (d) visionary

2. Leader power = _____ power × _____ power.

    (a) reward, punishment   (b) reward, expert   (c) legitimate, position   (d) position, personal

3. A manager who says "because I am the boss, you must do what I ask" is relying on _____ power.

    (a) reward   (b) legitimate   (c) expert   (d) referent

4. The personal traits now considered important for managerial success include _____.

   (a) self-confidence   (b) gender   (c) age   (d) personality

5. According to the Blake and Mouton model of leader behaviours, the most successful leader is one who acts with _____.

   (a) high initiating structure   (b) high consideration   (c) high concern for task and high concern for people   (d) low job stress and high task goals

6. In Fiedler's contingency model, both highly favourable and highly unfavourable leadership situations are best dealt with by a _____ leader.

   (a) task-oriented   (b) laissez-faire   (c) participative   (d) relationship-oriented

7. Directive leadership and achievement-oriented leadership are among the options in House's _____ theory of leadership.

   (a) trait   (b) path–goal   (c) transformational   (d) life-cycle

8. Vision, charisma, integrity, and symbolism are all on the list of attributes typically associated with _____ leaders.

   (a) contingency   (b) informal   (c) transformational   (d) transactional

9. _____ leadership theory suggests that leadership success is achieved by correctly matching leadership style with situations.

   (a) Trait   (b) Fiedler's   (c) Transformational   (d) Blake and Mouton's

10. In the leader behaviour approaches to leadership, someone who does a very good job of planning work, setting standards, and monitoring results would be considered a(n) _____ leader.

    (a) task-oriented   (b) control-oriented   (c) achievement-oriented   (d) employee-centred

11. When a leader assumes that others will do as she asks because they want to positively identify with her, she is relying on _____ power to influence their behaviour.

    (a) expert   (b) reference   (c) legitimate   (d) reward

12. The interactive leadership style, sometimes associated with women, is characterized by _____.

    (a) inclusion and information sharing   (b) use of rewards and punishments   (c) command and control   (d) emphasis on position power

13. A leader whose actions indicate an attitude of "do as you want, and don't bother me" would be described as having a(n) _____ leadership style.

    (a) autocratic   (b) country club   (c) democratic   (d) laissez-faire

14. Constructive feedback is _____.

    (a) general rather than specific   (b) indirect rather than direct   (c) given in small doses   (d) given any time the sender is ready

15. Cross-cultural communication may run into difficulties because of _____, or the tendency to consider one's culture superior to others.

    (a) selective perception   (b) ethnocentrism   (c) mixed messages   (d) projection

Short-Response Questions

16. Why does a person need both position power and personal power to achieve long-term managerial effectiveness?

17. What is the major insight of the Vroom–Jago leader–participation model?

18. How does Peter Drucker's view of "good old-fashioned leadership" differ from the popular concept of transformational leadership?

19. Briefly describe how a manager would behave as an active listener when communicating with subordinates.

Application Question

20. When Marcel Girard took over as leader of a new product development team, he was both excited and apprehensive. "I wonder," he said to himself on the first day in his new assignment, "if I can meet the challenges of leadership." Later that day, Marcel shared this concern with you during a coffee break. Based on the insights of this chapter, how would you describe to him the implications for his personal leadership development of current thinking on transformational leadership and moral leadership?

MANAGEMENT SKILLS AND COMPETENCIES

SELF-ASSESSMENT

Back to Yourself: Integrity

Even though we can get overly enamoured with the notion of the "great" or "transformational" leader, it is just one among many leadership fundamentals that are enduring and important. This chapter covered a range of theories and models useful for leadership development. Each is best supported by a base of personal integrity that keeps the leader above the "integrity line." Servant leadership represents integrity, Drucker's notion of good old-fashioned leadership requires integrity, and Gardner's concept of moral leadership is centred on integrity. Why is it, then, that in the news and in everyday experiences we so often end up wondering where leadership integrity has gone?

Further Reflection: Least-Preferred Co-Worker Scale

Instructions

Think of all the different people with whom you have ever worked—in jobs, in social clubs, in student projects, or whatever. Next think of the one person with whom you could work least well—that is, the person with whom you had the most difficulty getting a job done. This is the one person—a peer, boss, or subordinate—with whom you would least want to work. Describe this person by circling numbers at the appropriate points on each of the following pairs of bipolar adjectives. Work rapidly. There are no right or wrong answers.

Pleasant	8 7 6 5 4 3 2 1	Unpleasant	Gloomy	1 2 3 4 5 6 7 8	Cheerful
Friendly	8 7 6 5 4 3 2 1	Unfriendly	Open	8 7 6 5 4 3 2 1	Guarded
Rejecting	1 2 3 4 5 6 7 8	Accepting	Backbiting	1 2 3 4 5 6 7 8	Loyal
Tense	1 2 3 4 5 6 7 8	Relaxed	Untrustworthy	1 2 3 4 5 6 7 8	Trustworthy
Distant	1 2 3 4 5 6 7 8	Close	Considerate	8 7 6 5 4 3 2 1	Inconsiderate
Cold	1 2 3 4 5 6 7 8	Warm	Nasty	1 2 3 4 5 6 7 8	Nice
Supportive	8 7 6 5 4 3 2 1	Hostile	Agreeable	8 7 6 5 4 3 2 1	Disagreeable
Boring	1 2 3 4 5 6 7 8	Interesting	Insincere	1 2 3 4 5 6 7 8	Sincere
Quarrelsome	1 2 3 4 5 6 7 8	Harmonious	Kind	8 7 6 5 4 3 2 1	Unkind

Scoring

Calculate your "least-preferred co-worker," or LPC, score by totalling all the numbers you circled; enter that score here [LPC = ___].

Interpretation

The LPC scale is used by Fred Fiedler to identify a person's dominant leadership style. He believes that this style is a relatively fixed part of our personality and is therefore difficult to change. Thus, he suggests the key to leadership success is finding (or creating) good "matches" between style and situation. If your score is 73 or above, Fiedler considers you a "relationship-motivated" leader; if your score is 64 or below, he considers you a "task-motivated" leader. If your score is between 65 and 72, Fiedler leaves it up to you to determine which leadership style is most like yours.

Source: Fred E. Fiedler and Martin M. Chemers, *Improving Leadership Effectiveness: The Leader Match Concept*, 2nd ed. (New York: Wiley, 1984). Used by permission.

TEAM EXERCISE

Leading by Participation

Preparation

Read each of the following vignettes. Write in the margin whether you think the leader should handle the situation with:

- I—an individual or authority decision
- C—a consultative decision
- G—a group decision

Vignette I

You are the leader of a large team laying an oil pipeline. It is now necessary to estimate your expected rate of progress in order to schedule material deliveries to the next field site. You know the nature of the terrain you will be travelling and have the historical data needed to calculate the mean and variance in the rate of speed over the type of terrain. Given these two variables, it is a simple matter to calculate the earliest and latest times at which materials and support facilities will be needed at the next site. It is important that your estimate be reasonably accurate; underestimates result in idle teams, and overestimates result in materials being tied up for a period of time before they are to be used. Progress has been good, and your team stands to receive substantial bonuses if the project is completed ahead of schedule.

Vignette II

You are supervising the work of 12 engineers. Their formal training and work experience are very similar, permitting you to use them interchangeably on projects. Yesterday, your manager informed you that a request had been received from an overseas affiliate for four engineers to go abroad on extended loan for a period of six to eight months. He argued and you agreed that for a number of reasons this request should be filled from your group. All your engineers are capable of handling this assignment, and from the standpoint of present and future projects, there is no particular reason why any one should be retained over any other. The problem is complicated by the fact that the overseas assignment is in what is generally regarded in the company as an undesirable location.

Vignette III

You are the head of a staff unit reporting to the vice president of finance. She has asked you to provide a report on the firm's current portfolio, including recommendations for changes in the selection criteria. Doubts have been raised about the efficiency of the existing system in the current market conditions, and there is dissatisfaction with rates of return. Your own specialty is the bond market, and it is clear to you that a detailed knowledge of the equity market, which you lack, would greatly enhance the value of the report. Four members of your staff are specialists in different segments of the equity market and possess a vast amount of knowledge about the intricacies of investment. However, they seldom agree on the best way to achieve anything when it comes to the stock market. Although conscientious as well as knowledgeable, they have major differences when it comes to investment philosophy and strategy. The report is due in six weeks. You have already begun to familiarize yourself with the firm's current portfolio and have been provided by management with a specific set of constraints that any portfolio must satisfy. Your immediate problem is to come up with some alternatives to the firm's present practices and select the most promising ones for detailed analysis in your report.

Instructions

Form groups as assigned by the instructor. Share your choices with other group members and try to achieve a consensus on how the leader should best handle each situation. Refer back to the Vroom–Jago "leader–participation" theory presented in this chapter. Analyze each vignette according to their ideas. Do you come to any different conclusions? If so, why? Nominate a spokesperson to share your results in general class discussion.

Source: Victor H. Vroom and Arthur G. Jago, *The New Leadership* (Englewood Cliffs, NJ: Prentice-Hall, 1988). Used by permission.

CASE 11

Maple Leaf Foods—A Test of Leadership

In August 2008, Maple Leaf Foods would face the biggest crisis in its over-100-year history. The Canadian Food Inspection Agency (CFIA) began investigating Maple Leaf's Toronto processing plant as the suspected source of listeria bacteria contamination that had caused numerous illnesses and even death. Dealing with one of the worst outbreaks in Canadian history, CEO Michael McCain faced the toughest challenge of his life: ensure public safety, regain public trust, and salvage Maple Leaf's reputation.

THE CANADIAN PRESS/ Toronto Star - Tara Walton

History of Maple Leaf

Although its origins can be traced back over 170 years to Grantham Mills, built in 1836 in St. Catharines, Ontario, Maple Leaf Foods was created in 1961 through the amalgamation of the Maple Leaf Milling Company Limited, Toronto Elevators Limited, and Purity Flour Mills Limited. Since being bought by the McCain family in the mid-90s, Maple Leaf Foods has transformed into Canada's leading food processor and exporter, with approximately 23,500 employees and sales of $5.2 billion in 2009.

Michael McCain

Born in Florenceville, New Brunswick, Michael McCain grew up with business in his blood. Son of Wallace McCain, one

of the brother team that founded Canada's largest french fry producers—McCain Foods—Michael worked in the company in progressively senior positions until succession issues between his father and uncle set off a legal battle that ultimately ousted Wallace's family from McCain Foods Ltd. After a worldwide search for another company for Michael to run, in 1995 McCain took over meat processing giant Maple Leaf Foods Inc.

The Crisis

Despite his reputation for being smart, tough, and brash, or perhaps because of it, McCain quickly turned antiquated Maple Leaf around, upgrading the company's approach to leadership and management, and expanding operations and product lines. McCain and Maple Leaf were ready to face any challenges.

In 2008, McCain was put to the test. The CFIA informed Maple Leaf that it had confirmed the presence of *Listeria monocytogenes* in three products from its Toronto meat plant. McCain suddenly faced the daunting task of leading a company that was making its customers seriously sick. Nothing had prepared him for a crisis of this magnitude.

The Buck Stops Here

When he became President, driven by his own vision and values of leadership, McCain created 21 core corporate values to provide a foundation for the daily working life of all Maple Leaf employees. McCain exemplified the first value, "Do What's

Right", when he immediately put himself at the centre of the crisis and took complete ownership over what was happening.

Looking grim-faced and worn-down, McCain made heartfelt apologies at press conferences and in television commercials, taking full responsibility for the listeria outbreak. "This is not about the lawyers and the accountants. It's about public health and our consumers and people, that's where we're spending our time and attention," he told reporters, adding: "The buck stops here."

McCain quickly closed the plant and called in the purifiers. Although only three products were contaminated, at a cost of more than $20 million, he immediately recalled more than 200 Maple Leaf products. He took out ads in national newspapers, television, and radio, openly showing his distress at the situation and communicating step by step how Maple Leaf was dealing with the situation and reassuring the public that he, and all Maple Leaf workers, would remain resolutely committed to producing safe products.

Under his leadership, Maple Leaf remained completely transparent in its rapid and sweeping reaction to the crisis. From the initial announcement, to the shutdown of the Toronto plant and voluntary recall of all products processed on the suspected production lines, Maple Leaf made its actions and its contrition well known. The media were invited to cover sanitation efforts, the corporate website featured full information on the recall and on the listeria bacterium, and a consumer hotline was set up to field customer concerns and questions.

By the end of the crisis, the outbreak had caused 22 deaths, while about 5,000 other Canadians became ill. It quickly settled a $27-million class action law suit to provide for the victims of the contamination and implemented more than 200 new standard operating procedures to control the risk of something like this happening again.

CEO Michael McCain openly accepted the blame for the deaths and spoke clearly about what happened and the difficulties of moving forward. His genuine compassion, personal pain, and expression of guilt served to rebuild the reputation of Maple Leaf Foods and cemented his reputation as a leader with character and compassion.

Epilogue

A review by the Canadian government found that the Maple Leaf plant actually went beyond policy requirements by having an additional extensive environmental testing program. When there was a presence of listeria, the production line was cleaned. What was missing was the big picture: staff treated these occurrences as isolated incidents. As the positive results were never looked at holistically, no one identified the recurring pattern. "Both Maple Leaf Foods and the Canadian Food Inspection Agency (CFIA) have since acknowledged that, if the company had conducted meaningful trend analyses of its test results and shared these findings with the CFIA inspectors, the source of the contamination could have been identified sooner and the sale of unsafe foods may have been prevented."

Discussion Questions

1. Drawing from the leadership models in the chapter and using examples from the case, describe which model(s) you feel fits Michael McCain's leadership at Maple Leaf Foods.

2. How did McCain's leadership approach to the situation help Maple Leaf Foods regain customer confidence?

3. What leadership traits do you think best describe McCain as a leader? Why?

4. FURTHER RESEARCH—Compare and contrast Maple Leaf's response to the listeria contamination with BP's response to the 2010 oil spill in the Gulf of Mexico or Toyota's recall of the Corolla and Rav4 in 2010. Which company handled the situation best and why? Which was the worst?

5. FURTHER RESEARCH—Put yourself in a CEO's shoes during a crisis. Based on what you've learned in the chapter, how would you handle the situation?

The Drive to Be Number One

Video Summary and Discussion

Frank Stronach can lay claim to quite a "rags to riches" story. The video recounts how his family came to Canada in 1954 from Austria with no cash and no connections whatsoever. From these humble beginnings, Stronach created Magna International, a world-renowned auto parts maker, which has grown exponentially over the years. It is heavily relied upon by automobile manufacturers around the world.

Frank Stronach's personality is such that he is never satisfied. He also has insatiable ambition and many have described him as a "big dreamer" because of his vision and foresight, focusing not on what is but on what could be. It is not surprising, therefore, that in Wayne Lilly's book about Stronach entitled *Magna Cum Laude*, the author documents that Stronach was a leading bidder to purchase Chrysler when it became apparent that the once-mighty automobile manufacturer was potentially for sale.

Tony Faria, a professor of marketing at the University of Windsor, considered Stronach's reasoning for being interested in buying Chrysler. He theorized that Stronach was concerned that, as Chrysler was in a downward spiral, a new owner other than him might spell trouble for Magna, so doing nothing was a risk from Stronach's point of view.

However, Stronach's true motivation for pursuing one of the Big Three automakers likely goes back to his strong belief in himself, that he can face any challenge and solve any problem. In Stronach's view, becoming the best automobile manufacturer in the world in addition to being the best auto parts maker in the world would be his ultimate achievement.

On May 9, 2007, Frank Stronach confirmed that his company and Onex, a Canadian investment company, made a bid for Chrysler, the struggling American unit of DaimlerChrysler. But Magna International lost. On May 14, DaimlerChrysler announced the sale of 80.1 percent of Chrysler Group to American private equity firm Cerberus Capital Management, L.P.; the company would now be called Chrysler LLC. The deal was finalized on August 3, 2007.

But the new ownership did not end Chrysler's troubles. On April 30, 2009, Chrysler LLC filed for bankruptcy reorganization and announced a plan for a partnership with Italian automaker Fiat. In June 2009, Chrysler LLC sold some assets and operations to the newly formed company Chrysler Group LLC. The U.S. government financed the deal with US$6.6 billion in financing, paid to the "Old Chrysler."

Being squeezed out of a Chrysler deal didn't stop Stronach. In January 2009, Magna International signed an alliance with the Ford Motor Company to build electric vehicles for the Detroit automaker. Magna Steyr, a Magna International subsidiary, now assembles cars and trucks for several different manufacturers in Europe.

Questions for Students

1. What type(s) of power does Frank Stronach appear to possess?

2. Can Stronach be described as a visionary leader? If so, why?

3. Which of the classic leadership styles does Stronach appear to reflect?

4. Comment on whether Stronach is more likely a transformational or transactional leader.

LEARNING FROM OTHERS

There are personalities behind those faces

The headline reads: "Spanx queen leads from the bottom line." The story begins: woman, unhappy with the way she looks in white pants, cuts feet off panty hose, puts them on, and attends party. The story continues: Sara Blakely founds Spanx, Inc.

"I knew this could open up so many women's wardrobes," Blakely says, "All women have that clothing in the back of the closet that they don't wear because they don't like the way it looks." With US$5,500 and the idea for "body shaping" underwear, she set out to start a business. But the pathway to profits wasn't always a straight line; someone else with the same idea might not have succeeded. Yet Blakely did; her unique blend of skills and personality made it all work.

Courtesy Spanx, Inc.; www.spanx.com

Blakely had experience with and a passion for direct selling, and she was diligent in researching patents and trademarks. When her first attempts to convince manufacturers to make product samples met with resistance, with one calling it "a crazy idea," she persisted until one agreed. She aspired to place Spanx in "high-end" department stores. When store after store turned her down, Blakely kept at it. Persistence paid off again when she persuaded a buyer at Neiman Marcus to give Spanx its first big chance.

Blakely travelled extensively and energetically, some might say exhaustively. "I'm the face of the brand," she says, "and we didn't have money to advertise. I had to be out. Sitting in the office wasn't helping." She sent Oprah Winfrey samples; after Oprah voted Spanx "one of her favorite things," sales really took off—now over 5.5 million pairs. About this time, Blakely realized additional skills were needed to handle the firm's fast-paced growth. She recognized her limits and "was eager to delegate my weaknesses." So she turned day-to-day operations over to CEO Laurie Ann Goldman, leaving herself free to pursue creativity, new products, and brand development. She has since started the Sara Blakely Foundation with the express purpose of "supporting and empowering women around the world."[1]

> **BENCHMARK** Creative, outgoing, passionate, driven, persistent, and ambitious—these adjectives and more describe Sara Blakely and her personality. They can also go a long way in explaining how and why she was successful with Spanx. Any manager needs to understand people, both others and themselves. When you look in the mirror, what and whom do you see?

Ambition

When it comes to understanding people at work, one of the differences that is often heard in conversations is ambition. You can think of it as the desire to achieve or to accomplish something. Ambition shows through in personality as a sense of competitiveness and a desire to be the best at something.[2] Hopefully, you have it too.

Scholar and consultant Ram Charan believes that ambition is one of the personal traits that separates "people who perform from those who don't."[3] He calls these traits "personal differentiators." You shouldn't have any trouble recognizing that ambition was a differentiator in the success of Sara Blakely and Spanx. Less ambitious people might have had the same idea, yet failed to pursue it as a business venture; or they might have tried to make a business out of it, but ended up quitting when the first difficult challenge appeared.

Charan says that ambition "propels individual leaders and their companies to strive to reach their potential," and that "leaders need a healthy dose of it to push themselves and others." Ambition in this sense is a good thing, something to be admired and to be developed both in others and in ourselves.

Personal Differentiators
• Ambition—to achieve
• Drive—to solve
• Tenacity—to persevere
• Confidence—to act
• Openness—to experience
• Realism—to accept
• Learning—to grow
• Integrity—to fulfill

But, as you might expect, there's a potential downside to ambition as well. And this raises a word of caution, something to help us keep ambition in perspective. Charan points out that people can get blinded by ambition, that they can end up sacrificing substance for superficiality and even sacrificing right for wrong. People who are overly ambitious may overstate their accomplishments to themselves and others; they may also try to do too much and end up accomplishing little of real value. Ambitious people who lack integrity can also get trapped by corruption and misbehaviour.[4]

❖ Get to Know Yourself Better

Take a look at the "personal differentiators" in the small box. How do you score? Can you say that your career ambition is backed by a sufficient set of personal traits and skills to make success a real possibility? Ask others to comment on the ambition you display as you go about your daily activities. Write a short synopsis of two situations—one in which you showed ambition and one in which you did not. Consider the implications for your career development.

CHAPTER 12 STUDY QUESTIONS

- How do perceptions influence individual behaviour?

- What should we know about personalities in the workplace?

- How do attitudes influence individual behaviour?

- What are the dynamics of emotions, moods, and stress?

VISUAL CHAPTER OVERVIEW

CHAPTER 12 INDIVIDUAL BEHAVIOUR

Study Question 1	Study Question 2	Study Question 3	Study Question 4
Perception	**Personality**	**Attitudes**	**Emotions, Moods, and Stress**
■ Psychological contracts	■ Big five personality dimensions	■ Attitudes and behaviour	■ Emotions
■ Perception and attribution	■ Myers-Briggs Type Indicator	■ Job satisfaction	■ Moods
■ Perceptual tendencies and distortions	■ Additional personality traits	■ Job involvement, organizational commitment, and employee engagement	■ Stress
■ Impression management		■ Organizational citizenship	
✓ Learning Check 1	✓ Learning Check 2	✓ Learning Check 3	✓ Learning Check 4

In his books *Leadership Is an Art* and *Leadership Jazz*, Max DePree, former chairperson of furniture maker Herman Miller, Inc., talks about a millwright who worked for his father. When the man died, DePree's father, wishing to express his sympathy to the family, went to their home. There he listened as the widow read some beautiful poems which, to his father's surprise, the millwright had written. DePree says that he and his father often wondered, "Was the man a poet who did millwright's work, or a millwright who wrote poetry?" He summarizes the lesson this way: "It is fundamental that leaders endorse a concept of persons."[5]

Contrast that story with this one. Some years ago, Karen Nussbaum founded an organization called 9 to 5, devoted to improving women's salaries and promotion opportunities in the workplace. She started it after leaving her job as a secretary at Harvard University. Describing what she calls "the incident that put her over the edge," Nussbaum says: "One day I was sitting at my desk at lunchtime, when most of the professors were out. A student walked into the office and looked me dead in the eye and said, 'Isn't anyone here?'"[6] Nussbaum founded 9 to 5 to support her commitment to "remake the system so that it does not produce these individuals."

Such things as perceptions, personalities, attitudes, emotions, and moods influence individual behaviour. When people work under conditions that fail to provide them with respect, as in Nussbaum's story, their behaviour sets often tend toward low performance, poor customer service, absenteeism, and even antisocial behaviour. But when people work in supportive settings and with caring bosses, more positive behaviours—higher performance, less withdrawal and dysfunction, and helpful citizenship—are common. This relates to DePree's story. He says: "We need to give each other space so that we may both give and receive such beautiful things as ideas, openness, dignity, joy, healing, and inclusion."[7]

> **Individual Behaviour Sets**
>
> - *Performance behaviours*—task performance, customer service, productivity
>
> - *Withdrawal behaviours*—absenteeism, turnover, job disengagement
>
> - *Citizenship behaviours*—helping, volunteering, job engagement
>
> - *Dysfunctional behaviours*—antisocial behaviour, intentional wrongdoing

PERCEPTION

Perception is the process through which people receive and interpret information from the environment. It is the way we form impressions about ourselves, other people, and daily life experiences. It is also the way we process information to make the decisions that ultimately guide our actions.[8] Perception acts as a screen or filter through which information passes before it has an impact on communication, decision-making, and behaviour. Because perceptions are influenced by such things as cultural background, values, and other personal and situational circumstances, people can and do perceive the same people, things, or situations differently. And importantly, people behave according to these perceptions.

Perception is the process through which people receive, organize, and interpret information from the environment.

PSYCHOLOGICAL CONTRACTS

One way in which perception influences individual behaviour is through the psychological contract, or set of expectations held by the individual about what will be given and received in the employment relationship.[9] Figure 12.1 shows that a healthy **psychological contract** offers a balance between individual contributions made to the organization and inducements received. Contributions are work activities, such as effort, time, creativity, and loyalty. Inducements are what the organization gives to the individual in exchange for these contributions. Typical inducements include pay, fringe benefits, training and opportunities for personal growth and advancement, and job security.

A **psychological contract** is the set of individual expectations about the employment relationship.

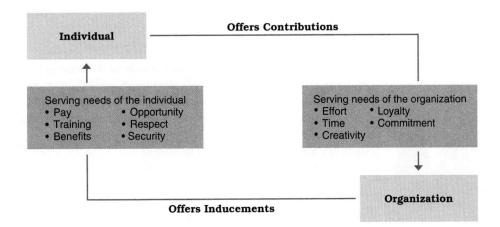

Figure 12.1 Components in the psychological contract.

The ideal situation is one in which the exchange of values in the psychological contract is perceived as fair. When the psychological contract is perceived as unfair, unbalanced, or broken, problems occur. Negative behaviours in the form of lower performance, withdrawal, and poor citizenship are likely when inducements are considered inadequate to compensate for contributions.

PERCEPTION AND ATTRIBUTION

Attribution is the process of explaining events.

Another way in which perception exerts its influence on individual behaviour is through **attribution**, the process of developing explanations for events. The fact that people can perceive the same things quite differently has an important influence on attributions and their ultimate influence on behaviour. In social psychology, attribution theory describes how people try to explain the behaviour of themselves and other people.[10] One of its significant applications is in the context of people's performance at work, particularly in how we try to explain bad behaviour and poor performance.

Fundamental **attribution error** overestimates internal factors and underestimates external factors as influences on someone's behaviour.

Fundamental **attribution error** occurs when observers perceive another person's performance problems as due more to internal failures of the individual than external factors relating to the environment. In the case of someone producing poor-quality work, for example, a team leader might blame a lack of job skills or laziness—an unwillingness to work hard enough. In response, the leader may try to resolve the problem through training, motivation, or even replacement. Because fundamental attribution error leads to the neglect of possible external explanations for the poor-quality work, such as unrealistic time pressures or substandard technology, opportunities to improve upon these factors through managerial action will probably be missed.

Self-serving bias explains personal successes by internal causes and personal failures by external causes.

Another confounding aspect of perception and attribution occurs as a **self-serving bias**. This happens when individuals blame their personal failures or problems on external causes and attribute their successes to internal causes. You might think of this the next time you "blame" your instructor for a poor course grade. Self-serving bias is harmful when it causes us to give insufficient attention to the need for personal change and development. While readily taking credit for successes, we are often too quick to focus on the environment to explain away our failures.

PERCEPTUAL TENDENCIES AND DISTORTIONS

In addition to the attribution errors just discussed, a variety of perceptual tendencies and distortions can also influence how people communicate and behave toward one another. They include the use of stereotypes, halo effects, selective perception, and projection.

Stereotypes

A **stereotype** occurs when attributes commonly associated with a group are assigned to an individual.

A **stereotype** occurs when someone is identified with a group or category, and then oversimplified attributes associated with the group or category are used to describe the individual. We all make use of stereotypes, and they are not always negative or ill-intended. But those based on such factors as

gender, age, and race can, and unfortunately do, bias perceptions. For example, the glass ceiling, mentioned in Chapter 1 as an invisible barrier to career advancement, still exists, and stereotypes may play a role in its perpetuation.

Legitimate questions can be asked about *racial and ethnic stereotypes* and about the slow progress of minority managers into North America's corporate mainstream.[11] A study of members of visible minorities in Canada by Catalyst in 2009 indicates that, while they make up 15 percent of Canada's labour force, they hold just 3 percent of senior-level management positions. A primary conclusion of Catalyst's research is that "A sizeable proportion of visible minority respondents with foreign educational credentials working for large employers felt their organizations did not recognize these credentials as being 'on par' with equivalent Canadian degrees, diplomas and certificates."[12]

While employment barriers caused by gender stereotypes are falling, even everyday behaviour may be misconstrued. Consider this example: "He's talking with co-workers" (interpretation: he's discussing a new deal); "She's talking with co-workers" (interpretation: she's gossiping).[13]

Ability stereotypes and *age stereotypes* also exist. A physically or mentally challenged candidate may be overlooked by a recruiter, even though her skills are perfect for the job. A talented older worker may not be promoted because a manager assumes older workers are cautious and tend to avoid risk. Interestingly, a Conference Board survey of workers aged 50 and older found that 72 percent felt they could take on additional responsibilities, and two-thirds were interested in further training and development.[14]

Halo Effects

A **halo effect** occurs when one attribute is used to develop an overall impression of a person or situation. When meeting someone new, for example, the halo effect may cause one trait, such as a pleasant smile, to result in a positive first impression; a particular hairstyle or manner of dressing may create a negative reaction. Such halo effects cause the same problem for managers as do stereotypes; that is, individual differences become obscured. This is especially significant in performance evaluations. One factor, such as a person's punctuality, may become the "halo" for a positive overall performance assessment, even though it may or may not be true.

A **halo effect** occurs when one attribute is used to develop an overall impression of a person or situation.

ISSUES AND SITUATIONS
What Millennials Want

There's a lot of buzz these days over the Millennial generation and what its members want from work and life. So-called Millennials were born between the mid-1980s and mid-1990s; many are now in university or are recent graduates. Perhaps you are one; perhaps you manage them. In any case, are you aware of how they are being described?

A CBS "60 Minutes" report depicts them as "raised by doting parents who told them they were special, played in little leagues with no winners or losers, or all winners . . . laden with trophies just for participating and they think your business-as-usual ethic is for the birds." An ad agency executive says this about Millennials as new hires: "You can't be harsh. You can't tell them you are disappointed in them. You can't really ask them to live and breathe the company. Because they're living and breathing themselves and that keeps them very busy." The lists of job preferences often attributed to Millennials include:

- meaningful work
- positive organizational culture
- personal attention
- sought-after opinions

- socially responsible employers
- learning opportunities
- supportive managers
- clear goals
- flexible schedules
- positive feedback
- lots of rewards
- tech-savvy setting

CRITICAL RESPONSE

What do you think? Are the descriptions, or stereotypes, accurate in terms of your observations and experiences? Are Millennials ready for workday realities in our current environment? Is corporate Canada ready for them?

Selective Perception

Selective perception is the tendency to single out for attention those aspects of a situation or person that reinforce one's existing beliefs, values, or needs.[15] Information that makes us uncomfortable is screened out; consistent information is allowed in. What this often means in organizations is that people from different departments or functions—such as marketing and manufacturing—see things from their own points of view and fail to recognize other points of view. One way to reduce this tendency and avoid the negative impact of selective perception is to be sure to gather and be open to additional opinions from other people.

Selective perception is the tendency to define problems from one's own point of view.

Projection

Projection is a perceptual error that involves the assignment of personal attributes to other individuals. A classic projection error is to assume that other persons share our needs, desires, and values. Suppose, for example, that you enjoy a lot of responsibility and challenge in your work. Suppose, too, that you are the newly appointed manager for people whose jobs you consider dull and routine. You might move quickly to expand their jobs so that they experience more responsibility and challenge. But this may not be a good decision. Instead of designing jobs to best fit their needs, you have designed their jobs to fit your needs; they may be quite satisfied doing jobs that, to you, seem routine. Projection errors can be controlled through self-awareness and a willingness to communicate and empathize with other persons—to try to see things through their eyes.

Projection is the assignment of personal attributes to other individuals.

IMPRESSION MANAGEMENT

Richard Branson, CEO of the Virgin Group, may be one of the richest and most famous executives in the world. One of his early business accomplishments was the successful start-up of Virgin Airlines, now a major competitor of British Airways (BA). In a memoir, the former head of BA, Lord King, said: "If Richard Branson had worn a shirt and tie instead of a goatee and jumper, I would not have underestimated him."[16] This shows how much our impressions can count—both positive and negative. Knowing this, scholars emphasize the importance of **impression management**, the systematic attempt to influence how others perceive us.[17]

Impression management is the systematic attempt to influence how others perceive us.

You might notice that impression management is a matter of routine in everyday life. We dress, talk, act, and surround ourselves with things that convey a desirable image to other persons. When well done, impression management can help us to advance in jobs and careers, form relationships with people we admire, and even create pathways to group memberships. And some basic tactics of impression management are worth remembering, as shown in Management Smarts 12.1.[18]

(AP Photo/Susan Montoya Bryan)

12.1 MANAGEMENT SMARTS
How to make a good impression at work and elsewhere

- Dress in ways that convey positive appeal in certain circumstances—for example, knowing when to "dress up" and when to "dress down."
- Use words to flatter other people in ways that generate positive feelings toward you.
- Make eye contact and smile when engaged in conversations to create a personal bond.
- Display a high level of energy suggestive of work commitment and initiative.

BE SURE YOU CAN
• define *perception* • explain the benefits of a healthy psychological contract • explain fundamental attribution error and self-serving bias • define *stereotype, halo effect, selective perception,* and *projection* and illustrate how each can adversely affect work behaviour • explain impression management

PERSONALITY

"Of course he's a bad fit for the job. With a personality like that, he'll never make it in this firm." "Put Laila on the project; her personality is perfect for the intensity that we expect from the team." These are examples of everyday conversations about people at work, with the key word being **personality**—the combination or overall profile of characteristics that makes one person unique from every other.

Personality is the profile of characteristics making a person unique from others.

BIG FIVE PERSONALITY DIMENSIONS

Although there are lots of personality traits, researchers have identified a short list of five that are especially significant in the work context. Known as the Big Five, these personality dimensions are described as follows.[19]

- **Extraversion**—The degree to which someone is outgoing, sociable, and assertive. An extravert is comfortable and confident in interpersonal relationships; an introvert is more withdrawn and reserved.

  Extraversion is being outgoing, sociable, and assertive.

- **Agreeableness**—The degree to which someone is good-natured, cooperative, and trusting. An agreeable person gets along well with others; a disagreeable person is a source of conflict and discomfort for others.

  Agreeableness is being good-natured, cooperative, and trusting.

- **Conscientiousness**—The degree to which someone is responsible, dependable, and careful. A conscientious person focuses on what can be accomplished and meets commitments; a person who lacks conscientiousness is careless, often trying to do too much and failing, or doing little.

  Conscientiousness is being responsible, dependable, and careful.

- **Emotional stability**—The degree to which someone is relaxed, secure, and unworried. A person who is emotionally stable is calm and confident; a person lacking in emotional stability is anxious, nervous, and tense.

  Emotional stability is being relaxed, secure, and unworried.

- **Openness to experience**—The degree to which someone is curious, open to new ideas, and imaginative. An open person is broad-minded, receptive to new things, and comfortable with change; a person who lacks openness is narrow-minded, has few interests, and is resistant to change.

  Openness to experience is being curious, receptive to new ideas, and imaginative.

A considerable body of literature links the personality dimensions of the Big Five model with work and career outcomes, as well as to life overall. For example, researchers find that conscientiousness is a good predictor of job performance for most occupations, and that extraversion is often associated with success in management and sales.[20] Indications are also that extraverts tend to be happier than introverts in their lives overall, that conscientious people tend to be less risky, and that those more open to experience are more creative.[21]

You can easily spot the Big Five personality traits in people with whom you work, study, and socialize. But don't forget, they also apply to you. Others form impressions of your personality, and respond to it, just as you do with theirs. Managers often use personality judgements when making job assignments, building teams, and otherwise engaging in the daily social give-and-take of work.

Even though the Big Five model adds some discipline to personality assessments, it should still be considered and used with caution. Doug Conant, CEO of Campbell Soup Co., for example, surprised an interviewer when she asked him this personality-based question: "You describe yourself as an introvert, which does not seem like the right personality for a CEO. How do you make that work for you?" He answered: "In my opinion, more than half of all CEOs are introverts. They're internally driven. The most effective CEOs are not the ones trying to please everybody. They're driving the agenda."[22]

MYERS-BRIGGS TYPE INDICATOR

Another popular approach to personality assessment is the Myers-Briggs Type Indicator, a sophisticated questionnaire that probes how people act or feel in various situations. Called the MBTI for short, it was developed by Katherine Briggs and her daughter Isabel Briggs-Myers from foundations set forth in the work of psychologist Carl Jung.[23]

Jung's model of personality included three main distinctions. First, extraversion and introversion were used to describe differences in ways people relate with others. Second, Jung described how people vary in the way they gather information: by sensation (emphasizing details, facts, and routine), or by intuition (looking for the "big picture" and being willing to deal with various possibilities). Third, he described how they vary in ways of evaluating information: by thinking (using reason and analysis) or by feeling (responding to the feelings and desires of others).

To Jung's model, Briggs and Briggs-Myers added a fourth distinction that describes how people vary in the ways they relate to the outside world: judging or perceiving. The resulting four dimensions of the Myers-Briggs Type Indicator can be briefly described as follows.[24]

- *Extraverted vs. introverted (E or I)*—whether a person tends toward being outgoing and sociable, or shy and quiet

- *Sensing vs. intuitive (S or N)*—whether a person tends to focus on details or on the big picture in dealing with problems

- *Thinking vs. feeling (T or F)*—whether a person tends to rely on logic or emotions in dealing with problems

- *Judging vs. perceiving (J or P)*—whether a person prefers order and control, or acts with flexibility and spontaneity

---

Sample Myers-Briggs Types

- ESTJ (extraverted, sensing, thinking, judging)—decisive, logical, and quick to dig in; common among managers.

- EITJ (extraverted, intuitive, thinking, judging)—analytical, strategic, quick to take charge; common for leaders.

- ISJF (introverted, sensing, judging, feeling)—conscientious, considerate, and helpful; common among team players.

- IITJ (introverted, intuitive, thinking, judging)—insightful, free-thinking, determined; common for visionaries.

There are 16 possible MBTI personality types that result from combinations of these four dimensions. A sample is shown in the small box. The neat and understandable nature of the classification scheme has made the MBTI very popular in management training and development, although it receives mixed reviews from researchers.[25] Employers and trainers tend to like it because, once a person is "typed" on the Myers-Briggs, for example as an ESTJ or ISJF, they can be trained to both understand their own style and learn how to better work with people having different styles.

ADDITIONAL PERSONALITY TRAITS

In addition to the Big Five dimensions and the Myers-Briggs Type Indicator, psychologists have long studied many other personality traits. As shown in Figure 12.2, those that have special relevance to people at work include locus of control, authoritarianism, Machiavellianism, self-monitoring, and Type A orientation.[26]

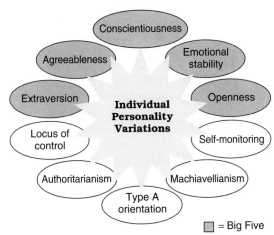

Figure 12.2 The Big Five and five more personality dimensions that influence human behaviour at work.

Locus of Control

Locus of control is the extent to which one believes that what happens is within one's control.

Scholars have a strong interest in **locus of control**, recognizing that some people believe they are in control of their destinies, whereas others believe that what happens to them is beyond their control.[27] "Internals" are more self-confident and accept responsibility for their own actions; "externals" are more prone to blame others and outside forces for what happens to them. Research suggests that internals tend to be more satisfied and less alienated from their work.

Authoritarianism

Authoritarianism is the degree to which a person tends to defer to authority.

Authoritarianism is the degree to which a person defers to authority and accepts status differences.[28] Someone with an authoritarian personality tends to act rigidly and be control-oriented when in a leadership capacity. This same person is likely to be subservient and follow the rules when in a follower capacity. The tendency of people with authoritarian personalities to obey orders can cause problems if they follow higher-level directives to the point of acting unethically—or even illegally.

Machiavellianism

Machiavellianism describes the extent to which someone is emotionally detached and manipulative.

In his sixteenth-century book, *The Prince*, Niccolo Machiavelli gained lasting fame for giving advice on how to use power to achieve personal goals.[29] **Machiavellianism** describes the extent to which someone is emotionally detached and manipulative in using power.[30] A person with a "high-Mach" personality is viewed as exploitative and unconcerned about others, often acting with the assumption that the end justifies the means. A person with a "low-Mach" personality, by contrast, would be deferential in allowing others to exert power over him or her.

Self-Monitoring

Self-monitoring is the degree to which someone is able to adjust behaviour in response to external factors.

Self-monitoring reflects the degree to which someone is able to adjust and modify behaviour in response to the immediate situation and to external factors.[31] A person high in self-monitoring tends to be a learner, comfortable with feedback, and both willing and able to change. Because high self-monitors are flexible in changing behaviour from one situation to the next, it may be hard to get a clear reading on where they stand. A person low in self-monitoring, by contrast, is predictable, tending to act consistently regardless of circumstances.

Type A Personality

A **Type A personality** is a person oriented toward extreme achievement, impatience, and perfectionism.

It's quite common to hear people being described as "Type A's." A **Type A personality** is high in achievement orientation, impatience, and perfectionism. One of the important tendencies of Type A persons is to bring stress on themselves, even in situations others may find relatively stress-free. You can spot Type A personality tendencies in yourself and others through the following patterns of behaviour.[32]

- Always moving, walking, and eating rapidly.
- Acting impatient, hurrying others, put off by waiting.
- Doing, or trying to do, several things at once.
- Feeling guilty when relaxing.
- Trying to schedule more in less time.
- Using nervous gestures such as tapping fingers or clenching fist.
- Hurrying or interrupting the speech of others.

ATTITUDES

"As an entrepreneur, you get up every day and you're always optimistic," says William Andrew, founder and president of Markham, Ontario's Elevate Sport Inc. and newly appointed president of Trimark Sportswear Group. "You always think tomorrow is going to be bigger and better and the sales are going to skyrocket." Having a positive attitude to combine with his entrepreneurial spirit has enabled Andrew to accomplish high levels of success in the sportswear industry, the height of which to date was landing the activewear licence for the Vancouver 2010 Olympic Games. Even though Elevate Sports is a relatively unknown company, Andrew was able to infuse his pitch to the Olympic committee with energy to illustrate the firm's ability to handle the exclusive account. His positive attitude has enabled Andrew to take his company and his employees to the next level.[33]

ATTITUDES AND BEHAVIOUR

An **attitude** is a predisposition to act in a certain way toward people and things in one's environment.[34] William Andrew was predisposed to take risks and embrace challenges. This positive attitude influenced his behaviour when dealing with the inevitable problems, choices, and opportunities of work and career.

An **attitude** is a predisposition to act in a certain way.

To fully understand attitudes, positive or negative, you must recognize their three components. First, the cognitive component reflects a belief or opinion. You might believe, for example, that your management course is very interesting. Second, the affective or emotional component of an attitude reflects a specific feeling. For example, you might feel very good about being a management major. Third, the behavioural component of an attitude reflects an intention to behave in a manner consistent with the belief and feeling. Using the same example again, you might say to yourself: "I am going to work hard and try to get an A in all my management courses."

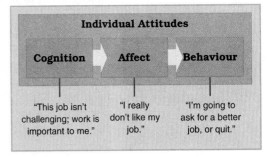

Importantly, the intentions reflected in an attitude may or may not be confirmed in actual behaviour. Despite having a positive attitude and all good intentions, for example, the demands of family, friends, or leisure activities might use up time you would otherwise devote to studying hard enough to get an A in your management courses. Thus, you might fail to live up to your own expectations.

The psychological concept of **cognitive dissonance** describes the discomfort felt when one's attitude and behaviour are inconsistent.[35] For most people, dissonance is very uncomfortable and results in changing the attitude to fit the behaviour ("Oh, I really don't like management that much anyway"), changing future behaviour to fit the attitude (dropping out of intramural sports to get extra study time), or rationalizing to force the two to be compatible ("Management is an okay major, but being a manager also requires the experience I'm gaining in my extracurricular activities").

Cognitive dissonance is discomfort felt when attitude and behaviour are inconsistent.

JOB SATISFACTION

Job satisfaction is the degree to which an individual feels positive or negative about a job.

People hold attitudes about many things at work—bosses, each other, tasks, policies, goals, and more. One of the most discussed work attitudes is **job satisfaction**, the degree to which an individual feels positive or negative about various aspects of work.[36]

If you watch or read the news, you'll regularly find reports on job satisfaction. You'll also find lots of job satisfaction studies in the academic literature. The results don't always agree, but they usually fall within a common range. When the *Wall Street Journal* asked a sample of American workers about job satisfaction, a majority were to some extent satisfied. The responses were 37 percent completely satisfied, 47 percent somewhat satisfied, 10 percent somewhat dissatisfied, 4 percent completely dissatisfied, and 2 percent not sure. Compare those numbers with Canadian workers. Statistics Canada found that the vast majority of Canadian workers are satisfied with their jobs, with only 1 in 12 workers offering that they were not satisfied.[37] Longitudinal research, though, finds that job satisfaction has been declining since 1995, that job satisfaction tends to be higher in small firms compared with larger ones, and that job satisfaction tends to run together with overall life satisfaction.[38]

Components of Job Satisfaction

Job satisfaction is something that we often express in conversations, it is something that managers often make assumptions about for people under their supervision, and it is an attitude that often gets measured through some form of questionnaire. These surveys usually probe beyond the more global questions of "job satisfaction—yes or no?" and make specific inquiries into just what aspects of a person's work are satisfying or not.

Two of the historically popular instruments that still underlie much of the job satisfaction research are the Minnesota Satisfaction Questionnaire (MSQ) and the Job Descriptive Index (JDI).[39] They measure various facets of job satisfaction that give rise to positive or negative attitudes. Presumably, managers can use the results of such surveys to take actions that increase levels of satisfaction. The following are among the job satisfaction facets most commonly measured.

- *Work itself*—does the job offer responsibility, interest, challenge?
- *Quality of supervision*—are task help and social support available?
- *Co-workers*—how much harmony, respect, friendliness exist?
- *Opportunities*—are there avenues for promotion, learning, growth?
- *Pay*—is compensation, actual and perceived, fair and substantial?
- *Work conditions*—do conditions offer comfort, safety, support?
- *Security*—are the job and employment secure?

Job Satisfaction and Its Outcomes

Back in Chapter 1, we identified two primary goals for an effective manager: to help others both achieve high performance and experience job satisfaction. Surely you can accept that job satisfaction is important on quality of work life grounds alone; that is, people deserve to have satisfying work experiences. But now we also have to ask: is job satisfaction important in other than a "feel good" sense?

RESEARCH BRIEF

Business students more satisfied with their lives overall perform at a higher level

Wondering if "a happy student is a high-performing student," Joseph C. Rode, Marne L. Arthaud-Day, Christine H. Mooney, Janet P. Near, Timothy T. Baldwin, William H. Bommer, and Robert S. Rubin hypothesized that satisfaction with both "life and student domains" would, along with cognitive abilities, have a positive influence on student academic performance. They created a predictive model from what they called "an integrative life" perspective, meaning that a person's performance is influenced by his or her overall state of life satisfaction.

A sample of 673 business students completed satisfaction and IQ questionnaires, and their academic performance was measured by self-reported GPAs and performance on a three-hour simulation exercise. The findings confirmed the expected relationships between students' leisure and family satisfaction and overall life satisfaction. Also confirmed were links between both life satisfaction and IQ scores, and self-reported GPA and simulation performance. Expected relationships between students' university and housing satisfaction and overall life satisfaction proved not to be significant.

Rode et al. point out that "it is time to more fully acknowledge that college students also live 'integrated lives' and are heavily influenced by the milieu that surrounds them."

Path analysis results

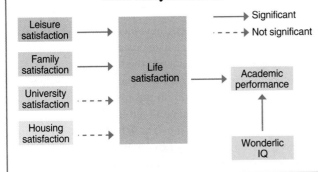

You be the researcher

Does your everyday experience as a student support these results or contradict them? Build a model that describes how you would predict student academic performance, not limiting yourself to directions used in this study. If it is true that students' academic performance is influenced by overall life satisfaction, what does this mean to an instructor or to a university administrator? How could any lessons of this study carry over to work situations?

Here is what we know. Job satisfaction influences absenteeism. Workers who are more satisfied with their jobs are absent less often than those who are dissatisfied. Job satisfaction also influences turnover. Satisfied workers are more likely to stay and dissatisfied workers are more likely to quit their jobs.[40] While intuitive, both of these findings are important. Absenteeism and turnover are costly in terms of the recruitment and training needed to replace workers, as well as in the productivity lost while new workers are learning how to perform up to expectations.[41]

When it comes to the job satisfaction and job performance relationship, however, things are a bit complicated.[42] There probably is a modest link between job satisfaction and performance.[43] But we shouldn't rush to conclude that making people happy on the job is a sure-fire way to improve their job performance. The reality is that some people will like their jobs and be very satisfied but still not perform very well. That's just part of the complexity of individual behaviour. A good reminder is a sign that once hung in a tavern near a Ford plant in Michigan: "I spend 40 hours a week here—am I supposed to work too?"

Arguments in the Job Satisfaction and Performance Relationship

"The happy worker is a productive worker."

Satisfaction ———→ Performance

"The productive worker is a happy worker."

Performance ———→ Satisfaction

"Performance followed by rewards creates satisfaction; satisfaction influences future performance."

Performance ——→ Rewards ——→ Satisfaction

There is also evidence that performance influences satisfaction; high-performing workers are likely to feel satisfied. Once again, however, a realistic interpretation is best. Some people may get their work done and meet performance expectations while still not feeling good about it. In fact, given that job satisfaction is a good predictor of absenteeism and turnover, managers might be well advised to worry about losing these highly productive but unhappy workers unless changes are made to increase their job satisfaction.

Finally, it is highly likely that job satisfaction and job performance influence one another. One of the more popular positions is that job performance followed by rewards that are valued and perceived as fair will create job satisfaction. This, in turn, will increase motivation to work hard to achieve high performance in the future. The pay-for-performance systems discussed in Chapter 10, merit pay and bonuses for example, are based on this management premise.

JOB INVOLVEMENT, ORGANIZATIONAL COMMITMENT, AND EMPLOYEE ENGAGEMENT

Job involvement is the extent to which an individual is dedicated to a job.

Two other attitudes that can influence individual behaviour at work are job involvement and organizational commitment. **Job involvement** is defined as the extent to which an individual is dedicated to a job. Someone with high job involvement psychologically identifies with her or his job, and, for example, would be expected to work beyond expectations to complete a special project.

Organizational commitment is the loyalty of an individual to the organization.

Organizational commitment is similar to job involvement, but reflects the degree of loyalty an individual feels toward the organization. Individuals with a high organizational commitment identify strongly with the organization and take pride in considering themselves a member. Also, researchers find that strong *emotional commitments* to the organization—based on values and interests of others—are as much as four times more powerful in positively influencing performance than are *rational commitments*—based primarily on pay and self-interests.[44]

Employee engagement is willingness to help others and do extra, and feeling positive about the organization.

Employee engagement is a positive work attitude that shows both high job involvement—being willing to help others and always try to do something extra to improve performance—and high organizational commitment—feeling and speaking positively about the organization. A survey of over 1,000 Canadian employees by the Gallup Organization and Carlson Marketing Group Canada suggests "engaged employees tend to generate high performance business outcomes as measured by increased sales, improved productivity, enhanced employee retention, and bottom line profitability." Things that counted most toward employee engagement in the Gallup research were believing one has the opportunity to do one's best every day, believing one's opinions count, believing fellow workers are committed to quality, and believing there is a direct connection between one's work and the company's mission.[45]

> ### Two Dimensions of Organizational Commitment
>
> 1. *Rational commitment*—feelings that the job serves one's financial, developmental, professional interests
>
> 2. *Emotional commitment*—feelings that what one does is important, valuable, and of real benefit to others

ORGANIZATIONAL CITIZENSHIP

Organizational citizenship is a willingness to "go beyond the call of duty" or "go the extra mile" in one's work.

Research also identifies a positive relationship between job satisfaction and **organizational citizenship**.[46] This is an attitude that basically represents a willingness to "go beyond the call of duty" or "go the extra mile" in one's work.[47] A person who is a good organizational citizen can be expected to do things that, although not required, help advance the performance of the organization. You might observe this as a service worker who goes to extraordinary lengths to take care of a customer, a co-worker who is always willing to take on extra tasks in a committee or task force, or a friend who is always working extra hours at no pay just to make sure things are done right for his employer.

GOING GLOBAL

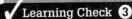

ENGAGING CANON SALESPEOPLE

There are few jobs in any workplace more focused on individual performance than the salesperson. For Canon, the global electronics firm, its goals for salespeople were, for years, based on volume. But without strong product differentiation, the company's competitive advantage started to disappear. Canon realized it needed to excel at customer service. Canon's European operations hired a consultant to create a customized sales academy where, for example, account managers honed their skills in relationship management and negotiation. The academy helped sales staff learn to think as consultants to Canon's retailers and taught them to work together with their customers to develop marketing plans to boost sales and in-store displays to increase customer satisfaction. The sales academy also linked employee development plans and performance appraisals together. Joris de Haas, the European HR Director for Canon's Consumer Business, offers that "The academy is at the heart of the business, creating effective development opportunities for our employees, together with the right motivation and spirit for world class customer partnership."

✓ **Learning Check ❸**

BE SURE YOU CAN

• define *attitude* and list the three components of an attitude • explain cognitive dissonance • define *job satisfaction* and list its components • explain the potential consequences of high and low job satisfaction • list and explain research findings on the satisfaction-performance relationship • define *job involvement, organizational commitment, employee engagement,* and *organizational citizenship*

EMOTIONS, MOODS, AND STRESS

A corporate scandal of recent note involved a spy operation conducted at Hewlett-Packard to uncover what were considered to be information leaks by members of its board of directors. When trying to explain to the media the situation and the resignation of Board Chair Patricia C. Dunn, CEO Mark V. Hurd called the actions "very disturbing" and said that "I could have and I should have" read an internal report that he had been given on the matter. The *Wall Street Journal* described him as speaking with "his voice shaking."[48]

Looking back on this situation, one might say that Hurd was emotional and angry that the incident was causing public humiliation for him and the company, that he was in a bad mood because of it, and that the whole episode was very stressful. In this one example, we have wrapped up three aspects of individual psychology that are of interest to management scholars—emotions, moods, and stress.

EMOTIONS

Emotional intelligence is an ability to understand emotions and manage relationships effectively.

Emotions are strong feelings directed toward someone or something.

Emotional intelligence was discussed in Chapter 1 as an important human relations skill for managers. Daniel Goleman defines "EI" as an ability to understand emotions in ourselves and in others and to use this understanding to manage relationships effectively.[49] But what is an emotion and how does it influence our behaviour—positively and negatively?

An **emotion** is a strong feeling directed toward someone or something. For example, you might feel positive emotion or elation when an instructor congratulates you on a fine class presentation; you might feel negative emotion or anger when an instructor criticizes you in front of the class. In both cases, the object of your emotion is the instructor, but in each the impact of the instructor's behaviour on your feelings is quite different. Your behaviour in response to the aroused emotions is likely to differ as well—perhaps breaking into a wide smile with the compliment, or making a nasty side comment in response to the criticism. Goleman's point, supported by research, is that we perform better in such situations when we are good at recognizing and dealing with emotions in ourselves and others. Such emotional intelligence allows us to avoid having our emotions "get the better of us."

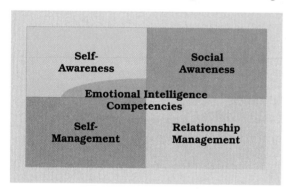

Goleman identifies four EI competencies that can and should be developed for managerial success.[50] *Self-awareness* is the ability to understand our own emotions and moods, and to understand their impact on our work and on others. *Social awareness* is the ability to empathize, to understand the emotions of others, and to use this understanding to better relate to them. *Self-management*, or self-regulation, is the ability to think before acting and to be in control of otherwise disruptive impulses. *Relationship management* is social insight, the ability to establish rapport with others in ways that build good relationships and influence their emotions in positive ways.

MOODS

Moods are generalized positive and negative feelings or states of mind.

Whereas emotions tend to be short-term and clearly targeted, **moods** are generalized positive and negative feelings or states of mind that may persist for some time.[51] Everyone seems to have occasional moods, and we each know the full range of possibilities they represent. How often do you wake up in the morning and feel excited, refreshed, and just happy, or feel low, depressed, and generally unhappy? What are the consequences of these different moods for your behaviour with friends and family, and at work or school?

Mood contagion is the spillover of one's positive or negative moods onto others.

Researchers are increasingly interested in the influence of emotions and moods on workplace behaviours, particularly **mood contagion**—the spillover effects of one's mood onto others. Findings indicate that positive and negative emotions of leaders can be "contagious," causing followers to display similarly positive and negative moods. When a leader's mood contagion is positive, followers display more positive moods, report being more attracted to their leaders, and rate the leaders more highly. Mood contagion can have inflationary and deflationary effects on the moods of followers, co-workers, and teammates, as well as family and friends.[52]

When it comes to CEO moods, a *BusinessWeek* article claims "harsh is out, caring is in"; in other words, it pays to be likable.[53] Some CEOs are even hiring executive coaches to help them manage emotions and moods to come across as more personable and friendly in relationships with others. If a CEO goes to a meeting in a good mood and gets described as "cheerful," "charming," "humorous," "friendly," and "candid," she or he may be viewed as on the upswing. But if the CEO is in a bad mood and comes away perceived as "prickly," "impatient," "remote," "tough," "acrimonious," or even "ruthless," she or he may be seen as on the downhill slope.

STRESS

Closely aligned with a person's emotions and moods is **stress**, a state of tension experienced by individuals facing extraordinary demands, constraints, or opportunities.[54] Any look toward the future and your work career would be incomplete without considering stress as a challenge that you are sure to encounter. In his book *The Future of Success*, for example, Robert Reich claims that "rewards are coming at the price of lives that are more frenzied, less secure, more economically divergent, more socially stratified."[55]

Stress is a state of tension experienced by individuals facing extraordinary demands, constraints, or opportunities.

Sources of Stress

Stressors are things that cause stress. Whether they originate directly from a change environment, other aspects of the work setting, or personal and non-work situations, stressors can influence our attitudes, emotions and moods, behaviour, job performance, and even health.[56] The Type A personality discussed earlier is an example of a personal stressor. Stressful life situations include such things as family events (e.g., the birth of a child), economics (e.g., a sudden loss of extra income), and personal affairs (e.g., a preoccupation with a bad relationship).

A **stressor** is anything that causes stress.

Work factors have an obvious potential to create job stress. In fact, Toronto-based consulting firm Watson Wyatt polled employees internationally and found that that the top reason for employees quitting their jobs was workplace stress.[57] We expe-

> **Work and Stress Facts**
>
> - 31 percent of university-educated people work 50+ hours per week.
> - 40 percent of adults get less than seven hours of sleep nightly during the workweek.
> - 60 percent of meals are rushed; 34 percent of lunches are eaten "on the run."
> - 33 percent of workers feel dead-ended in their jobs.
> - 47 percent of workers under 35 and 28 percent of those over 35 report having feelings of burnout.

rience stress from long hours of work, excessive e-mails, unrealistic work deadlines, difficult bosses or co-workers, unwelcome or unfamiliar work, and unrelenting change. It is also associated with excessively high or low task demands, role conflicts or ambiguities, poor interpersonal relations, or career progress that is too slow or too fast. Two common work-related stress syndromes are *set up to fail*—where the performance expectations are impossible or the support is totally inadequate to the task—and *mistaken identity*—where the individual ends up in a job that doesn't at all match his or her talents, or that he or she simply doesn't like.[58]

Constructive Stress

Stress actually has two faces—one constructive and one destructive.[59] Consider the analogy of a violin.[60] When a violin string is too loose, the sound produced by even the most skilled player is weak and raspy. When the string is too tight, however, the sound gets shrill and the string might even snap. But when the tension on the string is just right, neither too loose nor too tight, a beautiful sound is created. With just enough stress, in other words, performance is optimized.

Constructive stress acts in a positive way to increase effort, stimulate creativity, and encourage diligence in one's work.

Constructive stress, sometimes called *eustress*, acts in a positive way for the individual or the organization. It is personally energizing and performance-enhancing.[61] Constructive stress is sufficient to encourage increased effort, stimulate creativity, and enhance diligence in one's work, while still not over-whelming the individual and causing negative outcomes. Individuals with a Type A personality, for example, are likely to work long hours and to be less satisfied with poor performance. For them, challenging task demands imposed by

a supervisor may elicit higher levels of task accomplishment. Even non-work stressors such as new family responsibilities may cause them to work harder in anticipation of greater financial rewards.

Destructive Stress

Destructive stress impairs the performance of an individual.

Just like tuning the violin string, however, achieving the right balance of stress for each person and situation is difficult. **Destructive stress**, or *distress*, is dysfunctional. It occurs when intense or long-term stress overloads and breaks down a person's physical and mental systems, as shown in Figure 12.3.

When in Vancouver, Les Hammond, a 51-year-old chartered accountant, investment banker, and entrepreneur, works about 75 hours a week. But his four international mining and technology companies take him abroad often. When overseas, Hammond says, he works around 100 hours per week—a pace that he has maintained for over 10 years. Hammond calls it "running flat out," and admits his life lacks balance. "Business is extremely competitive, and you've got to be prepared to be at it 24 hours a day," he says. "I'm not saying it's right. I'm not saying it's healthy. I'm saying that's just the way it is." The way it is also predisposes executives like Hammond to health risks. Authors Darren Larose and Bernadette Schell indicate that not only is the present-day job of corporate officers stressful, it is also mentally and physically debilitating, with 88 percent of executives surveyed indicating elevated levels of stress.[62]

Job burnout is physical and mental exhaustion from work stress.

Destructive stress can lead to **job burnout**—a form of physical and mental exhaustion that can be personally incapacitating. Productivity suffers when people with burnout react through turnover, absenteeism, errors, accidents, dissatisfaction, and reduced performance. Another potential by-product of destructive stress is **workplace rage**—aggressive behaviour toward co-workers and the work setting in general. Lost tempers are common examples; the unfortunate extremes are tragedies that result in physical harm to others.[63]

Workplace rage is aggressive behaviour toward co-workers or the work setting.

Medical research is concerned that too much stress can reduce resistance to disease and increase the likelihood of physical and/or mental illness. It may contribute to health problems such as hypertension, ulcers, substance abuse, overeating, depression, and muscle aches, among others.[64] And excessive work stress can have spillover effects into one's personal life. A study of dual-career couples found that one partner's work experiences can have psychological consequences for the other; as one partner's work stress increases, the other is likely to experience stress, too.[65]

The bottom line is that any stress experienced at work is contagious; it can affect one's spouse, family, and friends. The wife of a company controller, for example, went through a time when her husband was stressed by a boss who was overly critical. "He was angry, really angry when he came home," she says. His mood affected her and their young child, and created what she called "one of the worst times in our seven-year marriage."[66]

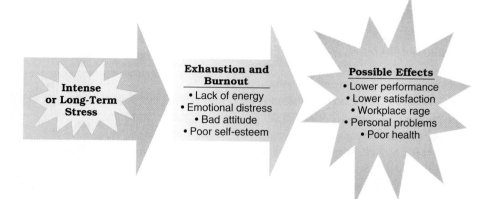

Figure 12.3 Potential negative consequences of a destructive job stress–burnout cycle.

Stress Management

The best stress management strategy is to prevent it from reaching excessive levels in the first place. A top priority is **personal wellness**, a term used to describe the pursuit of one's physical and mental potential through a personal health-promotion program. This form of preventive stress management recognizes the individual's responsibility to enhance his or her personal health through a disciplined approach to such things as smoking, alcohol use, diet, exercise, and physical fitness.

Actions can also be taken to cope with and, hopefully, minimize the impact of personal and non-work stressors. Family difficulties, for example, may be relieved by a change in work schedule, or the anxiety they cause may be reduced by an understanding supervisor. Also, people sometimes need help in combating the tendency toward "working too much." Reminders from bosses, co-workers, and friends not to forgo vacations or not to work excessive overtime can be very helpful. Work stress caused by role ambiguities, conflicts, and overloads can sometimes be dealt with by role clarification through a management-by-objectives approach. By facilitating the communication between supervisors and subordinates, MBO offers an opportunity both to spot stressors and to take action to reduce or eliminate them. Job redesign can also be helpful when there is a poor fit between individual abilities and job demands.

Personal wellness is the pursuit of one's full potential through a personal health-promotion program.

 Canadian Company in the News

THE "ROOTS" OF A HEALTHY WORK ENVIRONMENT

Today's managers are expected to help create work environments within which people have positive experiences while performing to high levels of expectation with minimum levels of stress. Here are Ed Cox's comments made on the anniversary of his 30 years of working for Roots Canada, a Toronto-based clothing company founded by Don Green and Michael Budman: "I love working at Roots because of the close-knit family and team atmosphere," said Cox. "Don and Michael really make me feel like part of the group. I appreciate their open-door policy. I can walk into their offices and get greeted like a friend rather than an employee. The Roots environment is so unique. That's why I enjoy working for Roots and look forward to each new workday." Established in 1973, Roots is one of Canada's leading brands and is known globally for producing quality leather goods and active athletic wear and, it would appear, motivated workers!

The Canadian Press Images/Francis Vachon

BE SURE YOU CAN

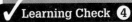 ✔ Learning Check ④

- define *emotion*, *mood*, and *stress* • explain how emotions and moods influence behaviour
- identify the common stressors found in work and in personal life • differentiate constructive and destructive stress • define *job burnout* and *workplace rage* • discuss personal wellness as a stress management strategy

MANAGEMENT LEARNING REVIEW

STUDY QUESTIONS SUMMARY

KEY TERMS

agreeableness, 361
attitude, 365
attribution, 358
attribution error, 358
authoritarianism, 364
cognitive dissonance, 365
conscientiousness, 361
constructive stress, 371
destructive stress, 372
emotion, 370
emotional intelligence, 370
emotional stability, 361
employee engagement, 368
extraversion, 361
halo effect, 359
impression management, 360
job burnout, 372
job involvement, 368
job satisfaction, 366
locus of control, 364
machiavellianism, 364
mood contagion, 370
moods, 370
openness to experience, 361
organizational citizenship, 368
organizational
    commitment, 368
perception, 357
personal wellness, 373
personality, 361
projection, 360
psychological contract, 357
selective perception, 360
self-monitoring, 364
self-serving bias, 358
stereotype, 358
stress, 371
stressor, 371
type A personality, 364
workplace rage, 372

1. How do perceptions influence individual behaviour?

- Perception acts as a filter through which people receive and process information from the environment.

- Because people perceive things differently, a situation may be interpreted and responded to differently by different people.

- A healthy psychological contract occurs with perceived balance between work contributions, such as time and effort, and inducements received, such as pay and respect.

- Fundamental attribution error occurs when we blame others for performance problems while excluding possible external causes; self-serving bias occurs when we take personal credit for successes and blame failures on external factors.

- Stereotypes, projection, halo effects, and selective perception can distort perceptions and result in errors as people relate with one another.

FOR DISCUSSION Are there times when self-serving bias is actually helpful?

2. What should we know about personalities in the workplace?

- Personality is a set of traits and characteristics that cause people to behave in unique ways.

- The personality factors in the Big Five model are extraversion, agreeableness, conscientiousness, emotional stability, and openness to experience.

- The Myers-Briggs Type Indicator profiles personalities in the extraversion-introversion, sensing-intuitive, thinking-feeling, and judging-perceiving dimensions.

- Additional personality dimensions of work significance are locus of control, authoritarianism, Machiavellianism, problem-solving style, behavioural self-monitoring, and Type A orientation.

FOR DISCUSSION What dimension would you add to make the "Big Five" the "Big Six" personality model?

3. How do attitudes influence individual behaviour?

- An attitude is a predisposition to respond in a certain way to people and things.

- Cognitive dissonance occurs when a person's attitude and behaviour are inconsistent.

- Job satisfaction is an important work attitude that reflects a person's evaluation of the job, co-workers, and other aspects of the work setting.

- Job satisfaction influences work attendance and turnover, and is related to other attitudes, such as job involvement and organizational commitment.

- Three possible explanations for the job satisfaction and performance relationship are: satisfaction causes performance, performance causes satisfaction, and rewards cause both performance and satisfaction.

FOR DISCUSSION What should a manager do with someone who has high job satisfaction but is a low performer?

4. **What are the dynamics of emotions, moods, and stress?**

- Emotions are strong feelings that are directed at someone or something; they influence behaviour, often with intensity and for short periods of time.

- Moods are generalized positive or negative states of mind that can be persistent influences on one's behaviour.

- Stress is a state of tension experienced by individuals facing extraordinary demands, constraints, or opportunities.

- Stress can be destructive or constructive; a moderate level of stress typically has a positive impact on performance.

- Stressors are found in a variety of personal, work, and non-work situations.

- Stress can be managed through both prevention and coping strategies, including a commitment to personal wellness.

FOR DISCUSSION Is a Type A personality required for managerial success?

SELF-TEST

Multiple-Choice Questions

1. In the psychological contract, security is considered a(n) _____, whereas loyalty is considered a(n) _____.

    (a) satisfier factor, hygiene factor   (b) intrinsic reward, extrinsic reward   (c) inducement, contribution   (d) attitude, personality trait

2. Self-serving bias is a form of attribution error that involves _____.

    (a) blaming yourself for problems caused by others   (b) blaming the environment for problems you caused   (c) poor emotional intelligence   (d) authoritarianism

3. If a new team leader changes job designs for persons on her work team mainly "because I would prefer to work the new way rather than the old," the chances are that she is committing a perceptual error known as _____.

    (a) halo effect   (b) stereotype   (c) selective perception   (d) projection

4. If a manager allows one characteristic of a person, say a pleasant personality, to bias performance ratings of that individual overall, the manager is falling prey to a perceptual distortion known as _____.

    (a) halo effect   (b) stereotype   (c) selective perception   (d) projection

5. Use of special dress, manners, gestures, and vocabulary words when meeting a prospective employer in a job interview are all examples of how people use _____ in daily life.

    (a) projection   (b) selective perception   (c) impression management   (d) self-serving bias

6. A person with a(n) _____ personality would most likely act unemotionally and manipulatively when trying to influence others to achieve personal goals.

    (a) extraverted   (b) sensation-thinking   (c) self-monitoring   (d) Machiavellian

7. When a person believes that he or she has little influence over things that happen in life, this indicates a(n) _____ personality.

   (a) low emotional stability   (b) external locus of control   (c) high self-monitoring   (d) intuitive-thinker

8. Among the Big Five personality traits, _____ indicates someone who is responsible, dependable, and careful with respect to tasks.

   (a) authoritarianism   (b) agreeableness   (c) conscientiousness   (d) emotional stability

9. The _____ component of an attitude is what indicates a person's belief about something, whereas the _____ component indicates a specific positive or negative feeling about it.

   (a) cognitive, affective   (b) emotional, affective   (c) cognitive, attributional   (d) behavioural, attributional

10. The term used to describe the discomfort someone feels when his or her behaviour is inconsistent with an expressed attitude is _____.

    (a) alienation   (b) cognitive dissonance   (c) job dissatisfaction   (d) person-job imbalance

11. Job satisfaction is known from research to be a good predictor of _____.

    (a) job performance   (b) job burnout   (c) conscientiousness   (d) absenteeism

12. A(n) _____ represents a rather intense but short-lived feeling about a person or a situation, whereas a(n) _____ describes a more generalized positive or negative state of mind.

    (a) stressor, role ambiguity   (b) external locus of control, internal locus of control   (c) self-serving bias, halo effect   (d) emotion, mood

13. Through _____, the stress people experience in their personal lives can create problems for them at work, and the stress experienced at work can create problems for their personal lives.

    (a) eustress   (b) self-monitoring   (c) spillover effects   (d) selective perception

14. As a stress management strategy, management by objectives would be especially useful in helping people deal with _____.

    (a) role conflicts   (b) workplace rage   (c) personal wellness   (d) resistance to change

15. At what level is stress most likely functional or positive in terms of impact on individual performance?

    (a) zero   (b) low   (c) moderate   (d) high

Short-Response Questions

16. What is a healthy psychological contract?

17. What is the difference between self-serving bias and fundamental attribution error?

18. Which three of the Big Five personality traits do you believe most affect how well people work together in organizations, and why?

19. Why is it important for a manager to understand the Type A personality?

Application Question

20. When Hassan Mohammed picked up a magazine article on how to manage health care workers, he was pleased to find some advice. Hassan was concerned about poor or mediocre performance on the part of several respiratory therapists in his clinic. The author of the article said that the "best way to improve performance is to make your workers happy." Hassan was glad to have read this and made a pledge to himself to start doing a much better job of making workers happy. But should Hassan follow this advice? What do we know about the relationship between job satisfaction and performance, and how can this apply to the performance problems at Hassan's clinic?

MANAGEMENT SKILLS AND COMPETENCIES

SELF-ASSESSMENT

Back to Yourself: Ambition

People are different; personal styles vary in the way we work and relate with others, and even in how we view ourselves. One of the differences you might observe when interacting with other people is in ambition, or the desire to succeed and reach for high goals. Ambition is one of those traits that can certainly have a big impact on individual behaviour. And as discussed in the chapter opener, it is evident in how we act and what we try to achieve at work, at home, and in leisure pursuits. The more we understand ambition in our lives, and the more we understand how personality traits like those in the Big Five model, the Myers-Briggs Type Indicator, and others influence our behaviour, the more successful we're likely to be in accomplishing our goals and helping others do the same.

Further Reflection: Internal/External Control

Instructions

Circle either (a) or (b) to indicate the item you most agree with in each of the following pairs of statements.

1. (a) Promotions are earned through hard work and persistence.
   (b) Making a lot of money is largely a matter of breaks.

2. (a) Many times, the reactions of teachers seem haphazard to me.
   (b) In my experience there is usually a direct connection between how hard I study and grades I get.

3. (a) The number of divorces indicates that more and more people are not trying to make their marriages work.
   (b) Marriage is largely a gamble.

4. (a) It is silly to think that one can really change another person's basic attitudes.
   (b) When I am right, I can convince others.

5. (a) Getting promoted is really a matter of being a little luckier than the next guy.
   (b) In our society, an individual's future earning power depends upon his or her ability.

6. (a) If one knows how to deal with people, they are really quite easily led.
   (b) I have little influence over the way other people behave.

7. (a) In my case, the grades I make are the result of my own efforts; luck has little or nothing to do with it.
   (b) Sometimes I feel that I have little to do with the grades I get.

8.   (a) People like me can change the course of world affairs if we make ourselves heard.
     (b) It is only wishful thinking to believe that one can really influence what happens in society at large.

9.   (a) Much of what happens to me is probably a matter of chance.
     (b) I am the master of my fate.

10. (a) Getting along with people is a skill that must be practised.
     (b) It is almost impossible to figure out how to please some people.

Scoring

Give yourself 1 point for 1a, 2b, 3a, 4b, 5b, 6a, 7a, 8a, 9b, 10a.

- 8–10 = high *internal* locus of control

- 6–7 = moderate *internal* locus of control

- 5 = mixed locus of control

- 3–4 = moderate *external* locus of control

Interpretation

This instrument offers an impression of your tendency toward an internal locus of control or an external locus of control. Persons with a high internal locus of control tend to believe they have control over their own destinies. They may appreciate opportunities for greater self-control in the workplace. Persons with a high external locus of control tend to believe that what happens to them is largely in the hands of external people or forces. They may be less comfortable with self-control and more responsive to external controls at work.

Source: Instrument from Julian P. Rotter, "External Control and Internal Control," *Psychology Today* (June 1971), p. 42.

TEAM EXERCISE

Job Satisfaction Preferences

Preparation

Rank the following items for how important (1 = least important to 9 = most important) they are to your future job satisfaction.

My job will be satisfying when it . . .
____ is respected by other people.
____ encourages continued development of knowledge and skills.
____ provides job security.
____ provides a feeling of accomplishment.
____ provides the opportunity to earn a high income.
____ is intellectually stimulating.
____ rewards good performance with recognition.
____ provides comfortable working conditions.
____ permits advancement to high administrative responsibility.

Instructions

Form into groups as designated by your instructor. Within each group, the men should develop a consensus ranking of the items as they think the women ranked them. The reasons for the rankings should be shared and discussed so they are clear to everyone. The women in the group should not participate in this ranking task. They should listen to the discussion and be prepared to comment later in class discussions. A spokesperson for the men in the group should share the group's rankings with the class.

Optional Instructions

Form into groups consisting entirely of men or women. Each group should meet and decide which of the work values members of the opposite sex will rank first. Do this again for the work value ranked last. The reasons should be discussed, along with the reasons why each of the other values probably was not ranked first . . . or last. A spokesperson for each group should share group results with the rest of the class.

Source: Adapted from Roy J. Lewicki, Donald D. Bowen, Douglas T. Hall, and Francine S. Hall, "What Do You Value in Work?" *Experiences in Management and Organizational Behavior*, 3rd ed. (New York: Wiley, 1988), pp. 23–26. Used by permission.

CASE 12

Facebook: It's Not Just for Kids

Social networking websites are a dime a dozen these days, so how does Facebook stay at the top? By expanding its user base and working with developers and advertisers to create fresh content that keeps users at the site for hours on end. But can Facebook handle the challenges of international expansion and stereotypes about its leadership?

The Perception Counts

Mark Zuckerberg wants you to think differently about Facebook, and unlike most other young Silicon Valley CEOs, he's got experience in managing the kind of changes in perception he hopes to bring about. Just like in 2006, when he opened Facebook to users of all ages to convince advertisers—and developers—that social networking was more than kids' stuff, Zuckerberg hopes to persuade these same two groups that Facebook is firmly seated at the top, successfully expanding into global markets.

Although users of Facebook and its social networking rival MySpace might trade barbs over whose site has the best features or the widest selection of friends, there's no denying that Facebook has been a runaway success. It is the sixth-most trafficked site on the Web, according to Internet research company comScore; it is also the second-most popular social networking site, trailing only MySpace. Now, more than half of Facebook users are outside college or university.[1]

Applications for Every User

Regardless of age or profession, what keeps users coming back to Facebook? The site relies on a host of internally and externally developed applications that integrate directly into the site to keep visitors' eyes glued to Facebook for hours on end. Games and a bevy of trivia contests give users entertaining ways to engage repeatedly with each other.

AP Photo/Paul Sakuma

Commercial marketers are paying more attention than ever to Facebook's propensity for attracting page views, hoping to benefit from the halo effect surrounding such a successful brand. Companies are integrating their logos and brands into Facebook's built-in culture of sharing and sending. Users can send one another a Walmart-branded ghost, a Ben & Jerry's ice cream cone, or even a virtual fedora to celebrate the opening of the new *Indiana Jones* movie. According to Derek Dabrowski, Sunkist brand manager at Dr. Pepper Snapple Group, it's a success. In a promotion to give away 250,000 virtual Sunkist sodas: "We got 130 million brand impressions through that 22-hour time frame. A Super Bowl ad, if you compare it, would have generated somewhere between 6 to 7 million."

But the best potential for amassing page views and click-throughs lies in Facebook's ability to integrate applications. The site's photo viewing app, for example—the number-one photo sharing application on the Web—receives more than 14 million photos a day from users. Some 400,000 developers and entrepreneurs are involved in developing what the company is calling the Facebook Platform. More than 24,000 apps have been developed so far, and Facebook receives another 140 per day. More than 95 percent of its members have used at least one application built on the Facebook Platform, and advertisers are betting that they can improve that statistic.[2]

As much as advertisers need Facebook users' page views, Facebook needs those advertisers as loyal customers. Last year, Facebook generated less than one-third the revenues MySpace earned. Facebook ads can sell as inexpensively as 15 cents (U.S.) per 1,000 impressions—compared with an estimated US$13 for a similar buy at Yahoo! The pressure is on Facebook to continue to differentiate itself from other social networking sites, according to Jeff Ratner, a managing partner at WPP's MindShare Interaction. If not, "Facebook doesn't look that different," he said. "It just becomes another buy, and there are cheaper, more efficient ways to reach eyes."[3]

Changing Perceptions

On several occasions during his reign at Facebook, the youthful Zuckerberg has fought the common Silicon Valley stereotype of young CEOs who are brash and unripe to lead. His flat rejection of Yahoo!'s US$1 billion bid to buy Facebook was criticized by some as a lost opportunity, so he's working to create a professional impression for his company by hiring some experienced web personalities. Zuckerberg persuaded Sheryl Sandberg to leave Google, where she had developed cash cows Adwords and Adsense, to join Facebook as chief operating officer. Fourteen years older than her boss, Sandberg is charged with bringing a mature personality to the laid-back, collegiate work environment. To do this, she'll integrate performance reviews, refine the recruiting model, and develop a mature, sustainable advertising program that will support Facebook as it evolves. "I'm hopeful that we play a significant role in pushing the envelope [with] awareness building," Sandberg said. "How we get there, I don't think we know yet."[4]

Noting that visitors to the site tripled after Facebook unveiled its international presence, the company is continuing its international growth.[5] In three months, Facebook translated its content into 15 different languages, with more languages—including Chinese—to come soon. This is critical, because more than 60 percent of Facebook's 110 million users live outside the United States—double MySpace's percentage. Whereas MySpace specializes in locally themed subsites, Facebook has opted to simply translate its entire site for non-English speakers. "Through the translations we are seeing mass adoption in those markets," said Javier Olivan, an international manager at Facebook, adding that because the site is by its nature a tool for communication, Facebook doesn't need to spend much energy localizing it. "The translation approach allows us to support literally every language in the world," Olivan said.[6]

And to head off the efforts of other social networking sites, Facebook plans to make data available to users from outside of the site with its Facebook Connect program. Like MySpace's Data Availability (which was announced one day before Facebook's data-sharing concept), Facebook Connect will allow users to import their Facebook profiles into other websites and synchronize their friend lists. Changes will appear in real time as users modify their Facebook profiles, and users will have "total control" of website permissions to access Facebook data, according to the company.[7]

Everyone from advertisers to users to Zuckerberg himself is hoping that Facebook Connect fares better than Beacon, Facebook's attempt to let users see their friends' activities on other websites. Like Facebook Connect, Zuckerberg promoted Beacon as a tool that would enhance the user experience. But it failed when too many users rejected the loss of privacy they felt it represented. Some users even signed a MoveOn.org petition to end Beacon. "We made mistakes in communicating about it," Zuckerberg admitted. "We made mistakes in the user interface. We made mistakes in responding to it after it was out there."[8]

What Do You Think?

Despite all its successes, Facebook's management team knows that they have serious work ahead in order to change the perception of advertisers, developers, and even some users regarding their ability to lead Facebook successfully and profitably into the future of social networking. Will adding experienced management alter advertisers' stereotypes about youthful Silicon Valley CEOs? Can Facebook attract enough development muscle to leave Beacon behind and launch Facebook Connect as a success?

Discussion Questions

1. In what ways can attribution error cause problems for Mark Zuckerberg as he wrestles with decisions that will determine the future of Facebook?

2. What personality types does Facebook most appeal to, and how does that affect its potential to broaden and diversify its user base?

3. Sheryl Sandberg is certainly under a lot of pressure to succeed in her new position at Facebook. What are the most significant stressors that she most likely faces, and how would you advise her to best deal with them?

4. FURTHER RESEARCH—Find as much information as you can about Mark Zuckerberg. Use the Big Five model to analyze his personality. How has his personality influenced, positively and negatively, his behaviour as founder and CEO of Facebook?

13 Information and Decision-Making

Decisions turn individual potential into achievement

Decisions . . . hunches . . . achievements? It's all about being tuned into the environment and oneself. That's a message that seems well learned by many of the top rappers of the day. Who's on your list? Are you listening to Jay-Z, Lil' Wayne, Drake, K'naan, or a local just breaking into the music scene? Each of these artists could have been doing something else today. But they're not; they're making urban music, turning themes into music successes.

(AP Photo/Jason DeCrow)

Jay-Z started as a street busker, built his own label, Roc-A-Fella Records, made lots more music, won Grammy awards, and became CEO of Def Jam Records and a part owner of the New Jersey Nets basketball team. He also started a clothing line. Was it luck that moved him toward fame and fortune, or something else? Raw talent alone isn't enough to succeed on the music stage. At some point, as with all occupations, talent has to be partnered with self-confidence, ambition, intuition, and an ability to make the right decisions.

Set rap aside for a moment and take a trip down music's memory lane with Berry Gordy and Motown Records. The songs he produced from the "Motor City" of Detroit were stepping stones to the Rock and Roll Hall of Fame. Browse your music library to a Motown jukebox and select the 1960s. You'll hear classics from Lionel Ritchie, Mary Welles, and Martha and the Vandellas. Stop in the 1970s to hear Marvin Gaye, Gladys Knight and the Pips, Stevie Wonder, and Diana Ross. For more, grab the award-winning DVD *Standing in the Shadows of Motown* to learn about the Funk Brothers, Uriel Junes, Joe Hunter, and other musicians who shaped the Motown sound at Gordy's "Hitsville U.S.A."

Gordy is mentioned in one of Jay-Z's songs, and his Motown story is a portfolio of decisions. An entrepreneur by nature, Gordy started Motown Records in 1957. He had been writing songs with his friend Smokey Robinson while working on the assembly line at a Detroit Ford plant. The writing progressed, the job did not, and it was decision time. Gordy took the risk and started his own studio to showcase local talent with a distinctive sound. His twist was to make a total package of background musicians available to new artists from the Detroit neighbourhoods. Gordy specialized in developing a type of soul music that became "The Motown Sound." And the rest, as they say, is history![1]

BENCHMARK There are lots of decisions underlying the successes of Jay-Z and Berry Gordy, ones that relied on reading social trends and spotting market opportunities. The next time you turn on your MP3 player, think about what lies behind the music. Think about the decisions that drive success in any occupation; think about what it takes to turn ideas and potential into real achievements.

Self-Confidence

Would you agree that confidence tends to put a spring in your step and a smile on your face? It's a powerful force, something to be nurtured and protected. Managers must have the self-confidence not only to make decisions but to take the actions required to implement them. Too many of us find all sorts of excuses for doing everything but that. Lacking confidence, we have difficulty deciding how to decide, we have difficulty deciding, and we have difficulty acting.

Look at the situation in the box and choose how you would proceed—option A, or B, or C?

Jeff McCracken was the chief engineer for the Norfolk Southern Railroad in this situation. He acted deliberately, with confidence, and in a collaborative fashion. After extensive consultations with the team, he decided to salvage the old track. They worked 24 hours a day and finished in less than a week. McCracken called it a "colossal job" and said the satisfaction came from "working with people from all parts of the company and getting the job done without anyone getting hurt."[2]

> *Situation:* Hurricane Katrina has damaged a railroad bridge over Lake Pontchartrain in New Orleans. You are leading a repair team of 100 people. The bridge is important for relief efforts in the devastated city. Two alternatives are on the table: rebuild using new tracks or rebuild with old track salvaged from the lake.
>
> *Question:* How do you proceed?
> A. Decide to rebuild with new tracks; move quickly to implement.
> B. Decide to rebuild with old tracks; move quickly to implement.
> C. Consult with team; make decision; move quickly to implement.

Self-confidence doesn't have to mean acting alone, but it does mean being willing to act. Management consultant Ram Charan says that self-confidence involves a willingness to "listen to your own voice" and "speak your mind and act decisively." It is, he says, an "emotional fortitude" that counteracts "emotional insecurities."[3]

Carole Clay Winters developed self-confidence in college when she joined Students in Free Enterprise and ended up on a team that taught business concepts to elementary schoolchildren. Her team was chosen to participate in a national competition judged by corporate leaders. They didn't win, but Carole did. "I felt my life had changed," she said. "I realized that if I could answer all the questions being posed by some of the country's most powerful executives, I had what I needed to become an executive myself." Carole went on to become a manager in the Washington, D.C., office of the accounting firm KPMG.[4]

❖ Get to Know Yourself Better

Opportunities to improve and develop your self-confidence abound, especially through involvement in student organizations and community activities. Do a self-check; make a list of things you could do to gain experience and add more self-confidence to your skills portfolio between now and graduation.

CHAPTER 13 STUDY QUESTIONS

- What is the role of information in the management process?

- How do managers use information to make decisions?

- What are the steps in the decision-making process?

- What are current issues in managerial decision-making?

VISUAL CHAPTER OVERVIEW

CHAPTER 13 INFORMATION AND DECISION-MAKING

Study Question 1	Study Question 2	Study Question 3	Study Question 4
Information, Technology, and Management	**Information and Managerial Decisions**	**The Decision-Making Process**	**Issues in Managerial Decision-Making**
■ What is useful information?	■ Managers as information processors	■ Step 1—Identify and define the problem	■ Decision errors and traps
■ Information needs in organizations	■ Managers as problem solvers	■ Step 2—Generate and evaluate alternative courses of action	■ Creativity in decision-making
■ How information technology is changing organizations	■ Types of managerial decisions	■ Step 3—Decide on a preferred course of action	■ Individual versus group decision-making
	■ Decision conditions	■ Step 4—Implement the decision	■ Ethical decision-making
		■ Step 5—Evaluate results	
✓ Learning Check 1	✓ Learning Check 2	✓ Learning Check 3	✓ Learning Check 4

Hurricane Katrina, the Haiti earthquake, floods in Pakistan, or tsunamis in Thailand are all devastating. People lost homes, jobs, and lives, while countries and organizations lost reputations after failing in their response capabilities. And in retrospect, it is clear that a lot of things could have been done differently to better prepare for natural disasters such as these and to handle these killer storms' or disasters' aftermaths. But when things are happening at the time, it's not easy to do everything right. Information gets missed or lost or poorly used, mistakes get made, and well-intended decisions can go wrong or prove inadequate to the task.

Anyone who practises management knows that decision-making is part of the job. They also know that quality decisions require good information, that not all decisions are going to be easy ones, and that some decisions have to be made under tough conditions. Case studies, experiential exercises, class discussions, and exam questions in university courses are intended to help students gain familiarity with the nature of decision-making, the potential problems and pitfalls, and even the pressures of crisis situations. From that point on, however, only you can determine whether you will be able to step forward and make the best decisions even in difficult circumstances, or collapse under the pressure.

INFORMATION, TECHNOLOGY, AND MANAGEMENT

Our society is information-driven, digital, networked, and continuously evolving. Career success requires two "must have" competencies: *computer competency*—the ability to understand computers and to use them to their best advantage; and *information competency*—the ability to use technology to locate, retrieve, evaluate, organize, and analyze information for decision-making. How about you—are you ready?

WHAT IS USEFUL INFORMATION?

This sign should be on every manager's desk: Warning: data ≠ information. **Data** are raw facts and observations. **Information** is data made useful and meaningful for decision-making. In the music industry, for example, lots of data are available on the demographic profiles of customers, such as age groups buying various CDs and music downloads. Not everyone with access to these data, however, turns them into useful information for decision-making. But those who do may gain a competitive advantage. In the example, that might mean changing advertising because younger customers buy mostly through the Internet while older customers still shop a lot in retail stores.

The management process of planning, organizing, leading, and controlling is driven by information. Managers need good information, and they need it all the time. Information that is truly useful in management meets the test of these five criteria:

1. *Timely*—the information is available when needed; it meets deadlines for decision-making and action.

2. *High quality*—the information is accurate and it is reliable; it can be used with confidence.

3. *Complete*—the information is complete and sufficient for the task at hand; it is as current and up to date as possible.

4. *Relevant*—the information is appropriate for the task at hand; it is free from extraneous or irrelevant materials.

5. *Understandable*—the information is clear and easily understood by the user; it is free from unnecessary detail.

INFORMATION NEEDS IN ORGANIZATIONS

An important key to managerial performance in this new world is **information technology**, or IT, and the way it helps us acquire, store, process, analyze, and transmit information. And in our IT-rich world, where continual advances in technologies make more information about more things available to more people more quickly than ever before, the question is: how well do we take advantage of it?

Information and the External Environment

Driven largely by IT, information serves the variety of needs described in Figure 13.1. At the organization's boundaries, information in the external environment is accessed. Managers use this

Data are raw facts and observations.

Information is data made useful for decision-making.

Information technology helps us acquire, store, and process information.

intelligence information to deal with customers, competitors, and other stakeholders such as government agencies, creditors, suppliers, and stockholders. Peter Drucker once said that "a winning strategy will require information about events and conditions outside the institution," and that organizations must have "rigorous methods for gathering and analyzing outside information."[5] This concern for the environment is an important part of our conversation about strategic management in Chapter 7.

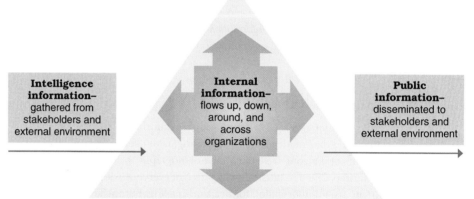

Intelligence information— gathered from stakeholders and external environment

Internal information— flows up, down, around, and across organizations

Public information— disseminated to stakeholders and external environment

Internal and external information flows are essential to problem solving and decision-making in organizations

Figure 13.1 Internal and external information needs in organizations.

Organizations also send vast amounts of *public information* to stakeholders and the external environment. This serves a variety of purposes, ranging from image building to product advertising to financial reporting. And the way organizations handle public information can be very strategic. When Boeing, for example, lost a contract to build a next-generation tanker for the U.S. Air Force, it published full-page newspaper ads. Why? Boeing's point was to inform the public why it believed its bid was unfairly denied and why its fierce competitors—Northrup Grumman and its European partner Airbus—should not have been awarded the contract. The ad was part of a massive public lobbying effort to gain support for having the decision overturned. The U.S. Auditor General eventually agreed with Boeing, and the Air Force reopened bidding; Boeing was given another chance.

(AP Photo/Laura Rauch, File)

Information and the Internal Environment

Silicon valley pioneer and Cisco Systems CEO John Chambers once pointed out that he always has the information he needs to be in control—be it information on earnings, expenses, profitability, gross margins, and more. He also says: "Because I have my data in that format, every one of my employees can make decisions that might have had to come all the way to the president . . . . Quicker decision making at lower levels will translate into higher profit margins . . . . Companies that don't do that will be noncompetitive."[6]

Within organizations, people need vast amounts of information to make decisions and solve problems in their daily work. They need information to act individually and in teams; they need information from their immediate work setting, from other parts of the organization, and from the organization's external environment. The ability of IT to gather and move information quickly within an organization can be a great asset to decision-making. It can help top levels stay informed, while freeing lower levels to make speedy decisions and take the actions they need to best perform their jobs.

HOW INFORMATION TECHNOLOGY IS CHANGING ORGANIZATIONS

In order to perform well, people in any work setting, large or small, must have available to them the right information at the right time, and in the right place. This is the function served by **information systems** that use the latest in information technology to collect, organize, and distribute data in such a way that they become meaningful as information. **Management information systems**, or MIS, meet the specific information needs of managers as they make a variety of day-to-day decisions. C. R. England Inc., a long-haul refrigerated trucking company, for example, uses a computerized MIS to monitor more than 500 aspects of organizational performance. The system tracks everything from billing accuracy to arrival times to driver satisfaction with company maintenance on their vehicles. Says CEO Dan England: "Our view was, if we could measure it, we could manage it."[7]

Organizations are not only using IT, they are being changed by its use. Information departments or centres are now mainstream features on organization charts. The number and variety of information career fields is rapidly expanding. And, as shown in Figure 13.2, IT is helping to break down barriers within organizations.[8] People working in different departments, levels, and physical locations now use IT to easily communicate and share information. The new IT-intensive organizations are "flatter" and operate with fewer levels than their more traditional organizational counterparts; computers replace people whose jobs were primarily devoted to moving information. This creates opportunities for faster decision-making, better use of timely information, and better coordination of decisions and actions.

Information systems use IT to collect, organize, and distribute data for use in decision-making.

Management information systems meet the information needs of managers in making daily decisions.

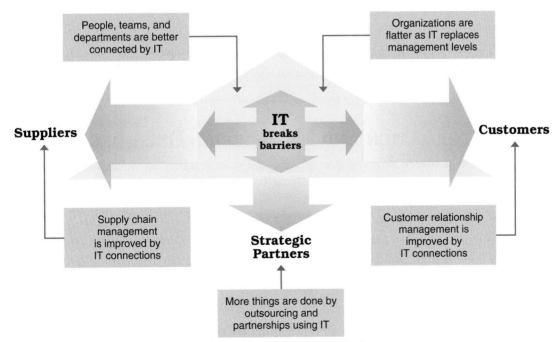

Figure 13.2 Information technology is breaking barriers and changing organizations.

CANADIAN MANAGERS

Heather Reisman: From Cyberspace to Your Bookcase

Simon Wilson©2003

Do you love books? Heather Reisman apparently does and she used this love in 1996 to launch Indigo Books, the first bookstore in Canada to sell music and gifts and have licensed cafés. The company's stated goal is "to create a true booklovers' haven—a place to discover books, music and more that might, in the rush of life, have gone undiscovered. A place that reflects the best of a small proprietor-run shop bundled with the selection of a true emporium." From this focused beginning and following an aggressive growth and acquisition strategy, Reisman has gone on to establish Chapters-Indigo, the largest bookstore chain in Canada. In growing and drawing upon information technology to make good decisions, Chapters-Indigo is able to deliver the right books to the right location, in the right quantities, at the right time. The on-line division, chapters.indigo.ca, is now one of Canada's top sites for books, music, videos, and DVDs. With the company's continuing growth reports, perhaps Reisman's love of books and decision tactics will result in long-term financial success as well.

IT is also breaking barriers between organizations and key elements in the external environment. It plays an important role in customer relationship management by quickly and accurately providing information regarding customer needs, preferences, and satisfactions. It helps in supply chain management to better manage and control costs everywhere from initiation of purchase, to logistics and transportation, to point of delivery and ultimate use.

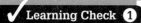

BE SURE YOU CAN

• differentiate data and information • list the criteria of useful information • describe the role of information systems in organizations • discuss how IT is breaking barriers within organizations and between organizations and their environments

INFORMATION AND MANAGERIAL DECISIONS

In a book entitled *Judgment: How Winning Leaders Make Great Calls*, scholars and consultants Noel M. Tichy and Warren G. Bennis discuss the importance of what leaders do before a decision is made, while making it, and when implementing it.[9] Information is the centre point in all three phases—information helps a leader sense the need for a decision, frame an approach to it, and communicate about it with others. As Bennis remarked in a *BusinessWeek* interview, "The source of many fatal judgments is the information pipeline. How do leaders get information that is relevant, has meaning, and is timely?"[10]

MANAGERS AS INFORMATION PROCESSORS

The manager's job in today's IT-enriched organizations can be depicted as a nerve centre of information flows, as shown in Figure 13.3. Managers in this sense are information processors—continually gathering information, giving it, and receiving it. All of the managerial roles identified by Henry Mintzberg and discussed in Chapter 1—interpersonal, decisional, and informational—involve communication and information processing.[11] So, too, do all aspects of the management process—planning, organizing, leading, and controlling. And in this regard, IT offers many advantages.

- *Planning advantages of IT*—better and more timely access to useful information, involving more people in the planning process.
- *Organizing advantages of IT*—more ongoing and informed communication among all parts, improving coordination and integration.
- *Leading advantages of IT*—more frequent and better communication with staff and diverse stakeholders, keeping objectives clear.
- *Controlling advantages of IT*—more immediate measures of performance results, allowing real-time solutions to problems.

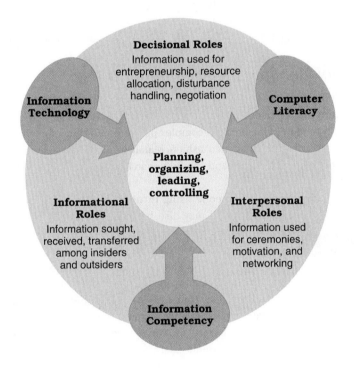

Figure 13.3 The manager as an information-processing nerve centre in the management process.

MANAGERS AS PROBLEM SOLVERS

Problem solving is the process of identifying a discrepancy between an actual and a desired state of affairs, and then taking action to resolve it. Success in problem solving depends on using information to make good **decisions**—choices among alternative possible courses of action. Managers, in this sense, make decisions while facing a continuous stream of daily problems. The most obvious problem situation is a *performance deficiency*. This is when actual performance is less than desired; for example, when turnover or absenteeism suddenly increases in the work unit, when a team member's daily output decreases, or when a customer complains about service delays. Another important problem situation emerges as a *performance opportunity*. This is when an actual situation either turns out better than anticipated or offers the potential to do so.

Problem solving involves identifying and taking action to resolve problems.

A **decision** is a choice among possible alternative courses of action.

Openness to Problem Solving

Managers often differ in their openness to problem solving; that is, in their basic willingness to accept the responsibilities that it entails. What you will see in observing the behaviour of others are approaches to problem solving that range from passive to reactive to proactive.

Some managers are *problem avoiders* who ignore information that would otherwise signal the presence of a performance opportunity or deficiency. They are passive in information gathering, not wanting to make decisions and deal with problems. Other managers are *problem solvers* who are willing to make decisions and try to solve problems, but only when forced to by the situation. They are reactive in gathering information and tend to respond to problems after they occur. They may deal reasonably well with performance deficiencies, but they may miss many performance opportunities.

There is quite a contrast between the latter two styles and *problem seekers*. These managers actively process information and constantly look for problems to solve. True problem seekers are proactive and forward-thinking. They anticipate performance deficiencies and opportunities, and they take appropriate action to gain the advantage. Success at problem seeking is one of the ways in which exceptional managers distinguish themselves from the merely good ones.

Systematic and Intuitive Thinking

Systematic thinking approaches problems in a rational and analytical fashion.

Intuitive thinking approaches problems in a flexible and spontaneous fashion.

Managers also differ in their use of "systematic" and "intuitive" thinking during decision-making. In **systematic thinking**, a person approaches problems in a rational, step-by-step, and analytical fashion. This type of thinking breaks a complex problem into smaller components and then addresses them in a logical and integrated fashion. Managers who are systematic can be expected to make a plan before taking action, and carefully search for information to facilitate problem solving in a step-by-step fashion.

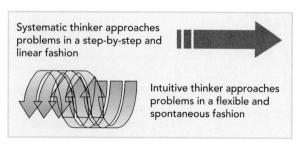

Systematic thinker approaches problems in a step-by-step and linear fashion

Intuitive thinker approaches problems in a flexible and spontaneous fashion

Someone using **intuitive thinking** is flexible and spontaneous, and may also be quite creative.[12] This type of thinking allows a person to respond imaginatively to a problem based on a quick and broad evaluation of the situation and the possible alternative courses of action. Managers who are intuitive can be expected to deal with many aspects of a problem at once, jump quickly from one issue to another, and consider "hunches" based on experience or spontaneous ideas. This approach tends to work best in situations where facts are limited and few decision precedents exist.[13]

Multidimensional Thinking

Multidimensional thinking is an ability to address many problems at once.

Strategic opportunism focuses on long-term objectives while being flexible in dealing with short-term problems.

Managers often deal with portfolios of problems that consist of multiple interrelated issues. This requires **multidimensional thinking**—the ability to view many problems at once, in relationship to one another and across both long and short time horizons.[14] The best managers are able to "map" multiple problems into a network that can be actively managed over time as priorities, events, and demands continuously change. They are able to make decisions and take actions in the short run that benefit longer-run objectives. And they avoid being sidetracked while sorting through a shifting mix of daily problems. Harvard scholar Daniel Isenberg calls this skill **strategic opportunism**—the ability to remain focused on long-term objectives while being flexible enough to resolve short-term problems and opportunities in a timely manner.[15]

Cognitive Styles

Cognitive styles describe the way people deal with information while making decisions. If you take the end-of-chapter self-assessment, it will examine your tendencies on the four master cognitive styles shown in the box.[16] These styles are based on a contrast of approaches toward information gathering (sensation vs. intuition) and information evaluation (feeling vs. thinking).

As the following descriptions suggest, people with different cognitive styles approach problems and decisions in quite different ways. It is important to understand our cognitive styles and tendencies, as well as those of others. In the social context of the workplace, the more diverse the cognitive styles of decision-makers, the more difficulty we might expect them to have while working together.

- *Sensation Thinkers* tend to emphasize the impersonal rather than the personal and take a realistic approach to problem solving. They like hard "facts," clear goals, certainty, and situations of high control.

- *Sensation Feelers* tend to emphasize both analysis and human relations. They tend to be realistic and prefer facts; they are open communicators and sensitive to feelings and values.

- *Intuitive Thinkers* are comfortable with abstraction and unstructured situations. They tend to be idealistic and prone toward intellectual and theoretical positions. They are logical and impersonal, but also avoid details.

- *Intuitive Feelers* prefer broad and global issues. They are insightful and tend to avoid details, being comfortable with intangibles; they value flexibility and human relationships.

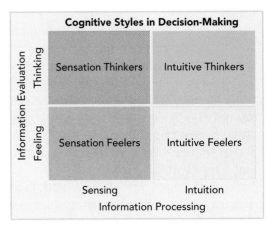

TYPES OF MANAGERIAL DECISIONS

Managers make many types of decisions while solving problems in their day-to-day work. Some decisions are quite structured and routine, while others are more unstructured and unique.

Programmed and Nonprogrammed Decisions

Managers sometimes face **structured problems**—ones that are familiar, straightforward, and clear with respect to information needs. Because these problems are routine and occur over and over again, they can be dealt with by **programmed decisions** that use solutions already available from past experience. Although not always predictable, routine problems can at least be anticipated. This means that decisions can be planned or programmed in advance to be implemented as needed. In human resource management, for example, problems are common whenever decisions are made on pay raises and promotions, vacation requests, committee assignments, and the like. Forward-looking managers use this understanding to decide in advance how to handle complaints and conflicts when and if they should arise.

Managers also deal with **unstructured problems** in the form of new or unusual situations full of ambiguities and information deficiencies. These problems require **nonprogrammed decisions** that craft novel solutions to meet the demands of the unique situation at hand. Most problems faced by higher-level managers are of this type, often involving the choice of strategies and objectives in situations of some uncertainty.

Structured problems are straightforward and clear with respect to information needs.

A **programmed decision** applies a solution from past experience to a routine problem.

Unstructured problems have ambiguities and information deficiencies.

A **nonprogrammed decision** applies a specific solution crafted for a unique problem.

ISSUES AND SITUATIONS
Lego's Wrong Turn

Surely you've played with Legos and maybe even given them as gifts. Many a childhood has been enriched by the multicoloured blocks and the many different forms, figures, and shapes into which they can be crafted at individual initiative. But how about the company that makes them—do its bits and pieces always fit together in ways that make good business sense?

It wasn't too long ago that the strategy at the firm seemed to shift. We saw advertisements for Legoland theme parks, and we could buy Lego-branded clothing. But the company saw huge losses. Chief Executive Jorgen Vig Knudstorp says: "It was the wrong strategy." It took seven years before the firm regained its focus with a "back-to-the-core" strategy based on plastic building blocks. Says Soren Torp Laursen, president of Lego Americas: "What I have learned the hard way is that Lego is not a lifestyle brand."

Look for Lego's new strategy in "Mindstorms," self-designed and programmable robots controlled by Lego brains—Spike, AlphaRex, and RobotArm, to name three. Knudstorp considers their software and electronic capabilities a doorway to the future. Look also for a new Lego video game

community and the multi-player on-line game, Lego Universe. Knudstorp is hoping a "right" turn in these directions will go a long way toward correcting the firm's "wrong" turns of the past.

CRITICAL RESPONSE

Why did this business run seven years with the wrong strategy? Are we talking about executive egos, with no one wanting to admit a mistake? Or are we looking at the sheer difficulty of disengaging from a strategy that was being implemented at very high costs? What decision-making checks and balances could help minimize the chances of such errors?

Crisis Decisions

A crisis is an unexpected problem that can lead to disaster if not resolved quickly and appropriately.

An extreme type of nonprogrammed decision occurs in times of **crisis**—an unexpected problem that can lead to disaster if not resolved quickly and appropriately. Terrorism in a post-9/11 world, outbreaks of workplace violence, IT failures and security breaches, ethical scandals, and environmental catastrophes are examples. Fred Sawyers knows the latter situation quite well. He was in New Orleans managing a Hilton hotel when Hurricane Katrina struck. But in what he describes as "the most harrowing week of his life," he excelled.[17] Using common sense, quick perception, and solid hard work, Sawyers moved from decision to decision—motivating staff, keeping the damaged hotel as safe as possible, and feeding and sheltering 4,500 persons from the storm. The *BusinessWeek* article carrying Sawyers's story led with the headline: "They don't teach this in B-School."[18] We might disagree a bit. Anyone who studies management knows that decision-making is part of the job. They also know that not all decisions are going to be easy ones; some will always have to be made under tough conditions.

The ability to handle crises may be the ultimate test of a manager's problem-solving capabilities.[19] Unfortunately, and unlike the Fred Sawyers case, research indicates that managers may react to crises by doing the wrong things: isolating themselves and trying to solve the problem alone or in a small "closed" group.[20] This denies them access to crucial information and assistance at the very time they are most needed. Management Smarts 13.1 offers, by contrast, guidelines on effective crisis management.

13.1 MANAGEMENT SMARTS
Six rules for crisis management

1. *Figure out what is going on*—Take the time to understand what's happening and the conditions under which the crisis must be resolved.

2. *Remember that speed matters*—Attack the crisis as quickly as possible, trying to catch it when it is as small as possible.

3. *Remember that slow counts, too*—Know when to back off and wait for a better opportunity to make progress with the crisis.

4. *Respect the danger of the unfamiliar*—Understand the danger of all-new territory where you and others have never been before.

5. *Value the sceptic*—Don't look for and get too comfortable with agreement; appreciate sceptics and let them help you see things differently.

6. *Be ready to "fight fire with fire"*—When things are going wrong and no one seems to care, you may have to start a crisis to get their attention.

It is getting more common for organizations to engage in formal **crisis management** programs. They are designed to help managers and others prepare for unexpected high-impact events that threaten an organization's health and well-being. Anticipation is one aspect of crisis management; preparation is another. People can be assigned ahead of time to crisis management teams, and crisis management plans can be developed to deal with various contingencies. Just as police departments and community groups plan ahead and train to best handle civil and natural disasters, so, too, can managers and work teams plan ahead and train to best deal with organizational crises.

Crisis management is preparation for the management of crises that threaten an organization's health and well-being.

DECISION CONDITIONS

There are three different decision conditions or environments: certainty, risk, and uncertainty. Although managers make decisions in each, the conditions of risk and uncertainty are common at higher management levels where problems are more complex and unstructured. Former Coca-Cola CEO Roberto Goizueta, for example, was known as a risk taker. One of his risky moves was introducing Diet Coke to the market—a success story. Another of his risks was changing the formula of Coca-Cola to create New Coke—a failure; Goizueta reversed direction after New Coke flopped.[21] When it comes to hybrid automobiles, General Motors wasn't a risk taker. Its hesitancy largely gave the market advantage to GM's Japanese rivals. The firm's vice chairman, Bob Lutz, now says: "GM had the technology to do hybrids back when Toyota was launching the first Prius, but we opted not to ask the board to approve a product program that'd be destined to lose hundreds of millions of dollars. We won't make that mistake again."[22] Figure 13.4 shows the three different decision environments.

Certain Environment

The decisions just described were made in conditions quite different from the relative predictability of a **certain environment**. This is an ideal decision situation where factual information is available about the possible alternative courses of action and their outcomes. The decision-maker's task is simple: study the alternatives and choose the best solution. Certain environments are nice and comfortable for decision-makers; however, very few managerial problems are like this.

A **certain environment** offers complete information on possible action alternatives and their consequences.

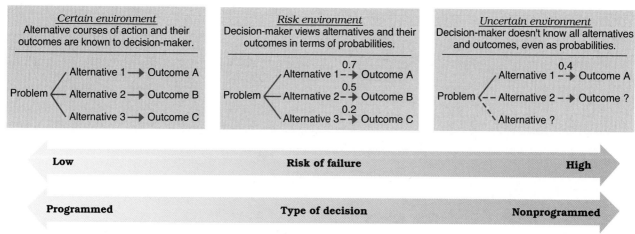

Figure 13.4 Three environments for managerial decision-making and problem solving.

Risk Environment

A risk environment lacks complete information but offers "probabilities" of the likely outcomes for possible action alternatives.

Many management problems emerge in **risk environments**—ones where facts and information on action alternatives and their consequences are incomplete. These situations require the use of probabilities to estimate the likelihood that a particular outcome will occur (e.g., 4 chances out of 10). Because probabilities are only possibilities, they introduce risk into the decision situation.

And some people deal better with risk than others. When considering possible investments in hybrid technologies, for example, GM executives either miscalculated the probabilities of positive payoffs or didn't believe the probabilities were high enough to justify the risk. Their Japanese competitors, facing the same risk environment, decided differently and gained advantage.

Entrepreneurs and highly innovative organizations have the capacities to make good decisions under risk conditions. Also, steps can sometimes be taken to reduce risk by gathering more and better information. In the case of new products, like Diet Coke, firms often make "go/no-go" decisions only after consumer preferences are identified by extensive market testing with focus groups.

Uncertain Environment

An uncertain environment lacks so much information that it is difficult to assign probabilities to the likely outcomes of alternatives.

When facts are few and information is so poor that managers are unable even to assign probabilities to the likely outcomes of alternatives, an **uncertain environment** exists. This is the most difficult decision condition.[23] The high level of uncertainty forces managers to rely heavily on creativity in solving problems. Because uncertainty requires unique, novel, and often totally innovative alternatives, groups are frequently useful for problem solving. But the responses to uncertainty depend greatly on intuition, judgement, informed guessing, and hunches—all of which leave considerable room for error. Perhaps no better example exists of the challenges of uncertainty than the situation faced by government and business leaders during the stock market crash of October 2008. The bank failures and dramatic worldwide stock market sell-offs left all decision-makers struggling to find the right pathways to deal with highly uncertain economic conditions.

✓ Learning Check ❷

BE SURE YOU CAN
• describe how IT influences the four functions of management • define *problem solving* and *decision-making* • explain systematic and intuitive thinking • list four cognitive styles in decision-making • differentiate programmed and nonprogrammed decisions • describe the challenges of crisis decision-making • explain decision-making in certain, risk, and uncertain environments

The Decision-Making Process

Figure 13.5 describes five steps in the **decision-making process**: (1) identify and define the problem, (2) generate and evaluate alternative solutions, (3) choose a preferred course of action and conduct the "ethics double-check," (4) implement the decision, and (5) evaluate results.[24] All five steps can be understood in the context of the following short but true case.

The **decision-making process** begins with identification of a problem and ends with evaluation of implemented solutions.

> *The Ajax Case. On December 31, the Ajax Company decided to close down its Murphysboro plant. Market conditions were forcing layoffs, and the company could not find a buyer for the plant. Some of the 172 employees had been with the company as long as 18 years; others as little as 6 months. All were to be terminated. Under company policy, they would be given severance pay equal to one week's pay per year of service.*

This case reflects how competition, changing times, and the forces of globalization can take their toll on organizations, the people who work for them, and the communities in which they operate. Think about how you would feel as one of the affected employees. Think about how you would feel as the mayor of this small town. Think about how you would feel as a corporate executive having to make the difficult business decisions.

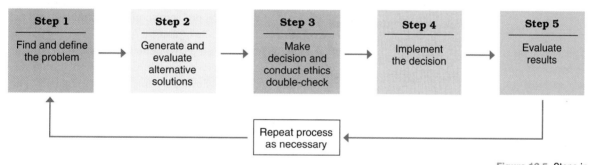

Figure 13.5 Steps in managerial decision-making and problem solving.

STEP 1—IDENTIFY AND DEFINE THE PROBLEM

The first step in decision-making is to find and define the problem. Information gathering and deliberation are critical in this stage. The way a problem is defined can have a major impact on how it is resolved, and it is important to clarify exactly what a decision should accomplish. The more specific the goals, the easier it is to evaluate results after the decision is actually implemented. Three common mistakes can occur in this critical first step in decision-making.[25]

Mistake number 1 is defining the problem too broadly or too narrowly. To take a classic example, the problem stated as "build a better mousetrap" might be better defined as "get rid of the mice." Managers should define problems in ways that give them the best possible range of problem-solving options.

Mistake number 2 is focusing on symptoms instead of causes. Symptoms are indicators that problems may exist, but they shouldn't be mistaken for the problems themselves. Although managers should be alert to spot problem symptoms (e.g., a drop in performance), they must also dig deeper to address root causes (such as discovering that a worker needs training in the use of a new computer system).

Mistake number 3 is choosing the wrong problem to deal with at a certain point in time. For example, here are three management problems. Which would you address first on a busy workday? *Problem*—An e-mail message from your boss is requesting a proposal "as soon as possible" on how to handle employees' complaints about lack of flexibility in their work schedules. *Problem*—One of your best team members has just angered another by loudly criticizing her work performance. *Problem*—Your working spouse has left a voice-mail message that your daughter is sick at school and the nurse would like her to go home for the day. Choices like this are not easy. But we have to set priorities and deal with the most important problems first. In this case, perhaps the boss can wait while you telephone school to learn more about your daughter's illness and then spend some time with the employee who seems to be having a bad day.

Back to the Ajax Case. Closing the Ajax plant will put a substantial number of people from the small community of Murphysboro out of work. The unemployment will have a negative impact on individuals, their families, and the town as a whole. The loss of the Ajax tax base will further hurt the community. The local financial implications of the plant closure will be great. The problem for Ajax management is how to minimize the adverse impact of the plant closing on the employees, their families, and the community.

STEP 2—GENERATE AND EVALUATE ALTERNATIVE COURSES OF ACTION

Once the problem is defined, it is time to assemble the facts and information that will be helpful for problem solving. It is important here to clarify exactly what is known and what needs to be known. Extensive information gathering should identify alternative courses of action, as well as their anticipated consequences. Key stakeholders in the problem should be identified, and the effects of possible courses of action on each of them should be considered.

Cost-benefit analysis involves comparing the costs and benefits of each potential course of action.

A useful approach for the evaluation of alternatives is a **cost-benefit analysis**, the comparison of what an alternative will cost in relation to the expected benefits. At a minimum, the benefits of an alternative should be greater than its costs. The following list includes costs, benefits, and other useful criteria for evaluating alternatives.

- *Costs:* What are the "costs" of implementing the alternative, including resource investments as well as potential negative side effects?

- *Benefits:* What are the "benefits" of using the alternative to solve a performance deficiency or take advantage of an opportunity?

- *Timeliness:* How fast can the alternative be implemented and a positive impact be achieved?

- *Acceptability:* To what extent will the alternative be accepted and supported by those who must work with it?

- *Ethical soundness:* How well does the alternative meet acceptable ethical criteria in the eyes of the various stakeholders?

Ultimately, any course of action can only be as good as the quality of the alternatives considered; the better the pool of alternatives, the more likely that any actions taken will help solve the problem at hand. A common error in this step is abandoning the search for alternatives too quickly. This often happens under pressures of time and other circumstances. But the fact that an alternative is convenient doesn't make it the best. It could have damaging side effects, or it could be less good than others that might be discovered with extra effort. One way to minimize this error is through consultation and involvement. It often works out that bringing more people into the decision-making process brings more information and perspectives to bear on the problem, generates more alternatives, and results in a choice more appealing to everyone involved.

Back to the Ajax Case. The Ajax plant is going to be closed. Among the possible alternatives that can be considered are (1) close the plant on schedule and be done with it; (2) delay the plant closing until all efforts have been made to sell it to another firm; (3) offer to sell the plant to the employees and/or local interests; (4) close the plant and offer transfers to other Ajax plant locations; or (5) close the plant, offer transfers, and help the employees find new jobs in and around Murphysboro.

STEP 3—DECIDE ON A PREFERRED COURSE OF ACTION

This is the point of choice where an actual decision is made to select a preferred course of action. Just how this is done and by whom must be successfully resolved in each problem situation. Management theory recognizes rather substantial differences between the classical and behavioural models of decision-making, as shown in Figure 13.6.

Classical Model

- Structured problem
- Clearly defined
- Certain environment
- Complete information
- All alternatives and consequences known

Optimizing Decision
Choose absolute best among alternatives

Rationality
Acts in perfect world

Manager as decision-maker

Bounded rationality
Acts with cognitive limitations

Behavioural Model

- Unstructured problem
- Not clearly defined
- Uncertain environment
- Incomplete information
- Not all alternatives and consequences known

Satisficing Decision
Choose first "satisfactory" alternative

Figure 13.6 Differences in the classical and behavioural models of managerial decision-making.

Classical Decision Model

The **classical decision model** views the manager as acting rationally in a certain world. The assumption is that a rational choice of the preferred course of action will be made by a decision-maker who is fully informed about all possible alternatives. Here, the manager faces a clearly defined problem and knows all possible action alternatives, as well as their consequences. As a result, he or she makes an **optimizing decision** that gives the absolute best solution to the problem.

The **classical decision model** describes decision-making with complete information.

An **optimizing decision** chooses the alternative giving the absolute best solution to a problem.

Behavioural Decision Model

Behavioural scientists question the assumptions of perfect information underlying the classical model. Perhaps best represented by the work of Herbert Simon, they instead recognize cognitive limitations to our human information-processing capabilities.[26] These limits make it hard for managers to become fully informed and make optimizing decisions. They create a **bounded rationality**, such that managerial decisions are rational only within the boundaries set by the available information and known alternatives, both of which are incomplete.

Bounded rationality describes making decisions within the constraints of limited information and alternatives.

The **behavioural decision model** assumes that people act only in terms of what they perceive about a given situation. Because perceptions are most often imperfect, the decision-maker has only partial knowledge about the available action alternatives and their consequences. Consequently, the first alternative that appears to give a satisfactory resolution of the problem is likely to be chosen. Simon, who won a Nobel Prize for his work, calls this the tendency to make **satisficing decisions**—choosing the first satisfactory alternative that comes to your attention. The behavioural model is considered most accurate in describing how many decisions get made in the ambiguous and fast-paced problem situations faced by managers.

The **behavioural decision model** describes decision-making with limited information and bounded rationality.

A **satisficing decision** chooses the first satisfactory alternative that comes to one's attention.

> *Back to the Ajax Case. Management at Ajax decided to close the plant, offer transfers to company plants in another state, and offer to help displaced employees find new jobs in and around Murphysboro.*

STEP 4—IMPLEMENT THE DECISION

Once a decision is made, actions must be taken to fully implement it. Nothing new can or will happen unless action is taken to actually solve the problem. Managers not only need the determination and creativity to arrive at a decision, they also need the ability and willingness to implement it.

The "ways" in which decision-making steps 1, 2, and 3 are accomplished can have a powerful impact on how well decisions get implemented. Difficulties encountered at the point of implementation often trace to the **lack-of-participation error**. This is a failure to adequately

Lack-of-participation error is failure to involve in a decision the persons whose support is needed to implement it.

involve in the process those persons whose support is necessary to implement the decision. Managers who use participation wisely get the right people involved in problem solving from the beginning. When they do, implementation typically follows quickly, smoothly, and to everyone's satisfaction. Participation in decision-making makes everyone better informed and builds the commitments needed for implementation.

> *Back to the Ajax Case. Ajax ran ads in the local and regional newspapers. The ad called attention to an "Ajax skill bank" composed of "qualified, dedicated, and well-motivated employees with a variety of skills and experiences." Interested employers were urged to contact Ajax for further information.*

STEP 5—EVALUATE RESULTS

The decision-making process is not complete until results are evaluated. If the desired results are not achieved or if undesired side effects occur, corrective action should be taken. Such evaluation is a form of managerial control. It involves gathering data to measure performance results and compare them against goals. If the results are less than what was desired, it is time to reassess and return to earlier steps. In this way, problem solving becomes a dynamic and ongoing activity within the management process. Evaluation is always easier when clear goals, measurable targets, and timetables were established to begin with.

> *Back to the Ajax Case. The advertisement ran for some 15 days. The plant's industrial relations manager commented, "I've been very pleased with the results." That's all we know. How well did Ajax management do in dealing with this very difficult problem? You can look back on the case as it was described and judge for yourself. Perhaps you would have approached the situation and the five steps in decision-making somewhat differently.*

 Canadian Company in the News

MAKING DECISIONS IN A POWERFUL ENVIRONMENT

Capital Power is an Edmonton-based independent power producer that is investing in renewable energy, in particular wind power. It currently has interests in 31 energy facilities (hydroelectric and coal-fired steam) across Canada and the United States, totalling 3,500 megawatts  of generation capacity. One of its facilities is Kingsbridge, a 40-megawatt wind farm located near the community of Goderich, Ont., which consists of 23 turbines. The Kingsbridge facility has been the best-performing wind farm in Ontario based on capacity factor. Capital Power receives incentive payments under the Wind Power Production Incentive Program offered by the Government of Canada. Under the program, Capital Power receives $10 per megawatt-hour for Kingsbridge up to a maximum of $1.1 million annually through to March 2016. The company, like other alternative energy producers, has made these decisions banking on either continued federal incentives or consumer support. Like any decision, only time will tell if this decision, made in an "uncertain environment," is a good one.

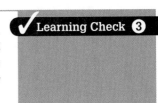

BE SURE YOU CAN
• list the steps in the decision-making process • apply these steps to a sample decision-making situation • explain cost-benefit analysis in decision-making • discuss differences between the classical and behavioural decision models • define *optimizing* and *satisficing* • explain how lack-of-participation error can hurt decision-making

ISSUES IN MANAGERIAL DECISION-MAKING

Most management situations are rich in decision-making challenges. By way of preparation, it helps to be aware of the common decision-making errors and traps, the advantages and disadvantages of individual and group decision-making, and the imperative of ethical decision-making.

DECISION ERRORS AND TRAPS

Faced with limited information, time, and even energy, people often use simplifying strategies for decision-making. These strategies or rules of thumb are known as **heuristics**.[27] Although they can be helpful in dealing with complex and ambiguous situations, they are also common causes of decision-making errors.[28]

> **Heuristics** are strategies for simplifying decision-making.

Availability Bias

The **availability heuristic** occurs when people use information that is "readily available" from memory as a basis for assessing a current event or situation. An example is deciding not to invest in a new product based on your recollection of a recent product failure. The potential bias is that the readily available information is fallible and irrelevant. For example, the product that recently failed may have been a good idea that was released to market at the wrong time of year.

> The **availability heuristic** bases a decision on recent information or events.

Representation Bias

The **representativeness heuristic** occurs when people assess the likelihood of something happening based on its similarity to a stereotyped set of occurrences. An example of representation bias is deciding to hire someone for a job vacancy simply because he or she graduated from the same school attended by your last and most successful new hire. The potential bias is that the representative stereotype masks factors that are important and relevant to the decision. For instance, the abilities and career expectations of the person receiving the offer may not fit the job requirements.

> The **representativeness heuristic** bases a decision on similarity to other situations.

Anchoring and Adjustment Bias

The **anchoring and adjustment heuristic** occurs when decisions are biased by inappropriate allegiance to a previously existing value or starting point. An example is a manager who sets a new salary level for an employee by simply raising her prior year's salary by a small percentage amount. Although the increase may appear reasonable to the manager, the prior year's salary may have substantially undervalued the employee relative to the market. The small incremental salary adjustment, reflecting anchoring and adjustment bias, may not satisfy her or keep her from looking for another job.

> The **anchoring and adjustment heuristic** bases a decision on incremental adjustments from a prior decision point.

REAL ETHICS

Left to Die

Some 40 climbers are winding their way to the top of Mt. Everest. About 300 metres below the summit sits a British mountain climber in trouble, collapsed in a shallow snow cave. Most of those on the way up just look while continuing their climbs. Sherpas from one passing team pause to give him oxygen before moving on. Within hours, David Sharp, 34, is dead of oxygen deficiency on the mountain.

A climber who passed by says: "At 28,000 feet it's hard to stay alive yourself . . . he was in very poor condition . . . it was a very hard decision . . . he wasn't a member of our team."

Someone who made the summit in the past says: "If you're going to go to Everest . . . I think you have to accept responsibility that you may end up doing something that's not ethically nice . . . you have to realize that you're in a different world."

After hearing about this case, the late Sir Edmund Hillary, who was one of the first two climbers to reach the top in 1953, said: "Human life is far more important than just getting to the top of a mountain."

YOU DECIDE

Who's right and who's wrong here? And, by the way, in our personal affairs, daily lives, and careers, we are all, in our own ways, climbing Mt. Everest. What are the ethics of our climbs? How often do we notice others in trouble, struggling along the way? And, like the mountain climbers heading to the summit of Everest, how often do we pass them by to continue our own journeys? Can you identify examples—from business, school, career, sports, and so on—that pose similar ethical dilemmas?

Framing Error

A **framing error** is trying to solve a problem in the context in which it is perceived.

Sometimes managers suffer from a **framing error** that occurs when a problem is evaluated and resolved in the context in which it is perceived—either positively or negatively. Suppose, for example, that data show a product has a 40-percent market share. A negative frame views the product as deficient because it is missing 60 percent of the market. The likely discussion and problem solving in this frame would focus on: "What are we doing wrong?" Alternatively, the frame could be a positive one, looking at the 40-percent share as a good accomplishment. In this case, the discussion is more likely to proceed with: "How do we do things better?" Sometimes people use framing as a tactic for presenting information in a way that gets other people to think inside the desired frame. In politics, this is often referred to as "spinning" the data.

Confirmation Error

A **confirmation error** occurs when focusing only on information that confirms a decision already made.

One of our tendencies after making a decision is to try to find ways to justify it. In the case of unethical acts, for example, Chapter 4 discussed ways in which we try to "rationalize" them after the fact. More generally in decision-making, we can fall prey to **confirmation error**. This means that we notice, accept, and even seek out only information that confirms or is consistent with a decision we have just made. Other and perhaps contrary information is downplayed or denied. This is a form of selective perception, in which we focus on problems from our particular reference or vantage point only; we neglect other points of view or information that might support a different decision.

Escalating Commitment

Another decision-making trap is **escalating commitment**. This occurs as a decision to increase effort and perhaps apply more resources to pursue a course of action that is not working.[29] Managers prone to escalation let the momentum of the situation overwhelm them. They are unable to "call it quits" even when facts and experience otherwise indicate that this is the best thing to do.

Consider the case of a start-up "no frills" airline called Skybus. The "bus" part of the name drove the business model, with fares advertised as low as US$10 for early reservations. Booking was only on-line, passengers retrieved their own luggage from trolleys, and food and drinks were sold on board—there were no "giveaways." Skybus launched in the summer and at first filled 80 percent of its seats. Even though passenger traffic soon fell to "loss" levels,[30] executives kept faith in the business model. They cut back some routes and redirected resources toward others they believed had profit potential. However, the airline failed when fuel prices soared and the economy went into recession.

Was it escalating commitment that contributed to the demise of Skybus? Did its executives stick with poor routes for too long or fail to admit flaws in the business model itself? Or was it just a case of choosing a bad time to launch a new airline? It's a tough call, but the likelihood of escalation is present. It's a common decision error, perhaps one that you are personally familiar with. Management Smarts 13.2 offers advice on how to avoid tendencies toward escalating commitments to previously chosen courses of action.

> **Escalating commitment** is the continuation of a course of action even though it is not working.

13.2 MANAGEMENT SMARTS
How to avoid the escalation trap in decision-making

- Set advance limits on your involvement and commitment to a particular course of action; stick with these limits.

- Make your own decisions; don't follow the lead of others, since they are also prone to escalation.

- Carefully assess why you are continuing a course of action; if there are no good reasons to continue, don't.

- Remind yourself of what a course of action is costing; consider saving these costs as a reason to discontinue.

- Watch for escalation tendencies in your behaviours and those of others.

CREATIVITY IN DECISION-MAKING

Lonnie Johnson is a former NASA engineer. You probably don't know him, but most likely you are familiar with something he invented—the Super Soaker water gun. Johnson didn't set out to invent the water gun; he was working in his basement on an idea for refrigeration systems that would use water rather than freon. Something connected in his mind, and

© AP/Wide World Photos

the Super Soaker was born. Johnson says: "The Super Soaker changed my life." He now heads his own research and development company and, among other things, the website says his firm has some 100 toys in development.[31]

Creativity is one of our greatest personal assets, even though it may be too often unrecognized. In fact, we exercise creativity every day in lots of ways—solving problems at home, building something for the kids, or even finding ways to pack too many things into too small a suitcase. But are we creative when it would really help in solving workplace problems? Just imagine what could be accomplished with all the creative potential that exists in an organization's workforce. How do you turn that potential into actual results—the Lonnie Johnson model, so to speak?

Personal Creativity Drivers

Creativity is the generation of a novel idea or unique approach that solves a problem or crafts an opportunity.

In management, we discuss **creativity** as the generation of a novel idea or unique approach to solving problems or exploiting opportunities.[32] One source of insight into personal creativity is the three-component model of task expertise, task motivation, and creativity skills.[33] The model is helpful because it points us in the direction of management actions that can be taken to build creativity drivers into the work setting, and thus facilitate more creativity in decision-making.

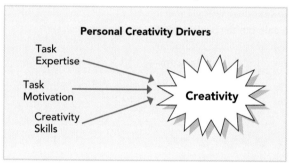

Creative decisions are more likely to occur when the person or team has a lot of *task expertise*. As with Lonnie Johnson, creativity is an outgrowth of skill, and it typically extends in new directions, such as something one is good at or knows about. Creativity is also more likely when the people making decisions are highly *task-motivated*. That is, creativity tends to occur in part because people work exceptionally hard to resolve a problem or exploit an opportunity. In the course of old-fashioned hard work, such as Lonnie Johnson spending hours in his basement, something new and different is accomplished.

Creative decisions are more likely when the people involved have stronger *creativity skills*. In popular conversations, you might refer to this as the contrast between "right brain" thinking— imagination, intuition, spontaneity, and emotion—and "left brain" thinking—logic, order, method, and analysis. But just what are we talking about here? Is creativity something that is built into some of us and not built into others? Or is creativity something that one can work to develop, along with other personal skills and competencies?

Researchers argue these points. But the debate is healthy and there is agreement that the following characteristics often describe creative people. As you read the list, why not use it as a personal test—a self-check of potential strengths and weaknesses in creativity skills?[34]

- Work with high energy

- Identify problems, plan, make decisions

- Hold ground in face of criticism

- Accept responsibility for what happens

- Resourceful, even in difficult situations

- Both systematic and intuitive in problem solving

- Think "outside of the box" (divergent thinking)

- Synthesize and find correct answers (convergent thinking)

- Look at diverse ways to solve problems (lateral thinking)

- Transfer learning from one setting to others

- Objective, willing to "step back" and question assumptions

The willingness to question assumptions is an important creativity skill. Creativity consultant Edward De Bono offers this example.[35] Elevator riders in a new high-rise building were complaining about long waiting times. Building engineers recommended upgrading the entire system at substantial cost. When De Bono was called in to offer his advice, he suggested placing floor-to-ceiling mirrors by the elevators. People, he suspected, would not notice waiting times because they would be distracted by their and others' reflections. He was right. His creativity broke the engineers' assumption that any solutions to slow elevators had to be mechanical ones.

Situational Creativity Drivers

If you mix creative people and traditional organization and management practices, what will you get? Perhaps not much; it takes more than individual creativity alone to make innovation a way of life in organizations.

Think creative whenever you use or see someone using an Apple iPhone. There's a lot of genius behind the product in concept, design, and marketing. But give the leadership credit too. They built an organizational culture where great ideas get attention and make their way into attractive new products.

Think creativity wasted the next time you watch TV on a beautiful, large, flat-panel screen. This is the story.[36] The year was 1964 when George H. Heilmeier showed his employers at RCA Labs his new discovery: a liquid-crystal display, or LCD. They played with it until 1968 and unveiled the new concept to the public. But RCA executives decided the firm was so heavily invested in colour TV tubes that they weren't really interested. Today the market is dominated by Japanese, Korean, and Taiwanese producers. Ironically, Heilmeier received the Kyoto prize, considered the Nobel Prize of Japan, for his pioneering innovation.

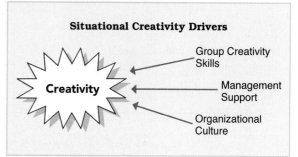

Innovative organizations like Apple operate with strong situational creativity drivers. Important among these are *group creativity skills*; teams are everywhere and they are well staffed with creative members. This becomes the basic fuel for new ideas and innovation. Also important are *management support* and *organizational cultures* that give the group creativity skills a chance to blossom. This can involve small things such as a team leader who has the patience to allow time for creative processes, and top management that is willing to provide supporting resources—things like money, technology, and space. It also involves valuing creativity organization-wide and making it a top priority in peer expectations, performance evaluations, and reward systems.

In later chapters, we'll be talking more about the link between creativity and management practices. For now, think of how far some organizations are willing to go in support of creative decision-making.

Fisher-Price Toys—*In a separate part of Fisher-Price headquarters, there is a place called the "Cave." It's not your typical office space; picture beanbag chairs, soft lighting, and couches. The Cave is for brainstorming, where designers, marketers, engineers, and others can meet and join in freewheeling discussions to come up with the next great toy for preschoolers. Consultants recommend that such innovation spaces be separated from the normal workplace and be large enough for no more than 15 to 20 people.[37]*

Motorola—*It may have seemed unremarkable when a group of Motorola engineers, designers, and marketers met in a Chicago loft office. But it became the innovation lab Moto City, a home away from corporate headquarters and its bureaucracy. The goal was to stimulate creativity.*

The group's task was simple but challenging: come up with a better cell phone. What they created together was the Motorola Razr, and 12.5 million sold the first year on the market.[38]

INDIVIDUAL VERSUS GROUP DECISION-MAKING

The prior examples remind us that groups and teams are important sources of creativity in decision-making—we wouldn't have the iPhone, Razr, or most of the other innovative products that enrich our daily lives without them. However, it is important to remember that the ways that managers use or don't use group decision-making can be real turning points in the results achieved. Basically, the issue boils down to this: in a problem situation, should the decision be made individually or with the assistance of a group?

Management scholars suggest that the best managers and team leaders switch back and forth among individual and group decisions to best fit the problems at hand.[39] The "right" decision method is one that provides for a timely and high-quality solution, and one to which people involved in the implementation will be highly committed.[40]

When Group Decisions Work Best

- Individual lacks expertise or information

- Problem is unclear and hard to define

- Acceptance by others is needed for effective implementation

- Time is sufficient for group involvement

Advantages of Group Decisions

Due to their potential advantages, group decisions are well worth pursuing whenever time and other circumstances permit. Decisions that involve team members make greater amounts of information, knowledge, and expertise available to solve problems. They expand the number of action alternatives that are examined; they help to avoid tunnel vision and consideration of only limited options. Team decisions also increase understanding and acceptance by members. And importantly, team decisions increase the commitments of members to work hard to implement the decisions they have made together.

Disadvantages of Group Decisions

The potential disadvantages of group decision-making trace largely to the difficulties that can be experienced in group processes. When many people are trying to make a team decision, there may be social pressure to conform. Some individuals may feel intimidated or compelled to go along with the apparent wishes of others. There may be minority domination, where some members feel forced or "railroaded" to accept a decision advocated by one vocal individual or a small coalition. Also, the time required to make team decisions can sometimes be a disadvantage. As more people are involved in the dialogue and discussion, decision-making takes longer. This added time may be costly, even prohibitively so, in certain circumstances.

ETHICAL DECISION-MAKING

In Chapter 4, we discussed the "ethics double-check"—asking and answering two straightforward but powerful *spotlight questions:*

> Spotlight Question 1 *"How would I feel if my family found out about this decision?"*

> Spotlight Question 2 *"How would I feel if this decision were published in the local newspaper or on the Internet?"*

The Josephson Institute model for ethical decision-making adds a third question to further strengthen the ethics double-check.[41]

> Spotlight Question 3 *"Think of the person you know or know of (in real life or fiction) who has the strongest character and best ethical judgement. Then ask yourself—what would that person do in your situation?"*

Although it adds time to decision-making, use of the spotlight questions helps ensure that the ethical aspects of a problem are properly considered. It is also consistent with the demanding moral standards of modern society. A willingness to pause to examine the ethics of a proposed decision may well result in both a better decision and the prevention of costly litigation. Ethicist Gerald Cavanaugh and his associates suggest that managers can proceed with the most confidence when the following criteria for ethics in decision-making are met.[42]

1. *Utility*—Does the decision satisfy all constituents or stakeholders?

2. *Rights*—Does the decision respect the rights and duties of everyone?

3. *Justice*—Is the decision consistent with the canons of justice?

4. *Caring*—Is the decision consistent with my responsibility to care?

RESEARCH BRIEF

Escalation increases risk of unethical decisions

That's the conclusion reached in an empirical study by Marc and Vera L. Street. They reviewed research confirming that escalating commitments to previously chosen courses of action can explain many poor decisions and undesirable outcomes in organizations. But they also point out that little has been done to investigate whether or not escalation tendencies lead to unethical behaviours.

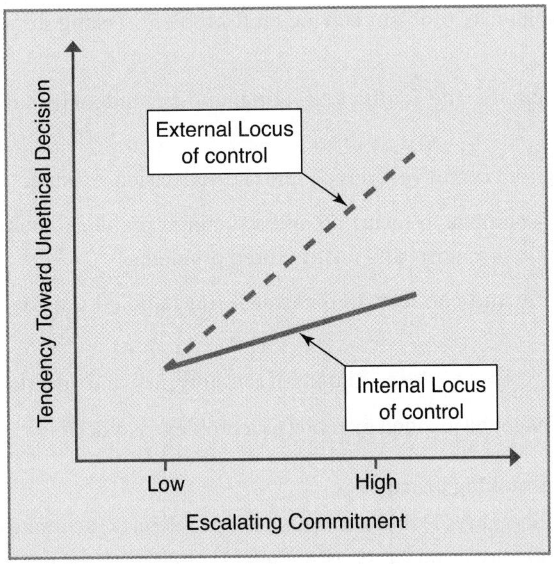

To address this void, the researchers conducted an experiment with 155 undergraduate students working on a computerized investment task. They found that exposure to escalation situations increases tendencies toward unethical acts, and that the tendencies further increase with the magnitude of the escalation. Street and Street believe this link between escalation and poor ethics is driven by desires to get out of and avoid the increasing stress of painful situations.

Additional findings from the study showed that students with an external locus of control had a higher propensity to choose an unethical decision alternative than their counterparts with an internal locus of control. This confirmed prior research findings reporting a link between locus of control and ethical behaviour.

[Figure: A line graph with vertical axis "Tendency Toward Unethical Decision" and horizontal axis "Escalating Commitment" ranging from Low to High. Two upward-sloping lines are shown: a dashed line labelled "External Locus of control" with a steeper slope, and a solid line labelled "Internal Locus of control" with a shallower slope.]

You be the researcher

This study was done in the classroom and under simulated decision conditions. How would you design a study that tests the same hypotheses in the real world? Also, is it possible to design a training program that would use the "Spotlight Questions" to help people better deal with unethical decision options in escalation situations?

BE SURE YOU CAN

• explain the availability, representativeness, anchoring, and adjustment heuristics • illustrate framing error, confirmation error, and escalating commitment in decision-making • identify key personal and situational creativity drivers • list questions that can be asked to double-check the ethics of a decision

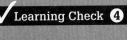
Learning Check ❹

MANAGEMENT LEARNING REVIEW

STUDY QUESTIONS SUMMARY

1.   What is the role of information in the management process?

• Competency in using technology to access, process, and share information is an essential career skill.

• Data are raw facts and figures; information is data made useful for decision-making.

• Information useful in management is timely, high-quality, complete, relevant, and understandable.

• Management information systems collect, organize, store, and distribute data to meet the information needs of managers.

• Managers play important roles in helping organizations meet their external and internal information needs.

• Information technology is breaking barriers within and between organizations to speed work flows and cut costs.

FOR DISCUSSION Are there any potential downsides to the ways IT is changing organizations?

2.   How do managers use information to make decisions?

• Managers serve as information nerve centres in the process of planning, organizing, leading, and controlling activities in organizations.

• Managers can display problem avoidance, problem solving, and problem seeking in facing problems.

• Managers vary in their use of systematic and intuitive thinking, and in tendencies toward multidimensional thinking.

• Managers must understand the different cognitive styles people use in decision-making.

• Programmed decisions are routine solutions to recurring and structured problems; nonprogrammed decisions are unique solutions to novel and unstructured problems.

• Crisis problems occur unexpectedly and can lead to disaster if not handled quickly and properly.

• Managers face problems and make decisions under conditions of certainty, risk, and uncertainty.

FOR DISCUSSION When would a manager be justified in acting as a problem avoider?

3.   What are the steps in the decision-making process?

• The steps in the decision-making process are (1) find and define the problem, (2) generate and evaluate alternatives, (3) decide on the preferred course of action, (4) implement the decision, and (5) evaluate the results.

• An optimizing decision, following the classical model, chooses the absolute best solution from a known set of alternatives.

• A satisficing decision, following the behavioural model, chooses the first satisfactory alternative to come to attention.

FOR DISCUSSION Do the steps in the decision-making process have to be followed in order?

4. **What are current issues in managerial decision-making?**

- Common decision errors and traps include the availability, representation, and anchoring and adjustment biases, as well as framing error, confirmation error, and escalating commitment.

- Creativity in decision-making can be enhanced by the personal creativity drivers of individual creativity skills, task expertise, and motivation.

- Creativity in decision-making can be enhanced by the situational creativity drivers of group creativity skills, management support, and organizational culture.

- Group decisions offer the potential advantages of greater information and expanded commitment, but they are often slower than individual decisions.

- Use of recommended spotlight questions as an ethics double-check is a good way for managers to ensure ethical decision-making.

FOR DISCUSSION Is it possible that use of the spotlight questions might still yield an unethical decision?

SELF-TEST

Multiple-Choice Questions

1. Among the ways information technology is changing organizations today, _____ is one of its most noteworthy characteristics.

   (a) eliminating need for top managers   (b) reducing information available for decision-making   (c) breaking down barriers internally and externally   (d) decreasing need for environmental awareness

2. Information technology assists with the management function of organizing because it _____.

   (a) gives more timely access to information   (b) allows for more immediate measures of performance results   (c) allows for better coordination among individuals and groups   (d) makes it easier to communicate with diverse stakeholders

3. A manager who is reactive and works hard to address problems after they occur is known as a _____.

   (a) problem seeker   (b) problem avoider   (c) problem solver   (d) problem manager

4. A(n) _____ thinker approaches problems in a rational and analytic fashion.

   (a) systematic   (b) intuitive   (c) internal   (d) external

5. The assigning of probabilities for action alternatives and their consequences indicates the presence of _____ in the decision environment.

   (a) certainty   (b) optimizing   (c) risk   (d) satisficing

6. The first step in the decision-making process is to _____.

   (a) identify alternatives   (b) evaluate results   (c) find and define the problem   (d) choose a solution

7. Being asked to develop a plan to increase international sales of a product is an example of the types of _____ problems that managers must be prepared to deal with.

   (a) routine   (b) unstructured   (c) crisis   (d) structured

8. Costs, timeliness, and _____ are among the recommended criteria for evaluating alternative courses of action.

   (a) ethical soundness   (b) competitiveness   (c) availability   (d) simplicity

9. A common mistake made by managers facing crisis situations is that they _____.

   (a) try to get too much information before responding   (b) rely too much on group decision-making   (c) isolate themselves to make the decision alone   (d) forget to use their crisis management plan

10. The _____ decision model views managers as making optimizing decisions, whereas the _____ decision model views them as making satisficing decisions.

    (a) behavioural, human relations   (b) classical, behavioural   (c) heuristic, humanistic   (d) quantitative, behavioural

11. When a manager makes a decision about someone's annual pay raise only after looking at their current salary, the risk is that the decision will be biased because of _____.

    (a) a framing error   (b) escalating commitment   (c) anchoring and adjustment   (d) strategic opportunism

12. When a problem is addressed according to the positive or negative context in which it is presented, this is an example of _____.

    (a) framing error   (b) escalating commitment   (c) availability and adjustment   (d) strategic opportunism

13. Among the environments for managerial decision-making, certainty is the most favourable, and it can be addressed through _____ decisions.

    (a) programmed   (b) risk   (c) satisficing   (d) intuitive

14. When a manager decides to continue pursuing a course of action that facts otherwise indicate is failing to deliver desired results, this is called _____.

    (a) strategic opportunism   (b) escalating commitment   (c) confirmation error   (d) the risky shift

15. Personal creativity drivers include creativity skills, task expertise, and _____.

    (a) emotional intelligence   (b) management support   (c) organizational culture   (d) task motivation

Short-Response Questions

16. What is the difference between an optimizing decision and a satisficing decision?

17. How can a manager double-check the ethics of a decision?

18. How would a manager use systematic thinking and intuitive thinking in problem solving?

19. How can the members of an organization be trained in crisis management?

Application Question

20. As a participant in a new mentoring program between your university and a local high school, you have volunteered to give a presentation to a class of Grade 10 students on the challenges in the new "electronic office." The goal is to sensitize them to developments in information technology and motivate them to take the best advantage of their high school academics so as to prepare themselves for the workplace of the future. What will you say to them?

MANAGEMENT SKILLS AND COMPETENCIES

SELF-ASSESSMENT

Back to Yourself: Self-Confidence

Managers are decision-makers. And if they are to make consistently good decisions, they must be skilled at gathering and processing information. Managers are also implementers. Once decisions are made, managers are expected to rally people and resources to put them into action. This is how problems get solved and opportunities get explored in organizations. In order for all this to happen, managers must have the self-confidence to turn decisions into action accomplishments; they must believe in their decisions and the information foundations for them. A good understanding of the many topics in this chapter can improve your decision-making skills. A better understanding of your personal style in gathering and processing information can also go a long way toward building your self-confidence as a decision-maker.

Further Reflection: Cognitive Style

Instructions

This assessment is designed to get an impression of your cognitive style based on the work of psychologist Carl Jung. For each of the following 12 pairs, place a "1" next to the statement that best describes you. Do this for each pair, even though the description you choose may not be perfect.

1. (a) I prefer to learn from experience.
   (b) I prefer to find meanings in facts and how they fit together.

2. (a) I prefer to use my eyes, ears, and other senses to find out what is going on.
   (b) I prefer to use imagination to come up with new ways to do things.

3. (a) I prefer to use standard ways to deal with routine problems.
   (b) I prefer to use novel ways to deal with new problems.

4. (a) I prefer ideas and imagination.
   (b) I prefer methods and techniques.

5. (a) I am patient with details, but get impatient when they get complicated.
   (b) I am impatient and jump to conclusions, but I am also creative, imaginative, and inventive.

6. (a) I enjoy using skills already mastered more than learning new ones.
   (b) I like learning new skills more than practising old ones.

7. (a) I prefer to decide things logically.
   (b) I prefer to decide things based on feelings and values.

8. (a) I like to be treated with justice and fairness.
   (b) I like to be praised and to please other people.

9. (a) I sometimes neglect or hurt other people's feelings without realizing it.
   (b) I am aware of other people's feelings.

10. (a) I give more attention to ideas and things than to human relationships.
    (b) I can predict how others will feel.

11. (a) I do not need harmony; arguments and conflicts don't bother me.
     (b) I value harmony and get upset by arguments and conflicts.

12. (a) I am often described as analytical, impersonal, unemotional, objective, critical, hard-nosed, rational.
     (b) I am often described as sympathetic, people-oriented, unorganized, uncritical, understanding, ethical.

Scoring

Sum your scores as follows, and record them in the parentheses. (Note that the *Sensing* and *Feeling* scores will be recorded as negatives.)

- (−   ) *Sensing* (*S Type*) = 1a + 2a + 3a + 4a + 5a + 6a
- (   ) *Intuitive* (*N Type*) = 1b + 2b + 3b + 4b + 5b + 6b
- (   ) *Thinking* (*T Type*) = 7a + 8a + 9a + 10a + 11a + 12a
- (−   ) *Feeling* (*F Type*) = 7b + 8b + 9b + 10b + 11b + 12b

Interpretation

This assessment contrasts personal tendencies toward information gathering (sensation vs. intuition) and information evaluation (feeling vs. thinking) in one's approach to problem solving. The result is a classification of four master cognitive styles and their characteristics. Read the descriptions provided in the chapter text and consider the implications of your suggested style, including how well you might work with persons whose styles are very different.

Source: Developed from Donald Bowen, "Learning and Problem-Solving: You're Never Too Jung," in Donald D. Bowen, Roy J. Lewicki, Donald T. Hall, and Francine S. Hall, eds., *Experiences in Management and Organizational Behavior*, 4th ed. (New York: Wiley, 1997), pp. 7–13; and John W. Slocum Jr., "Cognitive Style in Learning and Problem Solving," ibid., pp. 349–353.

TEAM EXERCISE

Lost at Sea

Consider This Situation

You are adrift on a private yacht in the South Pacific when a fire of unknown origin destroys the yacht and most of its contents. You and a small group of survivors are now in a large raft with oars. Your location is unclear, but you estimate that you are about 1,500 km south-southwest of the nearest land. One person has just found in her pockets five $1 coins and a packet of matches. Everyone else's pockets are empty. The items below are available to you on the raft.

	Individual ranking	Team ranking	Expert ranking
Sextant	_____	_____	_____
Shaving mirror	_____	_____	_____
25 litres of water	_____	_____	_____
Mosquito netting	_____	_____	_____
1 survival meal	_____	_____	_____
Maps of Pacific Ocean	_____	_____	_____
Floatable seat cushion	_____	_____	_____
10 litres oil-gas mix	_____	_____	_____
Small transistor radio	_____	_____	_____
Shark repellent	_____	_____	_____
2 square metres black plastic	_____	_____	_____

1 litre 20-proof rum	_____	_____	_____
5 metres nylon rope	_____	_____	_____
24 chocolate bars	_____	_____	_____
Fishing kit	_____	_____	_____

Instructions

1. *Working alone*, rank the 15 items in order of their importance to your survival ("1" is most important and "15" is least important).

2. *Working in an assigned group*, arrive at a "team" ranking of the 15 items. Appoint one person as team spokesperson to report your team ranking to the class.

3. *Do not write in Column C* until your instructor provides the "expert" ranking.

Source: Adapted from "Lost at Sea: A Consensus-Seeking Task," in the *1975 Handbook for Group Facilitators.* Used with permission of University Associates, Inc.

CASE 13

Spin Master: Turning Fun into Opportunities

Spin Master, Canada's most celebrated and largest toymaker, is the result of the desire of three young entrepreneurs to prove not only that they can grow a global corporation in a very competitive industry, but that they can stay human while doing so.[1] Over the past 15 years, Spin Master has become an internationally recognized company, selecting, developing, and marketing toys globally. Spin Master's success has stemmed largely from its willingness to take calculated risks, be innovative, and track what is selling across the globe.[2]

Winner of numerous Toy of the Year honours, as well as one of Canada's 50 Best Managed Private Companies, Spin Master is poised to develop the long-term brands and discipline that will assure it a permanent place in the global toy market alongside giants such as Hasbro and Mattel.[3] Even with sales of over $750 million and 900 employees spread throughout offices in Toronto, Los Angeles, Mexico City, Paris, London, Munich, Amsterdam, Hong Kong, and China,[4] that's no easy task.

Courtesy Spin Master

The Seeds of Growth

The roots of Spin Master date back to 1994, when three university friends, Ronnen Harary, Anton Rabie, and Ben Varadi, set out to build a business. Their first product was The Earth Buddy. This product was "a small, pantyhose-covered head filled with grass seeds that sprouted hair when watered."[5] With Earth Buddy's vaguely environmental cachet, Rabie figured it would be a perfect fit for the urban-adventurer image espoused by Roots Canada Ltd., a company founded by Michael Budman and Don Green. Budman allowed Rabie and Harary to test-market Earth Buddies in Roots stores. They were a hit! Next came a 500,000 order from K-Mart in the United States, so operations soon moved from Harary's kitchen to a factory staffed by 200 employees working around the clock.[6] With $1.8 million in sales within the first six months, the Earth Buddy was an unqualified hit.[7]

So how do you follow up a pantyhosed sprouting head? With Devil Sticks, of course! In a grassroots marketing campaign, students were enlisted to travel across North America and demonstrate the baton-like toy at public events. Spin Master once again had huge success, selling more than 250,000 Devil Sticks in just six months.[8]

In 1996, two British inventors introduced an air-pressured airplane to Spin Master. The prototype the inventors sent to

Toronto was, Harary says, "a Canada Dry ginger ale bottle with foam wings—it still had the label on it." But the partners at Spin Master saw opportunity. "The one thing that did appeal to me wasn't so much the item itself as the state of the category," Varadi says. On the top end were gasoline-powered planes; on the low end were $3 rubber-band-and-balsa-wood "aircraft." Varadi figured there had to be something in the middle. "If we could pull this off, we'd be like pioneers in this category," he said. "We also realized that this would elevate the level of the company in terms of how people saw us."[9] With time, effort, and faith, the Air Hogs brand was born in 1998, with the release of the Sky Shark. The toy was both a popular and critical success, earning a prestigious spot on *Popular Science's* annual list of the Top 100 Innovations in Science in Technology.[10]

Drawing on the success of Air Hogs, Spin Master continued to blend in-house creativity with innovative marketing partnerships and became adept at modernizing former toy classics such as the legendary Shrinky Dinks and refuelling toy-buyers' imaginations. Demonstrating that Spin Master had not forgotten its grassroots past, the collectible wiggly characters Mighty Beanz were introduced. Using the same philosophy and marketing techniques as Devil Sticks, Spin Master began distributing the Beanz across North America, and they have been flying off the shelves, with more than 10 million sold. Spin Master also created a Marshmallow children's furniture division, producing the successful Flip-Open Sofa and innovative new items such as the High-Back Chair and Cube Couch.[11]

Capitalizing on its considerable strengths, Spin Master also licenses some of the world's leading brands, which continues to be an integral part of its strategy to drive growth. Spin Master has teamed up with Disney, Nickelodeon, Dream Works, Marvel, Lucas Films, and Dairy Queen in delivering products ranging from Sponge Bob Square Pants–inspired Bounce 'Rounds to the Dairy Queen's Blizzard Maker. Further growth has been driven by other Spin Master best-selling brands, such as Air Hogs, Bakugan, Liv Fashion Dolls, Moon Dough, and Zoobles.[12]

Picking Winners

So how do you pick a winning toy? "It's the hardest thing in the world," says Varadi. "You have to look at the product line's history, trends, competition. Is it a basic improvement on something else or does it take it in a new direction? In the end, it's a gut feel."[13]

The US$20 billion North American toy market is highly competitive and contracting by 3 percent a year. Customers are fickle and easily bored, making the lifespan of a typical toy today just 18 months. As a result, Spin Master has to reinvent 60 percent of its product line every year.[14] To fuel growth, Spin Master has sought strategic relationships with a broad spectrum of industry players, from inventors to toy brokers, international distributors to manufacturers, all the way to retailers and brand licensors. As a result, Spin Master has been rewarded with growth and accolades in an industry that often leaves new participants reeling.[15]

There's a culture of "How do we do this?" not "Why we can't do this" at Spin Master. "It's really refreshing," says Professor Ken Wong of Queen's University's School of Business. He credits the Spin Master leaders trusting their instincts and listening to all available external inputs, rather than just to formal, conventional market research, in forging their consistent success.[16]

Strategic intelligence gathering also gives Spin Master an innovation edge. Rabie spends a few days every two months prowling retail stores, eyeing merchandise trends, and chatting up retailers. One frequent source is Jon Levy, co-founder of Mastermind Toys, a specialty retailer in Toronto. "They are fantastically connected to all areas of their business," says Levy. "They care about my market and really want to know what makes my market tick. That's very unusual." He says every conversation with Rabie starts with genuine personal warmth before moving quickly to rapid-fire questions such as "What's your best-selling item? What do you think is going to be hot this fall?"[17]

What's Next?

"We have such a large desire for growth," says Rabie, "we feel that if we can harness the world's ideas, we can grow faster than we would by growing on ideas developed internally."[18] But as COO Iain Kennedy relates, Spin Master had outgrown its IT infrastructure and it needed to better manage sales, inventory, and other crucial data. Information on Spin Master's products was fractured and inconsistent, which meant the company couldn't make effective decisions. That was a big problem in an industry that needs to react quickly as merchandise goes from hot to not. To move forward, Spin Master launched a program to transform the way it gathered and leveraged business intelligence. The results have been very positive; every morning, Spin Master's sales analysts know exactly what products sold each day at each of its worldwide retailers. The company's in-stock performance (its ability to keep an item on store shelves) is up more than 25 percent, while on-time delivery has jumped from 60 percent to 98 percent.[19]

Even with its runaway start and catch-up decision support system, the spirit in which the company was founded has not changed. Spin Master remains a youthful, hip, energetic organization, willing to take risks, eager to innovate, and always looking to pursue new and exciting ideas.[20]

Discussion Questions

1. Describe the key decisions that Harary, Rabie, and Varadi faced in the start-up of their company. Looking at the decision environment, were these more programmed or nonprogrammed decision types?

2. As a result of Spin Master's success, what decision errors and traps might be a problem for the company in the future?

3. The three founders have found a way to agree so far. What decision-making challenges might they face in the future?

4. FURTHER RESEARCH—How might Spin Master further use information technology to help fuel continuing global expansion?

Make people your top priority

The Butcher Company, a maker of floor-care products, made headlines when its owner, Charlie Butcher, at age 83, sold the firm to the family-owned S. C. Johnson Company. His grandfather had started the firm in 1880, creating a paste wax for polishing the wooden floors that he installed. As his wax grew in popularity, The Butcher Company blossomed as well; it lasted three generations. When grandson Charlie sold the firm, he said: "I am thrilled to be leaving The Butcher Co. in the hands of another great family company. This is a wonderful opportunity for my family, Butcher's employees and customers . . . ."

But the best part of the story took place after the sale. Butcher shared US$18 million of the proceeds with the firm's 325 employees, an average of US$55,000 per person. Each received about US$1.50 for every hour they had worked for the firm over the years.

The day after the sale, Butcher was at the plant handing out cheques. How did everyone react? The firm's president, Paul P. McClaughlin, said the employees "just filled up with tears. They would just throw their arms around Charlie and give him a hug." Butcher's administrative assistant, Lynne Ouellette, summed it up this way: "Charlie really wanted to take care of the hourly folks and people who put in a lot of years."

But this wasn't anything new; Butcher had always been a believer in people. It was just another chance to confirm the theory that he'd been practising for years—a belief that treating talented people well will create business success. "When people are happy in their jobs," said Butcher, "they are at least twice as productive." In an interview, he reminded the audience that he believed the employees were what made his business successful. "I meant it," he said, "and when the opportunity came to put my money where my mouth was, that's exactly what I did."

When, in retirement, Butcher published the book *How to Succeed in Business by Giving Away Millions*, it wasn't a bestseller. But he was proud to have lived his message. At his death in 2004, his obituary called him a businessman "known for his generosity and passion for knowledge and justice."[1]

| BENCHMARK | This is a unique example of management commitment to employees—considering each and every one an owner. There is no doubt that Charlie Butcher's respect for people paid off over the years; his company achieved success because of the motivation and accomplishments of the workers. Don't you sometimes wonder why more managers don't get this message? |

Engagement

One of the hot topics in management these days is *engagement*. You might think of it in terms of personal initiative and willingness to "go the extra mile" in your work. According to Tim Galbraith, vice president of people development at Yum Brands, Inc., "A person who's truly engaged says 'I'm willing to give a little bit more; I'm willing to help my team member when I see they're in need," Kim Bechtel, the president of Calgary-based consultants yourHRco, which helps small business with human resource issues, offers that employers need to "know who your people are, know what their talents are, have an ongoing conversation with them about how engaged they feel in the work and how that engagement makes them feel about working for the company, and then tie some reinforcement to that."[2]

Would you admit that the engagement of people at work varies greatly, just as it does among students? The Conference Board, in reviewing the literature on engagement, defined it as "a heightened emotional connection" with the organization that influences an employee to "exert greater discretionary effort in his or her work." The report also describes the positive impact of engagement as greater retention, lower turnover, higher productivity, more loyalty to the employer, and better customer service.[3]

Signs of High Employee Engagement

- Willing to look for problems and fix them
- Willing to do more than just meeting job requirements
- Willing to stay late, start early, do the "extras"
- Willing to help others who are stuck or overwhelmed
- Willing to do things better; not accept the status quo
- Willing to think ahead, craft ideas and plans for future

As you think about employee engagement, consider your experiences with airline travel. How well have you been taken care of by service workers when a plane is delayed, your bag is over the allowable weight, or your luggage is lost? Airline executives are complaining a lot about rising costs and falling profits these days; passengers are also doing lots of complaining about poor service.

A recent book on the airline industry, *Up in the Air: How the Airlines Can Improve Performance by Engaging Their Employees*, makes the point that "a high level of engagement and a good labor relations system are the keys to increasing productivity and service quality." When the authors talk about engagement, they link it to service workers' willingness "to use discretionary effort to solve problems for us as passengers." They further suggest that unlocking the powers of employee engagement requires two things: authority to act given from the company side, and motivation on the worker side.[4]

❖ Get to Know Yourself Better

How many of the signs of high engagement shown in the box apply to you—consistently, predictably? Draw up a set of examples that show you in "high-engagement situations" at work or school. Write a short journal entry that describes the types of jobs and job settings that can bring out the best from you in terms of work engagement.

CHAPTER 14 STUDY QUESTIONS

- How do individual needs influence motivation?

- What are the process theories of motivation?

- What role does reinforcement play in motivation?

- What are the alternative approaches to job design?

VISUAL CHAPTER OVERVIEW

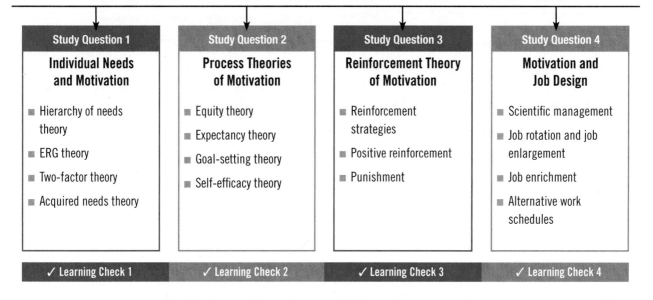

CHAPTER 14 MOTIVATION THEORY AND PRACTICE

Study Question 1	Study Question 2	Study Question 3	Study Question 4
Individual Needs and Motivation	**Process Theories of Motivation**	**Reinforcement Theory of Motivation**	**Motivation and Job Design**
■ Hierarchy of needs theory ■ ERG theory ■ Two-factor theory ■ Acquired needs theory	■ Equity theory ■ Expectancy theory ■ Goal-setting theory ■ Self-efficacy theory	■ Reinforcement strategies ■ Positive reinforcement ■ Punishment	■ Scientific management ■ Job rotation and job enlargement ■ Job enrichment ■ Alternative work schedules
✓ Learning Check 1	✓ Learning Check 2	✓ Learning Check 3	✓ Learning Check 4

Did you know that J. K. Rowling's first Harry Potter book

was rejected by 12 publishers, that their "sound" cost the Beatles a deal with Decca Records, and that Walt Disney once lost a newspaper job because he supposedly "lacked imagination"?[5] Thank goodness they didn't give up. In fact, we might say that their "motivation" to stay engaged and confident with their work paid off handsomely—to them and to those who have enjoyed the fruits of their labours over the years.

Why do some people work enthusiastically, persevering in the face of difficulty and often doing more than required to turn out an extraordinary performance? Why do others hold back, quit at the first negative feedback, and do the minimum needed to avoid reprimand or termination? What can be done to ensure that the best possible performance is achieved by every person, in every job, on every workday? These questions are, or should be, asked by managers in all work settings. Good answers begin when, as with the example of Charlie Butcher in the chapter opener, we are willing to respect people and make them a top priority. And when it comes to acting on this priority, there is no better place to start than by achieving a clear understanding of motivation theories and their implications for practice.

INDIVIDUAL NEEDS AND MOTIVATION

The term **motivation** is used in management theory to describe forces within the individual that account for the level, direction, and persistence of effort expended at work. Simply put, a highly motivated person works hard at a job; an unmotivated person does not. A manager who leads through motivation does so by creating conditions under which other people feel consistently inspired to work hard.

Most discussions of motivation begin with the concept of individual **needs**—the unfulfilled physiological or psychological desires of an individual. Although each of the following theories discusses a slightly different set of needs, all agree that needs cause tensions that influence attitudes and behaviour. Their advice to managers is to help people satisfy important needs through their work and try to eliminate obstacles that block need satisfaction.

> **Motivation** accounts for the level, direction, and persistence of effort expended at work.

> A **need** is an unfulfilled physiological or psychological desire.

HIERARCHY OF NEEDS THEORY

The theory of human needs developed by Abraham Maslow was introduced in Chapter 2 as an important foundation of the history of management thought. In his hierarchy, **lower-order needs** include physiological, safety, and social concerns, and **higher-order needs** include esteem and self-actualization concerns.[6] Whereas lower-order needs are desires for physical and social well-being, the higher-order needs are desires for psychological development and growth.

Maslow uses two principles to describe how these needs affect human behaviour. The *deficit principle* states that a satisfied need is not a motivator of behaviour. People are expected to act in ways that satisfy deprived needs—that is, needs for which a "deficit" exists. The *progression principle* states that a need at one level does not become activated until the next-lower-level need is already satisfied. People are expected to advance step by step up the hierarchy in their search for need satisfactions. This principle ends at the level of self-actualization; the more these needs are satisfied, the stronger they are supposed to grow.

> **Lower-order needs** are physiological, safety, and social needs in Maslow's hierarchy.

> **Higher-order needs** are esteem and self-actualization needs in Maslow's hierarchy.

Although research has not verified the deficit and progression principles, Maslow's ideas are still very helpful. Figure 14.1 illustrates how managers can use them to better meet the needs of the people with whom they work. Notice that higher-order self-actualization needs are served by things like creative and challenging work and job autonomy; esteem needs are served by responsibility, praise, and recognition. The satisfaction of lower-order social, safety, and physiological needs rests more with conditions of the work environment. Employee benefits are one example. An Aventis Health Care Survey of Canadian workers concluded that the majority of Canadians would not be willing to trade their employee health benefit plans for cash. In fact, when given the choice between their existing health benefits and an $8,000 yearly sum, 72 percent of Canadians surveyed chose their existing benefit package.[7]

Bettmann/© Corbis

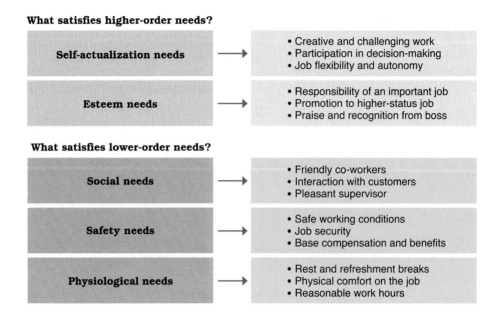

Figure 14.1 Opportunities for satisfaction in Maslow's hierarchy of human needs.

ERG THEORY

Existence needs are desires for physical well-being.

Relatedness needs are desires for good interpersonal relationships.

Growth needs are desires for personal growth and development.

One of the most promising efforts to build on Maslow's work is the ERG theory proposed by Clayton Alderfer.[8] This theory collapses Maslow's five needs categories into three. **Existence needs** are desires for physiological and material well-being. **Relatedness needs** are desires for satisfying interpersonal relationships. **Growth needs** are desires for continued psychological growth and development.

The dynamics among needs in ERG theory differ a bit from Maslow's thinking. ERG does not assume that certain needs must be satisfied before other ones become activated; any or all needs can influence individual behaviour at a given time. And Alderfer does not believe that satisfied needs lose their motivational impact. His ERG theory contains a *frustration-regression principle*, according to which an already-satisfied lower-level need can become reactivated and influence behaviour when a higher-level need cannot be satisfied. It might be argued, for example, that when labour unions representing factory workers bargain hard for things like shorter workweeks and better working conditions (responsive to existence needs), they are doing so partly out of the workers' dissatisfaction with boring assembly-line jobs (frustrated growth needs).

TWO-FACTOR THEORY

A **satisfier factor** is found in job content, such as a sense of achievement, recognition, responsibility, advancement, or personal growth.

A **hygiene factor** is found in the job context, such as working conditions, interpersonal relations, organizational policies, and salary.

The two-factor theory of Frederick Herzberg was developed from a pattern discovered in almost 4,000 interviews.[9] When asked what "turned them on" about their work, respondents talked mostly about things relating to the nature of the job itself. Herzberg calls these **satisfier factors**. When asked what "turned them off," they talked more about things relating to the work setting. Herzberg calls these **hygiene factors**.

As shown in Figure 14.2, the two-factor theory links hygiene factors with job dissatisfaction. That is, job dissatisfaction is likely when hygiene is poor. The hygiene factors are found in the job context and include such things as working conditions, interpersonal relations, organizational policies and administration, technical quality of supervision, and base wage or salary. Herzberg argues that improving them, such as by adding piped-in music or implementing a no-smoking policy, can make people less dissatisfied at work. But it will not increase job satisfaction and motivation.

Figure 14.2 links satisfier factors, sometimes called motivator factors, with job satisfaction. The satisfier factors include such things as a sense of achievement, feelings of recognition, a sense of responsibility, the opportunity for advancement, and feelings of personal growth. Herzberg believes that work motivation comes from satisfier factors found in job content. When these factors are present, jobs become sources of high-order need satisfactions. And to build such high-content jobs, Herzberg suggests the technique of *job enrichment*. It largely makes the job holder responsible for not just doing the work but also planning and controlling its accomplishment. This job design technique will be discussed in more detail later in the chapter.

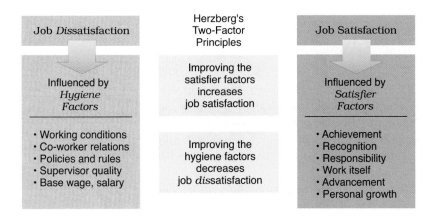

Figure 14.2 Elements in Herzberg's two-factor theory.

Scholars have criticized Herzberg's theory as being method-bound and difficult to replicate.[10] For his part, Herzberg reports confirming studies in countries located in Europe, Africa, the Middle East, and Asia.[11] At the very least, the two-factor theory remains a useful reminder that there are two important aspects of all jobs: *job content*—what people do in terms of job tasks; and *job context*—the work setting in which they do it. Herzberg's advice to managers is still timely: (1) always correct poor context to eliminate actual or potential sources of job dissatisfaction; and (2) be sure to build satisfier factors into job content to maximize opportunities for job satisfaction.

ACQUIRED NEEDS THEORY

In the late 1940s, David McClelland and his colleagues began experimenting with the Thematic Apperception Test (TAT) as a way of examining human needs.[12] The TAT asks people to view pictures and write stories about what they see. The stories are then content-analyzed for themes that display the strengths of three needs: achievement, power, and affiliation. According to McClelland, people acquire or develop these needs over time as a result of individual life experiences. Because each need can be linked with a distinct set of work preferences, he encourages managers to understand these needs in themselves and in others, and try to create work environments responsive to them.

Need for achievement is the desire to do something better or more efficiently, to solve problems, or to master complex tasks. People with a high need for achievement like to put their competencies to work; they take moderate risks in competitive situations, and they are willing to work alone. As a result, the work preferences of high-need achievers include individual responsibility for results, achievable but challenging goals, and feedback on performance.

Need for achievement is the desire to do something better, to solve problems, or to master complex tasks.

GOING GLOBAL

CIRQUE DU SOLEIL MEETS PERFORMERS' NEEDS TO SOAR HIGH

Canadian based but with a strong global presence, Cirque du Soleil is committed to making its performers' jobs both challenging and rewarding. Even with gruelling rehearsal and performance schedules, Cirque du Soleil is able to both attract and retain talented performers. In part, Cirque is an employer of choice because it allows performers to unleash their own creativity, giving a whole new meaning to "high performance." Performers have a large say about how shows are staged. They are also allowed to move across the globe to join other Cirque du Soleil shows. This flexibility allows performers to gain exposure to other top artists in their field and to fulfill their needs for achievement and affiliation.

Need for power is the desire to control, influence, or be responsible for other people.

Need for power is the desire to control other people, to influence their behaviour, or to be responsible for them. People with a high need for power are motivated to behave in ways that have a clear impact on other people and events. They enjoy being in control of a situation and being recognized for this responsibility. A person with a high need for power prefers work that involves control over other persons, has an impact on people and events, and brings public recognition and attention.

McClelland distinguishes between two forms of the power need. The *need for personal power* is exploitative and involves manipulation for the pure sake of personal gratification. This type of power need is not successful in management. By contrast, the *need for social power* is the positive face of power. It involves the use of power in a socially responsible way, one that is directed toward group or organizational objectives rather than personal gains. This need for social power is essential to managerial leadership.

Need for affiliation is the desire to establish and maintain good relations with people.

Need for affiliation is the desire to establish and maintain friendly and warm relations with other people. People with a high need for affiliation seek companionship, social approval, and satisfying interpersonal relationships. They tend to like jobs that involve interpersonal relationships and bring opportunities to receive social approval.

McClelland believes that people with a very high need for affiliation alone may have difficulty as managers because their desires for social approval and friendship interfere with decision-making. There are times when managers and leaders must decide and act in ways that other persons may disagree with. If the need for affiliation limits someone's ability to make these decisions, managerial effectiveness gets lost. The successful executive, in McClelland's view, is likely to possess a high need for social power that is greater than an otherwise strong need for affiliation.

✔ **Learning Check ①**

BE SURE YOU CAN

• define *motivation* and *needs* • describe work practices that satisfy higher-order and lower-order needs in Maslow's hierarchy • contrast Maslow's hierarchy with ERG theory • describe work practices that influence hygiene factors and satisfier factors in Herzberg's two-factor theory • explain McClelland's needs for achievement, affiliation, and power • describe work conditions that satisfy a person with a high need for achievement

Process Theories of Motivation

Although the details vary, each of the needs theories offers insights into individual differences and how managers can deal positively with them. Another set of motivation theories, the process theories, add to this understanding. The equity, expectancy, goal-setting, and self-efficacy theories focus on how people make choices to work hard or not, based on their individual preferences, the available rewards, and possible work outcomes.

EQUITY THEORY

The equity theory of motivation is best known in management through the work of J. Stacy Adams.[13] It is based on the logic of social comparisons and the notion that perceived inequity is a motivating state. That is, when people believe that they have been unfairly treated in comparison to others, they will be motivated to eliminate the discomfort and restore a sense of perceived equity to the situation. The classic example is pay, and the equity question is: "in comparison with others, how fairly am I being compensated for the work that I do?"

Equity and Social Comparison

Figure 14.3 shows how the equity dynamic works in the form of input-to-outcome comparisons. These equity comparisons are especially common whenever managers allocate things such as pay raises, vacation schedules, preferred job assignments, work privileges, and office space. The equity comparisons may be with co-workers, workers elsewhere in the organization, and even persons employed by other organizations.

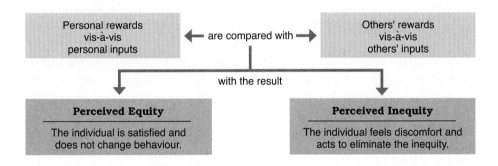

Figure 14.3 Equity theory and the role of social comparison.

A key point in the equity theory is that people behave according to their perceptions. What influences individual behaviour is not the reward's absolute value or the manager's intentions; the recipient's perceptions determine the motivational outcomes. Perceived inequities occur whenever people feel that the rewards received for their work efforts are unfair, given the rewards others appear to be getting. An individual who perceives that she or he is being treated unfairly in comparison to others will be motivated to act in ways that reduce the perceived inequity. For example, when *perceived negative inequity* exists, Adams predicts that people will try to deal with it by:

- Changing their work inputs by putting less effort into their jobs.
- Changing the rewards received by asking for better treatment.
- Changing the comparison points to make things seem better.
- Changing the situation by leaving the job.

REAL ETHICS

Information Goldmine

A worker opens the top of the office photocopier and finds a document someone has left behind. It's a list of performance evaluations, pay, and bonuses for 80 co-workers. She reads the document. Lo and behold, someone considered a "nonstarter" is getting paid more than others regarded as "super workers." New hires are being brought in at substantially higher pay and bonuses than are paid to existing staff. And to make matters worse, she's in the middle of the list and not near the top, where she would have expected to be. She makes a lot less money than some others are getting.

Looking at the data, she begins to wonder why she is spending extra hours working on her laptop evenings and weekends at home, trying to do a really great job for the firm.

"Should I pass this information around anonymously so that everyone knows what's going on? she wonders. "Or should I quit and

find another employer who fully values me for my talents and hard work?"

YOU DECIDE

What would you do? Obviously, you are going to be concerned, and perhaps upset. Would you hit "print," make about 80 copies, and put them in everyone's mailboxes—or even just leave them stacked in a couple of convenient locations? That would get the information out and right into the gossip chains pretty quickly. But is this ethical?

In the real case, our worker decided to quit, saying: "I just couldn't stand the inequity." She also decided not to distribute the information to others in the office. "I couldn't give it to people who were still working there because it would make them depressed, like it made me depressed," she said.

Equity Dynamics

Research on equity theory has largely been accomplished in the laboratory. It is most conclusive with respect to perceived negative inequity. Those who feel underpaid, for example, may try to restore perceived equity by pursuing one or more of the actions described in the prior list, such as reducing current work efforts to compensate for the missing rewards or even quitting the job.[14] There is also evidence that the equity dynamic occurs among people who feel overpaid. This time the perceived positive inequity is associated with a sense of guilt. The attempt to restore perceived equity may involve, for example, increasing the quantity or quality of work, taking on more difficult assignments, or working overtime.

Managers should probably anticipate perceived negative inequities whenever especially visible rewards, such as pay or promotions, are allocated. Then, instead of letting equity dynamics get out of hand, they can try to manage perceptions. This might involve carefully communicating the intended value of rewards being given, clarifying the performance appraisals upon which they are based, and suggesting appropriate comparison points. This advice is especially relevant in organizations using merit-based pay-for-performance systems. Just what constitutes "meritorious" performance can be a source of considerable debate. And any disagreement over performance ratings makes problems due to negative equity dynamics more likely.

EXPECTANCY THEORY

Victor Vroom's expectancy theory of motivation asks the question: what determines the willingness of an individual to work hard at tasks important to the organization?[15] The theory answers that "people will do what they can do when they want to do it." More specifically, Vroom suggests that a person's motivation to work depends on the relationships among the three expectancy factors depicted in Figure 14.4, and described here:

Expectancy is a person's belief that working hard will result in high task performance.

- **Expectancy**—a person's belief that working hard will result in a desired level of task performance being achieved (this is sometimes called effort-performance expectancy).

- **Instrumentality**—a person's belief that successful performance will be followed by rewards and other work-related outcomes (this is sometimes called performance-outcome expectancy).

Instrumentality is a person's belief that various outcomes will occur as a result of task performance.

- **Valence**—the value that a person assigns to the possible rewards and other work-related outcomes.

Valence is the value a person assigns to work-related outcomes.

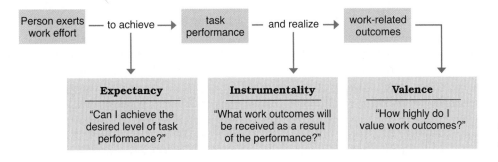

Figure 14.4 Elements in the expectancy theory of motivation.

Motivation = Expectancy × Instrumentality × Valence

In the expectancy theory, motivation (M), expectancy (E), instrumentality (I), and valence (V) are related to one another in a multiplicative fashion: $M = E \times I \times V$. In other words, motivation is determined by expectancy times instrumentality times valence. Mathematically speaking, a zero at any location on the right side of the equation (that is, for E, I, or V) will result in zero motivation.

Suppose, for example, that a manager is wondering whether or not the prospect of earning a promotion will be motivational to a subordinate. Expectancy theory predicts that a person's motivation to work hard for a promotion will be low if any one or more of the following three conditions apply. First, if expectancy is low, motivation will suffer. The person may believe that he or she cannot achieve the performance level necessary to get promoted. So why try? Second, if instrumentality is low, motivation will suffer. The person may lack confidence that a high level of task performance will result in being promoted. So why try? Third, if valence is low, motivation will suffer. The person may place little value on receiving a promotion; it simply isn't much of a reward. So, once again, why try?

Expectancy Theory Applications

Expectancy theory reminds managers that different people answer the question "why should I work hard today?" in different ways. The implication is that every person must be respected as an individual with unique needs, preferences, and concerns. Knowing this, a manager can try to customize work environments for high motivation.

To maximize expectancy, people must believe in their abilities; they must believe that, if they try, they can perform. Managers can build positive expectancies by selecting workers with the right abilities for the jobs to be done, providing them with the best training and development, and supporting them with resources so that the jobs can be done very well. To maximize instrumentality, people must perceive that high performance will be followed by certain outcomes. Managers can create positive instrumentalities by taking care to clarify the possible rewards linked with high performance, and by acting consistently in actually allocating rewards on a performance-contingent basis. To maximize positive valence, people must value the outcomes associated with high performance. Here, managers can use the content theories to help identify important needs. These needs can then be linked with rewards that offer positive valences and that can be earned through high performance.

GOAL-SETTING THEORY

As newly elected chair of the Wine Council of Ontario and president of Flat Rock Cellars, a winery co-founded with his father in 1999, Ed Madronich Jr. is an illustration of how influential the act of goal setting can be in accomplishing one's dreams. Starting his career as a brand manager for Vincor Canada, Madronich seized every opportunity he could to enhance his knowledge and experience in the wine industry, including spending a summer in France to increase his exposure to world-class wines. Madronich quickly worked his way from brand manager to director of marketing for Inniskillin before taking the leap to establish Flat Rock Cellars with his father. Ed used a strategic step-by-step approach to develop a thorough knowledge of his industry and embraced the challenges his dream presented to reach his final goal. Flat Rock Cellars is now known as a premier winery in the Niagara region with its high-quality wines and unique creative flair. Using expectancy theory, Victor Vroom would point out that Madronich's parents increased his motivation through their enthusiasm for the wine industry and by creating high positive expectancy surrounding hard work. Using goal-setting theory, Edwin Locke would add that Madronich found lots of motivation through career advancement goals he set prior to his entrepreneurial venture.[16]

Goal-Setting Essentials

The basic premise of Locke's goal-setting theory is that task goals can be highly motivating if they are properly set and if they are well managed.[17] Goals give direction to people in their work. Goals clarify the performance expectations in supervisory relationships, between co-workers, and across subunits in an organization. Goals establish a frame of reference for task feedback. Goals also provide a foundation for behavioural self-management. In these and related ways, Locke believes goal setting can enhance individual work performance and job satisfaction.

To achieve the motivational benefits of goal setting, research by Locke and his associates indicates that managers and team leaders must work with themselves and others to set the right goals in the right ways. Things such as goal specificity, goal difficulty, goal acceptance, and goal commitment are among the goal-setting recommendations provided in Management Smarts 14.1.

14.1 MANAGEMENT SMARTS
How to make goal setting work for you

- *Set specific goals:* They lead to higher performance than do more generally stated ones, such as "do your best."

- *Set challenging goals:* When viewed as realistic and attainable, more difficult goals lead to higher performance than do easy goals.

- *Build goal acceptance and commitment:* People work harder for goals they accept and believe in; they resist goals forced on them.

- *Clarify goal priorities:* Make sure that expectations are clear as to which goals should be accomplished first, and why.

- *Provide feedback on goal accomplishment:* Make sure that people know how well they are doing with respect to goal accomplishment.

- *Reward goal accomplishment:* Don't let positive accomplishments pass unnoticed; reward people for doing what they set out to do.

Goal Setting and Participation

Participation is often a key to unlocking the motivational value of task goals. The concept of management by objectives, described in Chapter 6 on planning, is a good example. When done well, MBO brings supervisors and subordinates together in a participative process of goal setting and performance review. MBO is most likely to increase motivation when participation allows for increased understanding of specific and difficult goals, and provides for greater acceptance and commitment to them. Along with participation, the opportunity to receive feedback on goal accomplishment also adds to the motivational impact of MBO.

Managers should be aware of the participation options in goal setting. It isn't always possible to allow participation when selecting which goals need to be pursued. But it can be possible to allow participation in deciding how best to pursue them. Also, the constraints of time and other factors operating in some situations may not allow for participation. Locke's research suggests that workers will respond positively to externally imposed goals if supervisors assigning them are trusted, and if workers believe they will be adequately supported in their attempts to achieve them.

SELF-EFFICACY THEORY

Closely related to both the expectancy and goal-setting approaches to motivation is self-efficacy theory, also referred to as social learning theory. Based on the work of psychologist Albert Bandura, the notion of **self-efficacy** refers to a person's belief that she or he is capable of performing a task.[18] You can think of self-efficacy using such terms as confidence, competence, and ability. From a manager's perspective, the major insight of self-efficacy theory is that anything done to boost feelings of confidence, competence, and ability among people at work is likely to pay off with increased levels of motivation.

Self-efficacy is a person's belief that she or he is capable of performing a task.

RESEARCH BRIEF

Positive psychological capital is an important influence on performance and satisfaction

A concept known as PsyCap, or psychological capital, is defined by Fred Luthans and his colleagues as "an individual's positive psychological state of development."

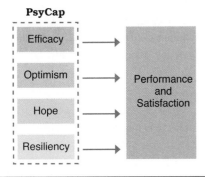

Psychological Capital

This positive state is composed of (1) high personal confidence and self-efficacy in working on a task, (2) optimism about present and future success, (3) hope and perseverance in pursuing goals and adjusting them as needed, and (4) resiliency in responding to setbacks and problems.

A briefings report from the Gallup Leadership Institute points out that psychological capital deals with "who you are" and "who you are becoming." They contrast this with human capital ("what you know") and social capital ("who you know"). It also summarizes studies that address the measurement of PsyCap, and the impact of PsyCap on work attitudes and performance.

In samples of management students and managers, researchers report success with a training intervention designed to raise the level of PsyCap for participants. When performance measures were taken among the

(*continued on next page*)

manager samples, increases in performance were associated with the PsyCap gains. In comparing the costs of the training intervention with the performance gains, the researchers calculated the return on investment as 270 percent. Overall conclusions for this stream of research are that the measurement of PsyCap is reliable and valid, and that PsyCap is positively related to individual performance and satisfaction.

You be the researcher

Does this concept of psychological capital make sense to you? Suppose you could rate others with whom you work or study on hope, optimism, efficacy/confidence, and resiliency. Is it reasonable to think that persons with high PsyCap will be more motivated and productive, whether we are talking about their work, academic performance, or approach to life overall?

Self-Efficacy Dynamics

Mahatma Gandhi once said: "If I have the belief that I can do it, I shall surely acquire the capacity to do it, even if I may not have it at the beginning."[19] The essence of self-efficacy theory is that, when people believe themselves to be capable, they will be more motivated to work hard at a task. The *Wall Street Journal* has called this "the unshakable belief some people have that they have what it takes to succeed."[20] But self-efficacy is not an undifferentiated feeling of confidence, according to Bandura. Rather, it is a capability-specific belief in one's competency to perform a task.

The link between Bandura's ideas, elements of Vroom's expectancy theory, and Locke's goal-setting theory should be clear. With respect to Vroom, a person with higher self-efficacy will have higher expectancy that he or she can achieve a high level of task performance; this increases motivation. With respect to Locke, self-efficacy links with a person's willingness to set challenging performance goals. In both respects, managers who help create feelings of self-efficacy in others should be boosting their motivation to work.

Enhancing Self-Efficacy

According to Bandura's work, there are four major ways in which self-efficacy can be enhanced.[21] First is *enactive mastery*—when a person gains confidence through positive experience. The more you work at a task, so to speak, the more your experience builds and the more confident you become at doing it. Second is *vicarious modelling*—basically, learning by observing others. When someone else is good at a task and we are able to observe how they do it, we gain confidence in being able to do it ourselves. Third is *verbal persuasion*—when someone tells us or encourages us that we can perform the task. Hearing others praise our efforts and link those efforts with performance successes is often very motivational. Fourth is *emotional arousal*—when we are highly stimulated or energized to perform well in a situation. A good analogy for arousal is how athletes get "psyched up" and highly motivated to perform in key competitions.

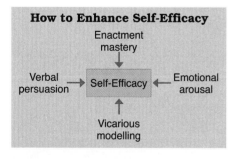

How to Enhance Self-Efficacy

BE SURE YOU CAN

• explain the role of social comparison in Adams's equity theory • describe how people with felt negative inequity behave • define *expectancy*, *instrumentality*, and *valence* • explain Vroom's expectancy theory equation: M = E × I × V • explain Locke's goal-setting theory • define *self-efficacy* and explain four ways of enhancing it

REINFORCEMENT THEORY OF MOTIVATION

The motivation theories discussed so far are concerned with explaining "why" people do things in terms of satisfying needs, resolving felt inequities, evaluating expectancies, and pursuing task goals. Reinforcement theory, by contrast, views human behaviour as determined by its environmental consequences. Instead of looking within the individual to explain motivation, it focuses on the external environment and its consequences. The basic premises of reinforcement theory are based on what E. L. Thorndike called the **law of effect**. It states: behaviour that results in a pleasant outcome is likely to be repeated; behaviour that results in an unpleasant outcome is not likely to be repeated.[22]

REINFORCEMENT STRATEGIES

Psychologist B. F. Skinner popularized the concept of **operant conditioning** as the process of applying the law of effect to control behaviour by manipulating its consequences.[23] You may think of operant conditioning as learning by reinforcement. In management, the goal is to use reinforcement principles to systematically reinforce desirable work behaviour and discourage undesirable work behaviour.[24]

Four strategies of reinforcement are used in operant conditioning. **Positive reinforcement** strengthens or increases the frequency of desirable behaviour by making a pleasant consequence contingent on its occurrence. Example: A manager nods to express approval to someone who makes a useful comment during a staff meeting. **Negative reinforcement** increases the frequency of or strengthens desirable behaviour by making the avoidance of an unpleasant consequence contingent on its occurrence. Example: A manager who has been nagging a worker every day about tardiness does not nag when the worker comes to work on time.

Punishment decreases the frequency of or eliminates an undesirable behaviour by making an unpleasant consequence contingent on its occurrence. Example: A manager issues a written reprimand to an employee whose careless work creates quality problems. **Extinction** decreases the frequency of or eliminates an undesirable behaviour by making the removal of a pleasant consequence contingent on its occurrence. Example: A manager observes that a disruptive employee is receiving social approval from co-workers; the manager counsels co-workers to stop giving this approval.

Figure 14.5 shows how the four reinforcement strategies can be used in management. Notice in the example how the supervisor can use each of the strategies to influence quality practices by employees. Note, too, that both positive and negative reinforcement strategies strengthen desirable behaviour when it occurs; punishment and extinction strategies weaken or eliminate undesirable behaviours.

The **law of effect** states that behaviour followed by pleasant consequences is likely to be repeated; behaviour followed by unpleasant consequences is not.

Operant conditioning is the control of behaviour by manipulating its consequences.

Positive reinforcement strengthens behaviour by making a desirable consequence contingent on its occurrence.

Negative reinforcement strengthens behaviour by making the avoidance of an undesirable consequence contingent on its occurrence.

Punishment discourages behaviour by making an unpleasant consequence contingent on its occurrence.

Extinction discourages behaviour by making the removal of a desirable consequence contingent on its occurrence.

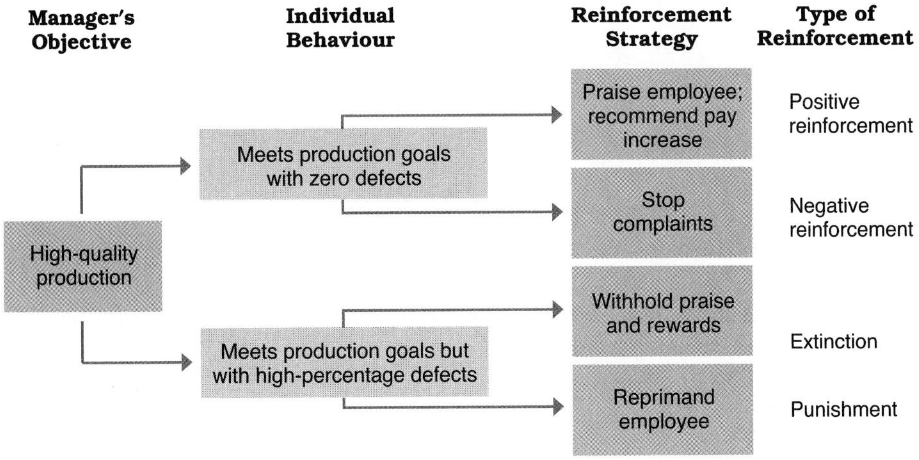

Figure 14.5 Four reinforcement strategies: case of total quality management.

ISSUES AND SITUATIONS
Executive Compensation

Chief executive officers' pay and bonuses are often set to positively reinforce desirable behaviour, such as increasing the company's share value.

The question for many corporate boards and shareholders is, though, are corporate CEOs and senior executives paid too much?

- In 2008, the average CEO in the United States took home about US$18 million in annual compensation, with perks adding another US$438,000.
- In 1965, average CEO pay was 24 times the average worker's, in 1994 it was 90 times, and in 2006 it was 364 times.
- CEOs in America outearn their counterparts in other advanced countries by 13 times.
- During the recent recession, corporate boards seemed to be reining in executive pay. For example, a review of Canada's 100 largest public companies shows top executives received, on average, almost no total compensation increase in 2009.

When Ford Motor Co. lost US$2.72 billion in 2007, its CEO Alan Mulally earned US$2 million in salary, US$4 million in bonus, and US$11 million in stock options. Peter Capelli, a professor at The Wharton School at the University of Pennsylvania, says: "If you're a plant manager and you have a good year, you can take a vacation, but if you're a CEO with options, you can cash out in a good year and your children are set for life." Ron Gettelfinger, president of the United Auto Workers union, said: "Our members at Ford agreed to substantial sacrifices in 2007 to help Ford survive so the company can rebuild and reinvest in the United States. We did not sacrifice so that management could find a way to reward themselves with higher compensation."

Most CEOs will likely say they deserve the high pay and perks, in return for extraordinary hours and years of hard work. But if you follow the news, you'll find a fair amount of "bad press" about the heights of executive pay. Some shareholders are putting resolutions about executive pay on annual meeting agendas, and many corporate boards are becoming more stringent in dealing with executive compensation. CEO pay even became an issue in the U.S. election campaign of 2008, with some calling for Congress to pass legislation giving shareholders more say over executive pay.

CRITICAL RESPONSE

Does astronomically high pay really motivate CEOs? Is there enough punishment for undesirable behaviour? Is it right to pay CEOs such high multiples of what the average workers in their firms earn? Is senior executive work worth such payouts? Are corporate America and corporate Canada doing the right things when it comes to executive pay?

POSITIVE REINFORCEMENT

Among the reinforcement strategies, positive reinforcement deserves special attention. It is governed by two important laws. First, the *law of contingent reinforcement* states that, for a reward to have maximum reinforcing value, it must be delivered only if the desired behaviour is exhibited. Second, the *law of immediate reinforcement* states that the more immediate the delivery of a reward after the occurrence of a desirable behaviour, the greater the reinforcing value of the reward. Additional guidelines for using positive reinforcement are presented in Management Smarts 14.2.

14.2 MANAGEMENT SMARTS
Guidelines for positive reinforcement and punishment

Positive Reinforcement

- Clearly identify desired work behaviours.

- Maintain a diverse inventory of rewards.

- Inform everyone what must be done to get rewards.

- Recognize individual differences when allocating rewards.

- Follow the laws of immediate and contingent reinforcement.

Punishment

- Tell the person what is being done wrong.

- Tell the person what is being done right.

- Make sure the punishment matches the behaviour.

- Administer the punishment in private.

- Follow the laws of immediate and contingent reinforcement.

One way to tap the power of positive reinforcement is through a process known as **shaping**. This is the creation of a new behaviour by the positive reinforcement of successive approximations to it. A **continuous reinforcement** schedule administers a reward each time a desired behaviour occurs. An **intermittent reinforcement** schedule rewards behaviour only periodically. In general, continuous reinforcement will elicit a desired behaviour more quickly than will intermittent reinforcement. Also, behaviour acquired under an intermittent schedule will be more permanent than will behaviour acquired under a continuous schedule. One way to succeed with a shaping strategy, for example, is to give reinforcement on a continuous basis until the desired behaviour is achieved. Then an intermittent schedule can be used to maintain the behaviour at the new level.

David Novak, CEO of Yum Brands, Inc., claims that one of his most important tasks as CEO is "to get people fired up." He adds: "You can never underestimate the power of telling someone he's doing a good job."[25] Viive Tamm, CEO of Toronto-based advertising agency Tamm Communications, recognizes that "money is only one of the things that talks" in keeping employees happy and engaged. As head of a small firm with limited financial resources, Tamm promotes positive reinforcement through employee barbeues, event tickets, and even free access to Tamm's vacation cabin near Montreal.[26] A classic example of positive reinforcement comes from the story of Mary Kay Cosmetics, where the legendary pink Cadillac has been a sought-after prize by top performers for many years. More recently, and to keep pace with changing times, the firm has added other vehicles and choices to the list of prizes. All are still awarded with great ceremony at gala parties where hundreds of co-workers join in the celebrations.[27] Another example of positive reinforcement is Sophos Inc., a computer programming company based in Vancouver. Sophos rewards top sales employees with an additional five days' paid vacation and $6,000 toward a trip of their choice.[28]

Shaping is positive reinforcement of successive approximations to the desired behaviour.

Continuous reinforcement rewards each time a desired behaviour occurs.

Intermittent reinforcement rewards behaviour only periodically.

PUNISHMENT

As a reinforcement strategy, punishment attempts to eliminate undesirable behaviour by making an unpleasant consequence contingent upon its occurrence. To punish an employee, for example, a manager may deny a valued reward, such as praise or merit pay, or administer an unpleasant outcome, such as a verbal reprimand or pay reduction. Like positive reinforcement, punishment can be done poorly or it can be done well. All too often, it is probably done poorly. Look again at Management Smarts 14.2; it offers advice on how best to handle punishment as a reinforcement strategy.

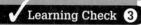

✓ **Learning Check ③**

BE SURE YOU CAN

• explain the law of effect and operant conditioning • illustrate how positive reinforcement, negative reinforcement, punishment, and extinction influence work behaviour • explain the reinforcement technique of shaping • describe how managers can use the laws of immediate and contingent reinforcement when allocating rewards

MOTIVATION AND JOB DESIGN

Job design is arranging work tasks for individuals and groups.

One area of practice in which the various motivation theories come into play is **job design**, the process of arranging work tasks for individuals and groups. Building jobs so that satisfaction and performance go hand in hand is in many ways an exercise in "fit" between the task requirements and an individual's needs, capabilities, and interests.[29] Figure 14.6 shows the job design alternatives of job simplification, job rotation and enlargement, and job enrichment.

	Job simplification	Job rotation and enlargement	Job enrichment
Job scope • number and variety of tasks	narrow	wide	wide
Job depth • extent of planning, controlling responsibility	low	low	high
Task specialization	high	moderate	low

Figure 14.6 Basic job design alternatives.

SCIENTIFIC MANAGEMENT

Job simplification employs people in clearly defined and specialized tasks with narrow job scope.

Job simplification involves standardizing work procedures and employing people in well-defined and highly specialized tasks. This is an extension of the scientific management approach discussed in Chapter 2. Simplified jobs are narrow in *job scope*—that is, the number and variety of different tasks a person performs. Many employees around the world earn their livings working at highly simplified tasks, often on assembly lines. The most extreme form of job simplification is **automation**, or the total mechanization of a job.

Automation is the total mechanization of a job.

The logic of job simplification is straightforward. Because the jobs don't require complex skills, workers should be easier and quicker to train, less difficult to supervise, and easy to replace if they leave. Furthermore, because tasks are well defined, workers should become good at them while performing the same work over and over again. Consider the case of Cindy Vang, on an assembly line for Medtronics Inc. She works in a dust-free room making a specialized medical component. She is certified on 5 of 14 job skills in her department. At any given time, however, she performs only one of them; for example, feeding small devices by tweezers into special containers. It is tedious work without much challenge, but Vang says: "I like it." Importantly, she notes that the job doesn't interfere with her home life with a husband and three sons. Her economic needs are met in a low-stress job and comfortable work environment.[30] Canadian-based multinational corporation Linamar uses scientific management principles in operating its 37 manufacturing facilities based in 8 countries. Through the standardization of line manufacturing and operational controls, Linamar has been able to produce consistent, efficient work practices across all of its international facilities.[31]

Things don't always work out this well in organizations using simplified job designs. The structured and repetitive tasks can cause problems of boredom and alienation. Productivity can suffer when unhappy workers do poor work, and when costs go up due to higher levels of absenteeism and turnover.

JOB ROTATION AND JOB ENLARGEMENT

A step beyond simplification in job design, **job rotation** increases task variety by periodically shifting workers between jobs involving different task assignments. Job rotation can be done on a regular schedule; it can also be done as opportunity or need exists. Such periodic or occasional job rotation is often used as a training approach, helping people learn about jobs performed by others. Another alternative is **job enlargement**: increasing task variety by combining two or more tasks that were previously assigned to separate workers. Often these are tasks that are done immediately before or after the work performed in the original job. This is sometimes called *horizontal loading*—pulling pre-work or later work stages into the job.

Job rotation increases task variety by periodically shifting workers between different jobs.

Job enlargement increases task variety by combining into one job two or more tasks previously done by separate workers.

CANADIAN MANAGERS

Tanbir Grover: Learning the Beverage Business from All Angles

After graduation, Tanbir Grover accepted a two-year rotational management position at the Toronto head office of the Coca-Cola Bottling Co. Drawing upon a job rotation strategy, Coca-Cola is offering highly motivated business graduates the chance to play musical chairs and test their skills in a number of different jobs. These graduates have a chance to work in different roles such as finance, sales, and supply-chain management before settling on a full-time management role within the company. "It's allowing me to practise what I've learned in smaller increments instead of being given a position in one department," says Grover. "In the end, it allows you to appreciate the business holistically."

JOB ENRICHMENT

Frederick Herzberg, whose two-factor theory of motivation was discussed earlier, questions the motivational value of job enlargement and rotation. "Why," he asks, "should a worker become motivated when one or more meaningless tasks are added to previously existing ones, or when work assignments are rotated among equally meaningless tasks?" By contrast, he says: "If you

Job enrichment increases job depth by adding work planning and evaluating duties normally performed by the supervisor.

want people to do a good job, give them a good job to do."[32] Herzberg believes this is best done through **job enrichment**, the practice of expanding job content to create more opportunities for satisfaction. In contrast to job enlargement and rotation, job enrichment increases *job depth*—the extent to which task planning and evaluating duties are performed by the individual worker rather than the supervisor.

Job Characteristics Model

Modern management theory adopts a contingency perspective that takes job enrichment a step beyond Herzberg's suggestions. Most importantly, it recognizes that job enrichment may not be good for everyone. This thinking is reflected in the job characteristics model developed by J. Richard Hackman and his associates, and shown in Figure 14.7.[33]

According to this diagnostic approach, job satisfaction and performance are influenced by three critical psychological states: (1) experienced meaningfulness of the work; (2) experienced responsibility for the outcomes of the work; and (3) knowledge of actual results of work activities. These, in turn, are influenced by the presence or absence of five core job characteristics. A job that is high in the following core characteristics is considered enriched; the lower a job scores on these characteristics, the less enriched it is.

1. *Skill variety*—the degree to which a job requires a variety of different activities to carry out the work, and involves the use of a number of different skills and talents of the individual.

2. *Task identity*—the degree to which the job requires completion of a "whole" and identifiable piece of work, one that involves doing a job from beginning to end with a visible outcome.

3. *Task significance*—the degree to which the job has a substantial impact on the lives or work of other people elsewhere in the organization, or in the external environment.

4. *Autonomy*—the degree to which the job gives the individual freedom, independence, and discretion in scheduling work and in choosing procedures for carrying it out.

5. *Feedback from the job itself*—the degree to which work activities required by the job result in the individual obtaining direct and clear information on his or her performance.

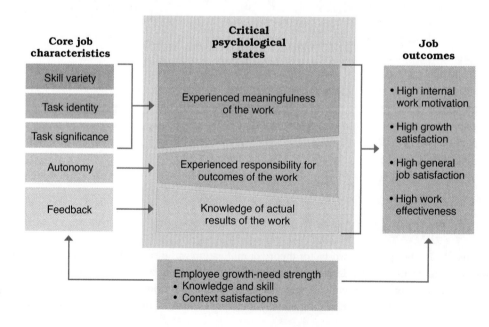

Figure 14.7 Designing jobs using the job characteristics model.

Source: Reprinted by permission from J. Richard Hackman and Greg R. Oldham, *Work Redesign* (Reading, MA: Addison-Wesley, 1980), p. 90.

In true contingency fashion, these core job characteristics will not affect all people in the same way. Generally speaking, people who respond most favourably to enriched jobs will have strong higher-order needs and appropriate job knowledge and skills, and will be otherwise satisfied with job context. The expectation is also that people who have strong growth needs, as described in Alderfer's ERG theory, will respond most positively to enriched jobs.

Improving Job Characteristics

For those situations when job enrichment is a good choice, Hackman and his colleagues recommend five ways to improve the core job characteristics. First, *form natural units of work.* Make sure that the tasks people perform are logically related to one another and provide a clear and meaningful task identity. Second, *combine tasks.* Expand job responsibilities by pulling together into one larger job a number of smaller tasks previously done by others. Third, *establish client relationships.* Put people in contact with others who, as clients inside or outside the organization, use the results of their work. Fourth, *open feedback channels.* Provide opportunities for people both to receive performance feedback as they work and to learn how performance changes over time. Fifth, *practise vertical loading.* Give people authority to perform the planning and controlling previously done by supervisors. In contrast to job enlargement and job rotation, which only make jobs bigger horizontally, job enrichment makes jobs vertically bigger as well.

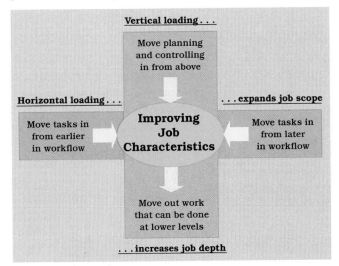

ALTERNATIVE WORK SCHEDULES

Not only is the content of jobs important, the context is too. Among the more significant developments is the emergence of a number of alternative ways for people to schedule their work time,[34] and "flexibility" is often the key word. Many employers are finding that providing alternative work schedules can help attract and retain motivated workers by offering flexibility that helps them deal with the many complications of work–life balance.

Flexible Working Hours

The term **flexible working hours**, also called *flextime*, describes any work schedule that gives employees some choice in the pattern of their daily work hours. Flexible schedules with choices of starting and ending times give employees greater autonomy while still meeting their work responsibilities. Some may choose to come in earlier and leave earlier, while still completing an eight-hour day; others may choose to start later in the morning and leave later. In between these extremes are opportunities to attend to personal affairs, such as dental appointments, home emergencies, visits to children's schools, and so on. All of the top 25 companies on Canada's Top Family Friendly Employers list offer flexible work arrangements and provide assistance with child care needs.[35] Reports indicate that giving employees flexibility in dealing with non-work obligations reduces stress—and job turnover.[36]

Flexible working hours give employees some choice in daily work hours.

Compressed Workweek

A **compressed workweek** is any work schedule that allows a full-time job to be completed in less than the standard five days of 8-hour shifts. Its most common form is the "4–40"; that is, accomplishing 40 hours of work in four 10-hour days. A key feature of the 4–40 schedule is that the

A **compressed workweek** allows a full-time job to be completed in less than five days.

employee receives three consecutive days off from work each week. The option of a compressed workweek is offered to many employees throughout the Canadian government. Employees of the Public Service Commission in the Yukon have the option of setting aside predetermined days off and leveraging their working hours over a two-week, three-week, or four-week basis.[37]

Reported benefits include improved employee morale, lower overtime costs, less absenteeism, fewer days lost to sick leave, as well as lower costs of commuting.[38] Potential disadvantages of the compressed workweek include increased fatigue and family adjustment problems for the individual, as well as increased scheduling problems, possible customer complaints, and union objections on the organization side.

Job Sharing

Job sharing splits one job between two or more people.

Another work scheduling alternative is **job sharing**, where one full-time job is split between two or more persons. This often involves each person working one-half day, but it can also be done on weekly or monthly sharing arrangements. Organizations benefit by employing talented people who would otherwise be unable to work. A parent, for example, may be unable to stay away from home for a full workday, but may be able to work half a day. Job sharing allows two such persons to be employed as one, often to great benefit.

Telecommuting

Telecommuting involves using IT to work at home or outside the office.

It is increasingly popular for people to work away from a fixed office location. **Telecommuting** is a work arrangement that allows at least a portion of scheduled work hours to be completed outside the office. It is often facilitated by computers and information technology that allow electronic

links with customers and co-workers. New terms are even becoming associated with telecommuting practices. We speak of "hotelling" when telecommuters come to the central office and use temporary office facilities; we also refer to "virtual offices" that include everything from an office at home to a mobile workspace in an automobile.

When asked what they like, telecommuters tend to report increased productivity, fewer distractions, the freedom to be your own boss, and the benefit of having more time for themselves. On the negative side, they cite working too much, having less time to themselves, difficulty separating work and personal life, and having less time for family.[39] One telecommuter's advice to others is this: "You have to have self-discipline and pride in what you do, but you also have to have a boss that trusts you enough to get out of the way."[40]

Part-Time Work

Part-time work is temporary employment for less than the standard 40-hour workweek.

Contingency workers are employed on a part-time and temporary basis to supplement a permanent workforce.

The growing use of temporary workers is a current employment trend. **Part-time work** is done on any schedule less than the standard 40-hour workweek that does not qualify the individual as a full-time employee. Many employers rely on such **contingency workers**—part-timers or "permatemps"—to supplement the full-time workforce, often on a long-term basis. There are now over 3.4 million part-time workers in the Canadian labour force.[41] No longer limited to the traditional areas of clerical services, sales personnel, and unskilled labour, these workers serve an increasingly broad range of employer needs. It is now possible to hire on a part-time basis everything from executive support, such as a chief financial officer, to special expertise in engineering, computer programming, and market research.

Because part-time or contingency workers can be easily hired, contracted with, and terminated in response to changing needs, many employers like the flexibility they offer in controlling labour costs and dealing with cyclical demand. On the other hand, some worry that temporary workers lack the commitment of permanent workers and may demonstrate lower productivity. Perhaps the most controversial issues affecting part-time workers are that they may be paid less than their full-time counterpart, and many do not receive important benefits such as health care, life insurance, pension plans, and paid vacations.

BE SURE YOU CAN

• illustrate a job designed by job simplification, rotation, and enlargement • list and describe the five core job characteristics • explain how a person's growth needs and skills can affect his or her responses to job enrichment • describe the advantages of compressed workweeks, flexible work hours, job sharing, and telecommuting as alternative work schedules • discuss the significance of part-time contingency workers in the economy

MANAGEMENT LEARNING REVIEW

STUDY QUESTIONS SUMMARY

1. How do individual needs influence motivation?

• Motivation predicts the level, direction, and persistence of effort expended at work; simply put, a highly motivated person works hard.

• Maslow's hierarchy of human needs suggests a progression from lower-order physiological, safety, and social needs to higher-order ego and self-actualization needs.

• Alderfer's ERG theory identifies existence, relatedness, and growth needs.

• Herzberg's two-factor theory describes the importance of both job content and job context to motivation and performance.

• McClelland's acquired needs theory identifies the needs for achievement, affiliation, and power, all of which may influence what a person desires from work.

FOR DISCUSSION Is a high need for achievement always a good trait for managers?

2. What are the process theories of motivation?

• Adams's equity theory recognizes that social comparisons take place when rewards are distributed in the workplace.

• People who feel inequitably treated are motivated to act in ways that reduce the sense of inequity; perceived negative inequity may result in someone working less hard in the future.

• Vroom's expectancy theory states that Motivation = Expectancy × Instrumentality × Valence.

• Locke's goal-setting theory emphasizes the motivational power of goals; task goals should be specific rather than ambiguous, difficult but achievable, and set through participatory means.

• Bandura's self-efficacy theory indicates that when people believe they are capable of performing a task, they experience a sense of confidence and will be more highly motivated to work hard at it.

FOR DISCUSSION Can goals be motivational if they are set by the boss?

3. What role does reinforcement play in motivation?

• Reinforcement theory recognizes that human behaviour is influenced by its environmental consequences.

KEY TERMS

automation, 430
compressed workweek, 433
contingency workers, 434
continuous reinforcement, 429
existence needs, 418
expectancy, 423
extinction, 427
flexible working hours, 433
growth needs, 418
higher-order needs, 417
hygiene factors, 418
instrumentality, 423
intermittent
   reinforcement, 429
job design, 430
job enlargement, 431
job enrichment, 432
job rotation, 431
job sharing, 434
job simplification, 430
law of effect, 427
lower-order needs, 417
motivation, 417
need, 417
need for achievement, 419
need for affiliation, 420
need for power, 420
negative reinforcement, 427
operant conditioning, 427
part-time work, 434

- The law of effect states that behaviour followed by a pleasant consequence is likely to be repeated; behaviour followed by an unpleasant consequence is unlikely to be repeated.

- Reinforcement strategies used by managers include positive reinforcement, negative reinforcement, punishment, and extinction.

- Positive reinforcement works best when applied according to the laws of contingent and immediate reinforcement.

FOR DISCUSSION Is it possible for a manager or a parent to rely solely on positive reinforcement strategies?

4. **What are the alternative approaches to job design?**
- Job design is the process of creating or defining jobs by assigning specific work tasks to individuals and groups.

- Job simplification creates narrow and repetitive jobs consisting of well-defined tasks with many routine operations, such as the typical assembly-line job.

- Job enlargement allows individuals to perform a broader range of simplified tasks; job rotation allows individuals to shift among different jobs with similar skill levels.

- The diagnostic approach to job enrichment involves analyzing jobs according to five core characteristics: skill variety, task identity, task significance, autonomy, and feedback.

- Alternative work schedules make work hours more convenient and flexible to better fit workers' needs and personal responsibilities; options include the compressed workweek, flexible working hours, job sharing, telecommuting, and part-time work.

FOR DISCUSSION Can you enrich someone's job without increasing their pay as well?

SELF-TEST

Multiple-Choice Questions

1. Lower-order needs in Maslow's hierarchy correspond to _____ needs in ERG theory.

   (a) growth   (b) affiliation   (c) existence   (d) achievement

2. A worker with a high need for _____ power in McClelland's theory tries to use power for the good of the organization.

   (a) position   (b) expert   (c) personal   (d) social

3. In the _____ theory of motivation, someone who perceives himself or herself as under-rewarded relative to a co-worker might be expected to reduce his or her performance in the future.

   (a) ERG   (b) acquired needs   (c) two-factor   (d) equity

4. Which of the following is a correct match?

   (a) McClelland—ERG theory   (b) Skinner—reinforcement theory   (c) Vroom—equity theory   (d) Locke—expectancy theory

5. The expectancy theory of motivation says that motivation = expectancy × _____ × _____.

   (a) rewards, valence   (b) instrumentality, valence   (c) equity, instrumentality   (d) rewards, equity

6. The law of _____ states that behaviour followed by a positive consequence is likely to be repeated, whereas behaviour followed by an undesirable consequence is not likely to be repeated.

    (a) reinforcement   (b) contingency   (c) goal setting   (d) effect

7. _____ is a positive reinforcement strategy that rewards successive approximations to a desirable behaviour.

    (a) Extinction   (b) Negative reinforcement   (c) Shaping   (d) Merit pay

8. In Herzberg's two-factor theory, base pay is considered a(n) _____ factor.

    (a) valence   (b) satisfier   (c) equity   (d) hygiene

9. When someone has a high and positive "expectancy" in the expectancy theory of motivation, this means that the person _____.

    (a) believes he or she can meet performance expectations   (b) highly values the rewards being offered   (c) sees a link between high performance and available rewards   (d) believes that rewards are equitable

10. In goal-setting theory, the goal of "becoming more productive in my work" would not be considered a source of motivation because it fails the criterion of goal _____.

    (a) acceptance   (b) specificity   (c) challenge   (d) commitment

11. B. F. Skinner would argue that getting a paycheque on Friday reinforces a person for coming to work on Friday, but it does not reinforce the person for having done an extraordinary job on Tuesday. This is because the Friday paycheque fails the law of _____ reinforcement.

    (a) negative   (b) continuous   (c) immediate   (d) intermittent

12. The addition of more planning and evaluating responsibilities to a job is an example of the _____ job design strategy.

    (a) job enrichment   (b) job enlargement   (c) job rotation   (d) job sharing

13. Workers in a compressed workweek typically work 40 hours in _____ days.

    (a) 3   (b) 4   (c) 5   (d) a flexible number of

14. Another term used to describe part-time workers is _____.

    (a) contingency workers   (b) virtual workers   (c) flexible workers   (d) secondary workers

15. Hotelling is a development associated with the growing importance of _____ in the new workplace.

    (a) personal wellness   (b) telecommuting   (c) compressed workweeks   (d) Type A personalities

Short-Response Questions

16. What preferences does a person with a high need for achievement bring to the workplace?

17. Why is participation important to goal-setting theory?

18. What is the common ground in Maslow's, Alderfer's, and McClelland's views of human needs?

19. Why might an employer not want to offer employees the option of a compressed workweek schedule?

Application Question

20. How can a manager combine the powers of goal setting and positive reinforcement to create a highly motivational work environment for a group of workers with high needs for achievement?

MANAGEMENT SKILLS AND COMPETENCIES

SELF-ASSESSMENT

Back to Yourself: Engagement

There's a lot of attention being given these days to the levels of engagement displayed by people at work. Differences in job engagement are evident in a variety of ways. Is someone enthusiastic or lethargic, diligent or lazy, willing to do more than expected or at best willing to do only what is expected? Managers obviously want high levels of engagement by members of their work units and teams, and the ideas of this chapter offer many insights on how to create engagement by using the content, process, and reinforcement theories of motivation. We also want engagement when our outcomes are dependent on how well others perform, say on a team project. Take a look around the classroom. What do you see and what would you predict for the future of your classmates based on the engagement they now show as students?

Further Reflection: Student Engagement Survey

Instructions

Use the following scale to write in the margin the number showing the degree to which you agree with the following statements.

1—No agreement
2—Weak agreement
3—Some agreement
4—Considerable agreement
5—Very strong agreement

1. You know what is expected of you in this course.

2. You have the resources and support you need to do your coursework correctly.

3. In this course, you have the opportunity to do what you do best all the time.

4. In the last week, you have received recognition or praise for doing good work in this course.

5. Your instructor seems to care about you as a person.

6. There is someone in the course who encourages your development.

7. In this course, your opinions seem to count.

8. The mission/purpose of the course makes you feel your study is important.

9. Other students in the course are committed to doing quality work.

10. You have a best friend in the course.

11. In the last six sessions, someone has talked to you about your progress in the course.

12. In this course, you have had opportunities to learn and grow.

Scoring

Score the instrument by adding up the numbers you assigned in all your responses. A score of 12–24 suggests you are "actively disengaged" from the learning experience; a score of 25–47 suggests you are "moderately engaged"; a score of 48–60 indicates you are "actively engaged."

Interpretation

This instrument is a counterpart to a survey used by the Gallup Organization to measure the "engagement" of American workers. The Gallup results are surprising—indicating that up to 19 percent of U.S. workers are actively disengaged, with the annual lost productivity estimated at some US$300 billion per year. One has to wonder: what are the costs of academic disengagement by students?

Source: This survey was developed from a set of "Gallup Engagement Questions" presented in John Thackray, "Feedback for Real," *Gallup Management Journal* (March 15, 2001), data reported from James K. Harter, "The Cost of Disengaged Workers," *Gallup Poll* (March 13, 2001).

TEAM EXERCISE

Why We Work

Preparation

Read this ancient story.

In days of old, a wandering youth happened upon a group of men working in a quarry. Stopping by the first man, he said: "What are you doing?" The worker grimaced and groaned as he replied: "I am trying to shape this stone, and it is backbreaking work." Moving to the next man, the youth repeated the question. This man showed little emotion as he answered: "I am shaping a stone for a building." Moving to the third man, our traveller heard him singing as he worked. "What are you doing?" asked the youth. "I am helping to build a cathedral," the man proudly replied.

Instructions

In groups assigned by your instructor, discuss this short story. (1) Ask and answer the question: "What are the motivation and job design lessons of this ancient story?" (2) Ask members of the group to role-play each of the stonecutters, respectively, while they answer a second question also asked by the youth: "Why are you working?" Have someone in the group be prepared to report and share the group's responses with the class as a whole.

Source: Developed from Brian Dumaine, "Why Do We Work?", *Fortune* (December 26, 1994), pp. 196–204.

CASE 14

Pixar: Animated Geniuses

Pixar has delivered a series of wildly successful animated movies featuring plucky characters and intensely lifelike animation. Yet some of the most memorable ones—Toy Story, Finding Nemo, and The Incredibles—were almost never made. Find out how Apple guru Steve Jobs, whose company struggled to stay alive during its early years, took these upstarts of animation to success.[1]

"The Illusion of Life"

Though the story is far from over, it might seem like a fairytale ending of sorts for John Lasseter, Pixar's creative head, who went from being fired from his position as a Disney animator in the early 80s to running Disney's animation wing with Pixar co-head Edwin Catmull. Lasseter provided the creative direction for Pixar as it grew from an offshoot of the Lucasfilm production company into the world's most successful computer animation company.

Pixar's movies—including *Monsters, Inc., Ratatouille,* and *Up*—have succeeded largely because of Lasseter's focus on

©Walt Disney Co./courtesy Everett Collection

employing computer graphics (CG) technology to make the characters, scenery, and minute details as realistic as possible. "Character animation isn't the fact that an object looks like a character or has a face and hands," Lasseter said. "Character animation is when an object moves like it is alive, when it moves like it is thinking and all of its movements are generated by its own thought processes . . . . It is the thinking that gives the illusion of life."[2]

This "illusion of life" is a direct result of the synergy between Pixar's creative teams, who develop the story and characters, and its technical teams who program—and frequently develop—the animation software used to breathe life into each movie. Each forces the other to innovate, and together they successfully balance the latest technology with a back-to-basics focus on interesting characters in compelling stories. "Pixar has such a thoughtful approach, both from a storyline and business perspective," said Ralph Schackart, analyst with William Blair & Co LLC. "I don't think anyone has quite figured out how to do it like them."[3]

In an industry abounding with *schadenfreude,* some might be surprised that Pixar's old-fashioned approach to moviemaking has succeeded. But Disney CEO Bob Iger believes the opposite. "There is not an ounce of cynicism in Pixar's films," Iger told *Fortune.* "And in a world that is more cynical than it should be, that's pretty refreshing. I think it's a critical ingredient to the success of Pixar's films."[4]

Another unique quality of Pixar is that—unlike competitor Dreamworks Animation SKG—it does not limit its creative products to the animated movies it releases. The studio shares its technical advances with the greater CG community through white papers and technology partnerships, such as its RenderMan software and hardware.[5]

Perhaps Pixar's closest competitor is Dreamworks, headed by former Disney impresario Jeffrey Katzenberg and backed by media luminaries Steven Spielberg and David Geffen. Other, smaller American animation companies such as Orphanage, Wild Brain Inc., and CritterPix Inc. face challenging budgets,

limited technology, and tighter deadlines. And in the event these upstarts do manage a theatrical release, they've got a hard act to follow—Pixar grosses an average of US$395 million per movie.[6]

An Uphill Battle

Pixar came to life in the early 1980s within a computer graphics division of Lucasfilm, George Lucas's production company.[7] The *Star Wars* director hired the brightest computer programmers he could find to fill the small but growing need in Hollywood for CG. Two of Lucas's programmers, Ed Catmull and Alvy Ray Smith, had developed a number of impressive CG technologies. Enter John Lasseter, just let go by Disney because his intense interest in computer animation wasn't shared by management. At an animation conference, Catmull and Smith tapped Lasseter to work with them on a number of digital animation shorts. One, *The Adventures of André & Wally B.,* was the very first character-animation cartoon done with a computer.[8]

Then came Steve Jobs, who had just left Apple Computer and was looking for a new technology venture. He purchased the division, which he named Pixar, for US$5 million, investing another US$5 million to make it financially soluble. During Jobs's tenure, Pixar created about one short film a year and slowly broke into producing television commercials. Jobs sought to capitalize on Pixar's inventive spirit by licensing its RenderMan software and selling its Pixar Image Computer. But at US$130,000 each, the rendering computers were a difficult sell, even in Hollywood. RenderMan sold only slightly better, earning it a reputation as niche software—especially because the program's primary customer was Disney.[9]

Although Jobs aggressively sought to build Pixar's reputation in the animation industry, it was still an uphill battle. He invested more than US$50 million in keeping the company afloat, refusing to concede defeat and even releasing Alvy Smith after repeated personality conflicts. Slowly, Hollywood began to take notice of Pixar. Disney expressed interest in having Pixar develop a feature-length animated movie, and Pixar agreed to animate and produce *Toy Story*. But, tired of pouring money into keeping it afloat, Jobs toyed with selling the company. He entertained offers from Oracle, Microsoft, and, curiously enough, the greeting-card company Hallmark.[10] But Jobs held out. "We should have failed," says Smith. "Steve just would not suffer a defeat."[11] The release of *Toy Story* proved his instincts right—the groundbreaking movie earned US$362 million worldwide, shattering records for box-office earnings by animated movies.[12] *A Bug's Life* followed, and although the movie did well, especially for an animated feature, it's worth noting that every Pixar release since has done even better.

Acutely aware of a string of failures for its own animated movies, Disney entered into talks to buy Pixar. Lasseter and Catmull were pleasantly surprised when Disney not only purchased Pixar, but also placed the Pixar honchos at the top of Disney's stagnant animation department. The sale went through for US$7.4 billion, and suddenly Steve Jobs became Disney's single largest shareholder.[13]

Pixar's future looks bright. Never one to rest on its laurels, the company continues to actively invest in software and technology, the tools that have made possible the life-like rendering that is the hallmark of Pixar movies. But Pixar will have to stay sharp to stave off competition from the junior animation firms that are quickly forging alliances with major production companies to put out feature-length films of their own. Wild Brain, for instance, inked a five-picture deal with Dimension Films, a unit of Miramax (owned by, of all companies, Disney).[14] Questions also remain about Pixar's future within the corporate umbrella of Disney. *Business Week* notes: "Many industry insiders wonder if the company will be able to maintain its string of hits now that it's part of the Magic Kingdom."[15]

But a good part of Pixar's success stems from its ability to generate intriguing stories that warm the hearts of audiences. And according to analyst Ralph Schackart, that's where Pixar has it made: "It all starts with the story. You or I can go buy off-the-shelf software and make an animated film. The barrier to entry for this industry is the story."[16]

Discussion Questions

1. For Steve Jobs, with all his wealth and success, how can the needs theories explain his motivation?

2. When Pixar was struggling and Jobs was investing more and more money to keep it afloat, he could have made the decision to sell and go off to invest his money and time in other pursuits. But he didn't. How can Jobs's decision to stick with Pixar be explained using (a) Vroom's expectancy theory and (b) Bandura's self-efficacy theory?

3. Pixar relies heavily on creative people who are motivated to do their best under production schedules that can sometimes be highly stressful. How could a human resource executive use the notion of "flexibility" to provide a highly motivating work environment for such people?

4. FURTHER RESEARCH—Some predict that Pixar's best days are over and that it will be hard for it to stay creative as a Disney business. Find out how Pixar is now doing. In what ways is its current performance consistent with or different from the predictions, and why?

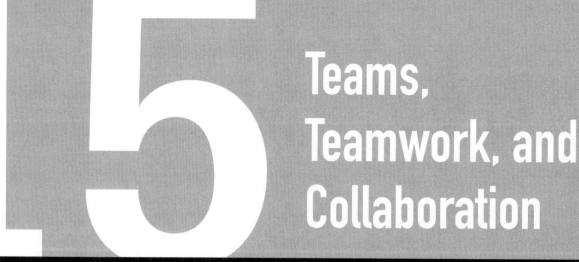

15 Teams, Teamwork, and Collaboration

LEARNING FROM OTHERS

The beauty is in the teamwork

What distinguishes a group of people from a high-performance team? For one, it's the way members work with one another to achieve common goals. A vivid example is a NASCAR pit crew. When a driver pulls in for a pit stop, the team must jump in to perform multiple tasks flawlessly and in perfect order and unison. A second gained or lost can be crucial to a NASCAR driver. Team members must be well trained and rehearsed to efficiently perform on race day.

When Ryan Newman won the Daytona 500 by a mere .092 seconds over runner-up Kurt Busch, it was time that could easily have been lost—not just on the track, but in the pits. "You can't win a race with a 12-second stop, but you can lose it with an 18-second stop," says Trent Cherry, the coach of Newman's pit crew.

Composed of former college and professional athletes, members of a pit crew are conditioned and trained to execute intricate manoeuvres while taking care of tire changes, car adjustments, fuelling, and related matters on a crowded pit lane. Each crew member is an expert at one task. But each is also fully aware of how that job fits into every other task that must be performed in a few-second pit stop interval. The duties are carefully scripted for each individual's performance and equally choreographed to fit together seamlessly at the team level. Every task is highly specialized and interdependent; if the jacker is late, for example, the wheel changer can't pull the wheel.

Robert Lesieur/Reuters/Landov LLC

Pit crews plan and practise over and over again, getting ready for the big test of race day performance. The crew chief makes sure that everyone is in shape, well trained, and ready to contribute to the team. "I don't want seven all-stars," Trent Cherry says, "I want seven guys who work as a team."[1]

> **BENCHMARK** We can't all be race car drivers or members of pit crews, but we're part of teams every day. The beauty of teams is accomplishing something far greater than what's possible for an individual alone. But like pit crews, great teams are built from a foundation of solid team contributors and leadership. Teams can be hard work, but they are worth it.

Team Contributions

No one can deny that teams are indispensable in today's organizations. But the benefits of team performance don't happen unless members make them happen through positive team contributions. These are the things people do to help teams succeed and help their members enjoy the team experience.

Scene—Hospital operating room: Scholars notice that heart surgeons have lower patient death rates for similar procedures performed in hospitals where they do more operations than those performed where they do fewer operations.

Why? Researchers claim the operations go better because the doctors spend more time working together with members of these surgery teams. It's not only the surgeon's skills that count, they say, "the skills of the team, and of the organization, matter."[2]

Scene—NBA basketball court: Scholars find that basketball teams win more games the longer the players have been together. Why? Researchers claim it's a "teamwork effect." Teams whose members play together longest win more because the players get to know each other's moves and playing tendencies.[3]

There is no doubt that a large part of your career success will depend on how well you work in and lead teams. Take a look at the list of "must have" team skills shown in the box. Do you have the skills portfolio and personal commitment to make truly valuable team contributions?

"Must Have" Team Skills
• Encouraging and motivating others
• Accepting suggestions
• Listening to different points of view
• Communicating information and ideas
• Persuading others to cooperate
• Resolving and negotiating conflict
• Building consensus
• Fulfilling commitments
• Avoiding disruptive acts and words

❖ Get to Know Yourself Better

When you speak with others who know and work with you, what do they say about your performance as a team member? What suggestions do they have for how you could improve your team contributions? Take the recommended self-assessments and think about the results. If you were to make a presentation to a potential employer describing your team skills, what would you say?

CHAPTER 15 STUDY QUESTIONS

- How do teams contribute to organizations?
- What are current trends in the use of teams?
- How do teams work?
- How do teams make decisions?
- How do you manage conflict?
- How can we negotiate successful agreements?

VISUAL CHAPTER OVERVIEW

CHAPTER 15 TEAMS, TEAMWORK, AND COLLABORATION

Study Question 1	Study Question 2	Study Question 3	Study Question 4	Study Question 5	Study Question 6
Teams in Organizations	**Trends in the Use of Teams**	**How Teams Work**	**Decision-Making in Teams**	**Conflict**	**Negotiation**
■ What is teamwork? ■ Teamwork pros ■ Teamwork cons ■ Meetings, meetings, meetings ■ Formal and informal groups	■ Committees, project teams, and task forces ■ Cross-functional teams ■ Virtual teams ■ Sell-managing teams ■ Team building	■ Team inputs ■ Stages of team development ■ Norms and cohesiveness ■ Task and maintenance roles ■ Communication networks	■ Ways teams make decisions ■ Team decision strategies ■ Groupthink ■ Creativity in team decision-making	■ Functional and dysfunctional conflict ■ Causes of conflict ■ Conflict resolution	■ Negotiation goals and approaches ■ Gaining integrative agreements ■ Negotiation pitfalls ■ Third-party dispute resolution

✓ Learning Check 1   ✓ Learning Check 2   ✓ Learning Check 3   ✓ Learning Check 4   ✓ Learning Check 5   ✓ Learning Check 6

"Sticks in a bundle are hard to break."—Kenyan proverb

"Teamwork is the fuel that allows common people to attain uncommon results."—Andrew Carnegie, industrialist and philanthropist

"Gettin' good players is easy. Gettin' 'em to play together is the hard part."—Casey Stengel, baseball manager

"Individual commitment to a group effort—that's what makes a team work, a society work, a civilization work."—Vince Lombardi, football coach

". . . in team sports or in business, a group working together can always defeat a team of individuals even if the individuals, by themselves, are better than your team."—John Chambers, corporate CEO

From proverbs to sports to business, teams and teamwork are rich topics of conversation and major pathways to great accomplishments.[4] But even so, we have to admit that just the words "group" and "team" elicit both positive and negative reactions in the minds of many people. Although it is said that "two heads are better than one," we are also warned that "too many cooks spoil the broth." The true sceptic can be heard to say: "a camel is a horse put together by a committee."

Teams are both rich in performance potential and very complex in the way they work; they can be great successes and they can also be colossal failures.[5] Even though most workers spend at least some time in teams, more than a third report dissatisfaction and less than half say they receive training in group dynamics.[6] Yet many people prefer to work in teams rather than independently. Over 60 percent of the average worker's time is spent in a team environment, and for white-collar workers the figure goes up to 82 percent.

TEAMS IN ORGANIZATIONS

Most tasks in organizations are well beyond the capabilities of individuals alone. Managerial success is always earned in substantial part through mobilizing, leading, and supporting people as they work together in groups and teams. The new organizational designs and cultures require it, as does any true commitment to empowerment and employee involvement.[7] The question for managers, and the guiding theme of this chapter, thus becomes: how do we make sure that teams and teamwork are used to everyone's best advantage?

WHAT IS TEAMWORK?

A **team** is a small group of people with complementary skills, who work together to accomplish shared goals while holding themselves mutually accountable for performance results.[8] **Teamwork** is the process of people working together to accomplish these goals.

As shown in Figure 15.1, managers must perform at least four important roles in order to fully master the challenges of teams and teamwork. These roles, along with examples, are *team leader*—serving as the appointed head of a team or work unit; *facilitator*—serving as the peer leader and networking hub for a special task force; *member*—serving as a helpful contributing member of a project team; and *coach*—serving as the external convener or sponsor of a problem-solving team staffed by others.

A **team** is a collection of people who regularly interact to pursue common goals.

Teamwork is the process of people actively working together to accomplish common goals.

Team leader

Network facilitator

Team member

External coach

How managers get involved with teams and teamwork

Figure 15.1 Team and teamwork roles for managers.

TEAMWORK PROS

Teamwork in our society makes available everything from aircraft to the Internet, from music videos to—as featured in the Learning from Others chapter opener—a successful pit stop for the

Synergy is the creation of a whole greater than the sum of its individual parts.

leader of a NASCAR race. It all happens because of **synergy**, the creation of a whole that is greater than the sum of its parts.

Synergy pools individual talents and efforts to create extraordinary results. It occurs when a team uses its membership resources to the fullest and thereby achieves through collective action far more than could otherwise be achieved by individuals acting alone. When Jens Voigt, one of the top racers on the Tour de France, was asked to describe a "perfect cyclist," for example, he created a composite of his nine-member team: "We take the time trial legs of Fabian Cancellara, the speed of Stuart O'Grady, the climbing capacity of our leaders and my attitude." Voigt was confirming that the tour is way too hard for a single rider to win on his own talents; like so many other things in any social setting, the synergies made possible by teamwork are the keys to success.[9]

GOING GLOBAL

WAVING THE TEAM FLAG

At the 2010 World Cup of soccer, a tournament that makes national heroes into global superstars, it was good old-fashioned teamwork that won the day. While individuals such as David Villa, Diego Forlan, Miroslav Klose, Bastian Schweinsteiger, and Thomas Mueller all had great games, the tournament's defining aspect was the superiority of team play over individual efforts. And the winning side, Spain, epitomized the approach better than anyone. It was their collective technical ability and team play that propelled them past all other nations. "It shows you that a team is not just one player," said goalkeeper Iker Casillas. "A player can win the tournament for you, like Argentina with (Diego) Maradona (in 1986), but, in the end, everything depends on teamwork." Portugal, England, Brazil, and Argentina were all unsuccessful partly due to the failure of their star players to overcome stronger teams.

Teams are good for organizations. According to a study conducted by Ipsos-Reid of business decision-makers in mid-sized Canadian firms (100 to 500 employees), 86 percent of business executives thought that teamwork is "very critical" to the overall success of their organization.[10] And teams are also good for their members. Just as in life overall, being part of a work team or social group can strongly influence our attitudes and behaviours. The personal relationships and connections can help people do their jobs better—making contacts, sharing ideas, responding to favours, and bypassing roadblocks. And being part of a team often helps satisfy important needs that may be difficult to meet in the regular work setting or life overall, providing things like social relationships, a sense of security and belonging, or emotional support.[11] The many benefits of teams and teamwork can be summed up as follows.

- More resources for problem solving

- Improved creativity and innovation

- Improved quality of decision-making

- Greater commitments to tasks

- Higher motivation through collective action

- Better control and work discipline

- More individual need satisfaction

TEAMWORK CONS

Experience has taught all of us that achieving synergy through teamwork isn't always easy, and that things don't always work out as intended. Teams are not free from problems. In his book *The Five Dysfunctions of a Team*, Patrick Lencioni outlines the characteristics of a broken team: absence of trust, fear of conflict, lack of commitment, avoidance of accountability, and inattention to detail. Lencioni explains that, without trust, people will be afraid to enter into disagreements or conflict with team members and especially with team leaders. As a result, decisions will be made that lack honest conversation and buy-in. The effect is that people will not feel committed to decisions made by the team. They will also fail to hold each other accountable and pay attention to results because they will feel apart from, rather than a part of, the team.[12]

As well, who hasn't encountered **social loafing**? This is the presence of "free-riders" who slack off because responsibility is diffused in teams and others are present to do the work.[13] What can a leader or other concerned team member do when someone is free-riding? It's not easy, but the problem can be addressed. Actions can be taken to make individual contributions more visible, reward individuals for their contributions, make task assignments more interesting, and keep group size small so that free-riders are more subject to peer pressure and leader evaluation.[14]

Social loafing is the tendency of some people to avoid responsibility by "free-riding" in groups.

Social loafing and other problems can easily turn the great potential of teams into frustration and failure.[15] Personality conflicts and individual differences in work styles can disrupt the team. Tasks are not always clear, and ambiguous agendas or ill-defined problems can cause teams to work too long on the wrong things. Not everyone is always ready to work. Sometimes the issue is lack of motivation, but it may also be conflicts with other deadlines and priorities. Low enthusiasm for group work may also be caused by a lack of team organization or success, as well as by meetings that lack purpose and members who come unprepared.[16]

MEETINGS, MEETINGS, MEETINGS

What do you think when someone says let's have a meeting? Are you ready and willing, or apprehensive and even perturbed? Meetings are a hard fact of the workplace, especially in today's horizontal, flexible, and team-oriented structures. But all too often, those who must attend do not enthusiastically receive the request to schedule another meeting.

A survey by Office Team found that 27 percent of respondents viewed meetings as their biggest time wasters, ranking ahead of unnecessary interruptions.[17] "We have the most ineffective meetings of any company," says a technology executive. "We just seem to meet and meet and meet, and we never seem to do anything," says another in the package delivery industry. "We realize our meetings are unproductive. A consulting firm is trying to help us, but we've got a long way to go," says a corporate manager.[18]

Consider the list of typical meeting problems described in Management Smarts 15.1.[19] You might even be able to add to the list from personal experience in student groups and work teams. But remember, meetings can and should be where information is shared, decisions get made, and people gain understanding of issues and one another. All of this can be accomplished without "wasting" time. But as with all group activities in organizations, good things don't happen by chance. People have to work hard and work together to make meetings productive and rewarding.

15.1 MANAGEMENT SMARTS
Spotting the seven sins of deadly meetings

1. People arrive late, leave early, and don't take things seriously.

2. The meeting is too long, sometimes twice as long as necessary.

3. People don't stay on topic; they digress and are easily distracted.

4. The discussion lacks candour; people are unwilling to tell the truth.

5. The right information isn't available, so decisions are postponed.

6. Nothing happens when the meeting is over; no one puts decisions into action.

7. Things never get better; the same mistakes are made meeting after meeting.

FORMAL AND INFORMAL GROUPS

A formal group is officially recognized and supported by the organization.

The teams officially designated and supported by the organization are **formal groups**. They fulfill a variety of essential roles within the formal organizational structure. Rensis Likert describes organizations as interlocking networks of formal groups in which managers and leaders serve as important "linking pins."[20] Each manager or leader serves as a superior in one work group and as a subordinate in the next-higher-level one. Such formal groups exist in various sizes and go by different labels. They may be called departments (e.g., market research department), units (e.g., audit unit), teams (e.g., customer service team), or divisions (e.g., office products division), among other possibilities.

An informal group is unofficial and emerges from relationships and shared interests among members.

Although they are not depicted on organization charts, **informal groups** are also present and important in all organizations. They emerge from natural or spontaneous relationships among people. Some informal groups are *interest groups*, in which workers band together to pursue a common cause such as better working conditions. Some emerge as *friendship groups* that develop for a wide variety of personal reasons, including shared non-work interests. Others exist as *support groups*, in which the members basically help one another do their jobs or cope with common problems.

Informal groups are very important for managers to understand. It's a mistake to assume they are necessarily bad; it's realistic to expect they can have a positive impact on work performance. The relationships and connections made possible by informal groups can help speed the workflow or allow people to "get things done" in ways not possible within the formal structure. Informal groups also help satisfy social needs that are otherwise thwarted or left unmet. Among other things, informal groups often offer their members social satisfactions, security, support, and a sense of belonging.

✔ **Learning Check ❶**   **BE SURE YOU CAN**
• define *team* and *teamwork* • identify four roles managers perform in groups • define *synergy* • explain teamwork pros and cons • discuss the implications of social loafing • explain the potential benefits of informal groups

TRENDS IN THE USE OF TEAMS

The trend toward greater empowerment in organizations includes an emphasis on committees, project teams, task forces, and cross-functional teams. Organizations today also increasingly use computer-mediated or virtual teams and self-managing teams.

REAL ETHICS

Social Loafing

1. *Psychology study:* A German researcher asked people to pull on a rope as hard as they could. First, individuals pulled alone. Second, they pulled as part of a group. The results showed that people pull harder when working alone than when working as part of a team. Such "social loafing" is the tendency to reduce effort when working in groups.

2. *Faculty office:* A student wants to speak with the instructor about his team's performance on the last group project. There were four members, but two did almost all of the work. The other two largely disappeared, showing up only at the last minute to be part of the formal presentation. His point is that the team was disadvantaged because two "free-riders" caused reduced performance capacity.

3. *Telephone call from the boss:* "John, I really need you to serve on this committee. Will you do it? Let me know tomorrow." In thinking about this, you ponder: "I'm overloaded, but I don't want to turn down the boss. I'll accept but let the committee members know about my situation. I'll be active in discussions and try to offer viewpoints and perspectives that are helpful. However, I'll let them know up front that I can't be a leader or volunteer for any extra work."

YOU DECIDE

Whether you call it "social loafing," "free-riding," or just plain old "slacking off," the issue is the same: what right do some people have to sit back in team situations and let other people do all the work? Is this ethical? And when it comes to John, does the fact that he is going to be honest with the other committee members make any difference? Isn't he still going to be a loafer, and yet earn credit with the boss for serving on the committee?

COMMITTEES, PROJECT TEAMS, AND TASK FORCES

A **committee** brings people together outside of their daily job assignments to work in a small team for a specific purpose. The task agenda is typically narrow, focused, and ongoing. For example, organizations usually have a variety of permanent or standing committees dedicated to a wide variety of concerns, such as diversity and compensation. Committees are led by a designated head or chairperson, who is held accountable for performance results.

Project teams or **task forces** bring people together to work on common problems, but on a temporary rather than on a permanent basis. The goals and task assignments for project teams and task forces are specific; completion deadlines are clearly defined. Creativity and innovation are sometimes important parts of the agendas. Project teams, for example, might be formed to develop a new product or service, redesign an office layout, or provide specialized consulting services for a client.[21]

A **committee** is designated to work on a special task on a continuing basis.

A **project team** or **task force** is convened for a specific purpose and disbands when its task is completed.

CROSS-FUNCTIONAL TEAMS

A **cross-functional team** operates with members who come from different functional units of an organization.

The **cross-functional team**, whose members come from different functional units, is indispensable to matrix organizations and those that emphasize horizontal integration. Members of cross-functional teams work together on specific projects or tasks, and with the needs of the whole organization in mind. They are expected to share information, explore new ideas, seek creative solutions, and meet project deadlines.

One of the expectations is that cross-functional teams will help avoid the functional chimneys problem discussed in Chapter 8 on organization structures. They are ways to knock down the "walls" that otherwise separate departments and people in the organization. At Tom's of Maine, for example, "Acorn Groups"—symbolizing the fruits of the stately oak tree—have been used to help launch new products. They bring together members of all departments to work on new ideas from concept to finished product. The goal is to minimize problems and maximize efficiency through cross-departmental cooperation.[22] Target CEO Gregg Steihafel also uses cross-functional teams in the "GO" apparel program. It unites talent from "merchandising, marketing, design, communications, presentation, supply chain and stores" to create and bring to customers new limited edition fashions.[23]

VIRTUAL TEAMS

Members of a **virtual team** work together and solve problems through computer-based interactions.

Virtual teams whose members work together largely through computer-mediated, rather than face-to-face, interactions are increasingly common. Their use is changing the way many committees, task forces, and other problem-solving teams function. Virtual teams operate like other teams in respect to what gets done; how things get done, however, is different. The electronic environment of virtual teamwork can be a source of both potential advantages and disadvantages.[24]

In terms of potential advantages, virtual teams can save time and travel expenses. At IBM, for example, programming teams work together around the clock and around the world, often chopping months off of tasks.[25] Virtual teams can also be easily expanded to include more members, and the discussions and information shared among members can be stored on-line for continuous updating and access. Also, computer mediation helps virtual team members work collectively in a time-efficient fashion and without interpersonal difficulties that might otherwise occur—especially when the issues are controversial. A vice president for human resources at Marriott, for example, once called electronic meetings "the quietest, least stressful, most productive meetings you've ever had."[26]

When problems do occur in virtual teams, they often arise because members have difficulty establishing good working relationships. A lack of face-to-face interaction limits the role of emotions and nonverbal cues in the communication process, and relations among team members can become depersonalized.[27] But following some basic guidelines can help keep these problems to a minimum. The keys are to do things that foster positive impressions and the development of trust among team members. Among tips for leading successful virtual teams are the following.[28]

- Select team members high in initiative and capable of self-starting.
- Select members who will join and engage the team with positive attitudes.
- Select members known for working hard to meet team goals.
- Begin with social messaging that allows members to exchange information about each other to personalize the process.

- Assign clear goals and roles so that members can focus while working alone and also know what others are doing.

- Gather regular feedback from members about how they think the team is doing and how it might do better.

- Provide regular feedback to team members about team accomplishments.

Recognizing the need for virtual cross-functional teams to work well together, Open Text, based in Waterloo, Ontario, built a secure on-line environment where its customers' employees, customers, and partners can interact. One client, with a Canadian federal department, found that "Open Text Social Media offers us central project sites with user profiles, discussion feeds, documents and wikis—everything in one place to keep everyone up to date. This alone is a huge timesaver."[29]

SELF-MANAGING TEAMS

In a growing number of organizations, traditional work units consisting of first-level supervisors and their immediate subordinates are being replaced with **self-managing work teams**. Sometimes called *autonomous work groups*, these are teams of workers whose jobs have been redesigned to create a high degree of task interdependence, who have been given authority to make many decisions about how they work, and who accept collective responsibility for results.[30]

Members of a **self-managing work team** have the authority to make decisions about how they share and complete their work.

Self-managing teams operate with participative decision-making, shared tasks, and responsibility for many of the managerial duties performed by supervisors in more traditional settings. The "self-management" responsibilities include planning and scheduling work, training members in various tasks, distributing tasks, meeting performance goals, ensuring high quality, and solving day-to-day operating problems. In some settings, the team's authority may even extend to "hiring" and "firing" members when necessary.

A key feature of any self-managing team is multitasking, in which team members each have the skills to perform several different jobs. And within a team, the emphasis is always on participation. The leader and members are expected to jointly decide how the work gets done. Figure 15.2 describes typical characteristics of self-managing teams as follows.

- Members are held collectively accountable for performance results.

- Members have discretion in distributing tasks within the team.

- Members have discretion in scheduling work within the team.

- Members are able to perform more than one job on the team.

- Members train one another to develop multiple job skills.

- Members evaluate one another's performance contributions.

- Members are responsible for the total quality of team products.

The expected advantages of self-managing teams include better performance, decreased costs, and higher morale. Of course, these results are not guaranteed. Managing the transition away from more traditional work settings isn't always easy. The process requires leadership committed to both empowerment and a lot of support for those learning to work in new ways. As the concept of self-managing teams spreads globally, researchers are also examining the receptivity of different cultures to self-management concepts.[31] Such cultural dimensions as high power distance and individualism, as discussed in Chapter 3, for example, may generate resistance that must be considered when implementing team-based organizational practices.

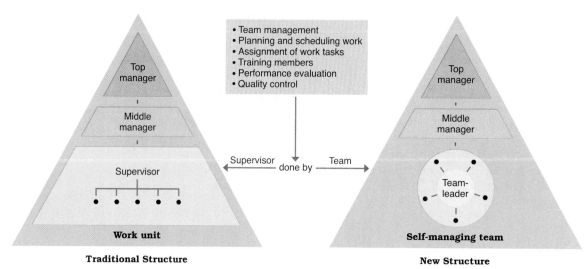

Figure 15.2 Organizational and management implications of self-managing work teams.

TEAM BUILDING

Team building is a sequence of activities to analyze a team and make changes to improve its performance.

Whichever type of group or team we are talking about, and wherever in an organization it may be located, high-performance results can't be left to chance. Just as in the world of sports, there are many things that can go wrong and cause problems for work teams.

Team building is a sequence of planned activities used to analyze the functioning of a team and make constructive changes in how it operates.[32] Most systematic approaches to team building begin with awareness that a problem may exist or may develop within the team. Members then work together to gather data and fully understand the problem, make and implement action plans, and evaluate results. As difficulties or new problems are discovered, the team-building process recycles.

There are many ways to gather data for team building, including structured and unstructured interviews, questionnaires, and team meetings. Regardless of the method used, the basic principle of team building remains the same: a careful and collaborative assessment of all aspects of the team, from how members work together to the results they achieve. And everyone should share the goal of creating a sustainable high-performance team with characteristics like those shown in the box.[33]

Characteristics of High-Performance Teams

- clear and elevating goals
- task-driven, results-oriented structure
- competent, hard-working members
- collaborative culture
- high standards of excellence
- external support and recognition
- strong, principled leadership

Team building can be done with consulting assistance or under managerial direction; it can also be done in the workplace or in outside locations. A popular approach is to bring team members together in special settings where their capacities for teamwork are put to the test in unusual and even physically demanding experiences. On one fall day, for example, a team of employees from American Electric Power went to an outdoor camp for a day of team-building activities. They worked on problems like how to get six members through a spiderweb maze of bungee cords strung a half metre above the ground. When her colleagues lifted Judy Gallo into their hands to pass her over the obstacle, she was nervous. But a trainer told the team this was just like solving a problem together at the office; the spiderweb was just another performance constraint, like the difficult policy issues or financial limits they might face at work. After "high-fives" for making it through the web, Judy's team jumped tree stumps together, passed hula hoops while holding hands, and more. Says one team-building trainer, "We throw clients into situations to try and bring out the traits of a good team."[34]

There are lots of team-building alternatives that break people out of their normal work settings and help them learn from entirely new experiences. Seagate Technology's CEO, Bill Watkins, takes this to the extreme. He spends some US$9,000 per person to send employees to New Zealand for a week at Eco Seagate. Participants engage in team building through participation in a variety of outdoor settings and activities. One includes a Maori *haka* dance with everyone chanting in the Maori language, "Seagate is powerful. Seagate is powerful." At the grand finale, teams compete in an all-day race of kayaking, cycling, swimming, and cliff rappelling.

Habit is a strong influence on behaviour, and the work habits of teams can become complacent and lackadaisical. It can be a real challenge to break people out of existing habits and switch into new mindsets that reinvigorate teamwork. Watkins says that one of the best ways to do this is to put people in team situations that are so novel and new that they're forced to learn new ways of working together. He says: "You put them in an environment where they have to ask for help."

CRITICAL RESPONSE

Is Bill Watkins onto something with Eco Seagate? Is there something special about these types of team experiences? And, if so, what's a manager to do? How can inspired teamwork be similarly achieved at less expense and in less sensational ways?

BE SURE YOU CAN ✔ Learning Check ❷
- differentiate a committee from a task force • explain the benefits of cross-functional teams
- explain potential advantages and disadvantages of virtual teams • list the characteristics of self-managing work teams • explain how self-managing teams are changing organizations
- describe the typical steps in team building

HOW TEAMS WORK

An **effective team** does three things well: perform its tasks, satisfy its members, and remain viable for the future.[35] On the *task performance* side, a work group or team is expected to transform resource inputs (such as ideas, materials, and information) into product outputs (such as a report, decision, service, or commodity). In respect to *member satisfaction*, members should take pleasure from both the team's performance accomplishments and their contributions toward making them happen. And as to *future viability*, the team should have a social fabric and work climate that makes its members willing and able to work well together in the future, again and again, as needed.

An **effective team** achieves high levels of task performance, membership satisfaction, and future viability.

Procter & Gamble's former CEO, A. G. Lafley, says that team effectiveness comes together when you have "the right players in the right seats on the same bus, headed in the same direction."[36] The open systems model in Figure 15.3 shows that a team's effectiveness is influenced by inputs— "right players in the right seats"—and by process—"on the same bus, headed in the same direction." You can remember the implications of this figure by the following Team Effectiveness Equation.[37]

Team effectiveness = Quality of inputs + (Process gains − Process losses)

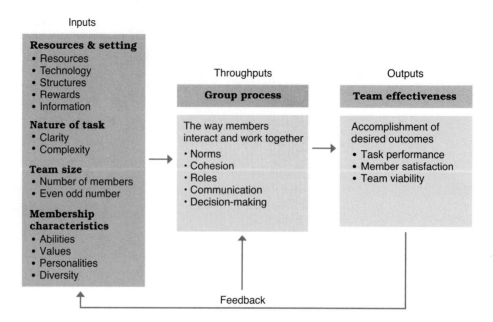

Figure 15.3 An open-systems model of team effectiveness.

TEAM INPUTS

Among the important inputs that can influence team effectiveness are such things as resources and setting, nature of the task, membership characteristics, and team size.[38] You can think of these as factors that "load" the team for action. A team with the right inputs has a greater chance of having a strong process and being effective.

Resources and Setting

The availability of resources and the nature of the organizational setting can affect how team members relate to one another and apply their skills toward task accomplishment. A key issue is the support provided in terms of information, material resources, technology, organization structures, available rewards, and work space. In this latter respect, many organizations are architecturally designed to directly facilitate teamwork. At SEI Investments, employees work in a large, open space without cubicles or dividers; each has a private set of office furniture and fixtures—but all on wheels; all technology easily plugs and unplugs from suspended power beams that run overhead. This makes it easy for project teams to convene and disband as needed, and for people to meet and converse within the ebb and flow of daily work.[39]

Nature of the Task

The nature of the task is always an important input. It affects how well a team can focus its efforts and how intense the group process must be to get the job done. Clearly defined tasks make it easier for team members to combine their work efforts. Complex tasks require more information exchange and intense interaction than do simpler tasks.[40] The next time you fly, check out the ground crews. You should notice some similarities between them and teams handling pit stops for NASCAR racers. In fact, if you fly United Airlines, there's a good chance the members of the ramp crews have been through "Pit Crew U." United is among many organizations that are sending employees to Performance Instruction & Training in North Carolina. At this facility, where real racing crews train, United's ramp workers learn to work intensely and under pressure while meeting the goals of teamwork, safety, and job preparedness. The goal is better teamwork to reduce aircraft delays and service inadequacies.[41]

Team Size

Team size affects how members work together, handle disagreements, and make decisions. The number of potential interactions increases geometrically as teams increase in size, and communications become more congested. Teams with odd numbers of members help prevent "ties" when votes need to be taken. Also, teams larger than about six or seven members can be difficult to manage for creative problem solving. Amazon.com founder and CEO Jeff Bezos is a great fan of teams. But he also has a simple rule when it comes to sizing the firm's product development teams: no team should be larger than two pizzas can feed.[42]

(AP Photo/Mark Lennihan)

Membership Characteristics

The blend of member characteristics on a team is also important. Teams need members with the right abilities, or skill mix, to master and perform tasks well. They must also have values and personalities that are sufficiently compatible for everyone to work well together. Renee Wingo, Chief People Officer at Virgin Mobile, believes that you make a mistake by filling teams with people just like you. "The power of any group is in the mix," she says. On her team, you'll find people of diverse ages, experiences, and personalities. While admitting that the more diverse the team, the harder it is to manage, Wingo also believes that the extra work pays off in better team performance.[43]

As the prior example suggests, team diversity—in the form of different values, personalities, experiences, demographics, and cultures among the membership—affects how teams work. The more homogeneous the team—the more similar the members are to one another—the easier it is to manage relationships. As team diversity increases, so, too, does the complexity of interpersonal relationships among members. But with the complications of membership diversity also come special opportunities. The more heterogeneous the team—that is, the more diversity among members—the greater the variety of ideas, perspectives, and experiences that can add value to problem solving and task performance.

STAGES OF TEAM DEVELOPMENT

Although having the right inputs is important, it doesn't guarantee team effectiveness. **Group process** counts too. This is the way the members of any team actually work together as they transform inputs into output. Also called *group dynamics*, the process aspects of any group or team include how members develop norms and cohesiveness, share roles, communicate with one another, and make decisions.[44]

Group process is the way team members work together to accomplish tasks.

We know that group process challenges tend to vary with the nature of a team's input foundations. In the international arena, for example, culturally diverse work teams have more difficulty learning how to work well together than do culturally homogeneous teams.[45] But once the process issues are mastered, the diverse teams eventually prove to be more creative than the homogeneous ones. We also know that process challenges vary based on just where a team is in its stage of development. A synthesis of research on small groups suggests that there are five distinct phases in the life cycle of any team.[46]

1. *Forming*—a stage of initial orientation and interpersonal testing.

2. *Storming*—a stage of conflict over tasks and working as a team.

3. *Norming*—a stage of consolidation around task and operating agendas.

4. *Performing*—a stage of teamwork and focused task performance.

5. *Adjourning*—a stage of task completion and disengagement.

RESEARCH BRIEF

Demographic faultlines have implications for managing teams

Membership of organizations is becoming more diverse, and teams are becoming more important. According to Dora Lau and Keith Murnighan, these trends raise some important research issues. They believe that strong "faultlines" occur when demographic diversity results in the formation of two or more subgroups whose members are similar to and strongly identify with one another. Examples include teams with subgroups forming around age, gender, race, ethnic, occupational, or tenure differences. When

Strong faultline team
members identify more with
subgroups than team

• more conflict
• less sense of safety
• less team satisfaction

Weak faultline team
members identify more with
team than subgroups

• less conflict
• more sense of safety
• more team satisfaction

strong faultlines are present, members tend to identify more strongly with their subgroups than with the team as a whole. Lau and Murnighan predict that this affects what happens within the team in terms of conflict, politics, and performance.

Using subjects from 10 organizational behaviour classes at a university, the researchers created different conditions of faultline strengths by randomly assigning students to case work groups based on sex and ethnicity. After working on cases, the students completed questionnaires about group processes and outcomes. Results showed members of strong faultline subgroups evaluated those in their subgroups more favourably than did members of weak faultline subgroups. Members of strong faultline subgroups also experienced less conflict, more psychological safety, and more satisfaction than did those in weak faultline subgroups.

You be the researcher

How might faultlines operate in groups of different sizes and in the contexts of different organizational cultures? Are faultlines influencing the processes and outcomes of groups in which you participate— at university and at work? And if you are a member or leader of a team with strong faultlines, what can you do to help minimize any negative effects?

Forming Stage

The forming stage involves the first entry of individual members into a team. This is a stage of initial task orientation and interpersonal testing. When people first come together, they ask questions: "What can or does the team offer me?" "What will I be asked to contribute?" "Can my needs be met while my efforts serve the task needs of the team?"

In the forming stage, people begin to identify with other members and with the team itself. They are concerned about getting acquainted, establishing relationships, discovering what is acceptable behaviour, and learning how others perceive the team's task. This may also be a time when some members rely on others who appear "powerful" or especially "knowledgeable." Such things as prior experience with team members in other contexts and individual impressions of organization philosophies, goals, and policies may also affect emerging relationships. Difficulties in the forming stage tend to be greater in more culturally and demographically diverse teams.

Storming Stage

The storming stage is a period of high emotionality and can be the most difficult stage to pass through successfully. Tensions often emerge over tasks and interpersonal concerns. There may be periods of outright hostility and infighting. Coalitions or cliques may form around personalities or interests. Subteams may form around areas of agreement and disagreement. Conflict may develop as individuals compete to impose their preferences on others and to become influential in groups.

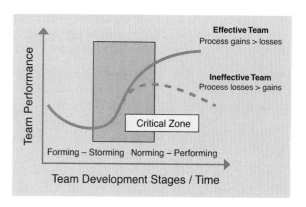

Important changes occur in the storming stage as task agendas become clarified and members begin to understand one another's styles. Attention begins to shift toward obstacles that may stand in the way of task accomplishment. Efforts are made to find ways to meet team goals while also satisfying individual needs. The storming stage is part of a "critical zone" in team development, where failures can create long-lasting problems, while success can set a strong foundation for later effectiveness.

Norming Stage

Cooperation is an important issue in the norming stage. At this point, team members begin to become coordinated and operate with shared rules of conduct. The team feels a sense of leadership, with each member starting to play useful roles. Interpersonal hostilities start to give way to a precarious balancing of forces as norming builds initial integration. Harmony is emphasized, but minority viewpoints may be discouraged.

The norming stage is also part of the critical zone of team development. Here, members are likely to develop initial feelings of closeness, a division of labour, and a sense of shared expectations. This helps protect the team from disintegration. In fact, holding the team together may seem more important than successful task accomplishment.

Performing Stage

Teams in the performing stage are more mature, organized, and well-functioning. They score high on the criteria of team maturity shown in Figure 15.4.[47] Performing is a stage of total integration in which team members are able to deal in creative ways with complex tasks and any interpersonal conflicts. The team operates with a clear and stable structure, and members are motivated by team goals. The primary challenge is to continue refining the operations and relationships essential to working as an integrated unit.

Adjourning Stage

The final stage of team development is adjourning, when team members prepare to achieve closure and disband. Temporary committees, task forces, and project teams should disband with a sense that important goals have been accomplished. But adjourning may be an emotional

	Very poor			Very good	
1. Trust among members	1	2	3	4	5
2. Feedback mechanisms	1	2	3	4	5
3. Open communications	1	2	3	4	5
4. Approach to decisions	1	2	3	4	5
5. Leadership sharing	1	2	3	4	5
6. Acceptance of goals	1	2	3	4	5
7. Valuing diversity	1	2	3	4	5
8. Member cohesiveness	1	2	3	4	5
9. Support for each other	1	2	3	4	5
10. Performance norms	1	2	3	4	5
	Where you don't want to be			Where you do want to be	

Figure 15.4 Criteria for assessing the maturity of a team.

period; when team members have worked together intensely for some time, breaking up may be painful. It is helpful here to acknowledge everyone for their contributions, praise them, and celebrate the team's success. Ideally, the team disbands with everyone feeling they would want to work with one another again sometime in the future.

NORMS AND COHESIVENESS

A **norm** is a behaviour, rule, or standard expected to be followed by team members.

A **norm** is a behaviour expected of team members.[48] It is a "rule" or "standard" that guides behaviour. The performance norm, which defines the level of work effort and performance that team members are expected to contribute, is an important example. Work groups and teams with positive performance norms are more successful in accomplishing task objectives than are teams with negative performance norms. Other team norms relate to such things as helpfulness, participation, timeliness, work quality, and creativity and innovation.

When violated, a norm may be enforced with reprimands and other sanctions. But team members vary in the degree to which they accept and adhere to group norms. Conformity to norms is largely determined by the strength of group **cohesiveness**, the degree to which members are attracted to and motivated to remain part of a team.[49] Persons in a highly cohesive team value their membership and strive to maintain positive relationships with other team members. Because they experience satisfaction from team identification, they tend to conform to the norms. In the extreme, violation of a norm can result in a member being expelled from a team or socially ostracized by other members.

Cohesiveness is the degree to which members are attracted to and motivated to remain part of a team.

Managing Team Norms

Team leaders should help and encourage members to develop positive norms. During the forming and storming steps of development, for example, norms relating to membership issues such as expected attendance and levels of commitment are important. By the time the stage of performing is reached, norms relating to adaptability and change become relevant. Guidelines for building positive group norms include the following.[50]

- Act as a positive role model.

- Reinforce the desired behaviours with rewards.

- Control results by performance reviews and regular feedback.

- Train and orient new members to adopt desired behaviours.

- Recruit and select new members who exhibit the desired behaviours.

- Hold regular meetings to discuss progress and ways of improving.

- Use team decision-making methods to reach agreement.

Managing Team Cohesiveness

The power of group cohesiveness is shown in Figure 15.5. When a team's performance norm is positive, high cohesion and the resulting conformity to norms has a beneficial effect on overall team performance. This is a "best-case" scenario. Competent team members work hard and reinforce one another's task accomplishments while experiencing satisfaction with the team. But when the performance norm is negative in a highly cohesive team, conformity to the norm can have undesirable results. The figure shows this as a "worst-case" scenario, where team performance suffers when members restrict their work efforts.

To achieve and maintain the best-case scenario shown in the figure, managers must be skilled at more than building positive norms. They must also be good at building high cohesiveness. This can be done in the following ways.

- Build agreement on team goals.

- Increase membership homogeneity.

- Increase interactions among members.

- Decrease team size.

- Introduce competition with other teams.

- Reward team rather than individual results.

- Provide physical isolation from other teams.

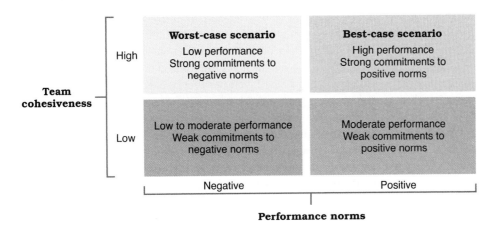

Figure 15.5 How cohesiveness and norms influence team performance.

TASK AND MAINTENANCE ROLES

Research on the social psychology of groups identifies two types of roles or activities that are essential if team members are to work well together.[51] **Task activities** contribute directly to the team's performance purpose, while **maintenance activities** support the emotional life of the team as an ongoing social system.

Although the team leader or supervisor should give them special attention, the responsibility for both types of activities should also be shared and distributed among all team members. Anyone can help lead a team by acting in ways that satisfy its task and maintenance needs. This concept of **distributed leadership** in teams makes every member continually responsible for both recognizing when task or maintenance activities are needed and taking actions to provide them.

Leading through task activities involves making an effort to define and solve problems and to advance work toward performance results. Without the relevant task activities, such as initiating agendas, sharing information, and others shown in Figure 15.6, teams will have difficulty accomplishing their objectives. Leading through maintenance activities, by contrast, helps strengthen the team as a social system. When maintenance activities such as encouraging others and reducing tensions are performed well, good interpersonal relationships are achieved and the team's ability to stay together over the longer term is ensured.

Both team task and maintenance activities stand in distinct contrast to the **disruptive activities** also described in the figure. Activities such as withdrawing and fooling around are self-serving and detract from, rather than enhance, team effectiveness. Unfortunately, very few teams are immune to dysfunctional behaviour by members. Everyone shares in the responsibility for minimizing its occurrence.

A **task activity** is an action taken by a team member that directly contributes to the group's performance purpose.

A **maintenance activity** is an action taken by a team member that supports the emotional life of the group.

Distributed leadership is when all members of a team contribute helpful task and maintenance behaviours.

Disruptive activities are self-serving behaviours that interfere with team effectiveness.

Distributed leadership roles in teams

Team leaders provide task activities	Team leaders provide maintenance activities	Team leaders avoid disruptive activities
• Initiating • Elaborating • Information sharing • Opinion giving • Summarizing	• Gatekeeping • Following • Encouraging • Harmonizing • Reducing tension	• Being aggressive • Competing • Blocking • Withdrawal • Self-confessing • Horsing around • Seeking sympathy • Seeking recognition

Figure 15.6 Distributed leadership helps teams meet task and maintenance needs.

COMMUNICATION NETWORKS

There is considerable research on the interaction patterns and communication networks used by teams. When team members must interact intensively and work closely together on tasks, this need is best met by a **decentralized communication network**. Sometimes called the *all-channel* or *star communication network*, this is where all members communicate directly with one another. At other times and in other situations, team members can work on tasks independently, with the required work being divided up among them. This creates a **centralized communication network**. Sometimes called a *wheel* or *chain communication structure*, its activities are coordinated and results pooled by a central point of control.

When teams are composed of subgroups experiencing issue-specific disagreements, such as a temporary debate over the best means to achieve a goal, the resulting interaction pattern often involves a **restricted communication network**. Here, polarized subgroups contest one another and may even engage in antagonistic relations. Communication between the subgroups is limited and biased, with negative consequences for group process and effectiveness.

A **decentralized communication network** allows all members to communicate directly with one another.

In a **centralized communication network**, communication flows only between individual members and a hub, or centre point.

In a **restricted communication network**, subgroups have limited communication with one another.

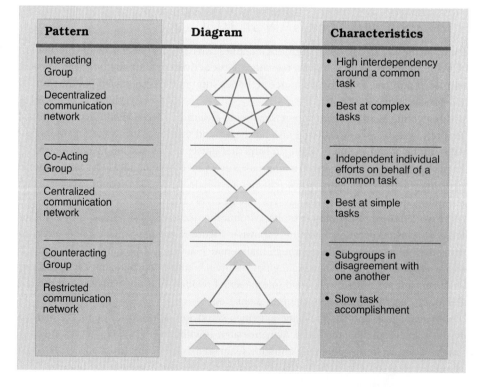

Pattern	Diagram	Characteristics
Interacting Group Decentralized communication network		• High interdependency around a common task • Best at complex tasks
Co-Acting Group Centralized communication network		• Independent individual efforts on behalf of a common task • Best at simple tasks
Counteracting Group Restricted communication network		• Subgroups in disagreement with one another • Slow task accomplishment

Figure 15.7 Interaction patterns and communication networks in teams.

Source: John R. Schermerhorn Jr., James G. Hunt, and Richard N. Osborn, *Organizational Behavior*, 8th ed. (Hoboken: Wiley, 2003), p. 347. Used by permission.

The best teams use communication networks, as shown in Figure 15.7, in the right ways and at the right times. Centralized communication networks seem to work better on simple tasks.[52] These tasks require little creativity, information processing, or problem solving and lend themselves to more centralized control. The reverse is true for more complex tasks, where interacting groups do better. Here, the decentralized networks work well because they are able to support the more intense interactions and information sharing required to perform complicated tasks. When teams get complacent, the conflict that emerges from co-acting groups can be a source of creativity and critical evaluation. But when subgroups have difficulty communicating with one another, task accomplishment typically suffers—for the short run at least.

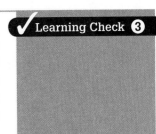

BE SURE YOU CAN

- define *team effectiveness* • identify inputs that influence group effectiveness • discuss how membership diversity influences team effectiveness • list five stages of group development • define *group norm* and list ways to build positive group norms • define *cohesiveness* and list ways to increase group cohesion • explain how norms and cohesiveness influence team performance • differentiate among task, maintenance, and disruptive activities • describe use of decentralized and centralized communication networks

DECISION-MAKING IN TEAMS

Decision-making, discussed extensively in Chapter 13, is the process of making choices among alternative possible courses of action. It is one of the most important group processes. But it is also complicated by the fact that teams can make decisions in different ways and face special decision-making challenges.

Decision-making is the process of making choices among alternative possible courses of action.

WAYS TEAMS MAKE DECISIONS

Edgar Schein, a respected scholar and consultant, notes that teams use at least six methods to make decisions. They are lack of response, authority rule, minority rule, majority rule, consensus, and unanimity.[53]

Lack of Response

In *decision by lack of response*, one idea after another is suggested without any discussion taking place. When the team finally accepts an idea, all others have been bypassed by simple lack of response rather than by critical evaluation.

Authority Rule

In *decision by authority rule*, the leader, manager, committee head, or some other authority figure makes a decision for the team. This can be done with or without discussion and is very time-efficient. Whether the decision is a good one or a bad one, however, depends on whether the authority figure has the necessary information and expertise, and on how well this approach is accepted by other team members.

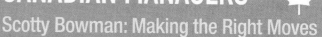

CANADIAN MANAGERS
Scotty Bowman: Making the Right Moves

(AP Photo/Dan Loh)

In sports teams, decisions by authority rule are made every minute of every game by the head coach. Clearly, the decisions made on and off the ice by former NHL hockey coach Scotty Bowman were usually the right ones. Bowman's winning numbers as a head coach are staggering: 9 Stanley Cups, 1,244 regular-season wins, and 223 playoff wins (all of these are NHL records). Add the respect accorded to him by players, media, and fans alike and it is easy to recognize him as the greatest NHL hockey coach of all time. Bowman's attention to detail and motivational coaching style kept his teams focused on what mattered most: winning the Stanley Cup. There hasn't been a professional coach in any league as successful with as many teams nor working with as many generations of athletes as Bowman did in his 34-year career.

Minority Rule

In *decision by minority rule*, two or three people are able to dominate or "railroad" the team into making a decision that they prefer. This is often done by providing a suggestion, and then forcing quick agreement by challenging the team with such statements as "Does anyone object? No? Well let's go ahead, then."

Majority Rule

One of the most common ways teams make decisions, especially when early signs of disagreement arise, is *decision by majority rule*. Formal voting may take place, or members may be polled to find the majority viewpoint. Although this method parallels the democratic political process, it is often used without awareness of its potential problems. The very process of voting can create coalitions as some people become "winners" and others "losers." Those in the minority—the "losers"—may feel left out or discarded without having had a fair say. They may be unenthusiastic about implementing the decision of the "majority," and lingering resentments may impair team effectiveness in the future. Such possibilities are well illustrated in the political arena, where candidates receiving only small and controversial victory margins end up struggling against entrenched opposition from the losing parties.

Consensus

Teams are often encouraged to achieve *decision by consensus*. This is where full discussion leads to one alternative being favoured by most members, and the other members agree to support it. When a consensus is reached, even those who may have opposed the decision know that their views have been heard by everyone involved. Consensus does not require unanimity, but it does require that team members be able to argue, engage in reasonable conflict, and still get along with and respect one another.[54] And it requires the opportunity for dissenting members to know that they have been able to speak and that they have been listened to.[55]

Unanimity

A *decision by unanimity* may be the ideal state of affairs. "Unanimity" means that all team members agree on the course of action to be taken. This is a logically perfect method, but it is also extremely difficult to achieve in actual practice. One of the reasons that teams sometimes turn to authority decisions, majority voting, or even minority decisions, in fact, is the difficulty of managing the team process to achieve consensus or unanimity.

TEAM DECISION STRATEGIES

The best teams don't limit themselves to just one decision-making method. Instead, they use a variety of methods over time as they face different kinds of problems. Indeed, an important team leadership skill is the ability to help a team choose the "best" decision method—one that provides for a timely, high-quality decision to which the members are highly committed. This was discussed in Chapter 11 on leadership and leadership development, under the Vroom-Jago model of leader participation.[56]

Teams must also learn to respect and manage the liabilities of group decisions, as pointed out when decision-making was examined in Chapter 13.[57] The potential problems largely trace to the difficulties that can be experienced in group processes. In team decision situations, there may be social pressure to conform. Individual members may feel intimidated or compelled to go along with the apparent wishes of others. There may be minority domination, in which some members feel forced or "railroaded" to accept a decision advocated by one vocal individual or a small coalition. Also, the time required to make group decisions can sometimes be a disadvantage. As more people are involved in the dialogue and discussion, decision-making takes longer. This added time may be costly, even prohibitively so, in certain circumstances.

> ### Keys to Consensus
>
> 1. Don't argue blindly; consider others' reactions to your points.
>
> 2. Don't change your mind just to reach quick agreement.
>
> 3. Avoid conflict reduction by voting, coin tossing, or bargaining.
>
> 4. Keep everyone involved in the decision process.
>
> 5. Allow disagreements to surface so that things can be deliberated.
>
> 6. Don't focus on winning versus losing; seek acceptable alternatives.
>
> 7. Discuss assumptions, listen carefully, and encourage inputs by all.

GROUPTHINK

While considering the potential downsides of team decision-making, there is a further issue to recognize. Although it may seem counterintuitive, a high level of cohesiveness can be a disadvantage when strong feelings of team loyalty make it hard for members to criticize and evaluate one another's ideas and suggestions. Members of very cohesive teams may feel so strongly about the group that they may not want to do anything that might detract from feelings of goodwill. This might cause them to publicly agree with actual or suggested courses of action, while privately having serious doubts about them. There can be times when the desire to hold the team together at all costs and avoid disagreements may result in poor decisions.

Psychologist Irving Janis calls this phenomenon **groupthink**, the tendency for highly cohesive groups to lose their critical evaluative capabilities.[58] You should be alert to spot the following symptoms of groupthink when they occur in your decision-making teams:

Groupthink is a tendency for highly cohesive teams to lose their evaluative capabilities.

- *Illusions of invulnerability:* Members assume that the team is too good for criticism, or beyond attack.

- *Rationalizing unpleasant and disconfirming data:* Members refuse to accept contradictory data or to thoroughly consider alternatives.

- *Belief in inherent group morality:* Members act as though the group is inherently right and above reproach.

- *Stereotyping competitors as weak, evil, and stupid:* Members refuse to look realistically at other groups.

- *Applying direct pressure to deviants to conform to group wishes:* Members refuse to tolerate anyone who suggests the team may be wrong.

- *Self-censorship by members:* Members refuse to communicate personal concerns to the whole team.

- *Illusions of unanimity:* Members accept consensus prematurely, without testing its completeness.

- *Mind guarding:* Members protect the team from hearing disturbing ideas or outside viewpoints.

Groupthink can occur anywhere. In fact, Janis ties a variety of well-known historical blunders to the phenomenon, including the lack of preparedness of U.S. naval forces for the Japanese attack on Pearl Harbor and the U.S. Bay of Pigs invasion under President John F. Kennedy. You could argue that groupthink may have been at work more recently during the financial crisis, when banks were quick to follow each other's lead into risky mortgage products. When and if you encounter groupthink, Janis suggests taking action along the lines shown in Management Smarts 15.2.

15.2 MANAGEMENT SMARTS
How to avoid groupthink

- Assign the role of critical evaluator to each team member; encourage a sharing of viewpoints.

- As a leader, don't seem partial to one course of action; do absent yourself from meetings at times to allow free discussion.

- Create subteams to work on the same problems and then share their proposed solutions.

- Have team members discuss issues with outsiders and report back on their reactions.

- Invite outside experts to observe team activities and react to team processes and decisions.

- Assign one member to play a "devil's advocate" role at each team meeting.

- Hold a "second-chance" meeting to review the decision after consensus is apparently achieved.

CREATIVITY IN TEAM DECISION-MAKING

Among the potential benefits that teams can bring to organizations is increased creativity. At Pixar Animation Studios, "collective creativity" is a core competency. Norms within Pixar's many teams encourage writers and artists to share their work with others when it's still in the developmental stages, and receive feedback. In other words, it's safe at Pixar to share something that isn't finished and may have flaws; that's how things are made better. Other norms that support creativity within teams are being helpful to others, free to communicate with anyone and everyone, and empowered to make decisions. Pixar teams are also mini learning organizations. Project "post-mortems" are used to learn what went right and wrong, and help team members make decisions on how to do things better in the future.[59]

Two techniques that are particularly helpful for tapping creativity during team decision-making are brainstorming and the nominal group technique.[60] Both can be pursued in computer-mediated or virtual team discussions, as well as in face-to-face formats.

Brainstorming

In **brainstorming**, teams of 5 to 10 members meet to generate ideas, usually following strict guidelines. All criticism is ruled out—judgement or evaluation of ideas must be withheld until the idea-generation process has been completed. "Freewheeling" is welcomed—the wilder or more radical the idea, the better. Quantity is important—the greater the number of ideas, the greater the likelihood of obtaining a superior idea. Building on one another's ideas is encouraged—participants should suggest how ideas of others can be turned into better ideas, or how two or more ideas can be joined into still another hybrid idea.

> **Brainstorming** engages group members in an open, spontaneous discussion of problems and ideas.

Brainstorming works best when it is organized and well managed. At the Aloft Group Inc., a small advertising firm, for example, president Matt Bowen teaches employees how to properly brainstorm as a way to foster creative thinking. His approach to brainstorming is: specify the goal—ideally in a sentence—and distribute it a day or two ahead of the session; limit the brainstorming session to an hour; keep the group small—ideally 5–7 members; allow no criticisms—there is no such thing as a "bad" idea; encourage everyone to build on one another's ideas; and, be sure to follow up by implementing something from the brainstorming session.[61]

Nominal Group Technique

By prohibiting criticism, the brainstorming method reduces fears of ridicule or failure on the part of individuals. This is supposed to generate more enthusiasm and a freer flow of ideas among members. But there are times when differences in opinions and goals are so extreme that a brainstorming meeting deteriorates into antagonistic arguments and harmful conflicts. In such cases, a **nominal group technique** can help.[62] This approach uses a highly structured meeting agenda to allow everyone to contribute ideas without the interference of evaluative comments by others. Participants are first asked to work alone and respond in writing with possible solutions to a stated problem. Ideas are then shared in round-robin fashion without any criticism or discussion, and all ideas are recorded as they are presented. Ideas are next discussed and clarified in another round-robin sequence, with no evaluative comments allowed. Finally, members individually and silently follow a written voting procedure that ranks all alternatives in priority order.

> The **nominal group technique** structures interaction among team members discussing problems and ideas.

BE SURE YOU CAN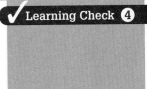
• illustrate how groups make decisions by authority rule, minority rule, majority rule, consensus, and unanimity • list advantages and disadvantages of group decision-making • define *groupthink* and identify its symptoms • illustrate how brainstorming and the nominal group technique can improve creativity in team decision-making

✔ Learning Check **4**

CONFLICT

Among your teamwork skills, the ability to deal with conflicts is critical. **Conflict** is a disagreement between people on substantive or emotional issues.[63] Managers and team leaders spend a lot of time dealing with conflicts of various forms. **Substantive conflicts** involve disagreements over such things as goals and tasks, allocation of resources, distribution of rewards, policies and procedures,

> **Conflict** is a disagreement over issues of a substance and/or an emotional antagonism.
>
> **Substantive conflict** involves disagreements over goals, resources, rewards, policies, procedures, and job assignments.

Emotional conflict results from feelings of anger, distrust, dislike, fear, and resentment, as well as from personality clashes.

and job assignments. **Emotional conflicts** result from feelings of anger, distrust, dislike, fear, and resentment, as well as from personality clashes and relationship problems. Both forms of conflict can cause difficulties. But when managed well, they can also be helpful in promoting creativity and high performance.

FUNCTIONAL AND DYSFUNCTIONAL CONFLICT

Not all conflict is bad; like stress, conflict can help boost creativity and performance. Thus, the absence of conflict is not always good. For example, groupthink, as described in the last section, is associated with highly cohesive groups whose members make bad decisions because they are unwilling to engage in conflict.

The inverted "U" curve depicted in Figure 15.8 shows that conflict of moderate intensity can be good for performance. This **functional conflict**, or constructive conflict, stimulates people toward greater work efforts, cooperation, and creativity. It helps groups achieve their goals. At very low or very high intensities, **dysfunctional conflict**, or destructive conflict, occurs. This makes it difficult for groups to achieve their goals. Too much conflict is distracting and interferes with other more task-relevant activities; too little conflict promotes complacency and the loss of a creative, high-performance edge. The goal is to keep conflict constructive and avoid its destructive consequences.

Functional conflict is constructive and helps task performance.

Dysfunctional conflict is destructive and hurts task performance.

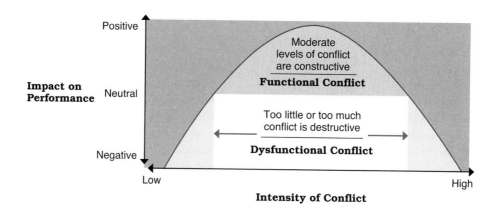

Figure 15.8 The relationship between conflict and performance.

CAUSES OF CONFLICT

A number of antecedent conditions can make the eventual emergence of conflict very likely. *Role ambiguities* set the stage for conflict. Unclear job expectations and other task uncertainties increase the probability that some people will be working at cross-purposes, at least some of the time. *Resource scarcities* cause conflict. Having to share resources with others or compete directly with them for resource allocations creates a potential conflict situation, especially when resources are scarce. *Task interdependencies* cause conflict. When individuals or groups must depend on what others do to perform well themselves, conflicts often occur.

Competing objectives are also opportunities for conflict. When objectives are poorly set or reward systems are poorly designed, individuals and groups may come into conflict by working to one another's disadvantage. *Structural differentiation* breeds conflict. Differences in organization structures and in the characteristics of the people staffing them may foster conflict because of incompatible approaches toward work. And *unresolved prior conflicts* tend to erupt in later conflicts. Unless a conflict is fully resolved, it may remain latent and later emerge to cause more conflict over the same or related matters.

CONFLICT RESOLUTION

When conflicts do occur, they can either be "resolved," in the sense that the causes are corrected, or "suppressed," in that the causes remain but the conflict behaviours are controlled. Suppressed conflicts tend to fester and recur at a later time. True conflict resolution eliminates the underlying causes of conflict and reduces the potential for similar conflicts in the future.

Structural Approaches to Conflict Resolution

Managers can use structural approaches to deal with conflicts between individuals or groups. There are times when *appealing to superordinate goals* can focus the attention on one mutually desirable end state. The appeal to higher-level goals offers all parties a common frame of reference against which to analyze differences and reconcile disagreements. Conflicts whose antecedents lie in the competition for scarce resources can be resolved by *making more resources available* to everyone. Although costly, this technique removes the reasons for the continuing conflict. By *changing the people*—that is, by replacing or transferring one or more of the conflicting parties— conflicts caused by poor interpersonal relationships can be eliminated. The same holds true for *altering the physical environment*. Facilities, workspace, or workflows can be rearranged to physically separate conflicting parties and decrease opportunities for contact with one another.

The integrating devices introduced in Chapter 8 as ways to improve coordination in an organization can also be used to deal with conflicts. Using liaison personnel, special task forces, cross-functional teams, and even the matrix form of organization can change interaction patterns and assist in conflict reduction. *Changing reward systems* may reduce competition between individuals and groups for rewards. Creating systems that reward cooperation can encourage behaviours and attitudes that promote teamwork and reduce conflict. *Changing policies and procedures* may redirect behaviour in ways that minimize the likelihood of problems in situations known to be conflict-prone. Finally, *training in interpersonal skills* can help prepare people to communicate and work more effectively in settings where conflict is likely.

Conflict Management Styles

People respond to interpersonal conflict through different combinations of cooperative and assertive behaviours.[64] Cooperativeness is the desire to satisfy another party's needs and concerns; assertiveness is the desire to satisfy one's own needs and concerns. Figure 15.9 shows five interpersonal styles of conflict management that result from various combinations of these two tendencies.[65]

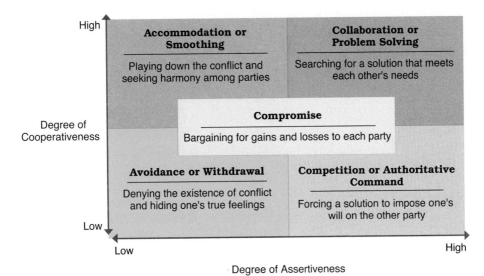

Figure 15.9 Alternative conflict management styles.

Avoidance or withdrawal pretends that a conflict doesn't really exist.

Accommodation or smoothing plays down differences and highlights similarities to reduce conflict.

Competition or authoritative command uses force, superior skill, or domination to "win" a conflict.

Compromise occurs when each party to the conflict gives up something of value to the other.

Collaboration or problem solving involves working through conflict differences and solving problems so everyone wins.

In **lose-lose conflict**, no one achieves his or her true desires, and the underlying reasons for conflict remain unaffected.

In **win-lose conflict**, one party achieves its desires, and the other party does not.

In **win-win conflict**, the conflict is resolved to everyone's benefit.

- **Avoidance** or *withdrawal*—being uncooperative and unassertive, downplaying disagreement, withdrawing from the situation, and/or staying neutral at all costs.

- **Accommodation** or *smoothing*—being cooperative but unassertive, letting the wishes of others rule, smoothing over or overlooking differences to maintain harmony.

- **Competition** or *authoritative command*—being uncooperative but assertive, working against the wishes of the other party, engaging in win-lose competition, and/or forcing through the exercise of authority.

- **Compromise**—being moderately cooperative and assertive, bargaining for "acceptable" solutions in which each party wins a bit and loses a bit.

- **Collaboration** or *problem solving*—being cooperative and assertive, trying to fully satisfy everyone's concerns by working through differences, finding and solving problems so that everyone gains.[66]

Avoiding or accommodating often creates **lose-lose conflict**. No one achieves her or his true desires, and the underlying reasons for conflict remain unaffected. Although the conflict appears settled or may even disappear for a while, it tends to recur in the future. Avoidance is an extreme form of non-attention. Everyone withdraws and pretends that conflict doesn't really exist, hoping that it will simply go away. Accommodation plays down differences and highlights similarities and areas of agreement. Peaceful coexistence is the goal, but smoothing may ignore the real essence of a conflict.

Competing and compromising tend to create **win-lose conflict** where each party strives to gain at the other's expense. In extreme cases, one party achieves its desires to the complete exclusion of the other party's desires. Because win-lose methods fail to address the root causes of conflict, future conflicts of the same or a similar nature are likely to occur. In competition, one party wins because superior skill or outright domination allows his or her desires to be forced on the other. An example is authoritative command where a supervisor simply dictates a solution to subordinates. Compromise occurs when trade-offs are made such that each party to the conflict gives up and gains something. But because each party loses something, antecedents for future conflicts are established.

Collaborating or true problem solving is a form of **win-win conflict**. It is often the most effective conflict management style because issues are resolved to the mutual benefit of all conflicting parties. This is typically achieved by confronting the issues and everyone being willing to recognize that something is wrong and needs attention. Win-win outcomes eliminate the underlying causes of the conflict; all relevant issues are raised and discussed openly.

✔ **Learning Check 5**

BE SURE YOU CAN

- differentiate between substantive and emotional conflict • differentiate between functional and dysfunctional conflict • explain the common causes of conflict • list the possible approaches to conflict resolution • explain the conflict management styles of avoidance, accommodation, competition, compromise, and collaboration • discuss lose-lose, win-lose, and win-win conflicts

NEGOTIATION

How would you behave and what would you do in the following situations?[67] You have been offered a job and would really like to take it. However, the pay being offered is less than you hoped. In another workplace scenario, there is enough money to order one new computer for your team, but two members have each requested new computers.

These are examples of the many work situations that lead to **negotiation**—the process of making joint decisions when the parties involved have different preferences. Stated a bit differently, negotiation is a way of reaching agreement. People negotiate over salaries, performance evaluations, job assignments, work schedules, work locations, and many other things. All negotiations are susceptible to conflict and negative aftermath, and test the communication and collaboration skills of those involved.

Negotiation is the process of making joint decisions when the parties involved have different preferences.

NEGOTIATION GOALS AND APPROACHES

There are two important goals to be considered in any negotiation. **Substance goals** are concerned with outcomes and are tied to content issues. **Relationship goals** are concerned with processes. They are tied to the way people work together while negotiating, and how they (and any constituencies they represent) will be able to work together again in the future.

Substance goals in negotiation are concerned with outcomes.

Effective negotiation occurs when issues of substance are resolved and working relationships among the negotiating parties are maintained, or even improved, in the process. The three criteria of effective negotiation are: (1) *quality*—negotiating a "wise" agreement that is truly satisfactory to all sides; (2) *cost*—negotiating efficiently, using a minimum of resources and time; and (3) *harmony*—negotiating in a way that fosters, rather than inhibits, interpersonal relationships.[68]

Relationship goals in negotiation are concerned with the ways people work together.

Effective negotiation resolves issues of substance while maintaining a positive process.

The way each party approaches a negotiation can have a major impact on its effectiveness.[69] **Distributive negotiation** focuses on "claims" made by each party for certain preferred outcomes. This emphasis on substance can take a self-centred and competitive form in which one party can gain only if the other loses. In such win-lose conditions, relationships are often sacrificed as the negotiating parties focus only on their respective self-interests.

Distributive negotiation focuses on win-lose claims made by each party for certain preferred outcomes.

Principled negotiation, often called **integrative negotiation**, is based on a win-win orientation. The focus on substance is still important, but the interests of all parties are considered. The goal is to base the final outcome on the merits of individual claims and to try to find a way for all claims to be satisfied, if at all possible. No one should lose in a principled negotiation, and positive relationships should be maintained in the process.

Principled negotiation or **integrative negotiation** uses a win-win orientation to reach solutions acceptable to each party.

GAINING INTEGRATIVE AGREEMENTS

In their book *Getting to Yes*, Roger Fisher and William Ury point out that truly integrative agreements are obtained by following four negotiation rules.[70]

1. Separate the people from the problem.

2. Focus on interests, not on positions.

3. Generate many alternatives before deciding what to do.

4. Insist that results be based on some objective standard.

Proper attitudes and good information are necessary foundations for integrative agreements. The attitudinal foundations involve the willingness of each negotiating party to trust, share information with, and ask reasonable questions of the other party. The information foundations involve both parties knowing what is really important to them and also finding out what is really important to the other party.

Figure 15.10 introduces a classic two-party labour–management negotiation over a new contract and salary increase.[71] Look at the figure and case from the labour union's perspective. The union negotiator has told her management counterpart that the union wants a new wage of $15.00 per hour. This expressed preference is the union's initial offer. However, she also has in mind a minimum reservation point of $13.25 per hour. This is the lowest that she is willing to accept for the union. Now look at it from the perspective of the management negotiator. His initial offer is $12.75 per hour. And his maximum reservation point, the highest wage he is prepared to eventually offer the union, is $13.75 per hour.

In such a two-party negotiation, the **bargaining zone** is defined as the space between one party's minimum reservation point and the other party's maximum reservation point. The bargaining zone in this case lies between $13.25 per hour and $13.75 per hour. It is a "positive" zone since the reservation points of the two parties overlap. If the union's minimum reservation point was greater than management's maximum reservation point, no room would exist for bargaining. A key task for any negotiator is to discover the other party's reservation point. Until this is known and each party realizes that a positive bargaining zone exists, it is difficult to negotiate effectively.

A **bargaining zone** is the space between one party's minimum reservation point and the other party's maximum reservation point.

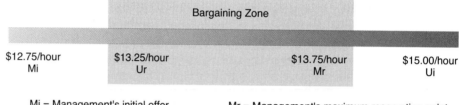

Bargaining Zone			
$12.75/hour Mi	$13.25/hour Ur	$13.75/hour Mr	$15.00/hour Ui

Figure 15.10 The bargaining zone in classic two-party negotiation.

Mi = Management's initial offer
Ur = Union's minimum reservation point

Mr = Management's maximum reservation point
Ui = Union's initial offer

NEGOTIATION PITFALLS

The negotiation process is admittedly complex, and negotiators must guard against common pitfalls. The first is falling prey to the *myth of the "fixed pie."* This involves acting on the distributive and win-lose assumption that, in order for you to gain in the negotiation, the other person must give something up. This approach to negotiating fails to recognize the integrative assumption that the "pie" can sometimes be expanded or used to everyone's advantage. A second negotiation error is *non-rational escalation of conflict.* The negotiator in this case becomes committed to previously stated "demands" and allows personal needs for "ego" and "saving face" to increase the perceived importance of satisfying them.

A third negotiating error is *overconfidence and ignoring the other's needs.* The negotiator becomes overconfident, believes his or her position is the only correct one, and fails to consider the needs of the other party or appreciate the merits of its position. The fourth error is *too much "telling" and too little "hearing."* The "telling" error occurs when parties to a negotiation don't really make themselves understood to each other. The "hearing" error occurs when they fail to listen well enough to understand what the other is saying.[72]

Another potential negotiation pitfall, and one increasingly important in our age of globalization, is *premature cultural comfort.* This occurs when a negotiator is too quick to assume that he or she understands the intentions, positions, and meanings being communicated by a negotiator from a different culture. Scholar Jeanne Brett says, for example, that negotiators from low-context cultures can run into difficulties when dealing with ones from high-context cultures. The low-context negotiator is used to getting information through direct questions and answers; the high-context negotiator is likely to communicate indirectly and not explicitly state positions.[73]

Finally, it is important to avoid the *trap of ethical misconduct.* The motivation to negotiate unethically sometimes arises from an undue emphasis on the profit motive. This may be experienced as a desire to "get just a bit more" or to "get as much as you can" from a negotiation. The motivation to behave unethically may also result from a sense of competition. This is a desire to "win" a negotiation just for the sake of winning it, or because of the misguided belief that someone else must "lose" in order for you to gain.

When unethical behaviour occurs in negotiation, the persons involved may try to explain it away with inappropriate rationalizing: "It was really unavoidable." "Oh, it's harmless." "The results justify the means." "It's really quite fair and appropriate."[74] Of course, these excuses for questionable behaviour are morally unacceptable. They can also be challenged by the possibility that any short-run gains will be offset by long-run losses. Unethical negotiators will incur lasting legacies of distrust, disrespect, and dislike, and they can be targeted for "revenge" in later negotiations.

ISSUES AND SITUATIONS
Canadian Negotiation Challenge

Under the terms of the Kyoto Protocol, the federal Canadian government committed to bringing emissions of greenhouse gases to below 1990 levels by 2012. As a country, we are not close to achieving this goal. As the third largest per capita producer of greenhouse emissions, the challenge is that the provinces and the federal government do not agree on the best way forward. Conservative Prime Minister Stephen Harper believes that the Kyoto Protocol should be dropped in favour of a "made-in-Canada" solution. Under a new Clean Air Act, Harper moved to regulate greenhouse-gas-emitting industries, allowing emission trading domestically. Alberta would like to see a go-slow policy which would allow emissions to rise until 2020 and then work to lessen emissions thereafter when appropriate technology has been developed. Alternatively, Ontario advocates the development of a "green" economy and to reach below 1990 levels by 2020.

CRITICAL RESPONSE

It would appear that there is no clear consensus on what should be the coherent Canadian policy on greenhouse gases. What negotiation approach would work best here?

THIRD-PARTY DISPUTE RESOLUTION

Even with the best of intentions, it may not always be possible to achieve integrative agreements. When disputes reach the point of impasse, third-party assistance with dispute resolution can be useful. **Mediation** involves a neutral third party who tries to improve communication between negotiating parties and keep them focused on relevant issues. The mediator does not issue a ruling or make a decision, but can take an active role in discussions. This may include making suggestions in an attempt to move the parties toward agreement.

Arbitration, such as salary arbitration in professional sports, is a stronger form of dispute resolution. It involves a neutral third party, the arbitrator, who acts as a "judge" and issues a binding decision. This usually includes a formal hearing in which the arbitrator listens to both sides and reviews all facets of the case before making a ruling.

Some organizations formally provide for a process called *alternative dispute resolution*. This approach uses mediation or arbitration, but does so only after direct attempts to negotiate agreements between the conflicting parties have failed. Often an ombudsperson, a designated neutral third party who listens to complaints and disputes, plays a key role in the process.

In **mediation**, a neutral party tries to help conflicting parties improve communication to resolve their dispute.

In **arbitration**, a neutral third party issues a binding decision to resolve a dispute.

Learning Check ⑥

BE SURE YOU CAN

• differentiate between distributive and principled negotiation • list four rules of principled negotiation • define *bargaining zone* • use this term to illustrate a labour-management wage negotiation • describe the potential pitfalls in negotiation • differentiate between mediation and arbitration

MANAGEMENT LEARNING REVIEW

STUDY QUESTIONS SUMMARY

KEY TERMS

accommodation, 468
arbitration, 471
avoidance, 468
bargaining zone, 470
brainstorming, 465
centralized communication
    network, 460
cohesiveness, 458
collaboration, 468
committee, 449
competition, 468
compromise, 468
conflict, 465
cross-functional team, 450
decentralized communication
    network, 460
decision-making, 461
disruptive activities, 459
distributed leadership, 459
distributive negotiation, 469
dysfunctional conflict, 466
effective negotiation, 469
effective team, 453
emotional conflicts, 466
formal groups, 448
functional conflict, 466
group process, 455
groupthink, 463
informal groups, 448
integrative negotiation, 469
lose-lose conflict, 468
maintenance activity, 459
mediation, 471
negotiation, 469
nominal group technique, 465
norm, 458
principled negotiation, 469

1. How do teams contribute to organizations?

• A team is a collection of people working together to accomplish a common goal.

• Teams help organizations perform through synergy—the creation of a whole that is greater than the sum of its parts.

• Teams help satisfy important needs for their members by providing sources of job support and social satisfactions.

• Social loafing and other problems can limit the performance of teams.

• Organizations operate as networks of formal and informal groups.

FOR DISCUSSION Why do people often tolerate social loafers at work?

2. What are current trends in the use of teams?

• Committees and task forces are used to accomplish special tasks and projects.

• Cross-functional teams bring members together from different departments, and help improve lateral relations and integration in organizations.

• New developments in information technology are making virtual teams commonplace at work, but virtual teams also pose special management challenges.

• Self-managing teams are changing organizations, as team members perform many tasks previously done by their supervisors.

• Team building engages team members in a process of assessment and action planning to improve teamwork and future performance.

FOR DISCUSSION What are some of the things that virtual teams probably can't do as well as face-to-face teams?

3. How do teams work?

• An effective team achieves high levels of task performance, member satisfaction, and team viability.

• Important team inputs include the organizational setting, nature of the task, size, and membership characteristics.

• A team matures through various stages of development, including forming, storming, norming, performing, and adjourning.

• Norms are the standards or rules of conduct that influence the behaviour of team members; cohesion is the attractiveness of the team to its members.

• In highly cohesive teams, members tend to conform to norms; the best situation is a team with positive performance norms and high cohesiveness.

- Distributed leadership occurs as members share in meeting a team's task and maintenance needs.
- Effective teams make use of alternative communication structures, such as the centralized and decentralized networks, to best complete tasks.

FOR DISCUSSION What can be done if a team gets trapped in the storming stage of group development?

4. How do teams make decisions?
- Teams can make decisions by lack of response, authority rule, minority rule, majority rule, consensus, and unanimity.
- Although group decisions often make more information available for problem solving and generate more understanding and commitment, the potential liabilities of group decisions include social pressures to conform and greater time requirements.
- Groupthink is a tendency of members of highly cohesive teams to lose their critical evaluative capabilities and make poor decisions.
- Techniques for improving creativity in teams include brainstorming and the nominal group technique.

FOR DISCUSSION Is it possible that groupthink doesn't occur only when groups are highly cohesive, but also when they are pre-cohesive?

5. How do you manage conflict?
- Conflict occurs as disagreements over substantive or emotional issues.
- Moderate levels of conflict are functional for performance and creativity; too little or too much conflict becomes dysfunctional.
- Conflict may be managed through structural approaches that involve changing people, goals, resources, or work arrangements.
- Personal conflict management styles include avoidance, accommodation, compromise, competition, and collaboration.
- True conflict resolution involves problem solving through a win-win collaborative approach.

FOR DISCUSSION When is it better to avoid conflict rather than engage it?

6. How can we negotiate successful agreements?
- Negotiation is the process of making decisions in situations in which the participants have different preferences.
- Substance goals concerned with outcomes and relationship goals concerned with processes are both important in successful negotiation.
- Effective negotiation occurs when issues of substance are resolved while maintaining good working relationships.
- Distributive negotiation emphasizes win-lose outcomes; integrative negotiation emphasizes win-win outcomes.
- Common negotiation pitfalls include the myth of the fixed pie, overconfidence, too much telling and too little hearing, and ethical misconduct.
- Mediation and arbitration are structured approaches to third-party dispute resolution.

FOR DISCUSSION How do you negotiate with someone trapped in the "myth of the fixed pie"?

SELF-TEST

Multiple-Choice Questions

1. When a group of people is able to achieve more than what its members could by working individually, this is called _____.
   (a) social loafing   (b) consensus   (c) viability   (d) synergy

2. In an organization operating with self-managing teams, the traditional role of _____ is replaced by the role of team leader.
   (a) chief executive officer   (b) first-line supervisor   (c) middle manager   (d) general manager

3. An effective team is defined as one that achieves high levels of task performance, member satisfaction, and _____.
   (a) resource efficiency   (b) future viability   (c) consensus   (d) creativity

4. In the open-systems model of teams, the _____ is an important input factor.
   (a) communication network   (b) decision-making method   (c) performance norm   (d) set of membership characteristics

5. A basic rule of team dynamics states that the greater the _____ in a team, the greater the conformity to norms.
   (a) membership diversity   (b) cohesiveness   (c) task structure   (d) competition among members

6. Groupthink is most likely to occur in teams that are _____.
   (a) large in size   (b) diverse in membership   (c) high-performing   (d) highly cohesive

7. Gatekeeping is an example of a _____ activity that can help teams work effectively over time.
   (a) task   (b) maintenance   (c) team-building   (d) decision-making

8. Members of a team tend to start to get coordinated and comfortable with one another in the _____ stage of team development.
   (a) forming   (b) norming   (c) performing   (d) adjourning

9. One way for a manager to build positive norms within a team is to _____.
   (a) act as a positive role model   (b) increase group size   (c) introduce groupthink   (d) isolate the team

10. When teams are highly cohesive, _____.
    (a) members are high performers   (b) members tend to be satisfied with their team membership   (c) members have positive norms   (d) the group achieves its goals

11. When members of a group share commitments to being on time for all meetings, on-time behaviour has become _____.
    (a) a symptom of groupthink   (b) synergy   (c) a norm   (d) activity maintenance

12. It would be common to find members of self-managing work teams engaged in _____.
    (a) social loafing   (b) multitasking   (c) centralized communication   (d) decision by authority rule

13. A conflict is most likely to be functional and have a positive impact on performance when it is _____.
    (a) based on emotions   (b) resolved by arbitration   (c) caused by resource scarcities   (d) of moderate intensity

14. In classic two-party negotiation, the difference between one party's minimum reservation point and the other party's maximum reservation point is known as the _____.

    (a) dispute resolution   (b) arena of indifference   (c) myth of the fixed pie   (d) bargaining zone

15. To increase the cohesiveness of a group, a manager would be best off _____.

    (a) starting a competition with other groups   (b) increasing the group size   (c) acting as a positive role model   (d) introducing a new member

Short-Response Questions

16. How can a manager improve team effectiveness by modifying inputs?

17. What is the relationship among a team's cohesiveness, performance norms, and performance results?

18. How would a manager know that a team is suffering from groupthink (give two symptoms), and what could the manager do about it (give two responses)?

19. Explain the "inverted U" curve of conflict intensity and performance.

Application Question

20. Marcos Martinez has just been appointed manager of a production team operating the 11 p.m. to 7 a.m. shift in a large manufacturing firm. An experienced manager, Marcos is pleased that the team members really like and get along well with one another, but they also appear to be restricting their task outputs to the minimum acceptable levels. What could Marcos do to improve things in this situation, and why should he do them?

MANAGEMENT SKILLS AND COMPETENCIES

SELF-ASSESSMENT

Back to Yourself: Team Contributions

If teams and teamwork are a major part of how organizations operate today, team contributions have to be considered one of the most essential career skills. We need to be able to contribute as team members in many different ways so that our teams can reach their performance potential. But experience proves time and time again that teams often underperform or, at least, lose time and effectiveness as members struggle with a variety of process difficulties. You can probably confirm this quite easily with a good, hard look at the teams that you participate in. While so doing, make a realistic self-assessment of your team contributions as well as those of others. Ask: How can the insights of this chapter help me build the team leader skills that can help turn teamwork potential into real team achievements?

Further Reflection: Conflict Management Strategies

Instructions

Think of how you behave in conflict situations in which your wishes differ from those of others. In the space to the left, rate each of the following statements on a scale of "1" = "not at all" to "5" = "very much."

When I have a conflict at work, school, or in my personal life, I do the following:

1. I give in to the wishes of the other party.

2. I try to realize a middle-of-the-road solution.

3. I push my own point of view.

4. I examine issues until I find a solution that really satisfies me and the other party.

5. I avoid a confrontation about our differences.

6. I concur with the other party.

7. I emphasize that we have to find a compromise solution.

8. I search for gains.

9. I stand for my own and the other's goals.

10. I avoid differences of opinion as much as possible.

11. I try to accommodate the other party.

12. I insist we both give in a little.

13. I fight for a good outcome for myself.

14. I examine ideas from both sides to find a mutually optimal solution.

15. I try to make differences seem less severe.

16. I adapt to the other party's goals and interests.

17. I strive whenever possible toward a 50-50 compromise.

18. I do everything to win.

19. I work out a solution that serves my own as well as other's interests as much as possible.

20. I try to avoid a confrontation with the other person.

Scoring

Total your scores for items as follows.
Yielding tendency: 1 + 6 + 11 + 16 = ___.
Compromising tendency: 2 + 7 + 12 + 17 = ___.
Forcing tendency: 3 + 8 + 13 + 18 = ___.
Problem-solving tendency: 4 + 9 + 14 + 19 = ___.
Avoiding tendency: 5 + 10 + 15 + 20 = ___.

Interpretation

Each of the scores above approximates one of the conflict management styles discussed in the chapter. Look back to Figure 15.9 and make the match-ups. Although each style is part of management, only collaboration or problem solving leads to true conflict resolution. You should consider any patterns that may be evident in your scores and think about how to best handle the conflict situations in which you become involved.

Source: This instrument is described in Carsten K. W. De Drew, Arne Evers, Bianca Beersma, Esther S. Kluwer, and Aukje Nauta, "A Theory-Based Measure of Conflict Management Strategies in the Workplace," *Journal of Organizational Behavior*, vol. 22 (2001), pp. 645–668. Used by permission.

Work Team Dynamics

Preparation

Think about your course work group, a work group you are involved in for another course, or any other group suggested by your instructor. Use this scale to indicate how often each of the following statements accurately reflects your experience in the group.

1 = always; 2 = frequently; 3 = sometimes; 4 = never

1.　My ideas get a fair hearing.

2.　I am encouraged to give innovative ideas and take risks.

3.　Diverse opinions within the group are encouraged.

4.　I have all the responsibility I want.

5.　There is a lot of favouritism shown in the group.

6.　Members trust one another to do their assigned work.

7.　The group sets high standards of performance excellence.

8.　People share and change jobs a lot in the group.

9.　You can make mistakes and learn from them in this group.

10.　This group has good operating rules.

Instructions

Form groups as assigned by your instructor. Ideally, this will be the group you have just rated. Have all group members share their ratings, and then make one master rating for the group as a whole. Circle the items for which there are the biggest differences of opinion. Discuss those items and try to find out why they exist. In general, the better a group scores on this instrument, the higher its creative potential. If everyone has rated the same group, make a list of the five most important things members can do to improve its operations in the future. Nominate a spokesperson to summarize the group discussion for the class as a whole.

Source: Adapted from William Dyer, *Team Building,* 2nd ed. (Reading, MA: Addison-Wesley, 1987), pp. 123–125.

NASCAR: Fast Cars, Passion, and Teamwork Create Wins

By only his second full year of NASCAR Winston Cup Series racing, the young Ryan Newman was rapidly becoming a racing phenomenon. He has since had spectacular consecutive racing seasons, including winning the Daytona 500.[1] What accounts for the success of a top NASCAR driver?

Racing Passion

In a sport that measures victory in hundredths of a second, NASCAR drivers need every competitive edge they can get. And Ryan Newman claims a unique advantage among his racing peers: his education. Newman graduated from Purdue University with a degree in vehicle structural engineering. He studied part-time while driving race cars. And did it make a difference? The season he graduated, Newman earned almost US$500,000 in NASCAR winnings. One year later, he'd earned nearly ten times as much.

A self-admitted car buff, Newman loves to drive cars and work on them.[2] His passion for fast cars developed at an early age. Encouraged by his parents, he started racing quarter midgets when he was only four-and-a-half years old. Newman amassed more than 100 midget car victories. Later he raced midget cars and sprint cars, achieving extraordinary success there as well.[3]

When Newman joined the Penske Racing Team, the co-owners hired Buddy Baker, a former top race car driver, to work with Newman. Being very selective about the drivers he works with, Baker insisted on meeting Newman and his family before accepting the job offer. Baker says: "When I started talking to Ryan, I could feel the energy that he had, and the passion he had for the sport. Then, I met his dad, and right there I knew, OK, he's got a good background. His father's been with him in go-carts, midgets. He turned the wrenches for his son. It was an automatic fit for me."

Baker thinks of Newman as though he were one of his own sons, both of whom briefly tried racing but neither of whom had a passion for it. Baker says that he never wanted to do anything but race, and Newman is just like him. Referring to Newman, Baker says: "From the time he was 5 years old until now, he's never wanted to be anything else."[4]

(AP Photo/Terry Renna)

High-Performance Team

About his pre–Winston Cup racing days, Newman says: "I always worked on my own cars and maintained them, did the set-ups, things like that. Obviously, I also drove them so I was always a hands-on, involved, seat of the pants driver." As a Winston Cup driver, Newman acknowledges that he "misses working on the cars, but when you have great guys doing that work, you don't feel like you have to do it yourself."[5]

"For all my life, my family has been my crew," Newman also says. "To come to an organization like Penske, and have so many more people behind you fighting for the same goals, it's like being in a bigger family. When you're with people you like, you have the confidence to do things well."[6] Most of the people who work on Newman's crew are engineers, and all of them are computer whizzes—significant talents for building and maintaining today's race cars.[7] Newman and the crew try to learn from the problem situations that they encounter so they can "keep the freak things from happening."[8]

Newman asserts that his racing team does the best job it can with what they have. "When there's an opportunity to try and stretch it to the end, we're going to try to stretch to the end," says Newman.[9] He enters every race with the attitude that he can and will win it.[10]

Working together as a team and optimizing every mechanical advantage, Ryan Newman and his team have beat the odds to generate a successful record in the ultracompetitive NASCAR circuit. And though victory brings the loyalty of fans and big prize winnings, it can also create tension among fellow racers, many of whom have been racing decades longer than Newman. What does it take for a young driver with talent, know-how, and commitment to create a NASCAR team that can win over the long haul?

Discussion Questions

1. What are the teamwork and team-building challenges that must be mastered to create synergy when a new NASCAR driver joins an established racing team and pit crew?

2. How can a NASCAR owner use insights from the open-systems model of team effectiveness to build a true high-performance racing team?

3. In what ways can a driver's behaviour help with or hinder a crew chief's efforts to build the right norms and a high level of cohesiveness in a pit crew? Or create conflict on a team?

4. FURTHER RESEARCH—Pit crews are often in the news. See what you can find out about pit crew performance. Ask: What differentiates the "high-performance" pit crews from the "also rans"? If you were to write a class lesson plan on "Pit Crew Insights for Team Success," what would you include in the lesson and why?

16

Control Processes and Systems

Best Buy: Discounting time, counting on you!

If it feels like a company owns your time, it means that you are likely working in a time-oriented office. However, a new type of workplace is emerging, one that is more results-oriented. These places of work focus on what you accomplish rather than how many hours you spend at work.

Going AWOL during "office" hours would be grounds for dismissal at many companies but not at Best Buy. One of North America's leading electronics retailers, Best Buy has embarked on a radical experiment to transform from a culture known for a focus on "face time" to a "results-only work environment," or ROWE. The ROWE program seeks to knock down the old business doctrine that long hours equate with high performance. The new goal at Best Buy is to judge performance based on output instead of hours. Rather than control people with the clock, Best Buy is looking to direct employee action by keeping track of results.

The ROWE experiment started at best Buy in 2003. Since then, 60 percent of the people at its U.S.A. headquarters have converted to results-only working. And it is working; Best Buy has found that under ROWE, employee productivity has increased by 35 percent.

ROWE completely alters the way people work, with employees now in control of everything. Not just where and when they work but, for example, whether they go to meetings. The only thing that an employee is judged on is results. It is total flexibility based upon total accountability. If you perform, golfing in the afternoon or going out for a long lunch is clearly okay!

Best Buy in Canada has not yet fully implemented the ROWE system. It is experimenting with ROWE to see if its results are similar to the ones found in the U.S.A. At present, employees in Canada are allowed up to two days a week where they can work from home. It is still a work in progress but time will tell![1]

| **BENCHMARK** | When Best Buy focuses on outcome performance rather than face time, it is offering control to its employees. What is interesting is that, by giving control away, while keeping track of results, it is actually following a strong control process—a lesson we can all benefit from. |

Strength and Energy

It may strike you as odd to talk here about personal strength and energy. But the fact is that it's not easy to always exercise the self-control needed to keep up with fast-paced work and personal responsibilities.

One national survey of North American workers found 54 percent feel overworked, 55 percent feel overwhelmed by their workloads, 56 percent say they do not have enough time to complete their work, 59 percent do not have enough time for reflection, and 45 percent have to do too many things at once. The Mayo Clinic points out that in our often "frenetically paced world" the boundaries between work and home have blurred. We work longer hours and stay constantly in touch with work with information technology. Combined with non-work responsibilities, these pressures take their tolls and create problems with fatigue—sheer physical breakdown; family—missing life events; friends—not nurturing friendships; and expectations—the more you work, the more is expected of you.

Just as with playing tennis or some other sport, we have to get and stay in shape, physically and mentally, so that we can not only perform well at work, but also maintain a positive work–life balance. This means building strength and energy to best handle the inevitable strains and anxieties of conflicts between work demands and personal affairs.[2]

Do you sometimes feel the need to "take back your life"? Think of all the meetings you attend, the projects that you are involved in, and your everyday work issues and responsibilities. Then think about your personal responsibilities—loved ones, family, friends, and more. How does everything balance out, or does it ever balance? Who's in control? You, someone else, or just the situations you find yourself in?

Mayo Clinic on Work–Life Balance

- *Learn to say no*—don't do things out of guilt or false obligation

- *Leave work at work*—set boundaries between work and personal affairs

- *Manage time*—be efficient and set priorities

- *Fight guilt*—remember it's okay to have a job and a family

- *Nurture yourself*—do something relaxing and enjoyable every day

- *Protect your day off*—spread chores so that a day off is free time

- *Get enough sleep*—give your system the chance to replenish its energy

---

❖ Get to Know Yourself Better

Check the Mayo Clinic tips in the box. How good are you, right now as a student, at satisfying both work and non-work demands? The chances are that present behaviour is a good predictor of how you'll do in the future. What are the lessons of a frank self-assessment? Are you in control or not? Do you have the strength and energy to do well at work and also have a healthy home life?

CHAPTER 16 STUDY QUESTIONS

- Why and how do managers control?

- What are the steps in the control process?

- What are the common control tools and techniques?

VISUAL CHAPTER OVERVIEW

CHAPTER 16 CONTROL PROCESSES AND SYSTEMS

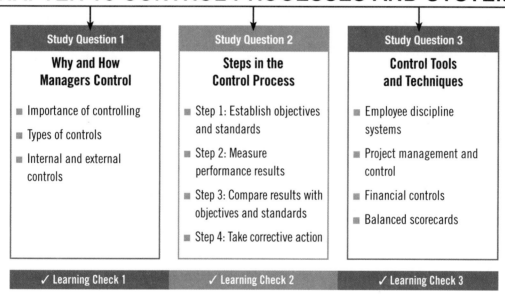

Study Question 1	Study Question 2	Study Question 3
Why and How Managers Control	**Steps in the Control Process**	**Control Tools and Techniques**
■ Importance of controlling ■ Types of controls ■ Internal and external controls	■ Step 1: Establish objectives and standards ■ Step 2: Measure performance results ■ Step 3: Compare results with objectives and standards ■ Step 4: Take corrective action	■ Employee discipline systems ■ Project management and control ■ Financial controls ■ Balanced scorecards
✓ Learning Check 1	✓ Learning Check 2	✓ Learning Check 3

Keeping in touch . . . Staying informed . . . Being in control. These are important responsibilities for every manager. But "control" is a word like "power." If you aren't careful when and how the word is used, it leaves a negative connotation. Yet control plays a positive and necessary role in the management process. To have things "under control" is good; for things to be "out of control" is generally bad.

WHY AND HOW MANAGERS CONTROL

In the ever-changing technology industry, CEO T. J. Rodgers of Cypress Semiconductor Corp. likes things in control. It goes along with his strong emphasis on performance and accountability. Cypress employees work with clear and quantified work goals, which they help set. Rodgers believes that this system helps find problems before they interfere with performance. He says: "Managers monitor the goals, look for problems, and expect people who fall behind to ask for help before they lose control of or damage a major project."[3]

Rodgers is all about planning, or setting goals, and controlling—keeping things on track to accomplish them. Control is important for any organization, and we practise a lot of control quite naturally. Think of fun things you do—playing golf or tennis or Frisbee, reading, dancing, driving a car, or riding a bike. Through activities such as this, you've already become quite expert in the control process. How? Most probably by having an objective in mind, always checking to see how well you are doing, and making continuous adjustments to get it right.

IMPORTANCE OF CONTROLLING

Controlling is a process of measuring performance and taking action to ensure desired results. Its purpose is straightforward: to make sure that plans are achieved, and that actual performance meets or surpasses objectives. The foundation of control is information. Henry Schacht, former CEO of Cummins Engine Company, once discussed control in terms of what he called "friendly facts." He stated: "Facts that reinforce what you are doing are nice, because they help in terms of psychic reward. Facts that raise alarms are equally friendly, because they give you clues about how to respond, how to change, where to spend the resources."[4]

> **Controlling** is the process of measuring performance and taking action to ensure desired results.

Figure 16.1 shows how controlling fits in with the other management functions. Planning sets the directions and allocates resources. Organizing brings people and material resources together in working combinations. Leading inspires people to best utilize these resources. Controlling sees to it that the right things happen, in the right way, and at the right time. It helps ensure that performance is consistent with plans, and that accomplishments throughout an organization are coordinated in a means-ends fashion. It also helps ensure that people comply with organizational policies and procedures.

Effective control is essential to organizational learning. It is a way of learning from experience. Consider, for example, the program of **after-action review** used by the Canadian military and now used in many corporate settings. This is a structured review of lessons learned and results accomplished in a completed project, task force assignment, or special operation. Participants answer questions such as: "What was the intent?" "What actually happened?" "What did we learn?"[5] The after-action review helps make continuous improvement a part of the organizational culture. It encourages those involved to take responsibility for their performance efforts and accomplishments. The end-of-chapter self-assessment is modelled on this approach.

> An **after-action review** identifies lessons learned through a completed project, task force assignment, or special operation.

Improving performance through learning is one of the great opportunities offered by the control process. However, the potential benefits are realized only when learning is translated into corrective actions. After setting up Diversity Network Groups worldwide, for example, IBM executives learned that male attitudes were major barriers to the success of female managers. They addressed this finding by strengthening controls: senior executives were required to report annually on the progress of women managers in their divisions. This action is credited with substantially increasing the percentage of women in IBM's senior management ranks.[6]

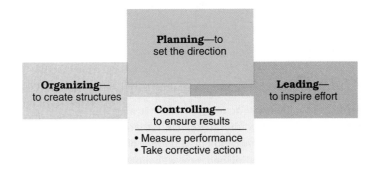

Figure 16.1 The role of controlling in the management process.

TYPES OF CONTROLS

One of the best ways to consider control is in respect to the open-systems perspective in Figure 16.2. It shows how feedforward, concurrent, and feedback controls link with different phases of this input-throughput-output cycle.[7] Each type of control increases the likelihood of high performance.

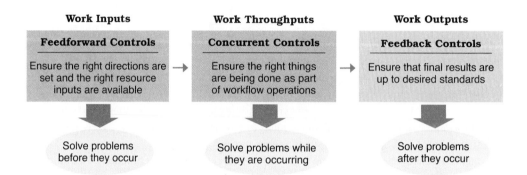

Figure 16.2 Feedforward, concurrent, and feedback controls.

Feedforward Controls

Feedforward control ensures that directions and resources are right before the work begins.

Feedforward controls, also called *preliminary controls*, take place before a work activity begins. They ensure that objectives are clear, that proper directions are established, and that the right resources are available to accomplish the objectives. The goal is to solve problems before they occur by asking an important but often neglected question: "What needs to be done before we begin?"

Feedforward controls are preventive in nature. Managers using them take a forward-thinking and proactive approach to control. At McDonald's, for example, preliminary control of food ingredients plays an important role in the firm's quality program. The company requires that suppliers of its hamburger buns produce them to exact specifications, covering everything from texture to uniformity of colour. Even in overseas markets, the firm works hard to develop local suppliers that can offer dependable quality.[8]

Concurrent Controls

Concurrent control focuses on what happens during the work process.

Concurrent controls focus on what happens during the work process. Sometimes called steering controls, they make sure things are being done according to plan. You can also think of this as control through direct supervision.

The goal of concurrent controls is to solve problems as they occur. The key question is "What can we do to improve things right now?" At McDonald's, ever-present shift leaders provide concurrent control through direct supervision. They constantly observe what is taking place, even while helping out with the work. They are trained to intervene immediately when something is not done right and to correct things on the spot. Detailed manuals also "steer" workers in the right directions as they perform their jobs.

Feedback Controls

Feedback control takes place after an action is completed.

Feedback controls, also called *post-action controls*, take place after work is completed. They focus on the quality of end results, rather than on inputs and activities. Feedback controls are largely reactive; the goals are to solve problems after they occur and prevent future ones. They ask the question: "Now that we are finished, how well did we do?"

We are all familiar with feedback controls and probably recognize their weak points, especially from a customer service perspective. Restaurants, for example, ask how you liked a meal after it is eaten; course evaluations tell instructors how well they performed after the course is over; a budget summary identifies cost overruns after a project is completed. In these and other circumstances, mistakes may already have been made, but the feedback provided by the control process can help improve things in the future.

INTERNAL AND EXTERNAL CONTROLS

Managers have two broad options with respect to control systems. First, they can manage in ways that allow and expect people to control their own behaviour. This puts priority on internal control, or self-control. Second, they can structure situations to make sure things happen as planned.[9] This is external control, and the alternatives include bureaucratic or administrative control, clan or normative control, and market or regulatory control. Effective control typically involves a mix of options.

Self-Control

We all exercise internal control in our daily lives; we do so in respect to managing our money, our relationships, our eating and drinking, and more. Managers can take advantage of this human capacity for **self-control** by unlocking and setting up conditions that support it. In essence, this means allowing and encouraging people to exercise self-discipline in performing their jobs. Any workplace that emphasizes participation, empowerment, and involvement will rely heavily on self-control.

Self-control, or internal control, occurs through self-discipline in fulfilling many responsibilities.

According to Douglas McGregor's Theory Y perspective, introduced in Chapter 2, people are ready and willing to exercise self-control in their work.[10] But McGregor also points out that they are most likely to do this when they participate in setting performance objectives and standards. Furthermore, the potential for self-control is increased when capable people have a clear sense of organizational mission, know their goals, and have the resources necessary to do their jobs well. It is also enhanced by participative organizational cultures in which everyone treats each other with respect and consideration.

An internal control strategy requires a high degree of trust. When people are expected to work on their own and exercise self-control, managers must give them the freedom to do so.

Bureaucratic Control

A classic form of external control is **bureaucratic control**. It uses authority, policies, procedures, job descriptions, budgets, and day-to-day supervision to make sure that people's behaviour is consistent with organizational interests. You can think of this as control that flows through the organization's hierarchy of authority. Organizations typically have policies and procedures regarding sexual harassment, for example, with the goal being to make sure that members behave toward one another respectfully and in ways that offer no suggestion of sexual pressures or improprieties. Organizations also use budgets for personnel, equipment, travel expenses, and the like to keep behaviour targeted within set limits.

Bureaucratic control influences behaviour through authority, policies, procedures, job descriptions, budgets, and day-to-day supervision.

Another level of bureaucratic control comes from the organization's external environment. Here, laws and regulations may govern behaviour of an organization's top executives. The best example is the U.S. Sarbanes-Oxley (SOX) Act, which establishes procedures to regulate financial reporting and governance in corporations that publicly trade in the United States, including those in Canada listed on U.S. exchanges.[11] The law was passed in response to major corporate failures, such as Worldcom and Enron, that raised serious questions regarding top management behaviour and the accuracy of financial reports provided by the firms. Under SOX, the chief executives and chief financial officers of firms must personally sign off on financial reports and certify their accuracy. Also put into place were special guidelines and procedures to be followed by the firm's audit committees. One of the important features of SOX in respect to control is the penalty provisions. CEOs and CFOs who misstate their firm's financial records can go to jail and pay substantial personal fines.

REAL ETHICS

Privacy and Censorship

Waterloo, Ontario—Research In Motion averts a ban on its BlackBerry services in India that would have affected more than a million users and frozen the Canadian company's expansion into the world's second-largest mobile-phone market. RIM says it will work to meet India's security needs while ensuring that clients' communications are secure.

Washington, D.C.—A U.S. spy agency secretly collects the phone records of millions of Americans as telephone companies turn over private data on their customers. International financial transfers are also electronically monitored in an attempt to detect terrorist networks. David Sobel of the Electronic Privacy Information Center says: "The climate has changed, and many companies give less weight to the privacy interests of their customers."

London, England—Amnesty International claims that Yahoo!, Microsoft, and Google are violating human rights in China by complying with government requests for censorship. Amnesty says that "corporate values and policies" are being compromised in the quest for profits. A spokesperson for Yahoo's China business, Alibaba.com, counters: "By creating opportunities for entrepreneurs and connecting China's exporters to buyers around the world, Alibaba.com and Yahoo! China are having an overwhelmingly positive impact on the lives of average people in China."

Beijing—Skype is told by the Chinese government that its software must filter words that the Chinese leadership considers offensive from text messages. If the company doesn't, it can't do business in the country. After refusing at first, company executives finally agree; phrases such as "Falun Gong" and "Dalai Lama" can no longer appear in text messages delivered through Skype's Chinese joint venture partner, Tom Online.

YOU DECIDE

Skype co-founder Niklas Zennstrom says: "I may like or not like the laws and regulations to operate businesses in the UK or Germany or the U.S., but if I do business there I choose to comply." What do you think? Do company executives have any choice but to comply with the requests of governments? When should business executives stand up and challenge laws and regulations used to deny customers the privacy they expect?

Clan Control

Whereas bureaucratic control emphasizes hierarchy and authority, **clan control** influences behaviour through norms and expectations set by the organizational culture. This is the power of collective identity, where persons who share values and identify strongly with one another tend to behave in ways that are consistent with one another's expectations. Just look around the typical university classroom and campus. You'll often see clan control reflected in dress, language, and behaviour as students tend to act consistently with the expectations of peers and groups they identify with. The same holds true in organizations, where clan control influences employees and members to display common behaviour patterns. The shared informality and ebullient attitudes of WestJet flight crews, for example, show the power of clan control as a critical benchmark of the airline.

> **Clan control** influences behaviour through norms and expectations set by the organizational culture.

Market Control

Market control is essentially the influence of market competition on the behaviour of organizations and their members. Business firms show the influence of market control in the way that they adjust products, pricing, promotions, and other practices in response to customer feedback and what competitors are doing. A good example is the growing emphasis on "green" products and practices. When a firm like Walmart starts to get positive publicity from its expressed commitment to eventually power all of its stores with renewable energy, for example, the effect is felt by its competitors.[12] They have to adjust their practices in order to avoid giving up the public relations advantage to Walmart. In this sense, the time-worn phrase "keeping up with the competition" is really another way of expressing the dynamics of market controls in action.

> **Market control** is essentially the influence of market competition on the behaviour of organizations and their members.

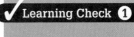

BE SURE YOU CAN
- define *controlling* as a management function • explain the benefits of after-action reviews
- illustrate how a fast-food restaurant uses feedforward, concurrent, and feedback controls
- discuss internal control and external control systems • give examples of bureaucratic, clan, and market controls

Steps in the Control Process

The control process involves the four steps shown in Figure 16.3. They are (1) establish performance objectives and standards; (2) measure actual performance; (3) compare actual performance with objectives and standards; and (4) take corrective action as needed. Although essential to management, these steps apply equally well to personal affairs and careers. Think about it. Without career objectives, how do you know where you really want to go? How can you allocate your time and other resources to take best advantage of available opportunities? Without measurement, how can you assess any progress being made? How can you adjust current behaviour to improve prospects for future results?

STEP 1: ESTABLISH OBJECTIVES AND STANDARDS

The control process begins with planning, when performance objectives and standards for measuring them are set. It can't start without them. Performance objectives identify key results that one wants to accomplish—and the word "key" deserves emphasis. The focus in planning should be on describing "critical" or "essential" results that will make a substantial performance difference. Once these key results are identified, standards can be set to measure their accomplishment.

Output Standards

An **output standard** measures performance results in terms of quantity, quality, cost, or time.

Output standards measure actual outcomes or work results. Businesses use many output standards, such as earnings per share, sales growth, and market share. Others include quantity and quality of production, costs incurred, service or delivery time, and error rates. Based on your experience at work and as a customer, you can probably come up with even more examples.

When Allstate Corporation launched a new diversity initiative, it created a "diversity index" to quantify performance on diversity issues. The standards included how well employees met the goals of bias-free customer service, and how well managers met the firm's diversity expectations.[13] When General Electric became concerned about managing ethics in its 320,000-member global workforce, it created measurement standards to track compliance. Each business unit reports quarterly on how many of its members attend ethics training sessions and signed the firm's "Spirit and Letter" ethics guide.[14]

How about output standards for other types of organizations, such as a symphony orchestra? When the Cleveland Orchestra wrestled with performance standards, the members weren't willing to rely on vague generalities like "we played well," "the audience seemed happy," or "not too many mistakes were made." Rather, they decided to track standing ovations, invitations to perform in other countries, and how often other orchestras copied their performance style.[15]

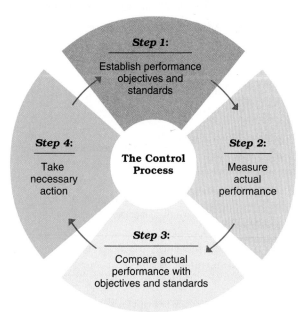

Figure 16.3 Four steps in the control process.

Input Standards

An **input standard** measures work efforts that go into a performance task.

The control process also uses **input standards** that measure work efforts. These are common in situations where outputs are difficult or expensive to measure. Examples of input standards for a university professor might be the existence of an orderly course syllabus, meeting all class sessions, and returning exams and assignments in a timely fashion. Of course, as this example might suggest, measuring inputs doesn't mean that outputs, such as high-quality teaching and learning, are necessarily achieved. Other examples of input standards at work include conformance with rules, efficiency in the use of resources, and work attendance.

STEP 2: MEASURE PERFORMANCE RESULTS

The second step in the control process is to measure actual performance. It is the point where output standards and input standards are used to carefully document results. When Linda Sanford, who is currently a senior vice president and one of the highest-ranking women at IBM, was appointed head of IBM's sales force, she came with an admirable performance record earned during a 22-year career with the company. Notably, Sanford grew up on a family farm, where she developed an appreciation for measuring results. "At the end of the day, you saw what you did, knew how many rows of strawberries you picked." At IBM, she was known for walking around the factory, just to see "at the end of the day how many machines were going out of the back dock."[16]

Measurements, as in the IBM example, must be accurate enough to spot significant differences between what is really taking place and what was originally planned. Without measurement, effective control is not possible. With measurement tied to key results, however, an adage often holds true: "What gets measured happens."

ISSUES AND SITUATIONS
Computer Addiction

Conversation starts—

"Do you ever turn off the computer at home? I don't mean for power saving; I mean for 'life saving.' Sometimes I wonder who's in control: is it me, or is it the computer? It used to be that we took work home in a briefcase, did a bit, closed the case up, and took it back to work the next day. Now work is always there, on the computer, on the Internet, in our e-mails. And it's habit-forming. I go home and turn the computer on—and it holds me captive for most of the night. I just can't seem to allocate a period of time for 'homework' and then shut the thing down and relax with the family."

Points to ponder:

- In San Jose, California, Elizabeth Safran works virtually. That's the way the 13-member public relations firm operates—by e-mails and instant messaging. But she is concerned about work–life balance, saying: "It [technology] makes us more productive, but everybody is working all the time—weekends, evenings. It's almost overkill."

- In London, England, Paul Renucci is managing director of a systems integration firm. He works at home on Fridays, saving two hours of traffic time and staying connected by computer. At 5 p.m. he turns the machine off, his workday over. He says: "I can work pretty hard, but at 5 p.m. exactly I stop working and the weekend starts."

- In Cambridge, Massachusetts, MIT Professor Lotte Bailyn notes that few people think about the impact of technology on personal lives when it arrives, but that "it is the top people that need to model the right behavior and set the example."

Conversation continues as friend responds—

"You're getting close to 'computer addiction.' You've got to get back in control; just use the 'off' button and take charge of your time. For me, technology is an office tool, not a lifestyle. But when it comes to our kids, the story may be different—they're always instant messaging. We'll have to see what happens when they enter the workforce. Maybe they'll be so comfortable with technology in their lives that they won't have any problems with it. But for people like us, we're learning how to deal with it at the same time we're learning how to use it."

CRITICAL RESPONSE

Who is in control when it comes to our personal time? Does technology creep into our lives and, before we know it, take control? Is the MIT professor correct? Is it up to those in charge—top managers—to set the norms and provide examples that show others how to use technology for work, but still stay in control of work–life balance?

STEP 3: COMPARE RESULTS WITH OBJECTIVES AND STANDARDS

Step 3 in the control process is to compare objectives with results. You can remember its implications by this *control equation*:

Need for action = Desired performance − Actual performance

The question of what constitutes "desired" performance plays an important role in the control equation. Some organizations use *engineering comparisons*. One example is United Parcel Service (UPS). The firm carefully measures the routes and routines of its drivers to establish the times expected for each delivery. When a delivery manifest is scanned as completed, the driver's time is registered in a performance log that is closely monitored by supervisors. Organizations also use *historical comparisons*, where past experience becomes the baseline for evaluating current performance. Also used are *relative comparisons* that benchmark performance against that being achieved by other people, work units, or organizations.

STEP 4: TAKE CORRECTIVE ACTION

The final step in the control process is to take the action needed to correct problems or make improvements. And **management by exception** is the practice of giving attention to situations that show the greatest need for action. It saves time, energy, and other resources by focusing attention on high-priority areas.

Managers should be alert to two types of exceptions. The first is a problem situation where actual performance is less than desired. It must be understood so that corrective action can restore performance to the desired level. The second is an opportunity situation where actual performance turns out higher than what was desired. It must be understood with the goal of continuing or increasing the high level of accomplishment in the future.

Management by exception focuses attention on substantial differences between actual and desired performance.

✔ **Learning Check ➋**

BE SURE YOU CAN
• list the steps in the control process • explain why planning is important to controlling • differentiate between output and input standards • state the control equation • explain management by exception

CONTROL TOOLS AND TECHNIQUES

Most organizations use a variety of control systems and techniques. They include employee discipline systems, special techniques of project management, and information and financial controls.

EMPLOYEE DISCIPLINE SYSTEMS

Absenteeism, tardiness, sloppy work. The list of undesirable conduct can go on to even more extreme actions: falsifying records, sexual harassment, embezzlement. All are examples of behaviours that can and should be formally addressed in human resource management through **discipline**—the act of influencing behaviour through reprimand.

When discipline is handled in a fair, consistent, and systematic way, it is a useful form of managerial control. And one way to be consistent in disciplinary situations is to remember the "hot stove rules" in Management Smarts 16.1. They rest on a simple understanding: "When a stove is hot, don't touch it." Everyone knows that when this rule is violated, you get burned—immediately and consistently, but usually not beyond the possibility of repair.[17]

Progressive discipline ties reprimands to the severity and frequency of the employee's infractions. Penalties for misbehaviour vary according to the significance of the problem. A progressive discipline system takes into consideration such things as the seriousness of the problem, how frequently it has occurred, how long it lasts, and past experience in dealing with the person who has caused the problem. The goal is to achieve compliance with organizational expectations through the least extreme reprimand possible. For example, the ultimate penalty of "discharge" would be reserved for the most severe behaviours (e.g., committing a crime) or for repeated infractions of a less severe nature (e.g., being continually late for work and failing to respond to a series of reprimands or suspensions).

Discipline is the act of influencing behaviour through reprimand.

Progressive discipline ties reprimands to the severity and frequency of misbehaviour.

16.1 MANAGEMENT SMARTS
"Hot stove rules" of employee discipline

- A reprimand should be immediate; a hot stove burns the instant you touch it.

- A reprimand should be directed toward someone's actions, not the individual's personality; a hot stove doesn't hold grudges, doesn't try to humiliate people, and doesn't accept excuses.

- A reprimand should be consistently applied; a hot stove burns anyone who touches it, and it does so every time.

- A reprimand should be informative; a hot stove lets a person know what to do to avoid getting burned in the future—"don't touch."

- A reprimand should occur in a supportive setting; a hot stove conveys warmth, but with an inflexible rule: "don't touch."

- A reprimand should support realistic rules. The don't-touch-a-hot-stove rule isn't a power play, a whim, or an emotion of the moment; it is a necessary rule of reason.

PROJECT MANAGEMENT AND CONTROL

It might be something personal, like an anniversary party for your parents, a renovation to your home, or the launch of a new product or service at your place of work. It might be the completion of a new student activities building on a campus, or the implementation of a new advertising campaign for a sports team. What these examples and others like them share in common is that they are relatively complicated tasks with multiple components that have to happen in a certain sequence, and that must be completed by a specified date. We call them **projects**, complex one-time events with unique components and an objective that must be met within a set time.

Projects are one-time activities with many component tasks that must be completed in proper order, and according to budget.

Project management is the responsibility for overall planning, supervision, and control of projects. A project manager's job is to ensure that a project is well planned and then completed according to plan—on time, within budget, and consistent with objectives. And two useful techniques for project management and control are Gantt charts and CPM/PERT.

Project management makes sure that activities required to complete a project are planned well and accomplished on time.

Gantt Charts

A **Gantt chart**, such as the one depicted in Figure 16.4, graphically displays the scheduling of tasks required to complete a project. This approach was developed in the early twentieth century by Henry Gantt, an industrial engineer, and it has become a mainstay of project management ever since. In the figure, the left column lists major activities required to complete a new cell phone prototype. The bars extending to the right indicate the time required to complete each activity.

A **Gantt chart** graphically displays the scheduling of tasks required to complete a project.

The Gantt chart provides a visual overview of what needs to be done on the project. This facilitates control by allowing progress checks to be made at different time intervals. It also assists with event or activity sequencing, making sure that things get accomplished in time for later work to build upon them. One of the biggest problems with projects, for example, is when delays in early activities create problems for later ones.

A project manager who actively uses Gantt charts is trying to avoid such difficulties. Obviously, the chart in the figure is oversimplified; an actual project to develop a new cell phone or even to complete a product modification such as the newest BlackBerry model is very complicated. However, with computer assistance, Gantt charts play a useful role in helping project managers track and control progress—even through high levels of complexity.

Activities

A Complete research and development work

B Complete engineering design

C Prepare budgets

D Build prototype

E Test prototype

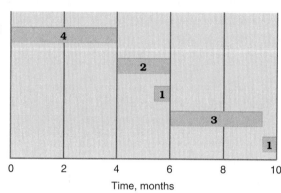

Time, months

Figure 16.4 Simplified Gantt chart for a new cell phone.

CPM/PERT Techniques

CPM/PERT is a combination of the critical path method and the program evaluation and review technique.

A companion to the Gantt chart is **CPM/PERT**, a combination of the critical path method and the program evaluation and review technique. Project planning based on CPM/PERT uses a network chart like the one shown in Figure 16.5. Such charts are developed by breaking a project into a series of small sub-activities that each have clear beginning and end points. These points become "nodes" in the charts, and the arrows between nodes indicate in what order things must be completed. The full diagram shows all the interrelationships that must be coordinated during the entire project.

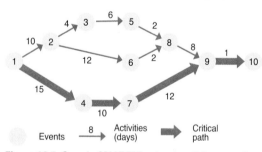

Figure 16.5 Sample CPM/PERT network activity-on-node diagram.

Use of CPM/PERT techniques helps project managers track and control activities, making sure they happen in the right sequences and on time. The activities can be listed on the arrows for tracking purposes, known as the activity-on-arrows (AOA) diagram; they can also be listed on the nodes, resulting in activity-on-nodes (AON) diagrams. The network in the figure is an AON diagram. If you look at it again, you should notice that the time required for each activity can be easily calculated and tracked. The pathway with the longest completion time from start to finish is called the critical path. It represents the shortest possible time in which the entire project can be completed, assuming everything goes according to plan. In the example, you will find that the critical path is 38 days.

FINANCIAL CONTROLS

The pressure is ever present for all organizations to use their financial resources well. And the global economic recession has left no doubt that the analysis of financial performance is an important part of managerial control.

Economic Value Added

Economic value added is a measure of economic value created by profits being higher than the cost of capital.

A basic starting point in financial control is the concept of **economic value added**, or EVA. This is a measure of the economic value being created by a firm. The logic is that any firm should use its assets well and earn a rate of return on its invested capital that is greater than the cost of that capital. A quick calculation of EVA takes operating profit after taxes and deducts typical capital costs, such as short-term debt, interest on bonds, and retained earnings. The more economic value added—that is, the higher the profits relative to the cost of capital investments—the more successful the firm. When EVA is fully calculated, the cost of capital includes not only things like money, machines, and physical facilities, but also the value of the human capital vested in the employees.

A related measure of a firm's overall financial performance is **market value added**, or MVA. This is the value of the firm as represented in the stock market relative to the cost of capital. MVA is a measure of wealth creation, and the higher the MVA the better. A firm is considered financially stronger the more its valuation in the stock market exceeds its capital costs.

> **Market value added** is a performance measure of stock market value relative to the cost of capital.

Basic Financial Ratios

Managers should be able to understand financial performance measures of *liquidity*—ability to generate cash to pay bills; *leverage*—ability to earn more in returns than the cost of debt; *asset management*—ability to use resources efficiently and operate at minimum cost; and *profitability*—ability to earn revenues greater than costs. Each can be assessed using financial ratios, like those listed here.

Liquidity—measures ability to meet short-term obligations

- *Current Ratio* = Current Assets/Current Liabilities
- *Quick Ratio* = Current Assets – Inventory/Current Liabilities

Higher is better: You want more assets and fewer liabilities.

Leverage—measures use of debt

- *Debt Ratio* = Total Debts/Total Assets

Lower is better: You want fewer debts and more assets.

Asset Management—measures asset and inventory efficiency

- *Asset Turnover* = Sales/Total Assets
- *Inventory Turnover* = Sales/Average Inventory

Higher is better: You want more sales and fewer assets or lower inventory.

Profitability—measures ability to earn revenues greater than costs

- *Net Margin* = Net Profit after Taxes/Sales
- *Return on Assets (ROA)* = Net Profit after Taxes/Total Assets
- *Return on Equity (ROE)* = Net Income/Owners' Equity

Higher is better: You want more profit for sales, assets, and equity.

Financial ratios are useful for historical comparisons within the firm and for external benchmarking. They can also be used to set financial targets or goals to be shared with employees and tracked to indicate success or failure in their accomplishment. At Civco Medical Instruments, for example, a financial scorecard is distributed monthly to all employees. They always know factually how well the firm is doing. This helps them focus on what they can do better to improve the firm's bottom line.[18]

RESEARCH BRIEF

Restating corporate financial performance foreshadows significant turnover among corporate executives and directors

Control and accountability are core issues in research by Marne L. Arthaud-Day, S. Travis Certo, Catherine M. Dalton, and Dan R. Dalton. Using a technique known as event history analysis, the researchers say that what happens subsequent to financial misstatements is an "opportunity to study the accountability of leaders for organizational outcomes, independent of firm performance."

Arthaud-Day et al. examined what happened in a two-year period for 116 firms that restated financials, in comparison with 116 others that did not. The firms were

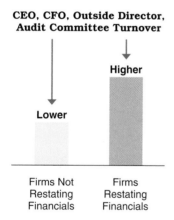

CEO, CFO, Outside Director, Audit Committee Turnover

Higher

Lower

Firms Not Restating Financials   Firms Restating Financials

chosen from the Financial Statement Restatement Database and matched in pairs by industry and size for control

purposes. Results showed that turnover of CEOs, CFOs, outside directors, and audit committee members was higher in firms that restated their earnings.

The researchers point out that financial misstatements harm a firm's legitimacy in the eyes of key stakeholders, and this threatens the firm's ability to obtain resources and external support. Because financial misstatements are considered to be direct management failures, executives are more likely to be held accountable for them than for poor performance of an organization overall—even for bankruptcy, which might be explained by adverse external factors.

The researchers note that "companies often couch involuntary departures in nice-sounding clichés (i.e., an executive 'retires'), making it nearly impossible to determine the true reason for turnover." In terms of future research, they recommend looking at what happens after "tainted" leadership is removed. Does the firm regain stakeholder legitimacy and do better in the future, or not?

You be the researcher

If one looked not just at financial misstatements, but also at share price declines, profit and loss trends, and product successes and failures, would similar patterns of control and accountability for top managers be found? Given the increased concern with tightening financial controls and holding business executives accountable for performance, are executives in governments, schools, and non-profits in your community being held accountable as well?

BALANCED SCORECARDS

A **balanced scorecard** tallies organizational performance in the financial, customer service, internal process, innovation and learning, and sustainability areas.

If "what gets measured happens," then managers should take advantage of "scorecards" to record and track performance results. If an instructor takes class attendance and assigns grades based on it, students tend to come to class; if an employer tracks the number of customers each employee serves per day, employees tend to serve more customers. Do the same principles hold for organizations?

Strategic management consultants Robert S. Kaplan and David P. Norton believe they do, and advocate using the **balanced scorecard** for management control.[19] It gives top managers, as they say, "a fast, but comprehensive view of the business." The basic principle is that, to do well and to win, you have to keep score. Developing a balanced scorecard for any organization begins with a clarification of the organization's mission and vision—what it wants to be, and how it wants to be perceived by its key stakeholders. Next, the following questions are used to develop specific scorecard goals and measures:

- *Financial Performance*—To improve financially, how should we appear to our shareholders? Sample goals: survive, succeed, prosper. Sample measures: cash flow, sales growth and operating income, increased market share, and return on equity.

- *Customer Satisfaction*—To achieve our vision, how should we appear to our customers? Sample goals: new products, responsive supply. Sample measures: percentage sales from new products, percentage on-time deliveries.

- *Internal Process Improvement*—To satisfy our customers and shareholders, at what internal business processes should we excel? Sample goals: manufacturing excellence, design productivity, new product introduction. Sample measures: cycle times, engineering efficiency, new product time.

- *Innovation and Learning*—To achieve our vision, how will we sustain our ability to change and improve? Sample goals: technology leadership, time to market. Sample measures: time to develop new technologies, new product introduction time versus competition.

- *Sustainability*—To integrate sustainability into our business model, what performance metrics should we incorporate? Sample goals: social return on investment, waste audits, environmental risk assessment, product life cycle audit, energy audits.

GOING GLOBAL

FROM $500 TO $5 BILLION

Infosys Technologies was started in India in 1981 by seven people who collectively invested less than US$500. Today, the company is a global leader in the next generation of IT and consulting, with revenues of over US$5 billion. As with other large organizations, Infosys faced performance challenges as it grew. By using the balanced scorecard approach and embedding it in its corporate governance systems, Infosys has achieved breakthrough performance and strengthened client relationships. It has used the balanced scorecard to forge a global footprint, with over 60 offices and 100,000 employees in India, China, Australia, the United Kingdom, Canada, and Japan. Not surprisingly, Infosys Technologies has been inducted into the Balanced Scorecard Hall of Fame.

When balanced scorecard measures are taken and routinely recorded for critical managerial review, Kaplan and Norton expect organizations to perform better in these five performance areas. Again, what gets measured happens. Think about the possibilities here. How can the balanced scorecard approach be used by the following organizations: an elementary school, a hospital, a community library, a mayor's office, a fast-food restaurant? How might the performance dimensions and indicators vary among these different types of organizations? And if balanced scorecards make sense, why is it that more organizations don't use them?

BE SURE YOU CAN
- explain progressive discipline • define *project management* • explain how Gantt charts and CPM/PERT analysis assist in project management • list and explain common ratios used in financial control • identify the four main balanced scorecard components

MANAGEMENT LEARNING REVIEW

STUDY QUESTIONS SUMMARY

KEY TERMS

after-action review, 483

balanced scorecard, 494

bureaucratic control, 485

clan control, 487

Concurrent control, 484

Controlling, 483

CPM/PERT, 492

discipline, 490

economic value added, 492

Feedback control, 484

Feedforward control, 484

Gantt chart, 491

input standards, 488

management by
    exception, 490

Market control, 487

market value added, 493

output standard, 488

progressive discipline, 490

project management, 491

projects, 491

self-control, 485

1. Why and how do managers control?

• Controlling is the process of measuring performance and taking corrective action as needed.

• Feedforward controls are accomplished before a work activity begins; they ensure that directions are clear, and that the right resources are available to accomplish them.

• Concurrent controls make sure that things are being done correctly; they allow corrective actions to be taken while the work is being done.

• Feedback controls take place after an action is completed; they address the question "Now that we are finished, how well did we do, and what did we learn for the future?"

• Internal control is self-control and occurs as people take personal responsibility for their work.

• External control is based on the use of bureaucratic, clan, and market control systems.

FOR DISCUSSION Can strong input and output controls make up for poor concurrent controls?

2. What are the steps in the control process?

• The first step in the control process is to establish performance objectives and standards that create targets against which later performance can be evaluated.

• The second step in the control process is to measure actual performance, and specifically identify what results are being achieved.

• The third step in the control process is to compare performance results with objectives to determine if things are going according to plan.

• The fourth step in the control process is to take action to resolve problems or explore opportunities that are identified when results are compared with objectives.

FOR DISCUSSION What are the potential downsides to management by exception?

3. What are the common control tools and techniques?

• Discipline is the process of influencing behaviour through reprimand; progressive discipline systems vary reprimands according to the severity of infractions.

• A project is a unique event that must be completed by a specified date; project management is the process of ensuring that projects are completed on time, on budget, and according to objectives.

• Gantt charts assist in project management and control by displaying how various tasks must be scheduled in order to complete a project on time.

• CPM/PERT analysis assists in project management and control by describing the complex networks of activities that must be completed in sequences for a project to be completed successfully.

• Economic value added (EVA) measures value creation relative to capital invested; market value added (MVA) measures stock market value relative to capital investment.

• Financial control of business performance is facilitated by a variety of financial ratios, such as those dealing with liquidity, leverage, assets, and profitability.

- The balanced scorecard measures overall organizational performance in five areas: financial, customers, internal processes, innovation, sustainability.

FOR DISCUSSION Should all employees of a business be regularly informed of the firm's overall financial performance?

SELF-TEST

Multiple-Choice Questions

1. After objectives and standards are set, what step comes next in the control process?

   (a) measure results   (b) take corrective action   (c) compare results with objectives   (d) modify standards to fit circumstances

2. When a soccer coach tells her players at the end of a losing game, "You really played well and stayed with the game plan," she is using a(n) _____ as a measure of performance.

   (a) input standard   (b) output standard   (c) historical comparison   (d) relative comparison

3. When an automobile manufacturer is careful to purchase only the highest-quality components for use in production, this is an example of an attempt to ensure high performance through _____ control.

   (a) concurrent   (b) statistical   (c) inventory   (d) feedforward

4. Management by exception means _____.

   (a) managing only when necessary   (b) focusing attention where the need for action is greatest   (c) the same thing as concurrent control   (d) the same thing as just-in-time delivery

5. When a supervisor working alongside an employee corrects him or her when a mistake is made, this is an example of _____ control.

   (a) feedforward   (b) concurrent   (c) internal   (d) clan

6. If an organization's top management visits a firm in another industry to learn more about its excellent record in hiring and promoting minority and female candidates, this is an example of using _____ for control purposes.

   (a) a balanced scorecard   (b) relative comparison   (c) management by exception   (d) progressive discipline

7. The control equation states: _____ = Desired Performance − Actual Performance.

   (a) Problem Magnitude   (b) Management Opportunity   (c) Planning Objective   (d) Need for Action

8. When a UPS manager compares the amount of time a driver takes to accomplish certain deliveries against a standard set through scientific analysis of her delivery route, this is known as _____.

   (a) a historical comparison   (b) an engineering comparison   (c) relative benchmarking   (d) concurrent control

9. Projects are unique one-time events that _____.

   (a) have unclear objectives   (b) must be completed by a specific time   (c) have unlimited budgets   (d) are largely self-managing

10. The _____ chart graphically displays the scheduling of tasks required to complete a project.

    (a) exception   (b) Taylor   (c) Gantt   (d) after-action

11. In CPM/PERT, "CPM" stands for _____.

(a) critical path method   (b) control planning management   (c) control plan map   (d) current planning method

12. In a CPM/PERT analysis, the focus is on _____ and the event _____ that link them together with the finished project.

(a) costs, budgets   (b) activities, sequences   (c) timetables, budgets   (d) goals, costs

13. A manager following the "hot stove rules" of progressive discipline would _____.

(a) avoid giving too much information when reprimanding someone   (b) reprimand at random   (c) focus the reprimand on actions, not personality   (d) delay reprimands until something positive can also be discussed

14. Among the financial ratios used for control, current assets/current liabilities is known as the _____.

(a) debt ratio   (b) net margin   (c) current ratio   (d) inventory turnover ratio

15. In respect to return on assets (ROA) and the debt ratio, the preferred directions when analyzing them from a control standpoint are _____.

(a) decrease ROA, increase debt   (b) increase ROA, increase debt   (c) increase ROA, decrease debt   (d) decrease ROA, decrease debt

Short-Response Questions

16. List the four steps in the controlling process.

17. How might feedforward control be used by the owner/manager of a local bookstore?

18. How does Douglas McGregor's Theory Y relate to the concept of internal control?

19. How does a progressive discipline system work?

Application Question

20. Assume that you are given the job of project manager for building a new student centre on your campus. List just five of the major activities that need to be accomplished to complete the new building in two years. Draw an AON network diagram that links the activities together in required event scheduling and sequencing. Make an estimate for the time required for each sequence to be completed and identify the critical path.

MANAGEMENT SKILLS AND COMPETENCIES

SELF-ASSESSMENT

Back to Yourself: Strength and Energy

Work–life balance is a major theme of the day. It really hits home when you consider how easy it is now to take our work with us anywhere we go, 24 hours a day and seven days a week. That's one of the offshoots of technology, as represented in our iPhones, BlackBerrys, high-speed Internet connections, and ultra-portable notebook computers. This penetration of technology into our lives raises issues of control. The chapter opener suggests that we take time to step back and ask: Who's in control of how and when I work? But at the same time as we try to get a better handle on control in our personal lives, we should be trying to use the insights of this chapter to do the best possible job with control as a management function.

Further Reflection: After-Meeting/Project Remorse

Instructions

Complete the following assessment after participating in a meeting or a group project.

1. How satisfied are *you* with the outcome of the meeting/project?
    Not at all satisfied   1   2   3   4   5   6   7   Totally satisfied

2. How do you think other members of the meeting/project group would rate you in terms of your *influence* on what took place?
    No influence   1   2   3   4   5   6   7   Very high influence

3. In your opinion, how *ethical* was any decision that was reached?
    Highly *un*ethical   1   2   3   4   5   6   7   Highly ethical

4. To what extent did you feel "*pushed into*" going along with the decision?
    Not pushed into it at all   1   2   3   4   5   6   7   Very pushed into it

5. How *committed* are *you* to the agreements reached?
    Not at all committed   1   2   3   4   5   6   7   Highly committed

6. Did you understand what was expected of you as a member of the meeting or project group?
    Not at all clear   1   2   3   4   5   6   7   Perfectly clear

7. Were participants in the meeting/project group discussions listening to each other?
    Never   1   2   3   4   5   6   7   Always

8. Were participants in the meeting/project group discussions honest and open in communicating with one another?
    Never   1   2   3   4   5   6   7   Always

9. Was the meeting/project completed efficiently?
    Not at all   1   2   3   4   5   6   7   Very much

10. Was the outcome of the meeting/project something that you felt proud to be a part of?
    Not at all   1   2   3   4   5   6   7   Very much

Interpretation

This assessment is a chance to look in the mirror and ask: "What are my thoughts about my team and my contributions to the team, now that the project is finished?" Ask what you could do in future situations to end up with a "perfect" score after a meeting, or after the project review.

Team Follow-Up Option

Have everyone in your group complete the same assessment for the project. Share results and discuss their implications (a) for the future success of the group on another project, and (b) for the members as they go forward to work with other groups on other projects in the future.

Source: Developed from Roy J. Lewicki, Donald D. Bowen, Douglas T. Hall, and Francine S. Hall, *Experiences in Management and Organizational Behavior,* 4th ed. (New York: Wiley, 1997), pp. 195–197.

TEAM EXERCISE

Defining Quality

Preparation

Write your definition of the word quality here. QUALITY = _____.

Instructions

Form groups as assigned by your instructor.

1. Have each group member present a definition of the word *quality*. After everyone has presented, come up with a consensus definition of quality. Write down the definition with which everyone most agrees.

2. Use the group's quality definition to state for each organization below a quality objective that can guide the behaviour of members in producing high-quality goods and/or services for customers or clients. Make sure that the objective is stated as a "key result" that can be measured for control purposes.

3. Elect a spokesperson to share group results with the class as a whole.

Organizations

1. university
2. hospital
3. on-line retail store
4. gourmet restaurant
5. Canada Post branch

6. coffee shop
7. student apartment rental company
8. used textbook store
9. grocery store
10. fitness centre

CASE 16

Four Seasons Hotels: Competitive Advantage through Quality

Treat your customers the way you would like to be treated. It's a simple but powerful philosophy that has helped create one of the top luxury hotel brands in the world. Ranked first by J. D. Power & Associates for luxury hotels and the top hotel chain in the United States, Four Seasons Hotels knows that "luxury" for guests is not about grand architecture and decor—any hotel can do that—but rather is about service that makes customers feel they are special. How does this Canadian-based hotel chain achieve the highest ratings and customer loyalty in the industry?

The Four Seasons Advantage

Isadore Sharp started the Four Seasons Hotel chain in 1961 by teaming up with his father to build a small hotel in a seedy neighbourhood in Toronto. Successfully integrating the amenities of a large hotel with the intimacy and warmth of home, Sharp set out to create "a reputation for service so clear in people's mind that Four Seasons' name would become an asset of far greater value than bricks and mortar." The results speak for themselves. The Four Seasons, now a global brand, has 82 hotels in 35 countries and more than 50 properties under development.

An innovator in guest services, the Four Seasons focuses on the "3 Ps": people, product, and profit. It believes that if employees focus on service, then the chain will have a good product, which will bring profit. In fact, it wants its employees to strive to go beyond expectations and beyond what training can deliver.

Sharp reasoned that, if the Four Seasons offered distinctly better service than its competitors, it could charge a substantial price premium, boosting revenue per room to the point where the hotel could afford top-of-the-line amenities. Before he could ask guests to pay a super-premium room rate, though, Sharp understood that Four Seasons Hotels would have to offer them an entirely different kind of service in return.

While Sharp considered factors such as location, staffing levels, room size, and furnishings, he also focused on what his customers really wanted from their Four Seasons experience. He asked what his guests, mostly travelling business executives, were looking for when they booked a hotel room. Sharp understood that the vast majority of executives travelled more frequently than they would have wanted and that the experience they longed for most was to feel as if they were at home or at their office.

The Four Seasons was the first to offer shampoo in the shower, 24-hour room service, bathrobes, make-up mirrors, hair dryers, and overnight cleaning and pressing, now standard in hotel rooms anywhere in the world. The Four Seasons was also the first to install a two-line phone in every guest room, as well as a big, well-lighted desk to make customers feel like they were in their own office. It was also the first to provide 24-hour secretarial services. It competitors eventually copied all of these initiatives, but not before Four Seasons established a singular reputation for providing service that its competitors couldn't match because it was literally unimaginable to them.

The Golden Rule

Everyone at the Four Seasons is guided by "the Golden Rule." It's a philosophy that encourages all employees to deal with others—partners, customers, co-workers, everyone—as they would want to be dealt with themselves.

The Golden Rule bound together all the parts of the strategy decisions at Four Seasons. Four Seasons' senior management treated employees the way the managers themselves would want to be treated. And employees would respond by treating guests in the same spirit. Every phase of hotel operations was bound to a strategy based on extraordinary service.

To drive this point home, the Four Seasons has no customer service department. Instead of making customer service a discrete responsibility, everyone at the Four Seasons is not just a member of the customer service function, but in charge of it.

The company became an innovator in building customer relationships by maintaining a complete history of communications with each guest. No matter which Four Seasons a guest stays at, the company knows how firm or soft they like their pillows, the normal time for their wake-up call, and how they like their eggs. Want another example of going beyond the expectation of traditional guest services? Recently, at the Four Seasons Resort in Whistler, B.C., a guest had broken a pair of sunglasses and left them on a table in his room with the intention of throwing them away. When he returned later that day, the sunglasses had been fixed, making his visit to the Four Seasons even more memorable.

When Times Are Tough

While the Four Seasons name is synonymous with luxury, quality, and service, there are problems in its marble lobbies.

Of the 82 hotels under the Four Seasons name, at least a dozen are in financial distress. In a recent year, occupancy levels at the luxury chain's U.S. hotels averaged just 57 percent, and revenue per available room fell 26 percent. Even with room rates that average $400 a night, some Four Seasons hotels couldn't generate enough cash to pay interest and operating costs and were close to delinquency on their mortgages; others have been forced to sell stakes in the hotel to keep them from foreclosure.

Recently, bowing to pressure by some of its property owners, the Four Seasons Hotels agreed to cut back on some of its regular features. Many hotels have stopped displaying the signature fresh flower arrangements in the lobby, closed their high-end restaurants on slow days, and are outsourcing laundry and other non-essential services. While the cuts may be good for the immediate bottom line, only time will tell how they will impact the iconic Four Seasons brand.

Discussion Questions

1. What are the core competencies that give Four Seasons a competitive advantage over its rivals in the luxury market? How sustainable do you think that competitive advantage is in the long run?

2. How does Four Seasons use control techniques to add value to customers' stays?

3. Do you think that the concept of project management applies to the service industry? How would this concept apply to the Four Seasons?

4. FURTHER RESEARCH—How does Four Seasons measure performance results? Are they using a balanced scorecard approach?

Operations and Services Management

Speed and flexibility rule global competition

Even in the world of high fashion, you can't be competitive if you aren't fast and flexible. Pressures from upstart retailers like Zara International and others that excel at "fast fashion"—getting new designs into stores quickly—have even brought changes to Louis Vuitton. The maker of high-fashion handbags and other accessories has revamped production techniques to increase speed without sacrificing quality.

A Louis Vuitton tote bag used to take up to 30 craftspersons some eight days to make. The bag was passed from hand to hand, with each worker performing a separate and highly specialized task.

That all changed when Vuitton executives, advised by consultants from McKinsey & Company, turned to the automobile industry, believe it or not, for ideas. They benchmarked Toyota's production processes and decided that things at the fashion house could be done a lot faster. The company reorganized workers into teams of 6 to 12 people, working at U-shaped workstations. Workers in each team perform more than one task and pass the in-process tote bag back and forth. They complete a tote bag in just one day.

(Photo by ChinaFotoPress)

Vuitton calls its production system "Pégase" after the mythical flying horse that is a symbol of speed and power. Since Pégase was introduced, Louis Vuitton has been able to ship new designs every 6 weeks, more than twice as fast as previously. Says Patrick Louis Vuitton of the founding family: "It's about finding the best ratio between quality and speed." Yves Carcelle, chief executive officer for the Pégase brand, says: "Behind the creative magic of Louis Vuitton is an extremely efficient supply chain."

This is quite a set of statements from a firm that thrived for years on fashion alone—a business strategy once described in the financial press as "celebrity advertising, lavish fashion shows, and the star-power of its top designer." To compete today with fast rivals and global competitors, even Louis Vuitton has now recognized that without the best execution, a great design can't guarantee success.[1]

> **BENCHMARK** Workers in Louis Vuitton's Pégase teams are less specialized than before, working on a broader set of individual tasks and as part of a team. They swap tasks and team roles while making different kinds of bags, allowing production to switch quickly from one design to another. Take a look around the next time you are in a service establishment or in a production facility. How much productivity could be gained by following similar ideas?

Self-Management

This chapter is about the management of operations—getting things right for organizations as they deal with lots of complexities. We face similar challenges in many ways; we're complex systems too, and we also need to be managed.

Career success today depends significantly upon one's capacities for self-management—the ability to understand yourself individually and in the social context, to assess personal strengths and weaknesses, to exercise initiative, to accept responsibility for accomplishments, to work well with others, and to adapt by continually learning from experience in the quest for self-improvement. Self-management is an essential skill that asks you to dig deep and continually learn from experience.

Some self-management ideas for career success are shown in the box. They are within everyone's grasp. But the motivation to succeed must come from within. Only you can make this commitment, and it is best made right from the beginning.

We all need to take charge of our destinies and become self-managers. You can help move your career forward by behaving like an entrepreneur, seeking feedback on your performance continually, setting up your own mentoring systems, getting comfortable with teamwork, taking risks to gain experience and learn new skills, being a problem solver, and keeping your life in balance.[2]

Self-Management for Career Success

- *Lesson one: There is no substitute for high performance. No matter what the assignment, you must work hard to establish and maintain your credibility and work value.*

- *Lesson two: Be and stay flexible. Don't hide from ambiguity; don't wait for structure. You must adapt to new work demands, new situations, and new people.*

- *Lesson three: Keep the focus. You can't go forward without talent. You must be a talent builder—someone who is always adding to and refining your talents to make them valuable to an employer.*

❖ Get to Know Yourself Better

One of the best ways to examine and demonstrate your capacity for self-management is in the way you approach everyday responsibilities and opportunities. Do a self-check. How well do you balance academic and non-academic activities? Do you miss deadlines or turn in assignments you aren't satisfied with? Do you learn from past mistakes? To what extent do you get things done, and done well, without someone telling you to do them or demanding a certain level of excellence?

CHAPTER 17 STUDY QUESTIONS

- What are the essentials of operations and services management?

- What is value chain management?

- How do organizations manage customer service and product quality?

- How can work processes be designed for productivity?

VISUAL CHAPTER OVERVIEW

CHAPTER 17 OPERATIONS AND SERVICES MANAGEMENT

Study Question 1	Study Question 2	Study Question 3	Study Question 4
Operations Management Essentials	**Value Chain Management**	**Service and Product Quality**	**Work Processes**
■ Manufacturing and services settings	■ Value chain analysis	■ Customer relationship management	■ Work process analysis
■ Productivity and competitive advantage	■ Supply chain management	■ Quality management	■ Process reengineering
■ Operations technologies	■ Inventory management	■ Statistical quality control	■ Process-driven organizations
	■ Break-even analysis		

✓ Learning Check 1	✓ Learning Check 2	✓ Learning Check 3	✓ Learning Check 4

As the opening example of Louis Vuitton suggests, organizations today operate in a world that places a premium on productivity, technology utilization, quality, customer service, and speed. Businesses large and small are struggling and innovating as they try to succeed in a world of intense competition, continued globalization of markets and business activities, and rapid technological change. Just how top executives approach these challenges differs from one organization to the next, but they all focus on moving services and products into the hands of customers in ways that create loyalty and profits.[3]

> At Xerox Corporation, *CEO Anne Mulcahy believes that competition is an opportunity to focus one's operations and keep employees' eyes on the target—winning ground against strong competitors. And she believes customers are centre stage, saying: "The toughest competitors are the ones that embed themselves in customer relationships—that's what we're trying to do." When in the field, she advises her sales force to emphasize Xerox's strengths rather than bad-mouthing the competition.*

> At BMW, *where customers are also foremost, a major thrust is on continuous innovation. CEO Norbert Reithofer says: "We push change through the organization to ensure its strength. There are always better solutions." One of those solutions is state-of-the-art manufacturing: the firm's facilities produce 1.3 million customized vehicles a year.*

At Ann Taylor stores, *when the firm was struggling to reassert its women's clothing brand and market position, CEO Kay Krill started with a 54-point action plan. It covered everything from processes to products to marketing. Although criticized for identifying so many things to address, she said: "There were 54 things we needed to fix. We fixed every one of them. All 54 were important to me."*

OPERATIONS MANAGEMENT ESSENTIALS

In one way or another, all organizations must master the challenges of **operations management**—getting work done by managing the systems through which organizations transform resources into finished products, goods, and services for customers and clients.[4] The span of operations management covers the full input-throughput-output cycle. Typical operations management decisions address such things as resource acquisition, inventories, facilities, workflows, technologies, and product quality.

> **Operations management** is the process of managing productive systems that transform resources into finished products.

MANUFACTURING AND SERVICES SETTINGS

The essentials of operations management apply to all types of organizations, not just to product manufacturers. Yes, Xerox transforms resource inputs into quality photocopy machines; BMW transforms them into attractive, high-performance automobiles; and Ann Taylor stores transform them into fashionable clothing and accessories. But in the services sector, WestJet transforms resource inputs into low-cost, dependable air travel; the Bank of Nova Scotia transforms them into financial services; Toronto's Hospital for Sick Children transforms them into health care services; and governments transform them into public services.

PRODUCTIVITY AND COMPETITIVE ADVANTAGE

The core issues in operations and services management boil down to how "productivity" and "competitive advantage" are achieved. This focuses management attention on the various processes and activities that turn resources—in the form of people, materials, equipment, and capital—into finished goods and services.

Productivity

Operations management in both manufacturing and services is very concerned with **productivity**—a quantitative measure of the efficiency with which inputs are transformed into outputs. The basic productivity equation is:

> **Productivity** is the efficiency with which inputs are transformed into outputs.

$$\text{Productivity} = \text{Output/Input}$$

If, for example, a local Canadian Blood Services centre collects 100 units of donated blood in one eight-hour day, its productivity would be 12.5 units per hour. If we were in charge of centres in several locations, the productivity of the centres could be compared on this measure. Alternatively, one might compare the centres using a productivity measure based not on hours of inputs, but on numbers of full-time staff. Using this input measure, a centre that collects 500 units per week with two full-time staff members (250 units per person) is more productive than one that collects 600 units per week with three (200 units per person).

When Microsoft studied the productivity of office workers in an on-line survey of more than 38,000 people across 200 countries, the results showed a variety of productivity shortfalls.[5] Although people reported working 47 hours per week, they were unproductive during 17 of the hours, and 69 percent of respondents said time spent in meetings was unproductive. Productivity obstacles

Competitive advantage is the ability to outperform one's competitors due to a core competency that is difficult to copy or imitate.

included unclear objectives and priorities, as well as procrastination and poor communication.

Competitive Advantage

Inefficiencies like those reported by Microsoft are costly; lost productivity by any measure is a drain on organizational competitiveness. Operating efficiencies that increase productivity, by contrast, are among the ways organizations may gain **competitive advantage**—defined earlier in the book as a core competency that allows an organization to outperform competitors.[6] Potential drivers of competitive advantage include such things as the ability to outperform based on product innovation, customer service, speed to market, manufacturing flexibility, and product or service quality. But regardless of how competitive advantage is achieved, the key result is the same: an ability to consistently do something of high value that one's competitors cannot replicate quickly or do as well.

Consider the example of Matsushita Electric Industries—maker of telephones, fax machines, security cameras, and other electronics. When productivity at Matsushita's plant in Saga, Japan, doubled in a four-year period, the executives didn't sit back and celebrate. They wanted still more. A huge set of conveyers was removed and robots were brought in along with sophisticated software to operate them. Plant manager Hitoshi Hirata says: "It used to be 2.5 days into a production run before we had our first finished product. But now the first is done in 40 minutes." And one might be tempted to compliment Hirata on a job well done and sit back to watch the results. Not so. He goes on to say: "Next year we'll try to shorten the cycle even more."[7]

GOING GLOBAL

QUALITY IS A UNIVERSAL LANGUAGE

Usually, when Canada and Russia are mentioned in the same sentence, you would naturally think of hockey. In this case, it is Tri Ocean, an engineering company based in Calgary, that brings these names together. Tri Ocean has been recognized by both the Russian Chamber of Commerce and the Canadian National Quality Institute for producing outstanding quality work. Through its award-winning Operational Excellence program, Tri Ocean has developed engineering protocols and procedures that enable the company to outperform industry norms. The Operational Excellence program focuses on continual improvement in leadership, planning, customer satisfaction, employee success, and process management. The company typically employs between 300 and 400 engineering, technical, project management, procurement, and administrative support staff, who have worked on projects across the globe including in Algeria, Australia, Brazil, Iran, Russia, the United Kingdom, and the United States.

Technology is the combination of knowledge, skills, equipment, and work methods used to transform inputs into outputs.

OPERATIONS TECHNOLOGIES

The foundation of any transformation process is **technology**—the combination of knowledge, skills, equipment, and work methods used to transform resource inputs into organizational outputs. It is the way tasks are accomplished using tools, machines, techniques, and human know-how. The availability of appropriate technology is a cornerstone of productivity, and the nature of the core technologies in use is an important element in competitive advantage.

Manufacturing Technology

It is common to classify manufacturing technology into three categories: small-batch production, mass production, and continuous-process production.[8] In **small-batch production**, such as in a racing bicycle shop, a variety of custom products are tailor-made to order. Each item or batch of items is made somewhat differently to fit customer specifications. The equipment used may not be elaborate, but a high level of worker skill is often needed. In **mass production**, such as manufacturing popular brands of recreational bicycles, the firm produces a large number of uniform products in an assembly-line system. Workers are highly dependent on one another as the product passes from stage to stage until completion. Equipment may be sophisticated, and workers often follow detailed instructions while performing simplified jobs.

Organizations using **continuous-process production** continuously feed raw materials—such as liquids, solids, and gases—through a highly automated production system with largely computerized controls. Such systems are equipment-intensive, but they can often be operated by a relatively small labour force. Classic examples are oil refineries and power plants.

Among the directions in manufacturing technology today, the following trends are evident.[9]

- There is increased use of *robotics*, where computer-controlled machines perform physically repetitive work with consistency and efficiency. If you visit any automobile manufacturer today, chances are that robotics is a major feature of the operations.

- There is increased use of *flexible manufacturing systems* that allow automated operations to quickly shift from one task or product type to another. The goal is to combine flexibility with efficiency, allowing what is sometimes called *mass customization*—efficient mass production of products meeting specific customer requirements.

- There is increased use of *cellular layouts* that place machines doing different work together, so that the movement of materials from one to the other is as efficient as possible. Cellular layouts also accommodate more teamwork on the part of machine operators.

- There is increased use of *computer-integrated manufacturing*, in which product designs, process plans, and manufacturing are driven from a common computer platform. Such approaches are now integrated with the Internet, so that customer purchasing trends in retail locations can be spotted and immediately integrated into production schedules at a manufacturing location.

- There is increased focus on *lean production* that continuously innovates and employs best practices to keep increasing production efficiencies. A master is Toyota, featured in the end-of-chapter case. A *BusinessWeek* headline once said "no one does lean like the Japanese."[10]

- There is increased attention to *design for disassembly*. The goal here is to design and manufacture products in ways that consider how their component parts will be recycled at the end of their lives.

- There is increased value to be found in *remanufacturing*. Instead of putting things together, remanufacturing takes used items apart and rebuilds them as products to be used again. One estimate is that using remanufactured materials saves up to 30 percent on costs.

Small-batch production manufactures a variety of products crafted to fit customer specifications.

Mass production manufactures a large number of uniform products with an assembly-line system.

In **continuous-process production**, raw materials are continuously transformed by an automated system.

Intensive technology focuses the efforts and talents of many people to serve clients.
Mediating technology links people together in a beneficial exchange of values.
In **long-linked technology**, a client moves from point to point during service delivery.

Service Technology

When it comes to service technology, the classifications are slightly different.[11] In health care, education, and related services, **intensive technology** focuses the efforts of many people with special expertise on the needs of patients, students, or clients. In banks, real estate firms, insurance companies, employment agencies, and others like them, **mediating technology** links together parties seeking a mutually beneficial exchange of values—typically a buyer and a seller. And **long-linked technology** can function like mass production, where a client is passed from point to point for various aspects of service delivery.

VALUE CHAIN MANAGEMENT

Whereas productivity may be considered the major efficiency measure in both manufacturing and services, "value creation" should be the target effectiveness measure. And in this sense, **value creation** means that the end result of a task or activity or work process is worth more than the effort and resources invested to accomplish it. In a manufacturing operation, for example, value is created when a raw material such as copper wire is combined with transistors and other electrical components to create a computer chip. In a service setting, value is created when a trained financial analyst provides a customer with advice that leads to profitable brokerage transactions in a stock portfolio.

Value creation occurs when the result of a work task or activity makes a product or service worth more in terms of potential customer appeal than at the start.

Figure 17.1 Elements in an organization's value chain.

VALUE CHAIN ANALYSIS

The **value chain** is the specific sequence of activities that creates products and services with value for customers.

You should recall that an organization's **value chain**, as shown in Figure 17.1, is the specific sequence of activities that results in the creation of products or services with value for customers. The value chain includes all *primary activities*—such as inbound logistics, operations, outbound logistics, marketing, sales, and after-sales service—as well as *support activities*—such as procurement, human resource management, technology development and support, and financial and infrastructure maintenance.[12]

Analysis of any organization's value chain will show an intricate sequence of activities that step by step adds value to inputs, right up to the point at which finished goods or services are delivered to customers or clients. Management Smarts 17.1 shows how to analyze each activity to add value.

17.1 MANAGEMENT SMARTS
A valuable chain reaction

The essence of value chain management is to manage each of the steps in the value chain for maximum efficiency and effectiveness. Part of the logic of being able to identify and diagram a value chain is to focus management attention on three major questions.

1. What value is being created for customers in each step?

2. How efficient is each step as a contributor to overall organizational productivity?

3. How can value creation be improved overall?

As the customer of an on-line retailer such as chapters.indigo.ca, you can think of this value in such terms as the price you pay, the quality you receive, and the timeliness of the delivery. From the standpoint of value chain management, Chapters-Indigo's value creation process can be examined from the point where books are purchased, to their transportation and warehousing, to electronic inventorying and order processing, and to packaging and distribution to the ultimate customer.

SUPPLY CHAIN MANAGEMENT

An essential element in any value chain is the relationship between the organization and the many people and businesses that supply it with needed resources and materials. All of these supplier relationships on the input side of the input-throughput-output action cycle must be well managed for productivity.

The concept of **supply chain management**, or SCM, involves strategic management of all operations linking an organization and its suppliers, including such areas as purchasing, manufacturing, transportation, and distribution.[13] The goals of supply chain management are to achieve efficiency in all aspects of the supply chain while ensuring on-time availability of quality resources and products. Walmart is still considered a master of supply chain management. As one example, the firm uses an advanced information system that continually updates inventory records and sales forecasts based on point-of-sale computerized information. Suppliers access this information electronically, allowing them to adjust their operations and rapidly ship replacement products to meet the retailer's needs.

Supply chain management strategically links all operations dealing with resource supplies.

Purchasing plays an important role in supply chain management. Just as any individual tries to control how much they spend, a thrifty organization must be concerned about how much it pays for what it buys. To leverage buying power, more organizations are centralizing purchasing to allow buying in volume. They are trimming supply chains and focusing on a small number of suppliers with whom they negotiate special contracts, gain quality assurances, and get preferred service. They are also finding ways to work together in supplier–purchaser partnerships. It is now more common, for example, that parts suppliers maintain warehouses in their customers' facilities. The customer provides the space; the supplier does the rest. The benefits to the customer are lower purchasing costs and preferred service; the supplier gains an exclusive customer contract and more sales volume.

Fair Trade Fashion

Perhaps you're one of a growing number of consumers who like to shop "fair trade." Doesn't it feel good when you buy coffee, for example, that is certified as grown by persons who were paid fairly for their labours? But can we say the same about clothing? How do we know that what we're wearing right now wasn't made under sweatshop conditions or by children?

There is at least one retailer that wants to be considered as selling fair trade fashion. Fair Indigo, launched by former executives of major fashion retailers, presents itself as "a new clothing company with a different way of doing business" that wants to "create stylish, high-quality clothes while paying a fair and meaningful wage to the people who produce them." Pointing out that there is no certifying body for fair trade apparel, Fair Indigo offers this guarantee: "We will therefore guarantee that every employee who makes our clothing is paid a fair wage, not just a legal minimum wage, as is the benchmark in the industry."

The firm's representatives travel the globe searching for small factories and cooperatives that meet their standards. By doing so, they're bucking industry trends in outsourcing and contract manufacturing. Fair Indigo's CEO, Bill Bass, says: "The whole evolution of the clothing and manufacturing industry has been to drive prices and wages down, shut factories and move work to countries with lower wages. We said, 'we're going to reverse this and push wages up.'"

YOU DECIDE

How do you define "fair," as in "fair trade"? Are you willing to pay a bit more for a fair trade product? And what do you think about Fair Indigo's business model? Is it "fashion" that sells apparel, or factory and conditions of origin? Will consumers pay more for fair trade fashion? Is Fair Indigo on the forefront of the next new wave of value creation in fashion retailing?

INVENTORY MANAGEMENT

Inventory is an amount of materials or products kept in storage.

Another important issue in the value chain is management of **inventory**, the amount of materials or products kept in storage. Organizations maintain a variety of inventories of raw material, work in process, and finished goods. Whenever anything is held in inventory, there is a cost associated with it, and controlling these costs is an important productivity tool.

Economic Order Quantity

Inventory control by **economic order quantity** orders replacements whenever inventory level falls to a predetermined point.

The goal of inventory control is to make sure that an inventory is just the right size to meet performance needs, thus minimizing the cost. The **economic order quantity** (EOQ) method of inventory control involves ordering a fixed number of items every time an inventory level falls to a predetermined point. When this point is reached, as shown in Figure 17.2, a decision is automatically made (typically by computer) to place a standard order to replenish the stock. The order sizes are mathematically calculated to minimize costs of inventory. The best example is the local supermarket, where hundreds of daily orders are routinely made on this basis.

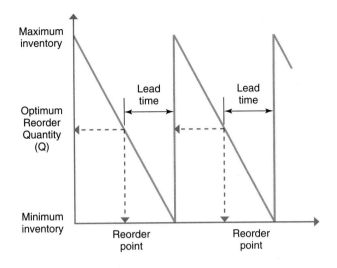

Figure 17.2 Inventory control by economic order quantity (EOQ).

Just-in-Time Systems

Another approach to inventory control is **just-in-time scheduling** (JIT), made popular by the Japanese. JIT systems reduce costs and improve workflow by scheduling materials to arrive at a workstation or facility "just in time" to be used. Since almost no inventories are maintained, the just-in-time approach is an important productivity tool. When a major hurricane was predicted to hit Florida, for example, Walmart's computer database anticipated high demand for, of all things, strawberry Pop-Tarts. JIT kicked in to deliver them to the stores "just in time" for the storm.[14]

Just-in-time scheduling minimizes inventory by sending out materials to workstations "just in time" to be used.

BREAK-EVEN ANALYSIS

Another important value chain management issue relates to capacity planning for the production of products or services, and the pricing of them for sales. In basic business terms: too much capacity raises costs, and too little capacity means unmet sales; too low a price fails to deliver revenues that cover costs, and too high a price drives away customers. Thus, when business executives are deliberating new products or projects, a frequent question is: "What is the 'break-even point'?"

The graph in Figure 17.3 shows that the **break-even point** is where revenues just equal costs. You can also think of it as the point where losses end and profit begins. The formula for calculating break-even points is:

The **break-even point** is where revenues = costs.

$$\text{Break-even point} = \text{Fixed costs}/(\text{Price} - \text{Variable costs})$$

Managers use **break-even analysis** to improve control and perform "what if" calculations under different projected cost and revenue conditions. See if you can calculate some break-even points, doing the types of analyses that business executives perform every day. Suppose the proposed target price for a new product is $8 per unit, fixed costs are $10,000, and variable costs are $4 per unit? What sales volume is required to break even? (Answer: the break-even point is at 2,500 units.) What happens if you are good at cost control and can keep variable costs to $3 per unit? (Answer: the break-even point is at 2,000 units.) Now, suppose you can only produce 1,000 units in the beginning and at the original costs. At what price must you sell them to break even? (Answer: $14.)

Break-even analysis calculates the point at which revenues cover costs under different "what if" conditions.

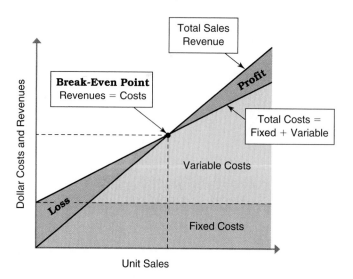

Figure 17.3 Graphical approach to break-even analysis.

BE SURE YOU CAN

• define *value creation* • describe the value chain for an organization • explain supply chain management • define *economic order quantity* • explain JIT • define *break-even point* and *break-even analysis* • use the formula to calculate break-even points

SERVICE AND PRODUCT QUALITY

Some years ago, at a time when North American industry was first coming to grips with fierce competition from Japanese products, American quality pioneer J. M. Juran challenged an audience of Japanese executives with a prediction. He warned them against complacency, suggesting that North America would bounce back in business competitiveness.[15] North American businesses have since done a lot to live up to Juran's prediction, but the challenges of delivering consistent quality are still apparent in the news and in our personal experiences. Have you ever heard conversations like this one?

> *"Here we go again—cut costs, cut costs, cut costs. How far can you cut costs and still have a viable operation? I think these top managers must have all graduated from the same MBA program, one that was dominated by 'number crunchers.' All they seem to know is how to cut costs. But where is it getting us? I see low morale, increasing problems meeting targets because we're all so overloaded, and corners being trimmed that could well turn into major quality problems at some point. I don't know about you, but I'm about fed up with it all."*

> *"I know, just look at the wait lines at some service establishments. How long does it take you to get to the car rental counter or to cash a cheque at the bank? Most service establishments these days are cutting back so far on staff that there are few people left to actually serve their customers. And the next time you're in a restaurant, keep your eyes open. The chances are that the servers are being run ragged because there just aren't enough of them. Don't you wonder how much could be added to the bottom lines of these firms if they would just pay more to add staff at levels that customers would appreciate?"*

A *Harvard Business Review* survey reports that American business leaders rank customer service and product quality as the first and second most important goals in the success of their organizations.[16] Notwithstanding the goals, there is often a disconnection between intentions and results—back to the prior conversations, so to speak. In a survey by the market research firm Michelson & Associates, poor service and product dissatisfaction were also ranked number 1 and number 2, respectively, as reasons why customers abandon a retail store.[17]

Reaching the twin goals of providing great service and quality products isn't always easy. But when they are pursued relentlessly, these goals can be an important source of competitive advantage. Bill Gates once said: "Your most unhappy customers are your greatest source of learning." Just imagine what would happen if every customer or client contact for an organization was positive. Not only would these customers and clients return again and again, but they would also tell others and expand the customer base.

ISSUES AND SITUATIONS
Bloggers Attack Poor Service

Bloggers have arrived in the world of customer service complaints. There are many people who take pleasure in sharing their travails and disasters with anyone who can type the offending company's name into a web address. And there's a lot of energy flowing through those stories.

When Justin Callaway didn't get satisfaction from Cingular (now AT&T) over a complaint that interference from his phone ruined his speakers, he used his experience as a freelance video editor to start a campaign. Along with friends, he recorded a song about Cingular and then added an animated bandit based on the company's logo to create a video short—"Feeling Cingular"—posted on YouTube. A vice-president from AT&T then wrote him offering to buy him new speakers to settle his complaint. Callaway refused, claiming the firm should do better at informing customers of potential interference problems. "It wasn't about the speakers anymore," he said.

A *BusinessWeek* report claims that "good customer service" isn't that hard to deliver: "Don't force customers to play 'call-center' tag . . . hire friendly people, train them well, and reward them with healthy pay and benefits."

CRITICAL RESPONSE

In the last chapter, we talked about "market control"—basically using responses from customers as a means of controlling behaviour in and by organizations. What do you think? In this age of YouTube and blogger mania, does market control mean that organizations hold themselves more accountable for customer service, and will the suggestions from *BusinessWeek* become everyday business realities? Or will firms continue to respond to situations like Callaway's case by case, and without any major adjustments to their operations?

CUSTOMER RELATIONSHIP MANAGEMENT

Without any doubt, customers put today's organizations to a very stiff test. Like you, most want three things: (1) high quality, (2) low price, and (3) on-time delivery of the goods and services they buy. The following are the types of customer stories that cause headaches for managers.[18]

- *Dell Computer* suffered a major customer backlash when some 3,000 callers to its customer service lines during one week had to wait at least 30 minutes before being able to speak with a real person.

- *Northwest Airlines* had a lot to explain to potential customers after leaving passengers stranded inside a plane for eight hours because of a snowstorm in Detroit.

- *Home Depot* saw customer satisfaction fall 8.2 percent while sales surged at its rival Lowe's, known for its top customer service.

- *Two Small Men with Big Hearts*, Canada's largest network of independent moving companies, has come under fire from customers in British Columbia. The Better Business Bureau has reported receiving more complaints about them than any other moving company in the province.

Essentials of Customer Relationship Management

Customer relationship management strategically tries to build lasting relationships with and to add value to customers.

Many organizations now use the principles of **customer relationship management** to establish and maintain high standards of customer service.[19] Known as CRM, this approach uses the latest information technologies to maintain intense communication with customers as well as to gather and use data regarding their needs and desires. At Marriott International, for example, CRM is supported by special customer management software that tracks information on customer preferences. When you check in, the likelihood is that your past requests for things like a king-size bed, no smoking room, and Internet access are already in your record. Says Marriott's chairman: "It's a big competitive advantage."[20]

There are probably many times in your experiences as a customer when you wonder why more managers don't get this message. Consider, for example, the case of Mona Shaw, a 76-year-old retired nurse. After arriving at a Comcast office to complain about poor installation of cable TV service to her home, she sat on a bench for two hours waiting to see a manager. She then left and came back with a hammer. She smashed a keyboard and telephone in the office, yelling: "Have I got your attention now?" It cost Shaw an arrest and a US$375 fine, but she became a media sensation and a rallying point for unhappy customers everywhere. As for Comcast, a spokesperson said: "We apologize for any customer service issues that Ms. Shaw experienced."[21]

Comcast's apology is nice, but don't you also wonder: Did the system change as a result of this incident? Was customer relationship management activated so that service improved for Shaw and other customers in the future? Was the experience of this branch incident reviewed by top management and the learning disseminated throughout Comcast operations nationwide? Or did things quickly slide back into business as usual?

External and Internal Customers

Customer relationship management applies equally well to external and internal customers. Figure 17.4 expands the open-systems view of organizations to depict the complex internal operations of the organization, as well as its interdependence with the external environment. In this figure, the organization's *external customers* purchase the goods produced or use the services provided. They may be industrial customers—other firms that buy a company's products for use in their own operations—or they may be retail customers or clients who purchase or use the goods and services directly. *Internal customers*, by contrast, are found within the organization. They are the individuals and groups who use or otherwise depend on one another's work in order to do their own jobs well.

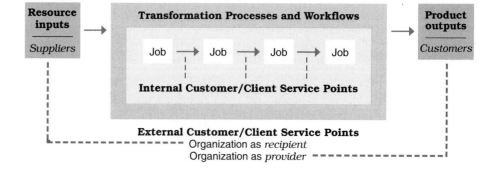

Figure 17.4 The importance of external and internal customers.

QUALITY MANAGEMENT

When the quality theme was first introduced in Chapter 2, we discussed how "world-class organizations" embed quality in all aspects of their operations.[22] Speaking of quality, what do 3M Canada, TELUS, Delta Hotels, Homewood Health Centre, and R. H. King Academy have in common? They are all past recipients of the Canada Awards for Excellence, one of Canada's highest levels of quality recognitions. These and other organizations make exceptional progress toward establishing Canada as a world leader in quality.[23]

The work of W. Edwards Deming is a cornerstone of the quality movement. His approach to quality emphasizes constant innovation, use of statistical methods, and commitment to training in the fundamentals of quality assurance. One outgrowth of his work is **total quality management**, or TQM. This is a process that makes quality principles part of the organization's strategic objectives, applying them to all aspects of operations and striving to meet customers' needs by doing things right the first time.

Most TQM approaches insist that the total quality commitment applies to everyone in an organization and throughout the value chain—from resource acquisition and supply chain management, through production and into the distribution of finished goods and services, and ultimately to customer relationship management. Both TQM and the Deming approach are also closely tied to the emphasis on **continuous improvement**—always looking for new ways to improve on current performance. Again, this applies throughout the value chain.[24] The basic notion driving continuous improvement is that one can never be satisfied; something always can and should be improved on.

One indicator of how embedded quality objectives have become in operations management is the importance of **ISO certification** by the International Standards Organization in Geneva, Switzerland. ISO certification has been adopted by many countries of the world as a quality benchmark. Businesses that want to compete as "world-class companies" are increasingly expected to have ISO certification at various levels. To do so, they must refine and upgrade quality in all operations and then undergo a rigorous assessment by outside auditors to determine whether they meet ISO requirements.

Total quality management is managing with an organization-wide commitment to continuous improvement, product quality, and customer needs.

Continuous improvement involves always searching for new ways to improve work quality and performance.

ISO certification indicates conformance with a rigorous set of international standards.

 Canadian Company in the News

TAKING A QUALITY APPROACH, ONE STEP AT A TIME

Winning the prestigious National Quality Institute's (NQI) Order of Excellence is a real honour for Diversicare Canada, which operates retirement homes and long-term care facilities in several provinces. The quest for quality began in 1990 when it established a committee to create a measuring tool or "scorecard" to identify quality problem areas. The quality committee developed a program that looked at 16 key indicators focusing on resident issues and employee performance. The company also paid attention to recruitment and retention strategies and designed programs to teach continuous improvement techniques to managers and employees. The company launched the program to great fanfare with a kickoff conference in 1993, but it languished for

Courtesy Diversicare

(*continued on next page*)

Canadian Company (*continued*)

two years because it was not championed across the whole organization. Yet the firm kept at it, by including quality initiatives in annual goals, cheering on early adopters of the program, and holding an annual quality conference. It worked. The quality program grew in strength and magnitude. In 2001, Diversicare was the first long-term health company to win the NQI's Gold Award. Now it is a double NQI Order of Excellence recipient. It fully lives up to its quality-inspired motto: "We Can Do It Better."

STATISTICAL QUALITY CONTROL

Statistical quality control measures work samples for compliance with quality standards.

Control charts graphically plot quality trends against control limits.

Six Sigma is a quality standard of 3.4 defects or fewer per million products or service deliveries.

For Deming, quality principles are straightforward: tally defects, analyze and trace them to the sources, make corrections, and keep records of what happens afterwards.[25] He championed **statistical quality control** that takes samples of work, measures quality in the samples, and determines acceptability of results. Unacceptable results trigger investigation and corrective action. An easy way to apply this notion is through control charts, such as the one shown in Figure 17.5.

Control charts are graphical ways of displaying trends so that exceptions to quality standards can be identified for special attention. In the figure, for example, an upper control limit and a lower control limit specify the allowable tolerances for measurements of a machine part. As long as the manufacturing process produces parts that fall within these limits, things are "in control." As soon as parts fall outside the limits, it is clear that something is going wrong that is affecting quality. The process can then be investigated—even shut down—to identify the source of the errors and correct them.

The logic of tallying and analyzing defects can be further extended with a variety of sophisticated statistical techniques. For example, many manufacturers now use a **Six Sigma** program, meaning that statistically the firm's quality performance standard will tolerate no more than 3.4 defects per million units of goods produced or services completed.[26] This translates to a perfection rate of 99.9997 percent.

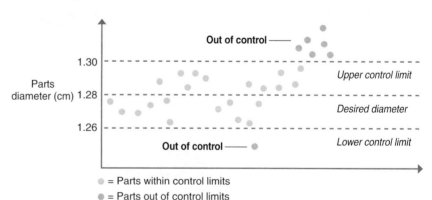

Figure 17.5 Sample control chart showing upper and lower control limits.

✓ **Learning Check** ❸ **BE SURE YOU CAN**

• discuss the importance of customer relationship management • differentiate internal and external customers of a firm • explain ISO certification • define *TQM* and *continuous improvement* • explain how control charts and Six Sigma programs are used in statistical quality control

WORK PROCESSES

The emphasis on productivity and competitive advantage through operations management includes business **process reengineering**.[27] This is defined as the systematic and complete analysis of work processes and the design of new and better ones.[28] The goal is to break old work habits and focus attention on better ways of doing things.

Process reengineering systematically analyzes work processes to design new and better ones.

WORK PROCESS ANALYSIS

In his book *Beyond Reengineering*, Michael Hammer defines a **work process** as "a related group of tasks that together create a result of value for the customer."[29] These tasks are what people do to turn resource inputs into goods or services for customers. Hammer highlights the following key words as essential elements of his definition: *group*—tasks are viewed as part of a group rather than in isolation; *together*—everyone must share a common goal; *result*—the focus is on what is accomplished, not on activities; *customer*—processes serve customers, and their perspectives are the ones that really count.

A **work process** is a related group of tasks that together create a value for the customer.

The concept of **workflow**, or the way work moves from one point to another in manufacturing or service delivery, is central to the understanding of processes.[30] The various parts of a work process must all be completed to achieve the desired results, and they must typically be completed in a given order. An important starting point for a reengineering effort is to diagram or map these workflows as they actually take place. Then each step can be systematically analyzed to determine whether it is adding value, to consider ways of eliminating or combining steps, and to find ways to use technology to improve efficiency.

Workflow is the movement of work from one point to another in a system.

RESEARCH BRIEF

How do you improve the productivity of a sales force?

That's the question asked by Dianne Ledingham, Mark Kovac, and Heidi Locke Simon. Writing in the *Harvard Business Review*, they use a series of case examples to illustrate how companies have used data and analytical methods to raise sales. They contrast the newer, data-driven approaches with what they call a "wing-and-a-prayer" style, in which salespersons are given goals and then simply told to go out and meet them.

One case involves U.S. Equipment Financing, a division of GE Commercial Finance headed by Michael Pilot. Pilot's approach was to focus on raising the performance of existing sales representatives by helping them sell more—the "productivity improvement approach"—in contrast to simply hiring more reps—the "capacity increase approach." Pilot attributes some US$300 million in new business to his scientific approach to sales force productivity. He began with

a new database that inventoried past transactions. He then asked sales reps to come up with criteria that would indicate the likelihood of a customer doing business with GE. He next ran regression analyses that tested these criteria against the past transactions. The result was a set of six criteria that correlated well with past successes.

When new prospects were scored using the criteria, Pilot found 50 percent more top-prospect sales candidates than had previously been identified. Using this set of top prospects, he redesigned the sales force to maximize attention to those prospects, and he provided reps with information and tools to better deal with their customers. The result was a 19-percent increase in the "conversion" rate, or sales closings.

Researchers consider Pilot's scientific method a "best practice" approach to improving sales force productivity. They recommend the TOPSales approach, focusing on (1) targeted offerings by market segment, (2) optimized technology tools and procedures, (3) performance

(*continued on next page*)

RESEARCH BRIEF *(continued)*

Sales Improvement Strategies

Productivity Improvement Approach: > sales per rep

$ Sales Goal

Capacity Increase Approach: < sales per rep

Sales Per Rep

Number of Sales Reps

management metrics and systems, and (4) systematic sales force deployment.

You be the researcher

This article by Ledingham et al. describes a vigorous productivity improvement approach to reaching a higher sales goal. Can you find examples in your experience or community where goals are reached, but the costs of doing so are very high? What would you propose so that the same goals could be reached with lower costs and higher productivity?

PROCESS REENGINEERING

Process value analysis identifies and evaluates core processes for their performance contributions.

Process reengineering can be used to regularly assess and fine-tune work processes to ensure that they directly add value to operations. Through a technique called **process value analysis**, core processes are identified and carefully evaluated for their performance contributions. Each step in a workflow is examined. Unless a step is found to be important, useful, and contributing to value-added results, it is eliminated. Process value analysis typically involves the following.[31]

1. Identify the core processes.

2. Map the core processes with respect to workflows.

3. Evaluate all core process tasks.

4. Search for ways to eliminate unnecessary tasks or work.

5. Search for ways to eliminate delays, errors, and misunderstandings.

6. Search for efficiencies in how work is shared and transferred among people and departments.

Figure 17.6 shows an example of how reengineering and better use of computer technology can streamline a purchasing operation. Ideally, a purchase order should result in at least three value-added outcomes: order fulfillment, a paid bill, and a satisfied supplier. For this to happen, things like ordering, shipping, receiving, billing, and payment must all be well handled. A traditional business system might have purchasing, receiving, and accounts payable as separate functions, with each function communicating with each other and with the supplier. As the figure shows, there are lots of inefficiencies here. Alternatively, process value analysis might result in reengineering the workflow and redesigning it to include a new purchasing support team. Its members can handle the same work more efficiently with the support of the latest computer technology.[32]

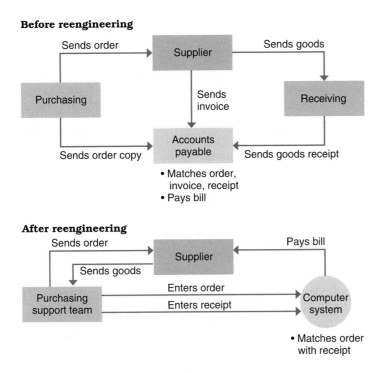

Figure 17.6 How reengineering can streamline work processes.

PROCESS-DRIVEN ORGANIZATIONS

Customers, teamwork, and efficiency are central to Hammer's notion of process reengineering. He describes the case of Aetna Life & Casualty Company, where a complex system of tasks and processes once took as long as 28 days to accomplish.[33] Customer service requests were handled in a step-by-step fashion by many different people. After an analysis of workflows, the process was redesigned into a "one and done" format, where a single customer service provider handled each request from start to finish. After the change was made, an Aetna customer account manager said: "Now we can see the customers as individual people. It's no longer 'us' and 'them.'"[34]

Hammer also describes reengineering at a unit of Verizon Communications. Before reengineering, customer inquiries for telephone service and repairs required extensive consultation between technicians and their supervisors. After process value analysis, technicians were formed into geographical teams that handled their own scheduling, service delivery, and reporting. They were given cellular telephones and laptop computers to assist in managing their work, resulting in the elimination of a number of costly supervisory jobs. The technicians enthusiastically responded to the changes and opportunities. "The fact that you've got four or five people zoned in a certain geographical area," said one, "means that we get personally familiar with our customers' equipment and problems."[35]

The essence of process reengineering is to locate control for processes with an identifiable group of people, and to focus each person and the entire system on meeting customer needs and expectations. It tries to eliminate duplication of work and systems bottlenecks so as to reduce costs, increase efficiency, and build capacity for change. The result is to create a process-driven organization that Hammer describes this way.

> *Its intrinsic customer focus and its commitment to outcome measurement make it vigilant and proactive in perceiving the need for change; the process owner, freed from other responsibilities and wielding the power of process design, is an institutionalized agent of change; and employees who have an appreciation for customers and who are measured on outcomes are flexible and adaptable.*[36]

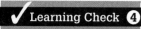 **Learning Check ④**

BE SURE YOU CAN

• define *process reengineering* and *work process* • draw a map of the workflow in an organization familiar to you • explain how process value analysis can be used to streamline workflows and improve work performance • explain the concept of a process-driven organization

MANAGEMENT LEARNING REVIEW

STUDY QUESTIONS SUMMARY

KEY TERMS

break-even analysis, 511
break-even point, 511
competitive advantage, 506
continuous improvement, 515
continuous-process,
    production, 507
control charts, 516
customer relationship,
    management, 514
economic order quantity, 510
intensive technology, 508
inventory, 510
ISO certification, 515
just-in-time scheduling, 511
long-linked technology, 508
mass production, 507
mediating technology, 508
operations management, 505
process reengineering, 517
process value analysis, 518
productivity, 505
Six Sigma, 516
small-batch production, 507
statistical quality control, 516
supply chain
    management, 509
technology, 506
total quality management, 515
value chain, 508
value creation, 508
work process, 517
workflow, 517

1. What are the essentials of operations and services management?

• The challenges of operations management relate to managing productive systems that transform resources into finished goods and services for customers and clients.

• Productivity measures the efficiency with which inputs are transformed into outputs: Productivity = Output/Input.

• Technology, including the use of knowledge, equipment, and work methods in the transformation process, is an important consideration in operations management.

FOR DISCUSSION Does the concept of productivity apply equally well in all types of organizations?

2. What is value chain management?

• The value chain is the sequence of activities that create value at each stage involved in producing goods or services.

• Value chain analysis identifies each step in the value chain to ensure it is efficient.

• Supply chain management, or SCM, is the process of managing all operations linking an organization and its suppliers, including purchasing, manufacturing, transportation, and distribution.

• Efficient purchasing and inventory management techniques such as just-in-time and economic order quantities are important forms of cost control.

• Break-even analysis identifies the point where revenues will equal costs under different pricing and cost conditions.

FOR DISCUSSION Can value chain analysis be helpful in service organizations such as banks?

3. How do organizations manage customer service and product quality?

• Customer relationship management builds and maintains strategic relationships with customers.

• Quality management addresses the needs of both internal customers and external customers.

• Total quality management tries to meet customers' needs—on time, the first time, and all the time.

• Organizations use control charts and statistical techniques such as the Six Sigma system to measure the quality of work samples for quality control purposes.

FOR DISCUSSION Is it realistic to speak of "total" quality management?

4. **How can work processes be designed for productivity?**

- A work process is a related group of tasks that together create value for a customer.

- Process engineering is the systematic and complete analysis of work processes and the design of new and better ones.

- In process value analysis, all elements of a process and its workflows are examined to identify their exact contributions to key performance results.

- Reengineering eliminates unnecessary work steps, combines others, and uses technology to gain efficiency and reduce costs.

FOR DISCUSSION Can process reengineering be overdone to the point where efficiency overwhelms effectiveness?

SELF-TEST

Multiple-Choice Questions

1. Productivity in a typical organization is calculated using the formula Productivity = _____ /Input.

    (a) Profit   (b) Cost   (c) Output   (d) Revenue

2. If you conducted a value chain analysis of a business, you would study _____.

    (a) customer satisfaction with products   (b) how much TQM affects profits   (c) the flow of activities that transform resources into goods and services   (d) the links between performance and rewards

3. New computer technologies have made possible _____ that quickly and efficiently produces individualized products for customers.

    (a) flexible manufacturing   (b) mass production   (c) mass customization   (d) design for disassembly

4. In remanufacturing, the focus is on _____.

    (a) breaking down used products and using the parts to make new ones   (b) arranging machines in cellular layouts   (c) mass customization   (d) replacing people with robots

5. Walmart's suppliers electronically access inventory data and sales forecasts in the stores and automatically ship replacement products. This is an example of IT utilization in _____.

    (a) supply chain management   (b) customer relationship management   (c) total quality management   (d) strategic constituencies analysis

6. An economic order quantity approach to inventory control _____.

    (a) uses computer control to accomplish JIT scheduling   (b) reorders inventory automatically when a certain point is reached   (c) allows for inventory to be purchased only when suppliers grant quantity discounts   (d) means that inventory levels never exceed a preset reorder amount

7. In a break-even analysis, the break-even point occurs when _____.

    (a) fixed costs = variable costs   (b) profits = expenses   (c) assets = liabilities   (d) revenues = total costs

8. Benchmarking, continuous improvement, and reduced cycle times are examples of organizational practices that show a commitment to _____.

    (a) affirmative action   (b) total quality management   (c) cost containment   (d) supply chain management

9. A quality standard that has become essential for world-class companies competing in global markets is _____.

    (a) the Deming prize   (b) upper control limit   (c) CRM   (d) ISO certification

10. _____ is an example of a statistical quality control technique.

    (a) Design for disassembly   (b) SCM   (c) Six Sigma   (d) Quality circle

11. A work process is defined as a related group of tasks that together create value for _____.

    (a) shareholders   (b) customers   (c) workers   (d) society

12. The first step in process value analysis is to _____.

    (a) look for ways to eliminate unnecessary tasks   (b) map or diagram the workflows   (c) identify core processes   (d) look for efficiencies in transferring work among people and departments

13. In addition to operating efficiency, competitive advantage is often pursued through operations management initiatives that _____.

    (a) increase use of minimum-wage workers   (b) provide for customer service improvements   (c) cut product quality to allow for lower pricing   (d) use the same product designs over and over again

14. A major difference between operations management in manufacturing and in services is that _____.

    (a) service organizations don't measure productivity   (b) manufacturing organizations don't offer services   (c) service organizations often use different technologies than do manufacturing organizations   (d) supply chain management doesn't work in services

15. The techniques of operations management are closely aligned with the concept of the organization as a(n) _____.

    (a) open system   (b) closed system   (c) top-down pyramid   (d) machine-driven rather than people-driven system

Short-Response Questions

16. What operating objectives are appropriate for an organization seeking competitive advantage through improved customer service?

17. What is the difference between an organization's external customers and its internal customers?

18. Why is supply chain management considered important in operations management?

19. If you were a reengineering consultant, how would you describe the steps in a typical approach to process value analysis?

Application Question

20. What would be possible productivity measures for the following organizations?

    (a) Canada Post   (b) university   (c) hospital   (d) amusement park   (e) restaurant

SELF-ASSESSMENT

Back to Yourself: Self-Management

Operations management tries to help organizations of all types best use resources and systems to achieve productivity. In many ways, our daily lives are similar quests for productivity. The way we utilize, or not, various opportunities to engage in positive self-management probably makes a substantial difference in the results we achieve in work and non-work settings alike. It might be helpful, for example, to pursue career development in the systematic ways that an operations specialist pursues supply chain management—identifying the players and key processes, examining the relationships, performing the analyses and calculations, and acting in ways that streamline behaviour for maximum efficiency and performance.

Further Reflection: Personal Numeracy

Instructions

In operations management and in other aspects of managerial and personal problem solving, we have to deal with numbers. But many of us struggle with basic math. How strong are your "numeracy" skills? Complete the following quiz. Compare your results with those of nearby classmates. Work together until you believe you have all the correct answers. Then, join in a class discussion addressing the question: "Why is personal numeracy so important as a life and career skill?"

1. How many zeros does it take to make a "googol"?

2. If there are two red, four green, and six blue M&Ms left in a packet, what is the probability of next picking a green one?

3. What is "pi" rounded to 4 decimal places?

4. How is a billion written in numbers?

5. What is 1/40 as a decimal?

6. If $7x + y = 9$ and $3x - y = 7$, what are x and y?

7. What is the perimeter of a triangular campus green if the bordering walkways measure 150, 540, and 450 metres, respectively?

8. Two angles in a triangle are 37 degrees and 64 degrees. What is the third angle?

9. Evie has $10,000 invested in a tax-free money-market account. The account pays 1.75 percent interest and her marginal tax rate is 28 percent. If this account was taxable, what would Evie's rate of interest be?

10. Salmah needs money for textbooks. She can get a paycheque loan of $200 for a fee of $30 every two weeks. What annual rate of interest is she paying for this loan?

Source: Developed in part from "Quiz: How's Your Maths?" BBC News: newsvote.bbc.co.uk (retrieved August 15, 2008).

Straw Towers

Materials Needed

One box of straws per group

Procedure

1. Form groups as assigned by the instructor. The mission of each group or temporary organization is to build the tallest possible straw tower. Each group should determine worker roles: at least four students will be builders, two others will be consultants who offer suggestions, and any remaining students will be observers.

2. Rules for the exercise:

   • Ten minutes allowed for planning for the tower.

   • Only 60 seconds can be used to build the tower.

   • No straws can be put together during the planning.

   • All straws must be put back in the box before the competition begins.

   • The completed tower must stand alone.

3. Discussion: What lessons for operations and services management are learned from this exercise?

Source: Adapted from Bonnie McNeely, "Using the Tinker Toy Exercise to Teach the Four Functions of Management" *Journal of Management Education,* vol. 18, No. 4 (November 1994), pp. 468–472.

Toyota: Looking Far into the Future

By borrowing the best ideas from North American brands and innovating the rest itself, Toyota has become a paragon of auto manufacturing efficiency. Its vehicles have been widely known for their quality and longevity—and until recently Toyota's sales numbers were the envy of the North American Big Three. Here is how Toyota became so efficient at producing high-quality automobiles and why it is now facing quality challenges.

Buy Domestic?

There used to be a sentiment encouraging Canadian and U.S. car buyers to purchase domestic models built and assembled in North America. Those who still tout the movement to buy domestic have likely done a good bit of head-scratching over how to classify Toyota—a Japanese company situated in Ontario that employs Canadian workers and that uses Canadian- and American-made parts to produce vehicles sold across North America. What to think when this Japanese brand achieves a product quality far superior to long-known North American brands? And Toyota has surged ahead of General Motors to rank number one in global auto sales.[1] Yet things have now changed. Toyota, once the model automotive manufacturing company, is now facing its own quality challenges. What happened?

Quality by Design

Toyota's success and growth in the North American auto market were based on strategies honed since the 1950s to earn and retain customer satisfaction by producing superior vehicles within a highly efficient production environment. From the home office to factories to showrooms, two core philosophies guided Toyota's business: (1) creating fair, balanced, mutually beneficial relationships with both suppliers and employees; and (2) strictly adhering to a just-in-time (JIT) manufacturing principle.

Collaboration over Competition

Over the decades, other North American auto manufacturers developed relationships with their suppliers that emphasized tense competition, price-cutting, and the modification of suppliers' production capacities with the changing needs of the domestic market. Year after year, parts suppliers had to bid to renew contracts in a process that valued year-to-year price savings over long-term relationships. Domestic manufacturers, notorious for changing production demands mid-season to comply with late-breaking market dynamics or customer feedback, forced suppliers to turn to double or triple shifts to keep up with capacity and thus avoid the problems—quality slips, recalls, line shutdowns, layoffs—that ultimately slow the final assembly of vehicles. When a carmaker doesn't know what it wants, suppliers have little chance of keeping up. This system of industry dynamics proved susceptible to new approaches from Japanese competitors.

Toyota's model of supply chain management displayed an exclusive commitment to parts suppliers, well-forecast parts orders that were not subject to sways in the market, and genuine concern for the success of suppliers. In the *Financial Times*, M. Reza Vaghefi noted that supply chain relationships among Asian manufacturers are based on a complex system of cooperation and equity interests. "Asian values, more so than in [W]estern cultures, traditionally emphasize the collective good over the goals of the individual," he said. "This attitude clearly supports the synergistic approach of supply chain management and has encouraged concern for quality and productivity."[2]

Visiting other North American auto plants and seeing months' worth of excess parts waiting to be installed taught Toyota the benefit of having only enough supplies on hand to fulfill a given production batch. Toyota plans its production schedules months in advance, dictating regularly scheduled parts shipments from its suppliers. Suppliers benefit by being able to predict long-range demand for products, scheduling production accordingly. This builds mutual loyalty between suppliers and the carmaker—almost as if suppliers were a part of Toyota. The fit and finish in Toyota vehicles is precise because its suppliers can afford to focus on the quality of their parts. And consumers notice: Toyota vehicles consistently earned high marks for customer satisfaction and retained their resale value better than almost any others.[3]

Keep It Lean

Early Toyota presidents Toyoda Kiichiro and Ohno Taiichi are considered the fathers of the Toyota Production System (TPS),

known widely by the JIT moniker or as "lean production." Emphasizing quality and efficiency at all levels, it drives nearly all aspects of decision-making at Toyota.[4]

Simply put, TPS is "all about producing only what's needed and transferring only what's needed," said Teruyuki Minoura, senior managing director at Toyota. He likened it to a "pull" system—in which workers fetch only that which is immediately needed—as opposed to a traditional "push" system.[5] "Producing what's needed means producing the right quantity of what's needed," he continued. "The answer is a flexible system that allows the line to produce what's necessary when it's necessary. If it takes six people to make a certain quantity of an item and there is a drop in the quantity required, then your system should let one or two of them drop out and get on with something else."[6]

To achieve maximum efficiency, workers at Toyota plants must be exceptionally knowledgeable about all facets of a vehicle's production, able to change responsibilities as needed. "An environment where people have to think brings with it wisdom, and this wisdom brings with it *kaizen* [the notion of continuous improvement]," noted Minoura. "If asked to produce only one unit at a time, to produce according to the flow, a typical line worker is likely to be flummoxed. It's a basic characteristic of human beings that they develop wisdom from being put under pressure."[7]

Keeping Up with the Times

No vehicle represents Toyota's innovation better than the Prius. The Prius has been wildly successful in North America and has come to represent a coming generation of fuel-sipping cars and the money- and environment-conscious consumers who clamour for them.[8] Worldwide, Prius sales recently topped the one-million mark, and the car sells in over 40 countries.[9]

On the other hand, no Toyota vehicle has come to represent the challenges of adapting to a changing sales landscape more than its Tundra pickup truck has. Hoping to make gains over the sales of domestic pickups, Toyota built a Tundra plant in Texas to prove that its trucks were as North American as those made by the Big Three. But bad became worse when—already 60 percent over budget—truck sales began to decline as the price of oil rose. Contractors and builders, prime candidates for pickups, began to think twice about new pickup purchases; the Tundra plants began to run well under capacity.[10]

Yet quality, and in turn Toyota's reputation, has began to suffer. Toyota is still dealing with the fallout from negative publicity the automaker received when it recalled 7.6 million vehicles because of acceleration problems, which led to dozens of accidents and some deaths in the United States. Now jittery from the allegations of cover-ups and public scrutiny, Toyota seems to be going to the other extreme: it issued more than 15 different recalls in Canada in 2010 alone.[11]

President Akio Toyoda reportedly attributed Toyota's quality and safety problems to its rapid growth, which outstripped its ability to maintain effective human resources. Toyoda said the company could not train enough people to keep pace with growth. The growing technical complexity of autos stretched the ability of too few Toyota engineers to adhere to their quality focus. He acknowledged a misguided focus in the "order of Toyota's traditional priorities" so that product safety and quality did not come first, with sales volumes and cost management becoming too important.[12]

Discussion Questions

1. How could Chrysler, Ford, or General Motors gain efficiencies through supply chain management?

2. What problems might a firm face when trying to implement and use the just-in-time systems found at Toyota?

3. How does Toyota's operations management approach show an understanding of the value chain?

4. **FURTHER RESEARCH**—Toyota now has to face the same quality challenges that its North American competitors (GM, Chrysler, Ford) have been facing. Do some investigation on how automobile manufacturers are incorporating quality into their cars and into their image. Who is doing the best job on both questions?

VIDEO CASE 6

Suppliers

Video Summary and Discussion

The video looks at the pressures on Canadian suppliers from consumers and retailers to cut prices.

It focuses on JAM Industries Ltd., a distributor of music equipment. Founded in 1972, the company began operating in Montreal under the trade name of Erikson Music, and it experienced rapid growth through the 1970s.

In the 1980s, JAM Industries widened its scope. It formed Korg Canada and Erikson Pro Audio. In 1986, JAM Industries purchased the full assets of Coast Wholesale Music Ltd. and proceeded to transform this Western Canadian company from a regional distributor into a full-fledged national marketing and sales force.

In the 1990s, building on established strengths, the company expanded. Erikson Pro Audio into the lighting market, distributing Martin Professional Lighting products in Canada, and into the consumer electronics field with the Erikson Consumer division.

Today, JAM Industries has consolidated its strengths into five main divisions: Coast Music (music accessories), Erikson Music (musical instruments including Korg keyboards), Erikson Pro (including pro lighting), Erikson Audio, and Erikson Consumer. Currently, it has more than $10 million in inventory.

Ed Schenker of JAM Industries describes music equipment distribution as a "tough business." He acknowledges that the significant increase in the Canadian dollar has helped Canadian wholesalers, who ultimately source their inventory from the United States. However, they have been reluctant to pass these savings on to consumers, since they argue that it takes time for them to reap the benefits of the stronger dollar, and because the increased costs of import taxes, duty, fuel, and wages prevent them from doing so. In addition, Schenker says Canadian standards for safety on electronic equipment are higher than those in the United States.

However, financial analysts are sceptical of the reasons put forth by JAM for not reducing prices as the Canadian dollar has strengthened. They cite statistics showing how profit margins in JAM's industry have skyrocketed with the strengthened dollar, which calls into question Schenker's "tough industry" claims.

At the same time, Canadian retailers face the same pressures to pass savings resulting from the stronger dollar on to consumers. Once again, they have been reluctant to do so amid higher profit margins deriving from reduced prices on imported goods. The end result, as Schenker explains, is that JAM Industries has been forced to cut prices regularly, squeezing the profit margins at the bottom end of the supply chain.

This controversy is not unlike that facing Canadian booksellers, who in particular are the focus of ire for many Canadian consumers because books, magazines, and paper products have both U.S. and Canadian prices printed on them in this country. Consumers are infuriated that, even at times when the Canadian dollar is trading above the U.S. greenback, books sold here often cost up to 30 percent more.

In response to the consumer outrage, Indigo Books and Music Inc. says that the price is to a large degree out of its hands. However, in order to address customer concerns, it has instituted a "sticker savings event" that gives a discount of 10 percent off any book in its stores.

In addition, some smaller, independent Canadian booksellers, such as Regina-based Book and Brier Patch and Audrey's Books in Edmonton, have begun selling at the American list price.

Large retailers like Walmart Canada Corp. have also joined the fray. It has announced that it will begin selling all books, magazines, greeting cards, and gift wrap at U.S. list prices, even though the new pricing has not been supported by cost concessions from suppliers. The retail giant is negotiating with vendors to bring prices down, but in the meantime it has signalled its willingness to reduce its own profit margins in its dedication to the absolute lowest prices.

That Walmart has taken this measure with books has exerted further pressure on Canadian booksellers to follow suit.

Questions for Students

1. JAM Industries has an inventory management challenge—with a rising Canadian dollar how might they manage their supply chain better?

2. Would you agree that inventory management is a significant issue for JAM Industries?

3. Would a supplier-purchaser partnership be in the best interests of JAM Industries and the music equipment retailers that it sells to? If so, how might such a partnership work, and how would each party benefit?

On a spring day in March 2009, Nadir Mohamed, the new CEO of Rogers Communications Inc., sat in his office and contemplated what was next for the $25-billion Canadian company.[1] After almost five decades at the helm, its indomitable founder, Ted Rogers, had passed away in December 2008. Mohamed had been with the company since 2000, but this was the first time he would be without the direction and vision of the man who had dedicated his life to making Rogers a Canadian icon.[2]

Rogers Communications Inc. (RCI), now Canada's largest wireless communications service,[3] began in 1960 when Ted Rogers bought a struggling radio station.[4] From this modest beginning, Rogers worked tirelessly to make his company a leader in the cable TV, wireless, and media industries. He was successful in his pursuit; at the time of Ted Rogers' death, RCI had over 8.9 million wireless subscribers, 2.3 million cable clients, over 400 branded retail stores, 55 radio stations, and 70 magazines and trade publications, bringing in a total of $12 billion in revenues.[5]

Nadir Mohamed knew that Ted Rogers would be a hard act to follow. He would have to be visionary, resourceful, inventive, and focused on results in order to lead RCI and its more than 28,000 employees forward.[6] In taking the company into a new era, Mohamed also knew that he had to keep in mind that RCI had been a family company. One of its chief advantages had always been the strength that came from understanding that there was a real person behind it. As founder and major shareholder, Ted Rogers had always had the final say in what happened.[7]

Mohamed also knew that, while he would be responsible for leading RCI into the future, the Rogers children, Edward III and Melinda, had inherited their father's 91 percent of RCI's class A voting shares, effectively ensuring continued control of the company to the Rogers family.[8] He wondered what problems, if any, would arise if his vision for RCI was not the same as the family's. As Mohamed prepared for his first day of work, the question was where to start and what to do first to ensure that Ted Rogers' legacy continued.

Rogers, the Company

Ted Rogers' father, Edward Rogers Sr., invented the alternating current (AC) radio tube, revolutionizing the industry by manufacturing radios that ran off ordinary household electricity. In what Ted Rogers called "another stroke of brilliance," his father then used his own radio station, CFRB, to increase the demand for more radios. Drawing upon his father's legacy, while still in law school, Ted Rogers fulfilled his mother's dream by re-establishing the Rogers name in broadcasting when he bought the radio station CHFI, renaming it CFTR (for Canada's First Ted Rogers).[9] A few years later, he entered the cable TV business by founding Rogers Cable. In the 1970s, Rogers focused on building his customer base by expanding to Toronto and acquiring rival Canadian Cable Systems to become the biggest cable company in Canada.[10] In a business world increasingly focused on the pursuit of short-term gain, Rogers decided early on that he was in it for the long haul. "There are people . . . who are not willing to put off the harvest," he said, "But I want to reinvest the harvest so there will be an even bigger harvest in the future."[11]

And a bigger harvest there was! The 1980s saw unprecedented growth for the company. Rogers Cable was re-formed into Rogers Communications Inc. with cable markets in Vancouver and the United States, including California, Minnesota, Oregon, and Texas[12] (the U.S. assets would be sold later for $1.5 billion profit).[13] During the 1980s, Rogers also acquired CFMT in Toronto and created Rogers Video, which has grown into the largest Canadian-owned chain of rental video stores.

After acquiring the Canadian Home Shopping Network, now The Shopping Channel, Rogers then collaborated with Canadian Pacific in CNCP (later renamed Unitel) to enter the long-distance telephone market.[14]

RCI did not slow down in the 1990s either, partnering with Viewers Choice Canada in 1991 to create a pay-per-view cable service. Rogers then acquired the publishing group Maclean Hunter, the largest takeover bid in Canadian history at the time, effectively creating Rogers Media. In 1994, RCI became the first cable company in North America to launch commercial high-speed Internet service, and it also launched pay-as-you-go cellular service. In the late 1990s, Rogers Cablesystems launched digital cable, which further enhanced services to customers.[15]

In 2000, RCI continued to branch out and bought the Toronto Blue Jays baseball team and acquired control of the Sportsnet channel from CTV, renaming it Rogers Sportsnet. It then launched high-definition and on-demand television in Canada as well as GSM (global system for mobile communications), the international standard in wireless networks. Personal video recorders were followed by the acquisition of wireless provider Microcell and a local telephone service provider called Call-Net. Rogers Yahoo! was next, followed by *Hello!* magazine, and five Citytv television stations. Perhaps one of Ted Rogers' last great moves was the partnership formed with Apple around the launch of the wildly popular iPhone in Canada.[16]

After the successful iPhone launch, the question on new CEO Mohamed's mind was: How would Rogers keep its reputation for leading innovation and technology in the rapidly changing, increasingly consolidated, wireless industry?

Rogers, the Man

Like his father, Ted Rogers was attracted to the communications industry and was an entrepreneur right from the start. While still in school, Rogers rigged a hidden rooftop antenna and connected it by a cable to his room in order to watch television. For a small fee, his fellow students could gather around and enjoy the marvels of television. Over the course of the next 50 years, Rogers would devote his life to building his business, starting with one fledgling radio station and ending with a $25-billion Canadian institution.[17]

Rogers was called an electronic visionary, a sleepless CEO, and a relentless entrepreneur by both his friends and competitors.[18] It was clear that Rogers was a hard worker, a consummate tactician, and relentless in his pursuit of growth. His colleagues remember him chasing new opportunities. "It was just on to the next thing," one of his executives remembers. "If we'd acquired a cable company, [Rogers]

would say, 'Have you called so and so? Have you called the 13 managers that you've taken over to tell them that we're with them? Have you called the CRTC to ensure they're happy? Have you called the shipping guy to make sure the trucks are painted?'"[19]

His daughter Melinda remembers that Rogers "was always an eternal optimist, and he summed this up with his signature line 'The best is yet to come.'" Perhaps his greatest gift was that he had a wonderful ability to envision technological change years before his competitors and the courage to act upon it. "It was not only his understanding of the potential in the early days of innovations such as FM radio, cable television, high-speed Internet, and wireless communications, but his confidence in himself and his ever-relentless perseverance that allowed him to succeed in much of what he did," Melinda says. "He was thoroughly prepared, ready to move at a moment's notice when the opportunity arose, and was able to think through various scenarios while negotiating to ensure that he got the outcome he was looking for."[20]

Over the years, as Rogers' business expanded, so did his debt. Many times, he came close to bankruptcy and he had to remortgage his Toronto home to make ends meet.[21] Rogers twice came very close to losing his debt-laden firm, once after a rapid U.S. cable expansion in the 1980s and the second time after a costly task of building Canada's first national wireless operation in the 1990s. "You don't deserve to be called an entrepreneur," Rogers once said, "unless you've mortgaged your house to the business." For Rogers, debt was a badge of honour, the mark of a true builder. After years of escaping out of tight financial situations, others recognized a certain successful inevitability about Rogers. He was somewhat of a modern renaissance man, equally conversant in engineering, law, tax policy, marketing, finance, and how to leverage, of course.[22]

Now it was Nadir Mohamed's turn; RCI was in his hands. To be successful, Mohamed knew he had to understand and compete across several different industries: wireless, cable, and media.

Wireless

The growing wireless industry in Canada contributes $39 billion annually and roughly 300,000 jobs to the Canadian economy. Wireless carriers invest more than $1 billion every year in mobile phone communications infrastructure. In Canada, wireless subscribers number 23.4 million, with half of all phone connections in 2010 being wireless.[23]

Competition in the industry is fierce as companies compete to recruit and then retain subscribers. Into this landscape new wireless companies have entered, seeking to challenge for market share and profits. With network technology now more evenly spread across the telecom industry, and as the market crowds with new competitors, it is apparent that distribution is becoming an even more important part of wireless companies' business.[24] Recently, Loblaw Cos. Ltd. announced that it would end its exclusive arrangement with Bell and begin selling phones from RCI, TELUS Corp., and new wireless entrants Wind Mobile and Public Mobile. Public Mobile is trying new approaches by offering phones in Gateway Newstand locations, at Ultramar gas stations, and at Eyeshot Media's 1,000 convenience stores across Ontario and Quebec. In 2010, in response to growing pressures, RCI began a trial retail arrangement with Shoppers Drug Mart Corp. to sell its products.

Canadian consumers recognized RCI for often being first with new gadgets, like the iPhone, or being more experimental than rivals with new technologies, like on-line video. However, RCI's main competitors, Bell Canada and TELUS, have teamed up to build an advanced network together, erasing one of Rogers' technological leads.[25]

Mohamed fully realized that it is a competitive place within which to do business, but also an important one for RCI. Looking at the company's balance sheets, he knows that RCI, with a total market capitalization of $20.64 billion,[26] has over 8.9 million wireless subscribers generating approximately $6.9 billion in revenue, making wireless and data account for approximately 56 percent of RCI's overall revenues.[27] In comparison, Bell, one of RCI's major competitors, has a larger market capitalization of $25.44 billion,[28] yet fewer wireless subscribers (7.15 million), and wireless represents only 27 percent of parent company BCE's overall revenues for 2010.[29] RCI's other main competitor, TELUS, has 6.85 million wireless subscribers and just over $14 billion in market capitalization, with wireless and wireless data representing approximately 74 percent of its $9.7 billion in overall revenues.[30]

Cable TV and Internet

When it first started, cable television was a poor cousin to the over-the-air television broadcasting system. Cable was concentrated in small communities that lacked a local television service. But with technological advances allowing more stations and the development of antenna-unfriendly high-rise buildings, the industry experienced rapid growth in larger cities, with penetration approaching 60 percent of Canadian households by 1975.[31]

Cable growth has been spurred particularly by an array of offerings not available on the air, such as specialty channels and pay television, which target specific viewer groups. The larger cable systems expanded capacity from 20 channels to, in some cases, hundreds of channels. As a result, the number of video channels supplied to the average Canadian home has increased continuously. Two-way (interactive) capability was introduced to facilitate non-programming services such as medical alerts, burglar alarms, and meter readings. By 1998, two-way services and capabilities had increased to such an extent that more than 40 percent of Canadian homes had access to the cable industry's high-speed Internet service.[32]

Also by 1998, 7.8 million homes (about 68 percent of homes with television) and a further 0.5 million commercial establishments now subscribed to cable. Three multisystem companies—RCI, Le Groupe Vidéotron, and Shaw—accounted for over 60 percent of cable subscriptions in Canada.[33]

Mohamed knows that RCI, with 2.3 million cable subscribers and 5 million Internet customers, now generates 33 percent of its overall revenue from its cable division, representing approximately $3 billion in revenues. In comparison, Shaw, with 7.6 million cable and Internet customers, realizes approximately $2.7 billion in revenues.[34]

Media

Despite its affinity for technology, RCI is heavily involved in a very old medium: print. But it's a risky business. RCI's 70 magazines and trade publications, along with its radio and TV stations, which form the media division, account for 11 percent of the company's revenues, but just 3 percent of operating profits.[35]

The global magazine publishing market was believed to be valued at US$ 72.8 billion in 2009; however, this was down 9.4 percent from the previous year. The future does not look bright; losses are anticipated for all regions during this period, though the biggest decline, 13.5 percent, is projected for North America. The Canadian magazine publishing market was estimated to be valued at $1.03 billion in 2009, which represents a 12.2-percent decrease. It is anticipated that the Canadian magazine publishing market will be valued at $1.11 billion by 2013, decreasing by 1.1 percent. The recession is largely responsible for this net decline, with 2009 showing the largest annual losses, at 13.5 percent.[36]

Mohamed realizes that reduced advertising spending due to the worldwide economic slowdown has had a detrimental impact on magazine revenue everywhere. Canadian run-of-press ad pages were down by 9.2 percent in 2008, with each of Canada's top 10 consumer magazines experiencing a loss. This has led to the recent closure of several Canadian magazines, including *Wish*, *Time Canada*, and *Gardening Life*, as well as layoffs at Rogers Publishing and other large Ontario-based publishing companies, such as Brunico Communications and St. Joseph Media.[37]

Moving Forward

Mohamed's path to the top of RCI was quite different from that of Ted Rogers. Mohamed, who comes originally from Tanzania, went to boarding school in England before moving to Vancouver to go to the University of British Columbia.[38] A chartered accountant by training, he has been in the communications industry from the start, as he began his career at TELUS Corp. and moved on to BCTel. After being hired away from BCTel by Rogers, he led RCI's wireless division through its takeover of Microcell Communications in 2004, a deal that made RCI the largest wireless provider in Canada.[39] Mohamed was with Rogers for nine years before taking the position of president and CEO.

For two years, Mohamed reported directly to Ted Rogers and he worked closely with him for more than a year while he was a key member of the Office of the President. Despite the differences in their personalities, he and Rogers shared the same objective: win in business. Mohamed has stated publicly that "We might have chosen to execute differently but we both had the same passion, the same sense of what it would take, the same work ethic. He valued debate. He liked being challenged, but of course he had the final vote." Although not known as a risk taker, throughout his career Mohamed had demonstrated the financial skills and mastery of the industry's technological complexities to give him a reputation for being a smart and innovative problem solver. A colleague stated that Mohamed "is simply the top telecom executive in the country. And the others are very good, believe me. Nadir has huge grey matter. He's always looking for an interesting way to approach a problem. That's part of why he rose through the ranks."[40]

As he was about to step into Ted Rogers' shoes for the first time, Mohamed reflected on the direction he felt the organization should go. What should RCI do to retain its leadership in the increasingly competitive wireless environment? How should it deal with the increasingly consolidated cable industry? Should RCI cut its losses and get out of the dwindling magazine industry? Preparing for his first board meeting as CEO, Mohamed quickly thought about his vision for RCI. He knew it was different than what Rogers would have done and wondered what would be the right way to sell it to the board and the Rogers family. He knew that, without their support, his days at RCI would be numbered.

Discussion Questions

1. What type of leader was Ted Rogers? Put yourself in Mohammed's shoes. Moving forward, what leadership strategies will you need to follow to keep both RCI's board of directors and family owners happy?

2. Do a SWOT analysis of Rogers. Describe the challenges you see RCI facing in the next five years. Knowing these, what opportunities should Mohammed pursue?

3. If he was to pursue these opportunities, prepare a "to do" list for Mohammed's first year in office. What things should Mohamed keep in mind when pursuing these strategies?

4. FURTHER RESEARCH—Examine what strategies Mohamed has undertaken since becoming the CEO. Do you agree or disagree with the direction he's taken?

Glossary

A

Accommodation or smoothing plays down differences and highlights similarities to reduce conflict.

An **accommodative strategy** accepts social responsibility and tries to satisfy economic, legal, and ethical criteria.

Accountability is the requirement to show performance results to a supervisor.

Action research is a collaborative process of collecting data, using it for action planning, and evaluating the results.

Active listening helps the source of a message say what he or she really means.

An **adaptive organization** operates with a minimum of bureaucratic features and encourages worker empowerment and teamwork.

An **administrator** is a manager in a public or non-profit organization.

An **after-action review** identifies lessons learned through a completed project, task force assignment, or special operation.

Agenda setting develops action priorities for accomplishing goals and plans.

Agreeableness is being good-natured, cooperative, and trusting.

An **ambidextrous organization** uses integrated creative teams to simultaneously be good at both producing and creating.

An **amoral manager** fails to consider the ethics of her or his behaviour.

The **anchoring and adjustment heuristic** bases a decision on incremental adjustments from a prior decision point.

An **angel investor** is a wealthy individual willing to invest in a new venture in return for equity in the venture.

In **arbitration**, a neutral third party issues a binding decision to resolve a dispute.

An **assessment centre** examines how job candidates handle simulated work situations.

An **attitude** is a predisposition to act in a certain way.

Attribution is the process of explaining events.

Fundamental **attribution error** overestimates internal factors and underestimates external factors as influences on someone's behaviour.

Authentic leadership activates positive psychological states to achieve self-awareness and positive self-regulation.

Authoritarianism is the degree to which a person tends to defer to authority.

An **authority decision** is made by the leader and then communicated to the group.

A leader with an **autocratic style** acts in a unilateral, command-and-control fashion.

Automation is the total mechanization of a job.

The **availability heuristic** bases a decision on recent information or events.

Avoidance or withdrawal pretends that a conflict doesn't really exist.

B

A **B2B business strategy** uses IT and web portals to link organizations vertically in supply chains.

A **B2C business strategy** uses IT and web portals to link businesses with customers.

A **balanced scorecard** tallies organizational performance in the financial, customer service, internal process, and innovation learning, and sustainability areas.

A **bargaining zone** is the space between one party's minimum reservation point and the other party's maximum reservation point.

Base compensation is a salary or hourly wage paid to an individual.

The **BCG matrix** analyzes business opportunities according to market growth rate and market share.

The **behavioural decision model** describes decision-making with limited information and bounded rationality.

A **behaviourally anchored rating scale** uses specific descriptions of actual behaviours to rate various levels of performance.

Benchmarking uses external and internal comparisons to plan for future improvements.

Best practices are things people and organizations do that lead to superior performance.

Biculturalism occurs when minority members adopt characteristics of majority cultures in order to succeed.

Bonus pay plans provide one-time payments based on performance accomplishments.

In **bottom-up change**, change initiatives come from all levels in the organization.

A **boundaryless organization** eliminates internal boundaries among subsystems and external boundaries with the external environment.

Bounded rationality describes making decisions within the constraints of limited information and alternatives.

Brainstorming engages group members in an open, spontaneous discussion of problems and ideas.

Break-even analysis calculates the point at which revenues cover costs under different "what if" conditions.

The **break-even point** is where revenues = costs.

A **budget** is a plan that commits resources to projects or activities.

A **bureaucracy** is a rational and efficient form of organization founded on logic, order, and legitimate authority.

Bureaucratic control influences behaviour through authority, policies, procedures, job descriptions, budgets, and day-to-day supervision.

Business model innovations result in ways for firms to make money.

A **business plan** describes the direction for a new business and the financing needed to operate it.

A **business strategy** identifies how a division or strategic business unit will compete in its product or service domain.

C

Centralization is the concentration of authority for most decisions at the top level of an organization.

In a **centralized communication network**, communication flows only between individual members and a hub, or centre point.

A **certain environment** offers complete information on possible action alternatives and their consequences.

The **chain of command** links all persons with successively higher levels of authority.

A **change leader**, or **change agent**, tries to change the behaviour of another person or social system.

Changing is the phase where a planned change actually takes place.

Channel richness is the capacity of a communication channel to effectively carry information.

A **charismatic leader** develops special leader–follower relationships and inspires followers in extraordinary ways.

Child labour is the full-time employment of children for work otherwise done by adults.

Clan control influences behaviour through norms and expectations set by the organizational culture.

The **classical decision model** describes decision-making with complete information.

The **classical view of CSR** is that business should focus on profits.

Coaching occurs as an experienced person offers performance advice to a less experienced person.

A **code of ethics** is a formal statement of values and ethical standards.

Coercive power is the capacity to punish or withhold positive outcomes as a means of influencing other people.

Cognitive dissonance is discomfort felt when attitude and behaviour are inconsistent.

Cohesiveness is the degree to which members are attracted to and motivated to remain part of a team.

Collaboration or problem solving involves working through conflict differences and solving problems so everyone wins.

Collective bargaining is the process of negotiating, administering, and interpreting a labour contract.

A **combination strategy** pursues growth, stability, and/or retrenchment in some combination.

Commercializing innovation turns ideas into economic value added.

A **committee** is designated to work on a special task on a continuing basis.

Communication is the process of sending and receiving symbols with meanings attached.

A **communication channel** is the pathway through which a message moves from sender to receiver.

Comparable worth holds that persons performing jobs of similar importance should be paid at comparable levels.

Comparative management studies how management practices differ among countries and cultures.

Competition or authoritative command uses force, superior skill, or domination to "win" a conflict.

Competitive advantage is the ability to do something so well that one outperforms competitors.

The **complacency trap** is being carried along by the flow of events.

A **compressed workweek** allows a full-time job to be completed in less than five days.

Compromise occurs when each party to the conflict gives up something of value to the other.

Growth through **concentration** is growth within the same business area.

A **conceptual skill** is the ability to think analytically to diagnose and solve complex problems.

Concurrent control focuses on what happens during the work process.

A **confirmation error** occurs when focusing only on information that confirms a decision already made.

Conflict is a disagreement over issues of substance and/or an emotional antagonism.

Conscientiousness is being responsible, dependable, and careful.

Constructive stress acts in a positive way to increase effort, stimulate creativity, and encourage diligence in one's work.

A **consultative decision** is made by a leader after receiving information, advice, or opinions from group members.

Contingency planning identifies alternative courses of action to take when things go wrong.

Contingency thinking tries to match management practices with situational demands.

Contingency workers are employed on a part-time and temporary basis to supplement a permanent workforce.

Continuous improvement involves always searching for new ways to improve work quality and performance.

Continuous reinforcement rewards each time a desired behaviour occurs.

In **continuous-process production**, raw materials are continuously transformed by an automated system.

Control charts graphically plot quality trends against control limits.

Controlling is the process of measuring performance and taking action to ensure desired results.

Co-opetition is the strategy of working with rivals on projects of mutual benefit.

A **core competency** is a special strength that gives an organization a competitive advantage.

Core values are beliefs and values shared by organization members.

Corporate governance is the system of control and performance monitoring of top management.

Corporate social responsibility is the obligation of an organization to serve its own interests and those of society.

A **corporate strategy** sets long-term direction for the total enterprise.

A **corporation** is a legal entity that exists separately from its owners.

Corruption involves illegal practices to further one's business interests.

Cost-benefit analysis involves comparing the costs and benefits of each potential course of action.

A **cost leadership strategy** seeks to operate with low cost so that products can be sold at low prices.

CPM/PERT is a combination of the critical path method and the program evaluation and review technique.

Creativity is the generation of a new idea or unique approach that solves a problem or crafts an opportunity.

Credible communication earns trust, respect, and integrity in the eyes of others.

A **crisis** is an unexpected problem that can lead to disaster if not resolved quickly and appropriately.

Crisis management is preparation for the management of crises that threaten an organization's health and well-being.

The **critical-incident technique** keeps a log of someone's effective and ineffective job behaviours.

A **cross-functional team** brings together members from different functional departments.

Cultural intelligence is the ability to accept and adapt to new cultures.

Cultural relativism suggests there is no one right way to behave; ethical behaviour is determined by its cultural context.

Culture is a shared set of beliefs, values, and patterns of behaviour common to a group of people.

Culture shock is the confusion and discomfort a person experiences when in an unfamiliar culture.

Customer relationship management strategically tries to build lasting relationships with and to add value to customers.

A **customer structure** groups together people and jobs that serve the same customers or clients.

D

Data are raw facts and observations.

Debt financing involves borrowing money that must be repaid over time, with interest.

Decentralization is the dispersion of authority to make decisions throughout all organization levels.

A **decentralized communication network** allows all members to communicate directly with one another.

A **decision** is a choice among possible alternative courses of action.

Decision-making is the process of making choices among alternative possible courses of action.

The **decision-making process** begins with identification of a problem and ends with evaluation of implemented solutions.

A **defensive strategy** seeks protection by doing the minimum legally required.

Delegation is the process of distributing and entrusting work to other persons.

A leader with a **democratic style** emphasizes both tasks and people.

Departmentalization is the process of grouping people and jobs into work units.

Destructive stress impairs the performance of an individual.

Differentiation is the degree of difference between subsystems in an organization.

A **differentiation strategy** offers products that are different from the competition.

Discipline is the act of influencing behaviour through reprimand.

Discrimination occurs when someone is denied a job or job assignment for reasons not job-relevant.

Disruptive activities are self-serving behaviours that interfere with team effectiveness.

Distributed leadership is when all members of a team contribute helpful task and maintenance behaviours.

Distributive justice is concerned that people are treated the same regardless of personal characteristics.

Distributive negotiation focuses on win-lose claims made by each party for certain preferred outcomes.

Growth through **diversification** is growth by acquisition of or investment in new and different business areas.

Divestiture sells off parts of the organization to refocus attention on core business areas.

A **divisional structure** groups together people working on the same product, in the same area, with similar customers, or on the same processes.

A **downsizing** strategy decreases the size of operations.

Dysfunctional conflict is destructive and hurts task performance.

E

An **e-business strategy** strategically uses the Internet to gain competitive advantage.

Early retirement incentive programs offer workers financial incentives to retire early.

The **ecological fallacy** assumes that a generalized cultural value applies equally well to all members of the culture.

Inventory control by **economic order quantity** orders replacements whenever inventory level falls to a predetermined point.

Economic value added is a measure of economic value created by profits being higher than the cost of capital.

In **effective communication**, the intended meaning is fully understood by the receiver.

An **effective manager** helps others achieve high performance and satisfaction at work.

Effective negotiation resolves issues of substance while maintaining a positive process.

An **effective team** achieves high levels of task performance, membership satisfaction, and future viability.

Efficient communication occurs at minimum cost.

Electronic grapevines use electronic media to pass messages and information among members of social networks.

An **emergent strategy** unfolds over time as managers learn from and respond to experience.

Emotional conflict results from feelings of anger, distrust, dislike, fear, and resentment, as well as from personality clashes.

Emotional intelligence is the ability to understand emotions and manage relationships effectively.

Emotional stability is being relaxed, secure, and unworried.

Emotions are strong feelings directed toward someone or something.

Employee assistance programs help employees cope with personal stresses and problems.

Employee engagement is willingness to help others and do extra, and feeling positive about the organization.

Employee stock ownership plans help employees purchase stock in their employing companies.

Employment equity is the right to employment and advancement without regard to race, sex, religion, colour, or national origin.

Empowerment allows others to make decisions and exercise discretion in their work.

An **entrepreneur** is willing to pursue opportunities in situations others view as problems or threats.

Entrepreneurship is risk-taking behaviour that results in new opportunities.

Environmental uncertainty is a lack of complete information about the environment.

Equity financing involves exchanging ownership shares for outside investment monies.

Escalating commitment is the continuation of a course of action even though it is not working.

Ethical behaviour is "right" or "good" in the context of a governing moral code.

An **ethical dilemma** is a situation that offers potential benefit or gain and is also unethical.

An **ethical framework** is a personal rule or strategy for making ethical decisions.

Ethical imperialism is an attempt to impose one's ethical standards on other cultures.

Ethics set standards of good or bad, or right or wrong, in one's conduct.

Ethics intensity or issue intensity indicates the degree to which an issue or situation is recognized to pose important ethical challenges.

Ethics mindfulness is enriched awareness that leads to consistent ethical behaviour.

Ethics training seeks to help people understand the ethical aspects of decision-making and to incorporate high ethical standards into their daily behaviour.

Managers with **ethnocentric attitudes** believe the best approaches are found at home and tightly control foreign operations.

Ethnocentrism is the belief that one's membership group or subculture is superior to all others.

The **euro** is the common European currency.

The **European Union** is a political and economic alliance of European countries.

Evidence-based management involves making decisions based on hard facts about what really works.

Existence needs are desires for physical well-being.

Expectancy is a person's belief that working hard will result in high task performance.

Expert power is the capacity to influence other people because of specialized knowledge.

In **exporting**, local products are sold abroad to foreign customers.

External recruitment seeks job applicants from outside the organization.

Extinction discourages behaviour by making the removal of a desirable consequence contingent on its occurrence.

Extraversion is being outgoing, sociable, and assertive.

F

A **family business** is owned and controlled by members of a family.

A **family business feud** occurs when family members have major disagreements over how the business should be run.

Family-friendly benefits help employees achieve better work–life balance.

Feedback is the process of telling someone else how you feel about something that person did or said.

Feedback control takes place after an action is completed.

Feedforward control ensures that directions and resources are right before the work begins.

Filtering is the intentional distortion of information to make it appear most favourable to the recipient.

A **first-mover advantage** comes from being first to exploit a niche or enter a market.

Flexible benefits programs allow employees to choose from a range of benefit options.

Flexible working hours give employees some choice in daily work hours.

A **focus strategy** concentrates on serving a unique market segment better than anyone else.

A **focused cost leadership strategy** seeks the lowest costs of operations within a special market segment.

A **focused differentiation strategy** offers a unique product to a special market segment.

A **force-coercion strategy** pursues change through formal authority and/or the use of rewards or punishments.

Forecasting attempts to predict the future.

Foreign direct investment is building, buying all, or buying part ownership of a business in another country.

A **foreign subsidiary** is a local operation completely owned by a foreign firm.

A **formal group** is officially recognized and supported by the organization.

Formal structure is the official structure of the organization.

Framing error is trying to solve a problem in the context in which it is perceived.

A **franchise** is a form of business where one business owner sells to another the right to operate the same business in another location.

In **franchising**, a fee is paid to a foreign business for rights to locally operate using its name, branding, and methods.

Fringe benefits are non-monetary forms of compensation such as health insurance and retirement plans.

The **functional chimneys problem** is a lack of communication and coordination across functions.

Functional conflict is constructive and helps task performance.

Functional managers are responsible for one area such as finance, marketing, production, personnel, accounting, or sales.

Functional plans indicate how different operations within the organization will help advance the overall strategy.

A **functional strategy** guides activities within one specific area of operations.

A **functional structure** groups together people with similar skills who perform similar tasks.

G

Gain-sharing plans allow employees to share in cost savings or productivity gains realized by their efforts.

A **Gantt chart** graphically displays the scheduling of tasks required to complete a project.

The **gender similarities hypothesis** holds that males and females have similar psychological properties.

The **general environment** is composed of economic, legal-political, technological, socio-cultural, and natural environment conditions.

General managers are responsible for complex, multifunctional units.

Managers with **geocentric attitudes** are high in cultural intelligence and take a collaborative approach to global management practices.

A **geographical structure** groups together people and jobs performed in the same location.

The **glass ceiling** is a hidden barrier to the advancement of women and minorities.

The **glass ceiling effect** is an invisible barrier limiting career advancement of women and members of visible minorities.

A **global business** conducts commercial transactions across national boundaries.

A **global corporation**, or MNC, is a multinational business with extensive operations in more than one foreign country.

In the **global economy**, resources, markets, and competition are worldwide in scope.

Global management involves managing operations in more than one country.

A **global manager** is culturally aware and informed on international affairs.

In **global sourcing**, materials or services are purchased around the world for local use.

A **global strategic alliance** is a partnership in which foreign and domestic firms share resources and knowledge for mutual gains.

Globalization is the worldwide interdependence of resource flows, product markets, and business competition.

A **globalization strategy** adopts standardized products and advertising for use worldwide.

A **graphic rating scale** uses a checklist of traits or characteristics to evaluate performance.

Green innovation is the process of turning ideas into innovations that reduce the carbon footprint of an organization or its products.

A **greenfield investment** builds an entirely new operation in a foreign country.

A **group decision** is made by group members themselves.

Group process is the way team members work together to accomplish tasks.

Groupthink is a tendency for highly cohesive teams to lose their evaluative capabilities.

Growth needs are desires for personal growth and development.

A **growth strategy** involves expansion of the organization's current operations.

H

A **halo effect** occurs when one attribute is used to develop an overall impression of a person or situation.

The **Hawthorne effect** is the tendency of persons singled out for special attention to perform as expected.

Heuristics are strategies for simplifying decision-making.

In a **hierarchy of goals** or **objectives**, lower-level objectives are means to accomplishing higher-level ones.

High-context cultures rely on nonverbal and situational cues as well as on spoken or written words in communication.

A **high-performance organization** consistently achieves excellence while creating a high-quality work environment.

Higher-order needs are esteem and self-actualization needs in Maslow's hierarchy.

Human capital is the economic value of people with job-relevant abilities, knowledge, ideas, energies, and commitments.

The **human relations movement** suggested that managers using good human relations will achieve productivity.

A leader with a **human relations style** emphasizes people over tasks.

Human resource management is the process of attracting, developing, and maintaining a high-quality workforce.

Human resource planning analyzes staffing needs and identifies actions to fill those needs.

A **human skill** or interpersonal skill is the ability to work well in cooperation with other people.

A **hygiene factor** is found in the job context, such as working conditions, interpersonal relations, organizational policies, and salary.

I

An **immoral manager** chooses to behave unethically.

Importing involves the selling in domestic markets of products acquired abroad.

Impression management is the systematic attempt to influence how others perceive us.

Improvement objectives describe intentions for specific performance improvements.

Incremental change bends and adjusts existing ways to improve performance.

Independent contractors are hired as needed and are not part of the organization's permanent workforce.

Individualism–collectivism is the degree to which a society emphasizes individuals and their self-interests.

In the **individualism view**, ethical behaviour advances long-term self-interests.

An **informal group** is unofficial and emerges from relationships and shared interests among members.

Informal structure is the set of unofficial relationships among an organization's members.

Information is data made useful for decision-making.

Information systems use IT to collect, organize, and distribute data for use in decision-making.

Information technology helps us acquire, store, and process information.

An **initial public offering**, or **IPO**, is an initial selling of shares of stock to the public at large.

Innovation is the process of taking a new idea and putting it into practice.

An **input standard** measures work efforts that go into a performance task.

Insourcing is job creation through foreign direct investment.

Instrumental values are preferences regarding the means to desired ends.

Instrumentality is a person's belief that various outcomes will occur as a result of task performance.

Integration is the level of coordination achieved between subsystems in an organization.

Integrity in leadership is honesty, credibility, and consistency in putting values into action.

Intellectual capital is the collective brainpower or shared knowledge of a workforce.

Intensive technology focuses the efforts and talents of many people to serve clients.

Interactional justice is the degree to which others are treated with dignity and respect.

Interactive leadership leaders are strong communicators and act in a democratic and participative manner with followers.

Intermittent reinforcement rewards behaviour only periodically.

Internal recruitment seeks job applicants from inside the organization.

Internet censorship is the deliberate blockage and denial of public access to information posted on the Internet.

Intuitive thinking approaches problems in a flexible and spontaneous fashion.

Inventory is an amount of materials or products kept in storage.

ISO certification indicates conformity with a rigorous set of international quality standards.

J

A **job analysis** studies exactly what is done in a job, and why.

Job burnout is physical and mental exhaustion from work stress.

A **job description** details the duties and responsibilities of a job holder.

Job design is arranging work tasks for individuals and groups.

Job enlargement increases task variety by combining into one job two or more tasks previously done by separate workers.

Job enrichment increases job depth by adding work planning and evaluating duties normally performed by the supervisor.

Job involvement is the extent to which an individual is dedicated to a job.

In **job rotation,** people switch tasks to learn multiple jobs.

Job satisfaction is the degree to which an individual feels positive or negative about a job.

Job sharing splits one job between two or more people.

Job simplification employs people in clearly defined and specialized tasks with narrow job scope.

Job specifications list the qualifications required of a job holder.

A **joint venture** operates in a foreign country through co-ownership by foreign and local partners.

Just-in-time scheduling minimizes inventory by sending out materials to workstations "just in time" to be used.

In the **justice view**, ethical behaviour treats people impartially and fairly.

K

Knowledge management is the process of using intellectual capital for competitive advantage.

A **knowledge worker** is someone whose mind is a critical asset to employers.

L

A **labour contract** is a formal agreement between a union and employer about the terms of work for union members.

A **labour union** is an organization that deals with employers on the workers' collective behalf.

Lack-of-participation error is failure to involve in a decision the persons whose support is needed to implement it.

A leader with a **laissez-faire style** displays a "do the best you can and don't bother me" attitude.

The **law of effect** states that behaviour followed by pleasant consequences is likely to be repeated; behaviour followed by unpleasant consequences is not.

Leadership is the process of inspiring others to work hard to accomplish important tasks.

Leadership style is the recurring pattern of behaviours exhibited by a leader.

Leading is the process of arousing enthusiasm and inspiring efforts to achieve goals.

Learning is a change in behaviour that results from experience.

A **learning organization** continuously changes and improves, using the lessons of experience.

Legitimate power is the capacity to influence other people by virtue of formal authority, or the rights of office.

In a **licensing agreement**, a local firm pays a fee to a foreign firm for rights to make or sell its products.

Lifelong learning is continuous learning from daily experiences.

A **limited liability corporation** is a hybrid business form combining advantages of the sole proprietorship, partnership, and corporation.

Line managers directly contribute to producing the organization's goods or services.

In **liquidation**, business operations cease and assets are sold to pay creditors.

Locus of control is the extent to which one believes that what happens is within one's control.

In **long-linked technology**, a client moves from point to point during service delivery.

In **lose-lose conflict**, no one achieves his or her true desires, and the underlying reasons for conflict remain unaffected.

Low-context cultures emphasize communication via spoken or written words.

Lower-order needs are physiological, safety, and social needs in Maslow's hierarchy.

M

Machiavellianism describes the extent to which someone is emotionally detached and manipulative.

A **maintenance activity** is an action taken by a team member that supports the emotional life of the group.

Management is the process of planning, organizing, leading, and controlling the use of resources to accomplish performance goals.

Management by exception focuses attention on substantial differences between actual and desired performance.

Management by objectives or **MBO** is a process of joint objective-setting between a superior and subordinate.

In **management by wandering around (MBWA)**, managers spend time outside their offices to meet and talk with workers at all levels.

Management development is training to improve knowledge and skills in the management process.

Management information systems meet the information needs of managers in making daily decisions.

Management science and **operations research** use quantitative analysis and applied mathematics to solve problems.

A **manager** is a person who supports, activates, and is responsible for the work of others.

A **managerial competency** is a skill-based capability for high performance in a management job.

Managing diversity is building an inclusive work environment that allows everyone to reach their full potential.

Market control is essentially the influence of market competition on the behaviour of organizations and their members.

Market value added is a performance measure of stock market value relative to the cost of capital.

Masculinity–femininity is the degree to which a society values assertiveness and materialism.

Mass production manufactures a large number of uniform products with an assembly-line system.

A **matrix structure** combines functional and divisional approaches to emphasize project or program teams.

A **mechanistic design** is centralized, with many rules and procedures, a clear-cut division of labour, narrow spans of control, and formal coordination.

Mediating technology links people together in a beneficial exchange of values.

In **mediation**, a neutral party tries to help conflicting parties improve communication to resolve their dispute.

Mentoring assigns early career employees as proteges to more senior ones.

Merit pay awards pay increases in proportion to performance contributions.

Middle managers oversee the work of large departments or divisions.

A **mission** statement expresses the organization's reason for existence in society.

A **mixed message** results when words communicate one message while actions, body language, or appearance communicates something else.

Modelling uses personal behaviour to demonstrate performance expected of others.

In **monochronic cultures**, people tend to do one thing at a time.

Mood contagion is the spillover of one's positive or negative moods onto others.

Moods are generalized positive and negative feelings or states of mind.

Moral leadership is always "good" and "right" by ethical standards.

A **moral manager** makes ethical behaviour a personal goal.

In the **moral rights view**, ethical behaviour respects and protects fundamental rights.

Most favoured nation status gives a trading partner most favourable treatment for imports and exports.

Motion study is the science of reducing a task to its basic physical motions.

Motivation accounts for the level, direction, and persistence of effort expended at work.

A **multicultural organization** is based on pluralism and operates with inclusivity and respect for diversity.

Multiculturalism involves pluralism and respect for diversity.

Multidimensional thinking is an ability to address many problems at once.

A **multi-domestic strategy** customizes products and advertising to best fit local needs.

A **multi-person comparison** compares one person's performance with that of others.

N

NAFTA is the North American Free Trade Agreement linking Canada, the United States, and Mexico in an economic alliance.

Necessity-based entrepreneurship takes place because other employment options don't exist.

A **need** is an unfulfilled physiological or psychological desire.

Need for achievement is the desire to do something better, to solve problems, or to master complex tasks.

Need for affiliation is the desire to establish and maintain good relations with people.

Need for power is the desire to control, influence, or be responsible for other people.

Negative reinforcement strengthens behaviour by making the avoidance of an undesirable consequence contingent on its occurrence.

Negotiation is the process of making joint decisions when the parties involved have different preferences.

A **network structure** uses information technologies to link with networks of outside suppliers and service contractors.

Networking is the process of creating positive relationships with people who can help advance agendas.

The **nominal group technique** structures interaction among team members discussing problems and ideas.

A **nonprogrammed decision** applies a specific solution crafted for a unique problem.

Nonverbal communication takes place through gestures and body language.

A **norm** is a behaviour, rule, or standard expected to be followed by team members.

O

Objectives are specific results that one wishes to achieve.

An **obstructionist strategy** avoids social responsibility and reflects mainly economic priorities.

An **OD intervention** is a structured activity that helps create change for organization development.

An **open system** transforms resource inputs from the environment into product outputs.

Openness to experience is being curious, receptive to new ideas, and imaginative.

Operant conditioning is the control of behaviour by manipulating its consequences.

Operating objectives are specific results that organizations try to accomplish.

An **operational plan** identifies short-term activities to implement strategic plans.

Operations management is the process of managing productive systems that transform resources into finished products.

An **optimizing decision** chooses the alternative giving the absolute best solution to a problem.

An **organic design** is decentralized, with fewer rules and procedures, open divisions of labour, wide spans of control, and more personal coordination.

An **organization** is a collection of people working together to achieve a common purpose.

An **organization chart** describes the arrangement of work positions within an organization.

Organization development is a shared power effort to improve an organization's ability to solve problems and improve performance.

Organization structure is a system of tasks, reporting relationships, and communication linkages.

Organizational behaviour is the study of individuals and groups in organizations.

Organizational citizenship is a willingness to "go beyond the call of duty" or "go the extra mile" in one's work.

Organizational commitment is the loyalty of an individual to the organization.

Organizational culture is the system of shared beliefs and values that guides behaviour in organizations.

Organizational design is the process of creating structures that accomplish mission and objectives.

Organizational effectiveness is sustainable high performance in using resources to accomplish a mission.

Organizational subcultures exist among people with similar values and beliefs based on shared work responsibilities and personal characteristics.

Organizing is the process of assigning tasks, allocating resources, and coordinating work activities.

Orientation familiarizes new employees with jobs, co-workers, and organizational policies and services.

An **output standard** measures performance results in terms of quantity, quality, cost, or time.

P

Part-time work is temporary employment for less than the standard 40-hour workweek.

Participatory planning includes the persons who will be affected by plans

and/or those who will implement them.

A **partnership** is a form of business where two or more people agree to contribute resources to start and operate a business together.

Perception is the process through which people receive, organize, and interpret information from the environment.

Performance appraisal is the process of formally evaluating performance and providing feedback to a job holder.

Performance effectiveness is an output measure of task or goal accomplishment.

Performance efficiency is an input measure of resource cost associated with goal accomplishment.

A **performance gap** is a discrepancy between a desired and an actual state of affairs.

A **performance management system** sets standards, assesses results, and plans for performance improvements.

Personal development objectives describe intentions for personal growth through knowledge and skills development.

Personal wellness is the pursuit of one's full potential through a personal health-promotion program.

Personality is the profile of characteristics making a person unique from others.

Persuasive communication presents a message in a manner that causes the other person to support it.

A **plan** is a statement of intended means for accomplishing objectives.

Planned change aligns the organization with anticipated future challenges.

Planning is the process of setting objectives and determining what should be done to accomplish them.

A **policy** is a standing plan that communicates broad guidelines for decisions and action.

Political risk is the potential loss in value of a foreign investment due to instability and political changes in the host country.

Political-risk analysis tries to forecast political disruptions that can threaten the value of a foreign investment.

Managers with **polycentric attitudes** respect local knowledge and allow foreign operations to run with substantial freedom.

In **polychronic cultures**, time is used to accomplish many different things at once.

A **portfolio planning** approach seeks the best mix of investments among alternative business opportunities.

A **portfolio worker** has up-to-date skills that allow for job and career mobility.

Positive reinforcement strengthens behaviour by making a desirable consequence contingent on its occurrence.

Power is the ability to get someone else to do something you want done or to make things happen the way you want.

Power distance is the degree to which a society accepts unequal distribution of power.

Pregnancy discrimination penalizes a woman in a job or as a job applicant for being pregnant.

Prejudice is the display of negative, irrational attitudes toward members of diverse populations.

Principled negotiation or integrative negotiation uses a "win-win" orientation to reach solutions acceptable to each party.

A **proactive strategy** meets all the criteria of social responsibility, including discretionary performance.

Problem solving involves identifying and taking action to resolve problems.

Procedural justice is concerned that policies and rules are fairly applied.

A **procedure** or **rule** precisely describes actions that are to be taken in specific situations.

Process innovations result in better ways of doing things.

Process reengineering systematically analyzes work processes to design new and better ones.

A **process structure** groups jobs and activities that are part of the same processes.

Process value analysis identifies and evaluates core processes for their performance contributions.

Product innovations result in new or improved goods or services.

A **product structure** groups together people and jobs focused on a single product or service.

Productivity is the quantity and quality of work performance, with resource utilization considered.

Profit sharing distributes to employees a proportion of net profits earned by the organization.

A **programmed decision** applies a solution from past experience to a routine problem.

Progressive discipline ties reprimands to the severity and frequency of misbehaviour.

Project management makes sure that activities required to complete a project are planned well and accomplished on time.

Project teams are convened for a particular task or project and disband once it is completed.

Projection is the assignment of personal attributes to other individuals.

Projects are one-time activities with many component tasks that must be completed in proper order, and according to budget.

Protectionism is a call for tariffs and favourable treatments to protect domestic firms from foreign competition.

Proxemics is how people use space to communicate.

A **psychological contract** is the set of individual expectations about the employment relationship.

Punishment discourages behaviour by making an unpleasant consequence contingent on its occurrence.

Q

Quality control checks processes, materials, products, and services to ensure that they meet high standards.

Quality of work life is the overall quality of human experiences in the workplace.

R

A **rational persuasion strategy** pursues change through empirical data and rational argument.

Reactive change responds to events as or after they occur.

Realistic job previews provide job candidates with all pertinent information about a job and organization.

Recruitment is a set of activities designed to attract a qualified pool of job applicants.

Referent power is the capacity to influence other people because of their desire to identify personally with you.

Refreezing is the phase at which change is stabilized.

Relatedness needs are desires for good interpersonal relationships.

Relationship goals in negotiation are concerned with the ways people work together.

Reliability means that a selection device gives consistent results over repeated measures.

A **renewal strategy** tries to solve problems and overcome weaknesses that are hurting performance.

The **representativeness heuristic** bases a decision on similarity to other situations.

In a **restricted communication network**, subgroups have limited communication with one another.

Restructuring changes the mix or reduces the scale of operations.

Reward power is the capacity to offer something of value as a means of influencing other people.

A **risk environment** lacks complete information but offers "probabilities" of the likely outcomes for possible action alternatives.

S

A **satisficing decision** chooses the first satisfactory alternative that comes to one's attention.

A **satisfier factor** is found in job content, such as a sense of achievement, recognition, responsibility, advancement, or personal growth.

Scenario planning identifies alternative future scenarios and makes plans to deal with each.

Scientific management emphasizes careful selection and training of workers and supervisory support.

Selection is choosing individuals to hire from a pool of qualified job applicants.

Selective perception is the tendency to define problems from one's own point of view.

Self-control, or internal control, occurs through self-discipline in fulfilling many responsibilities.

Self-efficacy is a person's belief that she or he is capable of performing a task.

A **self-fulfilling prophecy** occurs when a person acts in ways that confirm another's expectations.

Members of a **self-managing work team** have the authority to make decisions about how they share and complete their work.

Self-monitoring is the degree to which someone is able to adjust behaviour in response to external factors.

Self-serving bias explains personal success by internal causes and personal failures by external causes.

Servant leadership is follower-centred and committed to helping others in their work.

Sexual harassment is behaviour of a sexual nature that affects a person's employment situation.

Shaping is positive reinforcement of successive approximations to the desired behaviour.

A **shared power strategy** pursues change by participation in assessing change needs, values, and goals.

Six Sigma is a quality standard of 3.4 defects or less per million products or service deliveries.

A **skill** is the ability to translate knowledge into action that results in desired performance.

Small-batch production manufactures a variety of products crafted to fit customer specifications.

A **small business** has fewer than 100 employees, is independently owned and operated, and does not dominate its industry.

Social business innovation finds ways to use business models to address important social problems.

Social capital is a capacity to get things done with the support and help of others.

Social entrepreneurship has a mission to solve pressing social problems.

Social loafing is the tendency of some people to avoid responsibility by "free-riding" in groups.

Social network analysis identifies the informal structures and their embedded social relationships that are active in an organization.

A **social responsibility audit** assesses an organization's accomplishments in areas of social responsibility.

Socialization is the process through which new members learn the culture of an organization.

The **socio-economic view of CSR** is that business should focus on broader social welfare as well as profits.

A **sole proprietorship** is a form of business where an individual pursues business for a profit.

Span of control is the number of subordinates directly reporting to a manager.

The **specific environment**, or task environment, includes the people and groups with whom an organization interacts.

A **stability strategy** maintains current operations without substantial changes.

Staff managers use special technical expertise to advise and support line workers.

Staff positions provide technical expertise for other parts of the organization.

Stakeholders are individuals and groups directly affected by the organization and its strategic accomplishments.

Statistical quality control measures work samples for compliance with quality standards.

A **stereotype** occurs when attributes commonly associated with a group are assigned to an individual.

Stock options give the right to purchase shares at a fixed price in the future.

In a **strategic alliance**, organizations join together in partnership to pursue an area of mutual interest.

Strategic analysis is the process of analyzing the organization, the environment, and the organization's competitive position and current strategies.

A **strategic constituencies analysis** assesses interests of stakeholders and how well the organization is responding to them.

Strategic control makes sure strategies are well implemented and that poor strategies are scrapped or modified.

Strategic human resource management mobilizes human capital to implement organizational strategies.

Strategic incrementalism makes modest changes in strategy as experience builds over time.

Strategic intent focuses and applies organizational energies on a unifying and compelling goal.

Strategic leadership inspires people to continuously change, refine, and improve strategies and their implementation.

Strategic management is the process of formulating and implementing strategies.

Strategic opportunism focuses on long-term objectives while being flexible in dealing with short-term problems.

A **strategic plan** identifies long-term directions for the organization.

Strategic positioning occurs when an organization does different things or the same things in different ways from one's major competitors.

A **strategy** is a comprehensive plan guiding resource allocation to achieve long-term organization goals.

Strategy formulation is the process of crafting strategies to guide the allocation of resources.

Strategy implementation is the process of putting strategies into action.

Stress is a state of tension experienced by individuals facing extraordinary demands, constraints, or opportunities.

A **stressor** is anything that causes stress.

Structured problems are straightforward and clear with respect to information needs.

Substance goals in negotiation are concerned with outcomes.

Substantive conflict involves disagreements over goals, resources, rewards, policies, procedures, and job assignments.

Substitutes for leadership are factors in the work setting that direct work efforts without the involvement of a leader.

A **subsystem** is a smaller component of a larger system.

A **succession plan** describes how the leadership transition and related financial matters will be handled.

The **succession problem** is the issue of who will run the business when the current head leaves.

Supply chain management strategically links all operations dealing with resource supplies.

Sustainable business both meets the needs of customers and protects the well-being of our natural environment.

Sustainable competitive advantage is the ability to outperform rivals in ways that are difficult or costly to imitate.

Sustainable development meets the needs of the present without hurting future generations.

Sustainable innovation creates new products and production methods that have reduced environmental impact.

Sweatshops employ workers at very low wages for long hours and in poor working conditions.

A **SWOT analysis** examines organizational strengths and weaknesses and environmental opportunities and threats.

A **symbolic leader** uses symbols to establish and maintain a desired organizational culture.

Synergy is the creation of a whole greater than the sum of its individual parts.

A **system** is a collection of interrelated parts working together for a purpose.

Systematic thinking approaches problems in a rational and analytical fashion.

T

A **tactical plan** helps to implement all or parts of a strategic plan.

Tariffs are taxes governments levy on imports from abroad.

A **task activity** is an action taken by a team member that directly contributes to the group's performance purpose.

A **team** is a collection of people who regularly interact to pursue common goals.

Team building is a sequence of activities to analyze a team and make changes to improve its performance.

Team leaders report to middle managers and supervise nonmanagerial workers.

A **team structure** uses permanent and temporary cross-functional teams to improve lateral relations.

Teamwork is the process of people actively working together to accomplish common goals.

A **technical skill** is the ability to use expertise to perform a task with proficiency.

Technology is the combination of knowledge, skills, equipment, and work methods used to transform inputs into outputs.

Telecommuting involves using IT to work at home or outside the office.

Terminal values are preferences about desired end states.

Termination is the involuntary dismissal of an employee.

Theory X assumes people dislike work, lack ambition, act irresponsibly, and prefer to be led.

Theory Y assumes people are willing to work, like responsibility, and are self-directed and creative.

360° feedback includes superiors, subordinates, peers, and even customers in the appraisal process.

Time orientation is the degree to which a society emphasizes short-term or long-term goals.

In **top-down change**, the change initiatives come from senior management.

Top managers guide the performance of the organization as a whole or of one of its major parts.

Total quality management is managing with an organization-wide commitment to continuous improvement, product quality, and customer needs.

Traditional recruitment focuses on selling the job and organization to applicants.

Training provides learning opportunities to acquire and improve job-related skills.

Transactional leadership uses tasks, rewards, and structures to influence and direct the efforts of others.

Transformational change results in a major and comprehensive redirection of the organization.

Transformational leadership is inspirational and arouses extraordinary effort and performance.

A **transnational corporation** is an MNC that operates worldwide on a borderless basis.

A **transnational strategy** seeks efficiencies of global operations with attention to local markets.

A **turnaround strategy** tries to fix specific performance problems.

Two-tier wage systems pay new hires less than workers already doing the same jobs with more seniority.

A **Type A personality** is a person oriented toward extreme achievement, impatience, and perfectionism.

U

An **uncertain environment** lacks so much information that it is difficult to assign probabilities to the likely outcomes of alternatives.

Uncertainty avoidance is the degree to which a society tolerates risk and uncertainty.

Unfreezing is the phase during which a situation is prepared for change.

Universalism suggests ethical standards apply absolutely across all cultures.

Unstructured problems have ambiguities and information deficiencies.

In the **upside-down pyramid,** operating workers are at the top serving customers while managers are at the bottom supporting them.

In the **utilitarian view**, ethical behaviour delivers the greatest good to the most people.

V

Valence is the value a person assigns to work-related outcomes.

Validity means that scores on a selection device have demonstrated links with future job performance.

Value-based management actively develops, communicates, and enacts shared values.

The **value chain** is the specific sequence of activities that creates products and services with value for customers.

Value creation occurs when the result of a work task or activity makes a product or service worth more in terms of potential customer appeal than at the start.

Values are broad beliefs about what is appropriate behaviour.

Venture capitalists make large investments in new ventures in return for an equity stake in the business.

Growth through **vertical integration** is growth by acquiring suppliers or distributors.

A **virtual organization** uses IT and the Internet to engage a shifting network of strategic alliances.

Members of a **virtual team** work together and solve problems through computer-based interactions.

The **virtuous circle** occurs when CSR improves financial performance, which leads to more CSR.

A **vision** clarifies the purpose of the organization and expresses what it hopes to be in the future.

Visionary leadership brings to the situation a clear sense of the future and an understanding of how to get there.

W

A **whistleblower** exposes the misdeeds of others in organizations.

In **win-lose conflict**, one party achieves its desires, and the other party does not.

In **win-win conflict**, the conflict is resolved to everyone's benefit.

Work–life balance involves balancing career demands with personal and family needs.

A **work process** is a group of related tasks that collectively creates a valuable work product.

In **work sampling**, applicants are evaluated while performing actual work tasks.

Workflow is the movement of work from one point to another in a system.

Workforce diversity describes differences among workers in gender, race, age, ethnicity, religion, sexual orientation, and able-bodiedness.

Workplace privacy is the right to privacy while at work.

Workplace rage is aggressive behaviour toward co-workers or the work setting.

Workplace spirituality creates meaning and shared community among organizational members.

World Trade Organization member nations agree to negotiate and resolve disputes about tariffs and trade restrictions.

Wrongful dismissal is a doctrine giving workers legal protections against discriminatory firings.

Z

A **zero-based budget** allocates resources as if each budget were brand new.

Self-Test Answers

Chapter 1

1. d   2. c   3. a   4. b   5. a   6. a   7. c   8. a   9. b   10. b
11. c   12. a   13. b   14. c   15. c

16. Managers must value people and respect subordinates as mature, responsible, adult human beings. This is part of their ethical and social responsibility as persons to whom others report at work. The work setting should be organized and managed to respect the rights of people and their human dignity. Included among the expectations for ethical behaviour would be actions to protect individual privacy, provide freedom from sexual harassment, and offer safe and healthy job conditions. Failure to do so is socially irresponsible. It may also cause productivity losses due to dissatisfaction and poor work commitments.

17. The manager is held accountable by her boss for the performance results of her work unit. The manager must answer to her boss for unit performance. By the same token, the manager's subordinates must answer to her for their individual performance. They are accountable to her.

18. If the glass ceiling effect were to operate in a given situation, it would act as a hidden barrier to advancement beyond a certain level. Managers controlling promotions and advancement opportunities in the firm would not give them to African-Canadian candidates, regardless of their capabilities. Although the newly hired graduates might progress for a while, sooner or later their upward progress in the firm would be halted by this invisible barrier.

19. Globalization means that the countries and peoples of the world are increasingly interconnected and that firms increasingly cross national boundaries in acquiring resources, getting work accomplished, and selling their products. This internationalization of work will affect most everyone in the new economy. People will be working with others from different countries, working in other countries, and certainly buying and using products and services produced in whole or in part in other countries. As countries become more interdependent economically, products are sold and resources purchased around the world, and business strategies increasingly target markets in more than one country.

20. One approach to this question is through the framework of essential management skills offered by Katz. At the first level of management, technical skills are important, and I would feel capable in this respect. However, I would expect to learn and refine these skills through my work experiences.

Human skills, the ability to work well with other people, will also be very important. Given the diversity anticipated for this team, I will need good human skills. Included here would be my emotional intelligence, or the ability to understand my emotions and those of others when I am interacting with them. I will also have a leadership responsibility to help others on the team develop and use these skills so that the team itself can function effectively.

Finally, I would expect opportunities to develop my conceptual or analytical skills in anticipation of higher-level appointments. In terms of personal development, I should recognize that the conceptual skills will increase in importance relative to the technical skills as I move upward in management responsibility. The fact that the members of the team will be diverse, with some of different demographic and cultural backgrounds from my own, will only increase the importance of my abilities in the human skills area.

It will be a challenge to embrace and value differences to create the best work experience for everyone and to fully value everyone's potential contributions to the audits we will be doing. Conceptually I will need to understand the differences and try to use them to solve problems faced by the team, but in human relationships I will need to excel at keeping the team spirit alive and keeping everyone committed to working well together over the life of our projects.

Chapter 2

1. c   2. b   3. d   4. a   5. a   6. b   7. a   8. c   9. a   10. a
11. c   12. a   13. d   14. c   15. b

16. Theory Y assumes that people are capable of taking responsibility and exercising self-direction and control in their work. The notion of self-fulfilling prophecies is that managers who hold these assumptions will act in ways that encourage workers to display these characteristics, thus confirming and reinforcing the original assumptions. The emphasis on greater participation and involvement in the modern workplace is an example of Theory Y assumptions in practice. Presumably, by valuing participation and involvement, managers will create self-fulfilling prophecies in which workers behave this way in response to being treated with respect. The result is a positive setting where everyone gains.

17. According to the deficit principle, a satisfied need is not a motivator of behaviour. The social need will only motivate if it is not present, or in deficit. According to the progression principle, people move step by step up Maslow's hierarchy as

they strive to satisfy needs. For example, once the social need is satisfied, the esteem need will be activated.

18. Contingency thinking takes an "if-then" approach to situations. It seeks to modify or adapt management approaches to fit the needs of each situation. An example would be to give more customer contact responsibility to workers who want to satisfy social needs at work, while giving more supervisory responsibilities to those who want to satisfy their esteem or ego needs.

19. The external environment is the source of the resources an organization needs to operate. In order to continue to obtain these resources, the organization must be successful in selling its goods and services to customers. If customer feedback is negative, the organization must make adjustments or risk losing the support needed to obtain important resources.

20. A bureaucracy operates with a strict hierarchy of authority, promotion based on competency and performance, formal rules and procedures, and written documentation. Enrique can do all of these things in his store, since the situation is probably quite stable and most work requirements are routine and predictable. However, bureaucracies are quite rigid and may deny employees the opportunity to make decisions on their own. Enrique must be careful to meet the needs of the workers and not to make the mistake—identified by Argyris—of failing to treat them as mature adults. While remaining well organized, the store manager should still be able to help workers meet higher-order esteem and self-fulfillment needs, as well as assume responsibility consistent with McGregor's Theory Y assumptions.

Chapter 3

1. c   2. c   3. b   4. d   5. a   6. a   7. d   8. c   9. a   10. d
11. d   12. a   13. c   14. c   15. c

16. The relationship between an MNC and a host country should be mutually beneficial. Sometimes, however, host countries complain that MNCs take unfair advantage of them and do not include them in the benefits of their international operations. The complaints against MNCs include taking excessive profits out of the host country, hiring the best local labour, not respecting local laws and customs, and dominating the local economy. Engaging in corrupt practices is another important concern.

17. The power-distance dimension of national culture reflects the degree to which members of a society accept status and authority inequalities. Since organizations are hierarchies with power varying from top to bottom, the way power differences are viewed from one setting to the next is an important

management issue. Relations between managers and subordinates, or team leaders and team members, will be very different in high-power-distance cultures than in low-power-distance ones. The significance of these differences is most evident in international operations, when a manager from a high-power-distance culture has to perform in a low-power-distance one, or vice versa. In both cases, the cultural differences can cause problems as the manager deals with local workers.

18. In Project GLOBE, the cultural dimension of institutional collectivism describes the degree to which members of a society emphasize and reward group actions, rather than individual actions. In-group collectivism describes a society in which members take pride in family and their group or organizational memberships.

19. For each region of the world, you should identify a major economic theme, issue, or element. For example: Europe—the European Union should be discussed for its economic significance to member countries and to outsiders; the Americas—NAFTA should be discussed for its current implications, as well as its potential significance once Chile and other nations join; Asia—the Asia-Pacific Economic Forum should be identified as a platform for growing regional economic cooperation among a very economically powerful group of countries; Africa—the new nonracial democracy in South Africa should be cited as a stimulus to broader outside investor interest in Africa.

20. Monique must recognize that the cultural differences between Canada and Japan may affect the success of group-oriented work practices such as quality circles and work teams. Canada was among the most individualistic cultures in Hofstede's study of national cultures; Japan is much more collectivist. Group practices such as the quality circle and teams are natural and consistent with the Japanese culture. When introduced into a more individualistic culture, these same practices might cause difficulties or require some time for workers to get used to them. At the very least, Monique should proceed with caution; discuss ideas for the new practices with the workers before making any changes; and then monitor the changes closely, so that adjustments can be made to improve them as the workers gain familiarity with them and have suggestions of their own.

Chapter 4

1. b   2. a   3. d   4. c   5. c   6. d   7. b   8. a   9. c   10. b
11. d   12. c   13. d   14. b   15. d

16. The individualism view is that ethical behaviour is that which best serves long-term interests. The justice view is

that ethical behaviour is fair and equitable in its treatment of people.

17. The rationalizations are believing that: (1) the behaviour is not really illegal, (2) the behaviour is really in everyone's best interests, (3) no one will find out, and (4) the organization will protect you.

18. The socio-economic view of corporate social responsibility argues that socially responsible behaviour is in a firm's long-run best interest. It should be good for profits, it creates a positive public image, it helps avoid government regulation, it meets public expectations, and it is an ethical obligation.

19. A board of directors of a business is ultimately responsible for the decisions and actions of the top management and the performance of the organization as a whole. The board members would normally be involved in such decisions as hiring/firing top management, setting compensation of top management, verifying and approving financial records and reports, and approving corporate strategies.

20. The manager could make a decision based on any one of the strategies. As an obstructionist, the manager may assume that Bangladesh needs the business and that it is a local matter as to who will be employed to make the gloves. As a defensive strategy, the manager may decide to require the supplier to meet the minimum employment requirements under Bangladeshi law. Both of these approaches represent cultural relativism. As an accommodation strategy, the manager may require that the supplier go beyond local laws and meet standards set by equivalent laws in Canada. A proactive strategy would involve the manager in trying to set an example by operating in Bangladesh only with suppliers who not only meet local standards but also actively support the education of children in the communities in which they operate. These latter two approaches would be examples of universalism.

Chapter 5

1. c 2. a 3. b 4. b 5. b 6. a 7. d 8. a 9. b 10. a
11. b 12. d 13. c 14. b 15. d

16. Entrepreneurship is rich with diversity. It is an avenue for business entry and career success that is pursued by many women and members of minority groups. Data show that almost 45% of Canadian SMEs are owned by women. Many report leaving other employment because they had limited opportunities. For them, entrepreneurship made available the opportunities for career success that they had lacked. Minority-owned businesses are one of the fastest-growing

sectors of the Canadian economy, where members of visible minorities are entering the SME marketplace in great numbers.

17. The three stages in the life cycle of an entrepreneurial firm are birth, breakthrough, and maturity. In the birth stage, the leader is challenged to get customers, establish a market, and find the money needed to keep the business going. In the breakthrough stage, the challenges shift to becoming and staying profitable, and managing growth. In the maturity stage, a leader is more focused on revising/maintaining a good business strategy and more generally managing the firm for continued success, and possibly for more future growth.

18. The limited partnership form of small business ownership consists of a general partner and one or more "limited partners." The general partner(s) play an active role in managing and operating the business; the limited partners do not. All contribute resources of some value to the partnership for the conduct of the business. The advantage of any partnership form is that the partners may share in profits, but their potential for losses is limited by the size of their original investments.

19. A venture capitalist, often a business, makes a living by investing in and taking large ownership interests in fledgling companies, with the goal of large financial gains eventually, when the company is sold. An angel investor is an individual who is willing to make a financial investment in return for some ownership in the new firm.

20. My friend is right—it takes a lot of forethought and planning to prepare the launch of a new business venture. In response to the question of how to ensure that I am really being customer-focused, I would ask and answer for myself the following questions. In all cases, I would try to frame my business model so that the answers are realistic, but still push my business toward a strong customer orientation. The "customer" questions might include: "Who are my potential customers? What market niche am I shooting for? What do the customers in this market really want? How do these customers make purchase decisions? How much will it cost to produce and distribute my product/service to these customers? How much will it cost to attract and retain customers?" After preparing an overall executive summary, which includes a commitment to this customer orientation, I would address the following areas in writing up my initial business plan: a company description—mission, owners, and legal form—as well as an industry analysis, product and services description, marketing description and strategy, staffing model, financial projections with cash flows, and capital needs.

Chapter 6

1. d   2. a   3. b   4. d   5. b   6. c   7. a   8. d   9. a   10. b
11. a   12. c   13. c   14. d   15. a

16. The five steps in the formal planning process are: (1) define your objectives, (2) determine where you stand relative to objectives, (3) develop premises about future conditions, (4) identify and choose among action alternatives to accomplish objectives, and (5) implement action plans and evaluate results.

17. Benchmarking is the use of external standards to help evaluate one's own situation and develop ideas and directions for improvement. The bookstore owner/manager might visit other bookstores in other towns that are known for their success. By observing and studying the operations of those stores and then comparing her store with them, the owner/manager can develop plans for future action.

18. Planning helps improve focus for organizations and for individuals. Essential to the planning process is identifying your objectives and specifying exactly where it is you hope to get in the future. Having a clear sense of direction helps keep us on track by avoiding getting sidetracked on things that might not contribute to accomplishing our objectives. It also helps us to achieve discipline in stopping periodically to assess how well we are doing. With a clear objective, present progress can be realistically evaluated and efforts refocused on accomplishing the objective.

19. Very often plans fail because the people who make the plans aren't the same ones who must implement them. When people who will be implementing are allowed to participate in the planning process, at least two positive results may happen that help improve implementation: (1) through involvement, they better understand the final plans; and (2) through involvement, they become more committed to making those plans work.

20. I would begin the speech by describing MBO as an integrated planning and control approach. I would also clarify that the key elements in MBO are objectives and participation. Any objectives should be clear, measurable, and time-defined. In addition, these objectives should be set with the full involvement and participation of the employees; they should not be set by the manager and then told to the employees. That understood, I would describe how each business manager should jointly set objectives with each of his or her employees and jointly review progress toward their accomplishment. I would suggest that the employees should work on the required activities while staying in communication with their managers. The managers, in turn, should provide any needed support or assistance to their employees. This whole process could be formally recycled at least twice per year.

Chapter 7

1. a   2. b   3. c   4. c   5. d   6. b   7. c   8. a   9. b   10. a
11. d   12. c   13. d   14. b   15. a

16. A corporate strategy sets long-term direction for an enterprise as a whole. Functional strategies set directions so that business functions such as marketing and manufacturing support the overall corporate strategy.

17. A SWOT analysis is useful during strategic planning. It involves the analysis of organizational strengths and weaknesses, and of environmental opportunities and threats.

18. An e-business strategy uses the Internet to help achieve sustainable competitive advantage. This can be done through B2B strategies that link businesses electronically with one another in business-to-business relationships. A good example is B2B in supply chain management, where suppliers are linked by the Internet and extranets to customers' information systems. They follow sales and track inventories in real time and ship new orders as needed. The B2C approach is more of a retailing model linking businesses to customers. An example is Amazon.com, which uses on-line sales and on-line customer interaction to sell its products.

19. Strategic leadership is the ability to enthuse people to participate in continuous change, performance enhancement, and the implementation of organizational strategies. The special qualities of the successful strategic leader include the ability to make trade-offs, create a sense of urgency, communicate the strategy, and engage others in continuous learning about the strategy and its performance responsibilities.

20. Porter's competitive strategy model involves the possible use of three alternative strategies: differentiation, cost leadership, and focus. In this situation, the larger department store seems better positioned to follow the cost leadership strategy. This means that Tashlin may want to consider the other two alternatives. A differentiation strategy would involve trying to distinguish Tashlin's products from those of the larger store. This might involve a "made in Canada" theme, or an emphasis on leather, canvas, or some other type of clothing material. A focus strategy might specifically target university students and try to respond to their tastes and needs, rather than those of the larger community population. This might involve special orders and other types of individualized service for the student market.

Chapter 8

1. b   2. a   3. b   4. a   5. b   6. c   7. b   8. b   9. a   10. d
11. c   12. b   13. b   14. c   15. b

16. The functional structure is prone to problems of internal coordination. One symptom may be that the different functional areas, such as marketing and manufacturing, are not working well together. This structure is also slow in responding to changing environmental trends and challenges. If the firm finds that its competitors are getting to market faster with new and better products, this is another potential indicator that the functional structure is not supporting operations properly.

17. A network structure often involves one organization "contracting out" aspects of its operations to other organizations that specialize in them. The example used in the text was of a company that contracted out its mailroom services. Through the formation of networks of contracts, the organization is reduced to a core of essential employees whose expertise is concentrated in the primary business areas. The contracts are monitored and maintained in the network to allow the overall operations of the organization to continue, even though they are not directly accomplished by full-time employees.

18. The term "contingency" is used in management to indicate that management strategies and practices should be tailored to fit the unique needs of individual situations. There is no universal solution that fits all problems and circumstances. Thus, in organizational design, contingency thinking must be used to identify and implement particular organizational structures at particular points in time. What works well at one point in time may not work well at another, as the environment and other conditions change. For example, the more complex, variable, and uncertain the elements in the environment, the more difficult it is for the organization to operate. This situation calls for a more organic design. In a stable and more certain environment, the mechanistic design is appropriate, because operations are more routine and predictable.

19. Differentiation and integration are somewhat conflicting in organizational design. As differentiation increases—that is, as more differences are present in the complexity of the organization—more integration is needed to ensure that everything functions together to the betterment of the whole organization. However, the greater the differentiation, the harder it is to achieve integration. Thus, when differentiation is high, organization design tends to shift toward the use of more complex horizontal approaches to integration and away from the vertical ones, such as formal authority and rules or policies. In horizontal integration, the focus is on such things as cross-functional teams and matrix structures.

20. Faisal must first have confidence in the two engineers—he must trust them and respect their capabilities. Second, he must have confidence in himself, trusting his own judgement to give up some work and allow the others to do it. Third, he should follow the rules of effective delegation. These include being very clear on what must be accomplished by each engineer. Their responsibilities should be clearly understood. He must also give them the authority to act in order to fulfill their responsibility, especially in relation to the other engineers. And he must not forget his own final accountability for the results. He should remain in control and, through communication, make sure that work proceeds as planned.

Chapter 9

1. b   2. a   3. b   4. c   5. c   6. b   7. c   8. a   9. d   10. a
11. a   12. d   13. b   14. a   15. b

16. A product innovation is one that results in a new or substantially modified product that an organization can sell or offer to its customers. A process innovation is a new or improved way of getting work done in the organization. A business model innovation is a new way to earn money as a business, or to earn clients as a non-profit organization.

17. Lewin's three phases of planned change are: unfreezing—preparing a system for change; changing—moving or creating change in a system; and refreezing—stabilizing and reinforcing change once it has occurred.

18. In general, managers can expect that others will be more committed and loyal to changes that are brought about through shared power strategies. Rational persuasion strategies can also create enduring effects if they are accepted. Force-coercion strategies tend to have temporary effects only.

19. The statement that "OD equals planned change plus" basically refers to the fact that organizational development tries both to create change in an organization and to make the organization members capable of creating such change for themselves in the future.

20. In any change situation, it is important to remember that successful planned change occurs only when all three phases of change—unfreezing, changing, and refreezing—have been taken care of. Thus, I would not rush into the changing phase. Rather, I would work with the people involved to develop a felt need for change based on their ideas and inputs, as well as mine. Then I would proceed by supporting the changes and helping to stabilize them into everyday routines.

I would also be sensitive to any resistance, and I would respect that resistance as a signal that something important is being threatened. By listening to resistance, I would be in a position to modify the change to achieve a better fit with the people and the situation. Finally, I would want to take maximum advantage of the shared power strategy, supported by rational persuasion and with limited use of force-coercion (if it is used at all). By doing all of this, I would like my staff to feel empowered and committed to constructive improvement through planned change.

Chapter 10

1. a   2. c   3. c   4. d   5. b   6. c   7. d   8. b   9. b   10. c
11. a   12. a   13. b   14. a   15. d

16. Internal recruitment deals with job candidates who already know the organization well. It is also a strong motivator because it communicates to everyone the opportunity to advance in the organization through hard work. External recruitment may allow the organization to obtain expertise not available internally. It also brings in employees with new and fresh viewpoints who are not biased by previous experience in the organization.

17. Orientation activities introduce a new employee to the organization and the work environment. This is a time when the individual may develop key attitudes and when performance expectations will also be established. Good orientation communicates positive attitudes and expectations and reinforces the desired organizational culture. It formally introduces the individual to important policies and procedures that everyone is expected to follow.

18. The graphic rating scale simply asks a supervisor to rate an employee on an established set of criteria, such as quantity of work or attitude toward work. This leaves a lot of room for subjectivity and debate. The behaviourally anchored rating scale asks the supervisor to rate the employee on specific behaviours that had been identified as positively or negatively affecting performance in a given job. This is a more specific appraisal approach and leaves less room for debate and disagreement.

19. A subculture possesses beliefs, values, and customs that may set the group apart from other organizational members. A manager should understand the wishes and wants of subcultures to be able to relate to their needs; this will allow the manager to draw from this awareness to develop a positive work environment for all.

20. As Sy's supervisor, you face a difficult but perhaps expected human resource management problem. Not only is Sy influential as an informal leader, he also has considerable experience on the job and in the company. Even though he is experiencing performance problems using the new computer system, there is no indication that he doesn't want to work hard and continue to perform for the company. Although retirement is an option, Sy may also be transferred, promoted, or simply terminated. The latter response seems unjustified and may cause legal problems. Transferring Sy, with his agreement, to another position could be a positive move; promoting Sy to a supervisory position in which his experience and networks would be useful is another possibility. The key in this situation seems to be moving Sy out so that a computer-literate person can take over the job, while continuing to use Sy in a job that better fits his talents. Transfer and/or promotion should be actively considered, both in his and in the company's interest.

Chapter 11

1. d   2. d   3. b   4. a   5. c   6. a   7. b   8. c   9. b   10. a
11. b   12. a   13. d   14. a   15. b

16. Position power is based on reward; coercion, or punishment; and legitimacy, or formal authority. Managers, however, need to have more power than that made available to them by the position alone. Thus, they have to develop personal power through expertise and reference. This personal power is essential in helping managers to get things done beyond the scope of their position power alone.

17. Leader–participation theory suggests that leadership effectiveness is determined in part by how well managers or leaders handle the many different problem or decision situations that they face every day. Decisions can be made through individual or authority, consultative, or group-consensus approaches. No one of these decision methods is always the best; each is a good fit for certain types of situations. A good manager or leader is able to use each of these approaches and knows when each is the best approach to use in particular situations.

18. Drucker said that good leaders have more than the "charisma" or "personality" being popularized in the concept of transformational leadership. He reminded us that good leaders work hard to accomplish some basic things in their everyday activities. These include: (1) establishing a clear sense of mission; (2) accepting leadership as a responsibility, not a rank; and (3) earning and keeping the respect of others.

19. Active listening involves listening for both message content and emotions; active listeners respond to both the words and feelings expressed. They also check, by

paraphrasing or restating, to ensure that they have understood the message.

20. In his new position, Marcel must understand that the transactional aspects of leadership are not sufficient to guarantee him long-term leadership effectiveness. He must move beyond the effective use of task-oriented and people-oriented behaviours and demonstrate through his personal qualities the capacity to inspire others. A charismatic leader develops a unique relationship with followers, in which they become enthusiastic, highly loyal, and high achievers. Marcel needs to work very hard to develop positive relationships with the team members. In those relationships he must emphasize high aspirations for performance accomplishments, enthusiasm, ethical behaviour, integrity and honesty in all dealings, and a clear vision of the future. By working hard with this agenda and by allowing his personality to positively express itself in the team setting, Marcel should make continuous progress as an effective and moral leader.

Chapter 12

1. c 2. b 3. d 4. a 5. c 6. d 7. b 8. c 9. a 10. b
11. d 12. d 13. c 14. a 15. c

16. A psychological contract is the individual's view of the inducements he or she expects to receive from the organization in return for his or her work contributions. The contract is healthy when the individual perceives that the inducements and contributions are fair and in a state of balance.

17. Self-serving bias is the attribution tendency to blame the environment when things go wrong—"It's not my fault; 'they' caused all this mess." Fundamental attribution error is the tendency to blame others for problems that they have—"It's something wrong with 'you' that's causing the problem."

18. All the Big Five personality traits are relevant to the workplace. Consider the following basic examples. Extraversion suggests whether or not a person will reach out to relate and work well with others. Agreeableness suggests whether or not a person is open to the ideas of others and willing to go along with group decisions. Conscientiousness suggests whether or not someone can be depended on to meet commitments and perform agreed-upon tasks. Emotional stability suggests whether or not someone will be relaxed and secure, or uptight and tense, in work situations. Openness to experience suggests whether or not someone will be open to new ideas or resistant to change.

19. The Type A personality is characteristic of people who bring stress on themselves by virtue of personal characteristics. These tend to be compulsive individuals who are uncomfortable waiting for things to happen, who try to do many things at once, and who generally move fast and have difficulty slowing down. Type A personalities can be stressful for both themselves and the people around them. Managers must be aware of Type A personality tendencies in their own behaviour and among others with whom they work. Ideally, this awareness will help the manager take precautionary steps to best manage the stress caused by this personality type.

20. Hassan needs to be careful. Although there is modest research support for the relationship between job satisfaction and performance, there is no guarantee that simply doing things to make people happier at work will cause them to be higher performers. Hassan needs to take a broader perspective on this issue and his responsibilities as a manager. He should be interested in job satisfaction for his therapists and do everything he can to help them to experience it. But he should also be performance-oriented and should understand that performance is achieved through a combination of skills, support, and motivation. He should be helping the therapists to achieve and maintain high levels of job competency. He should also work with them to find out what obstacles they are facing and what support they need—things that perhaps he can deal with on their behalf. All of this relates as well to research indications that performance can be a source of job satisfaction. And finally, Hassan should make sure that the therapists believe they are being properly rewarded for their work, because rewards are shown by research to have an influence on both job satisfaction and job performance.

Chapter 13

1. c 2. c 3. c 4. a 5. c 6. c 7. b 8. a 9. c 10. b
11. c 12. a 13. a 14. b 15. d

16. An optimizing decision is one that represents the absolute "best" choice of alternatives. It is selected from a set of all known alternatives. A satisficing decision selects the first alternative that offers a "satisfactory" choice, not necessarily the absolute best choice. It is selected from a limited or incomplete set of alternatives.

17. The ethics of a decision can be checked with the "spotlight" questions: "How would you feel if your family found out?" "How would you feel if this were published in the local newspaper?" Also, one can test the decision by evaluating it on four criteria: (1) Utility—does it satisfy all stakeholders? (2) Rights—does it respect everyone's rights? (3) Justice—is it consistent with fairness and justice? (4) Caring—does it meet responsibilities for caring?

18. A manager using systematic thinking is going to approach problem solving in a logical and rational fashion. The tendency will be to proceed in a linear, step-by-step fashion, handling one issue at a time. A manager using intuitive thinking will be more spontaneous and open in problem solving. He or she may jump from one stage in the process to another and deal with many different things at once.

19. It almost seems contradictory to say that one can prepare for crises, but it is possible. The concept of crisis management is used to describe how managers and others prepare for unexpected high-impact events that threaten an organization's health and well-being. Crisis management involves both anticipating possible crises and preparing teams and plans ahead of time for how to handle them if they do occur. Many organizations today, for example, are developing crisis management plans to deal with terrorism and computer "hacking" attacks.

20. This is what I would say in the mentoring situation: continuing developments in information technology are changing the work setting for most employees. An important development for the traditional white-collar worker falls in the area of office automation—the use of computers and related technologies to facilitate everyday office work. In the "electronic office" of today and tomorrow, you should be prepared to work with and take full advantage of the following: smart workstations supported by desktop computers; voice messaging systems, whereby computers take dictation, answer the telephone, and relay messages; database and word processing software systems that allow storage, access, and manipulation of data, as well as the preparation of reports; electronic mail systems that send mail and data from computer to computer; electronic bulletin boards for posting messages; and computer conferencing and video-conferencing that allow people to work with one another every day over great distances. These are among the capabilities of the new workplace. To function effectively, you must be prepared not only to use these systems to full advantage, but also to stay abreast of new developments as they become available.

Chapter 14

1. c   2. d   3. d   4. b   5. b   6. d   7. c   8. d   9. a   10. b
11. c   12. a   13. b   14. a   15. b

16. People high in need for achievement will prefer work settings and jobs in which they have (1) challenging but achievable goals, (2) individual responsibility, and (3) performance feedback.

17. Participation is important to goal-setting theory because, in general, people tend to be more committed to

the accomplishment of goals they have helped to set. When people participate in the setting of goals, they also understand them better. Participation in goal setting improves goal acceptance and understanding.

18. Maslow, McClelland, Alderfer, and Herzberg would likely find common agreement in respect to a set of "higher-order" needs. For Maslow, these are self-actualization and ego; they correspond with Alderfer's growth needs, and with McClelland's needs for achievement and power. Maslow's social needs link up with relatedness needs in Alderfer's theory and the need for affiliation in McClelland's theory. Maslow's safety needs correspond to Alderfer's existence needs. Herzberg's "satisfier factors" correspond to satisfactions of Maslow's higher needs, Alderfer's growth needs, and McClelland's need for achievement.

19. The compressed workweek, or 4-40 schedule, offers employees the advantage of a three-day weekend. However, it can cause problems for the employer in terms of ensuring that operations are covered adequately during the normal five workdays of the week. Labour unions may resist, and the compressed workweek will entail more complicated work scheduling. In addition, some employees find that the schedule is tiring and can cause family adjustment problems.

20. It has already been pointed out in the answer to question 16 that a person with a high need for achievement likes moderately challenging goals and performance feedback. Participation of both manager and subordinate in goal setting offers an opportunity to choose goals to which the subordinate will respond, and that also will serve the organization. Furthermore, through goal setting the manager and individual subordinates can identify performance standards or targets. Progress toward these targets can be positively reinforced by the manager. Such reinforcements can serve as indicators of progress to someone with a high need for achievement, thus responding to their desire for performance feedback.

Chapter 15

1. d   2. b   3. b   4. d   5. b   6. d   7. b   8. b   9. a   10. b
11. c   12. b   13. a   14. b   15. a

16. Input factors can have a major impact on group effectiveness. In order to best prepare a group to perform effectively, a manager should make sure that the right people are put in the group (maximize available talents and abilities), that these people are capable of working well together (membership characteristics should promote good relationships), that the tasks are clear, and that the group has the resources and environment needed to perform up to expectations.

17. A group's performance can be analyzed according to the interaction between cohesiveness and performance norms. In a highly cohesive group, members tend to conform to group norms. Thus, when the performance norm is positive and cohesion is high, we can expect everyone to work hard to support the norm—high performance is likely. By the same token, high cohesion and a low performance norm will yield the opposite result—low performance is likely. With other combinations of norms and cohesion, the performance results will be more mixed.

18. The textbook lists several symptoms of groupthink, along with various strategies for avoiding it. For example, a group whose members censor themselves from contributing "contrary" or "different" opinions and/or whose members keep talking about outsiders as "weak" or the "enemy" may be suffering from groupthink. This may be avoided or corrected, for example, by asking someone to be the "devil's advocate" for a meeting, and by inviting in an outside observer to help gather different viewpoints.

19. The inverted "U" curve of conflict intensity shows that, as conflict intensity increases from low to moderate levels, performance increases. This is the zone of constructive conflict. As conflict intensity moves into extreme levels, performance tends to decrease. This is the zone of destructive conflict.

20. Marcos is faced with a highly cohesive group whose members conform to a negative, or low-performance, norm. This is a difficult situation that is ideally resolved by changing the performance norm. In order to gain the group's commitment to a high-performance norm, Marcos should act as a positive role model for the norm. He must communicate the norm clearly and positively to the group and should not assume that everyone knows what he expects of them. He may also talk to the informal leader and gain his or her commitment to the norm. He might carefully reward high-performance behaviours within the group and may introduce new members with high-performance records and commitments. And he might hold group meetings in which performance standards and expectations are discussed, with an emphasis on committing to new high-performance directions. If his attempts to introduce a high-performance norm fail, Marcos may have to take steps to reduce group cohesiveness so that individual members can pursue higher-performance results without feeling bound by group pressures to restrict their performance.

Chapter 16

1. a 2. b 3. d 4. b 5. b 6. b 7. d 8. b 9. b 10. c
11. a 12. b 13. c 14. c 15. c

16. The four steps in the controlling process are: (1) establish objectives and standards, (2) measure actual performance, (3) compare actual performance with objectives and standards, and (4) take necessary action.

17. Feedforward control involves the careful selection of system inputs to ensure that outcomes are of the desired quality and up to all performance standards. In the case of a local bookstore, one of the major points of influence over performance and customer satisfaction is the relationship between the customers and the store's employees who serve them. Thus, a good example of feedforward control is exercising great care when the manager hires new employees and then trains them to work according to the store's expectations.

18. Douglas McGregor's concept of Theory Y involves the assumption that people can be trusted to exercise self-control in their work. This is the essence of internal control—people controlling their own work by taking personal responsibility for results. If managers approach work with McGregor's Theory Y assumptions, they will, according to him, promote more self-control—or internal control—by people at work.

19. A progressive discipline system works by adjusting the discipline to fit the severity and frequency of the inappropriate behaviour. In the case of a person who comes late to work, for example, progressive discipline might involve a verbal warning after three late arrivals, a written warning after five, and a pay-loss penalty after seven. In the case of a person who steals money from the business, there would be immediate dismissal after the first such infraction.

20. There are a very large number of activities required to complete a new student centre building on a university campus. Among them, one might expect the following to be core requirements: (1) land surveys and planning permissions from local government, (2) architect plans developed and approved, (3) major subcontractors hired, (4) site excavation completed, (5) building exterior completed, and (6) building interior completed and furnishings installed. Use Figure 16.5 from the chapter as a guide for developing your AON diagram.

Chapter 17

1. c 2. c 3. c 4. a 5. a 6. b 7. d 8. b 9. d 10. c
11. b 12. c 13. b 14. c 15. a

16. Possible operating objectives reflecting a commitment to competitive advantage through customer service include: (1) providing high-quality goods and services, (2) producing at low cost so that goods and services can be sold at low prices, (3) providing short waiting times for goods and services, and (4) providing goods and services meeting unique customer needs.

17. External customers are the consumers or clients in the specific environment who buy the organization's goods or use its services. Internal customers are found internally in the workflows among people and subsystems in the organization. They are individuals or groups within the organization who use goods and services produced by others who are also inside the organization.

18. Supply chain management is important due to the costs of resources, the costs of holding things in inventory, and all the costs of transporting resources and supplies for the organization. SCM uses the latest technologies and systematic management to oversee all aspects of inbound logistics so that the various elements and activities in the organization's supply chains operate as efficiently and as effectively as possible.

19. The focus of process reengineering is on reducing costs and streamlining operations efficiency while improving customer service. This is accomplished by closely examining core business processes through the following sequence of activities:

(1) identify the core processes; (2) map them in a workflows diagram; (3) evaluate all tasks involved; (4) seek ways to eliminate unnecessary tasks; (5) seek ways to eliminate delays, errors, and misunderstandings in the workflows; and (6) seek efficiencies in how work is shared and transferred among people and departments.

20. Although the appropriateness of the measure would vary by department or area of each organization that one is addressing, possible productivity measures are:

(a) Canada Post—# letters delivered per day / # letter carriers on payroll

(b) University—# students enrolled / (# full-time + part-time faculty)

(c) Hospital—# patients per day / # available hospital beds

(d) Amusement park—# paid admissions per day / # available rides

(e) Restaurant—# meals served per day / # servers on payroll

Endnotes

CHAPTER 1

ENDNOTES

1. See monster.com; linkedin.com; Bridget Carey, "Old Resume Just the Start These Days," *The Columbus Dispatch* (March 16, 2008), p. D3; Joseph De Avila, "CEO Reorganizes Job-Search Pioneer," *Wall Street Journal* (May 12, 2008), p. B1.

2. Originally described by Joseph Luft and Harry Ingham, "The Johari Window, a Graphic Model of Interpersonal Awareness," *Proceedings of the Western Training Laboratory in Group Development* (Los Angeles: UCLA, 1955).

3. Information from the Fast Company website, www.fastcompany.com.

4. Leonard Brody and David Raffa, *Everything I Needed to Know About Business . . . I Learned from a Canadian* (Toronto: John Wiley & Sons, 2009), p. 282.

5. Many books popularize new examples and cases. See, for example, William C. Taylor and Polly LaBarre, *Mavericks at Work: Why the Most Original Minds in Business Win* (New York: William Morrow, 2006).

6. Max DePree's books include *Leadership Is an Art* (New York: Dell, 1990) and *Leadership Jazz* (New York: Dell, 1993). See also Herman Miller's website at www.hermanmiller.com.

7. Charles O'Reilly III and Jeffrey Pfeffer, *Hidden Value: How Great Companies Achieve Extraordinary Results with Ordinary People* (Boston: Harvard Business School Press, 2000), p. 2.

8. Thomas A. Stewart, *Intellectual Capital: The Wealth of Organizations* (New York: Bantam, 1998).

9. See Peter F. Drucker, *The Changing World of the Executive* (New York: T.T. Times Books, 1982), and *The Profession of Management* (Cambridge, MA: Harvard Business School Press, 1997), and Francis Horibe, *Managing Knowledge Workers: New Skills and Attitudes to Unlock the Intellectual Capital in Your Organization* (New York: Wiley, 1999).

10. *Workforce 2000: Work and Workers for the 21st Century* (Indianapolis: Towers Perrin/Hudson Institute, 1987); Richard W. Judy and Carol D'Amico (eds.), *Workforce 2020: Work and Workers for the 21st Century* (Indianapolis: Hudson Institute, 1997). See also Richard D. Bucher, *Diversity Consciousness: Opening Our Minds to People, Cultures, and Opportunities* (Upper Saddle River, NJ: Prentice-Hall, 2000); R. Roosevelt Thomas, "From Affirmative Action to Affirming Diversity," *Harvard Business Review* (March–April 1990), pp. 107–17; and *Beyond Race and Gender: Unleashing the Power of Your Total Workforce by Managing Diversity* (New York: AMACOM, 1992).

11. Phillip Toledano, "Demographics: The Population Hourglass," *Fast Company* (March 2006), p. 56; Conor Dougherty, "Nonwhites to Be Majority in U.S. by 2042," *Wall Street Journal* (August 14, 2008), p. 43.

12. Information from "Racism in Hiring Remains, Study Says," *The Columbus Dispatch* (January 17, 2003), p. B2.

13. Judith B. Rosener, "Women Make Good Managers. So What?" *BusinessWeek* (December 11, 2000), p. 24.

14. *BusinessWeek* (August 8, 1990), p. 50.

15. Thomas, op. cit.

16. Kenichi Ohmae's books include *The Borderless World: Power and Strategy in the Interlinked Economy* (New York: Harper, 1989); *The End of the Nation State* (New York: Free Press, 1996); *The Invisible Continent: Four Strategic Imperatives of the New Economy* (New York: Harper, 1999); and *The Next Global Stage: Challenges and Opportunities in Our Borderless World* (Philadelphia: Wharton School Publishing, 2006).

17. For a discussion of globalization, see Thomas L. Friedman, *The Lexus and the Olive Tree: Understanding Globalization* (New York: Bantam Doubleday Dell, 2000); Joseph E. Stiglitz, *Globalization and Its Discontents* (New York: W.W. Norton, 2003); and Joseph E. Stiglitz, *Making Globalization Work* (New York: W.W. Norton, 2007).

18. Alfred E. Eckes, Jr., and Thomas W. Zeiler, *Globalization and the American Century* (Cambridge, UK: Cambridge University Press, 2003), pp. 1–2.

19. Michael E. Porter, *The Competitive Advantage of Nations: With a New Introduction* (New York: Free Press, 1998).

20. Thomas L. Friedman, *The World Is Flat: A Brief History of the Twenty-First Century* (New York: Farrar, Straus and Giroux, 2005), p. 15.

21. Joe Biesecker, "What Today's College Graduates Want: It's Not All About Paychecks," *Central Penn Business Journal* (August 10, 2007).

22. Carey, op. cit.

23. Portions adapted from John W. Dienhart and Terry Thomas, "Ethical Leadership: A Primer on Ethical Responsibility in Management," in John R. Schermerhorn Jr. (ed.), *Management*, 7th ed. (New York: Wiley, 2002).

24. For discussions of ethics in business and management, see Linda K. Trevino and Katherine A. Nelson, *Managing Business Ethics* (Hoboken, NJ: John Wiley & Sons, 2006); and Richard DeGeorge, *Business Ethics*, 5th ed. (Englewood Cliffs, NJ: Prentice-Hall, 2005).

25. Daniel Akst, "Room at the Top for Improvement," *Wall Street Journal* (October 26, 2004), p. D8; Herb Baum and Tammy King, *The Transparent Leader* (New York: Collins, 2005).

26. Carey, op. cit.

27. Charles Handy, *The Age of Unreason* (Cambridge, MA: Harvard Business School Press, 1990).

28. For his latest work, see Charles Handy, *A Business Guru's Portfolio Life* (New York: AMACOM, 2008), and *Myself and other Important Matters* (New York; AMACOM, 2008).

29. Robert Reich, "The Company of the Future," *Fast Company* (November 1998), p. 124.

30. Tom Peters, "The New Wired World of Work," *BusinessWeek* (August 28, 2000), pp. 172–73.

31. For an overview of organizations and organization theory, see W. Richard Scott, *Organizations: Rational, Natural and Open Systems*, 4th ed. (Englewood Cliffs, NJ: Prentice-Hall, 1998).

32. Developed in part from Jay A. Conger, *Winning 'em Over: A New Model for Managing in the Age of Persuasion* (New York: Simon-Schuster, 1998), pp. 180–81; Stewart D. Friedman, Perry Christensen, and Jessica DeGroot, "Work and Life: The End of the Zero-Sum Game," *Harvard Business Review* (November–December 1998), pp. 119–29; Chris Argyris, "Empowerment: The Emperor's New Clothes," *Harvard Business Review* (May–June 1998), pp. 98–105; and John A. Byrne, "Management by Web," *BusinessWeek* (August 28, 2000), pp. 84–98. See also emerging reports such as O'Toole and Lawler, op. cit.; and Jon Nicholson and Amanda Nairn, *The Manager of the 21st Century: 2020 Vision* (Sydney: The Boston Consulting Group, 2008).

33. Robert Reich, *The Future of Success* (New York: Knopf, 2001), p. 7. Reich's recent book is *Supercapitalism: The Transformation of Business, Democracy and Everyday Life* (New York: Knopf, 2007).

34. Charles Forelle, "EU Fines Microsoft $1.35 Billion," *Wall Street Journal* (February 28, 2008), p. B2.

35. See Jane Spencer and Kevin J. Delaney, "YouTube Unplugged," *Wall Street Journal* (March 31, 2008), pp. BIB2.

36. Ibid.

37. Data in table from "List of the 13 Internet Enemies," Reporters Without Borders (July 11, 2006), retrieved from: www.rsf.org (August 27, 2008).

38. Information from "Durbin Says Internet Giants Close to Agreement on Code of Conduct," United States Senator Dick Durbin (August 4, 2008), retrieved from: www.durbin.senate.gov (August 27, 2008).

39. Peter Sayer, "Microsoft Corporation CEO Ballmer Says IT Is Entering Another Period of Revolution," *IDG News Service* (March 3, 2008), www.itvendorsdirectory.ca/online-resources/microsoft.

40. Bobby White, "The New Workplace Rules: No Video-Watching," *Wall Street Journal* (March 4, 2008), pp. B1, B3.

41. Hugh Mackenzie, *A Soft Landing: Recession and Canada's 100 Highest Paid CEOs*, Canadian Centre for Policy Alternatives (January 2010).

42. Rob Walker, "Sex vs. Ethics," *Fast Company* (June 2008), pp. 73–78.

43. Information from Remi Trudel and June Cotte, "Does Being Ethical Pay?" *Wall Street Journal* (May 12, 2008), p. R4.

44. See Rebecca Smith, "Where the Jobs Are," *Wall Street Journal* (March 24, 2008), p. R12.

45. Heather Green and Kerry Capell, "Carbon Confusion," *BusinessWeek* (March 17, 2008), pp. 52–56.

46. Definition from www.sustainablebusiness.com.

47. Ibid.

48. Ibid.

49. Information from Matthew Wheeland, "Selling Small, Thinking Big: P&G's Sustainable Innovations," www.greenbiz.com (retrieved August 27, 2008).

50. See Thomas Donaldson and Lee Preston, "The Stakeholder Theory of the Corporation," *Academy of Management Review*, vol. 20 (January 1995), pp. 65–91.

51. Mathew Rees, "The Fresh-Roasted Smell of Success," *Wall Street Journal* (November 7, 2007), p. D9.

52. "Ivory Tower: How an MBA Can Bend Your Mind," *BusinessWeek* (April 1, 2002), p. 12.

53. See Michael E. Porter, *Competitive Strategy: Techniques for Analyzing Industries and Competitors* (New York: Free Press, 1980); and *Competitive Advantage: Creating and Sustaining Superior Performance* (New York: Free Press, 1986); see also Richard A. D'Aveni, *Hyper-Competition: Managing the Dynamics of Strategic Maneuvering* (New York: Free Press, 1994).

54. Michael E. Porter, "Strategy and the Internet," *Harvard Business Review*, vol. 79, no. 3 (March 2001).

55. James D. Thompson, *Organizations in Action* (New York: McGraw-Hill, 1967); Robert B. Duncan, "Characteristics of Organizational Environments and Perceived Environmental Uncertainty," *Administrative Science Quarterly*, vol. 17 (1972), pp. 313–27. For discussion of the implications of uncertainty, see Hugh Courtney, Jane Kirkland, and Patrick Viguerie, "Strategy under Uncertainty," *Harvard Business Review* (November–December 1997), pp. 67–79.

56. Gareth N. Jones, *Organization Theory and Design*, 3rd ed. (Upper Saddle River, NJ: Prentice-Hall, 2001).

57. This is discussed in James L. Gibson, John M. Ivancevich, and James H. Donnelly Jr., *Organizations: Behavior, Structure, Processes*, 5th ed. (Homewood, IL: Richard D. Irwin, 1991).

58. Jeffrey Pfeffer and John F. Veiga, "Putting People First for Organizational Success," *Academy of Management Executive*, vol. 13 (May 1999), pp. 37–48; Jeffrey Pfeffer, *The Human Equation: Building Profits by Putting People First* (Boston: Harvard Business School Press, 1998).

59. George Anders, "Drucker's Teachings Find Following in Asia," *Wall Street Journal* (June 18, 2008), p. B2.

60. Henry Mintzberg, "The Manager's Job: Folklore and Fact," *Harvard Business Review*, Vol. 53 (July–August 1975), p. 61. See also his book *The Nature of Managerial Work* (New York: Harper-Row, 1973, and HarperCollins, 1997).

61. Matthew McClearn, "Laura Secord Comes Home," *Canadian Business* (April 12, 2010).

62. For a perspective on the first-level manager's job, see Leonard A. Schlesinger and Janice A. Klein, "The First-Line Supervisor: Past, Present and Future," pp. 370–82 in Jay W. Lorsch (ed.), *Handbook of Organizational Behavior* (Englewood Cliffs, NJ: Prentice-Hall, 1987). Research reported in "Remember Us?" *Economist* (February 1, 1992), p. 71.

63. McClearn, op. cit.

64. Mark Jones, "Core Values Make the Difference," *Financial Post* (January 12, 2009).

65. This running example is developed from information from "Accountants Have Lives, Too, You Know," *BusinessWeek* (February 23, 1998), pp. 88–90; Silvia Ann Hewlett and Carolyn Buck Luce, "Off-Ramps and On-Ramps: Keeping Talented Women on the Road to Success," *Harvard Business Review* (March 2005), reprint 9491; and the Ernst and Young website, www.ey.com.

66. Mintzberg (1973/1997), op. cit., p. 30.

67. See Mintzberg (1973/1997), op. cit.; Henry Mintzberg, "Covert Leadership: The Art of Managing Professionals," *Harvard Business Review* (November–December 1998),

pp. 140–47; and Jonathan Gosling and Henry Mintzberg, "The Five Minds of a Manager," *Harvard Business Review* (November 2003), pp. 1–9.

68. Mintzberg (1973/1997), op. cit., p. 60.

69. For research on managerial work, see Morgan W. McCall Jr., Ann M. Morrison, and Robert L. Hannan, *Studies of Managerial Work: Results and Methods. Technical Report #9* (Greensboro, NC: Center for Creative Leadership, 1978), pp. 7–9. See also John P. Kotter, "What Effective General Managers Really Do," *Harvard Business Review* (November—December 1982), pp. 156–57.

70. Kotter, op. cit., p. 164. See also his book *The General Managers* (New York: Free Press, 1986) and David Barry, Catherine Durnell Crampton, and Stephen J. Carroll, "Navigating the Garbage Can: How Agendas Help Managers Cope with Job Realities," *Academy of Management Executive*, vol. II (May 1997), pp. 43–56.

71. Robert L. Katz, "Skills of an Effective Administrator," *Harvard Business Review* (September–October 1974), p. 94.

72. See Daniel Goleman's books *Emotional Intelligence* (New York: Bantam, 1995); and *Working with Emotional Intelligence* (New York: Bantam, 1998); and his articles "What Makes a Leader," *Harvard Business Review* (November–December 1998), pp. 93–102; and "Leadership That Makes a Difference," *Harvard Business Review* (March–April 2000), pp. 79–90; quote from p. 80.

73. See Daniel Goleman, Richard Boyatzis, and Annie McKee, *Primal Leadership: Realizing the Power of Emotional Intelligence* (Boston: Harvard Business School Press, 2002).

74. Daniel Pink, *A Whole New Mind: Moving from the Information Age to the Conceptual Age* (New York: Riverhead Books, 2005), pp. 2–3.

75. See Richard E. Boyatzis, *The Competent Manager: A Model for Effective Performance* (New York: Wiley, 1982); and Richard E. Boyatzis, "Competencies in the 21st Century," *Journal of Management Development*, Vol. 27 (No.1), 2008, pp. 5–12.

FEATURE NOTES

Going Global: Marcia Almey, "Women in Canada: Work Chapter Updates," in *Women in Canada 2005* (Ottawa: Statistics Canada, 2006, Catalogue No. 89F0133XWE); "Labour Force Activity, Visible Minority Groups, Immigrant Status and Period of Immigration, Age Groups and Sex for the Population 15 Years and Over," table in 2006 Census of the Population, Statistics Canada, Catalogue No. 97-562-XCB2006013; "New Report Reveals a Widening Wage Gap between Men and Women in Canada," news release, Canadian Labour Congress, March 6, 2008.

Real Ethics: Information from Brian Bergstein, "Hundred Dollar Laptop Project: Founder Expects Distribution by 2007," *The Columbus Dispatch* (April 10, 2006), p. F5; and "Waking Up a Laptop Revolution," *Financial Times* (March 29, 2006), p. 1; Bruce Einhorn, "In Search of a PC for the People," *BusinessWeek* (June 12, 2006), pp. 40–41; Steven Levy, "The $100 Laptop Controversy," *Newsweek* (January 4, 2008), newsweek.com; Steve Hamm, "Wanted: One CEO for One Laptop Per Child," *BusinessWeek* (March 17, 2008), p. 64.

Canadian Managers: "Top 20 Business Women in Canada 2009," *Women's Post* (December 13, 2009).

Canadian Company in the News: RIM website and RIM news release, "AT&T and Research In Motion Ignite Customers with the new BlackBerry Torch," August 3, 2010.

Issues and Situations: Information from Nanette Byrnes, "Star Search," *BusinessWeek* (October 10, 2005), pp. 68–78.

Research Brief: Robert J. House, P. J. Hanges, Mansour Javidan, P. Dorfman, and V. Gupta (eds.). *Culture, Leadership and Organizations: The GLOBE Study of 62 Societies* (Thousand Oaks, CA: Sage Publications, Inc., 2004); Mansour Javidan, Peter W. Dorfman, Mary Sully de Luque, and Robert J. House, "In the Eye of the Beholder? Cross Cultural Lessons in Leadership from Project GLOBE," *Academy of Management Perspectives*, Vol. 20 (2006), pp. 67–90.

CASE ENDNOTES

1. Vancity website, www.vancity.com.

2. "Vancity Recognized as One of Canada's Top 100 Employers," news release, October 15, 2010.

3. Nick Rockel, "Luring Young Talent Sets Stage for the Future," *The Globe and Mail* (June 1, 2010).

4. *Vancity 2008–2009 Accountability Report*, pp. 11, 39–40.

5. Ibid., p. 40.

6. Brian Morton, "Vancity's Net Income Near Record Level," *The Vancouver Sun* (July 12, 2010), p. B6.

7. *Vancity 2008–2009 Accountability Report*, p. 40.

8. *Vancity 2008–2009 Accountability Report*, p. 33.

9. Frances Bula, "The Queen of Vancity," *Vancouver* (September 1, 2009).

10. *Vancity 2008–2009 Accountability Report*, p. 27.

11. *Vancity 2008–2009 Accountability Report*, p. 14.

12. Regan Ray, "Q&A: Vancity's Tamara Vrooman," *Canadian Business* (November 19, 2007).

13. *Vancity 2008–2009 Accountability Report*, p. 13.

14. "B.C.'s Top 100 Influential Women," *Vancouver Sun* (October 29, 2010).

15. "Vancity Believes We Can All Be Wealthy; New Accountability Report from One of Canada's Top Three Corporate Citizens," news release, July 8, 2010.

CHAPTER 2

ENDNOTES

1. Quotes from "How Good Is Google?" *The Economist* (November 1, 2003); Robert D. Hof, "Google: What Goes Up . . ." *BusinessWeek* (April 14, 2008), pp. 21–22; and "100 Best Companies to Work For," *Fortune:* cnnmoney.com. See also John Battelle, *The Search: How Google and Its Rivals Rewrote the Rules of Business and Transformed Our Culture* (New York: Penguin, 2005); www.google.com/corporate.

2. See David A. Kolb, *Experiential Learning: Experience as the Source of Learning and Development* (Englewood Cliffs, NJ: Prentice-Hall, 1984); and David A. Kolb, "Experiential Learning Theory and the Learning Style Inventory," *The Academy of Management Review* (Vol. 6, 1981), pp. 289–96.

3. Quote from Allan H. Church, *Executive Commentary, Academy of Management Executive* (February 2002), p. 74.

4. A thorough review and critique of the history of management thought, including management in ancient civilizations, is provided by Daniel A. Wren, *The Evolution of Management Thought*, 4th ed. (New York: Wiley, 1993).

5. Pauline Graham, *Mary Parker Follett—Prophet of Management: A Celebration of Writings from the 1920s* (Boston: Harvard Business School Press, 1995).

6. For a timeline of twentieth-century management ideas, see "75 Years of Management Ideas and Practices: 1922–1997," *Harvard Business Review*, supplement (September–October 1997).

7. For a sample of this work, see Henry L. Gantt, *Industrial Leadership* (Easton, MD: Hive, 1921; Hive edition published in 1974); Henry C. Metcalfe and Lyndall Urwick (eds.), *Dynamic Administration: The Collected Papers of Mary Parker Follett* (New York: Harper-Brothers, 1940); James D. Mooney, *The Principles of Administration*, rev. ed. (New York: Harper-Brothers, 1947); Lyndall Urwick, *The Elements of Administration* (New York: Harper-Brothers, 1943); and *The Golden Book of Management* (London: N. Neame, 1956).

8. References on Taylor's work are from Frederick W. Taylor, *The Principles of Scientific Management* (New York: W.W. Norton, 1967), originally published by Harper-Brothers in 1911. See Charles W. Wrege and Amedeo G. Perroni, "Taylor's Pig-Tale: A Historical Analysis of Frederick W. Taylor's Pig Iron Experiments," *Academy of Management Journal*, vol. 17 (March 1974), pp. 6–27, for a criticism; see Edwin A. Lock, "The Ideas of Frederick W. Taylor. An Evaluation," *Academy of Management Review*, vol. 7 (1982), p. 14, for an examination of the contemporary significance of Taylor's work. See also the biography, Robert Kanigel, *The One Best Way* (New York: Viking, 1997).

9. Kanigel, op. cit. See also Cynthia Crossen, "Early Industry Expert Soon Realized a Staff Has Its Own Efficiency," *Wall Street Journal* (November 6, 2006), p. B1.

10. Frank B. Gilbreth, *Motion Study* (New York: Van Nostrand, 1911).

11. Ben Worthen, "Do You Need to Work Faster? Get a Bigger Computer Monitor," *Wall Street Journal* (March 25, 2008), p. B8.

12. Information from Raymund Flandez and Kelly K. Spors, "Tackling the Energy Monster," *Wall Street Journal* (June 16, 2008), p. R1.

13. Available in English as *Henri Fayol, General and Industrial Administration* (London: Pitman, 1949); subsequent discussion is based on M. B. Brodie, *Fayol on Administration* (London: Pitman, 1949).

14. A. M. Henderson and Talcott Parsons (eds. and trans.), *Max Weber: The Theory of Social Economic Organization* (New York: Free Press, 1947).

15. Ibid., p. 337.

16. For classic treatments of bureaucracy, see Alvin Gouldner, *Patterns of Industrial Bureaucracy* (New York: Free Press, 1954); and Robert K. Merton, *Social Theory and Social Structure* (New York: Free Press, 1957).

17. M. P. Follett, *Freedom and Coordination* (London: Management Publications Trust, 1949).

18. Judith Garwood, "A Review of Dynamic Administration: The Collected Papers of Mary Parker Follett," *New Management*, vol. 2 (1984), pp. 61–62; eulogy from Richard C. Cabot, *Encyclopedia of Social Work*, vol. 15, "Follett, Mary Parker," p. 351.

19. The Hawthorne studies are described in detail in F. J. Roethlisberger and William J. Dickson, *Management and the Worker* (Cambridge, MA: Harvard University Press, 1966) and G. Homans, *Fatigue of Workers* (New York: Reinhold, 1941). For an interview with three of the participants in the relay–assembly test-room studies, see R. G. Greenwood, A. A. Bolton, and R. A. Greenwood, "Hawthorne a Half Century Later: Relay Assembly Participants Remember," *Journal of Management*, vol. 9 (1983), pp. 217–31.

20. The criticisms of the Hawthorne studies are detailed in Alex Carey, "The Hawthorne Studies: A Radical Criticism," *American Sociological Review*, vol. 32 (1967),

pp. 403–16; H. M. Parsons, "What Happened at Hawthorne?" *Science*, vol. 183 (1974), pp. 922–32; and B. Rice, "The Hawthorne Defect: Persistence of a Flawed Theory," *Psychology Today*, vol. 16 (1982), pp. 70–74. See also Wren, op. cit.

21. This discussion of Maslow's theory is based on Abraham H. Maslow, *Eupsychian Management* (Homewood, IL: Richard D. Irwin, 1965); and Abraham H. Maslow, *Motivation and Personality*, 2nd ed. (New York: Harper-Row, 1970).

22. Douglas McGregor, *The Human Side of Enterprise* (New York: McGraw-Hill, 1960).

23. This notion is also discussed in terms of the "pygmalion effect." See Dov Eden, *Pygmalion in Management* (Lexington, MA: Lexington Books, 1990); and Dov Eden, Dvorah Geller, and Abigail Gerwirtz, "Implanting Pygmalion Leadership Style Through Workshop Training: Seven Field Experiments," *Leadership Quarterly*, Vol. 11 (2) (2000), pp. 171–210.

24. Gary Heil, Deborah F. Stevens, and Warren G. Bennis, *Douglas McGregor on Management: Revisiting the Human Side of Enterprise* (New York: Wiley, 2000).

25. Information from Terry Stephan, "Honing Her Kraft," *Northwestern* (Winter 2000), pp. 22–25.

26. Chris Argyris, *Personality and Organization* (New York: Harper-Row, 1957).

27. The ideas of Ludwig von Bertalanffy contributed to the emergence of this systems perspective on organizations. See his article, "The History and Status of General Systems Theory," *Academy of Management Journal*, vol. 15 (1972), pp. 407–26. This viewpoint is further developed by Daniel Katz and Robert L. Kahn in their classic book, *The Social Psychology of Organizations* (New York: Wiley, 1978). For an integrated systems view, see Lane Tracy, *The Living Organization* (New York: Quorum Books, 1994). For an overview, see W. Richard Scott, *Organizations: Rational, Natural, and Open Systems*, 4th ed. (Upper Saddle River, NJ: Prentice-Hall, 1998).

28. Chester I. Barnard, *Functions of the Executive* (Cambridge, MA: Harvard University Press, 1938).

29. For an overview, see Scott, op. cit., pp. 95–97.

30. See, for example, the classic studies of Tom Burns and George M. Stalker, *The Management of Innovation* (London: Tavistock, 1961, and republished by Oxford University Press, London, 1994); and Paul R. Lawrence and Jay W. Lorsch, *Organizations and Environment* (Boston: Division of Research, Graduate School of Business Administration, Harvard University, 1967).

31. W. Edwards Deming, *Quality, Productivity, and Competitive Position* (Cambridge, MA:

MIT Press, 1982); Rafael Aguay, *Dr. Deming: The American Who Taught the Japanese about Quality* (New York: Free Press, 1997).

32. See Howard S. Gitlow and Shelly J. Gitlow, *The Deming Guide to Quality and Competitive Position* (Englewood Cliffs, NJ: Prentice-Hall, 1987).

33. See Joseph M. Juran, *Quality Control Handbook*, 3rd ed. (New York: McGraw-Hill, 1979); and "The Quality Trilogy: A Universal Approach to Managing for Quality," in *Total Quality Management*, ed. H. Costin (New York: Dryden, 1994).

34. Stephen Miller, "Joseph M. Juran: 1904–2008," *Wall Street Journal* (March 8–9, 2008), p. A7.

35. See Edward E. Lawler III, Susan Albers Mohrman, and Gerald E. Ledford Jr., *Employee Involvement and Total Quality Management: Practices and Results in Fortune 100 Companies* (San Francisco: Jossey-Bass, 1992).

36. Peter F. Drucker, "The Future That Has Already Happened," *Harvard Business Review*, vol. 75 (September–October 1997), pp. 20–24; Peter F. Drucker, Esther Dyson, Charles Handy, Paul Daffo, and Peter M. Senge, "Looking Ahead: Implications of the Present," *Harvard Business Review*, vol. 75 (September–October 1997).

37. See, for example, Thomas H. Davenport and Laurence Prusak, *Working Knowledge: How Organizations Manage What They Know* (Cambridge, MA: Harvard Business School Press, 1997).

38. Peter Senge, *The Fifth Discipline* (New York: Harper, 1990).

39. Ibid.

40. Eric Schmidt and Hal Varian, "Google: Ten Golden Rules," *Newsweek* (December 2, 2005).

41. Thomas J. Peters and Robert H. Waterman, Jr., *In Search of Excellence: Lessons from America's Best-Run Companies* (New York: Harper-Row, 1982).

42. For a retrospective on *In Search of Excellence*, see William C. Bogner, "Tom Peters on the Real World of Business" and "Robert Waterman on Being Smart and Lucky," *Academy of Management Executive*, vol. 16 (2002), pp. 40–50.

43. See Jim Collins and Jerry I. Porras, *Built to Last* (New York: HarperCollins, 1994); and Jim Collins, *Good to Great* (New York: HarperCollins, 2001).

44. See Gordon Binder, *Science Lessons: What the Business of Biotech Taught Me About Management* (Boston: Harvard Business School Press, 2008).

45. Jeffrey Pfeffer and Robert I. Sutton, *Hard Facts, Dangerous Half-Truths, and Total Nonsense: Profiting from Evidence-Based*

Management (Boston: Harvard Business School Press, 2006); Jeffrey Pfeffer and Robert I. Sutton, "Management Half-Truths and Nonsense," *California Management Review*, Vol. 48(3), 2006: 77–100; Jeffrey Pfeffer and Robert I. Sutton, "Evidence-Based Management," *Harvard Business Review* (January 2006), reprint R0601E.

46. Jeffrey Pfeffer, *The Human Equation: Building Profits by Putting People First* (Boston: Harvard Business School Press, 1998); and Charles O'Reilly III and Jeffrey Pfeffer, *Hidden Value: How Great Companies Achieve Extraordinary Results with Ordinary People* (Boston: Harvard Business School Press, 2000).

47. Denise M. Rousseau, "On Organizational Behavior," *BizEd* (May/June 2008), pp. 30–31.

48. John Gardner, *No Easy Victories* (New York, Harper & Row, 1968).

49. Peter F. Drucker, "Looking Ahead: Implications of the Present," *Harvard Business Review* (September–October 1997), pp. 18–32.

50. Quote from Ralph Z. Sorenson, "A Lifetime of Learning to Manage Effectively," *Wall Street Journal* (February 28, 1983), p. 18.

FEATURE NOTES

Going Global: Information from Justin Martin, "Mercedes: Made in Alabama," *Fortune* (July 7, 1997), pp. 150–58; "A Plant Grows in Alabama," *Mercedes Momentum* (Spring 1998), pp. 56–61; "Domestic Brands Surpass Imports in Initial Quality for the First Time in IQS history," news release, J. D. Power and Associates, June 17, 2010.

Real Ethics: This situation was reported in the *Columbus Dispatch* (March 8, 2006), p. D2.

Canadian Company in the News: Information from Four Seasons corporate website, www.fourseasons.com.

Research Brief: Jim Collins, *Good to Great: Why Some Companies Make the Leap . . . and Others Don't* (New York: Harper Business, 2001).

CASE ENDNOTES

1. Inditex Press Dossier: www.inditex.com/en/downloads/ITXDossier08_en.pdf (accessed May 19, 2008).

2. "The Future of Fast Fashion," *Economist* (June 18, 2005).

3. Inditex Press Dossier.

4. Cecile Rohwedder and Keith Johnson, "Pace-Setting Zara Seeks More Speed to Fight Its Rising Cheap-Chic Rivals," *Wall Street Journal* (February 20, 2008), page B1.

5. "The Future of Fast Fashion."

6. "Shining Examples." *Economist* (June 17, 2006).

7. Inditex Press Dossier.

8. "Zara Seeks More Speed."

9. Ibid.

10. Pitsinee Jitpleecheep, "Esprit Counters New Brands with Price Cut," *Bangkok Post* (Thailand) (September 19, 2007).

11. "New Look Hopes Paris Store Will Be Continental Bridgehead," *The Times* (United Kingdom) (June 13, 2006).

12. Diana Middleton, "Fashion for the Frugal," *The Florida Times-Union* (October 1, 2006).

13. Inditex Press Dossier.

14. "Our Group," www.inditex.com/en/who_we_are/our_group (accessed May 18, 2008).

15. "Who We Are," www.inditex.com/en/who_we_are/timeline (accessed May 18, 2008).

16. "Our Group."

17. Inditex Press Dossier.

18. Ibid.

19. Ibid.

20. "The Future of Fast Fashion."

21. "Westfield Looks to Zara for Fuller Figure of $1bn Australian," *The Australian* (September 3, 2007), p. 3.

22. Inditex Press Dossier.

23. "Ortega's Empire Showed Rivals New Style of Retailing," *The Times* (United Kingdom) (June 14, 2007).

24. "The Future of Fast Fashion."

25. "Zara Seeks More Speed."

26. "The Future of Fast Fashion."

CHAPTER 3

ENDNOTES

1. Jeff Sanford, "Beat China on Cost: Gildan Taps Other Labour Pool and Trade Pacts," *Canadian Business* (November 7, 2005); Jeff Sanford and John Gray, "Top CFO 2005: Lawrence Sellyn, Gildan Activewear Inc.," *Canadian Business* (April 25, 2005); Tavia Grant, "Swings in Dollar Spur Headaches," *The Globe and Mail* (May 27, 2010), p. B4; additional information from the Gildan website, www.gildan.com.

2. Richard D. Lewis, *The Cultural Imperative: Global Trends in the 21st Century* (Yarmouth, ME: Intercultural Press, 2002).

3. Information from Emily Parker, "The Roots of Chinese Nationalism," *Wall Street Journal* (April 1, 2008), p. A17.

4. Makoto Ohtsu, *Inside Japanese Business: A Narrative History 1960–2000* (Armonk, NY: M.E. Sharpe, 2002).

5. Sample articles include "Globalization Bites Boeing," *BusinessWeek* (March 24, 2008), p. 32; "One World, One Car, One Name," *BusinessWeek* (March 24, 2008), p. 32; Eric Bellman and Jackie Range, "Indian-Style Mergers: Buy a Brand, Leave It Alone," *Wall* *Street Journal* (March 22–23, 2008), pp. A9, A14.

6. See for example Kenichi Ohmae's books *The Borderless World: Power and Strategy in the Interlinked Economy* (New York: Harper, 1989); *The End of the Nation State* (New York: Free Press, 1996); *The Invisible Continent: Four Strategic Imperatives of the New Economy* (New York: Harper, 1999); and *The Next Global Stage: Challenges and Opportunities in Our Borderless World* (Philadelphia: Wharton School Publishing, 2006).

7. For a discussion of globalization, see Thomas L. Friedman, *The Lexus and the Olive Tree: Understanding Globalization* (New York: Bantam Doubleday Dell, 2000); John Micklethwait and Adrian Woodridge, *A Future Perfect: The Challenges and Hidden Promise of Globalization* (New York: Crown, 2000); and Thomas L. Friedman, *The World is Flat: A Brief History of the Twenty-First Century* (New York: Farrar, Straus and Giroux, 2005).

8. Rosabeth Moss Kanter, *World Class: Thinking Locally in the Global Economy* (New York: Simon-Schuster, 1995), preface.

9. Quote from Jeffrey E. Garten, "The Mind of the CEO," *BusinessWeek* (February 5, 2001), p. 106.

10. "Honda's Innovative Green Engine Plant Powered by Canadian Talent," Government of Canada, http://investincanada.gc.ca/eng/publications/honda.aspx.

11. Information from Mei Fong, "Chinese Refrigerator Maker Finds U.S. Chilly," *Wall Street Journal* (March 18, 2008), pp. B1–B2.

12. Quote from John A. Byrne, "Visionary vs. Visionary," *BusinessWeek* (August 28, 2000), p. 210.

13. Information from newbalance.com/corporate.

14. Information on hourly wage costs reported in "Breaking a Taboo, High Fashion Starts Making Goods Overseas," *Wall Street Journal* (September 27, 2005), pp. A1, A10.

15. Information in box from "Factory to the World," *National Geographic* (May 2008), p. 170. For how Chinese firms are being affected by the global economic slowdown see Dexter Roberts, "China's Factory Blues," *BusinessWeek* (April 7, 2008), pp. 78–82.

16. Information from Michael A. Fletcher, "Ohio Profits from Exports," *Columbus Dispatch* (December 30, 2007), p. B3.

17. "Survey: Intellectual Property Theft Now Accounts for 31 Percent of Global Counterfeiting," Gieschen Consultancy, February 25, 2005.

18. Information from "Not Exactly Counterfeit," *Fortune* (April 26, 2006).

19. "Foreign Direct Investment, Net Inflows," table from the World Bank, World Development Indicators, available at www.google.com/publicdata?ds=wb-wdi&met=bx_klt_ dinv_cd_wd&idim=country:CAN&dl=en&hl=en&q=foreign+direct+investment+canada.

20. John R. Baldwin and Wulong Gu, "Global Links: Multinationals, Foreign Ownership and Productivity Growth in Canadian Manufacturing," (Ottawa: Statistics Canada, 2005), Canadian Economy in Transition Working Paper.

21. Criteria for choosing joint venture partners developed from Anthony J. F. O'Reilly, "Establishing Successful Joint Ventures in Developing Nations: A CEO's Perspective," *Columbia Journal of World Business* (Spring 1988), pp. 65–71; and "Best Practices for Global Competitiveness," *Fortune* (March 30, 1998), pp. S1–S3, special advertising section.

22. Karby Leggett, "U.S. Auto Makers Find Promise—and Peril—in China," *Wall Street Journal* (June 19, 2003), p. B1; "Did Spark Spark a Copycat?" *BusinessWeek* (February 7, 2005), p. 64.

23. www.wto.org/English/thewto_e/whatis_e/tif_e/fact3_e.htm (March 25, 2008).

24. Information and quote from "WTO Takes up U.S. Complaint against China Patent Regime," AFP (September 7, 2007), afp.google.com/article/ALeqM5hASBbePC8gtbmtfzExtmfkdNDvKQ.

25. Pete Engardio, Geri Smith, and Jane Sasseen, "Refighting NAFTA," *BusinessWeek* (March 31, 2008), pp. 55–59.

26. Ibid.; Engardio, et al., op. cit.

27. *The Economist* is a good weekly source of information on Africa. See www.economist.com. See also James A. Austin and John G. McLean, "Pathways to Business Success in Sub-Saharan Africa," *Journal of African Finance and Economic Development*, vol. 2 (1996), pp. 57–76; and "Embracing Africa," *BusinessWeek* (December 18, 2006), p. 101.

28. Robert Farzad, "Can Greed Save Africa?" *BusinessWeek* (December 10, 2007), pp. 46–54.

29. Information from Chris Tomlinson, "Africa's New Hope: Entrepreneurs Lead Economic Growth," *The Columbus Dispatch* (December 9, 2007), p. G3.

30. www.sadc.int/about_sadc/vision.php

31. Data from "Sandwiched," *Economist* (July 26, 2008), p. 88.

32. Information from "Fortune Global 500," Fortune.com; "FT Global 500 2008," *FT Weekend* (June 28/29, 2008), pp. 34–41; and "The Rise of New Business Powers," *FT Weekend* (June 28/29, 2008), p. 14.

33. See Peter F. Drucker, "The Global Economy and the Nation-State," *Foreign Affairs*, vol. 76 (September–October 1997), pp. 159–71.

34. Information from Steve Hamm, "IBM vs. TATA: Which Is More American?" *BusinessWeek* (May 5, 2008), p. 28.

35. Michael Mandel, "Multinationals: Are they Good for America?," *BusinessWeek* (February 28, 2008): businessweek.com.

36. Ibid.

37. See, for example, www.corpwatch.org/article.php?id=377.

38. R. Hall Mason, "Conflicts between Host Countries and Multinational Enterprise," *California Management Review*, vol. 17 (1974), pp. 6, 7.

39. Mandel, op. cit.; Engardio, et al., op. cit.

40. Devon Maylie, "Alcoa Invests Near Planned Mines," *Wall Street Journal* (March 24, 2008), p. B4; Tom Wright, "Indonesia's Commodity Boom Is a Mixed Bag," *Wall Street Journal* (March 24, 2008), p. A8; James T. Areddy, "Tibet Unrest May Deter Foreign Investors," *Wall Street Journal* (March 24, 2008), p. A3.

41. Data in table from *Report on the Transparency International Global Corruption Barometer 2007* (Berlin: Transparency International, 2007). See also transparency.org. See also Blake E. Ashforth, Dennis A. Gioia, Sandra L. Robinson, and Linda K. Trevino, "Special Topic Forum on Corruption," *The Academy of Management Review*, vol. 33 (July 2008), p. 670.

42. Transparency International, "Persistently High Corruption in Low-Income Countries Amounts to an Ongoing Human Disaster," news release, Berlin (September 23, 2008). See also "Playing It Straight," *Wall Street Journal* (May 6, 2008), p. A18.

43. "Endgame: Hypocrisy, Blindness, and the Doomsday Scenario," *Fast Company* (June 2008), p. 121.

44. "An Industry Monitors Child Labor," *New York Times* (October 16, 1997), pp. B1, B9; Rugmark International website, www.rugmark.de.

45. Information from corporate website, www.nikeBiz.com/labor/toc_monitoring.html.

46. "Endgame: Hypocrisy, Blindness, and the Doomsday Scenario," op. cit.

47. Definition from World Commission on Environment and Development, *Our Common Future* (Oxford: Oxford University Press, 1987); reported on International Institute for Sustainable Development website, www.iisdl.iisd.ca.

48. Ibid.

49. www.global100.org.

50. www.iso.org/iso/iso_14000_essentials.

51. http://isotc.iso.org.

52. Examples reported in Neil Chesanow, *The World-Class Executive* (New York: Rawson Associates, 1985).

53. For alternative definitions of culture, see Martin J. Gannon, *Paradoxes of Culture and Globalization* (Thousand Oaks, CA: Sage, 2008), Chapter 2.

54. P. Christopher Earley and Elaine Mosakowski, "Toward Cultural Intelligence: Turning Cultural Differences into Workplace Advantage," *Academy of Management Executive*, vol. 18 (2004), pp. 151–57.

55. For a good overview of the practical issues, see Richard D. Lewis, *The Cultural Imperative: Global Trends in the 21st Century* (Yarmouth, ME: Intercultural Press, 2002); and Martin J. Gannon, *Understanding Global Cultures* (Thousand Oaks, CA: Sage, 1994).

56. Example from Fong, op. cit.

57. Edward T. Hall, *The Silent Language* (New York: Anchor Books, 1959).

58. Edward T. Hall, *Beyond Culture* (New York: Doubleday, 1976).

59. Edward T. Hall, *The Hidden Dimension* (New York: Anchor Books, 1969); and *Hidden Differences* (New York: Doubleday, 1990).

60. Ibid.

61. Geert Hofstede, *Culture's Consequences* (Beverly Hills, CA: Sage, 1984); and *Culture's Consequences: Comparing Values, Behaviors, Institutions and Organizations Across Nations*, 2nd ed. (Thousand Oaks, CA: Sage, 2001). See also Michael H. Hoppe, "An Interview with Geert Hofstede," *Academy of Management Executive*, vol. 18 (2004), pp. 75–79.

62. Geert Hofstede and Michael H. Bond, "The Confucius Connection: From Cultural Roots to Economic Growth," *Organizational Dynamics*, vol. 16 (1988), pp. 4–21.

63. See Geert Hofstede, *Culture and Organizations: Software of the Mind* (London: McGraw-Hill, 1991).

64. For another perspective, see Harry Triandis and M. Gelfand, "Convergent Measurement of Horizontal and Vertical Collectivism," *Journal of Personality & Social Psychology*, vol. 74, pp. 118–28.

65. This dimension is explained more thoroughly by Geert Hofstede et al., *Masculinity and Femininity: The Taboo Dimension of National Cultures* (Thousand Oaks, CA.: Sage, 1998).

66. Information for "Stay Informed" from "The Conundrum of the Glass Ceiling," *Economist* (July 23, 2005), p. 634; and "Japan's Diversity Problem," *Wall Street Journal* (October 24, 2005), pp. B1, B5.

67. Ibid.

68. See Hofstede and Bond, op. cit.

69. See, for example, Nancy Adler and Allison Gundersen, *International Dimensions of Organizational Behavior*, 5th ed. (New York: Thomson South-Western, 2008).

70. Geert Hofstede, "Motivation, Leadership, and Organization: Do American Theories Apply Abroad?" *Organizational Dynamics* (1980), p. 43; Geert Hofstede, "The Cultural Relativity of Organizational Practices," *Journal of International Business Studies* (Fall 1983), pp. 75–89. See also Hofstede's "Cultural Constraints in Management Theories," *Academy of Management Review*, vol. 7 (1993), pp. 81–94.

71. The classics are William Ouchi, *Theory Z: How American Business Can Meet the Japanese Challenge* (Reading, MA: Addison-Wesley, 1981); and Richard Tanner Pascale and Anthony G. Athos, *The Art of Japanese Management: Applications for American Executives* (New York: Simon-Schuster, 1981). See also J. Bernard Keys, Luther Tray Denton, and Thomas R. Miller, "The Japanese Management Theory Jungle—Revisited," *Journal of Management*, vol. 20 (1994), pp. 373–402.

72. See Chapters 4 and 5 in Miriam Erez and P. Christopher Early, *Culture, Self-Identity, and Work* (New York: Oxford University Press, 1993).

73. For a good discussion of the historical context of Japanese management practices, see Makoto Ohtsu, *Inside Japanese Business: A Narrative History 1960–2000* (Armonk, NY: M. E. Sharpe, 2002), pp. 39–41.

74. Robert J. House, Paul J. Hanges, Mansour Javidan, Peter W. Dorfman, and Vipin Gupta, eds., *Culture, Leadership and Organizations: The GLOBE Study of 62 Societies* (Thousand Oaks, CA: Sage Publications, Inc., 2004). Further issues on Project GLOBE are developed in George B. Graen, "In the Eye of the Beholder: Cross-Cultural Lessons in Leadership from Project GLOBE: A Response Viewed from the Third Culture Bonding (TCB) Model of Cross-Cultural Leadership," *Academy of Management Perspectives*, vol. 20 (November 2006), pp. 95–101; and Robert J. House, Mansour Javidan, Peter W. Dorfman, and Mary Sully de Luque, "A Failure of Scholarship: Response to George Graen's Critique of GLOBE," *Academy of Management Perspectives*, vol. 20 (November 2006), pp. 102–14.

75. This summary is based on Mansour Javidan, P. Dorfman, Mary Sully de Luque, and Robert J. House, "In the Eye of the Beholder: Cross-Cultural Lessons in Leadership from Project GLOBE," *Academy of Management Perspectives* (February 2006), pp. 67–90.

76. Data from Gannon, op. cit., p. 52.

77. For additional cultural models and research, see the summary in House, op. cit., as well as Fons Trompenaars, *Riding the Waves of Culture: Understanding Cultural Diversity in Business* (London: Nicholas Brealey Publishing, 1993); Harry C. Triandis, *Culture and Social Behavior* (New York: McGraw-Hill, 1994); Steven H. Schwartz, "A Theory of Cultural Values and Some Implications for Work," *Applied Psychology: An International Review*, vol. 48 (1999), pp. 23–47; and Martin J. Gannon, *Understanding Global Cultures*, 3rd ed. (Thousand Oaks, CA: Sage, 2004).

78. Discussion based on Howard V. Perlmutter, "The Tortuous Evolution of the Multinational Corporation," *Columbia Journal of World Business*, vol. 4 (January–February 1969).

79. Information from Daisy Nguyen, "McBack and Relax," *Columbus Dispatch* (March 28, 2008), pp. C12, C10.

80. See, for example, Mzamo P. Mangaliso, "Building Competitive Advantage from Ubuntu: Management Lessons from South Africa," *Academy of Management Executive*, vol. 15 (2001), pp. 23–33.

81. Information from Mei Fong, "Chinese Refrigerator Maker Finds U.S. Chilly," *Wall Street Journal* (March 18, 2008), pp. B1, B2.

82. Geert Hofstede, "A Reply to Goodstein and Hunt," *Organizational Dynamics*, vol. 10 (summer 1981), p. 68.

FEATURE NOTES

Going Global: "Eliminate Entry Test, Wind Mobile Chief Says," *National Post*, June 10, 2010, p. FP 6.

Real Ethics: Information from Raul Burgoa, "Bolivia Seizes Control of Oil and Gas Fields," *Bangkok Post* (May 3, 2006), p. B5.

Issues and Situations: Information from Peter Burrows, "Stalking High-Tech Sweatshops," *BusinessWeek* (June 19, 2006), pp. 62–63.

Research Brief: Margaret A. Shaffer, David A. Harrison, Hal Gregersen, J. Steward Black, and Lori A. Ferzandi, "You Can Take It with You: Individual Differences and Expatriate Effectiveness," *Journal of Applied Psychology*, vol. 91 (2006), pp. 109–25.

Canadian Managers: "Chris Viehbacher, Chief Executive Officer of sanofi-aventis as of December 1, 2008," available at http://en.sanofi-aventis.com/at-a-glance/organization/bio_viehbacher.asp.

CASE ENDNOTES

1. McCain Foods Limited website, "Our Company," www.mccain.com/company/Pages/default.aspx.

2. McCain Foods Limited website, "History," www.mccain.com/company/History/Pages/Default.aspx.

3. Grant Catton, "Repeat Issuer McCain Gets Funds via HSBC & BNP," *Private Placement Letter* (New York: August 31, 2009, Vol. 27, Iss. 35), p. 3.

4. McCain Foods Limited website, "Worldwide," www.mccain.com/worldwide/Pages/default.aspx.

5. Rebecca Penty, "McCain's Passion for China; Growth: French Fry Producer Is After a Lion's Share of the Asian Country's Fast Food Market," *The Telegraph-Journal*, Saint John (February 6, 2010), p. C1.

6. McCain Foods Limited website, "History."

7. McCain Foods Limited website, "McCain Food's Global Corporate Social Responsibility Report Fiscal 2009," http://www.mccain.com/company/socialresponsibility/Pages/default.aspx.

8. Rebecca Penty, "McCain to Cut Potato Sourcing by 20 Per Cent; Food: Low Demand, High Loonie, Leftover Crop and Competition behind Cutbacks," *The Telegraph-Journal*, Saint John (March 16, 2010), p. B1.

9. John Greenwood, "McCain Hopes Busy Chinese Like Fries; Asian Expansion," *National Post* (February 26, 2008), p. FP1.

10. Danielle Flavelle, "McCain to Build Fry Plant in China; Wants to Solidify Its Market There. Joins Influx of Foreign Firms," *Toronto Star* (June 24, 2004), p. D1.

11. Ben Shingler, "McCain's New Plant Has Latest Bells and Whistles; French Fries Company Looking to Strengthen Its Share of Foreign Markets," *The Telegraph-Journal*, Saint John (September 5, 2008), p. B1.

12. Penty, February 6, 2010.

13. Ibid.

14. Ibid.

15. Flavelle, op. cit.

16. Penty, February 6, 2010.

CHAPTER 4

ENDNOTES

1. See www.benandjerrys.com, including timeline, and J. M. Hirsch, "For Its 30th Birthday, Ben & Jerry's Offers 280th (or Is It 300th) Flavor," Associated Press (March 17, 2008).

2. Information on the Josephson Institute of Ethics from www.josephsoninstitute.org/MED/MED—2sixpillars.htm (retrieved September 10, 2006).

3. Desmond Tutu, "Do More Than Win," *Fortune* (December 30, 1991), p. 59.

4. For an overview, see Linda K. Trevino and Katherine A. Nelson, *Managing Business Ethics*, 3rd ed. (New York: Wiley, 2003).

5. See, for example, James Oliver Horter and Lois E. Horton, *Slavery and the Making of America* (New York: Oxford University Press, 2004).

6. Trevino and Nelson, op. cit.

7. Milton Rokeach, *The Nature of Human Values* (New York: Free Press, 1973). See also W. C. Frederick and J. Weber, "The Values of Corporate Executives and Their Critics: An Empirical Description and Normative Implications," in W. C. Frederick and L. E. Preston (eds.), *Business Ethics: Research Issues and Empirical Studies* (Greenwich, CT: JAI Press, 1990).

8. Philip Delves Broughton, "MBA Students Sway Integrity for Plagiarism," *Financial Times* (May 19, 2008), p. 13.

9. J. M. Christensen Hughes and D. L. McCabe, "Academic Misconduct within Higher Education in Canada," *Canadian Journal of Higher Education* (Vol. 36, No. 2), pp. 1–21.

10. See Gerald F. Cavanagh, Dennis J. Moberg, and Manuel Velasquez, "The Ethics of Organizational Politics," *Academy of Management Review*, vol. 6 (1981), pp. 363–74; Justin G. Locknecker, Joseph A. McKinney, and Carlos W. Moore, "Egoism and Independence: Entrepreneurial Ethics," *Organizational Dynamics* (Winter 1988), pp. 64–72; and Justin G. Locknecker, Joseph A. McKinney, and Carlos W. Moore, "The Generation Gap in Business Ethics," *Business Horizons* (September–October 1989), pp. 9–14.

11. Raymond L. Hilgert, "What Ever Happened to Ethics in Business and in Business Schools?" *The Diary of Alpha Kappa Psi* (April 1989), pp. 4–8.

12. The Universal Declaration of Human Rights was adopted by General Assembly resolution 217 A (III) 10 December 1948, in the United Nations. See un.org/Overview/rights.html.

13. Jerald Greenburg, "Organizational Justice: Yesterday, Today, and Tomorrow," *Journal of Management*, vol. 16 (1990), pp. 399–432; Mary A. Konovsky, "Understanding Procedural Justice and Its Impact on Business Organizations," *Journal of Management*, vol. 26 (2000), pp. 489–511.

14. For a review, see Russell Cropanzano, David E. Bown, and Stephen W. Gilliland, "The Management of Organizational Justice," *Academy of Management Perspectives* (November 2007), pp. 34–48.

15. Interactional justice is described by Robert J. Bies, "The Predicament of Injustice: The Management of Moral Outrage," in L. L. Cummings and B. M. Staw (eds.), *Research in Organizational Behavior*, vol. 9 (Greenwich, CT: JAI Press, 1987), pp. 289–319. The example is from Carol T. Kulik and Robert L. Holbrook, "Demographics in Service Encounters: Effects of Racial and Gender Congruence on Perceived Fairness," *Social Justice Research*, vol. 13 (2000), pp. 375–402.

16. Robert D. Haas, "Ethics—A Global Business Challenge," *Vital Speeches of the Day* (June 1, 1996), pp. 506–9.

17. This discussion is based on Thomas Donaldson, "Values in Tension: Ethics Away from Home," *Harvard Business Review*, vol. 74 (September–October 1996), pp. 48–62.

18. Ibid.; Thomas Donaldson and Thomas W. Dunfee, "Towards a Unified Conception of Business Ethics: Integrative Social Contracts Theory," *Academy of Management Review*, vol. 19 (1994), pp. 252–85.

19. Donaldson, op. cit.

20. Reported in Barbara Ley Toffler, "Tough Choices: Managers Talk Ethics," *New Management*, vol. 4 (1987), pp. 34–39. See also Barbara Ley Toffler, *Tough Choices: Managers Talk Ethics* (New York: Wiley, 1986).

21. See discussion by Trevino and Nelson, op. cit., pp. 47–62.

22. Steven N. Brenner and Earl A. Mollander, "Is the Ethics of Business Changing?" *Harvard Business Review*, vol. 55 (January–February 1977).

23. Survey results from Del Jones, "48% of Workers Admit to Unethical or Illegal Acts," *USA Today* (April 4, 1997), p. A1.

24. See Thomas M. Jones, "Ethical Decision Making by Individuals in Organizations: An Issue-Contingent Model," *Academy of Management Review*, vol. 16 (1991), pp. 366–95; Sara Morris and Robert A. McDonald, "The Role of Moral Intensity in Moral Judgments: An Empirical Investigation," *Journal of Business Ethics*, vol. 14 (9) (1995), pp. 715–26; and Tim Barnett, "Dimensions of Moral Intensity and Ethical Decision Making: An Empirical Study," *Journal of Applied Social Psychology*, vol. 31 (2001), pp. 1038–57.

25. Reported in Adam Smith, "Wall Street's Outrageous Fortunes," *Esquire* (April 1987), p. 73.

26. Lawrence Kohlberg, *The Psychology of Moral Development: The Nature and Validity of Moral Stages* (*Essays in Moral Development*, Volume 2) (New York: Harper Collins, 1984). See also the discussion by Linda K. Trevino, "Moral Reasoning and Business Ethics: Implications for Research, Education, and Management," *Journal of Business Ethics*, vol. 11 (1992), pp. 445–59.

27. The Body Shop came under scrutiny over the degree to which its business practices actually live up to this charter and the company's self-promoted green image. See, for example, John Entine, "Shattered Image," *Business Ethics* (September–October 1994), pp. 23–28.

28. The company story and information on Dame Anita Roddick from thebodyshop international.com/aboutThus.

29. Al Rosen, "Only in Canada, Eh?," *Canadian Business* on-line (November 6, 2006); "WestJet Apologizes to Air Canada for Snooping," *National Post*, n.d., available at www.finan cialpost.com/story.html?id=6ca8461a-fb61-4bcc-be49-002f092c337f&k=61096#ixzz0u WIPckav.

30. "Corporate Espionage: A By-Product of Today's Global Economy," Foreign Affairs and International Trade Canada, available at www.international.gc.ca/canadexport/ articles/384740.aspx.

31. Saul W. Gellerman, "Why 'Good' Managers Make Bad Ethical Choices," *Harvard Business Review*, vol. 64 (July–August 1986), pp. 85–90.

32. Items from new headlines, including "Canada's Technology Star Becomes Financial Black Hole," CBC News on-line (September 16, 2009); "EHealth Scandal a $1B Waste: Auditor," CBC News on-line (October 7, 2009); also Blake E. Ashforth, Dennis A. Gioia, Sandra C. Robinson and Linda K. Trevino, "Special Topic Forum on Corruption in Organizations," *Academy of Management Review*, vol. 33 (July 2008), p. 670.

33. See "Whistle-Blowers on Trial," *Business-Week* (March 24, 1997), pp. 172–78, and "NLRB Judge Rules for Massachusetts Nurses in Whistle-Blowing Case," *American Nurse* (January–February 1998), p. 7.

34. For a review of whistleblowing, see Marcia P. Micelli and Janet P. Near, *Blowing the Whistle* (Lexington, MA: Lexington Books, 1992); see also Micelli and Near, "Whistleblowing: Reaping the Benefits," *Academy of Management Executive*, vol. 8 (August 1994), pp. 65–72.

35. Information from Ethics Resource Center, "Major Survey of America's Workers Finds Substantial Improvements in Ethics": www. ethics.org/releases/nr_20030521_nbes. html.

36. "A Tip for Whistleblowers: Don't," *Wall Street Journal* (May 31, 2007), p. B6.

37. "Whistleblower Protection," Lang Michener LLP, available at www.langmichener. ca/index.cfm?fuseaction=content. contentDetail&id=9811&lid=0.

38. James A. Waters, "Catch 20.5: Mortality as an Organizational Phenomenon," *Organizational Dynamics*, vol. 6 (Spring 1978), pp. 3–15.

39. "Ethical Business Leadership," *BGS International Exchange* (Spring 2008), pp. 14–16.

40. Alan L. Otten, "Ethics on the Job: Companies Alert Employees to Potential Dilemmas," *Wall Street Journal* (July 14, 1986), p. 17; and "The Business Ethics Debate," *Newsweek* (May 25, 1987), p. 36.

41. Information from corporate website, www.gapinc.com/community sourcing/ vendor_conduct.htm.

42. Information from Joseph Pereira and Steve Stecklow. "Wal-Mart Raises Bar on Toy-Safety Standards," *Wall Street Journal* (May 14, 2008), p. B1; Presentation on Canadian Toy Safety Standards by CPS (www.bureau-veritas.com).

43. Kohlberg, op. cit.

44. Information from "Gifts of Gab: A Start-Up's Social Conscience Pays Off," *Business Week* (February 5, 2001), p. F38. See also "About Us" at madgabs.com.

45. Information from www.josephsoninstitute. org/MED/MED-2sixpillars.htm.

46. Archie B. Carroll, "In Search of the Moral Manager," *Business Horizons* (March/April 2001), pp. 7–15.

47. Kohlberg, op. cit.

48. See Terry Thomas, John R. Schermerhorn Jr., and John W. Dienhart, "Leading Toward Ethical Behavior in Business," *Academy of Management Executive*, vol. 18 (May 2004), pp. 56–66.

49. David Bornstein, *How to Change the World: Social Entrepreneurs and the Power of New Ideas* (Oxford, UK: Oxford University Press, 2004).

50. See Laura D'Andrea Tyson, "Good Works—With a Business Plan," *BusinessWeek* (May 3, 2004, retrieved from BusinessWeek Online, November 14, 2005, at www.businessweek. com); and John Wood, *Leaving Microsoft to Change the World* (New York: HarperCollins, 2006.)

51. Examples are from the David Suzuki Foundation website, www.davidsuzuki.org; Rick Hansen Foundation website, www.rickhan sen.com; Free the Children website, www. freethechildren.com; and Greenlite website, www.greenlite.ca.

52. Joe Biesecker, "What Today's College Graduates Want: It's Not All About Paychecks," *Central Penn Business Journal* (August 10, 2007).

53. Ibid.; Sarah E. Needleman, "The Latest Office Perk: Getting Paid to Volunteer," *Wall Street Journal* (April 29, 2008), p. D1.

54. Nanett Byrnes, "Heavy Lifting at the Food Bank," *BusinessWeek* (December 17, 2007), pp. SC08-SC09; and Michael E. Porter and Mark R. Kramer, "Strategy & Society: The Link Between Competitive Advantage and Corporate Social Responsibility," *Harvard Business Review* (December 2006), Reprint R0612D.

55. See Thomas Donaldson and Lee Preston, "The Stakeholder Theory of the Corporation," *Academy of Management Review*, vol. 20 (January 1995), pp. 65–91.

56. See tomsofmaine.com/about/environment. asp.

57. Mary Miller, "Ben Cohen's Hot Fudge Venture Fund," *Business Ethics*, vol. 16 (January–February 2002), p. 6.

58. See "The Socially Correct Corporate Business," *Fortune* special advertising section (July 24, 2000), pp. S32–S34; and Joseph Pereira, "Doing Good and Doing Well at Timberland," *Wall Street Journal* (September 9, 2003), pp. B1, B10.

59. See Joel Makower, *Putting Social Responsibility to Work for Your Business and the World* (New York: Simon-Schuster, 1994), pp. 17–18.

60. The historical framework of this discussion is developed from Keith Davis, "The Case for and against Business Assumption of Social Responsibility," *Academy of Management Journal* (June 1973), pp. 312–22; Keith Davis and William Frederick, *Business and Society: Management, Public Policy, Ethics*, 5th ed. (New York: McGraw-Hill, 1984). The debate is also discussed by Makower, op. cit., pp. 28–33. See also "Civics 101," *Economist* (May 11, 1996), p. 61.

61. The Friedman quotation is from Milton Friedman, *Capitalism and Freedom* (Chicago: University of Chicago Press, 1962). See also Henry G. Manne, "Milton Friedman Was Right," *Wall Street Journal* (November 24: 2006), p. A12. The Samuelson quotation is from Paul A. Samuelson, "Love That Corporation," *Mountain Bell Magazine* (Spring 1971). Both are cited in Davis, op. cit.

62. Davis and Frederick, op. cit.

63. Herb Greenberg, "How Values Embraced by a Company May Enhance that Company's Value," *Wall Street Journal* (October 27–28, 2007), p. B3.

64. See James K. Glassman, "When Ethics Meet Earnings," *International Herald Tribune* (May 24–25, 2003), p. 15.

65. See Makower, op. cit. (1994), pp. 71–75; Sandra A. Waddock and Samuel B. Graves, "The Corporate Social Performance–Financial Performance Link," *Strategic Management Journal* (1997), pp. 303–19; Michael E. Porter and Mark R. Kramer, "Strategy-Society: The Link Between Competitive Advantage and Corporate Social Responsibility," *Harvard Business Review* (December 2006), pp. 78–92.

66. The "compliance–conviction" distinction is attributed to Mark Goyder in Martin Waller, "Much Corporate Responsibility Is Box-Ticking," *The Times Business* (July 8, 2003), p. 21.

67. Archie B. Carroll, "A Three-Dimensional Model of Corporate Performance," *Academy of Management Review*, vol. 4 (1979), pp. 497–505. Carroll's continuing work in this area is reported in Mark S. Schwartz and Archie B. Carroll, "Corporate Social Responsibility: A Three Domain Approach," *Business Ethics Quarterly*, vol. 13 (2003), pp. 503–30.

68. See the discussion by Porter and Kramer, op. cit.

69. Elizabeth Gatewood and Archie B. Carroll, "The Anatomy of Corporate Social Response," *Business Horizons*, vol. 24 (September–October 1981), pp. 9–16.

70. Judith Burns, "Everything You Wanted to Know About Corporate Governance . . . But Didn't Know How to Ask," *Wall Street Journal* (October 27, 2003), pp. R1, R7.

71. Ibid.

72. Kevin Drawbaugh, "Congressional Panel Rips Subprime CEOs' Lavish Pay," *Reuters* (March 7, 2008), retrieved from reuters.com.

73. Ibid.

74. "Warming to Corporate Reform," *Wall Street Journal* (October 25, 2005), p. R2.

75. Giselle Weybrecht, *The Sustainable MBA* (West Sussex, UK: John Wiley & Sons, 2010).

76. Ling Woo Liu, "Water Pressure," *Time* (June 12, 2008).

77. Ibid.

78. Ibid.

79. Ibid.

80. Weybrecht, op. cit.

81. Ibid.

FEATURE NOTES

Going Global: Information from the Cirque du Soleil website, www.cirquedusoleil.com.

Real Ethics: Information from Cheryl Soltis, *Wall Street Journal* (March 21, 2006), p. B7.

Issues and Situations: Information from Erin White, "What Would You Do? Ethics Courses Get Context," *Wall Street Journal* (June 12, 2006), p. B3.

Research Brief: Cedric E. Dawkins, "First to Market: Issue Management Pacesetters and the Pharmaceutical Industry Response to AIDS in Africa," *Business & Society* (September 2005), pp. 244–82.

Canadian Company in the News: Information from Karen Bains, "Casebook of Environmental Best Practices Among Cooperatives: Mountain Equipment Co-op," Canadian Co-operative Association, September 2009.

CASE ENDNOTES

1. Laura Zinn, "Tom Chappell: Sweet Success from Unsweetened Toothpaste," *Business-Week* (September 2, 1991), p. 52.

2. Janet Bamford, "Changing Business as Usual," *Working Women*, vol. 18 (November 1993), p. 106.

3. Judy Quinn, "Tom's of Maine," *Incentive* (December 1993), p. A4.

4. Ibid.

5. Craig Cox, "Interview: Tom Chappell, Minister of Commerce," *Business Ethics*, vol. 8 (January 1994), p. 42.

6. Mary Martin, "Toothpaste and Theology," *Boston Globe* (October 10, 1993), p. A4.

7. Cox, op. cit.

8. Mary Martin, "A 'Nuisance' to Rivals," *Boston Globe* (October 10, 1993), p. A4.

9. Cox, op. cit.

10. Ibid.

11. "The Tom's of Maine Mission," at www.tomsofmaine.com/about/mission.asp.

12. Quinn, op. cit.

13. Ellyn E. Spragins, "Paying Employees to Work Elsewhere," *Inc.* (February 1993), p. 29.

14. Quinn, op. cit.

15. Ibid.

16. Martin Everett, "Profiles in Marketing: Katie Shisler," *Sales and Marketing Management* (March 1993), p. 12.

17. Quinn, op. cit.

18. Cox, op. cit.

19. Ibid.

20. Ibid.

21. www.cosmeticsdesign.com/news/ng.asp?n=84131-tom-s-of-maine-toothpaste-natural-glycyrrhizin

22. www.tomsofmaine.com/about/Colgate.asp

23. www.oregonlive.com/business/oregonian/index.ssf?/base/business/1191637537264110.xml&coll=7

24. Tom's of Maine website, www.tomsofmaine.com.

25. Ibid.

26. K. W. Meyers, "Tom's of Maine Business Plan Includes People," *Rocky Mountain News* (October 5, 2000), p. 3B.

CHAPTER 5

ENDNOTES

1. Information from "Vincent Cheung Wins Entrepreneur Competition," news release, University of Toronto, May 19, 2010; ACE website at www.acecanada.ca.

2. This list is developed from see Jeffery A. Timmons, *New Venture Creation: Entrepreneurship for the 21st Century* (New York: Irwin/McGraw-Hill, 1999), pp. 47–48; Robert D. Hisrich and Michael P. Peters, *Entrepreneurship*, 4th ed. (New York: Irwin/McGraw-Hill, 1998), pp. 67–70.

3. Information from "Women Business Owners Receive First-Ever Micro Loans Via the Internet," *Business Wire* (August 9, 2000); Jim Hopkins, "Non-Profit Loan Group Takes Risks on Women in Business," *USA Today* (August 9, 2000), p. 2B; and "Women's Group Grants First Loans to Entrepreneurs," *Columbus Dispatch* (August 10, 2000), p. B2.

4. Speech at the Lloyd Greif Center for Entrepreneurial Studies, Marshall School of Business, University of Southern California, 1996.

5. Information from the corporate websites and from The Entrepreneur's Hall of Fame, www.1tbn.com/halloffame.html.

6. Information from https://www.empireclub.org/foundation/index.html.

7. Information from www.chapters.indigo.ca.

8. Information from www.timhortons.com.

9. "Dame Anita Roddick Dies Aged 64," BBC News on-line (September 10, 2007).

10. For a review and discussion of the entrepreneurial mind, see Timmons, op. cit, pp. 219–25.

11. See the review by Hisrich and Peters, op. cit., and Paulette Thomas. "Entrepreneurs' Biggest Problems and How They Solve Them," *Wall Street Journal Reports* (March 17, 2003), pp. R1–R2.

12. Based on research summarized by Hisrich and Peters, op. cit., pp. 70–74.

13. Information from Jim Hopkins, "Serial Entrepreneur Strikes Again at Age 70," *USA Today* (August 15, 2000).

14. Timothy Butler and James Waldroop, "Job Sculpting: The Art of Retaining Your Best People," *Harvard Business Review* (September–October 1999), pp. 144–52.

15. "Smart Talk: Start-Ups and Schooling," *Wall Street Journal* (September 7, 2004), p. B4.

16. Data from *Paths to Entrepreneurship: New Directions for Women in Business* (New York: Catalyst, 1998); and Eve Hayek, "Report Shatters Myths About U.S. Women's Equality" (October 1, 2005); both available on the National Foundation for Women Business Owners website, www.nfwbo.org/key.html; and "Smart Talk: Start-Ups and Schooling," *Wall Street Journal* (September 7, 2004), p. B4.

17. Information from the Standing Committee on the Status of Women, "Parental Benefits for Self-Employed Women," www.wec.ca/taskforce.html, June 13, 2005.

18. Information from Industry Canada, Small Business Policy Branch, "Visible Minority Entrepreneurs," March 2005, SME Financing Data Initiative, Small Business Financing Profiles, www.strategis.ic.gc.ca.

19. *Key Small Business Statistics* (Ottawa: Industry Canada, July 2010).

20. Information reported in "The Rewards," *Inc. State of Small Business* (May 20–21, 2001), pp. 50–51.

21. "Small Business Expansions in Electronic Commerce," U.S. Small Business Administration, Office of Advocacy (June 2000).

22. Information from Will Christensen, "Rod Spencer's Sports-Card Business Has Migrated to Cyberspace Marketplace," *Columbus Dispatch* (July 24, 2000), p. F1.

23. Data reported by The Family Firm Institute: www.ffi.org/looking/factsfb.html.

24. Conversation from the case "Am I My Uncle's Keeper?" by Paul I. Karofsky (Northeastern University Center for Family Business) and published at: www.fambiz.com/contprov.cfm?ContProvCode=NECFB[ANGELO] ID=140.

25. *Survey of Small and Mid-Sized Businesses: Trends for 2000* (Arthur Andersen, 2000).

26. See U.S. Small Business Administration website, www.sba.gov.

27. George Gendron, "The Failure Myth," *Inc.* (January 2001), p. 13.

28. Discussion based on "The Life Cycle of Entrepreneurial Firms," in Ricky Griffin, ed., *Management*, 6th ed. (New York: Houghton Mifflin, 1999), pp. 309–10; and Neil C. Churchill and Virginia L. Lewis, "The Five Stages of Small Business Growth," *Harvard Business Review* (May–June 1993), pp. 30–50.

29. Developed from William S. Sahlman, "How to Write a Great Business Plan," *Harvard Business Review* (July–August 1997), pp. 98–108.

30. Brian Morton, "Award-Winning Victoria Grocery Store Passionate about Local Produce," *The Vancouver Sun* (August 4, 2010), p. C7.

31. Standard components of business plans are described in many text sources such as Linda Pinson and Jerry Jinnett, *Anatomy of a Business Plan: A Step-by-Step Guide to Starting Smart, Building the Business, and Securing Your Company's Future*, 4th ed. (Chicago: Dearborn Trade, 1999); and on websites such as American Express Small Business Services, Business Town.com, and Bizplanlt.com.

32. "You've Come a Long Way Baby," *BusinessWeek Frontier* (July 10, 2000).

FEATURE NOTES

Canadian Managers: Matt Powers, "Entrepreneurship Camp Aimed at Aboriginal Youth," *Leader-Post*, Regina (July 30, 2010), p. FNU2.

Real Ethics: Compiled with information from http://www.bbbc.org.uk/, http://www.rootsofempathy.org/Mary.html, *Meet the New Heroes: Muhammad Yunus* http://www.pbs.org/opb/thenewheroes/meet/yunus.html, and http://www.ashoka.org/social_entrepreneur. (Websites accessed November 11, 2010.)

Going Global: Anne Golden, "Canada's Innovation Malaise: The Cure's in Our Culture," *The Globe and Mail* (August 10, 2010), p. A15.

CASE ENDNOTE

1. www.originalcupcakes.com/cupcakes.php

CHAPTER 6

ENDNOTES

1. Information and quotes from Andrew Wall, "A Few Modest Proposals," *Canadian Business*, vol. 79 (December 26, 2005–January 15, 2006), p. 19; "Cognos Unveils New Blueprints for Initiative and Strategic Long Range Planning," *Al Bawaba* (October 19, 2005), p. 1; IBM/Cognos website, www-01.ibm.com/software/data/cognos/.

2. Data from "Hurry Up and Decide," *BusinessWeek* (May 14, 2001), p. 16; and *BusinessWeek* (June 23, 2008), p. 56.

3. Eaton Corporation Annual Report, 1985.

4. Henry Mintzberg, "The Manager's Job: Folklore and Fact," *Harvard Business Review*, vol. 53 (July–August 1975), pp. 54–67; and Henry Mintzberg, "Planning on the Left Side and Managing on the Right," *Harvard Business Review*, vol. 54 (July–August 1976), pp. 46–55.

5. Quote from Stephen Covey and Roger Merrill, "New Ways to Get Organized at Work," *USA Weekend* (February 6–8, 1998), p. 18.

Books by Stephen R. Covey include *The 7 Habits of Highly Effective People: Powerful Lessons in Personal Change* (New York: Fireside, 1990); and Stephen R. Covey and Sandra Merril Covey, *The 7 Habits of Highly Effective Families: Building a Beautiful Family Culture in a Turbulent World* (New York: Golden Books, 1996).

6. See Stanley Thune and Robert House, "Where Long-Range Planning Pays Off," *Business Horizons*, vol. 13 (1970), pp. 81–87. For a critical review of the literature, see Milton Leontiades and Ahmet Teel, "Planning Perceptions and Planning Results," *Strategic Management Journal*, vol. 1 (1980), pp. 65–75; and J. Scott Armstrong, "The Value of Formal Planning for Strategic Decisions," *Strategic Management Journal*, vol. 3 (1982), pp. 197–211. For special attention to the small business setting, see Richard B. Robinson Jr., John A. Pearce II, George S. Vozikis, and Timothy S. Mescon, "The Relationship Between Stage of Development and Small Firm Planning and Performance," *Journal of Small Business Management*, vol. 22 (1984), pp. 45–52; and Christopher Orphen, "The Effects of Long-Range Planning on Small Business Performance: A Further Examination," *Journal of Small Business Management*, vol. 23 (1985), pp. 16–23. For an empirical study of large corporations, see Vasudevan Ramanujam and N. Venkataraman, "Planning and Performance: A New Look at an Old Question," *Business Horizons*, vol. 30 (1987), pp. 19–25.

7. Information from Carol Hymowitz, "Packed Calendars Rule over Executives," *Wall Street Journal* (June 16, 2008), p. B1.

8. Quote from *BusinessWeek* (August 8, 1994), pp. 78–86.

9. See William Oncken, Jr., and Donald L. Wass, "Management Time: Who's Got the Monkey?" *Harvard Business Review*, vol. 52 (September–October 1974), pp. 75–80, and featured as an HBR classic, *Harvard Business Review* (November–December 1999).

10. Dick Levin, *The Executive's Illustrated Primer of Long Range Planning* (Englewood Cliffs, NJ: Prentice-Hall, 1981).

11. See Elliot Jaques, *The Form of Time* (New York: Russak Co., 1982). For an executive commentary on his research, see Walter Kiechel III, "How Executives Think," *Fortune* (December 21, 1987), pp. 139–44.

12. Information from "Skype: How a Startup Harnessed the Hoopla," *BusinessWeek* (September 26, 2005), p. 35.

13. Information from "Avoiding a Time Bomb: Sexual Harassment," *BusinessWeek*, enterprise issue (October 13, 1997), pp. ENT20–21.

14. Data from "Car Crazy," *National Geographic* (May 2008), p. 142.

15. For a thorough review of forecasting, see J. Scott Armstrong, *Long-Range Forecasting*, 2nd ed. (New York: Wiley, 1985).

16. "IOC President Backs Cypress Mountain Events," CBC News on-line (January 28, 2010).

17. Information from Associated Press, "Cola Jihad Bubbling in Europe," *Columbus Dispatch* (February 11, 2003), pp. C1, C2.

18. The scenario-planning approach is described in Peter Schwartz, *The Art of the Long View* (New York: Doubleday/Currency, 1991); and Arie de Geus, *The Living Company: Habits for Survival in a Turbulent Business Environment* (Boston, MA: Harvard Business School Press, 1997).

19. Information and quote from "The No. 2 Killer in Africa by Parasite," *Fast Company* (June 2008), pp. 102–3.

20. See, for example, Robert C. Camp, *Business Process Benchmarking* (Milwaukee: ASQ Quality Press 1994); Michael J. Spendolini, *The Benchmarking Book* (New York: AMACOM, 1992); and Christopher E. Bogan and Michael J. English, *Benchmarking for Best Practices: Winning Through Innovative Adaptation* (New York: McGraw-Hill, 1994).

21. Rachel Tiplady, "Taking the Lead in Fast-Fashion," *BusinessWeek Online* (August 29, 2006); and Cecile Rohwedder and Keith Johnson, "Pace-Setting Zara Seeks More Speed to Fight Its Rising Cheap-Chic Rivals," *Wall Street Journal* (February 20, 2008), pp. B1, B6.

22. Information from Peter Burrows and Manjeet Kripalani, "Cisco: Sold on India," *BusinessWeek* (November 28, 2005), pp. 50–51.

23. Sarka Halas, "All-Star Execs: Top COO: Geoffrey Martin," *Canadian Business*, n.d., available at http://list.canadianbusiness.com/rankings/best-managers/2008/geoffrey-martin/article.aspx?id=20081124_10012_10012.

24. Quote from Kenneth Roman, "The Man Who Sharpened Gillette," *Wall Street Journal* (September 5, 2007), p. D8.

25. T. J. Rodgers, with William Taylor and Rick Foreman, "No Excuses Management," *World Executive's Digest* (May 1994), pp. 26–30.

26. Example from Roman, op. cit.

27. See Dale D. McConkey, *How to Manage by Results*, 3rd ed. (New York: AMACOM, 1976); Stephen J. Carroll, Jr., and Henry J. Tosi, Jr., *Management by Objectives: Applications and Research* (New York: Macmillan, 1973); and Anthony P. Raia, *Managing by Objectives* (Glenview, IL: Scott, Foresman, 1974).

28. For a discussion of research, see Carroll and Tosi, op. cit.; Raia, op. cit.; and Steven Kerr, "Overcoming the Dysfunctions of MBO," *Management by Objectives*, vol. 5, no. I

(1976). Information in part from Dylan Loeb McClain, "Job Forecast: Internet's Still Hot," *New York Times* (January 30, 2001), p. 9.

29. See Douglas McGregor, *The Human Side of Enterprise* (New York: McGraw-Hill, 1960).

30. The work on goal-setting theory is well summarized in Edwin A. Locke and Gary P. Latham, *Goal Setting: A Motivational Technique That Works!* (Englewood Cliffs, NJ: Prentice Hall, 1984). See also Edwin A. Locke, Kenneth N. Shaw, Lisa A. Saari, and Gary P. Latham, "Goal Setting and Task Performance 1969–1980," *Psychological Bulletin*, vol. 90 (1981), pp. 125–52; Mark E. Tubbs, "Goal Setting: A Meta-Analytic Examination of the Empirical Evidence," *Journal of Applied Psychology*, vol. 71 (1986), pp. 474–83; and Terence R. Mitchell, Kenneth R. Thompson, and Jane George-Falvy, "Goal Setting: Theory and Practice," Chapter 9 in Cary L. Cooper and Edwin A. Locke (eds.), *Industrial and Organizational Psychology: Linking Theory with Practice* (Malden, MA: Blackwell Business, 2000), pp. 211–49.

31. Carol Hymowitz, "Two More CEO Ousters Underscore the Need to Better Strategize," *Wall Street Journal* (September 11, 2006), p. 81.

FEATURE NOTES

Real Ethics: Information from "Trial and Error," *Forbes* (June 19, 2006), pp. 128–30; Drake Bennett, "Measures of Success," *Boston Globe Online* (July 2, 2006).

Canadian Managers: "Top 40 under 40," *The Globe and Mail* (May 8, 2007); available at www.theglobeandmail.com/report-on-business/article758224.ece.

Research Brief: Michael C. Mankins and Richard Steele, "Stop Making Plans; Start Making Decisions," *Harvard Business Review* (January 2006), reprint R0601F.

Going Global: Information from the Brock Solutions website, www.brocksolutions.com.

Issues and Situations: Information from Moon Ihlwan, "Camp Samsung: To Develop Winning Products, the Korean Giant Isolates Artists and Techies for Months on End," *BusinessWeek* (July 3, 2006), pp. 46–48.

CASE ENDNOTES

1. Barry Silverstein, "Lands' End: Hard Landing?" *Brand Profile* (October 7, 2007).

2. "The Lands' End Principles of Doing Business," at www.landsend.com (accessed May 26, 2008).

3. "About Lands' End," at www.landsend.com (accessed May 26, 2008).

4. David Lidsky, "Basic Training," *Fast Company*, issue 108 (September 2006).

5. "History" at www.landsend.com (accessed May 26, 2008).

6. www.fundinguniverse.com/company-histories/Lands-End-Inc-Company-History.html (accessed May 27, 2008).

7. Ibid.

8. Kelly Nolan, "Sears Gives Lands' End New Beginning," *Retailing Today*, vol. 45, no. 18 (October 9, 2006).

9. Jim Tierney, "Sears Stores Find a Fit for Lands' End," *Multichannel Merchant* (October 2007).

10. "Dressed for Success?" *Uniforms* (May/June 2007), p. 50.

11. "Lands' End Elfs It Up," *Multichannel Merchant* (February 2006), p. 44.

12. *Multichannel Merchant*.

CHAPTER 7

ENDNOTES

1. Information from Curt Woodward, "Starbucks Strategy," *The Columbus Dispatch* (April 28, 2007), pp. C1–C2; Burt Helm, "Saving Starbucks' Soul," *BusinessWeek* (April 9, 2007), pp. 56–61; and Melissa Allison, "Starbucks Closing 5 Percent of U.S. Stores," *The Seattle Times* (July 2, 2008).

2. Information from Janet Adamy, "Coffee Clutch: McDonald's Brews a Test for Weakened Starbucks," *Wall Street Journal* (January 8, 2008), pp. 1617.

3. Helm, op. cit.

4. Allison, op. cit.

5. Examples from Edward De Bono, *Lateral Thinking: Creativity Step by Step* (New York: Harper & Row, 1970).

6. For an overview of Walmart, see Charles Fishman, *The Wal-Mart Effect* (New York: Penguin, 2006).

7. Michael Barbaro and Reed Abelson, "Despite Some Holes, Wal-Mart's Plan to Cut Drug Prices Is Lauded by Most," *The New York Times* (September 22, 2006), p. C3.

8. Michael E. Porter, *Competitive Strategy: Techniques for Analyzing Industries and Competitors* (New York: Free Press, 1980).

9. Ibid.; Michael E. Porter, *Competitive Advantage: Creating and Sustaining Superior Performance* (New York: Free Press, 1986); Richard A. D'Aveni, *Hyper-Competition: Managing the Dynamics of Strategic Maneuvering* (New York: Free Press. 1994).

10. Tony Wanless, "Going Long," *BCBusiness Online* (December 1, 2007).

11. Information and quotes from Marcia Stepanek, "How Fast Is Net Fast?" *BusinessWeek E-Biz* (November 1, 1999), pp. EB52–EB54.

12. Gary Hamel and C. K. Prahalad, "Strategic Intent," *Harvard Business Review* (May–June 1989), pp. 63–76.

13. www.pepsico.com/PEP_company.

14. For research support, see Daniel H. Gray, "Uses and Misuses of Strategic Planning," *Harvard Business Review*, vol. 64 (January-February 1986), pp. 89–97.

15. Peter F. Drucker, *Management: Tasks, Responsibilities, Practices* (New York: Harper-Row, 1973), p. 122.

16. Himani Ediriweera, "A Down to Earth Firm," *Toronto Star* (January 20, 2010); Canada Goose website, www.canada-goose.com.

17. Peter F. Drucker, "Five Questions," *Executive Excellence* (November 6, 1994), pp. 6–7.

18. See Laura Nash, "Mission Statements—Mirrors and Windows," *Harvard Business Review* (March–April 1988), pp. 155–56; James C. Collins and Jerry I. Porras, "Building Your Company's Vision," *Harvard Business Review* (September–October 1996), pp. 65–77; and James C. Collins and Jerry I. Porras, *Built to Last: Successful Habits of Visionary Companies* (New York: Harper Business, 1997).

19. Gary Hamel, *Leading the Revolution* (Boston, MA: Harvard Business School Press, 2000), pp. 72–73.

20. www.patagonia.com/web/us/patagonia.go?assetid=2047&ln=24.

21. Tim Hortons corporate website, www.timhortons.com.

22. Steve Ladurantaye, "Canada Goose Spreads the Warmth," *The Globe and Mail* (January 26, 2010).

23. For more on organizational culture, see Edgar H. Schein, *Organizational Culture and Leadership*, 2nd ed. (San Francisco: Jossey-Bass, 1997).

24. Terrence E. Deal and Allen A. Kennedy, *Corporate Cultures: The Rites and Rituals of Corporate Life* (Reading, MA: Addison-Wesley, 1982), p. 22.

25. Canada Goose website, www.canada-goose.com.

26. Peter F. Drucker's views on organizational objectives are expressed in his classic books: *The Practice of Management* (New York: Harper-Row, 1954); and *Management: Tasks, Responsibilities, Practices* (New York: Harper-Row, 1973). For a more recent commentary, see his article, "Management: The Problems of Success," *Academy of Management Executive*, vol. 1 (1987), pp. 13–19.

27. Grant Robertson, "Year of the Goose," *The Globe and Mail* (February 25, 2010).

28. C. K. Prahalad and Gary Hamel, "The Core Competencies of the Corporation," *Harvard Business Review* (May–June 1990), pp. 79–91; see also Michael A. Hitt, R. Duane Ireland, and Robert E. Hoskisson, *Strategic Management: Competitiveness and Globalization* (Minneapolis: West, 1997); pp. 99–103.

29. See Richard A. D'Aveni, *Hyper-Competition: Managing the Dynamics of Strategic Maneuvering* (New York: The Free Press, 1994).

30. For a discussion of Michael Porter's approach to strategic planning, see his books *Competitive Strategy* and *Competitive Advantage*; his article, "What Is Strategy?" *Harvard Business Review* (November–December 1996), pp. 61–78; and Richard M. Hodgetts's interview, "A Conversation with Michael E. Porter. A Significant Extension Toward Operational Improvement and Positioning," *Organizational Dynamics* (summer 1999), pp. 24–33.

31. The four grand strategies were described by William F. Glueck, in *Business Policy: Strategy Formulation and Management Action* (New York: McGraw-Hill, 1976).

32. Information from Vauhini Vara, "Facebook CEO Seeks Help as Site Suffers Growing Pains," *Wall Street Journal* (March 5, 2008), pp. A1, A14.

33. "Globe Plans to Shed 90 Positions," *Calgary Herald* (January 10, 2009).

34. Anne Kingston, "As the Globe Turns," *Maclean's* (July 9, 2009).

35. Information and quote from Rajesh Mahapatra, "Tata Group Catapults into Global Marketplace," *The Columbus Dispatch* (April 3, 2008), pp. C1, C9.

36. Hitt et al., op. cit., p. 197.

37. Information from Adamy, op. cit.

38. See William McKinley, Carol M. Sanchez, and A. G. Schick, "Organizational Downsizing: Constraining, Cloning, Learning," *Academy of Management Executive*, vol. 9 (August 1995), pp. 32–44.

39. Kim S. Cameron, Sara J. Freeman, and A. K. Mishra, "Best Practices in White-Collar Downsizing: Managing Contradictions," *Academy of Management Executive*, vol. 4 (August 1991), pp. 57–73.

40. This strategy classification is found in Hitt et al., op. cit.; the attitudes are from a discussion by Howard V. Perlmutter, "The Tortuous Evolution of the Multinational Corporation," *Columbia Journal of World Business*, vol. 4 (January–February 1969). See also Pankaj Ghemawat, "Managing Differences," *Harvard Business Review* (March 2007), Reprint R0703C.

41. McDonald's global strategy is described in Grant, op. cit., p. 383; www.mcdonalds.ca.

42. Adam M. Brandenburger and Barry J. Nalebuff, *Co-Opetition: A Revolutionary Mindset that Combines Competition and Cooperation* (New York: Bantam, 1996).

43. See Michael E. Porter, "Strategy and the Internet," *Harvard Business Review* (March 2001), pp. 63–78; and Michael Rappa, *Business Models on the Web* (www.ecommerce.ncsu.edu/business_models.html, February 6, 2001).

44. Richard G. Hammermesh, "Making Planning Strategic," *Harvard Business Review*, vol. 64 (July–August 1986), pp. 115–120; and Richard G. Hammermesh, *Making Strategy Work* (New York: Wiley, 1986).

45. See Gerald B. Allan, "A Note on the Boston Consulting Group Concept of Competitive Analysis and Corporate Strategy," Harvard Business School, Intercollegiate Case Clearing House, ICCH9-175-175 (Boston: Harvard Business School, June 1976).

46. Keith H. Hammond, "Michael Porter's Big Ideas," *Fast Company* (March 2001), pp. 150–56.

47. Information from www.polo.com.

48. Barbara Shecter, "Walmart Begins Canadian Banking Push," *Financial Post* (June 15, 2010).

49. James Brian Quinn, "Strategic Change: Logical Incrementalism," *Sloan Management Review*, vol. 20 (fall 1978), pp. 7–21.

50. Henry Mintzberg, *The Nature of Managerial Work* (New York: Harper-Row, 1973); John R. P. Kotter, *The General Managers* (New York: Free Press, 1982).

51. Henry Mintzberg, "Planning on the Left Side and Managing on the Right," *Harvard Business Review*, vol. 54 (July–August 1976), pp. 46–55; Henry Mintzberg and James A. Waters, "Of Strategies, Deliberate and Emergent," *Strategic Management Journal*, vol. 6 (1985), pp. 257–72; Henry Mintzberg, "Crafting Strategy," *Harvard Business Review*, vol. 65 (July–August 1987), pp. 66–75.

52. www.patagonia.com/web/us/patagonia.go?assetid=3351.

53. For research support, see Daniel H. Gray, "Uses and Misuses of Strategic Planning," *Harvard Business Review*, vol. 64 (January–February 1986), pp. 89–97.

54. See Judith Burns, "Everything You Wanted to Know About Corporate Governance . . . But Didn't Know How to Ask," *Wall Street Journal* (October 27, 2003), pp. R1, R7.

55. Information from "Persistent Pay Gains," *Wall Street Journal* (April 14, 2008), p. R1.

56. Quote from Joann S. Lublin, "Boards Flex Their Pay Muscles," *Wall Street Journal* (April 14, 2008), p. R1.

57. Paul Ingrassia, "The Auto Makers Are Already Bankrupt," *The Wall Street Journal* (November 21, 2008), p. A23.

58. Josh Levs, "Big Three Auto CEOs Flew Private Jets to Ask for Taxpayer Money," www.cnn.com (retrieved November 21, 2008). See also David Kiley, "Auto Execs in the Hot Seat," *BusinessWeek* (November 19, 2008).

59. See R. Duane Ireland and Michael A. Hitt, "Achieving and Maintaining Strategic Competitiveness in the 21st Century," *Academy of Management Executive*, vol. 13 (1999), pp. 43–57.

60. Hammond, op. cit.

61. Michael Dell quotes from Matt Murray, "As Huge Companies Keep Growing, CEOs Struggle to Keep Pace," *Wall Street Journal* (February 8, 2001), pp. A1, A6. See also Dell facts at www.dell.com.

FEATURE NOTES

Going Global: Peter Robison and Yalman Onaran, "Fuld's Subprime Bets Fueled Profit, Undermined Lehman," Bloomberg, September 15, 2008.

Real Ethics: Information from David Welch, "Go Bankrupt Then Go Overseas," *BusinessWeek* (April 24, 2006), pp. 52–54.

Issues and Situations: Information from Nick Wingfield, "Master of the Universe," *Wall Street Journal* (May 27–28, 2006), pp. A1, A8, "Will Wright: Game Designer," www.ted.com/-speakers/view/id/128.

Canadian Managers: Anne Kingston, "Bonnie of The Bay," *Maclean's* (March 12, 2009).

Research Brief: Richard A. Vernardi, Susan M. Bosco, and Katie M. Vassill, "Does Female Representation on Boards of Directors Associate with Fortune's '100 Best Companies to Work For' List?" *Business and Society*, vol. 45 (June 2006), pp. 235–48.

CASE ENDNOTES

The case was compiled using the following sources:

- Hudson's Bay Co., www.hbc.com/hbc/about/default.asp.

- Hudson's Bay Co., www.hbc.com/hbcheritage/history/overview.asp.

- Mark Anderson, Keith Howlett, Richard Talbot, and Lindsay Meredith, "Subject: Hudson's Bay Co.: Venerable Department Store and Discount Retailer. Problem: More Dynamic Competitors Are Eating Its Market. Question: Can CEO George Heller Beat Off the Big-box Innovators?", *National Post Business*, July 2002, p. 29.

- Rachel Giese, "The Bay's Cinderella Moment," *Canadian Business*, November 23, 2009, p. 42.

- "New Owner of The Bay Says No Major Layoffs Planned," Canada AM—CTV Television, January 27, 2006, p. 1.

- David George-Cash, "Hudson's Bay Co. Owner Dies, Wife Takes Key Role," Canwest News, April 13, 2008.

- David Moin, "Brooks on The Bay Watch," *WWD*, October 19, 2009, p. 5.

- David Moin, "Hudson's Bay Scores with Olympics," *WWD*, March 2, 2010, p. 19.

- Marina Strauss, "HBC's Wares Get Hot with the 'Coolness' Factor," *The Globe and Mail*, February 27, 2010, p. B.4.

CHAPTER 8

ENDNOTES

1. Information from "Information and Statistics Fact Sheet" and "Edward Jones Again Named One of the '50 Best Employers in Canada,'" www.edwardjones.com.

2. Henry Mintzberg and Ludo Van der Heyden, "Organigraphs: Drawing How Companies Really Work," *Harvard Business Review* (September–October 1999), pp. 87–94.

3. The classic work is Alfred D. Chandler, *Strategy and Structure* (Cambridge, MA: MIT Press, 1962).

4. See Alfred D. Chandler, Jr., "Origins of the Organization Chart," *Harvard Business Review* (March–April 1988), pp. 156–57.

5. Information from Jena McGregor, "The Office Chart That Really Counts," *BusinessWeek* (February 27, 2006), pp. 48–49.

6. See David Krackhardt and Jeffrey R. Hanson, "Informal Networks: The Company Behind the Chart," *Harvard Business Review* (July–August 1993), pp. 104–11.

7. See Kenneth Noble, "A Clash of Styles: Japanese Companies in the U.S.," *New York Times* (January 25, 1988), p. 7.

8. For a discussion of departmentalization, see H. I. Ansoff and R. G. Bradenburg, "A Language for Organization Design," *Management Science*, vol. 17 (August 1971), pp. B705–B731.

9. "Organization Structure: The Basic Conformations," in Mariann Jelinek, Joseph A. Litterer, and Raymond E. Miles, eds., *Organizations by Design: Theory and Practice* (Plano, TX: Business Publications, 1981), pp. 293–302; Henry Mintzberg, "The Structuring of Organizations," in James Brian Quinn, Henry Mintzberg, and Robert M. James, eds., *The Strategy Process: Concepts, Contexts, and Cases* (Englewood Cliffs, NJ: Prentice-Hall, 1988), pp. 276–304.

10. The focus on process is described in Michael Hammer, *Beyond Reengineering* (New York: Harper Business, 1996).

11. Excellent reviews of matrix concepts are found in Stanley M. Davis and Paul R. Lawrence, *Matrix* (Reading, MA: Addison-Wesley, 1977); Paul R. Lawrence, Harvey F. Kolodny, and Stanley M. Davis, "The Human Side of the Matrix," *Organizational Dynamics*, vol. 6 (1977), pp. 43–61; and Harvey F. Kolodny, "Evolution to a Matrix

Organization," *Academy of Management Review*, vol. 4 (1979), pp. 543–53.

12. Developed from Frank Ostroff, *The Horizontal Organization: What the Organization of the Future Looks Like and How It Delivers Value to Customers* (New York: Oxford University Press, 1999).

13. The nature of teams and teamwork is described in Jon R. Katzenbach and Douglas K. Smith, "The Discipline of Teams," *Harvard Business Review* (March–April 1993), pp. 111–20.

14. Susan Albers Mohrman, Susan G. Cohen, and Allan M. Mohrman, Jr., *Designing Team-Based Organizations* (San Francisco: Jossey-Bass, 1996).

15. See Glenn M. Parker, *Cross-Functional Teams* (San Francisco: Jossey-Bass, 1995).

16. Denise Deveau, "Animation Firm Grows One Frame at a Time," *Financial Post* (May 22, 2009).

17. See the discussion by Jay R. Galbraith, "Designing the Networked Organization: Leveraging Size and Competencies," in Susan Albers Mohrman, Jay R. Galbraith, Edward E. Lawler III, and associates, *Tomorrow's Organizations: Crafting Winning Strategies in a Dynamic World* (San Francisco: Jossey-Bass, 1998), pp. 76–102. See also Rupert F. Chisholm, *Developing Network Organizations: Learning from Practice and Theory* (Reading, MA: Addison-Wesley, 1998).

18. See Jerome Barthelemy, "The Seven Deadly Sins of Outsourcing," *Academy of Management Executive*, vol. 17 (2003), pp. 87–98.

19. See Ron Ashkenas, Dave Ulrich, Todd Jick, and Steve Kerr, *The Boundaryless Organization: Breaking the Chains of Organizational Structure* (San Francisco: Jossey-Bass, 1996).

20. Information from "Scott Livengood and the Tasty Tale of Krispy Kreme," *BizEd* (May/June 2003), pp. 16–20; Eloqua website, www.eloqua.com; Andrew Wahl, "The Virtual Office: Why Run Your Business Online?", *Canadian Business Online* (April 9, 2007).

21. Information from John A. Byrne, "Management by Web," *BusinessWeek* (August 28, 2000), pp. 84–97; see the collection of articles by Cary L. Cooper and Denise M. Rousseau, eds., *The Virtual Organization: vol. 6, Trends in Organizational Behavior* (New York: Wiley, 2000).

22. For a classic work, see Jay R. Galbraith, *Organizational Design* (Reading, MA: Addison Wesley, 1977).

23. This framework is based on Harold J. Leavitt, "Applied Organizational Change in Industry," in James G. March, ed., *Handbook of Organizations* (New York:

Rand McNally, 1965), pp. 1144–70; and Edward E. Lawler III, *From the Ground Up: Six Principles for the New Logic Corporation* (San Francisco: Jossey-Bass Publishers, 1996), pp. 44–50.

24. Max Weber, *The Theory of Social and Economic Organization*, A. M. Henderson, trans., and H. T. Parsons (New York: Free Press, 1947).

25. Ibid.

26. For classic treatments of bureaucracy, see Alvin Gouldner, *Patterns of Industrial Bureaucracy* (New York: Free Press, 1954); and Robert K. Merton, *Social Theory and Social Structure* (New York: Free Press, 1957).

27. Tom Burns and George M. Stalker, *The Management of Innovation* (London: Tavistock, 1961; republished by Oxford University Press, London, 1994).

28. See Henry Mintzberg, *Structure in Fives: Designing Effective Organizations* (Englewood Cliffs, NJ: Prentice-Hall, 1983).

29. See Rosabeth Moss Kanter, *The Changing Masters* (New York: Simon-Schuster, 1983). Quotation from Rosabeth Moss Kanter and John D. Buck, "Reorganizing Part of Honeywell: From Strategy to Structure," *Organizational Dynamics*, vol. 13 (winter 1985), p. 6.

30. See for example, Jay R. Galbraith, Edward E. Lawler III, and associates, *Organizing for the Future* (San Francisco: Jossey-Bass, 1993); and Susan Albers Mohrman, Jay R. Galbraith, Edward E. Lawler III, and associates, *Tomorrow's Organizations: Crafting Winning Strategies in a Dynamic World* (San Francisco: Jossey-Bass, 1998).

31. Peter Senge, *The Fifth Discipline: The Art and Practice of the Learning Organization* (New York: Doubleday, 1994).

32. Paul R. Lawrence and Jay W. Lorsch, *Organizations and Environment* (Boston: Division of Research, Graduate School of Business Administration, Harvard University, 1967); Burns and Stalker, op. cit.

33. See Jay R. Galbraith, op. cit., and Susan Albers Mohrman, "Integrating Roles and Structure in the Lateral Organization," Chapter 5 in Jay R. Galbraith, Edward E. Lawler III, and associates, *Organizing for the Future* (San Francisco: Jossey-Bass, 1993).

34. Ibid.

35. For a good discussion of coordination and integration approaches, see Scott, op. cit., pp. 231–39.

36. Leonard Brody and David Raffa, *Everything I Needed to Know About Business . . . I Learned from a Canadian* (Toronto: John Wiley & Sons, 2009), p. 300.

37. David Van Fleet, "Span of Management Research and Issues," *Academy of Management Journal*, vol. 26 (1983), pp. 546–52.

38. Example and figure data reported in George Anders, "Overseeing More Employees— With Fewer Managers," *Wall Street Journal* (March 24, 2008), p. B6.

39. Ibid.

40. Burns and Stalker, op. cit.

FEATURE NOTES

Issues and Situations: Information from Phred Dvorak, "Experts Have a Message for Managers: Shake It Up," *The Wall Street Journal* (June 16, 2008), p. B8.

Going Global: Ellen Byron, "Procter & Gamble Eyes 'Cultural Shift' with Revamped Grooming Division," *The Globe and Mail* (April 29, 2009), p. B14.

Canadian Managers: Don Carmody Productions website, www.doncarmody.com/biography.php.

Research Brief: William Ouchi, *Making Schools Work: A Revolutionary Plan to Get Your Children the Education They Need* (New York: Simon & Schuster, 2003); and Richard Riordan, Linda Lingle, and Lyman Porter, "Making Public Schools Work: Management Reform as the Key," *Academy of Management Journal*, vol. 48, no. 6 (2005), pp. 929–40.

CASE ENDNOTES

1. www.apparelandfootwear.org/Statistics.asp.

2. "Adidas-Reebok Merger Lets Rivals Nip at Nike's Heels," *USA Today* (August 4, 2005).

3. articles moneycentral.msn.com/Investing/CNBC/TVReports/NikeStarEndorsements.aspx.

4. adage.com/article?article_id=116309.

5. nikeresponsibility.com/#workers-factories/active_factories.

6. Aaron Bernstein, "Nike Names Names," *BusinessWeek Online* (April 13, 2005).

7. Ibid.

8. Stanley Holmes, "Green Foot Forward," *BusinessWeek* (November 28, 2005, Issue 3961).

9. "Nike Replaces CEO After 13 Months," *USA Today* (January 24, 2006).

10. "Just Doing It," *Economist* (August 6, 2005, Vol. 376, Issue 8438).

11. findarticles.com/p/articles/mi_m0EIN/is_2008_March_5/ai_n24363712.

12. premium.hoovers.com/subscribe/co/factsheet.xhtml?ID-14254

13. "Deal Sets Stage."

14. "Adidas-Reebok Merger."

15. Hollie Shaw, "Ambush League: Official Sponsors Gain Footing with TV Viewers," *National Post* (July 9, 2010), p. FP10.

CHAPTER 9

ENDNOTES

1. Quotes from Robert Berner, "How P&G Pampers New Thinking," *BusinessWeek* (April 14, 2008), pp. 73–74; information from pg.com/company; and money.cnn.com/magazines/fortune/globalmost admired/2007/snapshots/334.html

2. Michael Beer and Nitin Nohria, "Cracking the Code of Change," *Harvard Business Review* (May–June 2000), pp. 133–41.

3. Quotes from John A. Byrne, "Visionary vs. Visionary," *BusinessWeek* (August 28, 2000), p. 210; and Kim Shiffman, "High Five," *Canadian Business Online* (October 14, 2009).

4. Tom Peters, *The Circle of Innovation* (New York: Knopf, 1997).

5. R. Duane Ireland and Michael A. Hitt, "Achieving and Maintaining Strategic Competitiveness in the 21st Century: The Role of Strategic Leadership," *Academy of Management Executive* (February 1999), pp. 43–57.

6. See, for example, Roger von Oech, *A Whack on the Side of the Head* (New York: Warner Books, 1983); and *A Kick in the Seat of the Pants* (New York: Harper-Row, 1986); John S. Dacey and Kathleen H. Lennon, *Understanding Creativity* (San Francisco: Jossey-Bass, 1998); and Bettina von Stamm, *Managing Innovation, Design & Creativity* (Chichester, UK: John Wiley & Sons, 2003).

7. Theresa M. Amabile, Regina Conti, Heather Coon, Jeffrey Laxenby, and Michael Herron, "Assessing the Work Environment for Creativity," *Academy of Management Journal*, Vol. 39 (October 1996), pp. 1154–84.

8. See Peter F. Drucker, "The Discipline of Innovation," *Harvard Business Review* (November–December 1998), pp. 3–8.

9. See Cortis R. Carlson and William W. Wilmont, *Getting to "Aha"* (New York: Crown Business, 2006).

10. Information from Jena McGregor, "The World's Most Innovative Companies," *BusinessWeek* (April 24, 2006), pp. 63–74; and Jena McGregor, "Most Innovative Companies: Smart Ideas for Tough Times," *BusinessWeek* (April 28, 2008), pp. 61–63.

11. David Cooperrider, "Sustainable Innovation," *BizEd* (July/August 2008), pp. 32–38.

12. "Green Business Innovations," *BusinessWeek* (April 28, 2008), special advertising section; Cooperrider, op. cit.; "Cascades Invites You to Consult and to Reuse Its 2009 Report on Sustainable Development," company news release, April 22, 2010; Anne Kingston,

"Green Report: It's So Not Cool," *Maclean's* (May 14, 2007); and Richard Yerema, "Bayer: Chosen as One of Canada's Greenest Employers for 2010," Mediacorp Canada, available at www.eluta.ca/green-at-bayer.

13. Peter F. Drucker, *Management: Tasks, Responsibilities, and Practices* (New York: Harper-Row, 1973), p. 797.

14. Cooperrider, op. cit.

15. Ibid.

16. David Bornstein, *How to Change the World: Social Entrepreneurs and the Power of New Ideas* (Oxford, UK: Oxford University Press, 2004).

17. Example from Aubrey Henvetty, "Seeds of Change," *Kellogg* (Summer 2006), p. 13; and "Amid Turmoil, One Acre Fund Sows Hope in Africa," *Kellogg* (Spring 2008), p. 7.

18. Gary Hamel, *Leading the Revolution: How to Thrive in Turbulent Times* (Boston: Harvard Business School Press, 2002).

19. Robert Berner, "How P&G Pampers New Thinking," *BusinessWeek* (April 14, 2008), pp. 73–74.

20. "CN Says Its Precision Railroading Model and Customer-Centric Innovations Are Improving Rail Service," company news release, May 3, 2010.

21. "New Life for Old Threads," *BusinessWeek* (April 28, 2008), special advertising section.

22. Information and quotes from Nancy Gohring, "Microsoft: Stodgy or Innovative? It's All About Perception," *PC World* (July 25, 2008).

23. Kenneth Labich, "The Innovators," *Fortune* (June 6, 1988), pp. 49–64.

24. Brian Scudamore, "The Out-of-Towners: Going Global Is an MBA-Level Course in Reacting to Surprises," *Profit* (April 2007).

25. See Jack and Suzy Welch, "Finding Innovation Where It Lives," *BusinessWeek* (April 21, 2008), p. 84.

26. Information and quotes from Yukari Iwatani Kane, "Sony CEO Urges Managers to Get 'Mad,'" *Wall Street Journal* (May 23, 2008), p. B8.

27. Irene Lewis, "Women's Canadian Club of Calgary Luncheon Series: Inspiring Transformational Change," speech to SAIT Polytechnic, Calgary, November 6, 2009.

28. Reena Jana, "Brickhouse: Yahoo's Hot Little Incubator," *BusinessWeek* (November 2007), p. IN 14.

29. Charles O'Reilly III and Michael Tushman, "The Ambidextrous Organization," *Harvard Business Review* (2004), Reprint # R0404-D.

30. Information from Steve Hamm, "International Isn't Just IBM's First Name," *BusinessWeek* (January 28, 2008), pp. 36–40.

31. Jeff Jarvis, "The Buzz from Starbucks Customers," *BusinessWeek* (April 29, 2008), pp. 73–75.

32. Welch, op. cit.

33. Leonard Brody and David Raffa, *Everything I Needed to Know About Business . . . I Learned from a Canadian* (Toronto: John Wiley & Sons, 2009), p. 191.

34. "How Google Fuels Its Idea Factory," *BusinessWeek* (May 12, 2008), pp. 54–55.

35. For a review of scholarly work on organizational change, see Arthur G. Bedian, "Organizational Change: A Review of Theory and Research," *Journal of Management*, vol. 25 (1999), pp. 293–315; and W. Warner Burke, *Organizational Change: Theory and Practice*, 2nd ed. (Thousand Oaks, CA: Sage, 2008).

36. Reported in G. Christian Hill and Mike Tharp, "Stumbling Giant—Big Quarterly Deficit Stuns Bank America, Adds Pressure on Chief," *Wall Street Journal* (July 18, 1985), pp. 1–16.

37. Beer and Nohria, op. cit.; and "Change Management: An Inside Job," *Economist* (July 15, 2000), p. 61.

38. Ibid.

39. Katie Engelhart, "From the Bottom Up: How Employees Are Turning Their Bosses on to Sustainability," *Maclean's* (April 29, 2010).

40. Welch and Welch, op. cit.

41. See Bedian, op. cit.

42. This is based on Rosabeth Moss Kanter's "Innovation Pyramid," *BusinessWeek* (March 2007), p. IN 3.

43. For a discussion of alternative types of change, see David A. Nadler and Michael L. Tushman, *Strategic Organizational Design* (Glenview, IL: Scott, Foresman, 1988); John P. Kotter, "Leading Change: Why Transformations Efforts Fail," *Harvard Business Review* (March–April 1995), pp. 59–67; and W. Warner Burke, *Organization Change* (Thousand Oaks, CA: Sage, 2002).

44. Kevin Newman, "Car Trouble," Global News transcript, April 27, 2009.

45. Based on Kotter, op. cit.

46. See Edward E. Lawler III, "Strategic Choices for Changing Organizations," Chapter 12 in Allan M. Mohrman Jr., Susan Albers Mohrman, Gerald E. Ledford Jr., Thomas G. Cummings, Edward E. Lawler III, and associates, *Large Scale Organizational Change* (San Francisco: Jossey-Bass, 1989).

47. The classic description of organizations on these terms is by Harold J. Leavitt, "Applied Organizational Change in Industry: Structural, Technological and Humanistic Approaches," in James G. March, ed., *Handbook of Organizations* (Chicago: Rand McNally, 1965), pp. 1144–70.

48. Kurt Lewin, "Group Decision and Social Change," in G. E. Swanson, T. M. Newcomb, and E. L. Hartley, eds., *Readings in Social Psychology* (New York: Holt, Rinehart, 1952), pp. 459–73.

49. This discussion is based on Robert Chin and Kenneth D. Benne, "General Strategies for Effecting Changes in Human Systems," in Warren G. Bennis, Kenneth D. Benne, Robert Chin, and Kenneth E. Corey, eds., *The Planning of Change*, 3rd ed. (New York: Holt, Rinehart, 1969), pp. 22–45.

50. The change agent descriptions here and following are developed from an exercise reported in J. William Pfeiffer and John E. Jones, *A Handbook of Structured Experiences for Human Relations Training*, vol. 2 (La Jolla, CA: University Associates, 1973).

51. Ram N. Aditya, Robert J. House, and Steven Kerr, "Theory and Practice of Leadership: Into the New Millennium," Chapter 6 in Cary L. Cooper and Edwin A. Locke, *Industrial and Organizational Psychology: Linking Theory with Practice* (Malden, MA: Blackwell, 2000).

52. Information from Mike Schneider, "Disney Teaching Excess Magic of Customer Service," *Columbus Dispatch* (December 17, 2000), p. G9.

53. Teresa M. Amabile, "How to Kill Creativity," *Harvard Business Review* (September–October 1998), pp. 77–87.

54. For an overview, see Jeffrey D. Ford, Laurie W. Ford, and Angelo D'Amoto, "Resistance to Change: The Rest of the Story," *Academy of Management Review*, Vol. 33, No. 2 (2008), pp. 362–77.

55. Sue Shellenbarger, "Some Employers Find Way to Ease Burden of Changing Shifts," *Wall Street Journal* (March 25, 1998), p. B1.

56. These checkpoints are developed from Everett M. Rogers, *Communication of Innovations*, 3rd ed. (New York: Free Press, 1993).

57. John P. Kotter and Leonard A. Schlesinger, "Choosing Strategies for Change," *Harvard Business Review*, vol. 57 (March–April 1979), pp. 109–12. Example from *Fortune* (December 1991), pp. 56–62; additional information from corporate website, www.toro.com.

58. Wanda J. Orlikowski and J. Debra Hofman, "An Improvisational Model for Change Management: The Case of Groupware Technologies," *Sloan Management Review* (Winter 1997), pp. 11–21.

59. Overviews of organization development are provided by W. Warner Burke, *Organization Development: A Normative View* (Reading, MA: Addison-Wesley, 1987); William Rothwell, Roland Sullivan, and Gary N. McLean,

Practicing Organization Development (San Francisco: Jossey-Bass, 1995); Wendell L. French and Cecil H. Bell Jr., *Organization Development*, 6th ed. (Englewood Cliffs, NJ: Prentice Hall, 1998); and W. Warner Burke, "A Contemporary View of Organization Development," Chapter 2 in Thomas G. Cummings (ed.), *Handbook of Organization Development* (Los Angeles: Sage Publications, 2008).

60. See French and Bell, op. cit.

FEATURE NOTES

Real Ethics: Information from "Can Business Be Cool?" *The Economist* (June 10, 2006), pp. 59–60; and Aubrey Henretty, "A Brighter Day," *Kellogg* (Summer 2006), pp. 32–34; Competitive Enterprise Institute, www.cei.org/pages/co2.cfm (retrieved September 29, 2006); Joseph Stiglitz, *Making Globalization Work* (New York: Norton, 2006), p. 172; and Jim Phillips, "Business Leaders Say 'Green' Approach Doable," *The Athens News* (March 27, 2008).

Issues and Situations: Information from Jena McGregor, "The World's Most Innovative Companies," *BusinessWeek* (April 24, 2006), pp. 63–74, "Innovation: The View from the Top," *Business-Week* (April 3, 2006), pp. 52–53; "The Enemies of Innovation," *BusinessWeek* (April 24, 2006), p. 68.

Going Global: Mitsubishi corporate website, www.mitsubishicorp.com.

Canadian Managers: Leonard Brody and David Raffa, *Everything I Needed to Know About Business . . . I Learned from a Canadian* (Toronto: John Wiley & Sons, 2009).

Research Brief: Harry Sminia and Antonie van Nistelrooij, "Strategic Management and Organizational Development: Planned Change in a Public Sector Organization," *Journal of Change Management*, vol. 6 (March 2006), pp. 99–113.

CASE ENDNOTES

1. Apple Inc. website, www.apple.com.

2. Ibid.

3. Pixar website, www.pixar.com.

4. apple20.blogs.fortune.cnn. com/2008/04/01/analyst-apples-us-consumer-market-share-now-21-percent/.

5. apple20.blogs.fortune.cnn. com/2008/05/19/report-apples-market-share-of-pcs-over-1000-hits-66/.

6. Peter Burrows, "The Improbable Heroes of Toontown," *BusinessWeek* (May 26, 2008), pp. 81–82.

CHAPTER 10

ENDNOTES

1. Information from www.rim.com.

2. *CCHRA National Code of Ethics*, Canadian Council of Human Resources Associations, available at www.chrp.ca/i-am-a-chrp/national-code-of-ethics/code-of-ethics/.

3. See William E. Snizek, "Hall's Professionalism Scale: An Empirical Reassessment," *American Sociological Review*, vol. 37 (February 1972), pp. 109–14.

4. Jeffrey Pfeffer, *The Human Equation: Building Profits by Putting People First* (Boston: Harvard University Press, 1998), p. 292.

5. Lawrence Otis Graham, *Perversity: Getting Past Face Value and Finding the Soul of People* (New York: Wiley, 1997).

6. Quote from William Bridges, "The End of the Job," *Fortune* (September 19, 1994), p. 68.

7. Marty Parker, "M&A and Corporate Culture," *Canadian Business Online* (July 4, 2007).

8. James N. Baron and David M. Kreps, *Strategic Human Resources: Framework for General Managers* (New York: Wiley, 1999).

9. Quotes from Kris Maher, "Human Resources Directors Are Assuming Strategic Roles," *Wall Street Journal* (June 17, 2003), p. B8.

10. John Hobel, "An Ethical Boost for Staff Morale?", *Canadian HR Reporter* (March 22, 2004, Vol. 17, Issue 6), p. 14.

11. Edward E. Lawler III, "The HR Department: Give It More Respect," *Wall Street Journal* (March 10, 2008), p. R8.

12. Ibid.

13. Information and quotes from Jena McGregor and Steve Hamm, "Managing the Global Workforce," *BusinessWeek* (January 28, 2008), pp. 34–39.

14. SNC Lavalin corporate website, www.snclavalin.com.

15. Data from Jena McGregor, "The Right Perks," *BusinessWeek* (January 28, 2008), pp. 42–43.

16. Information from "Case Study: Microsoft's Canadian Solution," *BusinessWeek* (January 28, 2008), p. 51.

17. See R. Roosevelt Thomas Jr.'s books, *Beyond Race and Gender* (New York: AMACOM, 1999); and (with Marjorie I. Woodruff) *Building a House for Diversity* (New York: AMACOM, 1999); and Richard D. Bucher, *Diversity Consciousness* (Englewood Cliffs, NJ: Prentice-Hall, 2000).

18. Taken from the Employment Equity Act, http://laws.justice.gc.ca.

19. See the discussion by David A. DeCenzo and Stephen P. Robbins, *Human Resource Management*, 6th ed. (New York: John Wiley & Sons, 1999), pp. 66–68, 81–83.

20. Human Rights Program Part IV: Measures Adopted by the Governments of the Provinces: British Columbia, www.pch.gc.ca/progs.

21. Canadian Human Rights Commission, "Anti-Harassment Policies for the Workplace: An Employer's Guide," www.chrc-ccdp.ca.

22. Susan Pigg, "Labour Relations; Human Rights Advocates Say They've Seen a Surge in Number of Pregnant Women Being Fired," *Toronto Star* (April 28, 2009); Jeffery R. Smith, "Fired Pregnant Woman Awarded $35 K," *Canadian HR Reporter* (November 30, 2009).

23. "What to Expect When You're Expecting," *BusinessWeek* (May 26, 2008), p. 17; and Madeline Heilman and Tyler G, Okimoto, "Motherhood: A Potential Source of Bias in Employment Decisions," *Journal of Applied Psychology*, vol. 93 no. 1 (2008), pp. 189–98.

24. See Frederick S. Lane, *The Naked Employee: How Technology Is Compromising Workplace Privacy* (New York: AMACOM, 2003).

25. Quote from George Myers, "Bookshelf," *Columbus Dispatch* (June 9, 2003), p. E6.

26. See Ernest McCormick, "Job and Task Analysis," in Marvin Dunnette, ed., *Handbook of Industrial and Organizational Psychology* (Chicago: Rand McNally, 1976), pp. 651–96.

27. See John P. Wanous, *Organizational Entry: Recruitment, Selection, and Socialization of Newcomers* (Reading, MA: Addison-Wesley, 1980), pp. 34–44.

28. Reported in "Would You Hire This Person Again?" *BusinessWeek*, Enterprise issue (June 9, 1997), p. ENT32.

29. Loblaw Companies Ltd. corporate website, www.loblaw.com.

30. For a scholarly review, see John Van Maanen and Edgar H. Schein, "Toward a Theory of Socialization," in Barry M. Staw, ed., *Research in Organizational Behavior*, vol. 1 (Greenwich, CT: JAI Press, 1979), pp. 209–64; for a practitioner's view, see Richard Pascale, "Fitting New Employees into the Company Culture," *Fortune* (May 28, 1984), pp. 28–42.

31. This involves the social information processing concept, as discussed in Gerald R. Salancik and Jeffrey Pfeffer, "A Social Information Processing Approach to Job Attitudes and Task Design," *Administrative Science Quarterly*, vol. 23 (June 1978), pp. 224–53.

32. Boxed material developed from Alan Fowler, "How to Decide on Training Methods," *People Management*, vol. 25 (1995), pp. 36–38.

33. See Larry L. Cummings and Donald P. Schwab, *Performance in Organizations: Determinants and Appraisal* (Glenview, IL: Scott, Foresman, 1973).

34. Dick Grote, "Performance Appraisal Reappraised," *Harvard Business Review Best Practice* (1999), Reprint F00105.

35. See Mark R. Edwards and Ann J. Ewen, *360-Degree Feedback: The Powerful New Tool for Employee Feedback and Performance Improvement* (New York: AMACOM, 1996).

36. Timothy Butler and James Waldroop, "Job Sculpting: The Art of Retaining Your Best People," *Harvard Business Review* (September–October 1999), pp. 144–52.

37. Canada's Top 100 Employers website, www.canadastop100.com/national.

38. See Betty Friedan, *Beyond Gender: The New Politics of Work and the Family* (Washington, DC: Woodrow Wilson Center Press, 1997); and James A. Levine, *Working Fathers: New Strategies for Balancing Work and Family* (Reading, MA: Addison-Wesley, 1997).

39. Study reported in Ann Belser, "Employers Using Less-Costly Ways to Retain Workers," *The Columbus Dispatch* (June 1, 2008), p. D3.

40. Eluta website, www.eluta.ca.

41. "Canadian Employers Implement Workplace Strategies to Enable Employees to Achieve Better Work/Life Quality," news release, Hewitt Associates, June 30, 2010; Richard Yerema, "Omni Health Care: Chosen as One of Canada's Top 100 Employers for 2010," Mediacorp Canada, November 2, 2009, available at www.eluta.ca/top-employer-omni-health-care-limited-partnership.

42. A good overview of trends and issues is found in the special section on "Employee Benefits," *Wall Street Journal* (April 22, 2008), pp. A11–A17.

43. See Kaja Whitehouse, "More Companies Offer Packages Pay Plans to Performance," *Wall Street Journal* (December 13, 2005), p. B6.

44. Ibid.

45. Erin White, "How to Reduce Turnover," *Wall Street Journal* (November 21, 2005), p. B5.

46. Ibid.

47. Information from Susan Pulliam, "New Dot-Com Mantra: 'Just Pay Me in Cash, Please,'" *Wall Street Journal* (November 28, 2000), p. C1.

48. Jeff D. Opdyke, "Phasing Out the Annual Raise: More Firms Opt for Bonuses," *Career Journal Today* (January 2005)..

49. Whitehouse, op. cit.

50. WestJet corporate website, www.westjet.com.

51. Jeffrey Pfeffer and John F. Veiga, "Putting People First for Organizational Success," *Academy of Management Executive*, vol. 13 (May 1999), pp. 37–48.

52. Information from www.intel.com and "Stock Ownership for Everyone," Hewitt Associates (November 27, 2000).

53. For reviews, see Richard B. Freeman and James L. Medoff, *What Do Unions Do?* (New York: Basic Books, 1984); Charles C. Heckscher, *The New Unionism* (New York: Basic Books, 1988); and Barry T. Hirsch, *Labor Unions and the Economic Performance of Firms* (Kalamazoo, MI: W. E. Upjohn Institute for Employment Research, 1991).

54. Trade Unions Act, 1985 (http://laws-lois.justice.gc.ca/eng/T-14/index.html).

55. *Canada Labour Code* (R.S., 1985, c. L-2), Department of Justice; Canada Industrial Relations Board corporate website, www.cirb-ccri.gc.ca.

56. "Union Membership in Canada: A 2009 Update," Canadian Auto Workers Union, Unionization FactSheets, September 2009.

57. Canadian Union of Public Employees corporate website, http://cupe.ca/.

58. "CUPE Ratifies Deal with Sodexo Canada," news release, Canadian Union of Public Employees, August 6, 2010.

59. Ross Marowits, "CAW Says It Defeated Air Canada's Demands for Concessions in Deal," The Canadian Press, January 15, 2009.

60. R. Roosevelt Thomas Jr., *Beyond Race and Gender* (New York: AMACOM, 1992), p. 10. See also R. Roosevelt Thomas Jr., "From 'Affirmative Action' to 'Affirming Diversity,'" *Harvard Business Review*, (November–December 1990), pp. 107–17; R. Roosevelt Thomas Jr., with Marjorie I. Woodruff, *Building a House for Diversity* (New York: AMACOM, 1999).

61. Survey reported in "The Most Inclusive Workplaces Generate the Most Loyal Employees," *Gallup Management Journal* (December 2001), retrieved from http://gmj.gallup.com/press_room/release.asp?i=117.

62. In their book *Corporate Culture and Performance* (New York: Macmillan, 1992), John P. Kotter and James L. Heskett make the point that strong cultures have the desired effects over the long term only if they encourage adaptation to a changing environment. See also Collins and Porras, op. cit. (1994).

63. John P. Wanous, *Organizational Entry*, 2nd ed. (New York: Addison-Wesley, 1992).

64. Scott Madison Patton, *Service Quality, Disney Style* (Lake Buena Vista, FL: Disney Institute, 1997).

65. This is a simplified model developed from Schein, op. cit. (1997).

66. Schein, op. cit. (1997); Terrence E. Deal and Alan A. Kennedy, *Corporate Cultures: The Rites and Rituals of Corporate Life* (Reading, MA: Addison-Wesley, 1982); Ralph Kilmann, *Beyond the Quick Fix* (San Francisco: Jossey-Bass, 1984).

67. James C. Collins and Jerry I. Porras, "Building Your Company's Vision," *Harvard Business Review* (September–October 1996), pp. 65–77.

68. David Rocks, "Reinventing Herman Miller," *BusinessWeek eBiz* (April 2, 2000), pp. E88–E96; www.hermanmiller.com.

69. James Collins and Jerry Porras, *Built to Last* (New York: HarperBusiness, 1994).

70. Steve Hamm, "Big Blue Goes for the Big Win," *BusinessWeek* (March 10, 2008), pp. 63–65.

71. David Welch, David Kiley, and Moon Ihlwan, "My Way or the Highway at Hyundai," *BusinessWeek* (March 17, 2008), p. 51.

72. Ralph H. Kilmann, Mary J. Saxton, and Roy Serpa, "Issues in Understanding and Changing Corporate Culture," *California Management Review*, vol. 28 (1986), pp. 87–94.

73. See Robert A. Giacalone and Carol L. Jurkiewicz (eds.), *Handbook of Workplace Spirituality and Organizational Performance* (Armonk, NY: M. E. Sharpe, 2005).

74. This case is reported in Jenny C. McCune, "Making Lemonade," *Management Review* (June 1997), pp. 49–53.

75. See Mary Kay Ash, *Mary Kay: You Can Have It All* (Roseville, CA: Prima Publishing, 1995).

76. Thomas Kochan, Katerina Bezrukova, Robin Ely, Susan Jackson, Aparna Joshi, Karen Jehn, Jonathan Leonard, David Levine, and David Thomas, "The Effects of Diversity on Business Performance: Report of the Diversity Research Network," reported in *SHRM Foundation Research Findings*, retrieved from www.shrm.org/foundation/findings.asp. Full article published in *Human Resource Management* (2003).

77. Taylor Cox Jr., *Cultural Diversity in Organizations* (San Francisco: Berrett Koehler, 1994).

78. See Joseph A. Raelin, *Clash of Cultures* (Cambridge, MA: Harvard Business School Press, 1986).

79. Barbara Benedict Bunker, "Appreciating Diversity and Modifying Organizational Cultures: Men and Women at Work," chapter 5 in Suresh Srivastava and David L. Cooperrider, *Appreciative Management and Leadership* (San Francisco: Jossey-Bass, 1990).

80. See Gary N. Powell, *Women and Men in Management* (Thousand Oaks, CA: Sage, 1993) and Cliff Cheng, ed., *Masculinities in Organizations* (Thousand Oaks, CA: Sage, 1996). For added background, see also Sally Helgesen, *Everyday Revolutionaries: Working Women and the Transformation of American Life* (New York: Doubleday, 1998).

81. Joyce Gannon, "Young Workers Crave Praise," *The Columbus Dispatch* (December 30, 2007), p. D3.

82. Ibid.

83. "Gazprom Most Profitable Firm on Fortune Global 500," Reuters, July 8, 2010.

84. Stephanie N. Mehta, "What Minority Employees Really Want," *Fortune* (July 10, 2000), pp. 181–86.

85. "Bias Cases by Workers Increase 9%," *Wall Street Journal* (March 6, 2008), p. D6.

86. Sue Shellenbarger, "More Women Pursue Claims of Pregnancy Discrimination," *Wall Street Journal* (March 27, 2008), p. D1; and Rob Walker, "Sex vs. Ethics," *Fast Company* (June 2008), pp. 73–78.

87. Ibid.

88. Thomas, op. cit. (1992).

89. Based on ideas set forth by Thomas, op. cit. (1992), and Thomas and Woodruff, op. cit. (1999).

FEATURE NOTES

Issues and Situations: Michael Orey, "Trouble at Toyota," *BusinessWeek* (May 22, 2006), pp. 46–48; Joann S. Lublin, "U.S. Harassment Laws Are Strict, Foreigners Find," *Wall Street Journal* (May 15, 2006), pp. B1, B3.

Real Ethics: Information from Jennifer Saranow, "Car Dealers Recruit Saleswomen at the Mall," *Wall Street Journal* (April 12, 2006), pp. B1, B3.

Research Brief: Joseph M. Stauffer and M. Ronald Buckley, "The Existence and Nature of Racial Bias in Supervisory Ratings," *Journal of Applied Psychology*, vol. 90 (2005), pp. 586–91. Also cited: K. Kraiger and J. K. Ford, "A Meta-analysis of Ratee Race Effects in Performance Ratings," *Journal of Applied Psychology*, vol. 70 (1985), pp. 56–65; and P. R. Dackett and C. L. Z. DuBois, "Rater-Ratee Race Effects on Performance Evaluations: Challenging Meta-Analytic Conclusion," *Journal of Applied Psychology*, vol. 76 (1991), pp. 873–77.

Canadian Company in the News: Richard Yerema and Rachel Caballero, "Ontario Power Generation Inc., Chosen as One of Canada's Top 100 Employers and Greater Toronto's Top Employers for 2010," Mediacorp Canada Inc., November 2, 2009, available at www.eluta.ca/top-employer-ontario-power.

Going Global: "Canadian Banks," available at www.yourloan.ca/loan-articles/canadian-banks/; Bank of Nova Scotia corporate website, http://scotiabank.com/.

CASE ENDNOTES

1. Corporate Profile, RBC Financial Group corporate website, www.rbc.com/aboutus/index.html.

2. *2009 RBC Annual Report*, RBC Financial Group corporate website, www.rbc.com/investorrelations/ar_09/overview.htm.

3. Careers, RBC Financial Group corporate website, www.rbc.com/careers/who-we-are.html.

4. Ibid.

5. Richard Yerema and Rachel Caballero, "Royal Bank of Canada: Chosen as One of Canada's Top 100 Employers for 2010, Greater Toronto's Top Employers for 2010 and Top Employers for Canadians Over 50 for 2009," Mediacorp. Canada Inc., available at www.eluta.ca/top-employer-rbc.

6. Ibid.

7. Alan Kline, "The Business Case for Diversity," *US Banker* (May 2010), Vol. 120, Iss. 5, pp. 10–12.

8. Zabeen Hirji, "Growth and Innovation Rests on Diversity: A Look at How RBC Has Leveraged Its Diverse Workforce," *Canadian HR Reporter* (December 18, 2006), pp. 18–19.

9. Hirji, op. cit.

10. History: Quick to the Frontier: 1960 to 1979, RBC Financial Group corporate website, www.rbc.com/history/quicktofrontier/glbl_stage.html.

11. Hirji, op. cit.; History, RBC Financial Group.

12. Kline, op. cit.

13. Awards, RBC Financial Group corporate website, www.rbc.com/aboutus/awards.html.

14. Ibid.

15. Kline, op. cit.

16. Awards and Recognition, RBC Financial Group corporate website, www.rbc.com/aboutus/20091125fame.html; Diversity, RBC Financial Group corporate website, www.rbc.com/aboutus/20100323-diversity.html.

CHAPTER 11

ENDNOTES

1. Jennifer Reingold, "CEO Swap: The $79 Billion Plan," *Fortune* (November 20, 2009).

2. List developed from S. Bartholomew Craig and Sigrid B. Gustafson, "Perceived Leader Integrity Scale: An Instrument for Assessing Employee Perceptions of Leader Integrity," *Leadership Quarterly*, vol. 9 (1998), pp. 127–45; Drucker quotes from Robert Lenzner and Stephen S. Johnson, "Seeing Things as They Really Are," *Forbes* (March 10, 1997), retrieved from www.forbes.com/forbes/1997/0310/5905122a.html.

3. Quote from Marshall Loeb, "Where Leaders Come From," *Fortune* (September 19, 1994), pp. 241–42. For additional thoughts, see Warren Bennis, *Why Leaders Can't Lead* (San Francisco: Jossey-Bass, 1996).

4. Barry Z. Posner, "On Leadership," *BizEd* (May–June 2008), pp. 26–27.

5. Tom Peters, "Rule #3: Leadership Is Confusing as Hell," *Fast Company* (March 2001), pp. 124–40.

6. See Jean Lipman-Blumen, *Connective Leadership: Managing in a Changing World* (New York: Oxford University Press, 1996), pp. 3–11.

7. Abraham Zaleznick, "Leaders and Managers: Are They Different?" *Harvard Business Review* (May–June 1977), pp. 67–78.

8. Rosabeth Moss Kanter, "Power Failure in Management Circuits," *Harvard Business Review* (July–August 1979), pp. 65–75.

9. For a good managerial discussion of power, see David C. McClelland and David H. Burnham, "Power Is the Great Motivator," *Harvard Business Review* (March–April 1976), pp. 100–10.

10. The classic treatment of these power bases is John R. P. French Jr. and Bertram Raven, "The Bases of Social Power," in Darwin Cartwright, ed., *Group Dynamics: Research and Theory* (Evanston, IL: Row, Peterson, 1962), pp. 607–13. For managerial applications of this basic framework, see Gary Yukl and Tom Taber, "The Effective Use of Managerial Power," *Personnel*, vol. 60 (1983), pp. 37–49; and Robert C. Benfari, Harry E. Wilkinson, and Charles D. Orth, "The Effective Use of Power," *Business Horizons*, vol. 29 (1986), pp. 12–16; Gary A. Yukl, *Leadership in Organizations*, 4th ed. (Englewood Cliffs, NJ: Prentice-Hall, 1998); includes "information" as a separate, but related, power source.

11. James M. Kouzes and Barry Z. Posner, "The Leadership Challenge," *Success* (April 1988), p. 68. See also their books *Credibility: How Leaders Gain and Lose It; Why People Demand It* (San Francisco: Jossey-Bass, 1996); *Encouraging the Heart: A Leader's Guide to Rewarding and Recognizing Others* (San Francisco: Jossey-Bass, 1999); and *The Leadership Challenge: How to Get Extraordinary Things Done in Organizations*, 3rd ed. (San Francisco: Jossey-Bass, 2002).

12. Burt Nanus, *Visionary Leadership: Creating a Compelling Sense of Vision for Your Organization* (San Francisco: Jossey-Bass, 1992).

13. Lorraine Monroe, "Leadership Is About Making Vision Happen—What I Call 'Vision Acts,'" *Fast Company* (March 2001), p. 98; School Leadership Academy website, www.lorrainemonroe.com.

14. Loeb, op. cit.

15. A classic work is Robert K. Greenleaf and Larry C. Spears, *The Power of Servant Leadership: Essays* (San Francisco: Berrett-Koehler, 1996).

16. Jay A. Conger, "Leadership: The Art of Empowering Others," *Academy of Management Executive*, vol. 3 (1989), pp. 17–24.

17. Greenleaf and Spears, op. cit., p. 78.

18. DePree, op. cit., 1989, 1992, 2004.

19. Monroe, op. cit.

20. The early work on leader traits is well represented in Ralph M. Stogdill, "Personal Factors Associated with Leadership: A Survey of the Literature," *Journal of Psychology*, vol. 25 (1948), pp. 35–71. See also Edwin E. Ghiselli, *Explorations in Management Talent* (Santa Monica, CA: Goodyear, 1971); and Shirley A. Kirkpatrick and Edwin A. Locke, "Leadership: Do Traits Really Matter?" *Academy of Management Executive* (1991), pp. 48–60.

21. See also John W. Gardner's article, "The Context and Attributes of Leadership," *New*

Management, vol. 5 (1988), pp. 18–22; John P. Kotter, *The Leadership Factor* (New York: Free Press, 1988); and Bernard M. Bass, *Stogdill's Handbook of Leadership* (New York: Free Press, 1990).

22. Kirkpatrick and Locke, op. cit. (1991).

23. This work traces back to classic studies by Kurt Lewin and his associates at the University of Iowa. See, for example, K. Lewin and R. Lippitt, "An Experimental Approach to the Study of Autocracy and Democracy: A Preliminary Note," *Sociometry*, vol. 1 (1938), pp. 292–300; K. Lewin, "Field Theory and Experiment in Social Psychology: Concepts and Methods," *American Journal of Sociology*, vol. 44 (1939), pp. 886–96; and K. Lewin, R. Lippitt, and R. K. White, "Patterns of Aggressive Behavior in Experimentally Created Social Climates," *Journal of Social Psychology*, vol. 10 (1939), pp. 271–301.

24. The original research from the Ohio State studies is described in R. M. Stogdill and A. E. Coons, eds., *Leader Behavior: Its Description and Measurement*, Research Monograph No. 88 (Columbus, OH: Ohio State University Bureau of Business Research, 1951); see also Chester A. Schreisham, Claudia C. Cogliser, and Linda L. Neider, "Is It 'Trustworthy'? A Multiple-Levels-of-Analysis Reexamination of an Ohio State Leadership Study with Implications for Future Research," *Leadership Quarterly*, vol. 2 (Summer 1995), pp. 111–45. For the University of Michigan studies, see Robert Kahn and Daniel Katz, "Leadership Practices in Relation to Productivity and Morale," in Dorwin Cartwright and Alvin Alexander, eds., *Group Dynamics: Research and Theory*, 3rd ed. (New York: Harper-Row, 1968).

25. See Bass, op. cit., 1990.

26. Robert R. Blake and Jane Srygley Mouton, *The New Managerial Grid III* (Houston: Gulf Publishing, 1985).

27. See Lewin and Lippitt, op. cit., 1938.

28. For a good discussion of this theory, see Fred E. Fiedler, Martin M. Chemers, and Linda Mahar, *The Leadership Match Concept* (New York: Wiley, 1978); Fiedler's current contingency research with the cognitive resource theory is summarized in Fred E. Fiedler and Joseph E. Garcia, *New Approaches to Effective Leadership* (New York: Wiley, 1987).

29. Paul Hersey and Kenneth H. Blanchard, *Management and Organizational Behavior* (Englewood Cliffs, NJ: Prentice-Hall, 1988). For an interview with Paul Hersey on the origins of the model, see John R. Schermerhorn Jr., "Situational Leadership: Conversations with Paul Hersey," *Mid-American Journal of Business* (Fall 1997), pp. 5–12.

30. See Claude L. Graeff, "The Situational Leadership Theory: A Critical View," *Academy of Management Review*, vol. 8 (1983), pp. 285–91; and Carmen F. Fernandez and Robert

P. Vecchio, "Situational Leadership Theory Revisited: A Test of an Across-Jobs Perspective," *Leadership Quarterly*, vol. 8 (Summer 1997), pp. 67–84.

31. See, for example, Robert J. House, "A Path–Goal Theory of Leader Effectiveness," *Administrative Sciences Quarterly*, vol. 16 (1971), pp. 321–38; and Robert J. House and Terrence R. Mitchell, "Path–Goal Theory of Leadership," *Journal of Contemporary Business* (Autumn 1974), pp. 81–97. The path-goal theory is reviewed by Bass, op. cit., and Yukl, op. cit. A supportive review of research is offered in Julie Indvik, "Path–Goal Theory of Leadership: A Meta-Analysis," in John A. Pearce II and Richard B. Robinson Jr., eds., *Academy of Management Best Paper Proceedings* (1986), pp. 189–92. The theory is reviewed and updated in Robert J. House, "Path–Goal Theory of Leadership: Lessons, Legacy and a Reformulated Theory," *Leadership Quarterly*, vol. 7 (Autumn 1996), pp. 323–52.

32. See the discussions of path–goal theory in Yukl, op. cit.; and Bernard M. Bass, "Leadership: Good, Better, Best," *Organizational Dynamics* (Winter 1985), pp. 26–40.

33. See Steven Kerr and John Jermier, "Substitutes for Leadership: Their Meaning and Measurement," *Organizational Behavior and Human Performance*, vol. 22 (1978), pp. 375–403; Jon P. Howell and Peter W. Dorfman, "Leadership and Substitutes for Leadership Among Professional and Nonprofessional Workers," *Journal of Applied Behavioral Science*, vol. 22 (1986), pp. 29–46.

34. An early presentation of the theory is F. Dansereau Jr., G. Graen, and W. J. Haga, "A Vertical Dyad Linkage Approach to Leadership Within Formal Organizations: A Longitudinal Investigation of the Role-Making Process," *Organizational Behavior and Human Performance*, vol. 13, pp. 46–78.

35. This discussion is based on Yukl, op. cit., pp. 117–22.

36. Ibid.

37. Victor H. Vroom and Arthur G. Jago, *The New Leadership: Managing Participation in Organizations* (Englewood Cliffs, NJ: Prentice-Hall, 1988). This is based on earlier work by Victor H. Vroom, "A New Look in Managerial Decision-Making," *Organizational Dynamics* (Spring 1973), pp. 66–80; and Victor H. Vroom and Phillip Yetton, *Leadership and Decision-Making* (Pittsburgh: University of Pittsburgh Press, 1973).

38. Vroom and Jago, op. cit.

39. For a review, see Yukl, op. cit.

40. See the discussion by Victor H. Vroom, "Leadership and the Decision-Making Process," *Organizational Dynamics*, vol. 28 (2000), pp. 82–94.

41. For a related discussion, see Edgar H. Schein, *Process Consultation Revisited:*

Building the Helping Relationship (Reading, MA: Addison-Wesley, 1999).

42. Among popular books are Warren Bennis and Burt Nanus, *Leaders: The Strategies for Taking Charge* (New York: Harper Business, 1997); Max DePree, *Leadership Is an Art*, op. cit.; Kotter, *The Leadership Factor*, op. cit.; Kouzes and Posner, *The Leadership Challenge*, op. cit., 2002.

43. The distinction was originally made by James McGregor Burns, *Leadership* (New York: Harper-Row, 1978), and was further developed by Bernard Bass, *Leadership and Performance Beyond Expectations* (New York: Free Press, 1985) and Bernard M. Bass, "Leadership: Good, Better, Best," *Organization Dynamics* (Winter 1985), pp. 26–40.

44. This list is based on Kouzes and Posner, op. cit.; Gardner, op. cit.

45. Daniel Goleman, "Leadership That Gets Results," *Harvard Business Review* (March–April 2000), pp. 78–90. See also his books *Emotional Intelligence* (New York: Bantam Books, 1995) and *Working with Emotional Intelligence* (New York: Bantam Books, 1998).

46. Daniel Goleman, "What Makes a Leader?" *Harvard Business Review* (November–December 1998), pp. 93–102.

47. Ibid.

48. Information from "Women and Men, Work and Power," *Fast Company*, issue 13 (1998), p. 71.

49. Jane Shibley Hyde, "The Gender Similarities Hypothesis," *American Psychologist*, vol. 60, no. 6 (2005), pp. 581–92.

50. A. H. Eagley, S. J. Daran, and M. G. Makhijani, "Gender and the Effectiveness of Leaders: A Meta-Analysis," *Psychological Bulletin*, vol. 117 (1995), pp. 125–45.

51. Data reported by Rochelle Sharpe, "As Women Rule," *BusinessWeek* (November 20, 2000), p. 75.

52. Research on gender issues in leadership is reported in Sally Helgesen, *The Female Advantage: Women's Ways of Leadership* (New York: Doubleday, 1990); Judith B. Rosener, "Ways Women Lead," *Harvard Business Review* (November–December 1990), pp. 119–25; and Alice H. Eagley, Steven J. Karau, and Blair T. Johnson, "Gender and Leadership Style Among School Principals: A Meta-Analysis," *Administrative Science Quarterly*, vol. 27 (1992), pp. 76–102; Jean Lipman-Blumen, *Connective Leadership: Managing in a Changing World* (New York: Oxford University Press, 1996); Alice H. Eagley, Mary C. Johannesen-Smith, and Marloes L. van Engen, "Transformational, Transactional and Laissez-Faire Leadership: A Meta-Analysis of Women and Men," *Psychological Bulletin*, vol. 124 (4), (2003), pp. 569–91; Carol Hymowitz, "Too Many Women Fall for Stereotypes of Selves, Study Says," *Wall Street Journal* (October 24, 2005), p. B1.

53. Vroom, op. cit. (2000).

54. Eagley, et al., op. cit.; Hymowitz, op. cit.; Rosener, op. cit.; Vroom, op. cit.

55. Rosener, op. cit. (1990).

56. For debate on whether some transformational leadership qualities tend to be associated more with female than male leaders, see "Debate: Ways Women and Men Lead," *Harvard Business Review* (January–February 1991), pp. 150–60.

57. Quote from "As Leaders, Women Rule," *BusinessWeek* (November 20, 2000), pp. 75–84. Rosabeth Moss Kanter is the author of *Men and Women of the Corporation*, 2nd ed. (New York: Basic Books, 1993).

58. Hyde, op. cit.; Hymowitz, op. cit.

59. Julie Bennett, "Women Get a Boost Up That Tall Leadership Ladder," *Wall Street Journal* (June 10, 2008), p. D6.

60. Based on the discussion by John W. Dienhart and Terry Thomas, "Ethical Leadership: A Primer on Ethical Responsibility," in John R. Schermerhorn Jr., *Management*, 7th ed. (New York: Wiley, 2003).

61. James MacGregor Burns, *Transforming Leadership: A New Pursuit of Happiness* (New York: Atlantic Monthly Press, 2003); information from Christopher Caldwell, book review, *International Herald Tribune* (April 29, 2003), p. 18.

62. Fred Luthans and Bruce Avolio, "Authentic Leadership: A Positive Development Approach," in K. S. Cameron, J. E. Dutton, and R. E. Quinn, eds., *Positive Organizational Scholarship* (San Francisco: Berrett-Koehler, 2003), pp. 241–58.

63. Doug May, Adrian Chan, Timothy Hodges, and Bruce Avolio, "Developing the Moral Component of Authentic Leadership," *Organizational Dynamics*, vol. 32 (2003), pp. 247–60.

64. Peter F. Drucker, "Leadership: More Doing than Dash," *Wall Street Journal* (January 6, 1988), p. 16. For a compendium of writings on leadership, sponsored by the Drucker Foundation, see Frances Hesselbein, Marshall Goldsmith, and Richard Beckhard, *Leader of the Future* (San Francisco: Jossey-Bass, 1997).

65. Quotes from Hesselbein, et al., op. cit.

66. Jay A. Conger, *Winning 'Em Over: A New Model for Managing in the Age of Persuasion* (New York: Simon-Schuster, 1998), pp. 24–79.

67. Ibid.

68. *BusinessWeek* (February 10, 1992), pp. 102–08.

69. See Robert H. Lengel and Richard L. Daft, "The Selection of Communication Media as an Executive Skill," *Academy of Management Executive*, vol. 2 (August 1988), pp. 225–32.

70. Information from Sam Dillon, "What Corporate America Can't Build: A Sentence," *New York Times* (December 7, 2004).

71. See Eric Matson, "Now That We Have Your Complete Attention," *Fast Company* (February–March 1997), pp. 124–32.

72. Martin J. Gannon, *Paradoxes of Culture and Globalization* (Los Angeles: Sage, 2008), p. 76.

73. David McNeill, *Hand and Mind: What Gestures Reveal About Thought* (Chicago: University of Chicago Press, 1992).

74. Adapted from Richard V. Farace, Peter R. Monge, and Hamish M. Russell, *Communicating and Organizing* (Reading, MA: Addison-Wesley, 1977), pp. 97–98.

75. Tom Peters and Nancy Austin, *A Passion for Excellence* (New York: Random House, 1985).

76. This discussion is based on Carl R. Rogers and Richard E. Farson, "Active Listening" (Chicago: Industrial Relations Center of the University of Chicago, n.d.); see also Carl R. Rogers and Fritz J. Roethlisberger, "Barriers and Gateways to Communication," *Harvard Business Review* (November–December 2001), Reprint 91610.

77. Ibid.

78. Sue de Wine, *The Consultant's Craft* (Boston: Bedford/St. Martin's Press, 2001), pp. 307–14.

79. A useful source of guidelines is John J. Gabarro and Linda A. Hill, "Managing Performance," Note 996022 (Boston, MA: Harvard Business School Publishing, n.d.).

80. Carol Hymowitz, "Managers See Feedback from Their Staffers as Most Valuable," *Wall Street Journal* (August 22, 2000), p. B1.

81. Developed from John Anderson, "Giving and Receiving Feedback," in Paul R. Lawrence, Louis B. Barnes, and Jay W. Lorsch, eds., *Organizational Behavior and Administration*, 3rd ed. (Homewood, IL: Richard D. Irwin, 1976), p. 109.

82. A classic work on proxemics is Edward T. Hall's book, *The Hidden Dimension* (Garden City, NY: Doubleday, 1986).

83. Mirand Weill, "Alternative Spaces Spawning Desk-Free Zones," *Columbus Dispatch* (May 18, 1998), pp. 10–11.

84. "Tread: Rethinking the Workplace," *BusinessWeek* (September 25, 2006), p. IN.

85. Amy Saunders, "A Creative Approach to Work," *Columbus Dispatch* (May 2, 2008), pp. C1, C9.

86. See Lengel and Daft, op. cit. (1988).

87. Information from Susan Stellin, "Intranets Nurture Companies from the Inside," *New York Times* (January 21, 2001), p. C4.

88. Information and quotes from Sarah E. Needleman, "Thnx for the IView! I Wud Luv to Work 4 U!! ;)," *Wall Street Journal Online* (July 31, 2008).

89. Alison Overholt, "Intel's Got (Too Much) Mail," *Fortune* (March 2001), pp. 56–58.

90. Developed from *Working Woman* (November 1995), p. 14; and Elizabeth Weinstein, "Help! I'm Drowning in E-Mail!" *Wall Street Journal* (January 10, 2002), pp. B1, B4.

91. Example from Heidi A. Schuessler, "Social Studies Class Finds How Far E-Mail Travels," *New York Times* (February 22, 2001), p. D8.

92. Information from Esther Wachs Book, "Leadership for the Millennium," *Working Woman* (March 1998), pp. 29–34.

93. Example from Russell A. Eisenstat, Michael Beer, Nathaniel Foote, Tobias Fredberg, and Flemming Norrgren, "The Uncompromising Leader," *Harvard Business Review* (July-August 2008), Reprint R0807D.

94. Information from Hilary Stout, "Self-Evaluation Brings Change to a Family's Ad Agency," *Wall Street Journal* (January 6, 1998), p. B2.

95. Examples reported in Martin J. Gannon, *Paradoxes of Culture and Globalization* (Los Angeles: Sage Publications, 2008), p. 80.

96. Box examples from Gannon, op. cit.

97. See Edward T. Hall, *The Silent Language* (New York: Doubleday, 1973).

FEATURE NOTES

Canadian Managers: Colleen Johnston, Group Head Finance and Chief Financial Officer, Corporate Office, TD Bank Financial Group, Remarks to Schulich School of Business 2007 Women in Leadership Conference, Toronto, March 9, 2007, available at www.td.com/communicate/speeches/09mar07.jsp; "The Top 20 Business Women in Canada 2009," *Women's Post*, December 13, 2009; and Rebecca Sausner, "The 25 Women to Watch: #1 Colleen Johnston, Group Head Finance, CFO, TD Bank Financial Group," *US Banker*, October 2008.

Research Brief: Joyce E. Bono and Remus Ilies, "Charisma, Positive Emotions and Mood Contagion," *Leadership Quarterly*, vol. 17 (2006), pp. 317–34.

Going Global: "Only Health Care Company Honored on 2010 WorldBlu List of Most Democratic Workplaces," news release, April 13, 2010, DaVita; Reference for Business encyclopedia, www.referenceforbusiness.com/history/Ci-Da/DaVita-Inc.html.

Real Ethics: Suggested by Jeffrey Seglin, "Request Puts Employees in a Tough Spot," *Columbus Dispatch* (May 28, 2006), p. B3.

CASE ENDNOTES

This case was compiled using the following sources:

• Gordon Pitts, "The Testing of Michael McCain," *Report on Business Magazine* (November 2008), p. 60.

- Paul Brent, "Sorry Situation," *Marketing* (September 15, 2008, Vol. 113, Iss. 16), p. 6.
- "Maple Leaf History," Maple Leaf corporate website, www.mapleleaf.com/en/corporate/company-info/our-rich-history/.
- "Michael McCain Biography," Maple Leaf corporate website, www.mapleleaf.com/en/corporate/company-info/management-team/details/michael-h-mccain.
- Gordon Pitts, "Michael McCain: Man Under Fire," *The Globe and Mail* (August 30, 2008).
- "Our High Performance Culture," Maple Leaf corporate website, www.mapleleaf.com/en/corporate/careers/our-high-performance-culture/.
- Marty Parker, "Values-Based Leadership: Michael McCain at Maple Leaf Foods," *Financial Post* (December 9, 2009).
- Carolyn Cooper, "A Lesson for Us All," *Food in Canada* (September 2008, Vol. 68, Iss. 7), p. 7.
- George H. Condon, "When Tragic Things Happen, Take a Lesson From Michael McCain," *Canadian Grocer* (September 2008, Vol. 122, Iss. 7), p. 78.
- "Maple Leaf Marks Listeriosis Anniversary," *Edmonton Journal* (August 25, 2009), p. A5.
- "Maple Leaf Foods," CTV News, December 18, 2008.
- Bradley Bouzane and David Wylie, "Slicing Machines Blamed in Listeria Outbreak; Maple Leaf CEO Announces 'Likely Source' at Toronto Plant; 38 Confirmed Cases of Illness," *Edmonton Journal* (September 6, 2008), p. A5.
- Misty Harris, "Maple Leaf Winning Back Its Customers; Media Strategists Point to Meat-Processing Firm's Honest, Compassionate Response to Last Year's Listeriosis Crisis," *Edmonton Journal* (January 23, 2009), p. A17.
- "Maple Leaf Foods Voluntary Recall of Two Recalled Products Largely Complete," news release, Maple Leaf Foods, February 24, 2009.
- "Maple Leaf Initiates Precautionary Recall of Nine Wiener Products," news release, Maple Leaf Foods, August 4, 2009.
- *Final Report: Report of the Independent Investigator into the 2008 Listeriosis Outbreak* (Ottawa: Government of Canada, July 2009).

CHAPTER 12

ENDNOTES

1. Information from Andrew Ward, "Spanx Queen Firms Up the Bottom Line," *Financial Times* (November 30, 2006), p. 7; and Simona Covel, "A Dated Industry Gets a Modern Makeover," *Wall Street Journal* (August 7, 2008), p. B9.

2. See, for example, Ram Charan, *Know-How: The 8 Skills that Separate People Who Perform from Those That Don't* (New York: Crown Business, 2007); and Ram Charan, "Six Personality Traits of a Leader," www.

career-advice.monster.com (accessed August 6, 2008).

3. Ibid.

4. Quotes from Charan, op. cit., 2008.

5. Max DePree, "An Old Pro's Wisdom: It Begins with a Belief in People," *New York Times* (September 10, 1989), p. F2; Max DePree, *Leadership Is an Art* (New York: Doubleday, 1989); David Woodruff, "Herman Miller: How Green Is My Factory," *BusinessWeek* (September 16, 1991), pp. 54–56; and Max DePree, *Leadership Jazz* (New York: Doubleday, 1992); quote from www.depree.org/html/maxdepree.html.

6. This example is reported in *Esquire* (December 1986), p. 243. Emphasis is added to the quotation. Note: Nussbaum became director of the U.S. Labor Department's Women's Bureau during the Clinton administration and subsequently moved to the AFL–CIO as head of the Women's Bureau.

7. depree.org, op. cit.

8. See H. R. Schiffman, *Sensation and Perception: An Integrated Approach*, 3d ed. (New York: Wiley, 1990).

9. John P. Kotter, "The Psychological Contract: Managing the Joining Up Process," *California Management Review*, vol. 15 (Spring 1973), pp. 91–99; Denise Rousseau, ed., *Psychological Contracts in Organizations* (San Francisco: Jossey-Bass, 1995); Denise Rousseau, "Changing the Deal While Keeping the People," *Academy of Management Executive*, vol. 10 (1996), pp. 50–59; and Denise Rousseau and Rene Schalk, eds., *Psychological Contracts in Employment: Cross-Cultural Perspectives* (San Francisco: Jossey-Bass, 2000).

10. A good review is E. L. Jones, ed., *Attribution: Perceiving the Causes of Behavior* (Morristown, NJ: General Learning Press, 1972). See also John H. Harvey and Gifford Weary, "Current Issues in Attribution Theory and Research," *Annual Review of Psychology*, vol. 35 (1984), pp. 427–59.

11. See, for example, Stephan Thernstrom and Abigail Thernstrom, *America in Black and White* (New York: Simon-Schuster, 1997); and David A. Thomas and Suzy Wetlaufer, "A Question of Color: A Debate on Race in the U.S. Workplace," *Harvard Business Review* (September–October 1997), pp. 118–32.

12. Katherine Giscombe, Laura Jenfer, *Career Advancement in Corporate Canada: A Focus on Visible Minorities: Diversity & Inclusion Practices* (Toronto: Catalyst, 2009).

13. These examples are from Natasha Josefowitz, *Paths to Power* (Reading, MA: Addison-Wesley, 1980), p. 60. For more on gender issues, see Gray N. Powell, ed., *Handbook of Gender and Work* (Thousand Oaks, CA: Sage, 1999).

14. Survey reported in Kelly Greene, "Age Is Still More Than a Number," *Wall Street Journal* (April 10, 2003), p. D2.

15. The classic work is Dewitt C. Dearborn and Herbert A. Simon, "Selective Perception: A Note on the Departmental Identification of Executives," *Sociometry*, vol. 21 (1958), pp. 140–44. See also J. P. Walsh, "Selectivity and Selective Perception: Belief Structures and Information Processing, *Academy of Management Journal*, vol. 24 (1988), pp. 453–70.

16. Quotation from Sheila O'Flanagan, "Underestimate Casual Dressers at Your Peril," *Irish Times* (July 22, 2005). See also Christina Binkley, "How to Pull Off 'CEO Casual," *Wall Street Journal* (August 7, 2008), pp. D1–D8.

17. See William L. Gardner and Mark J. Martinko, "Impression Management in Organizations," *Journal of Management* (June 1988), p. 332.

18. Sandy Wayne and Robert Liden, "Effects of Impression Management on Performance Ratings," *Academy of Management Journal* (February 2005), pp. 232–52.

19. See M. R. Barrick and M. K. Mount, "The Big Five Personality Dimensions and Job Performance: A Meta-Analysis," *Personnel Psychology*, vol. 44 (1991), pp. 1–26.

20. Ibid.

21. For a good summary, see Stephen P. Robbins and Timothy A. Judge, *Organizational Behavior*, Twelfth Edition (Upper Saddle River, NJ: Prentice-Hall, 2007), p. 112.

22. Adrienne Carter, "Leading Indicators: Doug Conant," *STERNbusiness* (Spring/Summer 2008), pp. 22–24.

23. Carl G. Jung, *Psychological Types*, H. G. Baynes, trans. (Princeton, NJ: Princeton University Press, 1971).

24. I. Briggs-Myers, *Introduction to Type* (Palo Alto, CA: Consulting Psychologists Press, 1980).

25. See, for example, William L. Gardner and Mark J. Martinko, "Using the Myers–Briggs Type Indicator to Study Managers: A Literature Review and Research Agenda," *Journal of Management*, vol. 22 (1996), pp. 45–83; Naomi L. Quenk, *Essentials of Myers–Briggs Type Indicator Assessment* (New York: Wiley, 2000).

26. This discussion based in part on John R. Schermerhorn, Jr., James G. Hunt, and Richard N. Osborn, *Managing Organizational Behavior*, 4th ed. (New York: Wiley, 1991), pp. 54–60.

27. J. B. Rotter, "Generalized Expectancies for Internal versus External Control of Reinforcement," *Psychological Monographs*, vol. 80 (1966), pp. 1–28; see also Thomas W. Ng, Kelly L. Sorensen, and Lillian T. Eby, "Locus of Control at Work: A Meta-Analysis," *Journal of Organizational Behavior*, 2006.

28. T. W. Adorno, E. Frenkel-Brunswick, D. J. Levinson, and R. N. Sanford, *The Authoritarian Personality* (New York: Harper-Row, 1950).

29. Niccolo Machiavelli, *The Prince*, George Bull, trans. (Middlesex, UK: Penguin, 1961).

30. Richard Christie and Florence L. Geis, *Studies in Machiavellianism* (New York: Academic Press, 1970).

31. See M. Snyder, *Public Appearances/Private Realities: The Psychology of Self-Monitoring* (New York: Freeman, 1987).

32. The classic work is Meyer Friedman and Ray Roseman, *Type A Behavior and Your Heart* (New York: Knopf, 1974).

33. Trimark Sportswear Group corporate website, www.trimarksportswear.com; Kira Vermond, "Top 40 Under 40: William Andrew, 39, Ontario," *The Globe and Mail* (June 4, 2010).

34. Martin Fishbein and Icek Ajzen, *Belief, Attitude, Intention and Behavior: An Introduction to Theory and Research* (Reading, MA: Addison-Wesley, 1973).

35. See Leon Festinger, *A Theory of Cognitive Dissonance* (Palo Alto, CA: Stanford University Press, 1957).

36. Timothy A. Judge and Allan H. Church, "Job Satisfaction: Research and Practice," Chapter 7 in Cary L. Cooper and Edwin A. Locke, eds., *Industrial and Organizational Psychology: Linking Theory with Practice* (Malden, MA: Blackwell Business, 2000); Timothy A. Judge, "Promote Job Satisfaction Through Mental Challenge," Chapter 6 in Edwin A. Locke, ed., *The Blackwell Handbook of Organizational Behavior* (Malden, MA: Blackwell, 2004).

37. Linda Grant, "Happy Workers, High Returns," *Fortune* (January 12, 1998), p. 81; "Health Reports: Job Satisfaction, Stress and Depression," Statistics Canada, *The Daily*, October 17, 2006.

38. See Timothy A. Judge, "Promote Job Satisfaction Through Mental Challenge," Chapter 6 in Edwin A. Locke, ed., *The Blackwell Handbook of Organizational Behavior* (Malden, MA: Blackwell, 2004); "U.S. Employees More Dissatisfied with Their Jobs," Associated Press (February 28, 2005), retrieved from www.msnbc.com; and "U.S. Job Satisfaction Keeps Falling, The Conference Board Reports Today," The Conference Board (February 28, 2005), retrieved from www.conference-board.org.

39. For the JDI, see Jeffrey M. Stanton, Evan F. Sinar, William K. Balzer, Amanda L. Julian, Paul Thoresen, Shahnaz Aziz, Gwenith G. Fisher, and Patricia C. Smith, "Development of a Compact Measure of Job Satisfaction: The Abridged Job Descriptive Index," *Educational and Psychological Measurement*, Vol. 61, No. 6 (December 2001), pp. 1104–1122. The MSQ is available from Vocational Psychology Research, The University of Minnesota, www.psych.umn.edu/psylabs/vpr/orderform.htm.

40. Judge and Church, op. cit. (2000); Judge, op. cit., 2004.

41. Reported in "When Loyalty Erodes, So Do Profits," *BusinessWeek* (August 13, 2001), p. 8.

42. These relationships are discussed in Charles N. Greene, "The Satisfaction-Performance Controversy," *Business Horizons*, vol. 15 (1982), p. 31; Michelle T. Iaffaldano and Paul M. Muchinsky, "Job Satisfaction and Job Performance: A Meta-Analysis," *Psychological Bulletin*, vol. 97 (1985), pp. 251–73; Judge, op. cit., 2004; and Michael Riketta, "The Causal Relation Between Job Attitudes and Performance: A Meta-Analysis of Panel Studies," *Journal of Applied Psychology*, Vol. 93, No. 2 (March 2008), pp. 472–81.

43. This discussion follows conclusions in Judge, op. cit., 2004.

44. Information from Sue Shellenbarger, "Employers Are Finding It Doesn't Cost Much to Make a Staff Happy," *Wall Street Journal* (November 19, 1997), p. B1. See also, "Job Satisfaction on the Decline," The Conference Board (July 2002).

45. Rob MacLeod, "National Gallup Survey Finds Both Recognition and Performance Measurement Strongly Correlate to Engaged Employees," Canada Newswire, December 1, 1999, p. 1; see also "The Things They Do for Love," *Harvard Business Review* (December 2004), pp. 19–20.

46. Dennis W. Organ, *Organizational Citizenship Behavior: The Good Soldier Syndrome* (Lexington, MA: Lexington Books, 1988).

47. See Mark C. Bolino and William H. Turnley, "Going the Extra Mile: Cultivating and Managing Employee Citizenship Behavior," *Academy of Management Executive*, Vol. 17 (August 2003), pp. 60–67.

48. Damon Darlin and Matt Richtel, "Chairwoman Leaves Hewlett in Spying Furor," *Wall Street Journal* (September 23, 2006), pp. A1, A9.

49. Daniel Goleman, "Leadership That Gets Results," *Harvard Business Review* (March–April 2000), pp. 78–90. See also his books *Emotional Intelligence* (New York: Bantam Books, 1995) and *Working with Emotional Intelligence* (New York: Bantam Books, 1998).

50. Goleman, op. cit. (1998).

51. See Robert G. Lord, Richard J. Klimoski, and Ruth Knafer (eds.), *Emotions in the Workplace; Understanding the Structure and Role of Emotions in Organizational Behavior* (San Francisco: Jossey-Bass, 2002); Roy L. Payne and Cary L. Cooper (eds.), *Emotions at Work: Theory Research and Applications for Management* (Chichester, UK: John Wiley & Sons, 2004); and Daniel Goleman and Richard Boyatzis, "Social Intelligence and the Biology of Leadership," *Harvard Business Review* (September 2008), Reprint R0809E.

52. Joyce E. Bono and Remus Ilies, "Charisma, Positive Emotions and Mood Contagion," *Leadership Quarterly*, Vol. 17 (2006), pp. 317–34; and Goleman and Boyatzis, op. cit.

53. See "Charm Offensive: Why America's CEOs Are So Eager to Be Loved," *BusinessWeek* (June 26, 2006).

54. See Arthur P. Brief, Randall S. Schuler, and Mary Van Sell, *Managing Job Stress* (Boston: Little, Brown, 1981), pp. 7–8.

55. Robert B. Reich, *The Future of Success* (New York: Knopf, 2000), p. 8.

56. Data in Stay Informed from Michael Mandel, "The Real Reasons You're Working So Hard," *BusinessWeek* (October 3, 2005), pp. 60–70; "Many U.S. Employees Have Negative Attitudes to Their Jobs, Employers and Top Managers," The Harris Poll #38 (May 6, 2005), retrieved from www.harrisinteractive.com.

57. "Stress Is Top Reason Employees Quit Their Jobs, Survey Finds," *Vancouver Sun* (December 17, 2007).

58. Carol Hymowitz, "Impossible Expectations and Unfulfilling Work Stress Managers, Too," *Wall Street Journal* (January 16, 2001), p. B1.

59. Hans Selye, *Stress in Health and Disease* (Boston: Butterworth, 1976).

60. Carol Hymowitz, "Can Workplace Stress Get Worse?" *Wall Street Journal* (January 16, 2001), pp. B1, B3.

61. See Steve M. Jex, *Stress and Job Performance* (San Francisco: Jossey-Bass, 1998).

62. Tamsen Tillson, "Is Your Career Killing You?" *Canadian Business* (September 26, 1997. Vol. 70, Iss. 12), p. 78.

63. See "workplace violence" discussed by Richard V. Denenberg and Mark Braverman, *The Violence-Prone Workplace* (Ithaca, NY: Cornell University Press, 1999).

64. See Daniel C. Ganster and Larry Murphy, "Workplace Interventions to Prevent Stress-Related Illness: Lessons from Research and Practice," Chapter 2 in Cooper and Locke, eds., op. cit. (2000); "Long Working Hours Linked to High Blood Pressure," www.Gn.com/2006/Health (retrieved August 29, 2006).

65. Reported in Sue Shellenbarger, "Finding Ways to Keep a Partner's Job Stress from Hitting Home," *Wall Street Journal*, (November 29, 2000), p. B1.

66. Quote from Shellenbarger, op. cit.

FEATURE NOTES

Issues and Situations: "The 'Millennials' Are Coming," CBS 60 Minutes (November 11, 2007); Information and quote from "What's Different About the Ys," *BusinessWeek* (September 24, 2007), p. 56. See also Ron Alsop, *The Trophy Kids Grow Up* (New York: Dow Jones & Co., 2008).

Real Ethics: Information from Victoria Knight, "Personality Tests as Hiring Tools," *Wall Street Journal* (March 15, 2006), p. B3C.

Research Brief: Joseph C. Rode, Marne L. Arthaud-Day, Christine H. Mooney, Janet P.

Near, Timothy T. Baldwin, William H. Bommer, and Robert S. Rubin, "Life Satisfaction and Student Performance," *Academy of Management Learning & Education,* vol. 4 (2005), pp. 421–33.

Going Global: "Achieving High Performance by Transforming the Sales Organization," Accenture corporate website, www.accenture.com; "Accenture Helps Canon Rise Above Competitors," Accenture, n.d., available at http://www.accenture.com/NR/rdonlyres/680A24A7-1692-4813-A73C-D91452B99DC8/0/Canon_creds.pdf.

Canadian Company in the News: Roots corporate website, www.roots.com.

CASE ENDNOTES

1. Facebook Press Room, Statistics, at www.facebook.com/press/info.php?statistics (accessed June 27, 2008).

2. Ibid.

3. Jessi Hempel, "Finding Cracks in Facebook," *Fortune,* vol. 157, issue 11 (May 26, 2008).

4. Ibid.

5. Ibid.

6. Catherine Holahan, "Facebook's New Friends Abroad," *BusinessWeek Online* (May 14, 2008).

7. Bill Greenwood, "MySpace, Facebook, Google Integrate Data Portability," *Information Today,* vol. 25, issue 6 (June 2008).

8. Brian Morrissey, "FedEx Microsite Receives Second Act," *Adweek,* vol. 49, issue 19 (June 9, 2008).

CHAPTER 13

ENDNOTES

1. Information from www.jayzonline.com; and www.history-of-rock.com/motown_records.

2. Situation from Carol Hymowitz, "Middle Managers Are Unsung Heroes on Corporate Stage," *Wall Street Journal* (September 19, 2005), p. B1.

3. Ram Charan, "Six Personality Traits of a Leader," career-advice.monster.com/leadership-skills (retrieved August 6, 2008).

4. Example and quotes from Carol Hymowitz, "Independent Program Puts College Students on Leadership Paths," *Wall Street Journal* (January 14, 2003), p. B1.

5. Peter F. Drucker, "Looking Ahead: Implications of the Present," *Harvard Business Review* (September–October 1997), pp. 18–32. See also Shaker A. Zahra, "An Interview with Peter Drucker," *Academy of Management Executive,* vol. 17 (August 2003), pp. 9–12.

6. Information from John A. Byrne, "Visionary vs. Visionary," *BusinessWeek* (August 28, 2000), pp. 10–14.

7. Jaclyn Fierman, "Winning Ideas from Maverick Managers," *Fortune* (February 6, 1995), pp. 66–80.

8. See Susan G. Cohen and Don Mankin, "The Changing Nature of Work: Managing the Impact of Information Technology," Chapter 6 in Susan Albers Mohrman, Jay R. Galbraith, Edward E. Lawler III, and associates, *Tomorrow's Organization: Crafting Winning Capabilities in a Dynamic World* (San Francisco: Jossey-Bass, 1988), pp. 154–78.

9. Noel M. Tichy and Warren G. Bennis, *Judgment: How Winning Leaders Make Great Calls* (Knoxville, TN: Portfolio Hardcover, 2007).

10. Noel M. Tichy and Warren G. Bennis, "Judgment: How Winning Leaders Make Great Calls," *BusinessWeek* (November 19, 2007), pp. 68–72.

11. Henry Mintzberg, *The Nature of Managerial Work* (New York: Harper-Collins, 1997).

12. For a good discussion, see Watson H. Agor, *Intuition in Organizations: Leading and Managing Productively* (Newbury Park, CA: Sage, 1989); Herbert A. Simon, "Making Management Decisions: The Role of Intuition and Emotion," *Academy of Management Executive,* vol. 1 (1987), pp. 57–64; Orlando Behling and Norman L. Eckel, "Making Sense Out of Intuition," *Academy of Management Executive,* vol. 5 (1991), pp. 46–54.

13. See, for example, William Duggan, *Strategic Intuition: The Creative Spark in Human Achievement* (New York: Columbia Business School, 2007).

14. Daniel J. Isenberg, "How Senior Managers Think," *Harvard Business Review,* vol. 62 (November–December 1984), pp. 81–90.

15. Daniel J. Isenberg, "The Tactics of Strategic Opportunism," *Harvard Business Review,* vol. 65 (March–April 1987), pp. 92–97.

16. Based on Carl Jung's typology as described in Donald Bowen, "Learning and Problem-Solving: You're Never Too Jung," in Donald D. Bowen, Roy J. Lewicki, Donald T. Hall, and Francine S. Hall, eds., *Experiences in Management and Organizational Behavior,* 4th ed. (New York: Wiley, 1997), pp. 7–13; and John W. Slocum Jr., "Cognitive Style in Learning and Problem Solving," ibid., pp. 349–53.

17. "They Don't Teach This in B-School," *BusinessWeek* (September 19, 2005), pp. 46–47.

18. Ibid.

19. Developed from Anna Muoio, "Where There's Smoke It Helps to Have a Smoke Jumper," *Fast Company,* vol. 33, p. 290.

20. For scholarly reviews, see Dean Tjosvold, "Effects of Crisis Orientation on Managers' Approach to Controversy in Decision Making," *Academy of Management Journal,* vol. 27 (1984), pp. 130–38; and Jan I. Mitroff,

Paul Shrivastava, and Firdaus E. Udwadia, "Effective Crisis Management," *Academy of Management Executive,* vol. 1 (1987), pp. 283–92.

21. See David Greisling, *I'd Like to Buy the World a Coke: The Life and Leadership of Roberto Goizueta* (New York: Wiley, 1998).

22. Information and quotes from Terry Kosdrosky and John D. Stoll, "GM Puts Electric-Car Testing on Fast Track to 2010," *Wall Street Journal* (April 4, 2008), p. B2.

23. See Hugh Courtney, Jane Kirkland, and Patrick Viguerie, "Strategy under Uncertainty," *Harvard Business Review* (November–December 1997), pp. 67–79.

24. See George P. Huber, *Managerial Decision Making* (Glenview, IL: Scott, Foresman, 1975). For a comparison, see the steps in Xerox's problem-solving process as described in David A. Garvin, "Building a Learning Organization," *Harvard Business Review* (July–August 1993), pp. 78–91; and the Josephson model for ethical decision-making described at www.josephsoninstitute.org.

25. Peter F. Drucker, *Innovation and Entrepreneurship: Practice and Principles* (New York: Harper-Row, 1985).

26. For a sample of Simon's work, see Herbert A. Simon, *Administrative Behavior* (New York: Free Press, 1947); James G. March and Herbert A. Simon, *Organizations* (New York: Wiley, 1958); and Herbert A. Simon, *The New Science of Management Decision* (New York: Harper, 1960).

27. See Daniel Kahneman and Amos Tversky, "Psychology of Preferences," *Scientific American,* vol. 246 (1982), pp. 161–73.

28. This presentation is based on the discussion in Max H. Bazerman, *Judgment in Managerial Decision Making,* 6th ed. (Hoboken, NJ: Wiley, 2005).

29. Barry M. Staw, "The Escalation of Commitment to a Course of Action," *Academy of Management Review,* vol. 6 (1981), pp. 577–87; and Barry M. Staw and Jerry Ross, "Knowing When to Pull the Plug," *Harvard Business Review,* vol. 65 (March–April 1987), pp. 68–74.

30. See, for example, Amy Saunders and Matzer Rose, "Skybus Throttles Back on Growth," *The Columbus Dispatch* (March 13, 2008).

31. Information from "Lonnie Johnson," *USAA Magazine* (Fall 2007), p. 38; and www.johnsonrd.com.

32. See, for example, Roger von Oech, *A Whack on the Side of the Head* (New York: Warner Books, 1983); and *A Kick in the Seat of the Pants* (New York: Harper & Row, 1986).

33. Teresa M. Amabile, "Motivating Creativity in Organizations," *California Management Review,* vol. 40 (Fall 1997), pp. 39–58.

34. Developed from discussions by Edward DeBono, *Lateral Thinking: Creativity Step-by-Step* (New York: Harper-Collins, 1970); John S. Dacey and Kathleen H. Lennon, *Understanding Creativity* (San Francisco: Jossey-Bass, 1998); and Bettina von Stamm, *Managing Innovation, Design & Creativity* (Chichester, UK: John Wiley & Sons, 2003).

35. Example from Dayton Fandray, "Assumed Innocent: Hidden and Unexamined Assumptions Can Ruin Your Day," *Continental.com/Magazine* (December 2007), p. 100.

36. Information from Stephen H. Wildstrom, "Video iPod, I Love You," *BusinessWeek* (November 7, 2005), p. 20; "Voices of Innovation," *BusinessWeek* (December 12, 2005), p. 22.

37. Information from "Mosh Pits of Creativity," *BusinessWeek* (November 7, 2005), pp. 98–99.

38. Ibid.

39. This contingency notion is the foundation of Victor H. Vroom and Arthur G. Jago, *The New Leadership: Managing Participation in Organizations* (Englewood Cliffs, NJ: Prentice-Hall, 1988). This is based on earlier work by Victor H. Vroom, "A New Look in Managerial Decision-Making," *Organizational Dynamics* (Spring 1973), pp. 66–80; and Victor H. Vroom and Phillip Yetton, *Leadership and Decision-Making* (Pittsburgh: University of Pittsburgh Press, 1973).

40. The classic work is Norman R. Maier, "Assets and Liabilities in Group Problem Solving," *Psychological Review*, vol. 74 (1967), pp. 239–49.

41. Josephson Institute, op. cit.

42. Based on Gerald F. Cavanagh, *American Business Values*, 4th ed. (Upper Saddle River, NJ: Prentice-Hall, 1998).

FEATURE NOTES

Real Ethics: Information from *Economist* (June 17, 2006), vol. 379, issue 8482, pp. 65–66.

Issues and Situations: Lauren Fowster and David Ibison, "Spike the Robot Helps Lego Rebuild Strategy," *Financial Times* (June 22, 2006), p. 18; "Lego Fans of the World, Unite," *BusinessWeek* (April 7, 2008), p. 26.

Canadian Managers: Chapters-Indigo corporate website, www.chapters.indigo.ca; Ken Mark, "Indigo Books Starts a New Chapter," *Chain Store Age* (October 2005), pp. 22A–23A; Rebecca Harris, "Indigo Gets Its Wish . . . List," *Marketing* (November 28, 2005, vol. 110).

Canadian Company in the News: Capital Power Corporation corporate website, www.capitalpower.com.

Research Brief: Marc Street and Vera L. Street, "The Effects of Escalating Commitment on

Ethical Decision Making," *Journal of Business Ethics*, vol. 64 (2006), pp. 343–56.

CASE ENDNOTES

1. Rick Spence, "Inside the Tornado," *Profit* (December 2005), p. 40.

2. "About Spin Master," Spin Master corporate website, www.spinmastertoys.co.uk/sections.jsp?about.

3. Spence, op. cit.

4. Spin Master corporate website, www.spinmaster.com.

5. "A Brief History of Spin Master," Spin Master corporate website, www.spinmaster.com/spinHq/hr/aboutspinmaster.htm.

6. Shawna Steinberg and Joe Chidley, "Fun for the Money," *Canadian Business* (December 11, 1998), p. 44.

7. "A Brief History of Spin Master," op. cit.

8. Ibid.

9. Steinberg and Chidley, op. cit.

10. "A Brief History of Spin Master," op. cit.

11. Ibid.

12. "News and Promotions," op. cit.

13. Spence, op. cit.

14. Ibid.

15. Anthony Grnak, John Hughes, and Douglas Hunter, "Lessons from the Sandbox," *National Post* (January 28, 2006), p. FW2.

16. Maneesh Mehta, "Growth by Design: How Good Design Drives Company Growth," *Ivey Business Journal* (January/February 2006).

17. Spence, op. cit.

18. Grnak, Hughes, and Hunter, op. cit.

19. Nick Rockel, "How Spin Master Gets Hottest Toys to Market," *The Globe and Mail* (April 9, 2010).

20. "A Brief History of Spin Master," op. cit.

CHAPTER 14

ENDNOTES

1. Information and quotes from Julie Flaherty, "A Parting Gift from the Boss Who Cared," *New York Times* (September 28, 2000), pp. C1, C25; Business Wire news release, "Employees of the Butcher Company Share over $18 Million as Owner Shares Benefits of Success" (September 21, 2000); "Butcher, Charles," *The New York Times* (June 20, 2004), retrieved from nytimes.com; and "Putting His Money Where His Mouth Is" (September 26, 2000): www.timesizing.com.

2. Noreen Rasbach, "Money Talks, But So Do Other Forms of Compensation," *The Globe and Mail Report on Business* (July 2, 2010).

3. Conference Board research reported in Patricia Soldati, "Employee Engagement: What Exactly Is It?" *Management Issues*

(March 8, 2007). Yum Brands information from Erin White, "How Surveying Workers Can Pay Off," *Wall Street Journal* (June 18, 2007), p. B3.

4. Information from "Executive Briefing: A New Approach for Airlines," *Wall Street Journal* (May 12, 2008), p. R3. See also Greg J. Bamber, Jody Hoffer Gittel, Thomas A. Kochan, and Andrew Von Nordenflycht, *Up in the Air: How the Airlines Can Improve Performance by Engaging Their Employees* (Ithaca, NY: Cornell University Press, 2009).

5. Information from Melinda Beck, "If at First You Don't Succeed, You're in Excellent Company," *Wall Street Journal* (April 29, 2008), p. D1.

6. See Abraham H. Maslow, *Eupsychian Management* (Homewood, IL: Richard D. Irwin, 1965); and Abraham H. Maslow, *Motivation and Personality*, 2nd ed. (New York: Harper-Row, 1970). For a research perspective, see Mahmoud A. Wahba and Lawrence G. Bridwell, "Maslow Reconsidered: A Review of Research on the Need Hierarchy," *Organizational Behavior and Human Performance*, vol. 16 (1976), pp. 212–40.

7. John Elliot, "Canadian Employees Wouldn't Trade Health Benefit Plan for Cash, Survey Says," *Benefits & Compensation Digest* (September 2004, Vol. 41, Issue 9), pp. 26–28.

8. See Clayton P. Alderfer, *Existence, Relatedness, and Growth* (New York: Free Press, 1972).

9. The two-factor theory is in Frederick Herzberg, Bernard Mausner, and Barbara Block Synderman, *The Motivation to Work*, 2nd ed. (New York: Wiley, 1967); Frederick Herzberg, "One More Time: How Do You Motivate Employees?" *Harvard Business Review* (January–February 1968), pp. 53–62, and reprinted as an HBR classic (September–October 1987), pp. 109–20.

10. Critical reviews are provided by Robert J. House and Lawrence A. Wigdor, "Herzberg's Dual-Factor Theory of Job Satisfaction and Motivation: A Review of the Evidence and a Criticism," *Personnel Psychology*, vol. 20 (winter 1967), pp. 369–89; Steven Kerr, Anne Harlan, and Ralph Stogdill, "Preference for Motivator and Hygiene Factors in a Hypothetical Interview Situation," *Personnel Psychology*, vol. 27 (Winter 1974), pp. 109–24.

11. Frederick Herzberg, "Workers' Needs: The Same around the World," *Industry Week* (September 21, 1987), pp. 29–32.

12. For a collection of McClelland's work, see David C. McClelland, *The Achieving Society* (New York: Van Nostrand, 1961); "Business Drive and National Achievement," *Harvard Business Review*, vol. 40 (July–August 1962), pp. 99–112; David C. McClelland and David H. Burnham, "Power Is the Great Motivator," *Harvard Business Review* (March–April 1976), pp. 100–10; David C. McClelland, *Human Motivation* (Glenview, IL: Scott,

Foresman, 1985); David C. McClelland and Richard E. Boyatsis, "The Leadership Motive Pattern and Long-Term Success in Management," *Journal of Applied Psychology*, vol. 67 (1982), pp. 737–43.

13. See, for example, J. Stacy Adams, "Toward an Understanding of Inequity," *Journal of Abnormal and Social Psychology*, vol. 67 (1963), pp. 422–36; J. Stacy Adams, "Inequity in Social Exchange," in L. Berkowitz, ed., *Advances in Experimental Social Psychology*, vol. 2 (New York: Academic Press, 1965), pp. 267–300.

14. See, for example, J. W. Harder, "Play for Pay: Effects of Inequity in a Pay-for-Performance Context," *Administrative Science Quarterly*, vol. 37 (1992), pp. 321–35.

15. Victor H. Vroom, *Work and Motivation* (New York: Wiley, 1964; republished by Jossey-Bass, 1994).

16. Flat Rock Cellars corporate website, www.flatrockcellars.com/pages/winery/people; "Traceability Gives Winery a Leg Up on Its Competitors," Ontario Ministry of Agriculture, Food & Rural Affairs, available at www.omafra.gov.on.ca/english/food/foodsafety/traceability/flatrocktraceprofile.htm.

17. The work on goal-setting theory is well summarized in Edwin A. Locke and Gary P. Latham, *Goal Setting: A Motivational Technique That Works!* (Englewood Cliffs, NJ: Prentice Hall, 1984). See also Edwin A. Locke, Kenneth N. Shaw, Lisa A. Saari, and Gary P. Latham, "Goal Setting and Task Performance 1969–1980," *Psychological Bulletin*, vol. 90 (1981), pp. 125–52; Mark E. Tubbs, "Goal Setting: A Meta-Analytic Examination of the Empirical Evidence," *Journal of Applied Psychology*, vol. 71 (1986), pp. 474–83; Gary P. Latham and Edwin A. Locke, "Self-Regulation Through Goal Setting," *Organizational Behavior and Human Decision Processes*, vol. 50 (1991), pp. 212–47; and Terence R. Mitchell, Kenneth R. Thompson, and Jane George-Falvy, "Goal Setting: Theory and Practice," Chapter 9 in Cary L. Cooper and Edwin A. Locke, eds., *Industrial and Organizational Psychology: Linking Theory with Practice* (Malden, MA: Blackwell Business, 2000), pp. 211–49.

18. Albert Bandura, *Social Learning Theory* (Englewood Cliffs, NJ: Prentice-Hall, 1977); and Albert Bandura, *Self-Efficacy: The Exercise of Control* (New York: W. H. Freeman, 1997).

19. Quote from www.des.emory.edu/mfp/self-efficacy.html.

20. Beck, op. cit.

21. Bandura, op. cit., 1977 and 1997.

22. E. L. Thorndike, *Animal Intelligence* (New York: Macmillan, 1911), p. 244.

23. See B. F. Skinner, *Walden Two* (New York: Macmillan, 1948); *Science and Human Behavior* (New York: Macmillan, 1953); *Contingencies of Reinforcement* (New York: Appleton-Century-Crofts, 1969).

24. Fred Luthans and Robert Kreitner, *Organizational Behavior Modification* (Glenview, IL: Scott, Foresman, 1975); and Fred Luthans and Robert Kreitner, *Organizational Behavior Modification and Beyond* (Glenview, IL: Scott, Foresman, 1985); see also Fred Luthans and Alexander D. Stajkovic, "Reinforce for Performance: The Need to Go Beyond Pay and Even Rewards," *Academy of Management Executive*, vol. 13 (1999), pp. 49–57.

25. Richard Gibson, "Pitchman in the Corner Office," *Wall Street Journal* (October 24, 2007), p. D10. See also David Novak, *The Education of an Accidental CEO: Lessons Learned from the Trailer Park to the Corner Office* (New York: Crown Business, 2007).

26. Rasbach, op. cit.

27. For the Mary Kay story and philosophy, see Mary Kay Ash, *Mary Kay on People Management* (New York: Warner Books, 1985); see also information at the corporate website, www.marykay.com.

28. Richard Yerema and Rachel Caballero, "Sophos Inc.: Chosen as One of Canada's Top 100 Employers and BC's Top Employers for 2010," Mediacorp Canada Inc., available at www.eluta.ca/top-employer-sophos.

29. For a review, see Arne L. Kalleberg, "The Mismatched Worker: When People Don't Fit Their Jobs," *Academy of Management Perspectives* (February 2008), pp. 24–40.

30. Information from David Whitford, "A Human Place to Work," *Fortune* (January 8, 2001), pp. 108–20.

31. Dawn Calleja, "Linamar's Drive to $10-Billion," *The Globe and Mail* (May 27, 2010).

32. See Frederick Herzberg, Bernard Mausner, and Barbara Block Synderman, *The Motivation to Work*, 2nd ed. (New York: Wiley, 1967). The quotation is from Frederick Herzberg, "One More Time: Employees?" *Harvard Business Review* (January–February 1968), pp. 53–62, and reprinted as an HBR Classic in September–October 1987, pp. 109–120.

33. For a complete description of the core characteristics model, see J. Richard Hackman and Greg R. Oldham, *Work Redesign* (Reading, MA: Addison-Wesley, 1980).

34. See Allen R. Cohen and Herman Gadon, *Alternative Work Schedules: Integrating Individual and Organizational Needs* (Reading, MA: Addison-Wesley, 1978), p. 125; Simcha Ronen and Sophia B. Primps, "The Compressed Work Week as Organizational Change: Behavioral and Attitudinal Outcomes," *Academy of Management Review*, vol. 6 (1981), pp. 61–74.

35. "The Top 25 Family-Friendly Employers in Canada: Our Annual List of Canada's Top Family-Friendly Employers for 2010," *Today's Parent* (December 2009).

36. Sue Shellenbarger, "What Makes a Company a Great Place to Work," *Wall Street Journal* (October 4, 2007), p. D1.

37. Yukon Public Service Commission website, www.psc.gov.yk.ca.

38. Information from Lesli Hicks, "Workers, Employers Praise Their Four-Day Workweek," *Columbus Dispatch* (August 22, 1994), p. 6; and Walsh, op. cit. (2001).

39. For a review, see Wayne F. Cascio, "Managing a Virtual Workplace," *Academy of Management Executive*, vol. 14 (2000), pp. 81–90.

40. Quote from Phil Porter, "Telecommuting Mom Is Part of a National Trend," *Columbus Dispatch* (November 29, 2000), pp. H1–H2.

41. "Labour Force Survey, July 2010," Statistics Canada, *The Daily*, August 6, 2010.

FEATURE NOTES

Going Global: "Employee Motivation" by Nitin Nohria, Boris Groysberg and Linda-Eling Lee, *Harvard Business Review*, vol. 86, July–August 2008.

Real Ethics: Information from Jared Sandberg, "Why You May Regret Looking at Papers Left on the Office Copier," *Wall Street Journal* (June 20, 2006), p. B1.

Research Brief: "Psychological Capital (PsyCap) Measurement, Development, and Performance Impact," Briefings Report 2006-01 (Gallup Leadership Institute); and Fred Luthans, James B. Avey, Bruce J. Avoilio, Steven M. Norman, and Gwendolyn M. Combs, "Psychological Capital Development: Toward a Micro-Intervention," *Journal of Organizational Behavior*, vol. 27 (2006), pp. 387–93.

Issues and Situations: Jeanne Sahadi, "CEO Pay: 364 Times More Than Workers," *CNNMoney* (August 29, 2007); "2007 Trends in CEO Pay," AFL-CIO: aflcio.org/corporatewatch (retrieved August 10, 2008); Joe Bel Bruno, "Calls Against Big CEO Pay Grow Louder," Financial News, AP (April 12, 2008), biz.yahoo.com; Janet McFarland, "2009 Executive Compensation: Executive Compensation Set to Rise," *The Globe and Mail* (May 24, 2010); Matthew Dolan and Mike Spector, "Ford CEO's Pay in '07 Draws Fire from UAW," *Wall Street Journal* (April 5–6, 2008), p. A3; Carol Hymowitz, "Pay Gap Fuels Worker Woes," *Wall Street Journal* (April 28, 2008), p. B8.

Canadian Managers: Erin Pooley, "MBA Jobs: Grads Sample the Workplace," *Canadian Business* (October 24–November 6, 2005, Vol. 78), Iss. 21.

CASE ENDNOTES

1. See David A. Price, *The Pixar Touch* (New York: Knopf, 2008); and Ed Catmull, "How Pixar Fosters Collective Creativity," *Harvard Business Review* (September 2008), Reprint R0809D.

2. Doug Childers, "Pixar's Success Is More Than Just Pixel-Deep," in Rich.com (June 1, 2008).

3. Greg Sandoval, "New Competitors Challenge Pixar's Animation Domination," *The Sacramento Union* (December 2, 2005).

4. "How Disney Knew It Needed Pixar," *Fortune*, vol. 153, issue 10 (May 29, 2006).

5. Pixar Corporate Overview at www.pixar.com/companyinfo/about_us/overview.htm (accessed June 8, 2008).

6. www.worstpreviews.com/review.php?id=758&section=preview.

7. See Price, op. cit.; Peter Burrows, "The Improbable Heroes of Toontown," *Business-Week* (May 26, 2008), p. 82; and Paul Boutin, "An Industry Gets Animated," *Wall Street Journal* (May 14, 2008), p. A19.

8. Brent Schlender and Christopher Tkaczyk, "Pixar's Magic Man," *Fortune*, vol. 153, issue 10 (May 29, 2006).

9. David Price, "How Pixar Cheated Death," *Inc.*, vol. 28, issue 6 (June 2006).

10. Jia Lynn Yang, "How Disney Picked Up Pixar," *Fortune*, vol. 157, issue 9 (May 5, 2008).

11. Quote from Burrows, op. cit.

12. Childers, op. cit.

13. Peter Cohen, "Disney Buys Pixar," *Macworld*, vol. 23, issue 4 (April 2006).

14. Sandoval, op. cit.

15. Quote from Burrows, op. cit.

16. Sandoval, op. cit.

CHAPTER 15

ENDNOTES

1. Information and quotes from Allen St. John, "Racing's Fastest Pit Crew," *Wall Street Journal* (May 9, 2008), p. W4; and Bonnie Berkowitz, "Pit Crews Keep NASCAR Racers on Track," *Columbus Dispatch* (May 28, 2008), p. D6.

2. Information from Scott Thurm, "Teamwork Raises Everyone's Game," *Wall Street Journal* (November 7, 2005), p. B7.

3. Ibid.

4. Chambers quote from Charles O'Reilly III and Jeffrey Pfeffer, *Hidden Value: How Great Companies Achieve Extraordinary Results Through Ordinary People* (Boston, MA: Harvard Business School Publishing, 2000), p. 4; other quotes from www.quotegarden.com.

5. For a discussion, see Jon R. Katzenbach and Douglas K. Smith, *The Wisdom of Teams: Creating the High Performance Organization* (Boston: Harvard Business School Press, 1993).

6. Lynda C. McDermott, Nolan Brawley, and William A. Waite, *World-Class Teams:*

Working Across Borders (New York: Wiley, 1998), p. 5; "White Collar Workers Shoulder Together—Like It or Not," *BusinessWeek* (April 28, 2008), p. 58.

7. See, for example, Edward E. Lawler III, Susan Albers Mohrman, and Gerald E. Ledford Jr., *Employee Involvement and Total Quality Management: Practices and Results in Fortune 1000 Companies* (San Francisco: Jossey-Bass, 1992); Susan A. Mohrman, Susan A. Cohen, and Monty A. Mohrman, *Designing Team-Based Organizations: New Forms for Knowledge Work* (San Francisco: Jossey-Bass, 1995).

8. Katzenbach and Smith, op. cit.

9. Joe Lindsey, "Nine Riders, and Nearly as Many Jobs," *The Wall Street Journal* (July 9, 2008).

10. "Mid-Sized Canadian Business Executives Say Teamwork Is Critical to Overall Success of Their Organization," news release, Ipsos-Reid, October 21, 2003.

11. Leavitt, op. cit.

12. Patrick M. Lencioni, *The Five Dysfunctions of a Team: A Leadership Fable* (San Franciso: Jossey-Bass, 2002).

13. A classic work is Bib Latané, Kipling Williams, and Stephen Harkins, "Many Hands Make Light the Work: The Causes and Consequences of Social Loafing," *Journal of Personality and Social Psychology*, vol. 37 (1978), pp. 822–32.

14. John M. George, "Extrinsic and Intrinsic Origins of Perceived Social Loafing in Organizations," *Academy of Management Journal* (March 1992), pp. 191–202; and W. Jack Duncan, "Why Some People Loaf in Groups While Others Loaf Alone," *Academy of Management Executive*, vol. 8 (1994), pp. 79–80.

15. See Marvin E. Shaw, *Group Dynamics: The Psychology of Small Group Behavior*, 2nd ed. (New York: McGraw-Hill, 1976); Harold J. Leavitt, "Suppose We Took Groups More Seriously," in Eugene L. Cass and Frederick G. Zimmer, eds., *Man and Work in Society* (New York: Van Nostrand Reinhold, 1975), pp. 67–77.

16. For insights on how to conduct effective meetings, see Mary A. De Vries, *How to Run a Meeting* (New York: Penguin, 1994).

17. Survey reported in "Meetings Among Top Ten Time Wasters," *San Francisco Business Times* (April 7, 2003).

18. Quotes from Eric Matson, "The Seven Sins of Deadly Meetings," *Fast Company* (April/May 1996), p. 122.

19. Developed from Matson, op. cit.

20. The "linking pin" concept is introduced in Rensis Likert, *New Patterns of Management* (New York: McGraw-Hill, 1962).

21. See Susan D. Van Raalte, "Preparing the Task Force to Get Good Results," *S.A.M.*

Advanced Management Journal, vol. 47 (Winter 1982), pp. 11–16; Walter Kiechel III, "The Art of the Corporate Task Force," *Fortune* (January 28, 1991), pp. 104–6.

22. Information from Jenny C. McCune, "Making Lemonade," *Management Review* (June 1997), pp. 49–53.

23. Matt Golosinski, "With Teamwork, Gregg Steinhafel Hits the Bulls Eye at Target," *Kellogg* (Summer 2007), p. 32.

24. See Wayne F. Cascio, "Managing a Virtual Workplace," *Academy of Management Executive*, vol. 14 (2000), pp. 81–90; Sheila Simsarian Webber, "Virtual Teams: A Meta-Analysis," www.shrm.org/foundation/findings.asp; and Stacie A. Furst, Martha Reeves, Benson Rosen, and Richard S. Blackburn, "Managing the Life Cycle of Virtual Teams," *Academy of Management Executive*, vol. 18 (2004), pp. 6–20.

25. Example from Phred Dvorak, "How Teams Can Work Well Together from Far Apart," *Wall Street Journal* (September 17, 2007), p. B4.

26. William M. Bulkeley, "Computerizing Dull Meetings Is Touted as an Antidote to the Mouth That Bored," *Wall Street Journal* (January 28, 1992), pp. B1–B2.

27. R. Brent Gallupe and William H. Cooper, "Brainstorming Electronically," *Sloan Management Review* (Winter 1997), pp. 11–21; Cascio, op. cit.

28. Cascio, op. cit.; Furst, et al., op. cit.

29. "Open Text Adds Comprehensive Social Media Capabilities to the Open Text ECM Suite, Delivers on Enterprise 2.0," news release, Canada Newswire, June 23, 2009.

30. See, for example, Paul S. Goodman, Rukmini Devadas, and Terri L. Griffith Hughson, "Groups and Productivity: Analyzing the Effectiveness of Self-Managing Teams," Chapter 11 in John R. Campbell and Richard J. Campbell, *Productivity in Organizations* (San Francisco: Jossey-Bass, 1988); Jack Orsbrun, Linda Moran, Ed Musslewhite, and John H. Zenger, with Craig Perrin, *Self-Directed Work Teams: The New American Challenge* (Homewood, IL: Business One Irwin, 1990); Dale E. Yeatts and Cloyd Hyten, *High Performing Self-Managed Work Teams* (Thousand Oaks, CA: Sage, 1997).

31. Bradley L. Kirkman and Debra L. Shapiro, "The Impact of Cultural Values on Employee Resistance to Teams: Toward a Model of Globalized Self-Managing Work Team Effectiveness," *Academy of Management Review*, vol. 22 (1997), pp. 730–57.

32. A very good overview is William D. Dyer, *Team-Building* (Reading, MA: Addison-Wesley, 1977).

33. Schein, op. cit., pp. 69–75.

34. Dennis Berman, "Zap! Pow! Splat!" *BusinessWeek*, Enterprise issue (February 9, 1998), p. ENT22.

35. For a discussion of effectiveness in the context of top management teams, see Edward E. Lawler III, David Finegold, and Jay A. Conger, "Corporate Boards: Developing Effectiveness at the Top," in Mohrman, et al., op. cit. (1998), pp. 23–50.

36. Quote from Alex Markels, "Money & Business," *U.S. News online* (October 22, 2006).

37. For a review of research on group effectiveness, see J. Richard Hackman, "The Design of Work Teams," in Jay W. Lorsch (ed.), *Handbook of Organizational Behavior* (Englewood Cliffs, NJ: Prentice-Hall, 1987), pp. 315–42; and J. Richard Hackman, Ruth Wageman, Thomas M. Ruddy, and Charles L. Ray, "Team Effectiveness in Theory and Practice," Chapter 5 in Cary L. Cooper and Edwin A. Locke, *Industrial and Organizational Psychology: Linking Theory with Practice* (Malden, MA: Blackwell, 2000).

38. Ibid.; Lawler et al., op. cit., 1998; Linda Hill and Michel J. Anteby, "Analyzing Work Groups," Harvard Business School, 9-407-032 (August 2007).

39. Example from "Designed for Interaction," *Fortune* (January 8, 2001), p. 150.

40. See, for example, Lynda Gratton and Tamara J. Erickson, "Eight Ways to Build Collaborative Teams," *Harvard Business Review*, Reprint R0711F (November 2007).

41. Information from Susan Carey, "Racing to Improve," *Wall Street Journal* (March 24, 2006), pp. B1, B6.

42. Robert D. Hof, "Amazon's Risky Bet," *BusinessWeek* (November 13, 2006), p. 52.

43. Information from Carol Hymowitz, "Managers Err if They Limit Their Hiring to People Just Like Them," *Wall Street Journal* (October 12, 2004), p. B1.

44. Marvin E. Shaw, *Group Dynamics: The Psychology of Small Group Behavior* (New York: McGraw-Hill, 1976).

45. See Warren Watson, "Cultural Diversity's Impact on Interaction Process and Performance," *Academy of Management Journal*, vol. 16 (1993); Christopher Earley and Elaine Mosakowski, "Creating Hybrid Team Structures: An Empirical Test of Transnational Team Functioning," *Academy of Management Journal*, vol. 5 (February 2000), pp. 26–49; Jeanne Brett, Kristin Behfar, and Mary C. Kern, "Managing Multicultural Teams," *Harvard Business Review* (November 2006), pp. 84–91.

46. J. Steven Heinen and Eugene Jacobson, "A Model of Task Group Development in Complex Organizations and a Strategy of Implementation," *Academy of Management Review*, vol. 1 (1976), pp. 98–111; Bruce W. Tuckman, "Developmental Sequence in Small Groups," *Psychological Bulletin*, vol. 63 (1965), pp. 384–99; Bruce W. Tuckman and Mary Ann C. Jensen, "Stages of Small-Group Development Revisited," *Group-Organization Studies*, vol. 2 (1977), pp. 419–27.

47. See, for example, Edgar Schein, *Process Consultation* (Reading, MA: Addison-Wesley, 1988); and Linda C. McDermott, Nolan Brawley, and William A. Waite, *World-Class Teams: Working Across Borders* (New York: Wiley, 1998).

48. For a good discussion, see Robert F. Allen and Saul Pilnick, "Confronting the Shadow Organization: How to Detect and Defeat Negative Norms," *Organizational Dynamics* (Spring 1973), pp. 13–16.

49. See Schein, op. cit., pp. 76–79.

50. Ibid.; Shaw, op. cit.

51. A classic work in this area is K. Benne and P. Sheets, "Functional Roles of Group Members," *Journal of Social Issues*, vol. 2 (1948), pp. 42–47; see also Likert, op. cit., pp. 166–69; Schein, op. cit., pp. 49–56.

52. Research on communication networks is found in Alex Bavelas, "Communication Patterns in Task-Oriented Groups," *Journal of the Acoustical Society of America*, vol. 22 (1950), pp. 725–30; Shaw, op. cit.

53. Schein, op. cit.

54. See Kathleen M. Eisenhardt, Jean L. Kahwajy, and L. J. Bourgeois III, "How Management Teams Can Have a Good Fight," *Harvard Business Review* (July–August 1997), pp. 77–85.

55. Consensus box developed from a classic article by Jay Hall, "Decisions, Decisions, Decisions," *Psychology Today* (November 1971), pp. 55–56.

56. Victor H. Vroom and Arthur G. Jago, *The New Leadership: Managing Participation in Organizations* (Englewood Cliffs, NJ: Prentice-Hall, 1988); Victor H. Vroom, "A New Look in Managerial Decision-Making," *Organizational Dynamics* (Spring 1973), pp. 66–80; Victor H. Vroom and Phillip Yetton, *Leadership and Decision-Making* (Pittsburgh: University of Pittsburgh Press, 1973).

57. Norman F. Maier, "Assets and Liabilities in Group Problem Solving," *Psychological Review*, vol. 74 (1967), pp. 239–49.

58. See Irving L. Janis, "Groupthink," *Psychology Today* (November 1971), pp. 43–46; *Victims of Groupthink*, 2nd ed. (Boston: Houghton Mifflin, 1982).

59. Ed Catmull, "How Pixar Fosters Collective Creativity," *Harvard Business Review* (September 2008), Reprint R0809D.

60. These techniques are well described in Andre L. Delbecq, Andrew H. Van de Ven, and David H. Gustafson, *Group Techniques for Program Planning* (Glenview, IL: Scott, Foresman, 1975).

61. Information from Kelly K. Spors, "Productive Brainstorms Take the Right Mix of Elements," *The Wall Street Journal* (July 28, 2008).

62. Delbecq, et al., op. cit.

63. Richard E. Walton, *Interpersonal Peacemaking: Confrontations and Third-Party Consultation* (Reading, MA: Addison-Wesley, 1969), p. 2.

64. See Robert R. Blake and Jane Srygley Mouton, "The Fifth Achievement," *Journal of Applied Behavioral Science*, vol. 6 (1970), pp. 413–27; Alan C. Filley, *Interpersonal Conflict Resolution* (Glenview, IL: Scott, Foresman, 1975).

65. This discussion is based on Filley, op. cit.

66. See Kenneth W. Thomas, "Conflict and Conflict Management," in M. D. Dunnett, ed., *Handbook of Industrial and Organizational Behavior* (Chicago: Rand McNally, 1976), pp. 889–935.

67. Portions of this treatment of negotiation originally adapted from John R. Schermerhorn, Jr., James G. Hunt, and Richard N. Osborn, *Managing Organizational Behavior*, 4th ed. (New York: Wiley, 1991), pp. 382–87. Used by permission.

68. See Roger Fisher and William Ury, *Getting to Yes: Negotiating Agreement Without Giving In* (New York: Penguin, 1983); James A. Wall, Jr., *Negotiation: Theory and Practice* (Glenview, IL: Scott, Foresman, 1985); and William L. Ury, Jeanne M. Brett, and Stephen B. Goldberg, *Getting Disputes Resolved* (San Francisco: Jossey-Bass, 1997).

69. Fisher and Ury, op. cit.

70. Ibid.

71. Developed from Max H. Bazerman, *Judgment in Managerial Decision Making*, 4th ed. (New York: Wiley, 1998), Chapter 7.

72. Fisher and Ury, op. cit.

73. "A Choreographer's Cues," *Kellogg* World (Summer 2006), p. 40.

74. Roy J. Lewicki and Joseph A. Litterer, *Negotiation* (Homewood, IL: Irwin, 1985).

FEATURE NOTES

Going Global: "Individualism Trumped as Teamwork Triumphs," *The Province*, July 11, 2010, p. A58.

Real Ethics: For research see Bib Latané, Kipling Williams, and Stephen Harkins, "Many Hands Make Light the Work: The Causes and Consequences of Social Loafing," *Journal of Personality and Social Psychology*, vol. 37 (1978), pp. 822–32; and W. Jack Duncan, "Why Some People Loaf in Groups and Others Loaf Alone," *Academy of Management Executive*, vol. 8 (1994), pp. 79–80.

Research Brief: Dora C. Lau and J. Keith Murnighan, "Interactions within Groups and Subgroups: The Effects of Demographic Faultlines," *Academy of Management Journal*, vol. 48 (2005), pp. 645–59; "Demographic Diversity and Faultlines: The Compositional Dynamics of Organizational Groups," *Academy of Management Review*, vol. 23 (1998), pp. 325–40.

Issues and Situations: Information from Sarah Max, "Seagate's Morale-athon," *BusinessWeek* (April 3, 2006), pp. 110–11.

Canadian Managers: "Scotty Bowman: A Coach for the Ages," CBC Sports on-line, April 17, 2010, available at www.cbc.ca/sports/hockey/peterpuck/story/2010/04/17/sp-peter-puck-bowman.html#ixzz0zqgg2Ygp.

Issues and Situations: With information from "Canada Joins Anti-Kyoto Bloc," *National Post (April 19, 2007)*, International Energy Agency, Energy Policies of IEA Countries – Canada, 2010.

CASE ENDNOTES

1. "Ryan Newman: Career Statistics," Yahoo! Sports at racing-reference.info/driver?id=newmary01 (accessed June 28, 2008).

2. Mike Harris, "Baker: Newman the Perfect Protégé," Associated Press (April 10, 2003).

3. "Ryan Newman Biography" at www.penskeracing.com/newman.

4. Ibid.

5. Dave Rodman, "Conversation: Ryan Newman," Turner Sports Interactive (June 9, 2003) at www.nascar.com.

6. "Ryan Newman Biography," op. cit.

7. Harris, op. cit.

8. Rodman, op. cit.

9. Ibid.

10. "Newman Looking Forward to Speedweeks Experience" at www.nascar.com.

CHAPTER 16

ENDNOTES

1. Compiled using the following sources: John Byrne and Michelle Conlin "Smashing the Clock," *Bloomberg Businessweek* (November 30, 2006); Craig Silverman, "All the Vacation You Want—Paradise or Purgatory?" *The Globe and Mail*, (January 15, 2010); Patrick J. Kiger, "Throwing Out the Rules of Work," *Workforce Management* (September 25, 2006).

2. Mayo Clinic information from "Work-Life Balance: Ways to Restore Harmony and Reduce Stress," www.mayoclinic.com/heal/work-lifebalance (retrieved August 14, 2008).

3. Quote from Gary Hamel, "Today's Companies Won't Make It, and Why?" *Fortune* (September 4, 2000), p. 386.

4. "The Renewal Factor: Friendly Fact, Congenial Controls," *BusinessWeek* (September 14, 1987), p. 105.

5. Rob Cross and Lloyd Baird, "Technology Is Not Enough: Improving Performance by Building Institutional Memory," *Sloan Management Review* (Spring 2000), p. 73.

6. Information from Pep Sappal, "Integrated Inclusion Initiative," *Wall Street Journal* (October 3, 2006), p. A2.

7. Based on discussion by Harold Koontz and Cryril O'Donnell, *Essentials of Management* (New York: McGraw-Hill, 1974), pp. 362–65; see also Cross and Baird, op. cit.

8. See John F. Love, *McDonald's: Behind the Arches* (New York: Bantam Books, 1986); and Ray Kroc and Robert Anderson, *Grinding It Out: The Making of McDonald's* (New York: St. Martin's Press, 1990).

9. This distinction is made in William G. Ouchi, "Markets, Bureaucracies and Clans," *Administrative Science Quarterly*, vol. 25 (1980), pp. 129–41.

10. Douglas McGregor, *The Human Side of Enterprise* (New York: McGraw-Hill, 1960).

11. For an overview, see www.soxlaw.com.

12. Martin LaMonica, "Wal-Mart Readies Long-Term Move into Solar Power," *CNET News.com* (January 3, 2007).

13. Information from Leon E. Wynter, "Allstate Rates Managers on Handling Diversity," *Wall Street Journal* (October 1, 1997), p. B1.

14. Information from Kathryn Kranhold, "U.S. Firms Raise Ethics Focus," *Wall Street Journal* (November 28, 2005), p. B4.

15. Example from George Anders, "Management Guru Turns Focus to Orchestras, Hospitals," *Wall Street Journal* (November 21, 2005), pp. B1, B5.

16. Information from Raju Narisetti, "For IBM, a Groundbreaking Sales Chief," *Wall Street Journal* (January 19, 1998), pp. B1, B5.

17. The "hot stove rules" are developed from R. Bruce McAfee and William Poffenberger, *Productivity Strategies: Enhancing Employee Job Performance* (Englewood Cliffs, NJ: Prentice-Hall, 1982), pp. 54–55. They are originally attributed to Douglas McGregor, "Hot Stove Rules of Discipline," in G. Strauss and L. Sayles, eds., *Personnel: The Human Problems of Management* (Englewood Cliffs, NJ: Prentice-Hall, 1967).

18. Information from Karen Carney, "Successful Performance Measurement: A Checklist," *Harvard Management Update* (No. U9911B), 1999.

19. Robert S. Kaplan and David P. Norton, "The Balanced Scorecard: Measures That Drive Performance," *Harvard Business Review* (July–August 2005); see also Robert S.

Kaplan and David P. Norton, *The Balanced Scorecard* (Cambridge, MA: Harvard Business School Press, 1996).

FEATURE NOTES

Real Ethics: Paul Davidson, " 'Climate Has Changed' for Data Privacy," *USA Today* (May 12, 2006), p. B1; Ben Elgin, "The Great Firewall of China," *BusinessWeek* (January 23, 2006), pp. 32–34; Alison Maitland, "Skype Says Text Messages Censored by Partner in China," *Financial Times* (April 19, 2006), p. 15; and "Web Firms Criticized Over China," CNN.com (July 20, 2006).

Issues and Situations: Information from Alan Cane, "Are Virtual Offices a Benefit or Burden?" *The Irish Times* (July 14, 2006), p. 12.

Research Brief: Marne L. Arthaud-Day, S. Travis Certo, Catherine M. Dalton, and Dan R. Dalton, "A Changing of the Guard: Executive and Director Turnover Following Corporate Financial Restatements," *Academy of Management Journal*, vol. 49 (December 2006).

Going Global: "Infosys Receives 2007 Balanced Scorecard Hall of Fame Award for Executing Strategy," news release, November 28, 2007.

CASE ENDNOTES

The case was compiled using the following sources:

- Roger Martin, "Inventions Are Fine, but It's the Innovation That Matters," *The Globe and Mail* (June 11, 2010), p. B2.

- Roger Martin, "Creating the Four Seasons Difference: How Challenging the Status Quo of the Hotel Business Paid Off for Isadore Sharp, Founder of the Four Seasons Chain," *Bloomberg Businessweek*, January 23, 2008.

- "How He Thinks," *Canadian Business* (Winter 2007/2008, Vol. 80, Iss. 24), pp. 79–83.

- Andrew Willis, "At Four Seasons Hotels, Issy Sharp's Era Nears an End," *The Globe and Mail* (June 25, 2010).

- "Four Seasons Hotels and Resorts Named to Fortune List of the '100 Best Companies to Work for' for 12 Consecutive Years," news release, Marketwire, January 23, 2009.

- Stephen Shapiro, "Innovation at the Four Seasons Hotel," Stephen Shapiro's 24/7 Innovation, February 26, 2008; available at www.steveshapiro.com/2008/02/26/innovation-at-the-four-seasons-hotel/.

- Kris Hudson, "Luxury Chain Cuts the Flowers, Sends Out Wash at Some Hotels," *Wall Street Journal* (June 1, 2010).

- Scott E. Sidman, "Lessons Learned from the Hotel Business . . . How Stellar Customer Service Can Assist with Tenant Retention," Building Engines corporate website, www.buildingengines.com/resource-center/information-briefs/lessons-learned-hotel-business%E2%80%A6.

CHAPTER 17

ENDNOTES

1. Christina Passariello, "Louis Vuitton Tries Modern Methods on Assembly Line," *Wall Street Journal* (October 9, 2006).

2. Stephen Covey, "How to Succeed in Today's Workplace," *USA Weekend* (August 29–31, 1997), pp. 4–5.

3. Examples from Anne Mulcahy, "How I Compete," *BusinessWeek* (August 21/28, 2006), p. 55; Gail Edmondson, "BMW's Dream Factory," *BusinessWeek* (October 16, 2006), pp. 68–80; and Amy Merrick, "Asking 'What Would Ann Do?'" *Wall Street Journal* (September 16, 2006), pp. B1–B2.

4. Good overviews are available in R. Dan Reid and Nada R. Sanders, *Operations Management: An Integrated Approach*, 2nd ed. (Hoboken, NJ: John Wiley & Sons, 2006); and Roberta S. Russell and Bernard W. Taylor III, *Operations Management: Quality and Competitiveness in a Global Environment* (Hoboken, NJ: John Wiley & Sons, 2005).

5. "Survey Finds Workers Average Only Three Productive Days Per Week," www.microsoft.com/press/2005/mar05 (retrieved October 20, 2006).

6. See Michael E. Porter, *Competitive Strategy: Techniques for Analyzing Industries and Competitors* (New York: Free Press, 1998); and *Competitive Advantage: Creating and Sustaining Superior Performance* (New York: Free Press, 1990); see also Richard A. D'Aveni, *Hyper-Competition: Managing the Dynamics of Strategic Maneuvering* (New York: Free Press, 1994).

7. Information from D'Aveni, op. cit.

8. Joan Woodward, *Industrial Organization: Theory and Practice* (London: Oxford University Press, 1965; republished by Oxford University Press, 1994).

9. Brian Hindo, "Everything Old Is New Again," *BusinessWeek* (September 25, 2006), p. 70.

10. Kenji Hall, "No One Does Lean Like the Japanese," *BusinessWeek* (July 10, 2006), pp. 40–41.

11. This treatment is from James D. Thompson, *Organizations in Action* (New York: McGraw-Hill, 1967).

12. Porter, op. cit., 1998.

13. See Michael Hugos, *Essentials of Supply Chain Management*, 2nd ed. (Hoboken, NJ: John Wiley & Sons, 2006).

14. "Gauging the Wal-Mart Effect," *Wall Street Journal* (December 3–4, 2005), pp. A1, A9.

15. See Joseph M. Juran, *Quality Control Handbook*, 3rd ed. (New York: McGraw-Hill, 1979); and "The Quality Trilogy: A Universal Approach to Managing for Quality," in *Total Quality Management*, H. Costin, ed.

(New York: Dryden, 1994); W. Edwards Deming, *Out of Crisis* (Cambridge, MA: MIT Press, 1986) and "Deming's Quality Manifesto," *Best of Business Quarterly*, vol. 12 (Winter 1990–1991), pp. 6–10. See also Howard S. Gitlow and Shelly J. Gitlow, *The Deming Guide to Quality and Competitive Position* (Englewood Cliffs, NJ: Prentice-Hall, 1987), and Juran, op. cit. (1993).

16. Rosabeth Moss Kanter, "Transcending Business Boundaries: 12,000 World Managers View Change," *Harvard Business Review* (May–June 1991), pp. 151–64.

17. Dale Dauten, "Which One Would You Rather Be?" *St. Louis Dispatch* (October 8, 2006), p. C2.

18. Information from Brian Hindo, "Satisfaction Not Guaranteed," *BusinessWeek* (June 19, 2006), pp. 32–38; and Kathy Tomlinson, "Large Moving Company Faces Charges, Upset Customers," CBC News on-line, February 3, 2010.

19. See C. K. Prahalad, Patricia B. Ramaswamy, Jon R. Katzenbach, Chris Lederer, and Sam Hill, *Harvard Business Review on Customer Relationship Management* (Boston, MA: Harvard Business School Publishing, 1998–2001).

20. Information from "How Marriott Never Forgets a Guest," *BusinessWeek* (February 21, 2000), p. 74.

21. Example and quote from Jena McGregor, "Customer Service Champs," *BusinessWeek* (March 3, 2008), pp. 37–42.

22. For the classics, see W. Edwards Deming, *Quality, Productivity, and Competitive Position* (Cambridge, MA: MIT Press, 1982) and Juran, op. cit.

23. "Canada Awards for Excellence (CAE) Overview," National Quality Institute website, www.nqi.ca/Awards/Overview.aspx.

24. See Edward E. Lawler III, Susan Albers Mohrman, and Gerald E. Ledford Jr., *Employee Involvement and Total Quality Management: Practices and Results in Fortune 1000 Companies* (San Francisco: Jossey-Bass, 1992).

25. Rafael Aguay, *Dr. Deming: The American Who Taught the Japanese about Quality* (New York: Free Press, 1997); W. Edwards Deming, op. cit. (1986).

26. For pros and cons of this approach, see "Six Sigma: So Yesterday?" *BusinessWeek* (June 2007), Special Edition, p. IN 11.

27. Michael Hammer, *Beyond Reengineering* (New York: Harper Business, 1997).

28. Michael Hammer and James Champy, *Reengineering the Corporation: A Manifesto for Business Revolution*, rev. ed. (New York: Harper Business, 1999).

29. Hammer, *Beyond Reengineering*, op. cit., p. 5; see also the discussion of processes in

Gary Hamel, *Leading the Revolution* (Boston, MA: Harvard Business School Press, 2000).

30. Thomas M. Koulopoulos, *The Workflow Imperative* (New York: Van Nostrand Reinhold, 1995); Hammer, *Beyond Reengineering*, op. cit.

31. Ronni T. Marshak, "Workflow Business Process Reengineering," special advertising section, *Fortune* (1997).

32. A similar example is found in Hammer, *Beyond Reengineering*, op. cit., pp. 9–10.

33. Ibid., pp. 28–30.

34. Ibid., p. 29.

35. Ibid., p. 27.

36. Quotation from Hammer and Company website, www.hammerandco.com/WhatIsAProcessOrgFrames.html.

FEATURE NOTES

Going Global: Tri Ocean corporate website, www.tri-ocean.com/about.htm; Industry Canada company profile, Tri Ocean Engineering, available at www.ic.gc.ca/app/ccc/srch/nvgt.do?lang=eng&prtl=1&sbPrtl=&estblmntNo=123456114642&profile=cmpltPrfl&profileId=441&app=sold.

Real Ethics: Information and quotes from Susan Chandler, "'Fair Trade' Label Enters Retail Market," *Columbus Dispatch* (October 16, 2006), p. G6; and www.fairindigo.com/about.

Issues and Situations: Information and quote from Jena McGregor, "Customer Service Champs," *BusinessWeek* (March 3, 2008), pp. 37–42.

Canadian Company in the News: "Diversicare Canada Management Services Co., Inc.: Our Excellence Journey," available at www.oltca.com/axiom/DailyNews/2009/September/Our%20Excellence%20Journey.pdf.

Research Brief: Dianne Ledingham, Mark Kovac, and Heidi Locke Simon, "The New Science of Sales Force Productivity," *Harvard Business Review*, vol. 84 (September 2006), pp. 124–33.

CASE ENDNOTES

1. "Toyota Outsells GM, Ford Posts Eye-Popping Loss," *US News & World Report*, posted on-line (July 24, 2008); wsj.com/mdc/public/page/2_3022-autosales.html.

2. M. Reza Vaghefi, "Creating Sustainable Competitive Advantage: The Toyota Philosophy and Its Effects," Mastering Management Online, October 2001 (accessed January 13, 2006, at www.ftmastering.com/mmo/index.htm).

3. "Top 10 SUVs, Pickups and Minivans with the Best Residual Value for 2005," Edmunds.com (accessed January 14, 2006 at www.edmunds.com/reviews/list/top10/103633/article.html).

4. "Making Things: The Essence and Evolution of the Toyota Production System," Toyota Motor Corporation (www.toyota.com).

5. "The 'Thinking' Production System: TPS as a Winning Strategy for Developing People in the Global Manufacturing Environment," Toyota Motor Corporation (www.toyota.com).

6. Ibid.

7. Ibid.

8. money.cnn.com/magazines/fortune/fortune_archive/2006/03/06/8370702/index.htm.

9. www.toyota.com/about/our_news/product.html.

10. Rick Newman, "Toyota's Next Turn," *US News & World Report* posted online (June 16, 2008).

11. Greg Keenan, "Trigger-Happy Toyota Recalls 1 Million Corolla, Matrix Vehicles," *The Globe and Mail* (August 26, 2010).

12. Robert E. Cole, "No Big Quality Problems at Toyota?", *Harvard Business Review* blog, March 9, 2010, http://blogs.hbr.org/cs/2010/03/no_big_quality_problems_at_toy.html.

INTEGRATED CASE

ENDNOTES

1. Moira Welsh, "A Tough Act to Follow; Relentless in Pursuit of his Vision, Communications Icon Inherited Hunger for Success," *Toronto Star* (December 3, 2008), p. B1.

2. "Nadir Mohamed, Rogers Senior Leadership," RCI, n.d. Retrieved on November 24, 2010 from http://www.rogers.com/web/Rogers.portal?_nfpb=true&_pageLabel=IR_LANDING&_nfls=true&_nfls=true&setLanguage=en&setLanguage=fr&ZoneName=aaglan_rcsldetail_zone_9e&_eventName=showSLdetail&BizUnit=rci

3. "At a Glance: Rogers Communications," RCI, n.d. Retrieved on November 23, 2010, from www.rogers.com/web/Rogers.portal?_nfpb=true&_pageLabel=IR_LANDING.

4. "History of Rogers," RCI, n.d. Retrieved on November 23, 2010 from http://your.rogers.com/aboutrogers/historyofrogers/overview.asp.

5. "RCI Third Quarter 2010 Corporate Fact Sheet," RCI, n.d. Retrieved on November 18, 2010, from www.rogers.com/cms/investor_relations/pdfs/factsheet.pdf.

6. "At a Glance: Rogers Communications;" "RCI Second Quarter 2010 Corporate Fact Sheet," RCI, n.d.

7. Chris Sorensen, "Ted Rogers a Tough Act to Follow," *Toronto Star* (December 3, 2008), p. B1.

8. Greg Meckbach, "What's Next for Rogers?," *Network World Canada* (January 15, 2009), Vol. 25, Iss. 1; Michael Posner, "The New Mr. Rogers," *Toronto Life* (September 2009), Vol. 43, Iss. 9, pp. 33–36.

9. Welsh, op. cit.

10. "History of Rogers."

11. David Olive, "Homegrown Success Was True Builder," *Toronto Star* (December 3, 2008), p. B7.

12. "History of Rogers."

13. Etan Vlessing, "Ted Rogers: Consummate Tactician Built a Media Empire," *Playback: Canada's Broadcast and Production Journal* (August 17, 2009), p. 107.

14. "History of Rogers."

15. Ibid.

16. Ibid.

17. Welsh, op. cit.

18. Ibid.

19. Vlessing, op. cit.

20. Ibid.

21. Welsh, op. cit.

22. Olive, op. cit.

23. Canadian Wireless Telecommunications Association, "Wireless Communications Make Canada Stronger." Retrieved on November 10, 2010. from www.cwta.ca/CWTASite/english/index.html.

24. Iain Marlow, "Cell Firms, Retailers Shift Strategy," *The Globe and Mail* (October 8, 2010), p. B7.

25. Iain Marlow, "Telecom Philosopher? Try Lover of Sure Bets," *The Globe and Mail* (October 9, 2010), p. B3.

26. "RCI Competitor Information," Yahoo Finance, n.d. Retrieved on November 21, 2010, from http://finance.yahoo.com/q/co?s=RCI+Competitors.

27. "RCI Third Quarter 2010 Corporate Fact Sheet."

28. "RCI Competitor Information," op. cit.

29. "BCE Investor Fact Sheet—Q3 2010." BCE, n.d. Retrieved on November 18, 2010, from www.bce.ca/data/documents/reports/en/2010/q3/Fact_sheet_q3_10_En.pdf.

30. "TELUS Investor Fact Sheet—Q3 2010." TELUS, n.d. Retrieved on November 18, 2010, from http://about.telus.com/investors/downloads/20103Q/Factsheet.pdf.

31. "Cable Television," *Canadian Encyclopedia*. Retrieved on November 10, 2010, from www.thecanadianencyclopedia.com/index.cfm?PgNm=TCE&Params=A1ARTA0001150.

32. Ibid.

33. Ibid.

34. "Shaw Announces Third Quarter Financial and Operating Results," news release, June 30, 2010. Retrieved November 18, 2010, from www.shaw.ca/NR/rdonlyres/3D148C5C-D533-4FA3-9FF4-B336F1409DCA/0/3rdQtr10.pdf.

35. "RCI Third Quarter 2010 Corporate Fact Sheet."

36. "Industry Profile: Magazine Publishing." Ontario Media Development Corporation, n.d. Retrieved on November 10, 2010, from www.omdc.on.ca/AssetFactory.aspx?did=6565.

37. Ibid.

38. Marlow, October 9, 2010.

39. Chris Sorensen, "iPhone Sales Nearly Double Rogers Profit; CEO Says Cable Giant Well-Positioned to Ride Out Economic Downturn," *Toronto Star* (October 29, 2008), p. B1.

40. Posner, op. cit.

Organization Index

Name Index

Subject Index